PRIMITIVISMUS

in der Kunst des zwanzigsten Jahrhunderts

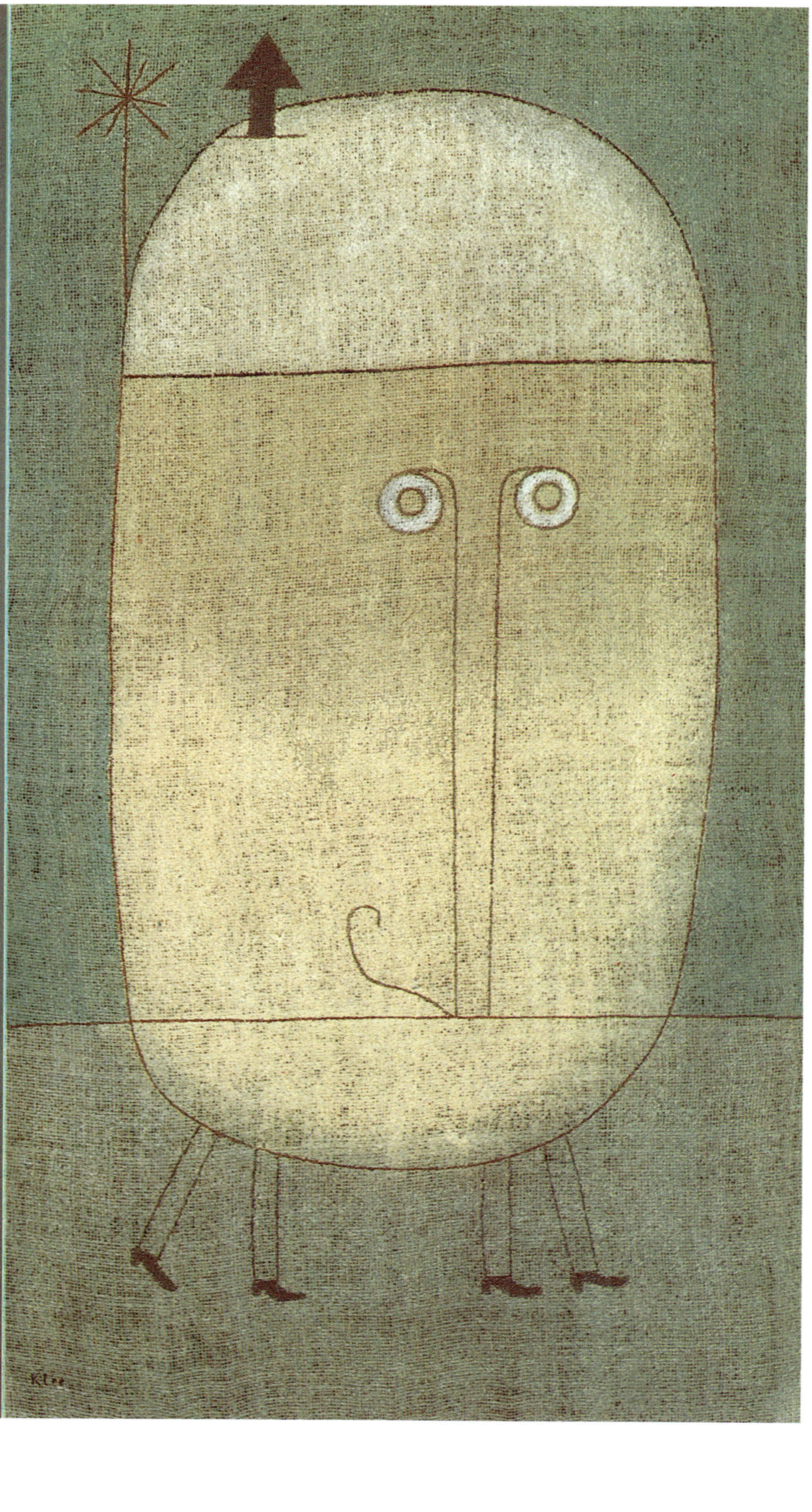
Klee

PRIMITIVISMUS

in der Kunst
des zwanzigsten Jahrhunderts

Herausgegeben von

William Rubin

Prestel-Verlag

Die amerikanische Originalausgabe dieses Buches erscheint unter dem Titel
»"Primitivism" in 20th Century Art« in 2 Bänden
als Publikation des Museum of Modern Art, New York

3. Auflage 1996

Fotonachweis siehe Seite 702

Redaktion der erweiterten deutschen Ausgabe: Peter Stepan
unter Mitarbeit von Gesine Hirsch.

Die Übersetzung besorgten:

Eine Einführung: Peter Stepan. Aus Nordamerika: Renate Langewiesche. Aus der Südsee: Renate Langewiesche.
Aus Afrika: Michael Hofmann. Gauguin: Katrin und Peter Mönch. Matisse: Katrin Mönch.
Picasso: Peter Stepan und Michael Hofmann. Brancusi: Peter Stepan. Deutscher Expressionismus: John Matheson.
Italienische Malerei: Nicolas Hepp. Paris und London: Gabriele Schickel.
Amerikanische Kunst: Christine Götz. Léger: Christine Götz. Klee: Magdalena Kilger.
Giacometti: Nicolas Hepp. Dada und Surrealismus: John Matheson. Henry Moore: Gabriele Schickel.
Abstrakter Expressionismus: Helga Tratz. Zeitgenössische Tendenzen: Gabriele Schickel.

Auf dem Schutzumschlag:

Vorderseite: Max Ernst, *Vogelkopf,* Bronze, 1934/35, Galerie Beyeler, Basel.
Maske, TUSYAN (Obervolta), Holz, Pflanzenfasern und Samen, Musée Barbier-Müller, Genf.

Rücken: Pablo Picasso, *Mädchen vor einem Spiegel,* Ausschnitt, 1932, Öl auf Leinwand, The Museum of Modern Art, Schenkung Guggenheim, New York.
Maske, KWAKIUTL, Britisch-Kolumbien (Kanada), bemaltes Holz, Höhe 34 cm, Museum für Völkerkunde, Berlin.

Auf dem Frontispiz:

Figur eines Kriegsgottes, ZUNI (Neu-Mexiko), bemaltes Holz und verschiedene Materialien, Museum für Völkerkunde, Berlin.
Paul Klee, *Maske der Furcht,* 1932, Öl auf Rupfen, The Museum of Modern Art, New York.

CIP-Kurztitelaufnahme der Deutschen Bibliothek

Primitivismus in der Kunst des zwanzigsten Jahrhunderts / hrsg. von William Rubin.
München: Prestel, 1984. Einheitssacht.: Primitivismus in modern art ‹dt.›
NE: Rubin, William S. [Hrsg.].

Printed in Czech Republic
Dieses Buch wurde aus der ›Times Antiqua‹ der Fa. D. Stempel AG, Frankfurt/Main, gesetzt.
(System Linotron 202)
Satz: Universitätsdruckerei Dr. C. Wolf & Sohn, München
ISBN 1716-4

Inhalt

Vorwort des Verlags

Der Primitivismus gehört zu den wichtigen konstituierenden Phänomenen der Kunst des 20. Jahrhunderts. Wie entscheidend der Einfluß von Werken der Naturvölker auf die deutschen Expressionisten, auf Max Ernst, Paul Klee, Matisse, Picasso und viele andere Klassiker der Moderne war, wird erst durch die hier vorgelegten Forschungsergebnisse deutlich. Die Bedeutung des Primitivismus als eines integralen Bestandteils des europäischen Kunstschaffens seit der Jahrhundertwende bildete für den Verlag den Anstoß, dieses große Unternehmen des Museum of Modern Art in einer deutschen Buchausgabe zugänglich zu machen. Sie wurde durch einen umfangreichen Registerteil erweitert, darunter ein Lexikon der Stämme Ozeaniens, Afrikas und Amerikas, die – seit ihrer Entdeckung immer mehr vom Untergang und dem Vergessen bedroht – damit aus der kunstwissenschaftlichen Anonymität heraustreten (siehe S. 707).

Wie sehr die Reichweite des Primitivismus in der Kunst unseres Jahrhunderts unterschätzt wurde, zeigt sich darin, daß dieser Begriff in der Kunstwissenschaft bislang kaum Verwendung fand (siehe Anmerkung auf S. 10). Der Verlag sah daher mit dieser Publikation und bei der schwierigen Entscheidung, für sie einen Titel zu finden, die Möglichkeit, dem Begriff Primitivismus als kunsthistorischem Terminus zur Durchsetzung zu verhelfen.

Die Idee des Primitivismus ist keine Erfindung des 20. Jahrhunderts, sondern kann auf eine lange geistesgeschichtliche Tradition zurückblicken. Jean-Jacques Rousseau ist der wichtigste Exponent primitivistischen Denkens im 18. Jahrhundert. Wie in Frankreich besannen sich auch deutsche Dichter und Philosophen auf die primitiven Völker, die sich ihr ursprüngliches Empfinden und eine innere Übereinstimmung mit der Natur bewahrt zu haben schienen.

Als der junge Goethe 1772 in seinem berühmten Aufsatz „Von deutscher Baukunst" das Straßburger Münster und seinen Baumeister überschwenglich pries, brachte er zum Ausdruck, wie fragwürdig ihm der überkommene Schönheitsbegriff war: *»Die Kunst ist lange bildend, eh' sie schön ist . . . Und so modelt der Wilde mit abenteuerlichen Zügen, gräßlichen Gestalten, hohen Farben seine Kokos, seine Federn und seinen Körper.«* Gegen die akademischen Kunstlehren und die Vorstellung, daß die bildende Kunst der Nachahmung der Natur und der „Schönheitelei" diene, setzte er das Bild eines aus inneren schöpferischen Impulsen gestaltenden Menschen. Als er diesen zivilisatorisch unverdorbenen Künstler schilderte, dachte Goethe wohl an die Bewohner der Südsee, die schon damals für ihre Masken, ihren Federschmuck und ihre Körperbemalung bekannt waren.

Diese vielzitierte Stelle aus Goethes Jugendschrift faßt die vitalistische Ästhetik einer ganzen literarischen Epoche zusammen. Es ist das erste Mal in der deutschen Geistesgeschichte, daß die kulturellen Leistungen der Naturvölker in dieser Weise geschätzt und verstanden wurden. Goethe stand mit dieser Auffassung nicht allein. Neben anderen Vertretern des Sturm und Drang war es vor allem Herder, der aus dem Überdruß an kultureller Überfeinerung *»die rohe, einfältige, aber große, zaubermäßige feierliche Art . . .«* in der abendländischen Vergangenheit und anderen Kulturen suchte: *»Sie wissen aus Reisebeschreibungen, wie stark und fest sich immer die Wilden ausdrücken. Immer die Sache, die sie sagen wollen, sinnlich, klar, lebendig anschauend . . . Sie schweigen entweder, oder reden im Moment des Interesses mit einer unvorbedachten Festigkeit, Sicherheit und Schönheit, die alle wohlstudierten Europäer allezeit haben bewundern müssen . . .«* (Aus dem Briefwechsel über Ossian und die Lieder alter Völker). Goethe und Herder schufen eine ideelle Grundlage für die über ein Jahrhundert später tatsächlich einsetzende Befruchtung und Bereicherung der europäischen Kunst durch Stile und Techniken der Naturvölker. Herders unmittelbares Interesse galt noch archaischen Zeugnissen der Literatur, die er übersetzte oder in eigenen Werken verarbeitete: Homer, Ossian, die nordische Dichtung. Übersetzungen oder Nachdichtungen afrikanischer oder ozeanischer Texte sollten erst im 20. Jahrhundert – vor allem im literarischen Primitivismus der Dadaisten – möglich sein.

Das Vorbild des Primitiven – und dies gilt nicht nur für die deutsche Kulturgeschichte – trat immer dann ins Bewußtsein, wenn die existentielle Wurzel, die menschliche Ganzheit künstlerischen Schaffens aus der Sicht zu geraten drohte, wenn vergessen wurde, *»wie eng die Schönheit mit der Kraft verschwistert ist und die Kraft mit allem Furchtbaren und Drohenden des Lebens . . .«* (G. Hauptmann). Primitive Kunst, das war und ist für viele der Ausdruck eines Seinszustandes, der um viele Dimensionen in der Erfahrung von Natur, Kosmos und geistiger Welt reicher ist. Neben der besonderen Relevanz des Themas Primitivismus für die Kunstgeschichte des 20. Jahrhunderts ist es gerade die Notwendigkeit, die Kunst mit der Totalität menschlicher Erfahrung zu konfrontieren, zu der die vorliegende Publikation einen wichtigen Beitrag leisten kann. So ist PRIMITIVISMUS IN DER KUNST DES ZWANZIGSTEN JAHRHUNDERTS mehr als ein Standardwerk zur Kunstgeschichte der Moderne. Die vielen und dabei so verschiedenen Begegnungen der Künstler unseres Jahrhunderts mit dem Primitiven zeigen Möglichkeiten der Erweiterung des künstlerischen Bewußtseins auf, die gerade heute von besonderer Aktualität sind.

Vorwort des Herausgebers

Daß Robert Goldwater in den dreißiger Jahren ein Buch über das heikle Thema des modernen Primitivismus schrieb, zeugt von Weitsicht und Mut. Damals waren Picassos *Demoiselles d'Avignon* praktisch noch unbekannt (das Bild wurde 1939 durch das Museum of Modern Art angekauft, ein Jahr, bevor Goldwaters *Primitivism in Modern Painting* erschien). Viele künstlerische und dokumentarische Zeugnisse, auf denen das vorliegende Buch aufbaut, waren in jener Zeit noch nicht zugänglich. Für die offizielle Fachwissenschaft hörte die Kunstgeschichte damals mit Cézanne, wenn nicht sogar schon mit Courbet, auf, und ernsthafte Untersuchungen zur modernen Kunst waren selten. Dessenungeachtet ist Goldwaters Buch, das 1967 als Neuauflage erschien, nach wie vor die unentbehrliche, richtungsweisende Publikation im Bereich primitivistischer Forschung.

Wenn Kunsthistoriker heutzutage von einzelnen Ergebnissen Goldwaters abweichen, so schmälert dies nicht die Bedeutung seiner Pioniertat, zumal es überraschend ist, wenn Forschungsmeinungen der Kunstgeschichte erst nach fünfzig Jahren revidiert werden. Was uns eher befremdet, ist die Tatsache, daß eine Publikation zu einem Schlüsselthema der Kunstgeschichte des 20. Jahrhunderts bislang ohne Nachfolge geblieben oder nie in Frage gestellt worden ist. Wohl haben Goldwaters Fachkenntnisse, die im Bereich moderner wie auch primitiver Kunst von einer seltenen Kompetenz zeugen, manch einen entmutigt oder gar abgeschreckt.

Trotzdem vermute ich, daß es noch andere Gründe gibt, weshalb der Primitivismus in der kunsthistorischen Forschung seit dem Erscheinen von Goldwaters Buch jahrzehntelang recht stiefmütterlich behandelt wurde, während man andere Aspekte der Kunst des 20. Jahrhunderts mit Untersuchungen nur so überhäufte. Nicht daß die Bedeutung der Stammesskulptur für die modernen Künstler unbeachtet geblieben ist. Ganz im Gegenteil, jede Geschichte der modernen Kunst wäre als unvollständig empfunden worden, hätte sie nicht der Bedeutung primitiver Einflüsse ihre Referenz erwiesen. Als Musterbeispiel galten immer die *Demoiselles d'Avignon,* zu denen eine Fülle abwegiger Klischees entstand, die den direkten Einfluß primitiver Skulpturen meist überbewerteten. (Demgegenüber wurde er von Goldwater, der Personifikation gelehrter Vorsicht, generell unterbewertet.)

Die ständige Wiederholung vertraut gewordener Klischeevorstellungen führte schließlich dazu, daß die eigentlichen Probleme unseres Themas übersehen wurden und keine ernsthafte Auseinandersetzung mehr stattfand. Keiner trägt eine größere Schuld an dieser Situation als der Herausgeber des vorliegenden Buches. Daß ich den Primitivismus in meinem Werk *Dada und Surrealismus* aus den sechziger Jahren – von einigen allgemeinen Äußerungen abgesehen – verschwieg, ist mein größter Irrtum als Historiker. Daß Marcel Jeans bahnbrechende *Geschichte der surrealistischen Malerei,* die kurz zuvor erschienen war, den Primitivismus ebenfalls nur beiläufig behandelt, bestätigt nur wieder einmal die Parabel, daß die Blinden von den Blinden geführt werden. Als junger Kunsthistoriker hatte ich Gelegenheit, den Surrealisten Matta zu besuchen. Doch nie wäre ich auf die Idee gekommen, seine figürlichen Schöpfungen mit Skulpturen aus Neuirland in Verbindung zu bringen (wie dies hier auf S. 10 und 11 getan wird); Matta selbst sprach davon, daß ihn Giacomettis Skulptur *Der Unsichtbare Gegenstand* □ 725 zu seinen Gestalten inspiriert habe, ohne auch nur ein Wort über Stammeskunst zu verlieren. Heute wissen wir, daß *Der Unsichtbare Gegenstand* seinerseits durch ozeanische Skulptur beeinflußt ist – und ich selbst bin etwas vorsichtiger geworden mit dem, was Künstler über Kunst sagen oder nicht sagen.

Die wenigen Male, da ich mich mit Picasso in seinen letzten Lebensjahren über primitive Kunst unterhalten konnte, führten eine Meinungsänderung meinerseits herbei, und mit Überraschung erkannte ich, daß seine Sicht dieser Skulpturen überkommenen Vorstellungen völlig widersprach. (Hinweise darauf finden sich schon in Françoise Gilots Memoiren, doch hatte ich sie übersehen; in der Folgezeit gab auch Malraux ein Gespräch mit Picasso wieder, das meine Erfahrungen bestätigte.) Schließlich faßte ich den Entschluß, daß die ganze Frage des Primitivismus neu zu untersuchen sei. Und gibt es eine bessere Möglichkeit als die Forschungen, die eine Ausstellung über dieses Thema nötig werden lassen?

Wie schon angesichts der spärlichen Information und Literatur zum Spätwerk Cézannes schien eine umfassende Publikation, in der die unterschiedlichsten Gesichtspunkte zum Thema Primitivismus sichtbar werden, unerläßlich – etwas wie ein Arbeitsbuch für diesen Bereich. Während meiner fünfjährigen Forschungsarbeit zeigte es sich, daß – wie mir schien – grundlegende Fragen niemals gestellt worden waren (warum etwa die Kubisten – im Gegensatz zu den Surrealisten – die afrikanische Skulptur der ozeanischen vorzogen). Leider war die verfügbare Zeit nicht ausreichend, um alle Fragen in gleicher Weise gründlich zu beantworten. Dennoch kann das vorliegende Buch, auch wenn noch viel Arbeit zu leisten ist, als der Beginn einer neuen Phase in der Erforschung des Primitivismus gelten.

William Rubin

Direktor der Abteilung Malerei und Plastik
im Museum of Modern Art, New York.

William Rubin

Preface to the Second Printing

The idea for this preface derived from an exchange of afterwords between the distinguished anthropologist Kenji Yoshida and myself in 1994 when, ten years after the appearance of *"Primitivism" in the 20th Century Art*, the Japanese publisher Tankosha, in part at the urging of Mr. Yoshida, undertook a translation of it. It was a daunting task, the overseeing of which Mr. Yoshida graciously accepted as a function of what he considered the book's importance to anthropology as well as art history. Much of his afterword was taken up with the problems of defining Japanese equivalents for an essentially unfamiliar terminology – one that has been partially confronted in Japan in the discipline of anthropology, but not in that of art history. Tankosha had felt, no doubt correctly, that some sort of context needed to be created for Japanese readers, inasmuch as primitivism – the influence of styles characterized in the West as "primitive" upon the history of occidental art – was a subject rarely discussed in Japan.

A significant part of Yoshida's text, however, was also devoted to the miniature *Kulturkampf* that developed around the exhibition and book in the United States, in particular between its authors and several anthropologists, as well as a few art critics and historians. One of the latter was Thomas McEvilley, whose discussion of *"Primitivism" in the 20th Century Art* led to a lengthy exchange of letters between him and Kirk Varnedoe (co-director of the exhibition and author of two of the book's essays) and myself.[1] McEvilley's criticism was less important for the intellectual community as a whole – certainly for those interested in primitivism in Japan – than the critique of the exhibition put forth by one of the leaders of the "new anthropology" in America, James Clifford, whose views were presented in his essay "Histories of the Tribal and Modern."[2]

As Clifford's text had wide circulation in the United States (at least in academic circles) and, according to Yoshida, was much read an discussed by Japanese anthropologists, he devoted much of his afterword to citations from, and discussions of, that essay. Yoshida's approach to the differences between Clifford and ourselves was in general fair-minded; he sought to explain them by proposing that the exhibition, which was conceived in the 1970s and elaborated from 1980 to 1986, was essentially projected from a structuralist point of view, while Clifford's criticisms derived from a poststructuralist angle that had come to characterize a variety of disciplines in the 1980s. While there is some truth to this analysis, I felt that the philosophical and critical differences that separated Clifford and ourselves were also otherwise motiviated, having a resonance with generational differences of an academic nature – not to say "turf battles" – that still uniquely dominate the American university world. Clifford's views extended well beyond the multiculturalism of my generation to positions that can only be described as "politically correct."[3] I therefore appended to Yoshida's text and afterword of my own, largely a critique of the Clifford material he cited. It is a version of *that* text which follows.

My colleague Kirk Varnedoe and I approached *"Primitivism" in 20th Century Art* as art historians attempting to clarify a particular phase in the development of modern painting. One would never guess from Clifford's text that "primitivism" has *never* meant "primitive" art. "Primitivism" is, by definition, an entirely Western cultural phenomenon, a term that refers to the history of (primarily) European reactions to – and passion for – whatever was considered "primitive" at any given moment. (Hence the absurdity of criticizing such projects as ours as "Eurocentric".) The popularity of Japanese prints among Western artists during the period 1860-90 is, for example, a chapter in the history of Western primitivism rather than a development in the history of Japanese art. During the earliest decades of the discipline of art history, the term "primitive" was used neither to describe what is now called tribal art nor – as would be the case around the turn of the century – certain arts of the Orient. On the contrary, it was attached to early Renaissance painters such as Jan van Eyck and Rogier van der Weyden, who were (and sometimes still are) called Flemish primitives.

Most art historians, moreover, and all vanguard artists have traditionally employed the word "primitive" in a *positive sense* – to connote *creators of new traditions*. This is what Cézanne meant when he described himself as "the 'primitive' of a new art" (which, in view of subsequent Cubism, he surely was). In Cézanne's day, however, the term "primitive art" did not yet refer to so-called tribal art. On the contrary, it was used then by artists and critics largely to characterize a variety of styles that were at once alien to traditional Western illusionism yet highly esteemed by the turn-of-the-century modernists. Many of these artistic traditions were non-Western – the Peruvian, Javanese, Cambodian, Egyptian, and Japanese, for example. But significantly, others, such as the Byzantine, Romanesque, and *maniera greca*, were Western. Only in the winter of 1905-6 (not "around 1910," as Clifford suggests) do some "tribal" objects escape their prior classifications exclusively as ethnological artifacts or curiosities, and begin to be spoken of, mostly by artists, as "primitive *art*" (or "negro art"). Within a few years, Picasso would insist that the greatest works of African art "surpassed even those of the Egyptians."[4]

Clifford's article does not treat these events in their historical context, but turns rather on present-day attitudes (especially as regards colonialism) towards the ethnic groups who actually executed the so-called tribal objects. In thus ahistorically orienting his discourse, however, he inverts the real cultural significance of the modernists' artistic interests (which were "elective affinities," to use Goethe's phrase) in such a manner that their primitivism appears not as the radical challenge to contemporary values that is actually was, but rather as an essentially colonialist syndrome: while he allows that "the modernist appropriation of tribal production is not simply imperialist," Clifford nevertheless insists, "the scope and underlying logic of the 'discovery' of tribal art [by the modernists] reproduces hegemonic Western assumptions rooted in the colonial and neocolonial epoch."[5] He presses this argument despite the fact that the artists in question were all in varying degrees anti-colonialist, Picasso especially. And despite the fact that – in contradistinction to the institutional and celebratory role of Western art in earlier periods – modernism can be convincingly interpreted as an implicit (and often explicit) critique of the very culture from which it emerged.

Colonialism and, more generally, "the West" are soon perceived as the devils of Clifford's particular morality tale – one in which primitivism becomes negatively redefined as "the restless desire and power of the modern West to collect the world."[6] Not surprisingly, Clifford describes modernist interest in tribal objects with that most notorious of jargon terms, "appropriation." No doubt this is the *mot juste* to describe much of what colonialism wrought. But its use in characterizing the work of modernist artists of the early twentieth century profoundly prejudices Clifford's discussion, in which these artists are pronounced guilty, in effect, by temporal association. In fact, the pioneer modernists'relation to tribal objects was no more a matter of appropriation than was the Archaic Greek sculptors' interest in Egyptian models, or fifteenth-century Italian painters' passion for the statuary of Classical Antiquity. Would Clifford have accused them of colonialist "appropriation"? As all art is made in part from art, its makers depend upon the work of others – near or far – to arrive at their own plastic languages.

The close resemblances between certain tribal and modern objects, as analyzed in our book, are declared by Clifford not to exist at all. He states no less peremptorily than mistakenly that the "tribal and modern artifacts [we compared] are similar only in that they do *not* feature the pictorial illusionism or sculptural naturalism that came to dominate Western European art after the Renaissance."[7] Pointing out that "abstraction and conceptualism" are pervasive in the arts of the non-Western world, he concludes that "to say that they share with modernism a rejection of certain naturalist projects is not to show anything like an affinity."[8] To be sure, abstraction and conceptualism *are* pervasive in the arts of the non-Western world; they are also, for that matter, pervasive in some earlier Western styles, such as the Byzantine and Romanesque. But such conceptual and plastic similarities as those on which we focused would certainly *not* have been evident (or only marginally so) had we juxtaposed twentieth-century vanguard objects with other non-illusionistic styles such as the Egyption, Aztec, and Cambodian – or, for that matter, with the Byzantine or Romanesque. Nor are they the product, as Clifford suggests, of statistical "coincidence."[9]

The correspondences we treated in our exhibition and book far transcend the "negative" similarities (absence of illusionism and naturalism) of which Clifford wrote. In my text, the latter were considered only a significant *precondition* of the configurational correspondences with which we dealt. But Clifford claims that eschewal of illusionism and naturalism are the "only" similarities between tribal and modern objects. This notwithstanding, anyone with a modicum of visual acuity who looked carefully at our exhibition or read our book would have understood – as we pointed out numerous times in the text – that the similarities in question involved many *particular configurational solutions* to the problems of representation common to the morphologies of both twentieth-century modernism and tribal art[10] (to say nothing of other similarities having to do with the scale, proportion, and the choice and handling of materials, especially the "collaging" of heterogeneous ones). Such particular features rendered the pairings – which in some cases were suggested in the sketchbooks of modern artists themselves – of an order and propinquity that could not conceivably have been matched in comparing examples of twentieth-century modernism with any *other* non-Western styles than the so-called tribal. Picasso had no affinity for Cambodian or Olmec sculpture – any more than for Byzantine art – and Clifford cannot get away with putting all non-illusionist and non-naturalist styles in the same basket.

Clifford argues with respect to *"Primitivism" in 20th Century Art* that "an equally striking collection [of comparisons] could be made demonstrating sharp dissimilarities between tribal and modern objects."[11] This, if true, is beside the point, since such an atypical selection would have to omit precisely those typologies of tribal sculpture which the modernists admired, sketched, collected, and were influenced by – in effect, the whole point of our exercise. "Indeed," Clifford goes on to say, "the 'tribalism' selected in the [Museum's] exhibition to resemble modernism is itself a construction designed to accomplish the task of resemblance. Ife and Benin sculptures, highly naturalistic in style, are excluded from the 'tribal.'"[12] Now, if our selection of objects was a "construction," it was one preemptively *dictated by the choices* made by those twentieth-century artists who went through primitivist phases. Our purpose was obviously not to cover the whole range of so-called tribal art. Benin sculpture – not really tribal anyway – was of little interest to modernists, though there were a few (mostly German) exceptions, whose works are, in fact, discussed and illustrated in our book; Ife sculpture was simply not available to the pre-World War II generations of artists in France with which our account primarily dealt, and was exceedingly scarce even in Germany.[13]

Clifford was most of all exercised by our use of the word "affinity." Indeed, as he claims to have no quarrel with the "focused story" we told – an "exact history... featuring individual artists and objects, their encounters in specific studios at precise moments" – his critique comes down to the way this story is "infused with another – a loose allegory of realtionship centering on the word *affinity*. The word is a kinship term," he continues, "suggesting a deeper or more natural realtionship than mere resemblance of juxtaposition," one in which the "tribal is modern"[14] (Clifford's words, not ours); and (what we had called) stylistic or structural "common denominators" in this relationship are interpreted by Clifford as an affront to the otherness of the other. "Why," he asks, "could one not learn as much about Picasso's or Ernst's creative processes by analyzing the *differences* separating their art from tribal models or by tracing the ways their art moved away from, gave new twists to, non-Western forms?"[15] The only answer to this astonishing question is: *One can and we did*. In the exhibition, such differences and transformations could only occasionally be alluded to in the necessarily brief wall labels,[16] though they were *manifest in the juxtaposed works themselves*, at least to a reasonably experienced viewer. In our book – as the reader will see for himself – we dealt with such differences time and time again.[17]

If I had harbored the least thought that anybody was going to take our use of the word "affinity" in Clifford's particular anthropological sense, I would – and perhaps should – have defined more precisely the intended limits of our *wholly correct* use of that word. We were, of course, applying it in its much more familiar *figurative* form, as linguist Umberto Eco did in a review of our exhibition.[18] The *Oxford English Dictionary* defines this usage as a "causal relationship or connexion (as flowing the one from the other...) [or] similarity of nature or character as might result from such relationship if it existed," and Webster renders it as a "causal connection or relationship: RESEMBLANCE." Whatever the figurative usage of "affinity" may imply *beyond* the above is in the realm of the subjective and intuitional, and Clifford can no more enter into Picasso's psyche than he can into that of a long-deceased tribal sculptor.

Clifford's definition of the word affinity in terms of kinship is, moreover, somewhat misleading, to the extent that kinship usually means commonality of blood, whereas the etymological (and biblical) definition of affinity is "relationship by marriage," as opposed to consanguinity, hence the relationship formed by the coming together – as in our exhibition – of two *different* things. By insisting on understanding affinity exclusively in his own kinship sense, Clifford furthermore implied that the relationship – which we dealt with in historical terms – was presented as a "two-way street," an *unthinkable*, indeed ludicrous, idea. "The affinity idea itself is wide-ranging and promiscuous," he says, "as are allusions to universal human capacities."[19] Can he really believe that our argument implied anything more than tribal artists were human beings endowed with capacity of informing the material world with an expressive, symbolic, and esthetic order?

But perhaps the notion that the African carvers – whatever their intentions – were *making art* is exactly what Clifford cannot accept; perhaps this is precisely what he meant in referring dismissively to "universal human capacities." In order for our thesis to hold, it is necessary to admit that tribal works – those that transcend being just artifacts – are, indeed, art. In his article, Clifford never describes African carvings with this word; he refers to them carefully only as "objects" or "artifacts." Our own references to African art-making capabilities are dismissed by Clifford as assumptions of "ahistorical 'human' capacities" (like speech and thought, one supposes).

To be sure, Clifford is nothing but consistent, insofar as he typically characterizes all art itself as a simple "category defined and redefined in specific historical contexts and relations of power." Hence, the "appreciation and interpretation of tribal objects takes place within a modern 'system of objects' which confers value on certain things and withholds it from others."[20] But such a definition of art as a fluctuating category – one in which an object may be art one day (year, decade, century) but not the next – is, historically speaking, irresponsible. For while the definition of art is constantly changing, it is changing only in that it is expanding. It expands lagely at the outer edge as artists invent new forms – even new arts – but also from within, as discovery and communication bring previously unfamiliar art from other cultures into our awareness, particularly into that of artists; they (rather than anthropologists) ultimately convince us what is art. Contrary to the implications of Clifford's fluctuation theory, nothing gets jettisoned or discarded from this definition. However much "relations of power" have altered over the centuries, nothing that has once been recognized as art has ever been, so to say, disenfranchised. Indeed, ever since the Greeks subsumed the paintings and sculptures of the Egyptians – who themselves *had no word for art* – under the umbrella of their concept, it has been clear that one does not have to know what art is in order to make it.

"The organizers of the MoMA exhibition have been clear about its limitations," Clifford asserts, "and they have repeatedly specified what they do not claim to show. It is thus in a sense unfair to ask why they did not construct a differently focused history of relations between 'the tribal' and 'the modern.'"[21] In fact, such a sense of fairness should have precluded Clifford from rolling out his own agenda. He proceeds to provide a rationale for his discussion by arguing that "the exclusions built into any collection or narration are legitimate objects of critique." Taken literally, this last sentence is nonsense, since no narration can acquire a form other than through countless exclusions. Thr real question is whether any particular exclusion is significant to the narrative in question. What Clifford discusses is *his* narrative, however, and not ours.

The putative "exclusion" for which we were most taxed by Clifford was that of not showing or discussing "the original cultural context" of the tribal objects. He writes: "Consideration of context, we are firmly told at the [MoMA] exhibition's entrance, is the business of anthropologists. Cultural background is not essential to correct esthetic appreciation and analysis... The pioneer modernists themselves knew little or nothing of these objects' ethnographic meaning. What was good enough for Picasso is good enough for MoMA. Indeed an ignorance of cultural context seems almost a precondidtion for artistic appreciation."[22] The rhetorical sleight-of-word in this passage is something to behold. After telling his reader that the statement concerning original cultural context being a matter for anthropologists is on a panel at the exhibitions entrance, Clifford continues with assertions about esthetic appreciation, Picasso, and MoMA, and concludes with a *non sequitur* about ignorance of context being almost a precondition for artistic appreciation; all the while leaving his reader with the (false) impression that the subsequent points are made "at the exhibition's entrance." In fact, however, they really constitute only Clifford's angry rhetorical riff in the face of facts he simply doesn't like:[23]

1) Our subject dealt with the reception among Western artists of *already decontextualized* tribal objects, and we intended that those objects would be understood as they had been, in effect, *recontextualized* within the studios, lives, and art of Europeans who knew little or nothing about their original cultural context. *What they made out of these objects in their own work and thought was the subject of our show*, which – since it did not necessitate the participation of anthropologists[24] – seems for Clifford to have been an unpardonable act.

2) When Picasso said with regard to some tribal sculptures, "all I have to know about Africa is in these objects," he did not mean – as I can testify from the context of our conversations – that he was uninterested in their original cultural context, but rather that none of the historical or iconographic facts one could learn about the context of a fine African or Oceanic sculpture (if, indeed, such information was then available) could give him as good, as deep, and as moving a sense of its author's world as the affective message of the work itself. As an art historian, I am committed to both approaches. I am personally interested in and, indeed, have studied some of the many cultural contexts of such tribal objects as we showed. But as a historian of modern art, the cultural context that interested me for our primitivism topic was Picasso's studio, his milieu, and the Paris of his day.

3) Given our aims, there was no reason to restore the tribal objects to their original (African, Oceanic, or Native American) contexts. And even if there had been, how, practically speaking, could this have been done with hundreds of objects from almost as many *different* tribal cultures – utterly differing objects whose only common denominator was the fact that they were of particular interest to modern artists?

Indeed, even when tribal objects are *all* drawn from a single culture, ethnological museums have their headaches re-creating "contexts" – which often end up looking more surreal than convincing.[25] Like Picasso, we are aware that certain qualities of any work of art are lost when its original context disappears. "Recapturing" that context is at best not only profoundly difficult and bound to incompleteness, but often wholly impossible, however hard we try. Such retrievals of context are all the more difficult in so-called tribal cultures, which had no written language, and hence left no historical records.

Picasso's (and our) assumption that great works of art not only contain the genius of their particular culture but at once subsume and transcend these particulars to speak across time and place to other cultures, is what Clifford rejects as an "ahistorical universal." Yet for those of us who deeply experience art, this power is self-evident. To be sure, even within the Western tradition, we do not "see" what Phidias's public saw any more than we "hear" Mozart with the ear of his time. But what we *do* see and hear nevertheless provides us with such a profound and satisfying ordering of experience that our sense of an ultimately common humanity is reinforced.

To digress for one paragraph about my personal experience: in Brooklyn, where I was born, I spent much of my free time – that not devoted to football and street-hockey – in the Brooklyn Museum, especially in its splendid Egyptian collection. Later, I studied ancient history and Egyptian art in graduate school and *in situ*, studied hieroglyphics and read substantially from surviving Egyptian texts – all of which served me in teaching Egyptian art on both the undergraduate and graduate levels. Much of this learning confirmed and enriched my feelings about Egyptian culture. Yet nothing I studied so convincingly communicated to me the sense of the Egyptian ethos, and the fundamentally static and wholly concrete nature of Egyptian thought, than those sculptures I had already seen and others like them. Clifford notwithstanding, "ignorance of cultural context" – whatever the context – could never be considered by me or my colleagues "almost a precondition for artistic appreciation." On the contrary, we are art historians rather than simply critics precisely because we believe context may enormously enhance our experience of art. This said, however, we cannot accept, as Clifford confidently does, that knowledge of a work's cultural context – whether tribal, Egyptian, or anything else – constitutes a *sine qua non* for its artistic appreciation

Although *"Primitivism" in the 20th Century Art* was the major whipping-boy for Clifford's article, he used the occasion to discuss exhibitions of tribal art in a number of other New York institutions. Collection installations and temporary exhibitions at the African Center, the American Museum of Natural History, the Metropolitan Museum of Art, and the IBM Gallery come in for varying citicisms. Only two exhibitions merited Clifford's unqualified approval. One was *The Asante*, at the American Museum of Natural History, which originated at London's Museum of Mankind.[26] "Although the Asante display centers on eighteenth- and nineteenth century artifacts," Clifford reported, "evidence of twentieth-century colonial suppression...is included, along with color photos and newly made "traditional" objects brought to New York as gifts for the museum. In this exhibition the *location* of the art on display – the sense of where, to whom, and in what time(s) it belongs – is quite different from the location of the African objects at MoMA or in the Rockefeller wing [of the Metropolitan Museum of Art]. The tribal is fully historical."[27]

Well, not quite. Nowhere in Clifford's appreciation, or in *The Asante* exhibition itself, or in its catalogue, is there any reference to the fact that the power of richness of that Gold Coast kingdom – which paid for its profusion of wrought gold works – was rendered possible in part by its role as one of the three or four major slave-exporting markets of Africa, or that some of the exquisite jewelry and regalia exhibited was, in effect, pruchased by this intra-African imperialist power with a significant share of proceeds from the sale to slave traders of some twenty million African blacks – surely a notable omission from the critique of a scholar who bends over backwards to cast Pablo Picasso as an unwitting tool of the imperial West.

1. Thomas McEvilley, "Doctor Lawyer Indian Chief: '"Primitivism" in 20th Century Art' at the Museum of Modern Art in 1984," *Artforum* 23, no. 3 (November 1984): 54-61; for Rubin's and Varnedoe's responses to McEvilley, and his reply, see "Letters: On "Doctor Lawyer Indian Chief: ""Primitivism" in 20th Century Art" at the Museum of Modern Art in 1984,""' *Artforum* 23, no. 5 (February 1985): 42-51; for the subsequent exchange between Rubin and McEvilley, see "Letters: On "Doctor Lawyer Indian Chief": Part II," *Artforum* 23, no. 9 (May 1985): 63-71; see also a related article: Kirk Varnedoe, "On the Claims and Critics of the "Primitivism" Show," *Art in America* 73, no. 5 (May 1985): 11-20.

2. In James Clifford, *The Predicament of Culture: Twentieth-Century Ethnography, Literature, and Art* (Cambridge: Harvard University Press, 1988).

3. This particular set of attitudes is widely (though by no means universally) shared in university anthropology departments. Indeed, the very concept of political correctness has developed largely as an American academic phenomenon. There is a certain irony in the fact that the philosophical ideas which form the background of political correctness are mainly French, and yet nothing comparable with Clifford's response to our book was seen in France, where *"Primitivism" in 20th Century Art* was widely praised and received – among other recognitions – the Vasari prize as the best book about art of the year.

4. André Salmon, "L'Art nègre," in *Propos d'ateliers* (Paris: G. Crès, 1922).

5. Clifford, 197.

6. Ibid., 196.

7. Ibid., 192.

8. Ibid.

9. Ibid. Clifford bases this assumption on a "principle" of the anthropological method he calls "limitation of possibilities," which presumably produces these "coincidences": "Invention," he argues, "while highly diverse, is not infinite. The human body, for example, with its two eyes, four limbs, bilateral arrangement of features, front and back, and so on, will be represented and stylized in a limited number of ways" (p. 191).

In anthropological theory such representations may appear "limited," but from a mathematical point of view the options for representing or symbolizing the human body in its different aspects and positions are so numerous as to be, practically speaking, infinite. Not a day goes by without artists finding new ways to figure (represent) the human body, as modern art in general and Picasso in particular have amply demonstrated. And why limit the invention of the human face, for example, to two eyes, when any number of tribal as well as modern artists (as was demonstrated in our exhibition) have posited three or more.

10. In my introductory chapter alone, there are numerous discussions of such configurational similarities; see, for instance, the comparison of a Dogon seated couple and Lipchitz's *Seated Man* (*"Primitivism"*, pp. 50-51), which refers to morphological similarities based on straight lines, right angles, and simple curves, a common frontality, the unusual but similar positioning of the hands and feet, the incising of details, the common monochrony, etc. Such configurational discussions abound in our book.

11. Clifford, 192.

12. Ibid.

13. German artists showed no interest, to my knowledge, in what little Ife material was in their museums. Greater familiarity with Ife objects began only with the large archeological find of 1938. The publication of this material – outside the purely scholarly literature – has all taken place since the end of World War II.

14. Clifford, 191.

15. Ibid., 193.

16. As, for example, our discussion, on such a label, of the "Creative misreading" by Klee of the support lozenges of Kota reliquaries as the legs of dancing figures.

17. To take just a few of the discussions in my opening chapter alone: the transformation of constituents from Hongwe reliquary figures in Brancusi's *Madame L. R.* (pp. 18-19); Picasso's transformation of the cylindrical eyes of Grebo masks into the protruding sound hole of his 1912 *Guitar* (pp. 18-21); Ernst's transformation of the Easter Island Bird-Man relief in the British Museum, in his stone sculpture *Oval Bird* and oil painting *Inside the Sight: The Egg* (pp. 25-29); the way in which the Zuni War God in the Museum für Völkerkunde, Berlin, in "a fascinating instance of modernist transformation," becomes Klee's *Mask of Fear* (pp. 29-32).

18. "Le affinità primitive," *L'Espresso* (October 28, 1984); Eco found *"Primitivism" in 20th Century Art* "one of the most beautiful and most fascinating shows I have had the fortune to come upon in recent years"; he characterized its book as "a precious reference work without which it would be impossible in the future to speak with any precision of the relationship of tribal art to the history of modernism."

19. Clifford, 193.

20. Ibid., 198.

21. Ibid., 212.

22. Ibid., 200.

23. For the record, the entrance-panel text to which Clifford referred read as follows:

"Primitivism" in 20th Century Art explores tribal art from the perspective of modern Western artists, most of whom knew little about the context or functions of the tribal objects they admired. As our focus is on the modernists' experience of tribal art, and not on ethnological study, we have not included anthropological hypotheses regarding the religious or social purposes that originally surrounded these objects. Prior to the 1920s, at which time a few Surrealists became *amateurs* of ethnology, artists generally did not know – nor evidently much care – about such matters. This is not to imply that they were uninterested in "meanings," but rather that the meanings which concerned them were the ones that could be apprehended through the objects themselves.

24. For our book, we solicited the paricipation of anthropologists and historians of tribal art, but not to discuss matters of African or Oceanic context. Their help was essential in establishing the dates at which various types of tribal art arrived in the West, and where they would or would not have been visible to modern artists. Chapters on this subject were contributed by Jean-Louis Paudrat, Philippe Peltier, and Christian F. Feest.

25. *The Asante*, an exhibition created by the Museum of Mankind, London (see below Clifford's admiration for this project), contained a wealth of magnificent material, but the "contextual recreation" – of the thatched hut/*son et lumière* variety – was so patently artificial that one might well have preferred no such "context" at all.

26. See Malcolm McLeod, *The Asante* (London: British Museum Publications, 1981).

27. Clifford, 210-11.

William Rubin

Der Primitivismus in der Moderne

Eine Einführung

Der Primitivismus – die Anregung des Denkens und Schaffens moderner Künstler durch Kunst und Kultur der Naturvölker[1] – gehört zu den Schlüsselthemen der Kunst des 20. Jahrhunderts. Wie sehr für das Verständnis der Moderne auch von Bedeutung, hat der Primitivismus allerdings bisher nur ein relativ geringes Interesse gefunden. Die unübersehbare Bibliographie zur modernen Kunst enthält lediglich zwei aufschlußreiche Publikationen zu diesem Thema: den vor einem halben Jahrhundert erstmals erschienenen Text Robert Goldwaters, der von wegweisender Bedeutung ist, sowie eine Abhandlung Jean Laudes. Sie wurde vor zwei Jahrzehnten verfaßt, ist in Umfang und Betrachtungsweise begrenzter und wurde – mittlerweile längst vergriffen – nie aus dem Französischen übersetzt.[2] Besondere und wichtige Sammlungen, zu denen jene PICASSOS gehört, waren den Autoren verschlossen; ebenso die bedeutenden Dokumentationen, die mittlerweile zugänglich sind. Die Notwendigkeit für eine wissenschaftlich fundierte Literatur, die der historischen Bedeutung des Themas gerecht wird, ist am außergewöhnlichen Umfang der gegenwärtigen Unternehmung zu erkennen, obwohl dieses Buch bestenfalls als ein Anfang gelten kann.

Nach eingehender Überlegung verwundert es eigentlich kaum, daß der Primitivismus so wenig Beachtung gefunden hat. Jede kluge Untersuchung dieses Phänomens setzt nämlich die Vertrautheit mit beiden Gebieten der Kunst voraus – primitiver Kultur und Moderne –, deren Überschneidung innerhalb der modernen westlichen Kultur diese Erscheinung des Primitivismus bedingt. Das Studium beider Bereiche blieb traditionell getrennt. Bis vor kurzem waren die Stammesobjekte – zumindest im Bereich der Forschung und des Museums – weitgehend eine Domäne der Völkerkundler. Erst seit dem Zweiten Weltkrieg hat das Fach Kunstgeschichte diesem Stoff seine Aufmerksamkeit zugewandt. Und doch sind Graduiertenprogramme über primitive Kunst[3] nach wie vor vergleichsweise selten und nur wenige Studenten dieser Programme betreiben zugleich Untersuchungen über die Moderne. Es überrascht daher keineswegs, daß vieles von dem, was Historiker des 20. Jahrhunderts über den Eingriff der Stammeskunst in die Entfaltung der Moderne gesagt haben, falsch ist. In Unkenntnis der Chronologie von Ankunft und Verbreitung primitiver Objekte im Westen haben sie in typischer Weise Thesen über Einflüsse aufgestellt, die unhaltbar sind. Als ein Beispiel verweise ich auf die Tatsache, daß keiner der vier Maskentypen, die von bedeutenden Gelehrten als mögliche Quellen für *Les Demoiselles d'Avignon* vorgeschlagen wurden, von PICASSO vor 1907 – als er das Bild schuf – in Paris gesehen werden konnte.[4] Auf der anderen Seite haben nur wenige Kenner der Kunst primitiver Völker mehr als nur ein flüchtiges Wissen über moderne Kunst. Ihre gelegentlichen Äußerungen über sie verraten manchmal eine überraschende Naivität.[5]

Die Blickwinkel, aus denen heraus Anthropologen sowie Historiker der Kunst Afrikas und Ozeaniens Stammesobjekte beleuchten, ergänzen sich letztlich stärker als daß sie sich widersprechen würden. Beide Forschungsrichtungen sind selbstverständlich darum bemüht, die Skulpturen der Eingeborenen in ihrem Entstehungszusammenhang zu verstehen. Bei der Beschäftigung mit der Geschichte des Primitivismus verfolge ich demgegenüber ganz andere Ziele: Ich möchte die primitiven Skulpturen im Sinne des westlichen Kontextes verstehen, innerhalb dessen sie von modernen Künstlern »entdeckt« wurden. Das Interesse der Völkerkundler gilt in erster Linie der spezifischen Funktion und Bedeutung jedes dieser Objekte, was aber für meine Fragestellung irrelevant ist, es sei denn, daß diese Tatsachen den fraglichen Künstlern aus der Moderne bekannt gewesen wären. Doch waren die Künstler vor den 20er Jahren, zu einer Zeit, als einige Surrealisten Amateur-Völkerkundler wurden, im allgemeinen über solche Dinge nicht informiert und kümmerten sich auch wenig darum.[6] Dies soll nicht heißen, daß sie an »Bedeutungen« nicht interessiert waren, sondern daß sie sich nur für solche Bedeutungen interessierten, die den Objekten selbst entnommen werden konnten. Wenn ich daher von der Perspektive der Moderne bei der Betrachtung dieser Skulpturen ausgehe (die wie jede Perspektive von ihrer Definition her Voreingenommenheit impliziert), werde ich gleichwohl versuchen, daraus eine Tugend zu machen, in der Hoffnung, daß diese Methode trotz ihrer Unvollständigkeit – es geht ja zunächst um die Beleuchtung der modernen Kunst – ein neues Licht auch auf die primitiven Objekte wirft.

Betrachtungen zu unserem Thema litten unter einiger Verwirrung über die Definition von Primitivismus. Der Begriff wurde erstmals im Frankreich des 19. Jahrhunderts gebraucht und fand als streng kunsthistorischer Terminus offizielle Aufnahme in das Französische über den siebenbändigen *Nouveau Larousse illustré*, der zwischen 1897 und 1904 erschien: »n. m. B.-arts. Imitation des primitifs.«[7] Obwohl der Hinweis des Larousse auf »imitation« gleichermaßen zu eng und zu weitgefaßt war, ist der Sinn dieser Definition – Malerei und Skulptur, die von früheren, »primitiv« genannten Künstlern beeinflußt

□ 1 *›Weibliche Figur‹ (Göttin Kawe), Nukuoro, Karolineninseln, Holz, Höhe 217 cm. Auckland Institute and Museum, Auckland, Neuseeland.*

☐ 2 *›Malanggan‹ (siehe Glossar), Neuirland, bemaltes Holz, Höhe 133 cm. Sammlung Serge Brignoni, Bern.*

wurde – seither von der Kunstgeschichte akzeptiert; nur die Identität der »Primitiven« hat sich gewandelt. Die Definition des Larousse spiegelt insofern den Gebrauch des Begriffs aus der Mitte des vorigen Jahrhunderts wider, als man unter den »Primitiven« zunächst die Italiener und Flamen des 14. und 15. Jahrhunderts verstand.

Bereits vor dem Erscheinen des *Nouveau Larousse illustré* hatten die Künstler den Begriff des »Primitiven« erweitert, so daß er nicht nur Romanik und Byzantinik einschloß, sondern eine ganze Reihe außereuropäischer Künste, angefangen von Peru bis hin zu Java. Entsprechend änderte sich der Sinn des »Primitivismus«. Kein Wort ließ aber bis jetzt an die Stammeskunst Afrikas oder Ozeaniens denken. Die Definitionen sollten diese Erdteile erst im 20. Jahrhundert berücksichtigen.

Während ›Primitivismus‹ zunächst als rein kunsthistorischer Begriff in Erscheinung trat, wurde seine Definition von einigen amerikanischen Wörterbüchern in der Folgezeit erweitert. Im *Webster* von 1934 taucht er erstmals als ein »Glaube an die Überlegenheit primitiven Lebens« auf, was eine »Rückkehr zur Natur« impliziert. Innerhalb dieses erweiterten Rahmens lautet die kunstbezogene Definition des *Webster* einfach: »die Verbundenheit mit oder Reaktion auf das, was primitiv ist«[8]. Dieses Verständnis des Begriffs setzte sich offenbar weiter durch, als ihn Goldwater 1938 im Titel seines Buches *Primitivism in Modern Painting* benutzte. Die allgemeine Übereinstimmung all dieser Definitionen von Primitivismus konnte dennoch einige Autoren nicht daran hindern, den Primitivismus (ein modernes Phänomen) mit der Kunst primitiver Völker zu verwechseln[9] (vgl. Anmerkung zur deutschen Ausgabe).

Primitivistische Maler des 19. Jahrhunderts schätzten die der Renaissance vorangegangenen Kunststile wegen ihrer »Einfachheit« und »Aufrichtigkeit«, Qualitäten, wie sie durch das Fehlen komplexer Hilfsmittel für illusionistische Beleuchtung und Perspektive bedingt schienen. Auch Strenge und Ausdruckskraft der Kunst vor der Renaissance suchten diese Künstler in der offiziellen Kunst ihrer Zeit vergeblich, die sich auf klassische und akademische Vorbilder berief. Je mehr die bürgerliche Gesellschaft Virtuosität und Finesse der Stile des Salons hochhielt, um so mehr fingen bestimmte Maler an, das Einfache und Naive wertzuschätzen, sogar das Rauhe und Grobe – bis zu dem Punkt, an dem einige primitivistische Künstler schließlich am Ende des 19. Jahrhunderts jene außereuropäische Kunst, die sie »wild« nannten, verehrten. Voller Bewunderung für diesen Begriff, verwendeten sie ihn zur Beschreibung praktisch jeder Kunst, die von der griechisch-römischen Linie des westlichen Realismus und seiner Neufassung und Systematisierung in der Renaissance abwich. Wenn wir vom heutigen Verständnis von »primitiv« und »wild« ausgehen, überrascht es uns, womit die Künstler im ausgehenden 19. Jahrhundert diese Adjektive in Verbindung brachten. Van Gogh verwies etwa auf die höfischen und theokratischen Stile der alten Ägypter und der Azteken Mexikos als »primitiv«, ja er charakterisierte sogar die von ihm verehrten japanischen Meister als »wilde« Künstler. Gauguin verwandte die Worte »primitiv« und »wild« für so unterschiedliche Stile wie jene Persiens, Ägyptens, Indiens, Javas, Kambodschas und Perus. Ein selbsternannter »Wilder«, fügte Gauguin später die Polynesier seiner bereits langen Liste von »Primitiven« hinzu. Er fühlte sich aber weniger von ihrer Kunst angezogen als von ihrer Religion und den Überresten ihrer Lebensweise. Jahr-

---

Anmerkung zur deutschen Ausgabe:

Nimmt man die Aufnahme in allgemeinbildende Lexika als Grundlage, so hat sich der Begriff ›Primitivismus‹ bis auf den heutigen Tag im deutschen Sprachgebrauch noch nicht ganz durchgesetzt. Bis in die jüngsten Ausgaben führen die klassischen deutschen Standardlexika ›Primitivismus‹ nicht auf. Erst im Duden von 1973 wird die streng kunstbezogene Definition gegeben: »moderne Kunstrichtung, die sich von der Kunst der Primitiven anregen läßt«. Selbst im engeren Bereich der Fachwissenschaft bediente man sich dieses Begriffes nur selten. Wie groß die Scheu ist, die in ihrer Bedeutung als ambivalent empfundenen Termini ›primitiv‹ oder ›Primitivismus‹ zu verwenden, belegt etwa der Titel der 1964 in der Berliner Akademie der Künste gezeigten Ausstellung *Das Ursprüngliche und die Moderne.* In den kurzen einleitenden Texten des Katalogs wird auf das Wort ›primitiv‹ zugunsten des synonym gebrauchten ›ursprünglich‹ konsequent verzichtet; ›Primitivismus‹ kommt gleichfalls nicht vor. Der Katalog der 1972 in München veranstalteten Ausstellung *Weltkulturen und moderne Kunst* folgte diesem recht gewählt wirkenden Wortgebrauch nicht. Werner Schmalenbach verwendet in seinem darin enthaltenen Artikel »Gauguins Begegnung mit der Welt der Naturvölker« ›Primitivismus‹ – ohne implizites Werturteil – innerhalb des deutschen Sprachraums als einer der ersten.

Früher – und in entschieden negativer Bewertung – taucht ›Primitivismus‹ im offiziellen Sprachgebrauch der DDR auf. Das Fremdwörterbuch des VEB-Verlags Leipzig von 1962 definiert den Begriff als eine »fortschrittsfeindliche künstlerische Richtung in kapitalistischen Ländern des 19. und 20. Jahrhunderts, die auf die Kunstäußerungen der auf niederer gesellschaftlicher Entwicklungsstufe stehenden Völker zurückgreift und sich dort neue Impulse verspricht«. Die ideologische Ächtung des Primitivismus bleibt in späteren Definitionen bestehen (»Tendenz zu gewolltem Archaismus und zu kindlich-naiver Darstellung«, Wörterbuch der deutschen Gegenwartssprache, 1974) und wird im Lexikon der Kunst von 1975 aus der Sicht der marxistischen Kunstphilosophie ausführlich begründet.

□ 3 *Roberto S.A. Matta, ›Eine ernste Lage‹, 1946, Öl auf Leinwand, 140 x 196 cm. Sammlung M. und E. Ludgin, in Aussicht gestellte Schenkung für das Museum of Contemporary Art, Chicago.*

zehnte bevor afrikanische und ozeanische Skulpturen für Künstler wichtig werden sollten, wurde die exotische Kunst – von GAUGUINS Generation noch als »primitiv« eingestuft – aufgrund vieler Eigenschaften bewundert, die die Künstler des 20. Jahrhunderts angesichts der Stammeskunst würdigt. Dazu gehörte vor allem eine Ausdruckskraft, die man in den letzten Phasen des westlichen Realismus, den die Avantgarde der Künstler als überfeinert und blutleer empfand, verloren glaubte. Mit Ausnahme von GAUGUINS Vorliebe für die Skulptur der Marquesas- und Osterinseln[10] zeigte doch kein Künstler des 19. Jahrhunderts irgendein künstlerisches Interesse an Stammeskunst, weder ozeanischer noch afrikanischer Provenienz. Unser heutiges Verständnis primitiver Kunst – weitgehend mit Stammesobjekten synonym – gehört ganz dem 20. Jahrhundert an.

Die ersten Jahrzehnte des 20. Jahrhunderts erlebten einen Wandel der Bedeutung wie auch eine Eingrenzung dessen, was als primitive Kunst galt. Mit der »Entdeckung« afrikanischer und ozeanischer Masken und Figurenplastiken durch MATISSE, DERAIN, VLAMINCK und PICASSO in den Jahren 1906–07 nahm eine streng moderne Interpretation des Begriffs ihren Anfang. Als sich der Schwerpunkt der Bedeutung auf Stammeskunst verlagerte, verschwand der ältere Gebrauch keinesfalls von heute auf morgen. »Primitive Kunst« wurde im folgenden Jahrhundertviertel einfach immer mehr mit Stammesobjekten identifiziert. Soweit es um avantgardistische Künstler des frühen 20. Jahrhunderts ging, war weitgehend afrikanische und ozeanische Kunst gemeint. Die Kenntnis der *INDIANER* (in Deutschland) und der *ESKIMOS* (auf die erst in den 20er und 30er Jahren Pariser Künstler näher eingingen) war nur oberflächlich.

In Paris wurde der Begriff »art nègre« (Negerkunst)[11] allmählich synonym für »primitive« Kunst gebraucht. Damit verengte sich offenbar das Spektrum der Bedeutung auf so etwas wie Stammeskunst.[12] Als ein Begriff, der afrikanischer Kunst hätte vorbehalten sein sollen, wurde er aber so locker angewandt, daß darunter auch die ozeanische Kunst fiel. Japanische, ägyptische, persische, kambodschanische und die meisten anderen nicht-westlichen höfischen Stile wurden erst in den 20er Jahren nicht mehr primitiv genannt. Das Wort fand allmählich nur noch auf die Stammeskunst Anwendung, für die es zum maßgebenden Gattungsbegriff wurde.[13] Das im folgenden Jahrzehnt von Goldwater verfaßte Buch verwendet »primitiv« synonym für afrikanische und ozeanische Kunst. Freilich wurden die präkolumbianischen höfischen Stile wie etwa die der *AZTEKEN*, *MAYAS* oder *INKAS* auch weiterhin primitiv genannt (und die Künstler unterschieden nicht immer zwischen diesen und der Stammeskunst). Doch handelt es sich hierbei um eine Inkonsequenz, die nunmehr als solche erkannt werden sollte. Von ihrem Stil, Charakter und ihren Voraussetzungen her ist die präkolumbianische höfische und theokratische Kunst Mittel- und Südamerikas mit den ägyptischen, javanesischen, persischen und anderen Stilen vergleichbar, die allesamt die Definition des Primitiven im ausgehenden 19. Jahrhundert

□ 4 *›Maske‹, DAN (Elfenbeinküste oder Liberia), Holz und Fasern, Höhe 23 cm. Sammlung Charles Ratton, Paris.*

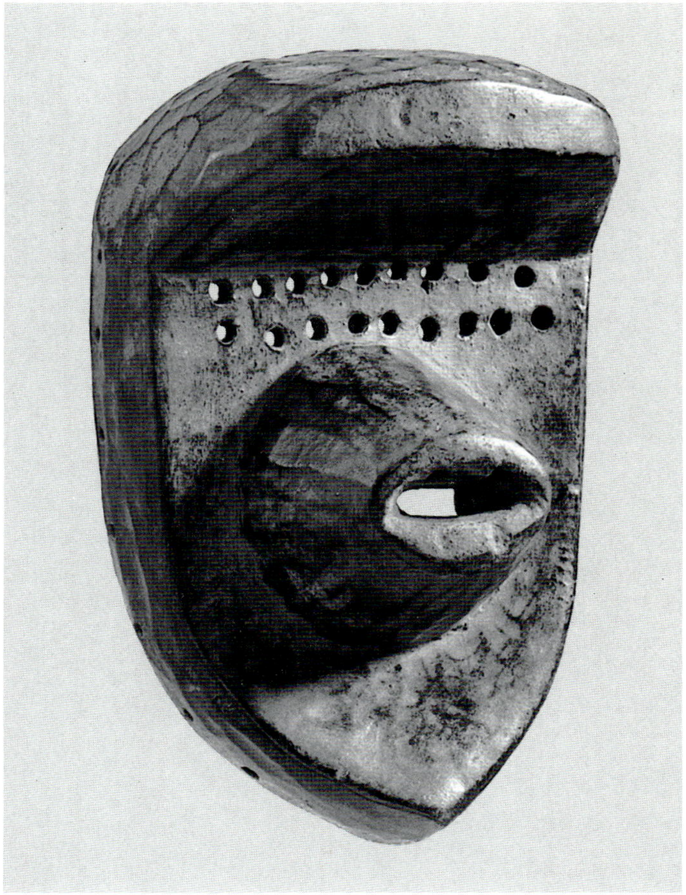

□ 5 *›Maske‹, DAN (Elfenbeinküste oder Liberia), Holz, Höhe 25 cm. Privatsammlung.*

□ 6 *›Maske‹, DAN (Elfenbeinküste oder Liberia), Holz, Höhe 22 cm. Privatsammlung.*

□ 7 *›Maske‹, DAN (Elfenbeinküste oder Liberia), Holz, Höhe 23 cm. Privatsammlung.*

trugen.[14] Der fortschreitende Bedeutungswandel des Begriffs nach 1906 ist Ergebnis eines Geschmackswandels. Ganz entsprechend erfreute sich die präkolumbianische Hofkunst – mit Ausnahme von MOORE, den mexikanschen Muralisten und in einem geringeren Maße von GIACOMETTI – im frühen 20. Jahrhundert nur eines relativ beschränkten Interesses seitens der avantgardistischen Künstler. PICASSO war nicht der einzige, der sie als zu monumental, hieratisch und anscheinend monoton in der Wiederholung empfand. Der bei der Stammeskunst wahrgenommene Erfindungsreichtum und ihre Vielfalt entsprachen mehr dem Pioniergeist moderner Künstler.[15]

Die gerade erwähnte Erfindungsgabe, die in einigen afrikanischen und ozeanischen Gesellschaften zu einer oft erstaunlichen künstlerischen Vielgestaltigkeit führte, gehört zu den großen Gemeinsamkeiten der Kunst der Eingeborenen und der Moderne. Nur wenige der erhaltenen Skulpturen der *DAN* sind älter als hundert Jahre, und doch übertrifft das in ihren Arbeiten erkennbare Spektrum an Erfindungen dasjenige der Hofkünste bei weitem □ 4–9, auch wenn diese über viel längere Perioden entstanden – im Falle Ägyptens seit dem Alten Reich sogar über Jahrtausende.[16] Anders als die ägyptische Gesellschaft, die in ihrer Bildersprache höchsten Wert auf Statik und Kontinuität legte, schätzten die *DAN* nicht nur ausdrücklich die Vielfalt, sondern erkannten auch den Wert der Originalität bis zu einem gewissen Grad an. Wie die faszinierende Studie des Völkerkundlers P.J.L. Vandenhoute zeigte, waren die *DAN* sogar dazu bereit, »einen höheren sozialen Nutzen (in solcher Originalität) zu erkennen«.[17] Obwohl sich die Bildhauer der Eingeborenen an einen traditionellen Typenvorrat hielten, bezeugen die erhaltenen Arbeiten selbst, daß die einzelnen Schnitzer viel mehr Freiheit bei der Abänderung und Weiterentwicklung solcher Typen hatten, als viele Interpreten bisher angenommen haben. Relative Vielfalt und Flexibilität zeichnen ihre Kunst neben den zusätzlich auftretenden Wandlungsprozessen besonders aus – im Gegensatz zu den statischeren, hieratischeren Stilen der erwähnten Hofkulturen (auf die ich mich der Einfachheit halber unter dem Gattungsbegriff ›archaisch‹ beziehen werde, wie schon Goldwater vor mir, wenn damit auch eine leichte Erweiterung des sonst üblichen kunsthistorischen Gebrauchs dieses Begriffs erfolgt).[18]

In den beiden letzten Jahrzehnten sind die Worte ›primitiv‹ und ›Primitivismus‹ von einigen Kommentatoren als ethnozentrisch und pejorativ kritisiert worden, ohne daß solche Kritiker alternative Vorschläge für einen anderen Gattungsbegriff akzeptiert hätten. Für ›Primitivismus‹ ist bisher nicht einmal ein solcher Vorschlag gemacht worden. Daß der abgeleitete Begriff ›Primitivismus‹ ethnozentrisch ist, stimmt gewiß – und durchaus mit Recht, da er sich nicht auf die Stammeskunst selbst bezieht, sondern auf das Interesse des Westens und seiner Reaktion auf sie. Der Primitivismus ist daher ein Aspekt der Geschichte der modernen Kunst, nicht der Stammeskunst. In diesem Sinne ist der Begriff daher vergleichbar mit dem französischen Wort »japonisme«, das sich nicht direkt auf die Kunst und Kultur Japans bezieht, sondern auf die Begeisterung, die Europa jener entgegenbringt. Die Vorstellung, daß »Primitivismus« pejorativ gemeint sei, kann gleichwohl nur auf ein Mißverständnis des Ursprungs und Gebrauchs des Begriffs zurückgehen, dessen Implikationen jedoch rein affirmativ gewesen sind.

Einwände gegen das Adjektiv ›primitiv‹ zielen andererseits nicht ganz ungerechtfertigt auf den pejorativen Nebensinn einiger seiner vielfachen Bedeutungen.[19] Diese Bedeutungen

□ 8 *›Maske‹*, DAN *(Elfenbeinküste oder Liberia), Holz und Fasern, Höhe 23 cm. Privatsammlung.*

□ 9 *›Maske‹*, DAN *(Elfenbeinküste oder Liberia), Holz, Höhe 26 cm. Privatsammlung.*

☐ 10 *Robert Bénard, ›Die Landung Kapitän Cooks auf den Tongainseln‹, 18. Jh., Radierung. Bibliothèque du Musée de l'Homme, Paris. Die Verbindung des »Mythos vom Primitiven« mit dem »Mythos der Antike« ist an der Kleidung, den Figuren- und Gesichtstypen dieser Radierung erkennbar, die für die französische Übersetzung des Reiseberichts von James Cooks zweiter Pazifikexpedition (1772–75) angefertigt wurde. Als Vorlage diente ein Gemälde von William Hodges, einem Begleiter Cooks auf seiner Seereise, über Cooks Landung auf den Tonga (»freundlich«)-Inseln.*

hatten aber keinen Platz in seiner Definition oder in seinem Gebrauch als kunsthistorischer Begriff. Als Picasso in einem äußersten Kompliment behauptete, daß »primitive Skulptur niemals übertroffen wurde«,[20] sah er nichts Widersprüchliches – und gewiß auch nichts Pejoratives – darin, daß er das vertraute und erst jetzt angefochtene Adjektiv ›primitiv‹ benutzte, um auf jene Kunst hinzuweisen. Es ist genau jener, Bewunderung ausdrückende Sinn, den er und seine Freunde diesem Wort verliehen und der auch für seinen Gebrauch in der Kunstliteratur charakteristisch ist. In diesem engeren Sinne verstanden, hat der Begriff keinen weniger positiven Sinn als jede andere ästhetische Bezeichnung (›Gotik‹ und ›Barock‹ eingeschlossen, die beide zunächst als Schmähwörter gemünzt waren).[21] »In Verbindung mit dem Wort ›Kunst‹«, so Robert Goldwaters Beobachtung, »ist das Wort ›primitiv‹ frei von verächtlichem Beigeschmack«.[22] Nach wie vor begrüßenswert wäre es, wenn sich ein befriedigender Gattungsbegriff fände[23] (vgl. Anmerkung zur deutschen Ausgabe). So schlug William Fagg, der Nestor der britischen Völkerkundler in Afrika, vor, ›primitiv‹ universell durch ›Stammes-‹ [engl. ›tribal‹] zu ersetzen.[24] Aber die Kritiker, die Einwände gegen ›primitiv‹ erheben, wehren sich mit der gleichen, wenn nicht größeren Heftigkeit gegen diesen Begriff.[25]

Es ist klar, daß die Kunstgeschichte nicht das einzige Fach ist, das den Versuch unternahm und dabei scheiterte, einen Gattungsbegriff für das Primitive zu finden, der die Kritiker zufriedengestellt hätte. Nachdem er sich längere Zeit mit dem Problem befaßt hatte, notierte Claude Lévi-Strauss, daß es »trotz aller Unzulänglichkeiten und der verdienten Kritik, die geäußert wurde, scheint, als habe ›primitiv‹ durch das Fehlen eines besseren Begriffs im zeitgenössischen anthropologischen und soziologischen Vokabular fest Fuß gefaßt«. »Der Begriff ›primitiv‹«, so fuhr er fort, »scheint jetzt vor der Verwirrung, die seiner etymologischen Bedeutung innewohnt und von einem überkommenen Evolutionismus verstärkt wurde, sicher zu sein.« Dem fügte Lévi-Strauss – für die Bewunderer der Stammeskunst kaum nötig – folgendes hinzu: »Ein primitives Volk ist kein rückständiges oder retardiertes Volk; tatsächlich kann es im einen oder anderen Bereich einen Genius für Erfindung oder Handlung besitzen, der die Errungenschaften anderer Völker weit in den Schatten stellt.«[26] Diesen letzten Punkt erkannten moderne Künstler zu Anfang dieses Jahrhunderts, noch bevor die Auffassungen, wie sie Lévi-Strauss zusammenfaßte, anthropologisches oder kunsthistorisches Denken bestimmten.

Für die bürgerliche Öffentlichkeit des 19. Jahrhunderts, wenn nicht sogar für die Kunstliebhaber des 20. Jahrhunderts, besaß das Adjektiv ›primitiv‹ dennoch eine pejorative Bedeutung. Die Öffentlichkeit betrachtetet jede Kultur außerhalb Europas, jede Kunst jenseits der Maßstäbe der Beaux-Arts und der Stile der Salons – somit alle nicht-westliche Kunst und manches aus dem Westen – von vornherein als minderwertig. (Selbst Ruskin war der Meinung, daß es »in ganz Afrika, Asien und Amerika keine Kunst« gebe.) Sofern die »Fetische« eingeborener Völker überhaupt bekannt waren, galten sie als die ungebildeten Absonderlichkeiten der Barbaren. Die Stammesobjekte wurden damals überhaupt noch nicht als Kunst betrachtet. Anfangs in den »cabinets de curiosités« versammelt, wurden Masken und figürliche Plastiken (neben anderem Sammlungsgut) im späteren 19. Jahrhundert mehr und mehr in Völkerkundemuseen verwahrt, die keine Unterscheidung zwischen Kunst und Artefakt trafen. Als Artefakte wurden Anzeichen kulturellen Fortschritts betrachtet. Die zunehmende Popularisierung der Darwinschen Theorien im späteren 19. Jahrhundert konnte die Vorurteile über die Erzeugnisse der Naturvölker nur verstärken, deren Schöpfer auf die unterste Stufe der Leiter kultureller Evolution verwiesen wurden.

Anmerkung zur deutschen Ausgabe:

Wenn der Begriff ›primitiv‹ im vorliegenden Buch ganz im Gegensatz zu früheren deutschsprachigen Publikationen durchgehend ohne Anführungszeichen erscheint, so versteht es sich, daß er wertungsfrei und ganz im kunsthistorischen Sinne verwendet wird.

In unserem Kapitel über GAUGUIN werden wir in aller Ausführlichkeit auf eine ganz konträre westliche Sicht des Primitiven eingehen, die sich bereits im 18. Jahrhundert – vor allem in Frankreich – herauszubilden begann. Doch betraf diese positive Einstellung, deren bekannteste Verkörperung Jean-Jacques Rousseaus »Edler Wilder« darstellt, nur einen Teil der schmalen Bildungsschicht. Mehr noch, ihrem Charakter nach blieb sie literarisch und philosophisch und erfaßte nie die plastischen Künste. Im Gegensatz zur landläufigen Meinung neigte sie dazu, primitives Leben zu idealisieren, worauf sich die Idee eines irdischen Paradieses gründete. Diese war vor allem durch Vorstellungen von Polynesien, besonders Tahiti, angeregt.[27] Wenn wir diese Einstellung bis zu ihrem Ursprung in Montaignes Essay »Über Kannibalen« zurückverfolgen, wird erkennbar, daß die fraglichen Autoren das Primitive von Anfang an in erster Linie als ein Instrument erkannten, um ihre eigene Gesellschaft zu kritisieren. Diese deformierte ihrer Ansicht nach den von Natur aus verehrenswürdigen Geist der Menschheit, der ihnen im Paradies der Inseln noch lebendig zu sein schien.

Es bedarf nicht des Hinweises, daß die meisten dieser Autoren kaum eine Ahnung vom Leben in Polynesien oder anderen entfernten Gegenden hatten. Zu Recht kann ihre Gedankenwelt als der »Mythos des Primitiven« bezeichnet werden. Selbst bei jenen, die über erste Kontakte zu eingeborenen Völkern verfügten, wurde die Realität oft von Phantasien über das Primitive überrannt. So fand etwa der französische Forscher Bougainville, einer der Entdecker Tahitis, Anhaltspunkte dafür, daß es auf dieser Insel Kannibalismus gab. Aber all das ist in der klassischen Beschreibung der Insel als »la nouvelle Cythére« – das neue Cythera – vergessen. Indem er Tahiti mit der Insel der griechischen Mythologie, auf der die Menschen unter der Herrschaft der Venus in ständiger Harmonie, Schönheit und Liebe lebten, gleichsetzte, stellte Bougainville den »Mythos des Primitiven« mit dem schon lange etablierten, aber fast genauso unwirklichen »Mythos der Antike« auf eine Stufe. Dabei war es von geringer Bedeutung, daß die positive Einstellung gegenüber dem Primitiven, die wir beschrieben haben, mit der Wirklichkeit genauso wenig zu tun hatte wie jene negative Sicht. Von Anfang an war der Mythos das treibende Moment. Bis in das dritte Jahrzehnt des 20. Jahrhunderts übte er auf Künstler und Schriftsteller einen weit größeren Einfluß aus als irgendwelche Tatsachen über das Leben der Eingeborenen, die selbst den ersten Sozialwissenschaftlern kaum bekannt waren.

Dieses zum kritischen Instrument gewordene Interesse am Primitiven – sozusagen ein gegenkultureller Sturmbock – bestand noch in veränderter Form, als frühe avantgardistische Künstler des 20. Jahrhunderts ihre Aufmerksamkeit vom primitiven Leben auf die primitive Kunst verlagerten. Die Moderne ist, verglichen mit den Kunstauffassungen vergangener Gesellschaften, durch ihre wesenhaft kritische Haltung einzigartig; hiermit stand auch ihr Primitivismus in Einklang. Anders als frühere Künstler, deren Werke die kollektiven institutionalisierten Werte ihrer Kultur feierten, war bei den Pionieren der modernen Kunst auch dann, wenn eine solche Verherrlichung stattfand, Kritik mindestens implizit enthalten. RENOIRS *Bootsfest* bejahte etwa den Wert der Freude, des Vergnügens und der Zwanglosigkeit, kurz: sinnenhaften

□ 11 *›Musikinstrument‹*, PERE *(Zaire), Holz und Eisen, Höhe 79,5 cm. Etnografisch Museum, Antwerpen.*

Lebens. Schon dadurch übte er aber Kritik an den repressiven und streng klassenbewußten Konventionen der zeitgenössischen viktorianischen Moral. Die Idee der Kubisten, daß von der Skulptur eingeborener Völker etwas Wichtiges zu lernen sei – einer Kunst, deren Erscheinung und Voraussetzungen den vorherrschenden ästhetischen Normen diametral entgegengesetzt waren –, konnte von der bürgerlichen Kultur nur als ein Angriff auf ihre Werte verstanden werden.

Daß die Bewunderung moderner Künstler für diese Stammesobjekte in den Jahren 1907–14 weit verbreitet war, belegen Photoaufnahmen von Ateliers, Schriften, überlieferte Aussagen und selbstverständlich ihre Werke selbst in ausreichendem, wenn nicht vollem Maße. Künstler wie PICASSO, MATISSE, BRAQUE oder BRANCUSI waren sich der konzeptuellen Komplexität und Subtilität der besten Stücke eingeborener Kunst bewußt. Diese ist nur im Sinne einer Reduktion der bildnerischen Mittel einfach und nicht im Sinne geistiger Simplizität, wie man gemeinhin glaubte.[28] Daß die Skulptur der Eingeborenen heutzutage für viele einen wesentlichen Aspekt der Weltkunst darstellt, daß ihr die Kunstmuseen in zunehmendem Maße Ausstellungsräume, ja ganze Abteilungen zur Verfügung stellen, erklärt sich letztlich aus dem Triumph der Kunst der Avantgarde.[29] Den Reisenden, Kolonisten und Völkerkundlern haben wir die Ankunft dieser Objekte im Westen zu verdanken. Ihren Aufstieg vom Rang des Kuriosen und Handwerklichen zu bedeutender Kunst, ja überhaupt zum Status der Kunst ist jedoch vor allem der bahnbrechenden Überzeugung moderner Künstler zu verdanken.

GAUGUIN wird zu Recht als der eigentliche Ausgangspunkt für die Untersuchung des Primitivismus in der modernen Kunst angesehen, doch ist dessen Rolle weithin zu stark vereinfacht und mißverstanden worden, da sein Primitivismus mehr philosophischer als ästhetischer Natur war. Darüber hinaus zeigte GAUGUIN, wie wir bereits beobachteten, nur ein geringes Interesse an der Kunst der pazifischen Völker, unter denen er lebte.[30] Ob ein abgeändertes Tiki (siehe Glossar) von den Marquesasinseln auf einem Hügel □ 230 oder ein vergrößertes »sprechendes Brett« von den Osterinseln, das als Hintergrund für ein Porträt verwandt wurde □ 226 – polynesische Kunstwerke dienten GAUGUIN mehr als Symbole und dekorative Hilfsmittel, weniger als Vermittler für Einflüsse auf seinen Stil. Zwar finden wir in seinen Plastiken und einigen Gemälden eine Anzahl von Hinweisen auf polynesische Kunst, doch sind diese seltener und peripherer als seine Andeutungen nicht-westlicher höfischer Stile – aus Ägypten, Persien, Kambodscha und Java –, von denen wir heutzutage keinen mehr als primitiv bezeichnen. GAUGUIN verschmolz diese unterschiedlichen Interessen zu einer eklektischen Vision, die es erlaubte, zeitgenössische Frauen aus Tahiti in einer stehenden Haltung, die von javanesischen Skulpturen stammte □ 224, oder sitzend wie in der ägyptischen Malerei darzustellen □ 229. Solche nicht über die Stammeskunst vermittelten Anregungen übten auf GAUGUINS Stil eine größere Wirkung aus als die polynesischen Gegenstände, die er gelegentlich zitierte. Angesichts der Erniedrigung und Auflösung tahitischen Lebens, wie es die französische Kolonialisierung mit sich brachte, ist es nicht unangebracht, GAUGUINS Bildbericht über sein »Inselparadies« als das etwas hilflose Beispiel eines Lebens, das die Literatur nachahmt und damit als eine mimetische Neuinszenierung des »Mythos vom Primitiven« zu betrachten.

Dieser Mythos sollte im frühen 20. Jahrhundert bis zu einem gewissen Grad in der Kunst der Fauvisten fortbestehen – so etwa in DERAINS 1906 vollendetem Gemälde *Der Tanz*, wie dies aus der Beimischung exotischer Stile ersichtlich ist □ 263. Obwohl sie Gegenstände der Eingeborenen sammelten, bedeuten die Fauvisten hinsichtlich des Primitivismus wie auch in bezug auf allgemeine Fragen des Stils eher eine Synthese von Ideen des ausgehenden 19. Jahrhunderts als einen radikalen Neuanfang. Erst mit PICASSO und den Kubisten, deren Arbeiten auf den Ausdrucksgehalt wie auch die plastische Eigenart ganz bestimmter Gegenstände der Eingeborenen direkt eingehen, trat der Primitivismus in seine dem 20. Jahrhundert angehörende Phase ein. Stärker als die Arbeit der Fauvisten erfüllten die Kubisten den Begriff des Primitiven mit einer neuen, konkreteren, enger gefaßten und mehr ästhetisch orientierten Bedeutung. Selbst im Winter 1906–07, als der Fauvismus seinen Höhepunkt erlebte, kreiste das Verständnis des Primitiven um die archaische Kunst. DERAINS blockhafte Plastik *Der Kauernde* aus dieser Zeit □ 261 ist präkolumbianischer Hofkunst oder theokratischen Kunstformen, wie in der aztekischen Kultur, ähnlicher als irgendeiner afrikanischen oder ozeanischen Skulptur, die er gesehen haben könnte.[31] PICASSOS *Akt eines Pferdeführers*, Anfang 1906 gemalt, enthält ein Echo griechischer Kouroi der Archaik, während sein Schaffen im Spätjahr 1906 und Anfang 1907 ein Interesse an archaischer Skulptur aus den provinziellen Zentren des alten Iberien erkennen läßt □ 317.

Zwar hatten die Fauvisten 1906 afrikanische Kunst »entdeckt« und damit begonnen, die eine oder andere Skulptur meist von Kuriositätenhändlern zu erwerben, doch überrascht es kaum, daß die meisten Stücke, denen ihr Interesse galt – wie etwa die Figurinen der *VILI* und *YOMBE* □ 22, 260, Masken der *SHIRA-PUNU* □ 13 oder die ägyptisch anmutende Gelede-Masken der *YORUBA* □ 14 (siehe Glossar) –, gerade jene afrikanischen Objekte waren, die teilweise wegen ihres verhältnismäßig ausgeprägten Realismus der aus dem 19. Jahrhundert überlieferten Definition des Primitiven am meisten entsprachen. Es ist vermutet worden, daß der stilisierte Realismus und die figürlichen Typen der *YOMBE*-Plastik ihrerseits auf irgendeine Weise durch frühe westliche Missionare beeinflußt sind. Frühe Anthropologen sahen eine Verbindung zwischen ägyptischen und westafrikanischen Stilen,[32] und wenn man den besonders orientalisierenden Charakter der *SHIRA-PUNU*-Masken bedenkt, die sich direkt an den Exotismus à la GAUGUIN anschließen, wird diese ganze frühe Auswahl begreiflich. So hören wir denn kaum mehr mit Überraschung, daß MATISSE, als er im Herbst 1906 PICASSO erstmals eine afrikanische Holzarbeit zeigte, »über ägyptische Kunst sprach«, wie sich PICASSO erinnerte.[33]

Die Auswahl an afrikanischen (und ozeanischen) Objekten war in den Pariser Geschäften und auf dem Flohmarkt immer noch sehr begrenzt. Obwohl einige der fremder anmutenden, abstrakteren Objekte wie etwa die Reliquiarfiguren (siehe Glossar) der *KOTA* □ 342, 343, 347, 349, 413 auch schon vor der Jahrhundertwende leicht zu finden waren, ist 1906 nichts über sie zu vernehmen und kein avantgardistisches Werk zeigt zu diesem Zeitpunkt ihren Einfluß. Erst als die Wirkung von PICASSOS revolutionärem Bild *Les Demoiselles d'Avignon* einschlug, das er im späten Juni oder frühen Juli 1907 fertiggestellt hatte, öffnete sich das fortgeschrittene geschmackliche Emp-

□ 12 *›Bemalte Figur aus Holz‹, Huon (Papua-Neuguinea), Höhe 47 cm. Sammlung Serge Brignoni, Bern.*

□ 13 *›Maske‹*, SHIRA-PUNU *(Gabun oder Volksrepublik Kongo), Holz, Höhe 28 cm. Privatsammlung, Paris. Ehemals Sammlung Maurice de Vlaminck.*

□ 14 *›Gelede-Maske‹ (siehe Glossar),* YORUBA *(Volksrepublik Benin), bemaltes Holz, Höhe 17 cm. Musée de l'Homme, Paris.*

finden allmählich den Stammesobjekten, die eine noch größere Herausforderung waren. Während ›primitiv‹ auf dem Höhepunkt des Fauvismus (1906) noch immer archaische Hofkunst und (in zweiter Hinsicht) die naturalistischeren Stile Afrikas bezeichnete, hatten die Kubisten seit dem Ersten Weltkrieg nicht nur die Bedeutung des Wortes verändert – so daß nun vorrangig die Kunst Afrikas und Ozeaniens gemeint war –, sondern auch einige der herausforderndsten und abstraktesten Formen dieser Kulturen erprobt. In der typisch synkretistischen Weise moderner Künstler waren jedoch Einflüsse der Stammeskunst manchmal mit jenen exotischer Stile, populärer Kunst und Aspekten früherer westlicher Kunst vermischt. In den *Demoiselles* etwa sind nicht nur Anspielungen auf afrikanische und ozeanische Skulptur anzutreffen, sondern auch auf archaische Kunst (Iberien), den Manierismus (EL GRECO) und auf die frühe Moderne (CÉZANNE und GAUGUIN). Daher zeugt es nicht unbedingt von schlechter wissenschaftlicher Arbeit, wenn Autoren einzelnen Werken der Moderne ganz verschiedene und scheinbar widersprüchliche Quellen primitiver Kunst zuschreiben. Wenn man von der Eigenart des modernen Synkretismus ausgeht, ist mit solchen Bezügen zu rechnen.

Jene Art des Primitivismus im 20. Jahrhundert, die auf einzelne Werke der Stammeskunst Bezug nimmt, verschwand nach dem Zweiten Weltkrieg. Die Künstler hörten nicht ganz auf, Skulpturen der Naturvölker zu sammeln oder in ihnen nach Ideen Ausschau zu halten. Doch wurde diese Objekt-Objekt-Beziehung gerade in den letzten fünfzehn Jahren durch einen loseren, indirekteren und vor allem stärker intellektuell geprägten Primitivismus ersetzt. Dieser erhält seine Inspiration primär von *Ideen* darüber, wie die Stammesobjekte wirksam waren, oder über die Gesellschaften, denen sie entstammen. Bis zu einem gewissen Grade durch surrealistische Einstellungen gegenüber dem Primitiven vorbereitet, nimmt dieser »konzeptuelle Primitivismus« – der bestimmte Zwitterbildungen, Earthworks, Environments, Happenings (Spielarten »schamanistischen« Theaters) und andere Aktivitäten einschließt – seine Inspiration mehr aus Texten als aus Kunstwerken: den Schriften von Bataille, Leiris u.a. sowie besonders aus dem Strukturalismus von Lévi-Strauss.

Nicht ohne Absicht wies ich zur Erläuterung der Bedeutung des Primitivismus an früherer Stelle auf den Japonismus hin. Ich tat dies, weil die Beliebtheit, der sich japanische Kunst im späten 19. Jahrhundert in Frankreich erfreute, in der Kunst der Impressionisten und Postimpressionisten eine große Rolle spielte. Diese ist in den äußeren wie tieferen Aspekten mit der Bedeutung vergleichbar, die die Stammeskunst in der ersten Hälfte des 20. Jahrhunderts genoß. In beiden Fällen wurde jene Rolle ebenso häufig übertrieben wie auch unterbewertet. Wir sollten in Erinnerung halten, daß sich moderne Kunst eine einmalig breite Vielfalt von Quellen nutzbar machte. Das Wachstum der Museen seit dem frühen 19. Jahrhundert und noch mehr der Gebrauch der Photographie zu Dokumentationszwecken haben eine Welt von Bildern zugänglich gemacht, die frühere Künstler nie zu Gesicht bekamen. Höhepunkt dieser Entwicklung ist Malraux' Idee des »Museums

□ 15 *›Maske‹,* Baule *(Elfenbeinküste), bemaltes Holz, Höhe 35 cm. Privatsammlung, New York.*

□ 16 *›Maske‹,* Yaure *(Elfenbeinküste), Holz, Höhe 23 cm. Privatsammlung.*

ohne Wände«. Diese totale Verfügbarkeit aller historischen Quellen, die die Periode der Moderne von allen anderen absetzt, ist im Œuvre Picassos beispielhaft eingeschlossen.

Unter den Myriaden von Einflüssen, die von modernen Künstlern absorbiert werden, ragen die japanischen Holzschneider im 19. Jahrhundert und die Bildhauer der Eingeborenen im 20. durch die Nachhaltigkeit und Bedeutung ihrer Wirkung besonders heraus.[34] Aber von wie großer Bedeutung war dieser Einfluß genau? Zumindest im Hinblick auf die Stammeskunst bleibt die Antwort ungewiß, da die Untersuchung dieses Problems noch in ihren Anfängen steckt. Doch wird es nie möglich sein, zufriedenstellende Klarheit in diese Zusammenhänge zu bringen, weil die präzise Beschreibung des Wesens künstlerischer Übermittlung sowie das Erkennen, ganz zu schweigen von der Messung dieses Vorgangs, schwierig sind. Doch wenn wir es einerseits gelten lassen, daß die Stammeskunst den wichtigsten, nicht-westlichen Einfluß auf die Geschichte der Kunst des 20. Jahrhunderts darstellt, müssen wir andererseits die oft zu hörenden Behauptungen, daß »Negerkunst den Kubismus hervorbrachte« oder »primitive Kunst den gesamten Verlauf moderner Kunst veränderte«, aufgeben. Wie noch zu sehen sein wird, waren die zur Frage stehenden Wandlungsprozesse in der modernen Kunst bereits in vollem Gange, als avantgardistische Künstler erstmals auf Stammeskunst aufmerksam wurden. Sie verspürten ein Interesse und fingen an, primitive Kunst zu sammeln, eigentlich *weil* ihre eigenen Erkundungen solche Objekte plötzlich für ihre eigene Arbeit relevant gemacht hatten. Von Anfang an stellte das Interesse an Stammesskulptur somit eine Wahlverwandtschaft dar.

Veränderungen im Wesen moderner Kunst zwischen 1906 und 1908 erklären, warum die »art nègre« von Künstlern der Avantgarde gerade damals und nicht früher in Paris »entdeckt« wurde. Es sei daran erinnert, daß die Stammeskunst kaum ein verborgener Schatz war. Das ›Musée d'Ethnographie du Trocadéro‹ (jetzt ›Musée de l'Homme‹), das 1882 eröffnet worden war, hatte schon vor der Jahrhundertwende eine ansehnliche Sammlung ozeanischer wie auch afrikanischer Objekte zusammengetragen. Internationale Ausstellungen wie die 1889 und 1900 in Paris boten didaktische Präsentationen eingeborener Kultur, ja ganze Anhäufungen solcher Dinge. Viele afrikanische und – wenn auch weniger zahlreiche – ozeanische Skulpturen waren Jahrzehnte, bevor sie moderne Künstler aufgriffen, in Kuriositätenläden zu finden. Die Stammeskunst wird dennoch für die von Grund auf realistischen Maler der impressionistischen und postimpressionistischen Generation mit Ausnahme von Gauguin keine ästhetische Relevanz gehabt haben. Daraus ergibt sich, daß die »Entdeckung« afrikanischer Kunst in dem Moment erfolgte, als sie von der aktuellen Kunstentwicklung her unabdingbar wurde.

Auch frühere Künstler hatten offenbar dann und wann auch Arbeiten der Eingeborenen gekauft, wie aus unserer Photographie des Ateliers von Gustave Boulanger hervorgeht, eines Salonmalers aus dem vorigen Jahrhundert, der mit Gérôme nach Afrika reiste □ 19. Aber solche Objekte waren nur bunter Zierat für das Atelier; ein ernsthaftes ästhetisches Interesse an

□ 17 ›Maske‹, Fang (Gabun), bemaltes Holz, Höhe 48 cm. Musée National d'Art Moderne, Centre National d'Art et de Culture Georges Pompidou, Paris. Ehemals Sammlung Maurice de Vlaminck, André Derain. Farbabbildung □ 257.

□ 18 ›Bronzereplik der Fang-Maske‹ □ 17 von F. Rudier, 41,5 x 29 x 14,5 cm. Musée des Arts Africains et Océaniens, Paris. Ehemals Sammlung Ambroise Vollard.

ihnen wurde durch die vorherrschenden künstlerischen Konventionen verhindert.

Es bleibt natürlich die Frage nach wie vor offen, was denn genau innerhalb der Entwicklung moderner Kunst geschehen war, daß die Künstler 1906–07 für Stammeskunst plötzlich aufnahmebereit waren. Zweifelsohne gibt es hierauf mehr als eine richtige Antwort, doch bin ich davon überzeugt, daß der wichtigste Grund in dem fundamentalen Wandel des größten Teils avantgardistischer Kunst liegt, einem Übergang von jenen Stilen, die in der optischen Wahrnehmung verwurzelt sind, zu solchen, die sich auf geistige Konzeptionen berufen. Die Stile der Impressionisten und Postimpressionisten (Gauguin wieder teilweise ausgenommen) entstanden aus der konzentrierten Beobachtung der realen Welt. Die Schärfe der künstlerischen Wahrnehmung führte dabei in mancher Hinsicht zu Wirklichkeitssuggestionen, die ältere Malerei übertraf. Sicherlich gibt es keine rein aus der Wahrnehmung schöpfende Malerei; die Daten der Retina werden erst durch den Geist erfahren. Es genügt jedoch, daß ein Maler wie Monet eine Kunst so nah an

□ 19 ›Blick in das Atelier von Gustave Boulanger‹, Paris, um 1880. Nach allgemeiner Überzeugung wurden Masken und figürliche Plastik der Eingeborenen durch Künstler um 1906 entdeckt. Trifft dies für die ästhetische Würdigung dieser Gegenstände zwar zu, so waren doch Künstler des 19. Jahrhunderts bereits im Besitz afrikanischen Materials. Solche Gegenstände könnten von den Häfen West- oder Zentralafrikas ausgeführt worden sein, oder sie kamen vielleicht über arabische Händler aus Nordafrika nach Europa. Die Photographie zeigt zwischen diversen Kunstgegenständen, Gipsabgüssen, Kostümen und anderen Atelierrequisiten eine Maske (Pfeil!), die vermutlich auf den Stamm der Bobo-Fing oder Marka zurückgeht.

der Wahrheit optischer Eindrücke wie irgend möglich hervorbringen wollte. Darum ging es den Postimpressionisten viel weniger. Und wenn CÉZANNE auch auf der Wahrheit seiner Eindrücke *devant le motif* bestand, waren doch gerade seine Kompositionen mit Badenden nicht aus der Natur entnommen, sondern aus der Vorstellung entstanden – gelegentlich unter Zuhilfenahme anderer Kunst oder der Photographie.

GAUGUIN unternahm jedoch die ersten entscheidenden Schritte hin zu einer konzeptuellen, daher »synthetischeren« und viel stärker stilisierten Kunst. (Es sollte nicht vergessen werden, daß die Konzeptualisierung der Seheindrücke – deren Gestaltung nach einer geistigen Vorstellung – jeweils nur gradweise erfolgt; selbst im »hermetischen«, hochentwickelt analytischen Kubismus gibt es viele aus der Wahrnehmung stammende Komponenten.) GAUGUIN warf keinesfalls den Realismus des Impressionismus über Bord, aber er vermochte diesen – zumindest in seinen besten Gemälden – mit flachen dekorativen Wirkungen und stilisierten Formen zu verbinden. Vorläufer dafür gibt es nicht innerhalb des westlichen Realismus, sondern in so verschiedener, nicht-illusionistischer Kunst wie jener Ägyptens, des Mittelalters, Persiens, Perus oder in bretonischer (volkstümlicher) Malerei, auch in den dekorativen Künsten (so den populären ›images d'Epinal‹) oder in der Skulptur Kambodschas, Javas oder Polynesiens. All das war für CÉZANNE zu viel, der GAUGUIN als einen Schöpfer »chinesischer« Bilder ablehnte.[35] Nicht ohne eine gewisse Ironie sollte der Höhepunkt der konzeptuellen Richtung in den ersten Jahrzehnten unseres Jahrhunderts – PICASSOS und BRAQUES Kubismus – mehr auf der Kunst CÉZANNES als auf etwas anderem aufbauen. Doch wurde die neue konzeptuelle Betrachtung CÉZANNES durch die Kubisten ganz entscheidend durch ihre Erfahrung des Archaischen gefärbt – der konzeptuelle Stil, den CÉZANNE, da er sich noch der Seherfahrung verbunden fühlte, verschmäht hatte. Noch mehr war die Beurteilung CÉZANNES seitens der Kubisten durch ihre Vertrautheit mit der Stammeskunst bestimmt, von deren Existenz dieser überhaupt keine Notiz genommen hatte.

Der Übergang vom Wahrnehmungsbetonten zum Konzeptuellen fing bei GAUGUIN an, obschon er sich bereits bei MANET ankündigt und sich im Japonismus, der seit 1860 Fuß faßte, spiegelt. In den ersten Jahren des 20. Jahrhunderts festigte sich diese Transformation und zeitigte 1906, im Anschluß an die große Retrospektive GAUGUINS im Salon des Indépendants, erste Wirkungen. In jenem Jahr kaufte sich VLAMINCK die berühmte *FANG*-Maske, die er bald darauf an seinen Freund DERAIN weiterverkaufte. Sie ist seither für den Primitivismus unseres Jahrhunderts die Hauptikone der Stammeskunst ☐ 17.[36] Viel Aufhebens wurde von dieser Maske gemacht, und keine Diskussion über unser Thema versäumte es, ihrer zu gedenken. Sie wurde schließlich so berühmt, daß Ambroise Vollard, der Händler avantgardistischer Kunst, von ihr eine Edition in Bronze gießen ließ ☐ 18. Das Ganze hat etwas Lächerliches. Einmal von der schlechten Qualität der Maske abgesehen, zeigen die Gemälde DERAINS und VLAMINCKS in den unmittelbar folgenden Jahren keinerlei Reflex von ihr oder irgendeinem anderen Stück eingeborener Kunst.[37] Erst die Anregung PICASSOS durch die Stammeskunst in *Les Demoiselles d'Avignon* signalisiert den eigentlichen Durchbruch – ein Werk, das eine neue Stufe im Prozeß der Konzeptualisierung

☐ 20 *›Maske‹, FANG (Gabun), bemaltes Holz und Fasern, Höhe 63,5 cm. Sammlung G. und F. Schindler, New York.*

☐ 21 *Juan Gris, ›Reliquiarfigur‹ (siehe Glossar), 1922, Karton. Zerstört.*

darstellt, die er während seiner iberischen Periode begonnen hatte. Der Ruhm dieses Bildes verbreitete sich im Spätjahr 1907 in der kleinen Welt fortgeschrittener Künstler rasch, und mit ihm wurde die Stammeskunst zu einer drängenden Frage.

Die *FANG*-Maske DERAINS ist meiner Ansicht nach insofern von Bedeutung, als sie über die Situation unmittelbar vor der Entstehung der *Demoiselles* Aufschlüsse zuläßt. Zunächst ist ihr relativ stark ausgeprägter Realismus wichtig, den man bemerkt, wenn sie mit der auffallenden Abstraktion und Stilisierung in besseren und authentischeren *FANG*-Masken, etwa jenen, die BRAQUE und PICASSO etwas später erwarben ☐ 409, 419, oder gerade mit den Meisterwerken unter den Masken der *FANG* verglichen wird ☐ 20, 392. Dieser untypische Realismus war der entscheidende Faktor dafür, daß DERAINS Maske so schnell aufgenommen und populär wurde, wie es nur noch bei der frühen Beliebtheit der Masken der *SHIRA-PUNU* (von denen jene aus dem Besitz VLAMINCKS zumindest ein hervorragendes Beispiel war ☐ 13) sowie den Figurinen der *KONGO* ☐ 178 und *YOMBE* vorkam ☐ 171. Weiterhin ist DERAINS Stück strenggenommen von nur mittelmäßiger Qualität – ein Typus, der in Gabun schon um die Jahrhundertwende für den Verkauf in Serie produziert wurde.[38] Daher ist dessen Berühmtheit in jenen frühen Jahren auch ein Hinweis darauf, wie schwer gutes Material am Anfang unseres Jahrhunderts zugänglich war.[39] Auch wenn solche Provenienzen wie »ehemals Sammlung Derain« oder »ehemals Sammlung Matisse«, die – wie sich herausstellte – oft falsch waren,[40] den Handelswert erhöhten, war der überwiegende Teil der Gegenstände aus dem Besitz aller bedeutenderen Maler zu Beginn dieses Jahrhunderts doch sehr mittelmäßig. Dies lehrt der Vergleich mit den besten Beispielen derselben Typen, die wir kennen und die erst in späteren Jahren aus Afrika zu uns gelangten. (Mit Ausnahme einiger Objekte von großer historischer Bedeutung werden im vorliegenden Buch nur die besten Arbeiten Eingeborener aus diesen frühen Sammlungen der Künstler gezeigt; doch sind auch einige der weniger bemerkenswerten in diesem Buch aus dokumentarischen Gründen abgebildet.)

Die Sammlungen der Wegbereiter der Moderne waren vergleichsweise zweitklassig teils wegen des Mangels qualitätvoller primitiver Skulpturen auf dem Markt jener Jahre, teils wegen der Mittellosigkeit der Künstler. (JUAN GRIS etwa war ganz besonders arm; dies mag der Grund sein, warum er sich ein *KOTA*-Reliquiar aus Karton anfertigte ☐ 21.) Wichtiger noch, diese Mittelmäßigkeit weist auf die Tatsache hin, daß die meisten Künstler zumindest im üblichen Sinne keine eigentlichen Sammler waren. PICASSO ist dafür ein ganz besonderes Beispiel. Ich hatte Gelegenheit, in seinen Ateliers und später in den Sammlungen seiner Erben fast siebzig der ungefähr hundert primitiven Objekte zu sehen, die PICASSO besaß, und mir sind die besten der übrigen Stücke durch Photoaufnahmen bekannt. PICASSOS Masken und figürliche Skulpturen waren im Durchschnitt zweitklassig oder schlecht. Unter den etwas über hundert Beispielen gibt es nur etwa ein halbes Dutzend wirklich guter Stücke. Diese werden nicht nur durch qualitätslose Schnitzereien, sondern auch einige kaum authentische[41] »Touristen«-Fabrikate überschattet, die eingeborene Künstler zum Verkauf statt für rituelle Zwecke hergestellt hatten. Tatsächlich zeigt das früheste Photodokument von PICASSOS Stammeskunst, eine Aufnahme des Ateliers von 1908 ☐ 402, eine *YOMBE*-Plastik, die ohne Zweifel im Auftrag eines Europäers angefertigt worden war.[42]

PICASSO hat sich nicht das geringste daraus gemacht. Angesichts eines zweitklassigen Beispiels äußerte er mir gegenüber: »Man braucht nicht das Meisterstück, um die Idee zu erahnen.« Hier kommen wir zum springenden Punkt der Frage. Ein Stilentwurf oder dessen Elemente können zur Genüge durch zweitrangige oder – wie PICASSO bei dieser Gelegenheit selbst bemerkte – sogar Fälschungen veranschaulicht werden. (Im Grunde genommen bestand die komplette Sammlung des Surrealisten WIFREDO LAM, ohne daß es dieser gewußt hätte, aus Fälschungen.) PICASSO häufte die Objekte eher an, als daß er sie sammelte, und beim Kauf dieser Dinge waltete mehr die Leidenschaft als die Sorgfalt. (»Je ne suis pas collectionneur«, sagte er, wobei er das ›r‹ am Schluß unbarmherzig rollte, um seine Geringschätzung auszudrücken.) Ein Sammler versucht eine Erwerbung unter allen Aspekten zu kennen (vgl. die etymologische Bedeutung des Wortes ›connaisseur‹) und würdigt sie um ihres Wertes willen. Unter den großen Künstlern stand MATISSE diesem Geist des Kunstgenusses am nächsten. Für PICASSO, der normalerweise nicht einmal zwischen afrikanischer und ozeanischer Kunst unterschied, stellte die Skulptur der Eingeborenen in erster Linie eine Wahlverwandtschaft und erst danach ein zur Einverleibung dienendes Material dar. Zum erfolgreichen Sammeln ist es unumgänglich, nach den Gegenständen zu forschen und ihnen auf der Spur zu bleiben, sie eingehend zu untersuchen und miteinander zu vergleichen. Dafür hatte PICASSO weder Zeit noch Geduld. Er erwarb das Gros seiner frühen primitiven Skulpturen, wie er mir anvertraute, bei sonntäglichen Spaziergängen mit Fernande über den Flohmarkt.[43] Einige wenige »chasses aux nègres«, wie etwa anläßlich seines Besuches in Marseille im Jahre 1912, bilden hier die Ausnahme. Anders als der ernsthafte Sammler kaufte er eine Maske schon einfach wegen der Form ihrer Ohren, des

□ 22 ›Mutter mit Kind‹, YOMBE (Zaire), Holz, Höhe 30,5 cm. Sammlung Arman, New York.

□ 23 ›Sitzender König‹ KUBA (Zaire), Holz, Höhe 54,5 cm. The Trustees of the British Museum, London.

□ 24 ›Hocker‹, LUBA (Zaire), Holz, Höhe 57 cm. Privatsammlung.

□ 25 ›Figur aus Holz‹, BAULE (Elfenbeinküste), Höhe 60 cm. Privatsammlung.

Profils der Nase oder weil ihm ein Moment ihrer Gesamtgestaltung gefiel – vielleicht auch, um seine Freunde zu amüsieren.

So war PICASSOS große Menge an primitiver Skulptur – weit davon entfernt, ein privates Museum für Stammeskunst zu sein – über das ganze Atelier verteilt und anderen Objekten, die er von ihrer Erscheinung her anziehend fand, gleichwertig. Seine Sammlung reichte von Gemälden, Skulpturen und Textilien über Musikinstrumente (eingeborenen wie modernen Ursprungs) bis hin zu Nippes, Andenken und Spielzeug. PICASSO bewahrte sein Leben lang mit fetischistischer Hingabe dieses Material. Die beiden in einer Aufnahme von 1908 erkennbaren afrikanischen Gegenstände waren etwa für gut ein halbes Jahrhundert nicht mehr in seinem Atelier gesehen worden. Als sie in seinem Nachlaß wieder ans Licht kamen, wurde meine Vermutung, daß sich PICASSO niemals von ihnen getrennt hätte, bestätigt.

PICASSO erwarb über die Jahre eine Handvoll wirklich erlesener Stammesobjekte – doch nicht vermöge einer besonderen Anstrengung. Als sich die ersten auf »art nègre« spezialisierten Pariser Kunsthändler meist zwischen 1908 und dem Ausbruch des Ersten Weltkrieges etablierten – Emile Heymann (MATISSE' »nègrier de la rue de Rennes«), der schon in den 1880er Jahren tätig war, Joseph Brummer (mehr über ihn s. S. 125) und Paul Guillaume –, häuften sich in deren Besitz immer mehr Objekte von höherer Qualität an, die sie PICASSO zum Kauf anboten.[44] Mit Ausnahme eines schönen Tiki von den Marquesasinseln □ 373 und der vermutlich besseren seiner beiden *GREBO*-Masken □ 417 wurde jedoch PICASSOS erste Garnitur in den Jahren nach dem Ersten Weltkrieg oder sogar später angekauft. Händler moderner und eingeborener Kunst wie Guillaume und Louis Carré boten ihm diese Objekte im Austausch gegen eigenhändige Werke PICASSOS an.

Angesichts der Intentionen und des Geistes, in dem sich PICASSO und andere Vertreter der Moderne der Stammeskunst näherten, überrascht es uns nicht, daß ihre Sammlungen – sofern sie diesen Namen verdienen – von solchen, die *amateurs* der »art nègre« aufgebaut hatten, verschieden waren. Dieser Geschmacksunterschied, der besonders bei PICASSO auffällt, ist in der Tat ein sehr aufschlußreiches Symptom. Es geht dabei weniger um die Qualität als um Charakter und Stil. Nicht nur die unterschiedlichen Interessenschwerpunkte hinsichtlich des Herkunftsgebietes und der von Künstlern und Sammlern bevorzugten Typen versetzen uns in Erstaunen, sondern fast noch mehr eine entscheidende Diskrepanz in Wesen und Machart der Objekte.[45] Bestimmte Kunstformen der *FANG* □ 383, *KOTA* □ 344, 347, 349, *BAMBARA* □ 354–357 und *SENUFO* □ 167, 168 wurden von beiden Gruppen bevorzugt. Doch schätzten die Sammler besonders die »klassischen« Arbeiten der *BAULE* □ 272, *GURO* □ 595, *KUBA*, *LUBA* und *VILI* □ 260. Den von PICASSO bevorzugten abstrakten Stilen, die das Erscheinungsbild radikal verändern und für die die Masken der *BAGA* □ 29, 417 und *GREBO* □ 365, 366 stellvertretend stehen mögen – wir beschränken uns auf die zu Beginn des Jahrhunderts in Paris leicht erhältlichen Beispiele –, schenkten sie im allgemeinen wenig Beachtung. Die von Sammlern geschätzte »klassische« afrikanische Kunst □ 13, 15, 16, 22, 24, 25, 56, 272 steht in ihrem stilisierten Realismus weitgehend den archaischen Kunstformen nahe, welche die frühere Bedeutung von »primitiv« – aus der Zeit vor PICASSO – bestimmt hatten.

□ 26 *›Kifwebe-Maske‹ (siehe Glossar), SONGGE (Zaire), bemaltes Holz, Höhe 63 cm. Privatsammlung.*

Es trifft zu, daß viele Sammler der neueren Zeit von den hoch abstrakten, stark durch die Phantasie bestimmten Kifwebe-Masken der *SONGGE* angezogen wurden □ 26, die in Frankreich erst einige Jahre nach dem Ersten Weltkrieg allmählich zu erhalten waren. Doch waren diese vor 1950 für die meisten Sammler kaum von Interesse. Als solche Masken in einer gewissen Anzahl in den späten Dreißigern in Paris auftauchten, wurden sie mißtrauisch betrachtet – weitgehend aus denselben Gründen, weshalb *Les Demoiselles d'Avignon* □ 301, die mit den Kifwebe-Masken einiges gemeinsam haben, allgemein von dem an moderner Kunst interessierten Publikum als zu häßlich erachtet wurden, als das Bild 1939 erstmals zu sehen war.[46] Der Geschmackswandel der letzten Jahre, der den *Demoiselles d'Avignon* zu legendärem Ansehen verholfen hat, ist auch für die derzeitige Beliebtheit der Kifwebe-Masken verantwortlich.

Der »klassische« Geschmack in der afrikanischen Kunst, wie er durch Paul Guillaume und Charles Ratton – den beiden wichtigsten Händlern von »art nègre« in Paris – vertreten wurde, ist von der Auswahl PICASSOS völlig verschieden, seine afrikanischen Schnitzarbeiten waren im allgemeinen weniger realistisch und vor allem weniger »poliert«. Gerne sah dieser die Spuren des Meißels, um den Prozeß der künstlerischen Entscheidung zu erfassen. Guillaumes und Rattons Vorliebe, die sich mehr oder weniger mit franko-belgischen Geschmacksvorstellungen deckt, legt besonderen Wert auf hochverfeinerte, oft komplizierte handwerkliche Ausführung, glatt polierte oder patinierte Oberflächen sowie einen zurückhaltenden, stilisierten Realismus.[47] Im Gegensatz dazu sind grober Eindruck, »non finito«, geometrischer Charakter und außergewöhnliche Erfindungsgabe diejenigen Qualitäten, die – kaum überraschend – für viele avantgardistische Künstler bei ihrer Auswahl von Stammeskunst ausschlaggebend waren. (Einige Händler und Sammler gingen sogar so weit und beseitigten die rauhe und »ungefällige« Oberfläche, die afrikanische Objekte durch ihren rituellen Gebrauch angenommen hatten, kratzten sie bis auf das natürliche Holz weg und rieben die Stücke mit Wachs ein, bis sie wie Möbel glänzten.) Das Weiterleben »klassischen« Geschmacks hat zur Folge, daß einige der außergewöhnlichsten und erfindungsreichsten afrikanischen Gegenstände, wie etwa die erlesensten Figuren der *MUMUYE* □ 60 und Masken der *WURKUN* (ursprünglich *WAJA* genannt □ 184), heute trotz ihrer vergleichsweise großen Seltenheit geringer eingeschätzt werden als besonders schöne Masken der *BAULE* oder Karyatidenhocker der *LUBA* □ 602.[48] Dies mag auch bis zu einem gewissen Grad erklären, weshalb Sammler die afrikanische der ozeanischen Skulptur deutlich vorziehen oder innerhalb der ozeanischen Werke die polynesische der melanesischen Plastik.

Daß viele Sammler diesem »klassischen« Geschmack mit seiner offenkundigen Nähe zum »déjà vu« westlicher und mittelöstlicher Kultur treu blieben, verwundert kaum, wenn man die Unsicherheit der Sammler und den geschmacksbestimmenden Einfluß des Kunsthandels in Rechnung stellt. Überraschend ist nur, daß er von Kennern wie Guillaume, der ein wichtiger Händler avantgardistischer Kunst war, und dem mit solcher Kunst ebenfalls vertrauten Ratton gefördert wurde. Dieses franko-belgische Vorurteil über das, was in der afrikanischen Kunst als gut zu befinden sei, war so mächtig, daß selbst ein Sammler wie René Gaffé, dessen Entscheidungen beim Ankauf moderner Malerei zu den kühnsten und hellsichtigsten in diesem Jahrhundert gehören, beim Ankauf von Stammes-

□ 27 ›*Reliquiarfigur*‹, *ONGWE (Gabun), Holz, Messing und Kupfer, Höhe 53 cm. Privatsammlung, Paris. Abbildung der Rückseite* □ *487*.

kunst sehr viel konservativer war. In seinem 1945 erschienenen Buch über die Plastik des Kongo bildete er weitgehend die weich geglätteten, relativ realistischen Typen von *LUBA*- und *KUBA*-Objekten ab □ 23, während er die erfindungsreicheren Schnitzereien derselben Völker vernachlässigte □ 678, 701 und die viel kühneren und abstrakteren kongolesischen Meisterwerke der *SONGGE* □ 107, 172, *BEMBE* □ 163, *PERE* □ 8, *MBOLE* □ 775 und *ZANDE* völlig übersah.[49]

Guillaume oder Gaffé hätten dem ohne Zweifel entgegengehalten, daß die von ihnen bevorzugten »klassischen« Stile qualitativ die besten seien, die Afrika anzubieten habe. Ich kann diese Ansicht nicht nur nicht teilen, sondern vermute, daß ihr Urteil unbewußt ein Überbleibsel der alten evolutionären Voreingenommenheit ist, welche die realistischeren Typenreihen – jene, die in ihrem Charakter westlicher Kunst näher und von daher auch zugänglicher waren – an die Spitze der Wertskala stellte. Wenn die selbst durch so hochrangige Beispiele verkörperte Skulptur »klassisch« afrikanischer Kunst wie die Masken der *YAURE* □ 16, *BAULE* □ 15 und *GURO* □ 595 oder die Figuren der *HEMBA* □ 56 und *KUBA* □ 23 alles wäre, was die Stammeskunst des Kontinents anzubieten hätte, würde Afrika sehr viel weniger zum ästhetischen Wortschatz der Weltkunst beigetragen haben, als es wirklich der Fall ist.

Das Interesse der Künstler galt erwartungsgemäß jenen afrikanischen Schnitzereien, die im Vergleich zu den »klassischen« Typen mit der Kunst westlicher oder östlicher Kulturen weniger gemeinsam haben. Sie verkörpern aus der Perspektive der gesamten Geschichte der Kunst genau das, was an der Kunst Afrikas von ihrer Definition her am unverwechselbarsten afrikanisch ist.[50] Als sich moderne Künstler, mit den Kubisten angefangen, stärker zur plastischen Idee, die das Werk verkörperte, hingezogen fühlten als zum einfachen »Genuß«, kümmerte es sie nur wenig, daß die zu Beginn des Jahrhunderts erhältlichen phantasievolleren Typen im allgemeinen alles andere als erlesen waren. Seit den 30er Jahren wurde es dann allerdings möglich, auch in diesem abstrakteren Stil Meisterwerke anzutreffen. Der »klassische« Geschmack sollte aber die vorherrschende Vorliebe beim Sammeln afrikanischer Kunst bleiben. Nur jene wenigen Sammler bilden hier eine Ausnahme, die über die moderne Kunst auf jene andere Richtung gestoßen sind.

Es steht außer Frage, daß PICASSO und viele seiner Kollegen durch die Stammeskunst nachhaltig beeinflußt wurden. Ebenso wahr ist, daß die Stammeskunst keinen fundamentalen Wandel in der Richtung moderner Kunst herbeiführte. PICASSO faßte es kurz und bündig zusammen: »Die afrikanischen Skulpturen, die sich über mein Atelier verteilen, sind *eher Zeugen als Modelle*.«[51] Dies bedeutet, daß sie mehr Zeugen seiner Unternehmungen als Ausgangspunkt seiner Bildwerke waren. Wie die japanischen Drucke, von denen MANET und DEGAS fasziniert waren, führten die primitiven Objekte kaum zu einer Umorientierung der Geschichte moderner Malerei, sondern sie verstärkten und sanktionierten bereits in vollem Gange befindliche Entwicklungen. Trotzdem wählte PICASSO, der einen Instinkt für das *mot juste* besaß, seine Worte sorgfältig aus; seine Konstruktion »eher . . . als« sollte behutsam bedacht werden. Obwohl eher »Zeugen« als »Modelle«, waren die Skulpturen zugegebenermaßen bis zu einem gewissen Grade auch Modelle. Zunächst aufgrund ihrer Verwandtschaft mit den Zielen des Künstlers ausgewählt, nahmen die Objekte der Eingeborenen – einmal im Atelier angekommen – eine zweifache Rolle an und machten einigen Einfluß geltend.

In welchem Maße und welche Art von Einfluß diese Objekte ausübten, ist, wie bereits bemerkt, sehr schwer einzuschätzen. Goldwater nahm in seinem klassischen Text eine sehr konservative Haltung zu dieser Frage ein, der sich auch Laudes späteres Buch weitgehend anschloß. Während er von »dem tiefreichenden Einfluß des Primitiven auf das Moderne«[52] in sehr allgemeinen Begriffen sprach (»Anspielung und Anregung«), bestand Goldwater auf der »extremen Seltenheit eines direkten Einflusses primitiver Kunstformen« auf die Kunst des 20. Jahrhunderts.[53] Wie unsere Untersuchung zeigen wird, hat Goldwater diesen Aspekt des Problems viel zu stark unterbewertet. Darüber hinaus betrachtete er den Einfluß der Stammeskunst größtenteils als poetisch, philosophisch und psychologisch, während er ihr nur einen »sehr beschränkten formalen Einfluß«[54] zugestand. Nach Goldwater übernahm etwa BRANCUSI nie »spezifische Formen der Negerplastik«, und »sein Werk weist zu keiner Zeit eine Beziehung zu irgendeinem besonderen Stammesstil auf«. Und doch scheinen mir Haltung, Gestalt und konvex-konkave Struktur des Kopfes und die gelängte Form des Halses (wie auch die schräg vorspringende Frisur oder der »Kamm«) bei BRANCUSIS *Madame L. R.* (1914–18) fraglos von Reliquiarfiguren (siehe Glossar) der *ONGWE* abgeleitet zu sein □ 27. Weiterhin geht der besonders gestaltete Mund jenes Kopfes, der von der im übrigen zerstörten Skulptur *Der erste Schritt* (1913) erhalten ist, gewiß auf eine Skulptur der *BAMBARA* im Trocadéro zurück, wie S. Geist gezeigt hat □ 482. Weitere Vergleichsbeispiele können für das Werk vieler Künstler angeführt werden, deren Primitivismus Goldwater nur sehr allgemein diskutierte.

In den oben angeführten Beispielen sprechen die Gegenüberstellungen von modernen und afrikanischen Arbeiten für sich. Doch bin ich der festen Meinung, daß ein ganzer Bereich anderer Einflüsse existiert, *die genauso auf bestimmte Formen in einzelnen Stammesobjekten zurückgehen* –, bei denen aber ein einfacher Vergleich zwischen modernen und eingeborenen Arbeiten keinesfalls eine Beziehung aufzeigen würde. Ich betrachte es geradezu als axiomatisch, daß viele der wichtigsten und tiefsten Einflüsse der »art nègre« auf das Werk jener Künstler, die Stammeskunst bewunderten und sammelten, nicht einmal erkennbar sind und wir nie etwas von ihnen wissen werden. Für Künstler aller Perioden gilt: Wenn sie eine Kopfform, eine Körperhaltung, eine bestimmte Gestaltungsweise oder ein dekoratives Muster dem Werk anderer Künstler entlehnten, so erhielt das Angeeignete eine kompliziertere, weniger leicht erkennbare Gestalt. Dies gilt besonders für das 20. Jahrhundert, wenn man von der vielfachen Metamorphose optischer Eindrücke in den meisten modernen Stilen ausgeht.[55] In dem Moment, da die plastische Idee, ob sie nun bewußt oder unbewußt abgelehnt wird, völlig verarbeitet ist und im Zusammenhang mit dem ganz unterschiedlichen Stil des Entleihers wieder hervortritt, wird sie oft »unsichtbar«. Der Einfluß der Stammeskunst bildet keine Ausnahme von diesem Prinzip.

Da *diese* Form direkter Einflußnahme anhand einer Gegenüberstellung bestimmter Objekte (zumindest ohne einige Hinweise) nicht erkennbar ist, mag der Leser mit Recht fragen, auf welcher Grundlage ich dies postuliere. Abgesehen von den Aussagen einiger Künstler liegt die Antwort auf die Frage, wie der künstlerische Geist arbeitet, für mich in den Nebenwegen und indirekten Pfaden, auf denen er sein Ziel erreicht. Doch können wir zum Glück die Wirkung dieser Gruppe von Einflüssen anhand eines idealen Beispiels aus dem Werk PICASSOS illustrieren: mit Hilfe der Rolle, die eine seiner *GREBO*-Masken (Elfenbeinküste)[56] bei der Formulierung einer *Gitarre* aus Blech, der ersten seiner kubistisch konstruierten Skulpturen □ 30, spielte. Wir haben von diesem »unsichtbaren« Fall nur deshalb Kunde, weil PICASSO ausnahmsweise selbst darüber sprach – eine Form von Zeugnis, die bei Künstlern selten ist. Ein späteres Beispiel für eine derartige direkte Aussage gibt uns HENRY MOORE, der seine Plastik *Mondkopf* von 1964 zu einer Abbildung einer *MAMA*-Maske aus Nigeria in Beziehung setzte □ 942.

Picassos *Gitarre* ist einer *GREBO*-Maske nicht unmittelbar ähnlich. Ihre Formen und ihre Syntax sind demonstrativ kubistisch. Worin besteht dann der Zusammenhang mit der Maske? Die *Gitarre* entstand zu einer Zeit (Ende 1912[57]), als die transparenten, rudimentär illusionistischen Flächen von PICASSOS hochanalytischer kubistischer Malerei von 1910–12 unter dem Eindruck der Collage Bildern mit größeren, einfacheren und vor allem opakeren Formen gewichen waren. Diese For-

□ 28 *Constantin Brancusi, ›Madame L. R.‹, 1914–18, Holz, Höhe 94 cm. Privatsammlung. Eine weitere Abbildung □ 488.*

☐ 29 *›Maske‹*, GREBO *(Elfenbeinküste oder Liberia), bemaltes Holz und Fasern, Höhe 64 cm. Musée Picasso, Paris. Ehemals Sammlung Pablo Picasso.*

☐ 30 *Pablo Picasso, ›Gitarre‹ (Guitare), Blech und Draht, 77,5 x 35 19 cm. The Museum of Modern Art, New York. Geschenk des Künstlers. Eine weitere Abbildung* ☐ *416.*

men stellten weniger Beschreibungen der dargestellten Objekte dar als Zeichen für sie – die Bestandteile einer konzeptuellen Sprache, die wir mittlerweile synthetischen Kubismus nennen. An diesem Punkt entschied sich PICASSO dafür, seine Ideen in dreidimensionale Reliefs zu übersetzen, womit er eine völlig neue Form von Skulptur begründete, die, statt geschnitzt oder modelliert, *konstruiert* wurde (weitgehend aus Materialien, die für die Kunst neu waren). Innerhalb dieses Prozesses ersetzte PICASSO den mehr oder weniger soliden Kern oder »Monolithen«, der seit alters her bei gemeißelter oder modellierter Skulptur üblich war, durch Bildungen, die das Auge durchdringen kann. Ihre besondere Art kennzeichnet einen Großteil der besten Skulptur unserer heutigen Zeit.

PICASSO kam zur afrikanischen Kunst, weil er sie als »raisonnable« betrachtete, d. h. als Ergebnis eines verstandesmäßigen Prozesses, also konzeptuell. In einer *GREBO*-Maske *ähneln* die paarweise vorspringenden Zylinder und horizontalen Parallelstangen nicht so sehr Augen und Mund wie sie als Begriffszeichen dafür *stehen.* Dasselbe gilt für den ornamentierten, nach oben gekurvten Vorsprung, der oft die Stirn darstellen soll. Die reduzierte Zeichensprache solcher afrikanischen Masken würde PICASSO in jedem Fall zugesagt haben. Daß jenes »Gesicht«, aus dem Augen, Nase und Lippen hervortreten, keine reliefierte dreidimensionale Form besitzt wie die meisten anderen Masken, sondern eine ungebogene flache Tafel ist – wie die Flächen der *Gitarre* –, ist eine der Besonderheiten der *GREBO*-Masken, die gerade in jenem Moment von PICASSOS Entwicklung von großer Relevanz waren. PICASSO richtete sein Augenmerk gerade auf diesen Aspekt der *GREBO*-Masken, als er darüber sprach, fuhr aber mit der Bemerkung fort, daß das für ihn interessanteste Merkmal gerade jenes zylindrische Auge gewesen sei.

Während Nase und Lippen offenbar vorspringende Gesichtszüge seien, habe er – so bemerkte PICASSO – die Augen immer als ein zurücktretendes, »höhlenartiges« Element in der Skulptur empfunden, besonders wenn er mehr den »Kreisbogen« – die Augenhöhle – als das Auge selbst ausarbeitete. Er erinnerte sich, daß er es als junger, mit Lehm modellierender Bildhauer durch Eindrücken seines Daumens geformt hatte. Der Bildhauer der *GREBO* hätte nun, so wies PICASSO darauf hin, die vor- *und* zurückspringenden Gesichtsmerkmale systematisch durch vorspringende Formen konsequent angezeigt. Dies wäre ihm deshalb möglich gewesen, weil er nicht ein Gesicht abgebildet, sondern in ideographischer Sprache dargestellt hätte – ein vollkommenes Beispiel dafür, was PICASSO unter »raisonnable« in der Stammeskunst verstand.

Als der Künstler dies erzählte (erst Kahnweiler und später in ausführlicherer Form mir),[58] kam ihm die Lösung für die

Darstellung des Schallochs der *Gitarre* – ein von der Fläche des Hintergrundes vorspringender Zylinder – aufgrund der Anregung durch die Masken der *Grebo*. Die Vorderfläche der *Gitarre* wird, obwohl sie ganz unten und auf der rechten Seite erscheint, in der Mitte des »Musikinstrumentes« weggeschnitten. Das Problem könnte folgendermaßen formuliert werden: wie ein Loch in einer Fläche (die Vorderseite seiner *Gitarre*) markieren, das als solches eigentlich nicht existiert? Die Lösung bestand im Fall der *Grebo*-Maske darin, das Negative ins Positive umzukehren und das Loch als einen Hohlzylinder nach vorne zu projizieren. Die Aushöhlung von Picassos Zylinder war bereits in den kreisförmigen Rändern, die der Künstler der *Grebo* auf die Augenzylinder gemalt hatte, vorweggenommen worden.[59]

Diese von Picasso gefundene Lösung stand völlig mit seinen anderen bei der Herstellung der *Gitarre* getroffenen Entscheidungen in Einklang, um nicht zu sagen mit der ganzen Struktur von Entscheidungen, die den synthetischen Kubismus ausmachten und die allesamt ihrer eigenen Logik folgten. Es wäre daher unsinnig, die Bedeutung dieses speziellen und beschränkten Eingriffs von Stammeskunst selbst in einem Objekt, das eine skulpturale Revolution auslöste, überzubewerten. Wichtiger als sein spezieller Beitrag zur *Gitarre* ist die Art, wie dieser Eingriff Zeugnis von der zugrundeliegenden Verwandtschaft zwischen der Kunst der Moderne und der Eingeborenenkunst auf der Ebene der konzeptuellen Form ablegt. Wichtiger ist auch der Beweis dafür, wie bestimmte moderne Lesarten in der kubistischen Periode Objekten der Stammeskunst eine besondere Resonanz verliehen. Diese spezifisch »formalistische« Lesart – viele Lesarten von Stammesobjekten durch Picasso oder andere Vertreter der Moderne waren alles andere als formal – hatte wahrscheinlich überhaupt nichts mit dem zu tun, was der afrikanische Künstler ausdrücken wollte, auch wenn wir freilich nicht wissen, welche künstlerischen Intuitionen den Künstler, der den Stil der *Grebo* initiierte, motivierten.[60] Die Behauptung, daß diese Bildhauer normalerweise im Rahmen religiöser Notwendigkeiten und Werte ihre Funktion ausübten, sagt nichts, was nicht auch weitgehend für bestimmte westliche Stile gültig wäre; auch das Problem plastischer Lösungen stellte sich den primitiven Künstlern nach wie vor, selbst wenn sie sich nicht vorstellen konnten, was solche Worte meinen.

Eine Maske der *Grebo* ist darüber hinaus keine für den Blick durchlässige Skulptur, worauf mehr als einmal hingewiesen wurde, seit Kahnweiler erstmals von »Transparenz« bei der Herstellung von Verhältnissen zwischen den Objekten sprach. Interessant genug ist allerdings, daß Afrikaner wirklich solche Skulpturen, durch die man hindurchsehen kann, schufen, auch wenn diese 1912 in Paris nicht zu sehen waren. Ich beziehe mich hierbei nicht in erster Linie auf die allzu bekannten Haartrachten der *Senufo*, die gewissen »transparenten« Skulpturen von David Smith nahestehen □ 954, 955. Die großen Aufbauten der Masken verharren in einer einzigen Fläche und wurden wie die offen gearbeiteten Malanggane Neuirlands □ 77 aus einem einzigen Holzblock gehauen. Der viel seltenere und zuweilen außerordentlich komplexe Vogel-Kopfputz der Bildhauer der *Baga* war hingegen zugleich geschnitzt und aus verschiedenen Holzstücken konstruiert. Ihre komplizierten Raumbildungen in offener Arbeit, die mit heiter dekorativen Farben bemalt wurden, erinnern an die Konstruktionen des synthetischen Kubismus, wie sie von Baranoff-Rossiné und anderen Pariser Künstlern im unmittelbaren Gefolge von Picassos Entdeckun-

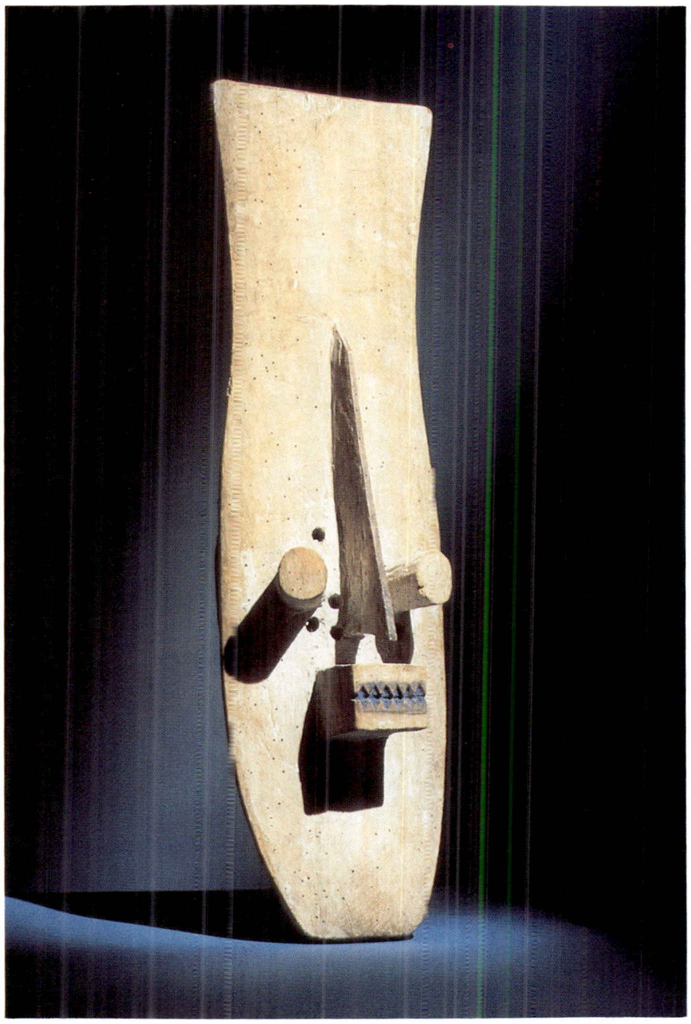

□ 31 *›Maske‹, Grebo (Elfenbeinküste oder Liberia), bemaltes Holz, Höhe 70 cm. The Metropolitan Museum of Art, The M. C. Rockefeller Memorial Collection, Vermächtnis N. A. Rockefeller, New York.*

gen geschaffen wurden □ 32, 33, 206. Wie würde der Vogel der *Baga*, den wir hier abbilden, in jenen Jahren Picasso interessiert haben! Aber dieser *rara avis* und andere seines Stammes gelangten erst in den 30er Jahren nach Paris.

Im Vergleich zu anderen Masken der *Grebo*, die um die Jahrhundertwende allmählich erhältlich wurden (Picasso wird das erlesene Exemplar, das 1901 in den Trocadéro gelangte, gesehen haben □ 332), stellt das hier abgebildete Beispiel aus dem Besitz Picassos eine Dutzendarbeit dar □ 29.[61] (Ein anderes, 1912 erworbenes Stück ist viel qualitätvoller; eine Zeichnung von 1917 zeigt es an einer Wand von Picassos Wohnung □ 418.) Wenn wir von dem ausgehen, was wir von Picassos Ansichten über die Objekte der Eingeborenen wissen, sollte es uns gleichwohl nicht überraschen, daß er sie trotz ihrer Mittelmäßigkeit in den höchsten Tönen lobte;[62] schließlich ist ihre »Idee« vollkommen klar. Dennoch ist es lehrreich, diese weniger bedeutende *Grebo*-Maske aus dem Besitz Picassos mit der Arbeit eines inspirierten Bildhauers zu vergleichen, etwa jener im Metropolitan Museum □ 31. Die grundlegenden stilistischen Bestandteile der *Grebo* sind beiden gemeinsam: eine stegartige Nase ohne Nasenlöcher, zylindrische Augen und parallele Lippen, wobei alles im rechten Winkel von einer sonst flachen Tafel vorspringt. Und doch, welch ein Unterschied! Das Beispiel aus dem Metropolitan Museum ist nicht

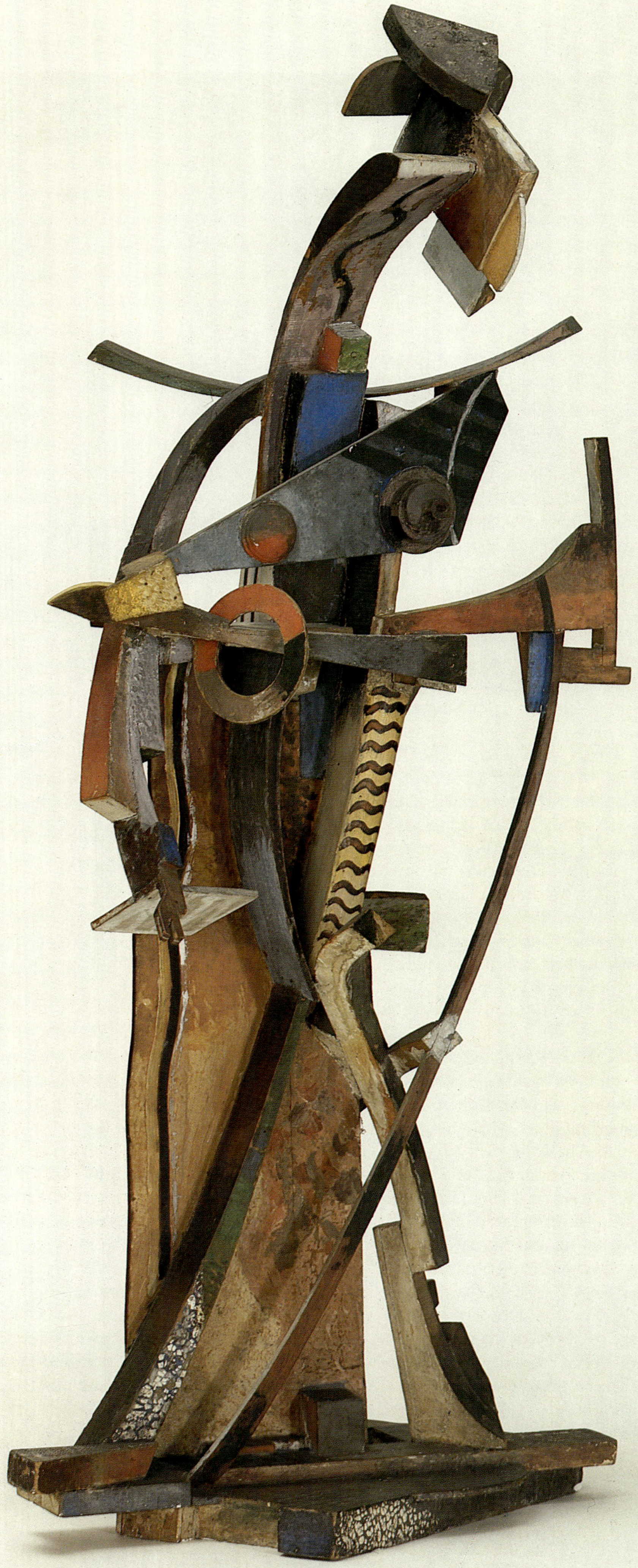

◁ ☐ 32 *Vladimir Baranoff-Rossiné, ›Symphonie Nummer 1‹, 1913, farbige Hölzer und verschiedene Materialien, 161 x 72 x 63 cm. The Museum of Modern Art, Katia Granoff Fund, New York.*

☐ 33 *›Vogel-Kopf-schmuck‹,* Baga *(Guinea), bemaltes Holz, Höhe 52 cm. Musée de l'Homme, Paris.*

nur subtiler in der Proportionierung und Verteilung der gemeinsamen Elemente und im Gebrauch der Farbe, sondern auch in der leicht konvexen Wölbung der Hauptfläche. Darüber hinaus enthält es etwas, das nur wirklich künstlerischer Phantasie entsprungen sein kann. Statt die Hörner darzustellen, hat der Künstler ihre Krümmung in der wunderbaren Verlängerung des Hauptplans absorbiert, wo sie nur zu erahnen sind. (Der Grad dieses künstlerischen Einfalls wird natürlich von solchen im Westen unbekannten Masken abhängen, die zwischen anderen gehörnten *Grebo*-Masken in der Art von Picassos Exemplar im Metropolitan Museum vermittelt haben könnten.)[63]

Es wird manchmal noch behauptet, daß die traditionelle Stammeskunst eher eine kollektive als eine individuelle Schöpfung darstelle, die ständiges Wiederholen bereits etablierter Formen einschließe, zu denen der einzelne Schnitzer außer handwerklichem Können nur wenig hinzufüge. Meine eigene Erfahrung im Umgang mit dieser Kunst hat mir ganz im Gegenteil bestätigt, daß gute Kunst nur von begabten Einzelnen geschaffen wird. Ich bin in der Tat verblüfft durch die Unterschiede, nicht durch die Ähnlichkeiten zwischen den Stücken ein und desselben eingeborenen Stils (zumindest bei Typen, die nicht für den europäischen Geschmack standardisiert wurden[64]), vor allem durch die Einzigartigkeit derjenigen Werke, die ich als Meisterwerke bezeichnen würde. Von den ungefähr ein Dutzend *Grebo*-Masken, die ich kenne, sind sich nicht zwei gleich, obwohl alle dieselben Grundformen enthalten.[65] Diejenige aus dem Metropolitan Museum ist die edelste aus der Gruppe und doch am wenigsten typisch. Die Unterschiede zwischen ihnen sind genauso ausgeprägt wie jene zwischen den Werken anonymer westlicher Künstler der Schulen des Mittelalters aus einer bestimmten Region – etwa einer romanischen Bildhauerschule. Die besten Arbeiten zeichnen sich in beiden Fällen durch

◁ ◁ □ 34 *Max Weber, ›Kongostatuette‹ (Congo Statuette, auch bekannt unter dem Titel African Sculpture), 1910, Gouache auf Karton, 34 x 267 cm. Privatsammlung, New York. Farbabbildung* □ *649.*

◁ □ 35 *›Figur aus Holz‹,* YAKA *(Zaire), Höhe 26 cm. Sammlung J. S. Weber, New York. Ehemals Sammlung Max Weber.*

□ 36 *Max Weber, ›Interieur mit Frauen‹ (Interior with Women), um 1917, Öl auf Leinwand, 46 x 60 cm. Forum Gallery, New York. Farbabbildung* □ *651.* ▷

besondere Qualität in Ausdruck und Erfindung aus. Skulpturen, die so erlesen sind wie die *GREBO*-Maske aus dem Metropolitan, sind unter primitiven Objekten freilich selten. Daß die Hauptmasse der Stammeskunst nicht sehr gut ist, sagt nichts aus, was nicht genauso für die Produktion irgendeiner anderen Periode gültig wäre, einschließlich – wenn nicht sogar gerade – unserer eigenen.

Die Geburt eines hochbegabten Künstlers ist in jeder Zivilisation eine Seltenheit, und nur bestimmte Kulturen stellen eine Umgebung für seine oder ihre Entfaltung bereit. Daß die gesamte afrikanische Skulptur – die gute wie die schlechte – nur aus einem Teil der von Stämmen besiedelten Gegenden stammt,[66] bedeutet keinesfalls, daß in den anderen Regionen keine Individuen mit einem großen künstlerischen Potential geboren worden wären. Eher machten dort die sozialen und religiösen Traditionen bildhauerische Tätigkeit nicht erforderlich oder ließen sie nicht zu (auch wenn in einigen dieser Gegenden ein hohes künstlerisches Niveau in anderen bildnerischen Kunstformen, etwa der Architektur und Körpermalerei, erreicht wurde).

Für die im allgemeinen geringe Qualität des größten Teils der Stammeskunst – zumindest jener, die sich im Westen erhalten hat – gibt es viele Erklärungen. In einigen Traditionen wurden etwa die Masken gerade für bestimmte Riten von allen männlichen Mitgliedern statt von ausgebildeten Künstlern angefertigt.[67] Wichtiger noch ist vielleicht die Tatsache, daß der Verlust bei der Stammeskunst nicht nur viel größer war als bei westlicher Kunst, sondern daß auch ihr Transport in den Westen und ihre Erhaltung vielfach dem Zufall überlassen blieben. Der Ausfall beginnt schon mit der beschränkten Haltbarkeit von Holzplastik in tropischem Klima. Außerdem wurden die Objekte in vielen primitiven Kulturen nach ihrer Entweihung aufgegeben, oft nachdem sie nur ein einziges Mal in Verwendung gewesen waren. Dies hat zur Folge, daß ein Großteil der Stammeskunst aus Holz, die sich in Afrika oder dem Westen erhalten hat, kaum älter als hundert Jahre ist und daher nur die Spitze des Eisbergs langer und (seit der Kolonialzeit) sich auflösender – zumindest aber einem tiefgreifenden Wandel ausgesetzter Traditionen darstellt.[68] Eine bestimmte Zahl afrikanischer Holzarbeiten ist viel älter, weil sie wie die ägyptische Holzplastik in trockenen Regionen südlich der Sahara aufbewahrt wurde (so die den *DOGON* zugeschriebenen »Tellem«-Figuren – siehe Glossar) oder weil religiöse oder gesellschaftliche Gründe eine Konservierung und Erhaltung garantierten.

Auch wenn bestimmte ältere Stücke besonders schön sind, war der Ausleseprozeß, der gerade diese vor dem Untergang bewahrte, *nicht vom Kriterium ästhetischer Qualität* bestimmt. Man hat auch vermutet, daß viele der frühesten afrikanischen Skulpturen, die in Europa ankamen, »Ersatzstücke« waren, in aller Eile für einen Europäer angefertigt, so daß die Stammesgemeinschaft ein sakrales Objekt nicht abzugeben brauchte.[69] Es erfolgte geradezu eine negative Auswahl, insofern als viele wichtige ältere Stücke von den frühen Missionaren als Götzenbilder zerstört wurden.[70] Die Hauptmasse der in Europa seit der Renaissance entstandenen Kunst ist gleichfalls verschwunden. Was übrig blieb, wurde weitgehend (wenn auch keineswegs vollständig) aufgrund einer kollektiven Übereinkunft über künstlerische Wertigkeit bewahrt, die in ihrer Gesamtwirkung wie ein Ausleseprozeß funktionierte. Für diesen Prozeß scheint eine Gesellschaft nicht nur begabte Künstler zu benötigen, sondern auch ein Konzept der bildenden Kunst, das von einer kritischen Tradition stetig unterstützt wird, die ihrerseits einer Schriftsprache bedarf. Das besaß die Skulptur, wie es sie in afrikanischen[71] und anderen analphabetischen Naturgesellschaften gab, nicht.

Bis in die 50er Jahre war die Auslese von Stammeskunst, wie sie der Westen bewahrte, nach qualitativen Maßstäben *rein zufällig*. Es gibt einige Meisterwerke unter den frühen primitiven Objekten, die von Seeleuten, Reisenden und Missionaren als Kuriositäten mitgebracht wurden. Und vereinzelt mögen sie auch von Menschen mit entwickeltem künstlerischem Geschmack aus der unübersehbaren Fülle von Möglichkeiten ausgewählt worden sein, obwohl dies sicherlich nicht immer der Fall war. Auch kann man sich kaum vorstellen, daß bei der Auswahl der Objekte, die von den Kolonisten als Souvenir mitgebracht wurden, Geschmacksfragen eine Rolle spielten (obzwar einige unter ihnen Kenner der Kunst ihrer Region wurden). Die Situation verbesserte sich ein wenig mit den frühen Völkerkundlern. Da die Ethnologen im allgemeinen zwischen Kunst und Artefakt keinen Unterschied machten – noch heute werden ästhetische Überlegungen als unwissenschaftlich und daher fachfremd abgelehnt –, ist die Mehrzahl der von ihnen mitgebrachten Objekte von nur geringem oder überhaupt keinem künstlerischen Interesse. Diese Ethnologen waren immerhin gezwungen, eine Auswahl zu treffen. Da sie mehr Erfahrung hatten und manchmal offenbar auch einen besseren Geschmack als die Reisenden oder Kolonisten, erwies sich die Qualität dessen, was sie zurückschickten, als etwas besser. Bestimmte Ethnologen der jüngeren Generationen verfügen über eine beträchtliche künstlerische Kultur, doch setzten sich diese Männer und Frauen in Afrika und Ozeanien mit Stammeskulturen auseinander, die durch den Kolonialismus und moderne Technologie in unterschiedlichem Ausmaß verändert worden waren. Dies hatte zur Folge, daß die traditionellen Kunstformen der letzten Jahrzehnte zu Übertreibungen, akademischer Kühle oder Qualitätsverlust neigten.[72] Obwohl gute ältere Stücke in Stammesregionen gelegentlich immer noch anzutreffen sind, fehlen den Völkerkundemuseen im allgemeinen die finanziellen Möglichkeiten, um sich für diese stark zu machen.

Es wäre an sich denkbar, daß die wichtigsten Händler von Stammeskunst, die in den Jahren unmittelbar vor und nach dem Ersten Weltkrieg in Erscheinung traten – Menschen von hoher Geschmackskultur wie Guillaume oder Ratton –, die Zufälligkeit, mit der solche Objekte auf westliche Märkte gelangt sind, durch ihre Einkaufsreisen in die Stammesgebiete behoben hätten. Dies war aber nicht der Fall. Soweit ich informiert bin, setzte kein Händler der Generation PICASSOS oder der darauf folgenden jemals auch nur einen Fuß auf afrikanischen Boden.[73] Die Händler schulten ihren Blick, indem sie aus dem Besten, was ihnen Reisende, Missionare, Kolonisten und die von ihnen finanzierten Zubringer zufällig mitbrachten, eine Auswahl trafen. Es stimmt, daß eine Reihe von Händlern, die nach dem letzten Krieg groß wurde, ausge-

□ 38 *Max Ernst, ›Vogel-Kopf‹ (Oiseau-tête), 1934–35, Bronze (Guß von 1955), 53 x 37,5 x 23 cm. Galerie Beyeler, Basel.*

◁ □ 37 *›Maske‹, Tusyan (Obervolta), Holz, Fasern und Samen, Höhe 67 cm. Musée Barbier-Müller, Genf.*

☐ 39 *›Relief mit einem Vogelmenschen‹, Osterinsel, bemalter Stein, Höhe 36 cm. The Trustees of the British Museum, London.*

☐ 40 ▷
Max Ernst, ›Ovaler Vogel‹ (Oiseau ovoïde), 1934, Stein, Höhe 30,5 cm. Verbleib unbekannt.

dehnte Reisen in Stammesgebiete unternahm und außergewöhnliche Stücke nach Europa mitbrachte, darunter Typen primitiver Skulptur, die bis dahin selten oder unbekannt waren ☐ 60, 197. In den 70er Jahren wurde jede längerfristige Wirksamkeit dieser Händler beeinträchtigt oder in Frage gestellt, als sich die einheimischen Autoritäten über den Wert älterer Objekte aus dem Besitz der Stammesgemeinschaften selbst klar wurden und die gerade neu entstandenen Nationen in Afrika und Ozeanien anfingen, solche Kunst als nationales Kulturgut zu behandeln.

Wenn auch die »unsichtbaren« Eingriffe von Stammesobjekten in die Geschichte der modernen Kunst, wie Picassos *Grebo*-Maske zeigt, weitgehend hypothetisch bleiben müssen, gibt es doch zur Genüge andere, ziemlich offenkundige Eingriffe, um unserer Definition von Primitivismus Substanz zu verleihen. Ihre Reichweite mag anhand von zwei frühen Gemälden Max Webers veranschaulicht werden.[74] Im ersten Fall, es ist Webers von Matisse beeinflußtes Stilleben *Kongostatuette* von 1910, wird eine kleine Figur der *Yaka* ziemlich realistisch dargestellt ☐ 34, 35. Dies bestätigt der Vergleich mit der originalen Skulptur des Malers. Wie bei den vielen Zitaten von Stammesobjekten in der Malerei des deutschen Expressionismus ☐ 546, 547, 556, 557 bekundet dieses Bild zwar Webers Interesse am Primitiven, aber – zumindest unmittelbar – keinerlei Einfluß der Stammeskunst auf seinen Stil. In diesem Sinne verhält sich die primitive Plastik wie jeder andere Gegenstand eines Stillebens. Doch werden in Webers *Interieur mit Frauen* von ca. 1917 ☐ 36, das dem synthetischen Kubismus verpflichtet ist, die afrikanischen Vorlagen weniger dargestellt als vielmehr von seinem mittlerweile kubistischen Stil absorbiert, der seinerseits mit Erinnerungen an Picassos »afrikanische« Gemälde von 1907–08 angereichert ist. Um nur ein Beispiel herauszugreifen, das Gesicht der in der Mitte sitzenden Frau ist eine Synthese von Elementen, die von länglich konkaven *Fang*-Masken ☐ 575 und den Masken der *Kuba* mit den konischen Augen stammen ☐ 701.

Die beiden Gemälde Webers bezeugen nacheinander ein Interesse an Stammeskunst seitens des Malers und seine Beeinflussung durch jenes Vorbild. Trotzdem sind viele bis heute geäußerte Vorschläge für eine solcherart direkte Einflußnahme, sei es in Texten oder Ausstellungen (etwa jener sehr ambitionierten, die zur Zeit der Olympischen Spiele in München stattfand),[75] ganz einfach irreführend. Denn es ist unwahrscheinlich, daß die fraglichen modernen Künstler die vorgeschlagenen Stammesobjekte in Abbildungen, geschweige denn im Original sehen konnten. Oft werden Einflüsse auf Werke der Moderne aus den frühen Jahrzehnten des Jahrhunderts behauptet, als viele der heute geläufigen Typen von Stammesobjekten in den Städten, in denen die Künstler arbeiteten oder in die sie reisten, nicht zu sehen waren und auch nicht abgebildet wurden (manchmal nur in höchst seltenen und teuren völkerkundlichen Publikationen, in die die vorsurrealistischen Generationen mit Ausnahme weniger deutscher Künstler keine Einsicht nahmen).

Wenn solche unhistorischen Gegenüberstellungen im Bilde überzeugend ausfallen, illustrieren sie eher *Verwandtschaften* als *Einflüsse*. Verwandtschaften sind alles andere als unwichtig und sagen auf lange Sicht insgesamt mehr über die Kunst des 20. Jahrhunderts aus als die viel selteneren Fälle einer direkten Einflußnahme (die man als Bestätigung der latenten Verwandtschaft betrachten könnte). Der dritte Abschnitt der Ausstellung, die das vorliegende Buch begleitet, widmet sich ganz der Untersuchung der tiefen Verwandtschaft, die die Kunst der Moderne und der Eingeborenen verbindet. Wie Picasso selbst beobachtete, kann dieses Phänomen in Analogie zur Vorliebe der italienischen Renaissancemalerei für die Kunst der klassischen Antike gesehen werden[76] – auch wenn die Maler der

□ 41 *Max Ernst, ›Das innere Gesicht: das Ei‹ (A l'intérieur de la vue: l'œuf), 1929, Öl auf Leinwand, 100 x 81 cm. Musée National d'Art Moderne, Centre National d'Art et de Culture Georges Pompidou, Paris.*

Renaissance (ähnlich wie die Kubisten bei der Stammesplastik) im Grunde genommen nur wenig von dieser anderen Kunst kannten. Eine saubere Unterscheidung zwischen Einflüssen und Verwandtschaften ist nichtsdestoweniger für die Analyse der modernen Kunst genauso entscheidend wie für die der Renaissance. Aber weil die Stammeskunst bis vor kurzem nicht als Teil der Kunstgeschichte behandelt wurde, sind die Spezialisten der Moderne wiederholt jenem Irrtum aufgesessen, dem ihre Kollegen aus der Kunstgeschichte der Renaissance nie unterliegen würden.

Um den Unterschied zwischen Verwandtschaft und Einfluß stärker zu beleuchten, möchte ich einige Werke von Max Ernst mit Stammesobjekten vergleichen, zu denen eine auffällige Ähnlichkeit besteht. Wenn wir etwa Ernsts *Vogel-Kopf* neben eine afrikanische *Tusyan*-Maske stellen □ 37, 38, erkennen wir – abgesehen von einer allgemeinen Ähnlichkeit der äußeren Erscheinung –, daß solche Einzelheiten wie der flache, rechteckige Kopf, der streng horizontale Mund, die kleinen runden Augen und der aus der Stirn hervortretende Vogelkopf beiden Arbeiten gemeinsam sind. Vergleicht man Ernsts reliefierte Steinskulptur *Ovaler Vogel* aus demselben Jahr (1934) mit dem Relief des Vogelmenschen von den Osterinseln aus dem Britischen Museum □ 39, 40, so stellt man fest, daß beide Male der Kontur eiförmig und ein zusammengesetzter Vogelmensch dargestellt ist, dessen gerundete Formen den Kontur des Bildfeldes nachklingen lassen.[77] Der Oberarm beider Figuren schwingt in einem Bogen herab, der Unterarm weist nach vorn; beide Vogelmenschen haben ein großes rundes Auge. Auch wenn die überdimensionierte Hand der Figur von den Osterinseln in Max Ernsts Steinplastik einen zweiten Vogelkopf vorbereitet (Vogelmenschen mit großen Händen sind allerdings auch in anderen Werken von Ernst anzutreffen) und der Kopf von Ernsts Figur wie auf dem Relief der Osterinseln vorragt, ist die Kopfform viel weniger schnabelartig. Dennoch entspricht diese Form einem anderen Vogelkopf von Ernst fast genau: Er steht ebenfalls in einem ovalen Feld und ist in dem Gemälde *Das innere Gesicht: das Ei* anzutreffen □ 41.

Eines der gefeiertsten polynesischen Objekte, wurde das Vogelmenschen-Relief von den Osterinseln 1915 ausfindig gemacht und 1920 vom Britischen Museum erworben; eine Reihe von Publikationen haben es seit 1920 abgebildet. Anders als seine kubistischen Vorgänger und in einem weit höheren Maße als die meisten seiner surrealistischen Freunde war Ernst ein großer Amateurvölkerkundler. Er besaß eine ansehnliche Bibliothek zu diesem Thema, in der sich – wie Maurer und Spies glauben[78] – eine oder mehrere jener frühen Publikationen befanden, in denen das Relief von den Osterinseln abgebildet war. Von daher ist die Annahme gerechtfertigt, daß hier ein Einfluß des Vogelmenschen auf Ernsts Werk vorliegt. Andererseits ist die Ähnlichkeit von Ernsts *Vogel-Kopf* mit der Maske der *Tusyan* – so auffällig sie auch sein mag – zufällig und muß daher als eine Verwandtschaft gelten. Der *Vogel-Kopf* wurde 1934 skulptiert – Masken der *Tusyan* scheinen vor dem Zweiten Weltkrieg in Europa nicht eingetroffen zu sein, noch wurden irgendwelche abgebildet.

Das Auftreten solch offenkundiger Verwandtschaften liegt teilweise darin begründet, daß moderne wie auch eingeborene Künstler in einer konzeptuellen, von Begriffszeichen bestimmten Weise arbeiten und dadurch gewisse Probleme und Möglichkeiten teilen. Heutzutage fällt es leicht, sich die Herstellung von Kunst in Begriffen einer Problemlösung vorzustellen. Doch trifft dies im wesentlichen ebenso auf die Stammeskünst-

□ 42 *Paul Klee, ›Maske der Furcht‹, 1932, Öl auf Rupfen, 100 x 57 cm. The Museum of Modern Art, N. A. Rockefeller Fund, New York.*

□ 43 ▷ *›Figur eines Kriegsgottes‹, Zuni (Neumexiko), bemaltes Holz und verschiedene Materialien, Höhe 77,5 cm. Museum für Völkerkunde, Berlin.*

ler zu, auch wenn sie – wie in westlicher Kunst häufig der Fall – erst über Generationen zu ihren Lösungen fanden.[79] Völkerkundler mögen argumentieren, daß ich den Stammeskünstlern fälschlich einen Sinn für westliche Kunstherstellung zuschreibe, indes der eingeborene Bildhauer, indem er rituelle Objekte für einen Kult schuf, nicht das geringste Bewußtsein für ästhetische Lösungen gehabt habe. (Letzteres ist natürlich lediglich eine Annahme, die sich darauf beruft, daß viele Stammeskulturen kein Wort für ›Kunst‹ kannten).[80] Auch wenn dies zutrifft, entsteht dennoch kein Widerspruch zu meiner Überzeugung, weil das Finden künstlerischer Lösungen letzten Endes eher einen intuitiven als intellektuellen Vorgang darstellt. Kunstschaffen hat unabhängig vom Ort bestimmte Generalnenner, und »der ästhetische Impuls ist eine der unveränderbaren Komponenten« der Menschheit, wie es der große Ethnologe Robert Lowie recht zutreffend beobachtete.[81] Die künstlerische Qualität der besten Stammesobjekte allein führt bereits vor Augen, daß große Meister am Werk waren und man zu einer Fülle ästhetischer Lösungen fand, wie wenig auch die Künstler selbst mit unserer Beschreibung dieser Vorgänge einverstanden gewesen wären. Weil diese Probleme allgemeiner Natur sind – welches Zeichen etwa für ›Nase‹ stehen soll –, ergaben sich Lösungen, die einander ähnlich waren, auch wenn keine Abhängigkeit von Einflüssen und Traditionen bestand. Daraus resultiert die Ähnlichkeit von eingeborenen Arbeiten unterschiedlichster Herkunft, aus Regionen, die in keiner Beziehung zueinander standen. Als Beispiele sei auf den Kopf einer Farnskulptur von den Neuen Hebriden (Melanesien) und eine afrikanische Maske der *Lwalwa* verwiesen ☐ 45. Ist es dann noch so überraschend, daß Picassos Lösung für den Kopf der in den *Demoiselles* rechts oben befindlichen Dame einer Maske aus der Region der *Etoumbi* ähnlich ist ☐ 337, eines Typus, den er damals gar nicht gesehen haben konnte?[82]

Die Feststellung, daß Picassos Lösung und die des Künstlers der *Etoumbi* einander ähneln, bedeutet nicht, diese gleichzustellen. Einmal ganz abgesehen von der Tatsache, daß der Kopf Picassos bemalt und die *Etoumbi*-Maske geschnitzt ist – so daß ganz andere künstlerische Konventionen in Anwendung kommen –, gibt es bei dem Bildwerk Picassos viele Aspekte, die ontogenetisch die gesamte Phylogenese der westlichen Kunst voraussetzen. Des weiteren erlauben es uns die ästhetischen Verwandtschaften zwischen solchen Bedeutungsträgern (signifiers) nicht, vergleichbare Beziehungen auf der Ebene der Bedeutung (signified) anzunehmen. Daher wurde Herbert Read zu Recht kritisiert, als er expressionistische ›Angst‹ – eine spezifisch moderne Erfahrung – mit afrikanischer Skulptur in Verbindung brachte.[83] Und Picassos Bemerkung über den exorzistischen Charakter afrikanischer Kunst, die nach seiner Meinung geschaffen wurde, um den Menschen »frei« zu machen, leitet sich von einem bestimmten Freiheitsbegriff aus dem Bedeutungsfeld privater psychologischer Emanzipation ab, der für ein Mitglied einer Stammesgesellschaft recht unverständlich wäre.

Das Relief des Vogelmenschen von den Osterinseln beeinflußte Max Ernst, die Maske der *Tusyan* spiegelt hingegen nur eine Verwandtschaft mit seinem Werk: Dies sind Entscheidungen, die eine Form wissenschaftlicher Untersuchung erforderlich machen, für die die Indizien in vielen Fällen leider nicht zugänglich sind. Wir sind uns zum Beispiel nicht sicher, wann bestimmte Typen afrikanischer Skulptur erstmals in Paris oder anderen Zentren auftauchten. Indem wir die maßgeblichen

Museen und frühen Privatsammlungen, Publikationen, datierte Photoaufnahmen oder Auktions- und Verkaufskataloge durchforschen, können wir aber noch vieles entdecken.[84] Das unersetzliche Werkzeug für den Historiker des Primitivismus im 20. Jahrhundert – eine chronologische Tabelle über die Ankunft verschiedener Typen von Stammeskunst in Europa – gibt es bis jetzt noch nicht (wenngleich ich Jean-Louis Paudrat gebeten habe, für Afrika einen Anfang zu machen; diese erste Fassung veröffentlichen wir im Anhang zu seinem Kapitel über die Ankunft und Verbreitung solcher Objekte im Westen im vorliegenden Buch, siehe S. 180–81).[85]

Selbst wenn wir sicher sind, daß ein moderner Künstler zu bestimmten eingeborenen Arbeiten oder ihren Abbildungen Zugang hatte, haben wir keine Gewißheit (es sei denn der Künstler selbst gesteht es offen ein), daß Ähnlichkeiten wirklich auf Einflüsse schließen lassen. Der Beweis erfolgt fast immer nach Indizien, wie er kunsthistorischer Beweisführung vielfach zu eigen ist. In keinem Dokument seiner Zeit steht etwa zu lesen, daß RAFFAEL einen bestimmten antiken römischen Sarkophag mit der Darstellung des Todes von Meleager sah. Und doch ist die Ähnlichkeit dieses Motivs mit der Komposition von RAFFAELS *Grablegung* (Galleria Borghese) so schlagend, daß der Einfluß des Sarkophags auf dieses Bild von Kunsthistorikern allgemein anerkannt wird.[86]

Das Problem, einen Einfluß aufgrund von Indizien nachzuweisen, ist in der Kunst des 20. Jahrhunderts wegen ihres sehr persönlichen und in hohem Maße metaphorischen Charakters besonders heikel. Mit Ausnahme der deutschen Expressionisten zitieren auch nur wenige Künstler solche Arbeiten, für die sie sich interessieren. Eine Reihe von Skizzen moderner Künstler nach eingeborenen Werken liegt uns vor, etwa HENRY MOORES Studie nach einer afrikanischen *MUMUYE*-Figur im Britischen Museum □ 912 oder GIACOMETTIS Zeichnung nach ozeanischen Objekten, die er in Museen oder als Abbildungen in den *Cahiers d'art* fand □ 759–762. Einzelheiten solcher Skizzen werden aber nur selten *direkt* in die kreative Arbeit dieser Künstler übersetzt. PICASSO hat freilich einen Holzarm von den Osterinseln buchstäblich seiner *Frau im langen Kleid* einverleibt, indem er ihn als ein *objet trouvé* wie eine Kleiderpuppe in derselben Skulptur behandelte □ 463 – doch handelt es sich hierbei um ein Zitat besonderer Art.

Die Untersuchung der Einflüsse führt uns meistens in Situationen, bei denen die Ähnlichkeiten zwischen eingeborenen und modernen Objekten zurückhaltender sind als im Falle von MAX ERNSTS vogelartigem Bildwerk und dem Relief von den Osterinseln. Die Beziehung von KLEES *Maske der Furcht* zum indianischen Kriegsgott der *ZUNI* im Berliner Völkerkundemuseum ist ein solcher Fall □ 42, 43. Ich bin davon überzeugt, daß KLEES Bild eine Erinnerung – bewußt oder unbewußt – an die *ZUNI*-Plastik enthält. Wir wissen, daß KLEE das Museum für Völkerkunde in Berlin bereits 1906 besuchte[87] und wiederholt während der folgenden Aufenthalte in Berlin in den Jahren 1913, 1917, 1918, 1922, 1929 und 1930. Von den Museumsleitern wissen wir, daß die *ZUNI*-Plastik, eine ihrer wichtigsten amerikanischen Exponate (erworben 1880), während des ganzen Zeitraums ausgestellt war, so daß die Wahrscheinlichkeit, von KLEE gesehen worden zu sein, sehr groß ist.

Ein Vergleich beider Werke wirft Licht auf einen faszinierenden Fall von Verwandlung in der Kunst der Moderne. Obgleich

□ 44 *›Figur eines Männerbundes‹, Banks Islands, Vanuatu (Neue Hebriden), Baumfarn, Höhe 185,5 cm. Museum für Völkerkunde, Basel.*

□ 45 *›Maske‹*, LWALWA *(Zaire), bemaltes Holz, Höhe 30,5 cm. Musée Barbier-Müller, Genf.*

□ 46 *›Figur eines Männerbundes‹, Banks Islands, Vanuatu (Neue Hebriden), Baumfarn, Höhe 182 cm. Musée de l'Homme, Paris.*

die Schnitzarbeit der *ZUNI* in dekorativen flachen Farben jener Art bemalt ist, die uns in KLEES Werk auch sonst häufig begegnet, ist die düstere Monochromie der *Maske der Furcht* von der Skulptur der *ZUNI* recht verschieden. Dies gilt auch für viele andere Aspekte von KLEES Bild. Die Übereinstimmungen sind gleichwie sehr auffallend, besonders wenn wir uns – wie in unserem Diagramm – auf die obere Hälfte der *ZUNI*-Figur beschränken. Ähnlich sind sich die nahezu ovale Form des oberen Kopfteils und vor allem der Pfeil, der oben herausragt. Eindrucksvoll ist auch die gleichartig lange und schmale Nase

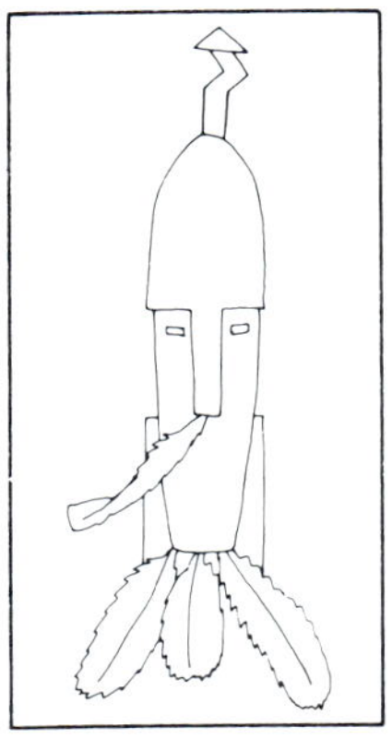

beider Figuren, wobei keine von ihnen einen Mund hat. Darüber hinaus bildet die horizontale Linie über der Stirn von KLEES Figur einen Widerhall jener Horizontalen, die den Kriegsgott an ähnlicher Stelle durchzieht. Die tiefer liegende Horizontale in KLEES Gemälde, die witzigerweise dazu dient, sowohl die Nase nach unten zu begrenzen wie auch die Horizontlinie zu bilden (und scheinbar einen Mund andeutet), erinnert indes an die waagrechte Linie, die das Kinn der *ZUNI*-Figur abgrenzt. Bei den Federn, die am Kinn des Kriegsgottes hervortreten, erfolgte, so glaube ich, eine noch viel subtilere Transformation. Sie regten wahrscheinlich die kuriose Vielbeinigkeit von KLEES Figur an, während die Arabeske, die den rechten Nasenflügel von KLEES Figur andeutet, durchaus von der Feder, die vom Nasenflügel des Kriegsgottes nach rechts absteht, inspiriert sein könnte.

Zweifelsohne finden Kenner eingeborener Kunst an Federn, die von einem Kinn oder Nasenflügel abstehen, nichts Besonderes. Ich wage aber zu behaupten, daß der junge KLEE derlei faszinierend und daher erinnerungswert fand – gerade den Pfeil, der vom Kopf absteht. Ob er an die Skulptur der *ZUNI* bewußt dachte, als er die *Maske der Furcht* schuf, können wir nicht wissen, doch ist dies sekundär, da KLEES Gebilde bis zu einem gewissen Grade immer über einen Prozeß automati-

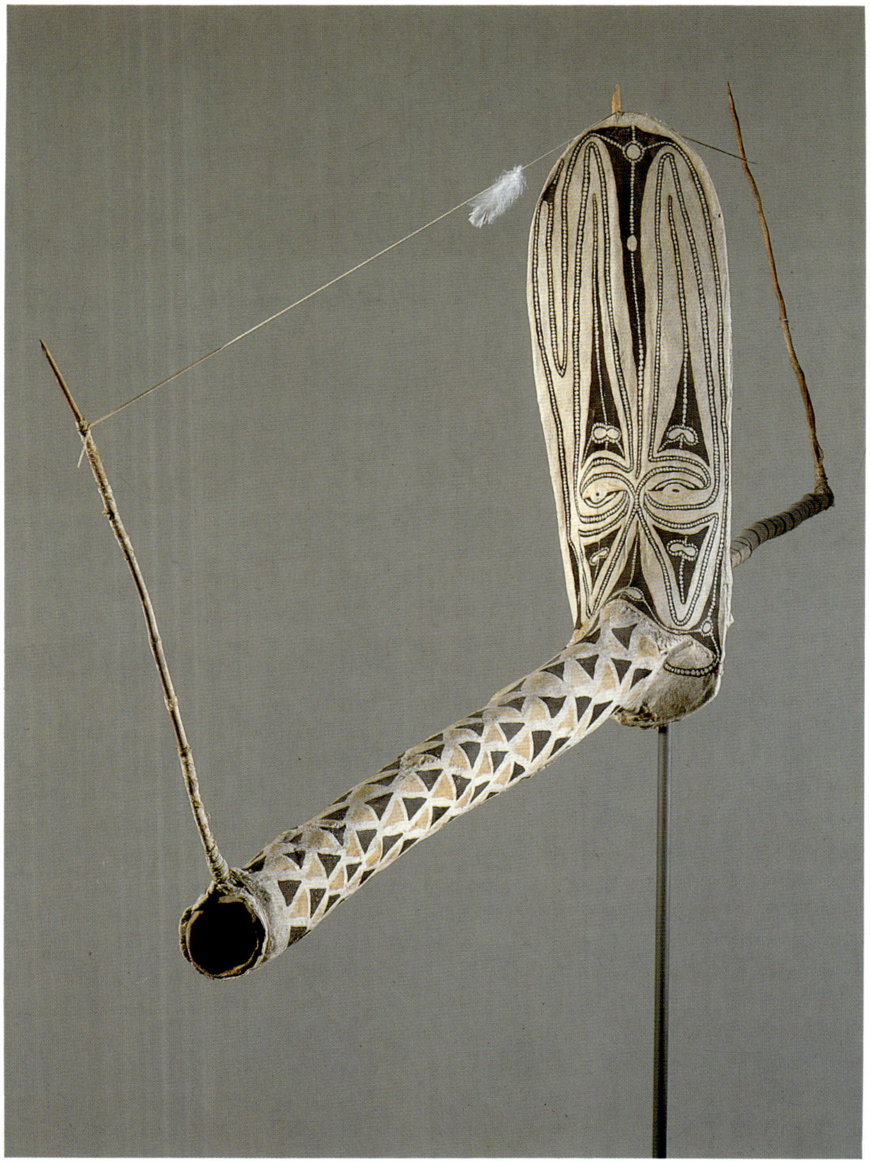

◁ ☐ 47 *›Helmmaske‹, Baining (Neubritannien), bemalter Bambus, Rindenstoff und Federn, Höhe 80 cm. Museum für Völkerkunde, Basel.*

☐ 48 ▷
Alberto Giacometti, ›Die Nase‹, 1947, Metall, Schnur und bemalter Gips, 82 x 42 x 40,5 cm. Alberto Giacometti-Stiftung, Kunstmuseum Basel.

☐ 49 *Alberto Giacometti, ›Kopf eines Mannes auf einer Stange‹ (Ausschnitt), 1947, Gips, Höhe 60 cm. Alberto Giacometti-Stiftung, Kunstmuseum Basel.*

schen Zeichnens aus jenem Bereich des Unbewußten heraufgeholt wurden, in dem eine »vergessene« Bildwelt ruhte.

Die Beziehung zwischen der *Zuni*-Skulptur und jener Klees offenbart über die Natur künstlerischer Übermittlung mehr als nur eine Umsetzung von Formen. Die *Maske der Furcht* wurde 1932, am Vorabend von Hitlers Machtergreifung in Deutschland, gemalt. Die faschistischen Schläger, unter ihnen die SS, die ihre gezackten »Blitz«-Abzeichen trugen, versetzten bereits Menschen auf der Straße in Schrecken.[88] Was wäre logischer gewesen als Klees Assoziation dieser Vorgänge mit einem Kriegsgott, dessen Kopf ein Zickzack-Pfeil krönte, der für die *Zuni* einen Blitz darstellte. Klees furchtsamer kleiner Mann, der auf Raupenfüßen die Straßen entlang kriecht, hat dennoch seine Antenne ausgefahren (links oben) und nimmt ohne Zweifel durch diese Vorrichtung den Terror wahr, den der Pfeil symbolisiert. Dieser ist – wie Klee zeigt – buchstäblich in seinem Kopf und von daher metaphorisch in seinem Geiste.[89]

Jene Form der Einflußnahme, wie sie zwischen der Schnitzarbeit der *Zuni* und dem Bild Klees stattfindet, steht in der Mitte zwischen zwei Extremen, die nur graduell verschieden sind: zwischen offen zutage tretenden Beziehungen einerseits –

☐ 50 *›Modellierter Kopf‹, Neuirland, menschlicher Schädel, Wachs, Kreide und Farbe, Höhe 17 cm. Museum für Völkerkunde, Basel.*

beispielhaft vertreten durch die Vogelmenschen der Osterinseln und Max Ernst – und den »unsichtbaren« Einflüssen andererseits, wie etwa jenen der *Grebo*-Masken auf Picassos *Gitarre*. Während wir nach meiner Überzeugung über die Existenz dieser drei Beziehungen begründete Gewißheit haben, gibt es einige Annahmen von Einflüssen, bei denen durch fehlende Nachweise zur Erhärtung der gezogenen Parallelen die geäußerten Hypothesen – sofern sie überhaupt überzeugend sind – eher geglückte Mutmaßungen darstellen. Eine davon war Reinhold Hohls Verbindung von Giacomettis Gipsskulptur *Die Nase* mit einer Maske der *Baining* aus Neuengland im Museum für Völkerkunde in Basel □ 47, 48. Diese bisher hypothetische Beziehung, die aber durch neue Informationen an Berechtigung gewonnen hat, führt einen besonders interessanten Aspekt in der Reaktion der Moderne auf Werke der Eingeborenen vor, ein Syndrom, das man »kreatives Mißdeuten« nennen könnte. Wir wissen, daß Giacometti völkerkundliche Museen, auch jenes in Basel, besuchte. Skulpturen wie *Löffelfrau* sind ohne Frage von Stammesobjekten angeregt – in diesem Fall von anthropomorphen Reislöffeln der *Dan* und benachbarter afrikanischer Völker □ 734–737. Daß *Die Nase* ein Echo seiner Begegnung mit der *Baining*-Maske darstellt, lassen die vergleichsweise überlangen Nasen vermuten (ein Motiv, das in Giacomettis Œuvre sonst nicht vorkommt), ferner die ornamentale Bemalung beider Nasen (ein seltener, wenn nicht einzigartiger Fall in Giacomettis Plastik), das Vorhandensein von Aufbauten an den Köpfen wie auch die Ähnlichkeit von Giacomettis Kopf – vor allem einer verwandten Kopfplastik aus dem gleichen Jahr □ 49 – mit einem bemalten Schädel aus Neuirland □ 50, der zusammen mit der *Baining*-Maske 1947 ausgestellt war, als *Die Nase* entstand.[91] Doch mißdeutete wahrscheinlich Giacometti die Maske der *Baining*. Denn was wir bislang als die Nase der Maske bezeichneten, ist in Wahrheit ein Sprachrohr und insofern ihr Mund[92] – wie ja auch eine Nase von ganz normaler Größe und Nasenflügel genau über dem Sprachrohr tatsächlich sichtbar sind. In gleicher Weise leiten sich die Beine der sogenannten »tanzenden Figuren« aus Picassos »afrikanischer« Periode – die, wie ich in einem späteren Kapitel noch zeigen werde, auf Ausdeutungen von Reliquiarfiguren der *Kota* zurückgehen □ 344 – von einer völlig verständlichen Mißdeutung der Raute ab, die den Kopf der Reliquiarfigur als ein Beinpaar mit nach außen gebeugten Knien stützt. Klees *Götzen* □ 720 sind ein Zeugnis dafür, daß diese besondere

Mißdeutung nicht ungewöhnlich war, denn auch diese Darstellung ist ganz klar von solchen Reliquiarfiguren angeregt.[93]

Von allen Mißdeutungen eingeborener Arbeiten durch die Moderne ist jene am häufigsten, die die manchmal steifen, frontalen und symmetrischen, dabei oft ungeschickten Haltungen vieler afrikanischer Figuren als Beispiele für Expressionismus begreift, so auch Reads zuvor erwähnte Assoziation mit ›Angst‹. Read führte die »Ähnlichkeiten« zwischen modernen und primitiven Objekten auf die Angst zurück, die er als ihre »gemeinsame psychologische Bedingung« ansah.[94] Diese weitverbreitete Fehlinterpretation, die auf eine überholte Deutung des Stammeslebens aus dem 19. Jahrhundert zurückgeht, ist ohne Zweifel irgendwie für die derzeitige Popularität afrikanischer Kunst bei bestimmten Künstlern, Psychiatern und Sammlern verantwortlich. Es macht natürlich wenig aus, wenn Künstler die besagten Objekte falsch interpretierten, sofern diese Mißdeutung für sie von Nutzen war. Im Interesse eines Verstehens der zwischen eingeborener und moderner Kunst bestehenden Unterschiede sollte es uns aber bewußt sein, daß eine Mißdeutung vorliegt.

Die Verzerrungen und Übertreibungen in modernen expressionistischen Darstellungen des menschlichen Körpers sind, wie es Meyer Schapiro formulierte, Funktionen eines »inwendigen« oder »gefühlten« Bildes vom Körper – im Gegensatz zu einem optisch wahrgenommenen.[95] (Das Gefühl von der Größe einer Anschwellung in unserem Gesicht ist bei Zahnschmerzen viel stärker als das tatsächliche Größenverhältnis). Dieses »gefühlte« Bild dient aber in der expressionistischen Kunst eher als ein Hinweis auf einen psychologischen als auf einen körperlichen Zustand. In HECKELS *Clown und Puppe* etwa □ 55 wird das Gefühl für Anspannung über die typisch expressionistische Übertreibung der Gliedmaßen mitgeteilt – Kopf, Hände und Füße –, die im Verhältnis zum Torso zu groß sind. Wie mühsam der Tanz für die männliche Figur ist – ganz im Gegensatz zur Freude und Anmut französischer Darstellungen des Tanzes –, zeigt der Kontrast zur völligen Ungezwungenheit, die in den kantigen Verzerrungen und der Leichtigkeit der lebensgroßen Puppe zum Ausdruck kommt, mit der die Hauptperson tanzt. Im Bilde HECKELS ist nicht nur ein allgemeines Gefühl des Unbehagens, sondern auch der Entfremdung der Geschlechter enthalten.[96]

Es wäre nicht schwer, die hier abgebildete Figur der *CHAMBA* als Verkörperung vieler dieser expressionistischen Themen falsch zu interpretieren □ 51. Die unbewegliche, frontale und scheinbar linkische Haltung des Körpers, dessen Hände, Kopf und Füße (von denen einer ganz gegen die Anatomie nach innen gerichtet ist) vergrößert sind, könnte als ein Bild der Verspannung gedeutet werden, wobei der übergroße Penis eine Verbindung dieser Verspannung mit Problemen der Sexualität nahelegt. Der ziemlich rundliche, geöffnete Mund würde dann Angst »aussprechen« (wie im Fall des offenen Mundes von EDVARD MUNCHS *Der Schrei* □ 53, eine der wichtigsten Ikonen des Expressionismus).

Doch Angst und Entfremdung sind bei der *CHAMBA*-Plastik genauso wenig Inhalt einer Konvention – hier der geöffnete Mund – wie bei der Maske der *SONGGE* □ 26 oder der Maske der *IBIBIO* □ 52, bei welcher der Mund Brennpunkt eines Musters ist, das – obwohl sehr viel regelmäßiger – an das Bild MUNCHS erinnert. Die Betonung des Geschlechts bei der *CHAMBA*-Figur,

□ 51 *›Männliche Figur‹, CHAMBA (Nigeria), Holz, Höhe 57 cm. Australian National Gallery, Canberra.*

☐ 52 *›Maske‹, Ibibio (Nigeria), Holz, Höhe 20 cm. Sammlung Jacques Kerchache, Paris.*

☐ 53 *Edvard Munch, ›Der Schrei‹, 1895, inschriftlich datiert 1896, Lithographie, 35 x 25 cm. The Museum of Modern Art, Matthew T. Mellon Fund, New York.*

☐ 54 *›Kultische Heilfigur‹, Montol (Nigeria), Holz, Höhe 37,5 cm. Indiana University Art Museum, Bloomington. Leihgabe der Sammlung R. und L. Wielgus.*

☐ 55 *Erich Heckel,* ▷ ▷ *›Clown und Puppe‹, 1912, Öl auf Leinwand, 100 x 70 cm. Zerstört.*

ein bekanntes Motiv der Stammeskunst, ist ebenfalls kein Zeichen sexueller Angst, sondern sexueller Identifikation und Fruchtbarkeit. Die Tradition der frontalen Darstellung, die die *CHAMBA*-Figur mit fast der ganzen übrigen Stammeskunst teilt, drückt genau das Gegenteil von dem aus, worauf MUNCH und KIRCHNER hinaus wollten, als sie – besonders in ihren Straßenszenen – Figuren frontal darstellten. Im Zusammenhang mit der bewegten und molekularen Welt der modernen Straße ist die Frontalität der Figuren MUNCHS eine Metapher für Angst und Entfremdung auf der öffentlichen, sozialen Ebene (das typisch moderne Gefühl der Platzangst). Diese Frontalität ergibt ein so ungewöhnliches Bild des modernen Menschen wie es ein gewohntes für den primitiven (oder archaischen) Menschen ist. Stammeskunst bringt eher ein kollektives Gefühl als ein individuelles zum Ausdruck, indem sie auf formalisierte und rituell geordnete Muster des Stammeslebens anspielt. Die Frontalität steht somit als eine künstlerische Konvention in Harmonie mit den Strukturen der Gesellschaft des Künstlers, wohingegen sich die Frontalität von MUNCHS Figuren mit der vorherrschenden Mobilität und der Dynamik modernen Lebens nicht deckt.

Darwin beschrieb die primitiven Völker wegen ihres Unvermögens, ihr Universum wirklich zu verstehen, als vollkommen unfrei, in der Gewalt ständiger Furcht und steten Zitterns. Genau diese überholte Ansicht führte zu Reads These. Damit Darwins Annahmen richtig gewesen wären, hätte allerdings der primitive Mensch bar jeglicher religiöser Überzeugungen sein müssen. Wie Lévi-Strauss beobachtete, stellen die Riten, auf die eingeborene Gesellschaften ihren Glauben gründen, ganz im Gegensatz dazu normalerweise eine substantielle psychologische Sicherheit bereit;[97] genau diese Sicherheit vermißt der expressionistische Mensch in der modernen Lebenssituation.[98] Dies will natürlich nicht heißen, daß Ordnung, Symmetrie und Frontalität der Stammesskulptur ein »Bild« eingeborenen Lebens vermitteln, genauso wenig wie die Starrheit der viel engeren Konventionen ägyptischer Skulptur. In beiden Zivilisationen – wie in jeder anderen – war das Leben Zufällen, Wandlungen und Störungen unterworfen. Daher vermitteln uns die Skulpturen weniger ein Bild des tatsächlichen Lebens als davon, wie es diese Gesellschaften wahrnahmen und bewerteten, wie sie die Dinge idealerweise haben wollten – ein Ziel, dessen Erfüllung teilweise durch die magischen Eigenschaften der Kunstobjekte selbst zugesichert werden sollte.

Jene Konventionen der *CHAMBA*-Figuren, die expressionistischen Fehldeutungen Vorschub leisten, sind in der afrikanischen Kunst wie auch in der Stammeskunst generell weit verbreitet. Daneben gibt es einige afrikanische Objekte, die von ihrem Charakter her noch viel ausgeprägter »expressionistisch« sind, die im Heilungskult verwendete Figur der *MONTOL* etwa □ 54 oder die »Krankheitsmaske« der *PENDE* □ 340. Während er eine konventionelle symmetrische Haltung beibehielt, scheint der Bildhauer der *MONTOL* den Wunsch gehabt zu haben, durch leichte Asymmetrien (wie in Händen und Armen) und zurückhaltende Artikulation des Körpers einen Eindruck von Anspannung und Unbeholfenheit zu erzeugen, der durch die Derbheit der Oberfläche und vor allem durch die Hebung des Kopfes und seinen leidenden Ausdruck noch verstärkt wird. Anders als im Fall der *CHAMBA*-Skulptur, bei der expressionistisches Unbehagen vom Künstler nicht beab-

□ 56 *›Figur aus Holz‹, HEMBA (Zaire), Höhe 68 cm. Sammlung Jacques Blanckaert, Brüssel.*

□ 57 *›Helmmaske‹, Makonde (Tansania), Holz, Höhe 27 cm. Sammlung Arman, New York.*

sichtigt war, mag es sich bei dem Exemplar der *Montol* um eine jener seltenen primitiven Arbeiten handeln, die die Darstellung körperlichen Leids zum Ziel hatte. Insofern bietet sich die fast paralytische Haltung der *Montol*-Figur zum Vergleich mit modernen expressionistischen Werken an. Es besteht aber ein fundamentaler Unterschied. Das Werk der *Montol* ist, wenn meine Lesart zutrifft, im wesentlichen realistisch und zur Ausstattung eines religiösen Spezialisten gehörig, die bei der Heilung Verwendung fand. Die Figur könnte einen Erkrankten darstellen. Die Art von Lähmung, die sie andeutet, existierte bestimmt auch in der Wirklichkeit. Vergleichbare Figuren in der modernen expressionistischen Kunst enthalten *Verzerrungen* der Realität, die einen inneren Zustand vermitteln sollen. Die »Verzerrungen« der assymmetrischen *Pende*-Maske – die in mancher Hinsicht der in den *Demoiselles* rechts unten befindlichen Figur ähnlich ist □ 339, 340 – sind nicht wie im Gemälde Picassos eine erdachte Metapher für einen psychischen Zustand, sondern die Darstellung eines Gesichts in den fortgeschrittenen Stadien solcher Krankheiten wie etwa Syphilis, *wofür das Modell in der Realität existierte* (obgleich die Darstellung der für die *Pende* charakteristischen Stilisierung unterworfen war).

Es gibt natürlich viele Stammesarbeiten, die (sofern wir sie nicht falsch deuten) von Grausamkeit, Angst und Schrecken handeln sowie eine gewisse Gewalttätigkeit ausdrücken, wie etwa das Gesicht einer Reliquiarfigur der *Ngumba* (Kamerun Fang □ 58) oder die außerordentlich beunruhigende *Makonde*-Maske □ 57. Anders als moderne expressionistische Werke, in denen solche Gefühle meistens mit psychischen Zuständen der dargestellten Figuren identifiziert werden, scheinen eingeborene Ausdruckswerte dieser Kategorie hingegen nach außen gerichtet zu sein in dem Sinne, daß sie böse Geister abschrekken und Reliquien schützen sollen. Daher zeigt sich beim Vergleich der *Ngumba*-Figur mit der ruhigen Darstellung des Menschen in der Bildhauerei der *Hemba* – deren Gelassenheit für afrikanische Kunst typischer ist –, daß beide Werke von

□ 58 *›Reliquiarfigur‹ (siehe Glossar), Ngumba (Kamerun), Holz, Höhe 68 cm. Musée de l'Homme, Paris.*

ihrer plastischen Wirkung wie von ihrem Ausdruck her viel mehr gemeinsam haben als die *NGUMBA*-Skulptur mit irgendeinem expressionistischen Bild von Angst oder Schrecken.

Die Tendenz der Moderne, bestimmte Zeichen in der Stammeskunst auf eine für primitive Kulturen fremde Weise zu interpretieren – ihren Bedeutungsträgern (signifiers) Bedeutungen (signified) aus dem 20. Jahrhundert zuzuordnen –, ist nur eine von vielen Möglichkeiten, wie wir auf Stammeskunst ethnozentrisch reagieren; diese zu unterschätzen, ist eine andere. Indem einige moderne Künstler (etwa MATISSE) Stammesobjekte sogar nur wegen ihrer plastischen Schönheit würdigten, entkleideten sie diese der symbolischen und thaumaturgischen Funktion, die für ihren Platz in der Matrix primitiver Kultur so bestimmend ist. Freilich haben einige Künstler – mit PICASSO angefangen und bis in unsere Tage – auf die animistischen Aspekte des Großteils der Stammeskunst intuitiv reagiert, auch wenn sie bald an die Grenzen ihrer ethnologischen Kenntnisse stießen.[99]

Mangelnde Vertrautheit mit dem kulturellen Kontext von Stammesobjekten ist nur einer von vielen Faktoren, die den modernen Künstler dazu verurteilen, diese Werke fragmentarisch zu betrachten. Wörtlich verstanden verweist der fragmentarische Charakter auf die Tatsache, daß Stammesobjekte im Westen oft unvollständig ankommen. Eine Maske kann etwa ihres »Bartes« aus Fasern, ihres Kopfputzes oder anderer symbolischer Attribute beraubt sein. Masken werden überdies isoliert von den Kostümen, deren Bestandteil sie ursprünglich waren, gesehen ☐ 807. Desgleichen stellen Kostüme »Fragmente« des Tanzes dar, der seinerseits wieder »Fragment« eines noch umfassenderen Ritus ist. Thompson beobachtete ferner, daß viele Formen afrikanischer Kunst dazu gedacht waren, in Bewegung gesehen zu werden.[100] Während dies für das Gros ritueller Figuren wahrscheinlich nicht zutrifft, entfernt es uns notgedrungen noch weiter von der Kunst, die am nachhaltigsten moderne Maler und Bildhauer beeinflußt hat.

Doch ist diese Situation kaum etwas Besonderes. Wir erfahren die gesamte Geschichte vergangener Kunst mehr oder weniger fragmentarisch und meistenteils ihres Umfeldes beraubt. Die wenigen Künstler, die ägyptische oder japanische Kunst schätzten, wußten über ihre Zweckbestimmung und den kulturellen Kontext kaum mehr Bescheid als über afrikanische oder ozeanische Kunst. Dieser Ethnozentrismus ist gleichwohl Funktion einer der größten Tugenden der Moderne: ihrer einzigartigen Anerkennung der Künste anderer Kulturen.[101] Die unsrige ist die *einzige* Gesellschaft, die die Vielfalt der Künste entfernter und fremder Kulturen gewürdigt hat. Eine konsequente Aneignung dieser Künste hat die Moderne um eine besondere Vitalität – Produkt wechselseitiger Befruchtung der Kulturen – bereichert.

Die kubistischen Künstler bekundeten bei ihrer Sammeltätigkeit eine deutliche Vorliebe für die Kunst Afrikas vor derjenigen Ozeaniens. Die Surrealisten waren andererseits enthusiastischer bei ozeanischen Objekten (und denen von *INDIANERN*, Völkern der Nordwestküste und *ESKIMOS*). Auf der »surrealistischen Weltkarte« ☐ 820 erscheinen die Osterinseln fast so groß wie Afrika. Dieser augenfällige Unterschied der Präferenzen wurde vielleicht durch die jeweilige Verfügbarkeit von Objekten aus den beiden Regionen relativiert, doch rührt er nach meiner Meinung primär von den grundlegenden Unterschieden zwischen Kubismus und Surrealismus her. Der Kubismus war wie die afrikanische Kunst trotz unterschiedlicher Abstraktionsgrade in der konkreten Realität der sichtbaren Welt verwurzelt. Der Surrealismus entschied sich wie vielfach die ozeanische Kunst (zumindest in Melanesien) für die Welt des Imaginierten, für die Verbildlichung des Phantastischen – mehr als für das aus dem Sichtbaren Entnommene.

Der Beweggrund für die Entscheidung der Kubisten und Surrealisten wird erkennbar, wenn wir die betonte Dreidimensionalität afrikanischer Bildhauerei – Maß ihrer Konkretheit und Tatsächlichkeit – mit der primär malerischen Struktur melanesischer und besonders neuguineanischer Skulptur vergleichen. Ihren malerischen Charakter offenbart gerade die rundplastische Skulptur, welche die Tendenz hat, von nur einem einzigen Betrachterstandpunkt ausreichend erfaßbar zu sein – normalerweise entweder direkt von vorn oder aus dem reinen Profil. Überraschend sind die relative Flächigkeit und »Körperlosigkeit« bestimmter ozeanischer Skulpturen, die unser Auge auf die äußeren Konturen oder die Zeichnung und ornamentale Bemalung der Oberfläche lenken. Jener Eindruck greifbarer, skulpturaler Masse, der die Essenz des Großteils afrikanischer Arbeiten ausmacht, wird nur geringfügig vermittelt. Weit mehr ozeanische als afrikanische Arbeiten werden auch in Rindentuch ☐ 806, Lehm ☐ 973 oder anderen »weichen« bildnerischen Materialien ausgeführt, die selbst ein Maß für das Malerische darstellen.

Während die beste afrikanische Plastik im allgemeinen aus fast jedem Blickwinkel interessant erscheint – die Figur der *MFUMTE* zwingt uns geradezu, sie zu umschreiten –, schränkt der malerische Charakter melanesischer Werke oft die günstigste Perspektive ein, die der Betrachter wählen würde. Die Frontansicht der Figur der *ABELAM* (Maprik) etwa zeigt nur sehr wenig von der Artikulation der Figur oder der verfeinerten Technik des Bildhauers ☐ 61. Nur der Blick auf das Profil läßt solche bemerkenswert subtilen künstlerischen Entscheidungen wie die Serie von fünf feinteilig abfallenden Stufungen erkennen, die den unteren Teil der Nase, Ober- und Unterlippe, Kinn bzw. Hals abgrenzen. Auch wird die formale Analogie zwischen der aus dem Halsschmuck tretenden Verzierung und der Form des Penis sichtbar.

Man vergleiche nun diese dekorativ bemalte Figur der *ABELAM* mit der zurückhaltenden Schnitzarbeit der *MUMUYE* aus Nigeria ☐ 60. Die *MUMUYE*-Figur ist in jeder Hinsicht so gestaltet, daß uns ihre dreidimensionale Plastizität beeindruckt – egal aus welchem Blickwinkel wir sie betrachten. Besonders bemerkenswert ist die Behandlung der Arme: Mit den Händen beginnend, bilden sie nach oben und nach hinten gleichzeitig einen Bogen um die Säule des Körpers, um dann wieder nach vorn zu treten, sich mit dem oberen Teil des Torsos zu verbinden und geradezu ein Oval zu bilden, das einem Zylinder eingeschrieben ist. Das obere Ende dieses Ovals erinnert außerdem an die Form der kappenartigen Haartracht, die auf geheimnisvolle Weise das Gesicht verhüllt. Der afrikanische Bildhauer vermeidet die für die *ABELAM*-Figur typische Ornamentierung von Fläche und flachem Relief. Seine Formen sind gering an der Zahl, einfach und kühn. Alles, was den Sinn für skulpturale Masse einschränken würde, ist vermieden worden. In anspruchsvoller afrikanischer Schnitzerei erscheint das Innere der Masse von der Plastizität her nie träge – wie beim überwiegenden Teil ägyptischer Skulptur und einigen anderen archaischen Stilen. Wie der archaische Bildhauer wählt der eingeborene Künstler die Frontalität zum Ausgangspunkt,

☐ 59 *›Figur aus Holz‹ (Seiten - und Vorderansicht), MFUMTE (Kamerun), Höhe 65 cm. Privatsammlung.*

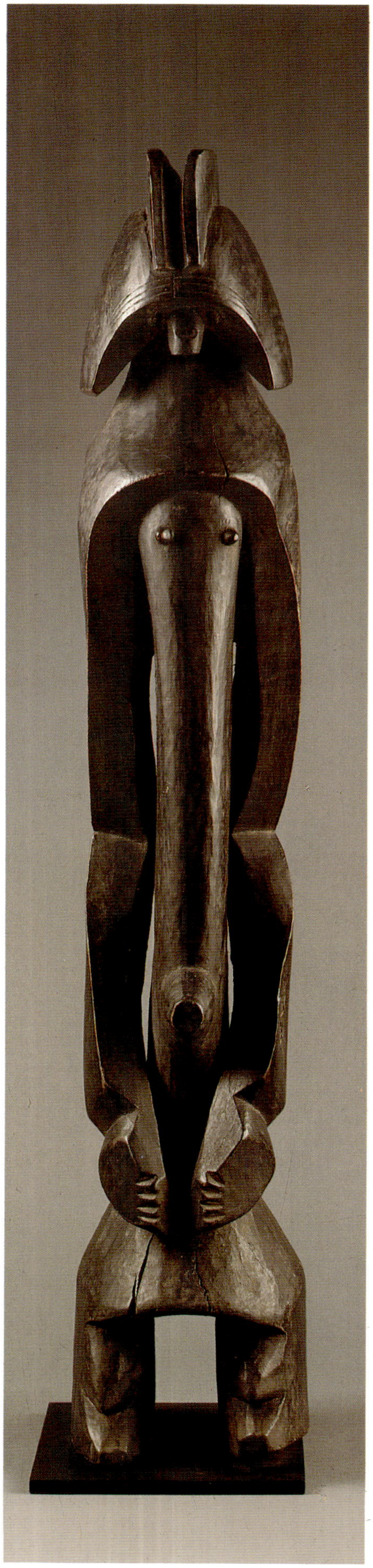

◁ ☐ 60 *›Figur aus Holz‹ (drei Ansichten), Mumuye (Nigeria), Höhe 120 cm. Sammlung Jack Naiman, New York.*

☐ 61 *›Bemalte Figur aus Holz‹ (Seiten- und Vorderansicht), Abelam, Maprik, Provinz Ost-Sepik (Papua-Neuguinea), Höhe 137 cm. Musée Barbier-Müller, Genf.*

◁ ☐ 62 *›Bemalte Figur aus Holz‹, Provinz Osthochland (Papua-Neuguinea), Höhe 150 cm. Privatsammlung.*

☐ 63 *Kenneth Noland, ›Tondo‹, 1961, Akrylfarben auf Leinwand, Durchmesser 148,5 cm. Sammlung A. E. Diamond, Toronto.*

doch geht er anders als jener über sie hinaus. Er fühlt sich frei, gegen das Gefüge solcher Formalität zu arbeiten, und es gelingt ihm, den Formen des Körpers eine plastische Lebendigkeit zu verleihen, die wir bei archaischer Kunst nur selten antreffen. Dort vermittelt rundplastische Skulptur oft den Eindruck, als seien vier Reliefs zusammengefügt; die Artikulation der Figur scheint sich direkt von der auf der Oberfläche des Stein- oder Holzblocks angebrachten Zeichnung herzuleiten, mit welcher der Bildhauer sein Werk begonnen hatte.[102]

Die einzigartigen Möglichkeiten der flächig-malerischen Formel, der melanesische Bildhauer den Vorzug geben, werden nirgendwo besser zur Entfaltung gebracht als in der Figur aus dem Hochland Neuguineas ☐ 62. Ihre Formen sind aus einem schmalen Brett gehauen, so daß die Skulptur zwar eine Vorder- und Rückseite, aber kein Profil hat. So faszinierend die konturierende Linie dieser Figur sein mag, ohne ihre Bemalung wäre viel von ihrem Reichtum verloren – die farbigen konzentrischen Kreise, die Kopf und Bauch bezeichnen und im Halbkreis der Stütze einen Widerhall finden. Es gibt nur wenige afrikanische Stücke, bei denen die Dekoration der Oberfläche und vor allem ein so reines Farbspiel eine derart wichtige Rolle spielen. Solche Eigenheiten würden dort die Plastizität beeinträchtigen, jenes Gefühl für skulpturale Masse, das der afrikanische Schnitzer gewöhnlich zu erreichen sich bemüht. Die Figur aus dem Hochland von Neuguinea ist nicht nur wegen ihres hohen Abstraktionsgrades bemerkenswert, sondern auch aufgrund der Autonomie dieser Abstraktion.

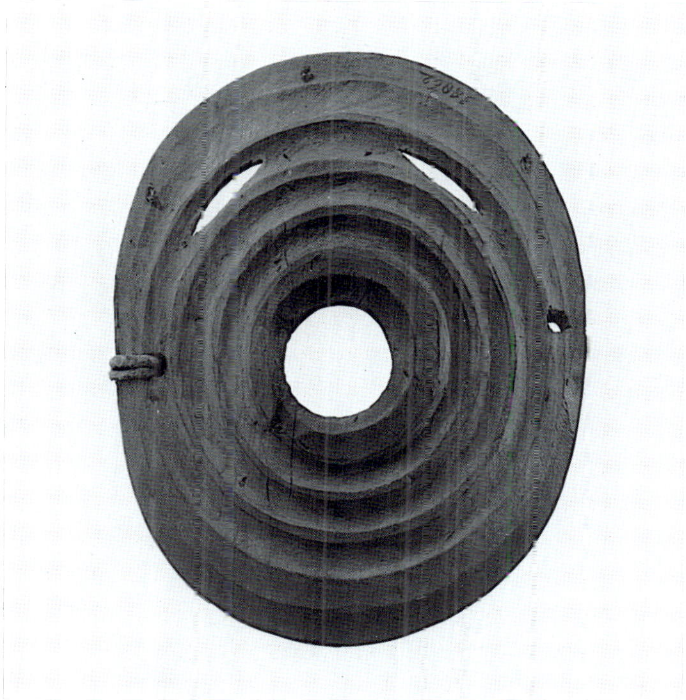

☐ 64 *›Eskimoische Maske‹, Unterer Yukon River (Alaska), bemaltes Holz und Leder, Höhe 18 cm. National Museum of Natural History, E. W. Nelson Collection, Smithsonian Institution, Washington.*

Man müßte auf die Malerei der letzten Jahrzehnte zurückgreifen – etwa einen *Tondo* von KENNETH NOLAND □ 63 –, um für das konzentrische Farbmuster, das der Künstler für Bauch und Kopf verwendete, ein Gegenstück in der westlichen Tradition zu finden. Das nächstliegende Beispiel für eine solch konzentrische Anordnung, die als Symbol für ein Körperteil benutzt wird, bietet sich mir in anderen Beispielen von Stammeskunst, etwa einer eskimoischen Maske vom Yukon □ 64. Da die Surrealisten Objekte der *ESKIMOS* wie auch aus Neuguinea bewunderten, ist diese Verwandtschaft vielleicht gar nicht überraschend.

Der »Kolorismus« melanesischer Kunst ist nicht nur eine Frage des wörtlichen Gebrauchs von Farbe oder der Gestaltung weicher Materialien, sondern auch der Raffinesse der Schnitzerei – kunstvolles Aushöhlen und komplizierte Durchdringung von Formen. Nirgendwo ist derlei besser verwirklicht als in dem Ungetüm, das einen Haarschmuck aus Neuguinea verziert, dessen ineinandergreifende Bestandteile an die Ornamentik der Stämme aus der osteuropäischen Völkerwanderung erinnern □ 67. Die genauso kleine Figur der *MAMBWE* aus Sambia □ 68, deren fleckiges Muster so streng und geometrisch wie die Gestaltung der Figur selbst ist – reduziert auf Torso, Geschlecht bzw. Nabel und »Kopf« –, ist abstrakt, sparsam und stellt eine wirkungsvolle afrikanische Grundlage für das Haarornament bereit. Es mag zutreffen, daß das Haarornament als Skulptur betrachtet in seiner Kleinteiligkeit schwelgt. Die Schnitzarbeit der *MAMBWE* hat wie viele Figürchen der *ZANDE* □ 200 von Natur aus eine solche Monumentalität, daß sie sich als Maquette für das große Werk eines modernen Bildhauers denken ließe.

Indem die ozeanischen Bildhauer die Masse oft dadurch opferten, daß sie auf einer einzigen Ebene mit malerischen Mitteln arbeiteten, verhalfen sie dem Raum, in dem sich ihre Figuren bewegten, zu einem Wirkungsgrad, den die afrikanische Kunst nie gekannt hat. Der Bildhauer Afrikas ist sich nur der Körpermasse gewahr; Raum wird eher gemessen als gestaltet, und wie in der klassischen Kunst dient er im wesentlichen als Mittel, um die Massen zu steigern. Gerade in der melanesischen Kunst hingegen wird der Raum zu einem wirkungsvollen Bestandteil der Ästhetik des Künstlers. Man beachte etwa, wie der Bildhauer vom Hochland Neuguineas die engen Räume zwischen den gebeugten Armen und Beinen der Figur ausnutzt. Noch eindrucksvoller ist die Funktion »verwahrter« Räume in der besten der *YIPWON*-Figuren aus der Region des Karawari auf Neuguinea □ 108. Hier werden die Zonen zwischen den wundervoll gekurvten »Rippen« so eindringlich empfunden wie die spitz zulaufenden Holzteile, die sie definieren. Leider sind diese Figuren, die zu den bemerkenswertesten Erfindungen eingeborener Künstler zählen, häufig so schlimm zerbrochen oder unvollständig, daß nur wenige Beispiele der innewohnenden bildhauerischen Idee gerecht werden.

Die Figur der *IATMUL* (Sepik) ist eines der schönsten Beispiele für den ausgeklügelten Gebrauch solcher verwahrter oder »negativer« Räume □ 65. Die Räume zwischen den Armen und dem Körper – vor allem der zwischen Beinen, Hüfte und Penis – zeigen ein autonomes ästhetisches Interesse, das den festen Körperbestandteilen, von denen sie eingegrenzt werden, zumindest ebenbürtig ist. Die ganze Skulptur ist mit

□ 65 *›Bemalte Figur aus Holz‹*, IATMUL, *Provinz Ost-Sepik (Papua-Neuguinea), Höhe 138 cm. Privatsammlung.*

einer außergewöhnlichen Ökonomie erfaßt, die sie gerade für den modernen Geschmack so anziehend macht. Die Verlängerung des im Umfang abnehmenden Torsos, der im Geschlechtsteil spitz zuläuft, zeigt dies besonders gut. Erst in den 20er Jahren, bei einigen Frühwerken GIACOMETTIS, waren moderne Bildhauer imstande, verwahrte Räume mit derartiger Einfachheit und Erfindungsgabe nutzbar zu machen. Man vergleiche jetzt diese Gestaltung des Künstlers der *IATMUL* mit der genauso einzigartigen und sparsamen Lösung, wie sie ein Bildhauer der *EKET* aus Nigeria für den Körper fand. Das Erfinderische liegt hier – ganz typisch für afrikanische Kunst – nicht im Wechselspiel fester Formen und gestalteter Räume, sondern in der Bewegung dieser festen Formen im Raum: die erstaunlich parallelen Bögen von Torso und Armen und der nach oben gerichtete Haken (das, was der Penis sein könnte), der gegen sie ausgespielt wird.

Die Wölfflinsche Verallgemeinerung, die ich zur Unterscheidung von »haptischer« afrikanischer Schnitzkunst und »optischer« bzw. malerischer ozeanischer Skulptur herangezogen habe, gilt nach meiner Überzeugung ganz allgemein für viele dreidimensionale Werke beider Bereiche. Da es sich aber um eine Verallgemeinerung handelt, gibt es zahlreiche Ausnahmen. Um nur ein Beispiel herauszugreifen hat die Figur der Göttin Kawe von Nukuoro □ 1 eine skulpturale Plastizität, die eines BRANCUSI würdig wäre. Wie PICASSOS Sepik-Figur □ 70 und die Tikis von Polynesien bezeugen □ 373, 382, ist eine Dreidimensionalität für Ozeanien auch nicht singulär. Umgekehrt ist die qualitätvoll geschnitzte und bemalte *TEKE*-Maske aus dem Kongo □ 69 – sie gehörte einmal *DERAIN* – durch ihren fast ozeanisch anmutenden malerischen Charakter für afrikanische Skulpturen ungewöhnlich (ich sage ›fast‹, weil die besondere Geometrie der Gestaltung entschieden afrikanisch bleibt).

Mit dem Bewußtsein, das wir für die Unterschiede zwischen afrikanischer und ozeanischer Skulptur geweckt haben, können wir nun Werke der Moderne zu diesen besser in Beziehung setzen. Die besondere Neigung der Kubisten zur afrikanischen

□ 66 *›Figur aus Holz‹ EKET (Nigeria), Höhe 73 cm. Privatsammlung, Paris.*

◁ ◁ □ 67
›Haarschmuck‹ (Ausschnitt), Yuat River, Provinz Ost-Sepik (Papua-Neuguinea), bemaltes Holz, Gesamthöhe 51 cm. Privatsammlung.

◁ □ 68
›Figur aus Holz‹, MAMBWE (Sambia), Höhe 30 cm. Museum für Völkerkunde, Berlin.

□ 69 *›Bemalte Maske aus Holz‹, Teke (Volksrepublik Kongo), Höhe 34 cm. Musée Barbier-Müller, Genf. Ehemals Sammlung André Derain.*

□ 70 *›Figur aus Holz‹, Provinz Ost-Sepik (Papua-Neuguinea), Höhe 45,5 cm. Musée Picasso, Paris. Ehemals Sammlung Pablo Picasso.*

□ 71 *Jacques Lipchitz, ›Sitzender‹, 1922, Bronze, 51 x 26 x 267 cm. Privatsammlung.*

Kunst ist anhand des Vergleichs eines DOGON-Paares mit LIPCHITZ' *Sitzendem* unmittelbar verständlich □ 71, 72.[103] Wie das Gros afrikanischer Kunst (und früher kubistischer Malerei) ist die Skulptur von LIPCHITZ monochrom. Polychromie hätte in afrikanischen wie in modernen Arbeiten das Gefühl für Volumina und die rein skulpturale Haptik verringert. Außerdem bleiben die wesentlichen Elemente des menschlichen Körpers trotz der starken Abstraktion in den Werken LIPCHITZ' und der DOGON eindeutig identifizierbar: Beide sind in reduzierenden geometrischen Formen erfaßt und betonen klare Linien, rechte Winkel und einfache Kurven. Die gemeinsamen parallelen Strukturen und Symmetrien demonstrieren eine innere geistige Verwandtschaft: die Plazierung von Füßen, Händen und der über die Schulter führenden Linie bei LIPCHITZ im Verhältnis zum linearen Zusammenschluß der gebeugten Knie, von Nabel und Köpfen bei der DOGON-Plastik. Weder die eine noch die andere Arbeit enthält viel bildhauerische »Zeichnung«. Die eingeschnittenen Linien der Frisuren und der Armbänder bei der DOGON weisen dieselbe geometrische Vereinfachung auf wie die Hände von LIPCHITZ' Figur. Auch bestehen die Augen in beiden Fällen aus einfachen Kreisen.

Obwohl die Bronze von LIPCHITZ nur eine Einzelfigur dar-

□ 72 *›Sitzendes Paar‹, Dogon (Mali), Holz und Eisen. Höhe 58 cm. Sammlung M. und B. Frum, Toronto.*

stellt, erinnert der Gegensatz von gekurvten und rechteckigen Formen innerhalb des Kopfes an den ästhetischen Kontrast von männlich und weiblich in der *Dogon*-Skulptur: die konischen Brüste der Frau im Gegensatz zum »kubischen« Oberkörper ihres Ehemanns oder das geschwungene Ohr und der Haarschopf im Gegensatz zum rechteckigen Ohr und der scharfkantigen Haarlinie des Mannes. Es ist bemerkenswert, daß Lipchitz' Kombination von runden und scharfkantigen Profilen innerhalb eines einzigen Kopfes eine Konvention des synthetischen Kubismus darstellt, die sich ursprünglich aus einer Konfrontation von männlichen und weiblichen Formen ableitet. Picasso hatte diese in seinem richtungsweisenden Bild *Harlekin* von 1915 eingeführt □ 74, bei dem die Einzelfigur aus einem tanzendem Paar – dem ursprünglichen Bildmotiv – herausgeschält und verdichtet wurde.

Die elementare Einfachheit, die Picasso zur Gleichsetzung des Männlichen mit dem Geradlinigen (und in der Folge mit Quadraten, Rechtecken und Kuben) und zur Assoziation des Weiblichen mit dem Krummlinigen (in der Folge mit Arabesken, Kreisen und Kugeln) veranlaßte, entsprach so ganz seiner Eigenart. (Sie wird parodiert in solchen Bonmots des Künstlers wie: »Wenn es einen Schnurrbart hat, dann ist es ein Mann«).

□ 73 *Pablo Picasso, ›Junge Akrobatin auf einem Ball‹ (Acrobate a la boule), 1905, Öl auf Leinwand, 147 x 95 cm. Puschkin-Museum der bildenden Künste, Moskau.*

Übrigens war diese Form reduzierenden analogischen Denkens, das PICASSO gerade für afrikanische Kunst so empfänglich machte, für ihn schon lange typisch, bevor er Stammeskunst sah oder bei der Entstehung des Kubismus mitwirkte. Bereits in *Junge Akrobatin auf einem Ball* von 1905 wird durch den Akrobaten und den Würfel, auf dem er sitzt – ebenso zwischen dem jungen Mädchen und dem Ball, auf dem sie balanciert –, eine klare Analogie hergestellt □ 73.

PICASSOS Elementarheit könnte leicht als banal bezeichnet werden. Aber gerade darin liegt der Grund für die größere Anziehungskraft seiner Kunst beim Publikum im Vergleich zu anderen großen Vertretern der Moderne. Denn erst wenn der größte Allgemeinplatz durch den Geist des Genies geadelt wird, erhalten wir das wirklich universale Kunstwerk. Im frühen 20. Jahrhundert war die Moderne so komplex und unverständlich geworden, daß ihr potentielles Publikum notgedrungen begrenzt war. Die hypertrophische Sensibilität, der die symbolistische Kunst vielfach huldigte – eine wichtige Quelle von PICASSOS »Blauer« und früher »Rosa Periode« –, stellte ein Extrem dieser Entwicklung dar. Mit dem Jahr 1906 war aber PICASSO zu einer Gegenreaktion imstande und sein nachfolgender Primitivismus – zunächst iberisch, danach von den Eingeborenen beeinflußt – wurde ihm zum adäquaten Werkzeug. Während die Stammeskunst in der öffentlichen Meinung dieser Jahre nach wie vor als Kuriosität abgetan wurde, besaß PICASSO einen besonderen Zugang zu ihr. Er hatte eine Vorliebe für ihre direkten, einfachen und reduzierten Lösungen. PICASSO erkannte nicht nur, wie diese zur Läuterung beitragen konnte, sondern auch zum Aufbau einer modernen Kunst, welche die essentiellen und universalen Eigenschaften, die er in der Stammesplastik erkannte, teilen würde. Die *Demoiselles* bilden den Höhepunkt seines achtzehn Monate währenden Kampfes gegen die farblos gewordene Modernität der symbolistischen Generationen. Nicht zufällig taucht PICASSOS »Afrikanismus« in dieser Zeit zum ersten Mal auf. Das »Elementare« der *Demoiselles* machte es zunächst erforderlich, Schichten überkommener Konventionen bis zum Kern plastischer Rudimente zu durchbrechen, ein Versuch, der PICASSO zur Stammeskunst eine Verbindung suchen ließ. Doch bedeuteten die *Demoiselles* mehr als nur eine Rückkehr zu formalen Grundlagen. Wie wir noch sehen werden (siehe S. 258ff.), verband PICASSO das Zurück zu den Grundlagen mit der Wiederentdeckung jener unmittelbaren magischen Potenz, von der er wußte, daß sie die inhärente Macht der Kunst darstelle, einer Kraft, zu der die westliche Tradition den Kontakt verloren hatte. Die »Offenbarung« dieser Magie war ihm bei seinem ersten Besuch des Musée d'Ethnographie du Trocadéro gekommen.

Die Ähnlichkeiten, die zwischen dem Bild *Eine ernste Lage* des Surrealisten MATTA □ 3 und so typisch ozeanischen Skulpturen wie den Malanggan von Neuirland bestehen □ 2, 77, sind in

□ 74 *Pablo Picasso, ›Harlekin‹ (Arlequin), 1915, Öl auf Leinwand, 183,5 x 105 cm. The Museum of Modern Art, L. P. Bliss Bequest, New York.*

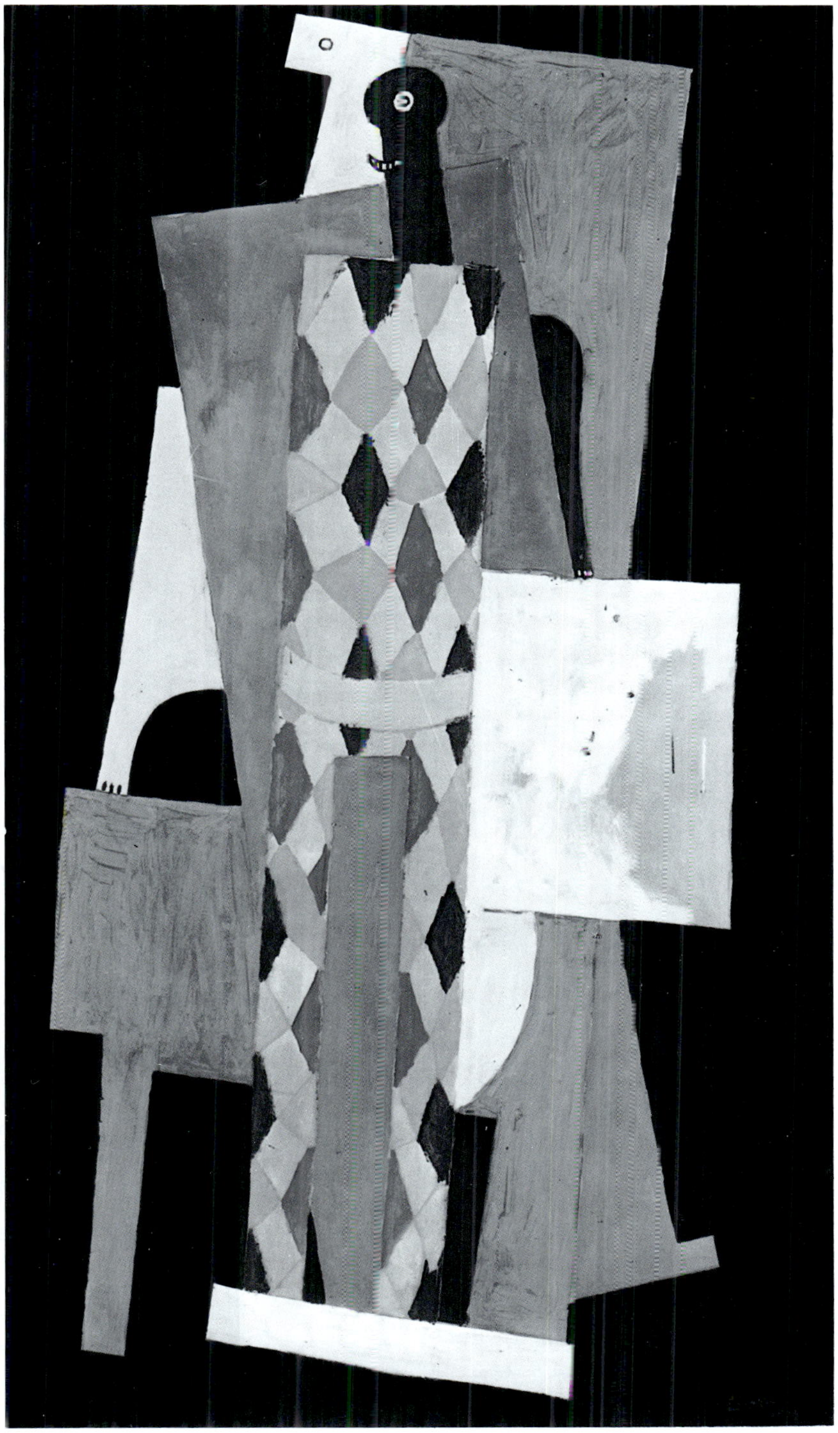

□ 75 *Pablo Picasso, ›Tanzendes Paar‹ (Couple de danseurs), 1915, Gouache und Bleistift, 14 x 12 cm. Sammlung Diane de Riaz, Val de l'Oise, Frankreich.*

jeder Beziehung der Verwandtschaft zwischen Werken der DOGON und LIPCHITZ' entgegengesetzt. Die Malanggan sind malerisch, d.h. mehr »optisch« als »haptisch«; mit MATTA teilen sie eine Sprache offener Formen und fließender »Zeichnung« (d.h. Silhouettierung). Beides wurde von Kubisten und afrikanischen Künstlern gemieden. Wie MATTA – aber wiederum anders als die afrikanischen oder kubistischen Bildhauer – mißt der neuirische Künstler der Farbe auf Kosten rein bildhauerischer Qualitäten eine große Bedeutung bei.

Die Beziehung zwischen MATTAS Figuren und den Malanggan führt uns über das Verwandte in den Bereich direkter Einflüsse, zumal MATTA wie ERNST und andere Surrealisten ein leidenschaftlicher Sammler dieser Skulpturen war. Obwohl die »kybernetischen« Strukturen MATTAS Figuren ein Aussehen wie ganz aus dem 20. Jahrhundert verleihen, spiegeln viele ihrer Aspekte seine Liebe für diese Stammesobjekte wider: die offen gearbeitete Struktur der Anatomie der Figuren, ihre steife Haltung und signalhaften Gesten, schließlich ihre Wildheit und Aggressivität. Wie die Malanggan werden auch MATTAS Figuren von monströsen Tieren angegriffen.

Geht man von einer Tendenz zu Frontalität und Symmetrie aus, so ist alle Stammeskunst eher »ikonenhaft« als »erzählerisch«. Daher ist es wohl gewagt, unter dem Gesichtspunkt des Erzählerischen zwischen afrikanischer und ozeanischer Kunst einen Unterschied zu machen. Dennoch scheint mit das Gros ozeanischer Plastik und die gesamte Skulptur der Nordwestküste Amerikas (die bei den Surrealisten in besonderer Gunst stand) eine offensichtlichere, wenn auch symbolische Beziehung zur erzählerischen Formulierung zu haben als afrikanische Kunst. Insofern können wir verstehen, warum es die Schöpfer des Kubismus, der eine »ikonenhafte« Kunst ist, nach Afrika zog, wohingegen der Surrealismus, der eine in symbolhafter Weise »erzählende« Kunst darstellt, seine Verfechter nach Melanesien, Mikronesien, Nord- und Südamerika führte.

Anders ausgedrückt wage ich verallgemeinernd zu behaupten, daß die Kunst Ozeaniens und der Nordwestküste im Vergleich eher zum Ausdruck des Mythos, während die afrikanische zum Ausdruck des Rituellen neigt. Ob die Riten aus dem Mythos abstrahiert sind oder, wie einige Anthropologen glauben, die Mythologie auf die Riten zurückgeht, braucht uns hier nicht zu interessieren, da wir aufgrund der unterschiedlichen Wesensart sagen können, daß den Riten eine größere »Abstraktheit« zu eigen ist als dem Mythos. Daher wird die in höherem Maße rituell orientierte afrikanische Kunst wiederum die Kubisten ansprechen, während die Surrealisten den mythischeren Inhalt ozeanisch/amerikanischer Arbeiten anziehend finden werden. Dies bedeutet natürlich nicht, daß in afrikanischer Kunst keine mythischen Figuren vorkommen; ganz im Gegenteil, es sind Beispiele dafür vorhanden.[104] Ihre Verbildlichung in der Kunst prägt allerdings mehr die Art und Weise wie sie in der Liturgie beschworen werden als die sequentielle Erzählweise des Mythos. Soweit in der Skulptur realisierbar,

◁ ◁ □ 76 *Roberto S. A. Matta, ›Wundbefragung‹ (Ausschnitt), 1948, Öl auf Leinwand, 150 x 196 cm. The Art Institute of Chicago, M. and E. Ludgin Collection. Gesamtabbildung* □ *875.*

◁ □ 77 *›Malanggan‹ (siehe Glossar), Neuirland, bemaltes Holz und verschiedene Materialien, Höhe 108 cm. Musée Barbier-Müller, Genf.*

□ 78 *›Schlangenfigur‹, BAGA (Guinea), bemaltes Holz, Höhe einschließlich Sockel 250 cm. Sammlung Jacques Lazard, Paris.*

□ 79 *›Figur aus Holz‹ (Vorder- und Rückansicht),* BOYO *(Zaire), Höhe 86 cm. Sammlung G. und F. Schindler, New York.*

□ 80 *›Fetisch‹ (siehe Glossar),* YOMBE *(Zaire), Holz und verschiedene Materialien, Höhe 59,5 cm. Musée Royal de l'Afrique Centrale, Tervuren.* ▷

☐ 81 *›Imunu‹ (siehe Glossar),* NAMAU, *Golf-Provinz (Papua-Neuguinea), Holz, Höhe 53 cm. Sammlung Friede, New York.*

☐ 82 *Alexander Calder, ›Apfelmonster‹ (Apple Monster), 1938, Apfelzweig und Drahtfeder, 165 x 81 x 128 cm. Privatsammlung.*

führt der Mythos zu zusammengesetzten oder totempfahlähnlichen Agglomeraten von der Art, wie sie in Ozeanien und an der Nordwestküste verbreiteter sind als in Afrika.[105]

Die Surrealisten zogen die Kunst Ozeaniens der afrikanischen teilweise wegen ihrer scheinbar größeren Naturnähe und des vielfältigeren, mehr aleatorischen Gebrauchs natürlicher Materialien vor. Mitunter wird behauptet, afrikanische Kunst sei klassisch, ozeanische hingegen romantisch. Auch wenn solche Verallgemeinerungen zur Verunklärung mindestens ebenso beitragen wie zur Klarstellung, kann man insofern sicher zustimmen, als melanesische Kunst wegen ihrer besonderen Identifikation mit der Naturwelt romantischer als die afrikanische ist. Während es bei afrikanischen Masken und figürlichen Skulpturen zahllose Zwitterbildungen von Menschen und Tieren gibt, neigen diese konzeptionell dazu, stärker als die geradezu allgegenwärtigen Monstren der melanesischen Völker von der Natur entfernt und abstrahiert zu werden. Im Vergleich zu vielen ozeanischen Kunstformen könnte die afrikanische Skulptur fast in Begriffen eines vorherrschenden Anthropomorphismus und Anthropozentrismus charakterisiert werden, die beide Merkmale des Klassischen sind.[106] Der Künstler Neuguineas neigt demgegenüber eher dazu, seine Monstren »ready-made« aus dem zu entnehmen, was ihm die Natur bietet. Wir finden etwa nirgends in afrikanischer Kunst etwas Vergleichbares für die böswillige Zwitterbildung des Imunu (siehe Glossar) aus der Region des Papua-Golfes, der weitgehend aus Zweigen oder Baumwurzeln besteht. Ergebnis dieser »natürlichen Auswahl« ist ein dem Zufall angepaßtes, gewundenes und dabei lineares Gebilde, dessen unförmige Konturen ästhetischen Idealen Afrikas diametral entgegengesetzt sind – nicht aber modernem Geschmacksempfinden und gerade dem der Surrealisten nicht, die solche Objekte ganz besonders schätzen. Ähnlichkeiten zu ihren Strukturen, wenn nicht sogar ein direkter Widerhall sind in vielen Arbeiten von ERNST oder MIRÓ genauso wie – in späterer Zeit – im Werk DUBUFFETS zu finden ☐ 974. Aber erst in der Kunst CALDERS, der den Surrealisten in den 30er Jahren nahestand, entdeckt man, wie es scheint, den direkten Einfluß eines Imunu. Schon früh an Stammeskunst interessiert,[107] hatte CALDER in den späten 30er Jahren eine recht umfangreiche Sammlung primitiver Kunst angelegt. Er war mit Pierre Loeb befreundet ☐ 160,[108] der Surrealisten wie GIACOMETTI und MIRÓ ausstellte und sich vor allem für die Sache der Stammeskunst aus der Südsee im allgemeinen und der *PAPUA* im besonderen einsetzte.[109] CALDERS *Apfelmonster* von 1938, das weitgehend aus den Zweigen eines Apfelbaumes besteht, ist innerhalb seines Œuvres ein ungewöhnliches Werk, das sich nach meinem Dafürhalten direkt von der Begeisterung des Künstlers für ein Imunu herleitet ☐ 81, 82. Wie die Imunus, deren aleatorischer Charakter geradezu prädestiniert war, avantgardistischem Geschmack zu gefallen, besteht CALDERS Stück größtenteils aus Fundstücken, die hernach nur minimalen Veränderungen unterworfen wurden. CALDER wie auch der Künstler Neuguineas verherrlichen das Monster, während es noch im rohen Material der Natur lauert. Solch hellseherisches Vorauswissen beeindruckte vor allem die Surrealisten, die sowohl den Imunu wie auch das *Apfelmonster* zu den »objets trouvés aidés« gerechnet hätten.

Das Objekt aus Neuguinea hat die beißende und wahrhaft halluzinatorische Eigenart einer Arbeit, deren Schöpfer tatsächlich an Monster glaubt. Nichts von dieser Bedrohung ist in

CALDERS Werk vorhanden, das eher einen wunderlichen und ausgesprochen unbedrohlichen Sinn für die Kräfte der Natur zum Ausdruck bringt. Wie die Monster KLEES und MIRÓS versetzt uns das Exemplar CALDERS nicht in Schrecken, weil sowohl sein Schöpfer als auch wir nicht mehr an Monster glauben – zumindest nicht an solche in der Natur. Für uns entspringt das wirklich Ungeheuerliche aus dem menschlichen Geist – in den 30er Jahren hat es PICASSOS Minotaurus so eindringlich beschworen (die Bestie im Kopf statt im Körper), der sich jetzt so unauslöschlich fest der modernen Psyche eingeprägt hat.

Die meisten formalen Eigenschaften, die die Kunst der Moderne und der Eingeborenen gemeinsam haben, können auf die dem 20. Jahrhundert geläufige Neigung zu konzeptuellen Darstellungsweisen zurückgeführt werden. Der Konzeptualismus eröffnete eine ganz neue Welt von Möglichkeiten, deren Realisierung zu einer so großen Übereinstimmung führte, wie sie zwischen den Bildzeichen von KLEES *Werbeblatt der Komiker* und einer afrikanischen Malerei auf Segeltuch aus Zaire besteht □ 83, 84. Das Ersetzen direkter Illustrationen durch reduzierte Zeichen bot dem modernen Künstler Gelegenheit, Formen der Analogie zu erkunden, mit denen eingeborene Künstler schon längst vertraut waren. Da Zeichen von Natur aus zu Ökonomie führen, überrascht es nicht, wenn Eingeborene wie auch moderne Künstler in ihrer Verwendung eine beachtliche Ökonomie erlangten.

Bei der Maske der *KWELE* etwa □ 87 wiederholt der Künstler im Grunde genommen dieselbe Form in drei vertikalen paarweisen Anordnungen um eine senkrechte Achse. Diese signaturartige Form ist für die *KWELE*-Plastik charakteristisch. Aus dem Zusammenhang gelöst, würde es wahrscheinlich als ein Auge (die von Kennern vorgeschlagene Interpretation) oder als Mund verstanden werden. Als wiederholtes Zeichen erhält es hingegen seine Identität durch die Plazierung auf der Fläche. Von daher mag dieselbe Form in Beziehung zur senkrechten Achse als Anspielung auf Augen, Nasenflügel oder Mund gelesen werden. Ähnlich ist die Achse als Nase lesbar. Aber die fragliche Form ist nicht mit irgendeinem dieser Merkmale direkt zu identifizieren, da sie nie ihre Selbständigkeit als Zeichen dem Zweck der Darstellung opfert. Eine ähnliche Zweideutigkeit herrscht in der Maske der *IGBO YAM* aus Nigeria □ 88. Obwohl das Auge hier als solches klar bezeichnet ist (wie auch die gekurvte Form des zeremoniellen Messers zum Schneiden der Yamswurzel, die oben fast als ein surreales Collageelement angebracht ist), könnten die drei in ihrer Bedeutung ungeklärten zapfenartigen Vorsprünge des Gesichts[110] aufgrund ihrer Lage mit Stirn, Nase, Mund oder Kinn assoziiert werden – gerade wenn man sie von vorn als Kreise sieht.[111] Aber wie bei der *KWELE*-Maske hängt das reiche Spiel dieser Formen von ihrer suggestiven Unbestimmtheit ab; daß sie trotz der Assoziationen, die sie erwecken, auf bestimmte Gesichtszüge nicht festgelegt werden können. Es wird zwar manchmal immer noch behauptet, in einem primiti-

□ 83 *›Muster mit figürlichen Elementen‹ (Ausschnitt), MANGBETU? (Zaire), bemalter Rindenstoff, Gesamthöhe 145 cm. Musée des Arts Africains et Océaniens, Paris.*

□ 84 *Paul Klee, ›Werbeblatt der Komiker‹, 1938, gefärbte Paste 48,5 x 32 cm. Privatsammlung, Schweiz.*

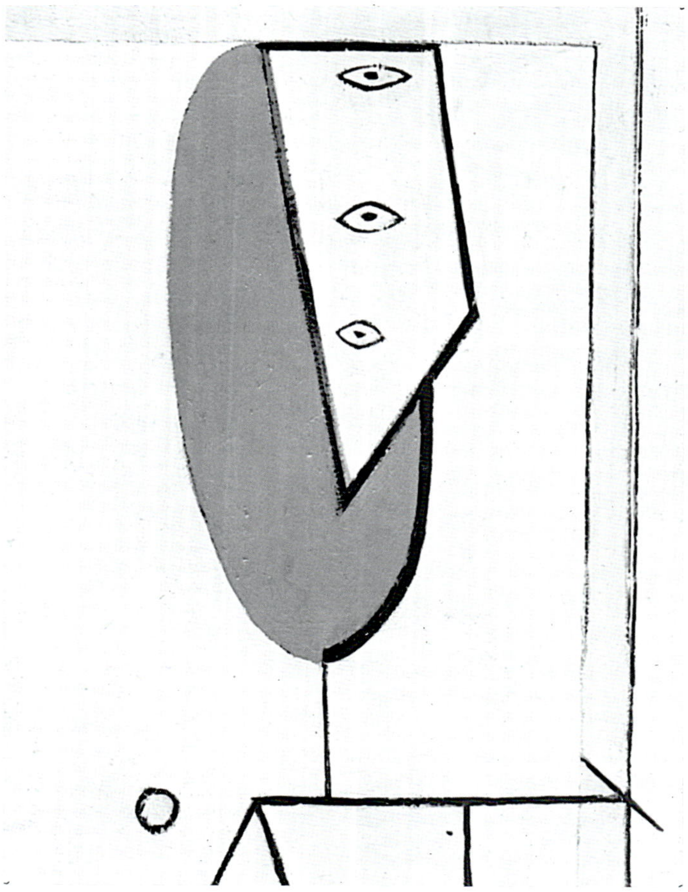

□ 85 *Pablo Picasso, ›Das Atelier‹ (L'atelier), Ausschnitt, 1927–28, Öl auf Leinwand, 150 x 231 cm. The Museum of Modern Art, Schenkung W. P. Chrysler, Jr., New York.*

□ 86 *Pablo Picasso, ›Kopf‹ (Tête), 1928, Öl auf Leinwand, 73 x 60 cm. Sammlung Jacqueline Picasso, Mougins.*

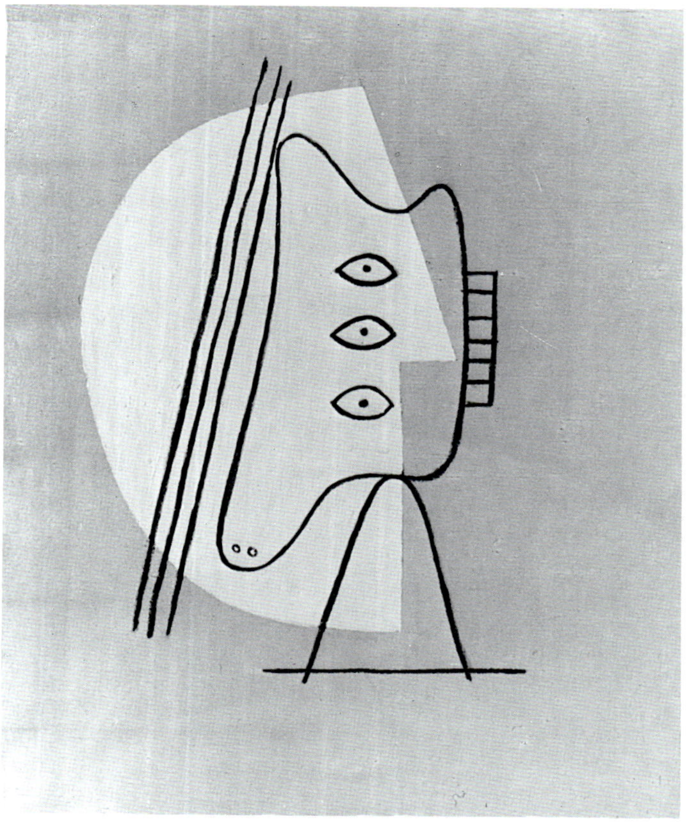

ven Werk habe alles eine besondere symbolische Bedeutung. Würde dies zutreffen, wäre die Freiheit, das Bild erst bei seiner Herstellung zu entwickeln, geringer als es bei eingeborenen Künstlern klar der Fall zu sein scheint. Auch bleibt die Frage unbeantwortet, warum gerade in einer traditionellen Gesellschaft viele Formen – wie die »Zapfenelemente« der *YAM*-Masken – offenbar nicht mehr gedeutet werden können. Tatsächlich sind andere ungedeutete Motive dieser Art Metamorphosen früherer, wörtlicherer Formen, deren ursprüngliche Identität im Laufe der Zeit verlorenging. Die besondere Projektionsfläche der abstrakten *JUKUN*-Maske □ 446 scheint sich etwa aus den Hörnern der Büffelmasken der *MAMA* entwickelt zu haben □ 941. Die Hörner verloren nicht nur ihre Identität, als sie in ein durchbohrtes dekoratives Oval übergingen, sondern die Maske wurde jetzt auch tiefer getragen: Früher von den *MAMA* auf den Kopf gesetzt, steht sie bei den *JUKUN* zwischen einer Kopfbedeckung und einer Gesichtsmaske.[112]

Das Spiel mit wiederkehrenden Motiven bei den Masken der *KWELE* und *IGBO* ist mit der häufigen Wiederholung von elementaren Zeichen vergleichbar, welche die Gesichter von vielen Figuren PICASSOS aus den 20er und 30er Jahren gliedern. In dem Gemälde *Kopf* □ 86 etwa wird eine augenähnliche Form dreimal auf dem weißen Profil des Gesichts senkrecht wiederholt; ähnlich im Kopf des Künstlers in dem Bild *Das Atelier* □ 85. Da dieses wiederholte Zeichen einfach als ein »drittes Auge« gedeutet werden kann, sind wir bei den afrikanischen Masken aufgefordert, es je nach Plazierung mit unterschiedlichen Gesichtsmerkmalen in Verbindung zu bringen – Augen, Nasenflügel und Mund –, auch wenn PICASSO dem Zeichen dieselbe Autonomie verlieh, derer sich auch die Formen afrikanischer Künstler erfreuen. Die »Verwechslung« anatomischer Merkmale bei eingeborenen und modernen Arbeiten dieser Art löst auch fruchtbare Assoziationen aus, die Wechselbeziehungen zwischen »Vorsprüngen« und »Löchern« am menschlichen Körper einschließen, mit denen sich Freud bei der Traumdeutung befaßte.

Im Bild mit dem Titel *Kopf* werden die poetischen Möglichkeiten der daraus resultierenden Unbestimmbarkeit noch weiter bereichert, indem PICASSO die Zeichen für »Auge« zugleich in zwei Systemen funktionieren läßt. Während sie den »geometrischen« weißen Profilkopf gliedern, haben sie auch an einem surrealeren »biomorphen« Kopf Anteil, der von schweren schwarzen Linien konturiert wird. Hier verursacht das Vorspringen der Zähne auf der rechten Seite und der Nase links unten in Verbindung mit den drei Linien, die für das Haar stehen, eine so halluzinatorische Vision, daß die drei Augen fast natürlich anmuten. Das beliebte Verfahren, zwei Ansichten eines Kopfes in einem einzigen Bild zu vereinen (normalerweise ein Profil innerhalb einer Frontalansicht), entwickelte PICASSO aus Möglichkeiten heraus, die im Kubismus latent vorhanden waren. Der *Kopf* ist insofern ungewöhnlich, als die beiden Ansichten in zwei unterschiedlichen Stilen gehalten sind, einem »klassischen« und einem surrealen. Indem es gleichzeitig an beiden Ansichten des Kopfes Anteil hat, verbindet das Motiv der gehäuften »Augen« die einander fremden Bilder der Konfiguration.

Ein einzelnes Zeichen, das innerhalb zweier verschränkter Systeme funktioniert – nicht zuletzt ein Aspekt der Ökonomie, von der ich bereits sprach –, ist in der modernen Kunst nicht ungewöhnlich. In KLEES *Vorhaben* □ 89 etwa gehört das Auge oben in der Mitte zu einer ein Muster bildenden Serie einzelner schwarzer Bildzeichen, die für Figuren, Bäume, Tiere und

□ 87 ›Maske‹, Kwele (Volksrepublik Kongo), Holz, Höhe 38 cm. Privatsammlung, Paris.

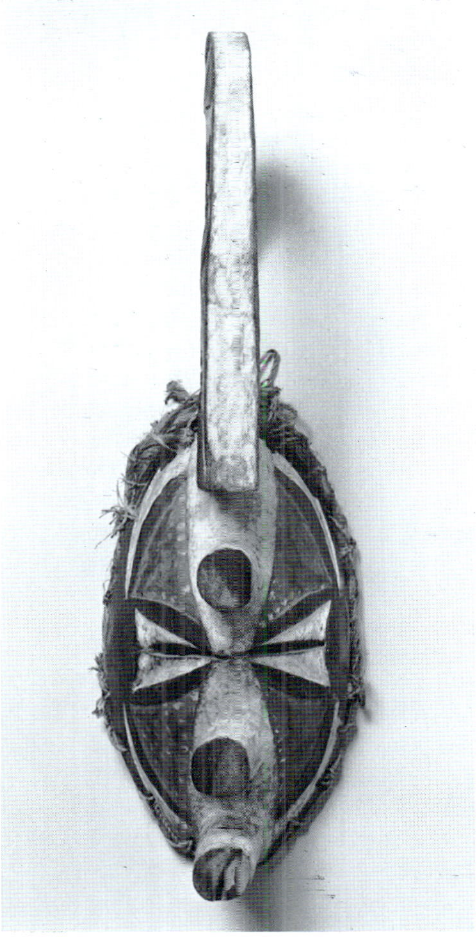

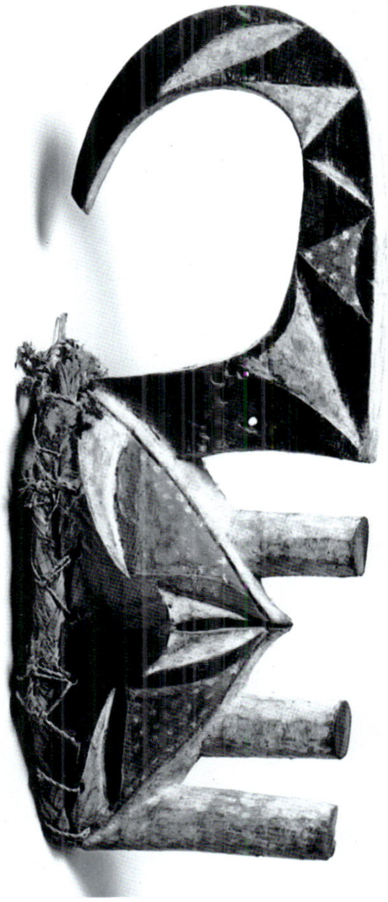

□ 88 ›Yam-Maske‹, (Vorder- und Seitenansicht), Igbo (Nigeria), bemaltes Holz, Höhe 37 cm. Sammlung R. und S. Sieber, Bloomington.

Häuser stehen, wie auch für unbestimmtere Formen, die gleichmäßig über die gesamte Fläche verteilt sind. Doch funktioniert dieses kompositionell isolierte Auge noch in einem weiteren System, da es zu einem Kopf gehört, dessen äußerer Kontur die Form eines ›C‹ bildet, darunter der Oberkörper einer in der Mitte der Bilder plazierten menschlichen Figur. Damit wir diesen Kameraden nicht übersehen, betonte Klee sein Kontur durch die unterschiedliche Farbigkeit des Hintergrundes. Die einzigartige duale Rolle des Auges signalisierte er, indem er es als einziges blaues Element innerhalb eines sonst roten, grünen und schwarzen Bildes hervorhob.

Das duale Funktionieren eines Zeichens, wie es in den Bildern Picassos und Klees zu beobachten ist, stellt eine Möglichkeit dar, die eingeborenen Künstlern nicht entging. Der Dekor auf dem Schild der *Asmat* □ 90 weist vergleichbaren »Witz« und Ökonomie auf. Die kleinen Zickzackformen, die beidseitig in Händen enden und sich über den Schild verteilen, sind Zeichen zwei verbundener Arme. Das an der Spitze des Schildes erkennbare Teilstück des gleichen Zeichens hat hingegen eine doppelte Funktion. Seine Verbindung mit dem dekorativen »Helm« einerseits und andererseits seine Umgrenzung durch den breiten Kontur, der ein Gesicht bezeichnet, haben zur Folge, daß sich das Zeichen klar als Nase und Oberlippe des Kopfes einer Ahnenfigur lesen läßt. In diesem neuen Kontext dient das »Hand«-Ende eher zur Bezeichnung eines »Mundes«.[113] Der Grad an Raffinesse im analogen Spiel von Formen, wie es dieser Schild der *Asmat* veranschaulicht, ist bei Stammesobjekten nicht selten. Vergleichbar komplexe Zusammenhänge anderer Art treten bei den paarweisen Vorsprüngen einer *Dogon*-Figur auf: konische Brüste und Nabel, gewinkelte Hände und Knie □ 352, 353; oder bei dem Analogie-Spiel von Kreismotiven, wie es bei den Augen, im Körperornament und den Armreifen einer *Boyo*-Skulptur zu beobachten ist □ 79, ebenso bei der scheinbaren Aufhängung des Oberkörpers in der Figur der *Pere* □ 11. Weitere Beispiele sind die Wechselwirkung zwischen Schnitzarbeit und Bemalung bei dem Dreiecksmotiv einer Schlange der *Baga* □ 78 oder das Streumuster aus kleinen Kinderfiguren (die manchmal Körperelemente ersetzen) auf Gesicht und Körper des Gottes A'a, wie es eine Skulptur von Rurutu (Australinseln) zeigt □ 465.

Die in der Literatur weitverbreitete Abneigung gegen das Analysieren eingeborener Arbeiten in solchen ästhetischen Kategorien (im Gegensatz zu statistischen und typologischen) ist vielleicht weniger das Ergebnis der allgemeinen Ansicht, daß eine solche kompositorische Raffinesse der primitiven Kunst fremd ist, als eines fast ausschließlichen Interesses für anthropologische und ikonographische Probleme bei jenen, die sich dieser Kunst am intensivsten widmen.[114]

Die im frühen 20. Jahrhundert erfolgte Emanzipation von den Einschränkungen einer rein wahrnehmungsbedingten Kunst schuf eine Vielfalt ästhetischer Möglichkeiten, die mit denen der Stammeskunst übereinstimmen. Nicht zuletzt gehört hierzu die Freiheit, die naturalistischen Proportionen zu vernachlässigen, an die sich die europäischen Künstler, wie verschieden ihr

□ 89 *Paul Klee, ›Vorhaben‹, 1938, gefärbte Paste und Zeitungspapier auf Leinwand, 75 x 112 cm. Paul Klee-Stiftung, Kunstmuseum Bern.*

□ 90 *›Schild‹,* Asmat, *Lorenz River (Irian Jaya – vormals Niederländisch-Neuguinea), bemaltes Holz, Höhe 40 cm. Sammlung Friede, New York.* ▷

□ 91 ›*Maske*‹, FANG (Gabun), *bemaltes Holz, Höhe 70 cm. Musée de l'Homme, Paris. Farbabbildung* □ *575.*

□ 92 ›*Doppelgesichtige Helmmaske*‹, FANG (Gabun), *bemaltes Holz, Höhe 30 cm. The Metropolitan Museum of Art, Rockefeller Memorial Coll., Verm. N. A. Rockefeller, New York.*

Stil auch gewesen sein mochte, seit der Gotik bis in den Neoimpressionismus (selbst den Fauvismus von 1905–06) gehalten hatten. Während dieser Jahrhunderte bewegten sich das Verhältnis von Höhe zu Breite des Körpers und jenes von Kopf und Gesamthöhe nur innerhalb bestimmter Grenzen.[115] Ein Wandel in Richtung auf extreme Maßverhältnisse wird im Spätjahr 1906 durch PICASSOS »iberischen« Stil – etwa in dem Bild *Zwei Frauen* □ 315 – vorweggenommen. Aber erst 1907 – in den *Demoiselles* (speziell der Figur rechts unten) und in Bildern von MATISSE wie *Luxus* – wurde die Befreiung von älteren Konventionen endgültig durchgesetzt. Bald machten sich die deutschen Künstler diese Freiheit für ein Verfahren »expressiver Disproportion« zu eigen. Wie Meyer Schapiro beobachtete, tendierte ihre Kunst dazu, sich in zwei figürliche Typen zu polarisieren, die vom Werk LEHMBRUCKS und BARLACHS vertreten werden: schlanke, langköpfige Figuren bzw. untersetzte Figuren mit gedrungenen Köpfen.[116] Ein vergleichbarer Kontrast tritt bei Masken der *FANG* auf, die die ovalen Proportionen des menschlichen Gesichts zu vollkommener Kreisform runden oder extrem in die Länge ziehen.

Der Tendenz der Moderne zu einer solchen Polarisierung konnte nur die Vertrautheit mit den erstaunlichen Proportionen einiger Stammesobjekte Rückhalt gewähren. GIACOMETTI kannte wahrscheinlich die außergewöhnlich dünne Figur der *NYAMWEZI* □ 94, eine Skulptur, die jahrzehntelang in Privatbesitz war – zuerst bei einem der großen Sammler moderner Kunst, André Lefevre, dem sie in den 30er Jahren gehörte. Doch stellt das Material der Eingeborenen nur einen von vielen möglichen Vorläufern für seine überlängten Figuren dar □ 93. GIACOMETTI war mit den dünnen etruskischen Figuren der Villa Giulia in Rom gründlich vertraut. Ich vermute daher, daß primitive und etruskische Modelle im Vergleich zu PICASSOS »Schirm«-Skulpturen von 1931 eher als Bestätigung denn als Inspiration für die ungewöhnlichen Proportionen von GIACOMETTIS späterem Werk dienten.[117]

Es erscheint mir ganz logisch, daß PICASSO die erste konstruierte Skulptur in demselben Jahr, als er die Collage einführte, geschaffen haben soll und daß diese voneinander abhängigen Entwicklungen zu einer Zeit einsetzten, als er sich eingehend mit Stammeskunst beschäftigte.[118] Die scheinbare Einfachheit und Roheit der Collage stellte bei PICASSO sicherlich eine zweite primitivierende Reaktion dar – in diesem Fall gegen das Hermetische und die *belle peinture* des hochentwickelten analytischen Kubismus. Sie findet ihre Parallele sechs Jahre früher, als er die spätsymbolistische Verfeinerung seiner Gemälde aus der »Blauen« und »Rosa Periode« vermittels des Primitivismus, der in den *Demoiselles* seinen Höhepunkt fand, überwand. Im Frühjahr 1912, als PICASSO auf sein *Stilleben mit Rohrstuhl* ein Stück Öltuch klebte und ein Endlosseil für Schiffe bestellte, das das Bild anstelle des Rahmens einfassen sollte, schränkte er nicht nur die verfeinerte malerische Sprache des hochentwickelten analytischen Kubismus ein. Er unterminierte auch dessen »klassische« Struktur, indem er ein Amalgam von Materialien einführte, die zuvor noch als unver-

□ 93 *Alberto Giacometti, ›Große Figur‹ (Grande figure), 1949, bemalte Bronze, 166 x 16,5 x 34,5 cm. The Museum of Modern Art, Vermächtnis James Thrall Soby, New York.* ▷

□ 94 ›*Figur aus Holz*‹, NYAMWEZI (*Tansania*), *Höhe 149 cm. Sammlung J. W. Mestach, Brüssel.* ▷ ▷

95

96

97

□ 95 *›Hundefetisch‹, VILI (Volksrepublik Kongo), Holz und verschiedene Materialien, Länge 80 cm. Museum für Völkerkunde, Berlin.*

□ 96 *Italo Scanga, ›Kartoffelmangel # 1‹, 1979, Horn, Kartoffeln und verschiedene Materialien, 132 x 30,5 x 20 cm. Sammlung des Künstlers; durch freundliche Unterstützung der Delahunty Gallery, New York.*

98

99

100

□ 97 *›Fetisch‹, Fon (Volksrepublik Benin), Horn, Holz und verschiedene Materialien, Höhe 38 cm. Sammlung Ben Heller.*

□ 98 *›Hundefetisch‹, Vili (Volksrepublik Kongo), Holz und verschiedene Materialien, Länge 88 cm. Musée de l'Homme, Paris.*

□ 99 *Lucas Samaras, ›Schachtel # 1‹, 1962, verschiedene Materialien, 23 x 42 x 43 cm. Sammlung Morton L. Janklow, New York.*

□ 100 *Arman, ›Kühle Hände blau‹, 1977, Handschuhe, 122 x 76 cm. Sammlung des Künstlers.*

einbar mit den schönen Künsten gegolten hatten. Die nachfolgende Anwendung der Collagetechnik auf die konstruierte Skulptur führte zu der unter dem Namen ›Assemblage‹ bekannten Zwitterbildung.

Auch wenn PICASSOS Hinzufügung von Stoff und Seil in der westlichen Tradition ohne Vorläufer ist, brachten ihm die Stammesskulpturen das Prinzip einer solchen Mischung näher, deren Schöpfer häufig Tuch, Bast, Schnur, Rinde, Metall, Lehm sowie Fundstücke in Verbindung mit Holz und anderen Materialien verwerteten (wie bei den Nagelfetischen und Emblemen ☐ 95–100, von denen Apollinaire ein bedeutendes Exemplar besaß ☐ 429, 430, oder den Masken ☐ 324, 333). PICASSOS Reliefs wurden außerdem so konstruiert, daß sie an der Wand hingen und dabei von ihr abstanden: Dies ist genau die Art, wie europäische Künstler ihre eingeborenen Masken präsentierten. Ich will damit nicht zum Ausdruck bringen, daß Stammesobjekte die ausschließliche Anregung der Collage und Assemblage darstellen, zumal es für die letztgenannten Kunstformen andere mögliche Vorläufer gibt. PICASSOS eingehende Beschäftigung mit Werken der Stammeskunst im Jahr 1912 vorausgesetzt, müssen sie aber in seinem Denken eine wichtige Rolle gespielt haben.

PICASSOS Verwendung abwechslungsreicher Materialien führte nicht zu Objekten, die der Stammeskunst ähnlich waren. Dies war nicht sein Weg. PICASSO pflegte das enthaltene Prinzip zu abstrahieren, machte es aber seinen eigenen Zwecken dienstbar. Der Gebrauch solcher Materialien durch die Dadaisten (JANCOS *Maske* ☐ 794) und Surrealisten (ERNSTS *Lustige Hunde* ☐ 849) spiegelt die Absicht, bewußt primitive Vorbilder zu evozieren. Dasselbe gilt sicherlich auch im Hinblick auf viele zeitgenössische Beispiele. ITALO SCANGAS *Kartoffelmangel* # 1 erinnert mit seinen Stoffstreifen an den Hundefetisch in Berlin ☐ 95, 96, während die Einbeziehung eines Tierhorns an die Fetische der *FON* ☐ 97 und *SONGGE* ☐ 172 denken läßt. CONNERS *Kreuz* ☐ 103, das mit einem assemblageähnlichen *EJAGHAM*-Emblem verglichen werden kann ☐ 101, gibt dem Ganzen

◁ □ 101 *›Ekpe-Stammesemblem‹*, EJAGHAM *(Kamerun), Holz und verschiedene Materialien, Höhe 89 cm. Privatsammlung, New York.*

□ 102 *›Fetisch‹*, FON *(Volksrepublik Benin), »Suze«-Flasche und verschiedene Materialien, Höhe 34,5 cm. Privatsammlung, Paris.*

□ 103 *Bruce Conner, ›Kreuz‹ (Cross), 1961, Holz, Metall und verschiedene Materialien, 94 x 49,5 cm. Sammlung R. und L. Dean, Los Angeles.*

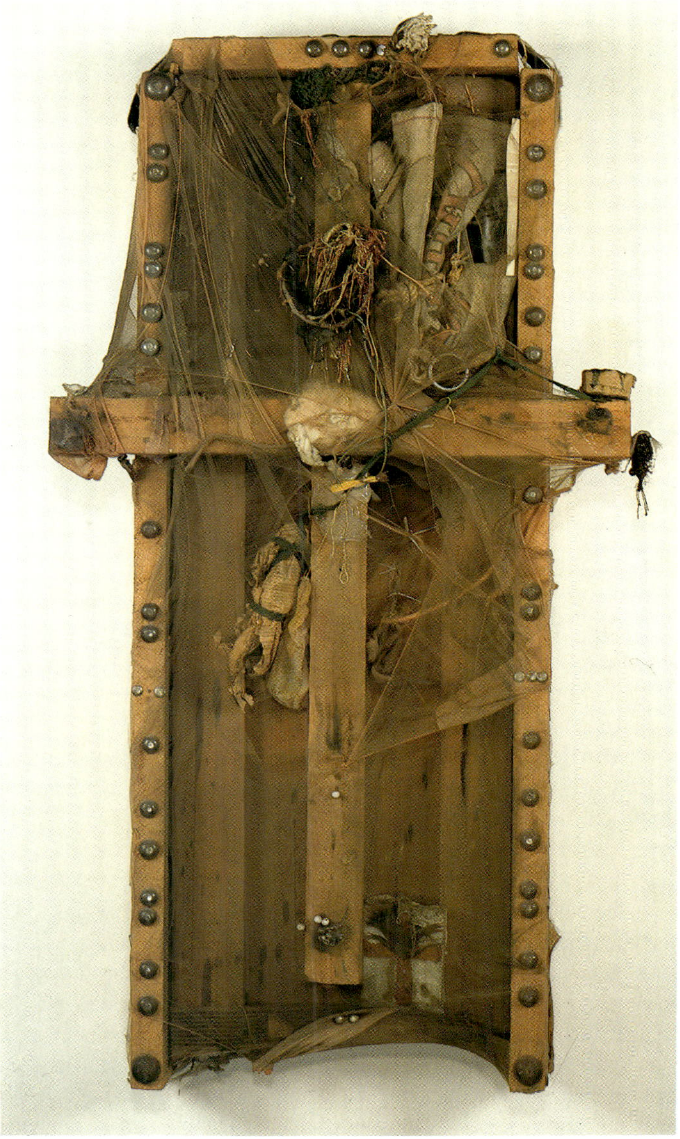

eine Wendung ins Christliche, wobei eine Umdeutung im Sinne des Animus eingeborener Religionen vorliegt (womit an den fetischhaften Charakter christlicher Devotion erinnert wird, der uns in Exvotos und dem Reliquienkult begegnet).

Afrikanische Fetische sind in ihrer Ideologie gemeinhin kollektiv, und die Bedeutung ihrer Aspekte wird von den Eingeweihten verstanden. Der moderne Künstler arbeitet mit privateren Symbolen. So wählte etwa LUCAS SAMARAS für *Schachtel # 1* □ 99 so ausschließlich häusliches Material aus, daß dessen Fetischismus auf fast freudianische Weise nach Innen lenkt. ARMANS *Kühle Hände Blau* □ 100 deckt sich mit dem fetischhaften Prinzip, das in allen »Anhäufungen« dieses Künstlers wirksam ist, wobei die Handschuhe einen spezifisch freudianischen Beiklang haben (DE CHIRICO hat dies für die moderne Malerei eingeführt). Und doch erweckt die Konfiguration von ARMANS Werk, die vor allem der ›allover‹-Malerei verpflichtet ist, einen relativ formalen Eindruck, der den »klassischen« Nagelfetischen wie dem Hund im Musée de

☐ 104 *›Seelenfänger‹, Pukapuka (Cookinseln), Fasern, Höhe ca. 100 cm. The Trustees of the British Museum, London.*

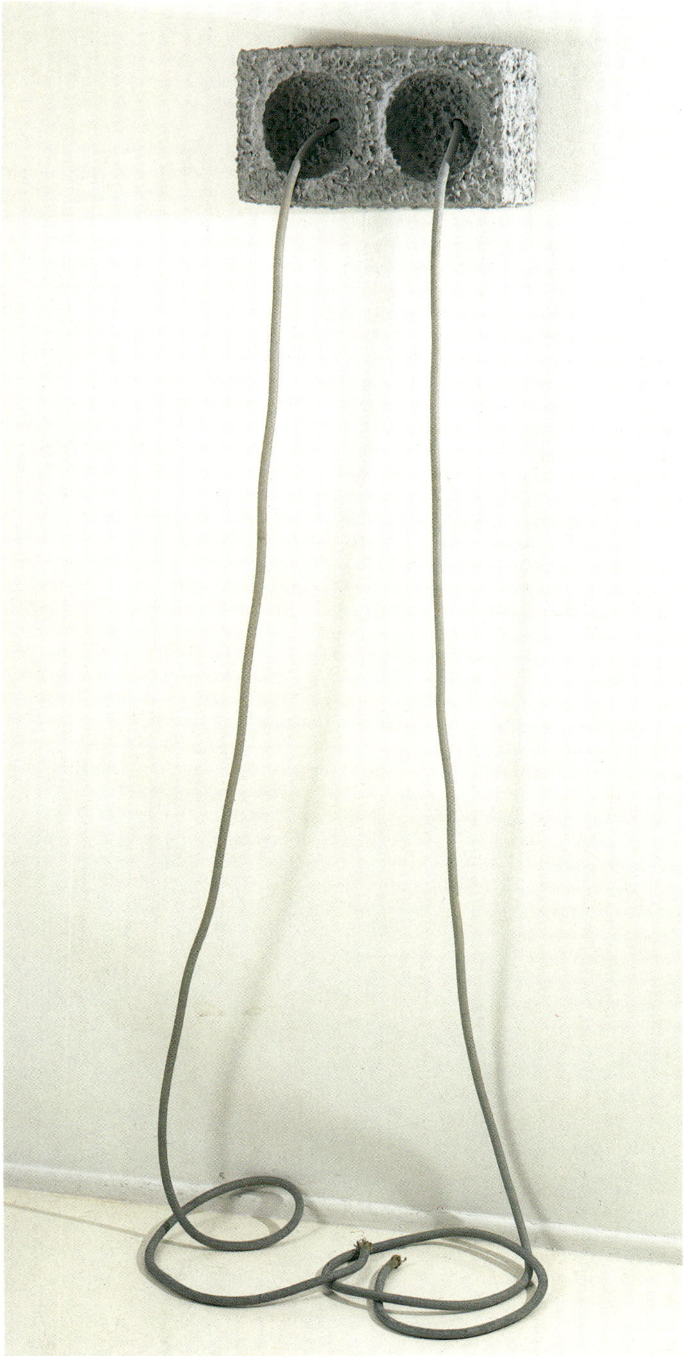

☐ 105 *Eva Hesse, ›Eines mehr als eins‹ (One more than one), 1967, Holz, Kunststoff, Papiermaché, Schnur und Akrylfarben, Größe der Schachtel 20 x 38 x 13 cm. Sammlung N. Spector und S. Antonakoś.*

l'Homme ☐ 98 näher steht als dem Exemplar im Berliner Museum für Völkerkunde ☐ 95. Als ein langjähriger Sammler afrikanischer Kunst fühlt ARMAN eine tiefe Beziehung zur Stammeskunst. Wie viele Künstler-Sammler macht er aber bei dieser keine direkten Anleihen. Sein Sammeln afrikanischer Kunst ist gleichwohl kein Zufall.

»Am Anfang meines Interesses für afrikanische Kunst«, so erinnert er sich, »wurde ich von Artefakten angezogen, die mit Material bedeckt und magischen Kräften geladen waren. Solche Fetische, die ein Gefühl des ›Angehäuften‹ verspüren ließen, standen einigen meiner eigenen Arbeiten durch ihre alles bedeckende Vervielfachung von Elementen und der daraus resultierenden suggestiven Kraft irgendwie nahe. Eine lange Beziehung zur afrikanischen Skulptur, die ich als Sammler hatte, gab mir ein klareres Verständnis, wie gute Kunst wirklich aussehen sollte.«[119]

Seit den frühen 60er Jahren stellen eine Reihe jüngerer Künstler Objekte her, die selbst die abstrakteren Formulierungen, wie sie vom Kubismus kommen, vermeiden – Lösungen, wie sie das Werk ARMANS bestimmten, ganz zu schweigen von JACKSON POLLOCK, DAVID SMITH oder ANTHONY CARO. Zunächst als »spezifische Objekte« geläufig, waren diese unfigürlichen und halbfigürlichen minimalistischen und postminimalistischen Schöpfungen oft von einer tiefen Poesie. EVA HESSES *Eines mehr als eins* etwa ☐ 105 berührt uns zum Teil durch die anatomischen und psychologischen Anspielungen der Formen und Materialien; die zwei konkaven Halbkugeln des Werkes sind als »eine augenförmige Umkehrung« der Brüste beschrieben worden und die dünnen Gummiröhren, die von ihnen ausgehen, als »Tränen«.[120]

Die meisten in diesem Buch besprochenen Stammesobjekte sind figürlich. Selbst Gebrauchsgegenstände wie Löffel, Stöcke oder Musikinstrumente sind meistens anthropomorph oder durch Bilder von Tieren oder Untieren bedeckt. Und doch findet man auch bei den eingeborenen Völkern eine Reihe »spezifischer Objekte«, die aufgrund ihrer Gestaltung, des Materials oder einer eigentümlichen Poesie dem Werk der Künstler aus Eva Hesses Generation und aus der unmittelbar folgenden sehr nahe stehen. Der bemerkenswerte »Seelenfänger« von der Pukapukainsel □ 104 teilt die Aleatorik von Hesses Arbeit aufgrund des freihängenden Seils, dem eine Serie paarweise angeordneter Ringe angeheftet ist, wie aufgrund der vergleichbar träumerischen Poesie. Man behauptet, daß er von »heiligen Männern« dazu benutzt worden sei, um die Seelen jener zu fangen, die gegen sie zürnten. Ein Insekt oder ein Vogel – durch eine der Schlingen dieser Falle geflogen – wäre als die Seele des Missetäters betrachtet worden, der dann um ihre Rückkehr hätte flehen müssen. Vor dem Ersten Weltkrieg hatte dieses Objekt bereits den dadaistischen Karikaturisten und Maler Marius de Zayas fasziniert, der hieraus die Anregung für sein Porträt von Stieglitz nahm □ 667.[121]

Die »Stabkarten« von den Marschallinseln □ 106, die man für zeitgenössische Skulpturen halten könnte, sind ausgeklügelte Navigationskarten, die die Reflexion, Brechung und das Wechselspiel des ozeanischen Seegangs vor und nach seinem Durchgang durch die Atolle anzeigen. Der erfahrene Navigator konnte anhand eines gegebenen Wellenmusters seine mutmaßliche Position inmitten der Gruppe dieser flachen, aufge-

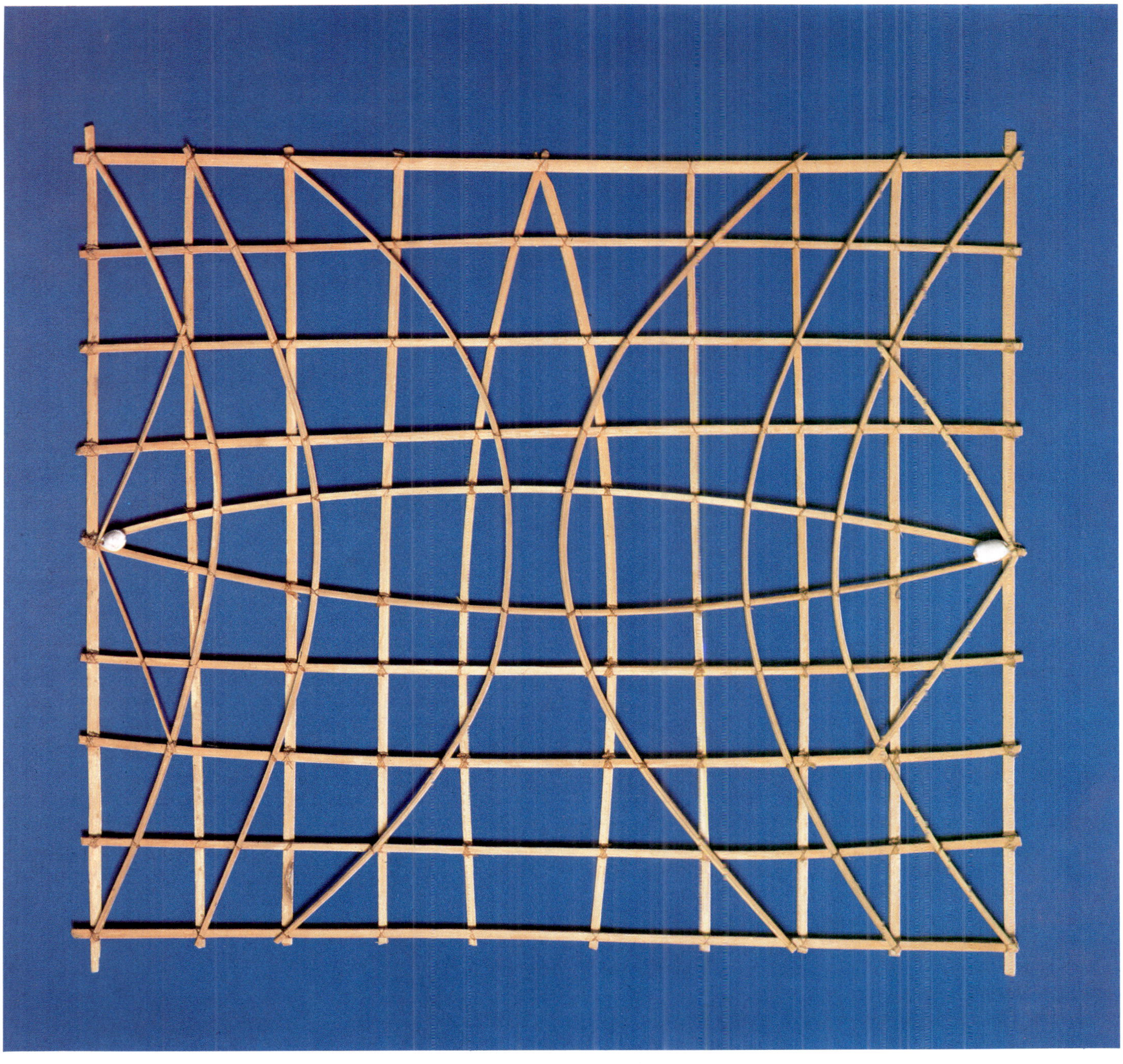

□ 106 *›Stabkarte‹, Marschallinseln, Holz, Fasern und Muscheln, Höhe 58 cm. The Trustees of the British Museum, London.*

reihten Inseln erschließen, deren Sichtweite von See aus nicht mehr als wenige Meilen betrug. Das bemerkenswerter Gitter aus geraden und gekurvten Stäben stellt ein Wellenmuster zwischen ganz bestimmten Atollen dar, die selbst durch kleine Muscheln angezeigt werden.

Die unerwartete Poesie, Schönheit und intellektuelle Faszination solcher Stammesobjekte erklären, warum sich viele junge Künstler in Völkerkundemuseen Anregung verschafft haben. Diejenigen, die das Museum of Natural History in New York, das Musée de l'Homme in Paris, das Museum für Völkerkunde in Berlin oder das Museum of Mankind (British Museum) in London besuchen, beschreiten damit einen Weg, der zu Beginn des Jahrhunderts von MAX WEBER, PABLO PICASSO, EMIL NOLDE und HENRY MOORE gebahnt wurde – auch wenn diese Künstler für ganz verschiedene Objekte empfänglich waren und jeder auf seine Weise reagierte.

Ein Unternehmen wie dieses Buch und die New Yorker Ausstellung von 1984 lassen im Veranstalter unvermeidlich die Frage nach deren Notwendigkeit aufkommen, sei es auch nur im Hinblick auf Zeitaufwand, Anstrengung und Kosten. Auch kann der Veranstalter, obwohl er die Werke über die Jahre in unterschiedlichem Zusammenhang einzeln sehen konnte, die Wirkung ihres Nebeneinanders eigentlich nicht voraussehen: die erhellende Einsicht – oder auch deren Ausbleiben –, zu der die Konfrontation der Werke führen kann. In einem bestimmten Sinne organisiert er die Ausstellung, um zu sehen, was passieren wird. Es wäre dennoch unredlich, wenn ich vorgeben würde, mir beim Einbringen des Vorschlags für ein solches Projekt nicht einigermaßen sicher gewesen zu sein, daß sie zu einer bedeutsamen Korrektur der bisher gültigen Geschichte moderner Kunst führen wird und das große Publikum dieser Kunst auf einige unbekannte, doch besonders relevante Meisterwerke anderer Kulturen aufmerksam machen kann. Es bestand auch der Gedanke, daß einige moderne Werke, die wir recht gut kennen, aus einer neuen Perspektive an Bedeutung gewinnen würden. Wie vermessen es auch erscheinen mag, liegt all dies im Bereich meiner Erwartungen.

Im Bereich meiner Hoffnungen existiert etwas weniger Explizites, etwas, das schwieriger in Worte zu fassen ist: daß die besondere Gegenüberstellung, die hier vorgeführt wird, nicht nur dazu verhilft, unsere Kunst, sondern in einmaliger Weise auch unsere menschliche Natur besser zu verstehen – wenn das nicht ein und dasselbe ist. Die Reste eines zweifelhaft gewordenen evolutionären Mythos sind noch in den Tiefen unserer Psyche lebendig. Die Avantgardisten der Moderne lehrten uns vor Jahrzehnten, daß die Eingeborenen eine Kunst hervorbrachten, die oftmals große Komplexität zu scheinbar einfachen Lösungen verdichtete. Es nimmt daher nicht Wunder, daß die Anthropologie in deren Kultur eine vergleichbare Komplexität aufgedeckt hat.[122] Ich hoffe unsere Bemühungen werden zeigen, daß das evolutionäre Vorurteil zumindest im Hinblick auf Werke des menschlichen Geistes ganz und gar absurd ist.

Die verschiedenen Metamorphosen von PICASSOS *Demoiselles d'Avignon* waren nichts als die sichtbaren Symbole einer Suche des Künstlers in seiner eigenen Psyche. Diese Selbstana-

◁ ☐ 107 *›Fetisch‹ (Detail),* SONGGE *(Zaire), Holz und verschiedene Materialien, Gesamthöhe 78 cm. Sammlung P. Dartevelle, Brüssel.*

☐ 108 *Yipwon-Figur (siehe Glossar),* ALAMBLAK, *Karawari River, Provinz Ost-Sepik (Papua-Neuguinea), Holz, Höhe 215 cm, Sammlung Friede, New York. Ehemals Sammlung Matta.*

□ 109 *›Figur aus Holz‹*, CHAMBA *(Nigeria), Höhe 57 cm. Sammlung Philippe Guimiot. Farbabbildung* □ *51.*

lyse, dieses Abschälen von Schichten des Bewußtseins wurde mit einer Untersuchung der Ursprünge menschlicher Selbstdarstellung in Verbindung gebracht. Nachdem er jene Entwicklung in seinen iberischen Studien über das Archaische zurückverfolgt hatte, war PICASSO für die »Offenbarung« primitiver Kunst im Trocadéro bereit, die ihn zur tieferen, ursprünglicheren Lösung führte, nach der er auf der Suche war. Im Trocadéro erfaßte PICASSO etwas von tiefer psychologischer Tragweite, dessen Entdeckung GAUGUIN in der Südsee verfehlt hatte.

Daß PICASSO die *Demoiselles* als sein »erstes von einem Bann befreiendes Bild« bezeichnete, gibt uns zu verstehen, daß er schon die eigentliche Herstellung des Gemäldes als analog zu jener Art psycho-spiritueller Erfahrungen oder Übergangsriten verstand, wofür seiner Ansicht nach die Werke im Trocadéro herangezogen worden waren. Die besondere Art persönlicher Freiheit, die er bei der Realisierung der *Demoiselles* erlebte – einer befreienden Kraft, die er mit der ursprünglichen Funktion der Stammesobjekte, welche er vor sich hatte, in Verbindung brachte –, wäre für den Eingeborenen ohne Bedeutung gewesen, worauf die Anthropologen als erste bestehen würden. Doch es existiert eine Verbindung. Denn was PICASSO in jenen Skulpturen erkannte, war letztlich ein Teil seiner selbst, seiner eigenen Psyche und von daher ein Garant für die mit den Bildhauern dieser Skulpturen geteilte Menschlichkeit. Außerdem erkannte er, daß die künstlerische Tradition des Westens viel von der Kraft verloren hatte, um den in diesen Skulpturen offenbarten inneren Menschen entweder direkt anzusprechen oder umzustimmen.

Wie jede große Kunst zeigen die erlesensten Stammesskulpturen Bilder des Menschen, die das individuelle Leben und die Zeit ihrer Schöpfer transzendieren. Dennoch erweckt der Kopf der abgebildeten afrikanischen Figur □ 107 im ersten Moment den fast schockierenden Eindruck psychologischer Andersartigkeit, während die Schnitzarbeit von Neuguinea □ 108 eine im Sinne unseres eigenen Körperverständnisses vergleichbare Andersartigkeit aufweist. Nichts aus der westlichen (oder östlichen) Kunst bereitet uns auf diese Skulpturen vor. Trotzdem berühren sie uns, weil wir in der Tat etwas von uns selbst in ihnen erkennen, einen Teil unserer selbst, den die westliche Kultur nicht bereit war zu tolerieren, geschweige denn vor dem 20. Jahrhundert zu verbildlichen. Wenn die Andersartigkeit primitiver Bildwerke unsere Menschlichkeit erweitern kann, dann deshalb, weil wir gelernt haben, diese Andersartigkeit in uns selbst zu erkennen. »Je est un autre«, wie Rimbaud erkannte.

Ich sprach an früherer Stelle über PICASSOS Idee einer Verwandtschaft zwischen moderner und eingeborener Kunst, die in gewisser Hinsicht dem Verhältnis zwischen der Kunst der Renaissance und der des klassischen Griechenland entspreche. Dieser Vergleich erfaßt indes die weitreichendsten Schlußfolgerungen aus der Übereinstimmung zwischen Primitivem und Modernem, die das vorliegende Buch untersucht, nicht. Denn während die Italiener des 15. Jahrhunderts in vielerlei Hinsicht den Griechen des 5. Jahrhunderts v. Chr. – materiell wie auch geistig – nicht überlegen waren, haben wir beide Kulturen in technologischer Hinsicht weit hinter uns gelassen und glauben im Bewußtsein dieser Überlegenheit, daß wir uns um Lichtjahre in der Entwicklung von den Naturvölkern entfernt haben. Insofern aber die Kunst ein konkreter Anhaltspunkt für die geistigen Errungenschaften der Zivilisationen ist, sollte uns die Verwandtschaft der Moderne mit der eingeborenen Kultur zu denken geben.

□ 110 *Arman, ›Anhäufung von Seelen‹, 1972, DAN-Masken in Polyester, 52 x 29 x 6,5 cm. Privatsammlung.*

□ 111 *›Maske‹, Kuba (Zaire), Holz, Höhe 33 cm. Privatsammlung, New York.*

□ 112 *›Maske‹, Kalabari Ijo (Nigeria), Holz, Höhe 38 cm. Sammlung Ernst Anspach, New York.*

□ 113 *›Affenschädel‹, Fon (Volksrepublik Benin), Schädel eines Affen, Unterkiefer eines Krokodils, Muscheln, Schnur und verschiedene Materialien, Länge 30,5 cm. Sammlung Ben Heller.*

Anmerkungen

1. In den vergangenen zwanzig Jahren wurde der Bezeichnung »Stammeskunst« [engl. tribal art] oft der Vorzug vor »primitiver Kunst« gegeben, um darunter eine große Vielzahl von Kunstrichtungen von mehr oder weniger nicht-zentralistischen Gesellschaften mit niedrigem technischen Entwicklungsstand zu fassen. Beide Bezeichnungen sind äußerst problematisch; wir verwenden sie in dieser Ausgabe nur widerstrebend (und gleichwertig), um überhaupt einen allgemeinen Sammelbegriff für die hier angesprochene Kunst zu haben. Bisher hat noch niemand befriedigende oder allgemein anerkannte Ersatzbegriffe für »Stammes-« oder »primitve« Kunst gefunden. Einige Experten geben »Stammeskunst« den Vorzug vor »primitive Kunst«, da ihnen in letzterer Bezeichnung zu viele negative darwinistische Nebendeutungen mitschwingen (siehe hierzu S. 13–14). Andere bevorzugen »primitive Kunst« gegenüber »Stammeskunst«, da viele der Kulturen, die man Stammeskulturen nennt (vor allem in Afrika), im ethnologischen Sinne gar keine sind.
Unser Gebrauch von »Stamm« kommt natürlich nicht von der Anthropologie her. Er entspricht in etwa Websters dritter und recht freier Definition von »tribe« [engl. Stamm] (New International Dictionary, 2. Aufl.): »Jede Ansammlung von Völkern, besonders auf einer primitiven oder nomadischen Stufe, von denen angenommen wird, daß sie gemeinsamer Herkunft sind und einer mehr oder weniger zentralistischen Herrschaft unterstehen, z. B. einem Häuptling oder Stammesoberhaupt.« Den Begriff des Stammes sollte man daher nur vom üblichen Sprachgebrauch her verstehen. Der Afrikanist Leon Siroto bemerkt dazu:
»Das Wort ›Stamm‹ wäre in diesem Zusammenhang nicht mehr als eine willkürliche Konvention, ein zweckmäßiger Allgemeinbegriff, um die Irrtümer des Ausdrucks ›primitiv‹ zu vermeiden. Es ist schon so lange und so weit verbreitet, daß es anscheinend volle Gültigkeit gewonnen hat.
Vorsicht ist geboten, denn viele, wenn nicht die meisten der durch den Ausdruck bezeichneten Völker bilden im engeren Sinne keine Stämme. Sie sprechen vielleicht dieselbe Sprache und pflegen mehr oder weniger die gleichen Bräuche, bilden aber keine politische Einheit und haben keinen Gemeinschaftssinn. Außerdem haben deshalb viele von ihnen eine unterschiedliche Ikonographie und ausgesprochen gegensätzliche Stile. Man sollte sich deshalb davor hüten, ihre Kunst als Stammeskunst zu verstehen (d. h. als ethnisch einheitlich und spezifisch) . . . Die Anthropologen neigen zur Ansicht, daß Stammesgruppen eher eine Erfindung der Europäer sind und weniger der Realität entsprechen« (Brief an W. Rubin vom November 1983).
Bis in die sechziger Jahre war der Terminus »Stamm« bei den Anthropologen noch allgemein in Verwendung, um einen über die Grenzen der Kulturen und Kontinente hinaus gültigen Ausdruck zu haben. So trug etwa die von Daniel Biebuyck 1969 herausgegebene Aufsatzsammlung den Titel *Tradition and Creativity in Tribal Art* (University of California Press). Heute würde man vielleicht einen anderen Titel wählen; aber das Problem der Nomenklatur ist noch nicht gelöst. William Fagg war der beredteste Fürsprecher einer »Stammesgebundenheit in der afrikanischen Kunst«. Diese Kunst sei »Ergebnis und Funktion des Stammessystems«, er fügt aber die Beobachtung hinzu, daß der »Stamm nicht ein statisches, sondern ein dynamisches Konzept« erfordere und »Stammesstile einem ständigen Wechsel unterworfen« seien (»The African Artist« in Biebuyck [Hrsg.], S. 45).
Nicht nur afrikanische Gelehrte haben den Stammesbegriff als »eurozentrisch« kritisiert (Ekpo Eyo, zitiert in der *New York Times* vom 12. Oktober 1980, S. 70), und ihr Standpunkt ist wohlbegründet, obwohl der Bann, mit dem der Ausdruck in Afrika belegt ist (er ist von einem afrikanischen Parlament ausdrücklich verboten worden), wahrscheinlich eine Reaktion auf das politische Problem ist, geeinte Nationen und ein nationales Bewußtsein aus ethnisch verschiedenen Völkerschaften zu bilden. Daß der erwähnte »Eurozentrismus« – trotz aller Versuche ihn zu überwinden – noch immer besteht, kann kaum überraschen, da die Fächer Kunstgeschichte und Anthropologie selbst europäische Erfindungen darstellen.
Wenn Kunsthistoriker einzelne Kulturen erörtern, können sie problematische Ausdrücke wie »Stammeskunst« leicht umgehen. Aber das Bedürfnis nach einem allgemeingültigen Ausdruck entspringt dem Wunsch, Charakteristika ansprechen zu können, die (zumindest in den Augen einiger westlicher Wissenschaftler) in einer Vielzahl von Kulturen in verschiedenen Teilen der Welt ähnlich zu sein scheinen. Selbst die allerneuesten Darstellungen der Weltkunstgeschichte verwenden noch, wenn auch zögernd, die Bezeichnungen »Stammes-« und »primitive Kunst« (z. B. Honour, H. / Fleming, J., *Weltgeschichte der Kunst*, München 1983, S. 563).
Einige Anthropologen würden argumentieren, daß Gemeinsamkeiten, die eine uneingeschränkte Anwendung des Stammesbegriffs suggerieren, reine Fiktion sind. Dies ist der Grund, warum das Wort aus der anthropologischen Literatur weitgehend verschwunden ist. Auch wenn der Einwand berechtigt ist, muß es für die Untersuchung des modernen Primitivismus nicht unbrauchbar sein. Da wir im Gegenteil die betreffenden Kulturen gerade nicht direkt ansprechen, sondern die Vorstellungen untersuchen, die sich in den letzten hundert Jahren im Westen über sie herausbildeten, ist der Stammesbegriff – der ein Ergebnis solcher Vorstellungen und ihres Entstehungskontexts ist – nicht irreführend. Der Abstand, den die Ethnologen von diesem Wort nahmen, ist insofern aufschlußreich, als er eine Aussage über die primitivistische Perspektive zuläßt.

2. Goldwaters *Primitivism in Modern Painting* wurde zum ersten Mal 1938 veröffentlicht; 1967 erschien eine überarbeitete und erweiterte Ausgabe unter dem Titel *Primitivism in Modern Art* in New York. Laudes *La Peinture française (1905–1914) et »l'art nègre«* erschien 1968 in Paris. Dies sind die einzigen wirklich ernsthaften und umfassenden Untersuchungen zu diesem Thema. Charles Wentincks populärwissenschaftliches Buch *Modern and Primitive Art*, Oxford 1979 (niederländische Originalausgabe 1974, Moderne und Primitive Kunst) ist unzulänglich und gibt keine befriedigende Unterscheidung zwischen tatsächlichen (oder möglichen) geschichtlichen Einflüssen und zufälligen Ähnlichkeiten. Das Fehlen dieser bedeutsamen Unterscheidung setzt sich fort in den Kapiteln über die Moderne und afrikanische bzw. ozeanische Kunst im Katalog *Weltkulturen und moderne Kunst. Die Begegnung der europäischen Kunst und Musik im 19. und 20. Jahrhundert mit Asien, Afrika, Ozeanien, Afro- und Indo-Amerika*, Ausstellung im Haus der Kunst, München 1972. Brauchbarer ist die auf die moderne Plastik beschränkte Erörterung unseres Themas in dem Katalog *Gauguin to Moore: Primitivism in Modern Sculpture* von Alan Wilkinson (Toronto, Art Gallery of Ontario, 7. November 1981 – 3. Januar 1982). Daneben könnte man noch nennen: Werner Schmalenbach, *Die Kunst der Primitiven als Anregungsquelle für die europäische Kunst bis 1900*, Köln 1961, und seinen Aufsatz »Grundsätzliches zur primitiven Kunst« in *Acta tropica* 15, Nr. 4, 1958, S. 289–323.

3. Wie erläutert (S. 13–14 und Anm. 19 unten), behalten wir den Ausdruck »primitiv« bei, betonen aber, daß er im kunsthistorischen Kontext eine vielfältige Bedeutung hat (im Gegensatz zum streng deskriptiven Gebrauch).

4. Siehe S. 272 ff.

5. Symptomatisch dafür ist, daß einer der führenden Autoren für afrikanische Kunst Masken nur deshalb als »kubistisch« einstuft, weil sie geradlinige geometrische Strukturen aufweisen.

6. Anthropologen, besonders diejenigen, die die Betrachtung von Stammesobjekten als Kunst für ihre Zwecke als irrelevant bezeichnen, tun oft so, als hätten nur die wissenschaftlich nachweis- oder verbalisierbaren anthropologischen Aspekte dieser Objekte eine Bedeutung. Die Interessen der Kunsthistoriker umfassen natürlich auch den Gehalt an Ästhetik und Ausdruck dieser Objekte, der gerade für Künstler den entscheidenden Zugang bildet. Dies zeigt sich etwa in einer Bemerkung, die Picasso mir gegenüber diesbezüglich machte: »Alles, was ich über afrikanische Kunst wissen muß, steckt in diesen Objekten.«

7. *Nouveau Larousse illustré*, 7 Bd. und 1 Suppl.bd., Paris 1897–1904, Bd. 7, S. 32.

8. *Webster's New International Dictionary*, 2. Aufl., unter dem Stichwort »primitivism«.

9. Ekpo Eyo, *Two Thousand Years of Nigerian Art*, Lagos 1977, S. 28, verwendet das Wort »Primitivismus« fälschlicherweise nur, um den europäischen Gebrauch des Wortes »primitiv« in bezug auf nicht-europäische Kunst zu bezeichnen. Er stellte (wie in der *New York Times* zitiert) fest, daß westliche Gelehrte »die Vorstellung des Primitivismus [sic] erfanden und sie verbreiteten, so weit ihr Einfluß reichte«.

10. Dies schloß nicht aus, daß sie solche Kunst als Kuriositäten sammelten, siehe S. 20 ff. Trotz seines beschränkten Interesses an polynesischer Kunst (siehe Anm. 30), besaß er möglicherweise auch zwei kleinere afrikanische Figuren (siehe S. 215, Anm. 49).

11. Dies ereignete sich in den Jahren vor dem Ersten Weltkrieg. »Nègre« (oder auch »travail de nègre«) hat im Französischen einen leicht abwertenden Klang. Dessenungeachtet gebrauchen viele gebildete Franzosen die Wendung »art nègre«, auch wenn sie das Wort »nègre« in anderen Zusammenhängen meiden.

12. Man sollte nicht vergessen, daß der Ausdruck »art nègre« zu Beginn des Jahrhunderts die Stammeskunst von Afrika wie auch von Ozeanien meinte. Das gleiche gilt für das Wort »Negerkunst« und seine Varianten. Beide Aus-

gaben von Carl Einsteins *Negerplastik* (1915 und 1920) enthalten Beispiele ozeanischer Plastik. Die Bezeichnung »art nègre« wurde sowohl für die Kunst am Königshof von Benin als auch für Stammesstile gebraucht.

13. In der Zeit zwischen den beiden Weltkriegen und noch einige Zeit danach wurde »primitiv« in Buchtiteln, Universitätskursen und zur Klassifizierung in Kunstmuseen verwendet (der Vorläufer des Michael C. Rockefeller-Flügels im Metropolitan Museum trug die Bezeichnung »Museum of Primitive Art« und die entsprechende Verwaltungsabteilung im Metropolitan Museum wird heute noch Abteilung für Primitive Kunst genannt). Bis vor kurzem wurde das Wort weitgehend, wenngleich zögernd, auch von Anthropologen verwendet (siehe das Zitat von Lévi-Strauss, S. 14). Eine 1973 von der Oxford University Press veröffentlichte Sammlung anthropologischer Aufsätze (hrsg. v. Anthony Forge) trug den Titel *Primitive Art and Society*.

14. Die Präkolumbianische Kultur wurde (und wird immer noch) von Künstlern und anderen zunächst mit der Kunst der großen und komplexen theokratischen Gesellschaften der Spätzeit gleichgesetzt, der *Maya*, *Tolteken* und *Azteken* in Mittelamerika und der *Inka* in Peru. Sie zeichneten sich durch einen hohen Grad an Spezialisierung und an sozialer, wirtschaftlicher und politischer Hierarchie aus, der sich in ihrer monumentalen Architektur und Plastik spiegelt, die ich dem Wesen nach eher als archaisch denn als primitiv bezeichnen würde. Weniger bekannt, aber einigen Künstlern sicher nicht unbekannt, waren viele einfachere präkolumbianische soziokulturelle Einheiten, die keine staatliche Regierung, auch keine öffentliche Monumentalkunst, Schriftsprachen (die auf jeden Fall nur die *Maya* besaßen) noch andere Merkmale komplexerer Gesellschaften vorzuweisen hatten. Bemerkenswert sind dabei die *Chrotega*, *Chiriqui*, *Chibcha* und viele andere Herrschertümer, die das Gebiet zwischen Mittelamerika und den nördlichen Anden bewohnten.
Wenn man die *Maya*, *Tolteken*, *Azteken* und *Inka* hinsichtlich ihrer Kunst mit Kulturen wie der Ägyptens oder Kambodschas in Verbindung bringt, unterscheiden sie sich insofern, als die gesellschaftliche und religiöse Ordnung aller präkolumbianischen Kulturen bestimmte Züge hat, die eher für primitive als für höfische Kulturen typisch sind. Da jedoch die modernen Künstler davon nur wenig oder gar nichts wußten und präkolumbianische Kulturen allein durch Kunstwerke (oder deren Reproduktionen) kannten, fanden diese Arbeiten im ausgehenden 19. Jahrhundert nicht zusammen mit der Stammeskunst Afrikas und Ozeaniens (die von den Künstlern der damaligen Zeit übersehen wurden) Eingang in die Moderne, sondern als archaische Kunst wie die anderer Hofkulturen, der ägyptischen etwa, die Gauguin und Van Gogh als »primitiv« betrachteten. Die »primitiven« Seiten der präkolumbianischen Technologie, Soziologie und Kommunikation sind der Grund, weshalb diese Kulturen hinsichtlich ihrer Kunst manchmal noch als primitiv eingestuft werden (sie befindet sich im Metropolitan Museum und in den meisten anderen Museen in derselben Abteilung wie die afrikanische und ozeanische Kunst).
Die monumentale mittelamerikanische Architektur und Plastik wurden in Museen und Weltausstellungen gezeigt (die Pariser Weltausstellung von 1889 rekonstruierte etwa ein »Haus der *Azteken*«) und erweckten das Interesse der Künstlergenerationen, bevor die »art nègre« bekannt wurde. Die Museumssammlungen enthielten auch Kunsterzeugnisse der entfernter gelegenen und weniger zentralisierten präkolumbianischen Gebiete, deren Kunst mehr Gemeinsamkeiten mit der Stammeskunst hatte. Doch bleibt offen, wieviel davon den Künstlern, zumindest vor den zwanziger und dreißiger Jahren, wirklich bekannt war.
Die präkolumbianische Kunst hatte unstreitig einen Einfluß auf die Moderne, der aber zunächst von der archaischen Plastik der *Azteken*, *Maya*, *Tolteken* und *Olmeken* ausging. Nach Gauguin und Van Gogh verbindet man das Interesse daran vor allem mit der Generation der dreißiger Jahre (obwohl den präkolumbianischen Kulturen auch von zeitgenössischen Künstlern Interesse entgegengebracht wird, allerdings mehr gedanklich als ästhetisch). Um festzustellen, wie nachhaltig und wie verbreitet dieser Einfluß war, bedarf es einer Untersuchung, die eine befriedigende Unterscheidung zwischen nachweisbaren Einflüssen und bloßen Ähnlichkeiten trifft. Barbara Braun, mit der ich über die Konzeption des Projektes Primitivismus in Kunst des 20. Jahrhunderts sprach, arbeitet derzeit an einem Buch über präkolumbianische Quellen der modernen Kunst.
Neben präkolumbianischen Objekten besaßen die meisten naturgeschichtlichen Museen auch Beispiele der Stammeskunst Mittel- und Südamerikas. Beispiele dieser jüngeren Objekte sind die *Mundurucú*-Kopftrophäe, die Nolde für sein Gemälde *Masken* verwendete □ 530, und die *Witoto*-Maske □ 972.

15. Picasso lag anscheinend mit sich selbst im Widerstreit über das, was er »l'art aztèque« nannte und womit er die Gesamtheit der ihm bekannten präkolumbianischen Kunst meinte. Meine Gesprächsnotizen enthalten eine Äußerung Picassos über diese Kunst, die ich aus dem Gedächtnis wiedergebe: »langweilige, unbewegliche, zu große . . . Figuren ohne Erfindung«. Er lobte jedoch die Schönheit eines »Aztekenkopfes« in einem Gespräch mit Brassaï, *Conversations avec Picasso*, Titel der engl. Ausgabe *Picasso and Company*, Garden City 1966, S. 242. Wie Brassaï für den 18. Mai 1960 vermerkt, schauten sich Picasso und er ein Photoalbum von ihm an. In einem Kapitel des Albums mit dem Titel »Primitive Bilder«, so berichtet Brassaï, »läßt ein Aztekenkopf Picasso plötzlich innehalten und dann ausrufen: ›Das ist so reich wie die Fassade einer Kathedrale‹.«
Picassos Gespür für den Erfindungsreichtum der Stammeskunst entspricht den Tatsachen, denn die afrikanische und ozeanische Kunst ist wirklich einfallsreicher als die präkolumbianische. Dies wird klar, wenn man das Museo Nacional de Antropologia von Mexiko mit der Ozeanienabteilung des Berliner Völkerkundemuseums vergleicht, die beiden schönsten und vollkommensten Darstellungen der jeweiligen Kunst, die ich kenne. Picassos Haltung hing teilweise aber auch von seiner Perspektive ab, daher meine Formulierung »wahrgenommener Erfindungsreichtum«. Was Picasso im Trocadéro und in den Kuriositätenläden als die Kunst der Neger zu Gesicht bekam, hielt er, grob gesagt, für die Leistung einer einzigen kulturellen Einheit Afrikas, während die afrikanische Stilfülle in Wirklichkeit u. a. das Ergebnis unzähliger ethnischer Gruppen mit unterschiedlichen Religionen, Sprachen und Traditionen ist, verteilt über ein Gebiet, das weitaus größer ist als Westeuropa.

16. Man beachte die Unterscheidung zwischen dem Alten Reich einerseits, dem Mittleren Reich und dem Neuen Reich andererseits. Die Kunst des Alten Reichs halte ich für besonders einfallsreich. Der »Akademismus« (im Gegensatz zum einfachen »Traditionalismus«), wie man ihn in der ägyptischen Kunst findet, wird erst nach dieser Zeit vorherrschend. Einfallsreichtum ist jedoch bei einem Kunstwerk ein quantitativer Aspekt, der nicht unbedingt etwas über die Qualität aussagt. In den Arbeiten des Alten Reiches mehr Erfindung zu entdecken, heißt nicht, die Qualität der Meisterwerke leugnen zu wollen, die uns aus dem Mittleren und dem Neuen Reich überliefert sind.

17. »Classification stylistique du masque dan et guéré de la Côte d'Ivoire Occidentale (A.O.F.)« in *Medelingen van het Rijksmuseum voor Volkenkunde, Leiden*, Nr. 4, Leiden 1948. Obwohl erst 1948 veröffentlicht, beruht diese eindrucksvolle Studie auf Forschungen aus der Zeit vor dem 2. Weltkrieg.

18. Goldwater, *Primitivism in Modern Art* (a.a.O., S. 150) verwendete »archaisch« zu Recht, um iberische Plastik zu charakterisieren, die Picasso interessierte und die dann »zu den ›Neger‹-Gemälden führt«. Picassos Interesse an dieser Plastik war wie sein noch älteres Interesse an der ägyptischen Kunst sehr dauerhaft. Letztere hat genügend Gemeinsamkeiten mit bestimmten außereuropäischen Hofstilen, so zumindest für Künstler des späten 19. und frühen 20. Jahrhunderts, um einen allgemein gültigen Begriff zu rechtfertigen. Nach meiner Ansicht erfüllt »archaisch« diesen Zweck besser als jedes andere Adjektiv.

19. Im *Larousse illustré* von 1897–1904 (in dem das Wort »primitivisme« zum ersten Mal auftauchte, siehe S. 9 und Anm. 7) sind für »primitif« (als französisches Adjektiv und Substantiv) sechzehn verschiedene Bedeutungen angegeben, die von algebraischen und geologischen bis zu historischen und kirchlichen reichen, ebenda S. 31–32. Zwei von ihnen waren abwertend, vor allem unter dem Stichwort »ethnologisch«: »Les peuples qui sont encore au degré le moins avancé de civilisation«. Die Primitiven im Hinblick auf die Kunst sind nach der Definition des *Larousse* einfach »Artistes, peintres ou sculpteurs qui ont précédé les maîtres de la grande époque«.

20. Bei einem Gespräch mit Sabartés in seinem Atelier in der Villa Les Voiliers, Royan 1940, siehe Jaime Sabartés, *Picasso, An Intimate Portrait*, New York 1949, S. 213, Originaltitel *Picasso, Retratos y Recuerdos*.

21. »Gotisch« wurde in der klassizistischen Kritik traditionell mit »barbarisch« gleichgesetzt. Erst im 19. Jahrhundert begann das Wort an Ansehen zu gewinnen. Die Geschwindigkeit, mit der pejorative Bedeutungen von Kunstbegriffen verschwinden können, läßt sich daran ermessen, wie schnell die Bezeichnung »impressionistisch« und mit ihr die Vertreter dieser Kunst von der Öffentlichkeit angenommen wurden, und das obwohl der Begriff, wie Meyer Schapiro bemerkt, abwertend war und an handwerkliche Hausdekoration erinnerte (»peinture d'impression«).

22. Goldwater, R., »Judgments of Primitive Art, 1905–1965« in *Tradition and Creativity in Tribal Art*, hrsg. v. Biebuyck, S. 25.

23. Ersatzlösungen wie »ethnisch« oder »eingeboren« haben so viele kunstgeschichtliche und/

oder soziologische Nachteile, daß kein ernstzunehmender Versuch unternommen wurde, »primitiv« durch sie zu ersetzen.

24. »The Dilemma Which Faces African Art« in *The Listener* 13, September 1951, S. 413–15.

25. Das gilt besonders für afrikanische Gelehrte aufgrund der politischen Ursachen, die ich in Anm. 1 ansprach.

26. *Structural Anthropology,* London 1963, S. 101–02.

27. Siehe den Beitrag Varnedoes, S. 188, 189.

28. »Einfachheit« war eine Vorstellung, auf die Picasso in meinem Gespräch mit ihm immer wieder zurückkam; manchmal bezog er sich dabei auf sein eigenes Schaffen, (häufiger) auf das anderer Künstler (z. B. Matisse'), zweimal auf die »art nègre«. Er meinte damit natürlich nicht einfach das Fehlen raffinierter Effekte, sondern eine Ökonomie, die die Verarbeitung komplexer Strukturen zur Voraussetzung hatte. »Einfachheit« tauchte in seinen Gesprächen im allgemeinen als Gegensatz zu jener Komplexität auf, die für den Salon-Illusionismus des 19. Jahrhunderts typisch ist. Picassos Kritik an der Kunst, die er in seiner Jugend kennengelernt hatte, galt den Künstlern, die es verlernt gehabt hätten, einfach zu sein. Gegenüber Sabartés und mir lobte er die primitiven Künstler für ihre Einfachheit, siehe Sabartés, a.a.O., S. 213.

29. Das klassische Beispiel dafür ist der Michael C. Rockefeller-Flügel des Metropolitan Museums. Er verdankt seine Entstehung Nelson Rockefellers Leidenschaft für Stammeskunst, die auch zu seiner früheren Gründung des Museums of Primitive Art geführt hatte. Diese Stiftung ist Ausdruck seiner Beschäftigung mit der Kunst des 20. Jahrhunderts und der Einsicht, daß die Stammeskunst für viele moderne Künstler von großer Bedeutung ist.

30. Mit der möglichen Ausnahme von *Parahi Te Marae* □ 230 enthält kein Gemälde Gauguins einen direkten Verweis auf die Kunst Tahitis oder der Marquesasinseln (die beiden Gebiete Polynesiens, in denen er lebte), obwohl seine Bilder voller Anspielungen auf andere außereuropäische Kunstformen sind. Das Gemälde *Tehamana hat viele Eltern* □ 226 zeigt im Hintergrund vergrößerte Schriftzeichen von der Osterinsel (die Gauguin nie besuchte). Andere Formen der Kunst der Osterinseln und der Marquesasinseln lassen sich in seinen Holzplastiken nachweisen. Aber selbst dort ist ihr Einfluß nicht der vorherrschende.

31. Flam (siehe S. 226) ist mit mir darüber einer Meinung. Es gab zwar im Trocadéro keine Objekte, die den *Kauernden* beeinflußt haben könnten, aber Derain hat vielleicht bei seinem Besuch im Britischen Museum im Jahre 1906 mehrere präkolumbianische Figuren gesehen, die mit seinem Werk gewisse Gemeinsamkeiten haben □ 114.

32. Über das Eindringen christlich-portugiesischer Formen in die kongolesische Kunst siehe Wingert, P. S., *The Sculpture of Negro Africa*, New York 1950, S. 54; Fagg, W., und Elisofon, E., *The Sculpture of Africa*, London 1958, S. 157. Delafosse ist mit anderen der Meinung, daß die *Baule*-Plastik von der ägyptischen Kunst (durch Wanderungen und Handelsbeziehungen) beeinflußt wurde. Seine wichtigste Veröffentlichung: »Sur les traces probables de civilisation égyptienne et d'hommes de race blanche à la Côte d'Ivoire« in *L'Anthropologie*, Bd. 2, 1900, S. 431–51.

33. Ich zitiere hier Malraux, *La Tête d'obsidienne*, Paris 1974, S. 17, obwohl ebenso Picasso mich und sicherlich auch andere darauf hinwies. Was er – zumindest im Gespräch mit mir – meinte, war nicht mit der Schlußfolgerung Malraux' aus dieser Bemerkung identisch, siehe meine Ausführungen S. 303 und S. 351, Anm. 142.

34. Es geht mir hier natürlich um Einflüsse der Kunst außerhalb von Europa und aus der Zeit vor der Renaissance. Die Kunst der Moderne ist trotz ihrer radikalen Ablehnung des aus der Renaissance stammenden Illusionismus letzendlich mehr durch Aspekte dieser Kunst geprägt als durch jede andere Tradition. Gleichgültig wieviel ein modernes Werk mit der Malerei Ägyptens, Roms, Byzanz' oder mit der primitiven Plastik gemein hat, der entscheidende Unterschied zu jenen besteht darin, daß die Sprache, die der Stil der Moderne zunächst abändert und vereinfacht, die des westlichen Illusionismus ist. Die älteren Stilrichtungen werden notwendigerweise aus der Perspektive gesehen, die von der dazwischenliegenden Tradition konstituiert wurde.

35. Bernard, *Souveniers sur Paul Cézanne* Paris 1925, S. 31.

36. Zu Besprechungen dieser Maske siehe Goldwater, a.a.O., S. 86–87, 102, Anm. 4, und Laude, a.a.O., S. 104–05, 109. Im vorliegenden Buch wird sie von Paudrat (S. 148), Flam (S. 221) und Bassani (S. 419) besprochen.

37. Obwohl ich selbst zu denen gehöre, die sich vor Jahren Goldings Ansicht anschlossen, daß der Kopf von einer der Figuren auf Derains *Badenden* aus dem Jahre 1907 □ 265 von der afrikanischen Kunst beeinflußt wurde, habe ich meine Meinung geändert, seitdem ich mit primitiver Kunst vertrauter bin. Ich stimme nun Flams Auffassung zu, S. 227, derzufolge kein Einfluß primitiver Kunst in diesem Gemälde vorliegt. Flam glaubt einen gewissen Einfluß afrikanischer Masken in den Bildern von Baden-den, die Vlaminck □ 258 und Derain □ 262 1908 malten, zu erkennen. Wenn überhaupt vorhanden, so ist der Einfluß nur geringfügig, zumal dies die einzigen Bilder der beiden Künstler sind, die solch eine Hypothese zulassen.

38. Ich habe mindestens ein halbes Dutzend Masken gesehen, die mit der Maske Vlamincks/Derains fast identisch sind, und es müssen sich noch mehr im Handel und in Privatsammlungen befinden. Das Museum of Fine Arts in Columbus, Ohio, veröffentlichte irrtümlicherweise das eigene Exemplar der Maske als die Maske Vlamincks/Derains; eine weitere befindet sich in der Sammlung des Völkerkundemuseums von Antwerpen.

39. Neben der qualitativ recht unbedeutenden Fang-Maske, die Vlaminck und Derain nacheinander besaßen, geben die von Matisse früh erworbene *Vili*-Plastik □ 260, die vier in Picassos Atelier Ende 1908 fotografierten Objekte □ 402, Picassos Reliquienwächter der *Kota* □ 411, seine *Baga*-Plastik □ 365, 366 einen allgemeinen Eindruck von der Qualität der zu Anfang dieses Jahrhunderts verfügbaren Objekte. Es ist bekannt, daß sowohl Matisse als auch Picasso relativ früh *Punu*-Masken besaßen. Zusammen mit den von der Avantgarde im ersten Jahrzehnt des Jahrhunderts erworbenen Gelede-Masken sind dies wahrscheinlich die bedeutendsten Erwerbungen (da die Qualität solcher Masken damals generell vergleichsweise hoch war). Das allgemeine Qualitätsniveau wurde erst gehoben, als Brummer und Guillaume Acquisiteure für den Erwerb dieser Objekte einsetzten. Davor war Qualität etwas rein Zufälliges; einige Objekte aus völkerkundlichen Expeditionen bilden hier eine Ausnahme

40. Mehrere Händler und Sammler haben manch ein Stammesobjekt absichtlich falsch als ehemaligen Gegenstand aus den Ateliers der wichtigsten Künstler der Avantgarde bezeichnet. Dies fördert die Legendenbildung, das Interesse an den Objekten und erhöht zweifelsohne ihren Wert. Bei allen sechs Objekten, die angeblich aus der Sammlung Picassos stammen und denen ich nachgegangen bin (d. h. denjenigen, die sich bei seinem Tod nicht in seinem Besitz befanden), hat sich ergeben, daß zwischen ihnen und dem Künstler keine nachweisbare Beziehung besteht. Das gleiche gilt für einige Objekte, die man mir als ehemalige Sammlungsstücke Matisse' anbot. Bei Objekten, die Vlaminck oder Derain gehört haben sollen, ist die Sache schwieriger, da beide vielfach in ihrem Leben mit Stammesobjekten regelrecht Handel trieben und Plastiken nur zum Wiederverkauf erwarben.

41. Es würde zu weit führen, die Frage der »Authentizität« hier in aller Ausführlichkeit zu behandeln. Um eine brauchbare Vorstellung zu gewinnen, genüge folgender Hinweis: Ein authentisches Objekt wird von einem Künstler für sein eigenes Volk geschaffen und für traditionelle Zwecke verwendet. Daher wären Werke afrikanischer und ozeanischer Künstler, die zum Verkauf an Fremde, wie Seeleute, Kolonisten oder Ethnologen hergestellt werden, als nichtauthentisch zu bezeichnen. Problematisch wird es, wenn an der Integrität der Tradition selbst zu zweifeln ist, dann nämlich wenn das Stammesleben unter dem Druck der modernen Technik und der gesellschaftlichen, politischen und religiösen Lebensformen des Westens verändert würde.

42. Zu Picassos *Yombe*-Objekt siehe S. 307, 308.

43. »La chasse aux œuvres nègres devint un réel plaisir pour lui« aus Fernande Olivier, *Picasso et ses amis*, Paris 1933, S. 169.

□ 114 *›Figur des Gottes Xochipilli‹, aztekisch (Mexiko) um 1300–1521, Stein, Höhe 55 cm. The Trustees of the British Museum, London.*

44. Ein solches Angebot ist in einem Brief Heymanns aus dem Jahr 1909 erhalten.

45. Während afrikanische und polynesische Kunstwerke für gewöhnlich poliert sind, besaß Picasso relativ viele Objekte mit rauher oder unpolierter Oberfläche.

46. Als die *Demoiselles* zum ersten Mal gezeigt wurden, war das Echo, von avantgardistischen Künstlern abgesehen, im allgemeinen kaum positiv und ihr Erwerb wurde von Freunden des Museum of Modern Art kritisiert. Diese Information verdanke ich Alfred Barr.

47. Wie Paudrat bemerkt (S. 173), war Rattons Geschmack kühner als der Guillaumes. Ihre Präferenzen, die geschmacksbildend waren, lassen sich dessenungeachtet unter einem einzigen, im wesentlichen »klassischen« Geschmack subsummieren.

48. Den Grad der Wertschätzung sehe ich hier letzlich im Preis der Objekte ausgedrückt.

49. Siehe Gaffé, R., *La Sculpture au Congo Belge*, Paris 1945. Der Mut Gaffés als Sammler moderner Kunst läßt sich an seinem Kauf von Mirós *Geburt der Welt*, nur ein Jahr nach der Entstehung, 1925, ermessen. Ihm gehörten auch einmal Picassos *Mädchen mit Mandoline (Bildnis Fanny Tellier)* und Chagalls *Ich und das Dorf*.

50. Das ist trotzdem eine andere Frage als »Was ist das *Charakteristischste* an der afrikanischen Kunst?« Die relativ naturalistische Kunst der *Yoruba* (ein Volk von mindestens zehn Millionen) ist weitaus typischer für Afrika als viele Stile, die meiner Meinung nach die Ästhetik der afrikanischen Kunst von der anderer großer Kulturen am stärksten unterscheidet.

51. Äußerung gegenüber Florence Fels im Verlauf der verschiedenen Gespräche, die zu dem von Fels veröffentlichten »Interview« führten, in *Les Nouvelles littéraires, artistiques et scientifiques* 42, 4. August 1923, S. 2: »Je vous ai déjà dit que je ne pouvais plus rien dire de 'l'art nègre' . . . . C'est ce qu'il me devenu trop familier, les statues africaines qui traînent un peu partout chez moi, sont plus des témoins que des exemples.« Mehr über diese Stellungnahme siehe S. 347, 348, Anm. 63, 64.

52. Goldwater, a.a.O., S. XVI.

53. Ebenda, S. XXI.

54. Ebenda, S. 254.

55. Wie ich zeigen werde, ist es kein Zufall, daß die Stammesvariante des modernen Primitivismus gleichzeitig mit dem Beginn des radikalen Wandelns der formalen Strukturen in der Moderne (bei den *Demoiselles* von 1907) auftritt. Daher erschwert es der Prozeß der Konzeptualisierung, der der modernen und der primitiven Kunst gleichermaßen eigen ist, die Schuld der Moderne gegenüber der primitiven Kultur zu identifizieren.

56. Diese beiden Masken, die in der Literatur früher irrtümlich den »*Wobé*« zugeschrieben wurden, befanden sich wahrscheinlich in Picassos Besitz, als er die Gitarre anfertigte. Eine der Masken □ 417 kaufte Picasso möglicherweise, als er sich im August 1912 mit Braque in Marseille nach Stammesobjekten umsah; die andere Maske □ 29 erwarb er zweifellos früher (siehe S. 313 ff.).
Ich fragte Picasso nach »*Wobé*«-Masken, als er die Gitarre dem Museum schenkte (Kahnweilers Bemerkung zu diesem Thema in dem in Anm. 58 genannten Aufsatz brachte mich darauf), aber er schob die Frage beiseite. Viele Monate später zeigte er mir eine »*Wobé*« *(Grebo)*-Maske und erweiterte und klärte dabei die Äußerungen, die Kahnweiler etwas verwirrend wiedergegeben hatte. Die wesentlichen Gedanken des Gesprächs bringe ich weiter unten im Haupttext. Die Maske, die mir Picasso zeigte, hatte zylindrische Augen, einen Bart und Hörner. Da ich mich damals mit afrikanischer Kunst überhaupt noch nicht auskannte, prägte sich mir die Maske nicht besonders gut ein. Daher vermag ich nicht zu sagen, ob es die Maske der Abbildung □ 29 war, aber ich bin mir ziemlich sicher. Diese Maske befand sich damals in der Villa La Californie (die Picasso 1955 gekauft hatte), wo Picassos Sekretär Miguel lebte. Wahrscheinlich brachte sie Miguel auf Picassos Geheiß nach Mougins in Le Mas Notre-Dame-de-Vie, wo Picasso von 1961 bis zu seinem Tod lebte. Daß sich eine solche Maske nicht in Notre-Dame-de-Vie befand, erklärt, warum Picasso nicht auf das Thema eingehen wollte, als ich ihn das erste Mal danach fragte.
Claude Picasso hat die Frage aufgeworfen, ob nicht die Maske, die ich zuerst sah, eine dritte *Grebo*-Maske aus Picassos Besitz war. Wenn dem so ist, dann tauchte sie nicht wieder auf. Zumindest wird keine derartige Maske in der groben, unvollständigen und oft fehlerhaften Liste der *objets de tiers* geführt (Objekte im Atelier Picassos, die er nicht selbst schuf), die nach seinem Tode erstellt wurde und die Claude Picasso für mich durchsah; außerdem stellte mir Lydia Gasman großzügigerweise eine Kopie davon zur Verfügung.
Daß die weniger qualitätsvolle der beiden *Grebo*-Masken Picassos □ 29 mit ziemlicher Sicherheit diejenige war, die er mir zeigte, heißt nur, daß es diejenige war, die Miguel mitbrachte. Hinsichtlich der *Gitarre* spielt sie deswegen noch keine größere Rolle als die Maske der Abbildung □ 417. Da die wesentlichen Züge der beiden Masken gleich sind und sich Picasso eher für die Konzeption solcher Masken als für bestimmte Einzelheiten interessierte, können wir die beiden Masken wie eine behandeln, wenn wir ihren Einfluß auf die *Gitarre* erörtern.

57. Picasso datierte die *Gitarre* aus dem Gedächtnis an den Beginn des Jahres 1912, noch vor das *Stilleben mit Rohrstuhl* (siehe meinen Aufsatz »Picasso in the Collection of the Museum of Modern Art«, Ausstellungskatalog, The Museum of Modern Art 1972, S. 74, 207–08, Anm. 4). Seitdem hat jedoch Edward Fry in einer Vorlesung (»Picasso's 1912 *Guitar*«, Referat zum 65. Jahrestreffen der College Art Association of America, San Francisco, 25.–28. Februar 1981) überzeugend dafür plädiert, die erste Fassung aus Karton in den Herbst 1912 zu datieren; die Umsetzung in Blech wäre demnach erst Anfang 1913 erfolgt. Fry ist der Überzeugung – ohne dafür allerdings einen Beweis zu haben –, daß die eine *Grebo*-Maske □ 417 im August 1912 in Marseille gekauft wurde (was durchaus der Fall sein kann) und sie Picasso zur Anfertigung der Gitarre motivierte. Problematisch an dieser These ist, daß Picasso mit ziemlicher Sicherheit seine andere *Grebo*-Maske bereits besaß □ 29 und daß die neuerworbene Maske, obwohl sie schöner ist, kein Gestaltungsprinzip aufweist, das nicht schon in der anderen Maske vorhanden gewesen wäre. Picasso dürfte auch die *Grebo*-Maske des Trocadéro □ 332 seit seinen ersten Besuchen im Jahre 1907 bekannt gewesen sein.

58. Kahnweiler spricht in seinem Aufsatz, der auf Englisch als »Negro Art and Cubism« in *Horizon*, London 1948, 18, Nr. 108, erschien, auf S. 418 von einer »*Wobé*«-Maske in Picassos Besitz und stellt zwischen ihr – insbesondere ihren zylindrischen Augen – und der Gitarre eine Beziehung her. Er sah außerdem in der Struktur solcher Masken ein Vorbild für die »Transparenz« des Kubismus, diese Idee nahm er später aber weitgehend zurück. Im Gespräch mit Picasso sagte ich, daß Kahnweiler eine sehr genaue Beobachtungsgabe bewiesen habe, indem er die *Gitarre* mit einer solchen Maske in Verbindung brachte. Picasso lachte und sagte, daß er selbst Kahnweiler darauf aufmerksam gemacht habe (eine Tatsache, die bei Kahnweiler, vielleicht aus Gründen der Diskretion, unerwähnt geblieben war).

59. Beide *Grebo*-Masken Picassos haben derartig bemalte Ränder.

60. Goldwater, a.a.O., S. 161, ist der Auffassung, daß das zylindrische Auge »den magischen, durchdringenden Blick des von der Maske symbolisierten oder zeitweise in ihr wohnenden Geistes ausdrückt«.

61. Wenn dies, wie ich vermute, die Maske ist, die Picasso mir zeigte (siehe Anm. 56), so beeinträchtigte ihre durchschnittliche Qualität nicht sein Interesse und seine Freude an ihr. Dafür spricht die Art, wie er von ihr sprach oder sie in die Hand nahm.

62. Obgleich *Grebo*-Masken am Anfang des Jahrhunderts keine Seltenheit waren (Oldmans Katalog bietet zwei zum Verkauf an) und viele von Picassos Freunden, wie Kahnweiler □ 412 und Apollinaire □ 429, Exemplare davon besaßen, gibt es meines Wissens keinen Beweis für die Existenz einer *Grebo*-Maske, die, sowohl von der Qualität als auch von ihren Besonderheiten her, der des Metropolitan Museum gleichkäme.

63. Die Literatur zu den *Grebo*-Masken, Frobenius, L., *Masken und Geheimbünde Afrikas*, Halle 1898, und Holas, B., *Tradition des Kru*, Paris 1980, kennt eine große Vielfalt von Typen, aber keine, die auf die Maske im Metropolitan Museum hinführen würde.

64. Da einige afrikanische Kunstwerke, wie etwa die *Fang*-Maske □ 17, die auf S. 21 ff. sowie in Anm. 38 erörtert wird, als Verkaufsobjekte standardisiert wurden, kamen gewisse Elemente der Standardisierung auch in Objekte, die zu kultischen Zwecken hergestellt wurden.

65. Dazu gehören die zylindrischen Augen, eine glatte Gesichtsfläche, parallele Lippen und in der Mehrzahl der Fälle eine »Stab«-Nase, aber nicht unbedingt die Hörner, die verschiedenartig gebogen sind, nur angedeutet werden oder ganz fehlen können.

66. Damit ist die breite geographische Zone von Westen nach Osten quer durch Zentralafrika gemeint. Eine Karte der bildhauerischen Regionen bei Leuzinger, E., *Africa: The Art of the Negro Peoples*, 2. Aufl., New York 1967, mit Faltplan.

67. Da die Afrikaner keinen Ausdruck für »Kunst« kennen, bezeichnen sie geschulte Hersteller von Objekten mit Handwerkernamen wie Schmied oder Schnitzer.

68. Wir wissen relativ wenig über die afrikanische Stammeskunst vor dem Ende des 19. Jahrhunderts, in dem der Kolonialismus im großen Ausmaß einsetzte. Die Experten sind sich über

den Umfang von Wandlungsprozessen und die Entwicklung neuer Formen vor dieser Zeit uneinig. Die Verfechter extremer Positionen behaupten sogar, daß die meisten der Objekte, die wir als authentische Stammeskunst betrachten, schon durch die Berührung mit dem Westen beeinflußt waren.

Da Afrika so groß ist und viele verschiedene religiöse und politische Richtungen kannte, war das Schicksal vorkolonialer Tradition von Ort zu Ort völlig verschieden. In bestimmten Küstengebieten gab es lange vor der Jahrhundertwende beträchtliche Kontakte mit Europäern. Dagegen leben in den meisten ländlichen Gebieten die animistischen Religionen und die mit ihnen einhergehenden Kunstformen noch immer weitgehend unverändert fort. In einigen dieser Gebiete ist es mit der Zunahme der Kontakte zum Westen und der Einflüsse von dort immer schwieriger geworden, die traditionellen Formen zu bewahren. Einige der unter diesen Bedingungen entstandenen Kunstwerke erscheinen mir ästhetisch steril – auch wenn sie von den Anthropologen für völlig authentisch erklärt werden, siehe etwa Ottenberg, S., *Masked Rituals of the Afikpo: The Context of an African Art,* Seattle und London 1975. Daß ich meine, die bei Ottenberg abgebildeten Masken seien älteren und gleichen Typen qualitativ unterlegen, sagt nichts über seinen erhellenden und geistreichen Text aus. Wem sich diese Frage durch den Umzug mit den Objekten stellt und wer sie eher als Kunstwerke, denn als gesellschaftliche und religiöse Zeugnisse ansieht, neigt zu der Ansicht, daß die meisten der jüngeren Objekte »tot« sind, d. h. bar jener Ausdruckskraft und ästhetischen Überzeugung, die man in früheren »authentischen« Objekten antrifft. Für ihn ist eine *Fang*-Maske aus den 50er Jahren weniger bedeutend – selbst wenn sie von einem Stammesbildhauer hergestellt und für kultische Handlungen verwendet wurde. Eine *Fang*-Maske der Dreißiger wäre vorzuziehen, weil der Glaube und das Vertrauen des *Fang*-Volkes damals noch unerschüttert waren. Dem noch vorzuziehen wäre – wenn es sie gäbe – eine Maske, die nachweislich aus der Zeit vor der westlichen Infiltration des *Fang*-Gebietes stammte.

Ich habe den Eindruck, daß die meisten Sammler von Stammeskunst zuviel Wert auf die Provenienz der Objekte legen (neben der Frage natürlich, ob es sich um regelrechte Fälschungen europäischen, afrikanischen oder ozeanischen Ursprungs handelt); dies geht oft soweit, daß ihnen dieser Punkt wichtiger erscheint als die künstlerische Qualität. Viele sehr alte, zweifellos »authentische« Objekte sind von geringem oder gar keinem künstlerischen Interesse. Umgekehrt mag ein großer eingeborener Künstler, der in der Übergangszeit nach den ersten Kontakten mit dem Westen auftrat, durchaus in der Lage gewesen sein, ein großes Kunstwerk hervorzubringen, wenn es vielleicht auch etwas von den traditionellen Formen abwich. Ein Beispiel für ein solches Objekt ist die Maske von der Torresstraße, die Picasso in den 20er Jahren erwarb. Während die traditionellen Masken in diesem Gebiet aus Muschelschalen oder Holz gefertigt wurden □ 143, hat dieses Exemplar □ 432 einen Sockel aus Metall, den wahrscheinlich Kaufleute hinterlassen haben. Trotzdem handelt es sich um ein außerordentliches Kunstwerk. Und obwohl es aus der Kolonialzeit stammt, leitet es sich doch aus einer Zeit her, in der die traditionellen Lebensformen der Torresstraße relativ unberührt waren. Jüngere Objekte eines Künstlers aus Neuguinea im Stil der Torresstraße, die zum Verkauf an Touristen in Port Moresby hergestellt werden, sind wieder etwas anderes.

69. Siehe Kerkache, J., *Chefs-d'œuvre de l'art africain*, Ausstellungskatalog, Grenoble, Musée de Peinture et de Sculpture, Nov.-Dez. 1982 ohne Seitenzählung.

70. Zerstörungen »heidnischer Idole« durch christliche Missionare fanden kontinuierlich statt, gelegentlich auch feierliche Autodafés wie etwa die Verbrennung, von der Peltier spricht, S. 110, 111. Ausgenommen davon wurden im allgemeinen die Objekte, die die Missionare aufhoben, um sie den Gemeinden in ihren Heimatländern als Beweis für den schrecklichen, von ihnen ausgelöschten Aberglauben zu zeigen. Die große Figur von den Australinseln ist hierfür ein Beispiel □ 465.
In jüngerer Zeit nehmen die Missionare gegenüber der Stammeskunst eine wohlwollende Haltung ein und zeigen sogar wissenschaftliches Interesse daran. Pater François Neyt ist Verfasser zahlreicher Texte über die Kunst des Kongo, wie dem kürzlich erschienenen *Arts traditionelles et histoire au Zaïre: Cultures forestières et royaumes de la Savane*, Brüssel 1981. Pater Joseph Cornet ist der Verfasser eines bedeutenden Werkes über die Kunst des Kongo, *Art de l'afrique noire au pays du fleuve Zaïre*, Brüssel 1972, und Direktor des Nationalmuseums von Zaïre.

71. Im Gegensatz zu einer weitverbreiteten Ansicht – die zweifellos z. T. daher kommt, daß Stammessprachen kein Wort für »Kunst« im westlichen Sinne kennen – gibt es bei diesen Völkern beträchtliche Diskussionen über den Charakter und die Qualität von Kunstwerken. Robert F. Thompson legte darüber vor kurzem eine wissenschaftliche Studie vor, »Yoruba Artistic Criticism« in *The Traditional Artist in African Societies,* hrsg. v. W. L. d'Azevedo, Bloomington 1979, S. 19–61. Ebenso Vogel, S. M., »Baule and Yoruba Art Criticism: A Comparison« in *The Visual Arts, Plastic and Graphic,* hrsg. v. Cordwell, J. M., Den Haag, Paris, New York 1979, S. 309–25; den Gesprächen mit ihr habe ich viel zu verdanken.
Die obengenannten Diskussionen sollten jedoch nicht mit der kumulativen, reflektierenden und in Wechselbezug stehenden Kunstkritik verwechselt werden, wie sie der Westen kennt. Daher ist es wahrscheinlich irreführend, Afrikaner mit einer traditionellen Lebensführung, die über Kunst diskutieren, als »Kritiker« zu bezeichnen (»Yoruba art critics are experts of strong mind . . .«, Thompson, S. [illegible]9). Meiner Meinung nach gibt diese afrikanische »Kunstkritik« oft die Dinge wieder, die westliche Gelehrte hören wollen.

72. Ich zeige hier ein Beispiel für eine solche »Übertreibung« des *Senufo*-Stils □ 115. Es handelt sich um einen Rhythmusgeber, der Picasso in den 60er Jahren von Jean Leymarie geschenkt wurde. Man vergleiche ihn mit den anderen *Senufo*-Rhythmusgebern □ 167, 168.

73. Der wahrscheinlich erste Händler, der sich persönlich in den Stammesgebieten nach Kunstwerken umsah, hieß Wirtz; er lebte in Basel und Neuguinea. Seine Tätigkeit fiel in die Zeit zwischen den beiden Weltkriegen, als er mehrere Objekte an das Museum für Völkerkunde in Basel verkaufte.

74. Mein Dank gilt Gail Levin, die mich auf diese Arbeiten aufmerksam machte. Sie erörtert sie im Zusammenhang des amerikanischen Primitivismus auf S. 266 ff.

75. *Weltkulturen und moderne Kunst,* siehe Anm. 2.

76. Im Gespräch mit dem Autor.

77. Dies gilt im Falle des Steines von der Osterinsel nur für die Oberfläche, die als Relief gearbeitet und bemalt ist (siehe Abbildung). Anders als der von Ernst bearbeitete Stein ist der Kantus des polynesischen sonst unregelmäßig.

78. Maurer und Spies im Gespräch mit dem Verfasser. Die Verbindung des Steins der Osterinsel mit dem Werk Max Ernsts wird meines Wissens erstmals von Lucy Lippard hergestellt,

□ 115 »*Weibliche Figur*«, *Senufo (Elfenbeinküste), Holz, Höhe 115 cm. Sammlung Jacqueline Picasso, Mougins. Geschenk an Picasso von Jean Leymarie, um 1962.*

»The Sculpture« im Ausstellungskatalog *Max Ernst: Sculpture and Recent Painting*, hrsg. v. Sam Hunter, New York, The Jewish Museum, 3.3.–17.4.1966, S. 38–39; dort sind Ernsts unbenannte Granitskulptur aus dem Jahre 1934 und die Steinskulptur eines Mannes mit Vogelkopf von der Osterinsel ohne weiteren Kommentar im Text einander gegenübergestellt.

79. Diese Ansicht ist allgemein akzeptiert. Wir verfügen aber nicht über genügend Stammeskunst, die unstreitig aus vorkolonialer Zeit stammt. Auch läßt sich das vorhandene Material nicht mit ausreichender Genauigkeit datieren, um das Ausmaß der Veränderungen, die die Stammeskunst im Lauf der Jahrhunderte erfuhr, bestimmen zu können.

80. Wie bereits erwähnt, gibt – und gab – es bei den Stammesvölkern Gespräche über wenigstens bestimmte Aspekte kultischer Plastik. Daß Stammeskünstler ästhetische Probleme zu lösen hatten, zeigen jedoch die Objekte auch selbst. In allen Kulturen ahmte die Mehrzahl der Künstler überlieferte Ideen lediglich nach, auch wenn diese Tatsache von vielen jüngeren Künstlern im Westen geschickt »getarnt« wird. Ein Unterschied liegt mit Sicherheit darin, wie sehr sich die Künstler darüber bewußt sind, daß gerade ästhetische Probleme gelöst werden. Doch die genialen Lösungen in der Bildhauerei werden im wesentlichen immer aus dem Instinkt geboren, gleich welcher intellektuelle Überbau nach ihrer Vollendung um sie errichtet wird, sei es von den Schöpfern selbst, von anderen Künstlern oder von Kritikern und Kunsthistorikern.

81. *Primitive Religion,* New York 1924, S. 260.

82. Zur Geschichte dieser Maske siehe Siroto, L., »A Mask from the Congo« in *Man* 54, Oktober 1954, S. 149–50, sowie eine unveröffentlichte Notiz aus den Akten des Museums. Siehe S. 273.

83. »Tribal Art and Modern Man« in *The Tenth Muse: Essays in Criticism*, London 1957. Dieser Aufsatz erschien ursprünglich in *The New Republic,* September 1953.

84. Diese Art von Untersuchung ist es wohl, die wir für die Geschichte der primitiven und auch der modernen Kunst am dringendsten brauchen. Einen ersten Schritt in diese Richtung unternahm Marie-Noël Verger-Fèvre in einer bei Jean Laude verfaßten Dissertation, *Présentation des objets de Côte d'Ivoire dans les expositions universelles de 1878 à 1937,* Université de Paris I, 1981–82, eine detaillierte Untersuchung über Ankunft und Verbreitung von Objekten von der Elfenbeinküste.

85. Siehe S. 180, 181.

86. Siehe Becatti, G., »Raffaello e l'Antico« in *Raffaello: L'opera, le fonti, la fortuna,* Novara 1968, S. 507–08. Für diesen Hinweis bin ich Creighton Gilbert zu Dank verpflichtet.

87. Einen Besuch im Museum für Völkerkunde in Berlin trägt Klee in sein Tagebuch ein: »Samstag, 14. 4. [1906] Vormittags im Zoo. Nachmittags im Museum für Völkerkunde«, in Klee, F. (Hrsg.), *Tagebücher von Paul Klee 1898–1918,* Köln 1957, S. 213.

88. 1929 ernannte Hitler Heinrich Himmler zum Führer der SS (Schutzstaffel), dem schwarzbehemdeten Elitekorps der Partei, das immer aktiver und rücksichtsloser wurde und von 1932 an in den Straßen stets präsent war.

89. Natürlich hat der Pfeil in Klees Werk eine Vielzahl von symbolischen Bedeutungen, die von den hier untersuchten abweichen, siehe Rosenthal, M., *Paul Klee and the Arrow,* Diss., University of Iowa 1979. Rosenthal hat mich darauf hingewiesen, daß eine ganze Reihe von Klees Bildtiteln aus dem Jahr 1932 seine Besorgnis über den Aufstieg Hitlers und die Allgegenwart seiner Legionen zum Ausdruck bringen, siehe etwa der *Barbarische Hauptmann* (Sammlung Felix Klee, Bern).

90. Beide Arbeiten Giacomettis, die wir Objekten aus dem Museum für Völkerkunde in Basel gegenüberstellen □ 47–50, kann man unter Angabe dieser Stammesquellen finden bei Hohl, R., *Alberto Giacometti,* Lausanne 1971, S. 295, Bildmaterial S. 61–62, 63–64; siehe auch S. 138 und 302, Anm. 50., deutsche Ausgabe Stuttgart 1971.

91. Mein Dank gilt Christian Kaufmann vom Basler Museum für Völkerkunde, der mich als erster auf die Beziehung zwischen Giacomettis *Kopf eines Mannes an einem Seil* und dem modellierten Kopf aus Neuirland aufmerksam machte, die ich bei Hohl übersehen hatte.

92. Diesen Hinweis verdanke ich Christian Kaufmann.

93. Diese Beziehung wurde zuerst bemerkt von James Smith Pierce in seiner Dissertation *Paul Klee and Primitive Art,* Harvard University 1961, überarbeitete Fassung, New York und London 1976, S. 42–43, 165.

94. Read, siehe Anm. 83.

95. Vorlesungen, Columbia University. Schapiro äußerte sich auch über Heckels unten erwähntes Bild *Clown und Puppe.*

96. Ein paar Jahre danach drückte Oskar Kokoschka in einem interessanten Beispiel »eines Lebens, das die Kunst nachahmt« sein Befremden darüber aus, daß Alma Mahler ihre Beziehung mit ihm beendete, indem sie ihn mit einer auf Bestellung angefertigten, lebensgroßen Puppe, die sie selbst darstellen sollte, durch die Stadt begleitete. Die Metapher, die die Entfremdung von einer Frau durch ihre wörtliche Reduzierung auf ein Objekt ausdrückt, hat eine lange literarische Geschichte, bis hin zu der weiblichen Puppe, die Tristan nach seiner Zurückweisung durch die weiße Isolde von seinen Handwerkern anfertigen ließ.

97. Dies ist eine der grundlegenden Thesen in Lévi-Strauss' *Structural Anthropology*, besonders in Kap. 3 »Magic and Religion«. Es handelt sich um das »Lindern der Träume«, durch das der primitive Mensch »geschützt wurde – und bis zu einem gewissen Maß von ihren Fesseln befreit war«, *Tristes Tropiques,* 1955, S. 513.

98. D.h. der Zusammenbruch stabiler und authentischer Vorstellungen der Gemeinschaft im Religiösen und Gesellschaftlichen. Die Impressionisten und viele französische Maler des 20. Jahrhunderts akzeptierten diese Atomisierung der Gesellschaft als einen freiheitlichen Aspekt und verliehen ihr in ihrer Kunst einen positiven Gehalt.

99. Nur wenige Künstler der Moderne haben völkerkundliche Bücher gelesen. Nolde und Kirchner scheinen einige Spezialwerke ihrer Zeit zu Rate gezogen zu haben, aber Carl Einsteins *Negerplastik,* 1915, die die Stammesplastik von einem rein ästhetischen Standpunkt aus diskutiert, interessierte sie viel stärker. Max Ernst stellt mit seiner breiten Kenntnis der völkerkundlichen Literatur eine Ausnahme dar. Picasso hingegen schöpfte seine Ideen über die Stammeskunst angesichts der Exponate im Trocadéro aus seiner Vorstellung und den Erläuterungen zu den Ausstellungsstücken. Obwohl Lydia Gasman in ihrer umstrittenen Dissertation *Mystery, Magic and Love in Picasso, 1925–1938,* Columbia University 1981, S. 476–82, das Gegenteil behauptet, hat Picasso sicherlich Mauss oder andere französische Ethnologen des frühen 20. Jahrhunderts nicht gelesen. Wie er mir gegenüber sagte, langweilte ihn wissenschaftliche Literatur über Kunst. Außerdem beherrschte er in dieser entscheidenden Phase (1907–08) nicht genug Französisch, um Mauss lesen zu können. Trotzdem ist es durchaus möglich, daß Picasso durch seine gelegentlichen Kontakte zu Mécislas Golberg und J. Deniker ein paar verallgemeinerte und verwässerte Versionen ethnologischen Gedankenguts übernahm, und in diesem Sinne hat Lydia Gasman recht. Vorstellungen der französischen Ethnologie können in den Ateliers einiger Pariser Künstler »in der Luft« gelegen haben, ähnlich wie für die abstrakten Expressionisten der »Existentialismus«, ein Schlagwort in den New Yorker Ateliers der späten 40er und der 50er Jahre. Picasso erfaßte das Wesen der primitiven Kunst hingegen ohne Zweifel instinktiv (siehe S. 264 und 347, Anm. 53).

100. Diese These liegt Robert Farris Thompsons *African Art in Motion: Icon and Art in the Collection of Katherine Coryton White*, Ausstellungskatalog, Washington, D. C., National Gallery of Art und Los Angeles, Fredrick S. Wight Art Gallery, University of California 1974, zugrunde, siehe vor allem S. XII–XIV, 1–5, 47–48, 111–12, 117, 152, 154.

101. Die westliche Gesellschaft ist nicht die erste, die die Kunst anderer Kulturen rühmt, aber die erste, die Kulturen rühmt, die (anders als die Antike im Verhältnis zur Renaissance) nicht mit den eigenen Traditionen in Übereinstimmung stehen. Sie ist die erste, die auch viele fremde Kulturen gleichzeitig schätzt, deren Wertsysteme einander widersprechen.

102. Es gibt Beispiele unvollendeter ägyptischer Plastiken, die beweisen, daß der Künstler die Arbeit begann, indem er auf die Vorderansicht und das Profil auf den Steinblock zeichnete. Picasso ging bei seiner *Karyatide* □ 391 auf die gleiche Weise vor. Die afrikanischen und ozeanischen Bildhauer arbeiteten ohne Zeichnungen, wenngleich sie vielleicht die Umrisse in den Stein ritzten.

103. Als Lipchitz seinen *Sitzenden* modellierte, hatte er bereits DOGON-Figuren im Trocadéro gesehen, der zu Beginn des Jahrhunderts Werke dieses Stammes besaß und ausstellte, siehe □ 352, 353. Die Ähnlichkeiten, die ich hier erörtere, gehen indes über solche Einflüsse hinaus und sind allgemeinerer Natur.

104. Die Afrikanisten sind sich nicht einig, ob in der afrikanischen Plastik mythologische Figuren überwiegen. Die meisten betrachten »mythologische Figuren« als Randerscheinungen der Ikonographie. Leon Siroto behauptet, daß eigentlich alle diese Figuren falsch gedeutet werden und daß, wenn überhaupt, nur wenige mythologischer Natur sind.

105. Man beachte, daß ich hier zwischen Totemfiguren und totemähnlichen Konstellationen unterscheide, die erzählerische Strukturen sein können ohne Stammestotems einzuschließen.

106. Susan Vogel führt die Analogie zwischen afrikanischer und antiker Plastik noch weiter als Fagg, »The African Artist«, und andere Auto-

ren. In »The Buli Master and Other Hands«, in *Art in America* 5, Mai 1980, S. 132–42, stellt sie fest: »Die traditionelle afrikanische Kunst ist . . . in der Tat eine klassische Kunst, was ihr Beharren auf Ordnung und Übereinstimmung mit der Tradition sowie ihre Verachtung radikaler Neuerungen und persönlichen Ausdrucks betrifft . . . Das Bemühen der afrikanischen Kunst um die Kontrolle von Affekten, um Ausgewogenheit und Proportion sowie ihre allgemeine Strenge machen sie dem Wesen nach klassisch.« In *African Aesthetics*, Mailand, unveröff., weist sie nachdrücklich darauf hin, daß afrikanische Wörter für Schönheit, die im Zusammenhang mit Kunstwerken gebraucht werden, eine moralische Komponente haben, wie das griechische *kalokagathia,* das zugleich das Schöne und Gute bezeichnet. Sie betont auch »die Kardinaltugend des Maßvollen, die allen afrikanischen Systemen der Ästhetik zugrunde liegt«; sie ist das Pendant zum griechischen Ideal der *sophrosyne*.

107. Siehe den Beitrag von Gail Levin, S. 465.

108. Mehr über Pierre Loeb, siehe den Beitrag von Philippe Peltier, S. 111–12.

109. Loeb finanzierte wichtige Reisen nach Ozeanien, vor allem an den Sentanisee, die J. Viot leitete.

110. Ich komme zu dieser Annahme, auch wenn die typischen Vorsprünge der Yam-Masken in der detailliertesten Untersuchung dieses Materials, Ottenbergs *Masked Rituals of Afikpo*, siehe Anm. 68, nicht erörtert werden.

111. Diese Art Maske konnte man beim Tanz nicht so sehen, da sie wie eine Mütze auf dem Kopf getragen wurde.

112. Wie vielfach behauptet, tragen die JUKUN solche Masken schräg aufgesetzt, wie ein Zwischending zwischen einer senkrecht getragenen Gesichtsmaske und der waagerechten Tragweise wie bei den *MAMA*-Masken, d. h. auf dem Kopf aufgesetzt; so wurden sie wohl ganz am Anfang getragen. Das Problem wurde von dem Kunsthistoriker Arnold Rubin untersucht. Mein Dank gilt Roy Sieber, der mir Photokopien der relevanten Stellen aus Rubins Doktorarbeit sowie andere Texte über *JUKUN*-Masken verschaffte.
Wir haben die Berliner *JUKUN*-Maske senkrecht stehend abgebildet (als ob es sich um eine Gesichtsmaske handelte) und nicht in einem Zwischenwinkel (so wie sie in Berlin aufgehängt ist und normalerweise abgebildet wird), um die Parallele zu Picassos *Kopf* zu verdeutlichen. (Wie Stammesobjekte ursprünglich gesehen wurden, interessierte die Künstler der Moderne nicht.) Es gibt jedoch Hinweise, daß wenigstens einige der *JUKUN*-Masken so getragen wurden. Obschon ich die Maske des Berliner Völkerkundemuseums □ 446 nicht genau untersuchen konnte, weil sie sich bei meinem Besuch in einer Vitrine befand, war es mir möglich, eine andere *JUKUN*-Maske aus dem Depot in die Hand zu nehmen, die, obgleich von etwas minderer Qualität, das Gegenstück zu ihr bildet. Ich beobachtete, daß die Markierungen, die innen zum Tragen angebracht waren, genau der Position der Augenhöhlen entsprechen, wenn man die Maske waagerecht wie eine Gesichtsmaske aufsetzt.

113. Douglas Newton verdanke ich diese Information, die aus A. A. Gerbrands (Hrsg.), *The Asmat of New Guinea: The Journal of Michael Clark Rockefeller,* New York, The Museum of Primitive Art 1967, S. 349 stammt.

114. Dies trifft leider für die Masse von Veröffentlichungen durch Historiker der primitiven Kunst und natürlich auch für die Arbeit der Anthropologen zu.

115. Die extremen Grenzen setzte die manieristische Kunst, vor allem El Greco. Die besondere Beliebtheit El Grecos zu Beginn unseres Jahrhunderts spricht für seine Nähe zu primitivistischen Überlegungen: er wurde von Autoren wie Salmon hervorgehoben, und die Verzerrungen und die Kantigkeit in seinen Werken beeinflußten Picasso bei seinen Arbeiten in Gosol im Jahr 1906 und bei den *Demoiselles*.

116. Kirk Varnedoe hat darauf hingewiesen, daß die typologische Betrachtungsweise von Proportionen in der nazistischen »Wissenschaft« parodiert wurde, in der die hockenden Stellungen moderner Skulpturen mit den Opfern der Elefantiasis verglichen wurden, siehe Lehmann-Haupt, H., *Art under a Dictatorship*, New York 1954, S. 38–41

117. Es ist fast unmöglich und niemand sollte versuchen, die vielen verschiedenen, im feinstofflichen kreativen Prozeß verbundenen Einflüsse auseinanderzudividieren, um ihnen verschiedene Grade der Wichtigkeit zuzuweisen. Mein eigener Eindruck ist, daß die von mir »Besenstiel«-Skulpturen genannten Arbeiten Picassos – die dieser laut Werner Spies tatsächlich aus dem Holz von Bilderrahmen schnitzte – für Giacometti von großer Bedeutung waren, wenn sich auch ihr Einfluß mehrere Jahre lang nicht geltend machte. Diese plastischen Typen Picassos (siehe Rubin, W. [Hrsg.], *Picasso: A Retrospective*, New York, The Museum of Modern Art 1980, S. 284), die teilweise aus natürlichen Motiven schöpfen und nicht wie Giacomettis Kunst des Jahres 1931 völlig der Phantasie entspringen, lieferten Giacometti in der Folge neben Cézanne Modelle für seine dünnen Figuren. Wenn diese, wie ich meine, zumindest in ihren Proportionen auch von der archaischen (etruskischen) und der primitiven Kunst beeinflußt sind, so gilt wohl das gleiche indirekt für die Figuren Picassos, die er zu einem Zeitpunkt schuf, als er in seinen größeren Skulpturen ein Interesse an der *BACA*-Plastik zeigte, siehe □ 457, 458.

118. Siehe S. 324ff.

119. Brief an W. R., September 1983.

120. Lippard, L., *Eva Hesse*, New York 1976, S. 86.

121. Siehe den Beitrag über amerikanische Kunst von Gail Levin im vorliegenden Buch, S. 477.

122. Dies ist der Nachteil von Lévi-Strauss' strukturalistischer Analyse des primitiven Zeichensystems, der Verwandtschaftsmuster und des Mythos. Ein Vergleich zwischen den Mechanismen des primitiven und modernen Geistes in *Structural Anthropology*, S. 230.

›Surrealistische Weltkarte‹, veröffentlicht in der franz. Zeitschrift „Variétés“, 1929

Die Ankunft primitiver Kunst im Westen

Christian F. Feest

Aus Nordamerika

Seit der Zeit, da es Kontakte zwischen Indianern und Weißen gibt, vom ersten Zusammentreffen bis zum heutigen Tag, wurden Erzeugnisse der nordamerikanischen Indianer gesammelt und geschätzt. Die Geschichte dieser Sammeltätigkeit ist unauflösbar mit anderen Aspekten interethnischer Beziehungen verbunden, mit ungläubiger Sprachlosigkeit über eine neue Welt oder alten Vorurteilen über ferne und fremde Völker. Wenn man schon nicht selbst in die Neue Welt reisen konnte oder wenigstens einige der meist kurzlebigen, nach Europa importierten Eingeborenen zu Gesicht bekam, stellten die ausgewählten Produkte der indianischen Völker noch immer den sichersten und schnellsten Weg dar, als Angehöriger einer Kolonialmacht am kolonialen Abenteuer teilzunehmen. Für Bewohner eines Staates ohne Herrschaft in Übersee wurde so immerhin die ständige Ausdehnung der bekannten Welt nachvollziehbar.

Man sollte nicht vergessen, daß Nordamerika erst spät Beachtung fand, nachdem sich Spanien und Portugal schon lange an den südlichen Teilen des Kontinents bereichert hatten. Statt Gold und Silber waren dort nur Fisch und Felle zu holen. Die Erfahrungen allerdings, die Europa im Süden der Neuen Welt gemacht hatte, übertrugen sich auf die Vorstellungen und Erwartungen von der ganzen Neuen Welt. Das erste und langlebigste Symbol der eingeborenen Amerikaner – der Federkopfschmuck – hat seinen Ursprung in Brasilien und fand erst später in den Norden. Der Federschmuck erscheint etwa auf Hans Burgkmairs Kupferstichen aus dem *Triumphzug Maximilians I.*, um 1519 □ 117, wo die Träger dieses Schmuckes noch heute als das »Volk von Calicut« bezeichnet werden. Ikonographisch sind jene »Indianer« in der europäischen Kunst des 16. Jahrhunderts mehr oder weniger leicht identifizierbar. Obwohl Berufsmaler erst seit der Mitte des 17. Jahrhunderts Portraits von Indianern in Öl nach dem lebenden Modell anfertigten, spielten Bilder von Indianern, die auf wenigen Tatsachen und vielen Vorurteilen beruhten, als Symbole des Überflusses und des Bösen in der europäischen Kunst schon viel früher eine bedeutende Rolle.

Die erste Schiffsladung indianischer Produkte, die Cortes aus Mexiko schickte – ihr folgten bald viele andere, von denen nur noch ein paar Dutzend Gegenstände erhalten sind –, bestand aus großen Mengen verarbeiteter Edelmetalle, aus Objekten mit eingelegten Türkismosaiken, bebilderten Manuskripten der Eingeborenen und vor allem Federwerk jeglicher Art. Als diese Gegenstände 1520 in Brüssel ausgestellt wurden, bekam sie auch Albrecht Dürer zu Gesicht. Seine Beschreibung dieser Objekte wurde irrtümlich als ästhetisches Werturteil aufgefaßt, indes ihn aber der enorme Wert dieser Dinge, das zuweilen exotische Rohmaterial, aus dem sie gefertigt waren, sowie die gute Ausführung der mexikanischen Arbeiten beeindruckt hatten.

Im Vergleich zu diesen esoterischen und fesselnden Stücken aus Mexiko waren die bekanntermaßen ältesten noch existierenden Gegenstände, die Jacques Cartier von Indianern Nordamerikas mitbrachte, recht prosaisch und anspruchslos: zwei Paar Mokassins, die als einzige Zier gefärbte Stachelschweinborsten aufwiesen. Wegen ihres unübersehbaren Gebrauchscharakters hatten Erzeugnisse nordamerikanischer Indianer damals noch nicht die Chance, mit Kunstwerken im europäischen Sinne verwechselt zu werden, wiewohl ihre feinsinnige Beschaffenheit berechtigte Bewunderung fand.

Obwohl sich manche Vorstellung von den Indianern über die Ländergrenzen hinweg herausbildete und verbreitete, entwikkelten doch die Nationen ihr jeweils typisches Bild von den Menschen der Neuen Welt. Die Masse der deutschen Veröffentlichungen über die Neue Welt im frühen 16. Jahrhundert dokumentiert für amerikanische Themen ein großes Interesse, das wohl in jenen Staaten, die aus dem einen oder anderen Grund von den kolonialen Beutezügen ausgeschlossen waren, eine kompensatorische Funktion besaß. Auch wird die aufkommende (stereotype) französische Mode des Lebens und Feierns mit Indianern anhand des brasilianisch-indianischen Dorfes Tupinamba deutlich, das 1550 anläßlich des Eintreffens König Heinrichs II. in Rouen, dem wichtigen Importhafen für Brasilholz, aufgebaut wurde □ 118. Innerhalb der durch die bestehenden Machtverhältnisse gesetzten Grenzen sah es das Königtum Frankreich nicht als unter seiner Würde an, mit Indianern Umgang zu pflegen. So schloß der junge Kronprinz Louis XIII mit dem Indianer »Kanada«, der 1604 nach Frankreich gebracht worden war, Freundschaft

Ein nicht so herzlicher Empfang wurde den ESKIMOS, der in Europa am häufigsten anzutreffenden Gruppe nördlicher Eingeborener, bereitet. Kajaks mitsamt ihren Insassen, oft ganze Familien, wurden von Schiffen christlicher Seefahrernationen eher unzeremoniell aus dem Wasser gefischt und nach Europa befördert, um zuerst über ihre Heimat ausgefragt und dann einem dankbaren Publikum als Menschenfresser vorgeführt zu werden. Es gibt noch zwei Handzettel aus dem Jahre 1566, die die Ankunft einer Eskimofrau mit ihrem Kind – ihr Mann war

◁ □ 116 *›Eskimoische Maske‹, Kuskokwim-Fluß (Alaska), bemaltes Holz, Federn, Höhe 51 cm. Museum of the American Indian, Heye Foundation, New York.*

□ 117 ›*Tupinamba-Indianer*‹ *(Brasilien), ›Die Leute von Calicut‹, Kupferstich von Hans Burgkmair aus dem ›Triumphzug Maximilians* I.‹, *ca. 1519.*

getötet worden – für eine Tour durch Bayern ankündigen □ 119. Ein Kajak, der sich einst in der Sammlung des Bayerischen Kurfürsten befand und heute im Völkerkundemuseum in München zu sehen ist, läßt auf ein ähnliches Ereignis im Jahre 1577 schließen. »Live« dargebotene *Eskimos* blieben wohl als ein alltäglicher Anblick in Deutschland bestehen – dies jedenfalls verraten uns die Kommentare Grimmelshausens aus dem 17. Jahrhundert über wiederholte Vorführungen von »Grönländern und Samoyeden« sowie andere Belege, die von diesen Spektakeln bis weit ins 19. Jahrhundert hinein berichten.

Angesichts der Tatsache, daß während des 16. Jahrhunderts Florida die einzige dauerhafte europäische Kolonie auf nordamerikanischem Boden blieb, nimmt es nicht Wunder, daß für die Mehrzahl nordamerikanischer Objekte in königlichen oder privaten Sammlungen diese Provenienz in Anspruch genommen wird. Da im späten 16. Jahrhundert die Heilige Inquisition das Sammeln von angeblich dämonenbehafteten eingeborenen Kunstprodukten öffentlich mißbilligte, bleibt Spanien eine ziemlich unergiebige Quelle für solche Gegenstände. Obwohl gleichfalls katholisch, hatte Italien in dieser Hinsicht kaum Probleme. Sammler wie Giganti oder Aldrovandi in Bologna verbuchten mit Stolz Federwerk aus Florida in ihren Katalogen. Der Bayerische Kurfürst besaß ein hölzernes Götzenbild aus Florida ebenso wie der spanische Sammler Lastanosa, dessen Äußerungen darüber (»unbeschreiblich häßlich«) klarmachten, daß er es nicht aus ästhetischen Gründen erworben hatte. Auf Seltenheit und kurioses Aussehen wurde beim Sammeln von Ethnographica in jenen Tagen geachtet.

Die Gründung englischer, französischer, niederländischer und schwedischer Kolonien entlang der atlantischen Küste zog ein rasches Anwachsen europäisch-indianischer Kontakte sowohl in der Neuen wie in der Alten Welt nach sich. Damit ging auch ein verstärktes Sammeln nordamerikanisch-indianischen Kulturgutes einher. Diese Entwicklung stieß kaum europäische Vorurteile über Amerikas Ureinwohner um, auf lange Sicht verhärteten sich diese eher noch. Ebensowenig änderten sich die Hauptmotive für das Sammeln eingeborener Erzeugnisse. Wenn sie überhaupt etwas sammelten, legten Kolonial-

□ 118 *›Scheingefecht zwischen zwei brasilianischen Stämmen‹ im Tupinamba-Dorf, das für den Einzug von Heinrich* II. *im Jahre 1550 in Rouen gebaut wurde.*

☐ 119 ›Eskimo-Frau mit ihrem Kind‹, die 1566 während einer Rundreise durch Bayern öffentlich zur Schau gestellt wurden. Dieser Handzettel ist der älteste erhaltene Druck mit einer Darstellung von Eskimos.

herren besonderen Wert auf praktisch nutzbare Erzeugnisse oder auf Objekte, die sie bei offiziellen Anlässen erhalten hatten (z.B. aus »Seidengras« gefertigte Taschen, Muschelgeld, Boote, Waffen von Eingeborenen oder Wampum-Gürtel). Missionare bevorzugten religiöse Utensilien der Indianer, darunter gelegentlich Objekte, die die christliche Ergebenheit ihrer neuen Pfarrkinder bezeugten. Andere wiederum sammelten Gegenstände, die einfach wunderlich und geheimnisvoll waren. Immer noch war künstlerische Qualität ein untergeordneter Aspekt beim Erwerb indianischer Erzeugnisse, so empfand man etwa das Götzenbild, das der Reverend Alexander Whitaker (der Pocahontas getauft hatte) 1615 aus Virginia mitbrachte, als ein »schlecht in einen Fliegenpilz geschnitztes Machwerk«.

Auch änderte sich die ambivalente Einstellung gegenüber dem Indianer als eines entweder edlen oder ruchlosen Wilden keinesfalls. Die in Kleidung und Manieren auf Englisch getrimmte Pocahontas wurde als eine Art eingeborene Adlige behandelt und so der englischen Königin vorgestellt ☐ 121. Fast zur gleichen Zeit stellte man zwei andere, noch »unzivilisierte« Indianer aus Virginia als lebende exotische Raritäten im Zoo des Londoner St. James-Parks aus ☐ 120. In England wurden Mode und Geschmack nachweislich von indianischer Kultur beeinflußt, und die französischen Adligen kleideten sich im 17. und 18. Jahrhundert nur allzugern als »amerikanische Könige«. Die Engländer sahen das »Indianerspiel« eher als Beschäftigung für ihre Kinder an, dies jedenfalls legt die Nachricht von einem Pelzhändler aus Virginia nahe, der 1689 einem Freund ein Indianerkostüm »für Deinen Sohn zum Spielen« nach England schickte.

Offenbar interessierte sich die englische Krone nicht ernsthaft für das Sammeln indianischer Objekte. Die frühen Sammlungen kamen alle durch Privatpersonen wie Sir Walter Cope oder John Tradescant (Vater und Sohn) zustande. In der Tradescant-Sammlung befand sich »Powhatans Umhang«. Er ist heute im Ashmolean Museum in Oxford zu sehen, kann aber wohl weder als Umhang noch als ehemaliger Besitz Powhatans gelten und illustriert die wachsende Tendenz zum Sammeln von Memorabilien auch wilder Völker. In Frankreich, Skandinavien und später auch in den deutschen Fürstentümern waren

□ 120 *›Ejakintomino‹, wie Pocahontas ein Indianer aus dem Küstengebiet Virginias. Er wurde zusammen mit heimischen und fremden Tieren im Zoo des St. James-Parks ausgestellt, während Pocahontas bei Hof als eine indianische Prinzessin eingeführt wurde. Aquarell von Michael van Meer, University Library, Edinburgh.*

□ 121 *›Pocahontas‹, Tochter von Powhatan, gekleidet für ihre Audienz bei der Königin von England als »Mrs. Rebecca Rolff«.*

die Herrscherhäuser bedeutende Sammler indianischer Artefakte. In Frankreich gab es private Sammlungen, etwa die von Nicolas-Claude Fabri de Peiresc, wovon Teile noch in der Bibliothèque Sainte-Geneviève in Paris zu sehen sind. Die Sammlungen des Adels wurden von denen der Krone jedoch weit in den Schatten gestellt. 1654 erwarb der dänische König die private naturgeschichtliche und völkerkundliche Sammlung des Ole Worm in Kopenhagen, die er später um die Sammlung des Herzogs von Gottrop erweiterte. Letztere umfaßte die niederländische Kollektion des Arztes Paludanus aus dem frühen 17. Jahrhundert.

Einige dieser frühen und recht buntgemischten Sammlungen waren wohl denen der zeitgenössischen nordamerikanischen Indianer nicht unähnlich. Archäologische Funde am Ort des ehemaligen Dorfes Patawomeke (südlich von Washington, D. C.) lassen auf Sammlungen von Fossilien schließen – sozusagen direkte Vorläufer der Smithsonian Institution. Die Schatzhäuser der eingeborenen Vornehmen im gesamten Küstengebiet von Virginia und Maryland beherbergten wertvolle, besondere exotische wie auch seltene Gegenstände (so das Bett und das Waschbecken, die der König von England Powhatan geschickt hatte). Genauso wie europäische Kolonialmächte mit der Herstellung bestimmter Güter für den Indianerhandel begannen, die speziell auf indianische Vorlieben abgestimmt waren, richteten sich indianische Handwerker auf das beginnende touristische Geschäft ein. Obwohl von den weißen Käufern nicht gleich zur Kenntnis genommen, steht es doch außer Zweifel, daß der europäische Geschmack Dekor und Ausführung aufwendig geschnitzter Holzkeulen, die offensichtlich zu Geschenkzwecken gemacht wurden, beeinflußte □ 123. Ähnliches gilt für andere, speziell für den Export gefertigte Stücke. Somit standen ästhetische Gesichtspunkte beim Sammeln indianischer Produkte zurück, doch übten sie allmählich einen indirekten Einfluß aus.

Besonders seit dem Anfang des 18. Jahrhunderts kamen immer mehr indianische Besucher nach Europa, und zwar nicht als unfreiwillige Kuriositäten – obwohl sie immer noch viel Neugier und wohl mehr allgemeines Interesse erregten als viele öffentlich ohnehin nicht zugängliche Sammlungen –, sondern als politische Abgesandte verbündeter Nationen. Dies traf vor allem auf England zu, wo der Besuch der »vier Könige von Kanada« (drei MOHAWKS und ein MOHIKANER) 1710 eine Serie ähnlicher Visiten von CHEROKESEN, CREEKS und anderen Indianern einleitete □ 122. Offenbar machten die MOHAWKS auf die Engländer einen solchen Eindruck, daß sie die Namenspatrone einer »Klasse aristokratischer Schurken, die die Straßen von London heimsuchten«, wurden (ähnlich verhielt es sich zwei Jahrhunderte später mit den »Apachen« in Paris). Es bleibt zu fragen, ob somit die englischen »Mohocks« als die ersten Vorläufer der italienischen »indiani metropolitani« des Jahres 1977 oder ihrer deutschen Vettern, der »Stadtindianer«, zu betrachten sind. Sicher ist, daß die MOHAWKS (wenn auch nicht die nach London abgesandten) im allgemeinen ihre Haare in dem hochgekämmten Stil trugen, der das Vorbild für die moderne »Punk«-Mode in ganz Europa wurde.

Trotz ihres zweifelhaften Rufes wurden die MOHAWKS in England würdig empfangen, erhielten eine Audienz bei Queen Anne und wurden von mehreren Malern porträtiert. So bekamen immer mehr professionelle Künstler – darunter Sir Joshua Reynolds – amerikanische Indianer in ihren Ateliers zu Gesicht. Besucher wie die »vier Könige« fanden in Europa immer Interessenten für eingeborenes Kunsthandwerk, das sie mit sich führten. Für diejenigen, die nicht selber nach Amerika reisen konnten, bot sich hier die Gelegenheit zum Sammeln.

□ 122 *›Stirn-Tragriemen‹, MOHAWK, New York (State), Hanf, Borsten, Elchhaar, Breite 4 cm, Dekor in falscher Elchhaar-Stickerei. Eines der Objekte, die die »vier Könige von Kanada« 1710 nach London mitbrachten. The Trustees of the British Museum, London.*

Drei Stücke, die man mit den »vier Königen« in Verbindung bringt und die sich in Sir Hans Sloanes großer Kollektion befanden, kamen schließlich ins Britische Museum (ähnlich wie die Tradescant-Sammlung ins Ashmolean nach Oxford wanderte). In Sloanes Sammlung gab es nur etwa 400 völkerkundliche Stücke, die mit ihrer Eintragung unter »Verschiedenes« noch nicht einmal separat inventarisiert waren. Gut die Hälfte dieser Gegenstände war nordamerikanischen Ursprungs, wobei ein Drittel aller Gegenstände mit sicherer Provenienz den *Eskimos* zugeschrieben werden konnte. Die Sammlung Sloane ist typisch für die Mehrheit europäischer Sammlungen, einschließlich jener, die zu naturwissenschaftlichen Institutionen gehörten, etwa der Royal Society, deren Sammlung kurz vor der von Sloane begründet wurde. Sie stellen zum einen keine eigentlichen Feldsammlungen dar, auch wenn sie von Feldsammlern zusammengetragen wurden, und bestehen zum anderen nicht ausschließlich aus indianischen Arbeiten. Es handelt sich eher um allgemeine Sammlungen, die nicht unbedingt besondere gefühlsbehaftete Neigungen der Öffentlichkeit, etwa gegenüber den Indianern, widerspiegeln.

Solche sentimentalen Interessen kommen viel deutlicher in den Feldsammlungen der britischen Armeeoffiziere zum Ausdruck, die entlang der »Zivilisationsgrenze« stationiert waren. Sir John Caldwell, dessen Kollektion kürzlich auseinandergerissen wurde, ließ ein Porträt von sich malen, das ihn mit seinen Indianersachen ausstaffiert darstellt. Er war im Gebiet der Großen Seen stationiert, ebenso Arent Schuyler de Peyster, der ein sehr lustiges und persönliches Gedicht über seine Indianerfreunde schrieb. Seine Sammlung, im Besitz von »The King's Regiment«, ist noch in Liverpool zu sehen.

Es nimmt kaum Wunder, daß das Interesse der Franzosen an indianischen Objekten um so nostalgischer wurde, je mehr ihr kolonialer Besitz schrumpfte und die Gelegenheiten zum Sammeln immer seltener wurden. In der Literatur erwuchs aus dieser Haltung das indianische Bild eines einfacheren, besseren und glücklicheren Lebens. Die indianische Moral wurde interpretiert, vor deren Hintergrund die Laster und Unzulänglichkeiten in der europäischen Zivilisation um so deutlicher hervortraten. Grundsätzlich ähnlich, wenn auch mit deutlicher Akzentverschiebung, war das Denken der zeitgenössischen britischen Sozial- und Wirtschaftsphilosophen, deren Evolutionstheorien den amerikanischen Indianer auf der frühesten, ursprünglichsten – aber auch primitivsten – Stufe ansiedelten (»Am Anfang«, so hieß es, »war die ganze Welt Amerika.«). Daß das französische Interesse an Indianern noch nach dem Verlust der nordamerikanischen Besitzungen anhielt, illustriert eine frühe Ausstellung kanadisch-indianischer Objekte, die der Marquis de Sérent in der Art eines Dioramas für den Unterricht der königlichen Kinder zu Versailles eingerichtet hatte.

Die amerikanische Revolution hatte nicht nur den Effekt, der deutschen Auswanderung nach Amerika für das 18. Jahrhundert neuen Auftrieb zu geben, sondern sie brachte auch eine deutliche Zunahme nordamerikanisch-indianischer Sammlungen in den deutschen Fürstentümern mit sich. Oft waren es Söldner aus Hessen oder Braunschweig, die den Grundstock späterer indianischer Sammlungen nach Deutschland schickten. Ihre Haltung gegenüber den amerikanischen Ureinwohnern war von wohlwollender Faszination. Noch

□ 123 *›Keule‹, irokesisch oder delawarisch (Nordöstliche USA), 17. Jahrhundert, Holz, eingelegte Wampum-Muscheln, Höhe 66 cm. Dänisches Nationalmuseum, Abteilung Völkerkunde, Kopenhagen.*

heute wird der deutsche Dichter Seume, der als Legionär in Amerika war, mit einer Zeile aus einem seiner Indianergedichte zitiert: »Wir Wilden«, deklamiert ein eingeborener Kanadier, »sind doch bessere Menschen.« Im größeren Zusammenhang betrachtet, führte die amerikanische Revolution zur Entstehung amerikanischer Sammlungen von indianischen Objekten – mithin fast drei Jahrhunderte nach den ersten europäischen Anfängen.

Inzwischen bahnte sich eine neue Art des Sammelns an. Die Entwicklung taxonomischer Ordnungen in den Naturwissenschaften (z. B. bei Linné) ebnete den Weg für eine wirklich systematische Sammeltätigkeit. Die großen Entdeckungsreisen des 18. Jahrhunderts boten dafür Gelegenheit auf weltweiter Basis. Das Sammeln völkerkundlicher Objekte wurde immer mehr von Naturwissenschaftlern betrieben und durch ihre neuen Ansätze bestimmt. Im Gefolge des gleichzeitig zunehmenden Handels mit naturhistorischen Gegenständen entstand im späten 18. Jahrhundert der erste reguläre Markt für Ethnographica. Der Mann, der am häufigsten mit den Forschungsreisen dieser Periode und neuen Formen des Sammelns in Verbindung gebracht wird, ist James Cook □ 124. Er ließ das Reisen, zuvor noch als Kunst angesehen, zur Wissenschaft werden. Während der letzten seiner drei Seereisen, auf denen er von vielen Wissenschaftlern verschiedenster Nationalität begleitet wurde, besuchte Cook die Nordwestküste Nordamerikas und veranlaßte den ersten großen Export indianischer Kunst und anderer Gegenstände aus dieser Region. Die Mehrzahl dieser Objekte wurde nach England verbracht, aber einige, die später nach Leningrad gelangten, wurden russischen Offizieren auf der Kamtschatka-Halbinsel übergeben. Wieder andere wanderten nach Kapstadt. Captain King nahm einige in sein heimatliches Irland mit, und John Webber, der offizielle Maler auf dieser letzten Reise, gab etliches an Bern, die Geburtsstadt seines Vaters. Händler verkauften Stücke aus dieser Reise nach Deutschland und Italien. Ein weiterer Teil der Gegenstände kam in das noch schlecht organisierte neue Britische Museum, aber die Mehrzahl in das private Museum des Sir Ashton Lever, das schließlich 1806 in einer öffentlichen Auktion verkauft wurde. Der Ruhm der aus der Cook-Reise stammenden Stücke sorgte in England und anderen Ländern für großes Aufsehen. So erwarb der österreichische Kaiser bei dieser Gelegenheit eine stattliche Anzahl von Objekten für sein Naturalienkabinett, innerhalb dessen sie den Kern für eine neue ethnographische Sammlung bildeten.

Nach Cooks Forschungsreisen und den gleichzeitigen französischen Reisen nach Ozeanien, organisierten auch andere Nationen ihre wissenschaftlichen Expeditionen. Von 1791 bis 1792 besuchte Admiral Alejandro Malaspina die Nordwestküste Amerikas, die seit Cooks Reise wegen des Seeotterhandels mit China ein besonders in wirtschaftlicher Hinsicht verlockendes Gebiet geworden war und von Spanien in Ausdehnung seiner südwestlichen Besitztümer nach wie vor beansprucht wurde. Malaspinas Sammlung, die jetzt im Museo de America in Madrid zu sehen ist, entstand zu einem Zeitpunkt, als sich Spanien wie in momentaner Erhellung ebenfalls für mexikanische Altertümer ernsthaft zu interessieren begann. Da des weiteren die Gebiete westlich des Mississippi von Spanien verwaltet wurden, konnte erstmals auch Material der *Plains-Indianer* seinen Weg nach Spanien finden.

Die große von Adam von Krusenstern geleitete russische Entdeckungsfahrt, der noch andere folgen sollten, ging 1805 zur pazifischen Nordwestküste Nordamerikas (eine von G. H. von Langsdorff angelegte Sammlung befindet sich heute in München, jene von Lisiansky in Leningrad). Dabei wurde

□ 124 *›Objekte von Indianern der Nordwestküste‹, 1778 von Captain Cook gesammelt und 1838 zusammen mit Objekten der Grönland-Eskimos in der K. u. K. ethnographischen Sammlung in Wien ausgestellt. Aquarell, Thomas Ender zugeschrieben.*

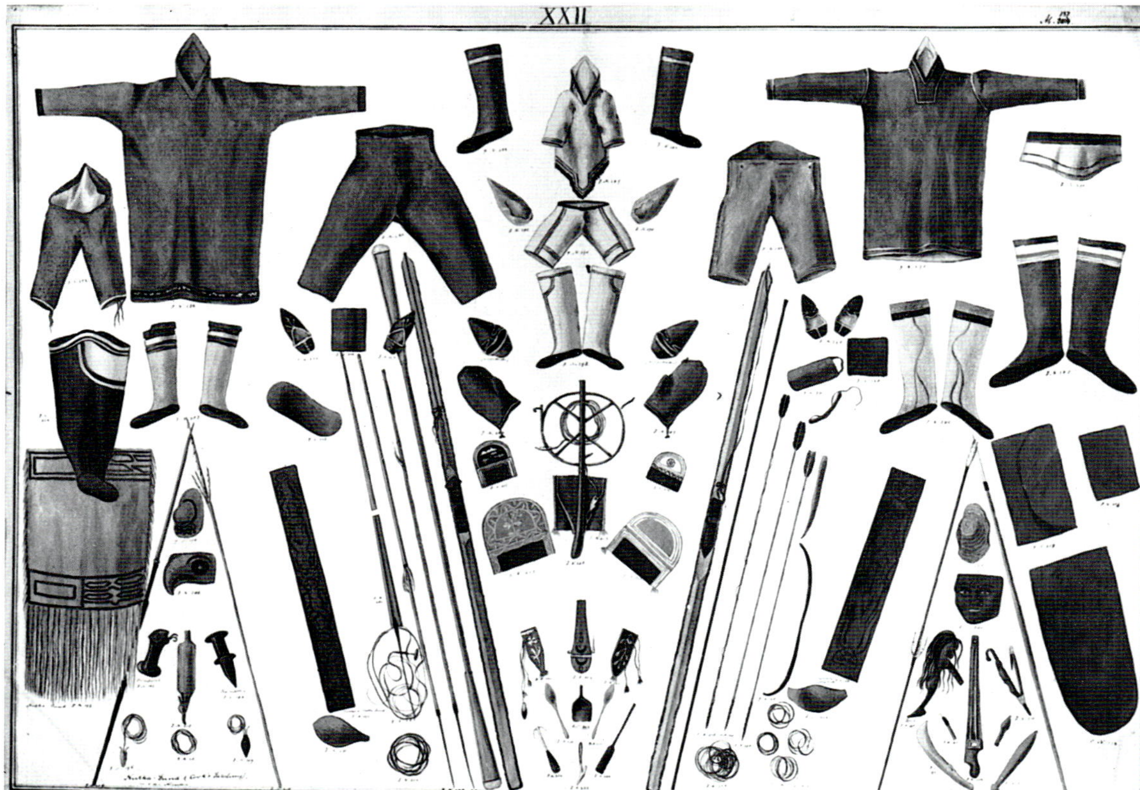

□ 125 *›George Catlins Iowa-Truppe beim Auftritt für Louis Philippe in den Tuilerien‹, 1845, Gemälde von Karl Girardet. Musée National du Château de Versailles.*

russisches Territorium berührt, weil nach der Mitte des 18. Jahrhunderts die russische Ostexpansion quer durch Sibirien bis zur Behringstraße und der Aleuten-Kette vorgestoßen war. Sammlungen wie die des Baron von Asch (heute in Göttingen) entstanden zur Zeit von Cooks dritter Seereise, kamen jedoch auf dem Landweg über Asien nach Europa.

Während die Mehrzahl der russischen Sammlungen von den Aleuten, den *Alaska-Eskimos* und den *Athapasken* nach Leningrad ging, bezogen andere europäische Sammlungen einen Anteil davon über Ausländer, die in russischen Diensten standen, oder durch dynastische Heiratsverbindungen. Arvid Etholens Sammlung in Helsinki, Generalgouverneur von Russisch-Amerika, gehört zur ersten Kategorie, zur letzteren zählt die von seinem Vorgänger Oberst Kouprianoff zusammengetragene und nun in Oldenburg befindliche Sammlung. Im allgemeinen legen die russischen Sammlungen wie auch die zu ihnen gehörenden ethnographischen Berichte Zeugnis von umsichtiger Planung ab, wozu auch die Verwendung von Fragebögen und Prüflisten gehörte.

Als eine Mischung aus kühnen Großtaten, politischen Verwicklungen und forscherischem Ehrgeiz ist die transkontinentale Expedition von Lewis und Clark durchaus mit den Entdekkungsreisen anderer Nationen zu vergleichen. Sie hatte nicht nur die Einrichtung eines der ersten amerikanischen Museen indianischen Kulturgutes zur Folge, sondern blieb auch für Generationen europäischer Bildungsreisender beispielhaft, die es in den amerikanischen Westen zog. Alexander von Humboldt stellte das andere große Vorbild dar. Sicherlich war eines der am besten vorbereiteten und erfahrensten Mitglieder dieser Gruppe Prinz Maximilian von Wied, dessen Sammlungen sich heute hauptsächlich in Berlin und Stuttgart befinden. Das deutsche Interesse an Nordamerika (und den Indianern) war auch im 19. Jahrhundert stark, zum Teil wegen der verstärkten deutschen Auswanderung, sicher aber auch wegen der ständig zunehmenden Flut trivialer, von James Fenimore Cooper und französischen Vorbildern beeinflußter Indianerromane.

Nur ein Jahr bevor Prinz Maximilian den Missouri in Begleitung des Schweizer Malers Karl Bodmer bis in das Kerngebiet der *Plains-Indianer* hinauffuhr, hatte der amerikanische Maler und ehemalige Anwalt George Catlin dieselbe Gegend besucht, um mit Leinwand und Pinsel die letzten Tage einer »verschwindenden Rasse« festzuhalten. Was Catlin an technischem Geschick und malerischer Qualität vermissen ließ, glich er durch Enthusiasmus und Quantität aus. Als die Regierung der Vereinigten Staaten kein Interesse am Kauf seiner »indianischen Galerie« zeigte, zog es Catlin nach Europa, wo er sich – wie sich herausstellte, zu Recht – einen wärmeren Empfang seiner Kunst und allem, was mit Indianern zu tun hatte, erhoffte. In Begleitung von wechselnden indianischen Tanzgruppen (*Ojibwas* und *Iowa* □ 125) eroberte Catlin zuerst London und dann Paris, wo seine Bilder im Louvre ausgestellt wurden und wo ihn König Louis Philippe beauftragte, eine Serie von Bildern über die französische Entdeckung Louisianas zu malen. Wie Bodmer und Catlin bereisten viele europäische und amerikanische Künstler des 19. Jahrhunderts den Westen und verbreiteten durch ihre Malerei Bilder von den (*Plains*-) Indianern. Manche von ihnen betätigten sich auch als Sammler. Catlin scheint sogar einige der Stücke, die er nach Hause mitgebracht hatte, »verbessert« zu haben; als Künstler traute er sich zu, es besser zu können als die Indianer – eine Haltung, die er mit Bürokraten, Missionaren und sogar manchen Ethnologen teilte.

Systematisches Beobachten und systematisches Sammeln legten im 19. Jahrhundert den Grundstein zur Begründung der Anthropologie als Wissenschaft. Während kleine, spezialisierte ethnographische Sammlungen, die normalerweise indianisches Material enthielten, entweder Universitäten angeschlossen waren (Göttingen, seit den 1780er Jahren) oder als

☐ 126 ›Bella-Coola-Indianer‹, von Kapitän Jacobsen nach Deutschland gebracht. Vorführung eines Tanzes aus dem Winterzeremoniell-Zyklus. Berlin, 1885.

☐ 127 ›Maske für ein Pferd‹, Cheyenne (Wyoming), Federn und Bast, Höhe 53 cm. Museum of the American Indian, Heye Foundation, New York.

☐ 128 *›Maske‹, von Inuk Elio aus Angmagssalik (Ostgrönland), 1934, Holz. Musée de l'Homme, Paris.*

separate Abteilungen zu naturhistorischen Museen (Wien, seit 1806) oder »Kunstkammern« gehörten (Berlin, seit 1829), entstanden die meisten europäischen Museen für Völkerkunde in der zweiten Hälfte des 19. Jahrhunderts als Abteilungen von naturhistorischen Museen (wie in Paris) oder als Teile noch allgemeinerer Sammlungen (wie das Britische Museum). Eine Ausnahme bildet Berlin, wo 1873 ein eigenes Museum für Völkerkunde eingerichtet wurde. Die meisten anderen Museen trennten sich – wenn überhaupt – erst im 20. Jahrhundert von dem Institut, dem sie ursprünglich angeschlossen waren. Fast alle waren öffentliche Einrichtungen und wurden staatlich finanziert und betrieben. Viele gaben den Völkerkundlern ihre ersten Anstellungen.

Nun sollte man aus dem Gesagten nicht den Schluß ziehen, daß alle oder zumindest die meisten Sammlungen, die von den neuen Museen aufgekauft wurden, systematisch wissenschaftlich bearbeitet waren. Sehr oft ging der Etat in der Errichtung von Prachtbauten und in Gehältern auf, so daß der weitere Ausbau der Sammlung zum Teil auf private Spenden angewiesen war. Manchen Museen war es oft nicht möglich, Gelder für den Kauf von systematischen Sammlungen aufzutreiben, die ihnen von einer immer größeren Zahl amerikanischer Feldsammler angeboten wurden. Sie mußten sich so mit dem begnügen, was Reisende an Spektakulärem mitbrachten und

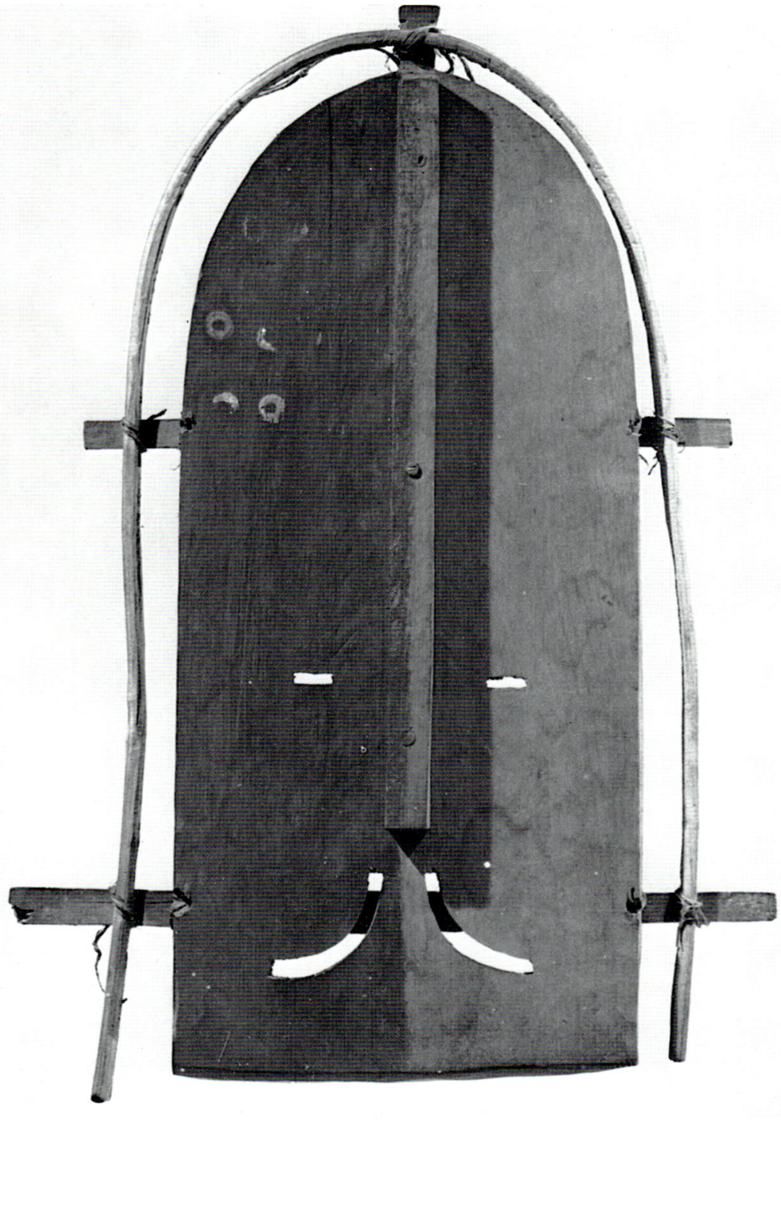

☐ 129 *›Eskimoische Maske‹, Kodiak-Insel (Alaska), Holz, Höhe 32,5 cm. Musée Municipal, Sammlung Pinart, Boulogne-sur-Mer.*

umsonst zur Verfügung stellten. Natürlich gaben solche Sammlungen weder eingeborene Kulturen noch eingeborene Ästhetik in adäquater Weise wieder – aber sie beeinflußten die Sicht anderer Völker in der Öffentlichkeit.

Die meisten europäischen Kolonialmächte finanzierten hauptsächlich wissenschaftliche Expeditionen in ihre eigenen kolonialen Besitzungen, und auch Staaten ohne kolonialen Besitz zeigten eher Interesse an Gebieten, die noch kolonialisiert werden konnten, als daran, Expeditionen in die Vereinigten Staaten oder Kanada zu unterstützen. Gelegentlich kam es vor, daß ein Europäer an einer amerikanischen Expedition teilnahm: So gesellte sich der Holländer H. F. C. Ten Kate zu der Hemenway-Expedition, die 1887 bis 1888 durch den Südwesten führte (vgl. die Sammlungen in Leiden und Rotterdam). Unter den französischen Erforschern des westlichen Nordamerika verdient Alphonse Pinard besondere Beachtung, dessen im Jahre 1871 aus den Aleuten zusammengetragene Sammlung (heute in Boulogne-sur-Mer) französische Künstler stark beeinflußte. Pinard ging später mit Léon de Cessac nach Südkalifornien (Sammlungen hiervon in Paris).

Wenn wissenschaftliche Sammlungen auch Kenntnisse erweitert haben, so waren sie doch oft nicht spektakulär. Weniger wissenschaftlich, dafür aber gut dokumentiert und vor allem umfangreich waren die Sammlungen, die der norwegische Schiffskapitän Adrian Jacobsen für verschiedene deutsche Museen (vor allem Berlin, aber auch Leipzig, Köln und Lübeck) sowie für sein heimatliches Oslo an der Norwestküste und in der Arktis zusammengestellt hatte. 1885 brachte Jacobsen eine *Bella Coola*-Truppe für ein Jahr nach Deutschland □ 93. Die Indianer führten nicht nur ihre Tänze, sondern auch ihre Schnitzkünste vor. Angezogen von diesen *Bella Coola*, reiste der deutschstämmige Franz Boas zur Nordwestküste. Er wurde einer der Gründerväter der professionellen amerikanischen Anthropologie und ist Verfasser des einflußreichen Werkes *Primitive Art*.

Trotz des enormen Eindrucks, den die *Bella Coola* auf das deutsche Publikum ausübten (besonders die Damen waren von ihnen angetan), blieben deutsche und europäische Vorstellungen von Indianern doch mit dem Bild verhaftet, das man sich über die *Plains-Indianer* gemacht hatte. Museen konnten nicht viel tun, um diesen unkorrekten Eindruck zu berichtigen, aber sie waren imstande, einer interessierten Minderheit – die Künstler eingeschlossen – eine große Vielfalt altamerikanischer Eingeborenenkunst darzubieten. Am Vorabend des Ersten Weltkriegs konnte etwa Berlin größere Sammlungen aus allen eingeborenen Kulturarealen Nordamerikas aufweisen; dies schloß Gegenstände der *Hopi-Indianer* aus dem Südwesten ein, die man von dem Indianer-Agenten bei den *Hopi*, Thomas V. Keam, erworben hatte, kalifornische Korbware von Samuel Barret und Wilcomb oder neuere *Plains*-Sammlungen von Clark Wissler. Zu erwähnen ist, daß die Gehege für eine Herde amerikanischer Bisons im Berliner Zoo im Stil von Werken der Nordwestküste geschnitzt waren.

Um die Jahrhundertwende standen die europäischen Museen beim Sammeln indianischen Materials vor einem großen Problem. Die intensive Feldsammeltätigkeit der Amerikaner erfolgte zusehends für die von Küste zu Küste errichteten heimischen Museen, nachdem die eingeborenen Gesellschaf-

□ 130 *›Figur‹, Salish (Washington), bemaltes Holz, Muscheln und Knochen, Höhe 91 cm. American Museum of Natural History, Department of Anthropology, New York.*

eröffnet, ist es nur wenige Jahre jünger als das Museum of the American Indian in New York.

Das Gebiet, in dem Europäer weiterhin Feldsammlungen erwarben, war die Arktis, vor allem Grönland, das natürlich die Hochburg der Dänen war. Aber auch die Franzosen richteten in Ostgrönland eine – noch heute betriebene – anthropologische Feldstation ein, aus der ebenfalls Sammlungen für Museen hervorgingen. Unter diesen befand sich eine prächtige Sammlung der grotesk verzerrten Angmagssalik-Masken, von denen ein Exemplar in André Malraux' imaginärem Museum Platz fand □ 128.

Die eigentliche »Entdeckung« indianischer Arbeiten als Kunst erfolgte offenbar in Amerika und Europa unabhängig voneinander zur gleichen Zeit. Als der amerikanische Maler John Sloan in New York die erste Ausstellung südwestlicher Indianermalerei organisierte, erschienen gleichzeitig zum ersten Mal auf dem europäischen Buchmarkt mehrere Werke, die indianische Objekte als Kunst vorstellten. Während aber die Amerikaner von zeitgenössischer Kunst und dem Südwesten ausgingen, fanden die Europäer über Museumsstücke und vor allem über die Nordwestküste Zugang. Leonhard Adams *Nordwestamerikanische Indianerkunst,* das die Berliner Sammlung zur Grundlage hatte, war eine bahnbrechende Studie. Sie erschien in den zwanziger Jahren, damit fast gleichzeitig mit dem weniger gelungenen Werk von Fuhrmann über die Kunst

ten den Verlust ihrer Unabhängigkeit wie einen Schock erlebt hatten. Durch diese Entwicklung benachteiligt, sahen es viele europäische Museen für unmöglich oder überflüssig an, Feldsammlungen oder zeitgenössische indianische Produkte zu erwerben. Man kaufte von Händlern wie Webster oder Oldman, die ihre Kataloge regelmäßig veröffentlichten, oder von den Erben der Reisenden des 19. Jahrhunderts. In ganz Europa war das private Sammeln indianischer Objekte ziemlich weit verbreitet, und vor allem zwischen den beiden Weltkriegen entstanden einige wichtige Sammlungen. Die Gründe für das Sammeln gerade indianischen Materials waren vor allem in einem romantischen Interesse an indianischer Kultur und Lebensart zu suchen; ästhetische Gesichtspunkte spielten nach wie vor eine untergeordnete Rolle. Unter diesem Aspekt ist auch die Gründung von Museen zu betrachten, die sich auf die Kulturen der Indianer spezialisierten. Die erste europäische Institution dieser Art war wohl das Karl-May-Museum in Radebeul bei Dresden, das ein deutscher »Squaw-Mann« aus Buffalo Bills Show zu Ehren des populärsten deutschen Verfassers von Indianerromanen ins Leben rief. Im Jahre 1928

□ 133 *›Decke‹*, Tlingit *(Alaska), gefärbte Wolle und Bast aus Zedernrinde, Höhe 56 cm. Museum of the American Indian, Heye Foundation, New York.*

◁ ◁ □ 131 *›Figur aus Holz‹, Nordwestküste (Britisch-Kolumbien), Höhe 117,5 cm. Museum für Völkerkunde, Berlin.*

◁ □ 132 *›Eskimoische Maske‹, Kodiak-Insel (Alaska), bemaltes Holz, Höhe 60 cm. National Museum of Natural History, Smithsonian Institution, Washington.*

der Nordwestküste, das aber wegen der Berücksichtigung anderer europäischer Sammlungen Beachtung verdient. Erwähnenswert ist, daß es vom Essener Folkwang, Schule für Kunst und Gestaltung, publiziert wurde.

Zu einer Zeit, in der die meisten europäischen Museen für Völkerkunde eingerichtet wurden, beherrschten revolutionäre Modelle die Kulturtheorie. Sehr oft reflektierte daher die Vorstellung einer voranschreitenden Entwicklung vom »Primitiven« hin zum »Zivilisierten« das gesamte Ausstellungskonzept. Auch als die meisten Völkerkundler dieses allzu simple Modell aufgegeben hatten, erfolgte die Korrektur in den Museen im allgemeinen erst ein oder zwei Generationen später. Das mehr oder weniger gebildete Publikum übernahm die neuen Sichtweisen erst allmählich. Die Vorstellung vom »Exotischen« blieb weitgehend gleichbedeutend mit »primitiv« und/oder »archaisch«. Unbeeindruckt von Kulturrelativismus, fanden viele Künstler auf ihrer Suche nach neuen alten Wurzeln eine fertige Lösung in primitiver Kunst und Kultur. Die immer noch lebendigen Kulturen Afrikas und Ozeaniens erhielten einen klaren Vorzug gegenüber dem mittlerweile nostalgisch verklärten und romantisierten Nordamerika der Indianer. Trotz aller Einflüsse bildeten die Indianer für europäische Künstler keine wesentliche Inspirationsquelle.

Philippe Peltier

Aus der Südsee

Bei der ersten Pazifiküberquerung im Jahre 1521 stieß Magellan auf keine Inseln. Sie wurden erst im späten 16. Jahrhundert von Spaniern und Portugiesen allmählich entdeckt. Diesen Seemächten folgten die Holländer, die ihre Rivalen durch die Gründung der Ostindischen Kompanie 1602 auf den Philippinen verdrängten. Da aber bei solchen Expeditionen – auch bei der Reise Tasmans nach Neuseeland (1642), wo er nicht an Land gehen konnte – die erhofften Erträge ausblieben, gab man sie ein Jahrhundert lang auf.

Aufwind erhielten die Seereisen erst wieder zu Anfang des 18. Jahrhunderts durch die (oft verklärenden) Berichte von Seereisen während der Renaissance, durch die Fortschritte in der Seefahrt, das Interesse des Jahrhunderts der Aufklärung an den Wissenschaften und durch die Theorie einer ›terra australis‹ als Gegengewicht zu den Kontinenten der nördlichen Halbkugel – eine Theorie, die in Frankreich von Charles de Brosses wiederbelebt worden war. Unter dem Vorwand wissenschaftlicher Forschung spielten nach wie vor wirtschaftliche Interessen, die Suche nach neuen Gütern und Bodenschätzen für Europa eine gewichtige Rolle. So ging 1765 John Byron auf die Reise, Samuel Wallis, Philip Cateret und Bougainville zwei Jahre später, und Captain Cook unternahm seine drei Fahrten zwischen 1768 und 1779. Obwohl sie alle jene mythischen südlichen Gefilde nicht fanden, erstellten sie doch immerhin die Karte des Pazifik. Dafür entstand ein anderer Mythos.

Die Seereisen Cooks und Bougainvilles sollten den Diskussionen der Denker des 18. Jahrhunderts über den Naturzustand des Menschen viele Anregungen liefern. Offenbar erinnerten sich aber die Gebildeten nach Lektüre dieser Reiseberichte nur an die Stellen, die von Polynesien handelten. Auch Bougainville, sonst eher zurückhaltend, wenn es um die Moral der »Wilden« ging, sowie Commerson, der ihn auf seiner Reise begleitet hatte, sollten ihrerseits die Wirklichkeit beschönigen. So wurde Tahiti – der eine nannte es Neu Cythera, der andere Utopia – zu einer Idylle, die mit dem edlen Charakter ihrer Einwohner, ihren einfachen Sitten, ihrer Verehrung des Liebesgottes und ihrer Sprache an die Georgica Vergils erinnerte.[1] Polynesien sah man als die pazifische Ägäis, und Maler stellten die Eingeborenen mit antikischen Zügen dar. Diderot trug mit seinem *Supplément au voyage de Bougainville* ebenso zum Mythos bei wie Restif de la Bretonne, dessen *La Découverte Australe* ein aus mittelalterlichen Fabeln abgeleiteter Initiationsroman ist, in dem alles in diesen Ländern das genaue Gegenteil zu Europa darstellt.

Aber bald schon sollte es Ärger im Paradies geben. Der »Edle Wilde« hatte nämlich einen infantilen und labilen Charakter, der ihn in die schlimmsten Exzesse trieb. Cooks Tod während eines Scharmützels auf Hawaii (1779) und der Tod des Franzosen Marion de Fresne auf Neuseeland ließen das Bild des »Bösen Wilden« entstehen.

Am Menschen in seinem ursprünglichen Zustand interessiert, den man wegen der Gesundheit der Natur für überlegen hielt, konzentrierten sich die Naturforscher mehr auf Sitten und Wesensart der Wilden als auf ihre Erzeugnisse. Die Illustrationen der Reiseberichte zeigen die Objekte der Eingeborenen nie in Anwendung, man sieht sie nur auf separaten Tafeln. Trotz des Aufsehens, das diese Objekte in Europa erregten, betrachtete man sie in erster Linie als »Kuriositäten«. Das ästhetische Urteil über sie fiel je nach Betrachter unterschiedlich aus. Während manche die gute Ausführung der Schnitzarbeit bewunderten, hielten andere diese Objekte einfach für krude Machwerke wie von Seeleuten. Und wiederum andere fühlten sich an antike Gegenstände erinnert, die in Europa gerade von Winckelmann wiederentdeckt wurden.[2]

Um die Jahrhundertwende war Europa auf der Suche nach seinen Ursprüngen, und die vom Tragischen und Erhabenen besessene Romantik war mehr vom Kannibalen als vom altehrwürdigen Wilden fasziniert. Man war auf der Suche nach der Welt, die die eigene Entwicklung widerspiegelte. Für die französischen Ideologen der Revolution und des Empire befand sich der »Wilde«, von der Natur geschwächt, nur auf einer unterentwickelten Stufe, seine Gesellschaft noch in einem Zustand der Unreife. In den nach England und Frankreich gebrachten Objekten sah man diese Auffassung bestätigt. Péron, der Baudin 1800–1804 auf einer Seereise zur südlichen Halbkugel begleitet hatte, verglich die auf Neuguinea gesammelten Objekte mit denen der antiken Kulturen des Westens.[3]

Die von den Seereisenden aufgebauten Sammlungen – zumindest in Frankreich scheint kein Objekt aus dem 16. Jahrhundert erhalten gewesen zu sein – wurden entweder auf verschiedene europäische Institutionen verteilt oder verblieben bei ihren Besitzern. Zwar wollte Jauffret in Frankreich ein naturgeschichtliches Museum einrichten, in dem umfassend Zeugnis von verschiedenen Kulturen abgelegt werden sollte, aber dieses zu utopische Projekt kam nie zustande. Die Sammlungen, die Bougainville mitgebracht hatte und die in der Bibliothek des Ordens Saint-Genevieve in Paris untergebracht waren, wurden während der Revolution geplündert.[4] Pérons

◁ ☐ 134 *›Maske‹, Wituinsel (Neubritannien), bemalter Baststoff und verschiedene Materialien, Höhe 65 cm. Musée Barbier-Müller, Genf.*

□ 135 *›Mannequin mit der Maske eines Kanakenhäuptlings‹ (Neukaledonien). Weltausstellung, Paris 1878, Stich nach einer Zeichnung von M. Vierge, veröffentlicht in „Le Monde illustré", 14. Dezember 1878.*

□ 136 *›Figur zur Bekrönung eines Daches‹,* ▷ Biwat, *Provinz Ost-Sepik (Papua-Neuguinea), Holz, Muscheln, Fasern und Federn, Höhe 122 cm. Musée Barbier-Müller, Genf.*

Schenkung an Joséphine Bonaparte scheint das gleiche Schicksal ereilt zu haben.[5]

Das Museum von Sir Ashton Lever in England war das erste überhaupt, in dem ein Teil der Sammlungen englischer Seereisender ausgestellt wurde. Ursprünglich in Manchester ansässig, kam es 1775 nach London und wurde 1806 in einer öffentlichen Versteigerung aufgelöst, wobei das Wiener Museum einen Teil der Sammlung erwarb.[6]

Diese frühen Sammlungen wurden durch weitere Pazifikreisen erweitert. Auch Handel und Missionseifer nahmen stark zu. Zunächst fuhren europäische und amerikanische Walfangschiffe der 1799 gegründeten East Indian Marine Society. Die von ihnen gesammelten Objekte bildeten den Grundstock für das Peabody Museum in Salem. Sie wählten Hawaii zu ihrem Stützpunkt, von wo aus ganz Polynesien bereist wurde. Seeleute auf der Flucht vor der drakonischen Borddisziplin blieben auf so mancher Insel, die ihnen gastlicher schien. Gegen Ende des 18. Jahrhunderts ließ sich die London Missionary Society in Polynesien nieder und dehnte sich in Konkurrenz zum Katholizismus bald über den gesamten pazifischen Raum aus. Missionare brachten Objekte zur Unterhaltung und als Beweis für ihre »seelsorgerischen« Aktivitäten nach Hause mit. Es kam immer häufiger zu Konversionen, und am 15. Februar 1815 wurden auf Tahiti (und ein paar Jahre später auf Hawaii) »Götzenbilder« auf dem Scheiterhaufen verbrannt. Die Gegenstände, die der Vernichtung entgingen, wurden nach London geschickt und im Missionsmuseum ausgestellt, bevor sie 1890 in das Britische Museum gelangten. Zur gleichen Zeit wurden in Europa noch andere Missionsmuseen eingerichtet. Gerade wissenschaftliche Expeditionen der Franzosen, Preußen und Briten stellten ozeanische Erzeugnisse zusammen, ebenso Kriegsschiffe der westlichen Mächte, die ihre Staatsangehörigen in den annektierten Territorien beschützen sollten, und schließlich auch Sklavenschiffe, die billige Arbeitskräfte für die Plantagen beförderten. Als wissenschaftliche Seereisen immer häufiger wurden, lockte es auch Abenteurer und Händ-

ler jedweder Couleur in die Südsee. Die Entdeckung des Sandelholzes 1804 auf den Fidschiinseln war das Startsignal für eine Plünderung, die Hawaii in den 1820er Jahren heimsuchte, die Neuen Hebriden 1825 und Neukaledonien 1840. Dann fing man Seegurken oder ›bêches-de-mer‹ und exportierte sie nach China. Aufgrund verbesserter Transportmöglichkeiten kam nach 1850 eine große Welle europäischer Siedler. Nach 1868 wuchs der Koprahandel ständig, und es wurden auf Kosten der Eingeborenen die Plantagen vergrößert, dies vor allem auf Queensland, den Fidschis, Neukaledonien, Tahiti, Hawaii und Samoa. Um 1863 brauchten diese Plantagen billige Arbeitskräfte, und so wurde die männliche Bevölkerung der Neuen Hebriden, der Gilbertinseln, Neukaledoniens und anderer Inseln zwangsrekrutiert. Nach und nach verloren die Inseln ihre Unabhängigkeit: Missionare, Handelshäuser und Konsuln spielten im Leben dieser Inseln (z. B. Hawaii) eine führende Rolle. 1840 wurden Neuseeland und die Fidschis annektiert, 1853 Neukaledonien, während die Salomoninseln, Samoa und die Neuen Hebriden später unter mehrere Staaten aufgeteilt wurden (jeweils 1877, 1879 und 1887). Gegen Ende des Jahrhunderts wurden die Tongainseln nach etlichen Bürgerkriegen ein Protektorat. Mit den Inseln Mikronesiens wurde unterschiedlich verfahren, bis sie 1880 ein für allemal annektiert wurden. Neuguinea, aus dem man keine Arbeitskräfte abgezogen hatte, wurde aufgeteilt: Schon 1828 annektierten die Niederlande den westlichen Teil, 1884 Deutschland den nordöstlichen, und im gleichen Jahr machten die Briten den Südosten zum Protektorat.

So brachte am Anfang des Jahrhunderts eine Vielzahl von Reisenden, Seeleuten, Wissenschaftlern, Siedlern und Abenteurern neben geologischen, botanischen und zoologischen Stücken auch einige Objekte oder größere Sammlungen, hauptsächlich aus Polynesien, mit. Aber kein Völkerkundemuseum stand bereit, um diese Sammlungen aufzunehmen. Sie landeten schließlich in den Kuriositätenkabinetten von Königen, Adligen oder Wissenschaftlern, die die Expeditionen finanziert hatten, oder in naturgeschichtlichen Museen. Die ersten mit Stiftungen beschenkten Museen befanden sich vor allem in Häfen und Hauptstädten: In Frankreich waren es das Museum in Boulogne, das Musée d'Histoire Naturelle in Caen, das die Sammlung Dumont-d'Urville erhielt, das Musée des Médailles der Bibliothèque Nationale in Paris und das 1850 eingerichtete Musée de la Marine, welches die königlichen Sammlungen bekam.[7]

Erst im letzten Drittel des 19. Jahrhunderts, als Europa seine koloniale Expansion massiv vorantrieb, nahm die Zahl der Völkerkundemuseen zu.[8] Oft bestanden ihre ersten Sammlungen aus ozeanischen Stücken, so etwa in Wien, Kopenhagen und Harvard. Eine wichtige Rolle spielten auch die Weltausstellungen, die regelmäßig dem industriellen Fortschritt huldigten und Erzeugnisse aus den Kolonien präsentierten. Dort konnte man auch Arbeiten aus der Südsee begutachten, z. B. 1851 in London und 1855 in Paris, wo Malereien australischer Aborigines ausgestellt waren.[9]

Im Januar 1878 eröffnete das Musée des Missions Ethnographiques in Paris mit der Ausstellung einer Sammlung hawaiischer Stücke, die Ballieu, damals französischer Konsul in

□ 138 *›Einrichtung der Eingangshalle des neuen Musée d'Ethnographie‹, Palais du Trocadéro, Paris 1882, Stich nach einer Zeichnung von De Haenon, veröffentlicht in „Le Monde illustré", 16. Mai 1882.*

Honolulu, gehörten. Dieses Museum war der Vorläufer des Musée d'Ethnographie de Paris, das unter der Leitung von E. Hamy im selben Jahr gegründet wurde, aber seine Türen erst 1882 öffnete □ 138, 327.

Auf der Pariser Weltausstellung von 1878 zeichneten sich drei verschiedene Interpretationsweisen primitiver Kunst ab durch die Aufstellung an drei verschiedenen Orten: nämlich im Palais des Sciences Anthropologiques, in den kolonialen Pavillons und schließlich im neuen Palais du Trocadéro mit seiner »Exposition des Arts Anciens« □ 135.

Im Palais sah man die Objekte neben Schädeln und behauenen Steinen aus prähistorischer Zeit. Waffen, vor allem aus Neukaledonien und Neuseeland, waren als Trophäen ausgestellt, zu denen sich zwei Korwar-Figuren aus Niederländisch-Neuguinea, Jade-Tikis aus Neuseeland und Objekte von den Tongainseln gesellten.[10] Es war eine unzulängliche Ausstellung, von Waffen aus dem ganzen pazifischen Raum beherrscht, die zusammen mit Gebrauchsobjekten eine Klassifikation der Gesellschaften ermöglichen sollten – von der am wenigsten entwickelten (Australien) bis zur aristokratischsten Kultur (Westpolynesien).

In den kolonialen Pavillons waren mehr Objekte ausgestellt. England zeigte Produkte aus Australien und Neuseeland, Frankreich aus Französisch-Polynesien und Neukaledonien. Aber es erschienen im britischen Teil der Ausstellung auch Stücke aus Neuguinea und von den Gilbert- und Salomoninseln

◁ □ 137 *›Schädelgerüst‹,* Kerewa, *Golfprovinz (Papua-Neuguinea), bemaltes Holz, Höhe 142 cm. The Metropolitan Museum of Art, The M. C. Rockefeller Memorial Collection, New York.*

□ 139 *›Osterinsel‹, Zeichnung von Pierre Loti, Sarah Bernhardt gewidmet, 7. Januar 1872.*

im französischen Teil – manchmal unter falschen Zuschreibungen. Jedes Objekt wurde einer festen Kategorie zugeordnet, die auf europäischen Erzeugnissen basierte, und neben diesen aufgestellt: So wurde eine neukaledonische Maske als »Nippes« eingestuft, während die wenigen Skulpturen mit »Geräten des täglichen Gebrauchs« vermischt wurden.[11] Erzeugnisse der Eingeborenen dienten als Beweis für den Wert westlicher Produkte und den Fortschritt der Zivilisation.

Die repräsentativste Ausstellung war die »Exposition des Arts Anciens«. Der Historienmaler JEAN-LÉON GÉRÔME war für die Abteilung »Ethnographie von Völkern außerhalb Europas« zuständig. Polynesien war mit Tikis aus Tahiti, Äxten von den Cookinseln, Keulen von den Marquesas und – das am meisten bewunderte Stück – einem Boot aus Neuseeland vertreten. Aus Melanesien kamen Skulpturen von den Salomoninseln, eine Maske und Zeremonienäxte aus Neukaledonien, Objekte aus der Geelvink-Bucht in Niederländisch-Neuguinea und – inmitten von kriegerischen Trophäen – einige »Schüsseln, Teller und Kopfputz«. Was den Kritikern an dieser »kindischen und barbarischen, naiven und furchterregenden« Kunst gefiel, waren lediglich »die Pracht des Holzes . . . die Ausführung, die handwerkliche Qualität, der ausgeprägte Hang zum Ornamentalen«, wobei schnell eine Verbindung dieser Erzeugnisse mit der Kunst des Orients hergestellt war.[12] So wurde die Ornamentik eher wahrgenommen als die bildhauerischen Qualitäten. Schon Racinets Buch *L'Ornament polychrome* von 1869 enthielt eine Abbildung mit Motiven, die von der Kunst Ozeaniens und der Plastik Neuseelands angeregt waren. Letztere wurde häufig dargestellt und besonders bewundert, denn sie zeichnete sich durch ein höchst kunstvolles ornamentales System von Verflechtungen aus, das keinerlei Imitationen bezweckte, sondern ganz aus der Phantasie entstand und daher als vollkommen dekorativ empfunden wurde.[13]

Auf dieser Weltausstellung dienten die Objekte vor allem der Dokumentation der Anfänge und Zivilisationsstufen. Die offizielle Malerei, einem eingefleischten Ideal von Schönheit und Wahrheit verschrieben, widmete sich bei der Darstellung »europafremder Völker« nach klassischer Tradition dem Studium von Physiognomie und Charakter. 1886 proklamierte Rochet, daß »Historienmalerei ethnographisch oder nichts sein wird«, und er träumte von einem Museum, das – anders als das Musée d'Ethnographie – nur Menschentypen, wie sie wirklich sind, zeigen würde.[14] Folglich würden statt der Skulpturen viel mehr Masken ausgestellt und studiert werden, die man für Portraits von Wilden hielt, wie sie waren oder wie sie sich selbst sahen. In diesem Sinne fanden sie als Kriegerpuppen im Musée d'Artillerie des Invalides Aufstellung, das für die Weltausstellung von 1878 umgestaltet wurde.[15]

Die einzelnen Südseeinseln waren in Art und Zahl ihrer Erzeugnisse in europäischen Sammlungen ganz unterschiedlich vertreten, je nachdem ob die Sammlung in der Provinz lag, sich in Privatbesitz befand oder kolonialen Agenturen gehörte, die bei der Verbreitung eine wichtige Rolle spielten. Jedes Land erhielt vorzugsweise Erzeugnisse aus seinen eigenen Kolonien.

So verkaufte 1878 in Toulouse das in Neukaledonien gegründete Maison Saves »Kuriositäten«. Ähnlich sammelte Le Mescam in jenen Jahren Objekte aus Neukaledonien (Masken, einen Türsturz) und von den Neuen Hebriden (u. a. einen geschnitzten Baumfarn und einige modellierte Schädel), die er 1895 dem Museum in Le Havre, Braques Geburtsstadt, überließ. 1857 errichtete das Maison Godeffroy in Hamburg seine erste Niederlassung auf Samoa, danach 1874 auf dem Bismarckarchipel. Seine Schiffe, die den Pazifik durchkreuzten, brachten Objekte nach Hamburg, von denen einige den Grundstock für ein 1881 gegründetes eigenes Museum bildeten. Die Firma Hernsheim ließ sich 1876 in Neuirland nieder und gab dem Berliner Museum einige Masken, die mit zu den ältesten seiner Sammlungen gehören.[16]

Museen waren nicht die einzigen Nutznießer von Schenkungen und Versteigerungen. Nehmen wir die 1878 im Trocadéro ausgestellte und 1887 in Paris verkaufte Sammlung Bertin. Außer den Objekten aus Tahiti besaß Bertin eine wichtige Serie von Stücken aus Deutsch- und Niederländisch-Neuguinea. Anläßlich des Verkaufs erschien ein Katalog. Dieses für Frankreich relativ seltene Ereignis läßt auf ein wachsendes Interesse an exotischen Objekten schließen. Die Sammlung fand mehrere Käufer, u. a. Hamy, Direktor des Musée d'Ethnographie, und Heyman, dem Händler in der Rue de Rennes, bei dem MATISSE seine erste afrikanische Skulptur erstand. Es ist anzunehmen, daß schon zu diesem recht frühen Zeitpunkt einige Antiquitätenhändler exotische Objekte an Sammler verkauften, die nicht unbedingt etwas mit Anthropologie zu tun hatten: Bertin war Juwelen-Großhändler.[17]

Im April 1882 wurden die Säle des Musée d'Ethnographie in Paris dem Publikum geöffnet. Die Sammlungen bestanden u. a. aus Stücken, die sich schon auf der Weltausstellung von 1878

□ 140 *›Kanakendorf‹ (Neukaledonien), Weltausstellung, Paris 1889, Stich nach einer Zeichnung von Louis Tinayre, veröffentlicht in „Le Monde illustré", 27. Juni 1889.* ▷

LOUIS TINAYRE

befunden hatten, darunter auch die aus England und den Niederlanden. Andere stammten von der Laglaize- und Raffray-Expedition zur Nordostküste von Neuguinea und der von Bourdil zur Südostküste. Wie Trophäen ausgestellte Waffen beherrschten den Gesamteindruck und repräsentierten die Hauptinseln des Pazifik. Nur Polynesien und Neukaledonien wurden durch vollständigere Serien illustriert. Im Jahre 1884 wurde die Sammlung Higginson mit Werken von den Neuen Hebriden, darunter auch Großplastiken, in der Eingangshalle des Musée d'Ethnographie aufgebaut. Diese Sammlung wurde durch einen Teil der Sammlung François nach einer Ausstellung in der Orangerie des Musée d'Histoire im Jahr 1890 ergänzt. Mit diesen beiden Sammlungen besaß Paris zu jener Zeit den vollständigsten Bestand von den Neuen Hebriden, der Skulpturen, Masken, Trommeln, Figuren sozial gestufter Gesellschaften und Totenstatuen umfaßte.[18] 1887 erwarb Roland Bonaparte die Sammlung Bertin und gab sie an das Musée d'Ethnographie, womit nun Stücke aus Deutsch- und Niederländisch-Neuguinea die Ausstellung ergänzten.[19] Nach einem Besuch der Kolonialausstellung in Amsterdam im Jahre 1883 erwarb Roland Bonaparte Werke aus Niederländisch-Neuguinea, vor allem von der Geelvink-Bucht, wo 1882 eine ständige Handelsvertretung gegründet worden war.[20] 1886 wurden auf der Londoner Kolonial-Ausstellung die ersten großen Tapa-Masken vom Papua-Golf gezeigt. Neuseeland war durch bedeutende Objekte aus der Sammlung Buller vertreten. Captain Cook gedachte man in einer eigens eingerichteten Sonderaustellung.

Nach der offiziellen Übernahme Neuguineas und des Bismarckarchipels durch die Deutsche Neuguinea-Companie im Jahre 1884 – wobei die Handelsabteilung der Firma mit der Verwaltung dieser Gebiete beauftragt wurde – eröffnete in Berlin eine Ausstellung der von dieser Vertretung gesammelten Stücke.[21] Die bis dahin noch weitgehend unerforschte Region wurde bald zum Ziel bedeutender Expeditionen. Der Russe Miklouho-Macklay, der sich als erster an der Nordküste Neuguineas aufhielt, legte dort Sammlungen an, die 1886 in St. Petersburg gezeigt wurden. Die Hansestädte, Berlin, Leipzig (das 1885 einen Teil des Godeffroy Museums erwarb) und Dresden erhielten Sammlungen aus den am stärksten kolonialisierten Gebieten: Palau, den Karolinen, Neuirland und Neubritannien. Besonderes Interesse scheint die Steinplastik aus Neuirland geweckt zu haben. Man besaß nur Stücke aus dem nordöstlichen Neuguinea, denn die Erforschung des Landesinneren ging nur mühsam voran, so daß die Objekte hauptsächlich von der Küste und den Inseln stammten. Nach 1895 wurden die wissenschaftlichen Forschungsreisen seltener.[22] Die von D'Albertis gesammelten Objekte (dieser war 1876 als erster den Fly River hinaufgefahren) stellte das Museo Ethnographico in Rom aus. Viele Objekte vom Golf von Papua bis hin zur Massim-Region gelangten in britische Museen, so Arbeiten aus dem Gebiet der Pitt-Rivers, die 1884 in Oxford ausgestellt wurden, oder Objekte aus der Expedition zur Torresstraße, die 1888 nach Cambridge kamen.

□ 141 *›Tahiti-Pavillon‹, Weltausstellung, Paris 1900.*

Budapester Museen wurden durch Sammlungen der Néprajzi-Mission, die man 1896 ausstellte, bereichert, ferner durch die zwischen 1896 und 1902 in Neuguinea und dem Bismarckarchipel angelegte Sammlung von Lajos Biró und schließlich durch Graf Rodolfe Festetics, der 1895/96 auf seiner Privatyacht eine Weltreise unternahm.[23]

Dieser knappe Überblick gibt einen Eindruck vom Umfang melanesischer Sammlungen, die die älteren polynesischen Bestände ergänzten. Diese Sammlungen wurden aufgrund des neuen Wohlstandes und der Einführung des Eisens in den Ursprungsgebieten und der damit steigenden handwerklichen Herstellung noch erweitert.[24]

In den Jahren 1880–95 stieg die Zahl der Veröffentlichungen, wobei sich zwei Interpretationen primitiver Kunst gegenüberstanden. Haddon, der eine evolutionistische Linie verfolgte, betrachtete nur die Motive, ihre Veränderung und ihren magischen Charakter; für die Objekte als solche interessierte er sich nicht. Gross hingegen setzt an die Stelle der formalen Interpretation die Interpretation der Objekte in ihrem gesellschaftlichen Zusammenhang und ermöglicht somit die Berücksichtigung aller Herstellungsweisen.

Im Frankreich jener Jahre richtete sich das öffentliche Interesse auf die koloniale Expansion in Afrika und Indochina. Bei der Pariser Weltausstellung des Jahres 1889 wurden für die Besucher auf dem Champ de Mars Hütten aus Tahiti und Neukaledonien in den »Eingeborenen-Dörfern« rekonstruiert. Zum ersten Mal waren ozeanische Objekte in ihrem eigentlichen Umfeld zu sehen. Wie aus einem »Niemandsland« kommend, erweckten sie ein befremdendes Gefühl: Vorherrschend waren ein Exotismus oder der Traum von einer frühen Welt, einer Rückkehr zu den Kindheitstagen der Zivilisation, einem für immer verlorenen Garten Eden. Es war ein Exotismus, der einem Synkretismus und einer »Ästhetik des Andersartigen« entsprang.[25] Von Louise Michel bis GAUGUIN war die Faszination durch steinzeitliche Mythen stärker als die Bereitschaft, sich mit künstlerischen Formen auseinanderzusetzen. Wir sehen Loti auf der Suche nach einer vergangenen Zivilisation, die er in der Osterinsel verkörpert glaubte. Diese ist gleichzeitig ein ›memento mori‹ des Pazifik für Captain Cook.[26] Exotisches Dekor kam hoch in Mode: Sarah Bernhardt legte ein Kabinett mit Maori-Skulpturen an, die ihr 1891 auf einer Weltreise geschenkt worden waren.

Nach der Weltausstellung von 1889 wurde das Musée d'Ethnographie in Paris neu gestaltet. Die aus Platzmangel auf den Treppenabsätzen zusammengepferchten Sammlungen der Südsee wurden 1892 in einem neuen Saal untergebracht. Aber der geringe Etat des Museums erlaubte es vorerst nicht, einen neuen Wärter anzustellen, so daß der neue Saal bis 1910 dem Publikum offiziell verschlossen blieb.[27]

Anders als in Deutschland und England gelangten in Frankreich nur noch wenige Objekte in die Sammlungen. Die Bevölkerung einiger pazifischer Inseln sank rapide.[28] Die Quelle für den Nachschub weiterer Objekte versiegte. Die Gesellschaftsinseln verwestlichten, doch ließen Missionare, die die alten Gebräuche verbannt hatten, Kopien von Objekten anfertigen. Auf der Pariser Weltausstellung von 1900 wurden in den kolonialen Pavillons u. a. »Kuriositäten« gezeigt, dies vor allem im Pavillon Tahitis □ 141.[29] Die koloniale Expansion brachte immer mehr Ausstellungen mit sich sowie die Eröffnung von Büros in großen Provinzstädten, wo einige Museen neben kommerziellen Erzeugnissen auch Stammeskunst ausstellten, die in manchen Fällen wohl auf Bestellung angefertigt

□ 142 *›Zwei Tikis‹ (siehe Glossar), Marquesasinseln, Holz, ehemals Sammlung Ambroise Vollard, veröffentlicht in Apollinaire und Guillaume, „Sculptures nègres", 1917.*

worden war. Nach Marseille, Bordeaux und anderen Städten transferierte man 1901 auch in Paris das Koloniale Büro in das Palais Royal, wo ein ständiges Museum eingerichtet wurde.[30]

In England und Deutschland hingegen fanden Unternehmungen größeren Stils statt. Deutsche Expeditionen wurden im Auftrag der Städte Hamburg und Berlin im Jahre 1905 fortgesetzt. Bessere Planung erlaubte es, eine enorme Anzahl von Stücken aus dem westlichen Pazifik einschließlich des Inneren Neuguineas auszuheben. So brachte die Hamburger Expedition von 1910/11 allein dieser Stadt 6667 Objekte ein. Als Brigham, der Direktor des Museums von Honolulu, 1913 in Hamburg Zwischenstation machte, fand er das Museum verschlossen, aus Platzmangel wurden die Sammlungen gerade in ein neues Gebäude verlegt. Aber er sah Teile der Sammlung Godeffroy beim »Händler Umlauff«. In Berlin begegneten ihm solche Mengen an Südseeerzeugnissen, daß er sich zu eingehenden Studien außerstande sah.[31] Mehr und mehr wurden wissenschaftliche Studien veröffentlicht. Emil Stephans Buch *Südseekunst* von 1907 ist ein wichtiger Schritt in der Ideenge-

schichte. Zum ersten Mal werden hier die Begriffe Naturtreue und Stilisierung in ihrem wechselseitigen Bezug angewandt.

Auf derselben Reise besichtigte Brigham die britischen Sammlungen in London, Oxford und Cambridge sowie die Sammler Fuller, Beasley und Edge-Partington. Aufgrund seiner maritimen und kolonialen Tradition war Großbritannien zu einem idealen Land für Sammler ozeanischer Kunst geworden, dementsprechend war der britische Markt belebter als alle anderen. Die Händler Webster und Oldman (letzterer war auf Waffen spezialisiert) veröffentlichten Kataloge, deren Analyse verrät, daß die Kunsterzeugnisse aus allen Gebieten des Pazifik kamen, wobei die britischen Kolonien, allen voran Neuseeland und der Golf von Papua, dominierten. Funde aus Hawaii und Französisch-Polynesien waren selten, und Objekte aus dem Inneren Neuguineas gab es überhaupt nicht. Schilde und vor allem Waffen waren zahlreicher als Skulpturen.[32]

Da es keine Quellen gibt, ist es kaum möglich, Anzahl und Art der Objekte einzuschätzen, die es im damaligen Frankreich gab.[33] In den ersten Sammlungen, die Künstler und Kenner zwischen 1906 und 1919 anlegten, zählte man mehr afrikanische als ozeanische Gegenstände. In Paris waren es die Fauvisten und Kubisten, in Dresden und dann in Berlin die deutschen Expressionisten, die sie sahen und sammelten. Anders als die Franzosen, die mit Ausnahme GAUGUINS nie in pazifische Gebiete gereist waren, begleiteten deutsche Künstler wie NOLDE und PECHSTEIN zwei wissenschaftliche Expeditionen in den Jahren 1913–14.[34] Aber das Beispiel GAUGUINS machte die Künstler für Polynesien aufgeschlossen; der Keramiker und PICASSO-Freund PACO DURRIO besaß einige Gemälde und Objekte von GAUGUIN (die Gemälde lieh er der Ausstellung des Salon d'Automne im Jahre 1906). Nach Angaben des Händlers Paul Guillaume war es der Maler FRANK BURTY HAVILAND, der als erster auf den architektonischen Charakter der Tikis hinwies. Von MATISSE wußte er zu berichten: »Wenn er Besuch in seinem Atelier hat, hält er Vorlesungen, wobei er Nietzsche und Claudel zitiert und auch Duccio, Cézanne und die Neuseeländer nicht unerwähnt läßt.«[35] 1907 erwarb PICASSO ein Tiki von den Marquesasinseln □ 373, 1908 befanden sich zwei neukaledonische Skulpturen in seinem Atelier □ 402–404.[36] Vollard besaß zwei große Tikis von den Marquesasinseln □ 142, die seinen Keller zierten, in dem er Maler und Schriftsteller zum Abendessen empfing. Somit kamen die ersten von französischen Künstlern beachteten Stücke hauptsächlich aus Polynesien. Schwieriger ist die Frage, welche Gegenstände von Level, einem frühen Sammler und Freund PICASSOS, Hessel oder Fénéon (die beide in der Galerie Bernheim arbeiteten) gekauft wurden. Nur die ersten Ausstellungen und die darauffolgenden Publikationen erlauben es, sich ein einigermaßen vollständiges Bild zu machen.

In jenen Jahren wurde kein Buch über Ozeanien verfaßt. Bis 1910 war der Südsee-Saal des Musée d'Ethnographie offiziell geschlossen, obwohl er in Ausnahmefällen in Begleitung einer Aufsicht betreten werden durfte (siehe S. 346, Anm. 49). Einige Objekte waren in der Eingangshalle, die Afrika und der Südsee gewidmet war, zu sehen. Auch stellte das Musée d'Artillerie und bis 1907 das Musée de la Marine im Louvre eine Reihe von Objekten aus. Die Sammlungen des Marinemuseums sollten später dem Musée de Préhistoire in Saint-Germain-en-Laye bei Paris angegliedert werden, wo sie ab

◁ □ 143 *›Maske‹, Saibaiinsel, Torresstraße, Holz, Muscheln, Fasern und Menschenhaar, Höhe 69 cm. Sammlung John A. Friede, New York.*

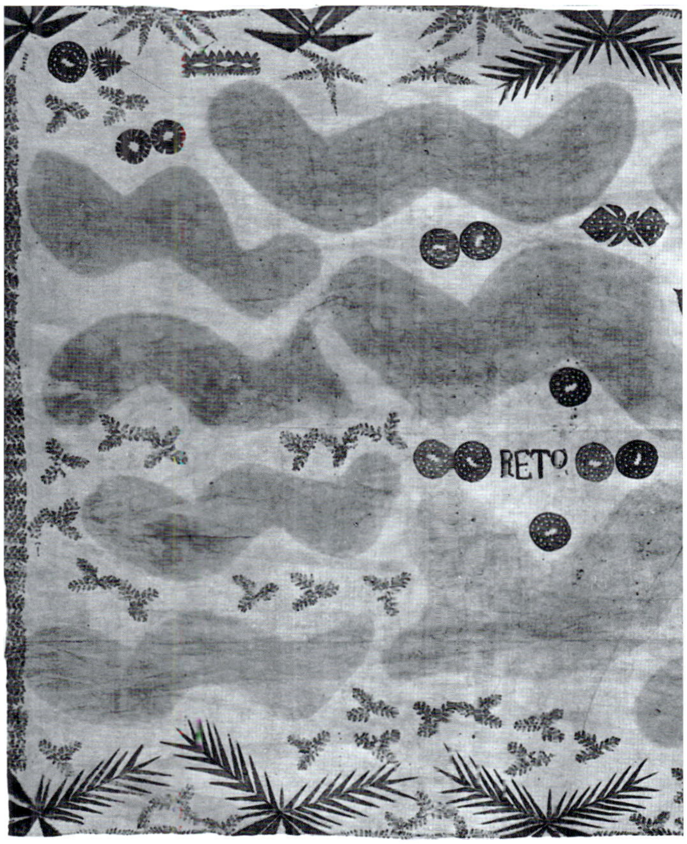

□ 144 *›Tapa‹, Ausschnitt (siehe Glossar), Tahiti (Gesellschaftsinseln), bemalte Rinde, Gesamtlänge 200 cm. Musée de l'Homme, Paris.*

□ 145 *›Tapa‹ (siehe Glossar), Tongainseln, bemalte Rinde, Länge 148,5 cm. Musée de l'Homme, Paris.*

□ 146 ›Masken‹, *entworfen von Louis Marcoussis für den »Bal Marin« des Grafen von Beaumont, 1928, Photographie von Marc Vaux. Veröffentlicht in „Variétés", 1928.*

1910 in der Salle des Comparaisons neu aufgebaut wurden – mit Ausnahme einiger hawaiischer Stücke, die ins Musée d'Ethnographie kamen.[37] Trotz äußerer Beschränkungen weist das Register des Musée d'Ethnographie eine gewisse Anzahl von Besuchern auf. Neben Reisenden und Anthropologen waren die prominentesten Besucher František Kupka, der hier 1907 Motive mexikanischer Stelen kopierte, sowie Robert Delaunay, der am 16. Oktober 1909 in Begleitung mehrerer anderer Personen kam, um den Südsee-Saal zu besichtigen.[38]

Bekannter als die deutschen Sammlungen waren die in London. So entstanden alle Abbildungen im Kapitel über die »Kunst der Tropen« im zweiten Band von Elie Faures *Histoire générale de l'art* nach Exponaten des Britischen Museums, dessen 1910 veröffentlichtes *Handbook to the Ethnographical Collection* für die frühen Liebhaber primitiver Kunst gedacht war.[39] Obwohl dieser Katalog unter ethnographischen Gesichtspunkten entstand, machte sich Elie Faure noch einmal eine Betrachtungsweise des 18. Jahrhunderts zu eigen und beschrieb die Kunst der Südsee – der Ägäis des Orients – als eine ungestüme und sogar entstellte Kunst, die erhöht sei durch die mit der Natur harmonierenden Farben. Er deutete sie als Kunst der Linie, des Dekorativen, das in Neuseeland auf die Spitze getrieben sei – ein Land, in dem durch Wildheit und Kannibalismus »eine hartnäckige Leidenschaft für Gleichgewicht und architektonischen Rhythmus« gäre – der Keim für eine entwickeltere Kunst, deren prähistorische Spuren man auch in der hieratischen Plastik der Osterinsel finden könne.[40]

Paul Guillaumes *Sculptures nègres* von 1917, anläßlich der Ausstellung primitiver Kunst zur Eröffnung seiner Galerie erschienen, enthält Anklänge an diesen Text.[41] Während Apollinaire im Vorwort dieses Katalogs jeden Versuch einer Klassifizierung und Interpretation angesichts des Fehlens präziser Informationen über Ursprung und Funktion der Objekte als zu gewagt ablehnt, stellt Guillaume einen Bezug zwischen ozeanischer und jungsteinzeitlicher Kunst Europas her. Die Rassen Ozeaniens, so Guillaume, schufen »monströse Gesichter, die fähig sind, böse Geister einzufangen oder abzuwehren; für sie ist die Furcht allgegenwärtig, und sie sind ganz damit beschäftigt, böse Geister zu verjagen . . . daher diese grimassenschneidenden Gesichter an den Türen oder auf den Hütten. Man hält sie für um so mächtiger, je schrecklicher sie sind.«[42]

Zwei Ausstellungen ozeanischer Kunst gingen Guillaumes Katalog voraus: eine im Juni 1913 in der Galerie Levesque und jene unter der Schirmherrschaft der Vereinigung »Lyre et Palette« von November bis Dezember 1916. In der ersten sah man neben afrikanischer Kunst nur eine Skulptur aus Neuguinea, in der zweiten ein Tiki von den Marquesasinseln, eine »dekorative Skulptur«, ein Götzenbild und eine Kanaken-Maske:[43] Gegenüber einer Vielzahl afrikanischer Objekte war Ozeanien nur schwach vertreten. So ist es kein Wunder, wenn Paul Guillaume in seinem Katalog von 1917, der lediglich vier Objekte von den Marquesasinseln gegenüber zwanzig afrikanischen aufführt, zu dem Schluß kommt, daß die skulpturalen Formen ozeanischer Objekte weniger mannigfaltig als die afrikanischen sind.

1919 organisierte Paul Guillaume eine Ausstellung in der Galerie Devambez. Clouzot und Level verfaßten das Vorwort zum Katalog und veröffentlichten *Art nègre et art océanien.* Diese Publikationen vermitteln eine bessere Vorstellung von den Sammlungen.[44] Level hatte der Ausstellung vierzehn Werke aus der Südsee zur Verfügung gestellt, davon waren sieben aus Polynesien (Hawaii, Osterinsel, Marquesasinseln) und sieben aus Melanesien (Neuguinea, Neukaledonien); hinzu kamen ein Tiki aus der Sammlung Paul Guillaume und eine Skulptur, die Léonce Rosenberg gehörte. Clouzot und Level vertraten Ansichten, die Guillaume Apollinaire fern lagen. Während dieser jeden analytischen Ansatz verwarf, schwankte ihre Interpretation zwischen einem Urteil aufgrund formaler Kriterien und der westlichen Ansicht, daß die Melanesier von Geistern beherrscht seien. Sie klassifizierten die Objekte nach ihren plastischen Eigenschaften – wobei die geometrischeren Stücke höher bewertet wurden – sowie nach Annahmen über den Grad der Wildheit der Gruppen, die sie produzierten. Demzufolge steht Australien auf der untersten Stufe: Nach Clouzot und Level ist dort keinerlei Kunstverständnis vorhanden und der einzige Ausdruck von Genialität sei die Erfindung des Bumerangs. Als nächstes folgt der Bismarckarchipel, dessen Erzeugnisse als dekorativer angesehen werden, danach Neukaledonien und die Neuen Hebriden, für die Objekte mit »reichen Formen« charakteristisch sind, deren Gesichter »geschnitzter Monster Grimassen schneiden, um das irreale Phantasiemonster der Eingeborenen zu verängstigen«. Endlich kommt Polynesien, dessen »ruhigeres und gelasseneres Marquesas-Tiki ein Monster aus dem Reich der Geometrie ist«. Polynesische Kunst befindet sich an der Spitze der Hierachie der Formen, die nach »Abstraktion und einer Art von Absolutheit« strebt. Diese Formen werden mit dem Werk junger Künstler, u.a. Picassos – »ein alter Adept des Tiki« – verglichen.[45] Entschiedener als Paul Guillaume unterstellen diese Autoren, daß die Leistungen der polynesischen Kunst einer Rasse kaukasischen Ursprungs zu verdanken seien, die einst diese Inseln besiedelt hätten. Dieser Interpretation, die sich mit den wissenschaftlichen Hypothesen jener Jahre deckt, folgt auch Réals 1922 erschienenes Buch über die Kunst Ozeaniens.[46]

Carl Einstein sollte im Gefolge der deutschen Ästheten Werke der Eingeborenen anhand ihrer Formen analysieren. Sein 1915 in Leipzig erschienenes Buch *Negerplastik* handelt von afrikanischer Kunst. Allerdings enthielt es irrtümlich auch Werke aus der Südsee, obwohl dieser Bereich mit keinem Wort angesprochen wurde. In der zweiten Auflage von 1920 sind einige Irrtümer korrigiert.[47]

Die Bücher Von Sydows hingegen, eines erschien 1921 in Leipzig, das andere 1923 in Berlin, ergeben ein vollständigeres Bild primitiver Kunst. Als Gegensatz zur afrikanischen betont

☐ 147 *Frau Pierre Loeb in der Wohnung ihrer Familie, Rue Desbordes-Valmore, Paris 1929.*

er die dekorative Qualität der ozeanischen Kunst, die die Oberfläche der Objekte, dem Kult der Sonne und des Todes gewidmet, in ein System von Linien und Farben verwandelt und damit eine stete optische Schwingung erzeugt.[48]

Mit ihren unterschiedlichen Ansätzen gelangten Clouzot und Level in Frankreich, Einstein (mit seiner Verbindung zum französischen Milieu) und Von Sydow in Deutschland zu einer neuen Sicht primitiver Kunst, die die ästhetischen Interessen der »Ismen« jener Epoche reflektierte. Man wandte sich wechselweise dem ozeanischen und dem afrikanischen Primitiven zu, und beide dienten als Vorbilder. In den zwanziger Jahren war seit Paul Guillaumes »Bal Nègre« – wo anscheinend nichts aus der Südsee vertreten war – eine von Afrika angeregte Mode gefragt. Der Geist Afrikas wurde nicht nur in Kunstwerken, sondern auch in Musik, Tanz und Lesungen beschworen.[49] Diese Tendenz griffen die Dadaisten in ihren öffentlichen Vorstellungen zu Beginn der zwanziger Jahre in Paris auf. 1917 veröffentlichte Tristan Tzara Übersetzungen von Maori-Liedern, die er auf den Dada-Soireen in Zürich vortrug. Er folgte damit dem Beispiel der Kabaretts deutscher Expressionisten, die ARP und ERNST besuchten. Diese Tradition lebte 1920 im Grand Palais wieder auf, als Breton einen Pilou-Pilou tanzte.[50] Damals begannen auch die Dadaisten Sammlungen aufzubauen. MAX ERNST erwarb während des Krieges Tapas, bemalte ozeanische Baststoffe, wozu Apollinaire schon 1916 Breton angeregt hatte; diese Leidenschaft verstärkte sich ein Jahr später durch die Lektüre der Zeitschrift *Dada*. In dieser Zeit interessierte man sich allerdings noch für ozeanische und afrikanische Objekte gleichermaßen, während Breton später feststellte, ihn berühre afrikanische Kunst nicht, er fände sie »zu plastisch«. 1924 enthielt Eluards Sammlung nur »Holzplastik von Negern«. Nach und nach wurde die Suche intensiver. Ihre Sammlungen kamen eher zufällig zustande – durch glückliche Funde und auf Reisen, vor allem nach England und Holland. Schon sprach Breton von der ›trouvaille‹, dem Zufallsfund, als einem Spiel – eine Idee, die er von Apollinaire übernommen hatte.[51]

1922 fand die Kolonial-Ausstellung in Marseille statt und 1923 im Musée des Arts Décoratifs die Ausstellung »Art indigène des colonies françaises«. Zusammen mit Stéphen Chauvet erstellten Clouzot und Level den Katalog zur Ausstellung im Pavillon de Marsan, wobei sie die Gestaltung exotischer Künstler zuweilen als vorbildlich lobten. Man machte den Betrachter auf Waffen, Gebrauchsgegenstände und vor allem auf Tapas aufmerksam, die sich zu »hinreißenden Farbsymphonien steigern . . . und diese Stoffe zu sehr dekorativen Stücken werden lassen«.[52] Die Ausstellung versammelte Gebrauchsgerät aus Polynesien und Melanesien (Schüsseln, Kämme und Stoffe aus Pflanzenfasern), so daß Vergleiche innerhalb derselben Gattung durchgeführt werden konnten. Als direktes Vorbild zog man polynesische Kunst wegen ihrer geometrischen Ornamentik eher in Betracht als die melanesische, die als zu

□ 148 *›Doppelfigur‹, Sentani-See (Westirian), Holz, Höhe 176 cm. Australian National Gallery, Canberra. Ehemals Sammlung Jacob Epstein. Feldphoto von Jacques Viot, 1929.*

wild empfunden wurde, als erotischer und bunter, also zu schrill und damit als entstellt. Diese Betrachtungsweise reduzierte selbst den auf vielen Objekten abgebildeten Tiki-Gott zu einem reinen Dekor. Trotzdem zog ozeanische Bildhauerei aus dem Vergleich mit zeitgenössischer europäischer Kunst Vorteile: Sahen Clouzot und Level 1919 noch »die Abstraktion des Tiki als ein zu beschränktes und formales Modell für fortgeschrittene künstlerische Experimente«,[53] so empfanden sie 1923 den stilisierten Kopf auf einer Waffe von den Neuen Hebriden als »ein Meisterstück, vor dem selbst der vollkommenste Kubist erblassen muß«.[54]

Der Text von Clouzot und Level wird von Illustrationen begleitet. Neue Namen erscheinen auf der Liste der Leihgeber: Zusätzlich zu MARCOUSSIS, PICASSO, Level, Hessel, Fénéon und Guillaume finden wir Moris, ein Händler, der sich vor dem Krieg auf dem Montmartre niedergelassen hatte, Ruppaley, ein ehemaliger Lehrer, der neben den Künstlern einer der ersten Sammler primitiver Kunstobjekte war, Angel Zarraga, der nur eine kleine Anzahl ozeanischer Stücke besaß, und schließlich G. Lecerf und Prudhome.

1926 sollte ein wichtiges Jahr werden. Zwei Ausstellungen, eine unter der Ägide der Surrealisten in Frankreich, die andere in der Galerie Flechtheim in Berlin, zeigten ausschließlich ozeanische Objekte.

Die von Roland Tual geleitete Galerie Surréaliste eröffnete im März 1926 mit einer Ausstellung von MAN RAYS »Bildern und Objekten von den Inseln«. Der Umschlag des Katalogs zeigte ein Photo MAN RAYS mit dem Titel *The Moon Shines on the Island of Nias,* auf dem eine *NIAS*-Skulptur aus Bretons Sammlung auf eine Mondlandschaft projiziert war.[55] Obwohl 21 Objekte, einschließlich der sieben von den Marquesasinseln, aus Polynesien kamen, wurde Melanesien ein noch größerer Raum reserviert, so daß hier fast alle Hauptinseln durch ein Objekt vertreten waren. In dieser Gruppe nahm Neuguinea mit acht Objekten den ersten Platz ein, gefolgt von Neuirland mit fünf. Neben der Osterinsel wurde die Kunst dieser Inseln von den Surrealisten am meisten bewundert und mit besonderem Enthusiasmus gesammelt. Die ausgestellten Stücke gehörten Ruppaley, Level, Morris, Delouis, Eluard und Tual sowie zwei Sammlern, die mit den Initialien L. A. und N. S. angegeben waren. Wenn die Anfangsbuchstaben L. A. für Louis Aragon stehen, läge es nahe, N. S. unter Annahme eines Druckfehlers auf Nancy Cunard zu beziehen – sie stand in Verbindung mit der Gruppe 24 und sollte bald darauf eine Affäre mit Louis Aragon haben. Auf zwei gemeinsamen Reisen gingen sie in britischen Häfen auf die Jagd nach primitiver Kunst, und als Nancy Cunard 1928 ihren Verlag in Paris gründete, war dieser mit Objekten aus Afrika und der Südsee dekoriert. Trotz seiner geringen Mittel hatte auch Tual, der seit 1921 mit Max Jacob befreundet war, schon kurz nach dem Krieg eine Sammlung begonnen, die eine der bedeutendsten werden sollte; sie wurde 1930 verkauft □ 149.[56]

Die zweite Ausstellung des Jahres 1926 wurde in der Galerie Flechtheim in Berlin unter dem Thema »Südseeplastiken« eröffnet. Später wanderte sie ins Kunstmuseum Zürich, um dann in die Düsseldorfer Galerie Flechtheim zu gelangen. Sie umfaßte 184 Stücke, die fast ausschließlich aus den im 1. Weltkrieg verlorenen deutschen Kolonien stammten (Neuguinea, Bismarckarchipel und Bougainville). Alle diese Stücke waren aus dem Privatbesitz Flechtheims, der in seiner Galerie mit Objekten aus der Südsee wie auch moderner Kunst handelte. Carl Einstein schrieb das Vorwort zum Katalog. Ausgehend von den Schriften deutscher Anthropologen nimmt er eine regionale Klassifizierung vor und gibt eine soziologische Erklärung. Er beschreibt die Südsee als ein Nebeneinander vieler Gemeinschaften, wobei jede ihre eigenen Symbole und Dämonen habe. Das einzige, was sie verbinde, sei die Verehrung der Geister der Vorfahren. Motive und Figuren wechseln sich auf Gegenständen ab, um über Mythen, Fabeln und die Kämpfe von Dämonen zu berichten – Dämonen allerdings, die den Menschen durch die Vermittlung des Totems auch beschützen. In den Bildern ist das Motiv des Todes vorherrschend: Oft wird der Schädel auf Körpern abgebildet, die »die Gestalt ornamentaler Skelette haben«.[57] Wie Von Sydow bemerkt, rührt die Gewalt dieser Bilder aber auch von der Tatsache her, daß die Figuren fest von einem Gitterwerk umschlossen sind.

Somit überwog in diesen Jahren, vor allem in Frankreich, die Kunst Ostmelanesiens. Zervos bemerkte 1927: »War es vor zwanzig Jahren noch die Negerskulptur, ist es heute melanesische und präkolumbianische Kunst, von der wir keine direkte Anregung, wohl aber ein Gefühl der Verwandtschaft erwarten.«[58] Da primitive Sammlungen in Mode kamen, stieg ihre Zahl an. In Frankreich nahmen die Intellektuellen, die surrealistische Unternehmungen bzw. die »Rückkehr zum Stil« in der Malerei finanziell unterstützten, diese neue Kunstform in ihre Sammlungen auf. Sie folgten dem Beispiel der Kunsthändler und stellten moderne Malerei und exotische Objekte Seite an Seite auf. Graf Etienne de Beaumont organisierte einen Bal Marin mit von MARCOUSSIS entworfenen Masken, die eine Synthese ozeanischer und afrikanischer Formen vorführten. Die von ozeanischer Kunst begeisterte Händlerin Madeleine Rousseau beriet Girardin bei seinen Ankäufen afrikanischer und ozeanischer Objekte (seine Gemäldesammlung sollte spä-

☐ 149 *Seite aus einem Auktionskatalog, anläßlich des Verkaufs der Sammlung Roland Tual, Paris, Februar 1930.*

ter den Grundstock für das Musée d'Art Moderne de la Ville de Paris bilden). Zwischen 1927 und 1930 gab es an vielen verschiedenen Orten Ausstellungen, und neue Ideen wurden entwickelt. Von 1928 an stieg die Zahl der Auktionen, dies vor allem in Paris, und der Höhepunkt wurde kurz vor der Weltwirtschaftskrise erreicht. Es kamen mehrere Bücher heraus, die sich an ein Publikum von Kunstliebhabern richteten. *L'Art chez les peuples primitifs* (1929) von A. Basler faßte die Ideen zusammen, die in den vorhergehenden Jahren entwickelt worden waren, wobei der Autor den Versuch einer Synthese unternahm, um kreative Prozesse zu erklären.[59] Den Theorien Freuds, denen Von Sydow folgte, steht er distanziert gegenüber, vielmehr neigt er zur Psychologie der Wahrnehmung des Raumes, die Otto Rank und Salomon Reinach in ihren Werken vertraten. Sie vergleichen die Wahrnehmung der Eingeborenen mit der von Kindern, »deren Wirklichkeitsempfinden weniger optisch als taktil ist«[60] (eine Analyse, die in Frankreich Luquet in *L'Art primitif*, 1930, weiterentwickelte, worin er seine Theorie des »visuellen und intellektuellen Realismus« erläuterte[61]). Für Basler entspringt Kunst einem magischen Naturgefühl, dem die Experimente GAUGUINS und PICASSOS nicht gerecht würden, da ihrer Kunst jene »ursprüngliche Wahrheit« fehle, die das Wesen religiöser Kunst ausmache. Maler hätten aus primitiver Kunst nicht nur ein formales System entnehmen können, sondern auch eine Schaffensweise – versperrte ihnen ihre Vernunftbetontheit hierzu nicht den Weg. Ähnlich dem Kinde besitzt der Wilde eine eigene Logik, die dem Westen auf ewig abhanden gekommen sei.

Basler bildete Objekte aus dem Besitz verschiedener Sammler ab: von Tual, BONDY, einem deutschen Maler, der Mitglied in der Académie von MATISSE war und mit der »Groupe du Dome« ausstellte, und schließlich von Chauvet, einem französischen Arzt, der später zwei Bücher veröffentlichte: eines über die Osterinsel; das andere trug den Titel *Art indigène de Nouvelle-Guinée* (1930) und war das erste Werk über dieses Gebiet, das, reichhaltig illustriert, in Frankreich erschien. Seine schon sehr bedeutende Sammlung wurde durch einige Stücke, die Graf Festetics mitbrachte, noch ansehnlicher.

In diesem Jahr (1929) befaßte sich die März/April-Nummer der *Cahiers d'art*, herausgegeben von Zervos, ausschließlich mit ozeanischer Kunst.[62] Zum ersten Mal wurde ein Panorama pazifischer Kunst, soweit sie bis dahin bekannt war, geboten. Polynesien nahm nach wie vor den ersten Platz ein. Mit Ausnahme je eines Vorwortes von Tristan Tzara und Zervos sowie zweier Artikel von Von Sydow und Fischer wurden die regionalen Studien von Spezialisten verfaßt, von Museumsdirektoren (Eichhorn, Speiser, Wölfel), einem Sammler (Chauvet) und Monseigneur Jaussen, der Bischof von Tahiti war. Alle Denkweisen sind hier vertreten, vom psychoanalytischen Ansatz (erläutert in einem Artikel über Von Sydow) bis zum ethnologischen. In seinem einführenden Text bespricht Christian Zervos die Theorien Baslers und verteidigt die Ansicht, die Kunst der Südsee sei Ausdruck visionärer Vorstellungskraft und der modernen Kunst verwandt. Jenseits der formalen Gestaltung seien es die graphischen Zeichen, die aus dem Dunkel der Vergangenheit hervortreten würden und das Wesen ozeanischer Kunst ausmachten. Die besten Beispiele für diese Zeichen gäbe es auf der Osterinsel, für die der Artikel des Monseigneur Jaussen eine erläuternde Tabelle bereithält (diese Illustrationen regten MAX ERNST ☐ 40, 41, 328, 830 und MIRÓ

☐ 150 *›Melanesische Masken‹, von André Breton und Paul Eluard auf einer Auktion zum Verkauf angeboten, 11. Juli 1931.*

an). Zervos' Ansicht teilen auch Poncetton und Portier in ihrem Werk *La Décoration: Océanie*.[63] Durch den Umgang mit Objekten und deren Anverwandlung in der surrealistischen Malerei wurden die Dämonen nach und nach vertrauter und die Kunst der Südsee universaler verständlich.

Viele Objekte waren in *Cahiers d'art* sowie dem Buch von Poncetton und Portier abgebildet. Sie stammten entweder aus großen Museen (Berlin, Basel) oder von privaten Sammlern: Breton, Eluard, Tzara, Flechtheim, Fénéon, Tual, Delois (ein Händler chinesischer Kunst, der zu primitiver Kunst übergegangen war), Ascher (ein ehemaliger Maler, der Bilderhändler geworden war und dessen Galerie sich damals am Montparnasse befand). Schließlich gehörten Carré und Ratton dazu, die mit zu den aktivsten Galeristen in Paris zählten (Ratton sollte mehrere Stücke aus der Sammlung Flechtheim zurückkaufen) sowie Pierre Loeb, dessen Tapas vom Sentani-See zum ersten Mal abgebildet wurden ☐ 151. Loeb war nicht nur Händler der

☐ 151 *›Tapa‹ (siehe Glossar), Sentani-See (Westirian), bemalter Baststoff, Länge 137 cm. Musée de l'Homme, Paris.*

surrealistischen Maler, sondern auch ozeanischer Kunst.[64] Seine private Sammlung war damals eine der bedeutendsten ☐ 147. PICASSO bot er einmal einen Arm von der Osterinsel an ☐ 475 (siehe S. 343). Gerade in seiner Galerie wurden viele Künstler mit der Kunst des Pazifik vertraut. 1929 schickte er Jacques Viot, der sich schon im pazifischen Raum auskannte, nach Neuguinea, um neue Objekte aufzusammeln. Viots besonderes Interesse galt der Kunst vom Sentani-See, die bis dahin in Frankreich fast gänzlich unbekannt war, und er brachte Tapas und Skulpturen mit. Nach seiner Rückkehr veröffentlichte er als Auszug aus einem Buch einen Artikel in der ersten Nummer der Zeitschrift *Le Surréalisme au service de la révolution*. Hierin beschreibt er mit den Worten D'Albertis' Neuguinea als ein verzaubertes Schloß, aber der Titel »N'encombrez pas les colonies« (Übervölkert die Kolonien nicht) war zugleich Anspielung auf die französische Kolonialpolitik und die für 1931 geplante Kolonialausstellung, die den Surrealisten ein Dorn im Auge war.[65]

1930 öffneten in Paris drei Ausstellungen die Tore. Die erste war von Tzara und Charles Ratton (der auch den Katalog erstellte) in der Galerie Pigalle organisiert worden, die zweite fand in der Galerie de la Renaissance, Rue Royale, statt und die dritte in der Galerie Mettler, wo einige Stücke von der Osterinsel zu sehen waren.[66] Diese drei Ausstellungen markieren einen wichtigen Wendepunkt: Zum einen waren sie die letzten privaten Initiativen vor der Wirtschaftskrise der dreißiger Jahre, zum anderen präsentierten sie zum ersten Mal in Frankreich einen Gesamtüberblick über die damals zugängliche Kunst der Südsee. Nicht zuletzt war es ein Novum, daß die Galerie de la Renaissance, die sich auf die Maler des »Zurück-zum-Stil« spezialisiert hatte, ozeanische Kunst ausstellte. Die Presse jedoch zeigte nur wenig Interesse an dieser Ausstellung. Dies waren auch die ersten Ausstellungen, die auf die Bestände vieler Sammler zurückgriffen, von denen manche hier zum ersten Mal namentlich erwähnt wurden. Die Ausstellung der Galerie Pigalle umfaßte 138 Objekte aus Ozeanien und britischen Kolonien, vor allem Neuseeland und der Südküste Neuguineas. Die Objekte waren aus den Sammlungen Loeb, Ratton, Tzara, Mettler, Ascher und Chauvet. Die Galerie de la Renaissance zeigte 180 Stücke, wobei sogar die Kunst der Salomoninseln, die bis auf einige Kanubuge und Kapkaps weitgehend unbekannt war, mit 13 Objekten aufwarten konnte. Melanesien und Polynesien waren gleich stark vertreten. Die Leihgeber deckten sich weitgehend mit denen der Galerie Pigalle: Lavachery (Direktor des Musée du Cinquantenaire in Brüssel und ehemaliger Anwalt, den die Leidenschaft für primitive Kunst zur Anthropologie geführt hatte), Chardenet, Lamart, die Journalistin Titayana, der Maler LHOTE, der Anwalt Pomaret; außerdem der Graphikhändler Le Veel, die beiden Brüder Stora (Händler von Wandteppichen und mittelalterlicher Kunst, von denen sich der jüngere für primitive Kunst interessierte), Yvon Helf (der auf antikes Silber spezialisiert war), der Schriftsteller Paul Morand zusammen mit Stéphen Chauvet, Louis Carré, Edouard und Pierre Loeb, Poncetton (Partner des Experten Portier, für den er Katalogbeiträge schrieb), Félix Fénéon und endlich Bela Hein (ein ehemaliger Journalist, der nun in Paris eine Antiquitätenhandlung betrieb). Die genannten Personen waren vorwiegend Händler und auch Sammler, die an Ausstellungen teilnahmen, und es ist

☐ 152 *›Kopfschmuck‹ (mit Ausschnitt),* BAINING *(Neubritannien), bemalter Baststoff und Gestell aus Schilfrohr, Höhe 720 cm. Hamburgisches Museum für Völkerkunde.* ▷

zu fragen, ob der Hauptzweck dieser Ausstellungen nicht im Kommerziellen lag, insofern eine Kunst gefördert wurde, die bis dahin nur einem kleinen Insiderkreis vorbehalten war. Aber die Wirtschaftskrise sollte diesem Trend zuvorkommen.

Kein Surrealist stellte für diese Ausstellungen eigene Stücke zur Verfügung (Tzara, der die Ausstellung in der Galerie Pigalle organisierte, hatte schon lange mit der Bewegung gebrochen, obwohl er noch mit einigen ihrer Mitglieder in Verbindung stand). Natürlich tauschten und verkauften Breton und Eluard Stücke ihrer Sammlung, während sie den Großteil behielten. Doch wurde ihre Auswahl nach besonderen Kriterien getroffen. 1929 befaßte sich eine Sonderausgabe der belgischen Zeitschrift *Variétés* mit der »Position des Surrealismus«. Sie enthält einen Artikel Eluards über die »Kunst der Wilden« (von dem sich bereits in seinem Notizbuch von 1927 erste Spuren finden[67]) und eine Weltkarte, die im Gegensatz zur normalen Darstellungsweise Ozeanien in den Mittelpunkt stellt (siehe S. 92, 93). Die Größe eines jeden Landes wurde in Abhängigkeit von seiner künstlerischen Bedeutung gesehen. Wichtigere Zonen sind u.a. der Bismarckarchipel und die Osterinsel, gefolgt von Neuguinea, Neuseeland und den Neuen Hebriden, Hawaii und den Marquesasinseln. Die Salomoninseln sind verkleinert und Neukaledonien, dessen Kunst Breton als entstellt empfand, fehlt. In der Kunst Ozeaniens sah Breton »den Triumph des Dualismus von Wahrnehmung und Darstellung« verwirklicht. Schon in der Vorliebe für bestimmte Objekte zeigt sich Bretons Begeisterung für die Idee des Dualismus. Voller Enthusiasmus sammelte er Kapkaps, Verkörperungen der »Synthese von Konkretem und Abstraktem«, sowie Uli-Figuren aus Neuirland, die man als Darstellungen von Hermaphroditen deutete, wie auch Skulpturen von Vogelmenschen der Osterinsel □ 821, 822, 825, 826, ein Ort, den er als das »moderne Athen der Südsee« ansah.

1931 wurde die Kolonialausstellung eröffnet. Einige Räume im neuen Musée des Colonies waren für die »Kunst des Pazifik« reserviert. Sie vereinigten alte und neue Stücke, die für diese Gelegenheit hergestellt worden waren. Zum ersten Mal nach dem Krieg wurde im Raum der Neuen Hebriden eine bedeutende Gruppe modellierter Objekte aus Malekula gezeigt. Aufgrund ihrer Ausführung, ihrer Farben, ihrer großen Totenabbildungen und Masken waren diese Objekte bei Sammlern genauso gefragt wie die Arbeiten aus der Sepik-Region. Mehrere Surrealisten reagierten auf diese Kolonialausstellung mit einer eigenen Schau, die Aragon, Thirion und Sadoul, damals Mitglieder der Kommunistischen Partei, organisierten. Mit Unterstützung Tanguys richteten Aragon und Eluard einen Raum ein, wo sie u.a. neuirländische Plastik aus der Sammlung Aragons und wohl auch Eluards ausstellten.[68]

In den dreißiger Jahren verschärfte sich der Gegensatz zwischen den Surrealisten auf der einen und Sammlern und Malern, die traditionellere Pfade eingeschlagen hatten, auf der anderen Seite. Westliche Kunst wurde an primitiver Kunst gemessen, und die Frage war: Ist die Malerei durch das Unbewußte oder durch »klassischen Formalismus« bestimmt? Emmanuel Berl verdammte den Fetisch-Kult als eine »Manifestation von ästhetischem Satanismus«.[69] Für Deutschland war die Ausstellung im Berliner Kunstgewerbemuseum von 1933, über die Hans Purrmann berichtet,[70] die letzte, bevor primitive Kunst wieder einmal zur »Geschichte der Wilden«

□ 153 *›Schild‹, Sulka (Neubritannien), bemaltes Holz, Fasern und Federn, Höhe 121 cm. Musée Barbier-Müller, Genf.*

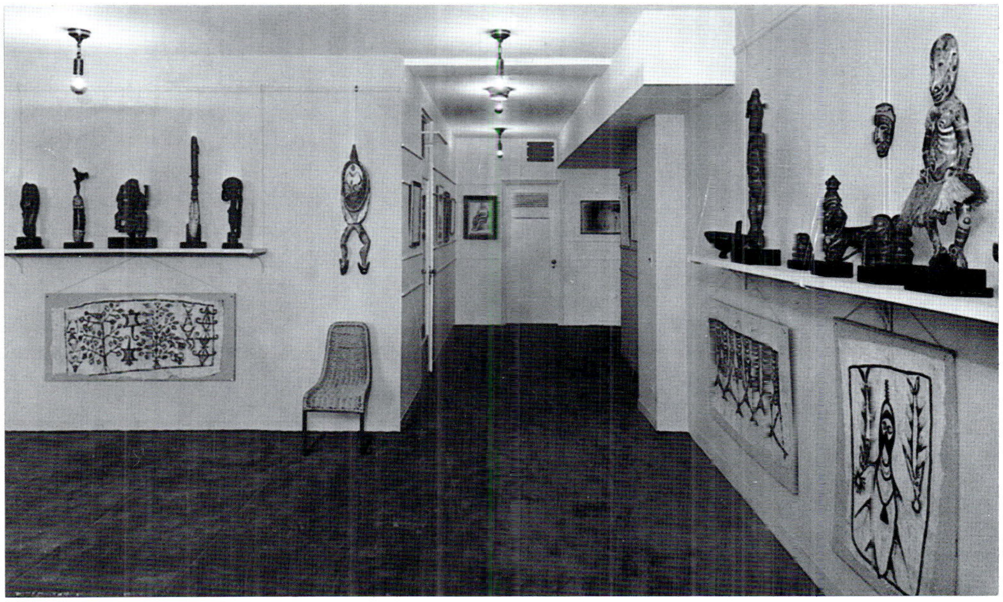

☐ 154 *Südseekunst, ausgestellt in der Galerie Pierre Matisse, New York 1934. Die Objekte wurden von Charles Ratton zur Verfügung gestellt.*

gehörte und unter Hitlers Kategorie der »entarteten Kunst« fiel, der sie Vorbild gewesen war.

Die Weltwirtschaftskrise, die Frankreich manche Härten auferlegte, ging auch an der Kulturentwicklung nicht spurlos vorüber. Verkäufe, die in den Jahren davor zugenommen hatten, ließen nun nach. Die auf Auktionen angebotenen Stücke folgten jetzt mehr dem Publikumsgeschmack. 1919 noch befanden sich Tapas und seltenere Objekte von den Marquesasinseln und Tahiti unter den teureren Stücken der seltenen Auktionen. Ihre Zahl fing seit 1928 an zu steigen. Die Sammlung Walter Bondy, bestehend aus fünfzig Objekten aus Neuguinea, dem Bismarckarchipel, Neukaledonien, den Marquesasinseln, der Osterinsel und Neuseeland, war eine der schönsten, die in jenen Jahren zum Verkauf stand. Eine weitere denkwürdige Auktion fand 1929 statt, wobei der Name des Sammlers unbekannt blieb. Die Sammlung Tual wurde 1930 verkauft ☐ 149. Sie bestand aus 119 ozeanischen Werken einschließlich einer Schildpattmaske von der Torresstraße. Schließlich organisierte Ratton 1931 eine Auktion, in der es ein Objekt gab, das Picasso erstand ☐ 70.[71] In London allerdings gingen Verkäufe weiter, wobei Erzeugnisse aus Neuseeland und Neuguinea stark vertreten waren. Die letzte große Auktion dieser Epoche war die der Sammlung Breton-Eluard, die Ratton im Juli 1931 durchführte ☐ 150. Der Umschlag des dazugehörenden Katalogs brach mit der Tradition, zum einen typographisch, zum anderen, weil die Formulierung »Skulptur aus Ozeanien, Afrika und Amerika« durch »primitive Kunst« ersetzt wurde – diese semantische Reduktion sollte die Einführung der Objekte in ein »universales Museum« begünstigen. Zum Verkauf standen 149 ozeanische Objekte, darunter zahlreiche Kapkaps und Masken aus Neuirland. Der erwartete Erfolg blieb indes aus. Manche Stücke wurden später nochmals in einem Geschäft angeboten, das Breton 1937 eröffnet hatte. 1938 übergab Eluard seine Sammlung Roland Penrose.[72]

☐ 155 *Objekte aus der »La Korrigane«-Expedition, 1934–35, in Neuguinea gesammelt. Feldphoto von Van de Broek. Musée de l'Homme, Paris.*

Auf der Suche nach einem neuen Kundenkreis organisierten die Händler Charles Ratton und Louis Carré Ausstellungen in New York. 1934 zeigte Ratton seine Ozeaniensammlung in der Galerie Matisse ☐ 154, 1936 präsentierte er »American, Oceanic and African«. In seiner Einführung zum Katalog unterschied Robert Goldwater ozeanische von afrikanischer Kunst mit Blick auf die dekorativen Qualitäten der Südsee und ihren Formenreichtum, bei dem Vögel und Menschen so vermischt würden, daß ein »paranoisches Bild« lange vor den Surrealisten entstanden sei.[73]

In diesen Krisenjahren in Frankreich wurde das Musée d'Ethnographie du Trocadéro neu konzipiert. Schon 1929 wurden die Exponate unter der wirksamen Leitung von Paul Rivet und der Assistenz von Georges-Henri Rivière neu präsentiert. In diesen Jahren stellten Kunstvereinigungen ethnologische Gegenstände aus und boten Gelegenheit, sich dem Studium der Riten und des Sakralen zu widmen.[74] Ein Beispiel für diese Neuorientierung war die bedeutende Ausstellung »La Danse sacrée« von 1934. Der neue Trend wurde im wesentlichen von den Mitarbeitern der Zeitschrift *Documents* getragen, die von Bataille gegründet und publiziert wurde und bei der Georges-Henri Rivière besonders engagiert mitwirkte. *Documents* unterstrich die Wichtigkeit von Grenzüberschreitung und Opfer und stand somit im Gegensatz zum Idealismus der Surrealisten.[75] In der fünften Nummer der *Documents* veröffentlichte Louis Clarke einen Artikel über die Kunst der Salomoninseln, die damals in Frankreich fast unbekannt war, und in der siebten Nummer analysierte Bataille Luquets Monographie über die Kunst Neukaledoniens. Er interessierte sich jedoch weniger für die neukaledonische Kunst als vielmehr für das Konzept eines von Luquet formulierten »psychologischen Realismus«, das es dem Autor erlaubte, die Logik von Kinder-

◁ □ 156 *›Figur eines Männerbundes‹, Vanuatu (vormals Neue Hebriden), bemalter Baumfarn, Höhe 203 cm. Field Museum of Natural History, Chicago.*

□ 157 ▷ *›Figur aus Holz‹, Provinz Ost-Sepik (Papua-Neuguinea), Höhe 77 cm. Sammlung Pierre Matisse. Ehemals Sammlung Henri Matisse.*

zeichnungen nachzuweisen. Inzwischen ein weltweiter Mittelpunkt mit engen Verbindungen zu Intellektuellenkreisen, organisierte das Musée d'Ethnographie wichtige Ausstellungen und erhielt zahlreiche Schenkungen. 1933 zeigte es die von Jacques Viot zusammengetragene Tapa-Sammlung. Diese Tapas hatten sich schon in den Amsterdamer Sammlungen befunden, aber nun erfolgte im Licht der surrealistischen Malerei eine neue Interpretation dieses Systems von kleinen Figuren – halb Fisch, halb Insekt – in einer Phantasielandschaft, die manchmal verzerrt ist, um ein System von Linien über der ganzen Fläche entstehen zu lassen. 1934 wurde der Saal der Marquesasinseln umgestaltet, um eine Schenkung aufzunehmen, die Michel Leiris in einem Artikel für *Cahiers d'art*[76] beschrieb. Im gleichen Jahr noch kam die Sammlung Von der Heydt hinzu.[77] Mit ihren zahlreichen Stücken aus Neuguinea und dem Bismarckarchipel füllte sie so manche Lücke, die zwanzig Jahre Nachlässigkeit in den Sammlungen hatten entstehen lassen. Vervollständigt wurden sie durch eine 1934 von dem Geographen Aubert de la Rüe auf einer offiziellen Expedition zusammengestellten Sammlung von den Neuen Hebriden. 1935 fand eine Osterinsel-Ausstellung statt, die 1936 in Brüssel wiederholt wurde. Diese Ausstellungen zeigten den Ertrag der von A. Métraux und Lavachery geleiteten franko-belgischen Fachexpedition, die mit dem Schiff *La Korrigane* den Pazifik durchquert hatte □ 155. Dank dieser Sammlung besitzt das 1938 in Musée de l'Homme umgetaufte Musée d'Ethnographie in seinem neuen Sitz eine bedeutende Anzahl hauptsächlich melanesischer Stücke.[78]

Vergleichbare Entwicklungen fanden auch in England statt. 1935 wurde im Burlington Fine Arts Club die Ausstellung »The Art of Primitive Peoples« eröffnet. Die Exponate kamen aus Neuseeland, den Fidschiinseln und Salomoninseln, der Massim-Region und aus Neuguinea; einige hatte der Anthropologe Gregory Bateson gesammelt. Der begleitende Katalog entstand nach völkerkundlichen Gesichtspunkten, und jeder Gegenstand erscheint in seinem wirtschaftlichen und sozialen Kontext.[79] Diesem Konzept folgt das ein Jahr später erschienene Werk von Raymond Firth *Art and Life in New Guinea.*[80] Im Juni 1937 wurde am Grosvenor Place eine Ausstellung mit über 300 Objekten aus der Sammlung Moyne eröffnet; sie zeigte Stücke von den Flüssen Fly, Eilanden (Asmat) und Ramu.

In den Vereinigten Staaten wurden 1895 auf der California Midwinter International Exposition, San Francisco, ozeanische Objekte (einschließlich einiger Beispiele aus Neuguinea, Neuseeland und Neuirland) ausgestellt. 1934 eröffnete im Fogg Museum (Harvard) die Ausstellung »Oceanic and African Art«; sie enthielt nur wenige polynesische Stücke. 1939 wiederum zeigte eine Ausstellung im Peabody Museum von Salem polynesische Sammlungen, in denen Gebrauchsgegenstände einen großen Platz einnahmen. Im gleichen Jahr war eine ganze Abteilung innerhalb der Golden Gate International Exposition in San Francisco der Präsentation Ozeaniens vorbehalten. Sie sollte der Öffentlichkeit demonstrieren, daß die Erzeugnisse dieser Region denen aus Europa und anderen Teilen der Welt gleichwertig waren.

Die Breton treugebliebenen Surrealisten mieden diese überdidaktische Welt aus Prinzip. Der völkerkundlichen Sichtweise setzten sie eine Vorstellung des Phantastischen entgegen, wissenschaftlichen Klassifikationen andere Kategorien, die ihre Absurdität bewiesen. Ozeanische Objekte traten in den Hintergrund, sie machten sich über amerikanische Objekte, Fertigprodukte, mathematische Objekte lustig und interpretierten ›objets trouvés‹ auf der »Exposition d'Objets Surréalistes« (1936) in der Galerie Charles Ratton.[81] Im selben Jahr präsentierte die internationale Surrealistenausstellung in London Objekte aus der Sepik-Region (Neuguinea), die das University

Museum of Archaeology and Anthropology, Cambridge, ausgeliehen hatte, sowie Abbildungen nach Stücken, die im Original nicht ausgestellt werden konnten. Keine dieser Ausstellungen zeigte jemals alle Sammlungen der Surrealisten. MAX ERNST, PAALEN, TANGUY und andere besaßen Objekte, die nie zu sehen waren.

Die frühen Seereisenden hatten nur einige wenige Objekte mitgebracht. Erst im Zuge der kolonialen Expansion Europas kamen vermehrt Objekte in den Westen, wobei sie in jener Zeit zum Beweis der Rückständigkeit dienten. In Museen, auf Weltausstellungen und in Privatsammlungen gezeigt, vermittelten sie einen Eindruck vom Leben und Brauchtum der Eingeborenen. Sie wiesen auf das Vorhandensein einer anderen Welt hin. Die französischen Surrealisten, indem sie die *trouvaille,* den Zufallsfund, feierten, stellten jenes System der Verschiebungen in den Mittelpunkt, in dem Objekte um so mehr Bedeutung annehmen, je tiefer die Betrachtung reicht. Zum Studium für Anthropologen wie von Künstlern herangezogen, waren sie vor allem der Anfang eines phantastischen Reiches, dessen Geschichte mit den ersten Pazifiküberquerungen beginnt und bis heute nicht abgeschlossen ist.

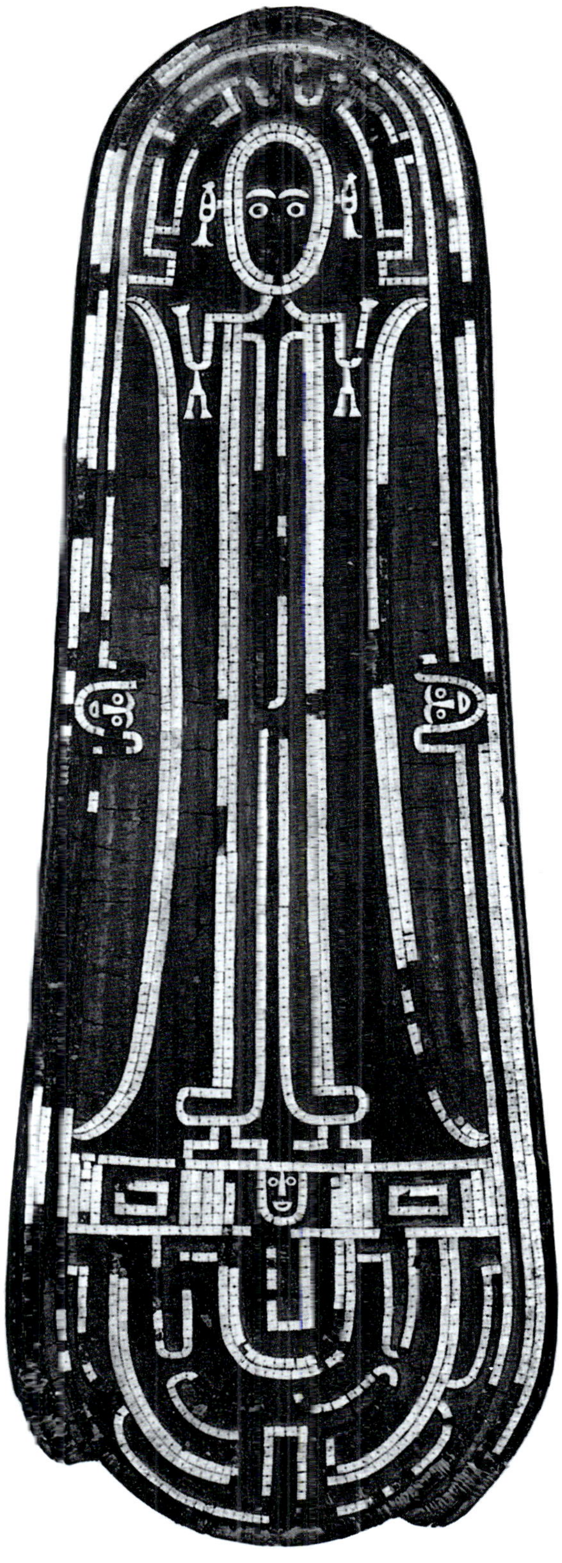

□ 158 *›Zeremonialschild‹, Malaita (Salomoninseln), Holz mit Perlmutteinlagen, Höhe 81 cm. The Australian Museum, Sidney.*

◁ □ 159 *›Jagdamulett‹,* ALAMBLAK, *Karawari-Fluß, Provinz Ost-Sepik (Papua-Neuguinea), Holz, Höhe 32 cm. National Museum of Natural History, Smithsonian Institution, Washington.*

Anmerkungen

Dieser Text wäre nicht entstanden ohne die wertvolle Mithilfe von Françoise Girard, Marie-Claire Bataille-Benguigi und Jean Jamin vom Musée de l'Homme, von Rosalind Krauss, Judith Cousins und Jean-Louis Paudrat, von Michel Leiris, Jean Laude und Charles Ratton. Diesen und Douglas Newton mit seiner kritischen, hilfreichen Lektüre des Textes gilt mein aufrichtiger Dank.

1. Siehe De Commerson, »Post-scriptum sur les îles de la Nouvelle-Cythère ou Tayti«, zuerst im *Mercure de France,* November 1769 veröffentlicht und danach in *Décade philosophique* des 30. Messidor, 4. Jahr, Band 18, S. 133–42.

2. Smiths, B., *European Vision and the South Pacific, 1768–1850,* Oxford 1960, analysiert die wechselnden Einstellungen gegenüber dem Pazifik und geht dabei vor allem von englischen Quellen aus.

3. Siehe Copans, J., und Jamin, J., *Aux origines de l'anthropologie française,* Paris, keine Jahresangabe; und Stocking, G., »French Anthropology in 1800«, in *Isis 65* Nr. 180, 1964, S. 134–50.

4. Etienne Taillemite veröffentlichte kürzlich die Logbücher Bougainvilles. Sie enthalten Karten, Tafeln und Zeichnungen. *Bougainville et ses compagnons autour du monde,* Paris 1977, 2 Bände.

5. Nicht alle diese Objekte sind von Péron gesammelt worden: Er erhielt 160 von dem Schiffsarzt Georges Bass, der sich in Sydney niedergelassen und die Objekte von Seefahrern erhalten hatte. Das o. g. Buch von Copans und Jamin enthält eine Liste über die Gegenstände entsprechend dem Manuskript Pérons, das sich in Le Havre befindet.

6. Die Sammlungen von Captain Cook und seinen Begleitern, deren Reiseberichte viele Male veröffentlicht wurden, sind auf viele europäische Museen verteilt. A. Kaeppler hat sie genau gelistet. Kaeppler, A. *Artificial Curiosities: An Exposition of Native Manufactures Collected on the Three Pacific Voyages of Captain Cook,* Honolulu 1978, und *Cook Voyage Artifacts in Leningrad, Berne and Florence Museums,* Honolulu 1978.

7. Die Caen-Sammlungen wurden von E. Deslomchamps publiziert, »Note sur les Collections Ethnographiques de Musée de Caen et sur deux haches en pierre polie provenant de la Colombie« in *Annuaire de Musée d'Histoire Naturelle de Caen,* 1884. Zu dieser Zeit besaß das Museum, ergänzt durch die Sammlungen von Vieillard, Marc und Deplanches, eine repräsentative Auswahl aus dem pazifischen Raum: aus Neuseeland ein Tiki und eine Kanuplanke; aus Tahiti einen Fliegenwedel; von den Marquesasinseln Ornamente, Keulen, Kronen aus Schildpatt und Ohrringe; von den Tongas und den Karolinen Waffen und Tapas; aus Neubritannien und Neuirland seltene Ohrringe; von den Salomoninseln ein »Krokodil«; aus Neukaledonien Masken, Skulpturen, Steinwaffen und Bambusstäbe; aus Niederländisch-Neuguinea Vogelskulpturen und Waffen; schließlich eine Schildpatt-Maske von der Torresstraße und Waffen aus Australien. Das Musée de la Marine des Louvre bestand aus Objekten verschiedener Reisender, u. a. von Dumont d'Urville und D'Entrecasteaux, wie auch aus Objekten, die Louis Philippe gehörten und die er von den Missionaren Pompallier und Douare sowie dem skandinavischen Antiquitätenhändler Rafn bekommen hatte. Im Musée de la Marine war Melanesien mit 253 Stücken vertreten, Mikronesien mit 38 und Polynesien mit 447. U. a. gehörten eine Trommel und eine Maske von den Neuen Hebriden dazu, Skulpturen aus Neukaledonien, »Götzenbilder« aus Neuguinea, eine kleine Skulptur von den Salomonen und eine mächtige Skulptur vom Gambier-Archipel, weiterhin mit Federn besetzte Dosen und Jaden aus Neuseeland, eine mit Federn besetzte Maske aus Hawaii oder geschnitzte Fliegenwedelgriffe aus Tahiti.

8. Zum Anwachsen der Völkerkundemuseen vgl. Goldwater, R., *Primitivism in Modern Art,* 2. Auflage, New York 1967, vor allem der erste Teil.

9. Das Musée d'Ethnographie du Trocadéro erwarb 1935 seine ersten australischen Malereien. Im 19. Jahrhundert hatten Forscher ihr Augenmerk noch mehr auf Fels- oder Höhlenmalereien gerichtet als auf Malereien auf Baumrinde. Smyth, R. B., war mit seinem Werk *The Aborigines of Victoria,* London 1878, einer der ersten, der sie untersuchte. Nach Smyth war aber »der eingeborene Künstler kein wilder Schwarzer. Er hatte die Gebräuche der Weißen beobachtet« (S. 286). In den 1890er Jahren war Baldwin Spencer, der das Arnhemland durchquerte, einer der ersten, die Rindenmalereien sammelten.

10. *Catalogue spécial de l'Exposition des Sciences Anthropolgiques,* Paris 1878. Die Objekte kamen aus dem Musée de Caen, dem Musée des Colonies du Palais de l'Industrie auf der Champs-Elysées (Dieses Museum wurde nach der Weltausstellung von 1855 gegründet; offenbar veröffentlichte es nie einen Katalog, und in den 1890er Jahren geriet es in Vergessenheit.), dem Museum in Bordeaux, der Pariser Sammlung Rivière und der Seidlerschen in Nantes sowie dem Royal College of Surgeons in London. Man könnte ebenfalls die *Actes du Congrès des Sciences Ethnographiques,* Paris 1878, konsultieren.

11. Jedes der Länder veröffentlichte einen Katalog. Zu Frankreich siehe *Catalogue des produits des colonies françaises,* Paris 1878. Die in den Katalogen aufgelisteten Aussteller waren sowohl Siedler als auch Handelsfirmen.

12. Liesville, *Coup d'œil général sur l'Expostion Historique de l'Art Ancien,* Palais du Trocadéro, Paris 1879, S. 82 ff. Dieses Werk beinhaltet eine Liste der Miglieder des »Aufnahme- und Klassifikationskomitees« und der Aussteller.

13. Racinet, A., *Ornament polychrome, Art ancien et asiatique, Moyen-Age, Renaissance, XVII, XVIII, XIX siècle: Recueil historique et préhistorique avec des notes explicatives,* Paris 1869, 2 Bde. Dieses Werk wurde 1885–86 und 1888 neu aufgelegt.

14. Rochet, C., *Traité d'anatomie d'anthropologie et d'ethnographie appliquées aux Beaux-Arts,* Paris 1886. Rochet lehrte an der École des Beaux-Arts in Paris Anatomie. Er war u. a. für die unverwüstliche Statue Karls des Großen, die den Vorplatz der Pariser Kathedrale ziert, verantwortlich. Sein Urteil über das von seinem »gelehrten Kollegen und ausgezeichneten Freund Doktor Hamy« geschaffene ethnographische Museum: ». . . es enthält zu viele Lumpen und wertlose Dinge.« (S. 250).

15. Die Galerie d'Ethnographie des Invalides in Paris stellt eine vollständige Serie von Kostümfiguren aus, die die Entwicklung des Kriegsgeräts demonstrierten. Die Galerie wurde im Lauf der Jahre einige Male verändert, aber die »Wilden« blieben zum Zweck des Vergleichs immer ausgestellt. 1917 wurde die Galerie aufgelöst, und die verbleibenden Objekte (Ornamente, Waffen usw.) sowie die Kostümfiguren kamen ins Musée d'Ethnographie.

16. Zum Maison Saves vgl. Astre, G., »Théophile et Alexis Saves, négociants toulousains en Nouvelle Calédonie et collecteurs d'objets d'Histoire Naturelle et d'Ethnographie à la fin du XIX siècle« in *Journal de la Société des Océaniens,* Nr. 18, Dezember 1962, S. 108. Das Maison Saves veröffentlichte einige Kataloge, von denen nur noch wenige Exemplare erhalten sind. Die Sammlung von Le Mescam erscheint in Lennier, G., *Description de la collection ethnographique océanienne qu'a offert à la Ville du Havre M. Le Mescam, négociant de Nouméa: Notes d'Ethnographie Océanienne,* Le Havre, 1886. Das Maison Godeffroy in Hamburg veröffentlichte eine völkerkundliche Zeitschrift, und Schmeltz, J. D., und Krause, R., gaben den Katalog zu den Sammlungen heraus, *Die Ethnographisch-Anthropologische Abteilung des Museum Godeffroy in Hamburg: Ein Beitrag zur Kunde der Südseevölker,* Hamburg 1881. Zu den Berliner Neuirland-Sammlungen siehe Helfrich, K., *Malanggan I,* Berlin, Museum für Völkerkunde, 1973.

17. Derzeit haben wir keine biographischen Daten über Bertin, und es ist nicht bekannt, wo er seine Sammlung kaufte. Aber wir können vermuten, daß er als Diamantenhändler nach Amsterdam und Antwerpen kam, Städte, in denen Objekte aus vielen nicht-französischen Besitzungen im Pazifik zu finden waren. Er wurde 1821 bei Paris geboren, und in seinem Todesjahr wurde seine Sammlung auseinandergerissen. Der Bericht über den Verkauf wurde von M. C. Bataille vom Musée de l'Homme in Paris entdeckt. Eine Kopie hiervon befindet sich in den Akten der Ozeanien-Abteilung. Neben Hamy (der Objekte für das Musée d'Ethnographie mit finanzieller Unterstützung von Prinz Roland Bonaparte erwarb) und Heyman wurden Objekte gekauft u. a. von Jonchery, Besnard, Pieret, Edwards, Dounelle (oder Daunelle) und Klein – Namen, von denen wir sonst keine Spur gefunden haben.

18. Die Südsee-Sammlungen wurden im Eingangsbereich aufgebaut. Kostümfiguren trugen »Ornamente«, und die wertvolleren Objekte befanden sich hinter Glas. Die Maske aus Neukaledonien ist nicht die älteste in den heutigen Sammlungen des Musée de l'Homme, eher jene, die Rochas 1861 der Société d'Anthropologie anbot und deren Museum im Quartier Latin gehörte. Ein in *La Nature,* Juni–September 1882, veröffentlichter Artikel interpretiert die Objekte als Bilderrätsel: »z. B. ist auf einer Stange, an deren Spitze sich ein Bär befindet, die Länge dieser Stange durch die Tatzenabdrücke des Tieres markiert; das Ganze bedeutet, daß der Eigentümer der Stange ›Kletternder Bär‹ genannt wurde«. Diese Deutung ist nicht weit entfernt von denen, die später Jarry oder manche Symbolisten vorbrachten.

19. In den 1880er Jahren entwickelte Prinz Roland Bonaparte, der später Präsident der

Société de Géographie wurde, ein starkes Interesse an Neuguinea, und er hoffte, Frankreich würde einen Teil davon annektieren. Er veröffentlichte *Les Derniers Voyages des Néerlandais à la Nouvelle Guinée Hollandaise,* Versailles 1885, und *Notices sur la Nouvelle Guinée,* Paris 1887. Er besaß eine bedeutende Sammlung von Objekten, vor allem Waffen. Als generöser Mäzen stiftete er dem Musée d'Ethnographie mehrere Sammlungen einschließlich der von Bertin, die aus 297 unterschiedlichsten Objekten bestand.

20. Zu dieser Ausstellung siehe *Catalogue de la Section Néerlandaise à l'Exposition Internationale Coloniale et d'Exportation Générale tenue du 1 mars au 31 octobre 1883 à Amsterdam,* Leiden 1883. Neuguinea war in erster Linie durch Alltagsgegenstände aus dem Museum in Utrecht und Korwar-Arbeiten vertreten. Die australische Sektion zeigte vor allem Waffen.

21. Siehe Finsch, O., »Die Ethnologische Ausstellung der Neu-Guinea Compagnie in Königlischen Museen für Völkerkunde« in *Original Mittheilungen aus der Ethnologischen Abtheilung der Königlichen Museen zu Berlin,* Jahr I, Heft 2.3, 1886, S. 92–100, und *Katalog der Ethnologischen Sammlungen der Neu-Guinea Compagnie ausgestellt im Königlichen Museum für Völkerkunde,* Berlin 1886.

22. Den allgemeinen Zustand der Sammlungen beschreibt Bahnson, K., »Ueber Ethnographische Museen« in *Mittheilungen der Anthropologischen Gesellschaft in Wien,* Band XVIII, 1888, S. 109 ff. siehe auch Brigham, W.M.T., »Report of a Journey around the World Undertaken to Examine Various Ethnological Collections« in *Occasional Papers of the Berenice Pauahi Bishop Museum,* Honolulu, Bd. 1, Nr. 1, 1898, S. 1–72. Brigham nennt einige private Sammlungen und skizziert ein Inventar der Sammlungen, die er in verschiedenen europäischen und amerikanischen Museen gesehen hatte.

23. Siehe die französische Ausgabe Bodrogi, T., *L'Art de l'Océanie,* Paris 1961. Zu Anfang des Jahrhunderts hatte Graf Festetics de Tolna seine Sammlung auf seinem Besitz bei Paris. Er veröffentlichte zwei Berichte über seine Reisen im Pazifik, in denen er schildert, wie er einige Objekte erwarb.

24. So scheint es, daß die Einführung traditioneller Währungen, die in Europa schon in den Jahren 1875–80 hergestellt wurden, ein vermehrtes Aufkommen von Objekten wie Malangganen in Neuirland mit sich brachte, die in großer Anzahl die Museen erreichten. In ähnlicher Weise ermöglichte der im pazifischen Raum traditionell unbekannte Gebrauch des Eisens nicht nur eine schnellere Produktion, sondern auch eine Vergrößerung mancher Objekte.

25. Segalen, V., *Essais sur l'exotisme: Une Esthétique du divers,* Montpellier 1978. Segalen ist auch Verfasser eines Aufsatzes über Gauguin, der ein paar Tage bevor Segalen auf Tahiti eintraf, verstarb, und des Buches *Les Immémoriaux,* das, wie Gauguins *Noa Noa,* den Tahiti-Mythos aufleben läßt. Über Exotismus und Malerei s. Laude, J., *La Peinture française (1905–1914) et »l'art nègre«,* Paris 1968.

26. 1898 wurde eine Adaption von Lotis frühem Roman *Le Mariage de Loti* unter dem Titel *L'Ile du rêve* auf der Bühne aufgeführt. In diesem von Reynaldo Hahn musikalisch unterlegten Versdrama geht es um die unglückliche Liebe zwischen einem Schiffskapitän und einer schönen Tahitianerin. Loti hatte 1872 als Leutnant auf der *Flore* den Pazifik durchquert. Auf der Osterinsel erwarb er zahlreiche Objekte, von denen einige im Musée de l'Homme in Paris zu sehen sind. Die *Flore* brachte noch einen Kopf aus Stein mit, der im Musée d'Histoire Naturelle ausgestellt wurde und später ins Musée d'Ethnographie du Trocadéro kam.

Die Anarchistin Louise Michel, die wegen ihrer Beteiligung an der Pariser Kommune 1871 in die Strafkolonie nach Neukaledonien verbannt worden war, veröffentlichte in den 1880er Jahren mehrere Erinnerungen über die dortigen Bewohner. Es stellt sich überhaupt die Frage, ob Anarchistenkreise nicht eine wichtige Rolle bei der neuen Bewertung primitiver Kunst spielten. So besaß Félix Fénéon, der u. a. ein herausragender Pointillist war, eine bedeutende Sammlung primitiver Kunst.

27. Siehe »L'Inauguration du buste du Docteur Hamy et de la salle d'Océanie au Musée d'Ethnographie du Trocadéro«, in *L'Anthropologie XXI,* 1910, S. 241–45. Zur materiellen und finanziellen Situation des Musée d'Ethnographie zu Beginn des Jahrhunderts siehe Verneau, »Le Musée d'Ethnographie du Trocadéro«, in *L'Anthropologie,* 1918–19, S. 547–60.

28. Dieser Bevölkerungsschwund war vor allem eine Folge von Epidemien europäischen Ursprungs, des Exports von billigen Arbeitskräften und einer psychischen Haltung, die von einem ohnmächtigen Gefühl der Ausweglosigkeit geprägt war.

29. Wahrscheinlich spezialisierten sich schon in den 1870er Jahren einige Gebiete Neukaledoniens auf den Verkauf von Objekten an Siedler und Reisende. In anderen Gegenden, etwa auf den Cookinseln, an der Nordküste Neuguineas und auf den Neuen Hebriden, hatte man bald mit der Herstellung von »Souvenirs« angefangen. In Papeete ließ Vater Colette Kopien nach Tafeln von den Osterinseln anfertigen. Eine Firma in Deutschland produzierte neuseeländische Jaden, wovon einige in den Pazifik geliefert wurden, um dort von skrupellosen Händlern als authentische Stücke feilgeboten zu werden.

30. 1893 gründete der frühere Oberst Heckel das Institut Colonial in Marseilles. Das Institut war mit der Handelskammer verbunden und hatte den Zweck, die Ressourcen der Kolonien zu studieren. Es gründete ein Museum, das u. a. Arbeiten aus Neukaledonien und Australien besaß. Zur gleichen Zeit wurden koloniale Gärten angelegt. Im Garten in Paris konnte man eine Kanakenhütte sehen. Das Musée des Colonies in Paris wurde im Palais Royal neu eingerichtet. Folgt man Florent Fels, so konnte man »dort billig originale melanesische Arbeiten kaufen«: Fels, F., »L'Art mélanien au Pavillon de Marsan« in *Nouvelles littéraires,* 27. Oktober 1923, S. 4.

31. Brigham, W. M. T., »Report of a Journey around the World to Study Matters Relating to Museums, 1912« in *Occasional Papers of the Berenice Pauahi Bishop Museum,* 1913. In dieser Zeit wurde das Berliner Museum durch die Sammlung aus der Sepik-Expedition von 1910/12 bereichert, siehe Kelm, H., *Kunst vom Sepik,* Berlin. Museum für Völkerkunde, 1966–68, 3 Bde. Die Hamburger Expedition ist das Thema einer neueren Studie von Fischer, H., *Die Hamburger Südsee Expedition: Über Ethnographie und Kolonialismus,* Frankfurt/Main 1981. Nach der Expedition wurde unter der Leitung von Thilenius ein umfangreiches Werk veröffentlicht und nach dem Krieg fortgesetzt.

32. Webster veröffentlichte seinen Katalog von Juni 1895 bis zum Herbst 1901, Oldman von Dezember 1903 bis Januar 1914. Von letzterem erwarben Breton und Eluard nach dem Ersten Weltkrieg einige Stücke. Edge-Partington veröffentlichte seine Sammlung auf eigene Kosten, siehe Edge-Partington, J., *Album of the Weapons, Tools, Ornaments, Articles of Dress of Natives of the Pacific Islands,* 3 Bde., Manchester 1890. Dies ist ein allgemeineres Werk über viele Museen und Privatsammlungen im United Kingdom und Australien, einschließlich seiner eigenen. Fullers gesamte Kollektion wurde vom Field Museum in Chicago aufgekauft.

33. Mehrere Händler, u. a. Heyman und Brummer, verkauften in Paris primitive Kunst, siehe dazu die Artikel von Paudrat, J.-L., und Rubin, W., im vorliegenden Buch. André Warnods Artikel über afrikanische Kunst (sie scheinen die ersten dieser Art gewesen zu sein, die ein Kunstkritiker verfaßte) bilden lediglich Stücke aus Afrika und Madagaskar ab. Warnod, A., »Curiosités esthétiques« in *Comoedia,* 27. Juni 1911 und 2. Januar 1912.

34. Zu erwähnen ist auch die Seereise des polnischen Schriftstellers und Malers Witkiewicz, der den Anthropologen B. Malinowski im Jahre 1914 als Maler und Photograph in den Pazifik begleitete. 1907 siedelte sich eine Gruppe deutscher Maler und Philosophen, die sich »Brüder der Sonne« nannten, in Neuguinea an. Zwei der »Brüder« starben allerdings und die Überlebenden wurden aus elenden Verhältnissen nach Europa zurückgebracht.

35. Guillaume, S. P., »Une Esthétique nouvelle, l'art nègre« in *Les Arts à Paris,* 15. Mai 1919, S. 1–3. In diesem Artikel gibt Guillaume eine Liste der ersten Sammler. Siehe auch Apollinaire, G., »Quelques Artistes au travail« in *Mercure de France,* 16. April 1911. Nachdruck bei Décaudin, *Œuvres complètes,* Paris 1966, S. 308.

36. Siehe Kahnweiler, *Juan Gris,* London 1947, Anm. 104. Die neukaledonischen Skulpturen erscheinen auf einem Photo, das Gelett Burgess 1908 in Picassos Atelier aufnahm, siehe *Pablo Picasso, A Retrospective,* New York, Museum of Modern Art, 1908, S. 87. Ein aufschlußreiches Photo von Picassos Sammelobjekten aus dem Jahr 1908 siehe □ 402.

37. Zu den Sammlungen des Musée de la Marine siehe Anmerkung 7.

38. Journal du Musée d'Ethnographie du Trocadéro, 1899–1910, Manuskript, Musée de l'Homme, Paris. Die Namen der Personen, die Delaunay begleiten, sind nicht aufgeführt, aber es kann vermutet werden, daß sich Apollinaire unter ihnen befand, der im *Paris-Journal* vom 18. Juli 1914 einen Artikel über das Musée d'Ethnographie veröffentlichte.

39. *British Museum Handbook to the Ethnographical Collection,* The Trustees, 1910, 1. Ausgabe.

40. Faure, E., *Histoire de l'art médiéval,* Paris 1912, besonders die Seiten 137–66. Die Tafeln zeigen Objekte von den Salomonen, Hawaii und der Osterinsel.

41. *Sculptures nègres, 24 photographies précédées d'un avertissement de Guillaume Apollinaire et d'un exposé de Paul Guillaume,* Paris, private, auf 63 Exemplare beschränkte Ausgabe. Dieses Buch erschien mit Unterstützung des Sammlers

Jacques Doucet, der Universität von Lausanne u. a. Über die Beziehung zwischen Apollinaire und Guillaume sowie die Veröffentlichung dieses Buches siehe Bouret, J., »Une Amitié esthétique au début du siècle: Apollinaire et Paul Guillaume, 1911–1918, d'après une correspondance inédite« in *Gazette des Beaux Arts 68,* Nr. 1223, Dezember 1970, S. 373–99. Einen Bericht über die Ausstellung in der Galerie Paul Guillaume, 108 Faubourg Saint-Honoré, schrieb Le Chevrel, M., »Devant l'Atlantique« in *Le Gaulois,* 18. Dezember 1917.

42. Guillaume, P., a. a. O., 1917.

43. *Collections de Monsieur Charles Vignier,* Galerie Leveque, 109 Faubourg Saint-Honoré, 16. Mai–15. Juni 1913. *Lyre et Palette, 6 rue Huyghens, XIVe, Première exposition du 19 novembre au 5 décembre 1916. Kisling, Modigliani, Ortiz de Zarate, Picasso, sculptures nègres.* Ein Text von Guillaume Apollinaire stellt die »Negerskulptur« vor. Die Galerie Lyre et Palette wurde von Emile Lejeune geleitet, einem Maler Schweizer Herkunft, der von Januar bis März 1964 seine Erinnerungen in der *Tribune de Genève* veröffentlichte.

44. Clouzot und Level, *L'Art sauvage – Océanie, Afrique: Catalogue de la première exposition d'art nègre et d'art océanien organisé par Paul Guillaume,* 10.–31. Mai 1919, Galerie Devambez. Der Katalog enthält Apollinaires Text aus *Album nègre* von 1917. Die Ausstellung präsentierte 147 Objekte.

Clouzot und Level, *L'Art nègre et l'art océanien,* Paris 1919. Die Abbildungen zeigen neben Beispielen aus dem Britischen Museum und dem Musée d'Ethnographie in Paris eine hawaiische Skulptur, eine Korwar-Figur, zwei neukaledonische Masken und einige Tikis aus Knochen und Holz von den Marquesasinseln sowie zwei Osterinsel-Statuen aus der Sammlung Level.

45. Clouzot und Level, a. a. O., 1919, S. 22.

46. Réal, D., *La Décoration primitive: Océanie,* Paris 1922. Die Abbildungen zeigen Objekte aus Indonesien und Ozeanien sowie Stücke aus der Sammlung Rupalley.

47. Einstein, C., *Negerplastik,* Leipzig 1915, 1. Auflage, München 1920, 2. Auflage. Südseeobjekte zeigen die Tafeln 43, 81, 82, 85, 86, 87. Die letzten beiden Tafeln (Nr. 107 und 111) mit einem neukaledonischen Türpfosten und einer Skulptur aus Neuirland sind in der 2. Auflage nicht mehr enthalten.

48. Sydow, E. von, *Exotische Kunst, Afrika und Ozeanien,* Leipzig 1921. Die abgebildeten Objekte, die vom Bismarckarchipel und aus Neuguinea stammen, gehörten den Museen in Leipzig und Dresden.

Sydow, E. von, *Die Kunst der Naturvölker und der Vorzeit,* Berlin 1923. Die Abbildungen zeigen Werke aus der gesamten Südsee.

Zu erwähnen sind noch zwei wichtige Bücher, die sich allgemein mit primitiver Kunst beschäftigen: Hausenstein, W., *Klassiker und Barbaren,* München 1923, und Kühn, H., *Die Kunst der Primitiven,* München 1923. Kühns Buch analysiert Goldwater, R., a. a. O., S. 30–31.

49. In der fünften Nummer seiner Zeitschrift *Les Arts à Paris* berichtete Paul Guillaume über dieses von ihm organisierte abendliche Fest, auch finden sich hier Pressekommentare darüber. Siehe auch Allard, »Fête nègre« in *Le Nouveau Spectateur,* Nr. 4, 25. Juni 1919, worin Fauconnets Kostümentwürfe im afrikanischen Stil abgebildet sind.

50. Duthuit, G., »Cinématographe et fêtes« in *Action,* Nr. 4, Juli 1920. Zur Geschichte der französischen Dada-Bewegung siehe Sanouillet, M., *Dada à Paris,* Paris 1965. »Pilou-Pilou« war die Bezeichnung der Siedler für die Tänze Neukaledoniens.

51. Über die frühen Jahre Bretons siehe Bonnet, M., *André Breton et la naissance de l'aventure surréaliste,* Paris 1975. Zu Eluard siehe Gatteau, J. C., *Eluard et la peinture,* Dissertation, Paris 1980, und den Katalog zur Ausstellung »Paul Eluard et ses amis peintres«, Paris, Centre Georges Pompidou, 14. November 1982 bis 17. Januar 1983.

52. Clouzot und Level, *Exposition d'art indigène des colonies françaises,* Musée des Arts Décoratifs, Palais du Louvre, Pavillon de Marsan, November–Dezember 1923, und Chauvet, S., *L'Art indigène des colonies françaises,* Paris 1924.

53. Clouzot und Level, a. a. O., 1919, S. 9.

54. Clouzot und Level, a. a. O., 1923, S. 22.

55. Siehe Katalog *Tableaux de Man Ray et objets des îles,* zur Eröffnung der Galerie Surréaliste, 16 Rue Jacques Callot, 26. März–10. April 1926. Im Katalog sind eine »Maske aus Neumecklenburg«, ein »gravierter Stein von den Loyalty Islands«, eine »Skulptur aus Hawaii« und eine »Maske aus Neuguinea« abgebildet.

56. siehe unten.

57. *Südseeplastiken,* Ausstellung im Mai 1926 in der Galerie Flechtheim, Berlin; im Juni 1926 im Kunsthaus, Zürich; im August 1926 in der Galerie Flechtheim, Düsseldorf; Berlin 1926. Vorwort von Carl Einstein. Im Katalog sind 29 der 184 ausgestellten Objekte enthalten. Eine illustrierte Übersetzung erschien in *Art und Archaeology* 1 (1927), S. 125–28.

58. Zervos, C., »Introduction« in *Cahiers d'art,* Nr. 7/8, 1927, S. 229. Der Artikel ist illustriert mit einem Photo einer Schildpatt-Maske von der Torresstraße aus der Sammlung Picassos □ 333.

59. Basler, A., *L'Art chez les peuples primitifs,* Paris 1929. Das Kapitel über Südseekunst wurde in *Les Arts à Paris,* Nr. 6, Januar 1929, S. 19–24, abgedruckt.

60. Basler, A., a. a. O., 1929, S. 23.

61. Luquet, *L'Art primitif,* Paris 1930. Dieses Problem des Realismus stand schon seit Jahren zur Diskussion. Neben Grosses Theorien in Deutschland kam dieses Thema im Anschluß an Breuils prähistorische Forschungen und seine Kontroverse mit S. Reinach in Frankreich zur Sprache. Die Frage war: Logischer Realismus oder visueller Realismus? Das Konzept des logischen Realismus, wie es die Aufsätze von Hamy über »La Figure humaine chez le sauvage et l'enfant« in *L'Anthropologie* 19, 1908, S. 385–407, und von Luquet, »Sur le caractère des figures humaines de l'art paléolithique« in *L'Anthropologie* 21, 1910, S. 409–23, darstellen, erlaubt den Vergleich der Kunst von Eingeborenen und Kindern. Somit nahm Luquet 1930 erneut Ideen auf, die schon seit Anfang des Jahrhunderts im Mittelpunkt einer breiten Diskussion gestanden hatten, und zwar nicht nur in Prähistoriker- und Anthropologenkreisen, sondern auch innerhalb der Psychologie, insbesondere der Entwicklungspsychologie.

62. *Cahiers d'art,* Nr. 2–3, 1929, S. 119, 189 Illustrationen.

63. Portier und Poncetton, F., *La Décoration: Océanie,* Paris ohne Jahresangabe (1931?), S. 8, 48 Tafeln.

64. Pierre Loeb schrieb einen Erinnerungsband, *Voyages à travers la peinture,* Paris 1946. Ihm wurde eine Ausstellung gewidmet. Siehe *L'Aventure de Pierre Loeb – La Galerie Pierre, Paris, 1924–1964,* Musée de l'Art Moderne de la Ville de Paris, Musée d'Ixelles, Brüssel 1979. Die Seiten 103–10 berichten über seine Sammlung primitiver Kunst.

65. Viot, J., »N'encombrez pas les colonies« in *Le Surréalisme au service de la révolution,* Nr. 1, Juli 1930, S. 43–45, und *Deposition de blanc,* Paris 1930. Dieses Buch ist eine antikolonialistische Satire. Viot veröffentlichte ebenfalls »La Baie de Geelwinck« in *Art vivant,* Nr. 147, April 1931, S. 172–73. Dieser Artikel ist mit Photos aus jenem Gebiet illustriert.

66. Katalog der *Exposition d'art africain et d'art océanien,* Paris 1930, S. 29, 15 Abbilungen, und der Katalog *Exposition des arts de l'Océanie, 23 mai–6 juin 1930, à la Renaissance, 11 rue Royalé,* S. 16. Einen Bericht über die Ausstellung in der Galerie Mettler schrieb Sautier, A., »Une Collection d'art d'Océanie« in *Formes,* Nr. 2, 1930, S. 13. Der Artikel enthält die Abbildungen zweier Steinstatuen von der Osterinsel.

67. Gatteau, J.-C., a. a. O., 1980, S. 244. Zu jener Zeit plante Eluard eine Reise nach Neuguinea. Allerdings erscheint seine Weltreise im Jahre 1924 ziemlich mysteriös.

68. Über diese Ausstellung gibt es wenig Informationen. Ein Photo davon war in *Le Surréalisme au service de la révolution,* Nr. 4, Dezember 1931, abgebildet, aber seine schlechte Qualität erlaubt nur eine ungefähre Identifizierung. Gatteau, J.-C., a. a. O., liefert einige ergänzende Angaben zur Organisation der Ausstellung, gibt aber keine Hinweise über die Objekte.

69. Berl, E., »Conformismes freudiens« in *Formes,* Nr. 5, Mai 1930, S. 3. Siehe auch Georges, W. »Le Crépuscule des idoles«, in *Les Arts à Paris,* Nr. 17. Mai 1930.

70. Purrmann, H., »Südseekunst« in *Kunst und Künstler,* 1933, S. 115. Zervos, C., veröffentlichte in *Cahiers d'art* seine »Reflexions sur la tentative d'esthétique dirigée du III Reich«, worin er auch seine Position zur Rolle der primitiven Kunst in der Malerei seiner Zeit formulierte.

71. Zwischen 1925 und 1939 fanden in Paris vierzig Auktionen statt. Dazu gab es Kataloge, die Südseeobjekte abbildeten. Sie enthielten ungefähr 900 Stücke, von denen manche mehrere Male zum Verkauf angeboten wurden. Die beiden letzten wichtigen Auktionen vor dem Krieg waren die aus dem Besitz von Frank Burty Haviland (1936) und Vlaminck (1937). Die Sammlung Level kam 1943 unter den Hammer. Diejenigen von Fénéon, Titayana (unter einem Pseudonym), Madeleine Rousseau, Paul Guillaume und La Korrigane wurden nach dem Krieg aufgelöst.

72. Siehe Penrose, »Un Œil de liberté« in *Paul Eluard et ses amis peintres,* a. a. O., 1983.

73. Goldwater, R., »American, Oceanic and African« im Ausstellungskatalog der Galerie Pierre Matisse, 20. April – 9. Mai 1936.

74. Zu diesen von dem Franzosen Mauss entwickelten Vorstellung und ihrer Anwendung auf die Plastik siehe den Beitrag von R. Krauss zu Giacometti im vorliegenden Buch.

□ 160 *Ausstellung ozeanischer und moderner Kunst in der Galerie Pierre Loeb, Paris 1949, Photographie von Denise Colomb. Von links nach rechts: ›Schädelgerüst‹, Provinz Ost-Sepik (Papua-Neuguinea); Alberto Giacometti, ›Die Hand‹, 1947, Bronze; Antonin Artaud, ›Selbstbildnis‹, 1946, Bleistift; ›Figur‹, wahrscheinlich Provinz Ost-Sepik (Papua-Neuguinea); ›Vieira da Silva in ihrem Atelier, Boulevard Saint-Jacques‹, Photographie von Denise Colomb; ›Figur zur Bekrönung eines Daches‹, Neukaledonien; ›Figur‹, wohl Provinz Ost-Sepik (Papua-Neuguinea); kleine Photographien mit den Eltern von P. Loeb; ›Pablo Picasso‹, Photographie von Man Ray, 1933, mit einer Widmung Picassos an S. und P. Loeb.*

75. Zur Gruppe *Documents* und dem Musée de l'Homme siehe Clifford, J., »On Ethnographic Surrealism« in *Comparative Studies in Society and History,* 23, Nr. 4, Oktober 1981, S. 539–65, und Jamin, J., »Un Sacré Collège, ou les apprentis sorciers de la sociologie« in *Cahiers internationaux de sociologie,* 68, 1980, S. 5–30. Zum Surealismus siehe u. a. Maurer, E., »In Quest of the Myth: An Investigation of the Relationship between Surrealism and Primitivism« Dissertation, University of Pennsylvania 1974, und Cowling, E., »An Other Culture« in *Dada and Surrealism Reviewed,* London 1978, S. 451–68.

76. Leiris, M., »L'Art des Iles Marquises« in *Cahiers d'art,* Nr. 5–8, 1934, S. 185–92. Dieser völkerkundliche Aufsatz untersucht die Erfindung des Tiki.

77. Die Sammlung des Schweizer Geschäftsmannes Von der Heydt beschrieb Sydow, E von; *Sammlung Baron Eduard von der Heydt,* Berlin 1932. Diese Publikation berücksichtigt allerdings nicht die reichhaltige Sammlung, die in das Musée de l'Homme kam und nach dem Krieg dem Züricher Museum Rietberg übergeben wurde, dessen Kern sie darstellt.

78. Die La Korrigane-Expedition wurde von den Familien De Ganay und Van den Broek organisiert. Beide Familien standen der Großindustrie nahe, und Madame de Ganay belegte in Paris Kurse bei Mauss.

79. *Catalogue of an Exhibition of the Art of Primitive Peoples,* London, Burlington Fine Arts Club, 1935. Einführung von A. D. Die Ausstellung zeigte 292 Objekte.

80. Firth, R., *Art and Life in New Guinea,* London 1936.

81. Die auf dieser Ausstellung gezeigten Objekte waren eine Schildpatt-Maske von der Torresstraße aus der Sammlung Georges Salle, eine geflochtene Maske aus der Sammlung Breton, eine Holzmaske, eine Ahnenfigur und eine Kopflehne aus Neuguinea, eine Skulptur aus Neuirland, eine Tapa-Maske Neubritanniens aus der Sammlung Pierre Loeb, eine aus Baumfarn geschnitzte Maske von den Neuen Hebriden und ein gravierter Kieselstein von den Loyaltyinseln aus der Sammlung Eluard.

Jean-Louis Paudrat

Aus Afrika

Zu Anfang dieses Jahrhunderts, als man den künstlerischen Rang völkerkundlicher Gegenstände zu erkennen begann, wurde Paris mehr als jede andere Stadt zum Sammelpunkt von Ideen und Aktivitäten, die der afrikanischen Kunst eine entscheidende Rolle bei der Entwicklung westlicher Gefühlskultur zuwiesen.

Über Jahrhunderte hinweg war eine bunte Vielfalt von Stammesobjekten in französische Sammlungen gelangt, deren Zahl sich nach 1880 durch den aufblühenden französischen Kolonialismus und die damit einhergehende Wissenschaftstätigkeit schließlich erhöhte. Von den Objekten, die noch vor der zweiten Hälfte des 19. Jahrhunderts mitgebracht wurden, gelangten jedoch nur einige wenige in öffentliche Sammlungen. Jene französischen »Wunderkammern«, die in der Renaissance von ein paar Fürsten und Schiffseignern eingerichtet wurden, haben keine Spuren hinterlassen. Sie horteten »fremdartige Götzenbilder«,[1] die aus einem Afrika kamen, das Rabelais als »seit jeher bekannt für die Herstellung neuer und monströser Dinge«[2] beschrieb. Nur fünf kunstvolle Jagdhörner, zwei Eßgeräte und ein Pulverhorn sind von der afro-portugiesischen Kunst des 16. Jahrhunderts, hergestellt von Elfenbeinschnitzern der *Scherbro, Edo* und *Kongo,* erhalten geblieben. Es ist sehr gut möglich, daß am Ende der Regierungszeit Ludwigs XIV. Graburnen der *Anyi* aus Afrika kamen,[3] doch ist in den Inventaren darüber nichts vermerkt. Es gibt jedoch Aufzeichnungen über eine »Statuette von der Guineaküste«,[4] deren Stammeszuordnung schwierig ist; sie wurde im 18. Jahrhundert an das Cabinet des Médailles der Bibliothèque Royale geschickt. Hatte der Comte de Caylus 1756 in seinem *Receuil d'antiquités égyptiennes, étrusques, grecques et romaines* einen Bronzeanhänger der *Kulango*[5] abgebildet, so veröffentlichte der Baron Denon, der an Napoleons Ägyptenfeldzug teilgenommen hatte, in *Les Monuments des arts du dessin chez les peuples tant anciens que modernes* ein Objekt, dessen Ursprung genauso weit von den Ufern des Nil entfernt lag. Schließlich wurden während der ersten Hälfte des 19. Jahrhunderts einige Goldstaubdosen der *Akan* ins Cabinet des Médailles aufgenommen.

Im Jahre 1850 wurde dann im Louvre das Musée Naval eingerichtet. Dieser Institution gehörten nach Angaben des 1856 erstellten Inventars[6] knapp fünfhundert Objekte; sie stammen von Überseegesellschaften, die unter dem Schutz der Marine standen: in erster Linie Waffen, Geräte für den Ackerbau, Leder- und Korbwaren, Kopfschmuck und Musikinstrumente. Einige Jahre später (1874) erdachte E.-T. Hamy, Assistent am Musée d'Histoire Naturelle, einen Plan, »um alle über verschiedene staatliche Einrichtungen verstreuten Stammesobjekte in einem einzigen Museum zu vereinigen«.[7] Seine Idee ähnelte den Vorschlägen Barthélemys aus dem späten 18. Jahrhundert und Jomards, Kurator des Dépôt de Géographie, aus dem Jahr 1828.

Die Eröffnung des Musée Ethnographique des Missions Scientifiques am 23. Januar 1878 in Paris – dem unmittelbaren Vorgänger des Museums, das eine so entscheidende Rolle in der Entwicklung der französischen Moderne spielen sollte – stellte das erste Ergebnis der Bemühungen Dr. Hamys dar, das Ministerium für öffentliche Bildung von der Notwendigkeit einer neuen wissenschaftlichen Einrichtung in der französischen Hauptstadt zu überzeugen. Ihre Aufgabe sollte das Sammeln und Klassifizieren nach einer vergleichenden Methode sein, um anhand typischer Stücke die Entwicklung menschlicher Techniken aufzuzeigen.

Im Unterschied zu den Sammlungen des Musée Permanent des Colonies, die seit der Weltausstellung von 1855 im selben Gebäude zu sehen waren, wurden die hastig zusammengestellten Sammlungen des Musée Ethnographique sechs Wochen lang in drei Räumen des zweiten Stocks des Palais de l'Industrie an den Champs-Elysées gezeigt. Die Ausstellung bestand hauptsächlich aus Kunstwerken alter Kulturen Asiens und Amerikas, beinhaltete aber auch eine kleinere Sektion für Ozeanien und Afrika. Was letzteres betrifft, so gab es zwei Vitrinen mit Exponaten aus Gabun, die von Hamy aus Material zusammengestellt worden waren, das Alfred Marche auf seiner zweiten Expedition zum Ogowe (1875–78) gesammelt hatte. Wahrscheinlich konnte man hier zum ersten Mal die Statue eines Reliquienwächters der *Kota* sehen.[8]

Aufgrund des Erfolgs, den dieser Vorläufer des Musée d'Ethnographie hatte, eröffnete der Baron de Watteville, Direktor der Akademie der Wissenschaften und schönen Künste, auf der Weltausstellung von 1878 eine »Halle der Reisen und wissenschaftlichen Expeditionen«; sie umfaßte mehr oder weniger die im Palais de l'Industrie gezeigten Objekte. Inzwischen wurde im rechten Flügel des Trocadéro eine Ausstellung von »ethnographischen Objekten der Völker außerhalb Europas«,[9] d.h. Amerikas und Afrikas, eingerichtet. Auch hier fanden sich mehr Objekte aus Alaska, Mexiko und Peru als aus Afrika: eine Reihe von kongolesischen Elfenbeinschnitzereien aus dem Besitz des Kaufmanns Conquy Senior, einige Textilien und Waffen aus dem Basutoland, eine Leihgabe Casalis' sowie

□ 161 *›Kopfschmuck‹, Kalabari Ijo (Nigeria), Holz, Höhe 47 cm. Sammlung R. und L. Wielgus.*

☐ 162 *Blick in das Musée d'Ethnographie du Trocadéro (Musée de l'Homme), drei* FON*-Figuren, Paris 1895.*

ein paar kleinere Objekte der *ASANTE.* Schließlich war die afrikanische Abteilung im Palais des Colonies, die ihre Exponate vor allem von Handelshäusern in Gabun und an der Goldküste bezog, mit Ausnahme von Kleidungsstücken und verschiedener Haushaltsgeräte auf Waagen und Gewichte zum Wiegen von Goldstaub beschränkt sowie auf einige Schmuckstücke der *AKAN* – einschließlich eines »Fetischs« des Herrschers der *FANTE* von Assinie.

Da die Weltausstellung von 1878 in erster Linie die öffentliche Meinung dafür gewann, Frankreichs koloniale Zukunft in Afrika zu sehen, eröffneten sich der Völkerkunde mit dem weiteren Vordringen nach Innerafrika neue Forschungsziele. Gleichzeitig fiel die endgültige Entscheidung, auch in Paris ein Völkerkundemuseum zu gründen, wie man es zum Teil schon im Ausland kannte. Die verschiedenen Beschlüsse dieses entscheidenden Jahres berücksichtigten allerdings nur einige afrikanische Stämme, die vor allem in Gebieten entlang der Atlantikküste beheimatet waren. Obgleich von einem gewissen Interesse, waren die Schenkungen, die Dr. Hamy für das zukünftige Museum entgegennahm, nicht besonders zahlreich:[10] eine *IGBO*-Ikenga (siehe Glossar) aus Onitsha, die man dem Händler Bishoffeim, der sie auf der Weltausstellung erworben hatte, abkaufte; einige Objekte aus dem Westsudan, die Solleilet von seiner Reise nach Ségou mitgebracht hatte; und eine Statuette von der Guineaküste, die im 18. Jahrhundert in den Besitz der Bibliothèque Nationale gelangt war. Das Musée Permanent des Colonies, das Musée Naval im Louvre, das Musée d'Artillerie, die Bibliothèque Nationale sowie einige gelehrte Gesellschaften (der Geographie, Anthropologie und Zoologie) verfügten damals über umfangreiche Sammlungen, zu denen auch Waffen, Textilien, Schmuck, Musikinstrumente sowie Haushalts- und Kultgegenstände gehörten. Zudem erweiterte das im September 1879 für ein paar Monate im Foyer des Théâtre du Châtelet eingerichtete »Musée Africain«[11] trotz seiner verwirrenden Präsentation das Spektrum der Stämme und Objekte um Stücke aus Zentral-, Ost- und Südafrika sowie um »Kultobjekte« (»afrikanische Gottheiten« aus der Sammlung Bertin, »bei religiösen Feiern verwendete Holzmasken, Opfermesser, verschiedene Fetische, Götzen, Hausgötter, Schönheitsembleme« aus der Sammlung Bouvier).

Die Ausstellung im Châtelet ließ auf ihre Weise einen spürbaren Wandel in der Einstellung zu Afrika erkennen. Adolphe Belots Drama *La Vénus noire,* das als Vorwand für die Ausstellung im Châtelet diente, folgte, von einigen freien Abweichungen abgesehen, getreu dem Bericht des deutschen Naturforschers Schweinfurth über seine Expedition (1860–71) durch die Gebiete der *SHILLUK, DINKA, BONGO, ZANDE* und *MANGBETU.*[12] Sein Reisebericht *Im Herzen Afrikas,* der 1874 in der Zeitschrift *Le Tour du monde* in elf reichillustrierten Folgen als *Au cœur d'Afrique* erschien, brachte der französischen Öffentlichkeit zu Bewußtsein, daß es im Innern Afrikas, fern von christlichen wie islamischen Einflüssen, Gesellschaften mit hohem kulturellem Niveau gab, die eine hochentwickelte Musik, Dichtung, bildende Kunst und Architektur hervorgebracht hatten. Auch bei der Darstellung des Pomps am Hof des Herrschers der *MANGBETU* betonte der Bühnenautor von sich aus die Wildheit ihres Verhaltens, um den Zuschauern zu verstehen zu geben, daß es von der westlichen Zivilisation noch nicht gemäßigt worden sei. Durch die Berichte von der Entdekkung unbekannter Länder, die Beschreibung der dortigen Bräuche und Abenteuergeschichten unerschrockener Forscher wurde das Interesse am Exotischen immer mehr angeregt. Über diese phantastischen Gegebenheiten vergaß man jedoch nie die eher pragmatische Realität der politischen und wirtschaftlichen Interessen Frankreichs.

Die Gönner des Musée Africain – die geographischen Gesellschaften von Paris und Marseille, die zoologische Gesellschaft, die Vertreter einiger Handelshäuser Marseilles, die Niederlassungen an der afrikanischen Küste unterhielten – sie alle suchten aus den Ergebnissen des vorangegangenen geographischen Kongresses Gewinn zu ziehen und die Öffentlichkeit davon zu überzeugen, daß den Wissenschaften bei der Eroberung neuer Territorien eine große Bedeutung zukam. Zoologie, Botanik und Ethnologie könnten genauere Informationen über zu erobernde Regionen ermitteln, über die dort lauernden Gefahren, über ihre Rohstoffe und alle Bräuche ihrer Bewohner, deren Kenntnis für den Aufbau einer zukünftigen Kolonialherrschaft nützlich sein könnte. Die Ausstellung im Châtelet entsprach diesem didaktischen Ziel, das vom Musée d'Ethnographie in größerem Rahmen wahrgenommen werden sollte. Die Sammlungen des Naturforschers Bouvier, der die Expeditionen von Marche und Compiègne nach Gabun, von Petit nach Kabinda, von Lucan nach Loango usw. finanzierte, machten deutlich, welchen Nutzen man aus der Unterstützung der Kolonialisierung ziehen konnte.

☐ 163 *›Doppelgesichtige Maske‹,* BEMBE *(Zaire), bemaltes Holz, Höhe 60 cm. Privatsammlung.*

□ 164 *›Hütte mit* KOTA*-Reliquiarfiguren‹, Zeichnung von Riou nach Angaben und Fundstücken von Jacques de Brazza aus der Westafrika-Expedition, veröffentlicht in „Le Tour du monde“, 2ᵉ semestre, 1887.*

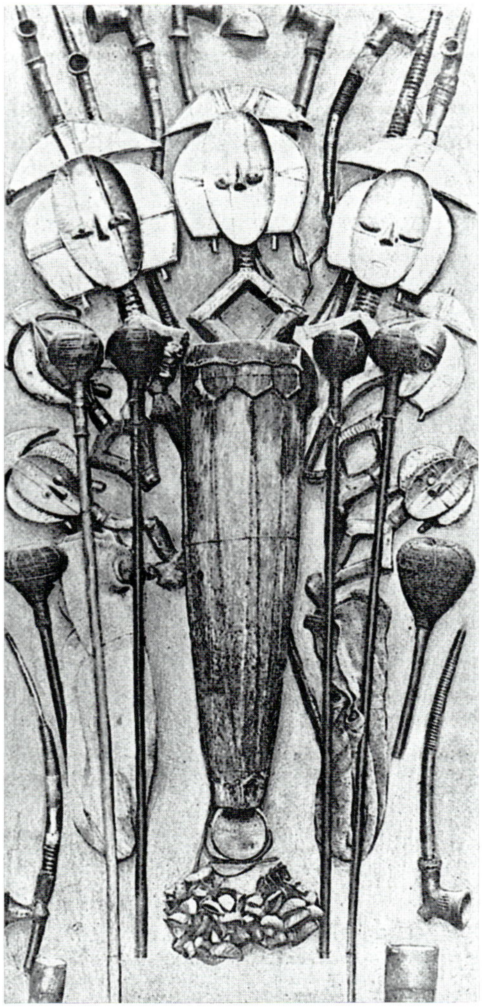

□ 165 *Reliquiarfiguren und andere Objekte der* KOTA*, erworben vom Musée d'Ethnographie du Trocadéro zwischen 1883 und 1886, Heliogravüre, veröffentlicht in „Le Tour du monde“, 1888.*

Der Kultusminister appellierte an Männer wie Charles Maunoir, den Generalsekretär der geographischen Gesellschaft von Paris, und Edouard Charton, den Herausgeber von *Le Tour du monde,* sich der Kommission anzuschließen, die zunächst ein Magazin für die seit 1878 zusammengestellten Sammlungen ausfindig machen und dann die Eröffnung des Musée d'Ethnographie am 12. April 1882 in den Ausstellungsräumen des Trocadéro ermöglichen sollte.

Von 1879 bis 1886, als einige der von den Teilnehmern der Westafrika-Expedition (1883–85) □ 164 gesammelten Stücke Eingang in das Museum fanden, scheinen nur äußerst wenige Neuerwerbungen hinzugekommen zu sein. Dennoch verdienen die geographischen und ethnischen Ursprünge der in dieser Zeit verzeichneten Objekte erwähnt zu werden. 1881 kam von der westafrikanischen Küste eine *BIJOGO*-Skulptur der Bissauinseln, die damals unter portugiesischer Herrschaft standen. 1883 wurden eine Elek-Figur und eine kleine Nimba-Büste (siehe Glossar) der *BAGA* aus dem Küstenbereich Guineas und fünf *IGBO*-Statuetten, die der Kommandeur der Compagnie Française d'Afrique Equatoriale, Kapitän Mattéi, im Nigerdelta gesammelt hatte, erworben. Hauptmann Archinard schickte aus dem Westsudan einen Antilopenkopfschmuck der *BAMBARA*, und 1885 trafen eine Nawa-Maske (siehe Glossar) desselben Volkes und eine *MALINKE*-Statuette, die Dr. Bellamy in der benachbarten Gegend erworben hatte, ein. Schließlich kam die Figur eines Reliquienwächters der *KOTA*, die Guiral als Mitglied der zweiten Expedition unter Führung Pierre de Brazzas gesammelt hatte.

Die wissenschaftliche Ausbeute von De Brazzas dritter, unter der Schirmherrschaft des Kultusministeriums stehenden Expedition nach Zentralafrika, genannt die Westafrikanische Expedition, wurde vom 1. bis 15. Juli 1886 in der Orangerie des Jardin des Plantes, einer Außenstelle des Musée d'Histoire Naturelle, fast dreißigtausend Besuchern gezeigt. Im Frühjahr 1886 trafen 101 Kisten, die verschiedene naturgeschichtliche und ethnographische Funde enthielten, ein. Sie kamen aus den Gebieten, in denen Teilnehmer der Expedition einen administrativen und politischen Apparat aufzubauen begonnen hatten, an der Loangoküste und im Gebiet Kouilou-niari, im Teke-Plateau, an den Ufern des mittleren und oberen Ogowe, des Alima und des Kongo. Einige waren von dem Naturforscher Jacques de Brazza und seinem Assistenten, Attilio Pecile, die 1883 beide vom Musée d'Histoire Naturelle einen entsprechenden Auftrag erhalten hatten, gesammelt worden. Den Rest trug ein Offizier namens Cholet ohne Auftrag zusammen; er schickte aus dem Gebiet der Koilou »144 Stücke, darunter 24 Metallarbeiten, 15 Musikinstrumente, 5 Geräte zum Rauchen, 38 Hausgeräte und 15 Fetische«, die er von dem Ingenieur Michaud (mittlerer Ogowe), von dem Arzt der Expedition, Dr. Schwebisch, und dem Naturforscher Tholon (oberer Ogowe) erhalten hatte. Einige Stammesobjekte, die von anderen Teilnehmern der Expedition (Dolisie, Chavannes, Beauguillaume) mehr zufällig mitgenommen wurden, machten die im Jardin des Plantes ausgestellte Sammlung von Objekten aus dem Gabun-Kongo-Gebiet komplett.[13]

Die aus diesem Anlaß von Emile Rivière verfaßte *Notice sur les collections de la Mission Scientifique*[14] zeigt, daß man trotz ihrer Bedeutung nur wenig über Zweck und Verwendung der Exponate wußte. Der Autor sah höchstens eine Beziehung zwischen den länglichen Streifen auf dem Gesicht einiger »Fetische« und dem Brauch der Hauteinritzung bei den *Teke*, zwischen den seitlichen Flügeln einiger anderer »Fetische« und dem Kopfschmuck der Frauen der *Mbamba*. Für die Technik, die Augen aus Glassplittern zu bilden, fand er ein ähnliches Verfahren bei den alten Ägyptern. Diese flüchtigen Überlegungen zeigen wie die von Hamy in seinem Vortrag vor der geographischen Gesellschaft, daß »Bräuche und Trachten, Glaube und Mythen kaum beobachtet wurden« von denen, die das Beweismaterial dazu lieferten.[15]

Nach Auflösung der Sonderausstellungen gelangten die Exponate vor allem an das Musée d'Histoire Naturelle, die geographischen Gesellschaften von Rom und Paris und an das Musée d'Ethnographie im Trocadéro. Letzterer, der schon 1884 von Schwebisch und Tholon drei Reliquiarfiguren der *Kota*, eine Maske der *Aduma* und zwei den *Ondumbo* zugeschriebene Statuetten erhalten hatte, bekam 1886 als Schenkung von De Brazza und Pecile drei weitere Reliquiarfiguren und einige Statuetten der *Vili*, von Pierre Michaud eine Reliquiarfigur der *Hongwe* und von Cholet eine bedeutende Gruppe von Objekten der *Vili* und *Kugni*. Eine Gesamtausstellung aller seit 1883 eingetroffenen Reliquiarfiguren wurde Ende 1886 im afrikanischen Saal gezeigt.[16]

Im März 1887 wurde die in fast dreißig Jahren zusammengetragene Sammlung des Juwelenhändlers Bertin versteigert.[17] Obwohl sie vor allem Objekte von den pazifischen Inseln enthielt, vermerkt der Katalog »eine Keule aus Zentralafrika und Gabun«. Es sei daran erinnert, daß sich in der Ausstellung des Musée Africain eine Glasvitrine und eine Reihe von Stammesobjekten, die Bertin gehörten, befanden, die außer einigen »Keulen« und »Stäben« auch ein paar »afrikanische Gottheiten« umfaßte. Unter den Käufern der Bertinauktion befanden sich Emile Heymann, der 1896 in der Rue de Rennes ein Geschäft mit exotischen und primitiven Objekten eröffnen sollte, und Fürst Roland Bonaparte, der spätere Vorsitzende des Exekutivkommitees der geographischen Gesellschaft; seine Großzügigkeit gestattete dem Musée d'Ethnographie im Trocadéro die Erweiterung der Ozeanienabteilung. Wahrscheinlich stammen die sieben afrikanischen Holzarbeiten, ebenso zwei Zeremonienstäbe der *Chokwe*, die 1888 unter Bonapartes Namen verzeichnet sind, aus derselben Auktion.

Die Weltausstellung von 1889 sollte, mehr noch als die vorausgegangene, den Wunsch ihrer Veranstalter nach Verbreitung des kolonialen Gedankens ausdrücken.[18] Frankreichs wirtschaftliche Entwicklung und politische Ausdehnung wurden damals als Ergebnis dreier Faktoren dargestellt: der Reform des Bildungssystems, des Fortschritts der angewandten Wis-

□ 166 *›Doppelgesichtige Figur‹, Lega (Zaire), bemaltes Holz. Höhe 50 cm. Privatsammlung.*

senschaften und der ersten Erfolge des Kolonialismus. So wurde in der großen Halle des Palais des Arts Libéraux, wo das Kultusministerium die Vorzüge des laizistischen, demokratischen Unterrichts feierte, den Beiträgen der unter seiner Regie erfolgten ersten »wissenschaftlichen« Expeditionen nach Afrika besondere Aufmerksamkeit geschenkt. Neben verschiedenen Dokumenten, die den erfolgreichen Aufbau der Verwaltung im Gabun-Kongo-Gebiet nachzeichneten, wurden einige der bedeutendsten Objekte aus der westafrikanischen Expedition besonders exponiert ausgestellt. Der auf der Exposition du Travail et des Sciences Anthropologiques vertretene komparatistische Ansatz wurde zum Teil mit Beispielen aus Ostafrika (Sammlung Roland Bonaparte) und dem südlichen Afrika (Sammlung Lombard) belegt. In den Hallen des Palais Central des Colonies, wo man Muster der für den Export nach Frankreich bestimmten Erzeugnisse zeigte, stellte außerdem jede afrikanische Abteilung ein paar für die jeweilige Region typische Objekte aus. Für den Sudan waren es Statuetten der *Malinke* und *Bambara;* für Guinea Skulpturen der *Baga* und *Landuma;* für die Goldküste einige Objekte der *Anyi*; für Dahome Masken der *Anago* (*Yoruba*) und Figuren der *Fon*; und für die Kolonie Gabun-Kongo 47 verschiedene »Fetische«. Obwohl der Herausgeber des offiziellen Katalogs des Palais Central ausdrücklich feststellt, daß man hinsichtlich der *Anyi*-Statuetten von »primitiver Kunst«[19] sprechen kann oder Pol-Neveux in der *Revue de l'Exposition Universelle*[20] von einer hochentwickelten Bildhauerei bei den *Baga* spricht und die Aufrichtigkeit des afrikanischen Künstlers mit der des anonymen Bildhauers der Kathedralen vergleicht, herrscht in den Aufsätzen ein amüsierter, herablassender Ton gegenüber allem vor, was man eigentlich als unbeholfen, archaisch und kindisch empfand.

Ein paar auf dem Place des Invalides nachgebaute Behausungen, die typisch für den Senegal, Gabun oder Kongo sein sollten, erregten ebenfalls die Phantasie des Publikums. Auf dem Platz des »Pahouin«-Dorfes konnte man ein paar Stammesangehörige der *Okande*, *Aduma* oder *Vili* sehen, wie sie tanzten oder handwerklich arbeiteten. Einige schnitzten auf Wunsch exotische Andenken aus Elfenbein.

Gleichzeitig mit dem erfolgreichen und in der Ausstellung von 1889 glorifizierten Bild des Ingenieurs (Eiffel) entstand allmählich das des Kolonialbeamten, des Eroberers des Hinterlands und ersten Organisators der Kolonie, Friedensstifters, aber auch Soldaten der christlichen Zivilisation, der die Macht der »Fetische« und den Brauch des Menschenopfers bekämpfte.

Der lange und mörderische Feldzug, den Frankreich nach 1877 in Dahome führte, um das Königreich Abome zu unterjochen, endete am 25. Januar 1894 mit der Kapitulation seines Herrschers. Für den einen Teil der französischen Presse war Behanzins Niederlage ein Sieg des Glaubens, für den andern ein Sieg der Vernunft über den »entwürdigenden Fetischismus«. Die von Oberst Dodds in der heiligen Stadt Kana und im Palast von Abome erbeuteten Machtinsignien wurden im Trocadéro zur Schau gestellt und waren gewissermaßen der Beweis für die Zivilisierung nicht nur religiöser, sondern auch politischer Häresie: der Königsthron, vier Türen mit Reliefs symbolischer Motive, drei allegorische Figuren – angeblich die Dar-

□ 167 *›Weibliche Figur, Rhythmusgeber‹, Senufo (Elfenbeinküste), Holz, Höhe 96,5 cm. Privatsammlung.*

stellungen des Ahnen, des Vaters und des Königs □ 162 –, zu denen später noch eine Statue des Donnergotts der *Fon* aus Metall □ 452 und zwei monumentale Thronsessel kamen. Dennoch waren die Kommentare zu diesen Trophäen nicht immer nur abschätzig oder herablassend. Der Kolumnist von *Le Monde illustré* etwa hielt sie für »die schönsten Exemplare des Negerhandwerks«, und er fügte hinzu: »Es besteht ein beträchtlicher Unterschied zwischen diesen interessanten Figuren und den rohen Fetischen Neukaledoniens.«[21] Ebenso wandte sich Maurice Delafosse (in zwei Artikeln in *La Nature*,[22] deren Überlieferung in *L'Anthropologie* René Verneau zu verdanken ist) gegen den Ausdruck »Fetisch«, den er als vulgär empfand, und gegen das Vorurteil, daß die Einwohner Dahomes zu künstlerischem Gefühl und jeder höheren Religiosiät unfähig seien. Für ihn als genauen und ehrlichen Beobachter waren diese Erzeugnisse historische Dokumente, die ideographischen Annalen des Königreichs. Als solche verlangten sie nach Entzifferung und Erläuterung. Seine Einstellung gegenüber der Kultur von Dahome steht in auffälligem Gegensatz zum Inhalt des patriotischen Stückes *Au Dahomey*, das im Théâtre de la Porte Saint-Martin gespielt wurde, oder zu den Kommentaren über den Auftritt von 150 männlichen und weiblichen Kriegern auf dem Marsfeld.

Gemessen an den Fortschritten innerhalb der Grenzen des französischen Kolonialreichs nach der Berliner Konferenz von 1884/85 und dem Anstieg der Zahl der Verwaltungs- und Handelsbeauftragten in den von Frankreich kontrollierten Gebieten sind die Neuzugänge der afrikanischen Abteilung des Musée d'Ethnographie während der neunziger Jahre eher gering. Mit Ausnahme des Königreichs Dahome (vor der Übernahme des Behanzin-Schatzes waren 1889 einige Objekte als Schenkung von dem Verwalter Albécas und 1891 die bedeutenden, von Edouard zwischen 1886 und 1890 im Land der *Anago* gesammelten Objekte erworben worden) und der Länder, die nicht unter französischer Kolonialherrschaft standen (von dort gibt es nur wenige registrierte Stücke), beschränken sich die Zugänge aus Westafrika auf die Elfenbeinküste (ein paar *Anyi*-Plastiken, ein vergoldetes Zierschwert der *Adjukru*, zwei Masken, zwei Statuetten und eine große Trommel der *Baule*), den Sudan (zwei Skulpturen der östlichen *Bambara* von Ouassoulou und eine *Malinke*-Figur) und den Senegal (eine *Balante*-Maske). Aus Gabun, dem Kongo und vom Ubangi kamen dagegen relativ viele Objekte. Von Ende 1889 bis 1900 erwarb das Museum etwa vierzig »Fetische« mit menschlichen und tierischen Zügen (»Nkonde« mit Nägeln, mit Spiegel und magischer Bedeutung): 35 von den *Vili* □ 98, einen von den *Woyo* (Kongo), vier von den *Teke* und einen von den *Ambete*. Außerdem erhielt es drei *Vili*-Masken, eine *Teke*-Maske und zwei Reliquiarfiguren der *Sango* und *Ondumbo*, eine *Ambete*-Büste und unter den Musikinstrumenten eine Pfeife der *Vili* und eine große *Yangere*-Trommel in Form eines Büffels, die De Brazza 1895 erworben hatte. Die einzige vor 1900 dem Museum einverleibte *Fang*-Skulptur wurde 1898 angekauft. Noch am Ende des 19. Jahrhunderts hatten die Sammlungen des Trocadéro keine Masken und Figuren der *Dogon*. Dasselbe gilt für Obervolta (*Mossi*, *Bobo*, *Bwa*, *Kurumba*) sowie die Gebiete an der Westgrenze (*Dan*, *Guere*) und im Nordosten (*Senufo*, *Lobi*). Aus Gabun und dem Kongo finden sich weder Holzarbeiten der *Kwele* und *Tsogo* noch

□ 168 *›Weibliche Figur, Rhythmusgeber‹, Senufo (Elfenbeinküste), Holz, Höhe 91,5 cm. Privatsammlung.*

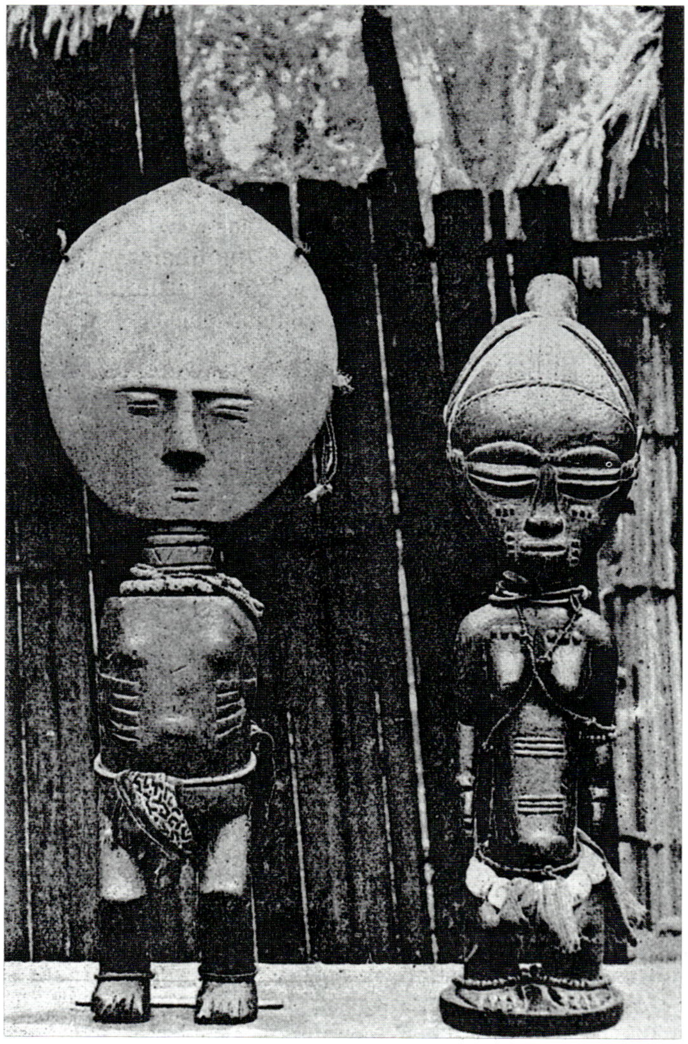

□ 169 *›Zwei Figuren aus dem Sudan‹, veröffentlicht unter der Bezeichnung Poupées fétiches des Nègres du Soudan in „Bibliothèque illustrée de voyages autour du monde“, 1888.*

verzeichnen die Inventare Masken der *Shira-Punu*, *Bembe*-Statuetten oder polychrome Köpfe von den *Mboshi*. Der Trocadéro kaufte auch keine der schon seit 1897 in England zugänglichen Bronze- und Elfenbeinplastiken aus dem Königreich Benin und auch keine Objekte aus den östlichen Savannen von Belgisch-Kongo mit Ausnahme zweier Zeremonienstäbe der *Chokwe*.

Nach dem Ende der Weltausstellung im Jahre 1900 machten die Organisationskomitees der Abteilungen Guinea und Elfenbeinküste dem Trocadéro einige Stiftungen zum Geschenk: eine Nalu-Initiationsmaske der Bruderschaft der Simo, etwa dreißig goldene Meßgewichte der *Akan*, eine Affenplastik der *Baule*, vier Grabplastiken der *Anyi* aus Ton, die so häufig reproduzierte *Grebo*-Maske aus dem Sassandragebiet □ 332 und einen Kopf aus Holz (Uhunmwun-elao) aus dem Benin, den man den *Baule* zuschreibt. Dazu kamen *Baule*-Masken und Statuetten als persönliche Schenkungen Clozels, des Generalsekretärs für die Elfenbeinküste, und Delafosse', des damaligen Verwaltungsbeauftragten der Kolonie. Im Hinblick auf einige seiner auf der Weltausstellung gezeigten Skulpturen formulierte Delafosse 1900 in *L'Anthropologie* die Hypothese von »möglichen Spuren ägyptischer Zivilisation und von Menschen der weißen Rasse im Gebiet der Elfenbeinküste«.[23]

Im letzten Viertel des 19. Jahrhunderts wurden in französischen Veröffentlichungen afrikanische Kunstwerke nur selten abgebildet. *Le Tour du monde* – neben der es bis zum Erscheinen von *La Bibliothèque illustrée des voyages autour du monde* im Jahre 1897 nichts Vergleichbares gab □ 169 – illustrierte zwar die Forschungsberichte über die bereisten Regionen und die Aktivitäten der dort ansässigen Völker mit zahlreichen Stichen □ 164. Auch wenn Abbildungen von Haushaltsgeräten, Ornamenten, Festgewändern und Musikinstrumenten vorkommen, sind doch Reproduktionen religiöser Objekte und politischer Symbole weitaus seltener. Nimmt man etwa den langen Reisebericht Bingers, *Du Niger au Golfe de Guinée*, der 1891 in *Le Tour du monde*[24] erschien und dann in zwei Bänden herauskam, so sind bei fast hundert Drucken nur sechs Masken und Plastiken abgebildet. Es gibt in Frankreich nichts Vergleichbares zu Schweinfurths *Artes Africanae* (1875),[25] den drei Bänden von Ratzels *Völkerkunde* (1875–88)[26] □ 170 oder Frobenius' *Die Masken und Geheimbünde Afrikas* (1898);[27] letzterer veröffentlichte nicht weniger als 130 Masken, die alle bekannten Gebiete Afrikas vertreten.

Die Fülle deutscher Publikationen steht offenbar in Zusammenhang mit dem Reichtum der völkerkundlichen Sammlungen in den meisten großen Städten des Landes. Berlin ist dafür

□ 170 *›Afrikanische Objekte‹, Lithographie, in Friedrich Ratzel, „Völkerkunde“, Band 1, Leipzig 1885.*

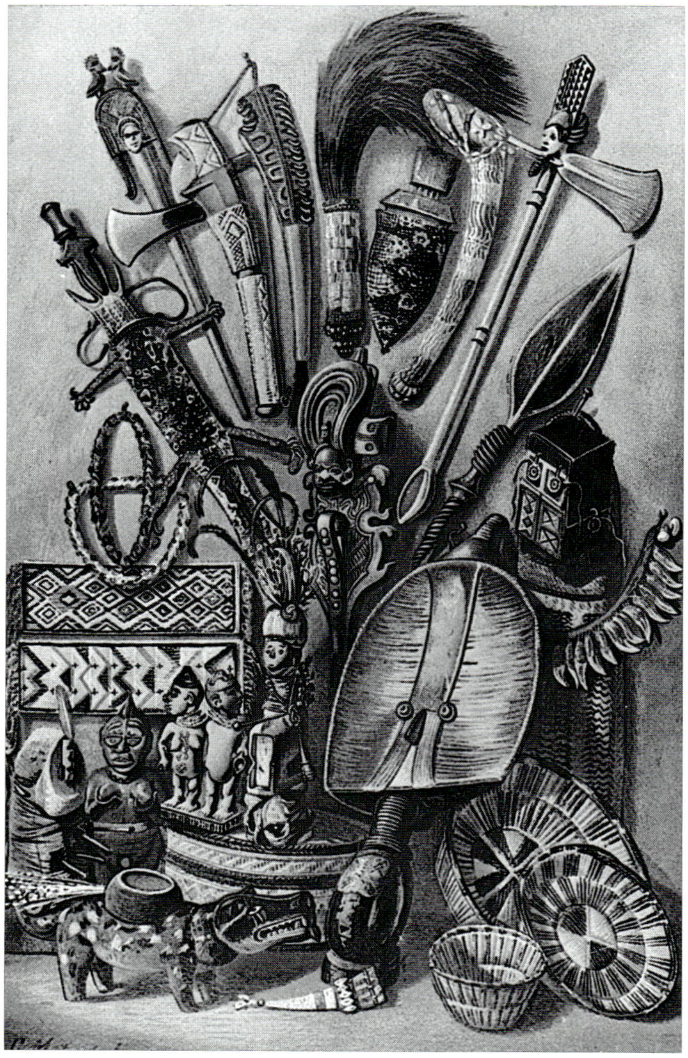

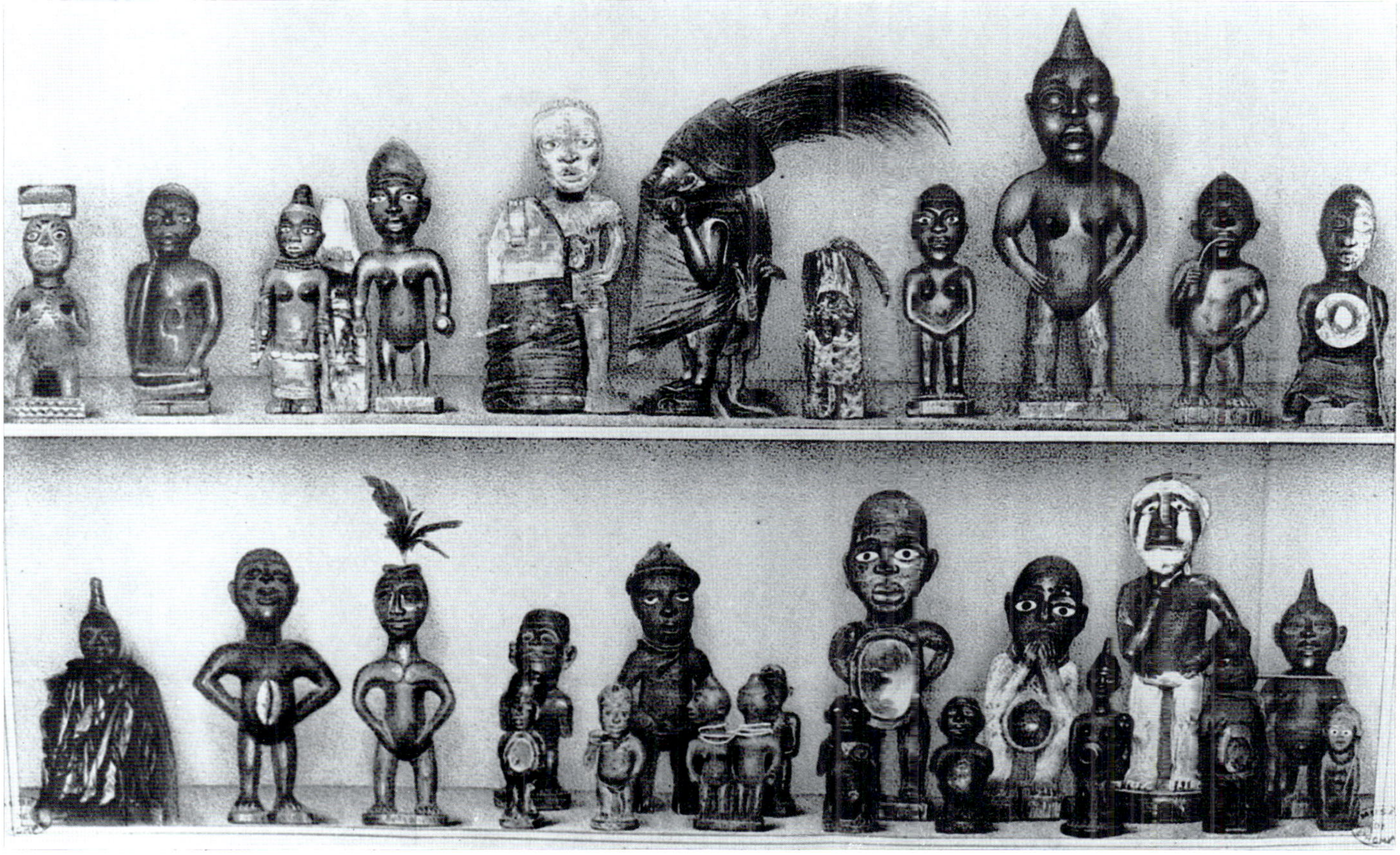

□ 171 ›Figuren von der Loangoküste‹, gesammelt von Bastian, Peschuel-Loesch und Gussfeldt, veröffentlicht in A. Bastian, „Die Deutsche Expedition an der Loangoküste“, 1874.

eines von vielen Beispielen.[28] Obwohl Deutschland zur Zeit Bismarcks nur zwei Jahre Kolonialpolitik betrieb, beherbergte das Berliner Museum für Völkerkunde bei seiner Eröffnung im Jahre 1886 fast zehntausend afrikanische Stammesobjekte. Die Sammlungen bestanden vor allem aus Stücken, die auf den großen Forschungsreisen Barths in den Zentralsudan (1850–55), von Rohlfs in das Gebiet zwischen Tripoli und der Guineaküste (1867) und kurz darauf nach Abessinien, von Nachtigal in den Ostsudan (1868–74) und von Schweinfurth in das Nilgebiet und an die Ufer des Uele (1868–71) zusammengetragen worden waren. Unter der entschlossenen Leitung von Adolf Bastian wurden die Sammlungen später erweitert. Die Teilnehmer der Deutschen Gesellschaft für die Erforschung Äquatorialafrikas (deren Gründer waren Bastian, Peschuel-Loesch und Güßfeldt) brachten zahlreiche »Fetische« der *Vili* zurück; sie hatten diese von 1872 bis 1876 an der Loangoküste gesammelt und auch wertvolle Beobachtungen über ihren Gebrauch gemacht.[29] Homeyer und Pogge schickten nach der Expedition, die nach Kimbundu und Luanda ging (1875–76), einige Objekte der *Chokwe*,[30] *Lunda* und *Luba* ein □ 568. Der österreichische Geologe O. Lenz, der 1877 für die deutsche Sektion der International Africain Association den Ogowe erforschte, stellte eine Reliquiarfigur der *Ongwe* sowie einige Stücke der *Kongo*, *Aduma* und *Ilanda* zur Verfügung. Schließlich kamen 1880 durch Flegel von allen Stationen seiner Reise Objekte der *Urhobo*, *Nupe*, *Tiv*, *Jukun*, *Mbum* und *Baya* in das Berliner Museum. Der Zeitraum von 1881 bis 1899 verzeichnet ein bedeutendes Anwachsen der Berliner Bestände; hier seien daher nur die wichtigsten Erwerbungen genannt. Der deutsche Beauftragte der International Association für den Kongo, Wissmann, erwarb auf seinen drei Expeditionen (1881–87) Arbeiten der *Songge*, *Luba*, *Kuba*, *Lulua* und *Ngombe* □ 570. Infolge der deutschen Annektion Kameruns im Jahre 1884 schickten die Soldaten und Verwalter des neuen Protektorats (Sand, Passavant, Zintgraf, Zenker, Conradt und Conrau) Objekte der *Duala*, *Kundu*, *Wute*, *Balong*, *Bafo* und *Bangwa*. Im Kongobecken sammelten für das Museum außerdem der im Dienst Leopolds II. stehende Leutnant Mikic, Buttner, Joest und Visser Objekte der *Sundi* und *Kongo* (insbesondere der *Vili*).

1897 wurde, zunächst mit dem persönlichen finanziellen Engagement Von Luschans, eine der bedeutendsten Sammlungen von Werken aus dem Benin aufgebaut □ 523. Wenige Wochen nach der Plünderung des Herrscherpalastes von Benin durch die Briten (zur Zeit der Strafexpedition, die im Februar 1897 ausgeschickt worden war, um das Massaker an fast allen Teilnehmern einer eindeutig friedlichen, den Ratgebern der *Oba* aber unerwünschten Mission zu rächen) wurde die offizielle Beute – fast tausend Bronzetafeln, die ursprünglich die Holzsäulen des Palastes zierten – vom Außenministerium in London zum Kauf angeboten. Außerdem kam bald ein großer Teil der von Soldaten des Expeditionskorps persönlich erbeuteten Objekte mit Hilfe geschäftiger Händler in Umlauf.[31] Für die ersten enthusiastischen Kommentatoren und eifrigen Käufer bedeutete diese große Zahl von Objekten mehr als nur eine Anhäufung von Kuriositäten. Nicht ohne Bewunderung erkannten sie in der vollkommenen technischen Handhabung seltener, wertvoller und dauerhafter Materialien und in dem Talent geschickter Handwerker, die es verstanden, der königlichen Machtfülle Ausdruck zu verleihen, sichere Zeichen einer großen Kunst in Afrika. Zum Beweis dienten auch die zahlreichen gelehrten Schriften, die sie schon vor 1900 teilweise beschreiben (Forbes, Pitt-Rivers, Roth, Read und Dalton in

□ 172
›Figur aus Holz, Metall und Federn‹ (Seiten- und Vorderansicht), Songge (Zaire), Höhe 112,5 cm. Sammlung J. W. Mestach, Brüssel.

Großbritannien; Carlsen, Brinkmann, Foy, Von Hagen und Von Luschan in Deutschland; Heger in Österreich; Peet in den Vereinigten Staaten). Zur selben Zeit setzt zwischen den Museen – und nicht nur völkerkundlichen – ein gewisser Wettbewerb um die charakteristischsten Beispiele dieser hochentwickelten Hofkunst ein. So kamen in den letzten drei Jahren des Jahrhunderts beträchtliche Neuzugänge in die englischen Museen Liverpool, Glasgow, Edinburgh und das Britische Museum, die kontinentaleuropäischen Hamburg, Stuttgart, Wien, Berlin, München, Leiden und Kopenhagen sowie das Field Museum in Chicago; einige erwarben nur Einzelstücke, andere ganze Serien. Die Händler (Webster, Cutter, Stevens, Bey und dann Oldman in England, Umlauff in Hamburg, Opperse in Amsterdam) spielten bei der Verbreitung dieser Kunstwerke ohne Zweifel eine entscheidende Rolle. Allein der Blick in die von W. D. Webster veröffentlichten Auktionskataloge genügt: In den 31 Ausgaben, die zwischen 1895 und 1901 erschienen, wurden nicht weniger als 546 Objekte aus Benin abgebildet und beschrieben.

So packend die Konfrontation westlicher Kunst mit den überraschenden Werken aus Benin auch gewesen sein mag, man kann wohl kaum William Faggs Feststellung folgen, daß »dieses Ereignis von unübersehbarer Bedeutung für die ersten Experimente moderner Kunst gewesen ist« und daß »es dazu beitrug, eine günstige Atmosphäre für die Anerkennung der Stammeskunst zu schaffen, unter deren Einfluß . . . die großen Neuerer unter den Künstlern in Paris und München direkte Impulse empfingen«.[32] Derain mag wohl die afrikanische Abteilung des Britischen Museums 1906 besucht haben, dennoch kann man kaum glauben, daß er gerade in der Kunst Benins eine »verblüffende« Kraft, »erstaunlich in ihrer Ausdrucksfähigkeit«, entdeckte.[33] Und aus der Tatsache, daß der Almanach des Blauen Reiters eine Bronzeplatte aus diesem Königreich abbildete,[34] läßt sich kaum auf einen Zusammenhang zwischen der Auffindung der Kunst Benins im Jahre 1897 und der »Entdeckung« afrikanischer Stammesplastik durch die Avantgarde im Jahre 1906 schließen.

Das Britische Museum entstand 1753 aus dem Nachlaß der riesigen Privatsammlung von Sir Hans Sloane, einem Arzt, der zunächst naturkundliche Objekte gesammelt hatte. Später kamen Bücher, Manuskripte, Münzen, Antiquitäten, Kunstwerke und auch völkerkundliche Objekte hinzu.[35] Von den ursprünglich 351 völkerkundlichen Sammlungsstücken waren nur 29 aus Afrika, darunter ein Gewebe aus dem Kongo und zwei elfenbeinerne Armreife aus Guinea – dies waren die ersten afrikanischen Objekte im Britischen Museum. Im Verlauf des 18. Jahrhunderts wuchs die afrikanische Abteilung langsam und ohne besondere Planung weiter an. Zu Neuerwerbungen kam es vor allem durch die Großzügigkeit von Privatleuten, wobei sich die wissenschaftlichen und kolonialen Interessen Großbritanniens widerspiegelten. Die berühmteste Expedition dieser Zeit war die Captain Cooks in den Pazifik; er kehrte mit vielen naturgeschichtlichen Funden und völkerkundlichen Gegenständen zurück, die in das Britische Museum (wie auch in viele andere europäische Museen) gelangten.

In der ersten Hälfte des 19. Jahrhunderts verzeichnete die afrikanische Abteilung zwei bemerkenswerte Neuzugänge. 1819 kehrte T. E. Bowdich aus Ghana von seiner »Mission vom

☐ 173 *›Figur aus Holz‹, Igbo (Nigeria), Höhe 98 cm. Privatsammlung, Paris.*

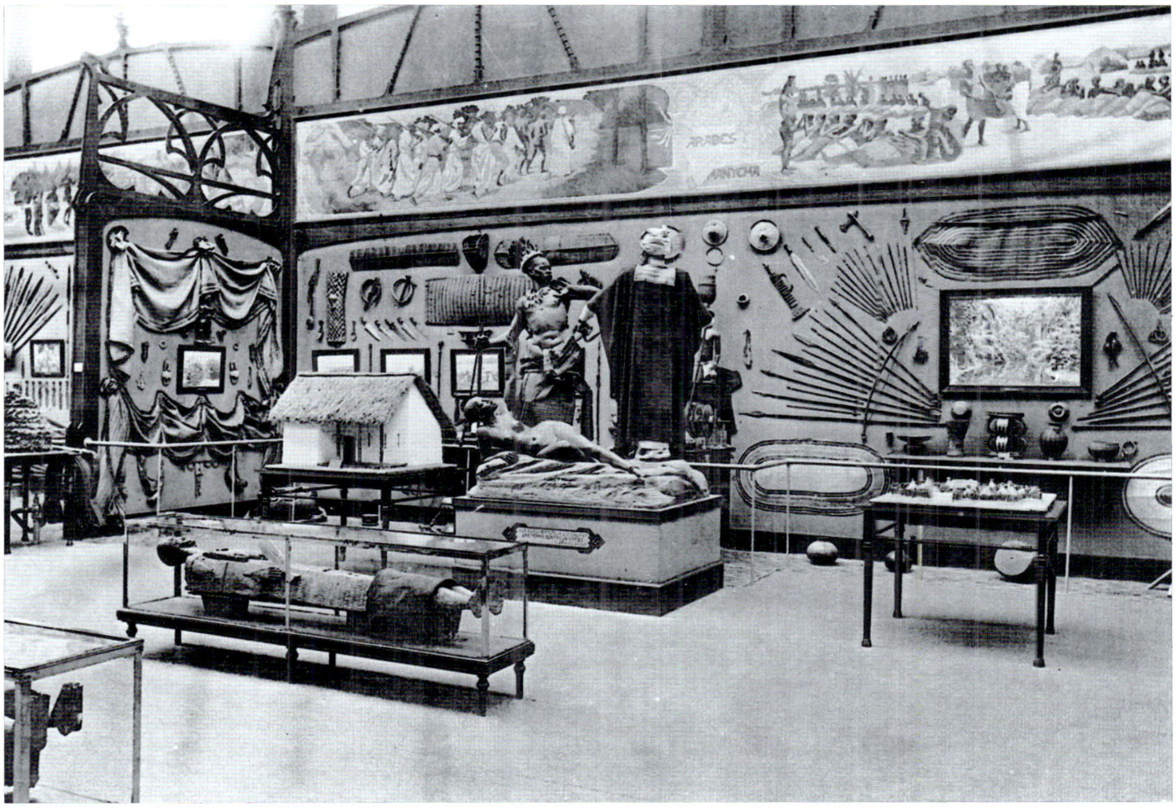

☐ 174 *Blick in Schauräume mit kongolesischen Objekten auf der Weltausstellung in Brüssel 1897, dem nachmaligen Musée Royal de l'Afrique Centrale.*

Cape Coast Castle nach Ashantee« zurück und legte neben Beispielen für Holz-, Metall- und Textilkunst »sechs Goldschmiedearbeiten« vor, die der Asantekönig für das Britische Museum vorgesehen hatte. Die anderen bedeutenden Erwerbungen aus dieser Zeit kamen 1843 mit der unglücklich verlaufenen Nigerexpedition zurück.

Unter der engagierten Leitung von Augustus Wollaston Franks entwickelte sich die gesamte völkerkundliche Abteilung in der zweiten Hälfte des 19. Jahrhunderts wesentlich schneller. Über die Verwalter und Beamten im britischen Kolonialdienst kamen zu dieser Zeit neue Exponate in die afrikanische Abteilung, so etwa Stücke aus Südafrika durch Sir Bartle Frere (1877–80), aus Nigeria durch Sir Harry Johnston (1885–87), aus Ostafrika durch Sir John Kirk (1888) und aus Mashonaland durch J. T. Bent (1893).

Im frühen 20. Jahrhundert entfalteten Amateure, Anthropologen, Reisende, Kolonialbeamte und Missionare eine rege Sammeltätigkeit. Von 1904 bis 1910 kaufte das Museum eine größere Zahl von Textilien und Skulpturen von Emil Torday, der den damaligen Belgisch-Kongo erforschte. Das Museum baute seine Bestände aus Ostafrika durch Schenkungen von Sir Claud Hollis aus Kenia (1908–10) und Sir Apolo Kagwa, des Katikiro von Uganda (1902), aus. Mr. und Mrs. Macleod Temple stifteten Objekte aus Nordnigeria und P. Amaury Talbot Stücke aus dem Südosten dieses Landes. Während der zwanziger Jahre erwarb das Museum T. R. O. Mangins Sammlung von Goldgewichten aus Messing von der Goldküste, H. S. Stannus' Sammlung aus dem Nyassaland und Objekte, die die Regierung von Tanganjika auf die British Empire Exhibition von 1924 geschickt hatte. 1933 erhielt die Völkerkunde den Status einer offiziellen Unterabteilung, und Thomas Athol Joyce wurde ihr Leiter. Die Ost- und Südafrikabestände vermehrten sich um Braunholtz' Sammlung tausender steinzeitlicher Geräte. 1934 kam die Sammlung C. A. Beving, die westafrikanische Textilien umfaßte, an das Museum ebenso wie Objekte, die Major und Mrs. P. H. G. Powell-Cotton in Französisch-Kamerun und dem englisch-ägyptischen Sudan gesammelt hatten. Ihre Tochter schenkte dem Museum bald Objekte, die sie in Somaliland und Angola gesammelt hatte.

Anhaltspunkte dafür, welche Aufmerksamkeit die modernen Künstler und ihr Umkreis von ca. 1890 bis 1905 der Stammeskunst schenkten (zu dieser Zeit besaß GAUGUIN vielleicht zwei kleine afrikanische Plastiken),[36] sind spärlich. 1905 ist das Jahr, das man im allgemeinen – doch, wie sich zeigen sollte, fälschlicherweise – als Schwelle des avantgardistischen Interesses für die »art nègre« betrachtet. Vermutungen über ein Interesse an afrikanischer Kunst vor diesem Zeitpunkt sind wenig überzeugend und mitunter widersprüchlich. So hat man etwa vorgeschlagen, daß JAMES ENSOR nach Vollendung des wichtigsten Teils seines Gesamtwerks vielleicht die Kunst des Kongo auf der Weltausstellung in Brüssel im Jahre 1897 entdeckte ☐ 174;[37] außerdem soll ein gewisser Zusammenhang zwischen den Plastiken, die der belgische Symbolist GEORGES MINNE 1890 mit Les Vingt ausstellte, und »den Fetischen wilder Stämme«[38] bestehen. Dagegen stellte CARLO CARRÀ bei einem Besuch des Trocadéro während seines ersten Aufenthalts in Paris im Jahre 1899 nur die Mittelmäßigkeit und Bedeutungslosigkeit des Museums fest.[39] JACOB EPSTEIN sah dort 1902 nur eine Masse armselig arrangierter primitiver Plastiken.[40] Ferner weist auch nichts darauf hin, daß PICASSO oder MATISSE ein besonderes Gefallen an einem der Exponate in den Kolonialpavillons der Weltausstellung von 1900 gefunden hätten.

Das Fehlen gesicherter Fakten für die Zeit um die Jahrhun-

□ 175 *Anzeige von Emile Heymanns Kuriositätengeschäft Au Vieux Rouet, Paris 1909.*

dertwende (1897–1903) kann jedoch nicht die Annahme rechtfertigen, daß die Anerkennung der primitiven Kunst durch die Künstler der Moderne ganz plötzlich und rein zufällig kam, wie uns viele Memoiren glauben machen wollen. Wie man nicht die historischen Bedingungen überschätzen sollte, die diese Anerkennung als Teil eines Prozesses erscheinen lassen, der schon vor dem Ende des 19. Jahrhunderts begann, so sollte man sich aber auch nicht auf Quellen verlassen, die die Neubewertung primitiver Kunst in die Zeit vor 1906 datieren.

Keiner der Berichte über die Ereignisse des Jahres 1904 ist glaubwürdig oder ausreichend gesichert.

Während Vlaminck selbst, der wohl kaum seine Rolle als Entdecker der Negerkunst schmälern wollte, diese Entdeckung in das Jahr 1905 legt,[41] datiert sie Goldwater aufgrund einer fragwürdigen Information Kahnweilers ein Jahr früher.[42] Andererseits nimmt Goldwater an, daß Matisse die ersten Objekte »vielleicht« 1904 erwarb, auf jeden Fall aber »vor 1906«.[43] Es sind drei Berichte des Künstlers überliefert, die dieser Hypothese widersprechen. Außerdem scheint keine der Sammlungen, die wenige Kenner aufbauten und deren Anfänge ins Jahr 1904 zurückgehen sollen, wirklich in diesem Jahr angelegt worden zu sein. André Level behauptet in einer privaten Mitteilung an Goldwater aus dem Jahre 1934[44] und später auch in seinen »Memoiren«, daß es im Jahre 1904 war, »als er beim Anblick der ersten Negerplastiken vor Anmut gerührt wurde«.[45] Doch fand diese Begegnung bei Matisse statt – was eine spätere Datierung ergibt, also auf 1906 oder wahrscheinlich danach. Jean Laude seinerseits nimmt an, daß Félix Fénéon mit dem Sammeln einiger afrikanischer Objekte »um 1904« begann.[46] Doch die beiden Herausgeber seiner Schriften, Françoise Cachin[47] und Joan Halperin,[48] stimmen darin überein, daß seine ersten Erwerbungen von »art nègre« in das Jahr 1919 fallen. Wahrscheinlich fing Fénéon schon vor 1919 zu sammeln an, doch keinesfalls in den ersten Jahren des Jahrhunderts. Wie William Rubin herausfand (siehe S. 291), bezeichnete Fénéon Picassos *Demoiselles* 1907 als Karikatur, erkannte in ihnen aber nichts Afrikanisches. Die Aussage Paul Guillaumes[49] über die eigene Entdeckung einer Bobo-Dioulasso-Figur – 1904 in einer Wäscherei im Montmartre –, die er sofort Apollinaire gezeigt haben will, verliert durch zwei Fakten an Glaubwürdigkeit: durch sein Alter (er war damals erst zwölfeinhalb) und dadurch, daß er den Dichter erst 1911 kennenlernte.

Daß Braque, André Lhote und Vlaminck 1905 afrikanische Plastiken erwarben, ist eher möglich, *wenn es dafür auch keinen sicheren Nachweis gibt.* Während des Sommers, den er zusammen mit Manolo und dem Kritiker Maurice Raynal zwischen Honfleur und Le Havre verbrachte, solle Braque von einem Matrosen eine Maske aus Gabun gekauft haben.[50] Im Juli desselben Jahres soll Lhote einem Trödler auf der Place Mériadeck in Bordeaux drei Francs für etwas bezahlt haben, das der Beschreibung nach eine Maske von der westlichen Elfenbeinküste gewesen sein muß.[51] Schließlich gibt es die oft erzählte Geschichte von Vlaminck, der wahrscheinlich Ende des Sommers dafür, daß er den Gästen eines Cafés in Argenteuil eine Runde spendierte, angeblich »zwei Statuetten aus Dahome, die mit rotem, gelben und weißem Ocker bemalt waren, sowie eine ganz schwarze Figur von der Elfenbeinküste« erhielt.[52] Wenn schon ein Zweifel an Vlamincks Vordatierung seiner Entdeckung besteht, muß es noch schwerer fallen, ihm abzunehmen, daß er 1905 von einem Freund seines Vaters »eine große Maske und zwei wunderbare Statuen von der Elfenbeinküste«[53] erhielt und die Maske noch im gleichen Jahr an seinen Freund Derain verkaufte □ 257. In den beiden Versionen Vlamincks von diesen Vorgängen[54] hebt er deren zeitliche Nähe ausdrücklich hervor; in einer gibt er sogar an, sie hätte im Abstand von nur wenigen Tagen stattgefunden. Beide Versionen geben die gleichen Gründe dafür an, weshalb Vlaminck schnell, aber mit Bedauern, ein Objekt verkaufte, das ihn beunruhigte und zugleich faszinierte: Er hatte damals mit großen finanziellen Problemen zu kämpfen. Die Aussage, daß Derain seine Erwerbung in sein Atelier in der Rue Tourlaque brachte, wo sie von Picasso und Matisse »beeindruckt«, »verwirrt und bewegt« betrachtet wurde, läßt sich stützen. Diese Informationen scheinen zu genügen, um den Erwerb der beiden Statuetten aus Dahome durch Vlaminck in das Jahr 1906 – wahrscheinlich Ende März – sowie seine Begegnung mit den Werken von der Elfenbeinküste in die erste Aprilhälfte zu datieren. Derain war nach seiner Rückkehr aus London Anfang April in die Rue Tourlaque gezogen. Die prekäre wirtschaftliche Situation Vlamincks und seiner Familie verbesserte sich zeitweise, als Vollard in der zweiten Aprilhälfte alle Gemälde in seinem Atelier aufkaufte.[55]

Was Matisse' damaligen Kauf eines »Negerobjekts« betrifft, stimmen alle Auskünfte des Künstlers selbst in drei Interviews – mit Pierre Courthion 1941,[56] André Warnod 1945,[57] E. Tériade 1952[58] – bis auf ein Detail überein. Auf dem Weg zu einem Besuch bei Gertrude Stein in der Rue de Fleurus bemerkte Matisse im Fenster von Emile Heymanns Geschäft für exotische Kuriositäten in der Rue de Rennes 87 ein »Negerobjekt« und kaufte es für ein paar Francs. Bei seiner Ankunft in der Wohnung Steins zeigte er es Picasso, der bei

□ 176 *›Maske‹, Ost-Bamileke (Kamerun), Holz, Höhe 76 cm. Privatsammlung.*

seinem Anblick eine gewisse Begeisterung erkennen ließ. Das Interview mit Courthion enthält einige Details, die bei den beiden anderen nicht auftauchen: MATISSE betonte, daß dies das erste Objekt gewesen sei, das er gekauft und mit fünfzig Francs bezahlt habe; es sei das erste Objekt gewesen, dem PICASSO einige Aufmerksamkeit geschenkt habe. Folgt man MATISSE, war dies der Anfang einer Begegnung, die primitive Kunst neu bewertete und der sich DERAIN erst anschloß, als er die große Maske von VLAMINCK bekommen hatte.

Es besteht allerdings ein Unterschied zwischen den drei Versionen: Gegenüber Courthion und Warnod sprach MATISSE von einer Statuette, gegenüber Tériade von einem kleinen Kopf. (Man sollte die oft gehörte Variante, wonach das Objekt eine Maske war, völlig ausschließen; diese Interpretation ist das Ergebnis einer schlechten französischen Übersetzung des Interviews mit Tériade, das ursprünglich auf Englisch veröffentlicht wurde.)[59]

Zwei indirekte Belege bestätigen diesen Bericht und runden ihn ab: Trotz eines falschen Datums stimmt das, was Max Jacob dem Schwiegersohn des Künstlers, Georges Duthuit, mitteilte, damit überein.[60] Gertrude Stein ihrerseits gab den historischen Augenblick genauer an: Es ereignete sich, nachdem PICASSO ihr Portrait vollendet hatte. Damit gewinnt die Datierung auf den Herbst 1906 an Gewißheit.[61] Untersucht man die verschiedenen Berichte Max Jacobs über seinen Besuch von MATISSE am Quai Saint-Michel in Begleitung PICASSOS, Apollinaires und Salmons offenbar ein paar Tage nach dem besagten Treffen bei Gertrude Stein, stellt man fest, daß immer von einer Statuette die Rede ist.[62] Alles legt die Vermutung nahe, daß der »kleine Kopf« in der Version Tériades nur Ausdruck für MATISSE' besonderes Interesse an diesem Teil des Ganzen ist. So gesehen galt die Parallele, die der Künstler zwischen der Statuette und den Porphyrköpfen der ägyptischen Abteilung des Louvre zog, nur in Hinblick auf den Kopf.

Die Zweideutigkeit der Version Tériades wäre durch eine genaue Beschreibung des Objekts zu vermeiden gewesen. Bisher zweifelt man noch an der Glaubwürdigkeit der einzigen existierenden Beschreibung, wahrscheinlich weil die Worte ihres Autors im allgemeinen nicht als sehr zuverlässig gelten. Max Jacob spricht von »einer kleinen, sitzenden Figur [bonhomme], die die Zunge herausstreckt«.[63] Hinter der scheinbaren Extravaganz dieser Feststellung zeichnet sich ein Umriß, eine Pose und eine Haltung ab, und auch die Größe wird erkennbar. Die Beschreibung paßt genau auf eine *VILI*-Statuette, die man in dem Teil von MATISSE' Hinterlassenschaft fand, der nach dem Tod seiner Tochter Marguerite deren Sohn zufiel □ 178, 260. Unzweifelhaft handelt es sich hier um die Plastik, von der in den eben zitierten, zahlreichen Berichten die Rede ist.

MATISSE' Begegnung mit der weißen Maske in DERAINS Atelier, die VLAMINCK so hervorhob, muß wie der Besuch im Atelier am Quai Saint-Michel nach dem Kauf der *VILI*-Statuette stattgefunden haben. Das heißt nicht unbedingt, wie MATISSE glaubte, daß DERAIN die *FANG*-Maske kaufte, nachdem MATISSE selbst seine Statuette erworben hatte. Während es einerseits nicht zu beweisen ist, daß PICASSO im Frühjahr die Maske im Atelier an der Rue Tourlague sah – dies ist sogar recht unwahrscheinlich –, ist es andererseits kaum vorstellbar, daß er sie ungefähr sechs Monate später übersah, als seine Kontakte zu MATISSE und DERAIN etwas enger wurden.

□ 177 *›Figur aus Holz‹*, *MBEMBE (Nigeria), Höhe 74 cm. Privatsammlung.*

□ 178 *›Figur aus Holz‹, VILI (Volksrepublik Kongo), Höhe 24 cm. Privatsammlung, ehemals Sammlung Henri Matisse. Vorderansicht* □ *260.*

Die Begegnung mit der afrikanischen Kunst fand also, von einigen denkbaren, aber nicht nachzuweisenden Einzelentdeckungen im Jahre 1905 abgesehen (durch BRAQUE, LHOTE und VLAMINCK), erst im Herbst 1906 statt. Dabei waren die *FANG*-Maske und die *VILI*-Statuette die Katalysatoren, DERAIN und MATISSE die Initiatoren. PICASSO sah vermutlich einige der Stücke zwischen dem August 1906 und dem Frühjahr des folgenden Jahres, er zeigte jedoch erst etwa Juni 1907 ein wirkliches Interesse an der Stammeskunst. Verschiedene Erfahrungen hatten jeden auf seine Weise darauf vorbereitet: Für MATISSE waren es im Sommer 1905 die Diskussionen bei Daniel de Montfreid mit MAILLOL über die Werke GAUGUINS – »es war vielleicht Maillol, der Matisse' Aufmerksamkeit auf die Negerplastik lenkte«;[64] für DERAIN waren es die Besuche des Trocadéro von 1904 und der Afrikaabteilung des Britischen Museums vom März 1906, dann vor allem seine Erwerbung im Monat darauf. Für PICASSO war es vermutlich die Entdeckung der iberischen Plastik aus Osuna im Louvre Anfang 1906.

Welche Objekte PICASSO vorher auch gesehen hat, man sollte die Bedeutung seines Besuchs im Trocadéro im Frühjahr 1907 nicht unterschätzen. Ohne im Widerspruch zu früheren Erfahrungen zu stehen, offenbarte sich PICASSO durch diese neue Erfahrung die primitive Kunst in einer Bedeutung und Dimension, die er bis dahin nicht wahrgenommen hatte. Der Bericht, den er dreißig Jahre später André Malraux darüber gab, ist in dieser Hinsicht sehr erhellend.[65] Als er allein die Räume des Trocadéro betrat, wünschte er sogleich der abstoßenden Atmosphäre des Ortes zu entfliehen, fühlte sich aber gleichzeitig unwiderstehlich angezogen: »Es war ekelhaft. Der Flohmarkt. Der Geruch . . . Ich wollte sofort wieder hinaus. Ich ging nicht. Ich blieb. Ich blieb.« Er fühlte, daß »sich in ihm etwas ereignete, . . . daß es sehr wichtig war«. Ihm wurde plötzlich

□ 179 *Afrikanische und ozeanische Objekte aus der Sammlung Henri Matisse im Haus eines seiner Erben, Paris 1976.*

klar, »warum er Maler war«. Denn anders als DERAIN, MATISSE und BRAQUE, für die »Fetische«, »les nègres«, nur einfach »gute Plastiken . . . wie andere auch« waren, hatte er erkannt, daß diese Masken vor allem »magische Dinge«, »Medien«, »Vermittler« zwischen dem Menschen und den dunklen Mächten des Bösen waren, genauso mächtig wie die »drohenden Geister« auf der ganzen Welt, »Werkzeuge« und »Waffen«, mit denen man sich von den Gefahren und Ängsten, die die Menschheit bedrohen, befreien konnte.

Ohne die Empfindungen PICASSOS in diesem »schrecklichen Museum« schmälern zu wollen, muß man einräumen, daß sie eine gewisse Berechtigung hatten. 1907 war der afrikanische Saal □ 162, 452 nicht, wie man sich heute vielleicht vorstellt, eine geräumige Halle für öffentliche Bildungszwecke, wo methodisch geordnete, sorgsam gepflegte und etikettierte Sammlungen unter publikumsfreundlichen Bedingungen ausgestellt waren. Es war vielmehr ein sehr kleines, überfülltes Depot, in dem einige der erstaunlichsten, je vom menschlichen Geist ersonnenen Werke hastig und ohne jedes Konzept aufgestellt worden waren. An den Wänden standen »vorübergehend« Glaskästen, die mitunter aus den schlecht zugeschnittenen Brettern von Versandkisten bestanden. Diese Schränke wankten unter dem Gewicht der ihnen aufgetürmten Objekte und unter mannigfachen Gerätschaften, die oben darauf gestellt waren, daß man kaum eines vom andern unterscheiden konnte. Diese waren ihrerseits mit Waffen aller Art und weniger sperrigen Stücken vermischt, die als »Wandtrophäen« aufgehängt waren. Man konnte sich kaum vom Rand zur Mitte bewegen, mußte bei jedem Schritt aufpassen, nicht zu stolpern: hier gegen eine lebensgroße menschliche Statue, dort gegen einen überladenen Ausstellungsschrank.

Dieses Durcheinander erschwerte jede objektive Einschätzung und verringerte jede kritische Distanz zwischen dem disparaten, unfreiwillig zusammengeratenen Ensemble und seinen überraschten und gebannten Betrachtern. Eine seltsame Vertrautheit, die nicht allein von der erzwungenen Enge ausging, stellte sich ein. Man konnte schon erschrecken vor den Mischwesen dieses phantastischen Bestiariums □ 162, vor der Gewalt und dem Schmerz, die von diesen geritzten oder mit Nägeln gespickten Körpern ausgingen, vor der Angst, die einem die wildblickenden, geisterhaften Erscheinungen einjagten, oder vor dem wie durch Zauberei belebten Material.

Dennoch bot dieses vom Sakralen geprägte Universum nicht die Bilder eines fernen, von rachsüchtigen Gottheiten und dämonischen Monstren bevölkerten Pantheons dar. Selten von überwältigender Monumentalität, verband es statt dessen chthonische Geister, lebendige Vorfahren, heilspendende Muttergottheiten und schützende Fetische. Damit wurde es möglich, die Vermischung des Heiligen mit der menschlichen Erfahrung, das Ineinanderfließen des kultischen und des alltäglichen Lebens zu betrachten.

Eine andere Welt wurde heraufbeschworen, eine Zwischenwelt zwar, die aber glaubwürdig, lebendig und vermenschlicht war. Man war eingeladen zum Übernatürlichen, aber zu einem gebändigten Übernatürlichen. Was PICASSO im Trocadéro entdeckte, was ihn durchdrang, hat sich vielleicht auf dieser Bewußtseinsebene abgespielt. Jedenfalls zog Christian Zervos, mit dem er darüber sprach, diesen Schluß daraus. »Die Kunst der primitiven Völker hatte tatsächlich nur insoweit einen Einfluß auf Picasso, als sie ihm eine Weltsicht erlaubte, die Erscheinungsbild und Charakter seines ästhetischen Erfahrungshorizonts veränderte, und sie ihm eine neue Darstellung der Welt anbot, in der sich die Erfahrung und das Übernatürliche durchdringen und dadurch als eine einzige Wirklichkeit erscheinen. Sie ermöglicht ihm, die ihn umgebenden Dinge sowohl im Zusammenhang ihrer Formen als auch in ihrer individuellen Verbundenheit mit dem Bereich des Übernatürlichen zu betrachten.«[66]

In den beiden letzten Monaten des Jahres 1906, nach dem Tod CÉZANNES und der zweiten Retrospektive von GAUGUINS Werk im Salon d'Automne, begann für ihn und einige der von ihm als avanciert eingestuften Künstler das, was MATISSE »die Zeit der künstlerischen Kosmogonien« nannte.[67] Die Zeit der »Entdeckung« war vorbei, das Gefallen an »les bois nègres« hatte sich bei allen – wenn auch nicht in gleicher Weise, so doch mit gleicher Intensität – durchgesetzt. Dies kann man an den Käufen sehen, die MATISSE, PICASSO, BRAQUE, VLAMINCK und DERAIN zwischen 1908 und 1914 tätigten.

□ 180 *Henri Rousseau, ›Bildnis Joseph Brummer‹, 1909, Öl auf Leinwand, 116 x 89 cm. Privatsammlung, Schweiz*

Nach Kahnweiler besaß Matisse 1908 »eine Sammlung von etwa 20 Stücken verschiedener Herkunft« □ 179.[68] André Level erinnert sich, etwa zur gleichen Zeit »im Besitz des Künstlers einige ziemlich zerbrechliche Objekte, Stäbe mit kleinen, klar erkennbaren und sauber gearbeiteten Köpfen« gesehen zu haben.[69] Wenn wir Pierre Schneiders Behauptung folgen, daß sich Matisse nur solcher Objekte entledigte, die er in seinem späteren Leben erworben hatte,[70] wie etwa der Südmalekula-Figur □ 466, 467, die in Picassos Besitz überging, oder des »äthiopischen« Sessels, der sich heute im Museum von Nizza befindet, können wir aus dem Besitz seiner Erben die wahrscheinlich vor dem ersten Weltkrieg geschaffene Sammlung rekonstruieren: Neben »zwei Stäben«, einer von den *Chokwe*, der andere von den *Kongo* mit einem menschenähnlichen Kopf aus Elfenbein, enthielt sie drei Reliquiarfiguren (eine der *Tsogo* und zwei der *Fang*), einige Statuetten (jeweils eine der *Vili* □ 178, *Bembe* und *Bambara* aus dem Segoubezirk, die 1917 von Paul Guillaume abgebildet wurde), eine weiße *Shira-Punu*-Maske, eine *Pende*-Maske, einen Becherhalter der *Kuba*, einen ausgehöhlten *Kuba*-Kopf von zweifelhafter Authentizität und eine weibliche Figur mit ausgestreckten Armen □ 285, die der Katalog der Ausstellung in der Galerie Pigalle 1930, wo sie gezeigt wurde, für eine Elfenbeinarbeit vom unteren Kongo ausgab.

Braque besaß damals die *Fang*-Maske und eine geschwungene Harfe, die auf einer Photographie von 1911 zu sehen ist □ 421,[71] sowie Objekte, die er wahrscheinlich im Sommer 1912 erwarb und die auf einer jüngeren Photographie erscheinen □ 181:[72] drei *Bambara*-Statuetten, ein Bildnis aus dem unteren Kongogebiet und zwei Plastiken, die nicht mit Sicherheit identifiziert werden können. Mit der schon genannten, 1905 gekauften *Tsogo*-Maske, dem *Dan*-Objekt und einigen *Kuba*-Textilien ist Braques Sammlung bereits komplett – so wie sie damals aussah und auch bleiben sollte. Sie war bei weitem nicht so umfangreich wie die Picassos, deren Zustandekommen William Rubin weiter unten bespricht (siehe S. 304ff.).

Da wir wissen, daß Vlaminck außer der Maske, die er an Derain abtrat, Jos Hessel alles verkaufte, was er seit seiner Entdeckung in Argenteuil[73] gesammelt hatte, läßt sich unmöglich sagen, was er nach 1908 erwarb, sei es in den Trödelläden des Montmartre, auf dem Pariser Flohmarkt oder in Marseille durch die Vermittlung Derains, der den Winter 1908/09 in dem nahegelegenen Martigues verbrachte.

□ 181 *Blick in das Atelier von Georges Braque, Paris um 1914.*

Trotz der ständigen Fluktuation von Derains Sammlung, die jede Annahme über ihren Charakter und Umfang vor 1914 zur reinen Spekulation macht, zeigt eine Photographie von 1912/13 □ 275,[74] daß sich in seinem Atlier drei *Fang*-Masken, einschließlich der von Vlaminck gekauften □ 257, zwei Reliquiarfiguren desselben Stammes, ein Antilopenkopfschmuck der *Bambara* und eine *Senufo*-Statue befanden.

Für die Zeit von 1908 bis 1914 stehen die Aktivitäten eines ungarischen Bildhauers, der kurz nach seiner Ankunft in Paris als Kunsthändler auftrat, mit unserem Thema in Zusammenhang. So war es Joseph Brummer, der neben der kleinen Schar von Künstlern, die die ersten Entdecker der »art nègre« waren, an ihrer Durchsetzung mitwirkte und der außerdem ihre Verbreitung in einigen mitteleuropäischen Metropolen noch vor dem ersten Weltkrieg vorantrieb.[75]

Nachdem Brummer in Budapest an der Schule für angewandte Kunst, in München bei Rühmann und in Nagybanya bei Istvan Réti studiert hatte, setzte er in Paris seine Ausbildung ohne großen Enthusiasmus fort; er besuchte den Unterricht bei Rodin, Matisse und in einigen Kunstakademien auf dem Montparnasse. Wenn er kein Geld mehr hatte, nahm er alle möglichen Arbeiten an, aber schon bald konnte er über den Verkauf japanischer Drucke im Auftrag etablierter Händler in einigen Secondhand-Läden »Negerobjekte« erstehen, die er dann den wohlhabenderen seiner Kommilitonen in den Akademien feilbot.

Nach einigem Erfolg mit diesen kleinen Geschäften, die er in seiner armseligen Behausung in der Rue Falguière angefangen

☐ 182 *Afrikanische Objekte aus der Sammlung Guillaume Apollinaire in seiner Bibliothek, Photographie um 1954. Eine Gesamtansicht der Bibliothek ☐ 429.*

hatte, legte er – wahrscheinlich 1909, vielleicht auch ein Jahr früher – seine ersten Gewinne in der Anmietung eines Ladens am Boulevard Raspail 6 an, wo er Plastiken aus Afrika und Ozeanien zusammen mit Gemälden des Zöllners ROUSSEAU verkaufte. Brummers erstaunliches Talent wurde offenkundig, als er zwischen den beiden Weltkriegen zu einem der reichsten und angesehensten Händler in New York wurde. Doch hier soll gezeigt werden, wie Brummer über viele freundschaftliche Beziehungen, die im günstigen Klima vor dem 1. Weltkrieg begonnen hatten, als junge Künstler aus den Vereinigten Staaten und aus ganz Europa nach den Grundlagen der modernen Kunst fragten, die Konfrontation mit einer ihrer wesentlichen Quellen förderte.

Die entscheidende Rolle, die damals der Kreis um Gertrude Stein spielte, ist zurecht hervorgehoben worden. Wir wissen nicht, ob Brummer dazugehörte oder nur Außenseiter blieb. Er verdankte jedenfalls seine Einschreibung in der von MATISSE 1908 eröffneten Akademie der Fürsprache Sarah Steins und des deutschen Malers HANS PURRMANN, an den er durch MAX WEBER, einen amerikanischen Kommilitonen an der Grande Chaumière, weiterempfohlen worden war. Über WEBER bzw. PURRMANN lernte er viele Künstler und Kritiker kennen, die seine Pläne unterstützten oder die er selbst von seinen Ansichten überzeugte. Es scheint, daß die meisten von ihnen auf die eine oder andere Weise mit dem Schicksal der »art nègre« im Westen verknüpft waren.

Wie PICASSO, dessen Werk und Atelier er kannte, formulierte MAX WEBER seine Konzeption des »Primitiven« in Beziehung zur afrikanischen Plastik, die er über Exponate der frühen Sammlungen des Trocadéro kennengelernt hatte,[76] und zur Malerei ROUSSEAUS, den er ob seiner durch und durch modernen Wahrheit bewunderte. So verhalf WEBER Brummer im März 1908 zu einer Begegnung mit ROUSSEAU. Etwa zur selben Zeit wurde, wieder über WEBER, der New Yorker Robert Coady ein häufiger Besucher in ROUSSEAUS Atelier. Ein paar Jahre später stellte er in seinen Galerien in der Fifth Avenue und am Washington Square, dann auch in seiner Zeitschrift *The Soil* Beispiele afrikanischer Kunst vor, nicht nur wegen ihres künstlerischen Werts, sondern auch, um damit für ein gleiches Ideal auf amerikanischem Boden einen Anstoß zu geben.[77] Brummer lernte auch einen anderen Freund WEBERS, Patrick Henry Bruce, kennen; dessen Sammlung war der Größe und der Qualität nach bedeutend genug, daß ihn die Veranstalter einiger wichtiger Ausstellungen der zwanziger und dreißiger Jahre um Leihgaben baten.[78] Außerdem freundete sich Brummer – ob über WEBER, wissen wir nicht – mit dem Maler FRANK BURTY HAVILAND an und beschaffte ihm Stücke für seine 1908 begonnene Sammlung afrikanischer und ozeanischer Kunst.[79] Andererseits machte Brummer über PURRMANN die Bekanntschaft von Karl Ernst Osthaus, einem Sammler aus Hagen, und Carl Einsteins, eines deutschen Schriftstellers, der auf seine Anregung hin das erste Buch über die Ästhetik der afrikanischen Kunst veröffentlichte.[80] Eine Gruppe Deutscher war ständig zu Gast im Café Dôme am Montmartre; dort konnte man Brummer zusammen mit Rudolf Levy, seinem einstigen Kompagnon im Laden am Boulevard Raspail, oder zusammen mit dem polnischen Kunstkritiker Adolphe Basler sehen, der regelmäßiger Besucher der »musikalischen Abende« bei ROUSSEAU war und der später ein Buch mit dem Titel *Art among Primitive Peoples* schrieb. Außerdem traf Brummer dort den tschechischen Maler WALTER BONDY und seine beiden Landsleute, die Bildhauer ERNST ASCHER und BELA HEIN (diese drei wurden Kunsthändler, BONDY in Berlin, letztere in Paris).

Obwohl es keinen Beweis dafür gibt, daß Brummer Guillaume Apollinaire vor 1911 kennenlernte, scheint es doch sicher, daß sie sich bereits Ende 1908, spätestens Anfang 1909 zum ersten Mal trafen. Es ist auch nicht auszuschließen, daß Brummer wenn auch nicht als erster (dies war wahrscheinlich PICASSO), so doch als einer der ersten Apollinaire dazu anregte, afrikanische Plastik zu sammeln.

Apollinaire war irgendwann zwischen April 1906 und November 1907 bei ROUSSEAU eingeführt worden. Zufällig wissen wir aus der ROUSSEAU gewidmeten Sonderausgabe von *Les Soirées de Paris,* wie die Entstehungsbedingungen für die Erstfassung von *Muse inspirant un poète* aussahen; das Werk stammt von 1909, aber Apollinaire mußte dem Maler dafür im November und Dezember 1908 Modell sitzen, als Brummer und WEBER, der vor seiner Heimreise in die Vereinigten Staaten stand, oft im Atelier in der Rue Perrel waren. Außerdem folgte auf die *Muse* als erstes Portrait dasjenige Brummers ☐ 180. ROUSSEAU malte es vor dem Frühjahr 1909, da es im Salon des Indépendants ausgestellt werden sollte. Daher wäre es unwahrscheinlich, wenn sich Brummer und Apollinaire nicht schon zu dieser Zeit gekannt hätten.

Der genaue Zeitpunkt, wann Apollinaire begann, afrikanische Kunst zu sammeln, ist bislang noch nicht ermittelt worden. Der französische Herausgeber seines Gesamtwerks, der auch

☐ 183 *›Maske‹, MBUNDA (Sambia), Holz, Höhe 43 cm. Privatsammlung.*

□ 184 *›Maske‹*, WURKUN *(Nigeria), Holz, Höhe 175 cm. Privatsammlung, Paris.*

einen Aufsatz »Guillaume Apollinaire devant l'art nègre«[81] verfaßt hat, äußert sich dazu nicht. Zu Apollinaires Umzug in die Rue Gros 37 in Argenteuil im Jahre 1910 merkt er lediglich an, daß dieser sich für Negerkunst zu interessieren anfing. Über die Identität seines ersten Kunsthändlers wurden mehrere Hypothesen aufgestellt: U.a. wird behauptet, es sei René Dupuy gewesen, ein Kindheitsfreund und Marineoffizier (daher mit Seehäfen vertraut), der später unter dem Pseudonym René Dalize für *Les Soirées de Paris* schrieb.[82]

Diese These, die von ihrem Urheber nicht belegt wird, ist unwahrscheinlich. Sie geht von der Reisetätigkeit des Fähnrichs Dupuy aus. Diese wurde durch seinen Abschied von der Marine im Jahre 1907 unterbrochen, und es ist mehr als unwahrscheinlich, daß Apollinaire schon vor diesem Zeitpunkt mit dem Sammeln afrikanischer Plastik begonnen hatte. Dafür gibt es nicht die geringsten Hinweise. Salmon, der den mittellosen Seemann bei seinen Landurlauben oft bei sich aufnahm, berichete, daß sich der Inhalt von Dupuys Kiste auf ein paar Bücher und das zum Opiumrauchen nötige Gerät beschränkte; das einzig Exotische darin war eine Pfeife aus Kanton.

Es wurde auch behauptet, daß Félix Fénéon derjenige war, der »Apollinaire um 1910 die ersten Stammesobjekte, die der Dichter erwarb, verkaufte«.[83] Sicherlich unterhielt Apollinaire schon seit 1904 freundschaftliche Beziehungen zu Fénéon. Doch wie wir bereits feststellten, ist allein die Datierung des Beginns von Fénéons Sammlung umstritten. Außerdem arbeitete Fénéon »um 1910« in der Galerie Bernheim mit Jos Hessel zusammen, der angeblich schon seit 1905 sammelte. Daher bedarf es sicherer Beweise, um diese voreilige Feststellung akzeptieren zu können. Es wurde auch auf eine frühe Version von *Le poète assassiné* aus dem Jahre 1907 hingewiesen, worin PICASSO im Hinblick auf eine *FON*-Bronze Apollinaires als »Vogel von Benin« bezeichnet wird. Dieser Hinweis soll beweisen, daß der Dichter damals ein Objekt afrikanischer Herkunft besaß.[84] Tatsächlich aber taucht das PICASSO gewidmete Epithet erst im späteren Manuskript von 1911 auf.[85]

Ich muß meinerseits gestehen, daß ich keinen schlüssigen Beweis für meine eigene Hypothese liefern kann. Es erscheint mir nur logischer, daß Brummer derjenige war, der Apollinaire wohl im Spätjahr 1909 die ersten afrikanischen Plastiken verkaufte oder schenkte. Die Rolle eines gelegentlichen Kundschafters, die der *flâneur* auf beiden Seiten des Seineufers für den Händler bald spielen sollte, läßt wohl den Schluß zu, daß sie gemeinsame Interessen hatten.

Wenn es auch nicht allein ihrer Initiative zu verdanken ist, so trugen Apollinaire und Brummer doch zur Verbreitung der Stammeskunst in den Prager Künstlerkreisen vor 1914 bei.[86] Afrikanische Plastiken gab es jedoch schon seit den achtziger Jahren in Böhmen, wenn auch nur durch die von dem Naturforscher Emil Holub auf seinen Expeditionen nach Zentral- und Südafrika zwischen 1872 und 1879 gesammelten Stammesobjekte. Am Ende des Jahrhunderts hatte Albert Sachs, ein deutscher Glasperlenhersteller mit einer Fabrik in Nordböhmen, der seine Erzeugnisse nach Nigeria und an die Goldküste ausführte, in einer Art Glaswarenmuseum in Jablonec eine Sammlung afrikanischer Objekte ausgestellt; einige davon hatten seine Vertreter in Afrika erworben, andere kamen von Webster und Opperse aus Amsterdam. Im Jahre 1900 begann der Schriftsteller Joe Hloucha, der vorher schon japanische

□ 185 *›Figur eines Vogels‹, SENUFO (Elfenbeinküste), bemaltes Holz, Höhe 145 cm. Privatsammlung, St. Louis.*

☐ 186 *›Baule-Maske‹ aus der »Orientalischen Ausstellung« in Budapest 1911, Haus der Künstler (Keleti Kiàllitàs a Müvészhàzban).*

Drucke gesammelt hatte, eine bemerkenswerte Sammlung afrikanischer Plastik. Aber die tschechischen Künstler wollten anscheinend nicht aus diesen »nationalen« Quellen schöpfen.

Die Gruppe plastischer Künstler (*Skupyna Vytvarny Umelcu*), die 1912 in Prag als Gegenpol zur Manès-Allianz gegründet wurde, zählte etwa 23 Schriftsteller, Maler, Bildhauer und Graphiker zu ihren Mitgliedern. Unter ihnen waren der Maler Josef Capek, sein Bruder Karel, ein Schriftsteller, der Bildhauer Otto Gutfreund und der Kunsthistoriker und Sammler Vincenc Kramar, der der Gruppe zwar nahestand, aber eine unabhängige Meinung vertrat. Parallel dazu gab Josef Capek im Oktober die 1911 ins Leben gerufene *Monatszeitschrift für Kunst* (*Umelecky Mesicnik*)[87] bis zum Frühjahr 1912 heraus. Nicht nur die Zeitschrift, sondern auch die Ausstellungen der Gruppe nahmen Bezug auf die primitive Kunst. So erscheinen in der Juniausgabe 1913 von *Umelecky Mesicnik* zusammen mit Gutfreunds »Fläche und Oberfläche«, einem der tiefgründigsten Aufsätze über moderne Bildhauerei aus jener Zeit, acht Photographien von »Negerobjekten«: Drei davon sollen Kahnweiler gehört haben (eine Maske, eine *Bambara*-Statuette und eine kleine *Baga*-Plastik), die übrigen Brummer (eine Doppelfigur von den Marquesasinseln, eine *Bambara*-, eine *Baule*- und eine *Teke*-Statuette sowie ein *Fang*-Kopf). In der Oktoberausgabe 1913 sind zwei *Senufo*-Masken aus Brummers Sammlung abgebildet. Von den Ausstellungen der Gruppe zeigten die dritte (Mai/Juni 1913) und vierte (Januar/März 1914) außer Werken ihrer Mitglieder und ausländischer Künstler, darunter Picasso, auch Negerskulptur.

Der Gedanke, Stammeskunst in Ausstellungen moderner Kunst zu zeigen, kam in Prag zwar mit Josef Capek, Gutfreund, Kramar oder auch Emil Filla auf; man darf aber nicht übersehen, daß diese Personen enge Verbindungen zu Pariser Künstlern und Händler unterhielten, die sie möglicherweise dazu ermutigten. Kramar stand über seine Erwerbungen mit Kahnweiler in Kontakt, der, ohne damit zu handeln, afrikanische Kunst besaß. Dies belegen Dokumente und auch Photographien, die 1913 in seiner Wohnung in der Rue George Sand aufgenommen und in der Zeitschrift veröffentlicht wurden ☐ 412.[88] Wir wissen nichts über Gutfreunds Verbindungen während seiner Zeit als Schüler an der Grande Chaumière in Paris in den Jahren 1909/10. Dagegen gibt es Genaueres über Josef Capek. Da die Familie Capeks im März 1902 Apollinaire in Prag empfangen hatte, waren Josef und Karel schon vor ihrem Aufenthalt in Paris mit den literarischen und künstlerischen Ideen des Dichters vertraut.[89] Als Apollinaire seinerseits 1910/11 Josef Capek gastfreundlich aufnahm, trat er als sein Mentor auf. So besuchte der junge Maler den Trocadéro und machte dort sogar Photographien von einigen Objekten, die ihn interessierten: von einer *Dogon*-Statue aus Westafrika ☐ 353 (die Leutnant Desplagnes vom Niger mitgebracht hatte) und von drei Weberschiffchen. 1918 veröffentlichte er dann in der Zeitschrift *Cerven* einen Artikel über Negerplastik und 1938 ein Buch über primitive Kunst. Diese Schriften gehen auf die frühe Begegnung mit den Plastiken im Musée d'Ethnographie du Trocadéro und denen im Besitz Apollinaires und des Kunsthändlers Brummer zurück.

☐ 187 *›Bambara-Figur‹ aus der »Orientalischen Ausstellung« in Budapest 1911, Haus der Künstler (Keleti Kiàllitàs a Müvészhàzban). Vgl.* ☐ *186.*

Wahrscheinlich fand 1911 in Brummers Heimat die erste Ausstellung statt, in der die Kunst Afrikas und Ozeaniens (unter einer Vielzahl außereuropäischer Werke) nicht nur als der klassischen Tradition ebenbürtig, sondern als die Hefe für die Erneuerung der zeitgenössischen Bildhauerei und Malerei dargestellt wurde. Die »Orientalische Ausstellung« (*»Keleti Kiàllitàs«*) fand im April und Mai im Budapester Künstlerhaus statt □ 186, 187. Die Schirmherrschaft hatten Joszef Rippl-Ronai und Karoly Kernstock, beide Ehrenmitglieder dieser Institution, die 1907 von der ungarischen Avantgarde für Künstler eingerichtet worden war. Neben persischen Miniaturen, japanischen Drucken, Ton- und Bronzestatuen aus dem alten China, Tibet, Kambodscha und Indien fanden sich 16 ozeanische und afrikanische Plastiken: sechs aus Neuguinea, zehn aus dem Kongo, dem Sudan und von der Elfenbeinküste. Letztere waren zum Teil Leihgaben des Schriftstellers und Journalisten Miklos Vitez, zum Teil stammten sie von dem Architekten und Dekorateur Lajos Kozma, der sie auf seinen Reisen durch Westeuropa erworben hatte. Der Katalog verzeichnet zwanzig chinesische Arbeiten als Leihgaben Brummers. Man darf daher annehmen, daß dieser von Paris aus einer der Förderer dieses historischen Ereignisses war.

Versucht man die Verbreitung der Stammeskunst in Rußland vor dem 1. Weltkrieg zu erfassen[90] und untersucht Shchukins Sammlung oder die Illustrationen in dem weiter unten besprochenen Buch von Markow, ist erkennbar, daß der Ursprung der

□ 188 *›Figur aus Holz‹,* CHOKWE *(Angola), Höhe 42 cm. Puschkin Museum, Moskau. Ehemals Sammlung Sergei Shchukin. Veröffentlicht in Carl Einstein, „Negerplastik", 1915. Eine andere Ansicht* □ *689.*

erworbenen Objekte oder die Quellen der abgebildeten Werke ausschließlich im Ausland zu suchen sind. Jedenfalls scheint es zu dieser Zeit in Petersburg oder Moskau keinen Spezialhandel für Stammesobjekte gegeben zu haben. Der Geograph und Sammler Anucin wurde vor allem von Umlauff in Hamburg und Oldman in London beliefert. Trotzdem tauchten seit den achtziger Jahren im Moskauer Völkerkundemuseum viele Zeugnisse der afrikanischen Kultur auf.

Ein Anfang 1914 in der Zeitschrift *Apollon* veröffentlichter Artikel Jakov Tugendholds über Sergei Shchukins französische Sammlung verweist darauf, daß in dem Teil von Shchukins Landhaus, wo etwa fünfzig Bilder PICASSOS hingen, sich auch »einige wunderbare Holzskulpturen aus Madagaskar und dem Kongo« befanden. Es waren mindestens sieben. Sie waren wahrscheinlich zwischen 1908 und 1912 bei Brummer oder bei FRANK BURTY HAVILAND in Paris über einen Mittelsmann gekauft worden. Vier davon wurden dann 1915 in *Negerplastik* abgebildet □ 188, 189, 192. Dem Eingreifen des Dichters Majakowskij unter dem Kommissariat Lunacharskijs ist es zu verdanken, daß *Die Kunst der Neger* (Iskusstvo Nergov) ungefähr fünf Jahre nach dem Tod des Verfassers, dem Dichter,

□ 189 *›Figur aus Holz‹,* BIJOGO, *Bissagos Inseln (Guinea-Bissau), Höhe 71 cm, Náprstkovo Muzeum, Prag. Ehemals Sammlung Sergei Shchukin. Veröffentlicht in Carl Einstein, „Negerplastik" 1915.*

□ 190 *›Reliquiarfiguren‹*, FANG *(Gabun oder Äquatorial-Guinea). Photographiert von **Vladimir Markow im Musée d'Ethnographie du Trocadéro** (Musée de l'Homme), Paris. Veröffentlicht in „Iskusstvo Negrov" (Negerkunst), 1919.*

Kunsttheoretiker und Gründungsmitglied der Petersburger Union der Jugend (Sojuz Molodezhi), Wladimir Markow, veröffentlicht wurde. 1919 sahen seine Gefährten V. D. Bubnowa und L. I. Zeerzewew das Manuskript für die Veröffentlichung durch, das in den letzten Monaten des Jahres 1913 und Anfang 1914 geschrieben worden war, ebenso die Photographien, die Markow selbst im Sommer 1913 in den Museen Westeuropas gemacht hatte □ 190. Die aus den *Annales du Congo belge* (1905) übernommenen Platten nicht mitgezählt, enthält das Buch 117 Originalphotographien von 72 Objekten, die sich mit einer Ausnahme alle in den öffentlichen völkerkundlichen Sammlungen von Leipzig, Berlin, Kiel, Kopenhagen, Oslo, Leiden, London und Paris befanden. Die einzige Ausnahme stellen die beiden Photographien einer Bambara-Statuette dar, die Brummer gehörte. Die Abbildungen zeigen deutlich, daß es sich hierbei nicht um irgendwelche Ethnographica handelte, die Markow zum Photographieren aus den Vitrinen nahm, sondern um wirkliche Kunstwerke, die er für die vollendeten Ergebnisse konsequent angewandter plastischer Prinzipien hielt. Da Markow die einzigartige Gesamtstruktur wie auch die vielfältige Formensprache im Detail gleichermaßen bewunderte, ließ er manchmal mit Absicht jedwedes Fetischmaterial oder Zusätze, die die Verständlichkeit des Objekts beeinträchtigen konnten, außer acht und entfernte sie. Nicht daß er solche Details, die oft nur als phantasievoll oder pittoresk gelten, unterschätzt hätte. Sie waren im Gegenteil für ihn echte plastische Symbole, deren Bedeutung in ihrer Eigenschaft als Teil eines Ganzen wie auch von ihrer ursprünglichen Verwendung her zu begreifen war. Außerdem diente die Montage verschiedener Ansichtsseiten desselben Objekts einer genauen Analyse, wie sie in Kapitel 4 seines Buches unternommen wurde. Als Markow den plastischen Gedanken, der hinter afrikanischer Plastik stand, untersuchte, definierte er in *Kunst der Neger* wie Gutfreund und Einstein gleichzeitig Prinzipien der Skulptur seiner Zeit.

Da die meisten Großstädte in Deutschland öffentliche völkerkundliche Sammlungen besaßen und »Kuriositäten« hier schon seit dem 19. Jahrhundert kommerziell verbreitet wurden, konnten die deutschen Avantgardisten wie etwa die Maler der Brücke und des Blauen Reiters unweit ihrer Ateliers die exotischen Quellen studieren. Es wäre daher verwunderlich, wenn der kleine ungarische Händler am Boulevard Raspail in Deutschland nur eine unbedeutende Rolle gespielt hätte. Wir wissen, daß Brummer dem Sammler Karl Ernst Osthaus einige afrikanische Plastiken lieferte, auch wenn es noch zu beweisen ist, daß er als Leihgeber hinter der Ausstellung primitiver Kunst stand, die 1912 im Privatmuseum des reichen Hagener Mäzens stattfand. Wenn einerseits Carl Einsteins *Negerplastik* als ein Buch ersten Ranges gelten kann – und zwar nicht nur, weil es ein Pionierwerk in der Auseinandersetzung mit afrikanischer Kunst war, sondern auch wegen der Bedeutung seiner Analysen und der Vielfalt seiner Abbildungen – und wir andererseits in Betracht ziehen, daß Brummer das Buch anregte wie auch finanzierte, ist er wohl kaum mehr als ein einfacher Händler von Kuriosa aus zweiter Hand einzustufen.

Carl Einstein[91] hatte bei seinem Studium in Berlin (1904–1907) die afrikanische Skulptur im Museum für Völkerkunde entdeckt. Er nahm auch sehr früh Kontakt mit der künstlerischen Avantgarde Deutschlands auf. Die Theoreme, die er in seinem Werk formuliert, zielen sowohl auf die evolutionistischen Thesen der Museologen als auch auf den gesteigerten Primitivismus der Expressionisten. Seine zuweilen

□ 191. *›Reliquienfigur‹*, Fang *(Gabun), Holz, Höhe 46 cm. Sammlung Arman, New York.*

als formalistisch eingestufte Perspektive sieht anders aus. Sie beruht auf breiten Kenntnissen der *Kunstwissenschaft* und auf dem, was er seit 1907 bei vielen Besuchen in den Ateliers Pariser Künstler sah. Seine 1901 begonnene Freundschaft mit Kahnweiler verschaffte ihm die Möglichkeit, u.a. Picasso, Braque und Gris zu treffen. Wie erwähnt, war zufällig Purrmann derjenige, der ihn in den Kreis der habitués des Dôme einführte. Dort lernte er auch Brummer kennen. Zweifellos erweckten die Originalität und Entschiedenheit seiner Äuße-

□ 192 *›Maske‹, Baule (Elfenbeinküste), in der Ausstellung der Galerie Levesque, Paris 1913. Veröffentlicht in Carl Einstein, „Negerplastik", 1915.*

rungen über Brummers Plastiken das Interesse und die Begeisterung des Händlers. Er bot Einstein nicht nur finanzielle Unterstützung für sein Buch an,[92] sondern stellte ihm auch die meisten Abbildungen zur Verfügung.

Wahrscheinlich wurde das Erscheinen von *Negerplastik* durch den Ausbruch des Krieges zwischen Frankreich und Deutschland um einige Monate verzögert. Dies stützt die Annahme, daß Einsteins Abfassung des Textes und Brummers Auswahl der Bilder in der ersten Hälfte des Jahres 1914 erfolgten. Die erste Auflage erschien 1915 in Leipzig, als Einstein schon im Elsaß in der Armee diente. Der einzige Unterschied zwischen der ersten und der 1920 in München herausgegebenen zweiten Auflage besteht in der Anzahl der Abbildungen (111 Photographien von 95 Objekten in der ersten Auflage, 108 von 92 in der zweiten). Leider gibt es in beiden Ausgaben keine Bildtexte, die die Stammeszugehörigkeit oder den Besitzer angeben würden. Zwar bezieht sich Einstein bei seinen Analysen nie auf bestimmte Objekte, eine schnelle Durchsicht macht jedoch klar, daß die Abbildungen nicht willkürlich gewählt sind. Schließt man die relativ kleine Zahl von Objekten aus dem Berliner Museum, die aus dem Britischen Museum – sie wurden aus dem Museumsführer von 1910 reproduziert – und die, von denen sich keine Spuren in den seither veröffentlichten Büchern und Katalogen finden, aus, kann man mit Sicherheit sagen, daß sich mehr als die Hälfte der in Einsteins Buch abgebildeten Objekte irgendwann einmal in Brummers Besitz befanden.

In Frankreich benutzte der Journalist und Kritiker André Warnod als erster schriftlich den allgemein verbreiteten Ausdruck »art nègre«, und zwar in einer Rezension in *Comoedia,* die am 2. Januar 1912 erschien. Unter den Bildbeispielen eingeborener Kunst, von der er behauptete, sie könne bei der Ausbildung junger Künstler bald die griechische Kunst ersetzen, befanden sich eine Maske, eine Baule-Statuette und ein Fang-Kopf aus der »Sammlung Brummer«. Im Jahr davor hatte Warnod in der gleichen Zeitschrift einen Begräbnispfahl aus Madagaskar vorgestellt, der »diesem intelligenten und gelehrten Antiquar« gehörte.

Die erste Ausstellung in Paris, in der afrikanische Plastik als solche in Erscheinung trat – obwohl sie ihr nicht ausschließlich gewidmet war –, fand vom 16. Mai bis 15. Juni 1913 in den Galeries Levesque statt. Sie zeigte die Sammlungen von Charles Vignier, die »Plastiken, Gemälde und antike Kunstwerke aus Asien sowie ein paar Exemplare der Kunst der Ägypter, der Neger und der Azteken« umfaßte. Vignier hatte als symbolistischer Dichter angefangen, der stark an Japan orientierten Kreisen nahestand. Sein Freund Fénéon bot ihm an, für die *Revue indépendante* zu schreiben. Später führte Vigniers Interesse an der Kunst des Fernen Ostens dazu, daß er damit Handel trieb; seine Kenntnisse der Bronzen und Keramiken des Alten China verschafften ihm die Anerkennung der erfahrenen Sinologen des Musée Guimet. Gleichzeitig verkaufte Vignier in kleinerem Rahmen Plastiken aus Afrika und Ozeanien in einem Laden der Pariser Rue Lamennais. Ende der zwanziger Jahre konnte er als Freund und ehemaliger Arbeitgeber Georges-Henri Rivières den nötigen Anstoß zur Reorganisation der Société des Amis du Musée d'Ethnographie du Trocadéro geben.

Im Katalog der Galerie Levesque werden unter der Überschrift »Art nègre« um die zwanzig afrikanische Objekte und ein »Fetisch aus geschwärztem Holz aus Neuguinea« beschrieben. Auf der gegenüberliegenden Seite findet sich eine einzige Abbildung: »eine schwarze Holzmaske mit Tätowierungen und dreiteiligem Haarschmuck von der Elfenbeinküste«. Diese Maske wurde später in Einsteins *Negerplastik* reproduziert

□ 193 *Blick in Edward Steichens Ausstellung der Werke von Braque, Picasso und primitiver Objekte in der Galerie 291, New York, 1914–15. Von links nach rechts: Pablo Picasso ›Flasche und Glas auf einem Tisch‹, 1912, Kota-Reliquiarfigur und Wespennest aus dem Besitz von Emil Zoler. Photographie von Alfred Stieglitz.*

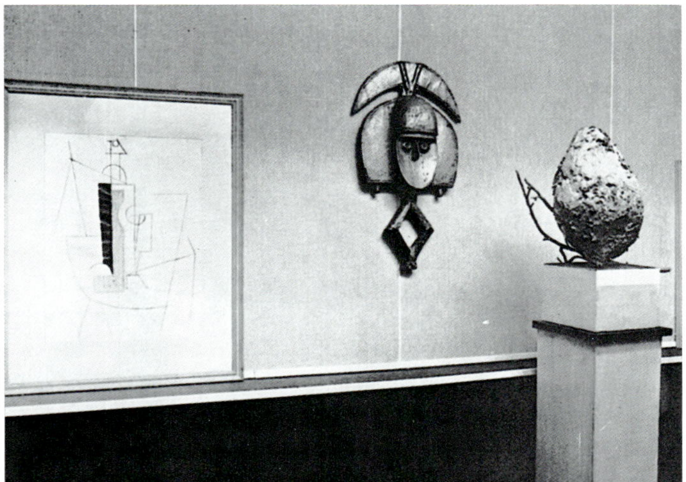

◻ 192, ebenso mindestens vier weitere Objekte, wenn man von ihrer Beschreibung im Katalog ausgeht: der berühmte »gefesselte Junge« der *Kanioka*, der sich heute im Museum Rietberg in Zürich befindet; eine *Teke*-Statuette, die das Universitätsmuseum in Philadelphia schon sehr früh erwarb; eine Schnabelmaske der *Dan* und ein Antilopenkopf unbekannter Herkunft. Die Plastiken in Vigniers Sammlung würden vielleicht bei Brummer erworben, doch ist auch das Umgekehrte möglich.

Nicht einer der geringsten Verdienste Brummers bestand darin, einen jungen Angestellten einer Gummireifenfabrik kurz nach 1910 zu veranlassen, ihm afrikanische Objekte zu besorgen. Obwohl die Zusammenarbeit der beiden nicht lange dauerte, prägte sie doch entscheidend die Laufbahn Paul Guillaumes, der zwischen den beiden Weltkriegen zum angesehensten Sammler und Händler afrikanischer Kunst wurde. Ein begeisterter Bewunderer traditioneller Erzeugnisse afrikanischer Zivilisationen, trug Guillaume dazu bei, den Graben zwischen den Vorstellungen der Ethnologen und der Museologen seiner Zeit zu vertiefen, aber auch zur wachsenden Wertschätzung des Wesens afrikanischer Plastik bei den Sammlern, die dank seiner immer zahlreicher wurden. Seine Aktivitäten und Schriften zeugen von dem Wunsch, die nach seiner Meinung schönsten Masken und Statuetten des »Schwarzen Kontinents« zu Meisterwerken der Weltkunst zu erheben. Paul Guillaumes Größe liegt in dieser Überzeugung, selbst wenn uns im Rückblick der von ihm favorisierte »klassische Geschmack« – verglichen mit der Vielfalt der afrikanischen Stilrichtungen – viel zu eklektisch erscheint. Neben seiner anekdotischen Interessantheit verdient es der Bericht Brummers über ein Treffen mit Paul Guillaume im Jahre 1911 erwähnt zu werden; er erlaubt uns auch, einige wichtige Dinge näher zu erläutern.[93]

Nachdem Apollinaire Brummer von einem qualitätvollen afrikanischen Objekt im Schaufenster eines Ladens für Autozubehör erzählt hatte, verhandelte dieser mit dem jungen Angestellten über einen Verkauf und brachte ihn dazu, ihm regelmäßig die »Fetische« zu zeigen, die die Firma des Angestellten durch ihre Kautschukimporte aus den Kolonien bekam. So verkaufte ihm der damals zwanzigjährige Guillaume mehrere dieser Plastiken aus Gabun und dem Kongo. Als er sie in Brummers Geschäft am Boulevard Raspail zur Schätzung anbot, machte er die Bekanntschaft Apollinaires, der von da an bis zu seinem Tod den jungen Händler durch die Tücken der Kunstwelt geleitete und ihn ständig unterstützte. Brummers Bericht wird auch von Basler bestätigt.[94] Dieser Kritiker stattete in Begleitung Frank Burty Havilands Guillaume einen Besuch ab, »vor seinem Militärdienst, in einer Autowerkstatt, wo er in einer Ecke Negerfetische lagerte«. Es ist begreiflich, daß Guillaume nach Abschluß der ersten Transaktionen mit Brummer zwar mit diesem erfahrenen Mann, der viele Beziehungen hatte, in Verbindung blieb, aber doch von einem eigenen Geschäft träumte. Trotz anderslautender Behauptungen von Paul Guillaume selbst ist der Beginn seiner Laufbahn als Kunsthändler und Sammler nicht vor 1911 anzusetzen. Die Behauptung, er habe die afrikanische Kunst 1904 entdeckt, wird auch durch die oben beschriebenen Ereignisse und die Schilderung von Alice Halicka eindeutig widerlegt.[95] Sie verbindet die Anwesenheit Marcoussis' mit den Käufen in der Rue Caulaincourt und datiert sie »um 1910«. Aller Wahrschein-

◻ 194 *›Figur aus Holz, Muscheln und Bast‹, Ngbandi (Zaire), Höhe 79 cm. Musée Royal de l'Afrique Centrale, Tervuren, Belgien.*

□ 195 ›*Maske*‹ *(Nigeria?), Holz, Höhe 22,5 cm. Privatsammlung.*

lichkeit nach knüpfte Guillaume seine Verbindungen zu Marcoussis ebenso wie zu Basler und Frank Burty Haviland über Brummer oder Apollinaire; dies kann also nicht vor 1911 geschehen sein.

Ein am 8. Oktober 1912 anonym in *Gil Blas* veröffentlichter Artikel kündigt für das Jahr 1913 die Eröffnung »der ersten Ausstellung von Stammeskunst, veranstaltet von einer neuen Gesellschaft von Sammlern« an. Es könnte sich hierbei um die Société des Mélanophiles handeln, die auf Anregung Paul Guillaumes gegründet wurde. Alberto Savinio, der in seinen Memoiren auf sie anspielt, gibt für die Gründung das Jahr 1913 an.[96] Obwohl die angekündigte Ausstellung überhaupt nicht stattfand und Zweifel an den Gründungsaktivitäten der Gruppe von Sammlern bestehen, deren Zahl und Identität zudem unbekannt ist, sind diese Tatsachen doch ein überzeugender Beweis für die Dynamik, mit der Guillaume seine Pläne bereits verfolgte. Er bat die Zulieferer seines früheren Arbeitgebers, Plastiken aus Gabun an seine Privatadresse zu verschiffen. Und schon 1912 gab er Anzeigen in der Kolonialpresse auf, um sein Lager aufzustocken. Mit seinem besonders ausgeprägten Unternehmergeist profitierte Guillaume von der Zusammenarbeit mit Apollinaire und mit einem großen Kreis von Verbindungen. Dies zeigt sich in mehr als einem der Briefe des Dichters an den Händler.

Die erste Ausstellung, auf der afrikanische Plastiken Guillaumes gezeigt wurden, fand außerhalb Frankreichs statt. In den USA wurden damit auch zum ersten Mal primitive Arbeiten »einzig unter dem Blickwinkel des Künstlerischen dargeboten«. Die Ausstellung wurde von Stieglitz' Kompagnon Marius de Zayas veranstaltet und war in der berühmten Galerie der Photo-Sezession an der Fifth Avenue Nr. 291 zu sehen. Dort wurden vom 3. November bis zum 8. Dezember 1914 achtzehn Objekte von der Elfenbeinküste und aus Gabun ausgestellt.[97] Trotz des etwas provozierenden Titels »Holzplastik von afrikanischen Wilden: Die Wurzel der modernen Kunst« gab es keinen Skandalerfolg; der Schau wurde aber viel ernsthaftes Interesse seitens der Presse zuteil. An den Wänden und auf den Sockeln der Galerie schienen diese Werke aus dem »Land des Schreckens«, wie De Zayas' mythischer Ausdruck lautete, völlig ihres exotischen Flairs beraubt – dies trotz Edward Steichens abstraktem Aufbau, der seiner Meinung nach »einen Hintergrund mit Buschtrommeln« evozieren sollte.[98] Die Auszüge aus den im Oktober 1916 von *Camera Work* veröffentlichten Rezensionen zeigen, daß die Kritiker der Kunst bzw. der gewagten Neuheit, wenn auch bisweilen feindselig, so doch keineswegs gleichgültig gegenüberstanden.

So konnte Paul Guillaume, der eben erst seine erste Galerie an der Rue Miromesnil in Paris eröffnet hatte, den ersten Erfolg auf internationaler Ebene verzeichnen. Es mag überraschen, daß sich De Zayas anstatt an einen anerkannten Händler wie Brummer oder auch Frank Burty Haviland an Guillaume wandte. Seine Freundschaft zu Havilands Bruder Paul[99] aus der Gruppe um die Galerie »291« und die Tatsache, daß Frank damals dort einige seiner eigenen Werke ausstellte, dürften ihn wohl auf diesen erfahrenen Sammler gebracht haben, den er wahrscheinlich schon kannte. Wir können nur vermuten, daß ihn ein zufälliges Treffen mit Guillaume bei Picabia, das zwischen dem 16. und dem 25. Mai 1914 anzusetzen ist, veranlaßte, mit dem begeisterten Protagonisten der afrikanischen Kunst, der außerdem von Apollinaire empfohlen wurde, zusammenzuarbeiten. De Zayas rühmt Guillaumes Selbstlosigkeit, mit der er ihm die Plastiken für die erste, sog. Propagandaausstellung anvertraute. Am 14. November desselben Jahres wurden von Guillaume über Le Havre an Stieglitz'

□ 196 ›*Maske*‹, *Lega (Zaire), Holz, Höhe 22 cm. Privatsammlung.*

◻ 197 *›Maske‹, Djibete (Nigeria), bemaltes Holz, Höhe 71 cm. Privatsammlung.*

Adresse siebzehn Öl- und Pastellgemälde verschifft, darunter fünf Bilder De Chiricos (u. a. *Liebeslied,* das auf vierhundert Francs taxiert wurde). Zu diesen modernen Gemälden kamen zwei »Bakoutas-Fetische [Reliquiarfiguren der *Kota* ◻ 193] aus Kupfer und Holz aus dem 17. Jahrhundert«, für die dreitausend Francs verlangt wurden.[100] Und das war sicher nicht die letzte Sendung über den Atlantik. Wenn man weiß, wie groß Paul Guillaumes Bekehrungseifer und Begeisterung waren, stellt man mit Überraschung fest, daß er vor Ende 1916 in Paris keine Ausstellung von Stammesplastik veranstaltete, obwohl er sie doch eifrig sammelte. Da er sowohl das Material als auch die Galerie, so klein sie auch war, schon vor dem Krieg besaß, kann man über die Gründe einer solchen Verzögerung nur Mutmaßungen anstellen. Einerseits hielt er sich vielleicht an ein Abkommen mit De Zayas, in dem letzterer das Vorrecht erhalten hatte, afrikanische Kunst zu zeigen (»zum ersten Mal . . . in diesem oder in jedem anderen Land«), und das er noch eine Zeitlang behalten wollte. Doch gibt es dafür keinen Beweis. Andererseits kann man davon ausgehen, daß Guillaume in der Zeit unmittelbar vor dem Krieg die Konkurrenz der Exposition d'Art Indigène Africain fürchtete; sie fand von Mai bis Juli 1914 mit der Unterstützung eines Wohltätigkeitsvereins, Le Souvenir Africain, statt. Diese Ausstellung hatte ein großes Echo in der religiösen und patriotischen Presse. Unter einem Gewirr ausgestopfter Tiere – dem Werk von Missionsschülern – und mittelmäßigen Bildern, die als Lotteriepreise ausgesetzt waren, entdeckte Apollinaire »einige wunderbare Idole, aufregende Statuen von unschätzbarem Wert, die von einem großen, unbekannten Künstler geschnitzt worden waren«.[101] Möglicherweise hatte Paul Guillaume auch nicht den Mut, sich in der Abwesenheit Apollinaires zwischen dem Dezember 1914, als dieser in die Armee eintrat, und dem August 1915, als er sich nur langsam von seiner Verwundung erholte, auf ein Unternehmen einzulassen, bei dem er der Hilfe seines getreuen Propagandisten bedurfte.

Anfang Winter 1916 schlug der chilenische Maler Manuel

□ 198 *›Kopfschmuck‹*, BAMUM *(Kamerun), bemaltes Holz und Bast, Höhe 30 cm. Sammlung Pierre Harter, Paris.*

ORTIZ DE ZARATE seinem Genfer Kollegen EMILE LEJEUNE,[102] der am Montparnasse, Rue Huyghens 6 ein Atelier hatte, das genügend Platz für Sommerkonzerte bot, vor, dort auch Ausstellungen einzurichten. ORTIZ und KISLING übernahmen die Organisation der ersten Ausstellung. So wurden zwischen dem 19. November und dem 5. Dezember unter dem Zeichen von Lyra und Palette nicht nur Bilder dieser beiden Künstler ausgestellt, sondern auch ein Ölgemälde und eine Zeichnung von MATISSE, zwei Stilleben von PICASSO und vierzehn Bilder von MODIGLIANI. Letztere hatte KISLING von Paul Guillaume ausgeliehen, der bei dieser Gelegenheit auch noch »25 Negerplastiken, Fetische aus Afrika und Ozeanien« zur Verfügung stellte. Der zur Ausstellung erschienene Katalog wurde wahrscheinlich von Guillaume finanziert. Neben Kurzbeschreibungen der ausgestellten Arbeiten enthielt er Gedichte von Cendrars und Cocteau zu Ehren Saties und eine kurze Notiz mit dem Titel »Art nègre« ohne Autorenangabe. LEJEUNE schreibt sie in seinen Memoiren Guillaume zu. Der Herausgeber des Briefwechsels zwischen Apollinaire und Guillaume sieht in ihr dagegen »die erste der Äußerungen und Erklärungen des Dichters zugunsten der Negerkunst«.[103] Wie dem auch sei, dieser Text faßt einige vom Schriftsteller und Händler anscheinend geteilte Vorstellungen zusammen: daß die dringende Notwendigkeit bestehe, diese Plastiken aus der Zwangsjacke der Völkerkundemuseen zu befreien, wo man ihre Schönheit nicht zu würdigen wisse und das Vorurteil hege, ihr ästhetischer Wert könne sich – entgegen der hohen Meinung der fortschrittlichsten Künstler der Zeit – nicht gegenüber den Meisterwerken der frühen Antike behaupten.

Wegen des nicht allein *mondänen* Erfolges dieser Ausstellung wurde sie für Paris zum Ausgangspunkt einer Modewelle, die die »art nègre« weit über die Künstlerkreise hinaus populär machte. Dadurch wurden Paul Guillaumes Überzeugungen gefestigt. Kurz darauf brachte er einen Bildband mit dem Titel *Sculptures nègres* heraus. Apollinaire schrieb das Vorwort, »A propos de l'art des noirs«, und gab besondere Ratschläge zum

Format des Buches. Außerdem half er den Ankündigungsprospekt zu gestalten. *Sculptures nègres* war im April 1917 gedruckt. Außer Apollinaires Anmerkungen und einer »Erläuterung« Paul Guillaumes enthält der Band 26 Abbildungen von 22 afrikanischen Objekten (aus Guinea, Gabun, dem Sudan, dem Kongo und von der Elfenbeinküste) und von vier polynesischen. Bei siebzehn Plastiken werden ihre Eigentümer genannt: Paul Guillaume – 5; Ambroise Vollard – 2; André Level – 1; Jos Hessel – 2; Alphonse Kann – 2; Comte de Gouy, Bernard d'Hendecourt, Vlaminck und Matisse je 1; der Trocadéro erscheint als Leihgeber einer Nimba der Baga. Apollinaire taucht in dieser Liste nicht auf; den Grund dafür findet man in einer Notiz an Guillaume: »Da ich für das Vorwort zeichne, erscheint mein Name besser nicht unter den Sammlern.«[104] Das berechtigt allerdings nicht zu der Annahme, daß alle nicht namentlich ausgewiesenen Objekte dem Dichter gehörten. Sein Bestreben, möglichst nicht genannt zu werden, läßt sich aus seinem Wunsch erklären, in den Augen der Kollegen als unabhängig und integer zu gelten, ein Image, das durch einen zu offenkundigen Zusammenhang mit Guillaume hätte gefährdet werden können. Die Frage, ob Apollinaire nicht doch gegen diesen Grundsatz verstoßen hat, stellt sich nach wie vor. Vergleicht man das Vorwort von *Sculptures nègres* mit einem ganz ähnlichen Artikel, den Apollinaire am 1. April 1917 im *Mercure de France* veröffentlichte und der sich stark von dem anderen unterscheidet, so wird klar, daß dieser Artikel dem Vorwort vorausging. Der Vergleich zeigt, daß das für Guillaume geschriebene Vorwort eine nicht nur gekürzte, sondern auch gemilderte Fassung der ironischeren und distanzierteren Gedanken des Artikels über die wachsende Beliebtheit primitiver Kunst ist. Schon die Überschrift des Artikels, »Mélanophilie ou mélanomanie«, bringt die Haltung Apollinaires klar zum Ausdruck. Dieses Auseinanderklaffen der tatsächlichen Auffassungen Apollinaires und Guillaumes setzte ihrer Zusammenarbeit aber kein Ende.

Guillaume hatte wahrscheinlich schon mehrere wichtige Ausstellungen in seinen Räumen in der Rue de Miromesnil und der Avenue de Villiers veranstaltet (Larionov, Gontscharowa, De Chirico, Picabia, Derain), doch erst mit der Eröffnung einer neuen Galerie im vornehmen Faubourg Saint-Honoré im Herbst 1917 gewann sein Name großes Ansehen. Seine damals in bestimmten Zeitschriften erschienen Anzeigen geben seine Ziele wieder. Er wollte neben den bedeutenden Werken »zeitgenössischer Meister« und den besten Beispielen der »neuen Malerei . . . Negerplastiken von erstklassiger Qualität« zeigen. Diese Stücke »von hohem Interesse«, die alle einer »frühen Periode« zugeordnet wurden, sollten mit einigen antiken Werken als Dauerausstellung in einer großen Vitrine dargeboten werden. In einem aufgeregten, am 18. Dezember 1917 in *Le Gaulois* erschienenen Artikel beschwor Madeleine Le Chevrel im Zusammenhang mit den hier ausgestellten »Völkern der Pahouin, Bahoulé, Bakoutos und Stämmen vom oberen Niger . . . das Strandgut des großen untergegangenen Atlantis«.

Während des Krieges wurde die Galerie in der Rue du Faubourg Saint-Honoré 108 eines der wenigen aktiven Zentren des künstlerischen und literarischen Paris. In dieser Zeit des gesteigerten Nationalismus erwies sie sich als eine Oase, wo man mit Ausnahme der deutschen Moderne von den avantgardistischen Bewegungen des Auslands hören konnte und wo der Kontakt zwischen Paris, New York und Zürich aufrechterhalten blieb. So trafen sich bei Paul Guillaume avantgardistische

□ 199 *Paul Guillaume, um 1930.*

Maler, Musiker und Schriftsteller. Vor seinen »Negergötzen« hatten einige die Gelegenheit, ihr Talent unter Beweis zu stellen. Auf dem »Abend der Dichtkunst und Musik« am 13. November 1917 spielte Satie nach einem Vortrag Apollinaires über neue Entwicklungen in der Bildhauerei seine *Parade* auf dem Klavier, und eine Schauspielerin las dazu Gedichte Apollinaires, Cendrars' »Le Profond Aujourd'hui« sowie »Façon« und »André Derain« des damals noch ziemlich unbekannten André Breton.[105] Im Programm des Abends erscheint als Faksimile vervielfältigt ein Schreiben Cocteaus an »Paul Guillaume, nègrier«. Es schließt: »Negerkunst hat nichts mit den trügerischen Blitzen der Kindheit oder der Wahnsinnigen zu tun, sondern mit den edelsten Zügen menschlicher Zivilisation.« Dies muß für Guillaume der Beweis gewesen sein, daß seine Botschaft verstanden worden war.

Guillaume hoffte, daß der »neue Geist«, der die Galerie und ihre Besucher anregte, in einer Publikation zum Ausdruck kommen würde, die den »künstlerischen und literarischen Neuigkeiten im Bereich der Kunst und verwandter Interessengebiete« gewidmet sein sollte. Zwischen der Matisse/Picasso- und der Van Dongen-Ausstellung erschien am 15. März 1918 die erste Ausgabe der großzügig illustrierten Zeitschrift *Les Arts à Paris*. Apollinaire arbeitete eng an den ersten beiden Ausgaben mit. Seine Biographen behaupten sogar, daß er »einen großen Teil davon selbst schrieb«. Man sollte ihm jedoch nur die unter den Pseudonymen »Paracelse«, »Docteur Passement« und »Louis Troëme« erschienen Artikel zuschreiben. Unter diesem letzten Pseudonym veröffentlichte er den Aufsatz »Sculptures d'Afrique et d'Oceanie«,[106] in dem er Guillaumes Ansichten zu entsprechen scheint: »Indem sie sich für Fetische interessieren, die alle der religiösen Leidenschaft – Quelle der reinsten Kunst – angehören, stärken . . . Künstler ihren Geschmack, die ihre Themen und Formen durch Hinwendung zu den Prinzipien großer Kunst erneuern wollen.«

Man kann sagen, daß Paul Guillaumes Jahre der Entwicklung mit dem Tod Apollinaires im November 1918 endeten. Er trat in die Nachkriegszeit mit entscheidenden Vorteilen ein:

□ 200 *›Figur aus Holz‹,* ZANDE *(Zaire), Höhe 26 cm. Sammlung M. und D. Ginzberg, New York.*

einer mittlerweile berühmten Galerie, bedeutenden Beständen, die er praktisch ohne Konkurrenten in den »schrecklichen Jahren« aufgebaut hatte, mit einer Zeitschrift, die sein Interesse förderte, und einem ausgedehnten Netz von Beziehungen. Da der Krieg für Frankreich erfolgreich ausgegangen war, konnte er außerdem von einem günstigen Klima profitieren. Das steigende Interesse an der Negerkunst, das er zu fördern hoffte, wurde durch eine veränderte Einstellung Frankreichs gegenüber Afrikanern begünstigt. Die hochmütige Verachtung, die die Mehrheit den Afrikanern entgegengebracht hatte, wurde u. a. wegen der Tapferkeit der afrikanischen Truppen im Kampf gegen den deutschen Feind durch ein neugieriges Interesse an den Sitten der Völker, die mutig gekämpft hatten und nun freudige Kameraden bei den Siegesfeierlichkeiten waren, ersetzt. Durch diese Welle wohlwollender Sympathie – die aber frei von Herablassung war – konnte Guillaume die Gelegenheit wahrnehmen, einen Werbe- und Verkaufsfeldzug zu starten, der in hohem Maße dazu beitrug, die »Negerkunst« als Mode einzuführen. Als ihm die großen Räumlichkeiten des Galerie-Verlagshauses Devambez in der Rue Malherbes zur Verfügung standen, veranstaltete er mit Hilfe Levels die Première Exposition d'Art Nègre et d'Art Océanien, die vom 10. bis 31. Mai 1919 stattfand. Obwohl dies eigentlich nicht die »erste« Ausstellung war, kann man doch zu Recht sagen, daß ihr aufgrund der zahllosen Reaktionen und der Massen von Besuchern nichts Vergleichbares vorausgegangen war. Der Katalog verzeichnet 150 Einträge. Zwei Drittel davon beziehen sich mittel- oder unmittelbar auf Objekte, die damals Guillaume gehörten. 39 Objekte kamen aus Levels Sammlung. Acht Skulpturen waren vermutlich wegen des Ansehens ihrer Besitzer aufgenommen worden: des Fabrikanten Louis Delafon, des Modeschöpfers und Kunstmäzens Jacques Doucet, des Malers und Nachfahren berühmter Schokoladenfabrikanten Georges Menier, des Orientalisten Victor de Goloubew, des Kunsthändlers Léonce Rosenberg und MAURICE DE VLAMINCKS. Obwohl die oft ungenauen, manchmal phantastischen Zuordnungen des Katalogs nicht unbedingt zuverlässig waren, wird man feststellen, daß die Arbeiten mit wenigen Ausnahmen (*ZANDE*- und *KUBA*-Objekte aus Belgisch-Kongo) aus den französischen Kolonien stammten. Daneben fällt auf, daß ein keineswegs unbedeutender Teil der Objekte nicht unter die Kategorie der Masken und Statuetten fällt, sondern in den Bereich der angewandten Kunst: Urnen und Schalen, Kämme und Armbänder, Löffel und Stühle. Außerdem enthält der Katalog neben dem Vorwort Apollinaires aus *Sculptures nègres* verschiedene kurze Aufsätze zur »Kunst der Wilden«, die die Autoren André Level und Henri Clouzot später in zahlreichen Aufsätzen ausarbeiteten.

Guillaume bereitete der Anerkennung seiner »neuen Ästhetik«, zu der die Schau in der Galerie Devambez beigetragen hatte, ein unerwartetes Nachspiel. Im Mai desselben Jahres inszenierte er auf einer denkwürdigen Soirée im Théâtre des Champs-Elysées die erste »Fête Nègre« für ein Publikum von Tout Paris.

Nach einer Eröffnungsrede, bei der der Zeremonienmeister zu zeigen suchte, daß das »Verständnis des modernen Menschen wie das der Neger werden sollte«, sahen die Zuschauer verschiedene choreographische und musikalische Darbietungen, deren Themen den Märchen und Legenden Afrikas entnommen waren, die Blaise Cendrars kurz zuvor für seine *Anthologie nègre* gesammelt hatte. Im Nachhinein ist es schwierig zu erkennen, inwieweit dieses Spektakel naive Belehrung oder bewußte Provokation war. Eine farblose Imitation eines Abends im Cabaret Voltaire, eine Vorwegnahme der *Erschaffung der Welt,* ein »Schauspiel von der Art der Exposition Coloniale, gelehrsam und gut bestückt«, eine »Bamboola-Burleske« – es war wahrscheinlich all dies gleichzeitig. Wie dem auch sei, die Presse berichtete ausführlich darüber, und Guillaume erwarb sich damit neuen Ruhm unter »der Elite der ewigen Heimat des Geschmacks«, wie er seine Nation zu bezeichnen beliebte.

Ganz allgemein trugen beide genannten Ereignisse des Jahres 1919, die Ausstellung bei Devambez und die »Fête Nègre«, dazu bei, eine Kunst, die einst nur das Interesse weniger Sammler erweckt hatte, zu einer Art Mode werden zu lassen; sollte man daraus auf den Beginn eines Desinteresses an exotischer Kunst seitens der Künstler schließen, da die Kraft, die Erneuerung oder der Bruch, die sie von ihr erhofften, nun irgendwie dem Zeitgeschmack angepaßt war? Die nostalgische Anrufung André Salmons aus dem Jahre 1919 etwa könnte darauf schließen lassen: »Den kannibalischen Göttern sei Dank, die uns den Mut zu heilbringenden Massakern einflößten.«[107] Würde nicht die Mode, indem sie sich die Waffen, die gegen die Tradition gerichtet worden waren, aneignete, diese allmählich stumpf machen und polieren, um sie dann zu Symbolen eines neuen Akademiedenkens zu machen? Tatsächlich nahm Roger Allard, einer der glühendsten Vorkämpfer des Kubismus, die Ausstellung bei Devambez zur Gelegenheit,[108] um die Haltung jener reichen Sammler zu verketzern, die, von schlauen Händlern manipuliert, die Qualität einer Plastik nach ihrem Verkaufswert einstuften und nicht ahnten, vielleicht »Nachahmungen afrikanischer Plastik« zu bewundern. Jedenfalls überdauerte die neue Mode nicht einmal eine Saison.

Primitive Kunst wurde dessenungeachtet zu einem Bestandteil des zeitgenössischen Möbels und der Dekoration □ 698–700. War sie früher einmal für einige ein Mittel zum Ausbruch aus der Gesellschaft gewesen, trug sie nun ironischerweise aufgrund ihres gesellschaftlichen Erfolges zur »Rückkehr zum Normalen« bei. Derain, der in dieser Hinsicht den Ansichten Guillaumes nahestand, sah darin den »ersten der Klassizismen«. Aus solchen Ansichten entstand in den frühen zwanziger Jahren die Frage: Darf die Stammeskunst auch in den Louvre Eingang finden?

Dies war der Hauptpunkt bei einer Umfrage, die Fénéon unter »zwanzig Ethnologen und Forschern, Künstlern und Ästhetikern, Sammlern und Händlern« durchführte. Die Ergebnisse erschienen zwischen dem 15. November und dem 15. Dezember 1920 in drei Ausgaben des *Bulletin de la vie artistique*, dem Organ der Galerie Bernheim-Jeune. Einige kurze Auszüge genügen, um einen Eindruck von den Antworten zu erhalten. Salomon Reinach, Kurator der Antiquités Nationales, hielt das Problem nicht für dringlich, da »die Holzplastik der Neger häßlich ist; sich an ihr zu erfreuen, schiene eine Verirrung, wenn es nicht einfach ein Witz ist«. Dagegen meinte die Malerin und Schriftstellerin Lucie Cousturier, eine enge Freundin Fénéons, daß, »sobald der Louvre die Negerkunst aufgenommen hat, er daran nicht eine Ergänzung, sondern sein Prinzip finden werde«. Jos Hessel, einer der ersten Sammler und mittlerweile angesehener Gemäldehändler, war davon überzeugt, daß die Lehren, die man aus der afrikanischen Kunst ziehen könne, um so wirkungsvoller wären, würde man »ein paar ganz reine Exemplare« in dem berühmten Museum ausstellen. Charles Vignier äußerte sich ironisch: daß der Louvre keine »Werke aus Peru, Polynesien, Dahome oder dem Sudan« enthalte, sei »kein ausreichender Grund, bei diesem Zustand zu bleiben. Andererseits befinden sich diese Werke u. a. im Britischen Museum, dem Metropolitan Museum in New York, dem Museum of Fine Arts in Boston und dem University Museum in Philadelphia.« Jean Guiffry, Kurator der Gemäldesammlung des geschmähten Louvre meinte tatsächlich: »Es wäre paradox, das Gestotter von Kulturen, die in ihrem Kindheitsstadium verharrten, so interessant es auch sein mag, mit den vollkommensten Werken des menschlichen Geistes zu vergleichen.« Léonce Rosenberg, der es sich nicht entgehen ließ, seinen Rivalen Paul Guillaume anzugreifen und die Überlegenheit der ozeanischen Kunst, die er vorzog, herauszustellen, meinte dennoch, daß »nur die zehn besten der bisher bekannten afrikanischen Arbeiten im Louvre einen kleinen Platz beanspruchen könnten.« Schließlich meinte Guillaume selbst, daß man nichts überstürzen solle, »denn im Augenblick gibt es noch keine offizielle Elite, die fähig wäre, mit aller notwendigen Entscheidungsgabe die Objekte auszuwählen, die am bedeutendsten und authentischsten sind und die aus sich heraus einer endgültigen Anerkennung wert sind«.

Einige Monate zuvor, im April 1920, hatte Florent Fels für seine Zeitschrift *Action* einige bekannte Zeugen für das Auftauchen der Stammeskunst befragt. Neben Picasso, der paradoxerweise behauptete, nichts davon zu wissen, und dem harten Urteil Cocteaus (»Die Negerkrise ist genauso langweilig geworden wie Mallarmés Japonismus.«) war auch Paul Guillaume offen: »Die Negerkunst ist die fruchtbringende Saat

□ 201 ›*Figur aus Holz und Metall*‹, Songye (Zaire), *Höhe 21 cm. Privatsammlung.*

des geistigen 20. Jahrhunderts ... es ist das Glück dieses Jahrhunderts, den Glanz einer Plastik, deren Herrschaft erst im Kommen ist, aus dem afrikanischen Altertum geborgen zu haben.«

Obwohl die Stammeskunst damals »in der Luft« lag, fand in Paris zwischen der Ausstellung in der Galerie Devambez und derjenigen im Pavillon de Marsan Ende 1923 keine weitere statt. In dieser Zeit wurde die Neugier dennoch durch Publikationen geschürt. Ein paar Bücher, aber vor allem zahlreiche Artikel, versuchten den afrikanischen Kunststilen ihre Eigenheiten und, gegenüber und über ihre Stellung in den Künstlerateliers hinaus, ihre Autonomie wiederzugeben. Der Sammler André Level erwies sich zusammen mit Henri Clouzot, einem Spezialisten für angewandte Kunst in Europa, in dieser Hinsicht als besonders produktiv. Ende 1920 veröffentlichten die Editions Devambez *L'Art nègre et l'art océanien*, das erste in Frankreich erschienene Buch, in dem der Versuch unternommen wurde, den künstlerischen Wert der Werke zur Konzeption ihrer Schöpfer in Beziehung zu setzen. Die Verfasser, die den Formen der von ihnen reproduzierten Objekte (ungefähr dreißig, von denen die Hälfte Level gehörte, der Rest Guillaume, Picasso, Louis Delafon, dem Trocadéro und dem Britischen Museum) viel Aufmerksamkeit schenkten, kamen zu Beobachtungen, die so erhaben wie Carl Einsteins Ansichten waren. So heißt es an einer Stelle: »Die Ausdrucksweise von Negermasken besteht sozusagen nie in einer Verzerrung von Gesichtszügen, einer Grimasse; sie lachen nicht, noch

weinen sie. Ihr Ausdruck rührt von ihrer Gestaltung her, von der Betonung der Flächen durch große Massen. Ihre Wirkung erzielen sie durch das Spiel von Linien. Nichts steht der Literatur ferner und der Plastik näher.« Einstein wird in diesem Buch übrigens nicht erwähnt, als Deutschen verdächtigte man ihn vielleicht der »Metaphysik«.

Da Clouzot und Level ganz disparate Quellen benutzten, sind ihre interessantesten Bemerkungen von einem Wirrwarr von Vorurteilen über die »Negermentalität« umgeben. Sie stützen ihre Behauptungen auf die – zumindest so zitierten – Schriften Arcins und Pater Baudins, die bedauerlichen Aussagen Professor Verneaus, Hamys Nachfolger als Leiter des Trocadéro, und die nicht weniger irrigen Analysen MARIUS DE ZAYAS'.[109] Das Ergebnis sind Absurditäten über »das physiologisch unterentwickelte Gehirn der Afrikaner« oder die den Afrikanern unterstellte Leichtgläubigkeit. Sie zitieren mit gewisser Hochachtung Verneau mit der Behauptung, daß in Loango Nägel in den Körper eines Fetischs geschlagen werden, so daß »die Empfindung, die er hat, dazu führt, daß er sich das von ihnen Verlangte fester ins Gedächtnis einprägt«.

Natürlich ist das Buch von Level und Clouzot typisch für die Denkmuster einer Zeit, in der es die kolonialen Interessen oft unmöglich machten, die kulturelle Relativierung, die allein für Artefakte gilt, auf andere Bereiche der Gesellschaft auszudehnen. Zwischen 1919 und 1923 erschienen etwa zehn Artikel unter dem Namen der beiden Autoren. Die Entdeckung der Hofkunst nach dem Waffenstillstand in Tervuren, das in den östlichen Savannen von Belgisch-Kongo liegt, erweckte Clouzots Interesse an der Geschichte der angewandten Kunst. Auch Levels Käufe bei dem Antwerpener Importeur H. Pareyn bezeugen ihre zahlreichen Untersuchungen über die Verzierung von Haushaltsgeräten und Kleidungsstücken.[110]

Die Schriften Levels und Clouzots, die vier Folianten von *La Décoration primitive*, die 1922/23 von der Librairie des Arts Décoratifs veröffentlicht wurden, und die Existenz so spezialisierter Sammlungen wie der Paul Rupalleys oder auch der des Kapitäns Lepage, des Verfassers des Bandes über Afrika aus dem genannten Reihenwerk, veranlaßten François Carnot, den Präsidenten der Union Central des Arts Décoratifs, gegen Ende 1923 im Pavillon de Marsan eine Exposition de l'Art Indigène des Colonies Françaises zu veranstalten. Sie umfaßte »die charakteristischsten Formen von Plastik, ornamentaler Plastik, Schmuck- und Textilkunst, von Gebrauchsgegenständen aus Holz, Metall oder Lehm, Musikinstrumenten, Flechtwerk usw.« Ihre Vorbereitung oblag einem Komitee bestehend aus Level, Clouzot, Verneau sowie den kolonialen Kreisen nahestehenden Journalisten und Schriftstellern Pierre Mille, Marius und Ary Leblond, außerdem dem Verwalter Delafosse, der damals Professor an der École Colonial und Leiter des Wirtschaftsbüros für Französisch-Westafrika war.

Die »Ornamente der Eingeborenen« wurden u.a. in der Absicht ausgestellt, Designern, Handwerkern und Herstellern verwertbare Beispiele vorzuführen. Es bot sich daneben den Befürwortern des Kolonialismus die Gelegenheit, ihre Propaganda aus einem kulturellen und einem wirtschaftlichen Blickwinkel zu führen. Die Ausstellung war nach geographischen Gesichtspunkten angelegt. Jede Kolonie war durch Erzeugnisse vertreten, die man für besonders typisch hielt. Unter den Leihgebern, die dem Aufruf des Kurators des Musée des Arts

□ 202 *›Figur aus Holz und Metall‹ (Vorderansicht),* LUBA *(Zaire), Höhe 35 cm. Sammlung J. B. Hautelet, Brüssel.*

Décoratifs für Afrika folgten, befanden sich sechs Institutionen und 43 Privatleute; darunter die Künstler Patrick Henry Bruce, Burty Haviland, Lhote, Georges de Miré und Angel Zarraga; die Schriftsteller Jean Giraudoux und Fénéon; die Händler und Sammler Guillaume, Hein, Ernest Brummer (der Bruder Josefs), Vignier, Antony Moris und Hessel; die privaten Sammler Alphonse Kann, André Lefèvre, Paul Poiret, Madame Tachard und Rupalley.

Die Zahl der dem Organisationskomitee von den Sammlern zur Verfügung gestellten Objekte war beträchtlich. Allein für die Abteilung Elfenbeinküste[111] sandte etwa Guillaume 79, Hessel 72 und Lhote 11 Objekte. Fénéon beteiligte sich mit 30 Weberschiffchen und 15 Masken.

Man kann sich leicht vorstellen, welches Interesse die Vorbereitung eines systematischen Katalogs der ausgestellten Objekte erregte. Doch der Widerstand einiger Leihgeber gegen die Veröffentlichung von Photographien ihrer Werke, die übergroße Zahl von Leihgaben (die wahrscheinlich die Erwartungen der Veranstalter bei weitem übertraf) und die begrenzte Zeit führten schließlich zum Verzicht auf eine Veröffentlichung. Daher muß man sich bei der Einschätzung der Exponate mit der hastigen Beschreibung zufriedengeben, die Dr. Stephen-Chauvet für ein 1924 erschienenes Bändchen verfaßte, oder mit den Illustrationen und dem Vorwort Levels und Clouzots, »La Leçon d'une exposition«, in ihrem Bildband *Sculptures africaines et océaniennes* (1925). Die Ausstellung im Pavillon de Marsan war die erste, die in dieser Größenordnung in Paris stattfand; sie war ein voller Erfolg. Für zwei Monate angesetzt, mußte sie um vier Wochen verlängert werden. Alexandre in *Le Renaissance des arts français*, Fels in *Nouvelles littéraires*, Janneau in *Bulletin de la vie artistique* und Tabarant in *L'Œuvre* und andere Kritiker schrieben wohlwollende Kommentare darüber.

Guillaume, der dem Organisationskomitee nicht angehörte und den offiziellen Exponenten »reiner« Ethnologie mißtraute, hatte zur Bedingung seiner Teilnahme gemacht, daß durch die Darbietung »der künstlerische Anspruch der Arbeiten weder gefährdet noch beeinträchtigt wird«. Als Hauptleihgeber der Ausstellung stand ihm in seiner neu eröffneten Galerie in der Rue La Boétie und in seiner Wohnung in der Avenue de Messine die größte Privatsammlung der damaligen Zeit zur Verfügung: Er besaß an die fünfhundert »antike« Plastiken afrikanischer Herkunft.[112] Der Umfang von Guillaumes Beteiligung an der Ausstellung im Pavillon de Marsan macht diese von ihm selbst genannte Zahl durchaus glaubwürdig.

Obwohl Guillaume über die Quellen seiner Käufe Stillschweigen bewahrte, kann man aus gutem Grund annehmen, daß er sie bei Kollegen wie Brummer und Moris tätigte und aus dem Ausland, vor allem aus England und wahrscheinlich aus Belgien, beliefert wurde. Außerdem enthielten die Anzeigen, die er in der literarischen und künstlerischen Presse aufgab wie auch seine Anzeigen in der Kolonialpresse stets Kaufangebote. Für solche Anzeigen bediente er sich auch des Nachrichtenbuchs im Bréhant, einem Café, in dem Kolonialbeamte auf Heimaturlaub verkehrten: »Paul Guillaume zahlt hohe Preise für alle Objekte und Sammlungen afrikanischer Herkunft.«[113] Man kann ziemlich sicher sein, daß er in Wirklichkeit einige seiner afrikanischen Lieferanten willkommen hieß, als er, wie er groß ankündigte, die Gesandten der Fama von Sassending

□ 203 *›Figur aus Holz und Metall‹, siehe* □ *202 (Seitenansicht).*

oder den Sohn des Dinah Salifou, »König der Baga und der Nalou«, empfing.[114]

Das Ansehen, das sich Guillaume aufgrund seines Erfolges als Sammler und Händler moderner wie auch primitiver Kunst bis in die frühen zwanziger Jahre erworben hatte, steigerte sich noch, als seine Transaktionen mit dem großen amerikanischen Sammler A. C. Barnes bekannt wurden. Er erhielt von Barnes nicht nur mehrere Meisterwerke moderner Kunst, sondern besorgte diesem 1922 und 1923 auch den wesentlichen Teil seiner in Merion, Pennsylvania, aufgebauten Sammlung afrikanischer Plastik. Geht man die Nummern von *Les Arts à Paris* durch, wird man schnell gewahr, daß vom Januar 1923 an die Zeitschrift der Galerie in der Rue La Boétie zum europäischen Organ der Barnes Foundation wurde und Paul Guillaume ihr bevorzugter, wenn nicht ausschließlicher Korrespondent. Er wurde zum Sprachrohr der philosophischen, gesellschaftlichen und ästhetischen Vorstellungen des Sammlers, von denen er sich verführen ließ. Außer Texten aus der Feder von Barnes findet man in Guillaumes Zeitschrift etwa die von Thomas Munro vorgenommene didaktische Bearbeitung seiner *Art of Painting* (1926), die Voranzeige eines Artikels von John Dewey – der zusammen mit William James und George Santayana einer von Guillaumes Hauptautoren war –, die Übersetzung der Statuten des Fleur de Lys Club in Philadelphia, der »einen neuen Bildungsplan für Neger« vorschlug, oder etwa einen Hinweis auf eine Ausgabe von *Opportunity, Journal of Negro Life*, ja sogar eine Photographie von »Paul Guillaume unter Negern in New Jersey«.

Primitive Negro Sculpture, eine Gemeinschaftsarbeit Guillaumes und Munros, der damals Bildungsbeauftragter der Barnes Foundation war, erschien 1926. Es sind darin 48 Objekte von der Elfenbeinküste, aus dem westlichen Sudan, aus Dahome, Gabun, Französisch-Kongo, Belgisch-Kongo und Nigeria (eine kleine Hüftmaske aus dem Benin) abgebildet. Alle entstammen der Sammlung in Merion; die meisten gehörten davon Guillaume. Drei davon waren jedoch im Besitz von MARIUS DE ZAYAS gewesen.[115] Als Guillaume 1923 in *Les Arts à Paris* »afrikanische Kunst in der Barnes Foundation« vorstellte, schrieb er: »In dieser Sammlung . . .

□ 204 *Pavillon von Französisch Äquatorial-Afrika auf der Kolonialausstellung in Paris 1931. Photographiert von M. Cloche.*

wurden die Epochen zum ersten Mal definitiv festgelegt.« In *Primitive Negro Sculpture* werden für die Objekte tatsächlich Epochen genannt: Keines wird darin auf das 20. Jahrhundert datiert und nur zwei auf das 19. Die Entstehung des berühmten *DOGON*-Paares wird zwischen dem 5. und dem 10. Jahrhundert, die einer Reliquiarfigur der *FANG* zwischen dem 8. und dem 10. Jahrhundert angesetzt. Solche Datierungen sind natürlich längst nicht mehr aufrechtzuerhalten.

1929 erschien eine französische Übersetzung des Buches von Guillaume und Munro, in der auf das dritte und vierte Kapitel verzichtet wurde. Gleichzeitig fand in der Galerie Bernheim-Jeune die Ausstellung einer hervorragenden Gemäldesammlung, die Guillaume angelegt hatte, statt. Guillaume befand sich damals auf dem Gipfel seiner Berühmtheit □ 199. Er hätte Paris gerne zu dem noch fehlenden großen Museum für moderne Kunst verholfen und daran ein Museum für »art nègre« angeschlossen. Aber seine Pläne wurden vom Kultusministerium abgelehnt, nicht ohne einen gewissen Groll bei Guillaume zu hinterlassen.

Seine Begeisterung für die Förderung der Kunst Afrikas begann etwas nachzulassen. Im Mai 1927 veranstaltete er eine bedeutende Ausstellung afrikanischer Plastik für den Salon du Sud-Est in Lyon. Damit ergriff er zum letzten Mal die Initiative. In der Maiausgabe 1930 von *Les Arts à Paris* veröffentlichte Waldemar George unter dem Titel »Le Crépuscule des idoles« einen offenen Brief, der Guillaumes Meinung über die Situation zu Beginn der dreißiger Jahre wiedergibt. Als Vorwand für den Brief hatte die »Exposition d'Art Africain et d'Art Océanien« der Galerie du Théâtre Pigalle gedient, in der

□ 205 *Charles Ratton, um 1935, Photographie. Archiv C. Ratton – G. Ladrillère, Paris.*

□ 206 *›Vogel-Kopfschmuck‹*, BAGA *(Guinea), bemaltes Holz, Höhe 54 cm. Musée de l'Homme, Paris.*

einige Objekte aus der Sammlung Guillaume gezeigt wurden, ohne daß dieser etwas mit der Organisation zu tun hatte. Der Verfasser des Briefes würdigte die Verdienste Guillaumes, der Maler und der »ersten Generation« von Sammlern eingeborener Kunst bei der Entdeckung der primitiven »Gestaltungsprinzipien«. Er beklagte aber, daß das ehemals schöpferische Element nun zu »Auflösungserscheinungen« führte. Er nannte die »surrealistischen Dichter, Händler und Maler« als Beispiel, deren »halluzinatorische Wünsche durch den Kontakt mit Götzenbildern verstärkt werden«. Er beschuldigte diese zweite Generation, »den Sinn eines Stils völlig verzerrt« zu haben, indem sie »ihn in den Dienst flüchtiger Leidenschaften stellten«, und ihn in »eine Art Akademiedenken« gezogen zu haben. Dies bedeute nicht, daß »der Negerkunst das Ende beschieden ist . . . Sie ist reif für den Louvre«, denn »sie sollte vom Standpunkt formaler Vollkommenheit betrachtet werden. Wenn die Pahouin [Fang] ihren Höhepunkt bilden, dann deswegen, weil sie den höchsten Grad an Meisterschaft und Kultur darstellen.« Was die neue Generation suchen solle, sei »eine Lektion der Neger über bildhauerisches Können, und nicht Unbeholfenheit . . ., Allgemeingültigkeit und nicht das Exotische und Wilde«. Zwei Monate später teilte Waldemar George seinen Lesern in *Formes* mit, daß er »vom Förderer der Stammeskunst in Europa und den Vereinigten Staaten« ein Geheimnis erfahren habe: »Paul Guillaume denkt daran, sich seiner bedeutenden Sammlung afrikanischer Plastiken zu entledigen.« Wäre dieser Plan ausgeführt worden, hätte wohl trotz Georges Wunschvorstellungen kaum das Musée du Louvre davon profitiert.

Paul Guillaume starb 1934. Am 18. März des folgenden Jahres wurde in New York im Museum of Modern Art die Ausstellung »African Negro Art« eröffnet □ 208. Außer Barnes und Coray beteiligten sich daran die wichtigsten europäischen und amerikanischen Sammler. Domenica Guillaume schickte 34 Objekte. Damit stand der Beitrag Guillaumes, nach der Anzahl der Leihgaben gemessen, an dritter Stelle. Mit fast der doppelten Zahl nahm der Pariser Händler Charles Ratton den ersten Platz ein □ 205.

Charles Ratton gehört zur zweiten Generation von Experten der Negerkunst, gegen die der Autor von »Le Crépuscule des idoles« seine harte Kritik richtete. Aufgrund etwas erweiterter ästhetischer Auffassungen, denen er zur Anerkennung verhalf, gehörte Ratton zu jener Bewegung, die vom Jahre 1930 an Meinungsverschiedenheiten mit Guillaume heraufbeschwor. Ratton war der letzte Händler und Sammler, der eine entscheidende Rolle bei der Verbreitung der afrikanischen Kunst und bei der Neuorientierung der Vorstellungen über sie spielte. Die Unterschiede zu seinem berühmten Vorgänger lassen sich wie folgt zusammenfassen: erstens die Anerkennung verschiedener Stilregionen, die bis dahin unterschätzt wurden oder nicht ausreichend bekannt waren; zweitens die Einbeziehung der amerikanischen Indianer und besonders Ozeaniens; schließlich die Verbesserung der Kontakte, wenn nicht zu den Anthropologen, so zumindest zu den Museumsleuten.

Im Jahre 1923 begann Charles Ratton auf Anregung des Malers ANGEL ZARRAGA einige afrikanische Objekte zu sammeln; das erste Stück hatte er bei Antony Moris in der Rue Victor Massé auf dem Montmartre gekauft.[16] Ratton besaß damals zwei Läden, einen in der Rue Laffitte 39, wo er Arbeiten aus dem europäischen Spätmittelalter verkaufte, und den anderen in der Rue de Rennes 76, wo er Antiquitäten, Fund-

□ 207 *›Maske‹*, PENDE *(Zaire), Holz und Bast, 46 cm. Privatsammlung.*

☐ 208 *Zusammenstellung von Objekten in der Ausstellung »Afrikanische Negerkunst« des Museum of Modern Art, New York 1935.*

stücke von Ausgrabungen im Orient und in Kolumbien, Keramik und Bronzen aus dem Fernen Osten sowie primitive Kunst feilbot. Eine Anzeige in *La Révolution surréaliste* vom Oktober 1927 läßt darauf schließen, daß Ratton schon damals mit der surrealistischen Bewegung in Verbindung stand.

Bei der Ausstellung »Les Arts Anciens de l'Amérique«, die im Jahr darauf im Musée des Arts Decoratifs stattfand, kam eine Reihe von Personen zusammen, die für unser Thema interessant sind. Als Leihgeber traten neben Ratton die Sammler Breton, Tual, Hein und Vignier auf.

Ratton lernte bei seinem Kollegen Vignier dessen Assistenten Georges-Henri Rivière kennen, der für die Aufstellung der präkolumbianischen Arbeiten im Pavillon de Marsan und zusammen mit Alfred Métraux für den Katalog verantwortlich war. Georges Salle, Michel Leiris, André Schaeffner und Georges Bataille hatten auf verschiedenen Gebieten alle mit Rivière zusammengearbeitet. Nachdem er den qualitätvollen Aufbau der Ausstellung gesehen hatte, berief der Amerikaner Paul Rivet, der eben zum Nachfolger Verneaus als Leiter des Trocadéro ernannt worden war, Rivière als Stellvertreter. In der ersten Ausgabe von *Documents*, deren Chefredakteur Georges Bataille unter den Herausgebern Rivet, Rivière und Einstein war, erschien Rivières Plan für die Neugestaltung dieser heruntergekommenen Einrichtung, die ihrem Auftrag überhaupt nicht mehr gerecht werden konnte. Unter einem Programmpunkt werden »Kontakte zu Sammlern und Händlern, von denen man Schenkungen, Nachlässe, Lagerbestände und Leihgaben bekommen könnte«, gefordert; unter einem anderen wird festgestellt, daß die Aufgabe des Völkerkundemuseums nicht die »eines Museums ist, wo die Objekte nur nach ästhetischen Gesichtspunkten präsentiert werden«. Charles Ratton gelang es dieses strenge Prinzip aufzulockern, wenn auch nicht unmittelbar durch die Zahl seiner Schenkungen (es waren zwischen 1930 und 1939 siebzig Objekte, zehn davon aus Afrika).

1930 wählte Ratton zusammen mit Tristan Tzara und Pierre Loeb[117] für die Ausstellung in der Galerie Pigalle fast dreihundert afrikanische Objekte aus den besten Sammlungen der Zeit aus. Nicht nur der bereits anerkannte Stil kam hier zu Wort, sondern auch Gebiete, aus denen der Trocadéro nur wenige oder keine Exemplare besaß: das Königreich Benin, die östlichen Gebiete Nigerias, Kamerun, Angola und sogar Tansania. Die 45 Leihgeber waren u. a. De Miré, Hein, Ratton, Tzara, die Galerie Percier und Stephen-Chauvet. Diese Ausstellung und eine weitere im Palais des Beaux-Arts von Brüssel bestätigen Rattons Ruf über Sammlerkreise hinaus.

1931, dem Jahr der Exposition Coloniale ☐ 204, war Ratton sowohl im Palais Permanent des Colonies, wo man eiligst Plastiken aus seiner Sammlung und Objekte von Carré, Hessel und Lefèvre zusammengestellt hatte, als auch im Trocadéro auf der Exposition Ethnographique des Colonies Françaises vertreten. Als Ergänzung zum Schatz von Behanzin aus dem Besitz des Museums wurde die *Fon*-Gruppe gezeigt, die Ratton von Achille Lemoine, dem Erben Oberst Dodds', erworben hatte. Außerdem nahmen Ratton und Carré an den sechs Versteigerungen des Jahres 1931, auf denen afrikanische Objekte angeboten wurden, als Experten teil: Eine fand mit 114 Objekten am 7. Mai, eine andere mit 30 Objekten aus dem Besitz Bretons und Eluards am 2. und 3. Juli, eine weitere am 16. Dezember statt; letztere versteigerte 112 Objekte aus dem Besitz De Mirés ☐ 760, darunter einige absolute Meisterwerke. Das Vorwort zum Katalog dieser Auktion schloß mit dem Eingeständnis des Verfassers Georges-Henri Rivière: »Möchten Sie wissen, was mir im Kopf herumgeht? . . . Irgendwie ärgere ich mich, daß der Trocadéro nicht reich genug ist, die ganze herrliche Sammlung aufzukaufen.« Da nur wenige Käufer kamen, wurden mehrere Objekte von den Veranstaltern der Auktion erworben. Im selben Jahr veröffentlichte Ratton auch *Masques africains*.

Am 15. Juni 1932 wurde nach der Ankündigung in einer Sondernummer der *Cahiers d'Art* im Trocadéro die »Exposition de Bronzes et d'Ivoires du Royaume du Bénin« eröffnet. Sie wurde ganz allein von Ratton organisiert. Er bestimmte

☐ 209 *›Figur aus Holz und Metall‹, Bambara oder Dogon (Mali), Höhe 69 cm. Privatsammlung.*

□ 210 *›Figur aus Holz‹*, OST-AKAN *(Ghana oder Elfenbeinküste), Höhe 61 cm. The Detroit Institute of Arts. E. C. Ford Fund for African Art.*

□ 211 ▷ *›Maske‹*, CHOKWE *(Zaire oder Angola), Holz und verschiedene Materialien, Höhe 27 cm, Privatsammlung.*

nicht nur die Auswahl und die Aufmachung des Katalogs, sondern half auch bei der Finanzierung.

Es wurden 130 Objekte aus etwa 30 öffentlichen und privaten Sammlungen in England, Frankreich und Deutschland gezeigt. Neben Ratton, der sich mit 14 Objekten beteiligte, finden sich unter den Leihgebern die Namen Carré (25 Objekte), Bernheim, Flechtheim, Ascher, Loeb, Moris, Tzara, DERAIN, Eluard und JACQUES LIPCHITZ. Anläßlich dieser Ausstellung wurde der »Schatz« des Museums für eine Zeitlang aufgebaut. Mit einer von LIPCHITZ konzipierten Installation wurden 12 präkolumbianische, afrikanische und ozeanische Meisterwerke besonders hervorgehoben.

Im Jahr darauf schickte Ratton über hundert zum Verkauf stehende Objekte auf die »All African Exhibition«, die vom 15. Juni bis 30. Oktober in Chicago stattfand.[118] Im Juli desselben Jahres wurde in Carrés Villa in Passy eine Auswahl aus den Sammlungen Rattons und Louis Carrés unter dem Titel »Sculptures et Objets de l'Afrique Noire, de l'Amérique Ancienne, de Mélanésie et de Polynésie« gezeigt. 1934 schrieb Ratton für Nancy Cunards monumentale *Negro Anthology* den kurzen Beitrag »The Ancient Bronzes of Black Africa«, der von Samuel Beckett aus dem Französischen übersetzt wurde.

Ratton erntete 1935 in New York Anerkennung, als gleichzeitig mit der Ausstellung der Galerie Pierre Matisse »African Art – Ratton's Collection« 62 seiner afrikanischen Plastiken im Museum of Modern Art gezeigt wurden. Die gefeierte »Exposition Surréaliste d'Objets«, die ein Jahr später in Rattons Galerie stattfand, enthielt ozeanische, aber keine afrikanischen Objekte und war damit sozusagen ein Hinweis auf den surrealistischen Geschmack. Zwei Jahre später aber richtete Ratton

□ 212 *›Kifwebe-Maske‹*, SONGGE *(Zaire) 48,5 cm. Sammlung A. L. Liebermann, St. Louis.*

mit der Unterstützung MAN RAYS und Eluards eine seltsame Ausstellung unter dem Titel »La Mode au Congo« aus. Sie zeigte Kopfschmuck und Haartrachten junger afrikanischer Frauen in Gegenüberstellung zu Photographien europäischer Modelle, die damit geschmückt waren.

Wir konnten hier nur einen groben Überblick der wichtigeren Aktivitäten Rattons in den späten zwanziger und den dreißiger Jahren geben. Durch die Zusammenstellung von Arbeiten außergewöhnlicher Qualität oder unbestreitbaren historischen Wertes verschaffte er seinen Kunden einige Meisterwerke afrikanischer Kunst. Die Sammlungen, die JACOB EPSTEIN, Baron von der Heydt und Helena Rubinstein vor dem 2. Weltkrieg besaßen, bezeugen seinen sicheren Geschmack.

Mit der glänzenden Ausstellung »African Negro Art«, die James Johnson Sweeney mit Unterstützung Robert Goldwaters und Rattons vorbereitete, kam eine große Zahl von Stammesobjekten (um die 600) in ein Museum moderner Kunst. Wie wir gesehen haben, wurden 1932 »bestimmte seltene und schöne Stücke« von Spiegelbildern einer anderen Lebensweise zu Meisterwerken der Kunst[119] – und dies trotz der »antiästhetischen«[120] Orientierung derjenigen, die den Trocadéro einige Jahre zuvor umgestaltet hatten. Im Jahre 1933 widmete *Minotaure*, das reichillustrierte Kunstmagazin Skiras und Tériades,

□ 213 ›*Figur aus Holz*‹, MAMBILA *(Nigeria), Höhe 45 cm. Musée Barbier-Müller, Genf.*

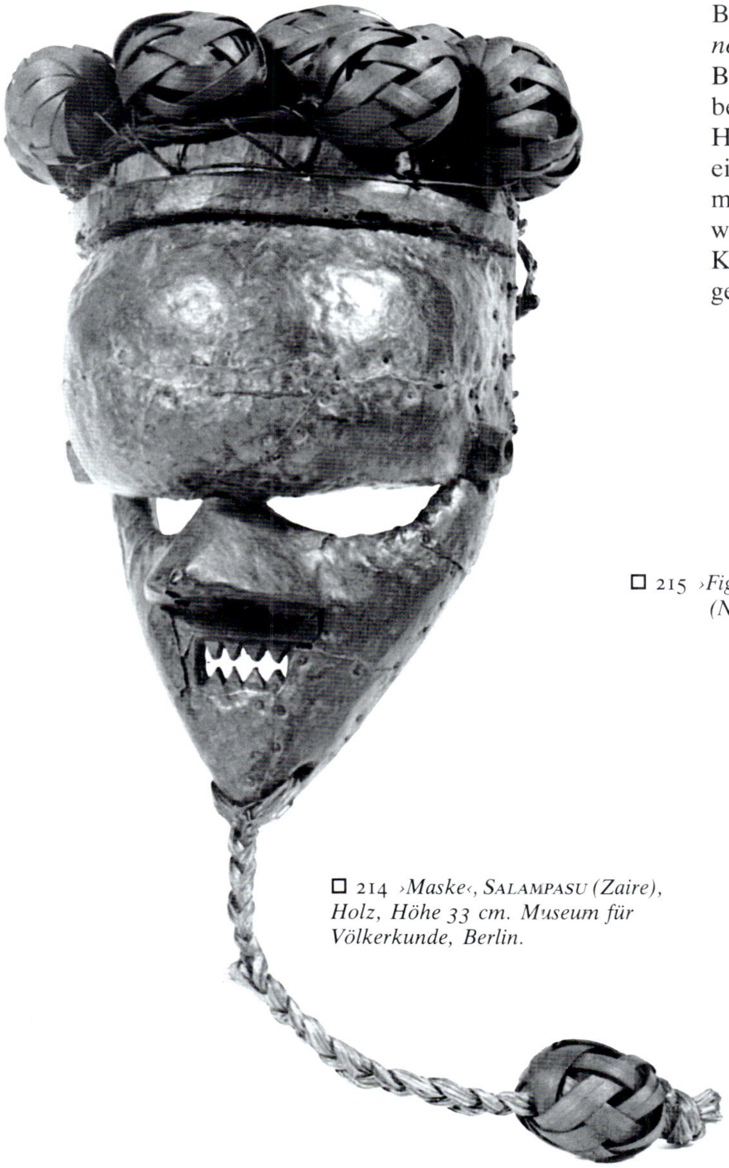

□ 214 *›Maske‹*, SALAMPASU *(Zaire), Holz, Höhe 33 cm. Museum für Völkerkunde, Berlin.*

der Dakar-Dschibuti-Expedition eine ganze Nummer; diese hatte gerade fast 3600 Objekte aus Afrika mitgebracht. Heißt dies, daß der Abstand zwischen den Verfechtern einer reinen Ethnologie und den Ästheten ständig geringer wurde? Eine Versöhnung dieser Gegenstände zu behaupten, wäre reine Rhetorik.

Einige Völkerkundler legten aber später den Grundstein für die Beschäftigung mit der Kunst jener Gesellschaften, die bis dahin nicht als Kunst betrachtet werden durfte, um als authentischer zu gelten. Am Ende seiner langen und minutiösen Monographie *Masques dogons* aus dem Jahre 1938 kommt Marcel Griaule, ein erbitterter Gegner der »Negermode«, zu einigen Schlußfolgerungen, wie sie in Einsteins *Negerplastik* auf seltsame Weise ähnlich vorkommen. Für ihn führte das Studium dessen, was er die Gesellschaft der Masken nennt, zu »neuen Tatsachen über die Entwicklung der afrikanischen Kunst oder sogar der Kunst im allgemeinen . . . Es ist nicht verfrüht festzustellen, daß in der Mentalität der Dogon die ästhetische Empfindung und der Bereich des Todes eng verknüpft sind.« Kann man in der Objektivierung schöpferischer Mittel noch weiter gehen? Zwischen 1935 und 1938 veröffentlichte der Kunstliebhaber und Amateurethnologe Carl Kjersmeier eine erste Typologie der afrikanischen Kunst in vier Bänden. Sie trug den Titel *Les Centres de style de la sculpture nègre africaine*. Anläßlich der Ausstellung »Les Arts du Congo Belge« gewährte Frans Olbrechts einen ersten Blick auf seine berühmte Karte der Stilregionen des riesigen Kongogebiets. Hinter der Tradition einer Gruppe hatte er schon die Existenz einer Werkstatt, das Talent und Geschick eines Meisters ausgemacht. Fern von seiner langen Geschichte, von der wir hier nur wenige Momente beleuchten konnten, trat der afrikanische Künstler endlich aus der Anonymität heraus, in die er verbannt gewesen war.[123]

□ 215 *›Figur aus Holz‹*, KEAKA *(Nigeria), Höhe 51 cm. Privatsammlung.*

Die folgende Tabelle von Jean-Louis Paudrat zeigt, zu welchem Zeitpunkt Objekte bestimmter afrikanischer Stämme erstmals in das Musée d'Ethnographie du Trocadéro (Musée de l'Homme) in Paris gelangten. Zugleich geht aus ihr hervor, wann Objekte derselben Stämme in Veröffentlichungen zur afrikanischen Kunst (siehe unten) erstmals auftauchten.

EINGANG IN DAS MUSÉE D'ETHNOGRAPHIE						STÄMME (NACH IHREM GEOGRAPHISCHEN STANDORT VON NORDEN NACH SÜDEN)	ZEITPUNKT DES ERSCHEINENS IN DEN PUBLIKATIONEN (SIEHE UNTEN)									
vor 1900	1900–07	1908–14	1915–20	1921–30	1931–33		1916	1917	1919	1925	1929 A	1929 B	1930	1931	1935	1938
	X					*Dogon*				X						
X						*Bambara*	X									
X						*Malinke/Marka/Bozo*				X						
	X					*Senufo/Minianka/Nafana/Kulango*	X									
		X				*Bobo/Bwa/Gurunsi/Kurumba*										X
					X	*Mossi*						X				
		X				*Lobi*						X				
X						*Baule/Yaure/Guro*	X									
X						*Anyi/Attie*		X								
						Asante							X			
X						*Balante*										
	X					*Susu*										
X						*Baga/Nalu/Landuma*		X								
X						*Bijogo*						X				
	X					*Koniagi*										
						Mende									X	
	X					*Sherbro/Kissi*						X				
					X	*Toma/Bassa/Kpelle*								X		
					X	*Dan/Mano/Gio/Kono*			X							
	X					*Kru/Guere/Kran/Grebo/Bete*	X									
X						*Fon/Ewe*				X						
X						*Yoruba*			X							
						Nupe									X	
	X					*Königreich Benin*			X							
X						*Igbo*										X
						Ibibio										X
						Ijo										X
						Cross River-Gebiet						X				

1916 MARIUS DE ZAYAS
African Negro Art: Its Influence on Modern Art, New York, Modern Gallery, 1916.

1917 GUILLAUME APOLLINAIRE und PAUL GUILLAUME
Sculptures nègres, 24 Abbildungen, Vorbemerkung von P. Guillaume, Paris 1917.

1919 ANDRÉ LEVEL und HENRI CLOUZOT
L'Art nègre et l'art océanien, Paris 1919.

1925 ANDRÉ LEVEL und HENRI CLOUZOT
Sculptures africaines et océaniennes, colonies françaises et Congo belge, Paris 1925.

Eingang in das Musée d'Ethnographie						Stämme (nach ihrem geographischen Standort von Norden nach Süden)	Zeitpunkt des Erscheinens in den Publikationen (siehe unten)									
vor 1900	1900–07	1908–14	1915–20	1921–30	1931–33		1916	1917	1919	1925	1929 A	1929 B	1930	1931	1935	1938
						Benue River-Gebiet							X			
					X	*Duala/Basa*										X
					X	*Grasland Kameruns*						X				
					X	*Sao*										
	X					*Sara*										
X						*Fang*	X									
X						*Kota*	X									
X						*Mbete*										
					X	*Kwele*				X						
X						*Kuyu*										X
X						*Teke*	X									
				X		*Bembe*			X							
X						*Shira-Punu/Tsogo/Vuvi/Aduma/Njawi*		X								
X						*Kongo/Vili/Woyo*		X								
				X		*Lulua*				X						
				X		*Luba*				X						
					X	*Kuba*			X							
						Mbala					X					
						Lega/Mbole						X				
				X		*Suku/Pende/Yaka*				X						
						Songge							X			
X						*Chokwe*					X					
X						*Yangere*										
				X		*Yakoma*										
	X					*Mangbetu/Zande/Ngbandi*										X
						Makonde						X				
X						*Zulu*										

1929 (A) A. PORTIER und FRANÇOIS PONCETTON
Les Arts sauvages. Afrique, Paris 1929.

1929 (B) PAUL GUILLAUME und THOMAS MUNRO
La Sculpture nègre primitive, Paris 1929.

1930 GALERIE PIGALLE
Katalog der *Exposition d'art africain et d'art océanien,* Paris 1930.

1931 CHARLES RATTON
Masques africains, Paris 1931.

1935 JAMES J. SWEENEY (Hrsg.)
African Negro Art, Katalog der Ausstellung im Museum of Modern Art New York, 18. März – 19. Mai 1935.

1935/38 CARL KJERSMEIER
Centres de style de la sculpture nègre africaine, 4 Bände, Paris und Kopenhagen 1935–38.

□ 215a
›Figur aus Holz‹, Dogon (Mali), Höhe 27 cm. Sammlung Dr. André, Frankreich.

□ 215b ▷
›Figur aus Holz‹, Zande (Zaire), Holz, Kupfer, Perlen und Muscheln, Höhe 20 cm. Sammlung W. Mestach, Brüssel.

Anmerkungen

Dieser Aufsatz ist dem Andenken meines Lehrers Jean Laude gewidmet. Mein Dank gilt Judith Cousins, Krisztina Passuth und Raoul Lehuard für das Material, das sie mir freundlicherweise zukommen ließen. Ich danke gleichfalls meinen Freunden Pierre Pitrou und Georges D. Rodrigues für ihre Hilfe.

1. Besson, M., *L'influence coloniale sur le décor de la vie française*, Paris 1944, zit. in: Laude, J., *La Peinture française et l'art nègre*, Paris 1968, S. 542.

2. Rabelais, *Œuvres complètes*, Paris 1973, S. 798.

3. Laude, J., *Les Arts de l'Afrique noire*, Paris 1979, S. 10.

4. Nach 1878 in den Sammlungen des Musée d'Ethnographie du Trocadéro.

5. Itzikovitz, M., »A propos d'un bronze abron« in *Arts d'Afrique noire*, Winter 1976.

6. Hamy, E.-T., *Les Origines du Musée d'Ethnographie,* Paris 1890, S. 49.

7. »Inauguration du buste du Dr. Hamy« in *L'Anthropologie* 21, Januar-Februar 1910.

8. Marche, A. A., »Voyage au Gabon et sur le fleuve Ogooué« in *Le Tour du monde,* 2. Semester 1878, S. 415.

9. Liesville, A. R. de, *Coup d'œil sur l'Exposition Historique de l'art ancien,* Paris 1879, S. 95 ff.

10. Bei der Darstellung der Sammlungsgeschichte des Trocadéro folgen wir dem Inventar.

11. Katalog des Musée Africain, Paris 1879.

12. Schweinfurth, G., »Au cœur de l'Afrique« in *Le Tour du monde,* 1. und 2. Semester 1874.

13. Über die Westafrikaexpedition siehe Coquery-Vidrovitch, C., *Brazza et la prise de possession du Congo,* Paris 1969.

14. Rivière, E., *Notice sur la mission de l'Ouest Africain,* Paris 1886.

15. Coquery-Vidrovitch, C., a.a.O., S. 16.

16. Sie ist abgebildet bei Brazza, S. de, »Voyages dans l'Ouest Africain« in *Le Tour du monde,* 2. Semester 1888, S. 39.

17. *Vente après décès d'une curieuse collection d'objets des îles de l'Océanie,* Paris, 4. März 1887.

18. S. Rousselet, L., *L'Exposition Universelle de 1889,* Paris 1890, und *Revue de l'Exposition Universelle de 1889,* Paris 1889.

19. *Colonies Françaises et pays de protectorats à l'Exposition Universelle* zit. in: Verger, M.-N., *Présentation des objets de Côte d'Ivoire dans les expositions universelles et coloniales,* Bericht, Universität Paris I, 1982, S. 7.

20. Pol-Neveux, »Le village sénégalais« in *Revue de l'Exposition Universelle,* S. 71.

21. Tomel, G., »Le trône de Béhanzin« in *Le Monde illustré,* 10. Februar 1894, S. 87.

22. Delafosse, M., »Statues des rois de Dahomé . . .« in *La Nature,* 24. März und 21. April 1894.

23. Delafosse, M., »Sur les traces probables . . .« in *L'Anthropologie,* Paris 1900, Bd. 11, S. 431–51.

24. Binger, L. G., »Du Niger au golfe de Guinée« in *Le Tour du monde,* 1. und 2. Semester 1891, S. 1–128 bzw. S. 34–144.

25. Schweinfurth, G., *Artes Africanae,* Leipzig/London 1875.

26. Ratzel, F., *Völkerkunde,* Leipzig 1885–88.

27. Frobenius, L., *Die Masken und Geheimbünde Afrikas,* Halle 1898.

28. Über das Museum für Völkerkunde in Berlin siehe Rumpf, A., und Tunis, I., *Afrika Abteilung,* Berlin o. J., und Krieger, K., *Westafrikanische Plastik* (Bd. 1, 2 und 3) und *Westafrikanische Masken,* Berlin 1960–69.

29. Bastian, A., *Die deutsche Expedition an der Loango-Küste,* Jena 1874–75.

30. Batin, M. L., »Quelques Œuvres tshokwe: Une perspective historique »in *Antologia di Belle Arti,* Rom 1981, 17/20.

31. S. Dark, P. J. C., »An Introduction to Its Discovery and Collection« in *Art of Benin,* Chicago 1962.

32. Fagg, W., *Merveilles de L'art nigérien,* Paris 1963, S. 9, 10.

33. Zit. bei: Laude, J., *La Peinture française,* S. 176.

34. Kandinsky, W., und Marc, F., *L'Almanach du Blaue Reiter,* Übersetzung der deutschen Ausgabe Paris 1981, S. 169.

35. Dieser und die folgenden Abschnitte wurden dem Text mit M. Paudrats Genehmigung angefügt. Sie beruhen auf den Forschungen Jean Wagners.

36. Goldwater, R., »L'Expérience occidentale de l'art nègre« in *Colloque sur l'art nègre,* Paris 1967, Bd. 1, S. 351.

37. Fraser, D., »The Discovery of Primitive Art« in *Anthropology and Art,* New York 1971, S. 28.

38. Zit. bei: Legrand, F. C., *Le Symbolisme en Belgique,* Brüssel 1971, S. 142.

39. Bassani, E., »Carrà e l'arte negra« in *Critica d'arte* 130, Juni 1973, S. 10.

40. Epstein, J., *An Autobiography,* London 1963, zit. bei: Wilkinson, A., *Gauguin to Moore,* Toronto 1981, S. 168.

41. Vlaminck, M., *Portrait avant Décès,* Paris 1943, S. 105.

42. Goldwater, R., *Primitivism in Modern Art,*

überarbeitete Auflage New York 1967, S. 102, Anm. 4.

43. Goldwater, R., a.a.O., S. 87.

44. Goldwater, R., a.a.O., S. 102, Anm. 4.

45. Level, A., *Souvenirs d'un collectionneur,* Paris 1959, S. 59.

46. Laude, J., *La Peinture française,* S. 323.

47. Fénéon, F., *Au-delà de l'Impressionisme,* Paris 1966, S. 27.

48. Fénéon, F., *Œuvres plus que complètes,* Genf/Paris 1970, S. XXVII.

49. Guillaume, P., »Une Estétique nouvelle, l'art nègre« in *Les Arts à Paris* 4, 15. Mai 1919, S. 1.

50. Habasque, G. im Katalog *Les Soirées de Paris,* Paris 1958, Anm. 37 und Laude, J., *La Peinture française,* S. 322.

51. Lhote, A., »Ce monde féerique de la plastique pure« im Katalog *Les Arts africains,* Paris 1955, S. 9.

52. Vlaminck, M., a.a.O., S. 105.

53. Vlaminck, M., a.a.O., S. 106.

54. Die zweite erschien in »Un Masque mère, Maurice de Vlaminck et l'art noir à Paris« in *Encyclopédie de la France d'outre-mer* 6, Paris Juni 1947, S. 12.

55. Crespelle, J.-P., *Vlaminck, fauve de la peinture,* Paris 1958, S. 135.

56. Das Interview mit P. Courthion, das C. Wentick teilweise zitiert, *Modern and Primitive Art,* Oxford 1978, S. 17, ist unveröffentlicht. Ich möchte Pierre Courthion für die Erlaubnis, in das Manuskript Einsicht zu nehmen, danken.

57. Warnod, A., »Matisse est de retour« in *Arts* 26, 27. Juli 1946.

58. Tériade, E., »Matisse Speaks« in *Art News Annual* 21 (1952), aus dem Englischen zurückübersetzt in: *Henri Matisse: Ecrits et propos sur l'art,* Paris 1972.

59. Laude, J., *La Peinture française,* S. 112.

60. Laude, J., a.a.O., S. 111.

61. Stein, G., *Autobiographie d'Alice Toklas,* Paris 1934, S. 71.

62. Jacob, M., *Chronique des temps héroïques,* Paris 1956, S. 71; ders., *Naissance du Cubisme et autres,* Paris 1932, zit. bei: Blachère, J.-C., *Le Modèle nègre,* Dakar 1981, S. 32; Dorgelès, R., *Bouquet de Bohème,* Paris 1947, S. 137.

63. Zit. bei Laude, J., *La Peinture française,* S. 111.

64. Stein, G., a.a.O., S. 71.

65. Malraux, A., *La Tête d'obsédienne*, Paris, S. 17ff.

66. Zervos, C., *Pablo Picasso,* Paris 1942, Bd. II, S. XLVII.

67. »Matisse Speaks« in *Henri Matisse,* a.a.O., S. 121.

68. Kahnweiler, D.-H., *Juan Gris*, Paris 1946, S. 156.

69. Level, A., a.a.O., S. 59.

70. Diese Information wurde freundlicherweise mitgeteilt von Pierre Schneider, Kunstkritiker und Autoriät für das Werk von Matisse.

71. Abgebildet bei Laude, J., *La Peinture française*, Abb. 80.

72. Abgebildet ebenda, Abb. 17.

73. Interview mit Jos Hessel von C. Zervos in *Feuilles volantes/Cahiers d'art* 4/5, Paris 1927, S. 2.

74. Die Photographie wurde dem Museum of Modern Art freundlicherweise von Michel Kellermann besorgt.

75. Zu Brummer siehe Devenyi, I., »Brummer Joszef« in *Muveszet,* Januar 1968, S. 16; Leonard, S., *Henri Rousseau and Max Weber,* New York 1970; Basler, A., *Henri Rousseau,* Paris 1927; Forsyth, W. H., »The Brummer Brothers: An Instinct for the Beautiful« in *Art News,* Oktober 1974.

76. La Beaumelle, A. de, »Max Weber« in *Paris/New York,* Paris 1977, S. 728.

77. Zu Coady siehe Zilczer, J. K., *The Aesthetic Struggle in America, 1913–1918,* Ann Arbor 1975.

78. Ebda.

79. Siehe Basler, A., a.a.O.

80. Göpel, B. und E., *Leben und Meinungen des Malers Hans Purrmann,* Wiesbaden 1961, S. 70–71, 133–34.

81. Decaudin, M., »Guillaume Apollinaire devant l'art nègre« in *Présence africaine 8,* 1958, S. 137ff.; Adéma, M., und Décaudin, M., *Album Apollinaire,* Paris 1971, S. 141.

82. Holman, V. J., *French Reactions to African Art 1900/1910,* Magisterarbeit, London 1980.

83. Salmon, A., *Souvenirs sans fins* (première époque), Paris 1955, S. 333.

84. Blachère, J.-C., *Le Modèle nègre,* S. 31.

85. Ebenda.

86. Zur Verbreitung afrikanischer Kunst in Böhmen siehe Herold, E., *Africké Umeni v Ceskoslovensku,* Prag 1983.

87. Zur Gruppe und zur Zeitschrift siehe Volavkova, Z., »La Revue mensuelle des arts« in *L'Année 1913,* Paris 1971, Bd. 2, S. 989ff.

88. Kahnweiler, D.-H., *My Galleries and Painters,* London 1971, Dok. 13 und 14.

89. Siehe bei Apollinaire, *Les Petites Flâneries de l'art,* Montpellier 1980, S. 164, Anm. 2.

90. S. Mirimanov, V. B., »L'Epoque de la découverte de l'art nègre en Russie« in *Quaderni Poro* 3, Juni-Juli 1981, S. 59ff.

91. Zu Carl Einstein siehe Meffre, L., *Carl Einstein et la problématique des avant-gardes dans les arts plastiques,* Diss., Paris 1980.

92. Devenyi, I., a.a.O., S. 16.

93. Eglington, L., »Untimely passing og P. Guillaume Evokes Memories« in *The Art News 33,* 4, 27. Oktober 1934, S. 1–4.

94. Basler, A., »Monsieur Paul Guillaume et sa collection de tableaux« in *L'Amour de l'art,* Juli 1929.

95. Zit. bei: Laude. J., *La Peinture française,* S. 117.

96. Savinio, A., *Souvenirs,* Palermo 1976, S. 265, Anm. 11.

97. Naumann, F. M., »How, When, and Why Modern Art Came to New York« in *Arts Magazine,* April 1980, S. 96ff.; Demé, F., *L'Approche de l'art Africain aux Etats-Unis d'Amérique 1914/1935,* Diss., Paris 1982.

98. Zit. bei: Seckel, H., im Katalog *Paris/New York,* Paris 1977, S. 228.

99. Nach seinem Abschluß an der Universität Harvard war Paul B. Haviland (1880–1950) einer der tatkräftigsten Mitarbeiter von Stieglitz in der Galerie »291« in den Jahren 1908 bis 1915; er arbeitete dort als Photograph, war Mitglied und Sekretär der Photo-Sezession, Mitherausgeber von *Camera Work*, zusammen mit Marius de Zayas Autor von *A Study of the Modern Evolution of Plastic Expression,* 1913, und einer der Gründer der Zeitschrift *291*. Sein jüngerer Bruder, Frank Burty Haviland (1886–1971), benutzte als Maler nur seine ersten beiden Namen; eine Einzelausstellung seiner Bilder und Zeichnungen fand in der Galerie »291« vom 6. April bis 6. Mai 1914 statt. Er sammelte schon vor dem 1. Weltkrieg primitive Kunst und legte eine wichtige Sammlung an, die auf der Versteigerung von 1936 zerstreut wurde.

100. Siehe Lieferschein an Stieglitz, aufbewahrt im Archiv der Beinecke Library, Yale University.

101. Apollinaire, G., »Arts d'Afrique« in *Paris-Journal,* 1. Juni 1914.

102. Lejeune, E., »Montparnasse à l'époque héroïque« in *La Tribune de Genève,* 8/9. Februar 1964.

103. Bouret, J., »Une Amitié ésthétique au début du siècle: Apollinaire et Paul Guillaume (1911–1918) d'après une correspondance inédite« in *Gazette des Beaux-Arts,* Dezember 1970.

104. Bouret, J., a.a.O., S. 390.

105. Zit. bei Bonnet, M., *André Breton, Naissance de l'aventure surréaliste,* Paris 1975, S. 116.

106. *Les Arts à Paris* 2, 15. Juli 1918, S. 10.

107. Salmon, A., *La Jeune Sculpture française,* Paris 1919, S. 92.

108. Allard, R. »Ménalisme« [sic] in *Le Nouveau Spectateur,* 25. Mai 1919, S. 22–28.

109. Zayas, M. de, *African Negro Art: Its Influence on Modern Art,* New York 1916, S. 12.

110. So in »L'Art du Congo Belge« in *Art et décoration,* 1920; »La Leçon de Tervuren« in *Bulletin de la vie artistique,* 1921; »A. E. F., Sculptures et objets d'usages« in *La Renaissance des arts français et des industries de luxe,* 1922, und »La Décoration des tribus du Congo Belge« in *L'Amour de l'art,* 1923.

111. Zit. von Verger, M.-N., a.a.O., S. 25.

112. Brief Paul Guillaumes im Archiv des Musée des Arts Décoratifs.

113. Zit. von Duncyer, J. M., in *Le Monde,* 7./8. November 1965.

114. Guillaume, P., »The Discovery and Appreciation of Primitive Negro Sculpture« in *Les Arts à Paris* 12, Mai 1926, S. 13.

115. Siehe die Tafeln 7, 10 und 19 in *African Negro Wood Sculpture,* New York 1918, photographiert von Charles Sheeler und mit einem Vorwort von Marius de Zayas.

116. Zu Moris siehe Lehuard, R., »La Collection du Père Moris« in *Arts d'Afrique noire* 46, Sommer 1983.

117. Tzara, T., *Œuvres complètes,* Paris 1976, Bd. 4, S. 674., Anm. 2.

118. Raoul Lehard teilte mir dies freundlicherweise mit.

119. Jamin, J., »Objets trouvés des paradis perdus« in *Collections Passion,* Neuchâtel 1982, S. 93.

120. Interview mit Georges-Henri Rivière in *Chefs d'œuvres du Musée de l'Homme,* Paris 1965, S. 15.

121. Siehe Vogel, S. M., »The Buli Master, and Other Hands« in *Art in America,* Mai 1980, S. 133ff.

Paul Gauguin, ›Geschnitzter Türrahmen‹, von dessen Haus auf den Marquesasinseln, um 1899, bemaltes Holz, linke Basis: 40 x 153 cm, linker Pfosten: 200 x 39 cm, Balken: 242 x 39 cm, rechter Pfosten: 195 x 40 cm, rechte Basis: 205 x 40 cm. Linke Basis in Privatbesitz, die übrigen Teile im Musée d'Orsay, Paris.

Der Primitivismus in der Kunst des zwanzigsten Jahrhunderts

□ 216 *Paul Gauguin, ›Gegrüßt seist Du Maria‹ (Ia Orana Maria* – Je vous salue Marie), 1891, Öl auf Leinwand, 113 x 87 cm.
The Metropolitan Museum of Art, Vermächtnis Sam Lewisohn, New York.

Kirk Varnedoe

Paul Gauguin

Paul Gauguin ist der Stammvater des modernen Primitivismus. Wohl haben vor ihm andere Maler die Kunst primitiver Gesellschaften gekannt, jedoch erkannte Gauguin als erster in diesen Kunstformen die Herausforderung an die europäische Tradition der Wirklichkeitsdarstellung. In den gedrängten und wunderlich proportionierten Formen der Stammeskunst sah er nicht den Ausdruck von Unvermögen, sondern einer freien, andersartig formenden Schöpferkraft. Diese Auffassung – eine Umkehrung der Wertmaßstäbe seines durch Technik und Fortschrittsglauben beherrschten Jahrhunderts – bestimmte Gauguins Leben und Werk.[1]

Sein Leben bietet Stoff für ein Familienepos. Gauguin war Einzelgänger, von Natur aus rastlos und unzufrieden. Sein Mischlingsblut war ihm ständig bewußt, und er trauerte seiner frohen Kindheit an fernen Küsten nach (bis zu seinem 9. Lebensjahr zog ihn seine verwitwete Mutter in Peru auf, 1856 kehrten sie nach Frankreich zurück). In den späten 80er Jahren des vorigen Jahrhunderts – Gauguin hatte seine ungeliebte bürgerliche Karriere in der Finanzwelt abgebrochen und sich von Frau und Kindern getrennt – fühlte er sich erneut herausgefordert: Er sah die Grenzen der impressionistischen Weltsicht und ihres Stils, die ihn doch einmal zum Künstlertum geführt hatten. Je mehr er seine Malerei Änderungen unterwarf, auf einfachere Zeichnung, flächigere Raumgestaltung und kühnere Farbgebung drängte, desto mehr erkrankte er an der städtischen Gesellschaft. Er fühlte sich nur heimisch in rauherer Umgebung wie der ländlichen Bretagne, wo er »wie ein Bauer« in groben Kleidern und mit geringen Mitteln leben konnte – er rühmte, daß er nicht »des Lebensgenusses beschuldigt werden kann«.[2] 1887 war sein erster Versuch fehlgeschlagen, Frankreich für immer zu verlassen: Er hatte zwar auf Martinique ein kurzes Idyll erlebt, mußte aber in Panama unter schlimmsten Bedingungen arbeiten. Aber 1891 vollzog er den endgültigen Bruch. Er schiffte sich ein, um auf Tahiti unter den »Wilden« zu leben (Tahiti gehört zu den polynesischen Gesellschaftsinseln und war seit 1843 französisches Protektorat). Nur einmal noch, 1893, kam Gauguin nach Frankreich zurück. Für die letzten Jahre seines Lebens zog er noch weiter fort – auf die Marquesasinseln, wo er 1903 starb. In einem seiner letzten Briefe an eine zivilisierte Welt, von der er sich zurückgezogen und entfremdet hatte, brach eine bittere, verteidigende und zugleich herausfordernde Selbsteinschätzung aus ihm hervor: »Ich bin am Ende, doch nicht besiegt. Ist der Indianer, der unter Martern lächelt, besiegt? Kein Zweifel, der Wilde ist besser, als wir es sind. Es ist Dein Fehler, wenn Du sagtest, ich hätte Unrecht zu behaupten, ich sei ein Wilder. Denn ich bin mir wirklich ein Wilder. Zivilisierte Menschen bezweifeln das, denn in meinen Bildern gibt es nichts, das so überraschend oder verwirrend ist wie dieses ›Wild-sein-trotz-meiner-selbst‹. Das macht sie so unnachahmlich.«[3]

Mit dieser launenhaften Abneigung gegen die Zivilisation und seiner Liebe zu außereuropäischer Kunst ist Gauguin scheinbar der unbestrittene Vorläufer des Primitivismus, der für das künstlerische Leben des 20. Jahrhunderts so wichtig werden sollte. Aber die Legende Gauguin wirft Probleme auf – sein Beitrag zum modernen Primitivismus muß überprüft werden. Steckt in seinem letzten Ausspruch nicht eine allzu pathetische Selbsteinschätzung? An Gauguins neuer Form- und Farbgebung ist leicht zu erkennen, daß sie eher von fortschrittlichen europäischen Künstlern wie Degas und Cézanne herstammen als von irgendeinem primitiven Vorbild. Sogar in seinen »wildesten« Visionen, ich denke an *Der Geist der Toten wacht* □ 249, bleiben die höchst erlesenen Farbharmonien und die Anmut der Linie auf völlig unbarbarische Weise dem europäischen Geschmack verbunden. Manet und Ingres spuken weit mehr durch diese Komposition als exotische Geister (teils ägyptische, teils polynesische) – von denen wohl die Gestalt im Hintergrund hergeleitet ist. Und der Traum vom friedlichen Arkadien des Puvis de Chavannes ist in tahitischen Meisterwerken wie *Woher kommen wir? Wer sind wir? Wohin gehen wir?* □ 218 trotz der (unpolynesischen) Götterfiguren allgegenwärtig und phantasievoll umgestaltet.

Man sollte den exotischen Gehalt solcher Bilder nicht wörtlich nehmen. Geduldiges Prüfen hat heute Fakten von Verdrehungen geschieden, Gauguins Lebenslegende zurechtgerückt und aufgedeckt, wie oft das »Primitive« in Gauguins Vorstellungen und Bildern aus Photoalben und Reiseführern stammt.[4] Gemessen an wirklichen Entdeckungen und echter Kulturflucht wirkt Gauguins Primitivismus wie eine Fassade aus Halbwahrheiten.

Es gibt bessere Möglichkeiten der Beurteilung. Der moderne künstlerische Primitivismus sucht nicht so sehr nach neuen Objekten als nach neuen Wegen, sich diesen zu nähern: Er ist vor allem eine Geisteshaltung. Gauguins Rolle als Wegbereiter liegt in seiner Denk- und Arbeitsweise und vorrangig in der Eröffnung neuer Möglichkeiten, um primitive mit moderner Kreativitätskraft zu verbinden. Eine Aufzählung der äußeren Einflüsse auf Gauguin – reine oder verfälschte – wirkt wie das Modell eines »wahren« Primitivzustandes, den Gauguin erreichte oder auch nicht; sie treffen nicht den Kern des Themas ›Gauguin und der Primitivismus‹. Will man Gauguins Begegnung mit bestimmten Formen primitiver Stammeskunst bestimmter Stammesgebiete verstehen, so muß man zunächst seine besondere geistige Situation betrachten, die eine solche Begegnung ermöglichte, auch das Ambiente, in dem seine Haltung Gestalt annahm und sich festigte. In diesen unscheinbaren Bereichen liegt tatsächlich eine unverfälschte primitivistische Persönlichkeitsstruktur, die nicht immer erkannt wurde. GAUGUINS Neuerungen, auf diese umfassendere und genauere Weise betrachtet, sind wiederum keine echten Entdeckungen. Sie sind mit einer breiteren Tradition des Primitivismus eng verbunden, die der Entwicklung von GAUGUINS Ästhetik vorausgeht und sie durchdringt.

In seiner ursprünglichen Form hat der Primitivismus – die Bewunderung der Tugenden materiell wenig entwickelter Gesellschaften – im europäischen Denken eine lange und weitverzweigte Geschichte. Schon in der klassischen Antike gab es Schriften, die den Verlust der Einfachheit beklagten und weniger verfeinerte Gesellschaften priesen.[5] Als im 16. und 17. Jahrhundert die Entdeckungsreisen zur Begegnung mit unbekannten Rassen und Gesellschaften führten, waren die Europäer über die große Vielfalt der Menschheit erstaunt. Sie bedachten von neuem die möglichen Vorzüge eines Lebens, unberührt von den Zwängen europäischer Zivilisation. Seit Montaignes satirischer Verteidigung der Kannibalen in einem Essay von 1592 kreist eine ganze philosophische und literarische Tradition um den Edlen Wilden, ein unverdorbenes Wesen, unschuldig und zugleich weise, oft asketisch abgehärtet, in anderen Varianten wieder höchst sinnlich. Seine reineren Tugenden und einfacheren Gedanken wurden als Gegenbild zur oberflächlichen, verweichlichten Künstlichkeit des zivilisierten Europa gepriesen. Diese Tradition erlebte gerade im 18. Jahrhundert eine Hochblüte, als die Philosophen der Aufklärung utopische Visionen von einem ursprünglichen Glückszustand und hoher moralischer Stärke des Menschen vor der zivilisatorischen Unterwerfung formulierten. Sie schmückten ihre Argumente mit optimistischen Berichten von den überseeischen Kulturen, die europäische Forscher noch immer entdeckten. Eine der letzten, aber die berühmteste Abhandlung ist Jean-Jacques Rousseaus »Discours sur l'origine et les fondements de l'inégalité parmi les hommes«. Rousseau geißelte den selbstgefälligen Glauben Europas an den Wert des Fortschritts und spottete über den Nutzen einer organisierten Gesellschaft (Voltaire antwortete mit »Dank für Eure Schrift gegen die Zivilisation«, als er eine Kopie des Essays erhalten hatte). Rousseaus Lobpreisung eines erfüllten Lebens auf einer früheren, einfacheren Stufe gab dem primitivistischen Denken erneut einen zwingenden und emotionalen Anstoß. Etwa 20 Jahre später schien eine Entdeckung den Traum von einer natürlichen Erfüllung des Menschen vor der modernen Verderbtheit zu bestätigen – die Entdeckung der Insel Tahiti im Jahre 1767.

□ 217 *Paul Jamin, ›Eine Entführung – Die Steinzeit‹, 1889, Öl auf Leinwand, Musée des Beaux-Arts, Reims.*

Die Berichte der ersten Entdecker Tahitis (wir werden uns noch genauer damit befassen) enthielten Visionen unverfälschten Vergnügens und natürlichen Glücks, die für viele jeden Anspruch auf die Vormachtstellung der modernen europäischen Gesellschaft endgültig untergruben. Ein Primitivismus, den solche Beweise stützten und der als Symbolfigur einen erdichteten, oft ganz und gar phantastischen Edlen Wilden vorwies, war ein zentraler Aspekt der fortschrittlichen politischen, philosophischen und religiösen Ideen im 18. Jahrhundert. Denker nahmen die Idee des primitiven Menschen als Markstein, um die Grundlagen sozialer Strukturen zu bestimmen, andere untersuchten die Berichte über die neuentdeckten Völker nach Anhaltspunkten über Biologie und Physiologie der menschlichen Rassen. Nicht allein das Wissen um die Überlegenheit des Lebens außerhalb der Zivilisation, auch die Verbindung des Studiums fremder Völker mit der Analyse der innersten Natur des Menschen trugen zu einer primitivistischen Tradition bei. Sie war das charakteristischste und folgenreichste Vermächtnis der intellektuellen Unruhe des 18. Jahrhunderts. GAUGUINS Wissen um die Werte primitiver Kunst wurzelte in dieser Gedankenwelt, die zu seiner Zeit wieder auflebte und sich weiterentwickelte. GAUGUIN, Vorfahr des modernen künstlerischen Primitivismus, war auch Erbe einer langen Tradition.

Das Erbe ist komplex, es beginnt schon mit dem Wort »primitif«. Im französischen Sprachgebrauch hat es viele mögliche Bedeutungen, für GAUGUIN mögen mehrere gleichzeitig wichtig gewesen sein. »Primitiv« bezeichnet u. a. einen ungebildeten Menschen, einen anfänglichen oder ursprünglichen Zustand, den Grundzustand einer Sache oder Erfahrung. So kann sich das Wort auf fremde Völker beziehen und zugleich auf das einem selbst zutiefst Angeborene. Der doppelsinnige Gebrauch des Wortes – als Begriff zur Stufung der Gesellschaften und für eine Philosophie, die sich mit dem menschlichen Wesen befaßt – gab dem Begriff »primitiv« eine besondere Bedeutung in der Gedankenwelt zu Zeiten GAUGUINS. Besonders in der Kunstbetrachtung des späten 19. Jahrhunderts fand das Etikett »primitiv« breitere Anwendung als heute. Frührenaissance und Volkskunst, japanische Drucke und Stammeskunst, alles fiel darunter. »Primitiv« stand der Bedeutung von »bäuerlich« und »archaisch« näher, als es heute der Fall ist.[6] Im weitesten Sinn hatte der Begriff »primitiv«, auf andere Künste und Kulturen angewandt, nie eine festumrissene Aussage – diese war nur in der Relation zu den wechselnden, gegenübergestellten Begriffen zu erkennen (»zivilisiert«, »modern« usw.). Das Wort »primitiv« wurde auch mit gegensätzlichen

□ 218 *Paul Gauguin, ›Woher kommen wir? Wer sind wir? Wohin gehen wir?‹ (D'ou venons-nous? Qui sommes-nous? Ou allons-nous?), 1897, Öl auf Leinwand, 139 x 374 cm. Museum of Fine Arts, Sammlung Tompkins, Boston.*

Begriffsgruppen verbunden, die seine Aussage und Wirkung klärten: heidnisch und christlich, natürlich und künstlich, irrational und rational usw. Jede Gruppe beinhaltete zugleich eine Wertung von hoch und niedrig, normativ und abweichend, gut und böse.[7] Das geläufige Bild von GAUGUIN als eines Veränderers dieser Ordnung hält solche simplen Gegensätze aufrecht: avantgardistischer Künstler gegen Gesellschaft, Wilder gegen Zivilisation und schließlich – ein Mann, in sich zerrissen, kämpft darum, eine zähe, instinkthaft vitale, »eingeborene« Person gegen die Schwächen seiner zivilisierten Überfeinerung zu behaupten (»Du mußt wissen«, schrieb er an seine Frau, »es gibt zwei Naturen in mir: den Indianer [d. h. den eingeborenen Amerikaner] und den Empfindsamen. Das Empfindsame ist verschwunden, nun kann der Indianer aufrecht und stark voranschreiten.«).[8]

In der Geschichte primitivistischer Ideen verdecken solche Dichotomien viel komplexere Verbindungen der scheinbar gegensätzlichen Begriffe. Jede Zivilisation erfindet das »Primitive«, das sie braucht, nicht nur als Antithese zu ihrer kulturellen Überfeinerung, sondern teilweise auch als Spiegelbild, um ihre Zweifel und Ideale auszugleichen oder zu kritisieren. Der zivilisierte Mensch hielt die primitive Welt – auch wenn er sie noch so sehr ausbeutete – für die Wiege seiner Kindheit. Neue Völker sah er als unverfälschte Abbilder seines ureigensten Wesens an. Die Geschichte des Primitivismus ist im europäischen Denken geprägt von einer Mischung erdachter Mythen und gesammelter Beweise. Wunschträume werden mit wirklichen Entdeckungen vermengt. Die Bewunderung anderer Gesellschaftsformen geht dabei Hand in Hand mit der Selbstkritik an der modernen europäischen Gesellschaft. Die Kontraste in der Legende GAUGUIN – wahrer Wilder und zivilisierter Künstler, Avantgardist und Konservativer, Indianer und Empfindsamer – sind in ähnlicher Weise nicht als »entweder – oder« zu verstehen, sondern als zusammengehörige Begriffe. Sie bergen Spannungen, die typisch sind für GAUGUINS rastloses Schwanken. Auch die europäische Begeisterung für die primitive Welt ist durch diese Ambivalenzen – Tatsache und Dichtung, Selbsttäuschung und Selbstkritik – charakterisiert. GAUGUINS Primitivismus, der auf eine Art folgerichtig in dieser Tradition steht, schöpft seine größte Kraft nicht nur aus der Flucht vor der Gesellschaft, sondern auch aus der Umsetzung der Interessen dieser Gesellschaft.

Das wissenschaftliche und kulturphilosophische Denken des 19. Jahrhunderts glaubte ein Phänomen – sei es eine Person, eine Sprache, eine Zivilisation – nur aus seinem Ursprung und organischen Wachstum verstehen zu können. In der 2. Hälfte des Jahrhunderts beschäftigte die Idee des Primitiven – im Sinne von Urzustand oder Urform – Biologen, Sozialtheoretiker, Linguisten und Psychologen (das wichtigste und folgenreichste Beispiel einer solchen Analyse ist Darwins *Entstehung der Arten*). In Frankreich wie überall untersuchten und verglichen die verschiedenen Wissenschaften »das Primitive« in Prähistorie, Kindheit und Stammesgemeinschaften, um ihre Theorien über die Grenzen und Möglichkeiten des Menschen und seinen Platz in der Naturordnung unter Beweis zu stellen. GAUGUINS Einstellung formte sich in diesem geistigen Klima, seine Wertschätzung der »primitiven« Kreativität war Teil einer Welle des Umdenkens, die auch die Wissenschaftler mitgerissen hatte. Besonders am Ende des Jahrhunderts wurde das Problem der biologisch begründeten Vorstellungen vom »Natürlichen« wichtig.[9]

Diese etablierten Vorstellungen stammten zum größten Teil aus einer Evolutionstheorie, die des Menschen Ursprung und Wesen vom Tier herleitete – aus dem Darwinismus und seinen Varianten. Ein anti-primitivistischer Pessimismus, der auf Darwin zurückging, ihn aber mißverstand, setzte sich in den 1860er und -70er Jahren durch und kam zur Zeit GAUGUINS in Gemälden des Salons zum Ausdruck, die die Brutalität der Urmenschen darstellten □ 217.[10] Mit verbissener »Genauigkeit« wies dieser Pessimismus alle Träumereien vom kindlichen Glück der Menschheit in einem Goldenen Zeitalter zurück, verteidigte eine rassisch bedingte Kulturhierarchie und schürte die Sorge um eine im Menschen latent vorhandene animalische Roheit (Ängste dieser Art kursierten in Frankreich, nachdem man 1871 die Gewalttätigkeit des Pöbels während des Aufstands der Kommune erlebt hatte).[11]

GAUGUINS Vorstellung von »Wildheit« (*sauvagerie*) widersprach dieser Sicht des Menschen, hielt aber auch von den optimistischen Idealen nichts, zu denen sich in den 1890er Jahren politisch bewußte Maler bekannten. Sie glaubten, der moderne Mensch könne ein utopisches Zeitalter der Harmonie mit der Naturordnung erlangen.[12] GAUGUIN vertrat von Anfang an einen kulturellen Primitivismus, der nichts mit einem verlo-

☐ 219 *Paul Gauguin, ›Der gelbe Christus‹ (Le Christ Jaune), 1889, Öl auf Leinwand, 92 x 73 cm. Albright-Knox Art Gallery, Buffalo.*

renen oder zukünftigen Naturzustand zu tun hatte. Im Gegenteil, GAUGUIN zog es zu Orten, wo das lange Vergangene in der Gegenwart zu überleben schien. Das Geheimnis, das ihn anzog, wohnte in den nichturbanisierten Menschen seiner Zeit. Frei von moderner Künstlichkeit verlief ihr Leben doch unter dem Joch überkommener Gesellschaftstraditionen. GAUGUINS anfängliche Begeisterung für bretonische Bauern war nicht einfach die Nostalgie nach dem Landleben, er war bezaubert von dem Geheimnisvollen – der Tracht, dem Aberglauben, den religiösen Bräuchen –, das die Bretonen zu atavistischen Außenseitern inmitten des modernen Frankreich machte.[13] Dort und später in Polynesien interessierten GAUGUIN Überbleibsel kultureller Determination immer mehr als das Ideal der natürlichen Freiheit.

In der landläufigen Betrachtung des Primitivismus, auch desjenigen GAUGUINS, wird dieser grundsätzliche Unterschied zwischen Sehnsucht nach einem Naturzustand und Begeisterung für ehrwürdige Kulturformen oft übersehen. Man sucht vielmehr nach einer ursprünglichen, leeren Unschuld. Tatsächlich ist das Zurückverfolgen »natürlicher«, biologischer oder animalischer Verhaltensweisen (wie in den Salondarstellungen zur Prähistorie) grundverschieden von dem Interesse, das GAUGUIN ländlicher Sitte und Gesellschaft in bretonischen Bildern entgegenbringt wie *Der gelbe Christus, Die bretonische Kreuzigung, Die Vision nach dem Gebet* ☐ 219, 221. Die erste Form der Regression sucht nach einer gegebenen, ursprünglichen Einheit des Menschen mit den Gesetzen des Organischen, während die zweite mit Hilfe der Folklore den Aufbau von Kulturen beobachtet und dabei die menschliche Natur außer acht läßt. Nach dieser Unterscheidung wird verständlich, wie GAUGUINS Primitivismus – der zu der Zeit Gestalt annahm, als der Künstler immer unzufriedener mit dem Impressionismus wurde – Teil einer antinaturalistischen Haltung war. Es ging hierbei nicht allein um eine ästhetische Auseinandersetzung mit der Nachahmung von Natureindrücken, sondern um eine deutliche Ablehnung des rein biologisch oder zu sehr organisch begründeten Denkens, eine für die Avantgarde seiner Zeit typische Ablehnung.

Naturalistische Kunst folgte dem Auge. Sie vertraute auf passive Beobachtung und die Wahrhaftigkeit der Sinneseindrücke, die in den 1880er Jahren seit Jahrzehnten Dogma materialistischer Wissenschaft und Philosophie war. GAUGUIN hatte den Eindruck, daß der Impressionismus aufgrund der Abhängigkeit von flüchtigen Eindrücken auf der Netzhaut des Auges letztlich den gleichen veralteten Grundsätzen verbunden war. Als GAUGUIN sagte, die Impressionisten arbeiteten »ohne Freiheit, da sie an die Augenscheinlichkeit gebunden sind«, wandte er sich gegen die Auffassung, das Hirn sei Sklave der Sinne. Und als er ihnen vorwarf, sie »forschten nur mit dem Auge und nicht in der geheimnisvollen Welt des Gedankens«, da trennte er das Sinnesorgan vom Intellekt und verwies auf eine Neubelebung der Idee durch eine dem Geist angeborene, selbsttätig schöpferische Kraft.[14] Diese Vorstellung von der Überlegenheit des Geistes gegenüber der Materie war Hauptgrund für die Ablehnung der rein biologischen Betrachtungsweise des Menschen und Anfang einer neuen Sicht des Primitiven. Die beiden Auffassungen davon, wie Kunst mit Erfahrung zusammenhängt – die alte »Netzhaut«-Idee und das neue Betonen des »Geistigen«, das GAUGUIN vorzog –, stehen nicht nur mit umfassenderen Vorstellungen über die Mechanismen des Geistes in Beziehung, sondern auch mit der negativen oder positiven Bewertung von Kulturentstehung und -entwicklung.

Die naturalistische Auffassung von Kunst als Nachahmung und die damit übereinstimmende Vorstellung, Denken sei das Resultat von Sinneswahrnehmungen, schien die bildliche Darstellung auf einen reinen Reflex zu reduzieren. Dieses Weltbild sah alle Darstellungsformen des Menschen – selbst Sprache, Religion und bildliche Darstellung – in der Nachahmung von Naturphänomenen verwurzelt. Zur Theorie über die Ursprünge der Kultur ausgeweitet, bot diese Weltansicht ein düsteres, unschönes Bild vom tastenden Beginnen der Menschheit und schloß so jede primitivistische Bewunderung für frühere, weniger entwickelte Erzeugnisse der Menschen aus: jede menschliche Leistung habe in unvollkommener Einheit mit der Natur begonnen und sei im Lauf der Zeiten wie eine Pflanze über verschiedene Stadien zu ständig zunehmender organischer Vielfalt gediehen.

Das Denken des späten 19. Jahrhunderts lehnte diese Behauptung des Naturalismus zusehends ab und wertete das Primitive damit auf. Als das neue Jahrhundert nahte, erkannte man immer deutlicher, daß die Mechanismen der menschlichen Intelligenz, Gesellschaft und Geschichte völlig un»natürlich« sind und wenig mit dem Wachstum von Pflanzen und Reflexbewegungen zu tun haben. Sehen und Denken hielt man nun im Einklang mit neuen Erkenntnissen der Psychologie mehr für einen Akt des Begreifens als des Wahrnehmens. Der Geist galt nicht mehr als passiver Behälter, den die Natur mit Eindrücken füllte, sondern als eine handelnde, organisierende Kraft, die von Anfang an das Chaos von Eindrücken ordnet.[15] Bildliche Darstellung war so gesehen eine Tat, keine Reaktion, ihr Wesen war Neubau, nicht Nachahmung. Infolgedessen entsprang Kultur – Sprache, Religion und Kunst – der Erfindung, nicht der Nachahmung. Am Anfang stand die expressive Äußerung von Tönen und Formen, die dann zu einem Verständigungsmittel geordnet wurden. Die Abwendung vom naturalistischen Denken ließ eine neue Betrachtungsweise des Primitiven zu: Es verkörperte nicht mehr die Unzulänglichkeit des Menschen der Urzeit und seine sklavische Bindung an die Natur, sondern barg in sich die schönste Kraft des Menschen, den Funken des Geistes, der ihn aus dem Bereich der Tiere und Pflanzen befreite.[16]

Gauguin besaß weiträumige, aber ziellose geistige Ambitionen. Er verkehrte in Kreisen, die stolz auf ihre wissenschaftlichen, pseudowissenschaftlichen wie auch philosophischen Erkenntnisse für eine neue Kunst waren. Der Wandel der geistigen Strömungen war Gauguin voll bewußt, besonders dann, wenn dieser Wandel seine Vorlieben und Wünsche zu begünstigen schien. Wenn sein Primitivismus auch Ursprung und Auslegung mit den umwälzenden Neuerungen des historischen und wissenschaftlichen Denkens gemeinsam hat, so ist er nicht als Erläuterung oder gar Reflex von aktuellen Theorien zu begreifen. Die neue antinaturalistische Sicht, von der ich gerade sprach, war das Umfeld für Gauguins Innovation. Das Manifest dieser Neuerung, die stilistische und konzeptionelle Wandlungen zu einem neuen künstlerischen Primitivismus verschmolz, ist das Bild *Die Vision nach dem Gebet* (*Jakobs Kampf mit dem Engel*) von 1889 □ 221.

□ 220 *Paul Gauguin, ›Die bretonische Kreuzigung‹ (Le calvaire breton), 1889, Öl auf Leinwand, 92 x 73 cm. Musées Royaux des Beaux-Arts de Belgique, Brüssel.*

Gerade wie die frühen Bilder aus der Bretagne stilistisch zunächst dem Impressionismus verpflichtet waren, so behandelte Gauguin Charakter und Kultur der Bretagne in konventionell pittoresker Manier, als wüchsen sie aus diesem eigenartig strengen, düsteren Boden. In der *Vision* aber entwickelte Gauguin einen neuen Formwillen, der stärker von der Phantasie als von Natureindrücken bestimmt war, und formulierte eine neue, ausgesprochen unirdische Sicht des ländlichen Themas. Auf die extrem flächige, zinnoberrote Landschaft projizierte er die Schau der frommen Frauen, die noch ganz ins Gebet versunken sind. Gauguin schrieb an Van Gogh, dieses Bild sei von »bäuerlicher und abergläubischer« Einfachheit und erklärte, es vereine zwei Welten in sich. Die *Vision* stelle eine vordergründige, natürlich abgebildete Welt der Sinne (»les gens nature«) gegen eine Landschaft und einen Kampf, der »nur in der Phantasie« der Frauen existiere und daher durch das Mittel starker Größenunterschiede als übernatürlich (»non nature«) gekennzeichnet sei. Das Bild verband in seiner grob vereinfachenden Gestaltung Sichtbares und Visionäres und verknüpfte Gauguins antinaturalistische, antiimpressionistische Stilisierung mit seiner Überzeugung, daß das Volk eine stark übersinnliche Vorstellungsgabe besäße.[17]

Auf den ersten Blick mag die *Vision* ein Bild der Gläubigkeit sein, aber im Gesamtzusammenhang von Gauguins Œuvre gesehen ist das Hauptthema die primitive Denkungsart. Aus diesem Bild spricht zum ersten Mal Gauguins Glaube an die Verwandtschaft zwischen dem unverkünstelten Geist und der Schöpferkraft des modernen Künstlers. Gauguin verfiel hier nicht in bloßen Mystizismus – er wählte im Gegenteil eine karikaturhafte Vereinfachung der Formen –, sondern ließ die primitivistische Tradition in aggressiv neuer und zeitgenössischer Art wieder aufleben. Seit Philosophen des 18. Jahrhunderts wie Condillac und Rousseau einfaches Leben mit vereinfachtem Denken gleichgesetzt hatten, war die Erforschung materiell weniger entwickelter Gesellschaften mit dem Studium des Geistes verknüpft. Primitive Ausdrucksweisen, so dachte man, erhellten in reinerer oder klarer umrissener Form die geistigen Funktionen des Menschen. Das romantische Vermächtnis Herders – die Annahme einer Verbindung zwischen »einfacheren« Menschen und geläuterter Wiedergabe geistiger Grundstrukturen – verwirklichte sich in einer besonderen Verehrung der Volkskunst als eines ungegängelten Kunstsinns, der als Beweis für einen angeborenen, universalen Ursprung der menschlichen Schöpferkraft genommen wurde. Diese Ansicht kam in so ungleichen künstlerischen Bereichen zum Ausdruck wie der romantischen »Natur-Poesie« und dem Realismus Courbets (seiner Bewunderung für das bodenständige Volkstum, bei dem er Anleihen machte), bis sie in Gauguins Tagen für das antinaturalistische Denken und Kunstschaffen eine neue Bedeutung gewann. Im späten 19. Jahrhundert wurde die alte Herdersche Begeisterung für den poetischen Gehalt der Einfachheit mit wissenschaftlichen Maximen von der Bedeutung und der angeborenen Überlegenheit einfacher menschlicher Ausdrucksformen untermauert. Fortschrittliche Denker verwarfen mehr und mehr die evolutionären Maßstäbe, die Überlegenheit mit größter Komplexität gleichgesetzt hatten. Die neue Glaubensregel besagte, das Grundlegende sei wichtiger als das Hochentwickelte. Wie von neueren Forschungen überzeugend dargelegt, erkannten Künstler der Generation Gauguins, daß ihre Auffassung von der überlegenen Kraft vereinfachter Formen – sie glaubten oft an eine verborgene Ordnung hinter der Vielfalt von natürlichen Erscheinungsformen – mit Aspekten der neuen Psychologie übereinstimmte, die sich mit den Grundlagen menschlicher Erfahrung befaßte. Rudimentäre Malereien ohne Abbildcharakter von Kindern oder unverbildeten Menschen (Graffiti

□ 221 *Paul Gauguin, ›Die Vision nach dem Gebet – Jakobs Kampf mit dem Engel‹ (La vision après le sermon), 1889, Öl auf Leinwand, 73 x 92 cm. National Gallery of Scotland, Edinburgh.*

eingeschlossen) galten der Psychologie, die den selbsttätigen Geist untersuchte, als Schlüssel zu den Grundstrukturen geistiger Vorgänge.[18] In diesem und in anderen Forschungsbereichen wurde dem Primitiven, als eine frühe Entwicklungsstufe oder weniger komplexe Form verstanden, eine erstrangige Bedeutung und Wertigkeit zugemessen.

Die seit langem bestehende Gleichsetzung von Einfachheit mit Tiefe, des unzivilisierten Geistes mit reinerer Schöpferkraft wurde somit für GAUGUINS Generation mit einem neuen Inhalt gefüllt. Neue psychologische Erkenntnisse verschmolzen mit Theorien der älteren primitivistischen Tradition wie auch einem wiedergewonnenen Idealismus und Okkultismus.[19] Diese Strömungen nährten die weitverbreitete Unzufriedenheit mit den Wertmaßstäben der biologisch begründeten und evolutionären Lehren von der Menschheitsentwicklung, insbesondere mit dem vorherrschenden Kunstideal der Mimesis. Diese geistige Wende bereitete den Boden für GAUGUIN, der bei der Verfolgung seiner ureigensten Interessen auch Elemente der alten Tradition neu belebte und ihnen avantgardistische Züge verlieh. Er schuf zur rechten Zeit eine sich aus den unterschiedlichsten Quellen speisende Mischung, die für ein höchst aufnahmebereites geistiges Klima voller Möglichkeiten für einen künstlerischen Primitivismus steckte.

Die formalen Vereinfachungen und das Thema der geistigen Schau lassen zusammen die *Vision* zu einem Manifest des Primitivismus auf all diesen konzeptuellen und stilistischen Ebenen werden. Und doch finden wir nichts in dem Gemälde, was wir heute primitive Kunst nennen würden, auch keine Vorbilder aus der Volkskunst. Wenn GAUGUIN die bretonische Volkskunst überhaupt beachtet hat □ 220, schöpfte er allenfalls allgemeine Stilanregungen aus deren ländlicher Naivität und vermengte diesen Gegenstand seiner Bewunderung mit einer seltsamen Vorliebe für orientalische, südamerikanische und frühe europäische Kunst.[20] Quellen für die *Vision* findet man bei DEGAS (Staffelung von Zuschauern und Szene), bei den volkstümlichen »Images d'Epinal« (hart gegeneinandergesetzte Farben ohne Schattierungen) und beim japanischen Holzschnitt (der Baumstamm, die Ringenden, die geballte graphische Ausdruckskraft) – alles vereint durch den cloisonnistischen Stil (benannt nach der Emaille-Malerei im Zellschmelzverfahren mit Stegen), in dem sich gerade ein jüngerer Kollege GAUGUINS versuchte, der Maler EMILE BERNARD.[21]

Die Neigung GAUGUINS, mehrere und völlig verschiedene Quellen zu vermischen, war nicht die Unsicherheit eines Anfängers, diese Neigung kommt in GAUGUINS reiferem Werk sogar verstärkt zum Ausdruck. Solch ein Eklektizismus machte geradezu das Wesen von Gauguins Primitivismus aus. Gauguin ist ein Beispiel für Voreingenommenheit in zweierlei Hinsicht. Zum einen erlebte er keinen »Schock des Neuen«, als er auf primitive Objekte traf und würdigte sie auch nicht in erster Linie unter formalen Gesichtspunkten. Statt dessen betrachtete er diese Objekte und ihren Stil von Anfang an unter Voraussetzungen, Wünschen und Erwartungen, die eingebettet waren in die philosophischen und historischen Gedanken, die wir schon ausführlich besprochen haben. Zum anderen verschmolz er den Einfluß primitiver Objekte, wenn sie ihm begegneten, ganz unorthodox mit europäischen und außereuropäischen Stilmitteln. In beiderlei Hinsicht nahm Gauguin viele charakteristische Züge des künstlerischen Primitivismus unseres Jahrhunderts in unterschiedlichem Maß vorweg.

Gauguins Integration japanischer Kunst, die in der *Vision* klar zutage tritt, ist ein typisches Beispiel für die Gestaltungsabsichten und stilistischen Verknüpfungen, die seinen Primitivismus formten. Gauguin, für den japanische Kunst zugleich primitiv und doch mit europäischer Kunst verwandt war, erkannte in ihr die Möglichkeit zu einer eigentümlichen Anregung. Zu seiner Zeit galt japanische Kunst allgemein als primitiv (obwohl manchen Europäern die Komplexität der japanischen Gesellschaft bekannt war), denn es fehlte ihr die Schattengebung und plastische Körpergestaltung, ihre Perspektive sah man als kindlich und ungeschult an.[22] Gauguin erweiterte ihre Bezüge zu europäischer Kunst radikal. Er sprach später einmal von einem Album, in dem er japanische Drucke neben »niedrigen« Karikaturen (von Daumier und Forain) und früher Renaissancemalerei (Reproduktionen nach Werken aus der Schule Giottos) gesammelt hatte. Er fand, daß alle diese Abbildungen »scheinbar so verschieden sind«, und hielt es für nötig, »zu zeigen, daß es Beziehungen zwischen ihnen gibt«. Lobenswert fand er besonders, wie japanische Künstler die Verkürzung anwandten, und betonte, Hokusai habe Menschen ebenso ausdrucksstark dargestellt wie Raffael, nur mit »wesentlich einfacheren Mitteln«. Gauguin verband diese Wertschätzung fremdländischer Fähigkeiten mit einem Appell, endlich die europäischen Karikaturisten als hochstehende Künstler anzuerkennen und auch die überlegene Kraft jener Aspekte von Giottos Stil zu würdigen, die andere bislang als »Irrtümer« seiner Perspektive und Darstellungsweise bemängelt hatten. Die künstlerischen Leistungen Japans und ihre Verwandtschaft mit diesen so verschiedenen europäischen Kunstformen sah Gauguin in den »ursprünglichen Werten« der »Ehrlichkeit« begründet. »Ehrlich zu malen«, so erläuterte er, »heißt nicht etwas bestätigen, was in der Natur wahr ist, sondern im Gegenteil, eine Bildsprache zu verwenden, die nicht die eigenen Gedanken verbirgt.«[23] Gauguin deutete die verschiedenen Möglichkeiten stilistischer Vereinfachung – außerhalb der vorherrschenden Tradition Europas (Hokusai), in geringerem Maße innerhalb der Tradition (Daumier) und im Werk eines der Väter dieser Tradition (Giotto) – als unterschiedliche Beweise für eine einzige, unterdrückte Wahrheit über die grundlegende vereinfachende Tendenz des Geistes, um Vorstellungskraft, Phantasie in die Kunst einzubringen. Um die Herrschaft des Naturalismus zu untergraben, begab sich Gauguin in die Rolle des Außenseiters, Hofnarrs und Pioniers mit dem Grundsatz, Vereinfachung sei Zeichen eines von Natur aus unverbildeten Geistes.

Das kleine Album Gauguins mit den Drucken und Reproduktionen bestätigt, was wir in der *Vision nach dem Gebet* erkannten, daß nämlich die Idee des Primitiven im Menschen, die Grundstrukturen des Denkens hinter einer Darstellung, Gauguin zu seiner Wertschätzung der Primitiven unter den Menschen führte. Das Album und das Gemälde machen deutlich, wie die Neubewertung vereinfachter, fremder Stilformen Gauguin zur Zerstörung und Umwälzung von Hierarchien in seiner eigenen Tradition ermutigte. Die Verbindungen zwischen der Ideenwelt und dem Verständnis für Stilformen zwischen lokalen und exotischen stilistischen Vorbildern verbieten die gewöhnliche Vorstellung eines »Einflusses« auf Gauguin, wenn damit eine externe Quelle mit völlig neuen, unbelasteten formalen Lehren gemeint ist. Es gibt keinen erkennbaren »Einfluß« fremder Vorbilder auf Gauguins Stil, nur auf sein Denken, das umfassender wurde und ihn mit der älteren Tradition des Primitivismus zusammenführte. Nur so kann seine Bedeutung für die wichtigsten Erscheinungen der Kunst des 20. Jahrhunderts erklärt werden.

Der Primitivismus zieht seine Kräfte im allgemeinen aus Verschiedenheiten und deren Aufhebung. Er schafft eine spannungsvolle Trennung, indem er die Bedeutung dessen erkennt, was anders ist. Eine Epoche, Kultur oder Psyche wird als herausfordernder Gegensatz zu unserer eigenen Lebensform betrachtet, deren Überlegenheit fraglich geworden ist. In einem schöpferischen Bruch, der das Diktat der Geschichte, Klassen und Rassen mißachtet, fordert der Primitivismus Auseinandersetzung über die Trennung hinweg, nachdem er Bezugspunkte erkannt hat. Gauguins »Eklektizismus« läßt diese Denkweise erkennen. Er führt nicht nur vor, wie der primitivistische Künstler außereuropäische Stilformen willkürlich und schöpferisch absorbiert, sondern auch, wie eine neue Einschätzung von »Außenseiter«-Kunst unweigerlich zu einer Neubewertung wichtiger Traditionen unserer eigenen Vergangenheit führt und von diesen selbst wieder angeregt wird. Daumier begegnet Giotto in Japan. In diesem Sinne legen Gauguins künstlerischer Primitivismus und seine modernen Nachkommen das Erbe des primitivistischen Denkens aus, das ich eingangs umrissen habe: zum Teil Entdeckung, zum Teil Erfindung, zum Teil Projektion einer neuen Sicht unserer selbst auf ein äußeres Bild von »ihnen«, um Selbstkritik und innere Rückbesinnung zu üben.

Doch ein Konzept und seine Realisierung sind zwei verschiedene Dinge. Die bisher besprochenen Grundsätze Gauguins stammten aus der späteren bretonischen Periode und werden durch seine Aufzeichnungen bestätigt, aber ihr Schwung ist in seiner Kunst abgefangen worden. Als Wegbereiter formulierte er eine in ihren Ansätzen radikale Vorstellung vom Primitiven. Aber als Mann des späten 19. Jahrhunderts schaute er lieber zweifelnd nach innen – wie in dem besonderen Fall der *Vision* –, anstatt die Gelegenheit für eine wirkliche Veränderung zu nutzen. So wurde Gauguin auch in weniger fruchtbaren Bereichen zu einem Beispiel für Voreingenommenheit. Sein Leben und seine Kunst waren voller Zwiespalt, und eine Aura von düsterer Doppeldeutigkeit umgibt seine schönen Primitiven.

Gauguins Glaube an den Vorrang des Geistes siegte etwa niemals über seine ebenso starke Bewunderung des »primitiven« Körpers. In der Südsee nimmt man Erotik lässiger als in der katholischen Bretagne. Gauguin war überwältigt von der Sinnlichkeit, die für ihn wie ein Traumbild von der sexuellen Unschuld war, ohne Scham und Schuldgefühle der Zivilisation. »Seid verliebt, Ihr werdet glücklich sein«, diesen Wahlspruch hatte er neben seinen Hauseingang auf der Marquesasinsel Hiva Oa geschnitzt (siehe S. 184, 185). Viele seiner in Polyne-

☐ 222 *Paul Gauguin, ›Selbstbildnis – Krug‹ (Auto-portrait), Steingut mit transparenter Glasur, 19 x 18 cm. Museum für angewandte Kunst, Kopenhagen.*

sien entstandenen Bilder drücken kaum mehr aus als diese starke, wenn auch kraftlose Erotik.

Das Schwanken zwischen geistigen und körperlichen Begriffen vom Primitiven wiederholt sich auch auf anderen Ebenen. GAUGUIN war mit sich uneins, nicht nur darüber was seine Werke, sondern auch wie sie es aussagen sollten. Einerseits wollte er den Intellekt ansprechen und schuf sich eine komplexe Symbolsprache, die sich auf die von ihm so benannte »*MAORI*-Mythologie« berief. Andererseits sollten Formen und Farben dieser Werke die Betrachter wie die unmittelbar sinnliche Kraft von Musik »instinktiv« anziehen. Dem Geschmack des 20. Jahrhunderts erschien seine Unentschlossenheit zwischen den, wie er es nannte, »literarischen« und »musikalischen« Gesichtspunkten als eine seiner schlimmsten Schwächen. Selbst im rein Formalen entfernen sich die späten bretonischen Bilder und die polynesischen Bilder von der einfältigen Derbheit in der *Vision*. Obwohl er weiter von Synthese und Einfachheit sprach, wurde GAUGUINS Primitivismus exotisch heterogen und oft disparat. Nach 1891 wirken seine Linienführung und Körper eher BOTTICELLIS Eleganz als HOKUSAIS knappem Stil oder GIOTTOS Wucht verpflichtet. Seine reifen Werke sind dämmrig verwoben mit eigenartig verfeinerten, seltsamen Farbkombinationen, sie haben kaum etwas mit den einfachen Farben der Volkskunst zu tun. Auf gedämpfte, eintönige Untergründe von dunklem Ocker, Rosa und Purpur werden Farben von verschwenderischer, sich gegenseitig ergänzender Kraft gesetzt, flächige Passagen gibt es nur ganz ähnlich in einem Gefüge von stark geschichteter Tiefe. Das *non finito* des Spätwerkes vermittelt schließlich keine Spontaneität, sondern eine erlesene, dekorative Vielfalt. DELACROIX, nicht mehr DAUMIER, ist tonangebend.

Diese Komplexität entsprang GAUGUINS grundlegendem Zwiespalt über die Natur des »Primitiven«, das er in seiner Kunst auszudrücken suchte. Von seinem inneren Empfinden her führte ihn seine Antipathie gegen den bürgerlichen Geschmack in gegensätzliche Richtungen: Auch wenn er den einfachen Handwerker verehrte, war ihm klar, daß große Kunst stets unter mächtigen Herrschern gedieh, und er verspürte in sich eine Sehnsucht nach Adelsherrschaft (daher vielleicht seine Vorliebe für Hof- statt für Stammesstile). Und wenn er auch bekannt hatte, daß sein Inneres gespalten war in eine »indianische« und eine »empfindsame« Natur, war ihm wohl die Verwirrung in seinem Kopf wenig bewußt, wenn er zugleich Indianer und Cowboys als Vorbilder reinen Mutes pries. In Paris hatte er 1889 Indianer in der Buffalo-Bill-Show gesehen, worauf er sich mit Pfeil und Bogen an der bretonischen Küste übte und in Tahiti als Urbild des Pfadfinders ankam: mit schulterlangem Haar und einem Cowboyhut. Diese Widersprüchlichkeit kommt erstmals in GAUGUINS wechselnden Aussagen über seine südamerikanischen Ahnen zutage. Obwohl von den höfischen Hochkulturen Altamerikas inspiriert, glaubte er, sich mit seiner Keramik als »Wilder aus Peru« bewiesen zu haben ☐ 222, 223. Als seine Vorfahren bezeichnete er ebenso widersprüchlich einmal die *INKAS*, ein andermal die spanischen Kolonialherren. Er identifizierte sich also abwechselnd mit der untergegangenen Zivilisation und den erobernden Granden.[24]

Sein Aufbruch nach Tahiti kann ganz widersprüchlich beurteilt werden, wobei jede Hypothese ihre Berechtigung hat. Auf dem Hintergrund des beispiellosen Imperialismus ist die Reise einerseits als ein Fall von feiger Ausbeutung zu betrachten. GAUGUINS »Flucht aus der Zivilisation« kann mit der jähen Entwicklung des französischen Kolonialismus in Analogie gebracht werden: 1881 war Tahiti gerade von einem Protektorat in eine Kolonie umgewandelt worden, und andere Orte, die er ins Auge gefaßt hatte (Tonkin, Madagaskar), waren ebenfalls Ziele französischen Abenteuertums. Seine Absicht auszuwandern weist möglicherweise noch tiefere Beziehungen zur imperialistischen Gesinnung auf. Der Kolonialismus hatte der literarischen und am Kauf von Kunst interessierten Pariser Gesellschaft Exotika schmackhaft gemacht. GAUGUIN wußte

☐ 223 *›Bügelkanne‹, Moche (Peru), Terrakotta, Höhe 32 cm. The Metropolitan Museum of Art, Schenkung Nathan Cummings, New York.*

das, und er wußte auch von dem wohlbekannten Privileg der Kolonisten, sich der reichlich vorhandenen »resources« (so sein Ausdruck) zu bedienen und damit billiger zu leben. Und wenn er von Stärkung (sein Ausdruck »nährende Milch«) spricht, die er in primitiven Ländern fern von europäischer Verrottung suchte, dann schwingt deutlich die offizielle französische Rhetorik mit, die Kolonisation als Schlüssel zur Wiederbelebung nationaler Kraft und zur Beseitigung der Dekadenz ausgab.[25] Diese aktuellen Beweggründe, die neben den Mythos von Tahiti als dem Ort sinnlicher Erfüllung und des Freiseins von Verantwortung traten, förderten GAUGUINS Vorstellung, die Insel sei ein Paradies für Kolonisten und ein Segen für seine Kunst. PISSARRO hatte in gewisser Weise recht, wenn er GAUGUIN vorwarf, er »wildert ständig in fremdem Land, jetzt plündert er die Wilden Ozeaniens«.[26]

Dieser Vorwurf trifft indes nicht den Kern: GAUGUIN reiste weniger um »die Wilden zu plündern« in die Südsee, sondern – und er hat sicherlich daran geglaubt – um sich selbst zu finden. In Übereinstimmung mit der langen Überlieferung romantischen primitivistischen Denkens hielt GAUGUIN die Kraft und Größe des ursprünglichen Lebens nicht für ein Vorrecht des einfachen Volkes und fremder Gesellschaften, sondern für ein Geburtsrecht, das er aus sich selbst heraus wiedererlangen könne.[27] Er war hochmütig, gesellschaftsfeindlich und egozentrisch bis zur Rücksichtslosigkeit, angetrieben von dem Gedanken, seine wahre innere Natur werde durch die Verhältnisse erstickt, sie harre nur der Erlösung von der negativen Umwelt und den Zwängen, um wieder rein zu erstrahlen. Das Wechselspiel zwischen innerer und äußerer Entdeckung, das sich in GAUGUINS Primitivismus anfangs in stilistischen Zusammenhängen angekündigt hatte, drückt sich auch in seinem Entschluß aus, nach Tahiti zu gehen.

GAUGUIN setzte Primitivismus mit Selbstverwirklichung gleich, nicht weil er den primitiven Völkern ihre schöpferische Art zu schaffen oder sich zu paaren neidete, sondern weil es ihm um Grundsätzlicheres ging. Er glaubte, der Schritt über die Grenzen der europäischen Kunst- und Lebenstraditionen würde ihn zu seiner Seele zurückführen, eine äußere Vereinfachung seiner Kunst und seines Lebens würde seine innere Verwirrung lösen und seine ursprüngliche Identität wiederherstellen. In seiner Keramik aus der Zeit vor Tahiti etwa entsteht das »Wilde« nicht durch Anleihen bei fremden Formen oder Glasuren (auch wenn südamerikanische oder orientalische Einflüsse zu erkennen sind), sondern durch sein seelisches Engagement bei dem körperlichen Prozeß. Er mied den Komfort der Töpferscheibe und bewahrte das natürliche Rot der gebrannten Erde, denn er glaubte, wenn er das Material widerstandsfähiger machte und dessen Natur im Feuer zutage trete, gliche das Resultat – wilde Physiognomie und leidenschaftliche Farben – am ehesten seiner Person □ 222.[28]

□ 225 *Ausschnitt eines Reliefs, Die Begegnung mit einem Ajīvaka-Mönch, Borobudur, Java.*

□ 224 *Paul Gauguin, ›Gegrüßt seist Du Maria‹, Farbabbildung* □ *216.*

GAUGUINS erste primitivistische Arbeiten bezeugen seine instinktive Vorliebe für elementare Einfachheit, die er ablehnen und zugleich sich aneignen konnte. Als er seine Liebe zur »wilden, primitiven« Bretagne beschrieb, sagte er, »wenn meine Holzschuhe auf dem Granitboden klappern, höre ich den gedämpften starken Ton, den ich in der Malerei wiederzugeben suche«.[29] Seine polynesischen Aufzeichnungen lassen ein weniger starres Bild der Einfachheit erkennen. Dort spricht er vom Aufgehen in einer sanften nährenden Umwelt und nicht von Widerstand. Die typisch europäische Vorstellung, primitive Völker seien ewige Kinder, wurde zu Träumen von der Rückkehr in ein kindliches Paradies verinnerlicht. Octave Mirbeau schrieb am Vorabend der Abreise seines Freundes, GAUGUIN sei getrieben von »einem wehmütigen Erinnern an jene Länder, wo einst seine ersten Träume reiften«, und von einem Verlangen zurückzukehren »zu seinen Dingen, die er dort zurückgelassen hatte«. Diese Verwechslung des Südamerika von GAUGUINS Kindheit mit der Südsee war mehr als zufällig. Tahiti dachte er sich als einen Ort, wo »sich die Natur seinem Traum besser anpaßt, wo er hofft, daß der Pazifik ihn zart liebkosen wird mit der alten und sicheren Liebe eines

□ 226 *Paul Gauguin, ›Die Ahnen von Tehamana‹ (Marahi Metua No Tehamana), 1893, Öl auf Leinwand, 76 x 54 cm. The Art Institute of Chicago.*

wiedergefundenen Vorfahren«.[30] Der Aufbruch nach draußen war eine Reise nach innen und zurück.

Gauguin erzählte einem Journalisten, er verlasse Frankreich, um »einfache, ganz einfache Kunst zu machen, um mich in die jungfräuliche Natur zu versenken, nur Wilde zu sehen, ihr Leben zu leben, keinen anderen Gedanken im Kopf zu haben als die Pläne, die sich in einem Hirn geformt haben, darzustellen, wie ein Kind es täte, und das nur mit primitiven Kunstmitteln, den einzigen Mitteln, die gut und wahr sind«.[31] Ironisch ist nur, daß sein Reiseziel kein einfacher Ort war und man ihn mit einfachen Mitteln nicht darstellen konnte. Man muß die Veränderungen in Gauguins Kunst wie die Inkonsequenzen, die an seinem Primitivismus oft kritisiert werden, an der Bedeutung messen, die Polynesien für ihn hatte – nicht einfach als persönliches Phantasiegebilde, sondern als vielschichtige Realität. Tahiti steht für die fundamentalen Gewißheiten, nach denen Gauguin immer gesucht hatte, und den unauflöslichen Zwiespalt, dem er unvermeidlich begegnete. In der Insel und dem Primitiven ganz allgemein fand Gauguin das Spiegelbild des schwierigen, gequälten, fragenden Menschen, der er war, und nicht des einfachen Menschen, der er sein wollte.

Tahiti hatte erst kurze Zeit Kontakt mit Europa und war schon zu einem Mythos geworden, um den sich widersprüchliche Vorstellungen rankten. Als die Insel 1767 entdeckt wurde, schien sie den uralten Traum von den »glückseligen Inseln« jenseits des Horizonts zu erfüllen, ein epochales Ereignis für eine Generation, die mit Büchern über den Edlen Wilden aufgewachsen war und gerade von Rousseaus Lobpreis der natürlichen Einfachheit angefeuert wurde. Zunächst hatte man die nordamerikanischen Indianer bewundert, aber Geschichten über ihre gewalttätige Feindseligkeit ließen sie ruchlos

□ 227 *›Tafel mit Schriftzeichen‹, Osterinsel. Holz. Höhe 9 cm. National Museum of Natural History, Smithsonian Institution, Washington.*

erscheinen. Die Tahitianer erfüllten die Vorstellungen des 18. Jahrhunderts von Empfindsamkeit und sinnlicher Anmut viel eher, waren sie doch »sanfte« Primitive von sorgloser, tropischer Gelassenheit und keine »harten« Primitiven im Kriegsgewand der kühleren Klimazonen. Andeutungen über dunklere Sitten der Tahitianer, wie Kannibalismus und Kindermord, überlasen eifrige Europäer und stürzten sich auf die Berichte, die vom Entzücken des französischen Entdeckers Louis-Antoine de Bougainville kündeten. Er hatte in sein Schiffstagebuch geschrieben:

»Die Natur hat [Tahiti] in das herrlichste Klima des Universums gelegt, es mit den schönsten Ansichten geschmückt, mit all ihren Gaben überschüttet, es mit Einwohnern besiedelt, die freundlich, groß und stark sind. Die Natur selbst hat ihnen ihre Gesetze gegeben. Sie folgen diesen Gesetzen in Frieden und bilden die vielleicht glücklichste Gesellschaft, die auf dem Globus existiert. Gesetzgeber und Philosophen, kommt her und seht hier vollendet, was Eure Vorstellungskraft nicht einmal hat träumen können . . . Dies Volk atmet nur Ruhe und Sinnesfreude. Venus ist die allgegenwärtige Göttin. Die Milde des Klimas, die Schönheit der Landschaft, die Fruchtbarkeit der Erde, die von Flüssen und Kaskaden durchspült ist, die Reinheit der Luft . . . alles erregt Wollust. So nenne ich den Ort Neu-Kythera [La Nouvelle Cythère, nach der erotisch-mythischen Insel, wo Venus geboren wurde], und hier wie auf der alten Insel benötigen wir die zügelnde Minerva, um uns vor dem verführerischen Klima und den Sitten dieser Gesellschaft zu schützen.«[32]

Tahiti wurde für immer mit der Erfüllung sinnlicher Phantasien gleichgesetzt. Für die Philosophie war sie hingegen Hauptzeuge gegen die Zivilisation: Diderot etwa verdammte in seinem »Nachtrag zu der Reise Bougainvilles« die Europäer, daß sie die Insel überhaupt betreten hätten; in einer mythischen Vision spricht er von übernatürlich weisen, schönen und tugendhaft freien Tahitianern. Die Insel wurde im europäischen Traum der Inbegriff einfachen, sonnendurchströmten Glücks und Anklage gegen die Künstlichkeit der modernen Gesellschaft mit ihren Zwängen und Sitten.[33]

Wie andere Symbole sinnenfreudigen Lebens gemahnte die Insel bald an die Vanitas: Dichter und Künstler beschworen das Bild eines »befleckten Paradieses«, dessen »fleischliche, launische und vergängliche« Gaben die Kurzlebigkeit irdischer Freuden zeigten.[34] Zu diesen moralischen Bedenken gesellten sich bald die tatsächlichen Übel einer schnell anwachsenden europäischen Präsenz: Krankheit, Bevölkerungsrückgang, kultureller Zusammenbruch. In weniger als einer Generation war kaum etwas von der Gesellschaft übriggeblieben, die Bougainville so gepriesen hatte. Mitte des 19. Jahrhunderts war Tahiti dafür berüchtigt, unter allen Südseeinseln von der »Zivilisation« am erbärmlichsten zugrunde gerichtet worden zu sein.[35] Mit dem neuen evolutionären Denken und dem erwachten Interesse an frühen Kulturen wurde Tahiti nicht des Philosophen Freud', sondern des Wissenschaftlers Leid: ein Rätsel, eine zerstörte, kaum lesbare Seite aus einem verlorenen Kapitel der Menschheitsgeschichte. Tahiti weckte Reue und blieb düsteres Geheimnis.

So war es das ganze 19. Jahrhundert, nur die Widersprüche verschärften sich im Laufe der Zeit: Einer Figur in Balzacs »La peau de Chagrin« genügte der Anblick des Lendenschurzes eines Tahitimädchens in einem Raritätenladen, um die Gedanken in ein Land der »wahren Reinheit« schweifen zu lassen, »in die für den Menschen so natürlichen Wonnen der Unschuld«. Melville äußerte herbe Kritik an der Erniedrigung der Tahitianer durch Missionare, und Henry Adams empfand tiefe Trauer über die teilnahmslosen, alkoholisierten Eingeborenen und berichtete von der melancholischen Untergangsstimmung in der Hauptstadt Papeete – nur einige Monate vor der Ankunft Gauguins. Papeete machte den Eindruck »verlorener Schönheit, recht ein Symbol des Paradieses«, wie Adams sagte.[36]

Sinnbild des Paradieses und des verlorenen Paradieses, Insel der Sehnsucht und des Schmerzes, all dies war Tahiti in den 1890er Jahren und mehr: noch immer ein wichtiges, aber inzwischen noch ambivalenteres Beweisstück für Fragen nach dem Ursprung des Menschen und nach dem Vor und Zurück in seiner Geschichte. Wer behauptet, Gauguins künstlerische Sicht habe wenig mit Polynesien zu tun und sei daher wertlos, hat diese schwierigen Gesichtspunkte der tahitischen Wirklichkeit nicht richtig beachtet und nicht verstanden, wie sehr Gauguin ihnen gerecht zu werden versuchte.

Gauguins Südseebilder entsprechen nicht den geläufigen Vorstellungen von tropischen Paradiesen oder von unverfälschter primitiver Kunst. Schon in dem sehr frühen tahitischen Bild *Gegrüßt seist Du Maria* □ 224 sind die widersprüchlichen Eindrücke voll ausgebildet: Üppige Farben von sprühender Kraft verbinden sich nicht zu heiterem Sonnenschein, sondern zu einem Gefühl sanft ersterbenden und müden Luxus. Die zarten, archaisch-eleganten Posen lassen die Rhythmik der unvollendeten Erzählung entstehen. Man erkennt leicht, daß viele Komponenten dieses Bildes weder aus der Beobachtung noch aus der Eingeborenenkunst stammen, sondern Anleihen aus Ost und West sind (die archaische Eleganz der Hintergrundfiguren etwa findet ihr Vorbild in den Reliefs des javanischen Buddha-Tempels von Borobudur □ 225). Es wäre völlig falsch, daraus zu schließen, die Pracht, das Raffinement und der fremde Stil seien Zeichen dafür, wie wenig sich Gauguin wirklich mit Tahiti auseinandergesetzt habe. Sie zeigen im Gegenteil das Ausmaß seiner Bereitschaft, nicht nur für seine Begegnung mit der Insel in den 1890er Jahren, für den Reiz und die Verlogenheit des Tahitimythos seit 1767, sondern auch für die grundsätzlichere Frage nach der Rolle Tahitis in der Menschheitsgeschichte. Sein tahitischer Primitivismus erwies sich als eine sorgsame Aufarbeitung dieses geistigen Reichtums und war keineswegs ein Ausweichen auf ein paar Grundwahrheiten.

Das Porträt seiner 14jährigen Geliebten Tehamana etwa geht von intimer, persönlicher Erfahrung aus und wendet sich über die Kolonialgeschichte zurück bis in eine rätselhafte Vergangenheit □ 226. In erdfarbenen Tönen gemalt, nach europäischer Sitte bekleidet (das Wickelgewand war eine Neuerung der Missionare), sitzt sie vor einer ruhigen Fläche voller phantastischer, verschwommener Hindu-Figuren und genau kopierter Piktogramme – stark vergrößerten Buchstaben aus der Rongorongoschrift von der Osterinsel □ 227, die nie entziffert oder mit einer anderen Schrift in Verbindung gebracht werden konnten.[37] Ein Kind von geschmeidiger und ergebener Sinnlichkeit, umringt von Zeichen eines alten, unerschlossenen geistigen Mysteriums, ist sie Polynesien in Person. Der Titel »Tehamana hat viele Eltern« bezieht sich auf die vielen Paten des Mädchens (Gauguin erzählt in seinen Aufzeichnungen davon) und auf die ungeklärten Ursprünge ihrer Rasse. Hier wird deutlich, wie Gauguin aus einem Erleben Tahitis Metaphern für die großen Probleme der Insel und ihres Volkes fand.[38]

□ 228 *Paul Gauguin, ›Studien nach Maori-Ornamenten‹, 1895–97 (?), Bleistift und Tusche, 20 x 15 cm. Privatsammlung.*

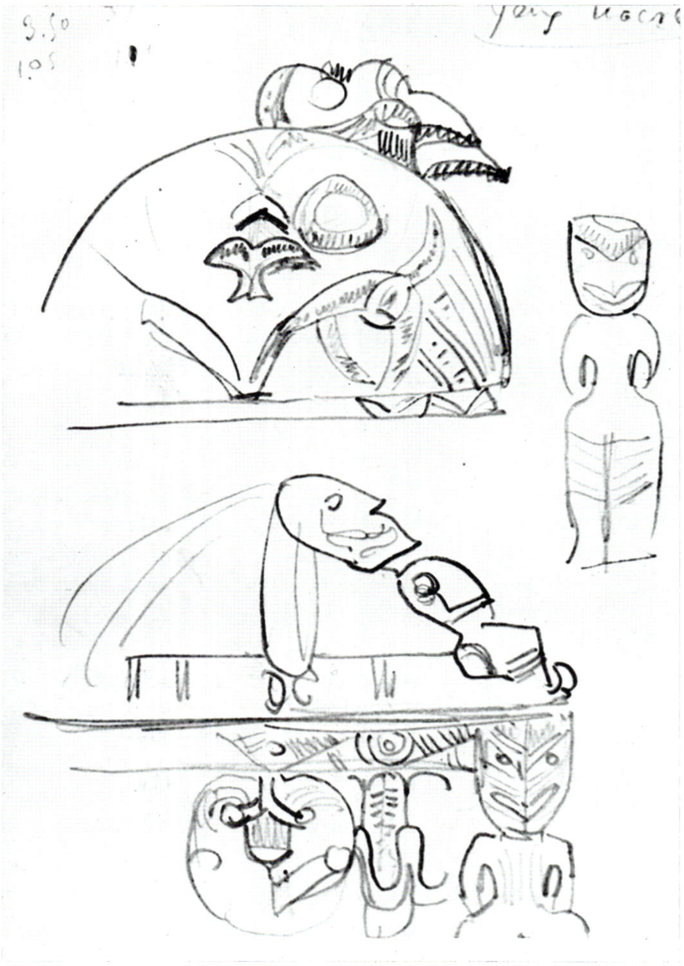

Gauguins Gesamtsicht von Polynesien geht wie dieses Bild auf verschiedene Erlebnisse, Untersuchungen und Spekulationen zurück. Wie unklar diese Anschauungen waren, erkennt man in seinen Bildern, wenn er unterschiedliche Stile und künstlerisch einander fremde Motive vermengte und ohne Zusammenhang nebeneinanderstellte. Diese Neigung zum mehrsprachigen Ausdruck zeigt Gauguins Unwillen und/oder Unvermögen, sich auf eine eindeutige und schlüssige Betrachtungsweise Polynesiens festzulegen, und bestätigt die Absicht, seine persönlichen Eindrücke von Tahiti mit einem Gewebe vielfältigster Assoziationen zu erweitern, um die Mysterien zu beschwören, die er intuitiv in Tahitis Vergangenheit erkannte. Andere Besucher der Insel hatten sich schon über die behäbige Ruhe der Tahitianer geäußert, hatten sie für Schwäche, Melancholie gehalten oder darin eine anmutig-trauervolle Sinnlichkeit gesehen – wie Pierre Loti in seiner Erzählung, die Gauguin vor seiner Abreise aus Frankreich gelesen hatte.[39] In Gauguin weckte diese Passivität Gedanken an hohe Kunst und verlorene Größe. Er schrieb über das Inselvolk: »Animalische Wesen, unbeugsam wie Statuen – etwas unbeschreibbar Altes, Erhabenes, Religiöses in ihrem Gebärdenspiel in ihrer seltsamen Unbewegtheit. Die verschwommene Oberfläche eines unklärbaren Rätsels in den träumenden Augen.«[40] Diese Andeutung einer unbekannten Vergangenheit, eingewoben in die Gegenwart, wollte er in seiner Kunst einfangen.

Die archaisierende Anmut und den langsamen Rhythmus in Gauguins spätem Stil hat man einem europäischen, wenn nicht gar präraffaelitischen Empfinden zugeordnet, eine wirkliche Verbindung zu Tahiti wurde darin nicht gesehen.[41] Aber gerade damit wollte Gauguin im Schweigen der Einwohner ein Echo des Vorzeitlichen beschwören und dieses Volk mit anderen, herrlicheren Kulturen verbinden. Schon bei der Weltausstellung von 1889 war Gauguin fasziniert gewesen von den starren Mienen javanischer Tänzer und ihrer monotonen Begleitmusik. Andere Begeisterte schrieben von einer tiefen Melancholie über vergangene Herrlichkeit, die von der Vorführung ausging, und verglichen die Tänzer mit Statuen des alten javanischen Tempels von Borobudur □ 225.[42] Gauguin brachte in seinen Tahitibildern eben diese musikalischen Elemente zum Ausdruck, um eine ähnliche Wirkung zu erreichen – er übernahm von Borobudur bestimmte Posen und entwickelte eine statische Choreographie der Gebärden und ungewöhnliche Palette kontrastierender Farbtöne. Auf den Einwand, daß diese Farbkontraste monoton seien, antwortete er, die Wirkung sei oft beabsichtigt: »Diese Wiederholungen von Tönen und monotonen Harmonien – ähneln sie von der musikalischen Bedeutung der Farbe nicht dem orientalischen Singsang in schriller, nasaler Stimme, der die schallenden Töne begleitet und als Kontrast bereichert?«[43]

Gauguins Umarbeitung der Polynesier in Javaner, für die er poetische Anleihen machte, um sein Erleben des alten tahitischen Rhythmus auszudrücken, spiegelt wohl auch Gedanken

□ 229 *Paul Gauguin, »Heute kein Markt« (TA MATETE), 1892, Öl auf Leinwand, 73 x 91 cm. Kunstmuseum, Basel.*

über die Vergangenheit Tahitis wider, denen auch die Ethnologen zugestimmt hätten. Die neuesten Forschungen erinnern uns daran, daß viele Theorien über die Herkunft der ozeanischen Rassen Malaysia und besonders Java als Ursprungsorte annahmen. So betrachtet wäre GAUGUINS häufiger Rückgriff auf die Plastik Borobudurs keine willkürliche Übertragung gewesen, sondern stand im Dienste der hypothetischen Rekonstruktion einer verlorenen Vergangenheit.[44] GAUGUIN ging genauso vor, wenn er europäische Kunst aus Photoalben für tahitische Szenen verwendete und damit lokale und fremdländische Symbole vermischte.

Für GAUGUIN waren die Tahitianer kindlich und Jahrtausende alt, zugleich sehr einfache und offene Wesen, die dennoch eine geheimnisvolle Würde angeborenen Adels in sich trugen. Einem solchen Volk gebührten nach seiner Meinung komplexe Bildkompositionen. In dieser Auffassung wurde er von einer gleichsam anthropologischen Überlieferung bestärkt. Die würdige und höfische Natur der tahitischen Gesellschaft war in den Berichten der ersten Entdecker besonders hervorgehoben worden. Wegen der Isolation der Insel und wegen der völligen Unkenntnis ihrer Geschichte löste diese Kultur eine noch heute andauernde Diskussion aus. Lange vor Thor Heyerdahls Reiseexperimenten und auch vor GAUGUINS Ankunft hatte man die Sprache und Bräuche der Inselbewohner nach Gemeinsamkeiten mit den verschiedensten Kontinenten und Kulturen untersucht – eine dieser Theorien hielt die Polynesier sogar für einen verlorenen Stamm des Volkes Israel.[45]

GAUGUINS Interesse für diesen kulturellen Synkretismus, die mutmaßliche Verbindung der Tahitianer mit den Traditionen anderer Völker, wird aus seiner Vermischung der *MAORI*-Mythologie mit Symbolen des Christentums und des Buddhismus offensichtlich. Das frühe *Gegrüßt seist Du Maria* wiederholt vielleicht noch das Klischee, daß naivere Eingeborene gläubigere Christen seien. Später jedoch, als er fremde religiöse Motive anspruchsvoll mit Figuren aus Tahiti zusammenfügte, sah GAUGUIN in den Polynesiern nicht nur unschuldige Geschöpfe, sondern verband sie im Geist der Theosophie auch mit uraltem Wissen.[46] Seine theosophischen Auffassungen, die in seinen Notizen nachzulesen sind, erklärten Parallelen zwischen den großen Weltreligionen als Reste einer verlorenen Einheit okkulten Wissens. Als er die äußerst lebendige *MAORI*-Religion studierte, ihre Schöpfungsmythen und ihren Streit zwischen männlichen und weiblichen Prinzipien, stieß er auf vertraute Töne, die ihn dazu veranlaßten, nach kulturellen Querverbindungen zu anderen religiösen Systemen zu suchen.[47] Die archaisierenden Tendenzen in GAUGUINS Südseeperiode, die die Kunst alter Zivilisationen wie die der Perser

☐ 230 *Paul Gauguin, ›Dort ist der Tempel‹ (Parahi Te Marae), 1892, Öl auf Leinwand, 68 x 91 cm. Philadelphia Museum of Art, Schenkung Mrs. Rodolphe Meyer de Schauensee.*

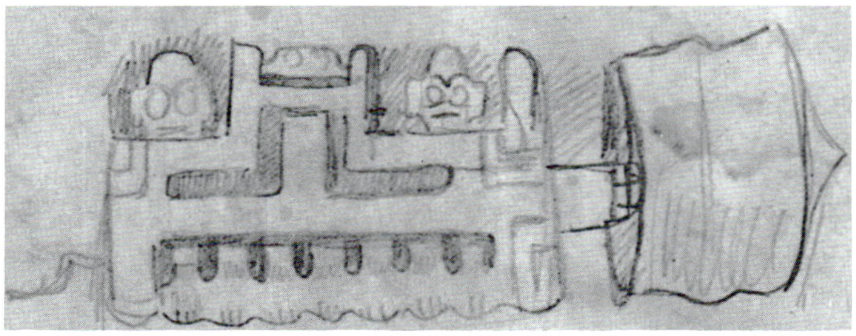

☐ 231 *Paul Gauguin, ›Studien nach einer Eingeborenen und marquesanischem Ohrschmuck‹, Ausschnitt, um 1893, Bleistift, Feder und Tusche auf Pergament, 24 x 32 cm. The Art Institute of Chicago, Sammlung D. Adler.*

☐ 232 *›Ohrschmuck‹, Marquesasinseln, Zeichnung aus Karl von den Steinen, „Die Marquesaner und ihre Kunst", 1925.*

und der Ägypter wieder aufleben lassen, erscheinen in diesem Zusammenhang weniger eigenartig. Das ägyptische Flair eines tahitischen Genremotivs, des Bildes *Heute kein Markt* ☐ 229, das auf eine Grabmalerei der 18. Dynastie zurückgeht, von der Gauguin eine Photographie besaß, resultiert aus Gauguins Gleichsetzung der tahitischen Vergangenheit – eine Analogie zu Atlantis – mit den großen alten Zivilisationen.

Diese besondere Sicht des Mysteriums der Südsee bestimmte nicht nur, was Gauguin aus fremden Kulturen auswählte, sondern auch, was ihm an polynesischer Kunst wichtig schien. Man hat lange behauptet, er habe kaum polynesische Vorbilder genutzt und daß solche Anleihen nur wenig Wirkung gehabt hätten.[48] Bevor er Frankreich 1891 verließ, hatte er sicherlich keine ozeanische Kunst gekannt noch etwas über sie gewußt. Eine Photographie von Objekten, die, wie es scheint, zu seiner Sammlung gehörten, zeigt auch zwei kleine Stammesfiguren, sie sind aber afrikanischer Herkunft, und ihr Erwerbsdatum ist ungewiß.[49] Gauguin wird sie in Paris gekauft haben, entweder vor 1891 oder, was wahrscheinlicher ist, bei seiner Rückreise 1893–95. Beide Daten würden bestätigen, daß er Stammeskunst früher als die Fauvisten sammelte. Diese Figuren hatten jedoch keine nachweisbare Wirkung auf seine Kunst, und nichts deutet darauf hin, daß er sich in Paris in ähnlicher Weise auch für polynesische Kunst interessierte. Einige polynesische Plastiken und Objekte waren im Trocadéro ausgestellt, aber er hat sie offensichtlich nie gesehen.[50] Er ging auch sicherlich nicht nach Tahiti, um in den wenigen Kunstwerken auf der Insel

□ 233 *Paul Gauguin, ›Studie nach einem Tiki‹, 1895–97 (?), Bleistift und indische Tusche, 20 x 15 cm. Privatsammlung.*

□ 234 *›Monumentale Steinfigur‹, Oipuna, Puamau Tal, Hiva Oa (Marquesasinseln), Höhe 259 cm.*

Anregungen zu finden. Was ihm tatsächlich an ozeanischer Kunst begegnete, sah er fast nie am Entstehungsort oder im lebendigen Gebrauch. Er war angewiesen auf Photographien, Museen (Auckland und Noumea besuchte er auf seinen Reisen) und auf seine Entdeckungen in den zusammengewürfelten Kuriositätensammlungen und Geschäften von Tahiti.[51] Eine der wenigen Zeichnungen nach polynesischer Kunst *in situ* – die Skizze einer Steinfigur auf der Marquesasinsel Hiva Oa – kann auch nach einer Photographie entstanden sein, bevor GAUGUIN das wirkliche Objekt sah.[52] Aus all dem ist zu schließen, daß GAUGUIN ein ziemlich zufälliges und bruchstückhaftes Bild von ozeanischer Kunst hatte. Doch aus den verschiedenen Berührungen läßt sich ein selektives stilistisches Interesse ablesen: eine Vorliebe für die Kunst der Marquesasinseln, die GAUGUINS künstlerischen Intentionen entgegenkam.

GAUGUINS primitivistischer Stil läßt expressives Ungestüm und Verzerrungen vermissen – aber nicht weil er von ozeanischer Kunst eingeschüchtert wurde oder sie mißverstand. Um in der Vielfalt polynesischer Kunst einen festen Orientierungspunkt zu finden, suchte er nach anderen Seiten der ihm bekannten Südseekunst. Wenn er sich für marquesische Ornamente entschied, so wählte er damit eine Ästhetik, die er als außergewöhnlich empfand[53] und die eine ambivalente Assoziation Adel-Barbarei hervorrief. Die Muster dieser Insel zeigen reiche geometrische und gegenständliche Motive von strenger Ordnung, sehr verschieden von der organischen Fülle und Ausdrucksstärke anderer ozeanischer Kunst, etwa Neuseelands oder Papua-Neuguineas. Hinzu kommt, daß die berühmt-berüchtigten marquesischen Tätowierungen □ 245, die GAUGUIN bewunderte und kopierte, lange für das Zeichen einer Adelskaste gehalten wurden. Auch die ähnlich gemusterten Ornamente auf Menschenknochen wurden mit diesen als besonders wild und kannibalisch geltenden Insulanern in Verbindung gebracht.[54] Diese Muster, etwa von marquesanischen Kriegerkeulen □ 244, 246, die er auch kopiert hatte, waren so kunstvoll, daß sie GAUGUINS Vermutung, es gäbe eine höhere Ordnung in Polynesiens kultureller Vergangenheit, entsprachen. Da sie von den wildesten Inseln stammten, die sich der europäischen Zivilisation am heftigsten widersetzt hatten, beschworen sie auch die dunkle Seite der Südsee, die Geschichte der Menschenopfer und blutiger Grausamkeiten, die der Anmut der Eingeborenen einen Beigeschmack barbarischer Bedrohung verlieh und ihre Rätselhaftigkeit steigerte.

GAUGUIN wollte mit seiner Kunst das Gefühl eines »certain luxe barbare d'autrefois« vermitteln – eine Kombination von Prunk und Wildheit, Pracht und drohenden Schatten des polynesischen Erbes. Seine Briefe sind voller Hinweise, wenn Zeugnisse nötig wären, daß die grellen Farbkontraste seiner Palette eine musikalische Synthese von Gewalt, religiösem Ernst und kindlichem Frohsinn vermitteln sollten.[55] Für diesen Zweck war marquesische Kunst ideal: Sie vereinte erlesene Formstrenge mit Zeichen des Grauens. Dieselbe Konstellation erkennt man in Werken wie *Idol mit Muschel* □ 237, 238, worin die entrückte Würde der Buddha-ähnlichen Pose durch das

☐ 235 *Paul Gauguin, Aquarell aus dem Manuskript „Ancien Culte Mahorie", 1892–93, Gesamtgröße 13 x 13 cm. Cabinet des Dessins, Musée du Louvre, Paris.*

☐ 236 *›Griff eines Paddels‹, Marquesasinseln, Holz, Höhe 6,5 cm. The Trustees of the British Museum, London.*

gefährliche Aufblitzen scharfer Zähne gebrochen wird, oder in *Dort ist der Tempel* ☐ 230, in dem strahlendes Sonnenlicht und prächtige Blumen einen *Marae* (Tempelbezirk) mit drohend aufragendem Götzenbild und einem mit Totenschädeln gespickten Zaun, der an Menschenopfer gemahnt, einrahmen. Diese Phantasie aus Pracht und Tod hat GAUGUIN marquesischen Kunstwerken nachempfunden. Der Götze ist ein Tiki (siehe Glossar), leicht ägyptisch zwar, aber trotzdem das seltene Beispiel für eine fast exakte Anleihe GAUGUINS bei der polynesischen Plastik ☐ 233, 234. Solche Tiki waren die einzigen tahitischen oder marquesanischen Monumentalplastiken. Der Zaun ist eine sehr freie und phantasievoll angereicherte Vergrößerung von kleinen Schmuckstücken aus Knochen, die die Inselbewohner am Ohr trugen ☐ 231, 232.[56]

Das *Idol mit Muschel, Dort ist der Tempel* oder andere Bilder aus GAUGUINS polynesischer Periode sind freie Erfindungen – keine zufälligen Fälschungen, teils faktische, teils hypothetische Konstruktionen, die die Wahrheiten der Imagination beschwören sollen und beabsichtigen Fragen zu stellen, nicht sie zu lösen. Wer in die Ikonographie dieser Bilder genaue Bedeutungen hineinliest, nimmt diese Werke zu wörtlich, ebenso wie jene, die solche Ikonographien als hoffnungslose Phantastereien abtun. Wir müssen sie als gültige Aussagen akzeptieren und versuchen, ihre Bedeutung aus dem Grundsätzlichen zu verstehen. GAUGUINS ozeanischer Primitivismus kreiste nicht nur um seine eigene Psyche oder ausschließlich um die Eingeborenen und ihre tatsächliche oder erträumte Kultur, sondern befaßte sich auch mit den Fragen nach dem Ursprung menschlicher Kreativität und Kommunikation, die sich bereits in seiner bretonischen Periode gestellt hatten.

Diese tiefere Auseinandersetzung mit dem Primitiven ist in manchen Werken hinter Schichten persönlicher und anthropologischer Bedeutungen zu erkennen. Die Holzplastik *Christus am Kreuz* ☐ 240, 241 und das Bild *Der Geist der Toten wacht* ☐ 249 muten etwa wie Gegensätze an: Die Plastik ist nach ozeanischen und traditionellen europäischen Vorbildern gearbeitet, das Gemälde nach einer modernen französischen Quelle und aus persönlichem Erleben. Beide zielen jedoch auf eine verwandte Aussage: die Holzplastik durch religiösen Symbolismus auf menschliche Urerfahrungen, das Gemälde durch zeitgenössische Erfahrungen auf den Ursprung von Religion und Symbolen.

Christus am Kreuz ist GAUGUINS reichste und konsequenteste primitivistische Plastik. Sie veranschaulicht seine Raumfeindlichkeit (horror vacui und anti-illusionistische Flächigkeit), die ihn bei seiner Auswahl primitiven Kunsthandwerks leitete. Das obere Ornament auf der einen Seite der Plastik ☐ 243 zeigt GAUGUINS Vorliebe für den flächenfüllenden späten Stil der marquesischen Kriegerkeulen ☐ 244. Wir haben ihn der eher »klassischen« und weniger reich gestalteten Form des gleichen Kunstwerkes gegenübergestellt ☐ 246. Auf derselben Seite erscheint direkt darunter eine Kreuzigung. Der stark abgemagerte Christus mit betont hervortretenden Rippen erinnert an einen Figurentypus der Osterinsel, den GAUGUIN vielleicht kannte, dessen hervorgehobener Brustkorb an Martyrien denken läßt ☐ 239. Eine Figur auf der anderen Seite von

Kunst kommt von Prestel
Bücher zur Kunst der Welt
Prestel
München · New York

Die PEGASUS *Bibliothek* ist ein Lesegenuß und Fest fürs Auge. Faszinierende Themen oder persönliche Aspekte im Schaffen berühmter Künstler werden von anerkannten Autoren neu und lebendig vorgestellt. Jeder Band ist seinem Thema entsprechend gestaltet und opulent farbig ausgestattet, so daß sich hier große Kunst im Buch mit Buchkunst in idealer Weise verbindet.

»Diese Kunstbände präsentieren sich nobel, mit diskret geprägtem Markenzeichen: dem Pegasus als ›beflügelndem‹ Motto für eine Reihe, die sich nicht dem Gesamt-Œuvre sondern einzelnen Aspekten im Künstler-Leben und Werk widmet. Publikumsfreundlich ist nicht nur die sorgfältige Gestaltung, auch die Thematik.« *SZ*

»Diese Bände wollen mehr die Freude an der Kunst fördern, als neue Schätze heben. Es sind Augenbücher.« *Die Welt*

TIZIAN

Nymphe und Schäfer. Von John Berger und Katya Berger Andreadakis. 120 Seiten mit 54 Farbtafeln und 23 einfarbigen Abb. ISBN 3-7913-1650-8. Geb DM 39,80/ÖS 291,–/SFr 38,80

Interessante Aspekte in Leben und Werk des großen Renaissancemalers Tizian werden in einem anregenden Briefwechsel zwischen dem Autor John Berger und seiner Tochter Katya an den Meisterwerken diskutiert.

PAUL GAUGUIN

Bilder aus der Südsee. Von Eckhard Hollmann. 116 Seiten mit 60 Farbtafeln und 30 einfarbigen Abb. ISBN 3-7913-1648-6. Geb DM 39,80/ÖS 291,–/SFr 38,80

Ab 1891 lebte Gauguin bis zu seinem Tod 1903 in der Südsee. Der Autor beschreibt lebendig das abenteuerliche Leben und Werk dieses Rebellen der Kunst.

AMEDEO MODIGLIANI

Akte und Porträts. Von Anette Kruszynski. 120 S. mit 74 Farbtafeln und 39 einfarb. Abb. ISBN 3-7913-1649-4. Geb DM 39,80/ÖS 291,–/SFr 38,80

Modigliani galt in Paris als Inbegriff des Bohemien. Einen Gegensatz dazu bildet sein künstlerisches Werk. Der Band zeigt ihn als großen Porträtisten und einfühlsamen Maler weiblicher Akte.

RENOIR

Augenblicke des Glücks. Von Karin Sagner-Düchting. 128 Seiten mit 71 Farbtafeln und 35 einfarbigen Abb. ISBN 3-7913-1712-1. Geb DM 39,80/ÖS 291,–/SFr 38,80

Renoirs idealisierte Darstellung des glücklichen Lebens im Paris der Belle Epoque, eingefangen in Bildern voller Heiterkeit und leuchtender Farbigkeit.

DALÍS BEGIERDEN

Von Ralf Schiebler. 128 Seiten mit 63 Farbtafeln und 40 einfarbigen Abb. ISBN 3-7913-1710-5. Geb DM 39,80/ÖS 291,–/SFr 38,80

Lust, Verlangen und Begierde sind Hauptmotive in Dalís Leben und Werk. Der Autor gibt eine eindrucksvolle Interpretation jener Bilder, deren zentrales Thema die Begierde in all ihren Facetten ist.

KOKOSCHKA UND ALMA MAHLER

Von Alfred Weidinger. 124 Seiten mit 91 Farbtafeln und 46 einfarbigen Abb. ISBN 3-7913-1711-3. Geb DM 39,80/ÖS 291,–/SFr 38,80

Die dreijährige Liebesbeziehung zwischen Alma Mahler und Oskar Kokoschka beeinflußte dessen künstlerisches Werk vehement. Der Autor beschreibt diese Begegnung und deren Ausstrahlung auf ein singuläres Werk.

CÉZANNE IN DER PROVENCE
Von Evmarie Schmitt
ISBN 3-7913-1444-0

CHAGALL – DAPHNIS UND CHLOE
ISBN 3-7913-1347-9

VAN GOGH – DAS DRAMA VON ARLES
Von Alfred Nemeczek
ISBN 3-7913-1479-3

EDWARD HOPPER – AMERIKA-BILDER
Von Wieland Schmied
ISBN 3-7913-1480-7

KANDINSKY UND GABRIELE MÜNTER
Von Annegret Hoberg
ISBN 3-7913-1348-7

KLIMT – MALER DER FRAUEN
Von Susanna Partsch
ISBN 3-7913-1404-1

MANET – PARISER LEBEN
Von Hajo Düchting
ISBN 3-7913-1445-9

MIRÓ AUF MALLORCA
Von Barbara Catoir
ISBN 3-7913-1478-5

MONET IN GIVERNY
Von Karin Sagner-Düchting
ISBN 3-791394-0

PICASSO – WELT DER KINDER
Von Werner Spies. ISBN 3-7913-1346-0

RODIN UND CAMILLE CLAUDEL
Von J. A. Schmoll gen. Eisenwerth
ISBN 3-7913-1392-4

SCHIELE – EROS UND PASSION
Von Klaus Albrecht Schröder
ISBN 3-7913-1393-2

Titelbild: Paul Gauguin, ›Zwei Tahitierinnen‹, 1899. (Photo: AKG, Berlin)

CLAUDE MONET

Von Stephan Koja. 224 Seiten mit 239 Abbildungen, 126 in Farbe. 24 x 30 cm. ISBN 3-7913-1643-5. Leinen DM 98,–/ÖS 715,–/SFr 91,–

Eine Monet-Monographie, die durch Kompetenz in der Auswahl und Schärfe der Interpretation besticht. Etwa 100 selten gesehene, sorgfältig reproduzierte Gemälde aus allen Schaffensphasen belegen die Meisterschaft des großen Impressionisten.

»Ein vorzüglicher Katalog: selten findet man farblich so originalgetreue Abbildungen wie in dem Band, der einen breiten Querschnitt präsentiert.« *Focus*

»Die außergewöhnliche Monographie zeigt selten gesehene Gemälde.« *Kunst aktuell*

LOVIS CORINTH

Herausgegeben von Peter-Klaus Schuster, Christoph Vitali und Barbara Butts.
392 Seiten mit 380 Abbildungen, 252 in Farbe.
24,5 x 30 cm. ISBN 3-7913-1645-1.
Leinen DM 98,–/ÖS 715,–/SFr 110.-

»Das Lebenswerk von Lovis Corinth: mit 150 Gemälden und rund 100 Werken auf Papier ist diese Monographie die bisher umfangreichste Würdigung. Sie distanziert sich vom Klischee des ›deutschen Impressionisten‹ und huldigt dem großen Einzelgänger, der den Sprung aus dem 19. Jahrhundert in die Moderne geschafft hat.« *Handelsblatt*

TIEPOLO IN WÜRZBURG

Der Himmel auf Erden. Zwei Bände.
Herausgegeben von Peter O. Krückmann.
Band I: 208 Seiten mit 337 Abbildungen, 139 in Farbe. 24 x 30 cm. ISBN 3-7913-1639-7.
Leinen DM 78,–/ÖS 569,–/SFr 73,–
Band II: 192 Seiten mit 205 Abbildungen, 52 in Farbe. 24 x 30 cm. ISBN 3-7913-1640-0.
Leinen DM 86,–/ÖS 628,–/SFr 80,–

»Tiepolos Deckenfresko in der Würzburger Residenz gilt als eines der größten Kunstwerke des Abendlands. Der ausführliche Katalog zur Ausstellung 1996 erhellt politische wie kunsthistorische Hintergründe des Dekorationsprojekts und referiert überraschende maltechnische Einsichten aus einer jüngeren gründlichen Untersuchung. Wie Tiepolo dieses Riesenwerk bewältigte, wird nach all dem klarer.« *Der Spiegel*

DAS EWIG WEIBLICHE

L'Eternel Féminin. Von Renoir bis Picasso.
Von Roland Doschka. 224 Seiten mit 151 Abb., 138 in Farbe. 24 x 30 cm. ISBN 3-7913-1749-0.
Leinen DM 78,–/ÖS 569,–/SFr 73,–

»Das Ewig Weibliche, ein Sujet in der Kunst, das zur Inspirationsquelle für ganze Malergenerationen wurde, zeigt Werke von 12 Künstlern der Klassischen Moderne von Cézanne über Degas, Renoir, Matisse bis hin zu Picasso. Mit diesen selten gesehenen Bildern werden Leckerbissen serviert: Eva in allen Facetten.« *Der Tagesspiegel*

RENÉ MAGRITTE

Herausgegeben von Volkmar Essers.
Ca. 240 Seiten mit ca. 200 Abbildungen, ca. 80 in Farbe. 24 x 30 cm. ISBN 3-7913-1747-4.
Leinen DM 98,–/ÖS 715,–/SFr 91,–

René Magrittes malerisches Œuvre hat sehr dazu beigetragen, den Surrealismus allgemein bekannt zu machen. Dieses Buch öffnet den Zugang zu dem vielschichtigen, rätselhaften und verschlüsselten Werk des großen belgischen Malers. Das ›Universum Magritte‹ wird mit den zentralen Themenkreisen durch zahlreiche Beispiele dargestellt und die tiefgründige, poetische Bedeutung seiner Wort-Bilder interpretiert.

PAUL KLEE

Die Zeit der Reife. Herausgegeben von Manfred Fath. 184 Seiten mit 166 Abbildungen, 121 in Farbe. 24 x 28 cm. ISBN 3-7913-1638-9.
Leinen DM 98,–/ÖS 715,–/SFr 91,–

»Bilder und Zeichnungen von Paul Klee zu sehen, wird man nie müde. Klees Phantasie – die reichste und umfassendste dieses Jahrhunderts – wird man wohl nie ergründen. Hier ist eine einmalige Möglichkeit, ausschließlich Arbeiten zu sehen, die Klee seit 1919/20 zurückgehalten und für seinen persönlichen Nachlaß bestimmt hatte.« *SZ*

Düstere Visionen und heitere Erinnerungen: erstmals wird diese spannende Dualität in Paul Klees dichtem Spätwerk deutlich.

MALEREI IN ÖSTERREICH 1945–1995

Die Sammlung Essl. Herausgegeben von Wieland Schmied. 296 Seiten mit 284 Abbildungen, 188 in Farbe. 23,5 x 30 cm. ISBN 3-7913-1642-7. Gebunden DM 98,–/ÖS 715,–/SFr 91,–

Wieland Schmied, einer der besten Kenner der österreichischen Kunst, führt die Entwicklung der zeitgenössischen Malerei in Österreich und ihren Durchbruch zu internationaler Bedeutung eindrucksvoll vor Augen. Die 250 Werke von 42 Künstlern stammen aus der Sammlung Essl, der bedeutendsten und mit mehr als 3000 Werken die umfangreichste mit moderner österreichischer Malerei ab 1945.

KUNST AUS ÖSTERREICH 1896–1996

Herausgegeben von der Kunst- und Ausstellungshalle der Bundesrepublik Deutschland, Bonn. Ca. 360 Seiten mit ca. 500 Abbildungen, ca. 250 in Farbe. 25 x 28 cm. ISBN 3-7913-1700-8. Leinen ca. DM 98,–/ÖS 715,–/SFr 91,–

100 Jahre Kunst aus Österreich: An herausragenden Vertretern der Malerei, Bildhauerei und Architektur – von Klimt, Schiele, Kokoschka bis Rainer und Attersee, von Wagner und Loos bis Hollein und Peichl – wird Österreichs Moderne in ihrem spannungsvollen Auf und Ab lebendig vorgestellt und ihre Bedeutung für die Kunst des 20. Jahrhunderts untersucht.

CHINESISCHE TUSCHMALEREI IM 20. JAHRHUNDERT

Herausgegeben von Heike Kotzenberg. 128 Seiten mit ca. 200 Abbildungen, ca. 45 in Farbe. 24,5 x 31 cm. ISBN 3-7913-1703-2. Leinen DM 78,–/ÖS 569,–/SFr 73,–

Das Standardwerk zur chinesischen Tuschmalerei in unserem Jahrhundert. Erstmalig in Deutschland wird ein Überblick gegeben über Maler, die in China als die größten Meister gelten. Er zeigt die Offenheit der chinesischen Maler, fremde Einflüsse in ihre traditionelle Kunst aufzunehmen und in einer Synthese von westlichen und östlichen Elementen das faszinierende Medium der Tuschmalerei zu modernisieren.

MAX KLINGER

Zeichnungen, Zustandsdrucke, Zyklen. Herausgegeben von Jo-Anne Birnie Danzker und Tilman Falk. 224 Seiten mit ca. 300 Abb., 13 in Farbe. 23 x 30 cm. ISBN 3-7913-1742-3. Leinen DM 98,–/ÖS 715,–/SFr 91,–

Einblicke in den künstlerischen Schöpfungsprozeß eines großen Graphikers. Vorzeichnungen, Studien, Zustandsdrucke und während der Arbeit verworfene druckgraphische Formulierungen ergänzen die endgültig edierte Form der Graphikzyklen. Sie dokumentieren spannend die bis ins Detail anspruchsvolle, akribische Stecherarbeit und machen den Entstehungsprozeß von Klingers Werk nachvollziehbar.

RILKE UND DIE KUNST

Herausgegeben von Gisela Götte und Jo-Anne Birnie Danzker. 192 Seiten mit ca. 166 Abb., ca. 53 in Farbe. 23 x 28 cm. ISBN 3-7913-1750-4. Leinen DM 78,–/ÖS 569,–/SFr 73,–

Ein doppelter Kunstgenuß: Werke von Rodin und Cézanne bis Picasso und den Worpsweder Künstlern, durch die Augen und mit der Feder Rainer Maria Rilkes vorgestellt. Ein Streifzug durch die frühe Kunst der Moderne, beschrieben von einem Dichter, der Zeit seines Lebens den »Kunstdingen« auf der Spur war. Ein Buch, das Kunstinteressierten ebenso willkommen sein wird wie den Freunden der Literatur.

FRANZ VON STUCK UND DIE PHOTOGRAPHIE

Inszenierung und Dokumentation. Herausgegeben von Jo-Anne Birnie Danzker, Ulrich Pohlmann und J. A. Schmoll gen. Eisenwerth. 192 Seiten mit 107 Abbildungen in Duoton und 210 einfarbigen Abb. 23 x 28 cm. ISBN 3-7913-1657-5. Fr. Preis Paperback DM 68,–/ÖS 496,–/SFr 64,–

»Erotik des Lichtbildes: Erstmals wird der vielschichtigen Beziehung Stucks zur Photographie nachgegangen. Von tausend überkommenen Ablichtungen werden ca. 300 gezeigt und mit den Gemälden konfrontiert. Erstaunlich bei den Photos, die nur als Hilfsmittel gedacht waren, ist die künstlerische Qualität.« *FAZ*

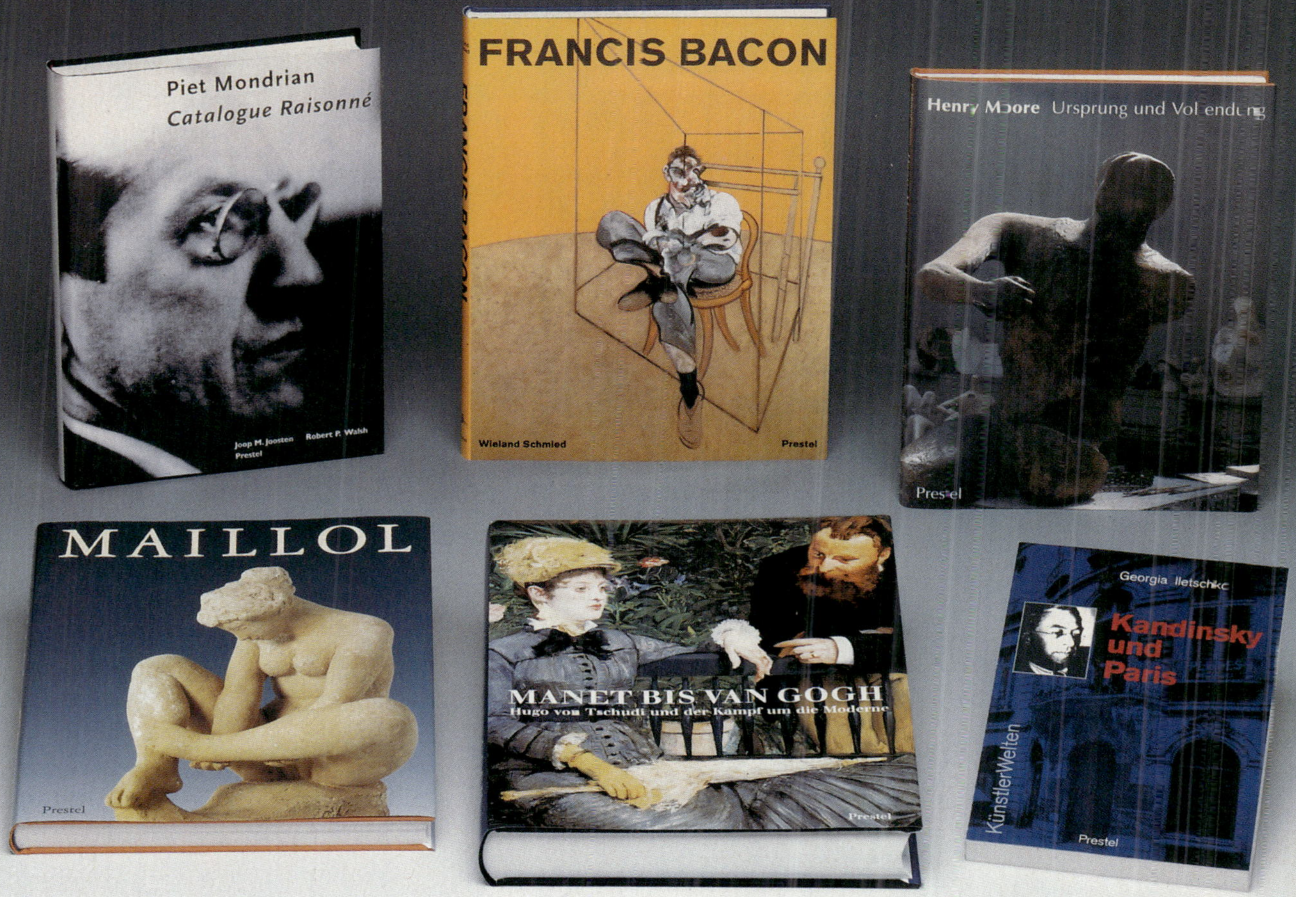

PIET MONDRIAN

Catalogue Raisonné. Von Joop M. Joosten und Robert P. Welsh. Englische Originalausgabe. Ca. 700 Seiten mit ca. 1300 Abbildungen, ca. 350 in Farbe. 23 x 31,5. ISBN 3-7913-1698-2. Leinen ca. DM 368,–/ÖS 2.686,–/SFr 332,– (Erscheinungstermin: Dezember 1996)

Das lange erwartete Œuvre-Verzeichnis zu den Gemälden von Mondrian, dem großen Pionier der geometrischen Abstraktion. Als Ergebnis jahrzehntelanger Forschungen legen die renommiertesten Kenner seiner Kunst mit diesem Werkverzeichnis die Dokumentation des Gesamtschaffens des bedeutenden niederländischen Malers vor.

ARISTIDE MAILLOL

Herausgegeben von Ursel Berger und Jörg Zutter. 232 Seiten mit 265 Abbildungen, 57 in Farbe. 24 x 28 cm. ISBN 3-7913-1641-9. Leinen DM 98,–/ÖS 715,–/SFr 91,–

Seit über 70 Jahren die erste deutschsprachige Publikation über den bedeutenden französischen Bildhauer, dessen Werk als Beginn der Abstraktion wie auch als Rückkehr zur Antike charakterisiert wurde. Der Band wartet mit einer Fülle neuer Erkenntnisse auf und zeigt auch unbekannte Werke, die ein authentisches Bild des Künstlers geben.
»Ein exzellenter Katalog, der mit vielen neuen Forschungsergebnissen aufwartet und die Werkdatierungen präzisiert.« *FAZ*

FRANCIS BACON

Von Wieland Schmied. 200 Seiten mit 272 Abbildungen, 89 in Farbe. 24,5 x 31 cm. ISBN 3-7913-1637-0. Leinen DM 98,–/ÖS 715,–/SFr 91,–

Ein Werk, das unter die Haut geht: Die gültige Monographie über einen der bedeutendsten Maler unseres Jahrhunderts und die verständliche Darstellung eines Œuvres von unvergleichlicher Kraft und Intensität. Bacons aufrüttelnde Malerei, die sich mit der Einsamkeit, dem Schmerz und der Erotik des Einzelnen befaßt, legt in einzigartiger Weise das Nervensystem des heutigen Menschenbilds frei.

MANET BIS VAN GOGH

Hugo von Tschudi und der Kampf um die Moderne. Herausgegeben von Johann Prinz von Hohenzollern und Peter-Klaus Schuster. 472 Seiten mit 482 Abbildungen, 173 in Farbe. 24 x 30 cm. ISBN 3-7913-1748-2. Leinen DM 98,–/ÖS 715,–/SFr 91,–

Tradition contra klassische Moderne – ein spannendes Kapitel deutsch-französischer Kunstgeschichte. Niemand hat moderne Kunst, speziell Meisterwerke des französischen Impressionismus, trotzt starker nationaler Vorurteile entschiedener gesammelt als Hugo von Tschudi. Der Kampf um die Moderne, den er mit Freunden in Deutschland um 1900 ausfocht, wird in einem lebendigen Epochen-Porträt vorgestellt.

HENRY MOORE

Ursprung und Vollendung. Zeichnungen und Skulpturen in Stein, Holz und Gips. Herausgegeben von Manfred Fath. 200 Seiten mit 189 Abbildungen, 78 in Farbe. 24,5 x 30 cm. ISBN 3-7913-1662-1. Leinen DM 98,–/ÖS 715,–/SFr 91,–

Das Werk des populärsten Bildhauers im 20. Jahrhundert, dokumentiert durch seine Entwürfe und die eigenhändig geformten Arbeiten aus Gips, Holz und Stein. In diesem opulent ausgestatteten Buch wird das Leben des englischen Künstlers und seine Arbeitsweise in allen Phasen vom Entwurf bis zur vollendeten Skulptur dargestellt und umfassend kommentiert. Ein wichtiges Buch für die Kunst unserer Zeit.

KÜNSTLERWELTEN: KANDINSKY UND PARIS

Die Geschichte einer Beziehung. Von Georgia Illetschko. Ca. 192 Seiten mit ca. 120 Abbildungen, ca. 20 in Farbe. 16,5 x 23,5. ISBN 3-7913-1740-7. Leinen ca. DM 39,80/ÖS 291,–/SFr 38,80

Der erste Band der neuen Prestel-Reihe ›KünstlerWelten‹, die das Spannungsfeld zwischen Leben und Werk berühmter Künstler ausleuchtet, ist Wassily Kandinsky und seinem mehrere Jahrzehnte währenden, spannenden Dialog mit der Kunstmetropole Paris gewidmet. Erstmals werden die vielschichtigen Einflüsse der Pariser Zeit auf sein Schaffen untersucht.

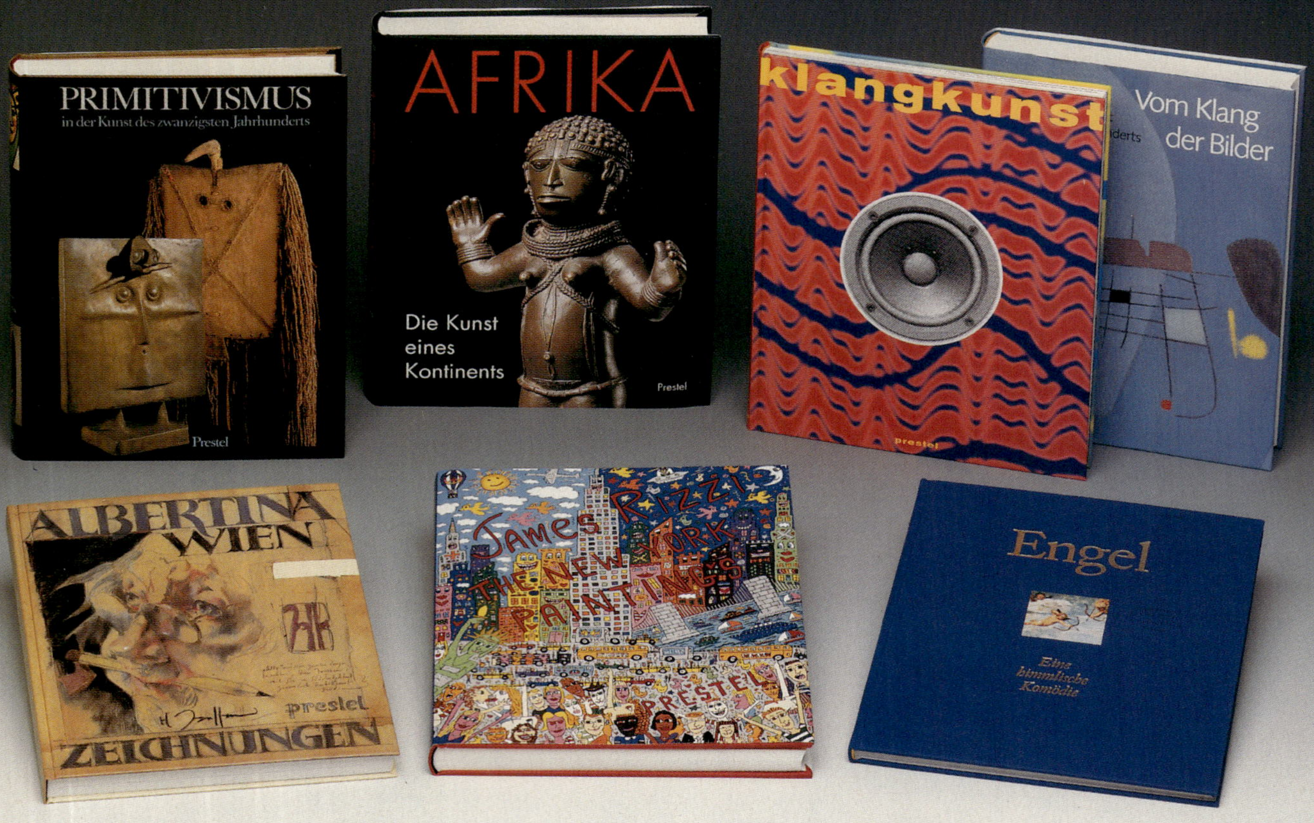

PRIMITIVISMUS IN DER KUNST DES 20. JAHRHUNDERTS

Herausgegeben von William Rubin. 742 Seiten mit 1056 Abbildungen, 369 in Farbe. 22,5 x 30 cm. ISBN 3-7913-1716-4. Sonderausgabe; Paperback DM 128,–/ÖS 934,–/SFr 119,–. Subskriptions-Preis bis 31.12.1996: DM 98,–/ÖS 715,–/SFr 91,–

»Dem ›Primitivismus‹ als einem grundlegenden Phänomen in der Kunst des 20. Jahrhunderts ist der Band gewidmet. Wo künftig von dem Thema die Rede ist, wird man diese gründliche, vielseitige Monographie zitieren müssen.« *Neue Zürcher Zeitung*

HORST JANSSEN

Zeichnungen. Herausgegeben von Walter Koschatzky. 192 Seiten mit 77 direkt nach den Originalen reproduzierten Farbtafeln und 72 einfarbigen Abbildungen. 22,5 x 28 cm. ISBN 3-7913-1693-1. Sonderausgabe; Gebunden DM 49,80/ÖS 364,–/SFr 47,80

»Eine großartige Auswahl von Arbeiten Janssens aus den Jahren 1965 bis 1983.« *SZ*

»Eine splendid besorgte Publikation.« *FAZ*

ENGEL

Eine himmlische Komödie. Von Gottfried Knapp. 96 Seiten, 125 Abb., 93 in Farbe. 23,5 x 30 cm. Geschenkausgabe. ISBN 3-7913-1758-X. Leinen mit Goldprägung DM 39,80/ÖS 291,–/SFr 38,80

»Ein ästhetischer und intellektueller Genuß. Ein erfolgreiches Geschenk für Kunst-Feinschmecker.« *Bayerischer Rundfunk*

AFRIKA

Die Kunst eines Kontinents. Herausgegeben von Tom Phillips. 620 Seiten mit 854 Abbildungen, davon 801 in Farbe. 24,5 x 30 cm. ISBN 3-7913-1692-3. Leinen DM 148,–/ÖS 1080,–/SFr 137,–

»Die über 800 Objekte und die mehr als 100 Beiträge bieten einen umfassenden Überblick über die Kunst des ganzen Kontinents und schlagen zugleich eine Brücke zwischen der Kultur des islamischen Nordens und der Kunst Schwarzafrikas.« *art*

»In der monumentalen Schau werden alle Disziplinen in die Pflicht genommen. Und alle haben zu der einzigartigen Huldigung an den Kontinent Afrika beigetragen.« *FAZ*

JAMES RIZZI

New York. 128 Seiten mit 100 farbigen Abbildungen. 24,5 x 32 cm. ISBN 3-7913-1644-3. Paperback DM 39,80/ÖS 291,–/SFr 38,80

Let's have fun! Das fröhliche, humorvolle und mitreißende New York-Porträt eines Großstadt-Kindes und Lebens-Künstlers. Ähnlich wie Keith Haring startete der New Yorker Rizzi seine Karriere sehr unkonventionell. Heute sind seine originellen, mit amüsanten Details vollgepackten, kindlich-naiv gemalten Werke sehr populär. In 60 großformatigen Gemälden zeichnet er mit großem Enthusiasmus sein persönliches Bild von New York: pulsierend, verrückt, unbeschwert und voller Energie.

KLANGKUNST

Herausgegeben von der Akademie der Künste, Berlin. 304 Seiten mit 374 Abb., 20 in Farbe. 25 x 30 cm. ISBN 3-7913-1699-0. Gebunden mit einer CD DM 98,–/ÖS 715,–/SFr 91,–

Das Abenteuer einer faszinierenden Grenzerfahrung: Kunst und Musik – zum Sehen und zum Hören. Dies Handbuch gibt erstmalig einen repräsentativen Querschnitt durch die atemberaubenden Entwicklungen im spannungsvollen Grenzbereich der Klangkunst. Das längst fällige Informations- und Nachschlagewerk zu diesem Thema mit einer ergänzenden CD: wichtig für Kunst- und Musikinteressierte.

VOM KLANG DER BILDER

Die Musik in der Kunst des 20. Jahrhunderts. Herausgegeben von Karin v. Maur. 488 Seiten mit 821 Abbildungen, 223 in Farbe. 22,5 x 30 cm. ISBN 3-7913-0727-4. Leinen DM 98,–/ÖS 715,–/SFr 91,–

»Dieser Überblick ist gigantisch! Eine unerschöpfliche Fundgrube weit über die Grenzen von Musik und Malerei hinaus.« *FAZ*

»Wie sich Musik und Bild inspirieren, welche Schlüsselrolle Musik beim Entstehen von Malerei spielt, ist im Pracht-Bildband nachzulesen.« *Kölnische Rundschau*

»Der Leser und Betrachter wird schnell merken, daß er hier einen wahren Schatz in Händen hält.« *Der Tagesspiegel*

ARCHITEKTUR IM 20. JAHRHUNDERT: ÖSTERREICH

Von Otto Wagner bis Coop Himmelblau. Herausgegeben von Wilfried Wang, Dietmar Steiner und Annette Becker. 352 Seiten mit 889 Abbildungen, 180 in Farbe. 23 x 32 cm. ISBN 3-7913-1613-3. Leinen DM 98,–/ÖS 715,–/SFr 91,–

»Der erste Band einer neuen Buchreihe zur Architektur im 20. Jh.. Ein chronologischer Teil, ein thematischer mit Merkmalen der Landesarchitektur sowie ein Projektteil gliedern das Standardwerk, das vorzüglich in Text, Bild und Layout ist.« *Der Architekt*

ARCHITEKTUR IM 20. JAHRHUNDERT: IRLAND

Hrsg. von Annette Becker, John Olley und Wilfried Wang. Ca. 200 Seiten mit ca. 460 Abbildungen, ca. 100 in Farbe. 23 x 32 cm. ISBN 3-7913-1706-7. Leinen DM 98,–/ÖS 715,–/SFr 91,– (Erscheinungstermin: November 1996)

BAUEN FÜR DIE SINNE

Gefühl, Erotik und Sexualität in der Architektur. Von Christian W. Thomsen. 184 Seiten mit 302 Abb., 205 in Farbe. 24 x 30 cm. ISBN 3-7913-1707-5. Gebunden DM 98,–/ÖS 715,–/SFr 91,–

Eine spannende, lustvolle Entdeckungsreise in die Geschichte der Wechselbeziehungen von Architektur und Erotik. Erstmalig legt der Autor eine Kulturgeschichte der erotischen Baukunst vor. Ein fulminantes Plädoyer für eine Architektur der Sinne.

GRÜN ZWISCHEN STÄDTEN

Emscher Landschaftspark (NRW), GrünGürtel Frankfurt / Regionalpark Rhein-Main, Grüne Nachbarschaft (Baden-Württemberg). Von Hermann Grub und Petra Lejeune. Ca. 160 S. mit ca. 150 Abb., 100 in Farbe. 24 x 30 cm. ISBN 3-793-1708-3. Paperback DM 58,–/ÖS 423,–/SFr 55,–

Landschaft als bedrohte Art: Drei spektakuläre Projekte zeigen, wie Architekten und Landschaftsplaner mit neuen Konzepten unsere Lebensqualität sichern wollen.

FILM ARCHITEKTUR

Von Metropolis bis Blade Runner. Hrsg. von Dietrich Neumann. 208 Seiten mit 219 Abb., 75 in Farbe. 24,5 x 30 cm. ISBN 3-7913-1656-7. Gebunden DM 98,–/ÖS 715,–/SFr 91,–

»Umfangreich bebilderte Beiträge zu 24 Filmen befassen sich mit der Rolle der Architektur im Kino und geben einen Überblick über die bedeutendsten Arbeiten für Meisterwerke in Europa und den USA.« *Stern*

DAM ARCHITEKTUR JAHRBUCH

1996. Hrsg. vom Deutschen Architektur-Museum, Frankfurt a. M., Annette Becker und Wilfried Wang. Ca. 200 Seiten mit ca. 400 Abb., ca. 100 in Farbe. 22 x 28 cm. ISBN 3-7913-1705-9. Paperback DM 58,–/ÖS 423,–/SFr 55,–

Die in jedem Jahr mit Spannung erwartete Bilanz der deutschen Architektur: 1996 steht die Denkmalpflege im Mittelpunkt.

SOL POWER

Die Evolution der solaren Architektur. Von Sophia und Stefan Behling. 240 S. mit 300 Abb. 420 in Farbe. 24 x 31 cm. ISBN 3-7913-1651-6. Leinen DM 98,–/ÖS 715,–/SFr 91,–

Wie in einem Film wird in dieser kommentierten Bilddokumentation die Weltgeschichte der Solararchitektur anhand vieler Beispiele eindrucksvoll aufgerollt

SOLAR ENERGY IN ARCHITECTURE AND URBAN PLANNING

Solarenergie in Architektur und Stadtplanung. Hrsg. von Thomas Herzog. Dreisprachige Ausgabe in Deutsch, Englisch, Italienisch. 224 S. mit 466 Abb., 290 in Farbe. 24 x 31 cm. ISBN 3-7913-1652-4. Leinen DM 98,–/ÖS 715,–/SFr 91,–

Das aktuelle, informative Handbuch für umweltbewußtes Planen und Bauen stellt ca. 50 Beispiele von Solararchitektur vor.

AWA AWARD WINNING ARCHITECTURE 1996

Hrsg. von Frantisek Sedlacek. Englische Originalausgabe. 232 Seiten mit 836 Abb., 4[illegible]9 in Farbe. 24,5 x 31 cm. ISBN 3-7913-1676-1. Paperback DM 78,–/ÖS 569,–/SFr 7[illegible],–

Ein unentbehrliches Nachschlagewerk: Das neue Architekturjahrbuch für preisgekrönte Bauten aus aller Welt macht die aktuellen Architekturtendenzen eines Jahres sichtbar.

AUF DEN FOLGENDEN SEITEN FINDEN SIE EINE AUSWAHL AUS UNSEREM UMFANGREICHEN PROGRAMM LIEFERBARER TITEL ZUR KUNST UND ARCHITEKTUR, ZUM DESIGN UND KUNSTHANDWERK

ALTNIEDERLÄNDISCHE MALEREI

Von Rogier van der Weyden bis Gerard David. Von Otto Pächt. Hrsg. von Monika Rosenauer. 264 Seiten mit 221 Abb., 33 in Farbe. 20,5 x 28 cm. ISBN 3-7913-1389-4. Leinen DM 118,–/ÖS 861,–/SFr 110,–

»Der Band ist für ein Publikum bestimmt, das bereit ist, sich um das ›Reifen des Sehens‹ zu bemühen. Methodisch fundierte Stilanalyse auf höchstem Niveau.« *Neue Zürcher Zeitung*

COSMAS DAMIAN ASAM

Hrsg. von Bruno Bushart und Bernhard Rupprecht. 360 Seiten mit 317 Abb., 61 in Farbe. 22,5 x 30 cm. ISBN 3-7913-0767-3. Leinen DM 98,–/ÖS 715,–/SFr 91,–

KUNST DES BIEDERMEIER 1815–35

Von Georg Himmelheber. 320 Seiten mit 598 Abb., 174 in Farbe. 22,5 x 30 cm. ISBN 3-7913-0885-8. Leinen DM 118,–/ÖS 861,–/SFr 110,–

»Eine Epoche wird rehabilitiert: mit diesem vorzüglichen Buch, das den Stilwandel exakt beschreibt, wird dem Biedermeier ein neues Profil gegeben.« *Süddeutsche Zeitung*

CARL BLECHEN

Hrsg. von Peter-Klaus Schuster. 309 Seiten mit 702 Abb., 222 in Farbe. 24 x 30 cm. ISBN 3-7913-1084-4. Leinen DM 118,–/ÖS 861,–/SFr 110,–

VAN EYCK

Die Begründer der altniederländischen Malerei. Von Otto Pächt. 224 Seiten mit 154 Abb., 28 in Farbe. 20,5 x 28 cm. ISBN 3-7913-1033-X. Leinen DM 98,–/ÖS 715,–/SFr 91,–

»Ein Meilenstein in der Van Eyck-Forschung.« *FAZ*

»Pächts Spurensuche ist ein wahres Lesevergnügen. Sie ist anspruchsvoll und dennoch gut lesbar.« *art*

DER GLANZ DER FARNESE

Kunst und Sammelleidenschaft in der Renaissance. Hrsg. von Christoph Vitali. 536 Seiten mit 380 Abb., 292 in Farbe. 24,5 x 29 cm. ISBN 3-7913-1626-5. Gebunden DM 148,–/ÖS 1080,–/SFr 137,–

»Kunstsammler par excellence: einen Eindruck von der großen Sammelleidenschaft der italienischen Adelsfamilie Farnese und ihren Schätzen verschafft diese glänzende Auswahl.« *Focus*

CASPAR DAVID FRIEDRICH

Von Helmut Börsch-Supan. 207 Seiten mit 132 Abb., 68 in Farbe. 23,5 x 29,5 cm. ISBN 3-7913-0835-1. Leinen DM 98,–/ÖS 715,–/SFr 91,–

GOYA

Das druckgraphische Werk. Von Alfonso E. Pérez Sánchez und Julián Gállego. 264 Seiten mit 298 einfarbigen Abb. 24 x 30 cm. ISBN 3-7913-1475-0. Bütten DM 118,–/ÖS 861,–/SFr 110,–

»Ein Kunstbuch mit gedruckten Meisterwerken von Goya: der Band bündelt alle graphischen Zyklen und Einzelblätter, sowohl die radierten als die lithographierten samt der zusätzlichen Blätter, die Goya dann nicht in die Bildfolgen einreihte.« *Die Welt*

DIE GROSSEN IMPRESSIONISTEN

Von Fritz Novotny. Mit einer Einführung von Artur Rosenauer. 152 Seiten mit 102 Abb., 78 in Farbe. 24 x 30 cm. ISBN 3-7913-1440-8 Gebunden DM 78,–/ÖS 569,–/SFr 73,–

»Ein Standardwerk, das den Bogen von Manet über Van Gogh bis Gauguin und Matisse spannt und die formalen und inhaltlichen Aspekte des Impressionismus gut beleuchtet.« *Berliner Morgenpost*

EDOUARD MANET

Augenblicke der Geschichte. Hrsg. von Manfred Fath und Stefan Germer. 212 Seiten mit 144 Abb., 32 in Farbe. 24 x 30 cm. ISBN 3-7913-1210-3. Leinen DM 98,–/ÖS 715,–/SFr 91,–

»Das Buch setzt Manets Historienbilder in einen geschichtlichen, kunsthistorischen und ikonographischen Zusammenhang.« *FAZ*

DIE NABIS

Propheten der Moderne. Hrsg. von Claire Frèches-Thory und Ursula Perucchi-Petri. 528 Seiten mit 618 Abb., 332 in Farbe. 23 x 30,5 cm. ISBN 3-7913-1283-9. Leinen DM 148,–/ÖS 1080,–/SFr 137,–

»Das Buch über die französische Künstlergruppe ›Nabis‹, unter ihnen Bonnard und Valloton, bringt neben den Farbwiedergaben der Bilder Aufsätze, die den Band zu einem wissenschaftlichen Instrumentarium machen.« *Neue Zürcher Zeitung*

REMBRANDT

Von Otto Pächt. Hrsg. von Edwin Lachnit. 256 Seiten mit 245 Abb., 64 in Farbe. 24 x 30 cm. ISBN 3-7913-1156-5. Leinen DM 98,–/ÖS 715,–/SFr 91,–

»Behutsam wie ein Außenseiter nähert sich der Wiener Kunsthistoriker Otto Pächt dem Thema Rembrandt. Ein großzügig bebildertes Buch, das vor allem eine Schule des Sehens ist.« *FAZ*

RODIN
Eros und Kreativität

Hrsg. von Rainer Crone und Siegfried Salzmann. 240 Seiten mit 357 Abb., 32 in Farbe und 140 in Duoton. 24 x 31 cm. ISBN 3-7913-1153-0. Leinen DM 98,–/ÖS 715,–/SFr 91,–

»Das große Rodin-Buch erfüllt hohe Ansprüche. Die brillante Präsentation vermittelt ein ungemein sinnliches Erlebnis.« *Augsburger Allgemeine*

DER TEPPICH VON BAYEUX

Triumphdenkmal der Normannen. Von Wolfgang Grape. 176 Seiten mit 134 Abb., 93 in Farbe. 24 x 28 cm. ISBN 3-7913-1336-3. Leinen DM 78,–/ÖS 569,–/SFr 73,–

»Der Band besticht durch die außerordentlich gute Reproduktion. Das Faszinosum des Originals wird so nachvollziehbar.« *Kölner Stadt-Anzeiger*

TITIAN (TIZIAN)

Englische Originalausgabe. 452 Seiten mit 311 Abb., 207 in Farbe. 21,5 x 29,5 cm. ISBN 3-7913-1102-6. Leinen DM 148,–/ÖS 1080,–/SFr 137,–

»Ehrung für das Genie der Farbe: dies ist die bislang größte Werkschau des berühmten Renaissance-Meisters Tizian.« *art*

TURNER IN DEUTSCHLAND

Hrsg. von Manfred Fath. 276 Seiten mit 276 Abb., 111 in Farbe. 24 x 28 cm. ISBN 3-7913-1490-4 Gebunden DM 98,–/ÖS 715,–/SFr 91,–

»Turner gilt als der größte englische Maler überhaupt: Die Landschaftsmalerei erhob er zur Königsdisziplin. Dieser Band zu Turners sieben Deutschland-Reisen bietet 150 Blätter, wasserfarbenes Wunderland, und profunde Betrachtungen.« *FAZ*

VIKTORIANISCHE MALEREI

Von Turner bis Whistler. Hrsg. von Robin Hamlyn, Christoph Heilmann, Christopher Newall und Julian Treuherz. 232 Seiten mit 140 Abb., 94 in Farbe. 24 x 30 cm. ISBN 3-7913-1244-8. Leinen DM 98,–/ÖS 715,–/SFr 91,–

»Der aufwendig gestaltete Band besitzt den Charakter eines Handbuches.« *Süddeutsche Zeitung*

FERDINAND GEORG WALDMÜLLER

Von Klaus Albrecht Schröder. 256 Seiten mit 240 Abb., 146 in Farbe. 24 x 30 cm. ISBN 3-7913-1078-X Leinen DM 108,–/ÖS 788,–/SFr 100,–

WIENER BIEDERMEIER

Malerei zwischen Wiener Kongreß und Revolution. Hrsg. von Gerbert Frodl und Klaus Albrecht Schröder. 368 Seiten mit 266 Abb., 186 in Farbe. 24 x 30 cm. ISBN 3-7913-1264-2. Leinen DM 98,–/ÖS 715,–/SFr 91,–

AMERIKANISCHE KUNST IM 20. JAHRHUNDERT

Malerei und Plastik 1913–1993. Hrsg. von Christos M. Joachimides und Norman Rosenthal.
524 Seiten mit 528 Abb., 252 in Farbe.
22,5 x 30 cm. ISBN 3-7913-1240-5.
Leinen DM 128,–/ÖS 934,–/SFr 119,–
»Ein reales Kunstereignis. Was den Kunstfreund erwartet, ist kein Lexikon der Modernen Kunst, sondern eine Art Sinfonie in drei Sätzen mit Vor- und Nachspiel.« *Focus*

MAX BECKMANN

Retrospektive. Hrsg. von Carla Schulz-Hoffmann und Judith C. Weiss. 480 Seiten mit 563 Abb., 165 in Farbe. 22,5 x 30 cm. ISBN 3-7913-1411-1.
Broschur DM 49,80/ÖS 364,–/SFr 47,80
»Die große Beckmann-Retrospektive: reich wie nie zuvor bietet dieses Lebenswerk sich als Panorama ohnegleichen dar.« *Der Spiegel*

BERLIN – MOSKAU MOSKAU – BERLIN 1900–1950

Bildende Kunst, Photographie, Architektur, Theater, Literatur, Musik und Film. Hrsg. von Irina Antonowa und Jörn Merkert. 709 Seiten mit 1013 Abb., 516 in Farbe. 24 x 30 cm. ISBN 3-7913-1488-2.
Gebunden DM 148,–/ÖS 1080,–/SFr 137,–
»Auftritt eines starken Doppels! Ein großes Thema: die regen kulturellen Wechselbeziehungen zwischen Rußland und Deutschland, zwischen Moskau und Berlin in der ersten Hälfte dieses Jahrhunderts werden mit einer Fülle von Bildern und Dokumenten in Erinnerung gebracht.« *art*

DER BLAUE REITER

im Lenbachhaus, München. Hrsg. von Armin Zweite. 288 Seiten mit 198 Abb., 121 in Farbe.
23 x 30 cm. ISBN 3-7913-1158-1.
Leinen DM 98,–/ÖS 715,–/SFr 91,–
»An 121 farbigen Bildbeispielen wird diese Künstlergruppe, von der ein wesentlicher Impuls für die Kunst ausging, gut vorgestellt.« *Die Welt*

FERNANDO BOTERO

Bilder, Zeichnungen, Skulpturen.
Hrsg. von Werner Spies. 196 Seiten mit 161 Abb., 85 in Farbe. 22,5x28cm. ISBN 3-7913-0774-6.
Leinen DM 49,80/ÖS 364,–/SFr 47,80

CHRISTO UND JEANNE-CLAUDE

Der Reichstag und urbane Projekte. Hrsg. von Jacob Baal-Teshuva. Photos von Wolfgang Volz. 168 Seiten mit 166 Abb., 125 in Farbe. 24 x 31 cm. ISBN 3-7913-1307-X.
Broschur DM 29,80/ÖS 218,–/SFr 29,80

SALVADOR DALÍ DAS DRUCKGRAPHISCHE WERK

Herausgegeben von Ralf Michler und Lutz W. Löpsinger.
Band I: Œuvrekatalog der Radierungen und Mixed-Media Graphiken 1924-1980. 272 Seiten mit 1070 Abb., 79 in Farbe. 24 x 30 cm.
ISBN 3-7913-1285-5.
Leinen DM 198,–/ÖS 1445,–/SFr 179,–
Band II: Œuvrekatalog der Lithographien und Holzstiche 1956-1980. 188 Seiten mit 693 Abb., 85 in Farbe. 24 x 30 cm. ISBN 3-7913-1492-0.
Leinen DM 178,–/ÖS 1299,–/SFr 161,–
»Die Benutzung dieses zweibändigen Dalí-Katalogs, dem Unentbehrlichkeit zukommt, ist im Handel und Auktionswesen, bei Sammlern und Verlegern dringend anzuraten.« *Die Weltkunst*

DEUTSCHE KUNST IM 20. JAHRHUNDERT

Malerei und Plastik 1905-1985. Hrsg. von Christos M. Joachimides, Norman Rosenthal und Wieland Schmied. 504 Seiten mit 629 Abb., 336 in Farbe. 22,5 x 30 cm. ISBN 3-7913-1462-9.
Paperback DM 49,80,–/ÖS 364,–/SFr 47,80
»Dieser qualitätsvolle Band ist ein ›Bilderbuch‹ zum Immer-wieder-in-die Hand-nehmen und genügt höchsten wissenschaftlichen Ansprüchen.« *Pan*

MAX ERNST

Hrsg. von Werner Spies. 388 Seiten mit 444 Abb., 250 in Farbe. 24 x 30 cm. ISBN 3-7913-1122-0.
Leinen DM 118,–/ÖS 861,–/SFr 110,–
»Die umfassende Werkübersicht dokumentiert eindrucksvoll sämtliche Werkphasen dieses Zauberers der kaum spürbaren Verrückungen.« *art*

LYONEL FEININGER

Von Ulrich Luckhardt. 188 Seiten mit 160 Abb., 60 in Farbe. 24 x 30 cm. ISBN 3-7913-0993-5.
Leinen DM 108,–/ÖS 788,–/SFr 100,–
»Die schön und sorgfältig ausgestattete Monographie füllt eine echte Lücke.« *Neue Zürcher Zeitung*

ALBERTO GIACOMETTI

Skulpturen, Gemälde, Zeichnungen. Hrsg. von Angela Schneider. 224 Seiten mit 216 Abb., 31 in Farbe und 114 in Duoton. 24 x 30 cm. ISBN 3-7913-1335-5.
Leinen DM 98,–/ÖS 715,–/SFr 91,–
»Nicht allein die Kunst, auch der Mensch wird vorgestellt. Erfrischend unpretentiöse Fotos illustrieren die Beiträge renommierter Kunsthistoriker.« *art*

KEITH HARING

Hrsg. von Germano Celant. 210 Seiten mit 227 Abb., 179 in Farbe. 24 x 30cm. ISBN 3-7913-1363-0.
Paperback DM 39,80/ÖS 291,–/SFr 38,80
»Eine Haring-Anthologie mit einem fast filmischen Querschnitt durch ein Werk von atemberaubender Sicherheit und pulsierender Vitalität.« *FAZ*

DAVID HOCKNEY

Gemälde. Von Paul Melia und Ulrich Luckhardt. 200 Seiten mit 190 Abb., 74 in Farbe. 24 x 31 cm. ISBN 3-7913-1388-6.
Leinen DM 98,–/ÖS 715,–/SFr 91,–
»Das differenzierte Bild eines vielseitigen Malers, dessen Werk sich kontinuierlich entwickelt hat. Die Interpretation seines Werks geschieht vor der Folie seiner Biographie und unter Verzicht auf psychologisierende Spekulationen.« *Die Welt*

HORST JANSSEN

Zeichnungen. Hrsg. von Walter Koschatzky.
192 Seiten mit 149 Abb., 77 in Farbe. 22,5 x 28 cm. ISBN 3-7913-1693-1.
Gebunden DM 49,80/ÖS 364,–/SFr 47,80

ANSELM KIEFER

Von Mark Rosenthal. Englische Originalausgabe. 216 Seiten mit 280 Abb.,105 in Farbe. 26 x 29,5 cm. ISBN 3-7913-0847-5.
Paperback DM 98,–/ÖS 715,–/SFr 91,–
»Fast umfassend wird hier – auf Wunsch des Malers in Englisch – das rätselhafteste und ambivalenteste Werk der deutschen Nachkriegszeit vorgestellt.« *Die Weltwoche*

PAUL KLEE

Wachstum regt sich. Klees Zwiesprache mit der Natur. Hrsg. von Ernst-Gerhard Güse.
192 Seiten mit 117 Abb., 60 in Farbe. 23 x 28 cm. ISBN 3-7913-1209-X.
Leinen DM 108,–/ÖS 788,–/SFr 100,–
»Der phantasievolle Paul Klee suchte immer eine Annäherung an die Natur, machte Unsichtbares sichtbar. Dies ist ein aufschlußreicher Band.« *FAZ*

OSKAR KOKOSCHKA

Hrsg. von Klaus Albrecht Schröder und Johann Winkler. 230 Seiten mit 189 Abb., 103 in Farbe. 24 x 30 cm. ISBN 3-7913-1123-9.
Leinen DM 108,–/ÖS 788,–/SFr 100,–
»Ein sehr übersichtlicher und ausgewogener Kunstband, der das malerische Werk in einer qualitätsbewußten Auswahl darstellt.« *FAZ*

DIE KUNST DER MODERNE

Zur Struktur und Dynamik ihrer Entwicklung. Von Goya bis Beuys. Von Sandro Bocola.
624 Seiten mit 440 einfarbigen Abb.
14,8 x 22,5 cm. ISBN 3-7913-1387-8.
Gebunden DM 58,–/ÖS 423,–/SFr 55,–
»Die Entwicklung der modernen Kunst in einem in sich geschlossenen, klar strukturierten und einleuchtenden Modell dargestellt.« *Foglio*

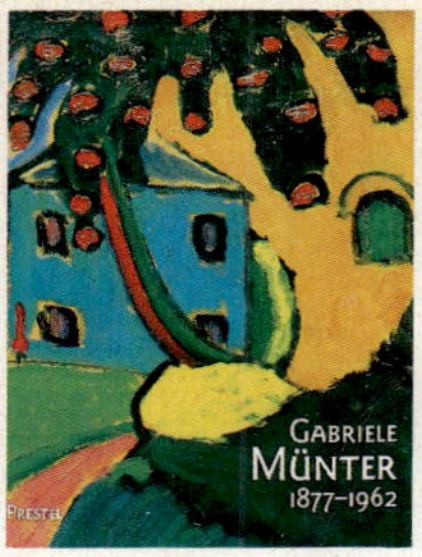

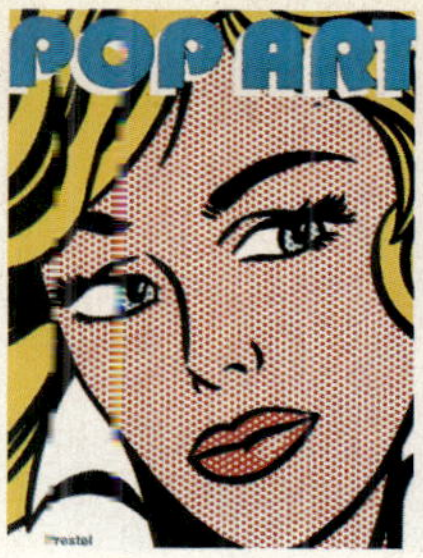

FERNAND LÉGER

1911–1924. Der Rhythmus des modernen Lebens. Hrsg. von Dorothy Kosinski. 256 Seiten mit 256 Abb., 103 in Farbe. 24 x 30 cm. ISBN 3-7913-1334-7. Bütten DM 98,–/ÖS 715,–/SFr 91,–

AUGUST MACKE
DIE TUNISREISE

Von Magdalena M. Moeller. 128 Seiten mit 32 Farbtafeln und 83 einfarbigen Abb. sowie 52 Photographien von August Macke. 23 x 30 cm. ISBN 3-7913-0990-0. Bütten DM 58,–/ÖS 423,–/SFr 55,–
»In dieser schönen Gesamtdarstellung ist Mackes berühmte ›Tunisreise‹ zu einem Fest fürs Auge geworden. Ein Buch für Kunstgenießer und Kenner.« *Der Tagesspiegel*

FRANZ MARC

Von Mark Rosenthal. 160 Seiten mit 94 Abb., 71 in Farbe. 24 x 29 cm. ISBN 3-7913-1215-4. Leinen DM 78,–/ÖS 569,–/SFr 73,–
»Die Monographie des amerikanischen Experten gibt einen repräsentativen Querschnitt durch das Werk von Marc.« *Bayerischer Rundfunk*

FRANZ MARC
ELSE LASKER-SCHÜLER

»Der Blaue Reiter präsentiert Euer Hoheit sein Blaues Pferd.« Karten und Briefe. Hrsg. von Peter-Klaus Schuster. 168 Seiten, 43 Farbtafeln und 74 Abb. 16 x 24 cm. ISBN 3-7913-0825-4. Gebunden DM 29,80/ÖS 218,–/SFr 29,80
»Ein schönes und exzellent gedrucktes Dokument einer legendären Künstlerfreundschaft.« *FAZ*

HENRI MATISSE

Zeichnungen und Skulpturen. Hrsg. von Ernst-Gerhard Güse. 256 Seiten mit 108 Abb., 98 in Duoton. 23,5 x 31,5 cm. ISBN 3-7913-1124-7. Leinen DM 98,–/ÖS 715,–/SFr 91,–
»Diese Blätter zu entschlüsseln, ist ein ebenso sinnliches wie intellektuelles Vergnügen.« *FAZ*

AMEDEO MODIGLIANI

Malerei, Skulpturen, Zeichnungen. Von Werner Schmalenbach. 228 Seiten mit 237 Abb., 94 in Farbe. 24 x 31,5 cm. ISBN 3-7913-1077-1. Leinen DM 118,–/ÖS 861,–/SFr 110,–

GABRIELE MÜNTER

Hrsg. von Annegret Hoberg und Helmut Friedel. 300 Seiten mit 384 Abb., 166 in Farbe. 24 x 29 cm. ISBN 3-7913-1216-2. Leinen DM 98,–/ÖS 715,–/SFr 91,–
»Ein hervorragendes Münter-Buch, das besondere Beachtung verdient.« *Neue Zürcher Zeitung*

EDVARD MUNCH

Von Reinhold Heller. 144 Seiten mit 114 Abb., 44 in Farbe. 24 x 31 cm. ISBN 3-7913-1301-0. Leinen DM 49,80/ÖS 364,–/SFr 47,80

NEUE SACHLICHKEIT

Bilder auf der Suche nach der Wirklichkeit. Figurative Malerei der zwanziger Jahre. Von Hans-Jürgen Buderer. Hrsg. von Manfred Fath. 248 Seiten mit 316 Abb., 143 in Farbe. 23 x 30 cm. ISBN 3-7913-1379-7. Leinen DM 98,–/ÖS 715,–/SFr 91,–
»Der empfehlenswerte Band führt 250 Arbeiten von 70 Künstlern zusammen. Ein Beleg dafür, wie weit der Bogen der ›Neuen Sachlichkeit‹ hier geschlagen wird.« *Stuttgarter Nachrichten*

PERFORMANCE – RITUAL – PROZESS

Handbuch der Aktionskunst in Europa. Von Elisabeth Jappe. 220 Seiten mit 173 Abb., 36 in Farbe. 19,5 x 27,2 cm. ISBN 3-7913-1300-2. Gebunden DM 78,–/ÖS 569,–/SFr 73,–
»Ein umfassendes Kompendium zum Thema Performance. Von der besten Expertin erfährt auch der Neuling ganz konkret, was sich abgespielt hat in diesem neuen Medium.« *art*

PICASSO

Die Sammlung Ludwig. Zeichnungen, Gemälde, Plastische Werke. Hrsg. von Evelyn Weiss und Maria Teresa Ocaña. 280 Seiten mit 326 Abb., 187 in Farbe. 24 x 31 cm. ISBN 3-7913-1235-9. Leinen DM 98,–/ÖS 715,–/SFr 91,–

PICASSOS WELT DER KINDER

Hrsg. von Werner Spies. 256 Seiten mit 270 Abb., 127 in Farbe. 24 x 30 cm. ISBN 3-7913-1491-2. Leinen DM 78,–/ÖS 569,–/SFr 73,–
»Werner Spies, der wohl gründlichste Kenner von Picassos Werk, hat aus dem Thema Kinderbilder ein Buch gemacht, das nicht nur vom Sujet her attraktiv und zum Publikumserfolg prädestiniert ist, sondern auch Entdeckungen offeriert, die kaum mehr möglich schienen.« *Die Zeit*

PABLO PICASSO

Wege zur Skulptur. Die Carnets Paris und Dinard von 1928. Von Werner Spies. 168 Seiten mit 206 einfarbigen Abb. 24 x 30 cm. ISBN 3-7913-1436-X. Bütten DM 78,–/ÖS 569,–/SFr 73,–

PICASSO UND BRAQUE

Die Geburt des Kubismus. Von William Rubin. 424 Seiten mit 551 Abb., 321 in Farbe. 23 x 29 cm. ISBN 3-7913-1046-1. Leinen DM 118,–/ÖS 861,–/SFr 110,–
»Ein hervorragend gestalteter Band, mit dem wir in Zukunft ein höchst nützliches Nachschlagewerk zum Kubismus zur Hand haben.« *SZ*

POP ART

Hrsg. von Marco Livingstone. 312 Seiten mit 315 Abb., 184 in Farbe. 24 x 29 cm. Leinen: ISBN 3-7913-1194-8. DM 98,–/ÖS 715,–/SFr 91,– Paperback: ISBN 3-7913-1414-9. DM 39,80/ÖS 291,–/SFr 38,80
»Was es des genaueren mit der Pop Art auf sich hatte, wie ihre Entstehung und Entwicklung verliefen, das wird in diesem Band so gründlich wie noch nie gezeigt.« *Der Spiegel*

GEORGES ROUAULT

Von Stephan Koja. 214 Seiten mit 200 Abb., 89 in Farbe. 24 x 30 cm. ISBN 3-7913-1294-4. Leinen DM 98,–/ÖS 715,–/SFr 91,–
»Diese neue, anschaulich verfaßte Monographie vermittelt einen gründlichen Einblick in Rouaults Schaffen.« *Neue Zürcher Zeitung*

RUSSISCHE AVANTGARDE
IM 20. JAHRHUNDERT

Von Malewitsch bis Kabakov. Die Sammlung Ludwig, Köln. Hrsg. von Evelyn Weiss. 280 Seiten mit 493 Abb., 321 in Farbe. 24 x 30 cm. ISBN 3-7913-1286-3. Leinen DM 98,–/ÖS 715,–/SFr 91,–
»Eine Sammlung der Superlative: von Kandinsky bis Rodtschenko, von El Lissitzky bis Popowa sind hier alle großen Namen vertreten.« *Der Tagesspiegel*

NIKI DE SAINT PHALLE

Bilder, Figuren, Phantastische Gärten. Hrsg. von Carla Schulz-Hoffmann. 160 Seiten mit 181 Abb., 66 in Farbe. 22,5 x 28 cm. ISBN 3-7913-0803-3. Leinen DM 98,–/ÖS 715,–/SFr 91,–
»Ein herausragendes Werk, dessen bunte Naivität und eruptive Phantastik uns in diesem Band weit mehr beschert als ein ›Kunsterlebnis‹.« *DU*

JEAN TINGUELY

Biographie und Werk. Von Heidi E. Violand-Hobi. 130 Seiten mit 170 Abb., 67 in Farbe. 24 x 31 cm. ISBN 3-7913-1473-4 Gebunden DM 78,–/ÖS 569,–/SFr 73,–
»Im Maschinenzauber: diese ausführliche Monographie ist dem 1991 verstorbenen großen Schweizer Künstler gewidmet. Die Autorin ist eine ausgezeichnete Kennerin von Tinguelys Biographie und Œuvre.« *Neue Zürcher Zeitung*

HANSJÖRG VOTH

Zeitzeichen – Lebensreisen. Hrsg. von Christian W. Thomsen. 160 Seiten mit 222 Abb., 57 in Farbe. 24 x 31 cm. ISBN 3-7913-1401-7. Broschur DM 49,80/ÖS 364,–/SFr 47,80

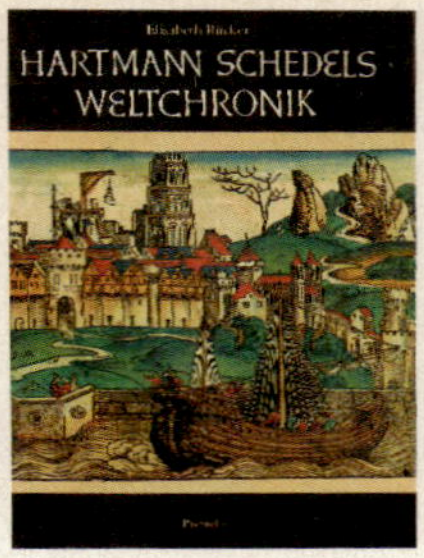

BUCHMALEREI DES MITTELALTERS

Eine Einführung. Von Otto Pächt. Hrsg. von Dagmar Thoss und Ulrike Jenni. 224 Seiten mit 32 Tafeln in Farbe und Gold und 210 einfarbigen Abb. 20,3 x 28 cm. ISBN 3-7913-0668-5.
Leinen DM 98,–/ÖS 715,–/SFr 91,–
»Wer diesen Band aufmerksam gelesen hat, der dürfte sich ein Rüstzeug erworben haben, Werken mittelalterlicher Buchmalerei mit vertieftem Verständnis zu begegnen.« *FAZ*

BUCHMALEREI DES FRÜHEN MITTELALTERS

Von Wilhelm Koehler. Fragmente und Entwürfe aus dem Nachlaß. Hrsg. von Ernst Kitzinger und Florentine Mütherich. 226 Seiten.
ISBN 3-7913-0308-2.
Leinen DM 48,–/ÖS 350,–/SFr 46,–

THE PAINTED PAGE

Italian Renaissance Book Illumination 1450–1550. Englische Originalausgabe. 280 Seiten mit 215 Abb., 198 in Farbe. 24 x 30 cm.
ISBN 3-7913-1385-1.
Leinen DM 128,–/ÖS 934,–/SFr 119,–
»Ein herrlicher Querschnitt durch die italienische Buchmalerei der Renaissance: 77 Handschriften und 60 handausgemalte Drucke aus 43 internationalen Sammlungen. Ein faszinierendes Buch durch seine hervorragenden Reproduktionen und die profunden Texte, die selbst zur Malweise in Zitaten der Künstler Auskunft geben.« *Illustration 63*

REGENSBURGER BUCHMALEREI

Von frühkarolingischer Zeit bis zum Ausgang des Mittelalters. 320 Seiten mit 180 Tafeln, 80 in Farbe. 21 x 28 cm. ISBN 3-7913-0802-5.
Leinen DM 118,–/ÖS 861,–/SFr 110,–
»Ein mit vorzüglichen farbigen Reproduktionen versehener einführender Band.« *SZ*

DAS KOSTBARE EVANGELIAR DES HEILIGEN BERNWARD

Hrsg. von Michael Brandt. 96 Seiten mit 31 farbigen Tafeln in Faksimilewiedergabe und 55 einfarbigen Abb. 23 x 30 cm. ISBN 3-7913-1224-3.
Leinen DM 78,–/ÖS 569,–/SFr 73,–
»Mit einer ausführlichen Darstellung der Text- und Kunstgeschichte wird der Einband sowie 29 Seiten in Originalgröße wiedergegeben.« *Die Welt*

DAS EVANGELIAR HEINRICHS DES LÖWEN UND DAS MITTELALTERLICHE HERRSCHERBILD

Hrsg. von Horst Fuhrmann und Florentine Mütherich. 84 Seiten mit 30 Tafeln in Farbe und Gold. 21 x 28 cm. ISBN 3-7913-0752-5.
Leinen DM 68,–/ÖS 496,–/SFr 64,–

DAS QUEDLINBURGER EVANGELIAR

Das Samuhel-Evangeliar aus dem Quedlinburger Dom. Hrsg. von der KulturStiftung der Länder und der Bayerischen Staatsbibliothek, München.
96 Seiten mit 35 Abb., 32 in Farbe. 21 x 27,7 cm.
ISBN 3-7913-1127-1.
Leinen DM 68,–/ÖS 496,–/SFr 64,–
»Diese kostbare Handschrift wurde für die Restaurierung zerlegt. Die Ergebnisse der dadurch möglichen wissenschaftlich fundierten Untersuchung sind hier nachzulesen.« *Darmstädter Echo*

JACOPO BELLINI
Der Zeichnungsband des Louvre

Hrsg. von Bernhard Degenhart und Annegrit Schmitt. 200 Seiten mit 119 Farbtafeln.
26,8 x 39 cm. ISBN 3-7913-0669-3.
Leinen im Schuber DM 298,–/ÖS 2175,–/SFr 269,–

GOETHE-FAUST Zweiter Teil
Zeichnungen von Max Beckmann

Text in Handsatz aus der Weiß-Antiqua, 143 faksimilierte Federzeichnungen von Max Beckmann. 412 Seiten. 24 x 29 cm. ISBN 3-7913-0328-7.
Leinen DM 198,–/ÖS 1445,–/SFr 179,–

REINHOLD METZ Don Quijote

96 Seiten mit 36 Farbtafeln und 8 einfarbigen Illustrationen. 21 x 30 cm. ISBN 3-7913-1191-3.
Bütten DM 68,–/ÖS 496,–/SFr 64,–

DAS GEBETBUCH KAISER MAXIMILIANS

Mit Randzeichnungen von Albrecht Dürer und Lucas Cranach d. Älteren. Der Münchner Teil in rekonstruierter Wiedergabe. Einführung von Hinrich Sieveking. 168 Seiten mit 124 zwölffarbigen Tafeln. 21 x 32 cm. ISBN 3-7913-0823-8.
Samtband mit Goldprägung im Schmuckschuber DM 148,–/ÖS 1080,–/SFr 137,–
»Die im Sinne eines Faksimiles erschienene ›Rekonstruktion‹ des berühmten Gebetbuches ist eine bemerkenswerte Publikation.« *SZ*

DAS LORSCHER EVANGELIAR

Faksimilie der karolingischen Handschrift. Hrsg. von Wolfgang Braunfels. 473 ganzseitige, randlose Reproduktionen, 54 in sechsfarbigem Buchdruck mit Silber und Gold. 26,8 x 36,8 cm.
ISBN 3-7913-0110-1. Halbpergament in Kassette DM 840,–/ÖS 6132,–/SFr 756,–

DAS WITTELSBACHER ALBUM

Hrsg. von Hans Ottomeyer. Bibliophile Ausgabe von 700 numerierten Exemplaren. 160 Seiten. 40 x 30 cm. ISBN 3-7913-0475-5.
Seideneinband mit Echtgoldprägung im Schmuckschuber DM 840,–/ÖS 6132,–/SFr 756,–

DIE REISEN DES RITTERS JOHN MANDEVILLE

Achtundzwanzig kolorierte Silberstiftzeichnungen auf Pergament. Hrsg. und kommentiert von Josef Krása. 136 Seiten, 28 Faksimileseiten in Farbe und Gold. 17,6 x 22,5 cm. ISBN 3-7913-0606-5.
Samtband im Schmuckschuber
DM 168,–/ÖS 1226,–/SFr 152,–
Das berühmteste und meistübersetzte Reisebuch des Mittelalters in einer schönen Ausgabe.

MUHAMMEDS WUNDERBARE REISE DURCH HIMMEL UND HÖLLE

Das Miradschname des Schah Ruch. Eine timuridische Handschrift des 15. Jahrhunderts. Einführung und Bildkommentare von Marie-Rose Séguy.
160 Seiten, die Miniaturen in Farbe und Gold.
20,5 x 29,5 cm. ISBN 3-7913-0412-7.
Kunstleder mit Goldprägung
DM 248,–/ÖS 1810,–/SFr 224,–

HARTMANN SCHEDELS WELTCHRONIK

Das größte Buchunternehmen der Dürerzeit.
Von Elisabeth Rücker.
236 Seiten mit 158 einfarbigen, 37 doppelseitigen farbigen Stadtansichten sowie einer beiliegenden Mappe mit 6 farbig faksimilierten Ausfalttafeln. 24 x 32 cm. ISBN 3-7913-0877-7.
Leinen DM 198,–/ÖS 1445,–/SFr 179,–
»Pracht und Anspruch der mittelalterlichen Drucke spiegeln sich auch im Erscheinungsbild dieser Publikation: Ein aufwendig ausgestattetes, vorzüglich gedrucktes, sorgfältig gestaltetes Buch, in einer ebenso lesbaren wie allen wissenschaftlichen Ansprüchen gerecht werdenden Diktion verfaßt: Eine zentrale Veröffentlichung über ein Spitzenwerk der Buchkunst – selbst Buchkunst.« *SZ*

DIE TRÈS RICHES HEURES DES JEAN DUC DE BERRY

Im Musée Condé in Chantilly. Begleittext von J. Longnon und R. Cazelles. Vorwort von M. Meiss. 139 faksimilierte Seiten mit 65 ganzseitigen und 65 Textminiaturen in Farbe und Gold. 21x29cm. ISBN 3-7913-0061-X. Leinen im Schmuckschuber DM 298,–/ÖS 2175,–/SFr 269,–
Sonderausgabe: 200 Seiten mit 131 Farbabb. 20,5 x 29 cm. ISBN 3-7913-1717-2.
Leinen DM 39,80/ÖS 291,–/SFr 38,80
Ein Klassiker des Prestel-Kunstbuchprogramms zusätzlich in einer preisgünstigen Sonderausgabe von hoher Qualität.
.»Ein Festbuch in Hinsicht auf die Malerei, die hier vorstellt wird, ist die Prestel-Edition der ›Très Riches Heures‹. Millard Meiss leitet die Ausgabe mit einem Vorwort ein, wie es nur ein souveräner Kenner schreiben kann.« *Neue Zürcher Zeitung*

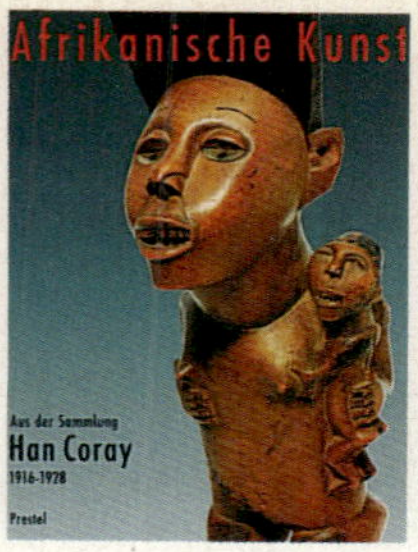

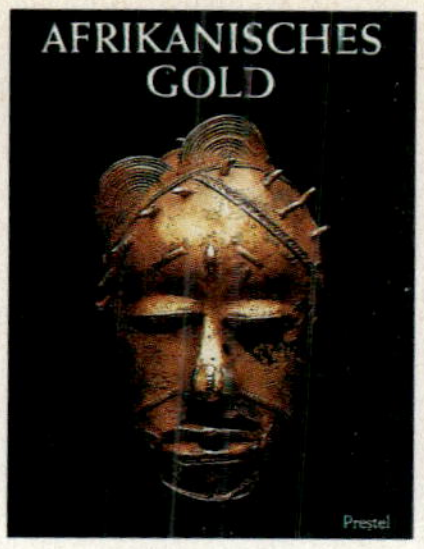

AFRIKA

Die Kunst eines Kontinents. Hrsg. von Tom Phillips. 620 Seiten mit 854 Abb., davon 801 in Farbe. 24,5 x 30 cm. ISBN 3-7913-1692-3.
Leinen DM 148,–/ÖS 1080,–/SFr 137,–
»Die Auswahl überzeugt durch die Ausstrahlung und formale Meisterschaft der Stücke, die in diesem prächtigen Band ausführlich kommentiert und sachkundig vorgestellt werden.« *Die Weltwoche*

AFRIKANISCHE KUNST

Hrsg. von Werner Schmalenbach. 320 Seiten mit 295 Abb., 71 in Farbe und 134 in Duoton. 22,5 x 30 cm. ISBN 3-7913-0848-3.
Leinen DM 118,–/ÖS 861,–/SFr 110,–
»Kompetent würdigt dieser mustergültige Band die hervorragenden und international bekannten Werke afrikanischer Kunst.« *Neue Zürcher Zeitung*

AFRIKANISCHE KUNST AUS DER SAMMLUNG HAN CORAY

1916-1928. Völkerkundemuseum der Universität Zürich. Hrsg. von Miklós Szalay. 260 Seiten mit 317 Abb., 117 in Farbe. ISBN 3-7913-1493-9.
Gebunden DM 98,–/ÖS 715,–/SFr 91,–

AFRIKANISCHES GOLD

Schmuck, Insignien und Amulette aus Ghana, Mali, dem Senegal und von der Elfenbeinküste. Von Timothy F. Garrard. 248 Seiten mit 225 Abb., 196 in Farbe. 23,5 x 30 cm. ISBN 3-7913-0913-7.
Leinen DM 118,–/ÖS 861,–/SFr 110,–

AFRIKANISCHE SITZE

Hrsg. von Sandro Bocola. 200 Seiten mit 414 Abb., 123 in Farbe. 23 x 29,7 cm. ISBN 3-7913-1386-X.
Leinen DM 98,–/ÖS 715,–/SFr 91,–
»Bei dieser Auswahl afrikanischer Sitze steht die künstlerische Dimension im Vordergrund: die hohe Kunstfertigkeit, der Einfallsreichtum und die große Formenvielfalt.« *Stuttgarter Nachrichten*

ASAFO

Fahnen aus Ghana. Hrsg. von Ernst-Gerhard Güse. 160 Seiten mit 101 Abb., 91 in Farbe. 26 x 30 cm. ISBN 3-7913-1437-8.
Gebunden DM 98,–/ÖS 715,–/SFr 91,–

BENIN

Kunst einer afrikanischen Königskultur. Von Armand Duchâteau. 136 Seiten mit 132 Abbildungen, 74 in Farbe. 24 x 30 cm. ISBN 3-7913-1448-3.
Leinen DM 78,–/ÖS 569,–/SFr 73,–
»Eine ausgewogene und informative Einführung in die Kunst einer ausgelöschten afrikanischen Königskultur.« *Foglio*

MASTERPIECES FROM CENTRAL AFRICA

The Tervuren Museum. Hrsg. von Gustaaf Verswijver u. a. Englische Originalausgabe. 200 Seiten mit 251 Abb., 126 in Farbe. 23 x 30 cm. ISBN 3-7913-1683-4.
Leinen DM 98,–/ÖS 715,–/SFr 91,–

ANIMALS IN AFRICAN ART

From the Familiar to the Marvelous. Von Allen F. Roberts. Katalog von Carol Thompson. Englische Originalausgabe. 192 Seiten mit 180 Abb., 150 in Farbe. 23 x 30 cm. ISBN 3-7913-1455-6.
Leinen DM 98,–/ÖS 715,–/SFr 91,–

AFRICA EXPLORES

20th Century African Art. Hrsg. von Susan Vogel. Engl. Originalausgabe. 300 Seiten mit 400 Abb., 228 in Farbe. 23 x 30 cm. ISBN 3-7913-1143-3.
Leinen DM 108,–/ÖS 788,–/SFr 100,–

ART/ARTIFACT

African Art in Anthropology Collections. Hrsg. von Susan Vogel. Englische Originalausgabe. 196 Seiten mit 160 Farbabb. 23 x 30 cm. ISBN 3-7913-0865-3.
Leinen DM 118,–/ÖS 861,–/SFr 110,–

CLOSEUP

Lessons in the Art of Seeing African Sculpture. Von Jerry L. Thompson und Susan Vogel. Englische Originalausgabe. 196 Seiten mit 185 Abb. 123 in Farbe. 23 x 30 cm. ISBN 3-7913-1150-6.
Leinen DM 98,–/ÖS 715,–/SFr 91,–
»Den Autoren ist etwas Seltenes geglückt: sie lehren den Leser sehen.« *Die Tageszeitung*

FACE OF THE GODS

Art and Altars of Africa and the African Americas. Von Robert Faris Thompson. Englische Originalausgabe. 336 Seiten mit 309 Abb., 282 in Farbe. 23 x 30 cm. ISBN 3-7913-1281-2.
Leinen DM 118,–/ÖS 861,–/SFr 110,–

SECRECY: AFRICAN ART THAT CONCEALS AND REVEALS

Hrsg. von Mary H. Nooter. Englische Originalausgabe. 256 Seiten mit 270 Abb., 160 in Farbe. 23 x 30 cm. ISBN 3-7913-1230-8.
Leinen DM 118,–/ÖS 861,–/SFr 110,–

SENEGAL BEHIND GLASS

Images of Religious and Daily Life. Von Anne-Marie Bouttiaux-Ndiaye. Englische Originalausgabe. 168 Seiten mit 181 Abb., 154 in Farbe. 24 x 30 cm. ISBN 3-7913-1424-6.
Leinen DM 108,–/ÖS 788,–/SFr 100,–

MEISTERWERKE AUS CHINA, JAPAN UND KOREA

Aus dem Museum für Ostasiatische Kunst, Köln. Hrsg. von Adele Schlombs. 296 Seiten mit 168 Abb., 163 in Farbe. 24,5 x 30 cm. ISBN 3-7913-1494-7.
Leinen DM 98,–/ÖS 715,–/SFr 91,–

CHINESISCHE TUSCHMALEREI IM 20. JAHRHUNDERT

Herausgegeben von Heike Kotzenberg. Ca. 128 Seiten mit ca. 200 Abbildungen, ca. 45 in Farbe. 24,5 x 31 cm. ISBN 3-7913-1703-2
Leinen ca. DM 78,–/ÖS 569,–/SFr 73,–

HUICHUN

Rückkehr in den Frühling. Chinesische Heilkunde in historischen Objekten und Bildern. Von Paul U. Unschuld. 220 Seiten mit 306 Abb., 147 in Farbe. 22,5 x 28 cm. ISBN 3-7913-1497-1.
Bütten DM 98,–/ÖS 715,–/SFr 91,–

HIROSHIGE

Blumen und Vögel. Einleitung und Bildkommentare von Cynthea Bogel und Israel Goldmann. 192 Seiten mit 102 Abb., 91 in Farbe. 24 x 36 cm. ISBN 3-7913-0884-X.
Leinen DM 178,–/ÖS 1299,–/SF 161,–

HOKUSAI

Von Matthi Forrer. Englische Originalausgabe. 224 Seiten mit 154 Abb., 126 in Farbe. 23 x 26,5 cm. ISBN 3-7913-1131-X.
Leinen DM 118,–/ÖS 861,–/SFr 110,–
»Das breite Spektrum des berühmten japanischen Künstlers: ein Muß für Hokusai-Freunde.« *SZ*

DIE GÖTTER DES HIMALAYA

Buddhistische Kunst Tibets. Die Sammlung G.-W. Essen. Von G.-W. Essen und T. T. Thingo. Geleitwort von S. H. dem Dalai Lama. 22,5 x 30 cm.
Band 1 (Tafelband): 300 Seiten mit 200 Farbabb. ISBN 3-7913-0994-3.
Leinen DM 98,–/ÖS 715,–/SFr 91,–
Band 2 (Bestandskatalog): 308 Seiten mit 459 einfarbigen Abb. ISBN 3-7913-0995-1.
Leinen DM 118,–/ÖS 861,–/SFr 110,–
Bd. 1+2 im Schuber: ISBN 3-7913-0996-X.
Leinen DM 198,–/ÖS 1445,–/SFr 179,–

POWER AND GOLD

Schmuck aus Indonesien, Malaysia und den Philippinen. Englische Originalausgabe. 370 Seiten mit 499 Abb., 361 in Farbe. 23 x 27 cm. ISBN 3-7913-0859-9.
Leinen DM 128,–/ÖS 934,–/SFr 119,–

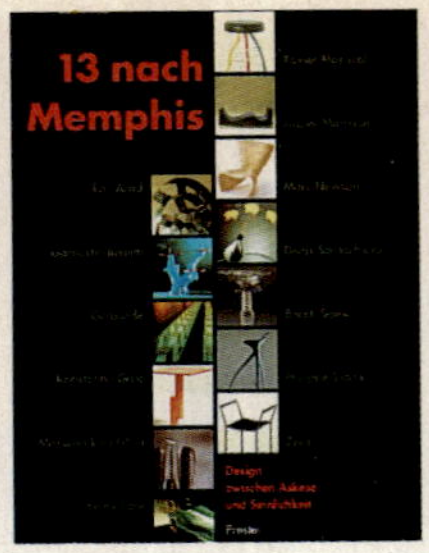

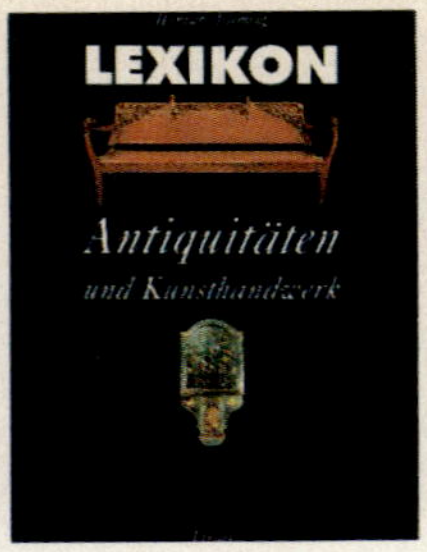

LUIGI COLANI

und die organisch-dynamische Form seit dem Jugendstil. Von Peter Dunas. 216 Seiten mit 316 Abb., 140 in Farbe. 24 x 30 cm. ISBN 3-7913-1663-X. Gebunden DM 39,80/ÖS 291,–/SFr 38,80
»Die erste vollständige Biographie über Werk und Wirken des Designers Colani ist eine spannende, bereichernde Lektüre, ein Stück Zeitgeschichte besonderer Prägung.« *Schöner Wohnen*

RAYMOND LOEWY

Pionier des Amerikanischen Industriedesigns. Hrsg. von Angela Schönberger. 264 Seiten mit 322 Abb., 31 in Farbe. 23 x 30 cm. ISBN 3-7913-1048-8. Leinen DM 78,–/ÖS 569,–/SFr 73,–

13 NACH MEMPHIS

Design zwischen Askese und Sinnlichkeit. Von Volker Albus und Volker Fischer. 200 Seiten mit 371 Abb. 136 in Farbe. 24 x 30 cm. ISBN 3-7913-1434-3.
Leinen DM 98,–/ÖS 715,–/SFr 91,–
»Die Zahl 13 steht für die vorgestellten internationalen Designer, die nach der richtungsweisenden Gruppe ›Memphis‹ höchst individuelle Formensprachen entwickelt haben. Eine wichtige Bestandsaufnahme für alle Design-Fans.« *Architektur*

DESIGN HEUTE

Maßstäbe: Formgebung zwischen Industrie und Kunst-Stück. Hrsg. von Volker Fischer. 328 Seiten mit 759 Abb., 308 in Farbe. 22,5 x 30 cm. ISBN 3-7913-0854-8.
Leinen DM 98,–/ÖS 715,–/SFr 91,–

INDUSTRIAL DESIGN – UNIKATE – SERIENERZEUGNISSE

Kunst, die sich nützlich macht. Die Neue Sammlung, München. Von Hans Wichmann. 524 Seiten mit 1.177 Abb., 131 in Farbe, ca. 8.000 Literaturangaben und 600 Künstlerviten. 22,5 x 30 cm. ISBN 3-7913-0684-7.
Leinen DM 178,–/ÖS 1299,–/SFr 161,–
»Eindrucksvoll katalogisiert dieser Prachtband die Designer-Höchstleistungen vom klassischen Kunstgewerbe bis hin zum Werkzeug.« *Der Spiegel*

DESIGN CONTRA ART DÉCO

1927–1932. Jahrfünft der Wende. Von Hans Wichmann. 388 Seiten mit 421 Abb., 114 in Farbe. 23 x 30 cm. ISBN 3-7913-1297-9.
Leinen DM 178,–/ÖS 1299,–/SFr 161,–

EIN STUHL MACHT GESCHICHTE

Von Werner Möller und Otakar Máčel. 128 Seiten mit 126 einfarbigen Abb. 22 x 28 cm. ISBN 3-7913-1192-1.
Pappband DM 78,–/ÖS 569,–/SFr 73,–

JUGENDSTILMÖBEL

Katalog der Möbelsammlung des Münchner Stadtmuseums. Von Hans Ottomeyer. 200 Seiten mit 291 Abb., 41 in Farbe. 22,5 x 26 cm. ISBN 3-7913-0855-6.
Leinen DM 178,–/ÖS 1299,–/SFr 161,–

MÖBEL DES NEOKLASSIZISMUS UND DER NEUEN SACHLICHKEIT

Katalog der Möbelsammlung des Münchner Stadtmuseums. Von Hans Ottomeyer und Alfred Ziffer. 236 Seiten mit 276 Abb., 51 in Farbe. 22,5 x 26 cm. ISBN 3-7913-1287-1.
Leinen .DM 198,–/ÖS 1445,–/SFr 179,–

ZOPF- UND BIEDERMEIERMÖBEL

Katalog der Möbelsammlung des Münchner Stadtmuseums. Von Hans Ottomeyer. 240 Seiten mit 321 Abb., 57 in Farbe. 22,5 x 26 cm. ISBN 3-7913-1082-8.
Leinen DM 198,–/ÖS 1445,–/SFr 179,–
»Diese Bestandsaufnahmen der Münchner Möbelsammlung, quasi ein Museum auf dem Papier, bringen gewichtige neue Erkenntnisse.« *SZ*

DIE MÖBEL DER RESIDENZ MÜNCHEN I: DIE FRANZÖSISCHEN MÖBEL DES 18. JAHRHUNDERTS

Hrsg. von Gerhard Hojer und Hans Ottomeyer. Bearbeitet von Brigitte Langer. 328 Seiten mit 435 Abb., 114 in Farbe. 24 x 31 cm. ISBN 3-7913-1591-9. Gebunden DM 168,–/ÖS 1226,–/SFr 152,–
Ab 1.1.1997: DM 198,–/ÖS 1445,–/SFr 179,–
»Der Katalog ist historisch gründlich recherchiert, umfassend dokumentiert, technisch analysiert und endlich perfekt photographiert. In der langen Reihe der großen Kataloge ist dieser die Krönung. Und außerdem auch eine Augenweide.« *FAZ*

DIE MÖBEL DER RESIDENZ MÜNCHEN II: DIE DEUTSCHEN MÖBEL DES 16. BIS 18. JAHRHUNDERTS

Hrsg. von Gerhard Hojer und Hans Ottomeyer. 312 Seiten mit 496 Abb., 137 in Farbe. 24 x 31 cm. ISBN 3-7913-1596-X.
Gebunden DM 198,–/ÖS 1445,–/SFr 179,–

DIE HÜTE DER ADELE LIST

Von Gerda Buxbaum. 168 Seiten mit 202 Abb., 71 in Farbe. 24 x 31 cm. ISBN 3-7913-1442-4.
Leinen DM 78,–/ÖS 569,–/SFr 73,–
»Die Hüte der legendären Wiener Hutmacherin Adele List werden hier präsentiert wie Kunstwerke und sie sind es auch: kleine Plastiken.« *Die Zeit*

LEXIKON ANTIQUITÄTEN UND KUNSTHANDWERK

Von Hugh Honour und John Fleming. 687 Seiten mit über 4000 Stichworten und 1000 einfarbigen Abb. 19,5 x 26,5 cm. ISBN 3-7913-0677-4.
Leinen DM 98,– /ÖS 715,– /SFr 91,–
»Das umfangreiche Lexikon bietet eine Fülle an Stoff und Anschaulichkeit.« *Neue Zürcher Zeitung*

GLASKUNST

Reflex der Jahrhunderte. Glasmuseum Hentrich des Kunstmuseums Düsseldorf im Ehrenhof. Von Helmut Ricke. 384 Seiten mit 584 Abb., 351 in Farbe. 22,5 x 27,5 cm. ISBN 3-7913-1592-7. Gebunden DM 148,–/ÖS 1080,–/SFr 137,–
»Die Reichhaltigkeit dieser Sammlung macht es möglich, an ausgewählten Gläsern die Geschichte der Glaskunst zu umreißen.« *Trödler & Sammeln*

ITALIENISCHES GLAS 1930–1970

Spitzenstücke aus Murano und Mailand. Die Sammlung der Steinberg Foundation. Hrsg. von Helmut Ricke und Eva Schmitt. Ca. 228 Seiten mit ca. 200 Abb., ca. 170 in Farbe. 24 x 30 cm. ISBN 3-7913-1709-1.
Leinen DM 98,–/ÖS 715,–/SFr 91,–

HANDBUCH DES EUROPÄISCHEN PORZELLANS

Von Ludwig Danckert. Umfassend bearbeitete und stark erweiterte Neuausgabe 1992. 980 Seiten mit über 3200 Stichworten und 5800 Marken. 12,5 x 21 cm. ISBN 3-7913-1173-5.
Kunstleder DM 178,–/ÖS 1299,–/SFr 161,–
»Der Danckert, das Standardwerk und unentbehrliche Handbuch für alle Porzellanliebhaber und -sammler.« *Süddeutsche Zeitung*

GLANZSTÜCKE

Modeschmuck vom Jugendstil bis zur Gegenwart. Hrsg. von Deanna Farneti Cera. 408 Seiten mit 768 Abb., 648 in Farbe. 25,5 x 28,5 cm. ISBN 3-7913-1176-X.
Leinen DM 128,–/ÖS 934,–/SFr 119,–
»Eine umfangreiche Dokumentation zur eingehenden Lektüre, zum Nachschlagen und zur Schmuckbestimmung.« *Der Tagesspiegel*

VOILÀ

Glanzstücke historischer Moden 1750 bis 1960. Hrsg. von Wilhelm Hornbostel. 192 Seiten mit 152 Abb., 87 in Farbe. 24 x 31 cm. ISBN 3-7913-1117-4.
Leinen DM 98,–/ÖS 715,–/SFr 91,–
»Ein ebenso opulentes wie witziges Journal über vergangenen Luxus und überholte Moden. Träume aus Samt und Seide.« *Süddeutsche Zeitung*

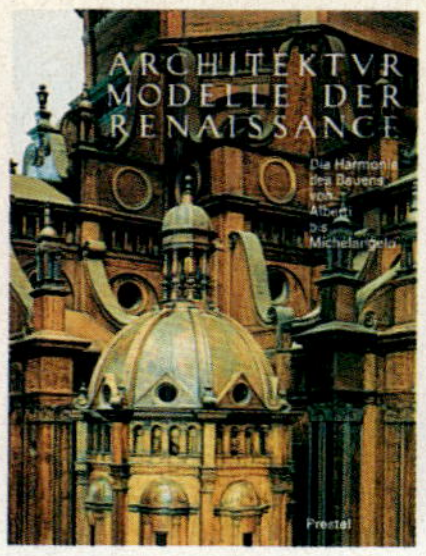

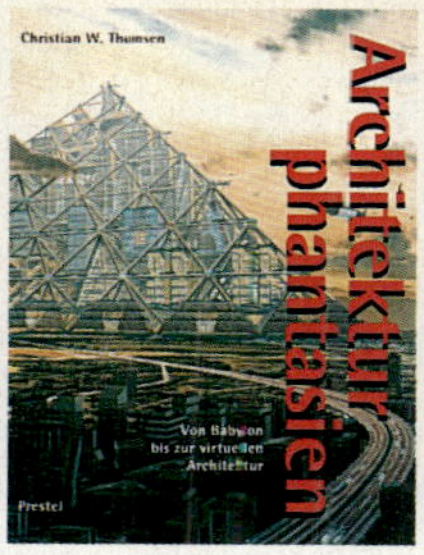

LEXIKON DER WELTARCHITEKTUR

Von Nikolaus Pevsner, John Fleming und Hugh Honour. 876 Seiten mit ca. 3500 einfarbigen Abb. und über 3000 Stichworten. 19 x 26,5 cm.
ISBN 3-7913-1238-3.
Leinen DM 178,–/ÖS 1299,–/SFr 161,–

ARCHITEKTUR IN DEUTSCHLAND 1919–1939

Die Vielfalt der Moderne.
Hrsg. von John Zukowsky.
256 Seiten mit 562 einfarbigen Abb.
23 x 30 cm. ISBN 3-7913-1339-8.
Leinen DM 98,–/ÖS 715,–/SFr 91,–

ARCHITEKTURMODELLE DER RENAISSANCE

Die Harmonie des Bauens von Alberti bis Michelangelo. Hrsg. von Bernd Evers.
416 Seitenmit 325 Abb., 26 in Farbe. 23,7 x 28 cm.
ISBN 3-7913-1396-7.
Leinen DM 128,–/ÖS 934,–/SFr 119,–

ARCHITEKTURPHANTASIEN

Von Babylon bis zur virtuellen Architektur.
Von Christian W. Thomsen. 192 Seiten mit 280 Abb., 154 in Farbe. 24 x 30 cm.
ISBN 3-7913-1397-5.
Leinen DM 98,–/ÖS 715,–/SFr 91,–

DIE ARCHITEKTURZEICHNUNG

Vom barocken Idealplan zur Axonometrie.
Hrsg. von Winfried Nerdinger.
212 Seiten mit 159 Abb., 95 in Farbe, 45 in Duoton. 22,5 x 28 cm. ISBN 3-7913-0721-5.
Bütten DM 98,–/ÖS 715,–/SFr 91,–

BAHNHOFSARCHITEKTUR

Deutsche Großstadtbahnhöfe des Historismus 1866-1906. Von Ulrich Krings.
480 Seiten mit 302 Abb., 12 in Farbe.
19 x 24 cm. ISBN 3-7913-0596-4.
Leinen DM 228,–/ÖS 1664,–/SFr 206,–

PETER BEHRENS

Umbautes Licht. Das Verwaltungsgebäude der Hoechst AG. Hrsg. von Bernhard Buderath.
192 Seiten mit 216 Abb., 40 in Farbe.
22,7 x 28,8 cm. ISBN 3-7913- 1059-3.
Leinen DM 98,–/ÖS 715,–/SFr 91,–

BERLIN AUF DEM WEGE ZU EINER NEUEN ARCHITEKTUR

Das Zeitalter Wilhelms II. Von Julius Posener.
644 Seiten mit 758 einfarbigen Abb. und über 200 Biographien. 23 x 24 cm. ISBN 3-7913-1476-9.
Paperback DM 98,–/ÖS 715,–/SFr 91,–

BUILDING FOR AIR TRAVEL

Architecture and Design for Commercial Aviation.
Hrsg. von John Zukowsky.
Englische Originalausgabe.
256 Seiten mit 370 Abb., 103 in Farbe, 53 in Duoton. 24 x 30 cm. ISBN 3-7913-1684-2.
Gebunden DM 98,–/ÖS 715,–/SFr 91,–

CASTEL DEL MONTE

Gestalt und Symbol der Architektur Friedrichs II.
Von Heinz Götze. 200 Seiten mit 257 Abb., 38 in Farbe, sowie 28 zweifarbigen Plänen.
22 x 28 cm. ISBN 3-7913-1130-1.
Leinen DM 98,–/ÖS 715,–/SFr 91,–

CHICAGO-ARCHITEKTUR 1872–1922

Die Entstehung der kosmopolitischen Architektur des 20. Jahrhunderts. Hrsg. von John Zukowsky.
480 Seiten mit 585 Abb., 54 Farbtafeln und 42 in Duoton. 22,5 x 30 cm. ISBN 3-7913-0820-3.
Leinen DM 128,–/ÖS 934,–/SFr 119,–

CHICAGO ARCHITECTURE AND DESIGN 1923–1993

Reconfiguration of an American Metropolis.
Hrsg. von John Zukowsky.
Englische Originalausgabe.
480 Seiten mit 634 Abb., 79 in Farbe.
22,5 x 30 cm. ISBN 3-7913-1251-0.
Leinen DM 128,–/ÖS 934,–/SFr 119,–

EUROPÄISCHE ARCHITEKTUR

Von Nikolaus Pevsner. 480 Seiten mit ca. 500 einfarbigen Abb. 16,5 x 23,5 cm.
ISBN 3-7913-1376-2.
Paperback DM 49,80/ÖS 364,–/SFr 47,80

GESCHICHTE DER ARCHITEKTUR

Von der Urhütte zum Wolkenkratzer. Von Heinrich Klotz. 264 Seiten mit 239 einfarbigen Abb.
16,5 x 23,5 cm. ISBN 3-7913-1487-4.
Paperback DM 39,80/ÖS 291,–/SFr 38,80

DAS GLASHAUS

Ein Bautypus des 19. Jahrhunderts.
Von Georg Kohlmaier und Barna von Sartory.
756 Seiten mit 745 einfarbigen Abb.
19 x 24 cm. ISBN 3-7913-1661-3.
Paperback DM 98,–/ÖS 715,–/SFr 91,–

HALLE 26

Deutsche Messe AG Hannover. Von Thomas Herzog. Dreisprachige Ausgabe in Deutsch, Englisch und Italienisch.
64 Seiten mit ca. 100 Abb., 80 in Farbe.
24 x 31 cm. ISBN 3-7913-1741-5.
Paperback DM 48,–/ÖS 350,–/SFr 46,–

HONG KONG ARCHITEKTUR

Die Ästhetik der Dichte.
Hrsg. von Vittorio Magnago Lampugnani.
160 Seiten mit 209 Abb., 92 in Farbe.
23 x 30 cm. ISBN 3-7913-1293-7.
Leinen DM 98,–/ÖS 715,–/SFr 91,–

DANIEL LIBESKIND

Radix – Matrix. Architekturen und Schriften.
Hrsg. von Alois Martin Müller, Museum für Gestaltung Zürich.
192 Seiten mit ca. 250 Abb., 35 in Farbe.
23 x 30 cm, ISBN 3-7913-1341-X.
Bütten DM 98,–/ÖS 715,–/SFr 91,–

MONOLITHIC ARCHITECTURE

Von Rodolfo Machado und Rodolphe el-Khoury.
Englische Originalausgabe. 176 S. mit 184 Abb., 32 in Farbe. 24 x 30 cm. ISBN 3-7913-1609-5.
Gebunden DM 98,–/ÖS 715,–/SFr 91,–

NIEDERLÄNDISCHE ARCHITEKTUR DES 20. JAHRHUNDERTS

Von Hans Ibelings. 192 Seiten mit 218 Abb., 108 in Farbe. 22 x 28 cm. ISBN 3-7913-1599-4.
Paperback DM 78,–/ÖS 569,–/SFr 73,–

PASSAGEN

Ein Bautyp des 19. Jahrhunderts. Von Johann Friedrich Geist. 560 S. mit 265 einfarbigen Abb., Katalog von 298 Passagen mit 200 Bauplänen.
19 x 24 cm. ISBN 3-7913-0487-9.
Paperback DM 98,–/ÖS 715,–/SFr 91,–

DAS SEMPER-DEPOT

Die Adaptierung des Semperschen Kulissendepots in Wien zum Atelierhaus der Akademie der bildenden Künste. Hrsg. von Carl Pruscha.
112 Seiten mit ca. 100 Abb. in Duoton, Skizzen und Plänen. 24 x 31 cm. ISBN 3-7913-1597-8.
Gebunden DM 67,–/ÖS 489,–/SFr 63,–

PHILIPPE STARCK

Architektur. Von Franco Bertoni.
224 Seiten mit 207 Abb., 200 in Farbe.
25,5 x 28,5 cm. ISBN 3-7913-1398-3.
Leinen DM 98,–/ÖS 715,–/SFr 91,–

TYRANNEI DES SCHÖNEN

Architektur der Stalin-Zeit. Hrsg. von Peter Noever. 256 Seiten mit 260 Abb., 106 in Farbe.
24 x 31 cm. ISBN 3-7913-1340-1.
Leinen DM 98,–/ÖS 715,–/SFr 91,–

DIE VILLEN DES FRIAUL

Geschichte und Kultur. Von Christoph Ulmer.
328 Seiten mit 290 farbigen Abb. und 64 Aufrissen und Plänen. 24,5 x 31 cm. ISBN 3-7913-1299-5.
Leinen DM 148,–/1080,–/SFr 137,–

Klaus Albrecht Schröder
Egon Schiele
Eros und Passion
Karin Sagner-Düchting
Renoir
Augenblicke des Glücks
Werner Spies
Picasso
Die Welt der Kinder
Susanna Partsch
Gustav Klimt
Maler der Frauen
Karin Sagner-Düchting
Monet in Giverny
Evmarie Schmitt
Cézanne in der Provence
Annegret Hoberg
Wassily Kandinsky und Gabriele Münter
Marc Chagall
Daphnis und Chloe
Alfred Weidinger
Kokoschka und Alma Mahler
Hajo Düchting
Manet
Pariser Leben
Alfred Nemeczek
Van Gogh
Das Drama von Arles
Anette Kruszynski
Amedeo Modigliani
Akte und Porträts
Barbara Catoir
Miró auf Mallorca
J.A. Schmoll gen. Eisenwerth
Rodin und Camille Claudel
Ralf Schiebler
Dalís Begierden
Eckhard Hollmann
Paul Gauguin
Bilder aus der Südsee
John Berger und Katya Berger Andreadakis
Tizian
Nymphe und Schäfer
Wieland Schmied
Edward Hopper
Bilder aus Amerika
Prestel

□ 237 *Paul Gauguin, ›Idol mit Muschel‹, Seitenansicht von* □ *238.*

Gauguins Skulptur □ 241 stammt direkt von einem anderen Typ der Plastik der Osterinsel □ 242, während sonst überall Körperpartien aus Holbeins *Toter Christus* vorkommen, die in ein Feld von Flächen, Mustern und Piktogrammen nach der Rongorongoschrift von der Osterinsel gepackt sind □ 227.[57] Dieser ganze verwickelte Symbolismus, der Leiden und Tod zum Thema hat, wird schließlich zu einem Bild des Lebens zusammengefaßt: dem Priapus-Stab aus Toa-Holz. Nach Rodins *Balzac* ist dies die phallischste Form in der Plastik des späten 19. Jahrhunderts.

Die primitivistische Aussage liegt hier weniger in den ozeanischen Einzelheiten als in der Gesamtform. Symbole des Martyriums bedecken das Urzeichen der Zeugung, so daß auch die phallischen Ursprünge der Religion beschworen werden – ein Gedanke, den Gauguin in seinen Schriften erörterte und in anderen phallischen Plastiken ansprach.[58] Auferstehung und Erektion werden miteinander in Beziehung gebracht, auch Gauguins Gleichsetzung des Primitiven mit persönlicher und kultureller Lebenskraft. Wie Gauguin sagte, wurde er angezogen von der »Leiblichkeit und Lebenskraft in den primitiven Kunstwerken«, fand aber griechische Kunst dekadent, widerlich und entmutigend, weil sie ihm »ein düsteres Gefühl von Tod ohne Hoffnung auf Wiedergeburt« gebe. Er schrieb Odilon Redon, in Europa könne der Tod unheilvoll und endgültig dargestellt werden, in Polynesien stünde er stets in Verbindung mit neuem Leben.[59]

Diese Vereinigung physischer und metaphysischer Triebkräfte zur Erneuerung der Lebenskraft war Hauptmotiv für

□ 238 *Paul Gauguin, ›Idol mit Muschel‹ (Idole à la cocquille), um 1893, Toa-Holz, Höhe 27 cm, Durchmesser 14 cm. Musée d'Orsay, Paris.*

Gauguins Ablehnung des dekadenten Europa und für seine Hinwendung zum primitiven Leben. Dieser besondere sexuelle Vitalismus wird in Gauguins Plastik von einer noch allgemeineren Aussage umschlossen, die auch seiner Begeisterung für die Polynesier entspringt: die Idee des gemeinsamen Urbeginns aller Kulturen. Im Spiel zwischen Oberfläche und darunter verborgener Gestalt leitet die Plastik Gauguins den Betrachter von unterschiedlichen kulturellen Systemen zur Erkenntnis ihres gemeinsamen Ursprungs. Dasselbe Thema gewinnt eine

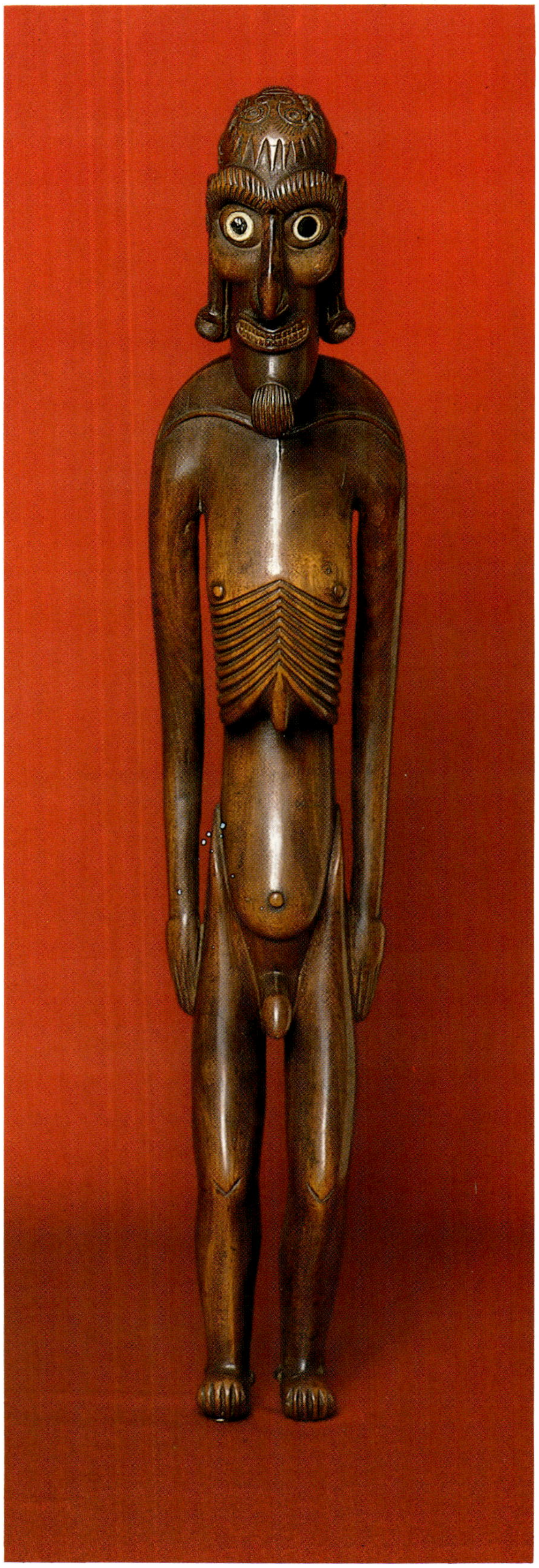

□ 239 *›Figur aus Holz‹, Osterinsel, Höhe 47 cm. The Trustees of the British Museum, London.*

□ 240 *Paul Gauguin, ›Christus am Kreuz‹, Zylinder aus Toa-Holz, 1891–92, Höhe 50 cm. Privatsammlung.*

□ 241 *Paul Gauguin, ›Christus am Kreuz‹, Rückansicht des Holzzylinders* □ 240.

□ 242 *›Figur aus Holz‹, Osterinsel, Höhe 4[illegible] cm.
The Trustees of the British Museum, London.*

□ 243 *Paul Gauguin, ›Christus am Kreuz‹, Ausschnitt des Holzzylinders* □ *240.*

□ 244 *Keule aus Holz (Späterer Stil), Ausschnitt, Marquesasinseln, Gesamthöhe 97,5 cm. Bernice Pauahi Bishop Museum, Honolulu.*

□ 245 *›Marquesanische Tätowierung‹ aus Karl von den Steinen, „Die Marquesaner und ihre Kunst", 1925.*

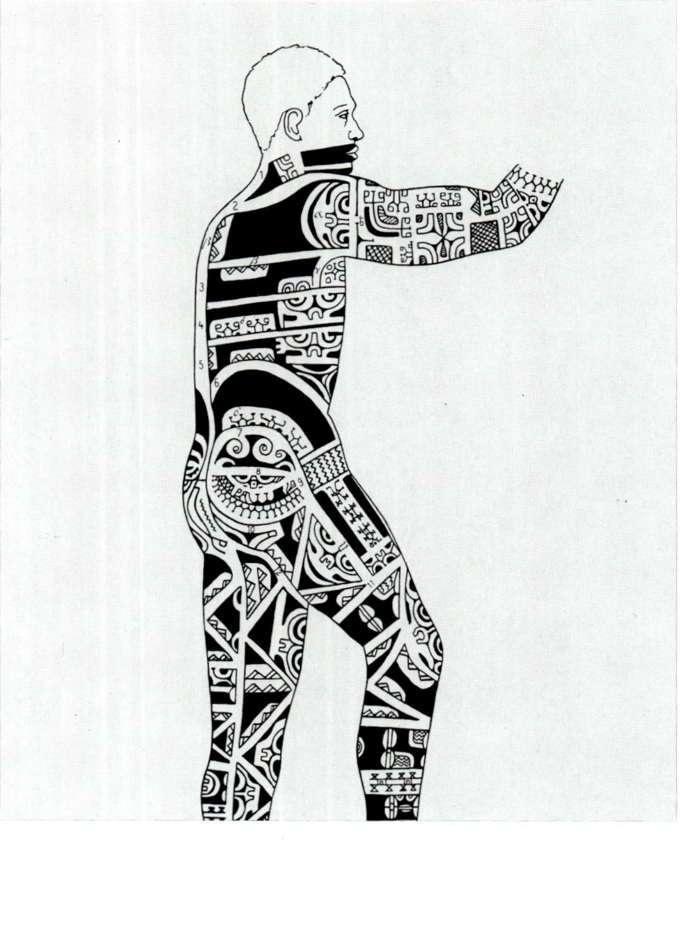

□ 246 *›Keule aus Holz‹ (Klassischer Stil), Ausschnitt, Marquesasinseln, Gesamthöhe 132 cm. Sammlung Valerie Franklin, Beverly Hills.*

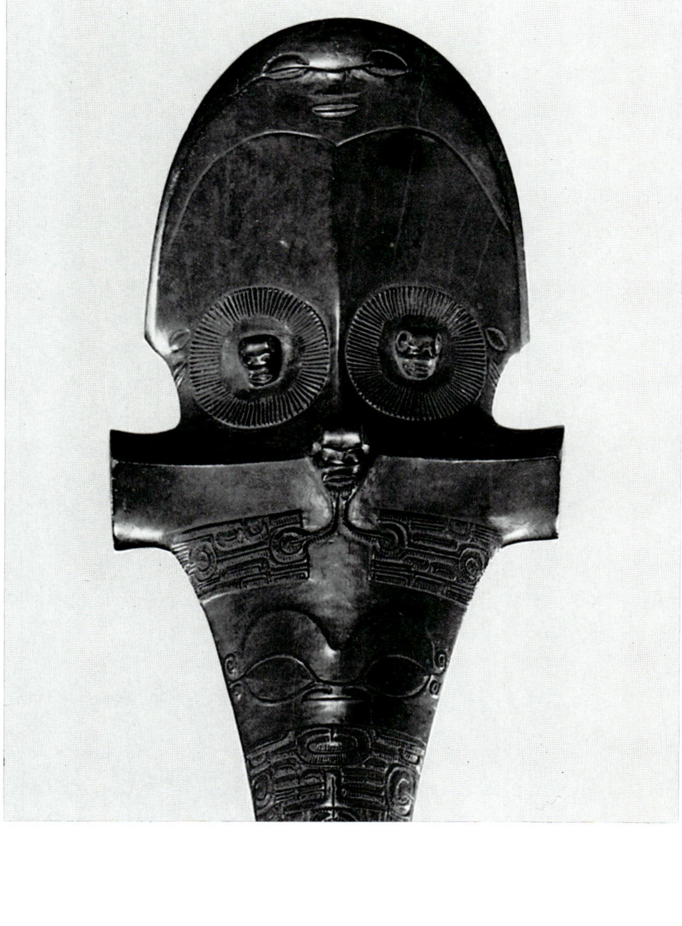

□ 247 *Paul Gauguin, ›Zwei Figuren zu seiten einer Statue‹, Aquarell aus „Ancien Culte Mahorie“, 1892–93, Gesamtgröße 10 x 17 cm. Cabinet des Dessins, Musée du Louvre, Paris. Farbabbildung* □ *305.*

□ 248 *›Steinfigur‹, Marquesasinseln, Höhe 46 cm. Musée Barbier-Müller, Genf.*

andere Bedeutung, wenn es GAUGUIN in *Der Geist der Toten wacht* □ 249 in umgekehrter Richtung betrachtet und mit einem menschlichen Urerlebnis beginnt.

Dieses Gemälde war für GAUGUIN ein Schlüsselbild, und seine Kommentare zu seiner Entstehung waren als exemplarische Hinweise zum Verständnis seiner Schaffensweise gedacht. Er sagte, begonnen habe es als »leicht anstößige« Aktdarstellung mit einem flüchtigen Blick auf die im Dunklen liegende Tehamana (das Bild ist tatsächlich eine Variante von MANETS *Olympia*, umarrangiert, mit exotischem Flair versehen, um noch verlockender zu wirken). Laut GAUGUIN gedieh das Werk durch naturalistische und anthropologische Sorgfalt (das geblümte »pareu«-Gewand über dem Bett ist ironischerweise als typisch tahitisches Attribut gewählt, obgleich es in Europa gefertigt wurde).[60] Es erhielt unterschiedliche Grade antinaturalistischer Farbkombinationen (Gelb, um »Lampenlicht anzudeuten«, Purpur für »Schrecken«), um schließlich mit der absonderlichen Hintergrundfigur des *Tupapau* abzuschließen (dieses gnomenhafte Schreckgespenst mit frontalem Auge in der Profilansicht des Kopfes hat in der ozeanischen Kunst kein Vorbild und ist eine weitere Anleihe, wahrscheinlich aus ägyptischen Quellen). Nach GAUGUINS Beschreibung gewann der *Tupapau* die Oberhand über die anfänglich geplante Nackte, wurde Hauptmotiv des Bildes und bestimmte die Aussage der Szene: das entsetzte Eingeborenenmädchen, hinter ihr ein Geist.[61]

Das resultierende Thema hatte GAUGUIN schon in der *Vision nach dem Gebet* □ 221 beschäftigt: naiver Aberglaube bezwingt die empirische Realität. Während das Sujet dort in bretonische Religiosität eingekleidet war, liegt es hier im wörtlichen Sinne entblößt, zurückversetzt in einen Zustand ohne den suggestiven Bann des Wortes, in einen Augenblick, wo sich die Vorstellungen des Mädchens, ausgelöst durch Furcht, vergegenständlichen. Tehamana vollzieht die Reaktion auf Urangst nach, die lange als Quelle des primitiven Animismus und somit letztlich der Mythologie galt.

GAUGUINS Schriften zeigen, daß ihm die Geschichte der Religionen und Sprachen vertraut war und daß er von der Diskussion um die Ursprünge dieser symbolischen Systeme des Menschen wußte. Der *Geist der Toten wacht* nimmt die klassische Hypothese von der Angst des Primitiven auf, der die Naturgeister anruft und so animistische bzw. totemistische Glaubensformen begründet. Aus diesem ursprünglichen Angstgefühl, so dachte man, entwickele sich durch Reaktion und Reflexion, Assoziation und Invention ein rudimentäres seelisches Leben bis hin zu unabhängigeren kulturellen Symbolen und zu einem vollständigen mythologischen System. GAUGUINS Beschreibung, wie er sein Gemälde von ursprünglichen Sinneseindrücken zu symbolischer Kunst entwickelt, folgt einem ähnlichen Muster und sieht seinen Schöpfungsprozeß als Analogie zur Entwicklung des Primitiven von primären Ausdrucksweisen zu entwickelter Sprache.[62]

In *Der Geist der Toten wacht* wie in der *Vision nach dem Gebet* ist das lautere Gemüt ein Bindeglied nach innen zum elementaren Denken und zurück zu den Ursprüngen der Kultur. Beide Male wird erkennbar, daß die primitive Geisteshaltung mit der GAUGUINS beim Ausführen des Bildes verwandt ist. Aber die Verbindung von karikaturhafter Einfachheit mit elementaren geistigen Strukturen in der *Vision* wird im späteren Bild nicht beibehalten, es vollzieht keine genaue Trennung zwischen Natur und Nichtnatur, zwischen Wahrnehmung und Projektion. Statt dessen ist er, wie GAUGUIN sagt, völlig verwoben mit zusammengewachsenen Schichten naturalistischer und nichtnaturalistischer Elemente und beruht letztlich auf einer Ambivalenz. GAUGUIN erläuterte die tahitischen Wörter: »Der Titel hat zwei Bedeutungen, entweder denkt sie

☐ 249 *Paul Gauguin, ›Der Geist der Toten wacht‹ (*MANAO TUPAPAU*), 1892, Öl auf Rupfen über Leinwand, 72 x 92 cm. Albright-Knox Art Gallery, Sammlung A. Conger Goodyear, Buffalo.*

an den Geist, oder der Geist denkt an sie.«[63] Als er weiter zur Quelle vordrang, beschäftigte sich GAUGUIN typischerweise weniger mit der Einfachheit und mehr mit der Vieldeutigkeit. Die Erlebniswelt der Primitiven verbindet nahtlos die Realität der Vorstellungen mit der Realität der Sinneswahrnehmungen. Primitive Sprache offenbart nicht felsenfeste Gewißheit, sondern essentielle, ursprüngliche Ungewißheit – die Wörter bedeuten zwei verschiedene Dinge, zwei gegensätzliche Realitäten.

Das verborgene Thema des Bildes *Der Geist der Toten wacht* und seiner Entstehungsgeschichte ist die angeborene Doppeldeutigkeit aller Darstellungen aus Menschenhand – Mythen, Wörter, Bilder –, die als Vermittler zwischen Natur und menschlichem Geist beiden Welten angehören. Für einen Künstler der symbolistischen Generation, der zwischen naturalistischer Treue gegenüber den Sinnen und dem Wunsch nach einem unabhängigen Zugang zum Geistigen balanciert, war diese oszillierende Doppeldeutigkeit das absolut Primitive, das Urmysterium. Für GAUGUIN, der davon besessen war, seine angeborene Ursprünglichkeit zu finden, und doch unleugbar vom Einfluß anderer geprägt war, enthielt der Spannungsbogen zwischen Geschaffenem und Nachgeahmtem auch eine ganz persönliche Bedeutung.

Es ist ein sehr moderner Gedanke, den Primitivismus mit dem Forschen nach dem Ursprung der Symbole zu koppeln, etwa protofreudianische Gleichsetzung sexueller Urkräfte in GAUGUINS Holzzylinder mit den Grundlagen kultureller Vielfalt. GAUGUIN jedoch sah diese Themen wiederum als Möglichkeit zur Darstellung düsterer symbolischer Zweifel und nutzte sie nicht zu einer dramatischen künstlerischen Wende. Eine andere Generation, die der Kubisten, sollte in der primitiven Kunst später einen Katalysator für entschiedenere Brüche mit der Nachahmung und für eine gründlichere Untersuchung der Grundlagen der Darstellung finden. Diese verwendeten den Primitivismus als eine Waffe gegen die mehrdeutigen und schummrigen Geheimnisse, die GAUGUIN so fesselten.

Diese Überlegungen bringen uns zur anfänglichen Behauptung, GAUGUIN sei der Stammvater des modernen Primitivismus, zurück. Wir haben GAUGUINS Intentionen und Leistungen überprüft, und wir haben versucht, seinen Primitivismus in bezug auf seine Themen und seine Gesellschaft neu zu definieren. Auch wurde die Rolle des Primitivismus in der europäischen Geistesgeschichte untersucht. Bei alledem ergab sich die Schwierigkeit, daß eine Neuinterpretation GAUGUINS unvermeidlich nach einer Neuinterpretation seines Einflusses rief, ein Gegenstand, der weiterer Erhellung bedarf. Es wurde oft

☐ 250 *Paul Gauguin, ›Die Worte des Teufels‹ (*Parau Na Te Varua Ino*), 1892, Öl auf Leinwand, 92 x 68 cm. National Gallery of Art, Schenkung W. A. Harriman, Washington.*

behauptet, Gauguins Werk sei sehr fruchtbar für die moderne Kunst gewesen, sowie er seinen Primitivismus vergaß und nur malte.[64] Diese Einsicht trifft teilweise zu, wurde aber mißbraucht. Diese Betrachtungsweise hat wichtige Eigenschaften des Künstlers verdunkelt und verzerrt, und es ist an der Zeit, das Gleichgewicht wiederherzustellen. Wie die Analyse des Bildes *Der Geist der Toten wacht* und der ganze Tenor dieser Ausführungen erkennen lassen, lag Gauguins Bedeutung für den Primitivismus des 20. Jahrhunderts nicht nur im Gebrauch seiner Formen und Farben durch seine unmittelbaren Nachfolger. Dies sind wichtige Gesichtspunkte für einen Vergleich, aber sie erschöpfen das Thema nicht.

Der moderne künstlerische Primitivismus ist, wie wir zu Beginn hervorgehoben haben, nicht nur eine Begegnung mit unvertrauten Formen, sondern auch eine neue Geisteshaltung, die bei dieser Begegnung zum Tragen kommt. So gesehen ist Gauguin eher von seinen Intentionen als von seiner Leistung her ein Wegbereiter. Er ist der fruchtbare Vermittler eigener Phantasie, durch den die lange Tradition primitivistischen Gedankenguts erstmals in eine moderne Vorstellung vom künstlerischen Schaffensprozeß eingeschlossen ist. Die Widersprüche, Abweichungen von der Norm und Unvollkommenheiten, die damit einhergehen, sind nebensächlich für Gauguins malerisches Werk, stehen aber in enger Beziehung zu seinem Ziel, das große Phänomen des Primitivismus in der modernen Kunst zu verankern.

Gauguin ist etwa als typischer Vertreter für die regressive Irrationalität des Primitivismus gesehen worden und galt daher als Kind romantischen Erbes. Doch seine Aufzeichnungen könnten die Bedeutung des Rationalen gar nicht stärker betonen. Er schließt ein Essay mit der Hoffnung, daß alle Hoffnung auf Fortschritt »allein auf der Vernunft« beruhe.[65] Das ist nicht nur Rhetorik. Man versteht sein Beharren auf Vernunft, wenn man es in Verbindung mit Primitivismus und ihren gemeinsamen Wurzeln im 18. Jahrhundert sieht. Die Philosophie der Aufklärung nannte die angeborene Denkstruktur »rational« im Gegensatz zu »empirisch«. Diese Dualität umschreibt genau das Verhältnis zwischen der ordnenden Kraft des Geistes und den Sinneswahrnehmungen, für die wir in Gauguins Werk Bezüge finden konnten. Das Insistieren Gauguins auf Vernunft in seinen Texten bekräftigt weiter, daß diese Vorstellung von der angeborenen, ursprünglichen Geistesstruktur einen ebenso integralen Bestandteil seines Werkes darstellt wie für die Blütezeit des Primitivismus im 18. Jahrhundert. Wiederholt bezog sich Gauguin auf den Begriff »rational«, um die elementare Wahrheit hinter dem trügerischen Wortsinn der Dinge zu bestimmen, die er bewunderte – von der Bibel bis zu Cézannes Aussprüchen. Sein Gebrauch des Wortes »rational« ist entscheidend zum Verständnis des Unterschieds zwischen dem Mysterium, das er liebte (das Rationale, verborgen in der Allegorie, unter dem Deckmantel des Wörtlichen), und der Mystifikation, die er verabscheute (daß etwa die Kirche die Christuswunder wörtlich nahm). Er sagte, daß er »wie die Bibel« vorgehe und tiefere rationale Bedeutungen seinen Allegorien zugrunde liegen würden, die er erdachte, um die »Wortgläubigen« zu ärgern.[66]

Aber es geht um mehr als eine semantische Auseinandersetzung über Irrationalität und Vernunft. Das Wiederaufleben der aufklärerischen Betrachtungsweise des Geistes, losgelöst von biologischen und historischen Erwägungen, brachte auf manchen Gebieten das Denken in den 1880er und -90er Jahren voran: Die moderne Kulturanthropologie erhob sich über die bloße Schädelvermessung und die schematische Klassifizierung

☐ 251 *Paul Gauguin, Studie für ›Die Worte des Teufels‹, 1892, Bleistift, 22 x 21 cm. Cabinet des Dessins, Musée du Louvre, Paris.*

□ 252 *›Tanzstab‹, Osterinsel, Holz, Höhe 68,5 cm. Sammlung J. W. Mestach, Brüssel. Ehemals Sammlung Jacob Epstein.*

der Rassen; Ethymologie und vergleichende Philologie traten hinter der modernen Linguistik zurück.[67] GAUGUINS Primitivismus schwamm nicht nur auf der großen antinaturalistischen Woge, von der oben gesprochen wurde, sondern gehörte auch zu dieser Übergangsphase, in der alte Vorstellungen, in neuem Zusammenhang wiederbelebt, zu radikal modernen Auswirkungen führten. GAUGUIN gehört viel stärker dieser Richtung an als dem Bereich des romantischen Erbes, denn zur gleichen Zeit bewiesen andere Spielarten des Primitivismus – Volksbewegungen mit nationalistischen Bestrebungen – engere Bindungen zur Romantik und hatten ganz andere Auswirkungen für das 20. Jahrhundert.[68]

Da GAUGUINS Primitivismus als irrational eingestuft wurde, galt er auch als wissenschaftsfeindlich. Auch diese Annahme ist falsch. Er setzte große Erwartungen in den Fortschritt und in die zukünftige geistige Erneuerung, die ihm möglich schien durch »diese strahlende Verbreitung der Wissenschaft, die heute von West nach Ost die ganze moderne Welt überleuchtet, so fesselnd, so großartig in ihrer Wirkung«.[69] Seine wissenschaftlichen Argumente sind ein Sammelsurium von Bruchstücken aus Physiologie und Physik – vom zentralen Nervensystem bis zu Antipartikeltheorien der Atomstruktur –, das Ganze verbunden mit metaphysischen Vorstellungen aus der Theosophie.[70] Das waren jedoch nicht seine einzigen Eigentümlichkeiten. GAUGUINS Meinung, die Alten hätten gewußt, was moderne Wissenschaftler erst entdeckten, entspricht seiner Gleichsetzung von primitiver und moderner Kunst. Solches Denken hat Vorläufer und Nachfolger. Der Primitivismus war vor GAUGUIN immer mit progressiven Reformgedanken einhergegangen. Diese Verbindung lebt in Hauptströmungen der Kunst des 20. Jahrhunderts weiter, denen der Primitive und seine Formen mit dem neuen Menschen und der Zukunft verwandt scheinen. Der Zusammenhang zwischen ursprünglicher und moderner Erfahrung, den GAUGUIN spürte, ist in zahllosen modernen Manifesten wiederzufinden, etwa der Proklamation »Wir sind die Primitiven eines neuen Zeitalters«.

GAUGUINS überraschende Aufgeschlossenheit für die Wissenschaft bestätigt, was sein Rationalismus andeutete: GAUGUIN ist ein geeigneteres Beispiel für den modernen künstlerischen Primitivismus, wenn er als Ganzes genommen wird, Ideen und Kunst in einem, alle Widersprüche inbegriffen; so betrachtet gibt er der gängigen Wahrheit, Primitivismus sei ein integraler Bestandteil der Moderne, eine neue Bedeutung. GAUGUINS Denkweise fordert uns heraus, die Frage nach der Beziehung zwischen dem modernen Primitivismus und der Entwicklung auf anderen Gebieten, besonders den wissenschaftlichen Erkenntnissen über den Menschen, neu zu stellen.

Die Revolution in der Annäherungsweise des modernen Menschen an die Kunst der Stammesgesellschaften begann mit GAUGUIN und fand durch Künstler des frühen 20. Jahrhunderts ihren Höhepunkt. Sie hatte zur Folge, daß aus den Stammesobjekten, die bislang nur wissenschaftliche Daten waren, Gegenstände ästhetischer Wertschätzung wurden und aus den naturhistorischen Museen in die Kunstmuseen wanderten. Somit wäre es vielleicht logisch, den künstlerischen Primitivismus als Antithese zur wissenschaftlichen Auffassung hinzustellen: Entweder feiert man die neue Bewertung der primitiven Kunst durch Künstler des 20. Jahrhunderts als Sieg über die ästhetische Blindheit der Anthropologie, oder man bezichtigt die moderne Vorliebe für Stammesobjekte imperialistischer Mißachtung der rituellen und sozialen Zusammenhänge, in denen solche Formen ihre wahre Bedeutung haben.

Doch wir verdrehen die Geschichte, wenn wir behaupten, es gäbe eine unversöhnliche Antipathie zwischen subjektiver Ästhetik und objektivem Wissen. Die Unterschiede zwischen der Sicht des Künstlers und der des Anthropologen sind außerordentlich groß, und die Entfernung zwischen naturhistorischen Museen und Kunstmuseen ist eine tiefe Kluft. Aber die so vollzogene Trennung zwischen solchen Kategorien und Institutionen geschieht innerhalb gemeinsamer Voraussetzungen, die beide Seiten als Träger der europäischen Kultur teilen. Es ist genauso wichtig, ihre Gemeinsamkeit zu verstehen wie ihre Gegensätzlichkeit hervorzuheben. Was die Einstellung des Europäers zum primitiven Menschen betrifft, ein zentrales Thema des europäischen Geisteslebens, darf kein Gesichtspunkt, besonders kein so folgenreicher wie die Aneignung der Stammeskunst durch moderne Künstler, im Hinblick auf seine Neuerungen isoliert oder polemisch betrachtet werden.

GAUGUIN löste die Verschiebung primitiver Objekte aus dem Rahmen der Naturwissenschaft in die künstlerische Bewertung zu einer Zeit aus, als die »Humanwissenschaften« begründet wurden. Seine fortschrittliche Einstellung stimmte mit der neuen geistigen Richtung dieser Disziplinen – Linguistik, Soziologie usw. – überein, worüber schon gesprochen wurde. GAUGUIN vertrat die Ansicht, daß der moderne künstlerische Primitivismus in seinem Ursprung nicht durch regressive emotionale Intuition, dem wissenschaftlichen Wissen konträr, beherrscht wird. Das Selbstverständnis des modernen Primitivismus wurzelt statt dessen bezeichnenderweise in einem rationalistischen und wissenschaftlichen Geist, der sich im späten 19. Jahrhundert aus einer neuen Systematisierung und Unabhängigkeit beim Studium menschlicher Gesellschaft und menschlichen Denkens entwickelte.

Seit dem 18. Jahrhundert war der Primitivismus bei der Analyse der Grundlagen von Wahrnehmung und Darstellung gegenwärtig und blieb weiterhin mit dem Studium dieser Fragen in der modernen Kunst verbunden, am offensichtlichsten bei der Sondierung des Unterbewußten durch die Surrealisten und im Versuch des abstrakten Expressionismus, universelle kommunikative Symbole zu finden (beide Themen werden später im vorliegenden Buch angesprochen). Unser Verständnis bleibt begrenzt, wenn wir den modernen Primitivismus in der Kunst von den Erkenntnissen der Anthropologie und Psychologie zu diesen Grundfragen des Menschen trennen.

Die Frage ist nicht, ob ein Anthropologe einen Blick für Ästhetik hat oder ein Künstler wissenschaftliche Fachbücher liest. Auch ohne solchen direkten Kontakt können Neuerungen in der künstlerischen Praxis und in den Natur- und Humanwissenschaften aus gemeinsamen Voraussetzungen, anregenden Ideen und historischen Ereignissen entstehen. Das bedeutet nicht, daß wissenschaftliche Objektivität auf einen Wandel der Denkweisen reduzierbar ist, und ganz bestimmt nicht, daß der primitive Künstler nur Illustrator neuer anthropologischer Erkenntnisse ist. Entscheidend für unsere Beobachtungen über den Primitivismus ist, daß die beiden Wege, sich dem Primitiven zu nähern – ästhetisch und wissenschaftlich –, voneinander unabhängig und im Einklang mit den Gesetzen ihres Faches sein sollten, doch vereinigt im gegenseitigen Austauschen von Erkenntnissen. Primitivismus zielt auf eine fruchtbare Beziehung zwischen Verschiedenem und Verwandtem ab. Als ein Weg, über menschliche Vielfalt nachzudenken, schafft der Primitivismus zuerst Hierarchien ab und erlaubt eine Pluralität von gültigen, unabhängigen und wirklich unterschiedlichen Wegen, die Welt zu gestalten. Dann sucht er die so entstandenen Unterschiede zu relativieren, indem er die fundamentalen Übereinstimmungen menschlichen Denkens und vor allem moderner Kreativität geltend macht. Dieser Prozeß hat schon zwischen unserer und anderen Kulturen stattgefunden. Nun müssen wir ihn auf unsere eigene Tradition anwenden, um klar zu machen, wie sehr beim Studium des Primitivismus Kunst, Wissenschaften und Humanwissenschaften zusammengehören – jede für sich ein gültiges, unabhängiges Mittel zur Erkenntnis, doch über grundlegende Ebenen einander verbunden. Wenn wir entweder die Verschiedenheiten oder die Verwandtschaften nicht beachten, wenn wir uns Hierarchien oder Polaritäten ausdenken, wo gegenseitige Abhängigkeit und Wechselbezüge wichtig sind, dann verkennen wir die Bedeutung GAUGUINS und die Kraft des Primitivismus als Gedanke und Kunst.

□ 253 *Paul Gauguin, ›Christus am Kreuz‹, postumer Reibedruck des Holzzylinders □ 240, um 1926, 40 x 13 cm. The Metropolitan Museum of Art, Harry Brisbane Dick Fund, New York.*

□ 254 *Paul Gauguin, ›Hina und Te Fatou‹, 1892–93, Tamanu-Holz, Höhe 33 cm, Durchmesser 14 cm. Art Gallery of Ontario, Toronto.*

□ 255 *›Stabgott‹, Raratonga (Cookinseln), Holz, Höhe 79 cm. Sammlung R. und L. Sainsbury, University of East Anglia, Norwich.*

Anmerkungen

1. Das Zustandekommen dieses Aufsatzes verdanke ich wesentlich der freundlichen Mitarbeit einiger Kollegen und Freunde. Frau Prof. Jehanne Teilhet-Fisk stellte mir dankenswerterweise die Druckfahnen ihrer Arbeit zur Verfügung, die inzwischen als »Paradise Reviewed«, Ann Arbor 1983, erschienen ist. Prof. Richard Field half mir in manchen Fragen weiter und stellte mir seine Arbeiten zur Verfügung, wenn mir die entscheidenden Artikel nicht zugänglich waren. Meine beiden Assistentinnen, Patricia Berman und Joan Pachner, arbeiteten unermüdlich und waren eine enorme Hilfe. Sehr zu Dank verbunden bin ich auch Elyn Zimmerman, Sam Varnedoe und Adam Gopnik, die meinen Aufsatz immer wieder lasen und wertvolle Vorschläge machten. Für viele wichtige Anregungen und Korrekturen in der Schlußphase danke ich William Rubin.

2. »Je suis au bord de la mer dans une auberge de pêcheurs près d'un village de 150 habitants, je vis là comme un paysan sous le nom de sauvage. Et j'ai travaillé journellement avec un pantalon de toile . . . Je dépense 1 fr par jour pour ma nourriture et deux sous de tabac. Donc on ne peut me reprocher de jouir de la vie.« Aus einem undatierten Brief von Paul Gauguin, Ende Juni 1889, in Malingue, M., *Lettres de Gauguin,* Paris 1946, S. 160. Englische Ausgabe von Guerin, D. (Hrsg.), *The Writings of a Savage, Paul Gauguin,* New York 1978, S. 29.

3. »Je suis par terre, mais pas encore vaincu. L'indien qui sourit dans le supplice est-il vaincu? Decidément le sauvage est meilleur que nous. Tu t'es trompé un jour en disant que j'avais tort de dire que je suis un sauvage. Cela est cependant vrai: je suis un sauvage. Et les civilisés le pressentent, car dans mes œuvres il n'y a rien qui surprenne, déroute, si ce n'estce'malgré-moi-le-sauvage'. C'est pourquoi c'est inimitable.« Paul Gauguin an Charles Morice im April 1903, in Malingue, a. a. O., S. 319. Guerin, a. a. O., S. 293.

4. Zwei ältere, doch nach wie vor wichtige Untersuchungen zu Gauguin stammen von Robert Goldwater, in *Paul Gauguin,* New York 1957, und *Primitivism in Modern Art,* New York 1967. Wesentlich zur Aufklärung der Legende Gauguin haben beigetragen: Bengt Danielsson, *Gauguin in the South Seas,* New York 1966, und Richard Field, »Plagiaire ou créateur?« in *Gauguin,* Paris 1961. Die Bezüge zum *Noa-Noa*-Manuskript hat als erster René Huyghe aufgezeigt: »La Clef de Noa-Noa« in *Ancien Culte Mahorie,* Paris 1951. Die erste systematische Analyse der künstlerischen Anleihen Gauguins nahm Bernard Dorival vor: »Sources of the Art of Gauguin from Java, Egypt and Ancient Greece« in *Burlington Magazine* 93, Nr. 577, April 1951, S. 118–122.

5. Arthur Lovejoy und George Boas, *Primitivism and Related Ideas in Antiquity,* New York 1980, Originalausgabe 1935.

6. Eine Untersuchung des Wortes »primitiv« als ein Begriff künstlerischer Klassifikation würde über die Möglichkeiten dieses Aufsatzes hinausgehen. Jede weitergefaßt Analyse müßte frühere Phänomene wie die radikalen Regressiven in J.-L. Davids Atelier, »les barbus« genannt, oder periodisch archaisierende Bewegungen wie die der Nazarener miteinbeziehen. Einen Überblick über die Veränderungen in der Vorstellung des 19. Jahrhunderts von den künstlerischen »Primitiven« der Frührenaissance gibt Francis Haskell, *Rediscoveries in Art,* Ithaca 1980.

7. White, H., »The Forms of Wildness: Archaeology of an Idea« in Dudley, E., und Novak, M. (Hrsg.), *The Wild Man Within: An Image in Western Thought from the Renaissance to Romanticism,* Pittsburgh 1972, S. 4–5: »Der Begriff ›Wildheit‹ gehört wie auch u. a. die Vorstellung von ›Verrücktheit‹ und ›Häresie‹ zu den Mitteln kultureller Selbstbestätigung. Diese Termini werden nicht nur benutzt, um eine bestimmte Bedingung oder einen Zustand zu bezeichnen, sondern auch, um den Wert ihrer dialektischen Antithesen zu bestimmen: ›Zivilisation‹, ›Gesundheit‹ bzw. ›Orthodoxie‹; . . . im historischen Ablauf solcher Anschauungen. . . sind sie Symbolkomplexe, deren Verweise sich in Reaktion auf die sich verändernden menschlichen Verhaltensweisen, die sie betonen sollen, wandeln.«

8. »Il faut te souvenir qu'il y a deux natures chez moi: l'Indien et la sensitive. La sensitive a disparu ce qui permet à l'Indien de marcher tout droit et ferment«, Gauguin an Mette im Februar 1888, Malingue, a. a. O., S. 126.

9. Lovejoy und Boas, *Primitivism and Related Ideas in Antiquity* und Boas, G., »Primitivism« in Weiner, P. (Hrsg.), *Dictionary of the History of Ideas,* New York 1973, Bd. 3, S. 557ff; Fairchild, H. N., *The Noble Savage: a Study in Romantic Naturalism,* New York 1928; Whitney, L., *Primitivism and the idea of Progress,* Baltimore 1934; Manuel, F. und F., *Utopian Thought in the Western World,* Cambridge 1979, besonders S. 425ff. Eine andere und wichtige Perspektive bietet Penniman, T. K., *A Hundred Years of Anthropology,* London 1965.

10. Angriffe auf den evolutionären Optimismus hatte es schon vor Darwin gegeben, als die historischen und materialistischen Werte des 19. Jahrhunderts auf das mehr ahistorische utopische Denken des 18. Jahrhunderts trafen. Siehe Penniman, ebda., und Stocking, G. W., *Race, Culture, and Evolution,* Chicago 1982, besonders das Kapitel »French Anthropology in 1800«. Zum intellektuellen Hintergrund des Rassismus siehe Mosse, G. L., *Toward the Final Solution,* New York 1978. Zu Darwin in Frankreich siehe Conry, Y., *Introduction du Darwinisme en France au XIXe siècle,* Paris 1974.

11. Eine weitere interessante semantische Untersuchung, die hier gleichfalls zu weit führen würde (siehe Anm. 6), könnte darin bestehen, die häufige Anwendung von Wörtern wie wild, barbarisch usw. im politischen Bereich zu analysieren. Gerade nachdem die Kommune Feuer an Pariser Monumente gelegt hatte, wurden die »gefährlichen Klassen« oft als rückschrittliche Lebewesen, unfähig zur Zivilisation eingestuft. Solche sozialen Ängste machten Theorien wie die Lombrosos populär, der biologische Rückschritte für die Ursache von Kriminalität hielt. Siehe hierzu Gould, S. J., *The Mismeasure of Man,* New York 1981, und Mosse, *Toward the Final Solution.*

12. Der Neoimpressionismus wurde häufig mit anarchistischen Idealen gleichgesetzt und diese

wiederum mit einer Neubelebung der Ideale Fouriers vom Goldenen Zeitalter oder der »temps d'harmonie«. Siehe Egbert, D., *Social Radicalism and the Arts: Western Europe,* New York 1970, und Herbert, E., *The Artist and Social Reform: France and Belgium, 1885–1898,* New Haven 1961.

13. Welchen Stellenwert die Bretagne in der französischen Gesellschaft und Vorstellungswelt einnahm, schildern Fred Orton und Griselda Pollock, »Les Données Bretonnantes la prairie de la représentation« in *Art History 3,* Nr. 3, September 1980, S. 314–344.

14. »Ils étudient la couleur exclusivement en tant qu'effet décoratif, mais sans liberté, conservant les entraves de la vraisemblance. . . ils cherchent autour de l'œil et non au centre mystérieux de la pensée.« Aus *Diverses Choses,* zitiert von Rotonchamp in *Gauguin,* Paris 1925, und von Cachin, *Gauguin,* Paris 1968, S. 257, und bei Guerin, a. a. O., S. 140.

15. Für die Psychologie und Sprachwissenschaft gibt es höchst anregende Forschungen, die Gauguin und die symbolistische Ästhetik mit Entwicklungen in der Wissenschaft in Verbindung bringen: Burhan, F. E., *Vision and Visionaries: Nineteenth Century Psychological Theory, the Occult Sciences, and the Formation of the Symbolist Aesthetic in France,* Diss., Princeton University, 1979. Burhan legt dar, wieviele idealistische Prämissen, zu denen sich symbolistische Künstler und Kritiker bekannten, auf Helmholtz und Taine zurückzuführen sind. Ich habe in diesem Aufsatz besonders auf das Kapitel »Theories of Original Language and the Concept of Symbolic Primitivism« zurückgegriffen und verdanke Burhan den Hinweis auf den Gebrauch der Metapher »Kunst ist Sprache« durch die Symbolisten.

16. Der durchgreifende Wandel im Denken kann in den Arbeiten früher Pioniere in verschiedenen wissenschaftlichen Disziplinen, besonders der Anthropologie und der Linguistik, beobachtet werden. Siehe Lowie, R., *The History of Ethnological Theory,* New York 1937, und Penniman, a. a. O. Zur Sprache siehe Cassirer, E., *The Philosophy of Symbolic Forms,* New Haven 1955; Jespersen, O., *Language,* New York, o. J.; Culler, J., *Ferdinand de Saussure,* New York 1977. In der Psychologie steht die stärkste Analogie zu William James, der die innere Strukturierung gegenüber den erhaltenen Daten stärker betont, *Principles of Psychology,* 1890; mehr über William James bei Pastore, N., *Selective History of Theories of Visual Perception, 1650 – 1950,* New York 1971.

17. Siehe die ausführliche Diskussion dieser Verbindung und ihrer Bezüge zu mystischen Schöpfungstheorien in Burhans Kapitel über *Die Vision nach dem Gebet*, S. 227–337. Burhan führt das Bild in allgemeiner Weise auf Gauguins Kunsttheorien zurück und hält es für ein symbolistisches Selbstporträt. Die Verbindung zwischen modernem Geist und primitiver Mentalität ist in Bastians Arbeiten über *Elementargedanken* erkennbar, die in *Völkergedanken* zum Ausdruck kommen, etwa in *Beiträge zur vergleichenden Psychologie: die Seele und ihr Erscheinungswesen in der Ethnographie,* 1868, und *Wie das Volk denkt,* 1892. Penniman, a. a. O., S. 110–112, faßt den Glauben an die »psychische Einheit der Menschheit« zusammen, der mit anderen Faktoren 1886 zur Gründung des Museums für Völkerkunde in Berlin geführt hat. Der moderne künstlerische Primitivismus wandelt auf dem schmalen Grat zwischen diesem Glauben und der Erkenntnis, daß Stammesangehörige und Künstler eine ganz eigene Mentalität haben, entsprechend Lévy-Bruhls Behauptung im 20. Jahrhundert, es gäbe eine große Kluft zwischen der primitiven und der rationalen Weltsicht. Lévy-Bruhls Aussage über den vorrationalen Bewußtseinszustand des Stammesmenschen wird innerhalb der Anthropologie durch die Theorien von Claude Lévi-Strauss angezweifelt. Er sieht unter dem primitiven Mythos und der primitiven Gesellschaft Strukturen einer hohen logischen Stufe. Die beiden Theorien – die eine schätzt den primitiven Menschen, weil er von der europäischen Logik weit entfernt ist, die andere erkennt seine verborgene gleichberechtigte Stellung auch nach westlichen Begriffen der Logik – entfachten eine lebhafte Auseinandersetzung innerhalb des primitivistischen Denkens des 20. Jahrhunderts. Jede Richtung findet ihren Niederschlag in der Kunst. Die Beziehung zwischen Lévi-Strauss' Auffassung und neuester primitivistischer Kunst wird von mir im Kapitel »Zeitgenössische Tendenzen« im vorliegenden Buch behandelt.

18. Burhan untersucht die Einstellung des späten 19. Jahrhunderts gegenüber den Malereien von Kindern und bringt sie besonders mit symbolistischer Ästhetik in Zusammenhang, a. a. O., S. 242–259. Sie erweitert und spezifiziert die von Goldwater in »The Evaluation of the Art of Primitive Peoples« in *Primitivism and Modern Art* behaupteten Bezüge. Zu Erweiterungen und Aktualisierungen von Goldwaters Forschung über Veränderungen in der Bewertung primitiver Kunst im 19. und frühen 20. Jahrhundert siehe Masheck, J., »Raw Art: ›Primitive‹ Authenticity and German Expressionism« in *Res* 4, Herbst 1982, S. 93–117. Zu Courbets Primitivismus siehe Meyer Schapiro, »Courbet and Popular Imagery: An Essay on Realism and Naivete« in *Journal of the Warburg and Courtauld Institutes* 4, 1940–41, S. 164–191. Über den romantischen Hintergrund für das Interesse an naiver Kunst siehe Sheon, A., »The Discovery of Graffiti« in *Art Journal* 36, Nr. 1, Herbst 1976, S. 16–22.

19. Zur Wechselbeziehung zwischen wissenschaftlicher Theorie und dem Okkulten siehe besonders Burhan, a. a. O. Burhan erweitert, klärt die bisherige Forschung über okkulte Vorstellungen und die Wiedererweckung des Schopenhauerschen Idealismus, in Rookmaker, H., *Gauguin und Nineteenth Century Art Theory,* Amsterdam 1972.

20. Zu den Einflüssen aus Südamerika und dem Orient siehe Bodelsen, M., *Gauguin's Ceramics,* London 1964, und Gray, C., *Sculpture and Ceramics of Paul Gauguin,* Baltimore 1963.

21. Zur Beziehung der *Vision* zu Degas' Caféhausszenen siehe Roskill, M., *Gauguin, van Gogh, and the Impressionist Circle,* Greenwich, Conn. 1970. Bogomila Welsh-Ovcharov bringt das Bild in Zusammenhang mit Bernard und dem Cloisonnismus, *Vincent van Gogh and the Birth of Cloisonism,* Toronto 1981.

22. Evett, E., »The Late Nineteenth-Century European Critical Response to Japanese Art: Primitivist Leanings« in *Art History* 6, Nr. 1, März 1983, S. 82–106. Weitere Untersuchungen zu diesem Thema bei Evett, *The Critical Reception of Japanese Art in Late Nineteenth Century Europe,* Ann Arbor 1982.

23. Aus dem Manuskript *Diverses Choses,* Guerin, a. a. O., S. 132–133. Eine Variante desselben Berichts erscheint in *Avant et après.*

24. Gauguins seelische Konflikte wurden häufig beschrieben, besonders durch Wayne Andersen in *Gauguin's Paradise Lost,* New York 1971, und in seiner Einführung zu Guerin, a. a. O. Gauguin schrieb in *Cahier pour Aline:* »Les grands monuments ont été faits sous le règne des Potentats. Je crois que les grandes choses aussi ne seront faites qu'avec des Potentats . . . Intuitivement, d'instinct sans réflexion, j'aime la noblesse . . . Je suis donc (d'instinct et sans savoir pourquoi) ARISTO«, siehe das Faksimile, Paris 1963. In seiner Lebensgeschichte *Avant et Après* erklärte er, zwei Rassen seien in ihm, S. 89, und im selben Text beanspruchte er für sich, von einem Borgia von Aragon, Vizekönig von Peru, abzustammen, während er sich zuvor als »un sauvage de Pérou« ausgewiesen hatte (Brief an Schuffenecker vom 8. Juli 1888 Malingue, a. a. O., S. 133).

Gauguins Begeisterung für Buffalo Bill ist in einem Brief vom Februar 1889 an Bernard nachzulesen, Malingue, a. a. O., S. 157. Gauguin schrieb im August 1890 an Bernard: »J'ai fait quelques flèches et je m'exerce sur le sable à les lancer comme chez Buffalo Bill. Voilà le soi-disant Jésus-Christ.« Abgedruckt in *Lettres de Paul Gauguin à Emile Bernard,* Genf, o. J., S. 117. Die rätselhafte und vielleicht selbstironische letzte Zeile erinnert daran, daß das Empfinden einer dualen Wesensart – Märtyrer und Messias – gleichfalls in Gauguins häufiger Identifikation mit dem (gleichfalls langhaarigen) Erlöser in seinen Selbstporträts zum Ausdruck kommt. Jehanne Teilhet-Fisk erwähnt in *Paradise Reviewed,* Ann Arbor 1983, S. 29, Gauguins Vorliebe für lange Haare, verbindet sie jedoch ausschließlich mit Gauguins Wunsch, den Wilden in der Wildwest-Show ähnlich zu sehen. Der Hut, den Gauguin nach Jenots Beschreibung beim Verlassen des Schiffs in Tahiti trug, erinnert eher an den ebenfalls langhaarigen Buffalo Bill: »Cheveux poivre et sel tombant en nappe sur les épaules au-dessous d'un vaste chapeau de feutre brun à larges bords, à la cowboy.« Jenot erwähnte ferner, daß er eine Winchester bei sich hatte. Siehe »Le Premier Séjour de Gauguin à Tahiti d'après le manuscrit Jenot« in Wildenstein, G. (Hrsg.), *Gauguin, sa vie, son œuvre,* Paris 1958, S. 117, 124.

25 Gauguin gebraucht das Wort *ressources* im Zusammenhang mit Madagaskar als möglichem Auswanderungsziel, wo es »plus de ressources comme types, religion, mysticisme, symbolisme« gebe, siehe Malingue, a. a. O., S. 198. Zum Thema Ausbeutung schrieb er an Bernard: »Je suis un peu de l'avis de Vincent, l'avenir est aux peintres des tropiques, qui n'ont pas encore été peints, et il faut du nouveau comme motifs pour le public, stupide acheteur.« Brief aus Arles, 1889, in *Lettres de Paul Gauguin à Emile Bernard,* S. 70–71.

Ein kurzer Überblick über die dramatische Expansion des europäischen Imperialismus seit 1870 bei Hayes, C. J., *A Generation of Materialism 1871–1900,* New York 1941. Eingehendere Untersuchungen zum französischen Kolonialismus bei Power, T., *Jules Ferry and the Renaissance of French Imperialism,* New York 1944; Roberts, S., *The History of French Colonial Policy 1870–1925,* London 1963; Brunschwig, *French Colonialism 1871–1914, Myths and Realities,* London 1960. Power merkt an, daß obwohl zwei Ereignisse das französische Interesse an

Polynesien erneuerten. Durch die Planung des Panamakanals erlangte Tahiti plötzlich neue Bedeutung als Stützpunkt . . . Gleichzeitig waren die Franzosen 1877 durch den Regierungsantritt eines neuen Eingeborenenherrschers beunruhigt, dessen Frau die Tochter eines Engländers war.« Diese Furcht vor möglichem englischen Einfluß ließ die Franzosen 1879 nach dem Status einer Kolonie drängen. Zu dieser Zeit war ein Zehntel des insularen Handels in französischer Hand, 1884 die Hälfte.

Power, S. 184, Anm. 203, erwähnt auch Argumente wie die von Arthur Bordier aus *La Colonisation scientifique et les colonies françaises,* 1881, der eine Stärkung der französischen Rasse durch Vereinigung mit Rassen aus den Kolonien vorschlägt, um eine Entvölkerung Frankreichs zu verhindern. Bordiers Gedanken spiegeln einmal das Vokabular der Regierung Ferrys wider, die den Franzosen nach der Niederlage auf dem Kontinent (durch Deutschland) kämpferische Aktivitäten außer Landes empfahl, um das nationale Bewußtsein wiederherzustellen. Zum anderen erinnern sie an die Ideen des Erzrassisten Gobineau, der in seinem *Essai sur l'inégalité des races humaines,* 1854, vorschlug, die europäischen Rassen sollten ihre höhere Kultur und Denkfähigkeit mit den größeren instinkthaften und künstlerischen Fähigkeiten der »niederen« Rassen mischen. All dies zusammen lieferte uns den Kontext, innerhalb dessen Gauguins Suche nach »Neubelebung« auf Tahiti erst richtig zu ermessen ist.

Gauguins Einstellung kommt in seiner eigenartigen Umkehrung des Herkules- und Antäusmythos exemplarisch zum Ausdruck, in dem Antäus die Erde berühren muß, um Kraft zu gewinnen. Vor seiner Abreise schrieb Gauguin an Bernard: »L'Occident est pourri en ce moment et tout ce qui est Hercule peut comme Antée prendre des forces nouvelles en touchant le sol de là-bas. Et on revient un ou deux ans après, solide«, Malingue, a. a. O., S. 193.

26. »Il est toujours à braconner sur les terrains d'autrui; aujourd'hui, il pille les sauvages de l'Océanie!« Camille an Lucien Pissarro am 23. November 1893, siehe Rewald, J. (Hrsg.), *Camille Pissarro, Lettres à son fils Lucien,* Paris 1950, S. 217.

27. Zur Tradition des »psychologisch orientierten Primitivismus« siehe Runge, E. A., *Primitivism and Related Ideas in Sturm und Drang Literature,* Baltimore 1946, besonders S. IX.

28. Gauguin schrieb Bernard über eine Vase, die er Madeleine Bernard geschenkt hatte: »C'est une chose bien sauvage, mais qui est plus l'expression de moi-même que les dessins des petites filles . . . Le pot est bien froid et cependant il a supporté intérieurement une chaleur de 1 600 degrés. En le regardant bien on pourrait peut-être trouver comme à son auteur un peu de cette chaleur.« Undatierter Brief vom Dezember 1888, Malingue, a. a. O., S. 155. In der Schilderung seines Selbstporträts hatte er die Farbe mit ähnlichen Ausdrücken beschworen: »Figurez-vous un vague souvenir de la poterie tordue par le grand feu! Tous les rouges, les violets, rayés par les éclats de feu comme une fournaise rayonnant aux yeux, siège des luttes de la pensée du peintre.« Brief vom 8. Oktober 1888 an Schuffenecker, Malingue, a. a. O., S. 141. Siehe auch seine Gedanken über dunkle Farben und Höllenqualen im Hinblick auf Keramik in »Notes sur l'art à l'Exposition Universelle« in *Le Moderniste illustré,* 4. und 11. Juli 1889.

29. »Vous êtes Parisianiste. Et à moi la campagne. J'aime la Bretagne. J'y trouve la sauvage, le primitif. Quand mes sabots résonnent sur ce sol de granit, j'entends le ton sourd, mat et puissant que je cherche en peinture.« Brief vom Februar 1888 an Schuffenecker, Malingue, a. a. O., S. 322.

30. »Et voilà la nostalgie lui revient de ces pays où s'égrenèrent ses premiers songes. Il voudrait revivre, solitaire, quelques années, parmi les choses qu'il a laissées de lui, là-bas . . . à Tahiti, où la nature s'adapte mieux à son rêve, où il espère que l'Océan pacifique aura pour lui des caresses plus tendres, un vieil et sûr amour d'ancêtre retrouvé.« Octave Mirbeau in *L'Echo de Paris* vom 19. Februar 1891 – ein Zeitungsausschnitt, den Gauguin in sein *Cahier pour Aline* klebte. Daß die Reise nach Tahiti eine Rückkehr zu Gauguins Kindheit gewesen sei, wurde von verschiedenen Autoren behauptet. Die bekannteste und ausführlichste Analyse des Künstlers in dieser Hinsicht ist Andersens *Gauguin's Paradise Lost.* Auch Field hat geschrieben, daß »seine Sicht Tahitis unentwirrbar mit seinem Bedürfnis verbunden war, seine Vergangenheit oder sein Unterbewußtsein zu objektivieren«, in *Gauguin and Exotic Art,* University of California at Santa Cruz, Center for South Pacific Studies, o. J. Beide Autoren verweisen auf Themen wie Mutter, Geburt, Tod, Rückkehr in seinen polynesischen Bildern.

31. Gauguin, zitiert von Jules Huret in »Paul Gauguin Discussing His Paintings« in *L'Echo de Paris* vom 23. Februar 1891. Siehe Guerin, a. a. O., S. 50.

32. Bougainvilles *Voyage autour du monde,* zitiert bei Martin-Allanic, J.-E., *Bougainville navigateur et les découvertes de son temps,* Paris 1964, S. 683, 668. Zum alten Traum von den »glückseligen Inseln« siehe Lovejoy und Boas, *Primitivism and Related Ideas in Antiquity,* S. 290.

33. Diderots *Supplément au voyage de Bougainville* wurde 1796 erstmals gedruckt, jedoch früher geschrieben. Siehe Diderot, *Œuvres,* 1951. Wichtig für die Geschichte Tahitis sind die Berichte der Entdecker: der erste von dem Engländer Wallis in Hawkesworth, J., *An Account of the Voyages Undertaken by Order of His Former Majesty* . . ., und dann Bougainvilles *Voyage autour du monde.* Beide Darstellungen sind ausgewogen in ihrer Einschätzung Tahitis und voller Details über die Bestechlichkeit und Feindseligkeit der Eingeborenen, was bei der Entstehung des tahitischen Mythos übergangen wurde. Diese Berichte der Entdecker waren gespickt mit warnenden Hinweisen auf Kämpfe, sogar Morde, die sich zwischen den europäischen Seeleuten und den Insulanern abspielten. Diderot und andere Mystifizierer Tahitis haben sicher Bougainvilles Bericht nicht gelesen. Die meisten Franzosen hatten sich schon ihr Urteil gebildet, ehe Bougainvilles *Voyage* veröffentlicht wurde, durch Zeitungsberichte und mündliche Aussagen von Leuten, die mit dem Forscher gesegelt waren, siehe etwa den frühen Artikel über Tahiti, den L. David Hammond bespricht, *News from New Cythera,* Minneapolis 1970. Tahiti spielt in einigen der unter Anm. 9 aufgeführten Bücher eine wichtige Rolle.

34. Smith, B., *European Vision and the South Pacific,* S. 31: »Von Dichtern und Künstlern wurde Tahiti von Anfang an als ein beflecktes Paradies gesehen – seine Freuden launenhaft, körperlich und vergänglich.« Und auf S. 27: »Tahiti bewies, daß es einst ein Goldenes Zeitalter gab, Tahiti bewies auch, daß es längst verflossen war. Die Insel war für die ernsthafte und nachdenkliche europäische Kunst- und Geisteswelt nicht Symbol des menschlichen Glücks, sondern Symbol für dessen Vergänglichkeit.« Smith fährt fort, an Tahiti nicht nur den Verfall des alten Primitivismus, sondern auch eine neue evolutionäre Betrachtungsweise zu konstatieren, S. 70.

35. Siehe die Bemerkung Powers', a. a. O., S. 74, über Polynesien als »vielleicht übelstes Beispiel französischer Kolonialherrschaft«. Die traurige Geschichte missionarischer Kämpfe, gewaltsamer Unterdrückung von Aufständen usw. wird aufgeführt von Henrique, L., *Les Colonies françaises,* Bd. 4, Paris 1889. Eine Ahnung von den Auseinandersetzungen erhält man auch bei Lutteroth, H., *O-Taiti, histoire et enquête,* Paris 1843, der die zweideutige Rolle des Belgiers Moerenhout erörtert. Moerenhouts eigenen Text *Voyage aux îles de Grand Océan,* Paris 1837, nutzte Gauguin als Quelle für tahitische Geschichte und Mythologie. Das Buch zeigt, daß schon in den 1830er Jahren das Gefüge der bodenständigen Kultur zusammengebrochen war. Siehe auch Roberts, *The History of French Colonial Policy,* besonders S. 510–514, der über das europäische Wirken auf der Insel ein vernichtendes Urteil fällt. Der Zeitraum von 36 Jahren – vom Protektorat seit 1843 bis zum Status als Kolonie 1879 – erlebte 15 Gouverneure. Hierzu bemerkte Roberts: »Die Verwaltung bedeutete Stillstand [auf den Gesellschaftsinseln], zerstörte beinahe völlig das Leben der Eingeborenen und führte das Wort *tracasserie* als Synonym für französisches koloniales Wirken ein.« (Nach 1880 gab es dann 31 Gouverneure in 40 Jahren.)

36. Für das Balzac-Zitat danke ich William Rubin, der seinerseits den Hinweis von Meyer Schapiro erhielt. *The Wild Ass's Skin* (La peau de chagrin), New York 1977, S. 37–38. Der Roman Melvilles heißt *Omoo,* siehe vor allem die Kapitel »A Missionary's Sermon; with Some Reflections« und »Tahiti As It Is«. Das Zitat von Adams stammt aus Ford, W. (Hrsg.), *Letters of Henry Adams,* New York 1930, S. 468. Adams' Briefe vom 6. und 23. Februar 1891 sind reiche Schilderungen von Papeete, wie es Gauguin vorfand, die es wert sind, in voller Länge gelesen zu werden.

37. Goldwater identifizierte die Schrift in *Primitivism and Modern Art,* S. 70. Die eigenartigen Zeichen waren bis 1864 unbekannt, und die Diskussion über ihre Herkunft und Bedeutung hält an. Siehe die Erörterung der Rongorongoschrift in diesem Bild und ihre Rolle als rätselvoller Gegenstand erregter Diskussionen in den 1890er Jahren in Teilhet-Fisk, a. a. O., S. 88. Allgemeines zu Rongorongo bei Doblhofer, E., *Voices in Stone,* London 1973. Die im Hintergrund von Gauguins Bild erscheinende Statue kann ein Hinweis sein, daß er von der Theorie, Rongorongo sei den Indussprachen sehr ähnlich, wußte, siehe Doblhofer, a. a. O., S. 301 ff.

38. Zur richtigen Lesung des tahitischen Titels *Merahi Metua No Tehamana* siehe Danielsson, B., »Gauguin's Tahitian Titles« in *Burlington Magazine* 109, Nr. 769, April 1967, S. 231.

In *Gauguin,* Art Institute of Chicago, 1959, zitieren die Anmerkungen von Samuel Wagstaff über das Bild folgende Passage aus Gauguins *Noa-Noa*: »Da ich nun Tehura [ein anderer

Name für die gleiche *vahine*] verstehen kann, in der ihre Ahnen schlafen und zuweilen träumen, ringe ich darum, durch dieses Kind zu sehen und zu denken und in ihr Spuren des längst Vergangenen wiederzufinden, das natürlich gesellschaftlich tot ist, aber in unbestimmten Erinnerungen fortlebt.« Teilhet-Fisk, a. a. O., S. 88, weitet die Frage nach den Ahnen aus, bezieht aber letztlich die Bildaussage auf das Tahiti der 1890er Jahre.

39. Henry Adams sagte es unverblümt, a. a. O., S. 466–467: »Sie sind still, ruhig, ziemlich traurig . . . Nie sah ich ein Volk, das so hoffnungslos gelangweilt schien wie die Tahitianer . . . Ihre Melancholie bedrückt mich sehr.« Pierre Loti war der *nom de plume* von Julien Viaud. Seine tahitische Erzählung *Rarahu* von 1881 gehört in die Reihe seiner exotischen Reiseromane. Später als *Le Mariage de Loti* veröffentlicht, liest sich die autobiographische Geschichte von der Liebe zu einer *vahine* fast wie ein Szenario für Gauguins erste Reise. Gauguin mochte die Nettigkeiten und Oberflächlichkeiten von Lotis schmerzlich parfümierter Prosa nicht, siehe Guerin, a. a. O., S. 138, 218; wenn wir jedoch seine Bilder oder *Noa-Noa* neben *Rarahu* und Victor Segalens *Les Immémoriaux* stellen, erkennen wir innerhalb des französischen Exotismus von der Südsee einen gemeinsamen Zug als Ort der traurigen Freuden und düsterer kultureller Auflösung. Eine Bewertung der musikalischen Seiten Lotis, seiner Beziehung zu Chateaubriand und seines Verhaltens gegenüber Zola bei Lebel, R., *Histoire de la littérature coloniale en France,* Paris 1931, S. 69.

40. »Figures animales d'une rigidité statuaire: je ne sais quoi d'ancien, d'auguste, religieux dans le rythme de leur geste, dans leur immobilité rare. Dans les yeux qui rêvent, la surface trouble d'un énigme insondable.« Brief an André Fontainas vom März 1899, Malingue, a. a. O., S. 288, Guerin, a. a. O., S. 184.

41. Das ist die Ansicht Goldwaters in *Primitivism in Modern Art,* bestätigt von Field in *Gauguin and Exotic Art:* »Es bleibt für das Verständnis seiner Malerei, seiner Plastik und seiner Graphik wesentlich, daß die Übernahmen primitiver Motive erstaunlich selten sind und ihre ausdrucksstarken, eckigen und unnaturalistischen Elemente in Gauguins Kunst sogar noch seltener feststellbar sind. Goldwater beschreibt genau Gauguins Position, wenn er sein Werk ganz entschieden mit der Einstellung des 19. Jahrhunderts zu flächigen, ornamentalen, archaischen und außereuropäischen Stilrichtungen in Verbindung bringt. . .«

42. ». . .ces danses javanaises qui, dans leur monotonie même et dans la lenteur hiératique de leurs mouvements, nous donnent l'impression de rites primitifs conservés à travers les âges. Il y a là les restes d'un art subtil et raffiné qui fait songer aux frises du temple de Borobudur . . . Un œil d'artiste ne saurait rester indifférent à ces cadences bizarres, à ces attitudes, à ces gestes, à ces inflexions de mains, à ces renversements, à ces déhanchements de corps, qui remontent aux origines même de bouddhisme.« Gonse, L., »L'Art à l'Exposition – l'Orient« in *L'Illustration,* 19. Oktober 1889. Ebenso Jourdain, F., »Le Kampong Javanais à l'Exposition Universelle« in *L'Illustration,* 6. Juli 1889: »Les danseuses . . . n'évoquent-elles tout un passé mort? . . . une mélopée monotone et mélancolique qui ne manque ni de charme ni de poésie.« Gauguin schrieb an Bernard: »Dans le village de Java il y a des danses hindoues. Tout l'art de l'Inde se trouve là et les photographies j'ai du Cambodge se retrouvent là textuellement.« Undatierter Brief vom März 1889, Malingue, a. a. O., S. 157.

43. »Ces répétitions de tons, d'accords monotones, au sens musical de la couleur, n'auraient-elles pas une analogie avec ces mélopées orientales chantées d'une voix aigre, accompagnement des notes vibrantes qui les avoisinent, les enrichissant par opposition . . .« Brief an André Fontainas vom März 1899, Malingue, a. a. O., S. 287, Guerin, a. a. O., S. 184.

44. Diese These vertritt Teilhet-Fisk, a. a. O., besonders S. 42, und nimmt sie zum Ausgangspunkt für eingehende Deutungen von buddhistischen Bezügen in Gauguins Werk. In einem Buch, das Gauguin gut gekannt haben könnte, Henriques *Les Colonies françaises*, 1889, werden die Theorien von Elisée Reclus und M. E. Raoul über die malaysische Herkunft der Polynesier besprochen, Bd. 4, S. 23, dabei geht der Autor besonders auf Java ein. In *Avant et après* zitiert Gauguin gerade Reclus' geographische Schriften (die eine neuartige Kombination von Geologie und Ethnologie waren) als Quelle einer Beschreibung der Marquesasinseln. Andererseits scheint es sicher, daß Gauguin die alte Theorie von einer Wanderung von Java nach Polynesien nicht teilte. Seine sarkastischen Kommentare über solche Theorien in *Avant et après* sind kein Widerruf (wie Teilhet-Fisk vermutet). Im Zusammenhang betrachtet sind sie statt dessen eine Forderung, die Verbindung beider Kulturen neu zu überdenken. Gauguin scheint die Vorstellung von einer großen ozeanischen Rasse geteilt zu haben (von der die Javaner und Polynesier Seitenlinien wären), was mit der Theorie eines untergegangenen australischen Kontinents in Zusammenhang steht, dessen Berggipfel als Südseeinseln geblieben wären. Gauguins Zustimmung zu dieser Sintfluttheorie der Ursprünge Tahitis wird deutlich in seiner Beschreibung der tahitischen Gipfel in den ersten Zeilen von *Noa-Noa.* Die Vorstellung von getrennten Schöpfungszentren, die durch gemeinsame Ideen und Symbole miteinander verbunden sind, entspricht Gauguins antidarwinistischem, synkretistischem Denken, das auch das Modell der Ausbreitung allein durch genaues Kopieren und rein mechanische Übermittlung ablehnt. Diese Überzeugung ist ganz zeitgemäß. Penniman erklärt, a. a. O., S. 177: »Die ganze Atmosphäre sozialer Untersuchungen, gleich ob sie Sachgüter der Kultur behandelten oder Soziologie, Religion und Gesetz, war [im späten 19. Jahrhundert] geprägt von Forschungen über die Sitten primitiver Völker mit dem Ziel, Ursprünge und Entwicklung der Zivilisation zu entdecken . . . Ein großer Teil der Forscher ging psychologisch an das Problem heran. Sie setzten voraus, Intellekt und Gefühle aller Völker unterschieden sich nur graduell, nicht in ihrem Wesen . . .« Auf S. 110–112 beschäftigt sich Penniman mit Bastians Schrift über primitive Psychologie und seinen antidarwinistischen Aussichten. Bastian glaubte, die ganze Menschheit sei durch fundamentale Gedanken verbunden. Gauguins Vorstellungen spiegeln dieses Denken über Herkunft und Vielfalt des Menschen.

☐ 255a *Angebliche Figuren von Paul Gauguin, Ausschnitt eines Photos aus „Zolotoye runo". Von Christopher Gray der Sammlung Emile Schuffenecker, Paris, zugeschrieben.*

45. In *Noa-Noa* schreibt Gauguin von »uralten Erinnerungen an große Anführer (eine Rasse, die ein solches Feudalsystem hatte)« Guerin, a. a. O., S. 81. Smith, a. a. O., S. 92, untersucht, wie Wandlungen im Denken des 18. Jahrhunderts zu dem Glauben führten, daß »vielleicht der Schlüssel zum Ursprung der Kunst wie überhaupt der Zivilisation . . . nicht zu finden ist, indem man die verschütteten Monumente in Griechenland und Italien ausgräbt, sondern indem man das Leben erforscht, wie es auf den Pazifikinseln gelebt wird«. Zur Idee des «verlorenen Stammes Israels« siehe La Farge, J., *Reminiscenses of the South Seas,* New York 1912, S. 317.

46 Teilhet-Fisk, a. a. C., S. 145, vereint theosophische Entlehnungen mit stilistischen Verschmelzungen: »In dem Maße wie seine Theosophie die Synthese der Religionen verlangte, verlangte Gauguins Kunst die Synthese von Stilen.« Gauguins Kenntnis theosophischer Literatur untersucht Andersen in seiner Einleitung zu Guerin, a. a. O., S. XX. Das in dieser Beziehung wichtigste Gauguin-Dokument ist sein Manuskript *L'Esprit moderne et le catholicisme* im St. Louis Art Museum.

47. Wie eine Pflichtübung tauchte dieser Religionsvergleich in Abhandlungen über die Südseeinsulaner immer wieder auf, wenn auch oft auf dem Niveau unfreiwillig komischer Metaphern. Moerenhouts Bericht über die *Maori*-Religion in *Voyage aux îles de Grand Océan* ist mit Blüten dieser Art gewürzt. Smith, a. a. O., analysiert das Phänomen religiöser Assoziationen mit den Polynesiern und das allgemeine Muster, wenn europäisches Denken auf Polynesien traf: Unbekanntes wird mit Begriffen des Bekannten eingestuft und angeglichen.

48. Siehe Anm. 41.

49. Christopher Gray veröffentlichte in *Sculpture and Ceramics of Paul Gauguin,* a. a. O., S. 316, den Ausschnitt einer Photographie, die zum ersten Mal 1909 erschienen war, um Objekte aus Gauguins Sammlung zu zeigen. 1909 waren diese Figuren noch Gauguin zugeschrieben worden, Gray erkennt sie aber völlig richtig als afrikanische Plastiken. In einer Vorlesung von 1966 (leider ohne genauere Beweisführung) sprach Robert Goldwater von »au moins deux exemplaires du Congo« in Gauguins Besitz um 1891 (siehe Goldwater, »L'Expérience occidentale de l'art negre« in *Colloque sur l'art nègre,* Dakar 1966, Bd. 1, S. 351). Goldwater bezieht sich eindeutig auf die bei Gray abgebildeten Figuren, aber offen ist, wie Goldwater seine

Datierung begründete. Ich verdanke Jean-Louis Paudrat die Kenntnis von Goldwaters Ausführungen über diese Objekte.

50. William Rubin hat die Inventare des Trocadéro durchgesehen und mehrere marquesische Tiki in Holz und Stein ausgemacht, die in den späten 1880er Jahren dem Museum gehörten, ebenso einige wenige hawaiische Plastiken.

51. Field behandelt den Besuch auf Auckland in »Plagiaire ou créateur?«, a. a. O., S. 148. Teilhet-Fisk fand in weiteren Zeichnungen Gauguins nach *Maori*-Kunst Vorbilder im dortigen Museum, a. a. O., S. 107–110.

52. In Kürze wird eine Arbeit über Gauguin erscheinen, zu der Alan Wilkinson Feldforschungen in Polynesien betrieb. In Zusammenarbeit mit Gilles Artur fand er auf den Marquesasinseln einen großen Stein-Tiki ☐ 234, den er für das Modell zu Gauguins Zeichnung hält. Ich bin Gilles Artur zutiefst dankbar, daß er mir eine Photographie dieses Objektes zukommen ließ und die Veröffentlichung im vorliegenden Zusammenhang gestattet.

53. In *Avant et après* pries Gauguin den »sens inouï de la décoration« der Marquesaner, ihre Fähigkeit, jede Oberfläche zu schmücken, sei sie auch noch so schwierig, und keine »vide choquant et disparate« zu hinterlassen. Besonders staunte er über den nahtlosen Wechsel zwischen Gesichtszügen und Mustern in ihren Werken. Als Gegensatz dazu verwendete Gauguin häufig den Ausdruck »papuanisch«, womit er sich auf die Kunst des Papuagolfes in Neuguinea bezog, und: als Synonym für besondere Derbheit, siehe Guerin, a. a. O., S. 186, 187, 221.

54. Zu den allgemeinen Vorstellungen über die Marquesasinseln siehe Melvilles Roman *Typee.* Lotis *Rarahu* enthält auch Hinweise auf den Kannibalismus, der angeblich dort noch praktiziert werde. Aber es gab noch andere Vorstellungen von den Marquesasinseln, die Gauguin noch vor seiner ersten Abreise nach Tahiti gekannt haben mag. Man denke an Van Goghs Jammer über die Zerstörung der Inseln durch den weißen Mann in seinem Brief an Bernhard vom Mai 1888 aus Arles (B 5[5]), *The Letters of Vincent van Gogh,* Boston 1978, Bd. 3, S. 483. Anlaß dafür war ein neues Buch über die Inseln. Über Marquesaskunst im allgemeinen siehe Karl von den Steinen, *Die Marquesaner und ihre Kunst,* Berlin 1925, 2 Bände, und Handy, W. C., *Tatooing in the Marquesas,* Honolulu 1922, mit ausgewählter Bibliographie. Handy stellt chronologisch dar, wie man über die Tätowierungen dachte. Die irrige Behauptung, die Reichen müßten sich tätowieren lassen, fußte auf einem Bericht von 1804, die die Zeichen als Statussymbole des Adels deuteten. Siehe auch Handy, *L'Art des Iles Marquises,* Paris 1938, S. 22.

55. »J'ai voulu avec un simple nu suggérer un certain luxe barbare d'autrefois [Beschreibung des Bildes *Nie wieder* von 1897 heute im Courtauld Institute, London]. Le tout est noyé dans des couleurs volontairement sombres et tristes . . .« Aus einem Brief an Daniel de Monfried vom 14. Februar 1897, Malingue, a. a. O., S. 101.

56. Siehe das Gedicht »Parahi Te Marae« in *Noa-Noa,* Paris 1924, S. 101, und die Beschreibung dieses Bildes von Charles Morice, S. 16. Zum Vergleich des Zaunes mit einem marquesischen Ohrschmuck siehe Wilkinson, A., *Gauguin to Moore: Primitivism in Modern Sculpture,* Toronto 1981, S. 60.

57. Zur Skulptur mit der Kreuzigung siehe Wilkinson, ebenda, S. 38–41, Amishai-Maisels, Z., »Gauguin's Early Tahitian Idols« in *Art Bulletin* 60, Nr. 2, Juni 1978, S. 331–341, Teilhet-Fisk, a. a. O., S. 128–133. William Rubin ist der Meinung, daß die beiden Hauptfiguren der Plastik – Christus mit den hervortretenden Rippen und die wesentlich kräftigere Gestalt auf der anderen Seite – den Gegensatz zwischen Sterblichkeit und Lebenskraft verkörpern. Er erfaßt damit die wesentliche Bedeutung dieser Skulptur Paul Gauguins.

58. Gauguin unternimmt in *L'Esprit moderne et le catholicisme* komparatistische Analysen verschiedener Religionen, besonders in bezug auf die Verbindung zwischen Kreuzigungssymbolismus und phallischen Gottheiten. Im Zusammenhang mit mexikanischen Göttern stellte Gauguin fest, daß die christliche Dornenkrone nicht von Anfang an Symbol des Leidens gewesen sei, sondern ein Abkömmling des Lebensbaums. Er fährt fort: »Dans son ›ascension‹ Witoba est dépeint comme une figure cruciforme étendue dans l'espace, avec les marques des clous sur sa main, ce qui indique la divinité virile assez puissante pour ressusciter de nouveau, et les clous sont les symboles de sa force pubescente. Cette vue est confirmée par le fait dans le Dekkan, Witoba est envisagé comme un avatar de Siva la Lingaique comme le Dieu qui se leva de nouveau, ou était ce que le Rituel appelle redressé. Il ne peut y avoir aucun doute qu'Orion a été jadis un type ›phallique‹ avec les trois étoiles pour l'emblème mâle.« S. 48 des Transkripts im St. Louis Art Museum.

59. »In primitiver Kunst werden wir immer Körperlichkeit und Lebenskraft finden (in der Kunst vollentwickelter Zivilisationen nichts als Wiederholung). Als ich die Ägypter studierte, fand ich in meinem Kopf immer die gesunde Gewißheit von etwas anderem, aber meine Studien griechischer und besonders dekadenter griechischer Kunst ekelten mich an oder entmutigten mich, denn sie gaben mir ein düsteres Gefühl von Tod ohne Hoffnung auf Wiedergeburt.« Aus *Diverses Choses,* in Guerin, a. a. O., S. 131.

Der Brief an Redon stammt aus Le Pouldu vom September (?) 1890 und bezieht sich auf ein Bild Redons zum Thema Tod: »En Europe, cette mort avec sa queue de serpent est vraisemblable, mais à Tahiti, il faut la voir avec les racines qui repoussent toutes les fleurs.« Malingue, a. a. O., S. 323.

60. Danielsson, *Gauguin in the South Seas,* a. a. O., S. 85, schreibt über die Kleidung der Tahitianer in den 1890er Jahren und erkennt in dem blumengemusterten Baumwollgewebe des typischen *pareu*-Gewandes Stoff aus europäischer Herstellung. Diese Art Stoff wurde in Textilmanufakturen wie Manchester nur für den Export hergestellt – daher fehlt jede Übereinstimmung mit europäischen Mustern dieser Zeit. Die Herkunft der großzügigen geblümten Muster (als wären sie von Matisse), die so sehr zu Gauguins Vision von Tahiti gehörten, bleibt im Dunkeln. Aber Adrienne Kaeppler von der Smithsonian Institution hat mir freundlicherweise mitgeteilt, daß Tahiti eine alte Tradition von pflanzlichen Mustern hatte. Das traditionelle *tapa*-Gewebe der Eingeborenen, aus dem der *pareu* früher hergestellt wurde, bedruckte man gerne mit Farnkrautmustern. Der Farn wurde in rote Farbe getaucht und dann auf das Gewebe gepreßt. Anfang des 19. Jahrhunderts führte dann der Einfluß der Missionare zur Verwendung einer Art Pikee, bei der auf den weißen Grund große rote Blumenmuster (oder umgekehrt) appliziert wurden. Colin Newbury vom Institute of Commonwealth Studies of Oxford University hat bei einem persönlichen Gespräch am 10. September 1983 auf Veröffentlichungen hingewiesen, die berichten, bedruckter Muslin und *pareu*-Stoff seien mindestens seit 1865 aus England und Frankreich importiert worden. Bengt Danielsson zitierte dazu am 4. Oktober 1983, ebenfalls in einem Gespräch, einen Brief aus Tahiti, den C. F. Gordon Cumming am 2. Dezember 1877 schrieb. Cumming geht ausführlich auf die »pareos« der Eingeborenen ein, die aus Stoff aus Manchester gearbeitet seien, »ausschließlich für diese Inseln mit herrlichen Mustern entworfen. Es ist wunderbar, daß man eine solche Vielfalt an Mustern herstellen kann, keines hat man je in England zu sehen bekommen.« C. F. Gordon Cumming, *A Lady's Cruise in a French Man-of-War,* London 1882, S. 288. Danielsson hat diesem Thema ausführliche Studien gewidmet und ein Photoarchiv von tahitischer Kleidung angelegt. Er kommt zu dem Schluß, daß bedruckter Stoff seit den 1850er Jahren importiert wurde mit dem Ziel, den traditionellen *pareu* aus Rindenfasergewebe zu ersetzen. Offenbar war der blumengeschmückte Stoff, den Gauguin so liebte, in Tahiti in den 1890er Jahren populär, aber es gibt keine Hinweise, daß auch diese Muster schon von Anfang an importiert worden waren. Photographien aus den 1850er Jahren zeigen *pareu* mit geometrischen Mustern. Danielsson glaubt, Gauguin habe die floralen Motive in seinen Bildern vielleicht erfunden – es gelang nämlich nicht, Gauguins tahitische Muster mit Mustern auf zeitgenössischen Photos in Verbindung zu bringen. Ich danke Herrn Danielsson für sein freundliches und informatives Eingehen auf meine Fragen, ebenso Mr. Newbury sowie Douglas Newton vom Metropolitan Museum und Adrienne Kaeppler.

61. Field untersucht in *Paul Gauguin: The Paintings of the First Voyage to Tahiti,* New York 1977, S. 109–115, Gauguins verschiedene Beschreibungen des Bildes *Manao Tupapau* und kommentiert die früheren Interpretationen der Texte durch Goldwater und Rey. Neben anderen Gesichtspunkten wird auch Gauguins Bezug zu Poes »Philosophy of Composition« behandelt. Field kommt zu dem Schluß, »das endgültige Essay zu *Manao Tupapau* in *Cahier pour Aline* ist eine Synthese aus dem aktuellen Tahitierlebnis, der formalen Analyse, wie sie aus den beiden Briefen vom Dezember 1892 hervorgeht, sowie aus einer dominierenden literarischen Komponente, die Gedanken Poes erkennen läßt, den Gauguin offensichtlich gerade gelesen hatte.«

62. Die Vorstellung, daß »das Gefühl der Angst der Anfang aller Religion« sei, geht auf Hume zurück und war ein Grundgedanke der Aufklärung, siehe Cassirer, E., *The Philosophy of Enlightenment,* Princeton 1968, S. 106–107. Zu Gauguins religionsgeschichtlichen Vergleichen siehe *L'Esprit moderne et le catholicisme.* In *Avant et après,* S. 55, geht Gauguin der Frage nach dem Anfang der Sprachen und nach Ähnlichkeiten in den verschiedenen Sprachen ausführlich nach, Guerin, a. a. O., S. 270–271. Dies kommt im gleichen Zusammenhang vor wie Gauguins Widerlegung der Immigrationstheorien über die Polynesier (siehe Anm. 44). In seinem Gedankenaustausch mit Strindberg

(1895) bediente sich Gauguin einer ausgefeilten linguistischen Analogie (er nannte sie »philologisch«), um die sprachlichen Uranfänge Europas und Ozeaniens zu vergleichen. Er stellte eine entwickelte »langue à flexion« rauheren Tönen, »isolés ou soudés sans nul souci du poli«, gegenüber. Gauguin muß also mit der linguistischen Theorie einigermaßen vertraut gewesen sein, denn die drei Termini, die er verwendet, hatte August Schleicher in seinen *Sprachvergleichenden Untersuchungen,* 1848–1850, gewählt: modulierend (à flexions), agglutinierend (soudés) und isolierend (isolés). Gauguins Brief an Strindberg ist Malingue entnommen, a. a. O., S. 263–264. Zu Schleichers Kategorien siehe Cassirer, *Philosophy of Symbolic Forms,* Bd. 1, S. 164–165. Cassirers Abhandlung, S. 186 ff., über Entwicklungstheorien der Darstellung in drei Stadien – nachahmend, analog, symbolisch – läßt Gauguins Ausführungen wie ein Paradebeispiel für ursprüngliches Denken erscheinen. Zur Beziehung von Sprache und Mythos siehe Cassirer, Bd. 2. In knapper Form beschreibt Cassirer diese Beziehung in *Language and Myth,* New York 1953. Über das Entstehen des ersten Wortes aus der ursprünglichen Vorstellung einer erschrekkenden Gestalt siehe S. 42–43. Cassirer kommt hier zu dem Schluß: »Offensichtlich ist, daß Mythos und Sprache in der Entwicklung des Denkens von momentanem Erleben zu bleibenden Vorstellungen, von sinnlichen Eindrücken zur Formulierung die gleiche Rolle spielen. Auch ihre entsprechenden Funktionen sind wechselseitig bedingt.« Vorher, S. 36, heißt es: »Die gleiche Funktion, die ein Götterbild erfüllt [Cassirer nimmt Bezug auf Useners Idee des ›vergänglichen Gottes‹ in der Furcht des frühen Menschen, 1896] . . . kann den Ausdrucksmitteln der Sprache zugeschrieben werden . . . Kaum war der Funke übergesprungen, kaum hatte sich die Spannung in einem Wort oder mythologischen Bild entladen, trat in der menschlichen Geisteshaltung eine Art Wendepunkt ein.« Siehe im selben Band auch »The Successive Phases of Religious Thought«, S. 62–83.

63. Gauguin erwähnt die Doppeldeutigkeit des Bildtitels zuerst in seinen Briefen vom 8. Dezember 1892 an Mette, Malingue, a. a. O., S. 61–62, und Daniel de Monfried, *Lettres de Gauguin à Daniel de Monfried,* Paris, o. J., S. 61–62. Zum Bildtitel siehe Danielsson, a. a. O., S. 228–233. Zum Abschnitt über die Frage, wie primitives Erleben subjektive Gewißheit und die Vieldeutigkeit der Worte in sich vereint, siehe Cassirer, *Philosophy of Symbolic Forms,* a. a. O., Bd. 1, S. 178.

64. Siehe etwa Reys These, Gauguin habe seine symbolistischen Auslegungen nur als sekundäre Rechtfertigungen für seinen mehr instinktiven Sinn für die reine Form benutzt, das ganze Drum und Dran sei unerheblich für uns, in Fields Aufsatz, oben Anm. 60. Diese Ansicht scheint Françoise Cachin zu teilen, die Gauguin immer dann für ausgezeichnet hält, wenn er beobachtet und nicht von geistigen Verwirrungen beeinträchtigt ist: »Il faut bien convenir que c'est dans l'observation et non dans une convention ambitieux que Gauguin retrouve sa grandeur«, in *Gauguin,* Paris 1968, S. 289.

65. »C'est donc à la *Raison* seul qu'appartient dèsormais le progrès . . .«, *L'Esprit moderne et le catholicisme,* a. a. O., S. 94.

66. Zum Gegensatz zwischen rationaler und wörtlicher Unterscheidung bei Gauguin siehe Guerin, a. a. O., S. 136, 142, 143; zu dem Gedanken, die Bibel arbeite mit Parabeln, S. 147; zu seiner Idee, er arbeite wie die Bibel, siehe den Brief an Fontainas vom August 1899, Malingue, a. a. O., S. 293.

67. Das Wiederaufleben von Ideen des 18. Jahrhunderts zeigt die Hinwendung von diachronischen zu synchronischen Denkweisen in den Geisteswissenschaften: in den Schriften von Dürkheim und seinen Nachfolgern, in Franz Boas' Denken, das zu *The Mind of Primitive Man* aus dem Jahre 1911 führte, auch im Denken von Michel Bréal und Ferdinand de Saussure, das in dessen revolutionärer Zeichentheorie seinen Höhepunkt fand. Zu Wandlungen in der Anthropologie und Völkerkunde im späten 19. Jahrhundert siehe Penniman, a. a. O., und Stocking, a. a. O. Die Essays von Hans Aarsleff untersuchen besonders das Wiederaufleben der Aufklärung, *From Locke to Saussure,* Minneapolis 1982, und vor allem »Bréal vs. Schleicher: Reorientation in Linguistics during the Latter Half of the Nineteenth Century«, S. 293–334. Aarsleff zeigt auf, daß zu seiner Zeit nicht nur Gauguin eine Vorliebe für frühere, »rudimentärere« Sprachformen besaß, siehe Gauguins Brief an Strindberg, Anm. 61.

68. Leider ist es mir innerhalb des vorliegenden Aufsatzes nicht möglich, auf die wichtige Frage eines völkischen Primitivismus einzugehen. Nordländische Kunstströmungen dieser Art werden teilweise behandelt in Varnedoe (Hrsg.), *Northern Light: Realism and Symbolism in Scandinavian Painting, 1880–1910,* New York, Brooklyn Museum, 1982; hervorragende historische Analysen in Mosse, G., *The Nationalization of the Masses,* New York 1975, und *The Crisis of German Ideology,* New York 1981, sowie in Stern, F., *The Politics of Cultural Despair,* Berkeley 1961.

69. ». . . cette étincelle, cette propagation lumineuse, immense, de la science, qui aujourd'hui d'occident en orient illumine tout le monde moderne d'une façon déjà si saisissante, si prodigieuse d'effets . . .«, *L'Esprit moderne et le catholicisme,* S. 77.

70. Erörterungen des zentralen Nervensystems und des Atoms in *L'Esprit moderne et le catholicisme,* S. 15–16. Beide Kommentare würde man heute als antireduktionistische Argumente gegen den mechanistischen Materialismus in Physik und Biologie betrachten. Gauguins Stellungnahme gegen die Wissenschaft wie in seinem Brief an Charles Morice vom April 1903, Malingue, a. a. O., S. 319, drückt lediglich die Ablehnung einer bestimmten Form materialistischer Wissenschaft aus, die in der Folge durch Entdekkungen in Gebieten wie der Strahlung von der Wissenschaft selbst überwunden wurde. Gauguins Formulierung gegenüber Morice – »Nous venons de subir en art une très grande période d'égarement causée par la physique, chimie mécanique et étude de la nature« – deckt sich völlig mit seiner Begrüßung der entstehenden modernen Wissenschaft. Kurioserweise könnte man wiederum Gauguin und Henry Adams als Menschen ihrer Zeit gegenüberstellen, wenn wir Gauguins Beobachtung des Todes der alten Wissenschaft mit Adams Kommentaren zu denselben Phänomenen in seinem berühmten Essay über die Lichtmaschine in Paris vergleichen, in *The Education of Henry Adams.*

□ 255 b
›Kopf‹, Bougainville, (Salomoninseln), bemaltes Holz, Höhe 43 cm. Museum für Völkerkunde, Basel.

Jack D. Flam

Matisse und die Fauvisten

Man ist generell der Ansicht, daß die primitive Kunst von einer Gruppe französischer Maler – den späteren »Fauvisten« MATISSE, DERAIN, VLAMINCK – um das Jahr 1905 »entdeckt« wurde. Der genaue Zeitpunkt, die Umstände und die Folgen dieser »Entdeckung« sind jedoch umstritten, wobei einige Fakten und Fragen nicht ausreichend beachtet wurden.[1] In diesem Aufsatz werde ich endgültig die Mitte des Jahres 1906 für die Entdeckung festlegen und die für das Verständnis ihrer Bedeutung wichtigen Umstände erläutern.

Mindestens ein Jahrhundert lang hatte man die Ausdrucksstärke und plastische Kraft primitiver Kunst nur erahnt, bis endlich die geistige und kulturelle Bereitschaft für ihre Entdekkung geschaffen war. Die Stammeskunst zog als eine der letzten außereuropäischen Kunstäußerungen die Aufmerksamkeit europäischer Künstler auf sich, wobei sich die französischen Künstler ziemlich spät der europäischen Verehrung der Primitiven anschlossen. Viele Charakteristika ließen die Stammeskunst für europäisches Empfinden fremdartiger als andere außereuropäische Kunstformen erscheinen. Erst nachdem sich grundsätzlich Veränderungen in der europäischen Tradition vollzogen hatten, konnten sich europäische Künstler der Stammeskunst mit Gewinn annehmen (siehe Einleitung S. 20ff.).

Stammesobjekte boten sich als solche der direkten Verwendung durch die Maler nicht unmittelbar an. Sie bestanden fast nur aus Einzelfiguren, die direkt aus dem Holz geschnitten waren. Den Gebrauch von Holz und das direkte Verfahren der Schnitztechnik sah man um die Jahrhundertwende als »primitiv« an.[2] Während Motive und bildnerische Mittel japanischer Drucke oder südostasiatischer Reliefs den Bedürfnissen europäischer Maler entgegenkamen, waren weder Motive noch Strukturprinzipien primitiver Kunst mit westlichen Traditionen so einfach in Einklang zu bringen. Diese Traditionen fußten auf den seit der Renaissance verbindlichen Raumauffassungen und jenen kanonischen Regeln für die Figur, die in die Antike zurückreichten. Die primitive Kunst bestand hauptsächlich aus Einzelfiguren, und diese Figuren zeigten die extremste Vereinfachung des menschlichen Körpers, der westliche Künstler bis jetzt begegnet waren. Verglichen mit einer *SENUFO*-, *FANG*- oder auch einer *BAULE*-Figur wirkt z. B. eine Statue aus der ägyptischen Königszeit, ein archaischer griechischer »Kouros« oder eine indische »Yaksha«-Figur anatomisch verhältnismäßig naturalistisch. Bei afrikanischen Objekten, die im allgemeinen die ersten Stammesformen sind, die französische Künstler beeinflußten, war der menschliche Körper vom Schnitzer oft völlig neu konzipiert.[3] Die bekannten afrikanischen Proportionen – sehr großer Kopf, großer Körper, auffallende Genitalien, ziemlich kleine Gliedmaßen – sind eher als »soziale« denn als anatomische Proportionen zu bezeichnen.[4] Die Betonung liegt mehr auf dem Plastischen als auf der anatomischen Artikulation, die dem Muskel- und Knochenbau oder dem wirklichen Aussehen des menschlichen Körpers ähnlich ist. Die Körperhaltungen dieser Figuren waren ebenfalls kaum in die europäische Bildsprache umzusetzen. Der Grund hierfür liegt in ihrem Mangel an einer besonderen Handlung, in ihrer Symmetrie und impliziten Abkehr von Raum, Zeit und vor allem der Schwerkraft. Die Plastik erkennt die Schwerkraft meist stillschweigend an, indem sie sich ihr entweder fügt oder dagegen ankämpft, und der überwiegende Teil figürlicher Malerei erzeugt unabhängig vom Grad ihrer Stilisierung einen Raum, in dem die Schwerkraft dann doch anerkannt wird. Die meisten afrikanischen Plastiken, die nur mäßig hoch und streng symmetrisch sind – die Knie sind angezogen und eine Standfläche fehlt oft – ziehen Schwerkraft, Zeit und umgebenden Raum einfach nicht in Betracht.[5] Afrikanische Holzfiguren sind meist bewegliche Objekte – im Gegensatz zur Monumental- oder Architekturplastik, wie sie in großen Teilen Europas und Asiens vorkommt. Ihr Entrücktsein aus der Zeit wird durch fehlende Bindung an einen besonderen Ort noch betont. Der Inhalt afrikanischer Kunst wurde ebenfalls nicht verstanden. Sie schien keinen erzählerischen Inhalt zu besitzen, anders als chinesische oder japanische Kunst, deren Entwicklung historisch faßbar war und die neben der häufigen erzählerischen Komponente auch ein Repertoire vertrauter Attribute und Symbole besaß. Demgegenüber waren afrikanische Figuren in keine erkennbare Aktivität verwickelt, sondern wurden außerhalb menschlicher Beschäftigungen, jenseits gewöhnlicher Zeit und gewohnten Raums gezeigt.[6] Auch wenn man sie für »mißgestaltet, scheußlich« und somit für »barbarisch« hielt, wurden sie als geheimnisvoll empfunden.

Die afrikanische Kunst war auch noch in einem anderen Sinne der Zeit entrückt: Da zu Beginn des Jahrhunderts ihre historische Entwicklung unbekannt war, schien sie in einer Art zeitlosem Raum zu existieren. Ihre namenlosen Schöpfer und deren unbekannte Kulturen konnten sich so der Tyrannei des Historizismus des 19. Jahrhunderts entziehen – obwohl sie nach dem populären Evolutionsmodell den »Anfang« der Menschlichkeitsentwicklung verkörperten.[7]

Doch zu Beginn des 20. Jahrhunderts entsprachen die ureigensten Merkmale afrikanischer Kunst, die ihr zuvor noch den

□ 256 *Henri Matisse, ›Madame Matisse‹, 1913, Öl auf Leinwand, 146 x 97 cm. Eremitage, Leningrad.*

□ 257 *›Maske‹, Fang (Gabun), bemaltes Holz, Höhe 48 cm. Musée National d'Art Moderne, Centre National d'Art et de Culture Georges Pompidou, Paris. Ehemals Sammlung Maurice de Vlaminck, André Derain.*

Zugang zu westlichem Empfinden versperrt hatten, zusehends Bedürfnissen und Strömungen, die man in Europa wahrzunehmen begann. Um 1906 suchten progressive Maler Alternativen zu einer Bildsprache, die mit optischen Effekten und allzu ausführlichen Detailschilderungen der äußeren Welt überladen war. Diese Suche entsprach der Sehnsucht nach neuen Wegen, um das Ideale dem Realen, die Vorstellung mit dem Wahrnehmbaren zu verbinden. Es gab zwei wichtige historische Quellen für dieses Interesse: die Kunst bestimmter Neoimpressionisten, die erfolgreich – wenn auch unsystematisch – eben eine solche Synthese gewagt hatten, zum anderen zahlreiche exotische und nichtnaturalistische Kunstformen, als Bilder (japanische Drucke und persische Minaturen) wie auch als Skulpturen (ägyptische, antike nahöstliche und vorrömisch-iberische Steinreliefs).[8]

Gauguin war der einzige bedeutende Künstler, der wirklich längere Zeit an Orten lebte, wo primitive Kunst geschaffen wurde. Ihr Einfluß auf seine Holzschnitte und Skulpturen ist oft ganz unmittelbar, in seinen Bildern hingegen selten und in der Regel indirekt. In dieser Gattung sind statt dessen die malerischen Traditionen der europäischen Kunst und die Kunst exotischer Hofkulturen vorherrschend.[9] Maillol erkannte diese Ambivalenz und bemerkte: »Gauguin . . . hätte schnitzen sollen wie er malte, um auch da die Natur nachzuahmen, anstatt Frauen mit großen Köpfen und winzigen Beinen zu machen. Er hatte zwei Auffassungen, eine in der Malerei, eine andere in der Plastik: er war in sich gespalten.«[10]

Dieser Gegensatz zwischen Plastik (dem häufigsten Ausdrucksmittel primitiver Kunst) und Malerei (der überragenden europäischen Ausdrucksform) ist charakteristisch für die frühe Berührung mit primitiver Kunst. Die Exotik von Gauguins Malerei hatte wohl kaum Einfluß auf seine Zeitgenossen, doch sollten seine Skulpturen und Holzschnitte für die Künstler der nachfolgenden Generation in Deutschland und Frankreich zu wichtigen Vorbildern für primitive Gestaltung werden. Die große Retrospektive seines Werkes im Salon d'Automne von

1906 wirkte wie ein Katalysator. Sie weckte ein merkliches Interesse für den einfachen Stil der Holzschnitte, und während der nächsten Jahre versuchten mehrere jüngere Künstler – besonders DERAIN, MATISSE und PICASSO – in einer GAUGUIN ähnlichen Weise zu schnitzen.

CÉZANNE spielte bei der Entdeckung der primitiven Kunst im Gegensatz dazu nur eine mittelbare Rolle. Er selbst zeigte kein Interesse an exotischen oder eingeborenen Kulturen. Während aber GAUGUIN mithalf, die Augen der jüngeren Künstler für die Ausdruckswerte der primitiven Kunst zu öffnen, war es CÉZANNE, der die Künstler für ihre plastischen Merkmale empfänglich machte.

Der sogenannte Fauvismus, der seinen Höhepunkt Mitte des Jahres 1905 bis Mitte 1906 erreichte, war im wesentlichen malerisch und an der Wahrnehmung orientiert. In dieser späten Phase des Neoimpressionismus wurden den rein optischen Wirkungen größere Bedeutung als den plastischen zugemessen, die Farbe übertrumpfte die Gestaltung der Form. Im Frühjahr 1906 suchten die fauvistischen Maler verstärkt ihren Bildern größere Ausgewogenheit zu verleihen und ein Gleichgewicht zwischen Farbe und plastischer Form herzustellen. Dieses neue Interesse für das Plastische (wie es auch in den Arbeiten PICASSOS auftritt) war am deutlichsten im Werk von MATISSE ausgeprägt, aber auch bei DERAIN und in geringerem Maße bei VLAMINCK erkennbar.[11]

Der Wegweiser zu dieser neuen Ausgewogenheit zwischen Flächengestaltung und Plastizität war CÉZANNE. Seine drastische Vereinfachung der Form und seine Fähigkeit, durch facettierte Farbflächen plastische Wirkungen zu erzielen, eröffnete den jungen Künstlern neue Möglichkeiten. Diese Herausforderung brachte sie aber zugleich in große Verlegenheit, denn während CÉZANNE den Weg zu einer neuen Sicht eröffnete, führten die fast überwältigende Kraft seiner Kunst und ihr mächtiger Einfluß in eine Art Sackgasse. Gerade an diesem Punkt konnte das Beispiel der afrikanischen Kunst hilfreich werden. Obwohl sie wie einige neoimpressionistische Bilder auf abstrakte Struktur und konzeptionelle Form größeren Wert legte als auf die äußere Wahrnehmung, war die afrikanische Kunst doch grundverschieden. Sie mißachtete optische Eindrücke viel stärker, war in der Beschreibung weniger wahrheitsgetreu und auch symbolischer als die Kunst der Nach-Impressionisten. Ihre Ikonographie und Geschichte waren nicht bekannt, deshalb wies sie nicht nur einen Weg, der den Neoimpressionismus, sondern auch Geschichte und kulturelle Traditionen umging. Von besonderer Bedeutung ist, daß es die Stammeskunst den jungen Künstlern erlaubte, sich jenseits der geschichtlichen Zwänge zu bewegen. Zu diesem Zwecke hielt sie ein Gegenmittel für deren Gefühl bereit, künstlerisch nachzuhinken, am Ende einer Tradition zu stehen, deren Möglichkeiten schon erforscht waren und die damit den Weg zu einer persönlichen Schöpferkraft versperrte.[12] In einer Zeit, da der Einfluß der großen Nach-Impressionisten die Entwicklung der Jüngeren zu hemmen schien und die meisten exotischen, außereuropäischen Künste schon ausgeschlachtet waren, verhieß die afrikanische Kunst die Aussicht auf einen Neubeginn.[13]

Viel Tinte wurde über die Frage vergossen, wer zuerst die Stammeskunst »entdeckt« und sie dem Dunkel der ethnographischen Museen entrissen habe – als ob solch eine »Entdekkung« eine Frage des Erstrechts wäre, das wir für gewöhnlich mit wissenschaftlichen Entdeckungen verbinden. Tatsächlich gab es keinen alleinigen »Entdecker«. Wie in allen Fällen, in denen wir es mit künstlerischem Einfluß zu tun haben, gilt es ein kompliziertes Gewebe von Impulsen und Reaktionen in Betracht zu ziehen. Wenn wir von der »Entdeckung« der primitiven Kunst sprechen, meinen wir den Augenblick, als die Künstler erkannten, daß die Stammesobjekte mehr sind als bloße Kuriositäten von rein ethnographischem Interesse, und sie in ihnen Züge bemerkten, die sie in ihre eigene Kunst aufnehmen konnten. Wenn wir von einem »Entdecker« der Stammeskunst sprechen, müssen wir uns fragen, wonach der Entdecker gerade suchte, was er entdeckt zu haben glaubte und welchen Nutzen er aus der Entdeckung ziehen konnte.

Den frühesten und hartnäckigsten Anspruch, der alleinige »Entdecker« gewesen zu sein, erhob MAURICE DE VLAMINCK – und seinem Recht auf diesen Ruhm wird noch immer großer Glaube geschenkt.[14] Nach seinen eigenen, leicht widersprüchlichen Darstellungen wurde ihm der ästhetische Wert afrikanischer Kunst erstmals irgendwann zwischen 1903 und 1905 bewußt.[15] Aus seinen zahllosen Erklärungen stellt sich der historische Verlauf folgendermaßen dar: Nachdem er an einem heißen, strahlenden Tag im Freien gemalt hatte, kehrte VLAMINCK in ein Bistro in Argenteuil ein. Er trank etwas, und da bemerkte er auf einem Wandbrett hinter der Bar drei afrikanische Objekte. Zwei davon – rot, ocker oder weiß bemalt – waren YORUBA-Skulpturen aus Dahome, das dritte, unbemalt und recht dunkel, kam von der Elfenbeinküste.[16] Er war so erschlagen von der Kraft dieser Objekte, daß er den Besitzer überredete, sie ihm zu überlassen; dafür spendierte er eine Lokalrunde. Wenig später zeigte VLAMINCK diese Stücke einem Freund seines Vaters, der ihm noch drei andere afrikanische Objekte schenkte – zwei Statuen und eine große weißliche *FANG*-Maske □ 257, welche die Frau des Freundes abstoßend gefunden hatte und damit drohte, sie in den Müll zu werfen. Als dann später DERAIN die Maske über VLAMINCKS Bett hängen sah, war er tief beeindruckt und bot zwanzig Francs dafür. VLAMINCK lehnte ab, als er aber eine Woche später knapp bei Kasse war, verkaufte er DERAIN die Maske für fünf Francs. Wie VLAMINCK erzählt, nahm DERAIN sie mit in sein Atelier in der Rue Torlaque, wo sie dann PICASSO und MATISSE sahen und sich wohl zum ersten Mal ihre Begeisterung für Stammeskunst entzündete.[17]

VLAMINCK berichtete, er habe zusammen mit DERAIN bei mehreren gemeinsamen Besuchen im Trocadéro schon früher

□ 258 *Maurice de Vlaminck, ›Badende‹ (Baigneuses), 1908, Öl auf Leinwand, 89 x 116 cm. Privatsammlung, Schweiz.*

□ 259 *Henri Matisse, ›Stilleben mit afrikanischer Skulptur‹ (Nature morte au sculpture africaine), 1906–07, Öl auf Leinwand, 105 x 70 cm. Privatsammlung.*

□ 260 *›Statuette aus Holz‹, Vili (Volksrepublik Kongo), Höhe 24 cm. Privatsammlung. Ehemals Sammlung Henri Matisse.*

afrikanische Bildwerke gesehen, hätte sie jedoch nur für »barbarische Fetische« ohne besonderen ästhetischen Reiz gehalten.[18] Im Bistro von Argenteuil habe er jedoch völlig anders reagiert. Er sei von den afrikanischen Objekten dort so erschüttert gewesen, daß er den Vorfall später als eine *Offenbarung* angesehen habe – ein Wort, das wahrscheinlich von Picasso stammt.[19]

Vlaminck machte es offensichtlich Spaß, ausgeschmückte Versionen dieser Geschichte zu erzählen. Sie gedieh zum meistzitierten Bericht von der Entdeckung der primitiven Kunst. Neben den eigenen, von ihm selbst veröffentlichten Schriften scheint Vlaminck auch anderen Darstellungen mit Auskünften dienlich gewesen zu sein, die ihm nicht nur eine Schlüsselrolle bei der »Entdeckung« der Stammeskunst zubilligten, sondern ihm auch zuschrieben, Matisse und Picasso die Augen dafür geöffnet zu haben.[20] Eine der hübschesten Versionen stammt von Francis Carco. Er berichtet, Vlaminck habe Derain eine afrikanische Plastik gezeigt und dabei gesagt, sie sei »fast so schön« wie die Venus von Milo. Derain antwortete angeblich, sie sei »so schön« wie die Venus. Die beiden beschlossen, Picasso die Plastik zu zeigen, dem Vlaminck wiederum sagte, sie sei »fast so schön« und Derain wiederholte, sie sei »so schön« wie die Venus von Milo. Picasso soll dann beide mit der Erklärung übertrumpft haben, die Maske sei »sogar noch schöner«.[21]

Wie Jean Laude herausfand, stecken Vlamincks Memoiren voller Selbsttäuschungen, Widersprüche und unverblümter Unwahrheiten.[22] Vlaminck lag es offenbar sehr am Herzen, als Entdecker zu gelten. Seine vermutlich entscheidende Rolle bei der »Entdeckung« der afrikanischen Kunst, die später so wichtig für die Entwicklung der modernen Kunst werden sollte, war ein Kalkül, um dem Part, den er spielte, mehr Gewicht zu verleihen. Wenn wir seine Erzählungen untersuchen, erkennen wir schnell: Was Vlaminck in der Bar beeindruckte, war genau dieselbe »Barbarei«, die er im Trocadéro beim Anblick der afrikanischen Objekte empfunden hatte. Aber im Museum waren die Objekte in Glaskästen eingesperrt und als »Kuriositäten« präsentiert. In Argenteuil war seine Gemütsverfassung offenbar völlig anders, das Innere der Bar wird wohl kühl und dunkel gewesen sein im Gegensatz zum strahlenden Sonnenlicht und der großen Hitze, in der er gerade mehrere Stunden gemalt hatte. Er war müde, seine Abwehrhaltung war gering, und er trank. Um ihn herum waren Matrosen und Arbeiter, nicht feinsinnige Kollegen. Nach seiner eigenen Darstellung war es nicht die plastische Ursprünglichkeit der afrikanischen Skulptur, die ihn so traf, sondern ihre eigentümliche Ausdruckskraft.[23]

Obwohl bemalte Plastik in Afrika ziemlich selten ist, waren außerdem zwei der drei Stücke, die VLAMINCK angeblich bei dieser Gelegenheit gesehen haben will, bunt bemalte *YORUBA*-Skulpturen aus Dahome mit einer Farbgebung, die er so ähnlich in seinen Bildern dieser Zeit anwendete. Mit anderen Worten, was VLAMINCK zunächst am stärksten beeindruckte, war eine Bestätigung seiner eigenen, von VAN GOGH beeinflußten expressionistischen Kunst sowie des von GAUGUIN geweckten Interesses für das Exotische und Mysteriöse.[24]

VLAMINCKS Interesse an afrikanischer Kunst war nur ein weiterer Beweis für die damals verbreitete Sympathie für primitive Einflüsse. Tatsächlich war VLAMINCK schon vor seiner fauvistischen Periode an Primitivem interessiert gewesen: Er sammelte Populär- und Volkskunst, Puppen und Bilderbögen aus Epinal, was ihn, wie er später andeutete, für die Aufnahme afrikanischer Kunst vorbereitet haben mag.[25] Die nachher einsetzende Anregung durch afrikanische Kunst erhärtet die These, daß ihm die Ausdrucksmöglichkeiten dieser Kunst, die er als besonders emotional und ausdrucksmächtig empfand, zwar als Katalysator zum Erreichen größerer Freiheit in seinem Werk diente,[26] darin andererseits aber keinen sichtbaren Niederschlag fanden. VLAMINCK war vor allem Landschaftsmaler, und die Möglichkeiten der primitiven Kunst waren am besten bei der Darstellung des menschlichen Körpers nutzbar. Als eine der wenigen Ausnahmen, wo überhaupt ein direkter afrikanischer Einfluß zu erkennen ist, kann sein Bild *Badende* von 1908 gelten □ 258. Die Gesichter der beiden vorderansichtig gegebenen Figuren haben hier eine erstaunlich wortgetreue und banale Ähnlichkeit mit der *FANG*-Maske, die er zwei Jahre zuvor an DERAIN verkauft hatte. Verglichen mit gleichzeitigen Werken von DERAIN, MATISSE oder PICASSO ist dieses Bild jedoch wegen seines geringen Verständnisses, das es für CÉZANNE oder die primitive Kunst aufbringt, besonders bemerkenswert.

Abgesehen von den Widersprüchen in VLAMINCKS so unterschiedlichen Berichten über seine »Entdeckung« und den Erzählungen anderer, für die er die Quelle war, bestehen hinsichtlich des Zeitpunktes dieser Begebenheit große Unstimmigkeiten. Sie ist oft undatiert,[27] dann wird 1903 angegeben[28] oder – in seinen ausgefeiltesten Berichten – 1905.[29] Dieser Zeitpunkt wird in der späteren Literatur gemeinhin anerkannt. Das richtige Datum ist wohl weder 1903 noch 1905, sondern das Jahr 1906 – etwa die Zeit, als sich auch MATISSE aus ganz anderen Gründen für die afrikanische Kunst intensiv zu interessieren begann.

Folgende Tatsachen sprechen für das Jahr 1906: Zunächst bezog DERAIN sein Atelier in der Rue Torlaque nicht vor dem Herbst 1906.[30] Folglich kann das Datum nicht 1905 gewesen sein, wenn DERAIN die *FANG*-Maske, gleich nachdem er sie von VLAMINCK gekauft hatte, in dieses Atelier brachte.[31] Des weiteren teilt MATISSE mit, der, wie wir aus zuverlässigen Quellen wissen, zum ersten Mal 1906 ernstlich an afrikanischen Plastiken interessiert war, daß DERAIN die berühmte *FANG*-Maske von VLAMINCK gekauft habe, *nachdem* er, MATISSE, sein erstes afrikanisches Stück im Herbst 1906 erworben hatte.[32] Das Jahr deckt sich außerdem mit wichtigen äußeren Indizien. Scheinbare Widersprüche in den Berichten von Autoren wie André Salmon und Max Jacob, die PICASSOS Bekanntschaft mit der primitiven Kunst auf die Initiative DERAINS zurückführen,[33] klären sich auf, ebenso wie die Frage, warum DERAIN in seinem Werk nicht vor dem Herbst 1906 auf afrikanische Kunst reagierte.[34] Es ist zu vermuten, daß DERAIN unbedingt VLAMINCKS *FANG*-Maske bekommen wollte, weil er die GAUGUIN-Retrospektive von 1906 gerade gesehen hatte und nun den Wert primitiver Kunst allmählich verstand.[35] Es ist auch durchaus einleuchtend, VLAMINCKS Bewunderung für afrikanische Kunst mit dem Konflikt zwischen Wahrnehmung und Vorstellung zu verknüpfen, der die Fauvisten 1906 so sehr beschäftigte – ein Problem, das sie jetzt viel deutlicher empfanden als im Jahr zuvor, als sie erstmals mit ihrer Befreiung vom Neoimpressionismus zu tun hatten.

Wenn wir für VLAMINCKS Entdeckung das Jahr 1906 festlegen, müssen wir auch DERAINS Rolle, die er bei VLAMINCKS beginnender Wertschätzung der afrikanischen Kunst spielte, überprüfen. Es kann als sicher gelten, daß die beiden vor dem Sommer 1906 über afrikanische Kunst ausführlich diskutiert hatten und VLAMINCK durch diesbezügliche Gespräche und Briefwechsel mit DERAIN auf seine Entdeckung vorbereitet war. In diesem Zusammenhang ist ein Brief DERAINS an VLAMINCK von besonderer Bedeutung, der nur das Datum »Londres, 7 mars«, aber keine Jahreszahl trägt.[36] DERAIN erwähnt seinen Besuch im »Musée nègre« (den ethnographischen Sammlungen des Britischen Museums) und schreibt über seine dortigen Erfahrungen:

»Ihr Ausdruck ist verblüffend und beunruhigend. Aber da ist eine zwiespältige Ursache hinter diesem Übermaß an Ausdruckskraft: Die Formen nehmen Gestalt an im hellen Tageslicht und sind dafür bestimmt, im Tageslicht zu wirken. Darauf sollten wir achten, wenn wir daraus lernen wollen. Somit ist klar, daß die Beziehungen der Massen eine Lichtwirkung oder die Übereinstimmung von Licht mit dieser oder jener Form hervorrufen können.«[37] Goldwater, der diesen Brief auf das

□ 261 *André Derain, ›Der Kauernde‹, 1907, Stein, 33 x 26 x 28 cm. Museum des 20. Jahrhunderts, Wien.*

Jahr 1910 datierte, führte ihn als Beispiel für jene Form der Bewunderung primitiver Kunst an, wie sie »nicht vor der Zeit der Kubisten auftrat . . .«.[38] Aber Laude hat überzeugend dargelegt, daß der Brief früher als 1910, wahrscheinlich 1906 geschrieben wurde – keinesfalls jedoch später als 1907.[39] Wenn er, wie es fast scheint, im März 1906 geschrieben wurde, dann geht er um einige Monate VLAMINCKS »Entdeckung« voraus und beweist, daß DERAINS Interesse für afrikanische Kunst schon vor dem Erwerb von VLAMINCKS *FANG*-Maske bestand. Nachdem wir wissen, daß es wahrscheinlich DERAIN war, der als regelmäßiger Besucher von Museen den gemeinsamen Besuch des Trocadéro anregte,[40] können wir weiter vermuten, daß er als erster VLAMINCKS Interesse für afrikanische Kunst weckte, obwohl VLAMINCK als erster solche Objekte erwarb. Wir wissen ohnehin, daß sich DERAIN und auch VLAMINCK schon einige Jahre zuvor mit primitiver Kunst anderer Art beschäftigt hatten: »Ich möchte die Kunst der Kinder studieren«, schrieb DERAIN 1902 an VLAMINCK, »die Wahrheit ist zweifellos dort zu finden.«[41]

Sehr bemerkenswert in DERAINS Brief aus London ist auch der Hinweis auf »Massen« und die Bemerkung, daß es unbedingt nötig sei, »den Kreis zu sprengen, in den uns die Realisten eingeschlossen haben«.[42] Hier verbindet sich DERAINS Interesse an der Stammeskunst mit dem Hauptanliegen seiner damaligen Malerei: der Suche nach mehr Plastizität und dem Bedürfnis, vom »Realistischen« abzurücken – der noch auf der Wahrnehmung beruhenden Grundlage des fauvistischen Stils von 1905. Man kann sich vorstellen, daß diese Anliegen im folgenden Herbst auch zu dem Wunsch beigetragen haben, die *FANG*-Maske von VLAMINCK zu kaufen.

MATISSE stieß wohl ungefähr zur selben Zeit wie VLAMINCK auf afrikanische Stammesplastik, wobei die Beweggründe und Folgen dieser Entdeckung in seinem Fall wesentlich interessanter und wichtiger sind. MATISSE' Interesse an afrikanischer Kunst scheint in das Frühjahr 1906 zurückzureichen – jener Zeit seiner ersten Reise nach Nordafrika, die im März dieses Jahres stattfand.[43] Vielleicht hatte MATISSE, der wie DERAIN häufig Museen besichtigte, schon vorher solche Plastik gesehen, denn sie war seit über zwei Jahrzehnten im Musée d'Ethnographie in Paris ausgestellt. Jedenfalls machten sie keinen sonderlichen Eindruck auf ihn, denn bis 1906 sah er keinerlei Bezugspunkte zwischen diesen Arbeiten und seinem eigenen Schaffen.[44] Zu Anfang des Jahres 1906 öffneten hingegen verschiedene Faktoren MATISSE die Augen für die Ausdruckswerte und plastischen Merkmale afrikanischer Skulptur. Er war zu dieser Zeit innerhalb der Avantgarde der einzige Maler, der CÉZANNE wirklich verstand. PICASSOS Vorstellung von dem Meister aus Aix war noch sehr bruchstückhaft. BRAQUE und DERAIN sollten den Gehalt seiner Kunst erst ein Jahr später voll begreifen. MATISSE aber hatte schon 1899 bei Vollard eine kleine, ausgezeichnete Fassung der *Drei Badenden* CÉZANNES gekauft. Schon seit Jahren hatte er mit Malerfreunden die Feinheiten von CÉZANNES Malerei diskutiert, die seit der Jahrhundertwende den stärksten Einfluß auf MATISSE' Werk ausübte. MATISSE' sogenannte fauvistische Periode endete im Winter 1906–07. Sie war eine kurze Übergangsphase von seinem früheren, dem Wahrnehmungseindruck unterworfenen – eigentlich nachimpressionistischen – Schaffen zu einem späteren synthetischen Stil. Erst gegen Ende seiner fauvistischen Periode, als seine Malerei wieder plastischer wurde und seine Farben an Intensität verloren, konnte MATISSE seine frühere Befruchtung durch CÉZANNE überdenken und dabei aus der Stammeskunst einen indirekten Nutzen ziehen. Während sich für VLAMINCK, ähnlich wie für GAUGUIN, die Stammeskunst vor allem mit einem gefühlsbetonten oder romantischen Primitivismus verband, erkannte MATISSE in der afrikanischen Kunst neue plastische Möglichkeiten für die Bildhauerei und über sie auch für die Malerei – und damit auch einen neuen Weg, mit dem Erbe CÉZANNES umzugehen.

□ 262 *›Derain in seinem Atelier‹, Winter 1908–09. Photographie aus G. Burgess, ›The Wild Men of Paris‹ in „Architectural Record", 1910.*

Während VLAMINCK seine eigene Bedeutung hochspielte und darauf pochte, MATISSE und PICASSO mit afrikanischer Kunst bekannt gemacht zu haben, waren MATISSE' Ansprüche bescheidener, sachlicher und sind sogar durch die Aussagen unabhängiger Dritter bestätigt worden. In der Autobiographie von Alice B. Toklas, die 1933 erschien – als die Freundschaft zu MATISSE schon lange nicht mehr bestanden hatte –, erklärte Gertrude Stein unmißverständlich, daß MATISSE »Picasso mit Negerplastik bekannt gemacht habe«, daß »Matisse als erster von den afrikanischen Statuen beeinflußt wurde – weniger in seiner Malerei als in seiner Bildhauerei –, daß Matisse Picassos Aufmerksamkeit darauf gelenkt habe, kurz nachdem Picasso Gertrude Steins Portrait vollendet hatte«.[45]

MATISSE ging 1941 in einem unveröffentlichten Interview auf diesen Bericht näher ein:

»Ich kam ganz direkt zur afrikanischen Plastik. Ich ging oft an einem Raritätenladen – er hieß »Le Père sauvage« – in der Rue de Rennes vorbei[46] und sah eine Menge Sachen dort im Schaufenster. Es gab eine ganze Ecke voll mit kleinen Negerstatuen aus Holz. Erstaunt sah ich, welch starken plastischen Ausdruck sie hatten, wie verwandt sie ägyptischen Plastiken waren. Verglichen mit europäischer Skulptur, die immer von der Muskulatur und der Beschreibung des Gegenstandes ausgeht, gehen diese Negerstatuen vom Material aus und finden eigene Flächen und Proportionen. Ich schaute sie mir häufig an. Jedesmal wenn ich vorüberging, hielt ich ohne die Absicht, eine Statue zu kaufen, an, und eines schönen Tages ging ich hinein und erstand eine für 50 Francs. Ich ging zu Gertrude Steins Haus in der Rue de Fleurus. Ich zeigte ihr die Statue, dann tauchte Picasso auf. Wir plauderten. Bei dieser Gelegenheit wurde Picasso auf Negerplastiken aufmerksam. Deshalb

□ 263 *André Derain, ›Der Tanz‹ (La Danse), 1905–06, Öl und Tempera auf Leinwand, 179,5 x 229 cm. Privatsammlung.*

spricht Gertrude Stein davon. Derain kaufte eine große Maske. Der Kreis der modernen Maler fand Interesse an ihr.«[47]

Als sich Picasso seiner ersten Begegnung mit afrikanischer Kunst erinnerte, erklärte auch er, daß Matisse sie ihm zuerst gezeigt habe. Er sagte auch, daß Matisse damals über ägyptische Kunst gesprochen habe. Als sich Picasso im folgenden Jahr dafür zu interessieren begann, sah er die primitive Kunst trotzdem völlig anders.[48]

Man hat häufig gesagt, die Fauvisten seien in ihrem Werk nicht wirklich von der primitiven Kunst beeinflußt worden. Nach Ettlinger etwa »sollte unterstrichen werden, daß Matisse und die Fauvisten – ihre Begeisterung in Ehren – wenig, wenn überhaupt irgend etwas unmittelbar aus der afrikanischen Kunst lernten, wie Guillaume Apollinaire schon 1907 darauf hinwies«.[49] Wie wir sehen werden, trifft dies für Derain und besonders Matisse einfach nicht zu. Der Einfluß afrikanischer Kunst auf diese Maler fällt mit dem Ende ihres Fauvismus zusammen.

Wie schon gesagt, gilt es bei der Frage nach der »Entdeckung« der primitiven Kunst zu berücksichtigen, was die Entdecker suchten, was sie entdeckt zu haben glaubten und welchen Nutzen sie aus der Entdeckung zu ziehen fähig waren. Vlaminck suchte, wie wir gesehen haben, Ausdrucksmächtigkeit und eine Art barbarischer Wildheit, die er auch fand. Aber über ein bestimmtes sentimentales Romantisieren hinaus – und hier hat Ettlinger ganz recht – scheint er wenig aus der afrikanischen Kunst gelernt zu haben.

Derain dagegen hat seine Eindrücke zu nutzen versucht. Er ging wie Vlaminck von Gauguin aus – aber eher vom Plastiker Gauguin als vom Maler. Dieser Einfluß ist vor allem in seinen Plastiken von Anfang 1907 offenbar. In seinen Bildern begegnete er, was nicht überrascht, größeren Schwierigkeiten, die strukturellen Eigenarten afrikanischer Kunst umzusetzen.

Ronald Johnson wies erstmals nach, daß Derain im Herbst 1906 ohne Vorlage zu schnitzen anfing, wahrscheinlich unter dem Eindruck der Gauguin-Retrospektive im Salon D'Automne, die einige Holzreliefs und Skulpturen des Künstlers gezeigt hatte.[50] Derain wandte diese Technik der direkten Holzbearbeitung in seinen Skulpturen an, die er vom Herbst 1906 bis Oktober 1907 schuf. Oft wurde behauptet, daß er dieses Verfahren vor allem dem Vorbild Gauguins verdanke. Genauso wichtig ist jedoch, daß Derain viele seiner Plastiken nicht wie Gauguin in Holz, sondern in widerstandsfähigerem Stein ausführte, auch wenn er dafür »Hausteinblöcke aus der Vordertreppe des Hauses seiner Familie« herausnehmen mußte.[51] Seine Entscheidung für Stein war konservativ. Seit Jahrtausenden war Stein das bevorzugte Material der europäischen Bildhauer, so daß sein Gebrauch DERAINS Unterfangen sozusagen eine innere Gültigkeit verlieh. Außerdem half ihm das widerstandsfähigere Material die sklavische Nachahmung GAUGUINS oder der primitiven Bildschnitzer zu vermeiden. Die Oberfläche des Steins konnte ziemlich roh belassen werden, ohne unvollendet zu wirken. Zugleich verstärkt die rohe Oberfläche von DERAINS Steinplastik den durchgängigen Eindruck ihrer »Primitivität«.

Obwohl Plastiken wie *Die Zwillinge* und *Stehender Akt*[52] in der Haltung ziemlich naturalistisch sind, ist letztere in Haltung, sinnlicher Formgebung und Material indischer Plastik näher als afrikanischer oder ozeanischer. Auch sind die Köpfe in beiden Werken archaisch vereinfacht. Der Kopf des Werkes *Stehender Akt* ist eine seltsame Mischung aus archaisch-griechischem Einfluß und DERAINS *FANG*-Maske – eine Mischung, die wiederum beweist, wie untypisch und fast «archaisch« die Gesichtszüge der Maske sind.

DERAINS bekannteste, einflußreichste, vielleicht interessanteste Plastik ist *Der Kauernde* □ 261, die BRANCUSIS *Kuß* direkt beeinflußt haben soll.[53] Die Blockhaftigkeit des *Kauernden*, die Kompaktheit seiner Formen und der Gegensatz zwischen angestauter Kraft der Figur und kubischer Form des Steins machen ihn zur originellsten und packendsten Plastik DERAINS. *Der Kauernde* wird häufig als Beispiel für den Einfluß der Stammeskunst auf DERAINS Plastik angeführt.[54] Die großen Hände, die geometrische Gestaltung der Finger und der kompakte Gesamteindruck sind mit den Steinfiguren von den Marquesasinseln und der Plastik GAUGUINS verglichen worden.[55] Doch hat die beherrschende körperliche und seelische Innerlichkeit der Figur nichts mit diesen Steinfiguren oder überhaupt primitiver Kunst zu tun. Das Betonen eines inneren Zustandes rückt die Figur, wie Johnson zeigt, in die Nähe der symbolistischen Kunst.[56] Die kubische Form des *Kauernden*, die eckigen, scharf hervortretenden anatomischen Einzelheiten und das Material weisen außerdem mehr Verwandtschaft mit aztekischer als mit Stammesplastik auf.

Leider sind die zwei Plastiken DERAINS, die anscheinend einen ganz unmittelbaren Einfluß der Stammeskunst zeigten, verlorengegangen. Eine Photographie vom Winter 1908–09, die Gelett Burgess 1910 veröffentlichte, zeigt den Künstler mit den beiden Werken □ 262.[57] Eine hält DERAIN auf seinen Armen, es ist seine kleine *Katze,* in Holz geschnitzt und hauptsächlich »grün bemalt, mit Spuren von Rot im Gesicht«.[58] Größe, Form und Farbgebung erinnern an PICASSOS kleine Skulpturen aus dem Jahr 1907[59] und auch an GAUGUINS zylindrische Schnitzereien. Die größere Plastik ganz rechts außen im Vordergrund ist der Stammeskunst noch stärker ähnlich. Sie könnte fast eine Imitation oder ein Pasticcio von Stammesobjekten sein – ihr Kopf gleicht bestimmten *FANG*-Masken, ihr Körper einem polynesischen Tiki.[60]

Die Beziehungen zur Stammeskunst sind in DERAINS primitivistischen Bildern spärlicher. *Der Tanz* von 1906 □ 263, ganz offenkundig ein Widerhall von GAUGUINS Bildern, ist ein seltsamer Mischmasch stilistischer Elemente. Die Gestalt rechts scheint als Typus an dieselben ostasiatischen Formen zu erinnern, die GAUGUIN in seinen Bildern aufgriff. Dieser Typus

□ 264 *André Derain, ›Badende‹ (Baigneuses), 1908, Öl auf Leinwand, 179 x 232 cm. Národní Galerie, Prag.*

zeigt einen Reflex in DERAINS *Stehendem Akt,* dessen Pose der Negerin rechts in DELACROIX' *Frauen von Algier* entnommen ist.[61] Die mittlere Gestalt ist gemessen am Stil des Bildes ziemlich naturalistisch, wenn man von der leuchtend roten Farbgebung absieht. Die Gestalt links mit ihren merkwürdigen Verrenkungen und dem wirbelnden, linear aufgefaßten Faltenwurf erinnert eher an so berühmte romanische Werke wie den Jesaja in Souillac als an Stammeskunst.[62]

Zwei hölzerne Paneele, die DERAIN 1906/07 für ein Bett schnitzte, weisen einen ähnlichen Eklektizismus auf. Die geschwungene Linienführung, die Verlagerung der Figuren in den Vordergrund sind gleichfalls von GAUGUIN angeregt.[63] Das Gesicht der Frau auf der kleineren Tafel gleicht GAUGUINS Frauen von Tahiti und erinnert entfernt an DERAINS *FANG*-Maske.

Das Bild *Badende* aus dem Jahre 1907 wird sicherlich am häufigsten angeführt, um einen direkten Zusammenhang zwischen DERAINS Malerei und der Stammesplastik nachzuweisen ☐ 265.[64] Wegen des vereinfachten Gesichts der mittleren Figur hat man DERAIN »den ersten Maler« genannt, »der in seinem Werk die Einflüsse beider, Cézannes und der Negerkunst, verknüpfte«.[65] Diese Behauptung, die oft zitiert wurde,[66] ist mit Sicherheit falsch, denn in diesem Bild gibt es nirgendwo einen direkten oder indirekten afrikanischen Einfluß. Die Flächen des Kopfes und des Halses sind wohl vereinfacht, die Art der Vereinfachung und die Haltung von Kopf und Hals jedoch ganz unafrikanisch. Sie teilen eher eine allgemeine Neigung zum Archaisieren, wie sie bei den 1906 geschaffenen Skulpturen von MATISSE zu beobachten ist ☐ 270, 271. Im übrigen sind die Figuren in DERAINS Bild anatomisch richtig und natürlich dargestellt. Ihre kontrapostischen Haltungen folgen der akademischen Tradition und scheinen aus Skizzen nach dem lebenden Modell entwickelt zu sein. Auch die Anklänge an CÉZANNE gehen nicht allzu weit. Trotz der CÉZANNE verwandten Kolorsitik, des leichten Cézanneschen Pinselstrichs und einer gewissen Härte der Formgebung sind diese Gestalten so nüchtern konstruiert, so statisch und so stark gegen den Hintergrund gestellt, daß sie fast nichts mit der inneren Dynamik von CÉZANNES *Badenden* gemein haben, von denen sie herstammen.[67] Erst im Jahr darauf gelang es DERAIN, »Cézanne und die Negerkunst« zu verbinden. In seinen *Badenden* aus dem Jahr 1908, die jetzt in Prag hängen ☐ 264, haben die drei oberen Köpfe wenigstens eine gewisse Beziehung zu afrikanischen Masken, wohingegen das Wechselspiel zwischen Hintergrund und Figuren sowie einige Haltungen deutlich an CÉZANNE erinnern. 1908 war aber PICASSO schon eine wesentlich drastischere Verbindung CÉZANNES mit der Stammeskunst gelungen, so daß keine von DERAINS *Badenden* als »ein echter Vorläufer des Kubismus«[68] gelten kann.

Die vorgenannte Photographie von DERAIN ☐ 262 bringt vielleicht deutlicher als alle anderen Zeitdokumente die unterschiedlichen Aspekte der damals aktuellen künstlerischen Probleme zur Anschauung. Die kleine *Katze* in DERAINS Armen und die ebenso primitivistische Figur am rechten Bildrand machen klar, wie unafrikanisch die beiden Steinfiguren, neben ihm *Stehender Akt* und unter ihr *Der Kauernde*, wirklich sind.

☐ 265 *André Derain, ›Badende‹ (Baigneuses), 1907, Öl auf Leinwand, 132 x 195 cm. The Museum of Modern Art, Paley-Rockefeller Funds, New York.*

☐ 266 *Henri Matisse, ›Stilleben mit Geranie‹ (Nature morte au géranium), 1906, Öl auf Leinwand, 98 x 80 cm. The Art Institute of Chicago, Slg. Joseph Winterbotham.*

☐ 267 *Henri Matisse, ›Rosa Zwiebeln‹ (Oignons roses), 1906, Öl auf Leinwand, 46 x 55 cm. Statens Museum for Kunst, Sammlung J. Rump, Kopenhagen.*

Über DERAIN hängt an der Wand eine Reproduktion von CÉZANNES *Fünf Badenden* aus den Jahren 1885–87 (jetzt im Kunstmuseum Basel, Venturi 542). Das Bild wirkt wie eine Ikone oder der Schrein eines Hausgottes. Das Nebeneinander dieser Objekte verkörpert DERAINS künstlerisches Anliegen seit 1906, als er einen Weg suchte, um die undingliche Festigkeit der Stammesplastik mit den heftigen Farben und der bisweilen hitzigen Leidenschaft seiner fauvistischen Gemälde zu verbinden. Er kannte einen Weg zu dieser Synthese: die vereinfachte plastische Qualität von CÉZANNES Figuren durch die radikalen Formen der primitiven Kunst neu zu deuten. Doch sein Ziel blieb ihm unerreicht. »Sogar im Jahr 1907«, schreibt John Elderfield, »war Derain unfähig, bei aller Bewunderung für afrikanische Plastik ihre Lehren in seinem Werk voll zu nutzen.«[69] Was er durch eine Verbindung primitiver Kunst und Neoimpressionismus wirklich leistete, war eine bescheidene Weiterentwicklung der Synthese, die GAUGUIN einige Jahre zuvor besser gelungen war. Trotz seiner Bemühung um skulpturale Bildwirkung und der Notwendigkeit, vom Realismus loszukommen, so wie es DERAIN in einem Brief des Jahres 1906 an VLAMINCK zum Ausdruck brachte, scheinen seine stärksten und originellsten Werke jene gewesen zu sein, die er direkt nach der Natur malte. Sowie er versuchte, seiner Kunst eine größere konzeptionelle Basis zu geben, wurde sie trocken und irgendwie leblos. Trotz seiner Entdeckerrolle übten Stammeskunst und andere konzeptuelle Stilrichtungen – besonders auch der Kubismus – ironischerweise keine belebende Wirkung auf sein Werk aus. Nach 1906 erreichte es nie wieder die Kraft und Ursprünglichkeit seiner fauvistischen Jahre.

Gelett Burgess führte im Winter 1908/09 mehrere Interviews, die einen geeigneten Ausgangspunkt für unsere Behandlung von MATISSE bieten. MATISSE, der Burgess die Namen von sieben später interviewten Künstlern gab,[70] war nach Burgess' Beurteilung der Künstler, der als erster die plastischen Werte afrikanischer Skulptur erkannte: »Seit Matisse' Hinweis auf ihre ›Volumina‹ durchstöbern alle Fauvisten die Kuriositätenläden nach Negerkunst.«[71] Burgess erkannte auch die in der Entdeckung der primitiven Kunst schlummernde ästhetische Revolution: »Ich habe über die Kunst vom Niger und aus Dahome gegrübelt«, schrieb Burgess zu Beginn seines Aufsatzes, »ich habe monströse Kunst der Hindu, asiatische Mysterien und viele andere primitive Grotesken genau angesehen: Es dämmerte mir, daß es da ein Prinzip des Häßlichen und ein Prinzip des Schönen gab, daß das eine vielleicht bloß die Verneinung des anderen war, ein umgekehrtes Bild, das seinen eigenen Wert und geheimnisvollen Sinn hat. Als die Erde jung war, malte und schnitzte der Mensch schreckliche und obszöne Dinge. War das Wiederaufleben (in der Moderne) Zeichen einer zweiten Kindheit der menschlichen Rasse oder eine echte Neugeburt der Kunst?« Er fährt ein paar Absätze weiter fort: »Es war Matisse, der den ersten Schritt in das unentdeckte Land des Häßlichen tat.«[72]

Aus heutiger Sicht muten Burgess' Bemerkungen, die in der Charakterisierung als »primitive Grotesken« so unvereinbare Kunstweisen zusammenwerfen, wunderlich an. Sie klingen wie andere geringschätzige Äußerungen seiner Zeit. Aber Burgess war selbst Maler und scheint ernsthafte Erkenntnisse über die damalige künstlerische Situation gesucht zu haben.[73] Seine Beobachtung über eine neue Ästhetik des Häßlichen berührt wichtige Zusammenhänge zwischen primitiver Kunst und moderner Malerei. Burgess scheint erkannt zu haben, daß mit der neuen, in Paris stattfindenden künstlerischen Revolution alte Schönheitsbegriffe durch neue Werte ersetzt wurden. 1906 war MATISSE der Kopf dieser Revolution, und die Stammesplastik, derer er damals gewahr wurde, sollte sich als wichtiger Katalysator zur Verwirklichung seiner Ziele erweisen.

Im Sommer 1906, nach seiner Rückkehr aus Nordafrika und vor dem ersten Kauf einer afrikanischen Plastik, suchte MATISSE einen neuen ästhetischen Ansatz für seine Kunst. Er wollte die Kunst CÉZANNES, die er damals wie kein zweiter

Maler verstand, mit der Kunst GAUGUINS und einem allgemeinen Primitivismus verbinden, wie ihn die Volks- und Kinderkunst kennt (auch die Malerei HENRI ROUSSEAUS, der beim »fauvistischen« Salon d'Automne 1905 dabei war).[74] Diese beiden Richtungen behandelten Form und Raum ganz unterschiedlich. CÉZANNE modelliert plastisch und reliefartig und schafft einen greifbaren, aber nichtperspektivischen Raum. GAUGUINS Richtung gestaltet Figuren, Objekte und Hintergrund in glatten, hellen Farben und dekorativer Flächigkeit. Die Polarität dieser Kunstweisen demonstrieren zwei in ihrer Thematik jeweils unterschiedliche Bildpaare, die MATISSE in Collioure kurz nach seiner Rückkehr aus Nordafrika malte: das *Stilleben mit Geranie* □ 266 und *Rosa Zwiebeln* □ 267 sowie die beiden Fassungen des *Jungen Matrosen* □ 268, 269.

Zunächst kommen in den zwei Stilleben gleiche Dinge vor: rosa Zwiebeln, nordafrikanische Keramik und eine Terrakotta nach MATISSE' Skulptur *Frau auf ihre Hände gestützt* aus dem Jahre 1905. Die formalen Unterschiede zwischen den Bildern sind indes so groß, daß man auf den ersten Blick kaum erkennt, wie stark die Motive übereinstimmen, *Stilleben mit Geranie* ist früher und entschieden traditioneller. Es ist von einem einzigen Blickpunkt aus gemalt (der Tisch und die Gegenstände darauf haben dieselbe Perspektive), weist einen klaren Schattenwurf auf und vermittelt ein starkes Raumgefühl. Umrisse, Pinselstrich und Tiefenwirkung sind ähnlich wie bei CÉZANNE. Das Bild ist noch, wie CÉZANNES Malerei, ganz der optischen Wahrnehmung verpflichtet und hat daher insgesamt einen recht naturalistischen Charakter.

In den *Rosa Zwiebeln* sind indes die Gegenstände vereinfacht und flächig wie in einer Kinderzeichnung.[75] In einen abstrakten Raum gestellt, beziehen sie sich auf keinen genauen Blickpunkt; Atmosphäre, Licht und Schatten werden vernachlässigt. MATISSE hat hier eine vereinfachte, primitivistische Technik angewandt, um den Wirklichkeitseindruck zu verringern und die symbolischen Beziehungen unter den Gegenständen zu betonen. Die Zwiebeln scheinen tatsächlich durch die sandige, erdähnliche Oberfläche des Tisches zu wachsen, während die Spiralen des großen Krugs dieses Wachstum symbolisieren. Die weibliche Gestalt und die Kamele auf der Vase vervollständigen das Quartett der Symbole – Frau, Tier, Spirale, Pflanzenwuchs. Dieser feinsinnige und verhaltene und dabei ganz malerische Symbolismus, bei dem Gegenstände und Darstellungsweise untrennbare Funktionen ihrer »Aussage« sind, ist eine der auffälligsten Neuerungen in MATISSE' Kunst während des Sommers 1906.

Eine ähnliche Polarität CÉZANNE – Primitivismus besteht zwischen den zwei Fassungen des Bildes *Junger Matrose*. Die erste ist von aggressiver, intensiver Wirkung (ähnlich MATISSE' Selbstportrait aus dieser Zeit, Statens Museum for Kunst, Kopenhagen). Die Gestaltung verknüpft Reste seines fauvistischen Stils mit deutlich an CÉZANNE erinnernder Farbgebung, Pinselarbeit und Raumaufteilung. Die zweite Fassung malte er kurze Zeit später, und zwar nicht nach dem Modell, sondern nach dem ersten Bild. Dieser Arbeitsweise, die MATISSE um 1904 aufnahm, sollten auch in der Folgezeit noch zahlreiche Bildpaare mit dem gleichen Motiv folgen.[76] Seine ersten Fassungen geben Gesehenes wieder, die zweiten – Bilder nach Bildern – sind mehr synthetisch. So konnte er seine starke Beziehung zur Natur aufrechterhalten und sich gleichzeitig von der völlig naturgetreuen Gestaltungsweise entfernen. Leo Stein erinnerte sich gut an ein frühes Beispiel für solches Vorgehen: »Es war Sommer, er brachte vom Lande die Skizze

□ 268 *Henri Matisse, ›Junger Matrose I‹ (Jeune marin à la casquette), 1906, Öl auf Leinwand, 100 x 79 cm. Privatsammlung.*

□ 269 *Henri Matisse, ›Junger Matrose II‹ (Jeune marin à la casquette), 1906, Öl auf Leinwand, 100 x 81 cm. Privatsammlung.*

□ 271 *Henri Matisse, ›Das Leben‹ (La Vie), 1906, Bronze, Höhe 23 cm. The Metropolitan Museum of Art, Sammlung Alfred Stieglitz, New York.*

□ 270 *Henri Matisse, ›Stehender Akt‹ (Nu debout), 1906, Bronze, Höhe 48 cm. Privatsammlung.*

eines jungen Fischers mit und eine freie Kopie davon mit extremen Verzeichnungen. Zunächst behauptete er, die habe der Briefträger von Collioure gezeichnet, aber dann gab er zu, daß sie ein Experiment von ihm selbst war. Es war das erste Mal, daß er mit übertriebenen Verzeichnungen arbeitete.«[77] Steins Ausdruck »übertriebene Verzeichnungen« ist treffend. Bis dahin waren die »Verzeichnungen« in MATISSE' Werk eine unmittelbar visuelle und gefühlsmäßige Antwort auf das, was er abmalte; sie entstanden in der Hitze des Gefechts. In diesem Fall jedoch war das Bild bewußt so angelegt. Die erste Fassung von *Junger Matrose* spiegelt die Erregung, die das dichte Zusammentreffen mit dem Motiv verursachte; MATISSE nannte es den Schock der Konfrontation.[78] Die zweite Version ist ein Meditieren über das Zusammentreffen und seine Gestaltung mit konzeptionellen Mitteln. Solches Vorgehen gewährte MATISSE den notwendigen Abstand zur Naturtreue des vorangegangenen Bildes und auch von CÉZANNES übermächtigem Einfluß. Anstatt seine Sinneseindrücke genau ins Bild zu übertragen, dabei die Spröde des Modells zu betonen, führt *Junger Matrose II* die rauhe Lebenswirklichkeit zu einer eleganten, anmutig geschwungenen Einheit. In der Einfachheit der Zeichnung und der strahlenden Farbflächen liegt fast etwas Kindliches, und doch zeigt das Bild ein tiefes Verständnis für GAUGUINS synthetischen Stil. Bezeichnenderweise datierte MATISSE nur die zweite Fassung von *Junger Matrose,* als wollte er damit andeuten, wie weit er 1906 war.

Nach seiner nicht ganz ernst gemeinten Verleugnung der beiden von der Flächigkeit her radikalsten Arbeiten dieses Sommers, die er einem erdichteten Landbriefträger unterschob, scheint MATISSE dennoch gemischte Gefühle über die Richtung gehabt zu haben, in die seine neuen Vereinfachungen und sein beginnender Primitivismus lenkten. Dieses Verleugnen mag ein Anzeichen der Unsicherheit und sogar der Verwirrung gewesen sein, die viele Künstler empfinden, wenn sie zum ersten Mal ihre radikalsten Werke zeigen. Ich meine aber, es ist auch ein Anzeichen für das Unbehagen an der Naivität, die solche Arbeiten bekunden. Sein neuer Stil war ja tatsächlich eine Verneinung der großen Renaissance-Tradition, in der er geschult worden war. PICASSO bemerkte scharfsinnig, daß MATISSE zu dieser Zeit die unkomplizierte Einfachheit der Kinderkunst erreichen wollte.[79] MATISSE mag die primitive und exotische Kunst für seine plastischen Neuerungen als Bestätigung gebraucht haben, die von außerhalb seiner eigenen Tradition kam.

Angeregt von afrikanischer Plastik hat sich MATISSE im Sommer 1906 verstärkt mit Bildhauerei beschäftigt. Mit der Skulptur *Stehender Akt* □ 270, für den seine Tochter Modell stand, wendet er sich völlig von seiner früheren Plastik ab, die auf einer Körperdarstellung mit Muskeln und Kontrapost ähnlich wie in seinen Bildern beruhte. Bei *Stehender Akt* ist die Haltung fast symmetrisch, der Hals verlängert, der Kopf unverhältnismäßig groß, und die Hände liegen wie bei Figuren der *BAULE* dicht am Körper □ 272. Auch der kleine Torso mit Kopf, *La Vie* □ 271, erinnert mit seinen ragenden Brüsten, emporgeworfenen Armen, dem überbetonten Gesäß und großen Kopf an Merkmale afrikanischer Statuetten.[80]

Im Herbst kehrte MATISSE nach Paris zurück. Sein Interesse an afrikanischer Kunst war nun so stark geworden, daß er eine kleine afrikanische Plastik erwarb. Wenig später – wahrscheinlich gegen Ende 1906 – begann er das einzige Stilleben mit der

□ 272 *›Weibliche Figur‹,* BAULE *(Elfenbeinküste), Holz, Höhe 48 cm. Sammlung Kelley Rollings, Tucson.*

Darstellung einer afrikanischen Figur □ 259, 260. Er ließ das Werk unvollendet. Vielleicht deutet dies auf einen Argwohn gegen das Exotische um seiner selbst willen und zeigt, wie wichtig es ihm war, eine Synthese anzustreben. Nicht um die bloße Darstellung oder Nachahmung afrikanischer Plastik ging es MATISSE, sondern um die Schaffung frei erfundener, afrikanisch beeinflußter formaler Strukturen. Die Entwicklung vollzog sich schnell, denn als er Anfang 1907 nach Collioure zurückkehrte, begann er an einer seiner bedeutendsten Skulpturen zu arbeiten, *dem Liegenden Akt* □ 274, und kurz darauf malte er den *Blauen Akt (Erinnerung an Biskra)* □ 273, der einen entscheidenden Wendepunkt in seiner Kunst markiert.

Bisher waren die meisten Skulpturen MATISSE' nach dem lebenden Modell gestaltet worden. Das Modellieren ging von der Oberflächenerscheinung des Körpers aus, die dem inneren Bau folgte. Mit der *Liegenden im Hemd*[81] schuf er 1906 eine plastische Fassung nach einer der ruhenden Figuren in der Mitte des Bildes *Die Lebensfreude* – eine dreidimensionale Verwirklichung der in dem Gemälde sehr unkörperlich wiedergegebenen Figur. Diese Plastik und ihr Vorbild im Gemälde haben dieselbe Grundhaltung wie die bekannte antike Plastik der *Schlafenden Ariadne* (die später immer wieder in den Bildern GIORGIO DE CHIRICOS auftaucht). Die Haltung mit den angezogenen Beinen und dem über den Kopf gebeugten Arm wurde seit dem späten 15. Jahrhundert u. a. zur Darstellung der Venus und anderer erotischer Figuren verwendet und um Sinnlichkeit auszudrücken.[82] Das Motiv kam bis ins 19. Jahrhundert immer wieder vor, als es INGRES für seine Odalisken heranzog und der akademische Maler CABANEL eine ähnliche Haltung für seine *Geburt der Venus* wählte. MATISSE entwickelte dieses Liegemotiv Anfang 1907 im *Liegenden Akt I* und im *Blauen Akt* weiter – Ausdruck seines Wunsches, nicht nur

□ 273 *Henri Matisse, ›Blauer Akt‹ (Nu bleu, Souvenir de Biskra), 1907, Öl auf Leinwand, 92 x 140 cm. The Baltimore Museum of Art, The Cone Collection, Maryland.*

□ 274 *Henri Matisse, ›Liegender Akt I‹ (Nu couché I), 1907, Bronze, 34 x 50 cm. The Museum of Modern Art, New York.*

☐ 275 *›Reliquiarfigur‹ (siehe Glossar),* FANG *(Gabun), Holz und Metall, Höhe 65 cm. The Metropolitan Museum of Art, M. C. Rockefeller Memorial Coll., New York. Ehemals Sammlung André Derain, Jacob Epstein.*

☐ 276 *›Ansicht des Ateliers von André Derain in Paris‹. Photographie um 1912–13.*

ein modernes Gegenstück zur antiken Venus, sondern, weit bedeutsamer wie wir sehen werden, eine Art afrikanischer Venus zu schaffen. Inwieweit diese Plastik für MATISSE die Bedeutung eines persönlichen Symbols hatte, ist daran zu erkennen, daß er sie seinen Bildern oft als prominentes Motiv einfügte.[83]

Der liegende Akt I war nicht direkt nach einem Modell, sondern aus der Erinnerung und der Vorstellung gestaltet, so daß MATISSE den menschlichen Körper viel freier nachbilden konnte. Einige Züge entsprechen den, wie er es nannte, »erfundenen Flächen und Formen« afrikanischer Plastik. Der ziemlich große Kopf, die kugelförmigen Brüste und das knollige Hinterteil erinnern an allgemeine Merkmale afrikanischer Plastik wie auch die starke Betonung der Masse der verschiedenen Körperpartien und die Art, wie diese Massen eher gegen als in Harmonie mit der Anatomie der Figur wirken. Obwohl die Pose der Figur europäischer Tradition folgt, entspricht sie in formaler Hinsicht durchaus dem imaginativen Nachbilden des menschlichen Körpers, das MATISSE an der afrikanischen Kunst so bewunderte.

MATISSE malte den *Blauen Akt,* als er schon einige Zeit am *Liegenden Akt I* gearbeitet hatte (der durch einen Unfall im Atelier fast zerstört wurde).[84] Seine Farbgebung gleicht der CÉZANNES, sie ist von gewollter Unbeholfenheit. Der *Blaue Akt* ist das erste wichtige Bild, das MATISSE nach dem Tode CÉZANNES im Oktober davor vollendete. Es ist eine Hommage an CÉZANNE und zugleich Ausdruck der Befreiung von dessen Konventionen, die MATISSE zum Teil seinem Studium der afrikanischen Plastik verdankt. In diesem Bild ist die Vereinfachung der Körperstruktur noch weiter getrieben als im *Liegenden Akt I.* Der Gebrauch afrikanisierender Stilelemente in der Formensprache ist noch stärker, obwohl wie bei fast allen Werken MATISSE' die fremden Einflüsse so gründlich und feinfühlig verarbeitet sind, daß sie nur bei genauem Hinsehen zu erkennen sind.

Die vielen Freiheiten, die sich MATISSE bei der Neugestaltung des weiblichen Körpers im *Blauen Akt* nahm, stammen letztlich von der afrikanischen Plastik. Der obere und untere Teil des Körpers etwa sind so sehr gegeneinander verdreht, daß sie zu verschiedenen Figuren gehören könnten. Der Körper ist von der Taille aufwärts frontal gesehen, während der untere Teil des Körpers auf den Bauch gedreht und von oben betrachtet erscheint. Verglichen mit den Freiheiten, die sich CÉZANNE bei der Wiedergabe des menschlichen Körpers erlaubte, sind die Verformungen hier extremer, anatomisch weniger motiviert und stehen damit afrikanischen Skulpturen viel näher.

Die vollen Brüste des *Blauen Akts,* der kurz geschorene, runde Kopf (ohne das fließende Haar oder den Nackenknoten, die typisch für europäische Vorbilder sind), schließlich der gelängte Körper, all dies erinnert an afrikanische Plastik. Auch das ausladende Gesäß ist für *BAULE-* und *FANG-*Skulpturen typisch, die damals in Paris sehr bekannt waren ☐ 272.[85] Im *Blauen Akt* schöpfte MATISSE die symbolischen Möglichkeiten weiter aus, die er seit einem Jahr erprobte. Das nordafrikanische Thema geht auf Erinnerungen an die Oase Biskra in Algerien zurück, zugleich ist die formale Prägung schwarz-

☐ 277 *Henri Matisse, ›Dekorative Figur‹ (Figure décorative), 1908, Bronze, Höhe 73 cm. Hirshhorn Museum and Sculpture Garden, Smithsonian Institution, Washington.*

☐ 278 *Henri Matisse, ›Zwei Negerinnen‹ (Deux négresses), 1908, Bronze, 47 x 26,5 x 19 cm. The Baltimore Museum of Art, The Cone Collection, Maryland.*

afrikanisch orientiert.[86] Das Gemälde ist keine wahrheitsgetreue Erinnerung an Geschehenes, sondern eher ein symbolisches Bild des starken Eindrucks der Afrika-Erlebnisse auf MATISSE' schöpferische Phantasie. Später erinnerte er sich an Biskra: » . . . eine herrliche Oase, ein lieblicher und erfrischender Ort inmitten der Wüste, mit sehr viel Wasser, das sich durch die Palmbäume schlängelte, durch die Gärten mit ihren grünen Blättern; ein überraschender Eindruck, wenn man aus der Wüste kommt.«[87] Das üppige Wachstum hatte MATISSE in Nordafrika tief beeindruckt. Der *Blaue Akt* wurde zur Verkörperung dieser Lebenskraft – ein bildliches Gegenstück zu André Gides begeisterten Worten über die Oase ein paar Jahre früher: »Diese afrikanische Erde . . . erwachend vom Winter, getränkt mit Wasser, sprudelnd von neuen Säften; sie jauchzte in diesem tobenden Frühling, dessen schallenden Widerhall auch ich in mir spürte.«[88]

MATISSE' Gemälde behält das Thema Erde im Frühling bei und hat eine außergewöhnliche Dynamik. Die Komposition beruht auf einer Reihe von Bögen, welche die Figur mit der umgebenden Landschaft verbinden. Sie unterstreicht so den unauflöslichen Kraftaustausch zwischen Frau und Erde. Neben dem Gleichklang der Bögen des Frauenkörpers mit der Landschaft hält der Farbauftrag das Bild zusammen: Die Figur strahlt Kraft aus in die Umgebung, die umgekehrt Armen, Brüsten, Gesäß und Beinen Resonanz verleiht. Auf keinen Betrachterstandpunkt beschränkt und auch in der Bewegung nicht fixiert, ist die Figur mit größerer Dynamik ausgestattet als es bei früheren Werken von MATISSE der Fall war. Die Wechselbeziehung zwischen Figur und Erde, zwischen Bild und Malfläche vermittelt einen Eindruck von Verdichtung und Auflösung

☐ 279 *Henri Matisse, ›Rückenakt III‹ (Nu de dos III), 1916–17, Bronze, 189 x 12 x 15 cm. The Museum of Modern Art, Mrs. Simon Guggenheim Fund, New York.*

des Raumes, gemahnt an den Fluß der Zeit: Die Realität wird als Wechselwirkung von Kraft und Materie wahrgenommen; die fruchtbare Fülle der Frau, zugleich aufgenommen und ausbrechend von der sie umgebenden Erde, scheint die Formen um sie zum Leben zu erwecken. Die Metaphern des Themas und seine formale Verkörperung sind untrennbar miteinander verbunden. Eher als in Derains *Badenden* sehen wir hier zum ersten Mal, »daß ein Werk den Einfluß Cézannes und der Negerkunst verbindet«.[89]

Der *Blaue Akt* war somit nicht nur ein wichtiger Schritt in Matisse' formaler Entwicklung, sondern auch in der Entwicklung seines symbolischen Repertoires. Das Gemälde weist auf die primitivistisch gestalteten Figurenbilder, etwa *Badende mit Schildkröte* und schließlich *Tanz,* voraus, mit denen sich Matisse in den nächsten Jahren beschäftigen sollte.[90]

Der *Blaue Akt* kündigte wie der *Liegende Akt I* mit seiner Beschwörung einer »afrikanischen« Venus auch eine neue Ästhetik in der Darstellung des weiblichen Körpers an. Die als Ausdrucksmittel eingesetzte »Häßlichkeit« des *Blauen Akts* war typisch für die neue Ästhetik der »afrikanischen« oder »barbarischen« Schönheit, über die sich später Gelett Burgess äußerte und auch Picasso, wenn wir dem Bericht Glauben schenken, daß er die afrikanische Figur für schöner erklärte als die Venus von Milo. Der *Blaue Akt* war unverkennbar als Affront gegen den Schönheitsbegriff der Salons konzipiert, damit nicht nur gegen Cabanels *Geburt der Venus,*[91] sondern auch gegen so bekannte Gemälde wie Ingres' *Grande Odalisque* und Manets *Olympia,* die gerade im Louvre nebeneinander gehängt worden waren.[92]

»Eine nackte Frau, häßlich, auf dunkelblauem Gras unter ein paar Palmen ausgestreckt«, schrieb Louis Vauxcelles über den *Blauen Akt*.[93] Matisse verteidigte das Bild in einer Erwiderung, deren Argumente von Braque und anderen aufgegriffen

☐ 280 *›Figürliche Verzierung eines Holzstabes‹, Luba (Zaire), Gesamthöhe 135 cm. Buffalo Museum of Science.*

☐ 281 *›Figürliche Verzierung eines Holzstabes‹, Baule (Elfenbeinküste), bemalt, Gesamthöhe 27 cm. Privatsammlung.*

werden sollten:[94] »Begegnete ich solch einer Frau auf der Straße, würde ich voll Schrecken davonlaufen. Ich erschaffe keine Frau, ich male ein Bild.«[95] Diese Vernachlässigung des Bildgegenstandes zugunsten des Formalen gilt auch für MATISSE' Wertschätzung afrikanischer Plastik mit ihren »erfundenen Flächen und Proportionen«. MAX WEBER erinnerte sich, wie MATISSE ungefähr ein Jahr später seinen Studenten afrikanische Stücke aus seiner Sammlung zeigte: »Er pflegte eine Figur in die Hand zu nehmen und erklärte uns die unverkennbaren und ureigensten plastischen Vorzüge, die wundervolle Kunstfertigkeit, das großartige Gefühl für die Proportionen, die feine, belebte Formfülle und die Ausgewogenheit darin.«[96]

Die wichtigsten Reaktionen auf den *Blauen Akt* kamen nicht von den Kritikern, sondern von den Malern.[97] Bei der Herbstausstellung der Indépendants von 1907 war der Einfluß von CÉZANNE stark spürbar, nur MATISSE ging mit seinem *Blauen Akt* über eine bloße Imitation CÉZANNES hinaus. Besonders PICASSO war von dem Bild tief beeindruckt. Möglicherweise wurden seine eigenen Gedanken, aus denen sich später die *Demoiselles d'Avignon* entwickelten, hiervon nachhaltiger angeregt als durch die *Lebensfreude*, mit der er ja wirklich wetteiferte, oder DERAINS *Badenden*, die – eine trockene Arbeit im Stil CÉZANNES – gleichfalls 1907 ausgestellt waren. PICASSO soll teils durch MATISSE' *Lebensfreude* im Frühling 1907 dazu angeregt worden sein, eine große mehrfigurige Komposition zu malen. Er hatte das Bild schon begonnen, und so interessierte ihn der *Blaue Akt* sicherlich viel mehr: ihr kräftiger Pinselstrich, ihre vielen Blickpunkte, der dynamische Raum und die heftigen anatomischen Verdrehungen, schließlich ihre »Häßlichkeit«. Der Primitivismus des »afrikanischen« Bildes *Der blaue Akt* hat bestimmt der Wirkung mehr entsprochen, die PICASSO in seinen Bildern Anfang 1907 anstrebte. Erst als MATISSE afrikanische Formen bzw. die Lehren CÉZANNES auswertete, wandte sie schließlich auch PICASSO – dann aber um so radikaler – in seiner Kunst an. Neben anderen Einflüssen bewogen die absichtliche Roheit und der Primitivismus des *Blauen Akts* PICASSO, rauher und kühner zu arbeiten als je zuvor.[98] Das Bild mag für PICASSO auch ein Anlaß gewesen sein, noch einmal die afrikanische Plastik im Trocadéro zu betrachten; im Anschluß daran malte er die zwei sogenannten »afrikanischen« Figuren auf der rechten Seite der *Demoiselles* neu.[99]

Da PICASSO afrikanische Quellen viel direkter als MATISSE gebrauchte und ihm radikalere und abstraktere afrikanische Objekte als Anregung dienten, sieht es so aus, als habe er von

□ 282 *Henri Matisse, ›Jeannette V‹ (Tête de Jeannette V), 1916, Bronze, 58 x 20 x 29 cm. Art Gallery of Ontario, Toronto.*

□ 283 *Henri Matisse, ›Jeannette V‹ (Profilansicht), siehe* □ *282.*

□ 284 *›Holzmaske‹*, BANGWA *(Kamerun), Höhe 20 cm. Privatsammlung. Ehemals Sammlung Tristan Tzara.*

nun an die führende Rolle bei der »Afrikanisierung« der französischen Malerei übernommen. MATISSE machte sich jedoch auch weiterhin primitive Formen und ihre strukturellen Konzepte in seiner Malerei und Plastik nutzbar. Da aber seine Kunst nach wie vor auf der Wahrnehmung gründete, wurden diese Quellen und andere konzeptionelle Einflüsse oft so stark integriert, daß sie in ihrer abgeschwächten Form oft nur schwer erkennbar sind.

Im Dezember 1907 veröffentlichte Guillaume Apollinaire einen Artikel über MATISSE, in dem er auf dessen Interesse an exotischer Kunst hinwies, einschließlich »der afrikanischen Negerstatuen, gemäß den Leidenschaften gestaltet, die ihre Schöpfer inspirierten . . .« Weiter sagte er: »Obwohl Matisse wißbegierig das Künstlertum aller menschlichen Rassen kennen wollte, bleibt er letztlich dem europäischen Schönheitsbegriff verbunden.«[100] Hieraus wurde die Bestätigung abgeleitet, MATISSE habe »wenig, wenn überhaupt etwas aus der afrikanischen Kunst gelernt«.[101] In Wahrheit war Ende 1907 die ästhetische Revolution, bei der die afrikanische Kunst und MATISSE eine bedeutende Rolle spielten, auf dem besten Wege, in den »europäischen Schönheitssinn« Eingang zu finden, zumindest unter vielen avantgardistischen Künstlern. Ende des folgenden Jahres war der Einfluß der Stammeskunst ziemlich weit verbreitet, der Einfluß CÉZANNES bei den progressiven Malern überall anzutreffen. Die Stammesplastik gehörte zum Repertoire der Formen und Ideen, mit denen ernsthafte Künstler arbeiteten.

Seit 1907 bis zum Ende des Ersten Weltkrieges machten PICASSO und BRANCUSI den radikalsten und phantasievollsten Gebrauch eingeborener Werke. Viele der einstigen Fauvisten waren weiterhin ernste Sammler primitiver Kunst, die jedoch kaum eine erkennbare Wirkung auf ihr Werk hatte. VLAMINCK blieb ein leidenschaftlicher Sammler der afrikanischen Kunst,

□ 285 *›Weibliche Sitzfigur‹*, BAMBARA *(Mali), Holz, Höhe 61 cm. Privatsammlung, Frankreich. Ehemals Sammlung Henri Matisse.*

□ 286 *Henri Matisse, ›Madame Matisse‹, Ausschnitt von* □ *256.*

□ 287 *›Maske‹, Shira-Punu (Gabun), bemaltes Holz, Höhe 31 cm. Sammlung Ernst Winizki, Zürich.*

widmete aber sein restliches Leben fast ganz dem Malen dramatischer Landschaften. Auch DERAIN sammelte weiter und behielt einige seiner afrikanischen Objekte bis an sein Lebensende. Mit Ausnahme einiger mehr oder weniger wörtlicher Zitate in seinen Bildern, auf die Jean Laude hinwies, zog er später ebenfalls wenig Nutzen aus der afrikanischen Kunst.[102]

Wieder einmal war MATISSE eine Ausnahme. Der große Kopf und die kugelförmigen Brüste seiner *Figure décorative* aus dem Jahr 1908 □ 277 sind von ihrer Tendenz her »afrikanisierend«; noch eindeutiger die *Zwei Negerinnen* □ 278, die nach einem Zeitschriftenphoto zweier *TUAREG*-Mädchen entstanden.[103] Sicher bewog die ansprechende Sinnlichkeit der Mädchen MATISSE, das Photo als Vorlage zu wählen. Diese Arbeitsweise entsprach seinem damaligen Wunsch, Photographien ins Dreidimensionale zu übertragen. Er drehte das in seiner Malerei längst angewandte Verfahren, aus dem Drei- ins Zweidimensionale zu gelangen, um, damit er auch in der Plastik mehr Abstand von der Natur gewinnen konnte. Die Skulpturen *Kniender Akt,* 1908, und *La serpentine,* 1909, entstanden nach recht gewöhnlichen Photos von Künstlermodellen aus Publikationen wie *Le nue esthétique.*[104] Die Photographie der zwei *TUAREG*-Mädchen wählte MATISSE wahrscheinlich auch deshalb, um das »Negerhafte« seiner Plastik zu verstärken.

Die *Zwei Negerinnen* ist die einzige mehrfigurige Plastik von MATISSE. Sie ist wohl teilweise von PICASSOS sehr skulpturaler Darstellung *Zwei Akte,* 1906, beeinflußt □ 315, die sich jedoch eher von iberischer als afrikanischer Kunst herleitet. Auch von afrikanischer Plastik, die das Kopfende von Stäben bekrönt und manchmal zwei fast identische, einander zugewandte weibliche Figuren zeigt, mag sie angeregt worden sein. *LUBA*-Plastik wie das hier abgebildete Beispiel □ 280 war allerdings wahrscheinlich zu dieser Zeit in Paris nicht zu sehen. Obwohl die Haltungen der *Zwei Negerinnen* recht genau der Photographie folgen, ist der Gesamteindruck völlig verändert. Die beiden Figuren erinnern, hauptsächlich im Verhältnis von Körper und Gesäß, in Brüsten und Frisuren, stark an afrikanische Werke, besonders an *BAULE*-Plastik □ 272.

Beim letzten Kopf der Jeannette-Serie, der *Jeannette v* □ 282, 283, tritt der afrikanische Einfluß noch deutlicher zutage. *Jeannette v* wird im allgemeinen zwischen 1910 und 1913 datiert, tatsächlich aber ist sie im Jahre 1916 entstanden.[105] Diesem radikalsten Kopf der Serie diente sehr wahrscheinlich die erlesene Sitzfigur der *BAMBARA* □ 285 als Anregung. MATISSE hatte sie unlängst erworben.[106] Sie ist auf dem Kaminsims der linken Tafel des Triptychons *Drei Schwestern* von 1916–17, Barnes Foundation, zu sehen. Des melancholischen

Charmes der ersten drei Jeannette-Köpfe und des Esprits des vierten beraubt, vermittelt *Jeannette v* den außergewöhnlichen Eindruck psychologischer Entblößung. Das primitive, geradezu urtümliche Wesen des Stücks ist seinem afrikanischen Prototyp ebenbürtig.

Der *Rückenakt III* □ 279, ungefähr zur selben Zeit wie *Jeannette v* entstanden, zeigt einen weitläufigeren afrikanischen Einfluß. Hier und in den gleichzeitig ausgeführten *Badenden am Fluß*[107] mag die afrikanische Kunst MATISSE zu einer eigenständigen Position gegenüber dem Kubismus, der die Körperstruktur aufbricht, verholfen haben. Diese Plastik ist ein Ergebnis interessanter stilistischer Versuche, in denen MATISSE zwischen 1913 und 1917 eine neuartige Synthese von Stammesformen und Elementen im Sinne CÉZANNES entwikkelt, um auf die Erneuerung der Kubisten einzugehen und ihnen gleichzeitig zu widerstehen. Im Vergleich zu den zwei früheren Rückenreliefs ist die Haltung der Figur *Rückenakt III* eher architektonisch als anatomisch. Die Körperteile sind eher durch lineare und ebene Rhythmen als durch Muskulatur verbunden, die Schwerkraft ist kaum zu spüren. Die Größe des Kopfes und die starke Betonung der Vertikalen durch das Rückgrat sind ebenfalls Reflexe der afrikanischen Plastik. Dieses Werk ist wohl die feinfühligste Übertragung bildhauerischer Prinzipien der afrikanischen Kunst in die eigene Plastik von MATISSE.

Auch in seiner Malerei hielt die Wirkung afrikanischer Formen im Jahrzehnt nach der Entdeckung der primitiven Kunst an. In einigen Fällen, so bei der stehenden Figur der beiden Fassungen von *Luxus,* 1907, gleichen etwa die Verhältnisse zwischen Oberkörper, gelängtem Hals und großem Kopf den allgemeinen Proportionen afrikanischer Plastik. Wenn sich

⊏ 288 *›Reliquiarkopf‹,* FANG *(Gabun), Holz. Höhe 35 cm. Privatsammlung. Ehemals Sammlung Maurice de Vlaminck.*

◁ ◁ □ 289
›Reliquiarfigur‹, FANG *(Gabun), Holz und andere Materialien, Höhe 25,5 cm. Privatsammlung, Paris.*

◁ ⊏ 290
Henri Matisse, ›Sitzende‹ (Femme assise), 1915, Öl auf Leinwand, 69 x 35 cm. Privatsammlung.

☐ 291 *Henri Matisse, ›Der Messerwerfer‹ (Le lanceur de couteaux), Ausschnitt, aus der Folge ›Jazz‹, 1947, Gouacheschnitt, 40,5 x 65 cm. The Museum of Modern Art, New York, Geschenk des Künstlers.*

MATISSE in den folgenden Jahren mit dem menschlichen Körper beschäftigte, war die Idee der »erfundenen Flächen und Proportionen« aus seinem Schaffen nicht mehr wegzudenken. In einigen Werken zitierte er sogar ganz bestimmte Formen der afrikanischen Kunst.

Das Gesicht der *Madame Matisse,* des Portraits seiner Frau aus dem Jahre 1913 ☐ 286, erinnert an Gabun-Masken. André Salmon lag nicht falsch mit der Kritik, das Gesicht sehe aus wie »eine Holzmaske, kreidebeschmiert . . . ein Wesen aus einem Alptraum«.[108] Die Symmetrie und Vereinfachung der Gesichtszüge, das maskenhafte Aussehen der Augen und sogar die Gestaltung von Haaren und Hut erinnern an die *FANG*- und kreideweißen *SHIRA-PUNU*-Masken aus Gabun ☐ 287, 288, die nach dem Glauben der Eingeborenen Geister und Gespenster verkörpern.

Die bisher unveröffentlichte *Sitzende* ☐ 290,[109] die auf 1915 datierbar ist, steht meines Erachtens ebenfalls gabunischer Kunst nahe – hier den Figuren der *FANG,* denen sie in vielen Einzelheiten ähnelt ☐ 289. Die Gestaltung des Kopfes und der Frisur, des Halses, der Schultern, der Brüste, von Armen und Oberkörper ähnelt so sehr dem Stil der *FANG,* daß dieses Gemälde wie kein zweites von MATISSE afrikanischer Kunst verpflichtet ist. Durch den Gegensatz zwischen der Strenge des Frauenkörpers und dem Reiz des Strumpfbandes auf ihrem Schenkel wirkt die Frau zugleich wie ein heidnisches Götzenbild und eine Kokotte, eine wunderbar vieldeutige Wirkung.

Wenn wir uns dem Spätwerk MATISSE' zuwenden, erkennen wir, daß sich der Künstler in den Ausschneidebildern, der letzten großen Synthese seiner Kunst, wiederum von afrikanischen Formen und Gegenständen anregen ließ. In einem herrlichen Bildspiel nimmt die Figur des *Messerwerfers* aus *Jazz* ☐ 291 eine Gestalt an, die an ein afrikanisches Wurfmesser erinnert. Eines der anspruchsvollsten der großen Ausschneidebilder, *Die Negerin* ☐ 299, wurde von einer Negerin, der Tänzerin Josephine Baker, angeregt und kennt zudem die Formensprache der afrikanischen Plastik. So steigert sich die »négritude« von Form und Thema gegenseitig – ähnlich wie bei dem Bild *Zwei Negerinnen* von 1908. In anderen Ausschneidebildern werden afrikanische Masken mehr oder weniger direkt dargestellt.[110] Während aber in MATISSE' früheren Bildern und Skulpturen primitive Anregungen hauptsächlich aus Afrika kamen, wird in den Ausschneidebildern auch der Einfluß ozeanischer Kunst erkennbar.

Die Anklänge ozeanischer Kunst in den »papier découpés« bilden einen interessanten Gegensatz zu MATISSE' früherem Gebrauch afrikanischer Formen. Seine Malerei und Plastik lassen vor allem anhand der Darstellung des menschlichen Körpers erkennen, was er aus der afrikanischen Kunst gelernt hat. In den Ausschneidebildern aus der Mitte der 40er Jahre scheinen ihm dekorative Formen Melanesiens zur Schaffung eines abstrakten, dematerialisierten Raumes verholfen zu haben, den ein die ganze Fläche bedeckendes Muster wiederholter Formen kennzeichnet. Der abstrakte Raum dieser »papiers découpés«, deren Motive häufig aus seinen Erinnerungen an die Südsee schöpften, unterscheidet sich weitgehend von der Raumauffassung in seiner Malerei.

☐ 292 *›Wurfmesser‹, ZANDE (Zaire), Eisen, Höhe 47,5 cm. Sammlung N. und S. Dinhofer, New York.*

□ 293 *Henri Matisse, ›Komposition grüner Hintergrund‹, 1947, Gouacheschnitt, 105 x 41 cm. Privatsammlung.*

□ 294 *›Schild‹, ASMAT (Westirian), bemaltes Holz und Fasern, Höhe 193 cm. Sammlung Serge Brignoni, Bern.*

□ 295 *›Maske‹*, NAMAU, *Golfprovinz (Papua-Neuguinea), bemalte Rinde, Stoff und Schilfrohr, Höhe 244 cm. National Museum of Ireland, Dublin.*

□ 296 *Henri Matisse, Umschlagentwurf für Baudelaires „Les Fleures du mal", 1947, Feder und Tusche, 27 x 21 cm. Eremitage, Leningrad.*

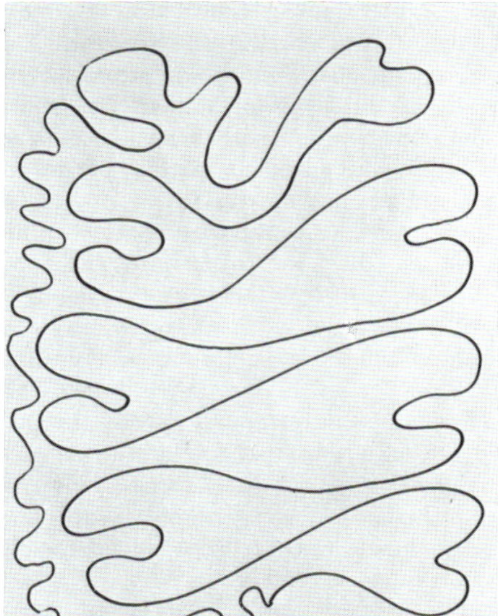

□ 297 *Henri Matisse, ›Ozeanien – der Himmel‹ (Océanie – le ciel), 1946, Siebdruck, 165 x 380 cm. Musée National d'Art Moderne, Centre National d'Art et de Culture Georges Pompidou, Paris.*

□ 298 *›Tapa‹ (siehe Glossar), Sentani-See (Westirian), bemalter Baststoff, Höhe 88 cm. Privatsammlung. Ehemals Sammlung Henri Matisse.*

MATISSE besuchte Tahiti im Jahre 1930, zu einer Zeit, als in seinem Leben und seiner Kunst vieles im Umbruch war. Von den Erfahrungen in Tahiti übertrug er nur wenig unmittelbar auf seine Kunst. Er war jedoch tief beeindruckt vom Licht, den Farben, dem üppigen Wachstum und dem Reichtum des Meeres,[111] und das Gedächtnis daran erhielt er sich bis an sein Lebensende. Mitte der 40er Jahre suchte er seine Eindrücke von der ozeanischen Flora und Fauna mit Elementen ozeanischer Dekorationskunst zu verbinden – so etwa in den Flächenmustern und dem abstrakten Raum der zwei *Ozeanien*–Kompositionen, die er 1946 als Entwürfe für Wandbehänge schuf.[112] Diese abstrakte, dekorative Tendenz wurde in einigen späteren Ausschneidebildern noch stärker, deren geschwungene Muster deutlich von melanesischen Objekten angeregt sind. Dies wird besonders in den Arbeiten um das Jahr 1947 deutlich, die oft an die Verzierungen melanesischer Schilde und Masken erinnern □ 294, 295.[113]

Wie die Erfahrungen mit der afrikanischen Kunst MATISSE 1906 halfen, Ideen seiner Bildwelt neue Gestalt zu verleihen, so scheint ihm das Vorbild ozeanischer Kunst geholfen zu haben, rund 40 Jahre später eine weitere Synthese zu finden. Damals wie zur Zeit seiner früheren »Entdeckungen« bot die Stammeskunst neue und einzigartige Lösungen für die formalen und expressiven Probleme, mit denen er sich auseinandersetzte.

Im Hinblick auf die Frühzeit der Entdeckung afrikanischer Kunst äußerte Gertrude Stein sehr scharfsinnig, daß PICASSO und MATISSE von der afrikanischen Kunst auf unterschiedliche Weise angezogen wurden: PICASSO »mehr durch seine Vision als durch seine Imagination« und MATISSE »mehr durch seine Imagination als durch seine Vision«.[114] Es sei dahingestellt, ob sich diese Deutung bei sorgfältiger Prüfung halten läßt. Wahr ist, daß MATISSE' Bildphantasie durch die Berührung mit afrikanischer und ozeanischer Kunst zutiefst beeinflußt wurde. Ihr Vorbild und ihre Anregung begleiteten ihn bis an das Ende seines Lebens.

Anmerkungen

Dieser Aufsatz ist Douglas F. Fraser gewidmet, der über 20 Jahre meine Forschungen über primitive Kunst förderte.

1. Bisherige Forschungsergebnisse zu diesem Thema bei Goldwater, R., *Primitivism in Modern Art,* New York 1967, besonders S. 86–103; Fraser, D. F., »The Discovery of Primitiv Art« in *Art Yearbook 1,* New York 1957, S. 119–33; Fry, E., *Cubism,* New York und Toronto 1966, S. 47–48; Laude, J., *La peinture française (1905–1914) et l'art nègre,* Paris 1968, besonders S. 83–239; Oppler, E. G., *Fauvism Reexamined,* New York und London 1976, S. 125–78; Wentinck, C., *Modern Art and Primitive Art,* Oxford 1979; Wilkinson, A. G., *Gauguin to Moore: Primitivism in Modern Sculpture,* Toronto 1981. In den folgenden Anmerkungen werden die Abhandlungen nicht mehr mit dem vollen Titel angegeben, sondern nur noch mit dem Namen des Autors gekennzeichnet.

2. Baudelaire hat in seinem Aufsatz über die Herbstausstellung von 1846 geschrieben: »Der Ursprung der Plastik hat sich im Dunkel der Zeiten verloren, auch in der karibischen Kunst. Wir können aber beobachten, daß alle Rassen mit großer Kunstfertigkeit Fetische schnitzten, lange bevor sie die Malerei entdeckten . . .«, aus: Mayne, J., *Art in Paris, 1845–1862: Salons and Other Exhibitions Reviewed by Charles Baudelaire«,* London und New York 1965, S. 111.

3. In Paris hatte afrikanische Kunst von Anfang an mehr Einfluß genommen als die ozeanische, zum einen wegen ihrer stärkeren plastischen Wirkung, zum anderen besaß Frankreich ja grosse Kolonien in Afrika. Donne, J. B., fand heraus (»African Art and Paris Studios, 1905–20«, in Greenlagh, M. und Megaw, V. [Hrsg.], *Art and Society,* New York 1978, S. 105–20), daß beinahe alle primitiven Objekte, die französische Künstler damals sammelten, aus französischen Territorien stammten. Faure, E., widmete im 2. Band seiner *Histoire de l'art, L'art médiéval,* Paris 1911 – worin erstmals in einer allgemeinen Kunstgeschichte der primitiven Kunst ein größerer Raum eingeräumt wurde – der afrikanischen Kunst weit mehr Aufmerksamkeit als der ozeanischen. Seine Betrachtung der ozeanischen Kunst beschränkte sich auf Polynesien (wo Frankreich Kolonien besaß), dessen Kunst größere plastische Ausstrahlung besaß als melanesische.

4. Siehe Firth, R., »The Social Framework of Primitive Art« in *Elements of Social Organisation,* Boston 1951, S. 175.

5. Der scheinbare Eindruck von Schwerelosigkeit bei afrikanischer Kunst stellte die europäischen Künstler vor große Probleme, da europäische Tradition wie der perspektivisch-illusionistische Raum und die auf Schwerkraft bezogenen Figuren so sehr miteinander verwoben waren. In Bildern wie Picassos *Akt* von 1907 (Daix, P., und Rosselet, J., *Picasso: The Cubist Years,* 1907–1916, Boston 1979, Nr. 40) werden typisch afrikanische Merkmale auf eine Figur übertragen, die wie das Modell für eine Akademiezeichnung anmutet. Auch im *Akt mit erhobenen Armen* (ebenda, Nr. 53), bei dem das Standmotiv weniger natürlich ist, spürt man noch Erdenschwere, die auch in einigen primitivistischen Plastiken Picassos von 1907 ähnlich zu beobachten ist (siehe auch Wilkinson, S. 103 und 109, und Penrose, R., *The Sculpture of Picasso,* New York 1967, S. 55). Darin besteht auch der Unterschied zu echter Stammeskunst.

6. Burgess, G., »The Wild Men of Paris« in *Architectural Record,* Mai 1910, S. 406.

7. Über die evolutionären Vorurteile in frühen Untersuchungen zur primitiven Kunst siehe Goldwater, S. 15–22, und Fraser, S. 119–20. Selbst Faure hegte in seinem sonst positiv zu beurteilenden Kapitel »Les Tropiques« in *L'art médiéval* ein solches Vorurteil: »Um eine primitive Kunst zu finden, die ihre Ursprünglichkeit bewahrt hat und doch neue, starke Gefühle mitteilen kann . . . müssen wir zu Völkern gehen, die primitiv geblieben sind.« (*Medieval Art,* Übersetzt von Pach, W., Garden City 1937, S. 166). Noch 1920 erklärte Vlaminck, afrikanische Kunst sei »die einzige, die man betrachten kann, ohne überschüttet zu werden mit Erklärungen und Lobpreisungen einer Literatur, die die Kunst der Gegenwart, der Vergangenheit, der Zukunft interpretiert«, und er betonte ihren »jungfräulichen« Wert (»Opinions sur l'art nègre« in *Action,* 3, April 1920, S. 26).

8. Das wachsende Interesse an nicht-naturalistischen Kunstrichtungen belegen die großen Ausstellungen im Paris jener Jahre, als sich der Fauvismus entwickelte: Islamische Kunst im Louvre 1903; Französische Primitive im Louvre 1904; Japanische Kunst im Salon d'Automne 1905; Alt-Iberische Kunst im Louvre 1906; Russische Kunst im Salon d'Automne 1906 mit mehr als 36 Ikonen (von Diaghilev organisiert). Die in solcher Kunst am meisten bewunderten Stilelemente waren gerade jene, die in der Folgezeit auch von der Avantgarde hervorgehoben werden sollten. Zugleich waren diese Stilelemente besonders gewürdigten Momenten in Werken bedeutender Neoimpressionisten ähnlich, die zu dieser Zeit ebenfalls in großen Ausstellungen gezeigt wurden: Van Gogh im Salon des Indépendants 1905; Gauguin in der Galerie Vollard 1903 und im Salon d'Automne 1906; Cézanne im Salon d'Automne von 1904 (nur fünf Bilder, aber drei »Badende« waren dabei) und 1907.

Die gemeinsamen Gestaltungsgrundlagen der exotischen Kunst, des Werks Gauguins und bis zu einem gewissen Grade auch Seurats traten in den ersten Jahren des 20. Jahrhunderts immer deutlicher zutage, und man wandte für diese oft ähnliche Kriterien an. Georges Lafenestre etwa schrieb in seiner Einführung zum Katalog der großen Primitiven-Ausstellung von 1904 über die »Echtheit des Gefühls« bei den frühen französischen Künstlern und ihre Fähigkeit, Reales mit Idealem zu verbinden (*Exposition des primitifs français au Palais du Louvre . . .,* Paris 1904, S. XVIII). Selbst ihre »Fehler« und »Plumpheiten« seien zu verzeihen wegen des »echten Ausdrucks eines reinen Gefühls« (ebenda S. XIX) – eine Formulierung, derer man sich auch zur Verteidigung von Van Gogh, Gauguin oder Cézanne hätte bedient haben können.

Im Sommer 1904 schrieb der neoimpressionistische Maler Henri-Edmond Cross an Charles Angrand über die französischen Primitiven. Nach einem Lob über Manet äußerte er: »Wenn ich Ihnen sage, ich sei von einer Kunst überwältigt gewesen – wenn nicht sogar mehr –, die das völlig Gegenteil [von Manets Kunst] darstellt, so werden Sie in mir den ewigen Widerstreit erkennen. Heute morgen ging ich in die Ausstellung der französischen Primitiven . . . Welch herrliche und erregende Kunst! Hier ist das so schwierige Problem gelöst, das Reale ins Imaginäre zu übertragen, und mit welch einfachen Mitteln: Die Verbindung fröhlicher und bunter Farben zu einer schönen Einheit reicht aus, um die prächtigsten Harmonien zu bezeugen« (Brief vom 7. Juli 1904, zitiert bei Bock, C. C., *Henri Matisse and Neo-Impressionism, 1898–1908,* Ann Arbor 1981, S. 67).

9. Siehe die Einführung von William Rubin im vorliegenden Buch, S. 16ff., und Varnedoes Aufsatz über Gauguin, S. 186ff.

10. Cladel, J., *Maillol, sa vie, son œuvre,* Paris 1937, zitiert im Katalog der Ausstellung »Arts primitifs dans les ateliers d'artistes«, Paris, Musée de l'Homme, 1967.

11. Siehe auch Derains Brief an Vlaminck aus dem Jahr 1906, von dem später noch zu sprechen sein wird, S. 223.

12. Über die Erinnerungen von Matisse an diese Zeit siehe Flam, J. D., *Matisse on Art,* London 1973, S. 55, 102, 126.

13. Interessanterweise brachte Vlaminck die Aneignung von Stammesformen später mit Künstlern in Verbindung, die zu »schwach waren, um sich in der Sprache ihrer Väter verständlich zu machen . . .« (*Poliment,* Paris 1931, S. 130). Demgegenüber äußerte Matisse 1945, ein Künstler könne, »um sich vor dem Bann des Werkes seines unmittelbaren Vorläufers, den er bewundert, zu schützen . . . in den Werken unterschiedlicher Zivilisationen nach neuen Quellen der Inspiration suchen, die seinen Neigungen entsprechen« (Flam, *Matisse on Art,* S. 102).

14. Siehe Wentinck, C., S. 16–17.

15. Vlamincks Berichte in *Tournant dangereux: Souvenirs de ma vie,* Paris 1929, S. 88–89; *Poliment,* S. 129–30; *Portraits avant décès,* Paris 1943, S. 105–07 – sein ausführlichster Bericht, auf dem das Folgende zum größten Teil beruht.

16. In *Poliment* und *Tournant dangereux* sind nur zwei Stücke erwähnt.

17. *Portraits avant décès,* S. 107, und ein Brief an M. A. Leblond aus dem Jahr 1944 (zitiert bei Laude, S. 104).

18. Ebenda, S. 106.

19. Ebenda; siehe auch Laude, S. 104.

20. Siehe Laude, S. 100–106.

◁ □ 299 *Henri Matisse, ›Die Negerin‹ (La négresse), Ausschnitt, 1952, Gouacheschnitt, 454 x 623 cm. National Gallery of Art, Ailsa Mellon Bruce Fund, Washington.*

□ 300 *Objekte aus dem Besitz von Henri Matisse während seines Aufenthaltes im Hôtel Régina, Nizza. Die Aufnahme entstand nach dem Tod des Künstlers.*

21. »De Montmartre au Quartier Latin« in *Mémoires d'une autre vie,* Genf 1942, S. 209–210.

22. Laude, S. 103.

23. In *Portraits avant décès,* S. 106, spricht Vlaminck von »Ausdruck instinktiver Kunst«. William Rubin hat in einem Gespräch (am 17.9.1983) dargelegt, daß Vlamincks Erfahrung in einem interessanten Gegensatz zu dem Picassos stand: Vlaminck war von afrikanischer Kunst nicht sonderlich beeindruckt, bis er sie *außerhalb* eines Museums sah, Picasso hatte ihre eigentliche Wirkung nicht voll erfaßt, bis er sie *in* einem Museum sah.

24. Guillaume Apollinaire hatte schon 1912 bemerkt, daß Vlaminck »in diesen grotesken und stark mystischen Werken zweifellos Analogien zu Schnitzereien und Plastiken Gauguins sah«. Gauguin selbst habe sich anregen lassen von »bretonischen Kreuzigungsgruppen oder wilden Plastiken Ozeaniens, zu denen er Zuflucht vor der europäischen Zivilisation genommen hatte« (»Art et curiosité, les commencements du cubisme« in *Le Temps,* 14. Oktober 1912; neuerlich bei Apollinaire, *Chroniques d'art, 1902–1918,* Paris 1960, S. 264).

25. *Tournant dangereux,* S. 88; *Portraits avant décès,* S. 106. Siehe Elderfield, E., *The ›Wild Beast‹: Fauvism and Its Affinities,* New York 1976, S. 109.

26. *Portraits avant décès,* S. 106.

27. *Tournant dangereux,* S. 88-89. Goldwater erklärt, S. 86: »Nach dem Gesamtzusammenhang zu urteilen, können wir sie auf das Jahr 1904 datieren, sicher nicht vor 1903.«

28. *Poliment,* S. 129–130.

29. *Portraits avant décès,* S. 105–107.

30. Oppler, S. 155, Anm. 3.

31. Siehe Vlamincks Berichte über Derains Kauf, Anm. 17.

32. Siehe Anm. 47.

33. Siehe Laude, S. 101–103.

34. Es gibt keine Spuren afrikanischer Einflüsse in Derains Malerei und Plastik vor dem Herbst 1906.

35. 1906 war der Salon d'Automne vom 6. Oktober bis zum 15. November geöffnet.

36. *Lettres à Vlaminck,* Paris 1955, S. 196–197. Der Brief wurde in London, Holland Park, Blenheim Crescent 65, abgeschickt.

37. Ebenda, S. 197.

38. Goldwater, S. 89.

39. Laude, S. 176. Frau Oppler sagt (S. 159, Anm. 2), der Brief »muß auf 1906, nicht 1910, datiert werden«, erwähnt aber nicht, warum sie 1907 ausschließt.

40. Siehe Oppler, S. 156.

41. »Lettres à Vlaminck«, S. 63.

42. Ebenda, S. 196.

43. Goldwater sagt (S. 87), Matisse habe »vielleicht schon 1904, sicherlich aber vor 1906« begonnen, afrikanische Plastik zu sammeln, aber ich habe keinen Beweis für diesen Ausspruch gefunden. Alfred F. Barr jr. schreibt im Zusammenhang mit der Plastik »Zwei Negerinnen« von 1908, Matisse habe damals »seit zwei oder drei Jahren« afrikanische Negerplastik gesammelt, belegt aber diese Behauptung nicht (*Matisse: His Art and His Public,* New York 1951, S. 159).

44. Ein ähnliches Phänomen hatte es in der Beziehung Matisse – Cézanne gegeben. Entgegen allen Behauptungen der Literatur über Matisse wissen wir heute, daß er schon 1895 Bilder von Cézanne gesehen hatte, aber erst vier oder fünf Jahre später Anregungen daraus zog. Matisse erwähnte dies in einem Interview mit Pierre Courthion im Jahre 1942, von dem mir Herr Courthion am 11. Dezember 1979 freundlicherweise berichtete. Matisse reagierte ähnlich verspätet auf islamische Kunst, die er 1903 in der Ausstellung im Louvre gesehen hatte.

45. *The Autobiography of Alice B. Toklas,* New York 1961, S. 63. Siehe auch Stein, *Picasso,* London 1938, S. 22: »Nach seiner Rückkehr von . . . Gosol . . . lernte er Matisse kennen, der ihn mit afrikanischer Plastik bekannt machte.«

46. »Le Père Sauvage«, auch bekannt als *»le négrier de la rue de Rennes«,* war Emile Heyman, dem ein Geschäft mit Namen »Au Vieux Rouet« gehörte. Siehe auch Kahnweiler, D. H., *Juan Gris, sa vie, son œuvre,* Paris 1946, S. 155–156, und Laude, S. 102.

47. So teilte mir Pierre Courthion mit (siehe Anm. 44). Eine schlecht übersetzte und auch sonst recht ungenaue Version gibt Wentinck, S. 17. In einer »Aussage« von 1951, zusammengestellt von Tériade, erwähnt Matisse, er habe »für ein paar Francs« einen afrikanischen Kopf gekauft (Siehe Flam, *Matisse on Art,* S. 134). Tériade hat diese Aussage willkürlich aus früheren Berichten zusammengeschrieben (»Matisse Speaks« in *Art News,* Vol. 58, Nov. 1951, S. 40–71), seine Genauigkeit ist in manchen Punkten recht fragwürdig.

48. Siehe Malraux, A., *Picasso's Mask,* New York 1976, S. 10–11.

49. »German Expressionism and Primitive Art« in *Burlington Magazine,* CX, April 1968, S. 191–192. Apollinaire hat in Wirklichkeit nicht darauf »hingewiesen«, sondern nur geschrieben, Matisse »bleibt bei allem dem europäischen Schönheitssinn verpflichtet« (»Henri Matisse« in *La Phalange,* Dezember 1907, übersetzt in Barr, *Matisse: His Art and His Public,* S. 102). Auch Kahnweiler meinte, daß Matisse nicht von afrikanischer Kunst beeinflußt wurde (»L'art nègre et le cubisme« in *Confessions esthétiques,* Paris 1963, S. 223).

50. Unveröffentlichter Aufsatz über Derains Plastik, 1969, S. 2. Ich möchte Herrn Johnson, der mir Einsicht in den Aufsatz gewährte, und William Rubin für diesen Hinweis danken.

51. Interview von Edward F. Fry am 26. März 1963 (siehe auch Fry, »Cubism 1907–1908: An Early Eyewitness Account« in *Art Bulletin,* XLVIII, März 1966, S. 73 und Anm. 59).

52. Abb. bei Elderfield, *The ›Wild Beasts‹,* S. 111.

53. Abb. ebenda; siehe auch Johnson, S. 8–9, und Wilkinson, S. 124.

54. Siehe Johnson, S. 5, wo eine direkte Verbindung festgestellt wird. Burgess, »The Wild Men of Paris«, zitiert bei Elderfield, *The ›Wild Beasts‹,* S. 111; Laude, S. 180 und Wilkinson, S. 124, deuten eine Verwandtschaft an.

55. Johnson, S. 5.

56. Ebenda.

57. »The Wild Men of Paris«, S. 414.

58. Johnson, S. 4, zitiert ein Gespräch mit Madame Derain 1969.

59. Siehe Abbildungen bei Wilkinson, S. 105, 107 und 113.

60. Meines Wissens wird diese Plastik in der Literatur über Derain nirgends erwähnt. Als ich sie Derain zuschrieb, habe ich ihren Mischstil in Betracht gezogen (soweit dies aus der unscharfen Aufnahme zu ersehen ist) und Burgess' Bemerkung (S. 406), Derain habe außer »afrikanischen Schnitzereien – schrecklichen kleinen, schwarzen Göttern und Göttinnen mit konischen Brüsten, deformiert und abscheulich«, auch seine eigenen »Nachbildungen in Holz und Gips besessen«.

61. Siehe auch Elderfield, *The ›Wild Beasts‹,* S. 107 und S. 157, Anm. 44.

62. Siehe auch Rubin, W., S. 262 im vorliegenden Buch, der die Frage behandelt, wie man romanische Plastik um die Jahrhundertwende als »primitiv« einstufte.

63. Verbleib unbekannt; Abbildung bei Elderfield, *The ›Wild Beasts‹.*

64. Die *Badenden* entstanden wohl 1907, etwa zur gleichen Zeit wie Matisse' *Blauer Akt.* Frau Oppler identifiziert die *Badenden* mit einem Bild (S. 289), an das sich Hans Purrmann erinnerte: Derain habe es in »freundschaftlichem Wettstreit mit Matisse« gemalt, »wer wohl die beste Figur in Blau zustande brächte (Barr, *Matisse: His Art and His Public,* S. 533, Anm. 3 zu S. 94), und sie weist Purrmanns Behauptung, das Bild sei zerstört worden, zurück. Elderfield (*The ›Wild Beasts‹,* S. 158, Anm. 75) stimmt dieser Identifizierung nicht zu und weist darauf hin, daß zwar Blau im ganzen Bild der *Badenden* vorherrsche, aber keine Figur blau sei.

65. Golding, J., *Cubism: A History and an Analysis,* London 1968, S. 139.

66. Siehe auch Elderfield, *The ›Wild Beasts‹,* S. 120, und Wilkinson, S. 124.

67. Rubin, W., (»Cézannism and the Beginnings of Cubism« in *Cézanne: The Late Work,* New York 1977, S. 156–157) untersucht ebenfalls die Cézannschen Elemente in diesem Bild (vor allem den Sinn für plastische Wirkung bei den Figuren) und betont Derains »außerordentliche Bedeutung als Bindeglied zwischen Cézanne und den avantgardistischen Malern um 1907«. Rubin glaubt, daß Picassos Konkurrenzeifer bei den *Demoiselles* (Frühjahr 1907) mehr von Derains *Badenden* angestachelt wurde, das in jenem Frühjahr gezeigt wurde, als von Matisse' *Lebensfreude,* das im Jahr davor ausgestellt worden war.

68. Golding, *Cubism,* S. 139. Über Picassos Synthese von Cézanne mit der Stammeskunst siehe Rubin »From Narrative to ›Iconic‹ in Picasso: The Buried Allegory in *Bread and Fruitdish on a Table* and the Role of *Les Demoiselles d'Avignon*« in *The Art Bulletin,* Dezember 1983, S. 615–649.

69. Elderfield, *The ›Wild Beasts‹,* S. 109.

70. »The Wild Men of Paris«, S. 401–414. Von diesen sieben wurden Braque, Derain, Czóbel, Friesz und Metzinger zu den Fauvisten gezählt, die beiden anderen waren Herbin und Picasso.

71. Ebenda, S. 410.

72. Ebenda, S. 402.

73. Siehe auch Fry, »Cubism 1907–1908«, S. 70.

74. Siehe auch Anm. 75.

75. Barr (*Matisse: His Art and His Public,* S. 77) meint, Matisse – der seinem Freund Jean

Puy zunächst erzählt hatte, das Bild sei vom Briefträger von Collioure gemalt worden – « hat dabei wohl an das Werk eines anderen kleinen Beamten, Henri Rousseau, gedacht«, dessen Bilder Matisse an eine »bis zur Naivität einfache Technik« erinnert hätten, die er in seinen *Rosa Zwiebeln* anwandte. Die Beziehung zwischen diesem Bild und Rousseaus Stilleben scheint mir jedoch nicht ganz ersichtlich.

76. Etwa die beiden Fassungen des *Stillebens mit Porree* von 1904 oder die beiden Fassungen von *Luxus* von 1907.

77. »More Adventures« erschienen in *Appreciation: Painting, Poetry and Prose,* New York 1947, neuerlich in *Four Americans in Paris: The Collections of Gertrude Stein and Her Family,* New York 1970, S. 98. Diese Episode gleicht derjenigen, die man sich über die *Rosa Zwiebeln* erzählt, siehe Anm. 75 oben.

78. Pierre Courthion im Gespräch (siehe Anm. 44 oben).

79. Ashton, D. (Hrsg.), *Picasso on Art,* New York 1970, S. 164. Picassos Verständnis der Ziele von Matisse ist daran erkennbar, daß er sich das Portrait *Marguerite* aussuchte (1906 oder 1907 gemalt), als er und Matisse um diese Zeit Bilder austauschten. Dieses Bild ist bewußt vereinfacht und viel kindhafter als die *Rosa Zwiebeln* oder der *Junge Matrose II* (siehe auch Barr, *Matisse: His Art and His Public,* S. 85 und 94).

80. Matisse' Interesse für archaische Kunstformen und primitive Plastik ist an den kleinen Köpfen aus jenem Sommer erkennbar. Bestimmte Gesichtszüge werden darin überzeichnet, und Matisse betonte mehr die Flächenstruktur als den Aufbau der Muskulatur: Vorbild waren hier wohl griechisch-archaische, etruskische, keltische und alt-iberische Arbeiten, in geringerem Maße Werke aus Afrika. Siehe auch die Abbildungen bei Legg, A., *The Sculpture of Matisse,* New York 1972, S. 14.

81. Abb. ebenda, S. 18.

82. Siehe auch Gewing, L., *Matisse,* London 1979, S. 77. Ein treffendes Beispiel für diese Haltung findet man in Tizians *Bacchanal* (jetzt im Prado). Siehe auch Clark, K., *The Nude,* New York 1956, S. 294–295, und Meiss, M., »Sleep in Venice: Ancient Myths and Renaissance Proclivities« in *Proceedings of the American Philosophical Society,* Vol CX, 1966; neuerlich in *The Painter's Choice: Problems in the Interpretation of Renaissance Art,* New York 1976, S. 215–217.

83. Aufgeführt bei Barr, *Matisse: His Art and His Public,* S. 100.

84. Siehe ebenda, S. 94, dort eine Darstellung dieses Zwischenfalls.

85. Siehe Donne, »African Art and Paris Studios«, passim.

86. Nordafrika unterscheidet sich zwar völlig von Schwarzafrika, Matisse hat aber später von seinen dortigen Erlebnissen als Erfahrungen in »Afrika« gesprochen, siehe Pierre Courthion, 11. Dezember 1979.

87. Ebenda.

88. *The Immoralist,* 1902, ins Englische übersetzt von Howard, R., New York 1970, S. 45.

89. Siehe auch Anm. 65 und 66 oben.

90. Die Beziehung zwischen Matisse' *Badende mit Schildkröte* und Picassos gleichzeitig entstandenem Bild *Drei Frauen* – beide haben Primitives und Urtümliches zum Gegenstand – wird in meinem Buch über Matisse ausführlich behandelt. Beide Werke sind ausgezeichnete Beispiele dafür, wie nah sich beide Maler in thematischer Hinsicht zu dieser Zeit standen, trotz ihrer oft unterschiedlichen formalen Ziele.

91. Der *Blaue Akt* war auch Reaktion auf ein so neues Bild wie Raphael Collins *Paresse,* 1906 im Salon der Société des Artistes Français ausgestellt, das in Haltung und Plazierung der Figuren sehr ähnlich war.

92. Genaueres bei Jean Puy, »Souvenirs« in *Le Point,* 21. Juli 1939, S. 36 (132).

93. »Le Salon des Indépendants« in *Gil Blas,* 20. März 1907, S. 1.

94. Siehe auch Burgess, »The Wild Men of Paris«, S. 405, 413–414.

95. »Notes of a Painter on His Drawing« in *Le Point,* Nr. 21, Juli 1939, S. 14 (110) – Übersetzung bei Flam, *Matisse on Art,* S. 82.

96. Niederschrift einer Vorlesung im Museum of Modern Art, New York, vom 22. Oktober 1951 (mit freundlicher Genehmigung der Archives of American Art).

97. Nach Vollendung der *Demoiselles* nahm Picasso tatsächlich auf die Haltung des *Blauen Akts* in seinen Serien mit liegenden Akten und ähnlichen Sujets Bezug (siehe Daix Rosselet, *Picasso,* Anm. 76, 77, 79–83). Dieser Dialog wurde bald noch vertieft: Im Laufe dieses Jahres malte Braque seinen *Großen Akt,* teils von Picassos *Demoiselles,* teils von Matisse' *Blauem Akt* angeregt, dem das Bild Braques kompositionell und von der Malweise her genau folgt. Im Herbst antwortete Matisse mit seinem *Stehenden Akt* (jetzt Tate Gallery).

98. Siehe Rubin, S. 255–57 im vorliegenden Buch.

99. Zur Chronologie der *Demoiselles* siehe Rubin, »From Narrative to ›Iconic‹ in Picasso . . .«, a.a.O.

100. »Henri Matisse« in *La Phalange,* Vol. II, Dezember 1907, S. 481–485 (englische Übersetzung bei Barr, *Matisse: His Art and His Public,* S. 101–102).

101. Ettlinger, »German Expressionism and Primitive Art«, S. 191–192 (siehe auch Anm. 49).

102. Einzelheiten über die Sammlungen von Derain und Vlaminck bei Laude, S. 113–124. Ein allgemein afrikanischer Einfluß ist in Werken Derains erkennbar, etwa in *Das letzte Abendmahl* (um 1913; Art Institut of Chicago), hier sind einige Köpfe, wenn auch kubistisch überformt, in afrikanischer Manier gehalten.

103. Siehe auch Elsen, A., *The Sculpture of Matisse,* New York 1972, S. 84

104. Über die photographischen Vorlagen für den *Kauernden Akt* und *La serpentine* siehe Elderfield, J., *Matisse in the Collection of the Museum of Modern Art,* New York 1978, S. 190, Abb. 43 und 46.

105. Pierre Matisse bestätigt in einem Gespräch vom 22. Juni 1983, daß Matisse *Jeannette V* gleichzeitig mit *Rückenakt III* schuf. Sein Erscheinen im *Stilleben mit Gipsbüste* (Barnes Foundation) bildet den Terminus ante quem für seine Entstehung. Dieses Bild wird irrtümlich auf 1912 datiert, tatsächlich stammt es jedoch aus dem Jahr 1916.

106. Pierre Matisse, ebenda, erinnert sich daran, daß Matisse dieses Stück zu Beginn des 1. Weltkrieges, um 1915, erwarb. Bei Paul Guillaume und Guillaume Apollinaire (*Sculptures nègres,* Paris 1917) wird es auf Tafel V als Bestandteil der Sammlung Matisse aufgeführt.

107. Art Institute of Chicago; Abb. bei Barr, *Matisse: His Art and His Public,* S. 408.

108. »Le Salon« in *Montjoie,* Nov.-Dez. 1913, S. 4.

109. Das Bild erscheint auf einem Photo von Matisse, das Anfang 1916 in seinem Atelier gemacht wurde: Elderfield, *Matisse in the Collection of The Museum of Modern Art,* S. 209, Abb. 90.

110. Siehe u. a. Cowart, J., Flam, J., Fourcade, D., Neff, J. H., *Henri Matisse, Paper Cut-Outs,* Saint Louis und Detroit 1977, Anm. 32, 70 und 108.

111. Siehe den Bericht von Matisse über seine Eindrücke von Tahiti, bei Flam, *Matisse on Art,* S. 110 und 145. Kurz nach seiner Rückkehr von Tahiti schuf er zwei Skulpturen: *Tiari* und *Venus in der Muschel* (abgebildet bei Elderfield, *Matisse in the Collection of The Museum of Modern Art,* S. 137–139). Beide enthalten bildliche Metaphern tropischer Vegetation: Der Frauenkopf in *Tiari* ist formal bestimmt von der exotischen Pflanze, die dem Werk den Namen gab; in der *Venus in der Muschel* wächst eine Frau aus der Muschel wie eine Pflanze aus einer Schale. Noch 1953, in seinem letzten Lebensjahr, tauchen Eindrücke von seiner Tahiti-Reise in *Erinnerung an Ozeanien* auf (abgebildet bei Elderfield, S. 168).

112. Cowart, Flam u. a., *Henri Matisse: Paper Cut-Outs,* Anm. 55 und 56

113. Siehe ebenda, Anm. 61–64, 66 und das Photo von S. 132–133. Matisse sammelte auch ozeanische Kunst, besaß eine Uli-Figur (siehe Glossar) aus Neuirland, eine große Figur von den Neuen Hebriden und ein Tapa (siehe Glossar) vom Sentani-See in Neuguinea □ 298, das einen interessanten Vergleich mit Matisse' Entwurf für ein Türgitter des Albert D. Lasker Mausoleums erlaubt (Abb. bei Elderfield, S. 265, Nr. 72).

114. *The Autobiography of Alice B. Toklas,* S. 63.

□ 301 *Pablo Picasso, ›Les Demoiselles d'Avignon‹, 1907, Öl auf Leinwand, 244 x 238 cm. The Museum of Modern Art, New York.*

William Rubin

Pablo Picasso

Der Primitivismus hat im Werk Picassos eine so zentrale und historisch so konsequente Rolle gespielt wie bei keinem zweiten Künstler.[1] In drei Phasen der Neuorientierung seiner künstlerischen Arbeit griff die primitive Kunst in jeweils unterschiedlichem Ausmaß in sein Werk ein: zwischen seiner Rückkehr aus Gosol im Jahr 1906 und der Auflösung seines frühen kubistischen Stils im Winter 1908–09; während der Entwicklung des synthetischen Kubismus (1912–13) im Zusammenhang mit der Collage und der Konstruktionsplastik; schließlich bei der modellierten und konstruierten Plastik, mit der Picasso in den frühen 30er Jahren neue Wege beschritt. Über solche punktuellen Einflußnahmen hinaus waren primitive Impulse in Picassos seelischer Existenz stets präsent. Sie gewannen Rückhalt durch die ständige Gegenwart primitiver Objekte in seinen Ateliers zwischen 1907 bis zu seinem Tod.

Picassos Empfänglichkeit für primitive Kunst war so stark entwickelt und offenkundig, daß ihn die frühen Kritiker als den Hauptvertreter des modernen Primitivismus betrachteten und dies trotz ihrer Einsicht, daß Matisse, Derain, Vlaminck und vielleicht auch andere Künstler noch vor Picasso die afrikanische Plastik »entdeckt« hatten.[2] Man hielt diese Verwandtschaft mit dem Primitiven für so stark verwurzelt, daß ein Mythos entstand, der Picasso über eine spanisch-maurische Herkunft afrikanisches Blut andichtete.[3] Diese Verbindung zwischen dem Kubismus und Afrika wurde rückwirkend sogar bis Cézanne angenommen.[4] Weniger auf der Ebene der Rassenzugehörigkeit als auf derjenigen der Psychologie – Picassos Aberglaube, seine übertriebene Todesangst, das frühe Konkurrenzverhältnis zu seinem Vater – sind die Wurzeln seiner besonderen Vorliebe für primitive Kunst zu finden. Da Picassos Vater von Beruf Maler war, verwandelte sich die Lust des Sohnes an der Herausforderung und Revolte, was sicherlich einmal auf einer psychosexuellen Ebene begonnen hatte, relativ leicht in Einstellungen gegenüber der Kunst.

Picassos Kindheit verlief in bürgerlichen und konventionellen Bahnen. Beherrschend in seiner Familie war der große, ungewöhnlich stattliche Vater, der nicht nur ein fähiger Maler war, sondern auch ein angesehener Professor an der Kunstakademie von Barcelona. Seine Malerei war, wenn auch keineswegs akademisch, so traditionell wie die Werte, die er seinen Kindern anzuerziehen gedachte. Das Bild *Erste Kommunion* des jungen Picasso (1895–96)[5] vermittelt einen guten Eindruck von der imposanten körperlichen Erscheinung seines Vaters – dies gerade im Zusammenhang mit jenem Thema, das diesem zu »wohlerwogenen« Überzeugungen und Lebenseinstellungen Anlaß gab. Mit der illusionistischen Bravour dieses Frühwerkes, für das sein Vater Modell stand, schlug ihn der junge Pablo sozusagen mit seinen eigenen Mitteln. Daß er es als 14jähriger Knabe schuf, dokumentiert nicht nur Picassos gewaltiges Talent, sondern auch seinen frühreifen ödipalen Triumph. (Nach der Überlieferung »legte sein Vater den Pinsel hin«, als er solche Bilder zu sehen bekam.) Unterstützt durch eine ungewöhnlich starke Bindung an seine Mutter (wie es sich in der frühen Übernahme ihres Mädchennamens, Picasso, anstelle des väterlichen Familiennamens, Ruiz, ausdrückt), ging der junge Künstler in der Ablehnung der Welt seines Vaters einen Schritt weiter, indem er mit dem Verlassen des Elternhauses eine Künstlerexistenz wie ein Bohemien führte.

All das ist recht unbedeutend und wäre auch so geblieben, hätte nicht Picasso intuitiv verspürt, daß eine dauerhafte symbolische Niederlage des Vaters und dessen, was er repräsentierte, nicht durch den Triumph auf dem Felde einer Kunst gelingen konnte, welche die väterlichen Werte verkörperte, sondern durch Ablehnung dieser Kunst zugunsten von etwas sehr Persönlichem und Einmaligem; eben nicht durch die Hypertrophie seines außergewöhnlichen Talents – Talent war ja die Stütze und der Maßstab traditioneller wie auch vom Salon diktierter Malerei –, sondern durch seine Aufopferung. Talent half die Tatsache verschleiern, daß der Illusionismus des 19. Jahrhunderts zu einer phrasenhaften und sentimentalen Kunst verkommen war. Indem er den Primitivismus 1906 bereitwillig aufnahm, sprengte Picasso die Kontinuität dieser tradierten Konventionen. Seine jahrelange Erkundung zusehends abgelegener und fremder ästhetischer Bezüge ermöglichte ihm die persönliche Wiederentdeckung der malerischen Authentizität.

Picassos Primitivismus ist kennzeichnend für die Erweiterung der künstlerischen Sprache des Westens, deren Unterscheidung zwischen »hoher« und »niederer« Kunst ungültig wurde. Er brachte auch eine Hinwendung zu Konzeption und Invention mit sich (d. h. Genialität) bei gleichzeitiger Vernachlässigung, ja Ablehnung von Technik und Virtuosität (Talent). Diesen Weg einzuschlagen bedeutete an sich nichts Neues, als Picasso damit experimentierte. Doch bei keinem zweiten Künstler der Moderne, der sich dafür entschied, war das Talent, das er aufopferte, so außerordentlich, die Neukonzeption so radikal und überkommenen Ideen derart fremd. Picassos Vater war nicht da, um schockiert zu sein, als der Primitivismus des jungen Malers in *Les Demoiselles d'Avignon*[6] ☐ 301 kulminierte, aber Picasso hatte schon seit langem Professor Ruiz mit der ganzen Gesellschaft der Künstler, ja eigentlich mit der gesamten bürgerlichen Welt psychologisch gleichgesetzt.

□ 302 *Paul Gauguin, ›Verliebt Euch und Ihr werdet glücklich sein‹ (Soyez amoureuses – vous serez heureuses), 1889. Lindenholz, geschnitzt, poliert und mehrfarbig gefaßt, mit Originalrahmen, 119,5 x 96,5 cm. Museum of Fine Arts, Stiftung A. T. Cabot, Boston.*

Picassos vorprimitivistische Malerei – beginnend mit den Stilmischungen von 1900–01 über die Bilder der oft farbenkräftigen ›Blauen› und frühen ›Rosa Periode‹ – stellte freilich eine Hinwendung zu einer gewissen Modernität dar. In den Augen seines Vaters hätte der Vorwurf der Häresie nur geringfügige Ansätze in dieser Malerei getroffen. Malerische Bravour war nach wie vor maßgebend, wenn auch von anderer Art als in den Bildern des Wunderkindes. Zudem waren sie von einer wenn auch ganz eigenen Sentimentalität durchtränkt. Die Distanz zwischen Picassos weitgehend vom Symbolismus angeregter gemäßigter Modernität der Jahre 1901–05 und der Kunst seines Vaters ist nur gering im Vergleich zu der Kluft, die dann zu den *Demoiselles* besteht.

In der Einleitung zum vorliegenden Buch wurde der Primitivismus als eine antibürgerliche, gegenkulturelle Kraft beschrieben. Solche Tendenzen Picassos sind schon vor 1906 in der Verherrlichung gesellschaftlicher Außenseiter zu erkennen – Arme, Blinde, Alte, abgelehnte und entmutigte Unterhaltungskünstler (bzw. verschiedenste Überlagerungen davon). Aber welche Gesellschaftskritik auch immer mit diesen Bildern beabsichtigt war, sie wird im Rahmen des Erzählerischen vorgetragen, weniger mit den Mitteln der Malerei. Erst mit dem Beginn von Picassos Primitivismus, als er aus Gosol zurückkehrte, setzt die eigentliche malerische Kritik ein – in Arbeiten, die zum ersten Mal von der robusten Persönlichkeit des jungen Künstlers künden.

Wie schon dargelegt, waren die Anfänge der primitivistischen Kritik literarisch und philosophisch ausgerichtet. Selbst in den Frühstadien moderner malerischer Form – bei Gauguin – blieb sie weitgehend auf Symbole und Ideen beschränkt. Gerade in diesem Primitivismus des *fin de siècle* liegen die Wurzeln Picassos. Ende des Jahres 1907 hatte er dann allerdings nicht nur die Erkennung archaischer[7] und exotischer Objekte, wie sie von der Generation der Symbolisten geleistet worden war, aufgearbeitet, sondern auch den Primitivismus fast im Alleingang neu und dabei ganz im Sinne des 20. Jahrhunderts definiert. Statt von Objekten der exotischen Hofstile ging Picassos Definition von Stammesobjekten aus, die bislang als Kuriositäten abgetan worden waren, und sie bezog ihre gefühlsorientierte »magische« Kraft wie auch ihr plastisches Potential ein.

Meine Aussagen über Picassos Psychologie gelten auch für beliebige andere moderne Künstler, deren syndromatische Seitenhiebe gegen Tradition und Autorität das Bürgertum provozieren sollten. Picassos eigentliche Bestrebungen gingen indes weit über die Revoltierlust von Bürgersöhnen hinaus. Er vertrat nicht nur die Überzeugung, daß die Kunst seiner Kindheit im Verein mit den darin enthaltenen religiösen, ethischen und sexuellen Überzeugungen nicht mehr lebensfähig war, sondern es ihm auch aufgegeben war, nach neuen Wegen Ausschau zu halten. Nur wer so früh und mühelos die von seinem Vater favorisierte Malerei nachahmen konnte, vermochte sie auch so schnell zu entlarven und sich sicher zu sein, daß ihre Positionen und wie sie diese vermittelte von Grund auf falsch waren. Was genau an ihr falsch war, sollte Picasso vollends erst mit dem »Schock« und der »Offenbarung« klar werden, die er angesichts der Stammesmasken und »Fetische« im Musée d'Ethnographie du Trocadéro erlebte: »In diesem Moment«, so sagte er später, »erkannte ich, um was es in der Malerei wirklich geht.«[8]

□ 303 *Pablo Picasso, ›Exotische Figuren‹ (Ausschnitt aus ›La Parisienne et figures exotiques‹), 1906 (?), Tusche, 30 x 42 cm. Musée Picasso, Paris.*

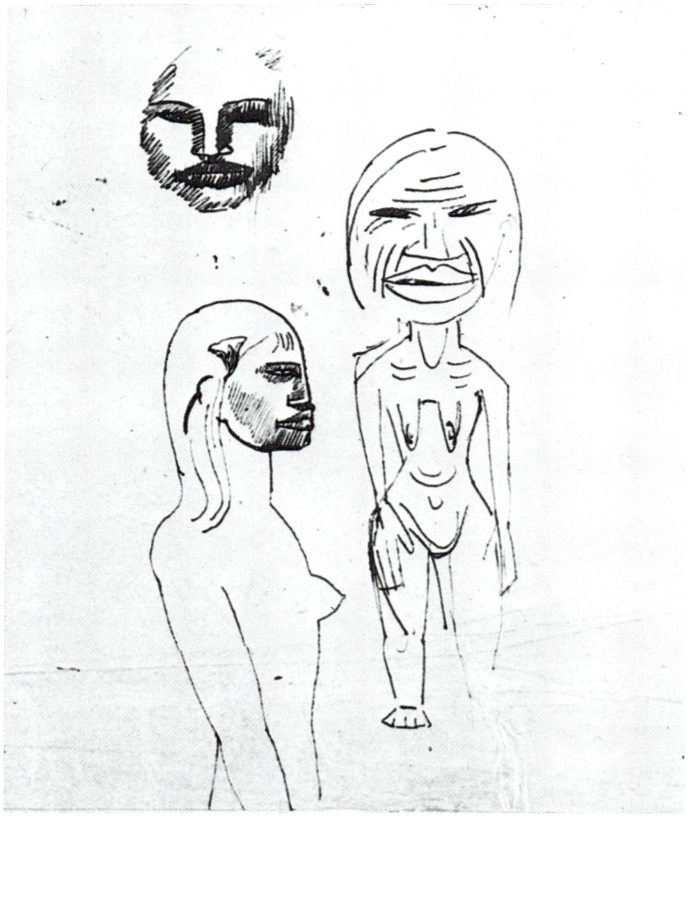

»Dieser Moment«, ein Offenbarungserlebnis des Juni 1907, von dem noch ausführlich zu sprechen ist, war erst durch jene ein Jahr dauernde Entwicklung möglich, die von einer Ausstellung iberisch-archaischer Reliefs aus Osuna im Louvre ausgelöst wurde.[9] Diese Skulptur regte PICASSO zu seinem »iberischen« Stil an, der im folgenden Frühjahr voll zum Durchbruch gelangte[10] und die erste entscheidende Stufe seines Primitivismus darstellt. Schon die Beschäftigung mit der Plastik Ägyptens im Louvre seit 1903 hatte den Weg für PICASSOS Iberianismus bereitet. (In der hieratischen Geste seiner *Frau mit einem Fächer*, 1905, ist wohl der Reflex eines ägyptischen Reliefs zu erkennen.) Die Samen seines Primitivismus – wie spät sie auch aufgingen – dürften noch sehr viel früher gesät worden sein: durch seine Kontakte mit GAUGUINS Kunst über die Freundschaft mit dem spanischen Bildhauer PACO DURRIO (1901).

PICASSOS Interesse galt zunächst GAUGUIN (dessen eigene primitive Vorbilder vor allem in archaischen Hofstilen zu suchen sind), sodann archaischer Kunst selbst (ägyptischer und iberischer Skulptur) und schließlich primitiver Kunst (afrikanischer und ozeanischer Plastik). Im frühen 20. Jahrhundert wurde diese Interessenverlagerung einfach als eine Reise zurück in die Vergangenheit gedeutet, zu den Anfängen der Kunst – und PICASSO selbst hat es wohl so verstanden. Ein solches Verständnis war vorherrschend trotz der Tatsache, daß Stammesobjekte viel später entstanden als irgendeine der nichtklassischen Kunstrichtungen, die PICASSO auf sich wirken ließ. Doch herrschte zur Zeit von PICASSOS Jugend noch Unkenntnis über diese Chronologie. Noch 1920 konnte André Salmon, ein Gründungsmitglied (1903) der »bande à Picasso«, irrtümlich behaupten, daß »eine Reihe der schönsten Stücke [afrikanischer Kunst], die auf uns gekommen ist, viel früher als das christliche Zeitalter entstand«. Er glaubte sogar den »Einfluß der Schnitzer von ›Fetischen‹« auf ägyptische und über sie auf griechische Kunst der Archaik erkennen zu können. Ausgehend von der Beschäftigung moderner Künstler mit den Grundprinzipien der Konstruktion kam Salmon zu dem Schluß, sie seien dazu bestimmt, »von den Ägyptern [zurück] zu den Negern zu gehen«.[11] Dieser durcheinander gebrachten Kunstgeschichte entsprach auf der anderen Seite die irrtümliche Spekulation bestimmter Anthropologen, ob die afrikanische Kunst von ägyptischer Plastik beeinflußt worden sei.[12] Es erübrigt sich der Hinweis, daß kein Stück Negerplastik, das PICASSO in den ersten Jahren seiner Begeisterung für die »art nègre« sah, älter als ein paar Jahrzehnte war, auch wenn die Ursprünge ihrer traditionellen Stile offenbar über Jahrhunderte zurückreichen.[13] Ob nun alt oder neu, die eingeborenen Erzeugnisse wurden von PICASSOS Generation mit den frühesten Zivilisationsstufen in Verbindung gebracht, dies in Übereinstimmung mit einem äußerst vereinfachten Modell der Weltgeschichte.

Ron Johnson hat zu Recht auf die Bedeutung von PICASSOS früher Berührung mit GAUGUIN Nachdruck gelegt,[14] dessen Einfluß den Hintergrund zu PICASSOS Primitivismus bildet und bis in die frühesten Phasen der *Demoiselles* hineinreicht. Hinweise in PICASSOS Werk auf GAUGUIN treten 1901 erstmals auf, als Sabartés und er DURRIO besuchten. »Da wurde viel über Gauguin gesprochen, Tahiti und das Gedicht *Noa-Noa,* über Charles Morice und tausenderlei andere Dinge.«[15] DURRIO besaß mehrere Arbeiten von GAUGUIN und kannte Charles Morice, der PICASSO bald darauf ein Exemplar seiner Edition

□ 304 *Pablo Picasso, ›Sich kämmende Frau‹ (Femme se coiffant), 1906. Bronze, 42 x 26 x 32 cm. The Baltimore Museum of Art, Sammlung Cone.*

von *Noa-Noa* überreichte (das offenbar verloren gegangen ist). In diesem Buch hinterließ PICASSO mindestens zwei Randzeichnungen.[16] GAUGUIN machte, wie Johnson zeigte, »einen tiefen Eindruck auf Picasso, so daß er seine erste Skulptur modellierte, eine *Sitzende Frau* (Z. II², 668, 1901), die nach Anregungen von Gauguins *Porträtvase Madame Schuffenecker* (1889) gestaltet war«. Johnson wäre jedoch der letzte, der der Meinung beipflichtet, daß in dem genannten Objekt GAUGUINS etwas Primitives oder gar Archaisches zu finden ist. Auch wenn eine Tuschzeichnung PICASSOS (Z. VI, 364), die sich auf GAUGUINS Werk bezieht, archaisierende Züge aufweist, gilt dies nicht für PICASSOS völlig im Stil RODINS gehaltene *Sitzende Frau*, die nur dem Motiv nach mit GAUGUINS Arbeit verwandt ist. Johnson stellt auch eine Beziehung her zwischen PICASSOS Plastik *Sich kämmende Frau* von Anfang 1906 □ 304 und GAUGUINS Relief *Verliebt Euch und Ihr werdet glücklich sein* □ 302 (1889). Spies bringt dieses Werk GAUGUINS in Zusammenhang mit dem im selben Jahr etwas später entstandenen Relief *Frauenkopf* von PICASSO (Spies 8).[17] Wenn PICASSO jedoch den gebeugten Arm der *Sich kämmenden Frau* aus GAUGUINS Relief übernahm, so beweist doch der Stil der Plastik – und der dazugehörigen Zeichnungen –, daß er gerade die in GAUGUINS Bild vorhandenen Archaisierungen zugunsten des klassischen Kontraposts, den man ihm auf der Kunstakademie beigebracht hatte, verwarf.[18]

□ 305 *Paul Gauguin, ›Zwei Figuren zu seiten einer Statue‹ (aus „Ancien Culte Mahorie"), 1892–93, Aquarell, Gesamtgröße 10 x 17 cm. Cabinet des Dessins, Musée du Louvre, Paris.*

Diese wenigen »gauguinesken« Werke PICASSOS aus den Jahren 1901 bis Anfang 1906 sind keine Vorläufer seines späteren Primitivismus. Die Einflüsse GAUGUINS, die in PICASSOS bemerkenswerten Stilwandel von Ende 1906 und 1907 eingehen sollten, lassen sich erst feststellen, nachdem er im Frühjahr 1906 dem Eindruck der iberischen Plastiken ausgesetzt gewesen war. Diese Erfahrung bereitete PICASSOS völlig neues Verständnis GAUGUINS vor, als er dessen große Gedächtnisausstellung nach seiner Rückkehr aus Gosol im Salon d'Automne besuchte.

Außer der Skizze einer tahitischen Schönheit – die PICASSO in seiner typischen Bosheit neben ein Phantasiebild (ihrer ?) Gebrechlichkeit im Alter stellte □ 303[19] – inspirierte ihn die GAUGUIN-Retrospektive meiner Meinung nach direkt zu einer ganz ungewöhnlichen Gouache, *Zwei Sitzende Frauen,* die bisher wenig Beachtung gefunden hat □ 306. In seinem Katalog der kubistischen PICASSO-Werke meint Daix, diese Gouache stehe in dem Werk des Künstlers »völlig isoliert« da (was großenteils auch stimmt). Er datiert sie unter Vorbehalt auf das Jahr 1909.[20] Daix' Zweifel an seiner Datierung entstehen aus der Beobachtung, daß sich in der Räumlichkeit, der Morphologie und dem Aufbau des Werks nichts findet, was eine Datierung auf 1909 sinnvoll erscheinen ließe, auch wenn die Grau-, Braun- und Grüntöne des Bildes auf dieses Jahr hindeuten.

Ich bin davon überzeugt, daß sich die Besonderheit von PICASSOS Gouache daraus erklärt, daß sie in gewisser Weise eine experimentelle oder Anerkennung ausdrückende Paraphrase eines ebenso ungewöhnlichen Aquarells GAUGUINS war, *Zwei Figuren zu seiten einer Statue* □ 305, das in der GAUGUIN-Retrospektive ausgestellt wurde.[21] *Zwei sitzende Frauen* verbindet dieses Aquarell mit Aspekten aus GAUGUINS *Heute kein Markt* □ 229 und seiner Plastik *Oviri* □ 309, die beide auf der Ausstellung von 1906 gezeigt wurden. Die Symmetrie in *Zwei sitzende Frauen*, die bei PICASSO überrascht, läßt ein bestimmtes Vorbild vermuten, als das sich GAUGUINS *Zwei Figuren zu seiten einer Statue* bestens eignet. GAUGUIN fertigte dieses Aquarell bald nach seiner Ankunft auf Tahiti eigens als Illustration für sein *Ancien Culte Mahorie* (er hielt die Tahitianer für MAORI; siehe S. 199). Der Verwendungszweck könnte den ebenso für GAUGUIN ungewöhnlichen symmetrischen und hieratischen Aufbau wie auch die Einzelheiten, die Tikis und ornamentale Formen von den Marquesasinseln vorstellen sollen, erklären.

Ende 1906 hatte PICASSO jedoch noch keine polynesischen Kunstwerke gesehen; daher überrascht es nicht, wenn er nur die allgemein archaischen Aspekte von GAUGUINS Aquarell übernahm – Symmetrie, Frontansicht, hieratische Gesten und Körperhaltungen –, während er alles spezifisch Ozeanische überging. Er ersetzte den Kopf des Tiki-haften Götzen im Zentrum von GAUGUINS Bild durch symmetrisch angeordnete Farne und Blumen (deren zwei Blüten die Stelle der Augen des Götzen einnehmen) und den Körper des Götzen durch eine Vase. PICASSO behielt die einfachen und schematisierten Köpfe, Hände und Füße von GAUGUINS Eingeborenenfrauen bei, während er ihre Körperhaltung veränderte. Die freien Seitenflächen in GAUGUINS Aquarell kehren vielleicht bei PICASSO in den Flächen für die Stühle wieder, auf denen die beiden Frauen sitzen.[22] Anstatt der von GAUGUIN gewählten marquesanischen Haltung der Arme und Hände malte PICASSO »ägyptisch«, d.h. er drehte die Schultern in die Bildfläche, während die Beine im Profil blieben. Jede von PICASSOS Figuren hat eine Hand auf den altarähnlichen Tisch gelegt und die andere in einer rituellen Geste erhoben, die ein »primitivistisches« Gegenstück zu der Geste der *Frau mit Fächer* bildet.

PICASSOS Zusammenstellung von fast frontal gesehenen Gesichtern und Schultern mit Beinen im Profil erinnert insbesondere an die Frau in der Mitte der Sitzbank von *Heute kein Markt* sowie an das seltsame Standmotiv von *Oviri*. Wenn auch *Oviri* in dieser Hinsicht als Vorbild weniger in Frage kommt, wurde PICASSOS Interesse an dieser Plastik doch, wie ich vermute, durch das Motiv der Beine, die keine Standfunktion haben, geweckt. Hier lag auch eine Verbindung mit MICHELANGELOS *Sterbendem Sklaven* nahe, einer Figur, die ihn seit seinen ersten Besuchen im Louvre tief beeindruckte □ 310. PICASSO erzählte mir, wie sehr ihn der *Sterbende Sklave* bewegte, als wir einen lebensgroßen Gipsabdruck von ihm betrachteten, der in einer Ecke seines Bildhauerateliers stand.[23] Der linke Arm der Figur ist über den Kopf zurückgeworfen und in einer Weise angewinkelt, wie es in PICASSOS Malerei wiederholt vorkommt. Der entspannte Unterkörper scheint nur halb getragen, ein Eindruck, der bei *Oviri* noch stärker ist. *Oviri* erinnert auch an die ambivalente halb sitzende, halb stehende Haltung, die durch die gebeugten Knie vieler Stammesskulpturen zustande kommt. Zusammen mit der Skulptur MICHELANGELOS und anderen Quellen beeinflußt *Oviri* unmittelbar die links von der Mitte stehende Ibererin in den *Demoiselles* □ 311. Zu ihrer besonderen Haltung, deren Widersprüchlichkeiten Leo Steinberg ausführlich erörterte,[24] gehört auch der erhobene und gebeugte Arm von MICHELANGELOS Marmorfigur. Dieser Aspekt des Bewegungsmotivs wird seit langem zu Recht mit vielen Vorbildern bei CÉZANNE in Verbindung gebracht (wie in *Fünf Badende*, v. 542), der sie seinerseits von MICHELANGELO hatte. PICASSO kannte allerdings MICHELANGELOS Skulptur schon Jahre, bevor er von deren Wirkungen auf das Werk CÉZANNES wußte.[25]

Daß die genannte Demoiselle in Zusammenhang mit dem Werk MICHELANGELOS sowie CÉZANNES und GAUGUINS zu sehen ist, wird durch die sexuelle Zweideutigkeit und den Konflikt im Zentrum von PICASSOS Bild unterstützt. Der neuplatonische Kampf zwischen der Körperlichkeit und der reinen Idee in der Arbeit MICHELANGELOS läßt sich leicht auf die weltlichere Auseinandersetzung Sexualität versus Liebe übertragen, wobei die Androgynität von MICHELANGELOS Figur die Assoziation mit dem Weiblichen erleichterte. Der erhobene und gebeugte Arm steht natürlich in unmittelbarem Zusammenhang mit der erotischen Offenbarung bei CÉZANNE (wie in *Die Versuchung des hl. Antonius*, v. 103). Daß PICASSO sie mit MICHELANGELO und GAUGUIN in Verbindung brachte, bereicherte diese Assoziationen nur. In den späteren Ausprägungen von PICASSOS »Afrikanismus«, etwa in den *Drei Frauen*, hat diese Geste deutlich die bildhauerische Ausdruckskraft eines MICHELANGELO.

□ 306 *Pablo Picasso, ›Zwei sitzende Frauen‹ (Deux femmes assises), 1906–07, Gouache, 25 x 32 cm. Privatbesitz.*

☐ 307 *Pablo Picasso, ›Bildnis Gertrude Stein‹ (Portrait de Gertrude Stein), 1905–06, Öl auf Leinwand, 99,5 x 81 cm. The Metropolitan Museum of Art, Vermächtnis Gertrude Stein, New York.*

☐ 308 *›Mann, von einem Löwen angegriffen‹, iberisch, Osuna, Ende 6.–3. Jh. v. Chr., Stein, Ausschnitt aus einem Relief, Höhe 41 cm. Museo Arqueologico Nacional, Madrid.*

Der Einfluß der iberischen Reliefs von Osuna ☐ 308, die Picasso im Louvre sah, zeigt sich schon zaghaft in den Werken, die er im Sommer 1906 in Gosol schuf, tritt aber erst in den Arbeiten nach seiner Rückkehr nach Paris vollends zutage.[26] Picassos Empfänglichkeit für das Archaische war jedoch schon Anfang 1906 deutlich geworden. So bilden in dem Gemälde *Knabe, ein Pferd führend* griechische Kouroi (archaische Jünglingsstatuen) die zweitwichtigste Anregung nach Cézanne. Die Stimmung und Ausführung dieser Arbeit kündigt ebenfalls den bevorstehenden Wechsel vom Sentimentalen zum Plastischen an. Die archaischen Gesichter der Osuna-Reliefs sind mit ihren stilisierten Zügen und Frisuren und den einfach modellierten Oberflächen sicherlich die Quelle für die maskenhaften Gesichter in Picassos Arbeiten dieses Herbstes. Aus vielen Gründen ist das klassische Beispiel dafür das überarbeitete Gesicht im *Bildnis Gertrude Stein* ☐ 307. Man braucht nur den Stil des Gesichts mit dem des Kleides – dem Mieder vor allem – oder des Stuhles zu vergleichen, um zu sehen, wie sehr sich Picassos Kunst seit seinem Weggang aus Paris im Frühjahr gewandelt hatte. Gertrude Stein behauptet verschiedentlich, im Winter und Frühjahr, bevor Picasso nach Gosol ging, genau zweiundneunzigmal Modell gesessen zu haben, ohne daß er eine befriedigende Ähnlichkeit erreichte; kurz bevor er Paris verließ, löschte er das Gesicht ganz aus.

Picasso malte Gertrude Steins Gesicht in iberischer Manier im folgenden Herbst aus dem Gedächtnis. Daher steht das Bild am entscheidenden Übergang von einer wahrnehmungsorientierten zu einer konzeptuellen Arbeitsweise (siehe S. 20ff.). Im Rückblick zeigt sich, daß damit der Weg für das frei war, was zwei Jahre später zum Kubismus werden sollte. Wie sehr sich auch Picassos Iberianismus von 1906–07 von seinem Afrikanismus von 1907–08 oder von seinem frühen Kubismus von 1908–09 unterscheiden mag, ein Prinzip blieb unverändert bestehen. Salmon – der es von Picasso selbst gehört haben mag – formulierte es später folgendermaßen: »Das die neue Ästhetik beherrschende große Gesetz lautet: Die Konzeption ist ausschlaggebender als die Wahrnehmung.«[27] Das Ende 1906 entstandene Bild *Zwei Frauenakte* ☐ 315 wurde als »Gipfelpunkt der ›iberischen‹ Phase« bezeichnet; es ist aber nur der Gipfel der ersten, »bildhauerischen« Phase von Picassos Iberianismus, die in die Monate unmittelbar nach Gosol fiel. In den ersten fünf Monaten des folgenden Jahres wurden die iberischen Formen flacher und nicht nur weniger plastisch, sondern gröber, einfacher, eckiger und schematischer. Wohl einen der wichtigsten Anstöße dafür erhielt Picasso im März 1907, als er zwei iberische Köpfe aus Cerro de los Santos kaufte, die, ohne daß er es wußte, aus dem Louvre gestohlen worden waren.[28] Obwohl archaisch, waren diese Köpfe roher und anscheinend »primitiver« als die Osuna-Reliefs (vor allem der männliche Kopf von Cerro, der auf einer Seite schwer beschädigt war ☐ 312, 317).[29]

Wie das Beispiel von *Zwei Frauenakte* zeigt, war der Figurentyp, den Picasso Ende 1906 malte, von gedrungener Gestalt, wie wir ihn in früheren Werken nicht finden. Diese Proportionen und die maskenhaften Gesichter – insbesondere die schwerlidrigen, fast rautenförmigen Augen – zeugen von dem fortgesetzten Einfluß der Osuna-Objekte, obschon das Massige in den knolligen und ungeschlachten Figuren von Cézanne herrührt. Mit der Gestaltung der Füße der rechten Figur von *Zwei Frauenakte* brach Picasso mit dem Realismus, wie er es nie zuvor getan hatte. Um dem massiven Rumpf des Aktes

☐ 310 *Michelangelo Buonarroti, ›Sterbender Sklave‹, 1513–16, Marmor, Höhe 226 cm. Musée du Louvre, Paris.*

☐ 311 *Pablo Picasso, ›Les Demoiselles d'Avignon‹, Ausschnitt von* ☐ *301.*

☐ 309 *Paul Gauguin, ›Oviri‹, ca. 1891–93, Terrakotta, Höhe 74 cm. Privatsammlung, Paris.*

□ 312 *›Kopf‹, iberisch, Cerro de los Santos, 5.–3. Jh. v. Chr., Stein, Höhe 21 cm. Musée des Antiquités Nationales, Saint-Germain-en-Laye. Vorderansicht siehe* □ *317.*

□ 313 *Pablo Picasso, ›Kopf‹ (Tête), 1907, Holz, behauen und teilweise bemalt, 39 x 25 x 12 cm. Sammlung Jacqueline Picasso, Mougins.*

□ 314 *Pablo Picasso, ›Frauenkopf‹ (Tête de femme), 1906–07, Bronze, 11 x 8 x 9 cm. Hirshhorn Museum and Sculpture Garden, Smithsonian Institution, Washington.*

□ 315 *Pablo Picasso, ›Zwei Frauenakte‹ (Deux femmes nues), 1906, Öl auf Leinwand, 151 x 93 cm. The Museum of Modern Art, Stiftung G. D. Thompson, New York.*

architektonisch einen größeren Halt zu verleihen, flachte PICASSO die Füße ab und verzichtete auf die vorderen Konturen des rechten Unterschenkels am Übergang zum Fuß. Er opferte damit den Eindruck einer dynamischen Wechselbeziehung zwischen der Figur und der Grundfläche, worauf sie steht, eine feste Konvention in der westlichen Kunst, die erstmals von MASACCIO überzeugend begründet wurde, als er das Gewicht des Körpers über den Knöchel auf einen Fuß verlagerte, der eindeutig auf festem Grund stand. Die schwerelose Weise, mit der die mächtige rechtsstehende Figur mit dem Boden verbunden ist, erinnert an die italienischen Primitiven, vor allem an GIOTTO, sowie an den unorganischen Stand afrikanischer Figurenplastik, von der PICASSO inzwischen mehrere Beispiele kannte.[30] Obgleich man *Zwei Frauenakte* nicht im gleichen Sinne als »primitiv« bezeichnen kann wie die Arbeiten der beiden darauffolgenden Jahre, zeigt die Ausführung des Bildes eine Einfachheit und erstaunliche Unfertigkeit – vor allem durch die flüchtige Schraffierung der Arme und die große Pinselarbeit im Hintergrund – sowie eine absichtlich unschöne Zeichnung, wodurch dieses Gemälde einen wichtigen Schritt in die genannte Richtung unternimmt.

PICASSOS Iberianismus stellt – zusammen mit seinem Interesse an GAUGUIN und an der ägyptischen Kunst – die erste, d. h. archaische Phase seines Primitivismus dar. Die späteren Stadien seines Iberianismus lassen sich im größeren Zusammenhang der *Demoiselles d'Avignon* untersuchen; sie bilden sowohl den Höhepunkt der archaischen Phase von PICASSOS Primitivismus als auch den Anfang des ihr folgenden Einflusses der Stammeskunst. Da selbst ein ganzes Buch kaum ausreichen würde, den kunsthistorischen Quellen und Implikationen die-

□ 317 *›Kopf‹, iberisch, Cerro de los Santos, 5.–3. Jh. v. Chr., Stein, Höhe 21 cm. Musée des Antiquités Nationales, Saint-Germain-en-Laye. Profilansicht siehe* □ *312.*

◁ □ 316 *Pablo Picasso, ›Kopf des Medizinstudenten‹, Studie zu ›Les Demoiselles d'Avignon‹, 1907, Gouache und Aquarell, 60 x 47 cm. The Museum of Modern Art, Stiftung A. Conger Goodyear, New York.*

ses Gemäldes gerecht zu werden, will ich versuchen, meine Untersuchung hier so weit wie möglich auf die Rolle des Primitivismus in diesem Gemälde zu beschränken – zugegebenermaßen eine etwas unorganische Trennung von miteinander verflochtenen kunsthistorischen Motiven und Einflüssen.

Im Gegensatz zu einer viele Jahre lang gültigen Chronologie (die sich größtenteils auf Kahnweilers *Weg zum Kubismus* zurückführen läßt), begann Picasso mit den großen Skizzen für die *Demoiselles* – ganz abgesehen von ihrer Ausführung auf Leinwand – erst gegen Mitte 1907. Kahnweiler erweckte den Eindruck, Picasso habe seit dem Spätjahr 1906 etwa sechs bis acht Monate an dem Bild gearbeitet. Ohne die aufgetretenen stilistischen Widersprüchlichkeiten lösen zu können, habe er das Bild im Frühsommer 1907 unvollendet gelassen. Die rechte, zuletzt entstandene Seite des Bildes stellte für Kahnweiler zudem »den Beginn des Kubismus« dar.

Ich hoffe, diesem kunsthistorischen Mythos andernorts überzeugend ein Ende bereitet zu haben.[31] Studien für die Gesamtkomposition der *Demoiselles* existieren erst vom März 1907 an. Das Gemälde wurde in seiner ersten, iberischen Fassung Ende Mai/Anfang Juni desselben Jahres ausgeführt. Während dieses Monats und wahrscheinlich bis in den Juli hinein nahm Picasso an dem Bild mehrere Veränderungen vor, und das, wie wir sehen werden, möglicherweise bei zwei verschiedenen Gelegenheiten. Das Bild war Anfang Juli 1907 fertig. (Der Kubismus wurde von Braque und Picasso erst in der zweiten Hälfte des Jahres 1908 entwickelt; auch brachte ihn Kahnweiler erst 1920 mit den *Demoiselles* in Verbindung.)

Die früheste große Gesamtskizze für die *Demoiselles* entstand Ende Februar oder Anfang März 1907 □ 319, wohl kurz bevor Picasso die Köpfe aus Cerro de los Santos erwarb. Sein Iberianismus hatte seit dem Bild *Zwei Frauenakte* stetig an Plastizität verloren, daher überrascht es nicht, daß weder seine Zeichnung im Basler Museum, in der sieben Figuren vorkommen, noch die zugehörigen Bilder von Einzelfiguren sehr stark modelliert sind. Die Hell/Dunkel-Beziehungen wirken oft abrupt, sogar brutal und werden in den weiteren Studien zu Streifen und Schraffierungen, die Picasso – allerdings erst ein paar Monate später – mit afrikanischen und ozeanischen Hautritzungen und Körperbemalungen in Beziehung setzte.

Wenn die kleine Bronzeplastik *Frauenkopf* □ 314 dem Höhepunkt der ersten Phase des Iberianismus (beispielhaft vertreten durch *Zwei Frauenakte*) angehört, so ist das für die letzte iberische Phase stehende Werk bezeichnenderweise ein Relief: *Kopf* □ 313. Der Geist dieses rohen und provozierenden Stückes, das grob in Holz gehauen und unbeholfen bemalt ist, erinnert an den männlichen Kopf von Cerro, auf den die eindeutig »primitive« Machart und die leicht karikierende Darstellungsweise zurückgehen.[32] Wie Golding schon vor langem feststellte,[33] steht der Cerro-Kopf sicher auch mit iberischen Entwürfen für die *Demoiselles* in Beziehung, etwa dem Aquarell des Medizinstudenten □ 316 mit seinem großen, eigenartig schneckenförmigen Ohr, der Asymmetrie seiner Augen[34] und der Grobheit der Gesamtauffassung. Die langen Streifen, die in PICASSOS Aquarell den Schatten der Nase bilden (sie haben eine gewisse Ähnlichkeit mit dem Frisurmuster der Cerro-Plastik), stellen eine Extrapolierung jener graphischen Kurzschrift dar, die man Schraffur nennt und deren typischere Beispiele im selben Blatt (rechts oben) als Schattierung der Draperie zu verstehen sind. Die kantige, primitivistische Art dieser Schraffierung veranlaßte einige Kritiker, sie mit Holzschnitten und aufgrund dieser Ableitung mit den Hautritzungen und Streifenmustern afrikanischer Plastik in Verbindung zu bringen. Allerdings gab es solche gewagten Streifenmuster in PICASSOS Werk längst vor seiner Juni-»Offenbarung« im Zusammenhang mit der Stammeskunst im Trocadéro, und sie waren im wesentlichen seine persönliche Primitivisierung einer traditionellen Schattierungstechnik. Nachdem PICASSOS Interesse für die afrikanische Plastik erwacht war, vermischte sich diese Musterbildung mit seinen Erinnerungen an die Ritzungen auf afrikanischen Masken und Figurenplastiken, an die parallelen Kupferstreifen der *ONGWE*-Reliquiarfiguren □ 342 sowie an die sog. »Tränenmuster« □ 413 und eingeritzten Parallellinien von *KOTA*-Reliquiarfiguren □ 347, 349.

Hunderte von Zeichnungen und Gemälden, die mit den *Demoiselles* in Beziehung stehen, müssen noch systematisch geordnet werden,[35] doch ist die Entwicklung in groben Zügen klar. Genese und Ausführung der Bildidee von den ersten Entwürfen bis zur vorläufigen »Vollendung« des Gemäldes im Mai oder Anfang Juni (wovon nur die beiden Mädchen in der Mitte, das Stilleben und einige andere Teile übrigbleiben) muß man in engem Zusammenhang mit der letzten, am wenigsten

□ 318 *Pablo Picasso, ›Büste eines Matrosen‹ (Buste d'homme), Öl auf Leinwand, 55 x 46 cm. Musée Picasso, Paris.*

□ 319 *Pablo Picasso, ›Medizinstudent, Matrose und fünf Frauenakte in einem Bordell‹, Studie zu ›Les Demoiselles d'Avignon‹, 1907, Kohle und Pastellkreide, 48 x 63,5 cm. Kunstmuseum Basel, Kupferstichkabinett.*

☐ 320 *Pablo Picasso, ›Fünf Akte‹, Studie zu ›Les Demoiselles d'Avignon‹, 1907, Aquarell, 17 x 22 cm. Philadelphia Museum of Art, Sammlung A. E. Gallatin.*

plastischen, schematischsten und kantigsten Phase von PICASSOS Iberianismus sehen (der auch sein großartiges Selbstbildnis in Prag angehört). Bis zum März 1907 hatte dieser Iberianismus zu einem Entwurf geführt, der den Empfangsraum eines Bordells zeigt ☐ 318, in dem ein sitzender Matrose von fünf nackten Prostituierten in verschiedenen Stellungen umgeben ist und von links ein Medizinstudent (je nachdem mit einem Buch oder einem Totenschädel) hereinkommt.[36] Bis Mitte Mai entstand nach einer Flut von Entwürfen in verschiedenen Techniken der Entwurf, der die Endfassung werden sollte; man kann sie in dem spätiberischen Aquarell des Philadelphia Museum of Art bereits erkennen ☐ 320, in dem die beiden männlichen Figuren verschwunden sind und das Bild hochformatiger geworden ist.[37] Die »erste Arbeitsphase« auf der Leinwand – die zu einem »vollendeten« Gemälde führte, das nur eine leicht abgeflachte und vertikalere Fassung des spätiberischen Aquarells war – fand Ende Mai und/oder Anfang Juni statt. Aber PICASSO war anscheinend mit dem Ergebnis seiner bisherigen künstlerischen Arbeit unzufrieden und nahm dann schon kurze Zeit später – im Juni und/oder Anfang Juli – einige Veränderungen auf der rechten und der linken Seite des Bildes vor. Im Licht dieser Veränderungen – ihrer psychologischen Beweggründe und ihres expressiven und plastischen Charakters – ist der Beginn der Stammesphase von PICASSOS Primitivismus zu verstehen.

Warum war PICASSO nicht mit der iberischen Fassung des Gemäldes zufrieden? Ich bin der Überzeugung, daß PICASSO bei der Umwandlung seiner Konzeption von einem narrativen Bild (d.h. anekdotischen) in ein eher »ikonisches« (frontaleres, in der Räumlichkeit dichteres und von Zeit und Ort vergleichsweise abstrahiertes Bild) bestimmte Aspekte der ursprünglich erzählerischen Bordellszene geopfert hatte, die in dem früheren Kontext durch die Begegnung der Mädchen mit dem Matrosen und dem Medizinstudenten vorhanden waren. PICASSO traf dann intuitiv die Entscheidung, in die *Demoiselles* verschiedene Konfigurationen einzuführen und brachte damit wirkungsvoll einige dieser Bedeutungen wieder ein – und zwar eher mit stilistischen als mit illustratorischen Mitteln. Der Rückgewinn der Aussage vollzog sich auf einer tieferen, obschon generellen Ebene, die der »ikonischen« Form, die das Bild angenommen hatte, entsprach. Die Demoiselles links und rechts von der Mitte vermitteln immer dunklere Einblicke in die Natur des Weiblichen. Nachdem PICASSO einmal die narrative Vermittlung verlassen hatte, machte sein Bild meiner Meinung nach diese Stilunterschiede erforderlich, um die Polarität zwischen Eros und Thanatos – dem Reiz des weiblichen Körpers und »der Abscheu« davor – zu überbrücken. Diese Polarität steckte, wie wir sehen werden, schon in seinem ursprünglichen Konzept. Man muß PICASSOS Umwandlung der

Demoiselles von einem narrativen in ein »ikonisches« Bild im Zusammenhang mit einer konsequenten Entwicklung auf einen statischen, frontalen und konzentrierten Bildtyp hin sehen, der für die Aus- und Umarbeitung der vier ehrgeizigsten Bilder Picassos aus den Jahren 1905–09 wie auch für die Entwicklung seiner Kunst von der ›Rosa‹ zur frühen kubistischen Periode bestimmend ist.

Das »Ikonisieren« der *Demoiselles* stand im Zentrum der stilistischen und symbolischen Neuerungen, die das Bild zu einem kunsthistorischen Wendepunkt werden ließen – allerdings aus Gründen, die sich von den üblicherweise genannten unterscheiden. Die *Demoiselles* sind, wie ich bereits sagte, nicht das »erste kubistische Gemälde«.[38] Sie stehen zwar vor Picassos Übergang von einer wahrnehmungsorientierten zu einer konzeptuellen Arbeitsweise und lassen etwas von dem flachen Reliefraum ahnen, der für den Kubismus charakteristisch werden sollte, doch ist dieses große und radikale Werk dem Wesen und der Struktur des Kubismus insgesamt konträr, obschon es ihm den Weg bereitete. Die *Demoiselles* verwischten die Spuren der Malerei des 19. Jahrhunderts, die noch im Fauvismus, dem avantgardistischen Stil der unmittelbar vorausgegangenen Jahre, nachwirkten. Es handelt sich also eher um eine Malerei der Abkehr von der Moderne des späten 19. Jahrhunderts – und von der nachmittelalterlichen Malerei des Westens im allgemeinen – als um einen Durchbruch zum Kubismus. Die ersten kubistischen Gemälde waren Braques Landschaften von L'Estaque vom Sommer 1908 und die Neufassungen, die Picasso im späteren Verlauf desselben Jahres an *Drei Frauen* und *Carnaval au bistrot* (in der Art von *Brot und Fruchtschale auf einem Tisch*) vornahm; dennoch erklärt die zentrale Stellung der *Demoiselles* ihre Bedeutung für das Verständnis des frühen Kubismus.

□ 322 *Henri Matisse, ›Marguerite‹, 1907, Öl auf Leinwand, 65 x 54 cm. Musée du Louvre, Schenkung Pablo Picasso, Paris.*

□ 321 *Pablo Picasso, ›Les Demoiselles d'Avignon‹, Ausschnitt von* □ *301.*

Seit den zwanziger Jahren wurden die *Demoiselles* überwiegend unter formalen Gesichtspunkten interpretiert, als Ausgangspunkt des Kubismus verstanden und sozusagen durch das verkehrte Ende des Teleskops betrachtet. Dies verhinderte nicht nur Untersuchungen zum tatsächlichen Beginn des Kubismus,[39] sondern führte auch zu einer grundlegenden Fehlinterpretation der *Demoiselles*. Die Lage veränderte sich durch Steinbergs Aufsatz über das Bild aus dem Jahre 1972,[40] der zu so etwas wie einer neuen Literatur über die *Demoiselles* anregte. Steinberg räumte mit dem weitverbreiteten Glauben auf, Picassos Umgestaltung der *Demoiselles* sei vor allem auf ein protokubistisches Interesse am Abstrakten zurückzuführen. Er wies nach, daß die Umarbeitung des Bildes stets von dem Wunsch nach einer immer deutlicheren Darstellung dessen, was Picasso von den ersten Entwürfen an ausdrücken wollte, getragen wurde: seine vielschichtigen und widersprüchlichen Empfindungen gegenüber den Frauen. Steinberg führte viele überzeugende Argumente an, um »das Trauma der sexuellen Begegnung« als Ursache für die Änderungen an dem Gemälde verständlich zu machen.

Die »afrikanischen« Figuren auf der rechten Seite der *Demoiselles* beurteilte Steinberg jedoch ausschließlich als Verkörperungen »rein sexueller Energie, als Abbild einer Lebenskraft«. Dies steht im Einklang mit seiner Gesamtdeutung des Gemäldes als einer Darstellung »orgiastischen Eintauchens« und »dionysischer Ausgelassenheit«. Diese Deutung Steinbergs erscheint mir zu enggefaßt, da die beiden »afrikanischen« Figuren (und in geringerem Maße die gauguineske »ozeanische« Demoiselle[41] auf der linken Seite) nach meinem Dafürhalten genauso, wenn nicht noch mehr, von der Furcht vor dem Tod als von der Lebenskraft inspiriert wurden. Nach freudianischem Verständnis wäre der Schatten der Sterblichkeit ja in jedem Bild enthalten, das eine »sexuelle Metapher« ist, – wie Steinberg die *Demoiselles* nennt. Ich bin aber der Überzeugung, daß dieser schon sehr explizit im ersten Entwurf des

Gemäldes vorhanden war, durch PICASSOS absichtliche Darstellung eines Medizinstudenten gleichzeitig mit einem Matrosen, und daß die Todesfurcht in der Endfassung in einer lebhafteren, obschon allgemeineren Form erhalten bleibt. Die Dimension der Todesfurcht in den *Demoiselles* bedurfte der Erläuterung nicht nur, weil sich dadurch bestätigt, daß die Endfassung des Gemäldes eher an Tiefe gewann und nicht von der ursprünglichen Intention abwich – und dadurch der Wert des Ikonischen (im Gegensatz zum Narrativen) zum Erreichen dieses Ziels deutlich wird –, sondern auch, weil ein neues Licht auf das Rätsel des primitiven Einflusses geworfen wird.

Die gleichzeitige Darstellung von Eros und Thanatos in den *Demoiselles* erinnert an eine besondere seelische Komponente PICASSOS: die ihm eigene, tief verwurzelte Furcht und Abneigung vor dem weiblichen Körper – die einherging mit seinem Verlangen nach ihm und seiner ekstatischen Idealisierung. Diese ambivalente Haltung trat ab und zu in PICASSOS Kunst wie in seinem Verhalten zutage; sie wird dadurch parodiert, daß er – wie er es zugab – die Frauen »entweder wie Göttinnen oder wie Fußabstreifer« behandelte. Natürlich sind vergleichbare Syndrome von Angezogen- und Abgestoßensein in der männlichen Psyche keine Seltenheit. Doch wie so oft im Werk eines großen Künstlers, werden in den *Demoiselles* solche banalen Vorgaben durch den Geist des Genies so erweitert, daß sich eine neue Einsicht ausdrückt – die obgleich so gewöhnlich, so universell ist.

PICASSOS Gefühle der Abscheu vor dem weiblichen Körper wurden im ersten Stadium der *Demoiselles* durch einen erzählerischen Kunstgriff dargestellt, der auf die Gefahr einer venerischen Krankheit, die zur damaligen Zeit oft tödlich verlief, anspielte (PICASSO hatte viele Jahre hindurch Bordelle besucht). Darin liegt die wahre Beobachtung der Gegenüberstellung von Matrose und Medizinstudent (der einen Totenschädel trägt) im ersten Entwurf.[42] Die Identität, die Attribute und die Stellung der männlichen Figuren tragen mehr als nur zur narrativen Bestimmung von Zeit, Ort und Handlung in dem Bordell bei. Das Bild erlaubt viele Lesarten, aber insofern der Matrose den verkörpert, der sich in einem Freudenhaus die Syphilis holt, und der Medizinstudent jenen, der sie heilt, spiegelt ihre Zusammenstellung einen selten erwähnten, doch sehr bedeutsamen Aspekt von PICASSOS Veranlagung – seine übertriebene Sorge vor der Geschlechtskrankkeit bei einer gleichzeitigen Faszination, wie sie sich in seinen Besuchen des Jahres 1902 im Hôpital Saint-Lazare ausdrücken, wo er Prostituierte, die an Syphilis behandelt wurden, studierte.[43] Dieser Beweggrund blieb nicht völlig unbemerkt. Mary Mathews Gedo, die zwar die wechselseitige Symbolhaftigkeit in der Zusammenstellung der beiden männlichen Figuren übersah, wagte dennoch die Behauptung, daß »der [von dem Medizinstudenten getragene] Schädel sich darauf beziehen könnte, daß PICASSO sich irgendwo und irgendwann in seiner jugendlichen Liebeslaufbahn mit einer Geschlechtskrankheit infiziert hat«.[44] Die Vermutung, daß PICASSO selbst infiziert war, ist unnötig, auch gibt es für eine solche Annahme keinen sicheren Beweis. Es ist mehr als ausreichend, daß der Maler eine solche durchaus mögliche tödliche Ansteckung zutiefst fürchtete.

Die Endfassung des Gemäldes stellt keinen erzählerischen Bezug mehr zu PICASSOS Furcht vor der Krankheit oder dem Tod her. Diese Furcht geht vielmehr in einer allgemeineren Furcht vor dem Sterbenmüssen auf, die durch direktere bildnerische Techniken vermittelt wird. Wir empfinden die Todesfurcht in dem vorzeitlichen Schrecken, der von den monströs verzerrten Köpfen der beiden Prostituierten auf der rechten Seite des Gemäldes ausgeht, die einen starken Gegensatz zu den vergleichsweise anmutigen iberischen Kurtisanen in der Mitte bilden. Man kann die Furcht, den Schock und das Grauen, die diese Köpfe im Jahr 1907 ausgelöst haben müssen, kaum ermessen, zieht man die Lebhaftigkeit, mit der wir sie noch heute empfinden, in Betracht. Diese »afrikanischen« Gesichter drücken, glaube ich, mehr aus als nur den »barbarischen« Charakter reiner Sexualität, wie Steinberg meint; im ersten Augenblick spielt ihre Brutalität auf die Frau als zerstörendes Wesen an – eine Nachwirkung der symbolistischen femmes fatales –, doch beschwören sie schließlich etwas, das über unseren zivilisierten Erfahrungshorizont hinausgeht, etwas Geheimnisvolles und Schreckliches, wie es Joseph Conrads Romanfigur Kurtz im *Herz der Finsternis* entdeckte.

Gerade weil PICASSO nach neuen Möglichkeiten der Vermittlung dieser vorzeitlichen Schreckenserfahrung suchte, nicht weil die Stammeskunst eine protokubistische Morphologie zur Verfügung stellte, ließ er sich von ihr in diesem besonderen Moment anregen. In dem Maße also, wie die *Demoiselles* auf der rechten Seite von Vorstellungen über die Stammeskunst angeregt wurden, die der Besuch im Trocadéro auslöste, öffnet sich ihr Bild den kollektiven Bedeutungen des Maskierens, wie sie Lévi-Strauss nachwies. Insofern aber diese Gesichter eigentlich durch PICASSOS Suche nach plastischen Entsprechungen zur Bannung seiner eigenen psychologischen Dämone zustande kamen, stellen sie eine Art visueller Abreaktion dar und bringen uns zu Freuds Deutung des Maskierens.

Sie besagt, daß ein Gefühl, dessen direkte Empfindung zu schmerzhaft wäre (hier die Furcht des Künstlers vor dem Tod durch Krankheit), durch seinen Austausch gegen ein »verhülltes« Bild verarbeitet wird.

Obwohl PICASSO seit dem 2. Weltkrieg ernsthaft das Gegenteil behauptete, hatte er, wie bereits erläutert, Beispiele der »art nègre« schon mindestens sechs Monate, bevor sie in die *Demoiselles* Eingang fanden, gesehen. Aber er hatte auf diese Eindrücke – genausowenig wie auf seine frühe Begegnung mit *ROUSSEAU* – nicht angesprochen, da sie mit seinen damaligen Bedürfnissen nicht korrespondierten. PICASSOS »Offenbarung« im Trocadéro soll laut Zervos und anderen, die in den *Demoiselles* keine Auswirkungen der »art nègre« sahen, Ende Juli 1907 stattgefunden haben, nachdem PICASSO das Gemälde vollendet hatte. Aber sie fand mit Sicherheit im Juni statt, als er nur die erste (iberische) Fassung der *Demoiselles,* von der nur die zwei Figuren in der Mitte übriggeblieben sind, fertiggestellt hatte. Auch stellte der Künstler in seinen Gesprächen mit André Malraux (1937) zwischen den *Demoiselles* und der »art nègre« eine Beziehung her.[45]

PICASSO begab sich eines Tages ins Musée de Sculpture Comparée, das in einem Flügel des Trocadéro untergebracht war, um die Gipsgüsse romanischer Plastik anzuschauen. Er war schon vorher dort gewesen, und die Tatsache, daß es ihn zu einer Kunst zog, die damals als »primitiv« galt, ist sicherlich symptomatisch – ein weiterer Fall von PICASSOS berühmter »Vorahnung«, die ihm hier Lösungen aufzeigte, um seine Unzufriedenheit mit den *Demoiselles* zu überwinden. Er war jedoch nie zuvor im Musée d'Ethnographie gewesen, das im zweiten Flügel des Trocadéro untergebracht war. Wie er später sagte, hatte er mehr Glück als Verstand, daß er dort hineinging. Im Nachhinein erscheint dies jedoch als eine logische Folge seiner Suche, die ihn ins Musée de Sculpture Comparée geführt hatte. Zwar sagte PICASSO, er sei praktisch über das ethnologische Material gestolpert,[46] doch sind die Gebäude so angelegt, daß er das eine Museum verlassen mußte, um das andere zu betreten.

Beim Eintritt in das Musée d'Ethnographie mußte er durch die große Rotundengalerie kommen, die damals der afrikanischen und ozeanischen Plastik gewidmet war und in der große, mit Masken und Kostümen bekleidete Puppen in kriegerischen oder rituellen Haltungen ausgestellt waren. Seine verschiedentlichen Bemerkungen über die Dunkelheit, den schlechten Geruch, den armseligen Aufbau und die allgemeine Schäbigkeit dieses Ortes[47] beziehen sich wohl mehr auf die einzelnen Räume als auf die Rotunde. Die afrikanische Galerie scheint damals in einem besonders schlechten Zustand gewesen zu sein (siehe ihre Beschreibung bei Paudrat, S. 151, 152). Sie war noch verwirrender präsentiert, als es sich auf den Photographien aus dem Jahre 1895 heute darstellt □ 162, 452. Man gelangte direkt von der Rotunde in diese Galerie, die, von kurzen, wenn anscheinend auch häufigen Ausnahmen abgesehen, dem Publikum offenstand.[48] Eine Treppe verband sie direkt mit der ozeanischen Galerie □ 327, 380, die sich wohl in einem besseren Zustand befand, da sie seit ihrer Einrichtung »offiziell« geschlossen war – obschon sie der wichtigste Museumsführer von Paris als regelmäßig geöffnet auswies. »Geschlossen« hieß lediglich, daß man sie nur mit Zustimmung oder in Begleitung des Wärters betreten durfte.[49]

Picassos Berichte von diesem Besuch (und von einigen nachfolgenden)[50] lassen vermuten, daß er sich ziemlich frei bewegen durfte. Wegen des Ekels, den er vor dem Ort empfand, wäre er am liebsten gleich geflohen. Aber irgend etwas hinderte ihn, sich von den Stammesobjekten abzuwenden, so daß er schließlich blieb. Als er das Museum später wieder verließ, verspürte er ein Gefühl der Erleichterung. Er dachte zunächst, dies liege nur an der frischen Luft, doch er merkte gleich, daß etwas nicht ganz Angenehmes, ja etwas zutiefst Beunruhigendes in ihm vorgegangen war.[51] Die Wörter – »Schock«, »Offenbarung«, »Belastung«, »Zwang« –, die er gegenüber Malraux, mir und anderen immer wieder gebrauchte, machen deutlich, daß er sowohl ein Trauma als auch ein Erweckungserlebnis erfahren hatte.

Insofern das Trauma mit den noch tastenden Versuchen auf dem Gebiet psychologischer Erfahrung zu tun hatte – der Selbstanalyse, die ihn beschäftigte, seitdem er die ›Summa‹ seines Lebens, zu der die *Demoiselles* werden sollten, in Angriff genommen hatte –, war es die »magische« Vorstellung von der Kunst als Katharsis, die zuerst Picassos Interesse an den Masken und Figurenplastiken weckte. Es fiel ihm später schwer, diesen Gedanken deutlich zu machen, u. a. vielleicht deswegen, weil seine Sicht der Stammeskunst lange als rein formalistisch fehlgedeutet worden war.[52] Er reagierte jedoch auch auf den reduktiven, ideographischen Charakter der Werke (die er Salmon gegenüber als »raisonnable« – d. h. vom konzeptuellen her logisch – beschrieb) sowie auf die ästhetischen Besonderheiten einiger Objekte; dies wird aus Zeichnungen der Jahre 1907 und 1908 evident. Picassos ambivalente Einstellung gegenüber den Objekten, die er sowohl »magicaux« als auch »raisonnables« nannte, bedeutet jedoch keinen Widerspruch. Das erste Wort beschrieb ihre Aufgabe und ihre Kraft; das zweite die Logik ihrer verschiedenen reduktiven und ideographischen (im Gegensatz zu deskriptiven) Darstellungsweisen.[53]

Picassos vehemente Reaktion auf den Besuch im Trocadéro war sicherlich der Auslöser für die »zweite Phase« der Arbeit

□ 323 *Pablo Picasso, ›Frauenbüste‹ (Buste de femme), 1907, Öl auf Leinwand, 81 x 60 cm. Privatsammlung, Schweiz*

an den *Demoiselles*, die damit aus einer erneuten und intensiveren Begegnung mit der Stammeskunst heraus aufgenommen wurde – gerade in dem Augenblick, als er nach einer angemessenen Visualisierung seiner dunklen Vorahnungen und geheimen Ängste suchte. Nicht zufällig nannte er die *Demoiselles* später sein »erstes Exorzismusbild«. »Für mich waren die [Stammes-] Masken nicht einfach Plastiken«, erklärte er Malraux. »Es waren magische Objekte . . . Vermittler . . . bei allem – bei unbekannten, drohenden Geistern . . . Es waren Waffen – um zu verhindern, daß die Leute von Geistern beherrscht wurden, um sich von ihnen zu befreien.« »Wenn wir diesen Geistern eine Gestalt verleihen«, sagte er (mit einer vollkommenen Definition dessen, was ich vorhin »visuelle Abreaktion« nannte), »dann werden wir frei.«[54]

Meine Überzeugung, daß der Besuch im Trocadéro der Umarbeitung der beiden Demoiselles auf der rechten Seite voranging, gründet sich zum Teil auf Aspekte dieser Figuren, die allein durch die Kenntnis von ein paar Objekten aus den französischen Territorien in Afrika nicht zu erklären sind, die er in den Ateliers von Derain, Vlaminck und Matisse in den sechs oder acht Monaten zuvor gesehen hatte. Bis 1907 hatte der Trocadéro eine große Zahl vielfältigster afrikanischer und ozeanischer Objekte erworben, von denen ich mit Hilfe meiner Kollegin Judith Cousins ein Verzeichnis angefertigt habe; bedauerlicherweise kann hier nur ein kleiner Teil des Materials abgebildet werden (die Eingangsdaten dieser Objekte sind mit

□ 324 *›Maske‹ (Gesamt- und Kopfansicht), Oba, Vanuatu (ehemals Neue Hebriden), Baumrinde und Holzfasern, bemalt, Höhe 15 cm. Musée de l'Homme, Paris. Erworben 1894.*

angegeben). Der Trocadéro präsentierte PICASSO nicht nur unzählige Objekte von größerer stilistischer Vielfalt als er sie bei Künstlerkollegen sah, sondern, was wichtiger ist, er stellte sie in einen anderen Kontext. Plastiken in einem Künstleratelier zu sehen, heißt, sie in einer Situation ästhetischen Genießens zu erfahren. Aus dieser Perspektive hinterließ die »art nègre« zwischen dem Herbst 1906 und dem Juni 1907 bei PICASSO überhaupt keinen Eindruck.[55] Dann betrachtet PICASSO diese Masken und »Fetische« plötzlich in einem anziehenden neuen Licht, und er erkennt, daß sie für seine Absichten, die er in den *Demoiselles* verfolgt, von Bedeutung sind. Er denkt nun in Kategorien von »Exorzismus«, »Vermittlung« und »Magie«. Was wäre logischer gewesen als die Tatsache, daß seine »Offenbarung« sich in einem Völkerkundemuseum ereignete, wo die isolierten Masken und Statuetten der Künstlerateliers durch Puppen in vollem Ornat ersetzt waren, umgeben von Kunstwerken, die ihre Kulturen lebendig machten und außerdem ihre rituelle Funktion anhand von Beschriftungen erklärt wurde?

Obgleich die magischen, exorzistischen Wurzeln der Kunst im Mittelpunkt von PICASSOS »Offenbarung« stehen, veranlaßt mich noch ein anderer Zug der »afrikanischen« Figuren in den *Demoiselles*, sie mit dem Besuch im Trocadéro in Verbindung zu bringen: ihre ironischerweise »ozeanische« Farbgebung. (Die afrikanischen Objekte sind meistens unbemalt oder wenn, dann nur leicht gefärbt – ausgenommen die folkloristische Palette der *YORUBA*; dies steht in Einklang mit dem prinzipiellen, vollplastischen Charakter afrikanischer Skulptur im Gegensatz zum vorwiegend malerischen Charakter der meisten ozeanischen Plastiken.) Die Greifbarkeit der maskenhaften Gesichter der rechts stehenden Demoiselles weist zwar nach Afrika, doch erinnern ihre satten Farben, die aufdringlich, ja sogar brutal miteinander kontrastieren, an die oft beißenden Zusammenstellungen von Orange, Blau, Weiß und Gelb bei bestimmten ozeanischen Objekten. Diese Farbkontraste stehen jedoch in keiner Beziehung zu Objekten aus Tahiti, von den Marquesasinseln oder aus Neukaledonien, die Pariser Künstler in den Jahren 1906–07 kaufen konnten, sondern zur Kunst aus anderen Gebieten wie den Neuen Hebriden (ein gemeinsam von Frankreich und England verwaltetes Protektorat) und aus Neuguinea, deren Plastik in Frankreich damals noch nicht im Handel war, wenngleich solche stark farbigen Stücke im 19. Jahrhundert in den Trocadéro Eingang gefunden hatten.[56] Plötzliche Stilveränderungen haben ihre Ursache bei Picasso oft in der Begegnung mit einer provozierenden, ihm bislang unvertrauten Kunst, die sein augenblickliches Denken und Fühlen spontan anspricht. Angesichts des plötzlichen Sprungs in einer Entwicklung, der in den rechts befindlichen Figuren der *Demoiselles* zum Ausdruck kommt, ist nach dem Auslöser zu fragen – und es gibt nicht nur keine besondere, sondern überhaupt keine andere Erklärung dafür als den Besuch im Trocadéro, den der Künstler selbst als »Schock« und als »Offenbarung« bezeichnete.

Die nie zuvor dagewesene grobe Farbgebung und der vernichtende malerische Angriff auf der rechten Seite der *Demoiselles* (und in den zugehörigen Gemälden □ 323) sind manchmal zu Unrecht mit dem Fauvismus in Verbindung gebracht worden. Dessen Farbigkeit blieb aber in seiner ganzen Entwicklung dem Wesen nach dekorativ und baute auf den drei Grundfarben auf. Außerdem war der Farbauftrag selbst beim »wildesten« Beispiel (Vlamincks *Holzfäller*) noch weit von der

□ 325 *Pablo Picasso, ›Les Demoiselles d'Avignon‹, Ausschnitt von* □ *301.*

□ 326 *›Maske‹, Malekula, Vanuatu (ehemals Neue Hebriden), Palmholz, bemalt, Höhe 63,5 cm. Field Museum of Natural History, Chicago.*

□ 327 *Exponate des Ozeaniensaals im Jahr 1895. Musée d'Ethnographie du Trocadéro (jetzt Musée de l'Homme), Paris.*

Kühnheit, der fast greifbaren Körperlichkeit einiger Pinselstriche in den *Demoiselles* entfernt. PICASSOS neuartige Farbgebung hat auch nichts mit GAUGUINS dekorativer Palette oder der expressionistischeren Chromatik der »Brücke«-Maler wie NOLDE und KIRCHNER zu tun, deren typische Farbskalen sich frühestens ein Jahr nach den *Demoiselles* herausbildeten (obschon nicht auszuschließen ist, daß sich eine gewisse Roheit ihrer Farbgebung gleichfalls aus ozeanischen Quellen ableitet). Die Expressionisten bevorzugten Farbtöne in dritter oder vierter Brechung, die ihren Bildern genau jene »kränkliche« psychologische Aura, jenes Angstgefühl, das sie auszudrücken suchten, verlieh. PICASSOS neue, »primitive« Koloristik von 1907 bleibt näher an primären und sekundären Farben als die der Deutschen, aber nicht so nahe an dem Primären wie die der Fauvisten. Die besonderen Orange-, Blau-, Rot-, Gelb- und Weißtöne, die er in den *Demoiselles* und verwandten Studien einsetzte, haben nichts mit den Farben, wie sie die französische Malerei jener Zeit kennt, zu tun. Die von PICASSO bevorzugten Farben sind insgesamt gesehen nicht nur satter, sondern die chromatischen Intervalle, die aneinandergrenzenden Farbtöne trennen, sind auch auf das Heftigste dissonant und somit völlig antidekorativ.

Dafür gibt es in der westlichen Kunst kein Vorbild. Aber die ozeanischen Kunstwerke, die im Trocadéro zur Zeit von PICASSOS Besuch ausgestellt waren, nehmen einiges davon vorweg. Eine Maske von denen Neuen Hebriden etwa □ 326 besteht aus Orange-, Blau- und Weißtönen, die denen der *Demoiselles* nahestehen, wobei ihre übertriebene Nase und ihr grimassenhaftes Grinsen – obschon PICASSO weit davon entfernt war, sie nachzuahmen – mit einer Art »schrecklichem« Expressionismus, den er einleitete, übereinstimmen. Dieser PICASSO eigene Expressionismus (den er in der Zeit von 1925 bis zum 2. Weltkrieg wiederbeleben sollte) und nicht so sehr der deutsche Expressionismus, wie so häufig angenommen, hat POLLOCK und DE KOONING in den frühen 40er Jahren angeregt und direkt zum grimassenhaften »Lächeln« auf dem Gesicht von DE KOONINGS *Frau I* geführt.

Gab es kein westliches Vorbild für die Farbpalette der rechten Seite der *Demoiselles*, so gab es auch keines für die maskenhaften Köpfe. Ihre »Verzerrungen« ergänzen die grobe Farbgebung, und diese beiden Eigenschaften zusammen verleihen den Figuren genau jenen Ausdruck von Ehrfurcht, Schock und Schrecken, den PICASSO anscheinend brauchte, um sich von seiner sexuell motivierten Angst vor Krankheit und Tod zu befreien. Sie bilden auch einen verräterischen Kontrast zum Bild der attraktiven Frau, das uns in den mittleren Figuren der *Demoiselles* entgegentritt.[57] Die »schrecklichen« Köpfe der

☐ 328 *Pablo Picasso, ›Stehende Figur‹ (Figure debout), 1907, bemaltes Holz, 37 x 6 x 6 cm, Basis 40 x 21 x 10 cm. Privatsammlung.*

☐ 329 *›Figur eines Männerbundes‹ (Ausschnitt), Malekula, Vanuatu (ehemals Neue Hebriden), bemaltes Farnholz, Gesamthöhe 270 cm. Musée de l'Homme, Paris. Erworben 1890.* ▷

rechten Figuren sind seit Entstehung des Gemäldes mit Stammesmasken – insbesondere afrikanischer Herkunft – in Verbindung gebracht worden. Tatsächlich haben ihr betont skulpturaler Charakter und einige Besonderheiten ihrer Erscheinung ein eindeutig afrikanisches Gepräge. Dennoch steht die »ozeanische« Farbgebung, die PICASSO den »afrikanischen« Köpfen verlieh, mit diesen Zügen in vollkommener Harmonie. PICASSO hatte natürlich keine Bedenken, Charakteristika unterschiedlichster Kulturen miteinander zu vermischen. Die ästhetische Einheit ist schließlich keine Frage der Quellen des Künstlers, sondern seines Werkes, und PICASSOS Vermischung von »afrikanischer« Plastizität mit »ozeanischer« Farbgebung auf der rechten Seite der *Demoiselles* war genial.

Außer vagen Vermutungen, daß Stammesplastiken mit Fruchtbarkeits- und Todesvorstellungen zu tun hätten (was nicht immer stimmt), wußten PICASSO und andere Maler seiner Zeit nichts Konkretes über ihren tatsächlichen Kontext, ihre Aufgabe und ihre Bedeutung. Ihre Unkenntnis war insofern von Vorteil, als sie dadurch frei waren, die Objekte je nach

□ 330 *›Holzfigur‹,* TEKE *(Volksrepublik Kongo), Höhe 30 cm. Musée de l'Homme, Paris. Erworben 1904.*

□ 331 *›Reliquiarfigur‹,* KOTA *(Volksrepublik Kongo), Holz, Kupfer und Messing, Höhe 50 cm. Musée de l'Homme, Paris. Erworben 1883 (siehe Anm. 84).*

□ 332 *›Maske‹,* GREBO, *Sassandra (Elfenbeinküste), bemaltes Holz, Federn, verschiedene Materialien, Höhe 29 cm. Musée de l'Homme, Paris. Erworben 1900.*

persönlicher Interessenlage zu deuten. Es bedarf auch kaum der Erwähnung, daß sich diese Unkenntnis auch auf die Geographie erstreckte. Wie andere Künstler seiner Generation unterschied PICASSO damals wie auch noch im späteren Leben nicht immer zwischen afrikanischer und ozeanischer Stammeskunst. Beide fielen unter den Begriff »art nègre«.[58] In dem Maß allerdings, wie eine Unterscheidung getroffen wurde, war das Ozeanienbild der Pariser Künstler von PICASSOS Generation, etwa bei MATISSE, eher ein Synkretismus aus der Lebenswelt der Polynesier (mehr noch als aus ihrer Kunst), ihrem Niederschlag im Werk GAUGUINS und den (vor allem literarischen) Voraussetzungen des französischen »Mythos vom Primitiven«, der GAUGUIN inspiriert hatte. So steckte in »ozeanisch« neben einem verdunkelnden Substrat an mysteriösem Ritual die üppige und unbedrohliche Naturwelt Polynesiens, wie sie Bougainvilles *Voyage autour du monde* feierte.

Solche Assoziationen erweckte das Wort »afrikanisch« nicht; dieser beschwor etwas Fetischistischeres, Magischeres und vor allem potentiell Bösartiges – das Conrads *Herz der Finsternis* viel näher stand als GAUGUINS *Noa-Noa.*[59] Die archetypische »Nachtfahrt« der Seele, wie sie in *Herz der Finsternis* mit der Metapher von Kurtz' Reise in den inneren Kongo unternommen wird, scheint mir mit PICASSOS Eintauchen in seine Psyche während der Arbeit an den *Demoiselles* geistig verwandt. Man könnte PICASSOS radikale Primitivisierung in den *Demoiselles* als eine malerische Formulierung von Conrads Worten ansehen: »Der Geist des Menschen ist zu allem fähig – weil alles in ihm steckt, die ganze Vergangenheit ebenso wie alle Zukunft.« Sicherlich sollten die »afrikanischen« Figuren auf der rechten Seite von PICASSOS Gemälde etwas Fremdes, Bedrohliches und im Grunde Unaussprechliches über »das Primitive« aussagen, wie Kurtz es in den Winkeln seines eigenen Unbewußten entdeckte, als er sich im Herzen des Kongo von den Zwängen der »Zivilisation« freimachte – ein Vorgang, den er in der Stunde seines Todes nur mit dem »Grauen« davor umschreiben konnte.

Die Rolle der »art nègre« in den *Demoiselles* wurde schon früh von Freunden PICASSOS wie Salmon, Stein und WILHELM UHDE eingehend diskutiert. Diese »Auslegung« des Gemäldes wurde bald so populär, daß die später zu Bildern verselbständigten Einzelmotive der *Demoiselles* »Afrikanischer Tänzer« oder »Afrikanischer Kopf« betitelt wurden, so als hätte PICASSO tatsächlich Bilder von Afrikanern gemalt oder zumindest afrikanische Figuren und Masken imitiert. Zu Beginn des 1. Weltkriegs erlebte diese Form der Kritik eine üppige Blüte in der Presse von Paris wie auch in New York, u. a. als Ergebnis der Aktivitäten des in Mexiko geborenen Karikaturisten, Künstlers, Unternehmers und vor allem Propagandisten MARIUS DE ZAYAS, der unter anderem als Mittelsmann zwischen Stieglitz und Paul Guillaume bei der Organisation der gefeierten Ausstellung afrikanischer Kunst in der Galerie »291« in New York im Jahre 1914 tätig war.[60] DE ZAYAS sah die ganze moderne Abstraktion als »Nachfahre« der Negerkunst,[61] von der er 1916 außerdem behauptete, sie sei der »Ausgangspunkt« der »ganzen Entwicklung« von PICASSOS Denken und Fühlen seit dem Jahre 1907 gewesen.[62] Er gab sich später gegenüber Alfred Barr offenbar als PICASSOS Gesprächspartner in dem heute berühmten Text aus, den Barr 1923 als »Statement gegenüber Marius de Zayas auf Spanisch«[63] in einem Nachdruck herausgab. In Wirklichkeit handelt es sich dabei aber um Äußerungen PICASSOS gegenüber Florent Fels.[64] Eine der Bemerkungen PICASSOS

□ 333 *›Maske‹,* SUSU *(Guinea), Stoff, Metall und Fasern, Höhe 60 cm. Musée de l'Homme, Paris. Erworben 1901.*

□ 334 *Pablo Picasso, ›Les Demoiselles d'Avignon‹, Ausschnitt von* □ *301.*

□ 335 *›Maske‹,* DAN *(Elfenbeinküste oder Liberia), Holz, Höhe 24,5 cm. Musée de l'Homme, Stiftung Baron von der Heydt, Paris. Erworben 1952.*

gegenüber Fels, die DE ZAYAS unterdrückte, weil sie seinen eigenen Theorien über die Rolle der »art nègre« zuwiderlief, geht auf die Frage nach der Wertigkeit primitiver Kunst ein. PICASSO äußerte, daß »die afrikanischen Plastiken, die überall in meinen Ateliers herumhängen, eher Zeugen als Vorbilder sind«.[65] Es steht außer Frage, daß die Art von Spekulationen, die DE ZAYAS und andere förderten, PICASSO verärgerten und ihn dazu provozierten, die Rolle der »art nègre« herunterzuspielen (und später sogar zu leugnen),[66] so weit, daß PICASSO seit dem 2. Weltkrieg hartnäckig behauptete, nicht nur keine Stammeskunst vor den *Demoiselles* gesehen zu haben, sondern auch, daß sein berühmter Besuch im Trocadéro eher nach als vor der Ausführung des Gemäldes stattgefunden habe. Wie um die »afrikanische« Deutung noch weiter zu erschüttern, äußerte sich PICASSO dann auch zum ersten Mal über die bis dahin unbeachtete Bedeutung der iberischen Kunst für die *Demoiselles*.[67]

Außer den Daten des Gemäldes selbst verdeutlichen jedoch die gemeinsamen Aussagen von Freunden, die ihn während der Entstehungszeit kannten, wie auch seine eigenen Bemerkungen im Gespräch mit Malraux im Jahre 1937, die sich auf die »art nègre« beziehen, daß PICASSOS spätere Kommentare eine Art Strategie waren (wie ich andernorts erläuterte),[68] um den vorherrschenden Theorien entgegenzuwirken und um der Diskussion um die *Demoiselles* und die ganze »afrikanische« Periode eine neue Richtung zu geben. Obwohl PICASSO bei gelegentlichen Besuchen in Künstlerateliers (bei MATISSE, VLAMINCK und DERAIN) in den sechs Monaten vor Inangriffnahme der *Demoiselles* ein paar afrikanische Objekte gesehen hatte und sein Besuch im Trocadéro eindeutig während und nicht nach ihrer Entstehung stattfand, hat PICASSO weder in diesem Gemälde noch in irgendeinem anderen, auch nicht in einer Zeichnung oder einer Skulptur irgendein Stammesobjekt regelrecht kopiert oder nachgeahmt. Entgegen der landläufigen Meinung spielte die Stammeskunst bei der Entstehung des Kubismus auch keine so große Rolle wie das Werk CÉZANNES. Das soll nicht heißen, daß Eindrücke von Stammesobjekten PICASSO nicht gelegentlich als Ausgangspunkt für seine Arbeit gedient hätten. Aber wenn dieser Fall eintritt, interessiert uns mehr noch als seine Quelle – sofern sie überhaupt zu erkennen ist – die Art, wie PICASSO sie umwandelte. Über die magische (d.h. psychologische und geistige) Kraft der Stammeskunst hinaus, war PICASSO von den Aspekten ihrer konzeptuellen Struktur beeindruckt, von Prinzipien, die er von ihren Trägern abstrahieren und in seinem Sinne gebrauchen konnte. Daher ähneln weder die beiden »afrikanischen« Köpfe auf der rechten Seite der *Demoiselles* noch der eine links außen, den ich als gauguinesk-»ozeanisch« bezeichnet habe, irgendeiner afrikanischen oder ozeanischen Maske, die PICASSO 1907 in Paris in den Ateliers seiner Freunde oder im Trocadéro gesehen haben könnte.[69]

Auch wenn sie von zu vereinfachten Vorstellungen von der Arbeitsweise PICASSOS ausgingen, haben Kunsthistoriker vier besondere Typen von Stammesmasken mit den *Demoiselles* in Verbindung gebracht. Nicht eine davon war *Picasso* jedoch im Jahre 1907 zugänglich. Alfred Barr[70] etwa kam auf eine (später auch von Laude[71] und anderen anerkannte) Beziehung zwischen dem Kopf rechts oben auf dem Gemälde – tatsächlich das maskenhafteste und »afrikanischste« der Gesichter – und einem Maskentyp aus dem *Etoumbi*-Gebiet im damaligen Französisch-Kongo □ 327. Dies bleibt ein sehr interessanter Vergleich, wenn er auch von einem Einfluß zu einer Verwandtschaft »degradiert« werden muß, weil keine der drei bekannten Masken dieses Typs vor 1929 nach Paris kamen.[72] Selbst wenn wir uns vorstellen, daß durch irgendeinen Zufall der Geschichte ein Matrose oder Kolonist eine solch seltene Maske aus dem *Etoumbi*-Gebiet nach Paris gebracht hätte, wären die Chancen, daß Picasso sie gesehen haben könnte, praktisch gleich Null. Wir wissen, daß sich keine solche Maske im Trocadéro befand (oder befindet), und wir wissen auch, daß dies überhaupt nicht die Art Objekt war, die seine drei Malerfreunde sammelten.[73] Diese besaßen damals wohl kaum mehr als dreißig afrikanische Plastiken, unter denen sich nur wenige Masken befanden. Diese vier Quellen stellen die Gesamtheit dessen dar, was Picasso bis zur Inangriffnahme und während der Arbeit an den *Demoiselles* an Stammeskunst zu sehen bekam. Da Picasso erst nach der Fertigstellung der *Demoiselles* mit dem Sammeln von Stammesobjekten begann,[74] hatte er noch keine entsprechenden Kunsthandlungen besucht; es wäre auch nur eine, Emile Heymanns ›Au Vieux Rouet‹, in Frage gekommen, die schon 1907 bestand. Wie ich bereits erläuterte, haben Ähnlichkeiten, wie die von Barr angedeuteten, nicht unbedingt den künstlerischen Kontakt zwischen den Urhebern dieser Objekte zur Voraussetzung. Alle Künstler, die den Menschen eher durch konzeptuelle Zeichen als deskriptiv darstellen, teilen viele formale Probleme und finden zum Teil auch gemeinsame Lösungen.

Beim Vergleich der Maske aus dem *Etoumbi*-Gebiet mit der Demoiselle rechts oben hob Laude die lange, dreieckige Nase der Maske hervor. Er sah sie als Quelle eines Nasentyps an, den man in Picassos Köpfen von Ende 1907 bis Anfang 1908 häufig findet und den die Franzosen *quart-de-brie* (Stück-Briekäse)-Nase nennen. Betrachten wir aber die anderen Nasen in Picassos Werken der »afrikanischen« Periode – zumindest die, die breit genug sind, um den Namen *quart-de-brie* zu verdienen –, erkennen wir, daß auf den meisten das Dreieck weniger von der Nase selbst – d. h. von der Vorderansicht der Nase wie bei der Demoiselle rechts oben und der *Etoumbi*-Maske – gebildet wird, als vielmehr von den Umrissen des Nasenprofils zusammen mit ihrem Schatten □ 323, 393. Diese Gestaltungsweise zeigen schon Köpfe aus der iberischen Phase der *Demoiselles* □ 316, die Picasso vor seinem Besuch im Trocadéro schuf. Das grobe Schraffieren, mittels dessen der Eindruck des Iberischen entstand, steht letztendlich am Anfang der parallel geführten komplementären Rot- und Grünstreifen, die den »Schatten« der Nase der Demoiselle rechts oben bilden. So liegt gerade der Ursprung der sog. *quart-de-brie*-Nase eher in der Malerei als in der Bildhauerei – eine Primitivisierung einer zweidimensionalen Schattierungsweise.

Dies sollte uns an einen Faktor erinnern, der bei der Suche einiger Kritiker nach primitiven Vorbildern von Picassos Werk oft vergessen wurde, daß nämlich diese mutmaßlichen Vorbilder Plastiken sind, während es sich bei den *Demoiselles* um ein Gemälde handelt, so daß ganz andere ästhetische Konventionen zum Tragen kommen. Indem Picasso die Konventionen der Malerei primitivisierte, verband er sie unstreitig mit Elementen der Flächengestaltung, Mustern von Hautritzungen

□ 336 *Pablo Picasso, ›Les Demoiselles d'Avignon‹, Ausschnitt von* □ *301.*

□ 337 *›Maske‹, Etoumbi-Gebiet (Volksrepublik Kongo), Holz, Höhe 35,5 cm. Musée Barbier-Müller, Genf.*

□ 338 *›Kifwebe-Maske‹*, SONGGE *(Zaire), bemaltes Holz, Höhe 50 cm. Sammlung J. W. Mestach, Brüssel.*

etwa, die ihm in primitiver Kunst begegnet waren. Aber in ihrer Gesamtheit setzt PICASSOS Primitivisierung in den *Demoiselles* die Verarbeitung der ganzen Tradition westlicher Malerei voraus. Tatsächlich ist trotz gegenteiliger Erscheinungen die moderne Malerei im allgemeinen stärker durch den westlichen Illusionismus als durch sonstige Vorbilder geprägt, denn ihre revolutionären Veränderungen operieren gerade aus dieser Gesamtheit überkommener Vorstellungen. So flacht etwa MATISSE häufig das Bild ab, als wolle er es von plastischen Elementen befreien, tut dies aber dennoch so, daß diese Elemente implizit erhalten bleiben. Daraus geht ein Bild mit plastischer Ausdruckskraft hervor, dessen spurenhafter Illusionismus sich von den Stilarten der Vorrenaissance, z. B. der ägyptischen Kunst, unterscheidet, da letztere von Anfang an flach waren. Dies gilt nicht in gleicher Weise für die Plastik PICASSOS (oder BRANCUSIS). Doch in der Phase von 1907–08 hat diese Plastik, von der das meiste unvollendet blieb, nur entfernte Beziehungen zu Stammesobjekten – und dann, wie wir noch sehen werden, zu ozeanischen genauso wie zu afrikanischen Vorbildern.

Der zweite der von den Gelehrten mit den *Demoiselles* in Verbindung gebrachten vier Maskentypen ist die DAN-Maske □ 335, die Golding in seinem klassischen Aufsatz zu den *Demoiselles* abbildet;[75] er vergleicht sie dort mit dem Kopf des dunklen Mädchens links außen □ 334. Natürlich behauptete er nicht, daß PICASSO gerade die Maske kannte, die sich in der Sammlung des Musée de l'Homme befindet. Sie gelangte auch erst 1952 dorthin. Aber jede Ähnlichkeit, die das Gesicht von PICASSOS Figur mit dieser oder einer anderen DAN-Maske haben könnte, wäre rein zufällig, da die ersten DAN-Masken erst ein paar Jahre nach der Fertigstellung der *Demoiselles* in Paris auftauchten. Die »Befriedung« der inneren Gebiete der Elfenbeinküste, wo die DAN leben, setzte erst 1908 ein und stieß auf heftigen Widerstand. Einige DAN-Masken könnten in den Jahren kurz vor dem 1. Weltkrieg in französische Häfen gelangt sein. Trotz ihrer späteren weiten Verbreitung kam die überwältigende Mehrzahl erst in der Zeit zwischen den Weltkriegen nach Europa. Eine DAN-Maske wurde 1919 bei Level und Clouzot abgebildet,[76] doch erwarb der Trocadéro sein erstes Exemplar erst 1931.

Trotz Goldings Vergleich des Kopfes der Figur links mit dem afrikanischen Werk schien mir dieses Gesicht dem Wesen nach durch und durch gauguinesk und über GAUGUIN wohl eher der ozeanischen oder der ägyptischen Kunst als irgend etwas Afrikanischem verpflichtet. Obgleich der Kopf dieser Demoiselle viele iberische Merkmale mit den Köpfen in der Mitte des Gemäldes teilt, vermitteln seine stärker summarischen und geometrischen Umrisse, die plastische Modellierung und die dunkle Farbe einen maskenhafteren Eindruck. Kopf und Hals scheinen, wie Golding beobachtete, sowohl stilistisch wie auch farblich eindeutig vom Rumpf losgelöst zu sein. Während die oberen Partien der beiden mittleren Figuren keine Spuren von Übermalung aufweisen, wurden Hals, Kopf, Haar, linke Hand und Teile des Körpers der Demoiselle links sicherlich umgearbeitet, nachdem PICASSO das Gemälde in seiner ursprünglich iberischen Form vollendet hatte. Dies geschah möglicherweise zur selben Zeit wie die Umarbeitung der beiden Demoiselles rechts oder doch etwas früher, wie mir scheint, so daß es wohl *zwei* Umarbeitungsphasen gab, zwischen die der Besuch im Trocadéro fiel. Auch Salmon scheint, wenn auch etwas verwirrend, in *La Jeune Peinture française* zwei Anläufe PICASSOS anzunehmen. Dies ist der einzige wirklich bedeutsame frühe Bericht eines Augenzeugen über die Fortschritte des Künstlers an seinem Bild.[77]

GAUGUINS Bild *Der Geist der Toten wacht* □ 249, das PICASSO wohl nur als Druck kannte (obwohl sich seine Elemente auch in *Noa-Noa* finden), enthält u.a. einen Tupapau (weiblicher Ahnengeist), halb Götze, halb Mensch, der auf der äußersten Linken plaziert ist und trotz einer reinen Profilansicht (nach rechts) ein Auge in Vorderansicht zeigt. Diese Besonderheiten weist auch PICASSOS Demoiselle, ebenfalls links im Bilde, auf. Und obwohl deren Gesicht maskenhafter und iberischer ist, scheint mir die Figur GAUGUINS in ihrer Aufnahme archaischer Einflüsse – vor allem aus Ägypten – derjenigen PICASSOS so nahe wie jede afrikanische oder ozeanische Maske. Auch gibt es keine Masken, die in der Profilansicht eine frontale Augenstellung haben. Dies ist eine Konvention der Malerei, die in der ägyptischen Tradition und anderen Formen archaischer Kunst, aus denen GAUGUIN schöpfte, ihren festen Platz hatte. Vom Poetischen und Psychologischen her ist *Der Geist der Toten wacht* für die *Demoiselles* sogar noch wichtiger. GAUGUIN zeigt ein verängstigtes junges Mädchen im Alter sexuellen Erwachens, das auf einem Bett liegt (GAUGUIN beschrieb diese Figur als »leicht unanständig«, und sie ist durchaus mit der Heldin seiner Paraphrase vom Verlust der Unschuld, *Nie wieder*, verwandt). Ihre »Angst« oder »Furcht« (GAUGUINS Worte) hat mit dem Tupapau in ihrer Vorstellung zu tun, also mit dem Tod. Die Verbindung von Eros und Thanatos in GAUGUINS Bild *Der Geist der Toten wacht* entspricht genau derselben Polarität, die ich als zentrales Anliegen der *Demoiselles d'Avignon* zu erkennen meine.

Daß PICASSO von einer ozeanischen (im Gegensatz zu einer afrikanischen) Vorlage bei den *Demoiselles* ausging, war eine von Ron Johnsons Thesen. Als mögliche Quelle für das Gemälde zog er eine Maske von der Torresstraße in Betracht □ 432, von der es hieß, daß sie in PICASSOS Sammlung gewesen sei.[78] PICASSOS Maske hat jedoch nicht den finsteren Blick der Schildkröten-Masken[79] dieser Region, die normalerweise das längliche Gesicht der eindrucksvollen Holzmaske, die wir unter □ 143 abbilden, aufweisen. PICASSOS Maske ist auch viel phantasievoller mit ihrem kleinen, aufgesetzten Zweitkopf und der Meeresmuschel-»Mütze«. Ihre runden Züge haben aber nichts mit den Gesichtern der *Demoiselles* zu tun, auch ihre blaßgrüne und rote Farbe ist dem Gemälde fremd. Wenn es auch nicht zu beweisen ist, soll PICASSO die Maske nach Aussagen seiner Freunde in den 20er Jahren erworben haben.[80] Charles Ratton, einer der Großen unter den französischen Händlern primitiver Kunst, versicherte mir auch, daß es nach seiner Kenntnis vor dieser Zeit in Paris keine Masken von der Torresstraße gab.

Die außergewöhnlichsten Masken, die mit den *Demoiselles* in Verbindung gebracht wurden, sind wohl die erstaunlich abstrakten Kifwebe-Masken der *SONGGE* □ 26, 338. Warren Robbins, ehemaliger Direktor des National Museum of African Art (Smithsonian Institution), gehört zu denen, die diese Masken – die sich normalerweise durch kühne Verzerrungen und einen großen Mund auszeichnen – mit dem Kopf der sitzenden Demoiselle rechts unten auf dem Gemälde in Verbindung brachten.[81] Aber PICASSO kann eine solche Maske unmöglich schon 1907 gesehen haben. Sogar heute besitzt das Musée de l'Homme nur ein Exemplar, das erst 1967 in die Sammlung kam. Außerdem sagte mir Ratton, daß die erste Kifwebe-Maske, die er in den späten 20er Jahren sah und dann 1935 auf der Ausstellung des Museum of Modern Art »African Negro Art« gezeigt wurde, die unter Abbildung □ 26 ist. Ratton teilte auch mit, daß Material aus dem damaligen Belgisch-Kongo, besonders aus dem Landesinneren, wo die *SONGGE* leben, bis nach dem 2. Weltkrieg auf den Pariser Märkten äußerst selten war. Sogar in Belgien, das 1908 den Kongo-Freistaat – bis dahin Privateigentum von Leopold II. – übernommen hatte, waren zu Beginn des Jahrhunderts Kifwebe-Masken der *SONGGE* selten. 1911 gelangte die erste Maske in das Musée Royal de l'Afrique Centrale in Tervuren, wo sich die größte Sammlung von Kifwebe-Masken befindet.[82]

□ 339 *Pablo Picasso, ›Les Demoiselles d'Avignon‹, Ausschnitt von* □ *301.*

□ 340 *›Mbuya-(Kranken-)Maske‹,* PENDE *(Zaire), bemaltes Holz, Fasern, Stoff, Höhe 26,5 cm. Musée Royal de l'Afrique Centrale, Tervuren, Belgien.*

Wie die meisten afrikanischen Objekte sind Kifwebe-Masken symmetrisch, wobei meistens der Mund (der oft das Kinn überdeckt) und nicht die Nase am deutlichsten absteht. Der Kopf der Demoiselle rechts unten hat einen kleinen Mund, der zur Seite verschoben und eher diagonal als horizontal verläuft; der expressionistische Ausdruck wird eher von der riesigen Knollennase, den asymmetrisch gesetzten, verschiedenfarbigen Augen sowie von den satten Orange- und Blautönen getragen. Die physische und psychische Gewalt, die in diesem Gesicht zum Ausdruck kommt, stimmt mit der im Fortgang des Malens immer stärker werdenden Torsion dieser Figur überein. Auf den frühen Entwürfen (Z. XXVI, 4) wird sie ganz von hinten und mit abgewandtem Blick gezeigt. Dann drehte sich ihr Kopf allmählich nach links, zunächst ins fliehende Profil □ 318, dann ins Vollprofil und schließlich in die Dreiviertelansicht zum

□ 341 *Stammesobjekte aus der Sammlung Picassos, wie er sie in seiner Villa La Californie, Cannes, lagerte. Photo von Claude Picasso, 1974.*

Betrachter □ 320. Aber immer zeigt ihr Körper dabei nach innen. In der Schlußfassung spiegeln die Formen mit einer fast perversen Wirklichkeitstreue die Gewaltsamkeit, mit der Picasso ihren Kopf gegen den gleichbleibend statischen Körper um 180° drehte – und ihr dabei den Hals »umdrehte«. Da Knollennasen mit grober Schattierung und asymmetrische Augen – wenn auch in gemäßigterer Form – bereits in den iberischen Entwürfen der *Demoiselles* vorkommen, boten die Objekte, die Picasso bei seinem ersten Besuch im Trocadéro sah, kaum mehr neue plastische Ideen an, sondern bestätigten nachträglich seine radikalen Schritte auf einem Weg, den er sich schon gebahnt hatte. Weder die rohesten Farben ozeanischer Kunst noch die gewagtesten Verzerrungen afrikanischer Plastik erreichen die Art expressionistischer Gewaltsamkeit, die Picasso in den sitzenden Demoiselles realisierte.

Obgleich Picasso keine Masken wie die Kifwebes der *Songge* oder die aus dem *Etoumbi*-Gebiet □ 337 gesehen haben konnte, interessieren uns Ähnlichkeiten als Ausdruck einer gemeinsamen bildnerischen Grundhaltung. Als solche sind sie ein Gradmesser dafür, wie weit Picasso die Prinzipien afrikanischer Plastik erfaßte. Diese Masken bezeichnen auch nicht die Grenzen von Picassos »Vorahnung« hinsichtlich afrikanischer Lösungen. Die stilisierten Asymmetrien einiger *Pende*-Masken □ 340 weisen noch mehr Analogien auf, auch in inhaltlicher Hinsicht, insofern als diese *masques de maladie* dem plastischen Charakter des Gesichts der sitzenden Demoiselle nicht nur ähnlicher sind, sondern auch Personen darstellen, die an fortgeschrittener Syphilis und anderen entstellenden Krankheiten leiden. Wie im Fall der anderen Masken kann Picasso jedoch keine *masque de maladie* im Paris des Jahres 1907 gesehen haben. Erst in den 20er Jahren kamen *Pende*-Masken in den Trocadéro, und noch heute gibt es dort keine Krankheitsmaske. Eine Picassos Figur viel weniger ähnliche Krankheitsmaske von der Elfenbeinküste (als »masque de guerre« mißdeutet) befand sich allerdings 1917 in der Sammlung André Level. Doch war sie Picasso mit Sicherheit ein Jahrzehnt früher nicht zugänglich.[83] Wir sollten allerdings nicht die Tatsache aus den Augen verlieren, daß sogar die gewaltsamsten Verzerrungen der afrikanischen *masques de maladie* reale Entstellungen des Gesichts wiedergaben; der Künstler brauchte nur die traditionelle Stilisierung seines Volkes auf physische Phänomene zu übertragen. Picassos Verzerrungen hingegen waren eine erfundene Projektion eines inneren, psychischen Zustandes. Sie stellen außerdem übersteigerte Formen von Asymmetrie dar, die sich schon in den ersten Projekten für die *Demoiselles* finden, die noch vor der Begegnung mit der Stammeskunst im Trocadéro entstanden sind.

Die Ähnlichkeiten zwischen den Köpfen der *Demoiselles* und den Masken, die man in kunsthistorischen Untersuchungen mit ihnen verglich, sind also rein zufällig – Ausdruck einer inneren Nähe von Kunstrichtungen, die sich durch konzeptuelle Zeichen mitteilen und nicht durch Konventionen der Malerei, die unmittelbar aus dem Sehen abgeleitet sind. Daß in Picassos Werk im Vergleich zu dem anderer Pioniere der Moderne weitaus mehr Ähnlichkeiten mit der Kunst der Stammesvölker zu erkennen sind, ist Beweis für eine tiefe geistige Übereinstimmung Picassos mit den Stammesvölkern sowie für seine allgemeine Assimilation der Prinzipien und des Charakters ihrer Kunst.

Obwohl die drei »maskierten« Demoiselles von Picassos Gemälde, abgesehen von den Hautritzungen, kaum direkte

Beziehungen zu irgendwelchen Masken aufweisen, die PICASSO damals gesehen haben könnte, äußert sich zumindest in der Kühnheit ihrer Abstraktion (auch in Aspekten der Oberflächengestaltung) die Verwandtschaft zu einem Typus primitiver Objekte, der im Trocadéro ausgestellt und schon vor der Jahrhundertwende in den Kuriositätenläden anzutreffen war, nämlich die mit Kupfer überzogenen Reliquiarfiguren (siehe Glossar) der *KOTA* und der *ONGWE*. Die *KOTA*-Figuren, die Golding und Barr mit den *Demoiselles* in Verbindung brachten, gibt es in einer eindrucksvollen Vielfalt, von der wir nur eine kleine Auswahl geben können □ 347, 349, 410, 411, 413, 721; schon zur Zeit von PICASSOS Besuch waren im Trocadéro die unterschiedlichsten Typen ausgestellt □ 342, 343. Die Gestaltung der Gesichter reicht von ziemlich realistischen Formen mit symmetrischen Diagonalstreifen, die keine Wundmale sind und manchmal stilisierte »Tränen« genannt werden, bis zu äußerst abstrakten Typen, bei denen das Gesicht nur aus einem abgesetzten Vertikalstreifen besteht, der zwischen zwei halbkreisförmigen Augen verläuft □ 344. Andere weisen eine große Vielzahl an Parallelmustern auf, die von Hautritzungen herrühren. Normalerweise haben die Köpfe eine ovale Form (manchmal laufen sie nach unten, nach oben oder nach beiden Seiten spitz zu) und können auch zu Rauten stilisiert sein.[84]

Die Köpfe der *ONGWE*-Reliquiarfiguren gehören im Gegensatz dazu einem einzigen Prototyp an – ein spitzes Oval, das unten waagerecht abgeschnitten ist □ 342, 487. In diesen *ONGWE*-Plastiken ist die konkave Kurve entlang der horizontalen Gesichtsachse manchmal perfekt im Gleichgewicht mit einer weniger ausgeprägten konkaven Kurve entlang der vertikalen. Typisch für die *ONGWE*-Gesichter ist ein Muster aus vielen dünnen Kupferstreifen, die horizontal und manchmal diagonal von der Mittelachse ausgehen. Dies erinnerte PICASSO zweifellos an Schraffuren, und viele seiner Skizzen aus den Jahren 1907–08 weisen ein solches afrikanisches Muster in den Schattierungen der Figuren auf, wie etwa die Ansicht von André Salmons Rücken □ 375. Auch hier hing die Übernahme eines besonderen Stammestyps davon ab, wie nahe dessen Gestaltungsmittel der Technik standen, die PICASSO bereits im Verlauf der radikalen Vereinfachungen nach Gosol entwickelte. Die *KOTA*- und *ONGWE*-Reliquiarfiguren sind sicherlich die abstraktesten Stammesskulpturen, die PICASSO kennenlernen konnte. Sie bilden zusammen mit den *BACA*-Figuren □ 365, 366, den *FANG*-Masken □ 392 und den Reliquiarköpfen □ 385 die wichtigsten afrikanischen Prototypen seiner Kunst in der Zeit vom Juni 1907 bis zum Sommer des folgenden Jahres. Der Maler besaß zwei *KOTA*-Reliquiarfiguren[85] □ 410, 411. Obwohl es weder photographische noch sonstige Zeugnisse über den Zeitpunkt des Erwerbs gibt, lassen die Einfachheit, die grobe Gestaltung und vor allem ihre Mittelmäßigkeit – von ihrem Einfluß auf sein Werk des Jahres 1907 einmal abgesehen –

□ 342 *›Reliquiarfigur‹, ONGWE (Gabun), Holz, Kupfer, Messing und Fasern. Höhe 49 cm. Musée de l'Homme, Paris. Erworben 1886.*

□ 343 *›Reliquiarfigur‹, KOTA (Gabun oder Volksrepublik Kongo), Holz, Kupfer und Messing, Höhe 40 cm. Musée de l'Homme, Paris. Erworben 1884.*

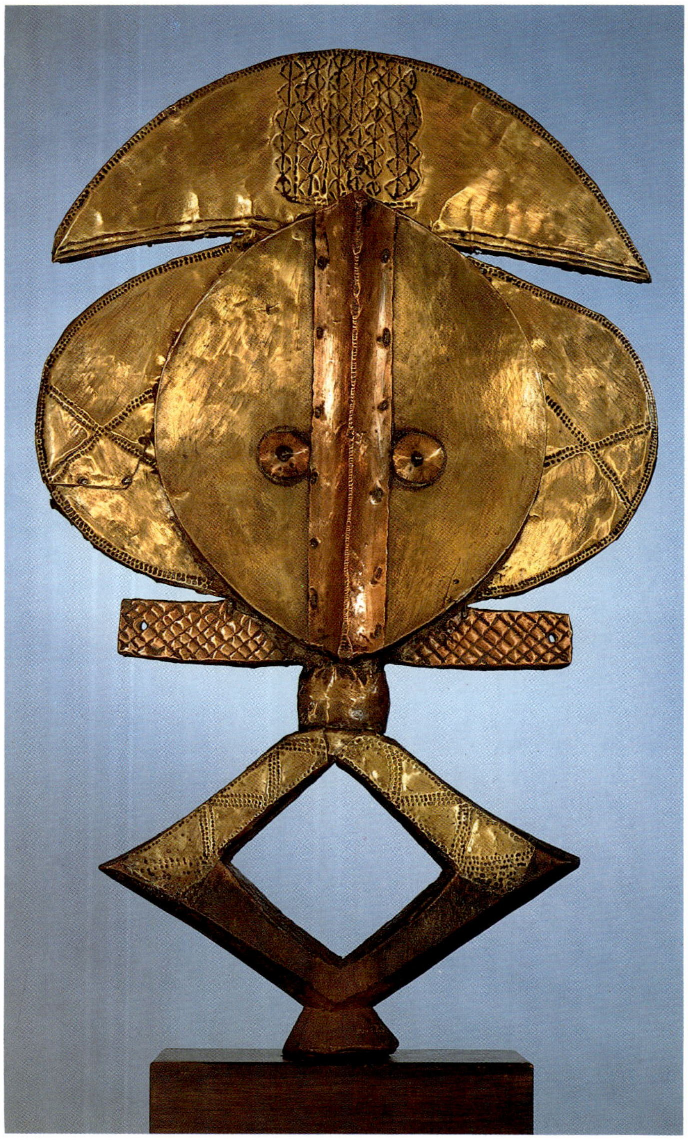

□ 345 *Pablo Picasso, ›Blatt mit Skizzen‹, 1907, Kohle, 60 x 40 cm. Privatbesitz, Frankreich. Auf der Rückseite die Kohlezeichnung ›Bildnis André Salmon‹, siehe □ 378.*

◁ □ 344 *›Reliquiarfigur‹, Kota (Gabun oder Volksrepublik Kongo), Holz, Kupfer und Messing, Höhe 57 cm. Privatbesitz.*

vermuten, daß sie den ersten Stammesobjekten, die er erwarb, zuzurechnen sind.[86] Zu Beginn des 1. Weltkriegs besaß Paul Guillaume einige sehr schöne *Kotas* □ 193, aber Picasso scheint sich nicht um sie bemüht zu haben (z. T. wohl deswegen, weil sie ziemlich teuer waren).[87]

Die rautenförmigen Stützen der *Kota*-Reliquienwächter wurden entgegen wissenschaftlicher Erkenntnis[88] oft und auch von modernen Künstlern für Beine gehalten. Wenn wir sie uns als Beine vorstellen, ergibt die Reliquiarfigur als Ganzes einen Tänzer – wie wir ihn in der kleinen hüpfenden Figur von Klees *Götzen* □ 720 erkennen. Die Fersen sind geschlossen und die Knie werden im Profil unterhalb des frontal gegebenen Kopfes nach außen gespreizt. Picasso war von dieser gebeugten Kniestellung offenbar fasziniert, da er sich in einer großen Zeichnung □ 345 damit beschäftigte, die ihrerseits in Gemälde einging, etwa in *Akt mit erhobenen Armen* □ 346, die im allgemeinen unter der Bezeichnung »Tanzende Figuren« oder »Afrikanische Tänzer« bekannt sind □ 351.

In dieser Zeit arbeitete Picasso ohne Modelle, ganz aus der Vorstellung, so daß er bei der Ausführung der genannten Kohlezeichnung eher von einer allgemeinen Erinnerung an *Kota*-Reliquiarfiguren als von einem bestimmten Objekt inspiriert war. Anders als Klee, der die rautenförmigen »Beine« der *Kota*-Figuren beibehielt, indem er die Knöchel zusammenließ, interessierte sich Picasso nur für die stark gebeugten Knie als Ausgangspunkt für eigene Gestaltungen. Bei der Figur rechts oben sind die Füße zwar zusammen, doch wurden die Knie asymmetrisch dargestellt – eine Asymmetrie, die alle aus diesem Motiv abgeleiteten Bilder kennzeichnet (sogar die, bei denen das gebeugte Knie nicht mehr vorkommt), so daß diese Bilder noch weiter von den Reliquiarfiguren entfernt sind. In diesen ungewöhnlichen Zeichnungen sehen wir, wie Picasso die flache Anlage der »Beine« der *Kota*-Figuren mit Ansätzen westlicher Raumperspektive zu verbinden suchte. Dieser flache, »zusammengebrochene« Reliefraum – Nebenprodukt des vormodernen westlichen Raums – war eben in den *Demoiselles* eingeführt worden und stellte den ersten Schritt zum anschließenden kubistischen Raum dar.

Wenn sich die Beine von Picassos »Tanzenden Figuren« indirekt auf die *Kota*-Reliquiarfiguren beziehen, so entspricht die Stellung ihrer Arme, die erhoben und über dem Kopf gebeugt sind, der mittleren Figur in den *Demoiselles* und gehörte damit schon während der spätiberischen Phase Picassos Vokabular an (Z. xxvi, 190). Sie ist wahrscheinlich Cézannes *Badenden* entnommen. Wie eine Zeichnung bezeugt □ 387, interessierten ihn offenbar Typen afrikanischer Karyatiden, wie er sie 1907 gesehen haben könnte □ 389, 390.[89] Doch kann man sie kaum als Vorbild für die Armhaltungen der

□ 346 *Pablo Picasso, ›Akt mit erhobenen Armen – Die Tänzerin von Avignon‹, 1907, Öl auf Leinwand, 150 x 100 cm. Privatbesitz.*

◁ ☐ 347 *›Reliquiarfigur‹,* KOTA *(Gabun), Holz, Kupfer und Messing, Höhe 75 cm. Privatbesitz, Schweiz.*

◁ ☐ 349 *›Reliquiarfigur‹,* KOTA *(Volksrepublik Kongo), Holz, Kupfer und Messing, Höhe 63,5 cm. Sammlung M. D. Simpson.*

◁ ☐ 348 *Pablo Picasso, ›Kopf‹ (Tête), 1907, Öl auf Leinwand, 18 x 14 cm. Sammlung Claude Picasso, Paris.*

☐ 351 ▷
Pablo Picasso, ›Akt mit erhobenen Armen‹ (Femme nue aux bras levés), 1907, Öl auf Leinwand, 63 x 42,5 cm. Sammlung Thyssen-Bornemisza, Lugano.

◁ ☐ 350 *›Maske‹, Mbole? (Zaire), bemaltes Holz, Höhe 24,5 cm. Sammlung J. W. Mestach, Brüssel.*

»Tänzer« ansehen. Das auffälligste Merkmal von Picassos »Tanzenden Figuren« ist überdies der Eindruck einer energischen, ja krampfhaften Bewegung, der nicht nur von den Stellungen, sondern auch von der kühnen und schnellen Machart erzeugt wird. Er steht im krassen Gegensatz zur Stasis der Stammeskunst (wie stark diese Bewegung auch immer mit den Vorstellungen des Künstlers von Stammestänzen zu tun haben mag).[90] Vielleicht ist dies der Anlaß für Lucy Lippards Beobachtung, daß der *Akt mit erhobenen Armen* zwar »als das wichtigste Beispiel afrikanischen Einflusses gilt, in Wirklichkeit aber zeigt, wie vergleichsweise oberflächlich Picassos Anleihen beim Afrikanischen waren«.[91] »Oberflächlich« würde ich durch »mittelbar« oder »fragmentarisch« ersetzen. Die Kraft von Picassos Phantasie und sein Gespür für Manipulation und Metamorphose waren so groß, daß direkte Anleihen bei den Primitiven, die man gelegentlich bei anderen Künstlern beobachtet, oder die unveränderte Darstellung von Stammesobjekten wie bei den Expressionisten, in seiner Malerei nur schwer vorzustellen sind.

Wichtiger als sichtbare Anleihen war jedoch Picassos Gespür für den starken emotionalen Gehalt von Stammesobjekten. Er erlebte sie als Träger einer magischen Kraft, die uns zutiefst zu beeinflussen vermag. Zugleich verstand er die konzeptionellen Prinzipien, die der afrikanischen Darstellungsweise zugrunde liegen. In dieser Hinsicht verdankt Picasso der afrikanischen Kunst nicht nur oberflächliche,

sondern tiefgreifende Anregungen. In der Kohlezeichnung von 1907 stellt PICASSOS Hand, die auf dem Blatt von unten her auftaucht, als würde sie die Handlungen der Figuren wie durch Zauberkraft lenken, ein bedeutsames Bindeglied zur primitiven Tradition dar. PICASSO hatte bereits eine Vorstellung von der Hand des Künstlers als eines Zauberstabes. In *Knabe, ein Pferd führend* aus dem Jahr 1906 scheint das ungezäumte Pferd dem Knaben wie durch die Gewalt seiner Geste hypnotisiert zu folgen. Wenn PICASSOS Vorstellungen von Stammesbräuchen – etwa vom Handauflegen der Schamanen oder Medizinmänner – vielleicht zu sehr vereinfacht und anthropologisch unkorrekt waren, so verstärkten sie doch sein eigenes Gespür für das Magische. Und da es sich bei den »Fetischen« um religiöse Gegenstände handelt, vereinigten sich für ihn die Vorstellungen vom künstlerischen Prozeß und von der Religion zu einem Bewußtsein von der Kraft der Hand des Künstler-Schamanen. In der genannten Zeichnung, einer der ersten von vielen Darstellungen seiner Hand, macht PICASSO diese Idee durch die »Kraftlinien«, die von ihr ausgehen, deutlich. Seine Hand ist in der Mitte der Zeichnung nochmals in einer anderen Stellung dargestellt; dort erwecken die von ihr ausgehenden Linien wieder den Eindruck, daß die Hand die Bewegungen der Figuren wie durch Zauberkraft »lenkt«, wodurch eine metaphorische Analogie zur Wirklichkeit entsteht, in der PICASSOS Hand tatsächlich ihr Schöpfer ist. Die isolierte Darstellung der Künstlerhand – die man von den Höhlenmalern bis POLLOCK antrifft □ 985 – ist immer Hinweis auf die Bildnerei als Ausdruck einer übernatürlichen, rituellen Kraft; genau dies ist die Vorstellung, die PICASSO bei seiner »Offenbarung« im Trocadéro überwältigte.

□ 352 *›Holzfigur‹, DOGON (Mali), Höhe 64 cm. Musée de l'Homme, Paris. Erworben 1935.*

□ 353 *›Holzfigur‹, DOGON (Mali), Höhe 60 cm. Musée de l'Homme, Paris. Erworben 1906.* ▷

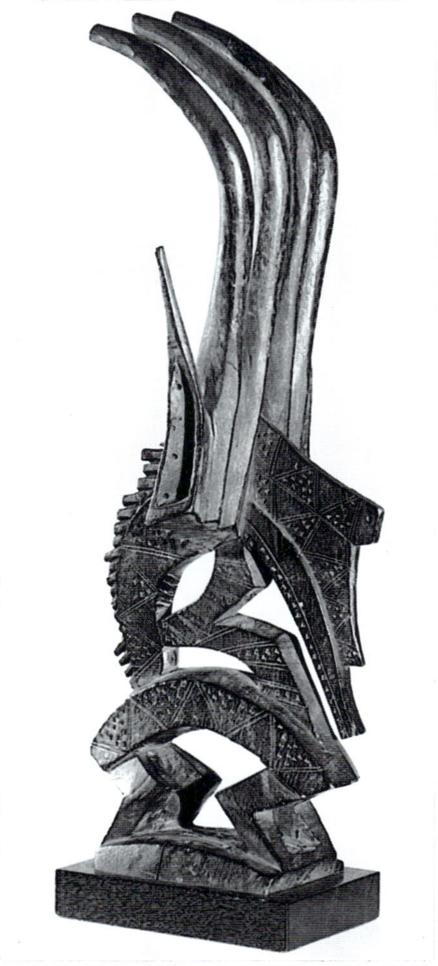

□ 354 *›Antilopenkopfschmuck‹*, BAMBARA *(Mali), Holz, 54,5 cm. Sammlung V. Franklin, Beverly Hills.*

□ 355 *›Antilopenkopfschmuck‹*, BAMBARA *(Mali), Holz, 60,5 cm. Privatbesitz.*

□ 356 *›Antilopenkopfschmuck‹* BAMBARA *(Mali), Holz, Fasern und Metall, Höhe 79 cm. Privatsammlung.*

□ 357 *›Antilopenkopfschmuck‹*, BAMBARA *(Mali), Holz und Baumwolle, Höhe 29 cm. Privatbesitz, Paris.*

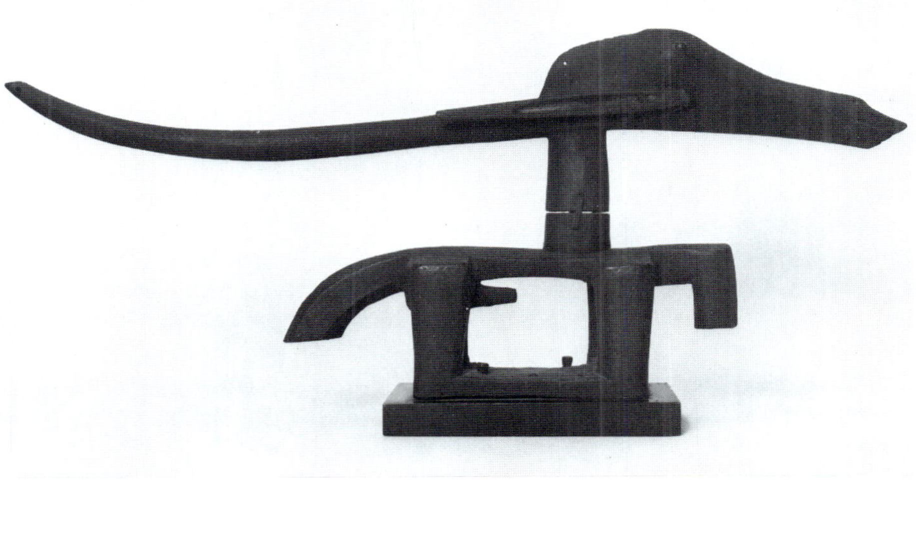

□ 358 *Pablo Picasso, ›Zwei Antilopen‹ (Deux antilopes), Ausschnitt, 1907, Bleistift, 15,5 x 21,5 cm. Privatbesitz.*

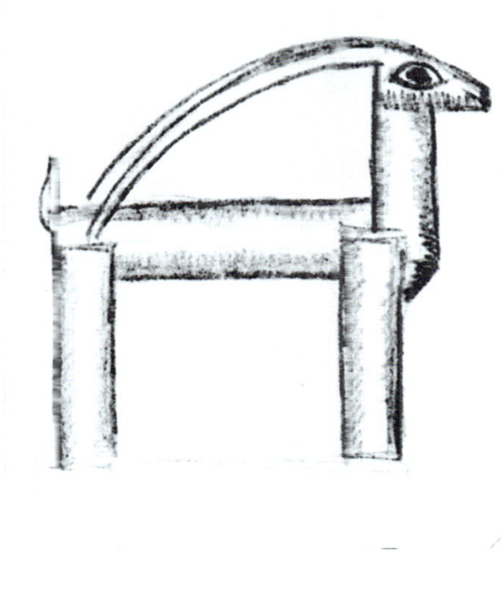

□ 359 *Pablo Picasso, ›Maske und Köpfe‹ (Masque et têtes), 1907, Bleistift, 22 x 16 cm. Sammlung Jacqueline Picasso, Mougins.*

Die für PICASSO typische Distanzierung von seinen primitiven Quellen läßt sich in vielen Zeichnungen aus dem Jahre 1907 erkennen. Von diesen möchte ich hier drei Beispiele untersuchen: eine Skizze, die eindeutig vom Kopfschmuck der *BAMBARA*, der beim Antilopentanz getragen wurde, beeinflußt ist □ 358; eine ganz ungewöhnliche Zeichnung, die ich *Maske und Köpfe* nennen möchte □ 359; und den Entwurf für eine Skulptur, die von »nimbaköpfigen« Figuren der *BAGA* angeregt ist □ 361, 362, 365–369.

Zieht man die vielfältigen, phantasievollen und manchmal hochabstrakten Formen, die diese Antilopenkopfbedeckungen in den Händen afrikanischer Künstler annahmen □ 354–357, in Betracht, so ist es interessant, daß sich PICASSOS Entwurf um einen größeren Realismus und eine stärkere Vereinfachung bemüht – als wäre eine *BAMBARA*-Antilope im strengen geometrischen Geist eines *DOGON*-Bildhauers umgearbeitet worden □ 352, 353. Die sparsame Geometrie des *DOGON*-Stils ist überhaupt das beste Vergleichsbeispiel für den frühen Kubismus der Jahre 1908–09. Es wird natürlich oft behauptet, daß die Kubisten die *DOGON*-Plastik nicht gekannt hätten, auch trifft es zu, daß bestimmte Typen von *DOGON*-Plastik – und nicht gerade die besten Stücke – erst nach der Dakar-Dschibuti-Mission von 1931–33 nach Frankreich kamen. Trotzdem gab es 1907, als PICASSO den Trocadéro besuchte, mehrere *DOGON*-Arbeiten, darunter eine große, typisch geometrische Figur □ 353, die der tschechische Kubist JOSEF CAPEK 1909 im Trocadéro sogar photographierte. Da der Einfluß solcher Arbeiten eher von ihrem Stil als von ihrer Qualität abhing (man denke an PICASSOS Ausspruch »Man bedarf nicht des Meisterwerks, um die Idee zu erfassen«), muß die *DOGON*-Plastik neben den damals besser bekannten Gattungen primitiver Kunst als Hintergrund von PICASSOS »Afrikanismus« gelten.

Die extreme Einfachheit von PICASSOS Antilope □ 358 ist u. a. dadurch zu erklären, daß PICASSO sie in Holz ausführen wollte und er in der Bildhauerei noch ein Anfänger war. Doch die Läufe als klar umrissene Zylinder zu gestalten und damit den Zylinder des Halses wiederaufzunehmen, war sicherlich eine ästhetische Entscheidung im Geist des afrikanischen Reduktio-

□ 360 *›Nimba-Maske‹*, *Baga (Guinea), Holz, Höhe 120 cm. Musée de l'Homme, Paris. Erworben 1902.*

nismus. Picassos Anliegen bestand darin, dieses reduktionistische Prinzip angemessen einzusetzen, es zu verstärken und auszuweiten; dies wurde zum Paradigma seiner Reaktion auf die Stammeskunst. Er kannte vielleicht schon 1907 einen Typus von *Bambara*-Plastik, der in Kahnweilers Sammlung anzutreffen war □ 372.[92] Die Ausführung der Schultern und Oberarme als Halbkreis hätte Picasso sicherlich interessiert. Aber es ist bezeichnend für ihn, daß er solche Lösungen noch weiter trieb, indem er Schultern, Arme und Hände einen vollständigen Kreis bilden ließ, um das Ganze dann gegen einen genauso geometrischen, dreieckigen Torso zu setzen □ 371.

Maske und Köpfe □ 359 ist eine der ungewöhnlichsten »primitiven« Zeichnungen Picassos des Jahres 1907. Sie ist um einen großen, mächtigen Kopf aufgebaut, der einer Maske ähnelt, so daß Laude annahm, sie beruhe auf einem afrikanischen Werk (»vraisemblement congolais«).[93] Aber man wird vergeblich nach einer Maske, ob ozeanisch oder afrikanisch, suchen, die ihr ähnlich ist. Man ist nämlich im Irrtum, wenn man glaubt, Picasso habe seine Bildsymbolik direkt auf einem bestimmten Prototyp aufgebaut.[94] Als ihn Pierre Daix über diese Zeichnung befragte, leugnete Picasso, daß sie von einem Stammesobjekt inspiriert sei, und behauptete, sie sei seiner Phantasie entsprungen – was sicherlich der Fall war.[95] Da sich die Phantasie aber aus demselben Unbewußten speist, das auch visuelle Eindrücke und »vergessene« Bilder speichert, überrascht es nicht, wenn verschiedene Züge dieser »Maske« zumindest indirekt an Elemente bekannter Stilarten denken lassen. Die Ohren sind das am leichtesten zu identifizierende Motiv, sie weisen überhaupt keinen Einfluß der Stammeskunst auf. Sie stellen eine rundere, symmetrische Fassung des muschelförmigen Ohrs des iberischen Kopfes aus Picassos Besitz dar. Das Ohr dieses Kopfes wirkt in weniger stilisierter Form auf der iberischen Aquarellstudie für die *Demoiselles* nach □ 319. Die streifigen, dreieckigen Schatten an den Seiten der Nase dieser »Maske« hatte Picasso schon in seinen iberischen Entwürfen vorweggenommen, obwohl die Strenge des Musters hier Picassos Erinnerungen an Hautritzungen der Stammeskunst und an die symmetrischen sog. »Tränen« bestimmter *Kota*-Reliquiarfiguren zur Voraussetzung hat. Andererseits ist die Form des Mundes – eigentlich eine Verlängerung der langen, schmalen Nase – ihrem Wesen nach eher melanesisch als afrikanisch.

Interessanter, wenn auch weniger auffallend als das zentrale Motiv von *Maske und Köpfe*, sind die Beweisstücke für den »Automatismus« von Picassos Zeichnung, die den Kopf umgeben. Sie halten die Kette seiner Denkprozesse fest, wodurch der Eindruck entsteht, daß Picassos Denken, wie Tzara es formulierte, »sich in der Hand vollzieht«.[96] Links unten hat Picasso das Muster der Diagonalen, die von der Nase seiner »Maske« nach unten weisen, so verkehrt, als wolle er einen Kopf schaffen, der zugleich ein Blatt ist. Dieser Blatt-Kopf, der Klee vorwegnimmt, führt durch dieselbe gedankliche Logik zu dem noch phantastischeren und größeren Kopf unten in der Mitte, dessen Mund ein Blumentopf, dessen Nase und Wangen Pflanzenstengel und dessen Augen kleine Palm- oder Papyruswedel sind – Elemente mit einer doppelten Aufgabe, die uns an seine Umwandlung des Götzen aus dem Gauguin-Aquarell erinnern □ 305, 306. Im Kontext solcher Bildsprache könnte man die trapezförmigen Objekte zu beiden Seiten des Hauptmotivs in *Maske und Köpfe* als Vasen deuten. Diesen Titel gab Zervos einer Einzelstudie zu dem Objekt links (Z. xxvi, 160). Angesichts des exotischen Gesamtcharakters der Zeichnung waren diese beiden Formen sicherlich, wenn auch nicht primär, als Stammesschilde gedacht. Bei Zeichnungen wie dieser schließt eine Interpretation die andere nicht aus. Im Gegenteil sagen die vielfältige Identität der Motive und die assoziativen Verknüpfungen zwischen ihnen mehr aus über Picassos geistige Prozesse und die Natur der Anverwandlung primitiver Vorlagen als die Gemälde dieser Periode. In diesen spüren wir die Vielschichtigkeit und den Reichtum seiner Vorstellungskraft, doch bei den Zeichnungen sehen wir sie klarer.

Unter den Zeichnungen des Jahres 1907, die man mit der Stammesplastik in Zusammenhang bringen kann, sind keine für Picassos Denk- und Arbeitsprozesse so aufschlußreich wie diejenigen, die sich auf Nimba (siehe Glossar), die man damals für die Fruchtbarkeitsgöttin der *Baga* hielt, beziehen.[97] In der *Baga*-Kunst findet sich der Nimba-Kopf bei riesigen Tanzmasken □ 360, 454, 458 und bei kleineren Figurenplastiken mit menschlichen Körpern □ 365, 366. Es steht außer Frage, daß Picasso die über einen Meter hohe Tanzmaske des Trocadéro

□ 361 *Pablo Picasso, ›Kopf‹ (Tête), 1907, Conté Crayon und Kohle, 65 x 50 cm. Sammlung Bernard Picasso, Paris.*

□ 362 *Pablo Picasso, ›Kopf‹ (Tête), 1907, Bleistift, 49 x 64,5 cm. Sammlung Jacqueline Picasso, Mougins.*

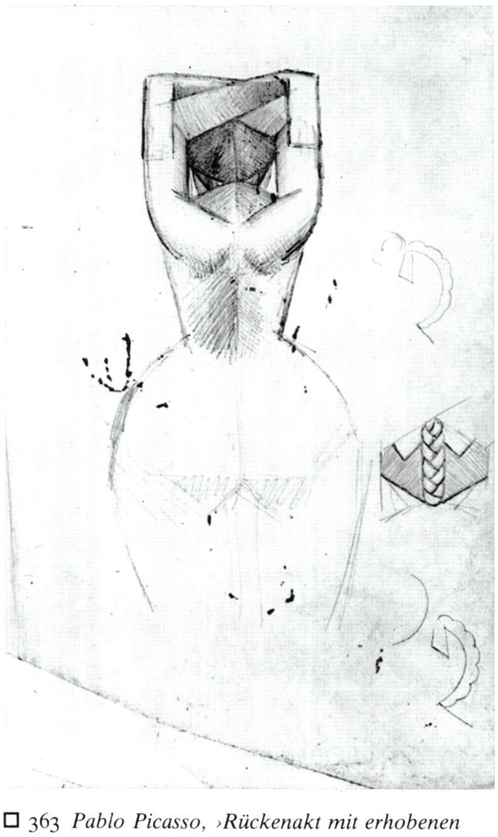

□ 363 *Pablo Picasso, ›Rückenakt mit erhobenen Armen‹ (Nue de dos aux bras levés), 1907, Bleistift, 48 x 31,5 cm. Sammlung Marina Picasso.*

□ 364 *Pablo Picasso, ›Frau in langem Kleid‹ (Femme vêtue d'une robe longue), 1907, Tusche, 64,5 x 49,5 cm. Sammlung Jacqueline Picasso, Mougins.*

☐ 365 *›Figur aus Holz‹, Baga (Guinea), Höhe 61 cm. Sammlung Paloma Picasso. Früher Sammlung Pablo Picasso.* ▷

bei seinem Besuch sah; im Jahr 1907 war sie das einzige derartige Stück in dem Museum. Diese Maske weist einige, wenn auch nicht alle typischen Merkmale »klassischer« Nimbas auf. Der lange, gebogene Kopf ragt – von der großen Nase noch verstärkt – weit nach vorn.

Den Kopf ziert ein flacher, leicht ausgehöhlter Kamm, der von der Stirn bis fast zum Nacken verläuft. Der Hals, ein langer Zylinder, trennt den Kopf vom Oberkörper, der große, aber flache Brüste hat, unter denen die vier vom Tänzer gehaltenen Stützen angebracht sind.[98] Beim Gebrauch bedeckte ein langes Bastkostüm, das unterhalb der Brüste ansetzte, den Tänzer vollständig. Er konnte nur durch kleine zwischen die Brüste gebohrte Löcher hindurchsehen.

Während die Nimba-Maske ausschließlich bei Tänzen Verwendung fand und so in Bewegung gesehen wurde, waren die kleineren Nimba-Figuren stationäre Objekte, deren Zweck nicht bekannt ist. Der Trocadéro besaß von ihnen im Jahr 1907 auch ein Exemplar. Als kleinere Objekte waren sie gelegentlich auch in Kuriositätenläden anzutreffen. Höchstwahrscheinlich kaufte Picasso das Paar »nimbaköpfiger« Figuren, das ihm

◁ ☐ 366 *›Figur aus Holz und Stoff‹, Baga (Guinea), Höhe 89 cm. Musée de l'Homme, Paris. Erworben 1904.*

gehörte (im Hintergrund des Photos ☐ 341 und ☐ 365), als die Zeichnungen mit diesen Motiven entstanden.

Die große Bleistiftzeichnung eines Kopfes ☐ 362 ist wohl zusammen mit einer ähnlichen, weniger detaillierten Studie (Z. VI, 907) Picassos erste Ausarbeitung eines von der Nimba abgeleiteten Motivs und doch recht weit von dem entfernt, was wir als ihren Ausgangspunkt betrachten. Dennoch überzeugt Reinhold Hohls Argument, daß ihr Kamm, eine Kette fast halbkreisartiger Formen, mit einer Nimba zu tun hat.[99] Hohl brachte Picassos Kamm jedoch einfach mit dem Kamm der Nimba-Maske aus dem Trocadéro in Verbindung, der die

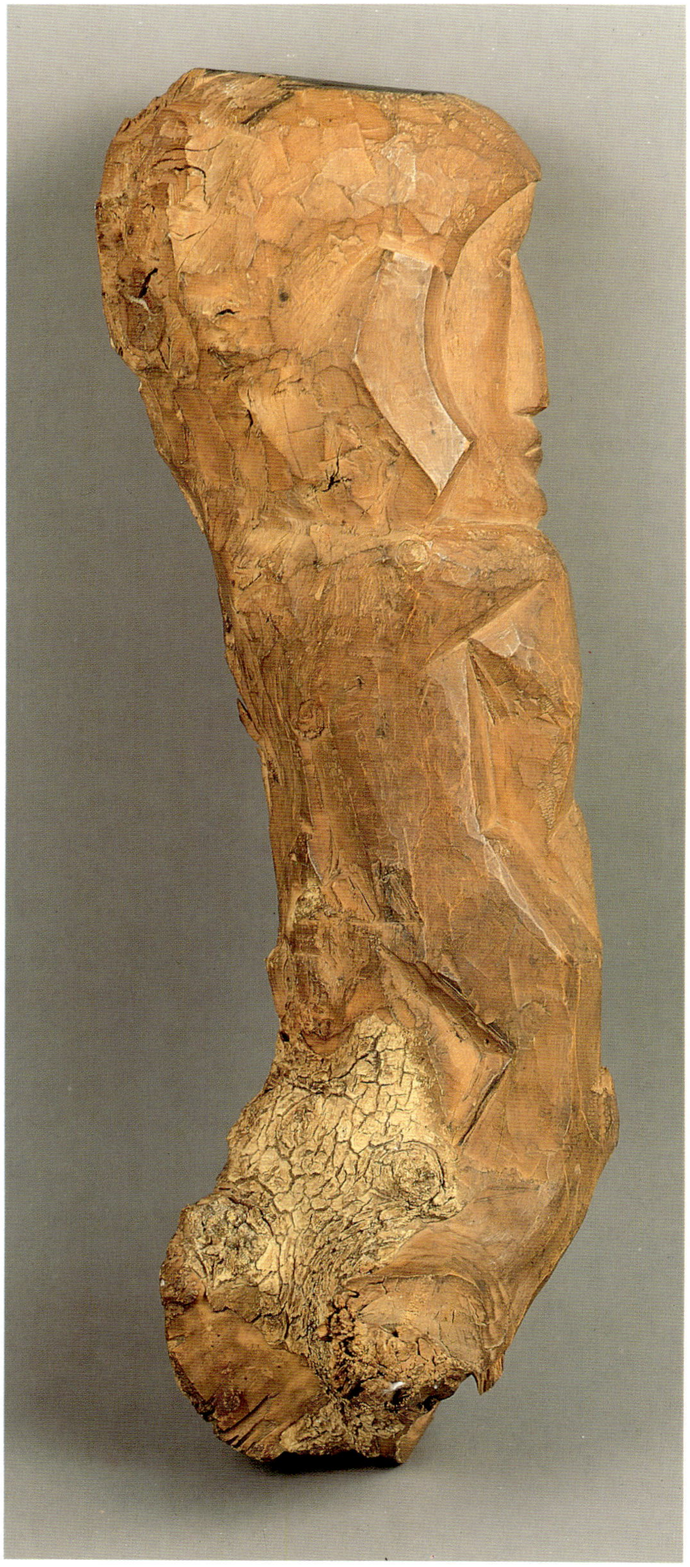

□ 367 *Pablo Picasso, ›Figur‹ (Figure), Vorder- und Seitenansicht, 1907, Holz, 35 x 12 x 10,5 cm. Musée Picasso, Paris.*

Haartracht umschließt wie der stärker ornamentale Kamm in der Zeichnung des *Kopfes*. Doch der Nimba-Kamm schließt gerade ab. Mir scheint, daß PICASSO zwar die Idee des Kamms von der Maske des Trocadéro oder von den kleineren »nimbaköpfigen« Figuren übernahm, die Rhythmik von fast halbkreisartigen Formen aber, wie sie in der Zeichnung *Kopf* auftritt, nicht einem Nimba-Kamm entlehnte, sondern einer Formenreihe aus der rundlichen Nase und der geschwungenen, vorspringenden Stirn. Diese Rhythmik erkennen wir im Profil seiner eigenen »nimbaköpfigen« Figuren wieder. Eine solche Formenreihe ließ sich der damals im Trocadéro ausgestellten *BAGA*-Maske oder *BAGA*-Figur nicht entnehmen. Seine eigenen Nimba-Skulpturen lieferten ihm eindeutig auch das Vorbild für die Nase in *Kopf*.

Diese Zeichnung ist keineswegs die Kopie einer Nimba. Wenn sich PICASSO von Motiven der Stammeskunst anregen ließ, griff er einzelnes heraus, wandelte es um und schuf neue

□ 368 *Pablo Picasso, ›Kopf im Profil‹ (Tête de profil), 1907, Bleistift, 21 x 13,5 cm. Musée Picasso, Paris.*

Verbindungen und damit seine eigene Version der Stammeskunst. Ein gutes Beispiel dafür ist die Tuschzeichnung *Frau in langem Kleid* □ 364, in der man bei genauem Hinsehen die vertraute Kette von Halbkreisen wiederum das Ende der Haartracht bilden sieht. Sollte es weiterer Beweise für die »afrikanische« Beeinflussung dieses Motivs bedürfen, braucht man sich nur die »unbekleidete« Version der Frau auf derselben Zeichnung anzusehen, die zeigt, wie sie als »afrikanische« Plastik vielleicht aussehen würde. Es gibt tatsächlich kaum deutlichere Beispiele für Picassos Verwendung der Schraffur in Analogie zu den Axt- und Meißelkerben, um die von afrikanischen Objekten vorgegebenen geometrisch exakten Flächen zu markieren. Einen weiteren Einblick in die assoziative Natur von Picassos Erfindungsgabe gewähren uns Hohls Beobachtungen zu der Bleistiftstudie *Rückenakt mit erhobenen Armen* □ 363, in der ein getrennt ausgearbeitetes Detail des Zopfes der Frau einem »Nimba-Kamm« dadurch angenähert ist, daß es Fragmenten der Haartracht von *Kopf* gegenübergestellt wurde.

Die Metamorphosen von *Kopf* und seinen Varianten fanden ihren Höhepunkt in der zwar unvollendeten, aber wunderbaren Holzplastik *Figur* □ 367. Daß Picasso schon die ganze Zeit eine Holzplastik geplant hatte, wird durch die Tatsache bestätigt, daß es neben der Profilansicht in *Kopf* eine Studie in Vorderansicht gibt □ 361. Picasso fing die Arbeit an seinen Holzplastiken aus dem Jahr 1907 mit Umrißzeichnungen an, die er auf einen Holzblock übertrug (ein Verfahren, das noch die unvollendete *Karyatide* erkennen läßt □ 387, bei der sich Spuren der orangefarbenen Umrißzeichnung erhalten haben). Als Picasso dann mit der Arbeit an der *Figur* begann, war der Kamm (»Zopf«) aufgegeben und das Vorspringen von Nase und Lippen leicht abgeschwächt, wie dies schon eine Skizze des Kopfes der Plastik zeigt □ 368, die wohl kurz vorher entstanden war. Obgleich wir aufgrund des unvollendeten Zustandes nicht genau wissen, wie Picasso den oberen und den hinteren Teil des Kopfes der *Figur* gestalten wollte, deutet diese Skizze darauf hin, daß die Nimba-Motive, die noch in *Kopf* auftauchen, hier völlig verschwinden sollten.

Es gibt vielleicht kein deutlicheres Zeichen für die assoziative Natur von Picassos Bildsprache als die Tatsache, daß er das große, karikaturistische Kohlebildnis seines Freundes André Salmon □ 378, einer der ersten Förderer der Stammeskunst, auf der Rückseite des Blattes zeichnete, das die Studie mit den gebeugten Knien nach den *Kota*-Reliquiarfiguren zeigt. Obwohl Salmon in der Literatur im Schatten der beiden anderen mit Picasso befreundeten Dichter, Max Jacob und Guillaume Apollinaire, steht, spielte er damals für Picasso eine bedeutende Rolle. Dies hatte zu einem nicht unerheblichen Teil mit seinem Interesse an der Stammeskunst zu tun, das vielleicht ein oder zwei Jahre länger als bei Apollinaire oder Picasso bestand.[100] Nachdem Picasso einmal seine »Offenbarung« im Trocadéro erlebt hatte, Stammesplastik kaufte und eingehend studierte, wurde Salmon – neben Apollinaire – sein wichtigster Gesprächspartner bei diesem Thema. Trotzdem berichtet Salmon, er habe bestimmte Objekte erst verstanden, als Picasso mit ihm darüber gesprochen und auf ihre »Logik« und »Reinheit«[101] hingewiesen hatte (»eine Reinheit im Aus-

□ 369 *Pablo Picasso, ›Stehender Akt im Profil‹ (Nu debout de profil), 1907, Pastellkreide und Gouache, 62,5 x 48 cm. Musée Picasso, Paris.*

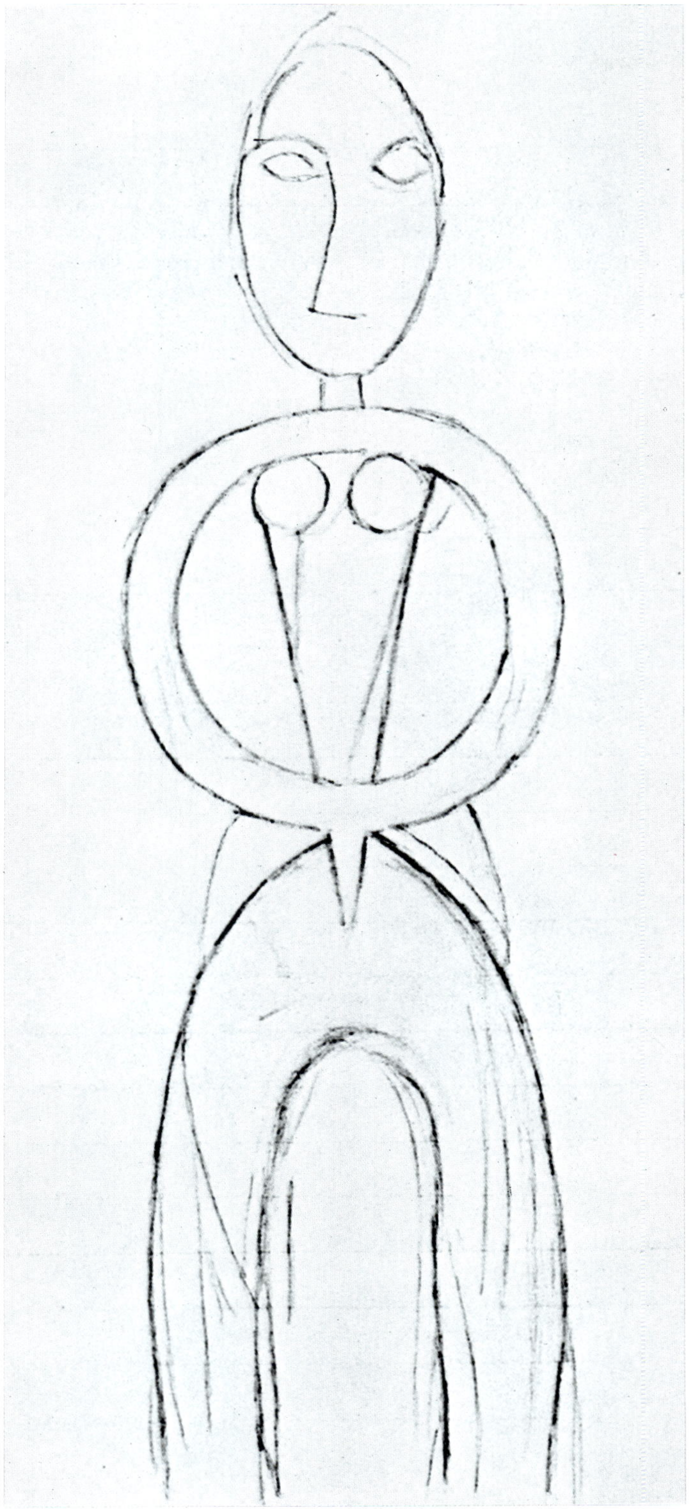

□ 371 *Pablo Picasso, ›Stehender Akt‹ (Nu debout), 1907, 22,5 x 17 cm. Privatbesitz.*

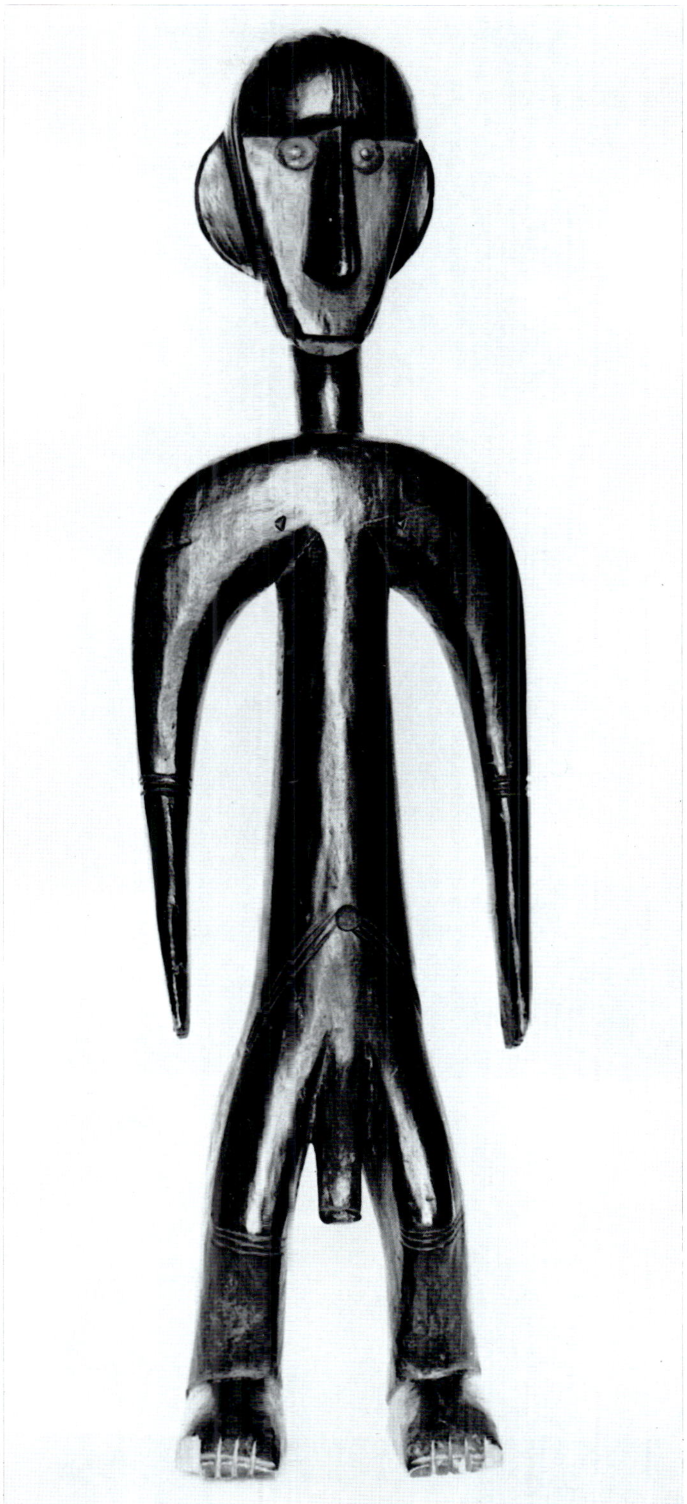

□ 372 *›Männliche Figur‹, Bambara (Mali), Holz, Höhe 59 cm. Privatbesitz, Frankreich.*

◁ □ 370 *›Maske‹, Fang (Gabun), Holz, Farbe und Fasern, Höhe 52 cm. Sammlung O. Dapper.*

druck, die die westliche Kunst nie erreichte«, sagte Picasso später zu Sabartés).[102] Anders als Apollinaire, der keine Bemerkungen zum Verhältnis zwischen Stammesplastik und Kubismus machte,[103] obwohl er afrikanische Kunst sammelte und darüber schrieb (siehe S. 154ff.), förderte Salmon nicht ausschließlich die Stammeskunst, sondern propagierte sie auch als Vorbild für zeitgenössische Künstler. So schrieb er auch als erster über Picassos Verhältnis zu ihr: »Schon [in den *Demoiselles*] begeisterte sich Picasso für die Schöpfer der Negerplastik, die er weit über die der ägyptischen Plastik stellte. Polynesische oder dahomeische Bildwerke erscheinen ihm ›vernünftig‹ [*raisonnable*] . . . Der Zauberlehrling holte sich bei den ozeanischen und afrikanischen Magiern ständig Rat.«[104] Trotz abwegigster Theorien über die Beziehungen zwischen afrikanischer, ägyptischer und griechischer Kunst (die damals

allerdings weitverbreitet waren) fand Salmons Aufsatz »L'Art nègre« genügend Anerkennung, um in *The Burlington Magazine* veröffentlicht zu werden.[105] Die häufige Bezugnahme auf plastische Qualitäten – ebenso wie auf die von Apollinaire hervorgehobenen magischen Eigenschaften – sollten uns daran erinnern, daß auch die Ästhetik der Stammeskunst auf Picasso eingewirkt hatte.[106]

Salmons frühe Beobachtungen zur Stammeskunst sind verstreut und fragmentarisch. Der umfassendere Aufsatz »L'Art nègre« erschien zwar erst 1920, doch fanden darin seine Gespräche mit Picasso ihren Niederschlag, die viele Jahre früher stattgefunden hatten. In einem der wichtigsten Abschnitte beschreibt Salmon die Stammeskunst als eine Form des »Realismus«, der eher auf einer Wahrheit gegenüber dem Gefühl als gegenüber den Erscheinungen beruht – ein Gedanke, den auch Picasso einmal mir gegenüber zum Ausdruck brachte.[107] Salmon schrieb:

»Der Schnitzer von Götzenbildern ist unstreitig der gewissenhafteste Realist . . . Seine Sorgfalt und Treue beim Studium menschlicher Vollkommenheit entspringen nicht dem gemeinen Fetischismus der Nachahmung, die akademisch eingestellte Europäer frohlocken läßt, sobald sie ein Gemälde mit einem Spiegel gleichsetzen können. Der Afrikaner und sein Rivale, der Polynesier, beziehen ihre ganze Inspiration aus der Vollkommenheit des Menschen, ohne ihr je das Kunstwerk unterzuordnen. Als Realisten achten sie mit peinlicher Genauigkeit auf die Gestaltung eines harmonischen Ganzen . . . [auf die] plastische Wiedergabe von Gefühlen, vorzugsweise wenn sie am intensivsten sind (woraus wir schließen können, daß der Negerkunst selbst die Psychologie nicht fehlt).«

Picassos Bildnis von Salmon war als Entwurfsskizze für eine Holzplastik gedacht. »Zur selben Zeit [als die *Demoiselles* entstanden]«, berichtet Salmon, »zeichnete Picasso ein Kohlebild von mir, das ein Vorentwurf für eine kleine Holzplastik sein sollte . . .«[108] Während sich die *Kota*-Skizzen auf der Vorderseite desselben Blattes in der für Picasso typischen Weise von ihren afrikanischen Quellen entfernten, kehrte sich der Prozeß bei der Entwicklung des Bildnisses von Salmon um – wohl wegen dessen Leidenschaft für die »art nègre«. Seine verschiedenen Umarbeitungen zeigen, wie Picasso Salmon zu einer Art Stammesplastik machte □ 376.[109]

Das Bildnis Salmons veranlaßt zum Nachdenken über die Rolle der Karikatur wie auch generell volkstümlicher Kunst[110] bei Picassos Reaktionen auf die Stammeskunst. Picasso hatte in den Jahren vor 1907 viele glänzende und unterhaltsame Karikaturen und karikaturhafte Zeichnungen angefertigt. Sie zeugen von seinem bemerkenswerten Talent in dieser Gattung. Einige davon waren regelrechte Karikaturen von Personen (und Bildern);[111] andere waren Phantasieprodukte, oft pornographischer oder »grotesker« Natur. Ich weiß allerdings von keiner Karikatur, die vor dem Bildnis Salmons entstand und auf großformatigem Zeichenpapier (die meisten fanden sich in den Notizbüchern) und mit der Absicht, sie in ein »seriöses« Medium umzusetzen, ausgeführt wurde.

Picassos Talent als Karikaturist war Voraussetzung für die frappierende Ähnlichkeit, die er noch in seinen abstraktesten Stilen zu erzeugen imstande war; vor ein paar Jahren machte ich diese Beobachtung bei seinen kubistischen Porträts aus dem Jahr 1910.[112] Die Fähigkeit, die wesentlichen Züge des

□ 373 *›Tiki‹, Marquesasinseln, Höhe 72 cm. Privatbesitz. Ehemals Sammlung Pablo Picasso.*

□ 374 *Guillaume Apollinaire in Picassos Atelier, Boulevard de Clichy. Das Photo wurde zwischen dem Frühjahr 1910 und dem Frühjahr 1912 aufgenommen.*

Gesichtsausdrucks einer Person zu isolieren, erlaubte es ihm, eine bemerkenswerte Ähnlichkeit mit Vollard, Uhde und Kahnweiler selbst bei so hochgradiger Abstraktheit zu erreichen, daß vieles andere auf den Gemälden unlesbar blieb.[113] Offensichtlich stand für Picasso die konzeptuelle Natur der Karikatur – die eher auf Ideen und Gefühlen als auf dem Wahrscheinlichkeitsprinzip beruhende Hierarchien der Darstellung begünstigt – den Lehren sehr nahe, die er aus der primitiven Kunst gezogen hatte. Es überrascht auch nicht, daß einige der frühen Betrachter der *Demoiselles*, wie der Kritiker Félix Fénéon, das Gemälde als karikaturistisch empfanden. So gab Fénéon, der später Stammeskunst sammeln sollte, dem jungen Picasso den Rat, sich der Karikatur zu widmen. Als Picasso dies später Roland Penrose erzählte, fügte er hinzu, daß »dies gar nicht so dumm war, da alle guten Porträts zu einem gewissen Grad Karikaturen sind«.[114] Die Verwandtschaft zwischen Picassos Karikaturen und seinen primitivistischen und kubistischen Werken läßt sich leichter fassen, wenn uns laut neuester Studien über die Wahrnehmung klar wird, daß »die äußeren Formen von Karikaturen in gewisser Weise die innere Struktur unserer geistigen Darstellungsweisen, die idealisierte und schematisierte innerliche Bildsymbolik widerspiegeln, die unsere Gehirne benutzen, um bei der Wahrnehmung eine ›Vorauswahl‹ zu treffen und sie zu strukturieren. Das ›geistige Auge‹ . . . sieht tatsächlich Karikaturen, keine Porträts . . . Unser Vorstellungssystem weiß, daß es Übertreibungen, Vereinfachungen und Verallgemeinerungen gebraucht, um unser Wissen von den Erscheinungen zu kodieren, und kann diese Abirrungen erkennen, wenn es mit einem Cartoon oder einer Karikatur konfrontiert wird.«[115]

Ohne Erstaunen bemerkt man, daß sich die »niedere« Kunst von Picassos Karikaturen mit seiner »hohen« Kunst genau in dem Moment zu vereinen beginnt, als sein Primitivismus anfängt: mit der Umarbeitung von Gertrude Steins Gesicht im iberischen Stil nach seiner Rückkehr aus Gosol. Adam Gopnick äußert in einer kürzlich erschienenen, brillanten Untersuchung zu diesem Thema: »Eine Ähnlichkeit [des Stein-Bildnisses], die . . . im großen Stil begann, wird durch die Verwen-

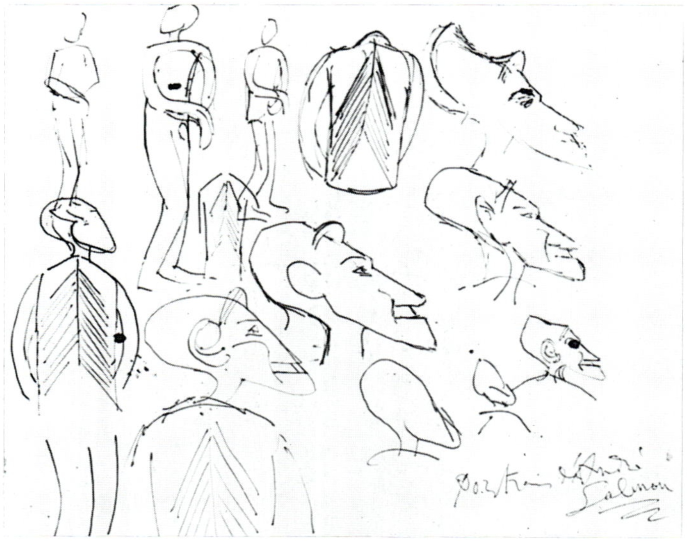

☐ 375 *Pablo Picasso, Skizzen zu ›Bildnis André Salmon‹, 1907, Tusche, 32,5 x 40 cm. Sammlung Jacqueline Picasso, Mougins.*

dung primitiver Formen in eine Studie physiognomischer Identifikation durch Verzerrung umgewandelt. Die Formen, die Picasso aus dem Vokabular der iberischen Kunst auswählt – die übergroßen Augen, die vergrößerten und hervortretenden Augenbrauen –, sind genau jene physiognomischen Merkmale, die jedes Lehrbuch dem jungen Karikaturisten zur Akzentuierung empfiehlt. Was Picasso vollbrachte, war die Erfindung einer Art Kreolsprache, eine Sprache, die ein fremdes Vokabular einer vertrauten Syntax anpaßt . . . Die Bewegung vom Niederen zum Höheren, der Sieg des Skizzenbuches über die Staffelei wird durch das Trojanische Pferd des Primitivismus errungen.«[116]

Bei Salmons Porträt beginnt Picasso mit der Karikatur und paßt sie allmählich dem graphischen Vokabular seines Primitivismus an. Die lockere Zeichnung des »unerschütterlichen Evangelisten des Primitivismus«[117] zeigt ihn von vorn mit einer Pfeife und einem Buch (wie ein Double für Picassos Medizinstudenten/Selbstporträt in den frühen Studien für die *Demoiselles*), den Kopf in Dreiviertelansicht, wie um seine lange Nase und sein vorspringendes Kinn besser in Pose zu setzen. Als Picasso mit diesem Bild in einer Studie zu spielen beginnt ☐ 375, wendet er Salmons Körper ins Profil und dann in die Rückenansicht (links oben). Die »Fischgräten«-Schraffierungen, die von Salmons Wirbelsäule ausgehen und von Picasso bislang als Hautritzungen ähnliche Kürzel für »primitive« Plastik eingesetzt worden waren, verraten die Tendenz des Porträts. Salmons Frisur ist zu einem hochstehenden Kamm vereinfacht, der zusammen mit der Verlängerung von Gesicht und Schädel geradezu ein pharaonisches Profil ergibt. In den nächsten Phasen entfällt dann der Kamm, um zu einer hervortretenden Braue zu werden. Als der Künstler eine endgültige Lösung gefunden hatte ☐ 376, sah der Entwurf zu einer Skulptur eher nach einer »Stammesplastik« als nach einer Karikatur aus. Der ursprüngliche sinusförmige Kontrapost des Salmon-Porträts ist dem massigen, flachfüßigen Bild eines ältlichen Aktes gewichen, dessen Frontalität und Symmetrie nur eine leichte Drehung des Kopfes auflockert.

Picassos Verwandlung eines jungen Mannes in einen alten, die seinem bösen Witz durchaus entspricht, wiederholt eine Art Metamorphose, die dem Künstler aus den berühmten sog. Karikaturen Leonardos bekannt war.[118] Im Verlauf der Arbeit wurden einige Attribute Salmons fallengelassen (die Haarfülle weicht einer Glatze); andere typische Züge wurden beibehalten (die lange Nase und das vorstehende Kinn) und neue kamen hinzu (die großen, abstehenden Ohren). An Salmons Verwandlung in eine »Stammesplastik« arbeitete Picasso mit großem Eifer; es gibt die verschiedensten Zeichnungen zu diesem Projekt. Im Laufe der Verwandlung hörte Salmon auf, Salmon zu sein und wurde wie viele Modelle Picassos ganz ein Wesen des Künstlers (Gertrude Stein bildet eine bemerkenswerte Ausnahme von dieser Regel).

Daß Picasso niemals dazu kam, Salmons Porträt ins Plastische umzusetzen, überrascht kaum. Mit jeder Skulptur, die er in Angriff nahm, blieben viele andere Skulpturprojekte im Entwurfsstadium stecken. Mangelnde Zeit und Geduld sind zwei von vielen Gründen.

Picasso interessierte sich für bildhauerische *Ideen*. Die damit verbundenen Probleme ließen sich auf dem Papier in Minuten lösen – und danach verlor Picasso vielfach das Interesse. Er scheute eindeutig die Anstrengung, die mit dem Schnitzen oder einer anderen dreidimensionalen Umsetzung seiner Ideen ver-

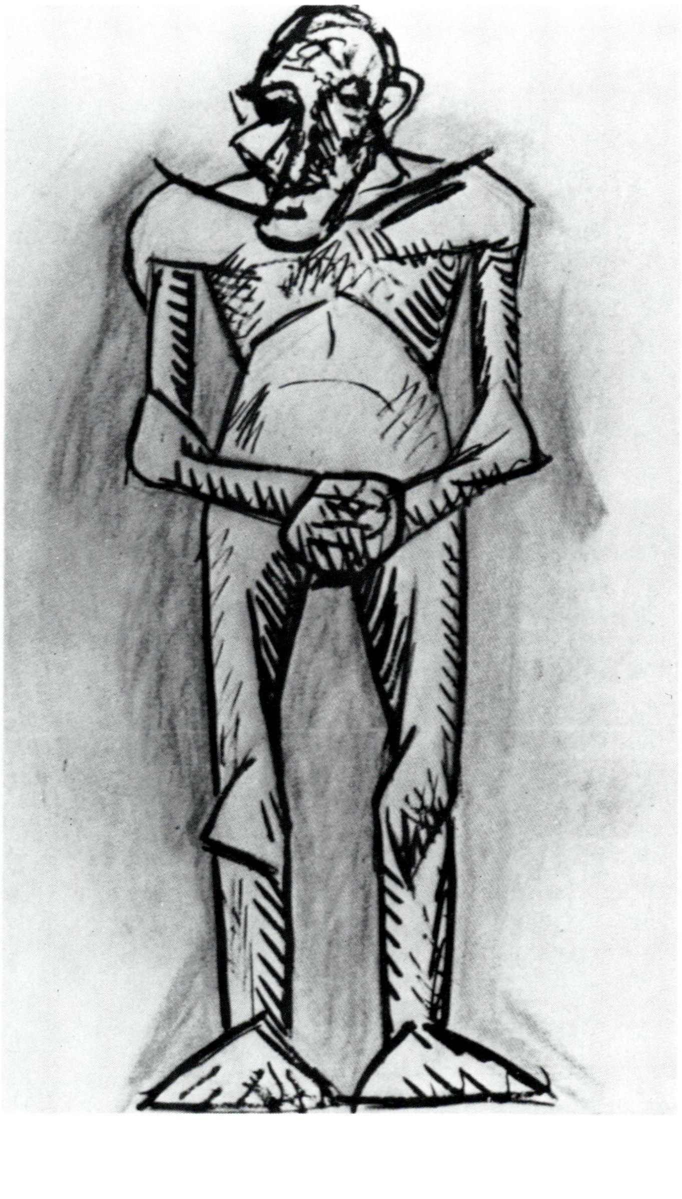

☐ 376 *Pablo Picasso, ›Bildnis André Salmon‹ (Portrait d'André Salmon), Endfassung, 1907–08, Tusche, 63 x 48 cm. Sammlung Jacqueline Picasso, Mougins.*

□ 377 *André Salmon, Photographie, Frontispiz von André Salmons Buch „Propos d'atelier", 1922 veröffentlicht.*

bunden war. Die Ausführung empfand er als langweilig und zeitraubend und überließ sie schließlich weitgehend anderen Personen. Gemessen an einem Brancusi war Picasso faul – und kümmerte sich kaum um die Werkstoffe oder die Feinheiten ihrer Oberfläche. Obwohl er der einfallsreichste und revolutionärste Bildhauer der Moderne war, dessen Werk – zumindest in qualitativer (d.h. stilistischer und konzeptioneller) Hinsicht – die Kunstgeschichte stärker veränderte als das Donatellos, Michelangelos oder Berninis, verlangen Picassos Leistungen auf diesem Gebiet eine Untersuchung, die mehr von seinen Zeichnungen als von den realisierten Objekten ausgeht. Letztere dienen in erster Linie als Überprüfungen der auf dem Papier erarbeiteten Konzepte. Selbst wenn Picasso die weniger arbeitsaufwendige Technik des Modellierens einsetzte – wie in den Skulpturen der 30er Jahre und später –, verkürzte er die dazu notwendige Zeit und Anstrengung durch die Verwendung von Fundobjekten, um seine Formen schnell auszufüllen. Daß diese Objekte vielen seiner Skulpturen ein poetisches, bisweilen surreales Moment verliehen, ändert nichts an der Tatsache, daß sie Picasso zunächst nur als Abkürzungen für die dreidimensionale Realisierung von graphischen Bildern betrachtete.[119]

Solchen Überlegungen sollte man bei der Erörterung von Picassos Plastiken aus dem Jahr 1907 – seiner augenfälligsten primitivistischen Phase – entsprechendes Gewicht beimessen. Kein Text zu diesen Plastiken berücksichtigt, daß die wenigen Objekte aus dem Jahr 1907 nur einen Bruchteil der Skulpturen ausmachen, die er in den Zeichnungen dieses Jahres konzipierte. Nur wenigen ist es aufgefallen,[120] daß von den Zeichnungen, die ein dreidimensionales Stadium erreichten □ 328, 367, 391, die Mehrzahl auf unterschiedlichen Stufen unvollendet blieb. Mit Ausnahme des Reliefs im iberischen Stil vom Frühjahr 1907 □ 313 gibt es keine festen Anhaltspunkte, um diese Objekte auf eine bestimmte Zeit des Jahres 1907[121] zu datieren; auch hat darüber keine fachliche Diskussion stattgefunden. Aber angesichts der Gemeinsamkeiten dieser Werke nicht nur mit der afrikanischen, sondern auch mit der ozeanischen Plastik (und es gibt keinen zwingenden Grund für die Annahme, Picasso habe letztere schon vor seinem Besuch im Trocadéro im Juni kennengelernt),[122] neige ich dazu, sie alle in die zweite Jahreshälfte 1907 zu datieren.

Die kleine *Stehende Figur* □ 328 ist ein typisches Beispiel für die Vielfalt der Quellen, die Picassos Plastiken verarbeiten. Die gestreckten Proportionen und die Kontur des Kopfes sind ein deutlicher Nachklang der großen, auffällig roten Plastik eines Männerbundes von den Neuen Hebriden (aus Farnholz), die das Herzstück der ozeanischen Abteilung des Trocadéro war □ 329. Die Proportionen der Arme, Beine und des Körpers von Picassos Plastik stehen hingegen der afrikanischen Bildhauerei näher. Johnson, der die *Stehende Figur* mit Gauguins *Saint Orang* verglich, sieht den »direkten Einfluß« dieses Neoimpressionisten auf Picasso.[123] Wenn dies zutrifft, dann ist eher Gauguins Interesse an der Holzplastik ausschlaggebend (die Picasso durch die Retrospektive des vorangegangenen Herbstes eindrucksvoll zur Kenntnis gekommen war) als deren besonderer Charakter, ihre Formen oder Ausarbeitung – es sei denn, man stellt die in ihr verarbeiteten Einflüsse polynesischer Plastik in Rechnung. Die gelbliche Farbe der *Stehenden Figur* sieht Johnson als »eine möglicherweise ironische Bezugnahme auf Gauguins Saint Orang und Gelber Christus«. Trifft dies zu, sind diese Assoziationen sicher mit den Erinnerungen an die bemalten Objekte von den Neuen Hebriden und aus Neuguinea im Trocadéro vermischt (vielleicht auch mit Erinnerungen

□ 378 *Pablo Picasso, ›Bildnis André Salmon‹ (Portrait d'André Salmon), 1907, Kohle, 60 x 40 cm. Privatbesitz, Frankreich.*

an einige bemalte *Yoruba*-Skulpturen, die er im Trocadéro, bei seinen Malerfreunden oder in Heymanns Laden gesehen haben könnte).

Johnson hat jedoch sicherlich recht, wenn er Picassos *Puppe* □ 381 als Beispiel für den wohl »direktesten Einfluß der Stammeskunst auf die Plastiken [Picassos] aus dem Jahr 1907« anführt. Er vergleicht die stilisierten Hände und den Mund, die gedrungenen Körperformen, den großen Kopf und die Glotzaugen mit den Figuren auf den Fächerhaltern von den Marquesasinseln □ 379. Bei der *Puppe* könnte es sich auch um eine für Picasso typische Umwandlung irgendeiner der vielen Arten von polynesischen Tikis (siehe Glossar) handeln □ 373, 382, die es damals im Trocadéro gab. Johnson macht auch darauf aufmerksam, daß das kleine Loch auf der Rückseite dieser Arbeit anzeigt, daß sie wie Picassos neukaledonische Figuren □ 402–404 an die Wand gehängt werden sollte – »einer der revolutionäreren Schritte, um die Unterschiede zwischen Malerei und Plastik durch die Art ihrer Aufstellung zu verwischen«. Die Puppe war offenbar rot, grün und blau bemalt, doch ist die Farbe heute weitgehend verschwunden.[124]

Die *Stehende Figur* und die *Puppe* gehören zu den wenigen vollplastischen Arbeiten dieser Zeit, die vollendet wurden. Bei der *Figur* □ 367 – die oben erörterte Plastik, die mit der Nimba in Beziehung stand – war nur die Vorderseite bearbeitet, diese dafür aber bis zur Schlußglättung. Die *Karyatide* □ 391, Picassos größte Holzskulptur von 1907, blieb im Rohstadium; ein großer Teil des Holzbalkens, aus dem sie gehauen ist, kam über die gröbsten Anfänge nicht hinaus. Auch die orangefarbige Umrißzeichnung, die Picasso zur Orientierung diente, ist noch erhalten.

Johnson nennt die *Karyatide* »grob gearbeitet« und vergleicht ihren Eindruck von »Brutalisierung, einer Art wilder Sexualität« mit den *Demoiselles*. Ich bin jedoch sicher, daß diese Figur trotz ihres geplanten kantigen Umrisses eine weiche Oberflächengestalt erhalten sollte – im Sinne der weiblichen Karyatiden □ 387, von denen eine offensichtlich der Entwurf für die *Karyatide* ist. In jedem Fall sollte sie eine glattere, nicht so roh bossierte Oberfläche, die sie jetzt dem Betrachter darbietet, erhalten. In diesem Sinne bestätigte Picasso gegenüber Werner Spies, daß er die mit der Axt bearbeitete Figur für unvollendet hielt.[125] Vielleicht hat ihr jetziger Zustand, der ihr einen der Stammeskunst fremden expressionistischen Charakter verleiht, Picasso schließlich gefallen; sonst hätte er sie wohl weggeworfen. Die Quelle für die *Karyatide* war anscheinend afrikanisch und nicht klassisch (wie für Modiglianis *Karyatide* □ 603). Da es aber die heute berühmten Karyatiden-Hocker der *Luba* □ 602 damals in Paris noch nicht gab, muß man die afrikanischen Vorbilder in den Plastiken von der Elfenbeinküste suchen oder in jenem Typ von Trommelträger-Figuren der *Senufo*, die schon nach Frankreich kamen. Obgleich Picassos Entwürfe keine direkte Ähnlichkeit mit den genannten Skulpturen aufweisen, haben sie mit ihnen den frontalen, ikonenhaf-

□ 379 *›Fächergriffe‹, Marquesasinseln, Holz, größte Höhe 27,5 cm. The University Museum, University of Pennsylvania, Philadelphia.*

□ 380 *Blick in den Ozeanien-Saal, Musée d'Ethnographie du Trocadéro (jetzt Musée de l'Homme), Paris 1895.*

□ 381 *Pablo Picasso, ›Puppe‹ (Poupée), 1907, bemaltes Holz und Metallaugen, Höhe 26 cm. Art Gallery of Ontario, Toronto.* ▷

□ 382 *›Figur aus Holz‹, Marquesas-inseln, mit Haar, Rindenstoff und Muscheln, Höhe 50 cm. Musée de l'Homme, Paris. Erworben 1887.* ▷ ▷

ten Zug sowie das Motiv der symmetrischen, vertikalen Vorderarme gemeinsam.

Zwei wesentliche Merkmale von Picassos Malerei des Jahres 1907, die sich 1908 fortsetzten, zeigen eine deutliche Verwandtschaft zur Stammeskunst: die blockhaften, symmetrischen Torsen und die konkaven Gesichter. Physiognomien wie der *Frauenkopf* von Anfang 1908 □ 393, die eine breite, konvexe Stirn und ein langes, spitz zulaufendes konkaves Untergesicht aufweisen, leiten sich aus dem rechts oben befindlichen Kopf der *Demoiselles* ab und sind unstreitig auch eine Reaktion auf die *Fang*-Plastik □ 385, 386, 392. Als Quelle avantgardistischen Interesses in den Vorkriegsjahren kommt die *Fang*-Plastik den *Kota*-Reliquiarfiguren an Bedeutung gleich. *Fang*-Masken befanden sich im Besitz Picassos □ 409, Braques □ 419, Derains □ 398 und anderer Künstler; Reliquienwächter der *Fang* □ 383 waren seltener und sehr begehrt. Picasso besaß eine Figur, und den grimmigen Kopf, den Einstein abbildete □ 386, hatte er wohl in den Jahren kurz vor dem 1. Weltkrieg kennengelernt.[126] Von den *Fang* beeinflußte, konkave Gesichtstypen erhalten sich bis ins Jahr 1908 in Picassos Werk, wie die *Studie zu Freundschaft* zeigt □ 384, sogar bis zu den *Drei Frauen*, deren Neufassung im Winter des folgenden Jahres das Ende von Picassos »Afrikanismus« bezeichnen sollte. Eine eigenartige Form von Konkavität findet sich in den *Studien zum Kopf einer Bäuerin* □ 395, die Picasso im Spätsommer 1908 während seines Aufenthaltes in La Rue des Bois schuf. Die Profilansichten des Kopfes erinnern jedoch weniger an die Konkavität der *Fang*-Masken (die normalerweise eine konvexe Stirn haben) als an die bestimmter *Bambara*-Masken □ 394, die im damaligen Frankreich wahrscheinlich anzutreffen waren.[127]

Der solide, reduktive und symmetrische Charakter der *Bäuerin* bestätigt die Annahme eines afrikanischen Einflusses auf Picassos Figurenmalerei in La Rue des Bois. Die dort entstandenen Landschaften sind hingegen von einer anderen Herkunft. Für sie gab es natürlich in der primitiven Kunst kein Vorbild, diese Rolle fiel Henri Rousseau zu.

Obwohl Picasso Rousseaus Werk schon früher kennengelernt hatte (höchstwahrscheinlich schon im Jahre 1901, aber mit Sicherheit 1905),[128] gewinnt es erst 1908 Einfluß auf ihn, als es seinen Absichten gelegen kam. Rousseaus Werk scheint 1906 für Matisse und Derain von einigem Interesse gewesen zu sein – als eine Art verallgemeinerter Primitivismus, der sich mit der Präsentation von *Le Lion ayant faim* . . . im Salon d'Automne des Vorjahres bei Rousseau durchgesetzt hatte.[129] Matisse' *Marguerite* □ 322 gewann unter dem Eindruck Rousseaus möglicherweise größere Einfachheit, ein Bild, das Picasso bei einem Bildtausch im Jahr 1907 ausgesucht hatte, als er noch iberisch malte.[130] Als Muster für Vereinfachung lieferte Rousseaus Werk Picasso nicht nur Prototypen für hochstilisierte,

☐ 383 *›Reliquiarfigur‹*, FANG *(Gabun oder Äquatorial-Guinea), Höhe 53 cm. Privatbesitz.*

□ 385 *›Reliquiarkopf‹, Fang (Gabun).*
Holz, Höhe 25 cm.
University of East Anglia, Sammlung R. und L. Sainsbury.

□ 384 *Pablo Picasso, Studie zu ›Freundschaft‹ (Etude pour l'amitié), 1908, Feder und Tusche, 48,5 x 31,5 cm. Musée Picasso, Paris.*

□ 386 *›Kopf‹, Fang (Gabun oder Äquatorial-Guinea),*
Holz, Höhe 27 cm.
The Philadelphia Museum of Art, Sammlung L. und W. Arensberg.

□ 387 *Pablo Picasso, ›Studien zu Karyatiden‹ (Etudes pour caryatides), 1907, Bleistift, 22,5 x 17,5 cm. Privatbesitz.*

□ 388 *Pablo Picasso, ›Akt mit erhobenen Armen‹ (Nue aux bras levés), 1907, Feder und braune Tusche, 26,5 x 19,5 cm. Musée Picasso, Paris.*

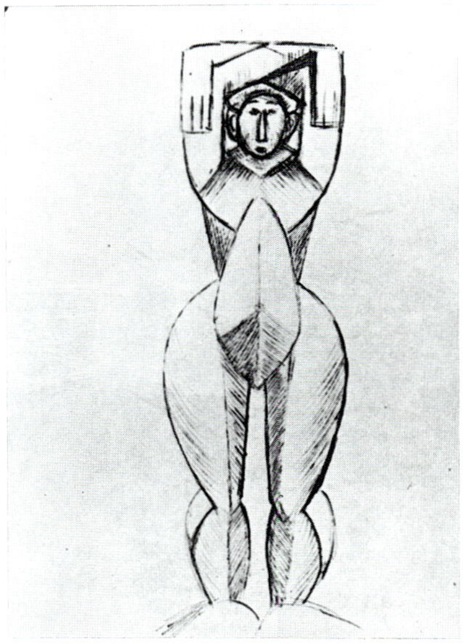

»geometrisierte« Landschaften, sondern auch für plastische Ordnung und Heiterkeit. Für ROUSSEAU konnte PICASSO aber erst in dem Moment empfänglich werden, als die gewaltsameren und expressionistischeren Effekte – grobe Farbgebung und energischer Pinselstrich – seiner »afrikanischen« Gemälde des Jahres 1907 einer monumentaleren und klassisch verhalteneren Kunst Platz machten. Diese Tendenz fand ihren Höhepunkt mit dem glatteren, »kontrollierteren« Pinselstrich und einer monochromeren Palette (Grün-, Braun- und Grautöne) in der Neufassung der *Drei Frauen*,[131] einem Übergangswerk, das Reste von PICASSOS »Afrikanismus« in den frühen Kubismus hinübernahm.

Zumindest im Rückblick erscheint es als vollkommen logisch, daß ROUSSEAUS Einfluß auf PICASSO dann am größten war, als dieser sich noch in seiner »afrikanischen« Periode befand, also vor seinem erneuten Interesse und seinem tieferen Verständnis für CÉZANNES Kunst, die in ihm erwachten, als er BRAQUES frühkubistische Bilder sah. Diese veranlaßten ihn, *Drei Frauen* völlig neu zu malen. ROUSSEAUS Archaismus, der der Stammeskunst in jeder Hinsicht näher stand als CÉZANNE, wurde so zum Bindeglied zwischen der »art nègre« und den Einflüssen von CÉZANNE und BRAQUE, die PICASSOS Entwicklung nach seiner Rückkehr aus La Rue des Bois immer mehr bestimmten. Ende 1908 war von PICASSOS »afrikanischen« Effekten nur das Facettenhafte seines frühen Kubismus geblieben □ 400, welches an die flächige Brechung einiger Stammesobjekte sogar dann erinnert, wenn CÉZANNE eine Wendung ins Primitive erhält.

Viele Freunde PICASSOS aus dieser Zeit sahen in Werken ROUSSEAUS und der Stammeskünstler eine vergleichbare Einfachheit und »Unschuld« und glaubten in ihrer Werkauffassung etwas Sakrales zu verspüren. »Der Zöllner«, schrieb Salmon, »malte seine ehrgeizigen Kompositionen so, wie der schwarze Bildermacher seine religiösen Bildnisse schnitzte.« Salmon verglich ROUSSEAU aber auch mit GIOTTO und UCCELLO und fügte hinzu: »Wir schätzen [ihn] nicht wegen des Barbarismus, sondern wegen seines Wissens.«[132] Wenn überhaupt, hat der Ausdruck *primitif* – im Sinne des 19. Jahrhunderts – für ROUSSEAU nur bezüglich der italienischen Primitiven eine Bedeutung.

ROUSSEAU selbst interessierte sich nicht für die Stammeskunst, und in seinem Werk lassen sich entsprechende Einflüsse auch nicht nachweisen. Er sah sich entschieden als zeitgenössischen Künstler und kann aus vielerlei Gründen auch als solcher gelten. Sein berühmter Ausspruch gegenüber PICASSO wurde oft zitiert, aber immer nur als Scherz verstanden: »Du, Pablo,

☐ 389 ›*Trommel*‹, SENUFO (*Elfenbeinküste*), *Holz und Haut, Höhe 123 cm. Privatbesitz.*

◁ ☐ 390 ›*Weibliche Figur*‹, *Elfenbeinküste, Holz, veröffentlicht in Marius de Zayas, „African Negro Art: Its Influence on Modern Art", 1916.*

☐ 391 *Pablo Picasso, ›Karyatide‹ (Caryatide), 1907, bemaltes Holz, 81 x 23 x 21 cm. Musée Picasso, Paris.*

□ 392 *›Maske‹*, FANG *(Gabun), bemaltes Holz, Höhe 50 cm. Sammlung Vérité, Paris.*

und ich«, sagte er, »wir sind die beiden größten Künstler der Zeit; du im ägyptischen Stil und ich im modernen.« Im Kontext des zeitgenössischen Wortgebrauchs betrachtet, erhält die Aussage Sinn. Am Ende des 19. Jahrhunderts war das Wort »ägyptisch« im Jargon der Kritiker ein Ersatz für »primitiv« geworden (und blieb es, bis »primitiv« in den Jahren kurz vor dem 1. Weltkrieg auf die Stammeskunst bezogen wurde). Als »ägyptisch« galt jede Kunst, die zum Exotischen, Hochstilisierten, Statischen, Einfachen, Geometrischen oder Frontalen tendierte. In seinen Briefen gebrauchte VAN GOGH »primitiv« zur Beschreibung der ägyptischen Kunst, und man erinnere sich, daß MATISSE von ägyptischer Kunst sprach, als er PICASSO zum ersten Mal eine afrikanische Plastik zeigte. Ein paar Jahre später kaufte LIPCHITZ sein erstes afrikanisches Objekt in der Meinung, es sei ägyptisch.[133]

Im Licht solcher Verwirrung scheint es verständlich, daß Louis Vauxcelles' Kritik von BRAQUES ersten kubistischen Gemälden im Herbst 1908 von dessen »Besessenheit vom Stil Cézannes und Reminiszenzen an die statische Kunst der Ägypter« sprach.[134] Vauxcelles wäre freilich im Recht gewesen, hätte er CÉZANNE zusammen mit der afrikanischen Kunst genannt, die BRAQUE bereits sammelte.[135] Doch im Jahr 1908 war die Kunst Afrikas und Ozeaniens selbst in Kritikerkreisen der Avantgarde kaum bekannt, und Vauxcelles wußte offenbar nichts von BRAQUES Interesse an ihr. Es überrascht nicht, daß ROUSSEAU PICASSOS Werk als »ägyptisch« bezeichnete, zumal er von PICASSOS Primitivismus wußte. Er kannte besonders die *Demoiselles* und ihre linke Figur, die selbst im Profil wie in der ägyptischen Kunst ein frontales Auge hat.

Wenn er von sich als einem Modernen sprach, dachte der Zöllner wohl an Motive wie Flugzeug, Ozeandampfer, den Eiffelturm, Fußballspiele, Fabriken – viele von ihnen sollte sein junger Freund ROBERT DELAUNAY im Kubismus wiederaufnehmen. ROUSSEAU, der »Primitive«, ist irrtümlicherweise oft nur

□ 393 *Pablo Picasso, ›Weiblicher Kopf‹ (Tête de femme), 1908, Öl auf Leinwand, 73 x 60 cm. Privatbesitz.*

als ein Künstler ganz eigener Art oder, noch schlimmer, als Gründer einer Schule von *naïfs* verstanden worden, die Maler wie Vavin und Bombois hervorbrachte. Demgegenüber gehört er mit seinen symbolistischen, dichterischen Ideen, der exotischen Ikonographie und seinem lichtarmen, achaisierenden und dekorativen Stil durchaus zur Generation der Postimpressionisten, der er chronologisch ohnehin zuzurechnen ist. Und es ist schlüssig, daß in den Jahren, als der Stil von Cézanne, Gauguin, Seurat und Van Gogh die jungen Kubisten und Fauvisten beeinflußte, auch die Kunst des Zöllners von Interesse war, zumal die vier führenden Vertreter des Postimpressionismus (Seurat, Van Gogh, Gauguin und Cézanne) bereits tot waren, während Rousseau 1908 ein aktives Mitglied im Kreise der jungen Maler war.

Einmal abgesehen von Picasso und seinen Malerfreunden, die den Zöllner verehrten, sahen es zwei ehemalige Schüler Matisse', der amerikanische Maler Max Weber[136] und der in Ungarn geborene Kunsthändler und vormalige Bildhauer Joseph Brummer, als ihre Lebensaufgabe, Rousseaus Werk bekanntzumachen. Brummers im Jahre 1908 eröffneter Laden am Boulevard Saint-Germain stellte die Bilder Rousseaus direkt neben den Stammesobjekten aus, für die Brummer zwischen 1908 und 1914 zum führenden Händler avancierte (siehe S. 153ff.).

Daß es nun neben dem Laden Heymanns in der Rue de Rennes, wo Matisse seine ersten afrikanischen Plastiken gekauft hatte, auch den Laden Brummers gab, verbesserte die Möglichkeiten, an Stammeskunst heranzukommen, beträchtlich, da man sie sonst in Paris nur hie und da in Kuriositätenläden und auf Flohmärkten finden konnte. Dies wirft die schwierige Frage auf, wie Picasso in der entscheidenden Zeit von 1907 bis zum 1. Weltkrieg zu seiner Sammlung kam. Zwar sind allgemeine Aussagen über Picassos frühere Sammeltätigkeit möglich – siehe hierzu meine Ausführungen in der Einleitung

□ 394 *›Maske‹, Bambara (Mali), Holz, Höhe 24 cm. Privatbesitz, Italien.*

□ 396 *Pablo Picasso, ›Stehende Akte und Studie eines Fußes‹ (Nus debout et étude de pied), 1908, Feder, Tusche, Aquarell, 30 x 22,5 cm. Musée Picasso, Paris.*

□ 395 *Pablo Picasso, Studie zum Kopf von ›Die Bäuerin‹, 1908, Kohle, 63 x 48 cm. Sammlung Marina Picasso.*

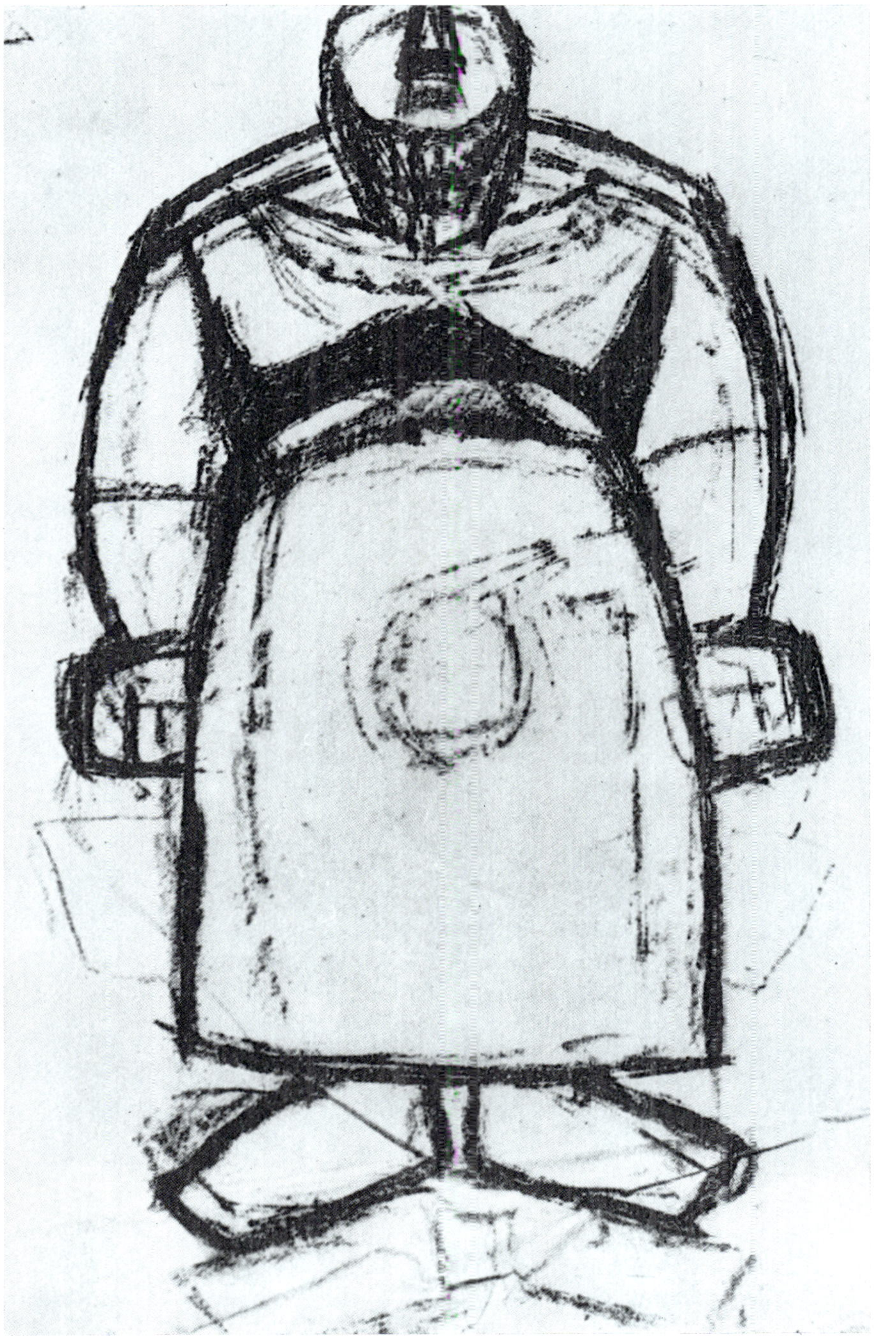

□ 397 *Pablo Picasso, ›Die Bäuerin‹ (La fermière), 1908, Kohle, 62,5 x 48 cm. Sammlung Jacqueline Picasso, Mougins.*

S. 25ff. –, doch macht es die schlechte Quellenlage schwierig, die Werke aus seinem Besitz jener Zeit genau zu bestimmen. Immerhin sind einige wenige Informationen vorhanden, und weitere Schlüsse lassen sich aus Picassos Werk selbst ziehen.

Nach unseren bisherigen Beobachtungen wurde Picasso die erste afrikanische Skulptur von Matisse bei einem Besuch Gertrude Steins im Herbst 1906 gezeigt.[137] Matisse berichtete später von seinem sich anschließenden Gespräch mit Picasso, und viele Autoren zogen daraus den Schluß, daß jener Besuch die Geburtsstunde von Picassos »Afrikanismus« gewesen sei.[138] In Picassos Werk des darauffolgenden halben Jahres finden sich jedoch keinerlei Anhaltspunkte, die diese Hypothese stützen würden.

Die geringe Bedeutung, die Picasso selbst diesem Treffen bei Gertrude Stein beimaß,[139] ist noch verständlicher, wenn Paudrat mit seiner These Recht behält (siehe S. 151), daß das von Matisse vorgezeigte Objekt jene anspruchsvolle *Vili*-Figur war, die Matisse kurz darauf in einem unvollendet gebliebenen Bild darstellte □ 259.[140] Matisse' Vorstellung von der afrikanischen Plastik, die hauptsächlich auf den konservativeren, »klassischen« Objekten der *Baule, Yombe, Yoruba, Vili* und *Punu* beruhte, führte ihn dazu, sie mit der ägyptischen Kunst gleichzusetzen.[141] Picasso, den die abstrakteren und phantasievolleren Objekte der *Baga, Kota* und *Ongwe* anzogen, muß Matisse' Gleichsetzung mißfallen haben.[142] Von ein paar Ausnahmen abgesehen,[143] interessierte Picasso an der afrikanischen Plastik vor allem das, was sie von der ägyptischen Kunst unterschied.

Wie ich bereits am Beispiel von Rousseaus Einfluß andeutete, ließ sich Picasso nicht auf die Kunst anderer ein, solange er keine Berührungspunkte zu seinem eigenen Schaffen sah; bevor sie nicht Fragen aufwarf oder beantwortete, die ihn beschäftigten – oder die ihm brauchbar erschienen. Noch ganz in seine am Iberischen orientierte Kunst vertieft, war er im

□ 398 *›Maske‹, Fang (Gabun), bemaltes Holz, Höhe 48 cm. Musée National d'Art Moderne, Centre National d'Art et de Culture Georges Pompidou, Paris. Ehemals Sammlungen Maurice de Vlaminck, André Derain.*

Herbst 1906 für die Objekte, die er während dieser Monate in den Ateliers von Matisse, Derain und Vlaminck sah, entweder noch nicht aufnahmebereit oder – was noch wahrscheinlicher ist – von ihnen nicht besonders berührt. Salmon meint freilich, Picasso habe schon 1906 Stammeskunst gesammelt. Doch schrieb er dies viele Jahre später und widersprach sich oft bei der Angabe von Daten.[144] Auch kann man dieser Quelle deshalb kein großes Gewicht beimessen, weil zusätzliche Beweise wie auch ein Niederschlag primitiver Kunst in Picassos Werken vom Winter 1906–07 fehlen. Ich neige daher dazu, Picassos Versicherung mir gegenüber Glauben zu schenken, er habe erst nach Vollendung der *Demoiselles* angefangen, Stammeskunst zu kaufen (d.h. im Sommer 1907). Seine Begeisterung über den Besitz solcher Objekte, die, wie er mir sagte, mit einer mysteriösen »Kraft aufgeladen« seien, kann sich nur nach seiner »Offenbarung« ihrer magischen Natur entwickelt haben.

Mit einer einzigen (möglichen) Ausnahme, die keine Stammeskunst zeigt, sind keine Photographien von Picassos Atelier aus der Zeit vor Ende 1908 bekannt.[145] Aufgrund mangelnder Hinweise, die aber noch unter den Dokumenten im Picasso-Archiv auftauchen können, lassen sich die frühesten Erwerbungen von »art nègre« seitens Picassos schlecht nachweisen.[146] Angesichts von Picassos Feststellung mir gegenüber besteht jedoch kein Grund, an Kahnweilers Aussage zu zweifeln, er habe das Tiki von den Marquesasinseln gegen Ende 1907 in dessen Atelier gesehen. Dieses Tiki □ 373 ist das einzige Objekt von hoher Qualität, von dem wir mit Sicherheit wissen, daß es Picasso vor dem 1. Weltkrieg besaß; er hat es vielleicht bei Heymann gekauft.[147] Daß seine erste ozeanische Erwerbung polynesisch war, erklärt der Hinweis auf die Plastizität solcher Tikis, die sich von der melanesischen Kunst unterscheidet und mit der afrikanischen vergleichbar ist. Gerade dieser Aspekt mußte Picasso vom Bildhauerischen her interessieren. Seine malerischen, melanesischen Objekte □ 432 erwarb er größtenteils nach 1920, als sich seine eigene Kunst in ähnlichen Bahnen bewegte.[148] Angesichts der hohen Qualität überrascht es nicht, daß Picassos Tiki die Jahre hindurch in seinem Atelier verblieb, während er viele frühe Erwerbungen von »art nègre« wegstellte. Wir erkennen es auf einem schönen, bislang unveröffentlichten Photo Apollinaires bei Picasso aus dem Jahre 1911 □ 374 und auf vielen Bildern des Ateliers aus späteren Jahren.[149]

Picasso sagte mir, daß er die meisten seiner frühen Stammesobjekte auf Spaziergängen mit Fernande erstand, besonders bei sonntäglichen Besuchen der Flohmärkte. Sein Nachlaß umfaßt eine große Zahl offenbar alter, aber recht unbedeutender Masken und Figuren, bei denen es möglich erscheint, daß sie auf solchen Spaziergängen gekauft wurden; ihr Kaufdatum läßt sich aber nicht feststellen.[150] Mir fällt es schwer zu glauben, er könnte solche Objekte nach dem 1. Weltkrieg ausgesucht haben, als sich die Auswahl an Stammesobjekten rasch vergrößerte und er die meisten seiner schöneren Stücke erwarb, einige im Austausch gegen eigene Werke. Sinnvoller ist die Vermutung, Picasso habe die vielen schwachen Stücke, die das Herzstück seiner »Sammlung« ausmachten,[151] zu einer Zeit gekauft, als die »art nègre« noch neu für ihn war und er schon aus Routinearbeiten Anregungen für sein Schaffen entnehmen

□ 399 *Pablo Picasso, ›Männerkopf‹ (Tête d'homme), 1908, Öl auf Holz, 27 x 21 cm. Kunstmuseum Bern, Herrmann- und-Margrit-Rupf-Stiftung.*

□ 400 *Pablo Picasso, ›Rückenakt‹ (Nu debout vu de dos), 1908, Gouache und Bleistift, 63 x 48 cm. Privatbesitz, dem Museum of Modern Art, New York, als Geschenk in Aussicht gestellt.*

konnte (siehe S. 27 ff.). Ein paar dieser anspruchslosen Stammesobjekte kann man zwischen guten Stücken auf den von Claude Picasso in der Villa La Californie gemachten Photos sehen □ 341. Tzara hatte diese Masse von Objekten gegen 1955 gesichtet und war von ihrer Mittelmäßigkeit überrascht.[152] Er verstand anscheinend nicht, wie und warum PICASSO »art nègre« anhäufte.

Man sollte sich auch vor Augen halten, daß wirklich qualitätvolle Stammesobjekte vor dem 1. Weltkrieg nicht billig angeboten wurden, und in den Jahren 1907–12 PICASSOS Kunst zu schwierig war, um sofort finanziellen Erfolg zu bringen. Noch vor dem 1. Weltkrieg verkaufte Paul Guillaume nachgewiesenermaßen ein afrikanisches Objekt für 20 000 Francs oder 6000 Dollar (nach heutiger Währung über 60 000 Dollar),[153] was etwa der Hälfte des Durchschnittspreises für einen guten CÉZANNE bei Vollard entsprach.[154] PICASSO war bei Ankäufen von Stammesobjekten außerdem recht sparsam, auch wenn er sich für sie begeisterte, und sein bekannter Widerwille, sich von Geld zu trennen, wirkte sich auf die Qualität seiner Erwerbungen nicht gerade vorteilhaft aus – dies gilt zumindest bis in die späten 20er Jahre. Noch 1918, als er geradewegs dabei war, ein berühmter Künstler zu werden und einen gewissen Wohlstand erworben hatte, schrieb er an Gertrude Stein, die in Nîmes interessante Stammesobjekte entdeckt und ihm vorgeschlagen hatte, sie zu kaufen: » . . . Ich würde mich freuen, sie zu bekommen, sofern sie nicht teuer sind.« Und zehn Tage später: »Bieten Sie dem Kerl für beide zusammen 100 Francs.« Der von Madame Stein vermittelte Handel kam zustande und PICASSO gefielen die Objekte. Die Plastiken, so schrieb er ihr, »m'ont plus« (ich behalte seine Schreibweise bei), und er schickte »avec cete letre« die 100 Francs, »que je vous doits pour les negres«.[155] Gewiß hatte PICASSO seinen Spaß an günstigen Kaufabschlüssen und vor allem an »chasses aux nègres«, die er unternahm, wann immer er in Hafenstädte reiste, wo mit Stammesobjekten zu rechnen war.

Die Durchschnittlichkeit der meisten Früherwerbungen PICASSOS bestätigt weitgehend das erste Atelierphoto, das Ende 1908 im Bateau-Lavoir aufgenommen wurde □ 402.[156] Soweit bekannt, tauchte nach dem 1. Weltkrieg keine der dort abgebildeten Stammesskulpturen in PICASSOS Ateliers oder Wohnungen später wieder auf. Doch da ich wußte, daß er sich nur ungern von solchen Objekten trennte – er hing mit einer abergläubischen, fast fetischistischen Besessenheit an ihnen[157] –, vermutete ich, daß sie in seinem Nachlaß wieder auftauchen würden. Die zwei an der Wand hängenden neukaledonischen Objekte wurden vom Musée Picasso ausgewählt □ 403, 404. Die zwei afrikanischen Stücke auf dem Tisch zwischen den Ateliersachen entdeckte ich bei zwei Erben. Zusammen mit dem Tiki, das von außergewöhnlicher Qualität war, gehören diese vier Stücke erwiesenermaßen zu der Sammlung, die PICASSO im Jahre 1908 besaß.

Die beiden neukaledonischen Figuren sind nach heutigen Maßstäben recht routinierte Stücke, wenn auch nicht schlechter als ihre Verwandten im Trocadéro □ 380. 1907–08 waren sie für Paris wohl sehr seltene Werke. Das größere läßt sich im Bildnis Kahnweilers von 1910, links neben dem Kopf des Dargestellten, nachweisen □ 426, so daß mindestens diese

□ 401 *›Maske‹, BOA (Zaire), bemaltes Holz, Höhe 25,5 cm. Sammlung J. W. Mestach, Brüssel.*

□ 403 *›Figur zur Bekrönung eines Daches‹, Neukaledonien, Holz, Höhe 118 cm, Musée Picasso, Paris. Ehemals Sammlung Pablo Picasso* ▷

□ 404 *›Figur zur Bekrönung eines Daches‹, Neukaledonien, Holz, Höhe 126 cm. Musée Picasso, Paris. Ehemals Sammlung Pablo Picasso. Farbabbildung siehe* □ *425.* ▷ ▷

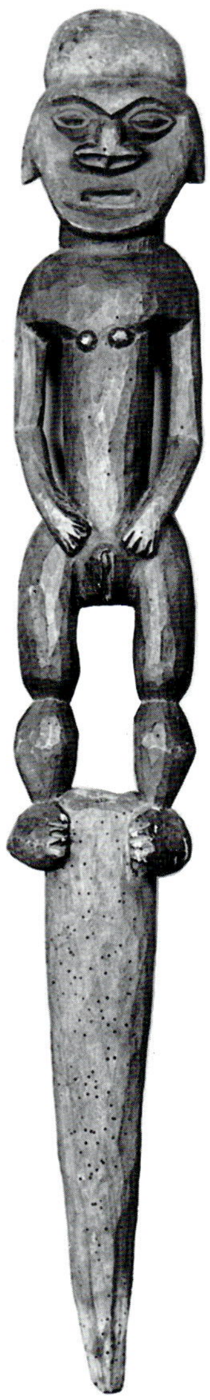

□ 402 *Picasso in seinem Atelier am Bateau-Lavoir. Photographiert für Gelett Burgess, 1908.*

□ 405 *›Harfe‹, Punu, evtl. auch Lele, Myene oder Fang (Gabun), bemaltes Holz, Höhe 80 cm. Sammlung Jacqueline Picasso, Mougins. Ehemals Sammlung Pablo Picasso.*

□ 406 *›Gruppe‹, Yombe (Volksrepublik Kongo, Cabinda oder Zaire), bemaltes Holz, 75,5 cm. Sammlung Marina Picasso. Ehemals Sammlung Pablo Picasso.*

Figur weiterhin bei Picasso blieb, als er vom Bateau-Lavoir an den Boulevard de Clichy umzog.

Das Photo von 1908 zeigt den berühmten Tisch mit herunterklappbaren Seitenteilen, auf dem eine große und seltsame afrikanische Plastik von der Loangoküste (damals Französisch-Kongo) steht, die man den *Yombe* zuschreibt; es handelt sich um ein mehrstufiges Objekt mit gewundenen Schlangen auf einem Elefantensockel. Von den sechs oder sieben Objekten dieser Art, die ich kenne – einschließlich des Objektes, das im Jahr 1900 in den Trocadéro kam und hier Picassos Wahl vielleicht beeinflußte –, dienten alle als Schmuckstützen für zeremonielle Handtrommeln.[158] Picassos Objekt wurde mit Sicherheit nicht für diesen Zweck hergestellt, es kann nie eine Trommel gehalten haben (am Kopf fehlt kein Teil und es gibt auch keine Stelle, wo man sinnvollerweise eine Trommel hätte aufsetzen können). Da es sich hier also um eine Variante handelt, die keinem traditionellen Zweck dienen sollte, könnte sie von einem Kolonisten in Auftrag gegeben worden sein, eine Vermutung, die durch das Vorhandensein von Europäern unter den Figuren gestützt wird. Somit fällt dieses Stück unter die Rubrik »Touristenware«, der viele der früh im Westen aufgetauchten Objekte angehören.[159] Da dieses Objekt, dessen folkloristischer Stil an viele *Yoruba*-Plastiken erinnert, weder vom Bildhauerischen her interessant ist noch eine magische »Ausstrahlung« hat, muß ich annehmen, daß Picasso dessen fast zirkushafte Verrücktheit Vergnügen bereitete.

Das Photo zeigt rechts neben der *Yombe*-Skulptur eine *Punu*-Harfe aus Gabun □ 405, die von einer kleinen weiblichen Figur gekrönt wird, die auf eine Trommel zwischen ihren Knien schlägt. Die Figur steht auf einer Art Sockel mit seltsamem Zackenmuster, darunter der Resonanzkörper, dessen Vorderseite mit bunten Rauten, die Picasso an ein Harlekinskostüm erinnert haben dürften, bemalt ist. Insgesamt war dieses Musikinstrument wohl ein ansehnliches Objekt, bevor es verstümmelt wurde, wobei auch die weibliche Figur verloren ging (unsere Abbildung gibt den restaurierten Zustand wie-

□ 407 *Ramon Pichot in Picassos Atelier, Boulevard de Clichy, Paris 1910.*

□ 408 *›Maske‹, Shira-Punu (Gabun oder Volksrepublik Kongo), bemaltes Holz, Höhe 28 cm. Musée Picasso, Paris. Ehemals Sammlung Pablo Picasso.*

□ 409 *›Maske‹, Fang (Gabun), bemaltes Holz, Höhe 33 cm. Sammlung Jacqueline Picasso, Mougins. Ehemals Sammlung Pablo Picasso.*

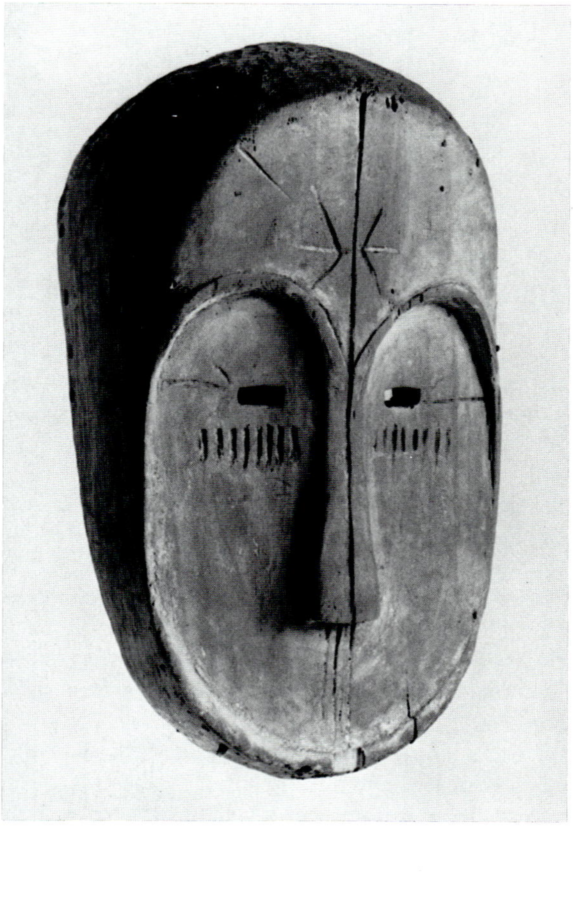

der). Eine Reihe von Figuren war von der *Yombe*-Skulptur abgebrochen, konnte aber aufgrund des Photos wieder am ursprünglichen Platz befestigt werden □ 406.

Das Photo von 1908 zeigt leider nur eine Ecke von Picassos kleinem Atelier, und es ist anzunehmen, daß sich dort außer dem Tiki noch andere Stammesobjekte befanden. Höchstwahrscheinlich hatte Picasso schon die weißgesichtige *Shira-Punu*-Maske □ 408 gekauft, die sich wohl unter den ersten Erwerbungen befand, da Fernande ihre Bedeutung unterstrich.[160] Sie ist jedoch erstmals auf einem Photo aus dem Jahr 1910 belegt □ 407, das den Freund des Künstlers Ramon Pichot in Picassos Atelier am Boulevard Clichy zeigt, wo die Maske rechts neben zwei Ölgemälden, einer Landschaft bei Horta von Picassos Kindheitsgefährten Manuel Pallerés und einem eigenhändigen Bild, hängt. Solche *Shira-Punu*-Masken gehörten zu den ersten Stücken, die die Fauvisten kauften (die schon ein halbes Jahr vor Picasso zu sammeln anfingen). Der stilisierte »Orientalismus« dieser Masken war nicht nur eingängig und ließ sich der von Gauguin ererbten Vorstellung vom Primitiven einpassen, sondern ihre Qualität war im Durchschnitt auch ziemlich hoch, und man konnte sie im Pariser Kunsthandel anscheinend leicht bekommen.

Unter den anderen Stücken, die wahrscheinlich zu Picassos früher »Sammlung« gehörten, befanden sich – neben den beiden im Zusammenhang mit der Zeichnung *Kopf* erwähnten kleinen *Baga*-Figuren – eine oder zwei seiner mit Kupfer überzogenen *Kota*-Reliquiarfiguren □ 410, 411. Dies bestätigt zum einen das anhand seiner Werke nachweisbare Interesse Picassos an solchen Objekten, besonders im Jahr 1907 (siehe S. 279–80); zum anderen eine Bemerkung Picassos über ihre

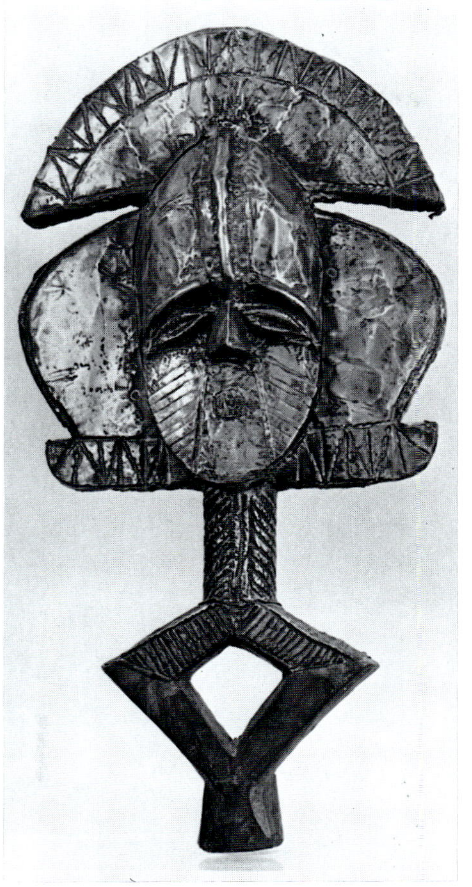

☐ 410 ›Reliquiarfigur‹, KOTA (Gabun oder Volksrepublik Kongo), Holz, Kupfer und Messing, Höhe 56,5 cm. Sammlung Marina Picasso. Ehemals Sammlung Pablo Picasso.

☐ 411 ›Reliquiarfigur‹, KOTA (Gabun oder Volksrepublik Kongo), Holz und Metall. Privatbesitz. Ehemals Sammlung Pablo Picasso. Photographiert von Claude Picasso in der Villa La Californie, Cannes 1974.

☐ 412 *Daniel-Henry Kahnweiler und seine Frau in ihrer Wohnung, Rue George Sand, Paris 1912–13.*

□ 414 *Pablo Picasso, ›Kopf‹ (Tête), 1907, Öl und Sand auf Holztafel, 17,5 x 14 cm. Sammlung Claude Picasso, Paris.*

□ 413 *›Reliquiarfigur‹, Kota (Gabun), Holz, Kupfer und Messing, Höhe 68 cm. Privatbesitz.*

□ 415 *Pablo Picasso, ›Frauenkopf-Fernande‹ (Tête de femme – Fernande), 1909, Bronze, Höhe 41 cm. Privatbesitz, Schweiz.*

□ 416 *Pablo Picasso, ›Gitarre‹ (Guitare), Blech und Draht, 77,5 x 35 x 19 cm. The Museum of Modern Art, New York. Geschenk des Künstlers.*

Originalität mir gegenüber;[161] drittens auch die Tatsache, daß seine beiden *Kota*-Reliquiarfiguren lange nicht die Qualität hatten, wie man sie bei Paul Guillaume und anderen Pariser Händlern in den Jahren vor dem 1. Weltkrieg bekommen konnte.[162] Als erste kaufte Picasso wohl die gröbere Figur, die in dem Zimmer der Villa La Californie photographiert wurde □ 411, wo Picasso viele seiner Stammesobjekte aufbewahrte. Picassos andere *Kota*-Reliquiarfigur □ 410, die typischer für ihre Art und sorgfältiger ausgearbeitet ist, kann auch nach heutigen Maßstäben als gute Arbeit gelten. Beide Figuren sind nicht so ansehnlich wie andere Stücke, die sich bereits 1907 im Trocadéro befanden □ 342, 343. (Eine recht eindrucksvolle *Kota*-Reliquiarfigur, die 1982 als ehemaliges Stück aus Picassos Sammlung deklariert wurde – sie soll sogar zur Entstehungszeit der *Demoiselles* zu seiner Sammlung gehört haben –, hat mit ihm überhaupt nichts zu tun.)[163] Von den beiden Objekten, die 1919 von Clouzot und Level unter der Provenienz »Sammlung Picasso« veröffentlicht wurden,[164] hatte Picasso die *Fang*-Maske □ 409 – stellt man seinen ausgeprägten Sinn für Wetteifer in Rechnung – wahrscheinlich vor Braque erworben, der spätestens 1911 eine bessere besaß □ 419. Man kann nicht einmal erraten, wann Picasso die bei Clouzot und Level abgebildete *Guere*-Maske erwarb.[165]

Das wohl bei weitem interessanteste afrikanische Stück, das Picasso in den Vorkriegsjahren kaufte, war die schönere seiner beiden *Grebo*-Masken □ 417, auf die er vielleicht bei seiner gemeinsam mit Braque unternommenen »chasse aux nègres« in Marseilles in der zweiten Augustwoche 1912 gestoßen war. In einer Postkarte an Kahnweiler spricht Braque davon,

□ 417 *›Maske‹, Grebo (Elfenbeinküste oder Liberia), bemaltes Holz und Fasern, Höhe 37 cm. Sammlung Claude Picasso. Ehemals Sammlung Pablo Picasso.*

□ 418 *Pablo Picasso, ›Das Speisezimmer des Künstlers in Montrouge‹ (La salle à manger de l'artiste à Montrouge), 1917, Bleistift, 27 x 22,5 cm. Musée Picasso, Paris.*

□ 419 *›Maske‹, Fang (Gabun), bemaltes Holz und Fasern, Höhe 32 cm. Sammlung C. Laurens, Paris. Ehemals Sammlung Georges Braque.*

Picasso die Stadt gezeigt und dabei »alle afrikanischen Objekte aufgekauft« zu haben (»avoir acheté tous les nègres«).[166] Eine Skizze in Picassos Skizzenbuch mit dem Datum 12. August 1912 □ 420 zeigt unter dem Cafétisch rechts unten vermutlich eine afrikanische Maske. Edward Fry, der darauf hinweist, glaubte in der Maske Picassos *Grebo* zu erkennen, die seiner Meinung nach damals gekauft wurde.[167] Doch trotz der Flüchtigkeit der Skizze ist immerhin erkennbar, daß die Maske – wenn es sich wirklich um eine solche handelt – keiner von Picassos beiden *Grebos* besonders ähnlich ist. Da Picassos qualitätvollere *Grebo*-Maske in einer Zeichnung aus dem Jahr 1917 an der Wand seiner Wohnung in Montrouge dargestellt ist □ 418, wäre der Ausflug nach Marseilles zwar ein einleuchtender, keineswegs aber zwingender Anlaß für Picassos Kauf der Maske. Selbst wenn man dieses Datum gelten ließe, wäre (im Gegensatz zu Frys Annahmen)[168] für die Datierung der *Gitarre* nichts gewonnen, einer Skulptur, die bekanntermaßen von einer oder beiden Masken der *Grebo* beeinflußt wurde (die man damals irrtümlich den *Wobe* zuschrieb), denn Picasso besaß mit hoher Wahrscheinlichkeit bereits die qualitativ mindere Maske □ 29. Es handelt sich bei ihr um den Typ eines mittelmäßigen, kaum gebrauchten Objekts, das man zu Anfang des Jahrhunderts antreffen konnte, als *Grebo*-Masken zu den relativ leicht käuflichen Typen gehörten.[169] Picasso hätte eine so durchschnittliche *Grebo*-Maske nie gekauft, nachdem er schon ein besseres Exemplar besaß □ 417. Auch hätte man ihm die schwächere Maske in den späteren Jahren kaum zum Geschenk gemacht.

Wegen der genannten Unsicherheiten ist nicht mit Gewißheit zu sagen, welche der beiden *Grebo*-Masken mit der *Gitarre* □ 416 mehr zu tun hat, wenn überhaupt einer von ihnen Priorität eingeräumt werden kann.[170] Da sowohl Kahnweiler □ 412 als auch Apollinaire □ 429 vor dem 1. Weltkrieg *Grebo*-Masken besaßen und beide später als Picasso zu sammeln begannen, erwarb Picasso die *Grebo*-Maske wahrscheinlich irgendwann zwischen Ende 1907 und 1912 und kaufte sich dann 1912 in Marseille die schönere, um seine Sammlung zu verbessern (obwohl nichts dagegen spricht, daß er sie in Paris während dieses Zeitraums gekauft haben könnte).

Da ich den Einfluß der *Grebo*-Masken auf die Gestaltung der *Gitarre* in der Einleitung recht ausführlich erörtert habe (S. 27–29), werde ich hier nicht nochmals darauf eingehen. Jene Form »unsichtbaren« Einflusses, die ich am Beispiel dieser Skulptur Picassos demonstrierte, ist nun für das Verhältnis von Georges Braques Kubismus zur Stammeskunst generell charakteristisch.

□ 420 *Pablo Picasso, ›Souvenir de Marseille‹, 1912, Tusche, 13,5 x 9 cm. Musée Picasso, Paris.*

□ 421 *Georges Braque in seinem Atelier in Paris, 1911.*

Obwohl BRAQUE in Zusammenhang mit der »art nègre« nur selten erwähnt wird, vor allem weil keines der Elemente seiner Bildsprache – auch nicht indirekt – an die Stammeskunst erinnert, war er doch in seinen frühen Jahren ein eifriger Sammler (siehe S. 153) und sparte nicht mit Worten, um die Bedeutung der afrikanischen Kunst für sich hervorzuheben: »Die afrikanischen Masken . . . eröffneten mir einen neuen Horizont. Sie ermöglichten mir, Kontakt zu instinktiven Dingen zu bekommen, zu ungehinderten Gefühlen, die der falschen Tradition [dem späten westlichen Illusionismus], die ich haßte, zuwiderlief.«[171]

Das Photo von BRAQUE in seinem Atelier aus dem Jahr 1911 zeigt an der Wand seine wundervolle *FANG*-Maske und eines seiner kubistischen Bilder auf dem Boden □ 419, 421. Nach außen haben beide Werke keine Gemeinsamkeiten, und dennoch sind die Gestaltungsprinzipien einer reduktiven Abstraktion und ideographischen Darstellung, die die Maske beherrschen, auch in dem Bild wirksam, wenn auch unter anderen geistigen Voraussetzungen. Wenn man die verhaltene Beziehung zwischen den beiden Werken begreift, versteht man BRAQUES Verhältnis zur Stammeskunst. Sein Verständnis für sie war jedoch formalistischer und in diesem Sinne beschränkter als bei PICASSO. Anders als der spanische Künstler interessierte er sich nicht für das »Magische« oder »Mysteriöse« dieser Objekte. Wie PICASSO später sagte, »verstand [Braque] die ›art nègre‹ nicht wirklich, weil er nicht abergläubisch war.«[172] BRAQUE schätzte auch die für die Stammeskunst so typische Materialmischung nicht, die den Hintergrund zu PICASSOS Erfindung von Collage und konstruierter Plastik bildet.[173]

Das Photo BRAQUES aus dem Jahr 1911 bezeugt auch die Allgegenwart von modernen wie eingeborenen Musikinstrumenten in den kubistischen Ateliers. Sowohl PICASSO als auch BRAQUE liebten Gitarren, Geigen, Lauten und Zithern nicht unbedingt wegen ihres Klangs, sondern wegen der Schönheit ihrer abstrakten und »lyrischen« Formen. PICASSO, dessen Phantasie und Gespür für die Metamorphose stärker entwickelt waren als bei BRAQUE, sah solche Instrumente mit Vorliebe analog zum menschlichen Körper oder Gesicht.[174] Der häufige Anthropomorphismus afrikanischer Instrumente regte dieses bildnerische Denken ständig an □ 422. (Ozeanische Instrumente sind häufig figürlich, wenn auch normalerweise in der Form von Tieren oder Ungeheuern wie bei den Reibetrom-

□ 422 *›Harfe‹, MANGBETU (Zaire), Holz, Tierhaut und Seil, Höhe 85,5 cm. Sammlung J. W. Mestach, Brüssel.*

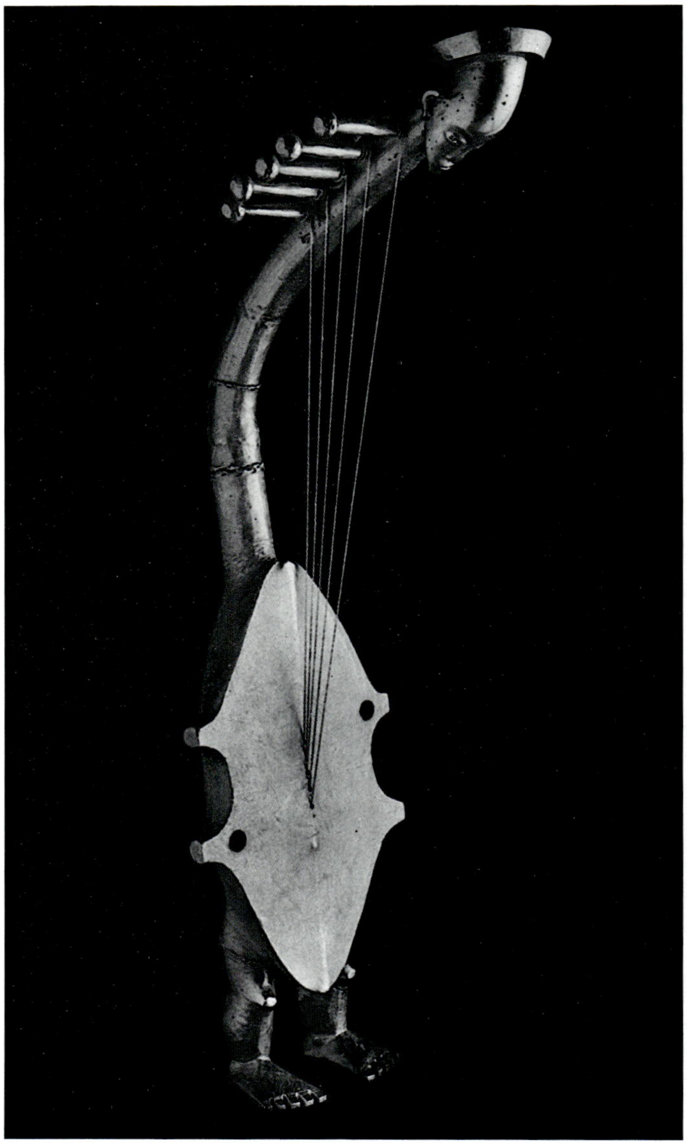

□ 423 *›Reibetrommel‹ (Neuirland), Holz, Höhe 53 cm. Sammlung J. W. Mestach, Brüssel.*

☐ 424 ›*Sanza*‹, ZANDE (*Zaire*), *Holz, Bambus und Harz, Höhe 66 cm. Musée Royal de l'Afrique Centrale, Tervuren.*

□ 426 *Pablo Picasso, ›Bildnis Daniel-Henry Kahnweiler‹ (Portrait de D. Henry Kahnweiler), Ausschnitt, 1910, Öl auf Leinwand, 100,5 x 73 cm. The Art Institute of Chicago. Schenkung G. W. Chapman.*

□ 427 *Pablo Picasso, ›Bildnis Daniel-Henry Kahnweiler‹, Ausschnitt, siehe □ 426.*

◁ □ 425 *›Figur zur Bekrönung eines Daches‹, Ausschnitt, Neukaledonien, Holz, Gesamthöhe 126 cm. Musée Picasso, Paris. Ehemals Sammlung Pablo Picasso, Gesamtansicht siehe □ 404.*

meln aus Neuirland, für die wir hier ein an der Grenze zur Abstraktheit stehendes Beispiel zeigen □ 423).

Da sich Picassos Kubismus 1910 von einer Sprache solide geformter Reliefformen zu einem »malerischen« Stil entwikkelte, bei dem Fragmente von immer transparenter werdenden Motiven in einem unermeßlichen lichten Raum schweben, wurde jede Beziehung, die sein Werk mit primitiver, ja mit jeder Art von Plastik haben konnte, notgedrungen schwächer. Das einzige Bindeglied, das ich in den Jahren 1909 bis 1912 zwischen seinem Werk und der Stammeskunst entdecken kann, ist der ihnen gemeinsame Konzeptualismus. Die ausgesprochen malerische Natur des hochentwickelten analytischen Kubismus steht in Stil und Geist nicht nur der Stammeskunst fern, sondern auch dem sachlicheren, greifbareren, »vernünftigeren« Kubismus von 1909,[175] ganz zu schweigen von Picassos »afrikanischem« Werk der Jahre 1907–08.

Picasso schätzte seine Stammeskunst gleichwohl auch in den Jahren 1910–11; die meisten frühen Atelierphotos dieser Jahre zeigen Arbeiten von Eingeborenen an den Wänden, auf den Tischen und auf dem Boden.

Die konzeptuelle Analyse, die von der Stammeskunst ausgegangen war, bildete zwar auch weiterhin die dialektische Grundlage von Picassos und Braques Entwicklung, doch konnte sie die auftauchenden künstlerischen Probleme nicht mehr direkt beeinflussen. Ein Stil, der die festen Formen des Kubismus in einer Weise auflöste, die eher an Cézannes späte Aquarelle und Ölbilder erinnerte als an die Gemälde seiner festen, »architektonischen« mittleren Periode, entsprach kaum noch den plastischen Ideen, die Picasso früher den Stammesobjekten entnommen hatte.

Der Hintergrund des Bildnisses von Kahnweiler zeigt, wie groß diese ästhetische Distanz geworden ist □ 426. Der Stil ist so abstrakt, daß die beiden Stammesobjekte an der Wand hinter dem Sitzenden – das schönere von Picassos beiden Stücken aus Neu-Kaledonien links □ 425 und rechts eine unidentifizierbare Maske □ 427 – wohl nie aufgefallen wären, hätte Picasso nicht selbst eine Anspielung auf sie gemacht.[176] Der obere Teil der neu-kaledonischen Figur ist an ihrer kronenartigen Haartracht zu erkennen (Pfeil), nicht aber an ihrem Gesicht, das bis zur Unkenntlichkeit »analysiert« wurde. Der untere Teil der Figur löst sich in einer Matrix abstrakter Formen auf, die sich von anderen Formen in ihrem Umkreis ableiten, etwa dem Likörglas, das an der Stelle auftaucht, wo der Mittelteil der Figur zu lokalisieren wäre.

□ 428 *Antoine Pevsner, ›Maske‹ (Masque), 1923, Zelluloid und Metall, 33 x 20 x 20 cm. Musée National d'Art Moderne, Centre National d'Art et de Culture Georges Pompidou, Paris.*

Die Maske auf der anderen Seite der Wand hinter Kahnweiler wird durch Flächen angedeutet, die sich aus einem ihrer äußeren Umrisse ergeben: ihrem dreieckigen Bart und der langen Nase sowie einer waagerechten Tafel quer über der Stirn, wie es auf der besseren von PICASSOS *GREBO*-Masken □ 417 ähnlich vorkommt.[177] Diese fragmentarischen Ebenen fließen in den ›Durchgängen‹ (*passages*) so stark mit ihrer Umgebung zusammen, daß man nicht sagen kann, welche Art Maske hier ursprünglich hing, geschweige denn, ob sie sich möglicherweise in PICASSOS Besitz befand. Es war gerade die Transparenz, der die *passage* als bildnerisches Mittel diente, die Kahnweiler später zum Thema eines wirren und verwirrenden Textes machte,[178] mit dem er zeigen wollte, daß der afrikanische Einfluß auf PICASSOS Kunst nicht zur Zeit der *Demoiselles*, sondern auf dem Höhepunkt des Kubismus am größten war. Zu diesem Zweck schrieb er den Masken der Elfenbeinküste und ihren Formen (insbesondere dem Typus, wie ihn die *GREBO* schufen) eine »Transparenz« zu, die diese nicht im mindesten aufweisen.[179]

Die illusionistische Transparenz des hochanalytischen Kubismus schuf eine Einheitlichkeit, die mehr auf dem Kontinuum des Lichts als dem der Formen beruht, die in diesem Licht auf- und untertauchen. PICASSO war sich offensichtlich darüber im klaren, daß sich dies nicht für die Plastik eignete.

Nach dem *Frauenkopf (Fernande)* aus dem Jahr 1909 □ 415 ließ er bis Ende 1912 von der Plastik ab, bis unter dem Eindruck der Collage eine neue, sachlichere Form eines nicht-illusionistischen Kubismus entstand. Wenn es eine plastische Entsprechung zum hochanalytischen Kubismus der Jahre 1910–11 gibt, dann nicht im Werk PICASSOS, sondern im späteren Werk PEVSNERS. Die durchscheinenden Ebenen von PEVSNERS Zelluloid-Reliefs leiten sich zweifelsohne vom Kubismus her, dem sie ihre Abstraktheit, ihre bräunliche Tonalität und ihre partielle Transparenz verdanken. Tatsächlich kann man sich PEVSNERS Maske als eine Realisierung von Ideen vorstellen, die in PICASSOS Behandlung der Maske im Bildnis Kahnweilers angelegt ist □ 428. Entgegen Kahnweilers späteren Theorien ist die »Transparenz«, die man einer GREBO oder einer anderen Stammesmaske zuschreiben kann, nicht optischer, sondern konzeptueller Natur und wirkt – wie bei PICASSOS *Gitarre* – eher wie ein »Ausschnitt« denn als illusionistische Methode, die die Lage von Ebenen in der Tiefe anzeigen soll.

So ist es kein Zufall, daß PICASSOS analytischer Kubismus kaum Plastik hervorbrachte – in der frühen, »taktilen« Phase

□ 429 *Ansicht von Guillaume Apollinaires Bibliothek, Paris, aufgenommen um 1954. Detailaufnahme siehe* □ *182.*

□ 430 ›*Fetischfigur*‹, YOMBE oder WOYO *(Zaire, Volksrepublik Kongo oder Cabinda), Holz und Metall, Höhe 100 cm. Privatbesitz. Ehemals Sammlung Guillaume Apollinaire.*

□ 431 *›Maske‹,* GUERE *(Elfenbeinküste), Holz, Fasern, Patronenhülsen und andere Materialien, Höhe 30,5 cm. Privatbesitz.*

□ 432 *›Maske‹, Torresstraße (Papua-Neuguinea), bemaltes Metall, Haar, Muscheln und andere Materialien, Höhe 49 cm. Sammlung Claude Picasso, Paris. Ehemals Sammlung Pablo Picasso.* ▷

des Jahres 1909 sogar überhaupt keine. Es scheint zunächst paradox, daß PICASSOS Malerei von Ende 1908 bis Anfang 1910 trotz ihrer latenten Plastizität so wenig dreidimensionale Werke hervorgebracht haben soll, während das antiplastische, flache Verfahren des synthetischen Kubismus, der im Jahre 1912 entstand, einige der größten Plastiken PICASSOS zeitigen sollte. Aber dieses Paradoxon besteht nur scheinbar. Zu verstehen, warum PICASSO sich 1912 wieder der Plastik zuwandte – und warum sich sein Werk damals und ein Jahr später wieder der Stammeskunst öffnete –, heißt, das Wesen jener tiefgreifenden Umwälzung zu verstehen, die PICASSO in der Bildhauerei gelang.

Mit dem *Frauenkopf (Fernande)* vom Herbst 1909 hatte PICASSO ein plastisches Gegenstück zu seinem frühen analytischen Kubismus geschaffen. Aber er war sich dessen bewußt, daß diese Neuschöpfung der in seinen Gemälden verwendeten Formen ironischerweise nur zu einer plastischen Illusion eines Mittels der Malerei führte. Vergleicht man den *Frauenkopf (Fernande)* mit den Gemälden des Jahres 1909, etwa *Frau mit Birnen,*[180] stellt man fest, daß die Gemälde eine größere plastische Wirkung entfalten als die Skulptur, bei der man den Eindruck von Schwere und Dichte des Materials vermißt (wie ihn etwa BRANCUSIS Plastiken vermitteln). Dies rührt daher, daß der *Frauenkopf (Fernande)* eigentlich nicht aus der Masse heraus entwickelt wurde, sondern ein um 360° gedrehtes Relief ist – eine zylindrische Oberfläche, die die zerfurchten Oberflächen von PICASSOS gemalten Formen vortäuscht. Die größere Plastizität der Gemälde war teils von PICASSOS Fähigkeit abhängig, jede Ebene so zu beleuchten, daß dabei ihr Reliefcharakter maximal zum Vorschein kam. Da das Licht auf den Gemälden reine Illusion ist, durfte es gegen logische Gesetze verstoßen, um die Plastizität der Formen zu steigern. Da natürliches Licht den Gesetzen der Physik unterworfen ist und infolgedessen nicht manipuliert werden kann, blieb diese Möglichkeit der Plastik versagt.[181] Der *Frauenkopf (Fernande)* war eine Sackgasse, die PICASSO wohl erkannte.[182] Damit war bewiesen, daß eine illusionistische modellierende Darstellungsweise im Sinne der Plastik RODINS[183] – der letzte Ausläufer antiker Bildhauerei – kein wirklich plastisches Gegenstück zur kubistischen Malerei hervorbringen konnte.

Angesichts des Rückschlages, den PICASSO mit dem *Frauenkopf (Fernande)* erlebte, überrascht es nicht, daß er drei Jahre

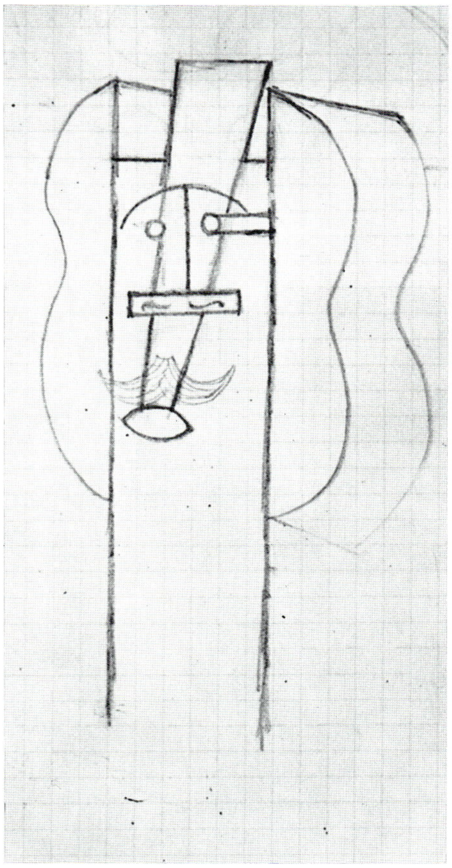

◁ ◁ ☐ 433 *Pablo Picasso, ›Kopf‹ (Tête), 1913, Bleistift, 14 x 9 cm. Musée Picasso, Paris.*

◁ ☐ 434 *Pablo Picasso, Studie zu ›Kopf‹, 1913, Bleistift, 14 x 9 cm. Musée Picasso, Paris.*

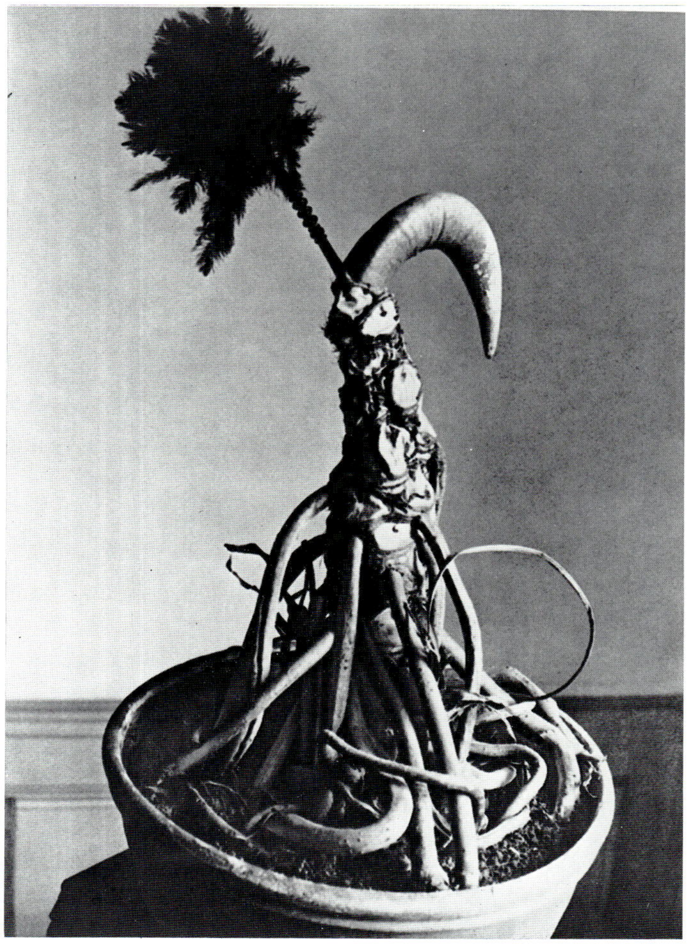

lang keine Skulptur mehr schuf. Als er 1912 mit der *Gitarre* wieder anfing,[184] ging es bereits um anderes. Jetzt sollte er eine Reliefkunst schaffen, die den Bildvorstellungen die Greifbarkeit wirklicher Gegenstände verlieh, die auf seinen Gemälden flach und körperlos geworden waren – also genau das Gegenteil der Situation, die 1909 herrschte. Masse, Gewicht und Dichte – zentrale Anliegen traditioneller Plastik – hatten keine Bedeutung mehr. Die neue Plastik verwendete ganz unorthodoxe Materialien, die bis dahin als hoher Kunst »unwürdig« erachtet worden waren.[185] Am Eindruck von Virtuosität völlig desinteressiert, schienen diese Objekte in Heimarbeit hergestellt worden zu sein. So ist die *Gitarre*, verglichen mit dem *Frauenkopf (Fernande)*, weniger anziehend. Aber sie verkörperte im Ansatz ein Konzept, das die Plastik revolutionierte: Die Technik des Modellierens und Meißelns in der »monolithischen« Tradition wurde durch die additive Konstruktion ersetzt.[186] Dies ebnete den Weg für flachere und linearere Konfigurationen in offener Technik, die konzeptuell verschlüsselte Objekte statt plastischer Illusionen von Objekten darstellten.

Wie ich in der Einleitung bemerkte, haben die *Gitarre* und andere kubistische Reliefs und Konstruktionen PICASSOS mit gewissen Typen von Stammesobjekten einige Züge gemeinsam. Ob diese Übereinstimmung in den Materialien und der Gestaltungsweise zufällig war oder dem – zuweilen unbewußten – Einfluß primitiver Kunst zugeschrieben werden muß, ist nicht zu entscheiden. Zumindest gibt es viele Parallelen. Viele der von PICASSO geschätzten Stammesobjekte wurden von Kupfer- oder Blechnieten zusammengehalten oder beinhalte-

☐ 435 *Pablo Picasso, ›Objekt‹ (Objet), 1931, Blumentopf, Wurzeln, Horn und roter Staubwedel. Wahrscheinlich zerstört.*

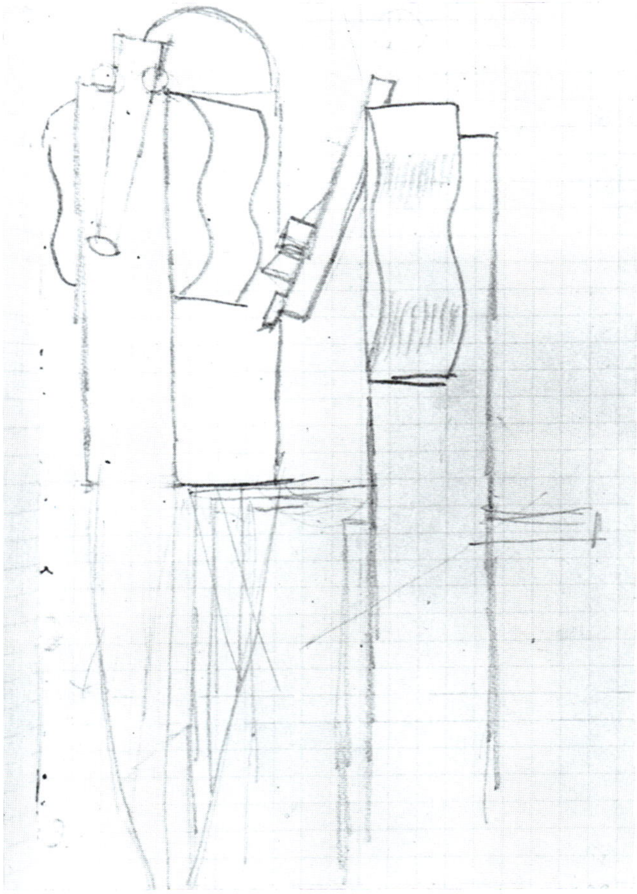

◁ ☐ 436 *Pablo Picasso, Studie zu ›Kopf‹, 1913, Bleistift, 14 x 9 cm. Musée Picasso, Paris.*

ten Teile verschiedenster Fundobjekte. Sie widersprachen damit westlichen Traditionen, die sowohl die Hierarchie als auch die Einheit der bildhauerischen Materialien verlangten.

Masken von der Elfenbeinküste, die in Paris zu Anfang des Jahrhunderts zu den verbreitetsten afrikanischen Objekten zählten, schlossen nicht selten Fundobjekte mit ein. Der Bildhauer der GUERE, der mit Patronenhülsen arbeitete ☐ 431, befrachtete seine Maske mit einem vorgefundenen (»ready-made«) Material, das sowohl individuelle als auch kollektive Macht symbolisiert und den Bronzen des Hofes von Benin so fremd ist wie die Fundmaterialien PICASSOs der Rodinschen Tradition des Westens. Wie der GUERE-Künstler hatte PICASSO bei integrierten Fundelementen das richtige Gespür. Sie sind Träger privater wie auch kollektiver Bedeutungen. Öltuch, Kieselsteine, Faden, Karton, Besenstiele, Draht, Nägel, Gartenwerkzeuge, Gummihandschuhe und Siebe aktivieren jeweils ein Feld kollektiv verständlicher Assoziationen. Aber für PICASSO hatten sie fast immer auch eine geheime, metaphorische Bedeutung. (Einmal erzählte er mir fast zwanzig Minuten lang von seinen Gefühlen zu den quastenförmigen Möbelfransen, die für die kubistischen Bilder und *papiers-collés* so typisch sind und im Werk der Tate Gallery regelrecht mit der bemalten Stilleben-Konstruktion aus Holz verwuchsen.)[187] Wie sich die Bedeutung der Patronenhülsen des GUERE-Künstlers ändert, sobald sie die Haartracht und den Bart seiner Maske

☐ 437 *›Maske‹, DOGON (Mali), Holz, Höhe 33 cm. Sammlung Folch, Barcelona.*

☐ 438 *Pablo Picasso, ›Kopf‹ (Tête), 1958, Holz, Nägel, Knöpfe, Gips und Kunstharz, bemalt, 50,5 x 20 x 22 cm. The Museum of Modern Art, Schenkung J. Picasso, New York.*

☐ 439 *Pablo Picasso, Kopf des Pferdes aus ›Parade‹, Rekonstruktion und Aufführung unter Leitung von Kermit Love, The Joffrey Ballet, 1974. Getanzt von Eric Dirk.*

☐ 440 *›Helmmaske‹,* BAULE *(Elfenbeinküste), Höhe 71 cm. Musée d'Art Moderne, Schenkung P. und D. Lévy, Troyes.*

☐ 441 *›Helmmaske‹,* BAULE *(Elfenbeinküste), Holz, Höhe 77 cm. Privatsammlung, Paris.*

☐ 442 *Pablo Picasso, ›Weiblicher Kopf‹ (Tête de femme), 1912, Tusche, 13,5 x 9 cm. Musée Picasso, Paris.*

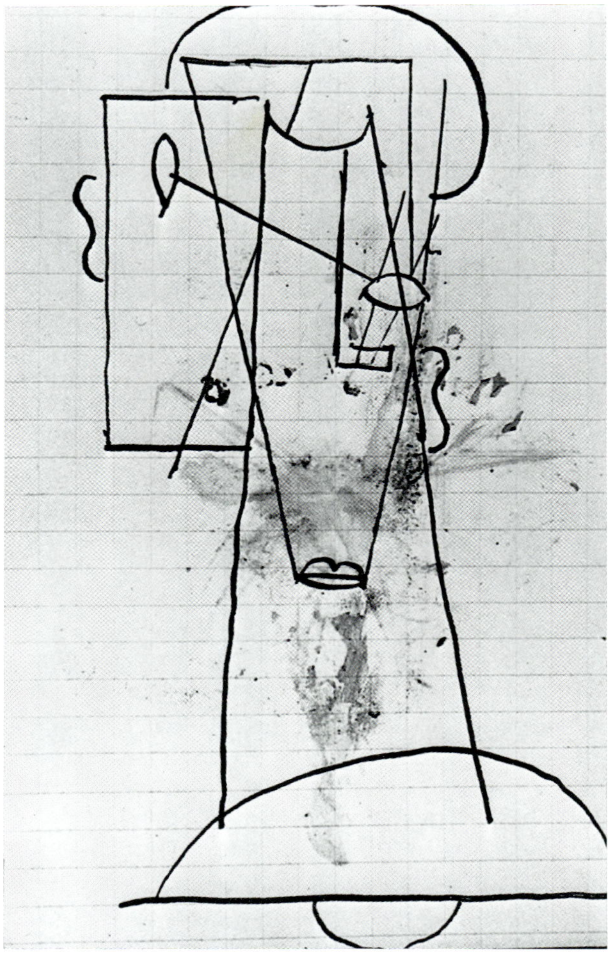

bilden, verwandelt PICASSO wie ein Zauberer einen Tennisball in das Auge eines Kriegers.[188] Oder er mißt seine Kräfte mit den Stammeskünstlern, indem er den Arm einer Skulptur von der Osterinsel als Fundobjekt für die aus einer Schneiderpuppe hergestellten *Frau in langem Kleid* benutzt □ 463.

Viele Stammesobjekte und PICASSOS Collage-Konstruktionen stehen sich in ihrer Einfachheit, Aufrichtigkeit und Unbeholfenheit nahe. Auch sind sie wohltuend unprätentiös. Vielleicht sind dies die Gründe, warum er gerade diese Werke seines Œuvres besonders schätzte. Natürlich ähneln nur wenige Konstruktionen oder Montagen PICASSOS primitiver Kunst, doch gelegentlich deutet er mit einer fast parodistischen Gestik an, daß er sich eingeborener Plastik bewußt ist. Das ist für mich die Aussage des »Fetischs«, den er schuf, indem er ein Horn und einen Staubwedel mit einem Bündel Philodendronwurzeln vereinte □ 435.

Nicht lange nach Vollendung der Metall-Fassung der *Gitarre* nahm PICASSO eine Serie von Skizzen für Skulpturen und Assemblagen in Angriff, in denen wir zum ersten Mal seit 1908 unverkennbare, wenn auch versteckte Bezüge zu Stammesobjekten finden.

Diese Zeichnungen werden mit der Studie eines länglichen Kopfes eingeleitet □ 442, der sich zu einem kinnlosen Mund verjüngt und damit an die Umrisse von *FANG*-Masken und *BAMBARA*-Tiermasken erinnert □ 443. Da PICASSO in Gedanken ja eine Gitarre auseinandernimmt, stellt er sich das schmaler werdende Griffbrett nach unten geknickt vor, so daß es als Nase dient, indes aus dem Resonanzkasten ein Kopf wird □ 434, 437. Diese Griffbrett-Nase wird dann auf den länglichen Kopf übertragen, der den *FANG*- und Tiermasken ähnlich sieht, und ergibt schließlich den außergewöhnlichen Entwurf für einen *Kopf* □ 433. Wäre diese Konstruktion je ausgeführt worden, hätte PICASSO mit einer Holzkiste angefangen. Die Vorderseite des Resonanzkastens einer Gitarre wäre in zwei Teile zerschnitten und dem vorderen Rand der Kiste angefügt worden, um die Seiten des Gesichts zu bilden; ein Segment des Griffbretts hätte PICASSO dazwischen als Nase befestigt. Hinter der Gesichtsfläche war eine Scheibe mit konzentrischen Kreisen vorgesehen; PICASSO verwendete eine solche Scheibe ein

□ 443 *›Maske‹, FANG (Kamerun), bemaltes Holz, Höhe 78 cm. Museum für Völkerkunde, Berlin.*

Links unten: □ 444 *Pablo Picasso, Pferd aus ›Parade‹, 1917. Photographiert von Oumansky und Novak, Privatbesitz.*

□ 445 *Pablo Picasso, Kostümentwürfe zu ›Parade‹, 1917, Aquarell und Bleistift, 20,5 x 28 cm. Musée Picasso, Paris.*

□ 446 *›Maske‹, Jukun (Nigeria), Holz, Höhe 26 cm. Museum für Völkerkunde, Berlin. Siehe S. 91, Anm. 112.*

□ 447 *Julio Gonzalez, ›Kopf‹ (Tête), 1929–30. Poliertes Eisen, Höhe 27 cm. Privatbesitz. Ehemals Sammlung A. Maguy, Paris.*

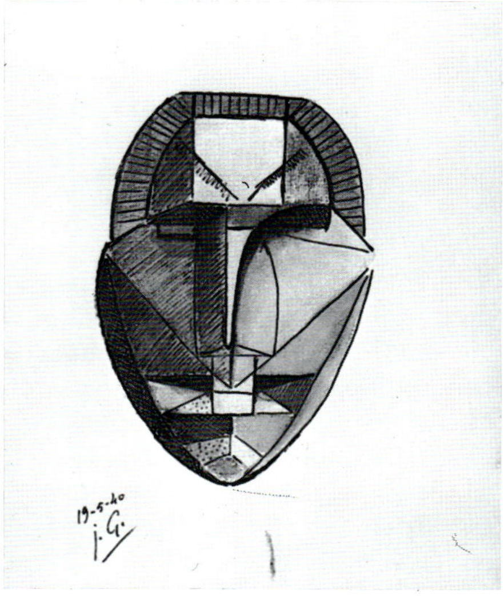

□ 448 *Julio Gonzalez, ›Ernste Maske‹, 1940, Tusche, laviert, 32 x 24 cm. Sammlung C. Martinez und V. Grimminger, Paris.*

□ 449 *Julio Gonzalez, ›Ernste Maske‹, um 1939, Bleistift, Tusche, laviert, 32,5 x 24 cm. The Trustees of the Tate Gallery, London.*

□ 450 *Pablo Picasso, ›Kopf‹ (Tête), 1930, Eisen, Messing und Bronze, 83,5 x 40,5 x 36 cm. Musée Picasso, Paris.*

Jahr später als Glocke für seine »Klarinette« in der Konstruktion *Mandoline und Klarinette.*

Solche Assoziationen mit *Fang-* oder *Bambara*-Tiermasken, die sich vielleicht in der Studie des Musée Picasso niederschlugen, verschwanden im Zuge der Ausführung von Picassos Projekt, gerade so wie sich die Spuren von Picassos Interesse an Nimba-Figuren bis zum Endstadium der *Figur* verloren hatten □ 367. Picasso versuchte jedoch nicht seine Quellen zu verwischen oder zu verstecken, als er eine Tiermaske als Vorbild für den Kopf des Pferdes in dem Kostüm für die *Parade* heranzog □ 444. Die Quelle geht ziemlich deutlich aus einer Zeichnung hervor, in der sich zwei Studien für den Kopf des Pferdes neben früheren Entwürfen für das Kostüm eines Zirkusdirektors finden □ 445. Wie man sich erinnert, kam bei letzterem eine kubistische Konstruktion heraus, die Anspielungen auf die Architektur und die Maschinentechnik enthielt. Der Eindruck drängt sich auf, Picasso habe besonderen Wert darauf gelegt, in diesem Kostüm Symbole der Moderne mit einer ganz anderen Quelle kubistischen Denkens – der Stammesmaske – in Verbindung zu bringen.[189]

In den späten 20er Jahren erlebte Picasso als Bildhauer eine neue schöpferische Phase, die damit begann, daß er 1928–29 Drahtstücke »in die Luft zeichnete«, zum Teil eine Nachwirkung der Drähte der *Gitarre* aus dem Jahr 1912. Diese neuen

□ 451 *Pablo Picasso, Studie zu ›Frauenbüste mit Selbstbildnis‹ und einer ›Skulptur‹, 1929, Bleistift, 23,5 x 30,5 cm. Musée Picasso, Paris.*

□ 452 *›Figur aus Metall‹, FON (Volksrepublik Benin), Höhe 165 cm. Musée de l'Homme, Paris. Erworben 1894. Aufnahme der Aufstellung im Musée d'Ethnographie du Trocadéro, Paris 1895.*

plastischen Arbeiten, die JULIO GONZALES nach PICASSOS Zeichnungen anfertigte, bildeten aufgrund ihrer Raumdurchlässigkeit Antipoden zur Stammeskunst. Sie verweigerten sich auch der leisesten Verfestigung der Formen, ob modelliert oder gemeißelt. Als PICASSO die Möglichkeiten der Metallskulptur erweiterte, realisierte er in den Jahren 1930–31 Ideen, die wiederum seine Liebe zur Stammeskunst offenbarten. Diese Beziehung wurde noch deutlicher, als er sich im Winter 1931–32 mit der außergewöhnlichen Serie großer Köpfe von Marie-Thérèse Walter zu einer plastischen Auffassung zurückkehrte, die von festen Formen ausging.

Schon 1930 besteht eine auffallende Affinität zwischen PICASSOS *Kopf* aus Eisen, Messing und Bronze □ 450 und einer afrikanischen Maske des *JUKUN*-Typs □ 446. In beiden Werken springen die vordersten Flächen des Kopfes weit in den Raum. Bei PICASSO bezeichnet diese konkave und vertikale Form den Mund;[190] bei der zum Vergleich herangezogenen *JUKUN*-Maske stellt das perforierte konkave Oval einen dekorativen Zusatz dar, der sich anscheinend über Jahre hinweg aus der Form der Hörner bei den Masken der benachbarten *MAMA* entwickelt hatte □ 941. Hier haben wir es wohl eher mit einer Verwandtschaft als mit einem Einfluß zu tun, denn PICASSO konnte, bevor er diese Plastik schuf, nicht einmal ein Photo einer solchen *JUKUN*-Maske gesehen haben, als er mit der Arbeit an dieser Plastik begann.[191] Nimmt man das spitze, konkave Oval, das den vorstehenden Mund von PICASSOS Kopf bildet, für sich, so erinnert es jedoch an einen seiner langjährigen Favoriten in der Stammesplastik, die *KOTA*-Reliquiarfigur. (GIACOMETTI war mit einer figürlichen Gipsplastik von 1926–27 □ 784, die unter dem Eindruck eines von einem Freund erhaltenen *KOTA*-Objekts entstand, zu einem ganz ähnlichen künstlerischen Ergebnis gekommen.)[192]

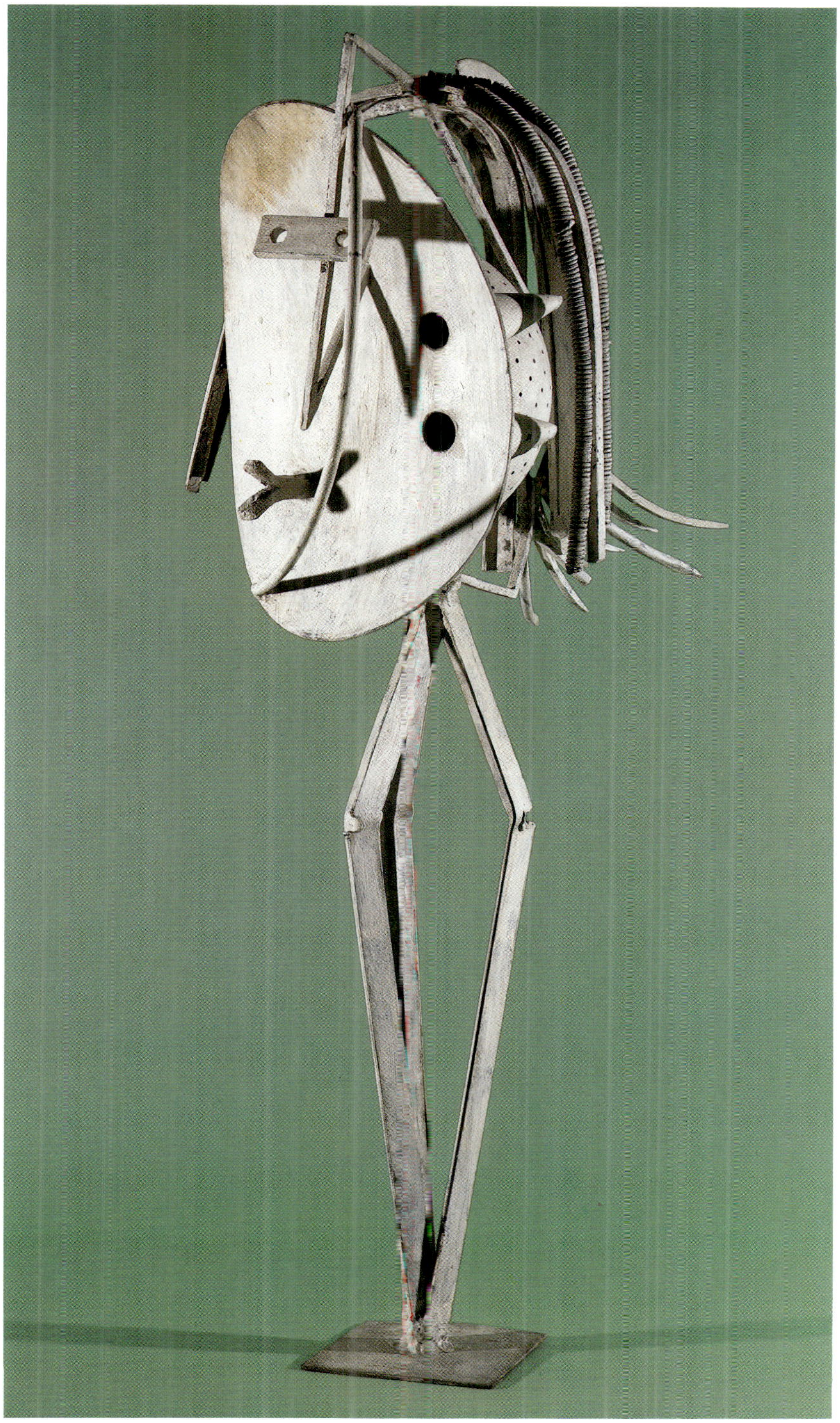

□ 453 *Pablo Picasso, ›Weiblicher Kopf – Olga Picasso‹ (Tête de femme), 1930–31, bemaltes Eisen, Blech, Siebe und Spiralfedern, 100 x 37 x 59 cm. Musée Picasso, Paris.*

Daß sich Picasso 1930–31 erneut mit diesen kupferüberzogenen *Kota*-Reliquiarfiguren beschäftigte, läßt sich auch aus dem konkaven Oval schließen, das er als Gesichtsfläche für den *Weiblichen Kopf* verwendete □ 453 (eigentlich ein Porträt Olga Picassos);[193] ebenso wie aus der langgestreckten Raute, die wie die Rauten der Reliquiarfiguren den Kopf trägt. Man könnte mutmaßen, daß sich Picasso aus zwei Gründen – die mit Olga zusammenhängen – mit diesen Reliquiaren auseinandersetzte (sie war nicht nur Thema des *Weiblichen Kopfes*, sondern inspirierte wahrscheinlich auch den *Kopf*). Ich sehe in den metallischen Beschichtungen der Reliquiarfiguren und ihren rautenförmigen Stützen eine Verbindung zu ihr.

Rufen wir uns zunächst ins Gedächtnis, daß Picasso wie einige andere Künstler der Moderne die Rauten der Reliquiarwächter als Beine fehlgedeutet und »tanzende Figuren« in ihnen gesehen hatte. Von daher bestünde eine mögliche Verbindung zwischen den Reliquiaren und Olga, die Berufstänzerin gewesen war. Selbst in Picassos glücklichen Jahren mit Olga (1917 bis 1924) betonen seine Zeichnungen und Gemälde von ihr meist die Härte und Schlankheit ihres Tänzerinnenkörpers und die eckigen Züge einer *danseuse noble*.

Als sich 1925 die Beziehung zwischen den beiden verschlechterte, verloren Picassos Bilder von Olga an Klassizität und Wirklichkeitsnähe und neigten zu einer Art surrealer Verzerrung,[194] die ihren Höhepunkt in den Jahren 1929–31 in einer Vielzahl von Entwürfen findet, die sie als knochenhartes, kantiges Unwesen darstellen.[195] Olga hatte sich nicht damit abfinden können, Picasso mit Marie-Thérèse zu teilen, und

☐ 455 *›Maske‹*, Lwalwa *(Zaire), Holz, Höhe 34 cm, Privatbesitz.*

☐ 454 *›Nimba-Maske‹*, Baga *(Guinea), Holz, Höhe 108 cm. Museum Rietberg, Zürich.*

□ 455 *Pablo Picasso, ›Frauenbüste – Marie-Thérèse Walter‹ (Buste de femme), 1931, Bronze, 68,5 x 42 x 43,5 cm. Musée Picasso, Paris.*

☐ 457 *Pablo Picasso, ›Frauenkopf – Marie-Thérèse Walter‹ (Tête de femme), 1931–32, Bronze, 85 x 37 x 48 cm. Galerie Louise Leiris, Paris.*

war immer mehr zerrüttet geworden. Als er in den späten 20er Jahren von ihr Urlaub genommen hatte, tauchte sie ab und zu irgendwo unerwartet auf – am Strand, auf der Straße – und überzog PICASSO mit Schmähungen. Viele Bilder PICASSOS von Olga aus den späten 20er Jahren verzeichnen den Wandel seiner Gefühle sehr anschaulich. Seit langem herrscht etwa Einigkeit darüber, daß die schreiende Frau mit wehendem Haar und herausgestreckter Zunge in der *Frauenbüste mit Selbstbildnis* Olga darstellt (1929, Z. VII, 248). Hier zeigt PICASSO, wie er distanziert und ruhig reagiert, während er von Olga beschimpft wird (dies die metaphorische Bedeutung des an der Wand gezeigten Selbstbildnisses). Andere Bilder PICASSOS von Olga spiegeln Ärger, Verdruß, ja sogar Angst wider. Olgas wachsende Entfremdung brachte sie wohl schließlich dazu, sein Leben zu bedrohen;[196] diese Tatsache inspirierte zweifellos ihre Darstellung als Charlotte Corday in *Frau mit Stilett (Marats Tod)* aus dem Jahr 1931.

Für die Darstellung von Olgas Körper als hart, kantig und aggressiv – wie in der berühmten *Sitzenden Badenden* aus dem Jahr 1930 (Z. VII, 306) – war Metall das adäquate Gestaltungsmittel in der Skulptur. Der Gedanke an *KOTA*-Reliquiarfiguren lag besonders nahe, da sie als einzige unter PICASSOS Stammesobjekten aus Metall waren.[197] Der *Weibliche Kopf* ☐ 453 läßt sich leicht als Darstellung Olgas interpretieren: aufgrund der

□ 458 *›Nimba-Maske‹*, BAGA *(Guinea), Holz und Fasern, Höhe 126 cm. Musée Picasso, Paris. Ehemals Sammlung Pablo Picasso.*

☐ 459 *Pablo Picasso, ›Mädchen vor einem Spiegel‹ (Jeune fille devant un miroir), Ausschnitt, 1932, Öl auf Leinwand, 162 x 130 cm. The Museum of Modern Art, Schenkung Guggenheim, New York.*

☐ 460 *Pablo Picasso, ›Frauenbüste‹ (Buste de femme), Ausschnitt, 1960. Öl auf Leinwand, 92 x 73 cm. Sammlung Jacqueline Picasso, Mougins.*

zackigen, wehenden »Haare« (wie in der *Frauenbüste mit Selbstbildnis*) und aufgrund der eleganten Raute, die den Kopf trägt, zugleich aber auch ein langer »Hals« oder die dünnen Beine einer Tänzerin sein kann. Die Assoziation zwischen dem *Weiblichen Kopf* und der *Frauenbüste mit Selbstbildnis* wird auch durch eine Zeichnung in einem Skizzenbuch bestätigt ☐ 451, die Studien zu beiden Arbeiten nebeneinanderstellt. Unter den Metallskulpturen dieser Zeit hat der *Weibliche Kopf* trotz seiner Härte und Kantigkeit eine gewisse Anmut und etwas Lyrisches. Er steht den aggressiv gemalten Darstellungen von Olga innerlich näher; das hervorstehende, zugespitzte Oval, das buchstäblich ihr Mundwerk darstellt, läßt die Schmähtiraden erahnen, die die Eifersüchtige auf den Künstler niederregnen ließ.

PICASSO wählte die Materialien für seine Skulpturen stets unter dem Gesichtspunkt aus, ob er damit seine Gefühle gegenüber einem Thema ausdrücken konnte, weniger um irgendwelche dem Material innewohnenden Möglichkeiten zu entfalten. Ein damit zusammenhängendes Interesse an ästhetischen Problemstellungen war gering. Wenn ihn seine Gefühle gegenüber Olga dazu veranlaßten, bei den eben erörterten Skulpturen Metall zu verwenden, so war sein Wechsel zum Modellieren mit Lehm und Gips bei der Serie monumentaler Köpfe der Jahre 1931–32 von seinen Gefühlen für Marie-Thérèse diktiert. Beide Skulpturengruppen haben Entsprechungen zu den frühesten Stücken von PICASSOS Sammlung primitiver Plastik. Beziehen sich die Skulpturen von Olga auf die *KOTA*-Reliquiarfiguren, so schuf er die monumentalen Köpfe von Marie-Thérèse unter dem Zeichen der Nimba ☐ 458, der Fruchtbarkeitsgöttin der *BAGA*.[198]

Die künstlerische Realisation der von Olga inspirierten Metallskulpturen war unpersönlich, insofern sie eigentlich GONZALES ausführte.[199] Im *Weiblichen Kopf* wurde Olga noch weiter von dem Künstler entfernt, indem sie dieser buchstäblich zu einem Objekt machte: PICASSO baute Siebe, Federn und Nägel ein, die als solche erkennbar und in einigen Fällen im Originalzustand belassen waren. Andererseits führten ihn seine Liebe für die weichen und sinnlichen Formen von Marie-Thérèse und seine Vertrautheit mit ihrem Körper zu einer Methode, bei der die Tonmasse der Skulptur von seiner eigenen Hand geknetet und geformt wurde.

Wir wissen nicht genau, wann und wie PICASSO zu der wundervollen, klassischen Nimba-Maske kam, es ist aber zu vermuten, daß sie ihm seit den späten 20er Jahren gehörte.[200] Er besaß wohl schon lange seine *BAGA*-Figuren ☐ 365,[201] die zu seinen ersten Erwerbungen gehört haben dürften. Wie wir sahen, stehen schon die 1907 entstandenen Zeichnungen mit der *BAGA*-Göttin Nimba in Beziehung ☐ 368, 369. Am Anfang des Jahrhunderts waren die größeren und schwereren Nimba-Masken äußerst selten, und obwohl PICASSO ein Exemplar im Trocadéro sah ☐ 360, hatte er sicher vor 1918 keine Gelegenheit, eine solche Maske noch zu kaufen.

Wenn PICASSO jene Schultermaske kaufte ☐ 458, nachdem er 1925 seine langjährige Beziehung mit Marie-Thérèse begonnen hatte, so ist dies nicht ohne einen gewissen tieferen Sinn. Marie-Thérèse war für PICASSO die Verkörperung von Sinnlichkeit, ja von Fruchtbarkeit schlechthin. Die vollen Formen, die vorspringende Nase und die großen Brüste der klassischen Nimbas werden PICASSO sicherlich an Marie-Thérèse erinnert haben, auch wenn er sich der Herkunft der Masken aus dem Fruchtbarkeitskult nicht bewußt gewesen wäre – was er aber war.[202] Es ist kein Zufall, daß PICASSOS Nimba wie ein Clan-

□ 461 *›Maske‹*, Kwakiutl *(Britisch-Kolumbien, Kanada), bemaltes Holz, Höhe 34 cm. Museum für Völkerkunde, Berlin.*

□ 462 *Picasso in seinem Atelier in der Villa La Californie, Cannes, mit dem Bronzeabguß der Rurutu-Skulptur. Aufnahme von E. Quinn, ca. 1960.*

□ 463 *Pablo Picasso, ›Frau in langem Kleid‹ (Femme vêtue d'une robe longue), 1943, Bronze, 161 x 50 x 36,5 cm. Privatbesitz.*

Totem am Eingang des Schlosses von Boisgeloup stand, wo er die großen Gipsbüsten und -köpfe von Marie-Thérèse schuf.[203] Wenn Brassaï, der diese Skulpturen photographierte, »Ähnlichkeiten mit einer barbarischen Göttin« feststellte, so hatte er vielleicht PICASSOS Nimba vor sich.

Die Umsetzung von PICASSOS Nimba in seine bildhauerischen Arbeiten ist bei der *Frauenbüste* □ 456 und dem *Frauenkopf* □ 457 am deutlichsten. Wie wir es von ihm gewohnt sind, übernahm er das Motiv auf eine persönliche Weise. Von den beiden genannten Skulpturen steht die *Frauenbüste* den Nimba-Masken näher, da sie Marie-Thérèse' volle Büste betont, obschon die fast durchgängige Silhouette von der Frisur über Stirn und große Nase stärkere Ähnlichkeiten mit dem Typus von Nimba-Masken hat, der sich im Museum Rietberg befindet □ 454, als mit dem klassischen, den PICASSO besaß. Geht man von der Umsetzung des halbkreisförmigen Vorsprungs auf ihrer Stirn aus, findet sich ein deutlicheres Echo von PICASSOS Nimba im *Frauenkopf* – zumindest was den oberen Teil ihrer Silhouette betrifft. (PICASSO hat vielleicht auch eine langnasige *LWALWA*-Maske gesehen □ 455, obwohl

□ 464 *Pablo Picasso, Zeichnung nach einem Arm von der Osterinsel, den P. Loeb Picasso vor 1940 schenkte. Veröffentlicht in Pierre Loeb, „Voyages à travers la peinture", 1945 (siehe Anm. 208 und* □ *375).*

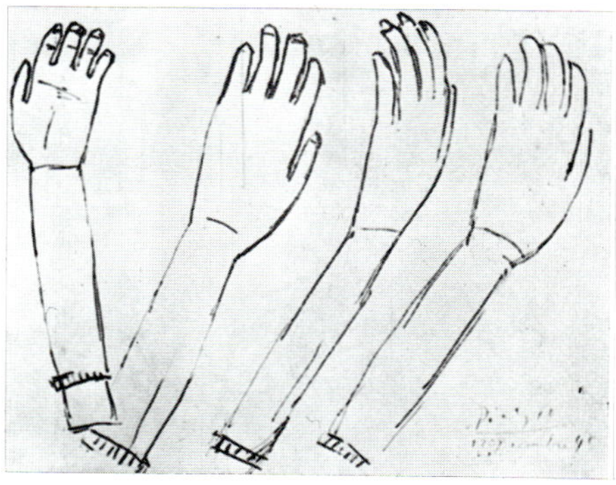

☐ 465 *›Figur aus Holz (Gott A'a)‹, Rurutu (Australinseln), Holz, Höhe 118 cm. The Trustees of the British Museum, London. Seitenansicht siehe* ☐ *873.*

solche Stammesmasken in Frankreich vor dem Zweiten Weltkrieg äußerst selten waren.)

Die spezifische Formensprache klassischer Nimba-Masken schließt sexuelle Nebenbedeutungen ein, die PICASSO nicht nur übernahm, sondern auch ausweitete. Einer solchen Symbolik war sich die Stammeskunst weniger bewußt und erlebte sie weniger persönlich als es bei PICASSO der Fall ist. Das geschwungene Profil der Nase der Nimba erweckt zusammen mit ihrer extrem schmalen Vorderansicht unausweichlich Assoziationen mit dem *mons veneris* und dem weiblichen Geschlecht, besonders in Verbindung mit dem ungewöhnlich kleinen Knospenmund, der darunter herausragt. Die Erotik der Nimba scheint PICASSO inspiriert zu haben, diese Assoziationen im *Frauenkopf* zu bereichern und komplexer zu gestalten. Dort überlagert er die prachtvolle Weiblichkeit von Marie-Thérèse mit einer Anspielung auf seine männlichen Genitalien – in Form einer phallischen Nase, die zwischen einem Paar kugelförmiger Augen hervorragt.

Indem PICASSO einen Bezug zwischen Marie-Thérèse und einer Maske, der Verkörperung einer afrikanischen Gottheit, herstellte, hob er das Bild der von ihm geliebten Frau auf eine wirklich mythische Ebene. Diese Verallgemeinerung seiner

□ 466 *Ansicht von Picassos Atelier in der Villa La Californie, Cannes, mit der Körpermaske von den Neuen Hebriden, um 1955.*

Gefühle sollte auf ganz andere Weise kurz darauf in einem Bild von Marie-Thérèse, *Mädchen vor einem Spiegel*, eine Nachfolge finden □ 459. Die Synthese aus einem lavendelfarbenen Profil und einer Vorderansicht in sattem Gelb, die zusammen ein ovales Gesicht ergeben, geht auf die kubistischen Stilisierungen der Schattenpartien eines Gesichts zurück. In den 20er Jahren verband PICASSO diese anfangs rein formale Entdeckung mit einer Vielzahl poetischer Assoziationen. Doch nur im *Mädchen vor einem Spiegel* tat er dies in einem allgemeinen, fast mythischen Sinn. Meyer Schapiro spricht in seiner außergewöhnlichen Beurteilung dieses Gemäldes von dem kühlen lavendelfarbenen Profil als einer »Mondsichel« und von der gelben Vorderansicht des Gesichtes als der »Sonne«.[204] Schapiros »Symbolismus« von »Sonne und Mond« zeigt, wie PICASSO aus den Urgründen seiner Phantasie schöpft, um genau die Art kosmischer Bildlichkeit zu erreichen, die wir in Stammesobjekten wie der Maske der *KWAKIUTL* aus dem Museum für Völkerkunde in Berlin erkennen □ 461.

Diese Maske ist fast genau in der Mitte gespalten worden, so daß man den entstandenen Querschnitt, der schwarz bemalt ist, als ein in der überwiegend frontal angelegten Maske enthaltenes Profil liest. Masken von der Nordwestküste Amerikas und eskimoische Masken teilen oft frontale Gesichter in eine dunkle und eine helle Hälfte, die auf Gegensätze wie Sonne und Mond, Tag und Nacht oder die dunkle und die Sonnenseite des Mondes anspielen. Diese »gespaltenen« oder auch verwandelten Wesen aus der Mythologie der Nordwestküste stehen unauflöslich mit dem Kosmischen in Beziehung,[205] wie aber bei solchen Polaritäten meist der Fall, ist auch die zugrundeliegende Dualität der menschlichen Psychologie und Sexualität in ihnen enthalten. PICASSO hat mit allergrößter Wahrscheinlich-

□ 467 *›Körpermaske‹, Malekula, Vanuatu (ehemals Neue Hebriden), bemaltes Farnholz und verschiedene Materialien, Höhe der Figur 114 cm. Musée Picasso, Paris. Ehemals Sammlung Henri Matisse und Sammlung Pablo Picasso.*

keit eine »durchschnittene« Maske wie die der Nordwestküste nie zu Gesicht bekommen, doch weist sie auf die Affinität seines poetischen Denkens in dem Bild *Mädchen vor einem Spiegel* mit den mythischen Universalien hin, die die Stammesobjekte versinnbildlichen. Für Picasso kommen als Quellen eher die Bilder einer runden Sonne und eines Viertelmondes mit Gesichtern in Frage, wie sie sich in Manuskripten des Mittelalters finden.[206] Daß sowohl Luna und Sol, die kosmischen Verkörperungen des männlichen und des weiblichen Prinzips, im Gesicht von Marie-Thérèse vereint sein sollen, kann man als Erweiterung jener Poesie verstehen, die Picasso dazu brachte, phallische und weibliche Formen im *Frauenkopf* zu verschmelzen □ 457. Ob mit bewußter Absicht gestaltet oder nicht, sie lassen seinen Wunsch nach seelischer und auch körperlicher Vereinigung mit seiner Geliebten ahnen.

Picassos Kunst der Jahre 1930–32 ist die letzte erkennbar primitivistische Phase seines Schaffens. Aber er schätzte und kaufte bis zu seinem Tod Stammesobjekte. So erwarb er einige der besten Stücke seiner Sammlung – etwa die mächtige Figur vom Sepik □ 70 und eine auffällige *Lega*-Maske, die verloren-

□ 468 *›Mutter und Kind‹*, URHOBO *(Nigeria), Holz, Höhe 145 cm. Sammlung P. Guimiot.*

◁ □ 469 ›*Kifwebe-Maske*‹, SONGGE *(Zaire), bemaltes Holz, Höhe 56 cm. Sammlung J. Naiman, New York.*

□ 470 ▷ ›*Maske*‹, SENUFO? *(Elfenbeinküste oder Mali), Holz, Höhe 28 cm. Sammlung Jacqueline Picasso, Mougins. Ehemals Sammlung Pablo Picasso.*

ging[207] – in den 30er Jahren und später. Irgendwann kurz vor Ausbruch des 2. Weltkriegs bewunderte PICASSO einen Holzarm von der Osterinsel in der Galerie von Pierre Loeb, worauf sie ihm Loeb prompt schenkte.[208] Nach seiner Flucht aus dem besetzten Paris erhielt Loeb 1942 von einem Freund (der den Künstler telefonisch über Neuigkeiten von Loeb unterrichtete) die Mitteilung, daß PICASSO »in diesem Augenblick« den Holzarm in der Hand halte.[209] Tatsächlich fertigte er gerade die Skizzen nach diesem Objekt von der Osterinsel an, das er als »objet trouvé« für den linken Arm der *Frau in langem Kleid* verwenden wollte, einer lebensgroßen Figur aus einer ausgedienten Schneiderpuppe □ 463, 464.

Zwei Objekte, die später in PICASSOS Atelier einen besonderen Platz einnehmen sollten, haben keine gewöhnliche Herkunft. Bei dem ersten handelt es sich um einen Bronzeguß des berühmten Gottes A'a von der Australinsel Rurutu. Als PICASSO 1950 ROLAND PENROSE' Atelier besuchte, sah er einen Gipsabguß dieser außergewöhnlichen Plastik – vielleicht das großartigste Stammesobjekt im Britischen Museum – und war davon überwältigt.

Natürlich hatten sie vor ihm schon die Surrealisten bewundert, und sechzehn Jahre früher war sie von VICTOR BRAUNER als Modell für das Bild *Die Konzentrationskraft des M. K.* benutzt worden □ 872. PENROSE kaufte den Gipsabguß vom Britischen Museum für die Ausstellung »40,000 Years of Modern Art«.[210] Das Museum hatte die Gußform und das Original im 19. Jahrhundert von der London Missionary Society geerbt, die von dem Gott A'a so viele Abgüsse wie möglich anfertigen ließ, um seinen Anhängern zu zeigen, »wie häßlich heidnische Götzen sein konnten«.[211] Für PICASSO wurde ein Sonderguß angefertigt, mit dem er eine eigene Bronze herstellen ließ □ 462.

Anläßlich eines Besuches bei MATISSE im Hôtel Régina in Nizza hatte PICASSO eine Körpermaske mit Armen und Beinen von den Neuen Hebriden bewundert □ 467, die MATISSE von einem Freund, der Schiffskapitän war, als Geschenk erhalten hatte.[212] (Anders als bei einer eigenen Erwerbung drückt sich in diesem Werk MATISSE' Geschmack im Zusammenhang mit

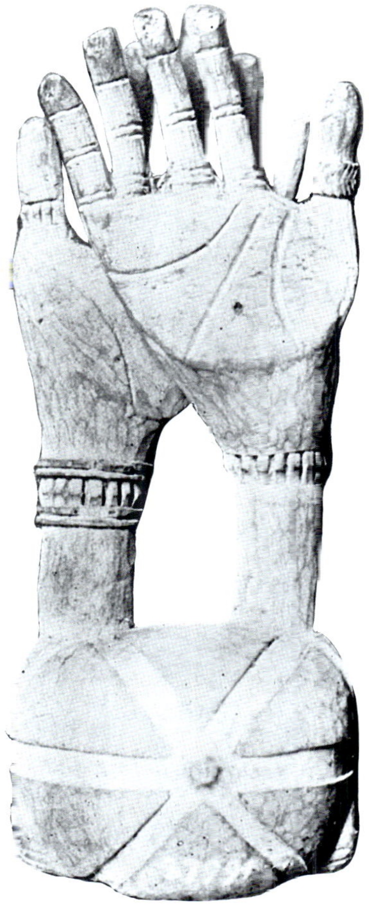

□ 471 ›*Bekrönung eines Stabes*‹, AKAN *oder* EWE *(Ghana, Elfenbeinküste oder Togo), Holz. Veröffentlicht in Marius de Zayas, „African Negro Art: Its Influence on Modern Art", 1916.*

□ 472 *›Tierkopf‹, Bozo (Mali), Holz, Metall und Fasern, Höhe 30 cm. Musée Picasso, Paris. Ehemals Sammlung Pablo Picasso.*

□ 473 *›Figur aus Holz‹, Kasingo (Zaire), Höhe 47 cm. Sammlung G. und F. Schindler, New York.*

primitiver Kunst, der ein völlig entgegengesetzter war, nicht aus.) Mit ihrem phantastischen Wesen mußte die Figur Picasso gefallen, die ihm Matisse schenkte, als er dessen Begeisterung sah. Nachdem Pierre Matisse sie nach dem Tod seines Vaters Picasso übergeben hatte, war sie jahrelang Blickfang in einem Atelier der La Californie □ 466.

Oft wird behauptet, daß der Haupteinfluß der »art nègre« auf Picasso die Entstehung des Kubismus betreffe – ein Urteil, das auf der irrtümlichen Annahme beruht, die *Demoiselles* seien ein kubistisches Gemälde. Demgegenüber spielte die Stammeskunst im analytischen Kubismus nur eine untergeordnete Rolle, die sich auf die Konzeptualisierung visueller Eindrücke erstreckte. Dies war der einzige Aspekt der »art nègre«, den zwei so verschiedene Künstler wie Braque und Picasso teilen konnten. Die afrikanische Plastizität und die ozeanische Farbgebung, die Picasso bewegten, gehören, wie auch seine Wiederentdeckung des Kunstschaffens als eines »magischen« Aktes, seiner vorkubistischen Kunst der Jahre 1907–08 an. Als Picasso und Braque im Winter 1908–09 im Wettstreit zu arbeiten begannen, nahm Picassos Kunst einen abgeklärteren, klassischeren Ausdruck an, der für den analytischen Kubismus charakteristisch wurde und mit Picassos unmittelbar vorausgegangenem »afrikanischen« Werk wesensmäßig nicht viel gemein hatte. Gerade diese Form von Klassizismus ließ er in seiner zweiten primitivistischen Phase hinter sich, als er die Collage und Assemblage schuf – antiklassische Verfahren, an denen Braque bezeichnenderweise nicht teilnahm.

Diese neuen Techniken, die mit der Stammeskunst viele Gemeinsamkeiten hatten, blieben Garanten der Abenteuerlichkeit und Offenheit von Picassos Kunst, der damit – über mehr als vierzig Jahre seit dem Beginn seines Primitivismus im Jahr 1906 – in der vordersten Front der Avantgarde blieb und im hohen Alter zum einsamsten aller Langstreckenläufer der modernen Kunst wurde.

Anmerkungen

Da das Werk Picassos in der Einleitung ausführlich erörtert wird (S. 22ff., S. 59ff., S. 67ff., S. 72ff., S. 81ff.), setze ich die Vertrautheit des Lesers mit diesen früheren Passagen für das folgende Kapitel voraus.

1. Der Primitivismus spielte bei Max Ernst eine ebenso zentrale Rolle, war aber für die Kunstgeschichte insgesamt weniger folgenreich.

2. Das gilt allgemein für so frühe Zeugen wie Apollinaire, Salmon und Stein und trifft in der zweiten Hälfte des Jahrzehnts immer mehr für Autoren wie De Zayas zu.

3. Picasso fragte mich danach im Lauf einer Unterhaltung, die sich an seine Frage nach der damaligen Situation der Schwarzen in Amerika anschloß. Ich weiß nicht, wer diese Vorstellung aufbrachte oder wie weit sie verbreitet war. Picasso schien von der Idee entzückt gewesen zu sein.

4. Exemplarisch findet sich diese Ansicht bei R. J. Coady, dem Kunstredakteur der Zeitschrift *The Soil* und Direktor der Washington Square Gallery und der Coady Gallery in New York (1914–19). Er schrieb: »Cézanne war kein Franzose. Das Negerblut mütterlicherseits beeinflußte seine Gemälde am meisten«, Zilczer, J., *The Aesthetic Struggle in America, 1913–1918: Abstract Art and Theory in the Stieglitz Circle*, Diss., University of Delaware 1975, S. 151.

5. Abgebildet bei Rubin, W. (Hrsg.), *Picasso: A Retrospective*, Ausstellungskatalog, The Museum of Modern Art, New York 1980, S. 14.

6. Picassos Vater starb am 3. Mai 1913, sah aber nie die *Demoiselles* oder ein anderes Gemälde der »afrikanischen« Periode und wohl auch kein kubistisches Gemälde. Für letztere könnte die einzige Ausnahme das Bildnis von Manuel Pallarès sein, das Picasso bei seinem kurzen Aufenthalt in Barcelona auf dem Weg nach Horta (Frühjahr-Sommer 1909) malte. Falls Picassos Vater das Bild sah, ist keine Reaktion überliefert.

7. Zu meiner Verwendung des Begriffs siehe S. 11ff.

8. Das vollständige Zitat in Gilot, F., und Lake, C., *Life with Picasso*, New York, Toronto, London 1964, S. 226: »In diesem Augenblick wurde mir klar, daß es das ist, worum es beim Malen überhaupt geht.« Ich habe diese Fassung von Picassos Bericht gewählt, da sie meinen eigenen Notizen zu Gesprächen mit ihm – bei denen er über dasselbe sprach – nähersteht als die Fassung André Malraux', *La Tête d'obsidienne*, Paris 1974, wo Picasso sagt: »Ich begriff, warum ich Maler war.«

9. Die im Frühjahr 1906 (oder nach Daix, P., *La Vie de Peintre de Picasso*, Paris 1977, S. 72, schon Ende 1905) ausgestellte Serie von Flachreliefs war von einer französischen Expedition im Jahr 1903 in der spanischen Festung bei Osuna ausgegraben worden. Die Ergebnisse dieser Ausgrabungen wurden erstmals veröffentlicht von Engel, A., und Paris, P., *Une Forteresse ibérique à Osuna*, Paris 1906. Das Buch und die gleichzeitige Ausstellung im Louvre trugen viel dazu bei, die damalige Begeisterung für die iberische Plastik zu entfachen.

10. Es bestehen Meinungsverschiedenheiten darüber, ob Picasso schon in Gosol seine bildhauerische, frühe iberische Phase entwickelte, obschon sein Iberianismus sicher dort begann. Einige Kritiker (Barr, Leymarie) datieren *Brotträgerin*, Philadelphia Museum of Art, – wo der Kopf in den neuen, maskenhaften Stil umgearbeitet wurde – in die Zeit in Gosol. Ich bin der Meinung, daß der Kopf in diesem Bild, wie bei dem Bildnis von Gertrude Stein, nach Picassos Rückkehr nach Paris umgearbeitet wurde.

11. Siehe Salmon, A., »L'Art nègre«, 1920, in seinen *Propos d'ateliers*, Paris 1922, S. 116, 123, 128.

12. Siehe S. 87, Anm. 32.

13. Dies wird von den meisten Afrikanisten angenommen, obwohl – wie schon bemerkt, S. 88–89, Anm. 68 – wir wenig über das wissen, was vor der Mitte des 19. Jahrhunderts geschah. Was wir aus dem wenigen erhaltenen und ausgegrabenen Material (Nok, Djenné, Benin), das z. T. mehr als tausend Jahre alt ist, wissen, ist, daß einige Aspekte der Stammeskunst schon vorgeprägt waren.

14. Johnson, R., »Primitivism in the Early Sculpture of Picasso« in *Arts Magazine* 49, Nr. 10, Juni 1975, S. 64–68.

15. Ebenda, S. 64.

16. Picasso hatte P. Daix davon erzählt, doch der Band fand sich in seinem Nachlaß nicht.

17. In Spies, W., und Piot, C., *Picasso: Das plastische Werk*, Ausstellungskatalog, Nationalgalerie Berlin, 7. Oktober – 27. November 1983 und Kunsthalle Düsseldorf, 11. Dezember 1983 – 29. Januar 1984, S. 33.

18. Aus diesem Grund bleibe ich skeptisch gegenüber der von Johnson vorgeschlagenen Beziehung zwischen der Tafel Gauguins und der Bronze *Sich kämmende Frau.*

19. Dies ist lediglich eine Vermutung meinerseits, ich stütze mich dabei auf Picassos Phantasien der Abscheu vor alten Frauen und den »Vanitas«-Charakter gewisser Gegenüberstellungen alter und junger Frauen, die sich in seinem Werk immer wieder finden.

20. Daix, P., und Rosselet, J., *Le Cubisme de Picasso: Catalogue raisonné de l'œuvre 1907–1916*, Neuchâtel 1979, S. 247, Kat. Nr. 304. Eine rasche Bleistiftskizze auf der Rückseite bezieht sich auf Studien zu *Ernteszene* von Anfang 1907.

21. Obwohl im Katalog der Gauguin-Retrospektive von 1906 nicht aufgeführt, schien mir *Zwei Frauen zu seiten einer Statue* so sehr Picassos Gouache vorwegzunehmen, daß ich meinte, Picasso müsse sie gesehen haben. G. Monnier, Kuratorin im Cabinet de Dessins du Louvre, die das Aquarell freundlicherweise überprüfte, teilt mir mit, daß sich in *Ancien Culte Mahorie*, dessen Mittelstück es war, ein Aufkleber befindet, der besagt, daß es in der Retrospektive des Salon d'Automne von 1906 gezeigt wurde.

22. Ich habe den Verdacht, daß der Raum unter dem linken Stuhl ursprünglich freigelassen war, wie das rechts noch der Fall ist. Picasso scheint mir auf die Gouache zurückgegriffen zu haben, um die seltsame, verkürzte Darstellung der Beine des linken Stuhls zu studieren. Diese räumliche Darstellung steht eindeutig im Widerspruch zu der sonst im Bilde vorherrschenden seitlichen Darstellungsweise. Die dadurch entstehende grelle Wirkung erklärt wohl, warum Picasso den entsprechenden Raum rechts frei ließ.

23. Die beiden Gipsabgüsse in Originalgröße (nach Michelangelos Marmorplastiken *Gefesselter Sklave* und *Sterbender Sklave* im Louvre) waren trotz der frühen Bewunderung für die Originale in Picassos Atelier ein Novum. Die Abgüsse hatten sich anscheinend im Château Grimaldi befunden, das das Musée Antibes beherbergte, als Picasso dort 1946 zu arbeiten begann, und wurden ihm von R. Dor de La Souchère, dem Kurator des Museums, geschenkt, kurz nachdem er sich 1961 in der Villa Notre-Dame-de-Vie in Mougins niedergelassen hatte. Penrose, R., *Picasso: His Life and Work*, New York 1973 (Erstauflage London 1958), S. 452.

24. »The Philosophical Brothel, Part 1« in *Art News* 71, Nr. 5, September 1972, S. 24, 29, Anm. 15–20.

25. Meinen Aufzeichnungen zufolge sagt Picasso, daß er die Statue Michelangelos seit seiner Kindheit liebte. Aus dem Zusammenhang geht jedoch nicht hervor, ob er Reproduktionen, die er in den spanischen Kunstschulen gesehen haben könnte, oder das Original meinte, das er – wie aus dem Gespräch ersichtlich – bei seinem ersten Besuch in Paris sah. Ein Photo, das die »Salle Michelange« im Louvre im Jahr 1906 zeigt, ist bei Berthold, G., *Cézanne und die alten Meister*, Stuttgart 1958, abgebildet, Bildtafel 38. Nach Berthold, S. 49, 59, Anm. 4[illegible], befanden sich Michelangelos *Sklaven* seit 1877 in dieser Galerie, die als Ersatz für die »alte« Galerie Michelangelos, wo die Skulpturen bis 1875 gestanden hatten, gebaut wurde.

26. Siehe Anm. 10.

27. »L'Art nègre« (wie in Anm. 11), S. 125.

28. Picasso hatte sie von Géry Pieret (auch Géry-Pieret, Gérard Pieret, Guy Pieret usw. genannt), Apollinaires Sekretär, gekauft. Siehe Golding, J., *Cubism: A History and an Analysis 1907–1914*, London 1968, S. 53, Anm. 1 (1. Aufl. London 1959).

29. Eine Abbildung des weiblichen Kopfes, den Picasso von Géry Pieret kaufte und der ihn weit weniger zu interessieren schien als der hier abgebildete, in Golding, J., »The ›Demoiselles d'Avignon‹« in *The Burlington Magazine* 100, Nr. 662, Mai 1958, S. 158, Abb. 24. Hier ein paar weitere Beispiele für Cerro-Skulpturen:

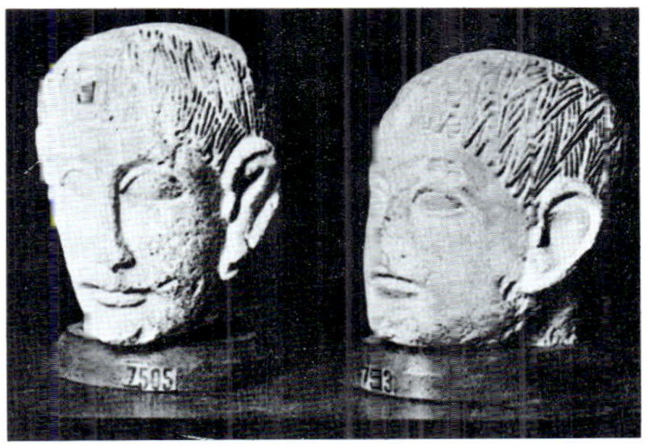

□ 474 *›Zwei Köpfe‹, iberisch, Cerro de los Santos, 5.–3. Jh. v. Chr., Stein, links: Höhe 23 cm, rechts: Höhe 22 cm. Museo Arqueológico Nacional, Madrid.*

30. Er hatte mehrere Stücke in den Ateliers Matisse', Derains und wohl auch Vlamincks im Frühherbst 1906 gesehen.

31. Siehe Rubin, W., »From Narrative to ›Iconic‹ in Picasso: The Buried Allegory in *Bread and Fruitdish on a Table* and the Role of *Les*

Demoiselles d'Avignon« in *The Art Bulletin* 65, Nr. 4, Dezember 1983, S. 615–49.

32. Mehr über die Karikatur siehe S. 290ff.

33. Golding, *Cubism: A History and an Analysis* (wie in Anm. 28), S. 53–54.

34. Die Asymmetrie der Cerro-Plastik geht fast ganz auf die Beschädigung einer Gesichtshälfte zurück. Dies scheint den zutiefst abergläubischen Picasso fasziniert zu haben, der wohl das übriggebliebene Auge mit dem volkstümlichen Glauben an den »bösen Blick« in Verbindung brachte. Die Asymmetrie der Augen des Matrosen (*Büste eines Matrosen* □ 318) und des Medizinstudenten (*Kopf eines Medizinstudenten* □ 316) sind jedoch nicht mit einäugigen Figuren wie der *Celestina* (1903) vergleichbar, die deutlichere Anspielungen zur Literatur aufweisen.

35. In Zusammenhang mit M. Richet, M.-L. Bernadac und H. Seckel vom Musée Picasso hoffen P. Daix und ich alle veröffentlichten und unveröffentlichten Skizzen, die mit den *Demoiselles* in Beziehung stehen, einander gegenüberzustellen, um die Entwicklung des Gemäldes und seine Chronologie genau nachzuzeichnen. Unsere Schlußfolgerungen sollen im Katalog der Ausstellung »Autour des *Demoiselles d'Avignon*« veröffentlicht werden, die im Musée Picasso für das Jahr 1986 vorgesehen ist.

36. In der Basler Skizze □ 319, der Endfassung der ersten Phase, trägt der Medizinstudent ein Buch und nicht einen Totenkopf. Es gibt jedoch viele Studien (etwa Z. XXVI, 45), die beweisen, daß er ursprünglich einen Totenkopf tragen sollte. So beschrieb ihn auch Picasso gegenüber Kahnweiler, Barr und mir.

37. Eine ausführliche Erörterung in meinem Aufsatz »From Narrative to ›Iconic‹ in Picasso« (wie in Anm. 31).

38. Ebenda. Siehe vor allem Anhang 5: »The *Demoiselles* and Cubism.«

39. Daß es Picasso- und Kubismusforscher versäumt haben, sich des Zeitraums zwischen dem Sommer 1908 und dem Sommer 1909 anzunehmen, ist daran erkennbar, daß in der Literatur bis vor wenigen Jahren Untersuchungen (und sogar Abbildungen) von zwei wichtigen Zeugnissen für Picassos frühen Kubismus fehlten: *Drei Frauen* (Eremitage Leningrad) und *Brot und Fruchtschale auf einem Tisch* (Kunstmuseum Basel).

40. »The Philosophical Brothel«, veröffentlicht in zwei Teilen in *Art News*, September 1972, S. 22–29, und Oktober 1972, S. 38–47. Alle weiteren Zitate von Steinberg im Haupttext sind diesem Aufsatz entnommen.

41. Eine Erörterung dieser Figur in meinem Aufsatz »From Narrative to ›Iconic‹ in Picasso« (wie in Anm. 31), S. 627–32, und vor allem Anhang 6: »The Left-Hand Figure in the *Demoiselles*«.

42. Siehe Anm. 36.

43. Anläßlich einer Reihe längerer Besuche in Picassos Villa erörterte ich mit ihm verschiedene Themen. Die Häufigkeit, mit der Picasso (oft in einem witzigen Ton) Geschlechtskrankheiten erwähnte, schien mir bemerkenswert. Unter seinen Freunden war Picasso lange dafür bekannt, daß er eine übertriebene, besessene Todesfurcht hatte. Da er in jungen Jahren häufig in Bordelle ging, mag diese Furcht eine verständliche Angst vor einer tödlichen Geschlechtskrankheit verstärkt haben. In Picassos Werk sind direkte oder versteckte Verweise auf Geschlechtskrankheiten sicherlich häufiger als bei jedem anderen bedeutenden Maler. Ein Überblick darüber würde einen eigenen Aufsatz erfordern.

44. Mathews Gedo, M., *Picasso: Art as Autobiography*, Chicago und London 1980, S. 75–80, 270–72, sowie »Art as Exorcism: Picasso's Demoiselles d'Avignon« in *Arts Magazine* 55, Nr. 2, Oktober 1980, S. 70–83. Gedo ging auf den Matrosen ein (von dem sie meint, er symbolisiere Picassos Ich der frühen Kindheit und seine erste Erfahrung mit einem Bordell in der frühen Jugend), den Medizinstudenten und die Prostituierten – besonders die Assoziation zwischen Ärzten und geschlechtskranken Prostituierten – und gelangte über die Interpretation, sie spiegelten Aspekte von Picassos eigener Geschichte, zur Hypothese, daß die erste Konzeption der *Demoiselles* Picassos eigenen »zweischneidigen Erfahrungen als objektiver Beobachter und als subjektives Opfer verseuchter Prostituierter« entsprach. So könne der Totenschädel ein Hinweis darauf sein, daß Picasso sich an einer Geschlechtskrankheit, wahrscheinlich Syphilis, angesteckt habe, vielleicht bei Fernande Olivier. (Gedo, die den geschwätzigen und notorisch unzuverlässigen Pierre Cabanne zitiert, bemerkt, daß Fernande gerüchteweise eine promiskuitive Vergangenheit hatte und sich tatsächlich prostituiert haben soll, als sie zuvor mit einem anderen Künstler zusammenlebte.) An anderer Stelle in *Art as Autobiography*, S. 53, 267, bezieht sich Gedo auf das vorherrschende Motiv der Blindheit in Picassos Arbeiten des Jahres 1903 und die vielen Deutungen seines Ursprungs; sie spekuliert dabei, daß dieses Motiv »aus Picassos Schuld- und Angstgefühlen wegen einer Geschlechtskrankheit, die er sich geholt hatte, resultiert«. Dabei zitiert sie Berger, J., *The Success and Failure of Picasso*, New York 1980 (Reprint der Ausgabe von 1965, Harmondsworth, England), S. 43–44. Berger meint, der Künstler »habe wohl an einer Geschlechtskrankheit gelitten« und »als Ergebnis dieser Krankheit« habe er befürchtet, zu erblinden.

45. *La Tête d'obsidienne,* S. 17–19. Malraux' Bericht über seine Unterhaltung mit Picasso beruht auf Notizen von einem Treffen im Jahr 1937. Wie ich schon bemerkte, sprach Picasso zum größten Teil auch mit mir über diese Themen. Als ich ihn zum zweiten Mal dazu bewegen konnte, über die *Demoiselles* zu sprechen, sagte er, daß sein Besuch im Trocadéro im Jahr 1907 ihn zutiefst bewegt hatte. Im Gesprächszusammenhang kann sich diese Bemerkung aber genausogut auf die »afrikanischen« Bilder der Jahre 1907–08 im allgemeinen bezogen haben wie auf die *Demoiselles* im besonderen. Da meine Aufzeichnungen im allgemeinen mit dem übereinstimmen, was Picasso gegenüber Malraux hinsichtlich der *Demoiselles* weit ausführlicher sagte, habe ich mir erlaubt, seinen Text zu verwenden, obwohl zu hören ist, daß bestimmte Passagen von *La Tête d'obsidienne* ganz oder teilweise Malraux' Erfindung sind.

46. In meiner Mitschrift der Unterhaltung mit Picasso führt er seinen ersten Besuch im Musée d'Ethnographie darauf zurück, daß er sich in der Tür geirrt habe; andernorts sagt er jedoch, Derain habe ihm geraten, das Museum zu besuchen.

47. » . . .c'était dégoûtant. Le marché aux Puces. L'odeur«, *La Tête d'obsidienne*, S. 17.

48. Da es zeitweise im Musée d'Ethnographie nur zwei Wächter gab, genügte die Abwesenheit oder Krankheit eines Wächters, daß alle Räume mit Ausnahme der Rotunde am Eingang geschlossen waren.

49. 1910 schreibt ein Kommentator, daß die ozeanische Hauptgalerie vierzehn Jahre lang geschlossen gewesen sei, obwohl sie der wichtigste Führer der Zeit, Joannes *Les Musées de Paris* von 1903, als geöffnet ausweist (wie auch die überarbeitete Ausgabe von 1905). Des Rätsels Lösung liegt vielleicht in den Angaben des Baedecker in diesem Zeitraum. Die Wächter scheinen ein noch heute nicht unbekanntes System genutzt zu haben, das in gewissen Kirchen, Baudenkmälern und Provinzmuseen gilt. Baedecker führt die Ozeanien-Abteilung als offiziell geschlossen, gibt aber an, daß man sie, sogar zu üblichen Schließungszeiten, gegen ein Trinkgeld besichtigen konnte – oder wie die englische Ausgabe sagt «by feeing the guardian«. Während der regulären Öffnungszeiten zumindest war die Rotunde am Eingang nicht geschlossen, die eine Auswahl ozeanischer und afrikanischer Kunst zeigte. Daß der Zugang zu unbewachten Räumen des Museums irgendwie dem Zufall überlassen war, läßt sich aus der ungewöhnlichen Zahl von Diebstählen im Trocadéro ersehen. In seiner Charakterisierung des Museums weist M. Mauss auf »beträchtliche Diebstähle« hin, in »L'ethnographie en France et à l'étranger« in *Revue de Paris*, 20. Jg., V, September–Oktober 1913, S. 537–60, 815–37.

50. Picasso sagte mir, daß er in seinen frühen Jahren mehr als einmal in den Trocadéro zurückkehrte und dabei des öfteren von Freunden begleitet wurde; bei seinem ersten Besuch war er allein. Es gibt einen eindeutigen Hinweis darauf, daß ihn bei einem Besuch Apollinaire begleitete, Samaltanou-Tsiakma, E., *Guillaume Apollinaire: Catalyst for Primitivism, for Picabia and Duchamp*, Diss., University of Virginia 1981, S. 31–37. Nach meinen Aufzeichnungen scheint Picasso den Trocadéro zum letzten Mal in den 30er Jahren besucht zu haben. Der Anlaß war wohl ein besonderes Ereignis im Museum, vielleicht die Ausstellung von Material der Dakar-Dschibuti-Expedition im Jahr 1933, an der sein enger Freund Michel Leiris teilgenommen hatte.

51. Meinen Aufzeichnungen nach erfuhr Picasso seine »Offenbarung« mit voller Gewalt, *gleich nachdem* er das Museum verlassen hatte.

52. Wie Picassos späte Behauptung, er habe vor der Fertigstellung der *Demoiselles* keine Stammeskunst gesehen, in gewissem Sinne die Vorstellungen, die sich mittlerweile um das Bild rankten, kompensieren sollten, siehe »From Narrative to ›Iconic‹ in Picasso« (wie in Anm. 31), Anhang 7: »Picasso's Equivocations with Respect to *Art Nègre*«, waren auch seine wiederholten Äußerungen über das Magische der Stammesobjekte (in Gesprächen mit C. Zervos, F. Gilot, A. Malraux, mir und zweifellos auch anderen) von der Absicht geleitet, die weitverbreitete Ansicht zu überwinden (exemplarisch bei Goldwater, *Primitivism in Modern Art*, New York 1967, S. 144–63; überarbeitete und erweiterte Auflage von *Primitivism in Modern Painting*, 1938), daß sein Interesse an der Kunst im wesentlichen formalistischer Natur war. Picassos entschiedene Reaktion sollte uns jedoch nicht zu dem Glauben verleiten, sein Interesse habe sich nur auf das Magische gerichtet. Ganz abgesehen vom Tenor seiner Bemerkungen gegenüber Salmon (Picasso habe die afrikanische Kunst »raisonnable« gefunden, »L'Art nègre«, wie in

Anm. 11, und »Picasso hat sich Gedanken zur Geometrie gemacht und dabei die wilden Künstler als Führer gewählt«, »Histoire anecdotique du cubisme« in *La Jeune Peinture française*, Paris 1912, S. 46) und einigen Beobachtungen mir gegenüber, die den Erfindungsreichtum der Stammesobjekte und ihres Materials betrafen und die leider in meinen Aufzeichnungen nur ungefähr wiedergegeben sind, geht aus dem hier untersuchten Material eindeutig hervor, daß Picassos Einstellung zur Stammeskunst sehr facettenreich war. *Worüber Künstler sprechen, muß man nicht notwendigerweise mit dem gleichsetzen, was sie tun.*

53. L. Gasmans Kapitel über Picasso und die Magie in ihrer Dissertation *Mystery, Magic and Love in Picasso, 1925–1938*, Columbia University 1981 (eine überarbeitete und erweiterte Auflage wird 1985 in der Yale University Press erscheinen) stellt eine glänzende Ansammlung von Material dar, das die Vorstellung stützt, Picasso habe eine magische Einstellung gegenüber der Stammeskunst gehabt. Gegen den von Goldwater verwandten Begriff »intellektueller Primitivismus« setzt sie den Ausdruck »magischer Primitivismus«. Während meine eigene Beurteilung von Picassos Reaktion auf die Stammesobjekte den Ansichten Gasmans viel näher steht als denen Goldwaters, suggerieren »intellektueller« und »magischer« Primitivismus eine Dichotomie, die nach meiner Ansicht Picassos Denk- und Arbeitsweise in ein falsches Licht setzt. Gasman scheint »intellektueller Primitivismus« und »magischer Primitivismus« als Alternativen und sich abwechselnde Erscheinungsformen anzusehen: »Natürlich ersetzte Picasso als ›Magiker‹ nicht den kühlen Picasso, der nach neuen Formen und Konzeptionen in den frisch entdeckten Schätzen der Primitiven suchte. Dieser ›intellektuelle Primitivismus› war so ernst zu nehmen wie sein ›magischer Primitivismus‹ und verlief parallel zum modernistischen Primitivismus seiner Zeitgenossen. ›Man ist nicht den ganzen Tag über ein Zauberer!‹ rief er Malraux gegenüber aus.« S. 472. Picasso hatte für die Stammeskunst nicht zwei verschiedene Denkmuster parat. Was Goldwater als »intellektuellen Primitivismus« bezeichnet, hängt mit der von Salmon überlieferten Sentenz Picassos zusammen, die afrikanische Kunst sei »raisonnable«, d. h., daß sie dem Intellekt unterworfen, infolgedessen logisch und konzeptuell sei. Die Bemerkung bezog sich so auf die ideographische Darstellungsweise primitiver Objekte. Der Ausdruck »magischer Primitivismus«, der von vielen Äußerungen Picassos angeregt und jetzt von vielem von Gasman gesammelten Belegmaterial unterstützt wurde, meint Picassos psychologische Einstellungen und bezieht sich auf seine verallgemeinerte Deutung dessen, was die Objekte für die Stammesvölker bedeuteten. So sind die beiden »Primitivismen« eigentlich zwei Seiten einer Betrachtungsweise. Als etwa Picasso in einem Gespräch die im wesentlichen formalen Probleme seiner GREBO-Maske besprach, verlor er keineswegs sein Gefühl für die Funktion des Objekts als eines magischen Vermittlers aus den Augen.

Das Material in Gasmans Dissertation macht Goldwaters Fehler wett, das Denken in der französischen Ethnologie mit der englischen und deutschen Anthropologie in eins gesetzt zu haben. Ihr Text steckt voller wichtiger Materialien, die sie M. Mauss und anderen entnommen hat und die uns einen guten Eindruck von dem hohen Niveau der französischen Ethnologie innerhalb des geistigen Lebens zu Anfang des Jahrhunderts vermitteln. Davon nehme ich nur ihren Hinweis aus, daß Picasso Mauss' Aufsatz von 1903–04 über die Magie gelesen haben könnte oder daß Lévy-Bruhls Text von 1910 über das Magische in der primitiven Kunst »Picassos Aufmerksamkeit erregt hätte«. Ganz abgesehen vom Stand der Französischkenntnisse Picassos im ersten Jahrzehnt dieses Jahrhunderts waren dies nicht die Dinge, die er las. Gasmans Darlegung von Analogien zwischen dem Denken Picassos und Mauss' ist ein faszinierendes Beispiel für das Wirken des Zeitgeists. Aber es bleiben eben Analogien. Außerdem wäre wohl Picassos Erlebnis im Trocadéro kaum eine »Offenbarung« gewesen, hätte er den frühen Aufsatz von Mauss tatsächlich gelesen. Nach seiner »Offenbarung« brauchte er Mauss nicht mehr zu lesen.

54. *La Tête d'obsidienne* (wie Anm. 8), S. 18.

55. Dies bestätigt nicht nur das Fehlen jedes sichtbaren Einflusses afrikanischer Kunst auf Picassos Werk dieser Zeit, sondern auch seine Bemerkungen über das afrikanische Objekt, das ihm Matisse bei Gertrude Stein zeigte. Siehe S. 270, 303 und Anm. 138, 139.

56. Die Mitarbeiter des Musée de l'Homme teilten mir mit, daß eigentlich alle Masken und Figuren sowie die Mehrzahl der Waffen und Gebrauchsgegenstände in den frühen Ausstellungen des Museums präsentiert waren, was auch der überladene Charakter der Photos aus dem Jahre 1895 bestätigt. Die abgebildete Maske von den Neuen Hebriden □ 324 ist eine von zwei einander sehr ähnlichen Stücken, die 1894 in das Museum gelangten; zumindest eine davon – wahrscheinlich aber beide – war bei Picassos erstem Besuch ausgestellt.

57. Wie auch ihr Eindruck bei jenen ausfallen mag, die mit Picassos iberischem Stil nicht vertraut sind, es besteht kein Zweifel, daß die mittleren Frauen attraktiv und sexuell anziehend aussehen sollten. Dies geht eindeutig aus der Farbgebung hervor, den verführerischen Stellungen, dem lyrischen Charakter ihrer Konturen und den relativ unverzerrten Gesichtszügen. Mit der allmählichen Fertigstellung des Bildes wurden sie durch den Kontrast mit den seitlichen Figuren um so anziehender, die sich zum Bedrohlichen und Monströsen entwickelten.

58. Siehe S. 85, Anm. 11.

59. Sowohl *Noa-Noa* (was »stark duftend« bedeutet) als auch *Herz der Finsternis* beruhen auf fast gleichzeitigen Erfahrungen mit den Tropen und wurden etwa gleichzeitig veröffentlicht. Gauguin kam im Juni 1891 auf Tahiti an, gerade ein Jahr, nachdem Conrad seine lange Reise den Kongo aufwärts unternommen hatte. *Noa-Noa* wurde in veränderter Fassung 1901 veröffentlicht; *Herz der Finsternis*, das 1899 als Serie erschienen war, kam 1902 als Buch heraus.

Ich habe Conrads Roman mit *Noa-Noa* verglichen, weil man damit eine gute Vorstellung von den Gegensätzen europäischer Ansichten über Polynesien und über Afrika erhält. Picasso konnte damals natürlich *Herz der Finsternis* nicht gelesen haben, da es erst 1926 unter dem französischen Titel *Au cœur des ténèbres* erschien. Doch die französische Haltung gegenüber Afrika zu Beginn des Jahrhunderts – die durch frühere Kommentare zu Stanleys Forschungsreisen und durch nachfolgende Reiseberichte beeinflußt war, noch mehr aber durch die schweren Verluste der Franzosen bei ihren militärischen Abenteuern in Zentralafrika – unterschied sich sehr von der Einstellung gegenüber den pazifischen Besitzungen. Picasso, ein eifriger Zeitungs- und Zeitschriftenleser, machte sich sicher die Stimmungen und Gefühle zu eigen, die in Paris in der Luft lagen. F. Ndiaye, Kuratorin für afrikanische Kunst im Musée de l'Homme, teilt mir mit, daß Franzosen, die über Afrika schreiben, nicht selten *Herz der Finsternis* zitieren, da es dazu in der französischen Literatur nichts Vergleichbares gibt. Tatsächlich kleidet Malraux den Satz »cœur des ténèbres« in seiner Behandlung Picassos und der afrikanischen Kunst in eine eindeutige Verbeugung vor dem älteren Romancier, *La Tête d'obsidienne*, S. 158.

60. Die Objekte für diese Schau wurden von Guillaume ausgesucht, doch die Aufstellung besorgte De Zayas. Zu seiner Rolle siehe Naumann, F. M., Einführung und Anmerkungen zu »How, When, and Why Modern Art Came to New York« von Marius de Zayas, in *Arts Magazine* 54, Nr. 8, April 1980, S. 96–126.

61. Zayas, M. de, *African Art: Its Influence on Modern Art*, New York 1916, S. 41. Dieses Buch brachte De Zayas' Bewunderer ständig in Verlegenheit, nicht nur weil es – trotz seines Titels – eigentlich nichts über den Einfluß der afrikanischen auf die moderne Kunst aussagt, sondern auch wegen seines verstiegenen Rassismus. Trotz der Bewunderung De Zayas' für die afrikanische Plastik hielt er die Afrikaner für Beispiele stagnierender Entwicklung: »Analysiert man die Kunst der verschiedenen menschlichen Rassen, stellt man fest, daß jede Rasse ein bestimmtes Darstellungsprinzip hat und daß der Grad der Entwicklung ihrer Kunst auf den Naturalismus hin unmittelbar mit der intellektuellen Entwicklung der Rasse, die sie hervorbringt, zusammenhängt . . . Die geringe Zahl direkter Nachahmungen – die fast abstrakte Form plastischer Darstellung des afrikanischen Negers – ist nichts weiter als das logische Ergebnis des Zustandes seines Gehirns . . . [S. 7]. Sie [die Neger] verharren auf einem geistigen Stand der dem von Kindern der weißen Rasse sehr ähnlich ist. Ihr Leben ist rein sensorisch. Wie weiße Kinder sind sie Egozentriker . . . [S. 10]. Man kann sagen, daß die zerebrale Verfassung eines Negerwilden besonders primitiv ist und sein Gehirn auf der untersten Stufe der menschlichen Entwicklung steht . . . [S. 10]. Der Grund für den Stillstand der geistigen Fähigkeiten des Negerwilden liegt in seinem natürlichen und gesellschaftlichen Milieu . . . Der Neger ist deshalb jeder intellektuellen Regung eigentlich unfähig und sucht nur, seine körperlichen Bedürfnisse zu befriedigen . . . [S. 13]. Obwohl das Auge des Negers die Formen in ihrer natürlichen Weise sieht ist sein Gehirn nicht in der Lage, sie zu verstehen und in dieser Weise zu speichern. . . Er denkt nicht nach und zieht keine Vergleiche um relative Werte zu bekommen, weil er der Analyse nicht fähig ist [S. 32].«

62. »Cubism?« in *Arts and Decoration*, April 1915, S. 284–86, 308. Zitiert bei Naumann, »How, When, and Why Modern Art Came to New York« (wie in Anm. 60), S. 104.

63. Barr, A. H. Jr. (Hrsg.), *Picasso: Forty Years of His Art* (mit zwei Stellungnahmen des Künstlers), Ausstellungskatalog, The Museum of Modern Art, New York, in Zusammenarbeit mit The Art Institute of Chicago, 1939, S. 9–12, 200. Die Stellungnahme von 1923 wurde unter

dem Titel »Picasso Speaks« in *The Arts* 3, Nr. 5, Mai 1923, S. 315–26, veröffentlicht. Barrs Nachdruck von »Picasso Speaks« in *Picasso: Forty Years of His Art* als Interview, das der Künstler De Zayas gewährte, ist das erste Mal, daß De Zayas' Name mit dieser Stellungnahme in Verbindung gebracht wird. Der Herausgeber von *The Arts* gab bei der Erstveröffentlichung im Mai 1923 lediglich an, daß »Picasso dieses Interview der Zeitschrift *The Arts* auf Spanisch gab und dann den spanischen Text autorisierte, den wir hiermit übersetzen«, ohne dabei De Zayas' Namen zu nennen, S. 315. Noch im Jahr 1936 ist kein Zusammenhang zwischen »Picasso Speaks« und De Zayas erkennbar, weder in M. Armitages kleinem Buch (worin das Interview mit Picasso von 1923 und ein späteres abgedruckt sind), noch in dem Brief, den Armitage an Barr schrieb, um ihn auf das Buch aufmerksam zu machen.

64. Ein zusätzliches Problem betrifft den bibliographischen Verweis in *Picasso: Forty Years of His Art,* S. 200, wo es heißt: »Eine französische Fassung [dieses Interviews] erschien mit zusätzlichen Abschnitten zu . . . Rousseau, der Negerkunst und der Literatur in Florent Fels, *Propos d'artistes,* Paris, Renaissance du Livre, 1925, S. 139–45.« Was hier (und auch andernorts) nicht berücksichtigt wird, ist die Tatsache, daß ein früheres Interview von Picasso mit F. Fels existiert, das unter dem Titel »Propos d'artistes: Picasso« in *Les Nouvelles littéraires, artistiques et scientifiques* Nr. 42, 4. August 1923, S. 2, veröffentlicht wurde. Dieses Interview ist als Quelle für die von Fels in *Propos d'artistes* 1925 veröffentlichte Fassung viel wahrscheinlicher als das De Zayas zugeschriebene »Picasso Speaks«.

Fels erläuterte die Genese des »longue interview«, das in *Les nouvelles littéraires* erschien, in einem anderen Text zu Picasso in einer späteren Aufsatzsammlung, *Le Roman de l'art vivant*, Paris 1959, S. 172–75, wo er feststellte, mit Picasso viele Gespräche geführt zu haben. (Er besuchte dessen Atelier erstmals, als der Künstler in den Jahren 1913–1916 in der Rue Schoelcher lebte, und dann Anfang Oktober oder November 1918 in der Rue La Boétie.) Picasso sagte in dem Interview des Jahres 1923 zu Fels: »Je vous ai déjà dit que je ne pouvais plus rien dire de 'l'art nègre'. Vous avez répondu pour moi, en une précédente enquête: 'L'art nègre, connais pas'.« Dies bezieht sich auf die »Opinions sur l'art nègre«, die im April 1920 in *Action* veröffentlicht wurden, und ist ein zusätzlicher Beweis für ihren damaligen vertrauten Umgang.

65. Picassos Bemerkung gegenüber Fels schließt an die genannte Äußerung direkt an: »C'est qu'il [»l'art nègre«] m'est devenu trop familier, les statues africaines qui traînent un peu partout chez moi, sont plus des témoins que des exemples«, *Les Nouvelles littéraires* (wie in Anm. 64, S. 2).

66. Picasso machte dies gegenüber P. Daix sehr deutlich, der es mir berichtete.

67. Zervos, C., *Pablo Picasso: Œuvres de 1906 à 1912*, Bd. 2, Teil 1, Paris 1942, S. XXXVII-III, 10. Siehe auch Johnson Sweeney, J., »Picasso and Iberian Sculpture« in *The Art Bulletin* 23, Nr. 3, September 1941, S. 191–98.

68. »From Narrative to ›Iconic‹ in Picasso« (wie in Anm. 31), Anhang 7: »Picasso's Equivocations with Respect to *Art Nègre*«.

69. Die engste Beziehung besteht zwischen dem Kopf der Figur rechts und – nicht den Masken, sondern den Köpfen der *FANG*-Reliquiarfiguren. Diese Ähnlichkeit ist jedoch ziemlich beiläufig, verglichen mit Ähnlichkeiten mit Masken, die Picasso nicht gesehen haben kann □ 337. Obwohl es im Trocadéro mindestens eine *FANG*-Figur gab, als Picasso seinen ersten Besuch dort machte, nehmen seine Köpfe erst gegen Anfang 1908 eine deutliche *FANG*-Physiognomie an (S. 295 ff.). Picasso besaß schon ziemlich früh eine *FANG*-Reliquiarfigur, sicherlich nicht später als 1910; man kann ihre Silhouette in einem Atelierfenster auf einem unveröffentlichten und undatierten Photo der Archive des Musée Picasso sehen, das im Atelier am Boulevard de Clichy aufgenommen wurde, wohin Picasso im September oder Oktober 1909 zog. (Er blieb bis zum Herbst 1912 dort.)

70. Barr, A. H. Jr., *Picasso: Fifty Years of His Art*, New York, The Museum of Modern Art, 1946, S. 55, 257.

71. Laude, J., *La Peinture française (1905–1914) et »l'Art nègre«*, Paris 1968, S. 254–55.

72. Siehe S. 90, Anm. 82.

73. Matisse scheinen die meisten Stammesobjekte gehört zu haben; um 1907 waren es etwa zwanzig. Es gibt keinen Hinweis darauf, daß Derain und Vlaminck zu diesem Zeitpunkt mehr als vier oder fünf Stücke besaßen.

74. Er stellte dies mir gegenüber sehr deutlich fest, und aus weiter unten erläuterten Gründen (S. 303–304) sehe ich keinen Anlaß, daran zu zweifeln.

75. Golding, »The ›Demoiselles d'Avignon‹« (wie in Anm. 29), S. 57, Tafel 19.

76. Clouzot, H., und Level, A., *L'Art nègre et l'art océanien*, Paris 1919, Tafel XXXVI: »Masque lunaire«, Elfenbeinküste, Sammlung A. Level, Höhe 25 cm.

77. Salmon, A., »Histoire anecdotique du cubisme« (wie in Anm. 52), S. 42–50.

78. Johnson, R., »Picasso's ›Demoiselles d'Avignon‹ and the Theatre of the Absurd« in *Arts Magazine* 55, Nr. 2, Oktober 1980, S. 104–05. Die Maske von der Torresstraße wurde von C. Zervos unter der Provenienz ›Sammlung Picasso‹ veröffentlicht in »L'Art nègre« in *Cahiers d'Art* 2, Nr. 7–8, 1927, S. 231.

79. Dies sind die typischen Masken der Region. Sie sind jedoch selten und sehr teuer; daher ist es zweifelhaft, ob Picasso eine gekauft hätte, wäre sie ihm angeboten worden. Ein hervorragendes Exemplar befand sich in den 30er Jahren in der Sammlung seines Freundes Georges Salles. Diese Maske wurde später von Kenneth Clark gekauft und ist von einem Vertreter seiner Erben fälschlicherweise als ehemaliger Besitz Picassos ausgegeben worden.

80. Dies wurde mir von P. Daix mitgeteilt.

81. In Vorlesungen in der National Gallery (»Picasso, Cubism and African Art«, 28. Februar 1982) und andernorts.

82. Brief an mich von Frau H. van Geluwe vom Musée Royal de l'Afrique Centrale, Tervuren. Sie bezieht sich hier auf die sog. »vollen« Kifwebes mit hervortretenden Zügen, um die es auch hier geht.

83. Selbst heute noch gibt es in französischen Sammlungen wenige wertvolle *masques de maladie*. Solche Masken sind im Handel selten und C. Ratton bemerkt, daß sie vor dem Geschmackswandel nach dem 2. Weltkrieg als zu häßlich galten, um verkauft zu werden. Der hier abgebildete Maskentyp □ 340 ist nach Susan Vogel stark von den fortgeschrittenen Stadien der Syphilis oder Gangosa beeinflußt. Diese besondere Krankheitsmaske der *PENDE*, auf die ich in den Beständen des Museums von Tervuren stieß, ist schöner und abstrakter als durchschnittlich der Fall. Sie wurde erst 1954 aus Afrika mitgebracht, und wenn man auch ihr Alter nicht datieren kann, so wurde sie doch aller Wahrscheinlichkeit nach später als die *Demoiselles* geschaffen.

Level behauptet, 1904 mit dem Sammeln begonnen zu haben, doch ist dieser Aussage widersprochen worden. Wie dem auch sei, es gibt keinen Hinweis darauf, daß er Picasso vor 1908 – ein Jahr nach den *Demoiselles* – begegnete. (In seinen *Souvenirs d'un collectionneur* sagt Level, daß er Picasso 1908 bei einem Besuch im Atelier des Künstlers in der Rue de Ravignan 13 kennenlernte und daß er dabei die *Gauklerfamilie* für die Sammlung La Peau de l'Ours kaufte. Siehe Level, A., *Souvenirs d'un collectionneur*, postum veröffentlicht, Paris 1959, S. 23.) Es gibt auch keine Berechtigung für die Annahme, Level habe die Maske ein Jahrzehnt vor ihrer Veröffentlichung besessen. Schließlich hat seine *masque de maladie* von der Elfenbeinküste viel weniger Ähnlichkeit mit dem Kopf der sitzenden Figur in den *Demoiselles* als die *PENDE*-Masken.

84. Unsere Zuschreibung bestimmter mit Metall überzogener Reliquienwächter aus dem Kongo und aus Gabun an die *KOTA* folgt einer alten, aber mißverstandenen Konvention, die von der französischen Kolonialverwaltung begonnen und dann aufgegeben wurde. L. Siroto machte mich darauf aufmerksam, daß viele der zuerst bekanntgewordenen Figuren von den *NDASA* und den *WUMBU* hergestellt wurden, Völkern, die eine Sprache pflegten, die der der nördlich von ihnen lebenden *KOTA* verwandt war. Diese eigentlichen *KOTA* hatten jedoch nicht ihren bildhauerischen Stil. Seitdem haben die Völkerkundler viel, wenn auch noch nicht alles, über die sekundären Stile in Erfahrung gebracht, die innerhalb dieses Korpus unter den *MBAMBA* entstanden, einem Volk, das – obwohl in der Nachbarschaft der *KOTA*-sprechenden Völker wohnhaft – sich von seiner Geschichte, seiner Sprache und seiner Sozialstruktur her von ihnen deutlich unterscheidet.

Streifen unter den Augen metallüberzogener *KOTA*-Figuren aus dem Mossendjo-Gebiet entsprechen nicht den Hautritzungen (die von den *KOTA* nicht praktiziert wurden); sie werden von bestimmten Händlern und Laien gerne als Tränen gedeutet. Diese Deutung, die dem Wert- und Zeichensystem der betreffenden Gesellschaft zuwiderläuft, findet seitens der Ethnologie keine Zustimmung. Nach Siroto könnte das Motiv von kleinen senkrechten Tätowierungen stammen, die früher in Mode gewesen waren (man findet sie in einigen Bildwerken anderer im Nordwesten lebender Völker) oder auch nur zum Schmuck dienen.

85. Bei diesen Plastiken handelt es sich zweifelsohne um diejenigen, die auf der oben erwähnten unzureichenden Liste, S. 88, Anm. 56, unter Nr. 69 als »Masques [sic], Plat cuivre et bois, effigie funéraire, Gabon, Bakota. Ht. 50 [cm]« bezeichnet werden. Es ist nicht sicher, ob Picasso mehr als die beiden *KOTA*-Reliquiarfiguren besaß, die ich in seinem Nachlaß entdeckte □ 410, 411. Ein Erbe, Bernard Picasso, zeigte

sich gegenüber Wissenschaftlern im allgemeinen und dem Museum im besonderen als unaufgeschlossen; daher kann man seine Bestände nicht überprüfen.

86. Hätte Picasso seine *Kota*-Figuren in den 20er Jahren oder danach gekauft, wären sie bestimmt viel qualitätvoller gewesen; erstens, weil die Auswahl größer war, und zweitens, weil Picasso für den Ankauf von primitiver Kunst etwas bereitwilliger Geld ausgab. Das von Claude Picasso photographierte Objekt □ 411 ist so grob gearbeitet, daß es eher auf das zu Anfang des Jahrhunderts käufliche Material hindeutet, das vor den Aktivitäten Brummers und Guillaumes im Umlauf war.

Als Antwort auf meine Frage nach Matisse, der ihm bei Gertrude Stein ein afrikanisches Objekt gezeigt hatte, stellte sich Picasso gegen Matisse. Dabei wies er auch darauf hin, daß ihm ganz andere afrikanische Objekte als Matisse gefielen, Objekte, die Matisse' Gleichsetzung von afrikanischer und ägyptischer Kunst als falsch oder töricht auswiesen. (Obwohl ich mich nicht an den genauen Wortlaut der Bemerkungen Picassos erinnern kann, deuten meine Aufzeichnungen darauf hin, daß er sich »spöttisch« äußerte.) Picasso erwähnte dann einige Objekte, die ihm gefielen. Dabei benutzte er vielleicht einige geläufige Bezeichnungen wie Nimba oder *Kota*. Doch da ich damals im Grunde nichts über afrikanische Kunst wußte, vergaß ich sie wieder. Meinen Aufzeichnungen entnehme ich jedoch, daß Picasso von »kleinen Metallfiguren, die sehr abstrakt sind«, und »großnasigen Masken« sprach. Rückblickend glaube ich, daß es sich hierbei nur um die *Kota*-Reliquiarfiguren und die »nimbaköpfigen« Figuren und/oder Nimba-Masken der *Baga* handeln kann. Diese beiden Arten von Objekten lassen sich unmittelbar mit den Arbeiten des Jahres 1907 in Verbindung bringen (S. 279 ff., 283 ff.). Diese Tatsache und Picassos Bemerkungen berechtigen zu der Annahme, daß sie zu den ersten Objekten gehörten, die ihn interessierten, wie auch zu den ersten Objekten, die er sammelte (obwohl der erste Nachweis für *Baga*-Figuren in seinem Atelier oder seiner Wohnung ein Photo von Olga ist, Archiv des Musée Picasso, das er für das Bildnis von ihr im Jahre 1917 benutzte, Z. III, 83).

87. In den Jahren vor dem 1. Weltkrieg waren Guillaumes (und wohl auch Heymanns und Brummers) schöne *Kota*-Reliquiarfiguren erstaunlich teuer – u. a. deswegen weil sie irrtümlich als mehrere Jahrhunderte alte Objekte galten. Paudrat, S. 165, merkt an, daß die beiden Reliquiarfiguren, die Guillaume zur Ausstellung von 1914 an Stieglitz sandte, auf je 3000 Francs geschätzt wurden, das ist sechsmal mehr als er für De Chiricos *Liebeslied* verlangte, eines der Meisterwerke des Künstlers (das heute mindestens das Zehnfache einer hervorragenden *Kota*-Figur wert ist).

Unter Sammlern und Historikern herrscht der falsche Eindruck, daß gute Stammesobjekte zu Beginn des Jahrhunderts gar nicht teuer waren. Man konnte natürlich armseliges, konventionelles Material sehr billig kaufen – wie das heute auch der Fall ist. Doch die Spitzenstücke waren extrem teuer und sind es noch immer (wenn auch nicht mehr im Vergleich mit den Meisterwerken der Moderne: Gemessen an den Preisen, die man für diese zahlen muß, sind Meisterwerke der Stammeskunst verhältnismäßig billig, auch wenn sie für gewöhnlich Hunderttausende von Dollars kosten).

88. Die erste Begegnung von Kunsthistorikern mit metallbedeckten *Kota*-Reliquiarfiguren verleitete sie dazu, die rautenförmigen Sockel willkürlich als Beine zu interpretieren. Diese Deutung ist falsch. Einige spätere Untersuchungen, die auf »*Kota*-Informanten« beruhten, Andersson, E., »Contributions à l'éthnographie des Kuta I in *Studia Ethnographica Upsaliensia* 6, 1953, S. 340, sowie auf stilistischen Vergleichen, Siroto, L., »Notes on the Bakota, Pangwe, and Balumbo Sculpture of the Gabon and the Middle Congo« in *Masterpieces of African Art*, Ausstellungskatalog, Brooklyn Museum, 21. Oktober 1954 – 2. Januar 1955, S. 26–30, argumentieren überzeugender, daß die Form wohl Arme darstelle. Photos von ganzen Reliquiaren zeigen den unteren Teil der Raute für gewöhnlich im Schrein versenkt, so daß er nicht zu sehen ist.

89. Es gibt nicht den geringsten Hinweis darauf, daß die heute berühmten Karyatidenhocker der *Luba* im ersten Jahrzehnt des Jahrhunderts in Frankreich greifbar waren (und sie befanden sich mit Sicherheit nicht in den Sammlungen des Trocadéro). Trotzdem waren einige Autoren versucht, sie mit Werken Pariser Künstler der damaligen Zeit in Verbindung zu bringen (so stellt etwa M. Schneckenburger in *Weltkulturen und moderne Kunst*, Ausstellungskatalog, München, Haus der Kunst, 16. Juni – 30. September 1972, S. 492–93, eine solche Verbindung mit Modiglianis gemalter Karyatide von ca. 1910 her). Ich habe meine Beispiele aus französischen Territorien gewählt, deren Skulptur sich in Paris schon in Umlauf befand.

90. Die verkrampfte und ausladende Bewegung der Glieder von Picassos tanzenden Figuren steht in keiner Beziehung zu irgendeinem afrikanischen oder ozeanischen Kunststil, den er gesehen haben könnte, oder zu frühen Stichen von Stammestänzen, wie sie in *Le Tour du monde* und anderen populären Zeitschriften abgebildet waren, die Picasso kannte. Sicherlich machte er sich Vorstellungen von solchen Zeremonien und dachte sich die Tänze als Ausdruck von großer Gewalt und Energie. Er sah sie eher als stoßhafte Gestik, die Martha Grahams Choreographien auszeichnet, denn als regelmäßige und beherrschte Bewegungen, wie wir sie aus Filmen über afrikanische Tänze kennen.

91. »Heroic Years from Humble Treasures: Notes on African and Modern Art« in *Art International* 10, Nr. 7, September 1966, Neudruck in *Changing: Essays in Art Criticism*, New York 1971, S. 38.

92. Obwohl sich die abgebildete *Bambara*-Figur □ 372 zum Zeitpunkt von Kahnweilers Tod in dessen Sammlung befand (und man sie in einem Photo aus dem Jahr 1913 auf einem Bücherregal in Kahnweilers Wohnung in der Rue George Sand sehen kann, abgebildet in Kahnweiler, D.-H., und Crémieux, F., *My Galleries and Painters*, Documents of Twentieth Century Art series, aus dem Französischen von H. Weaver, Einleitung von J. Russell, New York 1971, zwischen S. 15 und S. 17), läßt sich nicht feststellen, ob er sie bereits 1907 besaß. Es handelt sich allerdings um einen Typus von Objekt, den er schon so früh gekauft haben kann.

93. Laude, *La Peinture française* (wie in Anm. 71), S. 253.

94. Es gibt keine Zeichnung und kein Bild Picassos, das ein Stammesobjekt direkt kopieren würde.

95. Dies teilte mir Daix in einem Gespräch mit.

96. *Artes*, Antwerpen, Nr. 3–4, 1947–48, S. 3, zitiert von Gasman, L., *Mystery, Magic and Love in Picasso* (wie in Anm. 53), S. 456.

97. Michel Leiris teilt mir mit, daß Picasso mit Sicherheit wußte, daß seine Nimba-Maske □ 453 eine Fruchtbarkeitsgöttin darstellte. Im allgemeinen wurden die »nimbaköpfigen« Figuren der *Baga* □ 365, 366 ebenfalls – wenn auch irrtümlich – in dieser Richtung interpretiert.

Leon Siroto teilt mir 1982 mit: »Unser gegenwärtiger Wissensstand erlaubt uns nicht, mehr als eine stilistische Verwandtschaft zwischen der riesigen Nimba-Maske und den weiblichen und männlichen Statuen, die eine identische Gestaltung des Kopfes aufweisen, anzunehmen. Alten Berichten zufolge waren solche Statuen für bestimmte *Baga*-Gemeinschaften wichtig, aber sie erwähnen in diesem Zusammenhang keine Nimba-Masken. Das Feldstudium der *Baga*-Ikonographie ist weitgehend vernachlässigt worden.«

98. Vermutlich wegen des enormen Gewichts dieser Masken wird manchmal behauptet, sie seien unter dem Bastrock von mehr als einem Tänzer getragen worden. Doch in Wirklichkeit konnte ein einziger Tänzer die Maske kontrollieren, indem er sie sowohl mit dem Kopf abstützte als auch an dem runden Reifen um die »Beine« am Joch (der bei Picassos Maske noch erhalten ist □ 453).

99. R. Hohl, Katalogtext für Nr. 52 (Blatt mit Zeichnungen vom Frühsommer 1907) in *Pablo Picasso: Eine Ausstellung zum hundertsten Geburtstag, Werke aus der Sammlung Marina Picasso*, Ausstellungskatalog, Spies, W. (Hrsg.), Haus der Kunst, München, 13. Februar bis 20. April 1981; Josef-Haubrich-Kunsthalle, Köln, in Zusammenarbeit mit dem Museum Ludwig, 11. August – 11. Oktober 1981; Städtische Galerie im Städelschen Kunstinstitut, Frankfurt am Main, 21. Oktober 1981 – 10. Januar 1982, S. 235–236.

100. Salmon weist an verschiedenen Stellen darauf hin, daß er 1905 und 1906 die Stammeskunst bewußt wahrnahm. Sollte dies der Fall gewesen sein, hätte er sich schon zwei Jahre vor Picassos Berührung mit der Stammeskunst (1907) für diese interessiert. Da Salmon diese Erfahrung Picassos andernorts fälschlich auf 1906 datiert, ist es möglich und geradezu wahrscheinlich, daß seine frühen Daten allesamt auf einem Irrtum beruhen und dem, wie sich inzwischen herausgestellt hat, mystischen Datum 1905, das häufig als Zeitpunkt der »Entdeckung« der Stammeskunst durch die Moderne bezeichnet wird.

101. «L'Art nègre« (wie in Anm. 11), S. 124.

102. Picasso sagte zu Sabartés: »On n'a jamais dépassé la sculpture primitive«, Sabartés, J., *Picasso, portraits et souvenirs*, aus dem Spanischen von P.-M. Grand und A. Chastel, Paris 1946, S. 223.

103. In Apollinaires *The Cubist Painters* findet sich nur ein kurzer Hinweis auf die Stammeskunst, die im selben Atemzug mit der ägyptischen Kunst genannt wird. Siehe Apollinaire, G., *Méditations esthétiques – Les Peintres cubistes*, Paris 1913, S. 16–17: »Ajoutons que cette imagination: *la quatrième dimension*, n'a été que la manifestation des aspirations, des inquiétudes d'un grand nombre de jeunes artistes regardant les sculptures égyptiennes, nègres et océaniennes.« Diese Passage geht vermutlich z. T. auf das Interview des Autors mit Matisse zurück – weniger auf Bemerkungen Picassos, »Henri Matisse« in *La Phalange*, Nr. 2, 15.–18. Dezember 1907,

Nachdruck unter dem Titel »Matisse interrogé par Apollinaire« in *Henri Matisse: Ecrits et propos sur l'art*, Fourcade, D. (Hrsg.), Paris 1972, S. 56–57: »Je n'ai jamais évité l'influence des autres . . . Par conséquent toutes les écritures plastiques: les Egyptiens hiératiques, les Grecs affinés, les Cambodgiens voluptueux, les productions des anciens Péruviens, les statuettes des nègres africains proportionnées selon les passions qui les ont inspirées peuvent intéresser un artiste et l'aider à dévolopper sa personnalité.«

Eine Analyse der Bedeutung Apollinaires für die Verbreitung des Primitivismus bei Samaltanou-Tsiakma, *Guillaume Apollinaire: Catalyst for Primitivism* (wie in Anm. 50), passim, Untersuchungen über die damalige Tendenz, die Plastik der Neger und der Ägypter mit »der vierten Dimension« in Verbindung zu bringen, siehe ebda., S. 48–50.

104. Salmon, A., »Histoire anecdotique du cubisme« (wie in Anm. 52), S. 43–44.

105. Salmon, A., »Negro Art«, Übers. v. Brinton, D., *The Burlington Magazine*, Nr. 205, April 1920, S. 164–72.

106. Die notwendige Kritik an der (von Goldwater eingeleiteten) traditionellen Sicht von Picassos Primitivismus, für die Gasmans eindrucksvoller Text ein Musterbeispiel ist, könnte dazu führen, daß das Pendel zu weit in die andere Richtung ausschlägt. Vieles in dieser Schrift beruht auf Aussagen (Zitaten von Picasso und verschiedenen Autoren) und nicht so sehr auf der direkten Konfrontation mit dem Kunstwerk. Anders als Matisse sprach Picasso selten über Formfragen. Selbst seine Aussagen zum Kubismus hatten einen poetischen Duktus, siehe meine Veröffentlichung *Picasso in the Collection of The Museum of Modern Art*, Ausstellungskatalog, The Museum of Modern Art, New York 1972, S. 72, 206, Anm. 3. Dennoch beweist sein Werk, daß Picasso sich sehr mit der Lösung formaler Probleme auseinandersetzte – und wir sollten dies mit Blick auf seinen Primitivismus nicht aus den Augen verlieren.

107. In meinen Aufzeichnungen notierte ich Äußerungen Picassos wie folgt: »Der größte Realismus ist die engste Entsprechung zwischen den Zeichen, die der Künstler schafft – in welchem Stil auch immer –, und dem Wesen . . . seines stärksten Gefühls.« In anderen Worten: Realismus ist nicht eine Frage der Illusion oder Illustration, sondern der Kommunikation.

108. Salmon, A., »La Semaine artistique. Cubisme: Exposition Metzinger (Galerie Rosenberg)« in *L'Europe Nouvelle*, 2. Jg., Nr. 3, 18. Januar 1919, S. 139–40.

109. Aus Platzmangel können hier mehrere Zwischenentwürfe nicht abgebildet werden, etwa Zervos VI, 966 und XXVI, 180.

110. Obwohl ich hier vor allem von der Karikatur spreche, sollten wir nicht vergessen, daß Picasso die »niedere« Kunst liebte, wie Nippes, alte Zeitschriften usw. beweisen, die er stets um sich hatte (und für *papiers collés* und Konstruktionen verwandte).

111. Etwa seine gleichzeitige Parodie von Manets *Olympia* und Cézannes *L'Après-midi à Naples* in Zervos, C., *Pablo Picasso,* Paris 1954, Bd. 6, Suppl. zu Bde. 1–5, Nr. 343.

112. Rubin, *Picasso in the Collection* (wie in Anm. 106), S. 66.

113. Erst Picasso selbst wies darauf hin, daß sich eine seiner neukaledonischen Figuren (die den Kunsthistorikern durch das Photo von Burgess längst bekannt war) links oben im Bildnis Kahnweilers befindet □ 425. Zu Picassos Bemerkung gegenüber J. Richardson siehe Anm. 176.

114. Penrose, R., *Picasso: His Life and Work*, London 1958, S. 126.

115. Gopnik, A., »High and Low: Caricature, Primitivism, and the Cubist Portrait« in *Art Journal* 43, Nr. 4, Winter 1983, S. 371–76.

116. Ebenda, S. 374.

117. Ebenda, S. 375.

118. Wie etwa die Blätter mit der Gegenüberstellung der Profile des strengen, alten Kriegers und des femininen Jünglings mit gelocktem Haar, abgebildet in Popham, A. E., *The Drawings of Leonardo*, New York 1945, Bildtafeln 24, 127, 141.

Als Picasso, Jacqueline und ich einmal einige seiner frühen Karikaturen durchsahen, die ein Händler bei ihm gelassen hatte (und von denen Picasso fürchtete, sie seien im Museum von Barcelona gestohlen worden), fragte ich ihn, ob er die sog. Karikaturen von Puvis de Chavannes kenne. Er verneinte dies, sagte aber, er möge die von Leonardo.

119. Diese Methode diente später Max Ernst in seinen Plastiken mehr poetischen und ikonographischen Zwecken.

120. Meines Wissens hat nur Spies darauf hingewiesen, *Picasso: Das plastische Werk* (wie in Anm. 17), S. 37–47.

121. Dieses Relief wurde von Spies in den Winter 1906–07 datiert, *Picasso: Das plastische Werk* (wie in Anm. 17), S. 326, Abb. 11, S. 372. Doch die Ähnlichkeit der Haarfrisur und vor allem der roheren Ausführung mit dem Cerro-Kopf, den Picasso im Frühjahr 1907 erwarb □ 312, zwingen mich, es in diese Zeit zu datieren.

122. Wenn Picasso ozeanische Kunst gesehen hat, dann in den Sammlungen Derains, Matisse' oder Vlamincks. Bei Untersuchungen zu ihren ersten Erwerbungen wird die ozeanische Kunst nie erwähnt. Insofern aber der Ausdruck »art nègre« sowohl ozeanische als auch afrikanische Kunst umfaßt und die beiden häufig verwechselt wurden, ist nicht auszuschließen, daß auch ozeanische Kunst gekauft wurde.

123. Johnson, »Primitivism in the Early Sculpture of Picasso« (wie in Anm. 14), S. 66, 67.

124. Als Johnson das Stück untersuchte, waren nur Spuren der Farbe übrig, vielleicht weil das Kind, dem sie geschenkt worden war (die spätere Mme. André Masson), damit wirklich als Puppe spielte. Heute scheinen noch weniger Farbreste erhalten zu sein.

125. Spies, *Sculpture by Picasso* Übersetzung des dt. Katalogs (siehe Anm. 17), New York 1971, S. 23.

126. Diesen Kopf soll Arensberg von F. B. Haviland gekauft haben, der ein Freund Picassos und Brancusis war und über De Zayas mit dem Kreis um Guillaume in Verbindung stand. Picassos *FANG*-Figur ist in einem Photo seines Ateliers am Boulevard de Clichy in ihrer Silhouette vor einem Fenster zu sehen (Musée Picasso).

127. Seit 1908 fand sich eine beträchtliche Zahl *BAMBARA*-Objekte in Frankreich, obwohl es keinen Hinweis auf den spezifischen Maskentyp gibt, der unter □ 394 zu sehen ist.

128. Siehe »From Narrative to ›Iconic‹ in Picasso« (wie in Anm. 31), S. 620–22.

129. In einem Brief an mich vom 15. Dezember 1982 ist Daix der festen Meinung, daß sich Matisse seit 1905 für Rousseaus Kunst interessierte, und zitiert im Hinblick auf eine mögliche Verbindung zwischen Matisse' *Rosa Zwiebeln* von 1905 und den Stilleben Rousseaus Barr, *Matisse: His Art and His Public*, New York, The Museum of Modern Art, 1951, S. 77.

Offenbar spielte das Werk Rousseaus zumindest eine gewisse Rolle für den durch Vereinfachung der Mittel gekennzeichneten Übergang Matisse' vom Fauvismus zu seinem ganz persönlichen Stil im Spätjahr 1906 (der eigentliche Unterschied zwischen den beiden Fassungen des *Matrosen*). Sie war jedoch nicht so entscheidend wie die Rolle Gauguins oder Cézannes sowie unterschiedlichster »primitiver« Kunst, die Matisse bereits sammelte.

Das Werk, das für mich am besten Matisse' verallgemeinerten Primitivismus des Winters 1906–07 verdeutlicht, ist *Marguerite* □ 322, das sich Picasso bei einem Austausch von Gemälden kurz nach der Vollendung auswählte. Einige Kritiker deuteten Picassos Wahl dieses scheinbar unbeholfenen, einfachen und naiven Porträts von Matisse als einen Versuch, Matisse bloßzustellen, indem er (Picasso) in seinem Atelier einen schwachen Matisse zur Schau stellte. Man braucht aber nur Margueritas Kopf auf diesem ganz außergewöhnlichen kleinen Gemälde mit den nach Gosol entstandenen Arbeiten Picassos zu vergleichen, ja mit den iberischen Köpfen in der Mitte der *Demoiselles*, um zu erkennen, warum Picasso dieses Gemälde anderen Werken Matisse' vorzog. Matisse' *Marguerite* entstand zu einem Zeitpunkt (Anfang 1907), als »primitiv« für die Fauvisten eine Vielzahl »archaischer«, oft exotischer Stile, »art nègre«, Gauguin und Rousseau umfaßte, während damit für Picasso zunächst die archaische iberische Kunst und erst in zweiter Linie Gauguin gemeint war. Erst später, über ein Jahr nach seinem Offenbarungserlebnis im Zusammenhang mit der »art nègre« (Juni 1907), wurde Picassos Werk von Rousseau beeinflußt; wie schon bei Matisse war das Werk Rousseaus als Muster einer Vereinfachung im Moment eines größeren stilistischen Übergangs wirksam. Daix erkennt völlig richtig, daß das Interesse Matisse' und Picassos für Rousseau »ganz natürlich aus ihrem Interesse für die ›primitive‹ Kunst resultiert«.

130. Die Verwandtschaft der letzten Phase von Picassos Iberianismus (Frühsommer 1907) mit dem Stil von Matisse' *Marguerite* wird noch deutlicher, wenn man dieses Bildnis mit einem der Köpfe in der Mitte der *Demoiselles* vergleicht □ 301, 321. Die beiden Werke liegen höchstens ein paar Monate auseinander.

131. Eine Untersuchung der Überarbeitung der *Drei Frauen* bei Rubin, W., »Cézannism and the Beginnings of Cubism« in *Cézanne: The Late Work*, Rubin (Hrsg.), New York, The Museum of Modern Art, 1977, S. 184–88.

132. »L'Art nègre« (wie in Anm. 11), S. 119.

133. Zu Lipchitz' Bericht siehe Wilkinson, S. 436 ff. im vorliegenden Buch.

134. Vauxcelles, L., »Exposition Braque: Chez Kahnweiler, 28 rue Vignon« in *Gil Blas*, 14. November 1908, Nachdruck in Fry, E. F., *Cubism*, London 1966, S. 50.

135. Es steht außer Frage, daß Braque um 1908 eine Reihe afrikanischer Plastiken besaß. Dennoch ist die von Habasque geäußerte und von Paudrat zitierte Vermutung, S. 148, S. 182,

Anm. 50, Braque habe sein erstes afrikanisches Objekt 1905 gekauft, äußerst fragwürdig. Dies hieße, er hätte schon vor Matisse mit dem Sammeln begonnen, während doch wohl Matisse' 1906 begonnene Sammlung Braque als Vorbild diente. Die allgemein übliche Datierung solcher »Erstsammlungen« in das Jahr 1905 kommt daher, daß das Jahr 1905 jahrzehntelang als der Zeitpunkt galt, an dem Matisse, Derain und Vlaminck zu sammeln anfingen. Heute wissen wir, daß es das Jahr 1906 war.

136. Siehe Leonard, S. E., *Henri Rousseau and Max Weber*, New York 1970.

137. Eine eingehende Besprechung bei Paudrat, S. 148ff., und Flam, S. 225ff.

138. Diese Meinung vertritt u. a. Laude, und die meisten Autoren sind ihm gefolgt. Sie geht zurück auf Tériades 1951 erschienene Fassung von Matisse' Bericht über die Ereignisse bei Gertrude Stein im Sommer 1906. In diesem Interview, »Matisse Speaks« in *Art News Annual* 21, 1952, Nachdruck in Flam, J. D., *Matisse on Art*, London 1973, S. 134, wird behauptet, daß Picasso von dem afrikanischen Objekt in Erstaunen versetzt war, das ihm Matisse zeigte (sehr wahrscheinlich die *Vili*-Figur □ 260, siehe Paudrat, S. 151). Das Interview Tériades, das Flam mir gegenüber als »unzuverlässig« bezeichnete, zeigt Matisse ohne die für ihn kennzeichnende Diskretion; Flam betrachtet es als »verderbten Text«. Er glaubt, daß das Interview Courthions aus dem Jahr 1942 zuverlässiger ist. Sowohl Flam als auch Paudrat hatten Zugang zu unveröffentlichten Teilen dieses Interviews, das von Matisse »gelesen und gebilligt« wurde. Matisse sagt darin nur: »Picasso est arrivé. Nous avons causé. C'est là que Picasso a remarqué la sculpture nègre. C'est pourquoi Gertrude Stein en parle« (mein Dank gilt Flam für diesen Hinweis). Siehe auch Flam, S. 246, Anm. 44, 47.

Wenn Picasso über das afrikanische Objekt »erstaunt« gewesen wäre (was besonders unwahrscheinlich ist, wenn es wirklich die *Vili*-Figur war), hätte er sich sicherlich damals schon für afrikanische Kunst zu interessieren begonnen. Stattdessen dauerte es noch ein halbes Jahr – und solange sind auch keinerlei Anzeichen für primitive Einflüsse in seinem Werk feststellbar –, bis er mit dem Sammeln anfing.

139. Als ich Picasso nach dieser Zusammenkunft fragte, antwortete er, er habe Matisse' afrikanischem Objekt keine besondere Bedeutung beigemessen, und er wies darauf hin, daß seine »Offenbarung« später stattgefunden habe (wobei er dann für die unterschiedlichsten Formen afrikanischer und ozeanischer Objekte aufgeschlossen war).

140. Die Entstehungszeit dieses unvollendeten Gemäldes ist nicht dokumentiert, doch aufgrund stilistischer Erwägung vermute ich im Winter 1906–07, was mit Matisse' damaligem Interesse für die *Vili*-Figur übereinstimmen würde. Pierre Schneider wird es in seinem in Kürze erscheinenden Buch über Matisse auf 1907–08 datieren.

141. Wie ich in der Einleitung anmerkte, war Matisse' Geschmack in Bezug auf afrikanische Kunst konservativ. Die von ihm bevorzugten »klassischen« Objekte hätte man fast für ägyptisch halten können (was auch geschah) statt als Werke der *Baga*, *Kota* und *Grebo*, die Picasso so schätzte.

142. Nach meinen Aufzeichnungen, siehe Anm. 86, spottete Picasso über Matisse' Gleichsetzung des Afrikanischen mit dem Ägyptischen und sagte etwa folgendes: »Matisse wußte nicht, was an der afrikanischen Kunst wirklich gut war.«

143. Picasso besaß und bewunderte eine weiße *Shira-Punu*-Maske, eine *Shango*-Maske und einige andere Objekte in dem mehr »klassischen« Geschmack Matisse'. Man sollte auch nicht vergessen, daß Matisse – zumindest später, einige Zeit nach der hier besprochenen Phase – zwei *Baga*-Figuren und eine Plastik aus Neuirland erwarb, Objekte also, die dem »Klassischen« fernstehen. Dennoch wies mich L. Delectorskaya nachdrücklich darauf hin, daß die Megapode-Geistermaske von den Neuen Hebriden □ 467, die Matisse von einem Freund erhalten hatte und dann an Picasso weitergab, für Matisse' Geschmack bei primitiver Kunst nicht typisch gewesen sei.

144. In »Histoire anecdotique du cubisme« (wie in Anm. 52), S. 41–61 (nach Fry, *Cubism*, wie in Anm. 134, S. 90, wurde *La Jeune Peinture française* bis zum April 1912 geschrieben und im Herbst veröffentlicht) gab Salmon so zu erkennen, daß die *Demoiselles* (die als »grande toile« angesprochen werden) nach der Vollendung des Gemäldes *Knabe mit Pfeife* (Ende 1905) angefangen wurden und sechs Figuren umfaßten. In *L'Art vivant*, 1920, S. 109–18, sagt er über die Anfänge nichts Genaues und spricht von »aux environs de 1908« wie von »dès 1906«, wohingegen er in seinem Aufsatz zur »Exposition Metzinger« in *L Europe nouvelle*, Januar 1919, S. 139, die »grande toile« auf »un peu après 1906« datiert. In *Souvenirs sans fin* datiert Salmon sein von Picasso 1907 gemaltes Porträt falsch, Paris 1961. S. 185.

145. Die einzige Ausnahme bildet ein von C. Zervos undatiert veröffentlichtes Photo, das Picassos Atelier, Rue Ravignan 13, zeigt. Man erkennt darauf das neben zwei Zeichnungen und einem Gemälde vermerkte Datum »1907«, »Œuvres et images inédites de la jeunesse de Picasso« in *Cahiers d'art* 25, Nr. 2, 1950, S. 278. W. Spies bildet in *Picasso: Das plastische Werk* (wie in Anm. 17, S. 42) ein Photo aus Claude Picassos Archiven ab, das – wenn auch ohne Datumsvermerk – mit dem von Zervos identisch ist, das er »um 1907« datiert.

146. Als ich mit den Mitarbeitern des Musée Picasso an der geplanten Ausstellung »Autour des *Demoiselles d'Avignon*« arbeitete, kamen mir alle Photos aus den Archiven, die Stammesobjekte zeigen, zu Gesicht. Das Musée Picasso wird diese Photos später veröffentlichen. Angesichts ihrer geringen Zahl und ihrer Entstehung nach Bateau-Lavoir sagen sie nicht viel über Picassos erste Erwerbung aus. Die Archive des Musée Picasso umfassen jedoch Briefe und weiteres Material aus diesen Jahren (das vom Archivar noch durchgesehen wird), das weiteres Licht auf Picassos frühe Käufe von Stammesobjekten werfen könnte.

147. Heymann war 1907 der einzige Händler, der auf Stammeskunst spezialisiert war. Irgendwann bevor Picasso das Tiki kaufte, erhielt der deutsche Ethnologe K. von den Steinen eine Aufnahme davon; er veröffentlichte sie später in seinem monumentalen Kompendium der Kunst der Marquesasinseln, *Die Marquesaner und ihre Kunst*, Berlin 1928, Bd. 3, nicht paginiert, Abb. 13a und b, als »in Händlerbesitz«. Da K. von den Steinen das Photo von einem Händler bekam – und es mußte ein Händler sein, von dem er wußte, daß er Stammeskunst führte –, kann eigentlich nur Heymann in Frage kommen.

148 Da melanesische Objekte weniger plastisch, dafür aber phantastischer und »surrealer« sind, überrascht es nicht, daß Picasso Objekte wie seine Maske von der Torresstraße □ 432 in den 20er und 30er Jahren gekauft haben soll, als sein eigenes Werk dem Surrealismus nahestehende Ziele verfolgte.

149 Duncan, D. D., *The Private World of Picasso*, New York 1958, S. 36–37, 41, 67, 72, 109 *Besuche bei Picasso* (Photos von S. und A. Rosengart), Luzern, Galerie Rosengart, 1973, S. 17.

150 Keine Nachweise gibt es für Käufe auf Flohmärkten. Möglicherweise tauchen einige Dokumente (etwa schriftliche Angebote) in den Archiven des Musée Picasso auf, die mit bekannten Objekten in Beziehung stehen. Die Wahrscheinlichkeit dafür ist gering, u. a. weil die geographischen und Stammesbezeichnungen, die die Händler vor dem 1. Weltkrieg benutzten, fast immer falsch sind – was es äußerst schwierig macht, Namen und Objekte einander zuzuordnen

151. Zu meinen Vorbehalten, Picassos Gruppe von Stammesobjekten »Sammlung« zu nennen, siehe S. 22.

152. Laude, *La Peinture française* (wie in Anm. 71), S. 116–17, Anm. 92. Laude gibt kein genaues Datum an, sondern sagt lediglich, daß Tzara die Objekte in Picassos Atelier in »Antibes« gesehen habe. Höchstwahrscheinlich sah Tzara Picassos Objekte in dessen Villa La Californie in Cannes (und nicht in Antibes, wo er nie ein Atelier hatte); sie waren bis zu seinem Umzug nach La Californie im Jahr 1955 in Kisten gelagert worden.

153. Verkäufe einzelner Stücke für bis zu 30000 Francs erwähnte F. W. Eddy in der *Sunday World* vom 29. Oktober 1916 bei seiner Besprechung der Ausstellung afrikanischer Negerplastik, die M. de Zayas für The Modern Gallery eingerichtet hatte; zitiert von Naumann, Einleitung und Anmerkung zu »How, When, and Why« (wie in Anm. 60), S. 110.

154. Nach J. Rewald zahlte die Familie Meyer 1912 und nochmals 1917 je 10000 Dollar an Vollard für große, bedeutende Bilder Cèzannes (heute in der National Gallery, Washington, D. C.).

155. In dem von Gertrude Stein der Yale University nachgelassenen Briefwechsel, der jetzt in der Beinecke Rare Book and Manuscript Library aufbewahrt wird, finden sich sechs Briefe und eine Postkarte von Picasso an Gertrude Stein (die damals in Nîmes lebte) aus dem Zeitraum vom Dezember 1917 (?) bis zum 8. Juni 1918, die seinen Wunsch, sie möge »statues nègres« für ihn kaufen, betreffen. Mein Dank gilt Margaret Potter, die mich auf diesen Briefwechsel aufmerksam machte.

156. Dies ist das allgemein anerkannte Datum, obwohl das Photo möglicherweise Anfang 1909 aufgenommen wurde. Siehe Fry, E. F., »Cubism 1907–1908: An Early Eyewitness Account« in *The Art Bulletin* 48, Nr. 1, März 1966, S. 70–73.

157. Es steht außer Frage, daß Picassos besitzergreifende Art gegenüber diesen Objekten mit dem zu tun hatte, was er ihre magische »Befrachtung« nannte. Ein Objekt, das zu seinem innersten Lebenskreis gehörte, einem andern zu geben, hätte in den Augen dieses abergläubischen

Künstlers bedeutet, dieser Person eine Art Macht über ihn zu verleihen. Meines Wissens wurde kein Objekt, daß Picasso besaß, je verschenkt oder verkauft – wenn er sich wohl auch leichter von einem spät erworbenen Objekt getrennt hätte (oder einem Objekt, das ihm geschenkt worden war) als von seinen ersten Erwerbungen.

158. Eine Abbildung eines solchen Objekts bei Wassing, R. S., *African Art: Its Background and Traditions,* übers. v. D. Imber, New York 1968, S. 46.

159. Meine Besuche in den Depots der wichtigsten europäischen Museen für Völkerkunde ließen den Eindruck entstehen, daß eine große Zahl (wenn nicht sogar die Mehrzahl) der in der Frühzeit erworbenen Stammesobjekte nicht für rituelle Zwecke verwendet wurde. Wieviele davon ungebraucht waren, weil sie für Kolonialbewohner, Seeleute oder Ethnologen angefertigt wurden, läßt sich unmöglich sagen.

160. Olivier, F., *Picasso et ses amis*, Paris 1933, S. 170 (der Zeitraum 1910–14): »Picasso aimait particulièrement un petit masque de femme à qui la peinture blanche du visage, ressortant sur la couleur bois de la coiffure, donnait une expression étrangement douce.«

161. Dies in dem Gespräch, bei dem er Matisse' Ansicht über die afrikanische Kunst abschätzig beurteilte und einige »kleine, sehr abstrakte Metallfiguren« und »großnasige Masken« als »einfallsreich« herausstellte (meine Umschreibung). Diese Bemerkung, siehe Anm. 86, ist nach meiner Ansicht auf die *Kota*-Reliquiarfiguren sowie die Nimba-Masken und -Figuren der *Baga* zu beziehen.

162. Ein Beispiel für die Qualität der letztgenannten Werke ist die von Guillaume an Stieglitz übersandte Reliquiarfigur, die man auf dem Photo ☐ 193 unten sieht.

163. *Primitive Art Newsletter* 5, Nr. 6, Juni 1982, S. 7.

164. Clouzot und Level, *L'Art nègre et l'art océanien* (wie in Anm. 76), Tafel xx: Masque pahouin [*Fang*], Höhe 35 cm; und Tafel xxxiv: Masque Côte d'Ivoire [*Guere*], Höhe 25 cm; beide unter »Sammlung Picasso« aufgeführt.

165. Wenn auch grundsätzlich möglich, ist es zu bezweifeln, daß ein Dokument, das mit diesen Masken in Beziehung steht, in den Archiven auftaucht. Beide Werke gehören zu einem Typ, der schon vor 1914 in Umlauf war. Eine *Guere* dieses Typs, die Picasso gehörte, Clouzot und Level, ebenda, Tafel xxxiv, die dieser so ähnlich ist, daß sie wohl vom selben Künstler stammt, wurde von De Zayas (der sie zweifellos von Guillaume hatte) in The Modern Gallery, New York, im Jahr 1916 zum Verkauf angeboten. Sie ist abgebildet bei Naumann, »How, When, and Why« (wie in Anm. 60), S. 73.

166. Zitiert in »Braque 1912–1918: Repères chronologiques« in *Georges Braque: Les Papiers Collés*, Ausstellungskatalog, Musée National d'Art Moderne, Centre Georges Pompidou, Paris, 17. Juni – 27. September 1982, S. 180.

167. Fry, E. F., »Les Dimensions du modernisme«, Mitschrift einer Reihe von vier Vorlesungen vom Mai–Juni 1982 am Musée National d'Art Moderne, Centre Georges Pompidou, Paris, in *CNAC Magazine*, hrsg. v. Centre National d'Art et de Culture Georges Pompidou, Nr. 16, Juli–August 1983, S. 18.

168. Fry nahm an, daß die angebliche »Entdeckung« einer »Wobé«-(*Grebo*-) Maske Picasso zu seiner Gestaltung des Schallochs der *Gitarre* anregte.

Doch abgesehen davon, daß Picasso seine weniger gute *Grebo* sicherlich schon besaß, kannte er weitere im Trocadéro, in der Sammlung Kahnweilers und anderswo. *Grebo*-Masken gehörten zu den in Paris im ersten Jahrzehnt des Jahrhunderts bekannteren Typen.

169. J. Kerchache, der Gelegenheit hatte, die Maske ☐ 29 zu untersuchen, bestätigte mir dies.

170. Da kreisförmige Augen allen *Grebo*-Masken dieses Typs gemeinsam sind und Picasso diese Idee abstrahierte, kann man zwischen den Objekten keine einfache Eins-zu-Eins-Beziehung herstellen.

171. Vallier, D., »Braque, la peinture et nous« in *Cahiers d'art* 29, Nr. 1–2, Oktober 1954, S. 14.

172. Malraux, *La Tête d'obsidienne* (wie in Anm. 8), S. 19.

173. Das Wort »Collage« wird oft sowohl für *papiers collés* als auch für das Zusammenkleben fremden Materials (Öltuch auf Leinwand wie bei Picassos *Stilleben mit Rohrstuhl*) sowie das Montieren verschiedener Materialien gebraucht (das Seemannsseil, das für dasselbe Werk als Rahmen verwendet wurde). Das *papier collé* ist aber, insoweit einheitliches Material verwendet wird, klassischer als die anderen Formen der Collage und sollte von diesen unterschieden werden. Für Braques Konservatismus und Klassizismus ist typisch, daß er ausschließlich mit dem *papier collé* arbeitete. Alle anderen Varianten der Collage sind allein Picassos Erfindung – es sind diejenigen, die Ähnlichkeiten mit der Stammeskunst aufweisen.

174. Solche Analogien finden sich in Braques Werk seltener und werden nie so weit geführt. Als Picasso mir die *Gitarre* für das Museum of Modern Art übergab, baute er sie wie eine sitzende Figur in einem Stuhl auf, und Jacqueline mußte sie so photographieren.

175. Der mehr bildhauerische, taktile, »sachliche« Kubismus von Ende 1908 und von 1909 steht im Vergleich zu Picassos Arbeiten von 1907–08 der Stammeskunst zwar ferner, ist ihr aber dennoch enger verbunden als die malerischen Formen des hochanalytischen Kubismus, bei dem der Reduktionismus seinem Wesen nach dem – wie es Picasso nannte – »Realismus« der Stammeskunst ferner steht. In den Jahren 1911–12 gewinnt eine andere Art Realismus die Oberhand, siehe Rubin, *Picasso in the Collection* [wie in Anm. 106], zu Äußerungen des Künstlers über die »Realität« im Hochkubismus, S. 72.

176. Siehe Richardson, J. (Hrsg.), *Picasso: An American Tribute*, Ausstellungskatalog, New York, Public Education Association, 1962, nicht paginiert.

177. Trotz der Ähnlichkeit machen es die anderen Formen dieser vorgetäuschten Maske recht deutlich, daß es sich nicht um die Grebo-Maske ☐ 417 gehandelt haben kann.

178. Kahnweiler, D.-H., »L'Art nègre et le cubisme« in *Présence africaine* Nr. 3, 1948, S. 367–77.

179. Kahnweiler verwechselt hier die ideographische Reduktion (der Stammeskunst) mit dem Verjahren des Anschneidens (im Kubismus).

180. Abgebildet bei Rubin, *Picasso in the Collection* (wie in Anm. 106), S. 60.

181. Daß damit die Gestaltungsmöglichkeiten eingeschränkt waren, wurde Picasso in diesem Moment klar, und eigentlich arbeitete keine seiner späteren Plastiken trotz ihrer Vielfalt mit dem vom Impressionismus und von Rodin angeregten Spiel malerischen Lichts.

182. In meinen Aufzeichnungen findet sich folgender (von mir paraphrasierte) Satz Picassos: »Es war sinnlos, mit dieser Art Plastik weiterzumachen.« Jahrelang habe ich untersucht, was er damit genau meinte. Er war eindeutig von Aspekten des modellierten *Weiblichen Kopfes (Fernande)* enttäuscht, und seine Bemerkung spiegelt vielleicht nur seine Ermüdung über ein Projekt, das sich als Sackgasse erwies, wider.

183. Goldwater charakterisierte einmal den *Weiblichen Kopf (Fernande)* zu Recht als »Rodins Kunst der Vertiefung und der Erhebung«, *What is Modern Sculpture?*, New York, The Museum of Modern Art, 1970, S. 42.

184. Ich akzeptiere Frys Korrektur des Datums für das Modell der *Gitarre* (Herbst 1912 statt Anfang 1912, wie Picasso meinte).

185. Siehe Einleitung, S. 72ff.

186. Siehe Einleitung, S. 27ff.

187. Abgebildet bei Spies, *Picasso: Das plastische Werk* (wie in Anm. 17), S. 329, Abb. 47.

188. Abgebildet bei Spies, Sculpture by Picasso (wie in Anm. 125), S. 132, 133.

189. Ich will damit sagen, daß sich Picasso sicherlich dessen bewußt war, daß der frühe Kubismus zwei wichtige unmittelbare Quellen hatte: Die bedeutendere davon war Cézannes Malerei, die vom ideographischen Reduktionismus der Stammeskunst abgewandelt wurde.

190. Obwohl dies nicht gleich auffällt, da der Mund vergrößert und senkrecht gestellt wurde, steht die Identität dieses Zuges außer Frage. Die Nase bildet ein Dreieck, das ungefähr von der oberen Mitte des Gesichtsvierecks ausgeht, die Augen sind runde Höhlen zu seiten der Nase.

191. Ich konnte keine Abbildungen dieses Maskentyps finden, die in Paris vor 1930 in Gelehrtenkreisen und noch weniger in Künstlerkreisen verfügbar gewesen wären.

192. Dies war die *Kota*-Reliquiarfigur, die Giacometti von Serge Brignoni gekauft hatte, siehe Krauss, S. 542, Anm. 13.

193. Diese Deutung, die mir schon früher aufgrund von Ähnlichkeiten zwischen *Frauenkopf* ☐ 453 und den »knochigen« Badenden, die Olga darstellten, klar wurde, wird durch die Skizze bestätigt ☐ 451, in der eine Frühform vom *Frauenkopf* (rechts auf der Skizze) »spiegelbildlich« als schreiende Olga erkennbar ist (Picasso bezeichnete sie gegenüber Penrose so), die fast so aussieht wie in *Frauenbüste mit Selbstbildnis* von 1929, *Picasso: A Retrospektive* (wie in Anm. 5), S. 272.

194. Die erste davon ist *Die Umarmung*, 1925, ebenda, S. 257.

195. Etwa in *Sitzende Badende*, 1930, ebenda, S. 279.

196. Penrose vertraute mir an – er verlangte ein heute nicht mehr nötiges Stillschweigen darüber (Picasso lebte damals noch) –, daß Olga in Phasen, wo sie außer sich war, Picassos Leben bedrohte.

197. Diese Feststellung beruht darauf, daß ich etwa siebzig von Picassos mehr als hundert Stammesobjekten gesehen und Photos von einigen weiteren untersucht habe.

Metallene und metallüberzogene Stammesobjekte sind verhältnismäßig selten. Picasso hat zwar vielleicht eine *Kota*-Reliquiarfigur mehr besessen, als wir meinen, man kann sich aber kaum vorstellen, welches andere metallene oder metallverkleidete Objekt er in den frühen Jahren bei sich gehabt haben könnte, sieht man einmal von den *Marka*-Masken ab – von denen er nach meinen Untersuchungen keine besaß.

198. Die große weibliche Nimba-Maske wurde – im Gegensatz zu den »nimbaköpfigen« *Baga*-Figuren, die beiderlei Geschlechts sein können, siehe Anm. 97 – weitgehend als Symbol jahreszeitlicher Wiedergeburt und menschlicher Fortpflanzung verstanden. Im allgemeinen gab Picasso wenig auf ethnologische Besonderheiten, doch M. Leiris versicherte mir, daß Picasso die übliche Deutung der Nimba-Figur kannte.

199. Gonzalez begann 1928 Picassos Metallfiguren meist nach Zeichnungen auszuführen. Die Ausführung des *Frauenkopfes* □ 453 wurde für Gonzalez der Ausgangspunkt seiner neuen Karriere als avantgardistischer Metallbildhauer. Die meisten seiner Arbeiten haben mit Picassos »in die Luft gezeichneten« Skulpturen zu tun. Gonzalez schuf jedoch auch eine Reihe von »Masken« □ 447–449, die weniger Picasso verpflichtet sind und Gonzalez' eigenes Interesse an der Stammeskunst widerspiegeln.

200. In meinen Aufzeichnungen findet sich ein Hinweis darauf, daß Picasso sie 1928 erwarb, aber ich kann die Quelle dafür nicht wiederfinden. J. Kerchache weist darauf hin, daß sie auf der Exposition d'Art Africain et d'Art Océanien in der Galerie du Théâtre Pigalle, Paris 1930, unter »Sammlung Pablo Picasso« ausgestellt wurde (Katalog Nr. 18).

201. Siehe S. 285.

202. Siehe Anm. 97.

203. Penrose bemerkt, *Picasso: His Life and Work* (wie in Anm. 114), S. 242: »Diese [Nimba]

□ 475 *›Arm mit Hand‹, Osterinsel, Holz, Länge 44,5 cm. Privatbesitz. Ehemals Sammlung Pablo Picasso. Ausschnitt aus einer Aufnahme von Brassaï, 1943.*

hatte ihr Echo in den monumentalen Gipsköpfen in den Ställen über den Hof.«

Für Picasso waren der formbare Charakter des Tons, aus dem diese Skulpturen modelliert wurden, und des Gipses, in den man sie umarbeitete, eine wichtige Ausdrucksdimension, wie ich im Text andeutete. Trotz ihrer Größe haben die Gipsskulpturen etwas Schwereloses und Heiteres, das Picassos Bild von Marie-Thérèse widerspiegelt (wie es dann in *Badende mit Strandball*, 1932, fast metaphorisch zum Ausdruck kommt, siehe Rubin, *Picasso: A Retrospective* (wie in Anm. 5), S. 295. Die Bronzen verlieren einen großen Teil dieser Wirkung. Picasso war sich dessen bewußt, wie das folgende Zitat belegt, aus Brassaï, *Picasso and Company*, Garden City 1966, S. 51. Übersetzung der französischen Originalausgabe *Conversations avec Picasso* von F. Price. Picasso: »Sie [die modellierten Skulpturen der frühen 30er Jahre] waren in Gips schöner. Zuerst wollte ich gar nichts davon hören, sie in Bronze gießen zu lassen. Aber Sabartés sagte immer wieder: ›Gips verdirbt . . . Es muß etwas Haltbares sein . . . Bronze hält ewig . . .‹ Er überredete mich, sie in Metall gießen zu lassen. Und schließlich gab ich nach. Was halten Sie davon?«
Brassaï: »Einige haben bei dem Wechsel verloren. Besonders Ihre monumentalen Köpfe.«

204. »A *Life* Round Table on Modern Art«, veranstaltet im Penthouse des Museum of Modern Art von R. W. Davenport in Zusammenarbeit mit W. Sargent, in *Life Magazine*, 11. Oktober 1948, S. 64.

205. Mein Dank gilt Dr. G. MacDonald, Direktor des National Museum of Man, National Museum of Canada, der meine Fragen nach der Ikonographie der Objekte von der Nordküste beantwortete.

206. Wie Meyer Schapiro in einem Gespräch mit mir bemerkte.

207. Abgebildet in *Arts primitifs dans les ateliers d'artistes*, Ausstellungskatalog, einführende Texte von G. Picon und J. Laude, Musée de l'Homme, Paris 1967, Tafel 41.

208. Loeb, P., »Une main« in *Voyages à travers la peinture*, Paris 1946, S. 29–30: »Je ne m'en serais jamais séparé, mais Picasso la vit et la désira.«

209. Ebenda, S. 30.

210. »40,000 Years of Modern Art. A Comparison of Primitive and Modern Art«, The Institute of Contemporary Arts, London 1949.

211. Brief R. Penrose' vom 30. September 1982 an mich.

212. Dies ist der »Temes Malau« oder »Megapode Geist«. Die Maske, bei der das Oberteil in dem Beispiel von Matisse/Picasso fehlt, ist normalerweise 2,5 m hoch. Die Zeichnung einer vollständigen Maske bei Harrison, T. H., *Savage Civilization*, New York 1937, S. 340 (mein Dank gilt D. Newton für diesen Hinweis).

□ 476 *Constantin Brancusi, ›Karyatide‹ (Caryatid), Zwei Ansichten, 1914–26, Holz, Höhe 166 cm. Fogg Art Museum, Harvard University, Cambridge.*

Sidney Geist

Constantin Brancusi

Der in einer 1913 entstandenen Holzskulptur Brancusis sichtbare afrikanische Einfluß wird im allgemeinen als der Beginn seines Primitivismus betrachtet. Doch ist bereits in einer Serie von Steinarbeiten, die Brancusi 1907–08 ausführte, eine Tendenz zu einem allgemeineren Primitivismus zu erkennen. Ende April 1907 hatte er ein Atelier im Parterre eines Hauses gemietet, um einen Auftrag für ein Grabdenkmal in Rumänien auszuführen. Nach Beendigung der modellierten Skulptur *Das Gebet*, die Teil dieses Auftrags war, und der Ausführung verschiedener Köpfe in Ton widmete er sich für den Rest des Jahres der Bildhauerei mit dem Meißel, die ihn von da an eigentlich fast ausschließlich interessierte.[1]

Die 1907 entstandenen Arbeiten in Stein und Marmor umfassen sechs Köpfe und Büsten, von denen fünf realistische Kinderporträts sind.[2] Vier der letztgenannten Werke weisen eine grobe Behandlung auf, die vom Spitzmeißel herrührt, ein Werkzeug, mit dem normalerweise eine Skulptur begonnen oder im groben behauen wird. Der *Mädchenkopf* muß wohl gegen Ende des Jahres 1907 entstanden sein □ 477, ein Werk, das Brancusi als »Première pierre directe, 190« – mit fehlender Jahresangabe – kennzeichnete.[3] Danach entstand anscheinend *Der Kuß*, wohl Ende des Jahres begonnen und Anfang 1908 vollendet □ 348.[4] Diese Aufzählung soll zeigen, daß Brancusi, als erst einmal *Das Gebet* vollendet war, in der zweiten Hälfte des Jahres 1907 intensiv nach einer »direkten« Form der Bildhauerei suchte und daß er diese in dem frischen, sicher gearbeiteten *Mädchenkopf* realisierte (die fünf Kinderköpfe sind verschwunden). Die volle künstlerische Verwirklichung gelang mit der Skulptur *Der Kuß.*

Es ist durchaus möglich, daß Brancusis Gedanken nach dem Besuch der Gauguin-Retrospektive im Salon d'Automne, die vom 6. Oktober bis 15. November 1906 dauerte, in diese neue Richtung gingen.[5] In dieser umfassenden und außerordentlich einflußreichen Ausstellung wird er Gauguins primitivistische Arbeiten in Stein und Holz gesehen haben, ein plastisches Werk, für das Künstler der jüngeren Generation, Matisse, Picasso und Derain, voller Bewunderung waren. 1907 schuf Picasso die Holzplastik *Stehende Figur* □ 328 und nach Angaben D.-H. Kahnweilers[6] Derain den *Kauernden* □ 261, eine kompakte Plastik in Kalkstein, die die Methode direkten Meißelns – die *taille directe* –, wie sie auch Gauguin anwandte, beispielhaft vorführte. Die Anziehungskraft dieses Verfahrens, in der das Kopieren eines Modells, sei es mechanisch oder nach Augenmaß, vermieden wird, liegt gerade in seiner Direktheit, der unumgänglichen Ehrlichkeit sowie der Überzeugung, daß damit eine neue, ganz dem Wesen des Steins entspringende Form entstehen könne. Es bot darüber hinaus die Möglichkeit, Rodin zu umgehen.

Wie wir sahen, arbeitete Brancusi 1907 vorwiegend an ziemlich realistischen Darstellungen, deren Oberfläche roh und grobkörnig gelassen wurde. Wenn er die Idee der *taille directe* nicht so schnell wie Picasso oder Derain aufgriff, so deshalb, weil er noch seiner langen und gründlichen Akademieausbildung in der Bildhauerei verhaftet blieb, einer strengen Disziplin, der sich weder Picasso noch Derain unterworfen hatten. Wie ich glaube, wurde ihm die Bedeutung der *taille directe* anläßlich der Ausstellung von Derains *Kauerndem* bewußt, die im September 1907 in Kahnweilers neuer Galerie an der Rue Vignon stattfand.[7]

Der Kuß und *Der Kauernde* sind sich in verschiedener Hinsicht ähnlich. Von vergleichbarer Größe, bestehen beide aus Kalkstein und sind blockhaft und symmetrisch konzipiert. Beide behandeln die nackte Figur, betonen die Hände und enthalten das Motiv der Arme, die eine Einfassung bilden. Gleichzeitig steht *Der Kuß* Gauguins primitivierendem Relief *Hina und Te Fatou* nahe □ 254, das die Retrospektive ausstellte. Brancusis *Weisheit* 1908,[8] die dem *Kuß* folgte, geht auf Figuren von Gauguin zurück, die *Bretonische Eva* und die sehr ähnliche alte Frau auf der linken Seite von *Woher kommen wir? . . .* □ 218 auf Arbeiten, die ihrerseits primitive Vorläufer haben.[9] Ich bin der Ansicht, daß der primitive Einfluß auf Brancusi, auch wenn er aus zweiter Hand kam oder sich auf dem Hintergrund einer mystischen Anschauung vollzog, nichts von seiner Bedeutung einbüßt. Die große und umfangreiche Retrospektive Gauguins, der der klangvolle Name des Künstlers und seine Flucht in ein scheinbares Paradies einen besonderen Glanz verlieh, gab den Fauvisten eine neue Orientierung und stand der Geburt von zwei Werken Brancusis hilfreich zur Seite. Sie veranlaßte Derain, Picasso und Brancusi zur *taille directe*, der wichtigsten Errungenschaft der Skulptur im ersten Jahrzehnt dieses Jahrhunderts. Rückschlüsse erlauben es, die *taille directe* – mit ihrem Verzicht auf das traditionelle Punktiergerät, der Rückkehr zur Spontaneität von Entwurf und Ausführung, ihrem Interesse an den Materialqualitäten des Steins – als ein Ergebnis primitiver Impulse zu Beginn des 20. Jahrhunderts zu betrachten.

Während Brancusi die *taille directe* nie mehr aufgab, entwickelte er nach und nach eine Kontrolle und verfeinerte Methodik, wodurch die Unmittelbarkeit seines Ansatzes verschleiert und die primitivistischen Residuen seiner Anfänge entfernt wurden. 1913 meißelte er die Holzplastik *Der erste Schritt* □ 481, womit er eine lange Reihe von Arbeiten im Werkstoff

□ 477 *Constantin Brancusi, ›Mädchenkopf‹ (Tête de Jeune Fille), 1907, Stein. Verbleib unbekannt.*

Holz einleitete, von denen die meisten im darauffolgenden Jahrzehnt entstanden. Von Anfang an ist in Form und Beschaffenheit der Holzplastiken Brancusis ein neuer Geist sichtbar: eine Rückkehr zum Primitivismus der frühesten Steinarbeiten in *taille directe*, die aber jetzt von einer in der Zwischenzeit erworbenen Kontrolle beherrscht werden. Die Einflüsse, die bei diesen Holzplastiken wirksam werden, sind allerdings nicht aus zweiter Hand vermittelt; sie spiegeln ein seit langem bestehendes Interesse an der Kunst Afrikas wider.

Eine Diskussion über afrikanische Einflüsse auf Brancusi hat nur selten stattgefunden, da sie oft als gegeben hingenommen oder einfach übergangen wurden. Ein Autor bestritt primitive Einflüsse aus zwei Gründen: wegen einer »Ablehnung« afrikanischer Kunst durch Brancusi und wegen der Ähnlichkeit, die zwischen rumänischer Volkskunst und afrikanischer Stammeskunst bestehe, eine Ähnlichkeit, die den Ursprung des Einflusses auf Brancusi fraglos von Afrika in seine Heimat Rumänien verlagere. Doch sind weder die Reichweite einzelner Einflüsse noch der Zeitpunkt von Brancusis »Ablehnung« untersucht worden.[10] Dieser Vergleich afrikanischer mit rumänischer Volkskunst beschäftigt sich auch überhaupt nicht mit dem Problem des Einflusses, das bestimmte Werke Brancusis stellen.[11] In der ersten eingehenden Untersuchung dieser Fragen von Katherine Jánszky Michaelsen[12] wird die These eines afrikanischen Einflusses durch eine Reihe von sprechenden Vergleichen unterstützt, aber zugleich überbewertet, um ein klassizierendes Werk wie *Schlafende Muse* aufgrund oberflächlicher Gemeinsamkeiten – Robert Goldwater nannte sie »lookalikes« – einzubeziehen. Leider hat Goldwater in der Frage von Brancusis Afrikanismus selbst einige Verwirrung gestiftet, indem er ein Schlüsseldokument zu diesem Komplex falsch las: Jacob Epsteins 1940 erschienene Memoiren *Let There Be Sculpture*. Nach Goldwater verwahrte sich Brancusi »1912 gegenüber Epstein vor einem [afrikanischen] Einfluß, ja zerstörte fast Arbeiten, die ihm gewisse afrikanische Züge aufzuweisen schienen«.[13] Ein genaues Lesen der Stelle bei Epstein verrät aber, daß Brancusis Ausfälle gegenüber afrikanischer Skulptur nicht 1912 stattfanden, also dem Datum von Epsteins erstem Besuch in Brancusis Atelier, sondern »zwanzig Jahre später«, als er Brancusi abermals besuchte.[14] Über dieses Treffen schreibt Epstein: »Brancusi, in dessen Frühwerk einige Arbeiten von afrikanischer Kunst beeinflußt waren, erklärt jetzt kategorisch, daß man nicht vom Afrikanischen beeinflußt werden darf; er ging sogar soweit, daß er fast eigene Werke, die ihm afrikanisierend erschienen, zerstörte.«[15] Das »jetzt« in diesem Satz, geschrieben nach dem Besuch in den frühen 30er Jahren, stellt die tatsächliche Abfolge der Ereignisse wieder her: Brancusis Interesse an afrikanischer Kunst, wie es sich erstmals 1913 zeigte, seine nachweisliche Zerstörung einiger seiner Arbeiten und seine Absage an afrikanische Einflüsse in den frühen Dreißigern.

Die ganze Frage des Afrikanismus, die Vorstellung eines von afrikanischer Kunst beeinflußten Brancusi, wird von rumänischen Kunsthistorikern geschlossen zurückgewiesen, die eigentlich jeden Einfluß außer rumänischer Volkskunst und Rodins in Abrede stellen. Es gibt keinen Anhaltspunkt bei Brancusi – weder als Mensch noch in seinem Charakter –, der eine Aversion gegen afrikanische oder primitive Kunst erklären würde. Er hatte Abgüsse klassischer Bildwerke in Bukarest kopiert und war dann zur persönlichen Weiterbildung nach Paris gegangen. Dort angekommen, war er für Anregungen stets offen. Er arbeitete eklektisch, und es zeigt sich, daß er nicht nur typische Elemente des übermächtigen Rodin, sondern auch von anderen zeitgenössischen Künstlern, von der Vielzahl öffentlicher Monumente sowie den Museen, die an Gegenständen verschiedenster Kulturen so reich waren, in sich aufnahm. Bei seiner raschen Auffassungsgabe wird er sofort die Bedeutung der Stammeskunst erkannt haben, deren Entdeckung – vergleichbar dem Japonismus etwa 50 Jahre früher – von den aufgeschlossenen Künstlern wie eine Offenbarung erlebt wurde. Wenn er sich dem direkten Einfluß afrikanischer Kunst vom Moment ihrer Entdeckung an noch fünf Jahre verschloß, so deshalb, weil ihn eine als revolutionär erlebte Methode der Steinbearbeitung ganz in Anspruch nahm.

Der erste Schritt von 1913 □ 481 ist Brancusis erste freistehende Figur. Ihre neuartige Konzeption täuscht darüber hinweg, daß sowohl Titel wie auch Thema – ein trollendes Kind – aus dem Salon stammen. Sie offenbart eine Stilisierung, die radikaler ist als bei der dritten Fassung von *Der Kuß* (1910), seinem bis dahin abstraktesten Werk.[16] *Der erste Schritt* ist eigentlich Brancusis erster Vorstoß in Richtung auf eine vollkommene Formalisierung, die er sicher von afrikanischer Skulptur erlernt hatte. Mit großer Gewißheit kann eine *Bambara*-Figur im Musée de l'Homme als unmittelbares Vorbild angesprochen werden □ 482. In beiden Arbeiten weisen die Arme, der Körper, Kopf und Hals Achsen auf, die der Maserung des Holzes folgen. Beide haben einen ausgehöhlten Mundraum mit spitz nach oben laufender Oberlippe, auch ist

□ 478 *Constantin Brancusi, ›Der Kuß‹ (Le Baiser), 1907–08, Stein, Höhe 28 cm. Muzeul de Artă, Craiova, Rumänien.*

der Kopf in beiden Fällen eiförmig. Die *Bambara*-Figur hat einen unsicheren Stand, als sei sie in dem etwas linkischen Moment einer gerade ansetzenden Bewegung erfaßt. Der erste Schritt stellt natürlich den zögernden Ablauf, wie ihn der Titel angibt, dar. Da die *Bambara*-Figur in einer von Marius de Zayas verfaßten und 1916 in New York veröffentlichten Studie über afrikanische Kunst abgebildet ist,[17] kann man darüber spekulieren, ob De Zayas aufgrund eines Hinweises von Brancusi auf das Stück aufmerksam wurde, bevor er Paris verließ. Die beiden Männer waren miteinander bekannt: Im Juli 1914 besuchten sie ein Gartenfest bei Edward Steichen außerhalb von Paris,[18] und De Zayas verkaufte später einige Arbeiten Brancusis in der Modern Gallery, New York, deren Leiter er damals war.

Der erste Schritt wurde Anfang des Jahres 1914 in der Galerie der Photo-Sezession gezeigt, deren Leiter, Alfred Stieglitz, den Mittelpunkt eines Kreises darstellte, dem auch De Zayas angehörte. Gleich bei der Rückkehr der Skulptur nach Paris zerstörte sie Brancusi und hob nur den Kopf auf □ 480, während Körper und Schenkel für den *Jünglingstorso* Vorbild waren (ca. 1917). *Der erste Schritt* ist somit der erste uns bekannte Kandidat für ein Werk, das Brancusi – wie wir annehmen – wegen seines afrikanischen Eindrucks zerstörte: es gibt keine Anhaltspunkte für eine Arbeit, die aus demselben Motiv irgendwann davor zerstört worden wäre. Wenn *Der erste Schritt* afrikanischer Plastik viel verdankt, ist diese Anleihe um so bedeutungsvoller, als sie in einem Werk gemacht wird, bei dem Brancusi ein für ihn neues Medium anwandte: Es war sein erster Schritt in der Holzbildhauerei. Ist diese Anleihe erst einmal erkannt, gilt es, das Gesamtwerk und seine Elemente zu würdigen, die darin erreichte technische Perfektion und gestalterische Eleganz, wie man sie nur selten bei primitiver Kunst und schon gar nicht bei der *Bambara*-Figur antrifft. Als es Brancusi müde war, mit prähistorischen und primitiven Bildhauern verglichen zu werden, sagte er, die Primitiven hätten es nicht verstanden, »mit so hoher Präzision bis zum Schluß zu arbeiten, wie ich es jetzt tue«.[19] Elegant entworfene und perfekt ausgeführte Beispiele afrikanischer Skulptur hatte er offenbar bis dahin noch nicht gesehen.

Der erste Schritt setzt voraus, daß sich der Bildhauer lange Zeit mit Stammeskunst beschäftigte und lange damit im Geiste

☐ 479 *Constantin Brancusi, ›Stehende Figur‹, 1914, Höhe 124 cm. Später zu ›Kleines französisches Mädchen‹ umgearbeitet.*

☐ 480 *Constantin Brancusi, Kopf von ›Der erste Schritt‹, 1913, Holz, Höhe 26 cm. Musée National d'Art Moderne, Centre National d'Art et de Culture Georges Pompidou, Paris.*

◁ ☐ 481 *Constantin Brancusi, ›Der erste Schritt‹ (Le Premier Pas), 1913, Holz, Höhe 111 cm. Mit Ausnahme des Kopfes zerstört.*

»schwanger« gegangen ist. 1955 erinnerte er sich an einen Besuch im Naturhistorischen Museum Wien, der 50 Jahre zurücklag. Wie Münsterberger vermerkte, »fielen ihm schnell wieder einige Nachzeichnungen afrikanischer Felsmalereien und verschiedene Beispiele afrikanischer . . . und ozeanischer Stammeskunst ein«. »Ihre eigentliche Wirkung«, so berichtete Brancusi Münsterberger, »entfaltete diese Kunst in Paris, wahrscheinlich zuerst bei Apollinaire oder im Atelier von Matisse«.[20] 1909, vier Jahre vor *Der erste Schritt,* hatte Brancusi Modigliani kennengelernt, der von afrikanischer Kunst begeistert war. Wie Modigliani machte auch er bald die Bekanntschaft von Dr. Paul Alexandre.[21] Wahrscheinlich sprach er 1912 auch mit Jacob Epstein über afrikanische Skulptur, der diese Kunst seit 1902 bewunderte und viel später eine umfangreiche und erlesene Sammlung zusammentrug. Als Brancusi im Juli 1913 die Allied Artists Exhibition in London besuchte,[22] wird er wohl Epsteins Besuch aus dem Vorjahr erwidert und mit ihm afrikanische Kunst gesehen haben (ebenso eigene Arbeiten von EPSTEIN, die ungeachtet späterer Dementi von afrikanischer Skulptur beeinflußt waren). Es ist auffällig, daß die Manifestation afrikanischen Einflusses in *Der erste Schritt*, obwohl seit langem vorbereitet, innerhalb weniger Monate nach den Begegnungen mit EPSTEIN erfolgte.

Der erste Schritt wurde vermutlich 1914 zerstört, weil die Figur in keiner der späteren Aufnahmen des Ateliers mehr zu sehen ist. Wenn das afrikanische Aussehen der Grund für die Zerstörung war, was ist dann von dem 1914–18 entstandenen Werk *Kleines französisches Mädchen* zu halten □ 486? Mit

□ 482 *›Figur aus Holz‹, BAMBARA (Mali), Höhe 65 cm.* ▷ *Musée de l'Homme, Paris.*

□ 483 *Constantin Brancusi, Studie zu ›Der Erste Schritt‹, 1913, Kreide, 82 x 38 cm. Museum of Modern Art, Stiftung B. und D. Scharps, New York.*

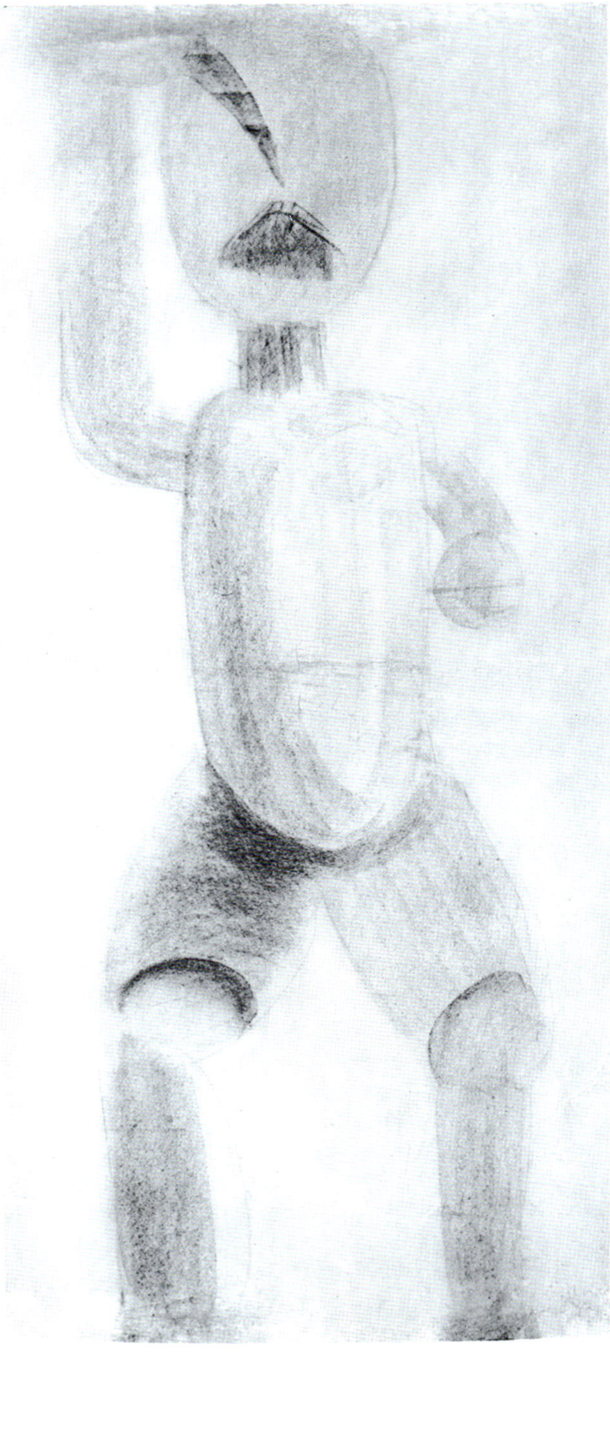

Sicherheit zeigt diese Arbeit einen noch deutlicheren afrikanischen Einfluß als die vorangegangene. *Der erste Schritt* hielt u.a. an zwei traditionellen Merkmalen fest, die in *Kleines französisches Mädchen* und überhaupt in allen späteren Arbeiten nicht mehr auftauchen: dem bruchlosen Übergang zwischen Figur und Basis sowie den großen Volumina, deren Achsen zur Maserung des Holzes nicht parallel laufen; der Verzicht auf diese Eigenheiten begünstigte BRANCUSIS Afrikanismus. (Während die Schenkel der zerstörten Figur *Der erste Schritt* diagonal gegen die Maserung des Holzes geschnitten sind, verlaufen sie in dem späteren *Jünglingstorso*, der auf dem früheren Werk aufbaut und aus einer Astgabel geschnitten ist, parallel zur Maserung.) Ungeachtet einer allgemeinen Vertikalität ist *Der erste Schritt* nach rechts geneigt, wie dies besonders an seinem vorgesetzten rechten Bein zu sehen ist. Auch dieses Charakteristikum sollte verschwinden, die Arbeiten in Holz werden von da an und über Jahrzehnte – mit Ausnahme von

□ 484 *›Helmmaske‹, SENUFO (Elfenbeinküste), Holz, Höhe 99 cm. Museum Rietberg, Zürich.*

□ 485 *›Puppe aus Holz und Perlen‹, BIJOGO, Bissagosinseln (Guinea-Bissau), Höhe 71 cm, Náprstkovo Muzeum, Prag.*

Der verlorene Sohn – wie im Falle afrikanischer Figuren genau vertikal und symmetrisch konzipiert.

Die erste Entwurfsstufe von *Kleines französisches Mädchen* □ 479 – ein Titel, der nicht von BRANCUSI stammt[23] – weist eine allgemeine Ähnlichkeit mit *Der erste Schritt* auf. Im vollendeten Werk sind die Arme verschwunden, Hals und Kopf werden durch ein sich verjüngendes Rückgrat verbunden, das über die ganze Länge mit Furchen bedeckt ist – BRANCUSIS ökonomische Lösung eines Aufbaus in Ringen, wie er in der afrikanischen Skulptur allgemein üblich ist. Obwohl nur aus wenigen und ungewöhnlichen Elementen bestehend, suggeriert die Figur in rührender Weise ein kleines Mädchen mit kurzem Rock; und doch ist sie unverkennbar afrikanisch. Der Kopf wiederholt Schädel, Augen und Nase von *Der erste Schritt*, und die Behandlung von Mund und gezacktem Haar vertieft noch dessen Afrikanismus. Wie William Rubin beobachtete, werden BRANCUSI die abstehenden Ohren und der ringartig gebildete Hals und Körper von den Helmmasken der *SENUFO* bekannt gewesen sein □ 484, die ebenfalls für den glockenähnlichen Rock von BRANCUSIS Figur als Vorbild in Frage kommen. *Kleines französisches Mädchen* hat, wie Rubin bemerkt, noch mehr Ähnlichkeit mit einer Fruchtbarkeitspuppe der *BIJOGO* in Prag □ 485, obwohl zu bezweifeln ist, daß BRANCUSI eine solche Puppe damals sehen konnte. Abbildungen dieses Werkes waren nicht erhältlich, und andere Versionen einer solchen Puppe sind viel weniger im Sinne BRANCUSIS gestaltet. Das Fehlen der Arme von BRANCUSIS Figur ist in dieser Form für eine europäische Arbeit sicherlich radikal, wohingegen es einigen Stilen Westafrikas und Zaires durchaus vertraut ist. Nicht das Fehlen der Arme ist hier schlechterdings afrikanisch – das gab es schon in einigen berühmten Fällen Rodinscher Plastik –, sondern daß sie in keiner Weise vorgesehen waren. Sie fehlen nicht als Ergebnis eines tatsächlichen oder implizierten Abschneidens wie bei RODIN, sondern es fehlt auch eine passende Stelle, an die sie zurückkehren könnten. Ebenso afrikanisch sind die steifen, runden Beine, die ähnlich wie bei der Fruchtbarkeitsfigur der *BIJOGO* zu Segmenten geschnürt erscheinen. Die einfache Form der Füße läßt die Figur stehen, ohne daß sie an einer Basis befestigt ist. Daß die Vorstellung von einem Mädchen mit dieser Holzplastik zusammenfällt (die keinerlei Anspielung auf eine Basis oder Stütze enthält), verbindet *Kleines französisches Mädchen* genauso mit der Figur der *BAMBARA* und mit einer Darstellungsweise der menschlichen Figur, wie sie überhaupt der afrikanischen Skulptur geläufig ist. Die Figur als ein unabhängiges Objekt, das auf eigenen Beinen steht, besitzt – unabhängig von der Größe – eine magische Ausstrahlung. BRANCUSI erreicht diese Magie, indem er die europäische Gewohnheit aufgibt, eine Kontinuität zwischen der menschlichen Figur und der von ihr bewohnten Umgebung herzustellen. Die Kontinuität des Materials kaschiert die Tatsache, daß Figur und Grundfläche eigentlich stofflich verschieden sind – etwa Fleisch und Erde. BRANCUSI hat diese Illusion bereits in verschiedenen Fassungen von *Der Kuß*, einer breitlagernden, autonomen Form, verworfen. In *Kleines französisches Mädchen* verwirft er sie auf eine typisch afrikanische Weise und von da an mit einer Konsequenz, wie man sie nicht immer bei afrikanischer Skulptur antrifft. Während *Der Kuß* die Umarmung, die Verschlingung zweier Lebewesen darstellt – nicht weniger Illusion wie die Berührung der Füße mit dem Boden –, wird kein neues Bild nach 1913 die Illusion von zwei oder mehr Dingen, die miteinander in Kontakt stehen, beinhalten. Seit 1914 zeigt BRANCUSIS Plastik Einzelobjekte, die wie Ikonen in unserem Raum magisch gegenwärtig sind.

Das Mittelstück der 1914 begonnenen Skulptur *Karyatide* □ 476 war bis zu diesem Zeitpunkt BRANCUSIS größte bildhauerische Arbeit. Die Füße ruhen – aber nicht in einem bruchlosen Übergang – auf der darunter befindlichen Basis. Hierdurch wird das Prinzip figuraler Unabhängigkeit, wie es sich in *Kleines französisches Mädchen* manifestiert, bestätigt. Wie bereits jene Arbeit ist die *Karyatide* im mittleren Bereich regelmäßig gefurcht, ein typisch afrikanisches Merkmal, wie bereits dargelegt, was dann auf zwei Seiten in der bekannteren Form der Zahnung auftritt. Zugleich kommt auf der Rückseite das in Afrika geläufige Motiv der Ringe in einer flächigen Variante vor. Bei der *Karyatide* wurden die afrikanischen Elemente in ein kompaktes dekorativ-architektonisches Ganzes eingebunden. Die Illustration menschlicher Anatomie ist einer Konzeption gewichen, die auf Körperlichkeit nur noch anspielt.

1914 begann BRANCUSI mit der Arbeit an der »afrikanischsten« seiner Skulpturen, *Madame L. R.* □ 488, die er nicht vor 1918 vollenden sollte. Das Werk ist radikal abstrakt und steht auf einem einzigen, genau in der Mitte plazierten »Bein«. (Auch wenn der Sockel jetzt vom Rest getrennt und rekonstruiert ist, war die Arbeit ursprünglich aus einem einzigen Holzblock gehauen.) Obwohl nicht ein einziges anatomisches Element erkennbar ist, hat das Objekt insgesamt einen sehr femininen Charakter und dies nicht nur wegen des »Kammes« auf dem Kopf und der konkaven Form am unteren Rand. Wie bei *Kleines französisches Mädchen* kommen keine Arme vor. Man wüßte auch nicht, wo sie ansetzen sollten. Der Anschein des Afrikanischen geht vor allem vom Kopf aus, einer kubistischen Variante der kupferüberzogenen Reliquiarfiguren der ONGWE (Gabun) □ 487, von denen BRANCUSI nicht nur den äußeren Kontur übernahm, sondern auch die Mittelachse und die vorspringende Spitze, aus der sein »Kamm« wurde. Diese Reliquiarfiguren haben anders als die bekannteren Figuren der KOTA eine Stütze, die senkrecht zum Kopf steht, und – wie William Rubin erkannt hat – von vorne betrachtet wie ein einziges Bein aussieht. Ungeachtet einer möglichen Themenvorgabe[24] ist *Madame L. R.* vom Entwurf her abstrakt komponiert. »Können Sie sich einen afrikanischen Künstler vorstel-

□ 486 *Constantin Brancusi, ›Kleines französisches Mädchen‹, 1914–18, Holz, 124 x 22 x 21 cm. The Solomon R. Guggenheim Museum, Nachlaß K. S. Dreier, New York.*

□ 487 *›Reliquiarfigur‹ (Vorder- und Rückansicht),* ONGWE *(Gabun), Holz, Messing und Kupfer, Höhe 53 cm. Privatsammlung, Paris.*

len, der ein Modell benutzt?« fragte BRANCUSI 1955[25] – auch er selbst brauchte bei seinen eigenen Werken keines.

BRANCUSI fertigte Zweitfassungen von *Kleines französisches Mädchen* und *Madame L. R.* an. Beiden widerfuhr dasselbe Schicksal wie dem *Ersten Schritt,* der Körper ging verloren, während der Kopf jeweils erhalten blieb. Die Zerstörung dieser Arbeiten, das Umarbeiten anderer und die jahrelange Beschäftigung mit wieder anderen Werken sind ein Zeichen dafür, daß die unter der Wirkung afrikanischer Vorbilder stehende Bildhauerei für BRANCUSI voller Probleme steckte. Aus seinen Skulpturen dieser Jahre gingen auch nur sehr wenige Serien hervor, wohingegen er sonst viele Serien entwickelte, die im Falle der Arbeiten in Stein sehr umfangreich sein können.[26]

Die Marmorplastik *Prinzessin X* □ 494 wurde durch ein primitives Werk angeregt. Die Skulptur ist eigentlich eine Neufassung der großen gegenständlichen Büste einer Frau mit geneigtem Kopf, die er anscheinend 1909 vollendete. Einige Zeit später arbeitete BRANCUSI aber wieder an ihr und vereinfachte sie.[27] Wir vermerkten bereits seinen Besuch in London im Juli 1913; er könnte damals einen Steinstößel aus Neuguinea gesehen haben □ 490, den das Britische Museum kurz zuvor angekauft hatte. Wie sich Kopf und Hals über zwei markante brustähnliche Formen wölben, dürfte BRANCUSI sicherlich interessiert haben, zumal eine Ähnlichkeit mit seinem 1910 entstandenen Werk *Pasarea Maiastra* bestand (ein Vogel aus Marmor, der Kopf und Hals über eine Brust beugt). Der Stößel könnte seine gerade aktuelle Arbeit angeregt haben, die erst nach 1916 ihre endgültige Fassung erhielt. Abgesehen von der großformatigen Gestaltung der *Prinzessin X* ist die Hand, die neben der Brust liegt, wenn auch ein Unikum in BRANCUSIS Œuvre, in afrikanischer Skulptur durchaus nicht selten.

Unentschlossenheit, radikale Umkehr und Neukonzeptionen begleiten die Entstehung von *Adam und Eva*, 1916–21 □ 489, eine hohe Struktur, die zwischen bearbeiteten oberen und unteren Teilen einen großen Holzblock einschließt. Die massive Gestalt des Blocks vermag wie durch ein Wunder die anderen Abschnitte, deren Stil voneinander völlig verschieden ist, zu integrieren. Tatsächlich entstanden sie auch in unterschiedlicher Zeit und mit Themen, die mit dem ersten Menschenpaar nichts zu tun hatten. Nach der »Hochzeit« dieser Formen wird sich BRANCUSI über das Verführerische der Eva und die Verantwortlichkeiten Adams verbreitet haben. Einem Reporter, der ihn 1926 interviewte, erklärte BRANCUSI die Bedeutung verschiedener formaler Merkmale der *Eva*,[28] angesichts seiner sonstigen Zurückhaltung eine Exegese von seltener Detailliertheit und so phantastisch wie andere seiner Erklärungen.

Denn wer war *Eva*, bevor sie mit *Adam* verbunden wurde? Auf einer Photographie von 1916 □ 491 erleben wir sie bei ihrem ersten Auftritt als eine gerade vollendete Skulptur, die

□ 488 *Constantin Brancusi, ›Madame L. R.‹ (Vorder- und Rückansicht), 1914–18, Holz, Höhe 94 cm. Privatsammlung.* ▷

wie *Madame L. R.* und der spätere *Sokrates* auf einem Bein steht. Formal gesehen ist die Arbeit afrikanisch, angefangen bei dem gewölbten Kopf, über den flanschenähnlichen Fuß bis zu den fehlenden Armen. In graphischer Hinsicht steht uns eine Frau afrikanischer Abstammung vor Augen: Die vollen Lippen entsprechen ganz denjenigen des Marmorkopfes von 1920, den BRANCUSI später *Weiße Negerin* nennen sollte. Somit handelte es sich um eine schwarze Frau mit prononcierten Lippen (Mund) und betonten Brüsten. Eine solche wörtliche Lesart kann nur ein Bein nicht akzeptieren: Der lange Zylinder muß eine komprimierte oder verdeckte Version der Hüfte und der (beiden) Beine sein. Ich nehme natürlich an, daß die *Eva* ihre Karriere als skulptierte Darstellung der schwarzen Sängerin eines Nachtklubs begann und daß sie ihre Identität vertauschte, um sich *Adam* anzuschließen, wobei sie den tragenden Zylin-

□ 489 *Constantin Brancusi, ›Adam und Eva‹, 1919–21. Holz und Kalkstein, Höhe 239 cm. The Solomon R. Guggenheim Museum, New York.*

□ 490 *›Stößel aus Stein‹, Papua-Neuguinea, Höhe 36 cm. The Trustees of the British Museum, London.*

□ 491 *Photographie der ›Eva‹. Veröffentlicht in einer unbekannten Zeitung, New York, Februar 1926.*

□ 492 *Constantin Brancusi, ›Stehende Frau‹, 1916, Holz, Höhe 81 cm. Später überarbeitet.*

□ 493 *Constantin Brancusi, Holzarbeit ohne Titel, um 1920, Höhe 162 cm. Später überarbeitet.*

der und die untere Kurve ihrer Brüste aufgab. Es ist wohl kaum denkbar, daß durch das Entfernen dieser Elemente den verbliebenen Teilen ein Paradies-Symbolismus zuteil werden würde. Hierbei handelt es sich sicher um eine nachträgliche Rationalisierung wie bei dem Märchen, das Brancusi erfand, um seine *Pasarea Maiastra* zu erklären, oder bei der Revision griechischer Mythologie, wie er sie in der Erklärung seiner *Leda* anbot. Und doch war es für Brancusi zweckmäßig, dieses Bild einer schwarzen Sängerin auf afrikanische Art zu gestalten, genauso wie es ihm später angemessen schien, sich Eva als Schwarze vorzustellen.

Der *Adam* war ursprünglich der untere Teil einer säulenförmigen Arbeit in Holz von ungefähr 1920. Als ihn Brancusi für *Adam und Eva* hernahm, behielt er seine formale Position zwar bei, wechselte aber wie bei der *Eva* seinen symbolischen Status. Die kantige Form des *Adam*, die Furchung am Hals und die Zahnung darunter sind alle ausgesprochen afrikanisch. Gleichzeitig erinnert die Plastik an Epsteins *Sonnenblume* von 1910 □ 614, die Brancusi gekannt haben muß. Während *Adam und*

□ 494 *Constantin Brancusi, ›Prinzessin X‹, 1916, Marmor, 56 x 8 x 23 cm. Sheldon Memorial Art Gallery, University of Nebraska, Lincoln.*

□ 495 *Constantin Brancusi, ›Die Endlose Säule‹ (La Colonne sans Fin), 1918, Holz, Höhe 211 cm. Später überarbeitet.*

Eva und die meisten anderen Arbeiten in Holz im Gesamteindruck und der Motivik afrikanische Skulptur beschwören, demonstrieren sie zugleich die feinsinnige Art, wie BRANCUSI den afrikanischen Einfluß aufnimmt – ein Feinsinn, den seine französischen und deutschen Kollegen nur selten erreichten. Die *Endlose Säule* □ 495, die abstrakteste unter seinen Schöpfungen, ist dafür ein ganz besonders gutes Beispiel.

1966 veröffentlichte die mit BRANCUSI befreundete CECILIA CUŢESCU-STORCK, eine der führenden rumänischen Malerinnen im frühen 20. Jahrhundert, ihre Erinnerungen, worin sie davon spricht, »die erste Fassung« der *Endlosen Säule* und »Teile von schräg behauenen Baumstämmen« 1909 in BRANCUSIS Atelier gesehen zu haben.[29] Barbu Brezianu, ein BRANCUSI-Spezialist, nahm diese Behauptung wörtlich und machte darüber hinaus darauf aufmerksam, daß ein 1911–12 entstandenes *Bildnis Dr. Paul Alexandre* von MODIGLIANI □ 496, das in einer Zeit der Nähe zu BRANCUSI gemalt worden war, ein Motiv enthält, das der *Endlosen Säule* ähnlich ist. Es zieht sich über das ganze Bild und rechtfertigt seiner Meinung nach eine Datierung der *Säule* in das Jahr 1909.[30] Diese Analyse ist in zweifacher Hinsicht zu bemängeln: Zum einen ist ihr Autor nicht bereit, auch nur irgendeinen außerrumänischen Einfluß auf BRANCUSI zuzulassen; daraus entsteht der Glaube, daß aller Einfluß von BRANCUSI ausgehe, keiner auf ihn einwirkte mit Ausnahme von RODIN. Zum anderen datiert BRANCUSI die *Endlose Säule* genau in das Jahr 1918,[31] und es ist für uns nachvollziehbar, wie er in den Jahren davor darauf zusteuert. Weder die *Säule* noch eine andere Arbeit in Holz taucht in Aufnahmen von BRANCUSIS Atelier vor 1914 auf. Auch sieht das Atelier in den wenigen Photos von 1910 nicht so aus, als könnten sich darin außerhalb des Blickfeldes der Kamera »Teile von Baumstämmen« und eine Arbeit vom Abstraktionsgrad der *Endlosen Säule* befinden. Man erinnere sich, daß in der Periode 1909–10 *Torso, Frau schaut in einen Spiegel, Baroness R. F.* □ 596, *Schlummernde Muse, Narziß* und *Der Kuß* (Friedhof Montparnasse) entstanden – Arbeiten in Stein und Marmor mit figurativem

□ 496 *Amedeo Modigliani, ›Bildnis Dr. Paul Alexandre‹, 1911–12, Öl auf Leinwand, 92 x 60 cm. Privatsammlung.*

Charakter, die die Vorstellung einer gleichzeitigen Entstehung der *Endlosen Säule* aus Holz schwerlich glaubhaft erscheinen lassen. C. Cuţescu-Storcks Behauptung ist somit unhaltbar, wenn auch nicht unerklärlich. Fast sechzig Jahre nach ihrem ersten Besuch in Brancusis Atelier schreibt sie über dieses so, als habe es ein Werk enthalten, das in seiner ersten Fassung sechs Jahre später auftaucht. Indem sie ihre Erinnerungen an verschiedene Besuche und wahrscheinlich verschiedene Ateliers durcheinanderbrachte, geht es ihr wie anderen Autoren von Memoiren über Brancusis frühe Jahre, die das Inventar der Ateliers in der Impasse Ronsin dem Atelier an der Rue de Montparnasse zuschreiben und sich dabei oft auf Photographien der ersteren beziehen.

Wie ist das Motiv in Modiglianis Porträt zu erklären? Anfang 1968 erhielt ich einen Brief der Familie Alexandre als Antwort auf meine Bitte um mehr Information über jenes Portrait. Georges Bréfort gab in diesem Brief Informationen seiner Mutter weiter, der Tochter Dr. Alexandres, die selbst nicht mehr schreiben konnte. Madame Bréfort ließ verlauten: »Es ist sehr wohl möglich, daß Modigliani beim Malen des vertikalen Streifens und des darauf sichtbaren Motivs von einem Wandbehang oder einem Tuch marokkanischen oder afrikanischen Ursprungs angeregt wurde, das sich in dem Haus befand, in dem Dr. Alexandre zum Zeitpunkt, als ihn Modigliani porträtierte, wohnte. Es überrascht nicht, daß Modigliani von diesem Behang angetan war. Wir wissen, daß ihn die ›art nègre‹ begeisterte, und es ist sehr wohl möglich, daß er den Behang dazu hernahm, um dem Gemälde seine Vorliebe für afrikanische Kunst mitzuteilen. Bis jetzt konnten wir den originalen Behang nicht wieder finden, doch ist meine Mutter davon ziemlich überzeugt, daß es keine Frage einer Erfindung seitens des Künstlers war, sondern ein Behang tatsächlich existierte.«[32]

Angesichts der Freundschaft Brancusis mit Modigliani und Dr. Alexandre ist anzunehmen, daß er den Behang von dem Gemälde her kannte, durch Besuche bei der Familie Alexandre

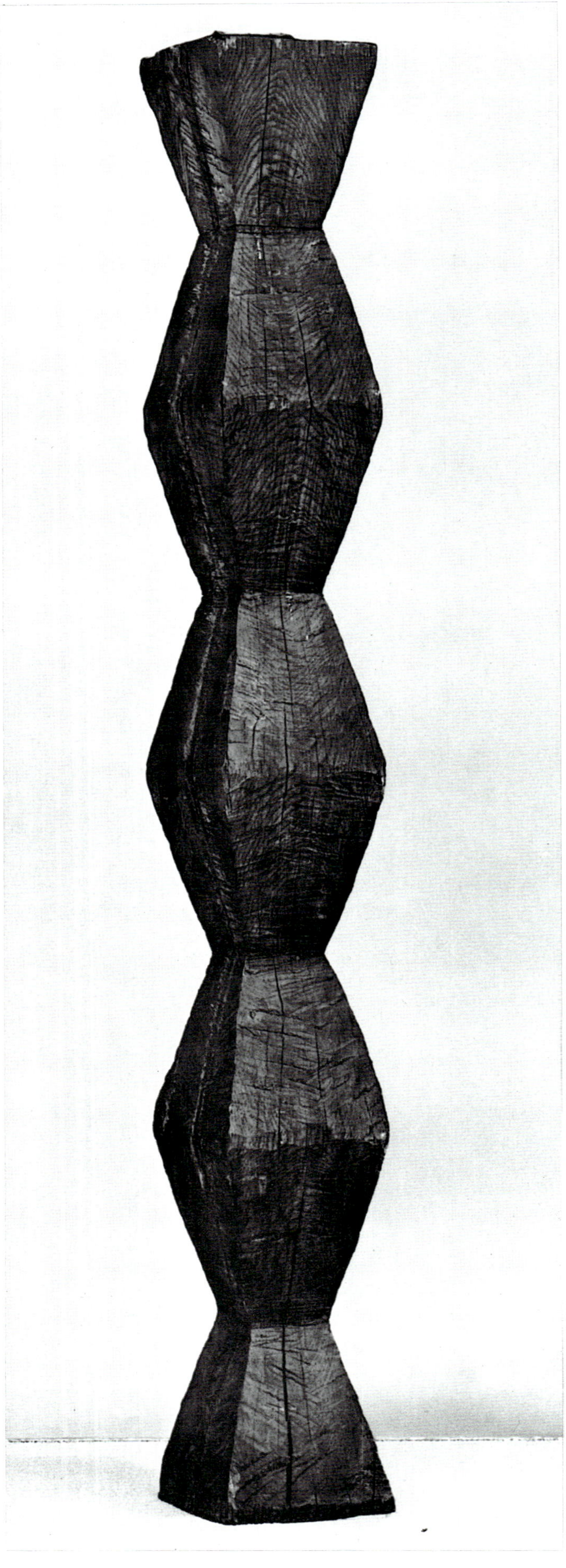

oder über beide Wege. Das Muster auf dem Behang mag durchaus der Keim für die *Endlose Säule* gewesen sein. Es wäre nicht das erste Mal, daß BRANCUSIS Phantasie die Tiefe einer flächigen Gestaltung ergründet hätte. Obwohl in Volkskunst vielfach anzutreffen, sieht das Motiv selten wie in MODIGLIANIS Gemälde aus. Statt der auseinanderstoßenden Rhomben, die dann auch in der *Säule* vorkommen, sind dort Quadrate üblich. Kein Verfechter der These eines rumänischen Vorbildes konnte bisher aus dem großen Bilderbogen rumänischer Säulen etwas der *Endlosen Säule* Vergleichbares finden. Mehrere Autoren bilden den oberen Teil eines Torpfostens aus der Provinz ab, der als Quelle sehr fragwürdig ist.[33] Der *Säule* steht von ihrem Wesen her eine eigenhändige Arbeit BRANCUSIS aus Marmor viel näher: die Basis von *Maiastra* (1912), die eine klare Zähnung aufweist und sehr wahrscheinlich durch den Behang in Alexandres Haus angeregt ist.[34]

Als BRANCUSI dieses Motiv ein paar Jahre später in Holz umsetzen wollte, war es sicherlich für eine Basis bestimmt. So stützt ein 167 cm hohes Beispiel von 1915, das in *L'Enfant au monde, groupe mobile* von 1917 nur auf zwei Seiten bearbeitet ist und später auseinandergenommen wurde, eine *Tasse*. Wie anhand der weißen Kreidezeichnung auf einer Seite der *Säule* erkennbar ist, beschäftigte sich BRANCUSI mit der Idee, runde Löcher zu bohren (er zog die Kreise sogar nach, als er die flachen Seiten in Facetten anlegte). Die Säule verschwand. Auf die Frage, was auf die *Säule* von 1918 zu stellen sei, antwortete Henri-Pierre Roché dem Sammler John Quinn: »[Brancusi] sagt, daß die Säule keine Basis brauche, bis sie für immer an einen besonderen Ort gelangt und einen besonderen Gegenstand trägt . . .«[35] Wenn die *Säule* von 1918 als eine Basis ihren Anfang nahm, wurde sie erst durch einen weiteren Schritt der Imagination zur Skulptur. 1927 erreichte sie endgültig den Status einer Plastik, als BRANCUSI das Zapfenloch beseitigte, mit dem die *Säule* in einem Steinblock befestigt war. Er verlieh ihr damit jene formale Unabhängigkeit, die für seine übrigen Skulpturen charakteristisch ist. Das Stück war über seine Ursprünge als Basis, über das aus Wiederholungen bestehende Dekorative hinausgewachsen und wurde bei 203 cm Höhe eine Metapher für die Gegenwart des Menschen.

Die 6,10 m hohe *Endlose Säule*, die 1920 in Edward Steichens Garten in Voulangis aufgestellt wurde, war aus einem Baumstamm aus jenem Garten gehauen; sie ist ein Sinnbild menschlichen Bewußtseins inmitten der Natur. Von der über 29 m hohen, aus Eisen gegossenen Säule von 1938 in Tîrgu Jiu wird gelegentlich behauptet, sie habe eine Sepulkralfunktion, was ihre angebliche Abhängigkeit von alten rumänischen Grabsäulen bestätigen würde. Doch hat das ganze Ambiente von Tîrgu Jiu, keineswegs nur seine Bestandteile, eine sepulkrale Bedeutung. Die *Säule* enthielt in den verschiedenen Fassungen, die ihr vorausgingen – 1915, 1918 □ 497 und 1920 –, nie auch nur eine Andeutung von einer sepulkralen Funktion oder Bedeutung. In Tîrgu Jiu wurde eine Säule, die bisher keine sepulkrale Bedeutung trug, mit einem Tisch und einem Tor vereinigt, deren Vergangenheit davon ebenso unberührt war – das Ganze für ein Monument zu Ehren der Gefallenen des Ersten Weltkrieges. In diesem Kontext erweckten die große Höhe des Werkes sowie der weite und offene Raum der Umgebung die Symbolik der *axis mundi*. Die *Säule* ist hier eine pulsierende Verbindung zwischen Himmel und Erde. Sie läßt die üblichen

□ 497 *Constantin Brancusi, ›Die Endlose Säule‹ (La Colonne sans Fin), 1918, Holz, 203 x 25 x 24 cm. The Museum of Modern Art, Schenkung Mary Sisler, New York.*

erdgebundenen Monumente hinter sich, wie auch das Motiv selbst über seine Ursprünge in der Volks- oder Stammeskunst hinausgeht.

Es ist trotz seiner komprimierten, symmetrischen Verwendung in der *Säule* eine Zackung oder Zähnung und in seiner Essenz ganz afrikanisch. Die Holzplastik vieler eingeborener Völker kennt dieses Motiv in vielen Formen und unterschiedlicher Häufigkeit. BRANCUSI wendet es in einer späteren Holzarbeit an, die nicht weniger afrikanisch ist, dem *Hahn* von 1924, und dessen Bronzen und monumentalen Fassungen in Gips ☐ 499. In dieser Arbeit hat die Zähnung erstmals statt einer dekorativen eine expressive Funktion und erzählt uns, wie sich das Tier des Bauernhofes rekelt und kräht. Der *Hahn* in Bronze und seine gezackte Steinbasis verstärken eine leichte ästhetische Akzentverschiebung, insofern als das Verständnis des Motivs als einer Dekoration von seiner Interpretation als Bedeutung begleitet oder überlagert wird. Insgesamt kommt die Zähnung mit ihrem afrikanischen Beigeschmack in den Basen von mindestens zehn Arbeiten vor, die meistens Vögel darstellen, zu denen aber auch *Exotische Pflanze* und *Prinzessin X* gehören. Weniger eindringlich wirkt die Zähnung in den großen Basen der sieben Fassungen von *Vogel im Raum* sowie in den Basen so verschiedener Werke wie *Chimère* ☐ 501, *Schlafendes Kind, Der Kuß* und *Der Fisch*. Unter den für BRANCUSI besonders typischen Gestaltungselementen ist die Zähnung sicherlich das häufigste, da es oft den Berührungspunkt zwischen Skulptur und Basis, zwischen kantigen Formen unten und fließenden Kurven oben bildet. Eine gesteigerte Wirkung des Motivs erzielte eine Installation anläßlich der BRANCUSI-Retrospektive des Art Institute of Chicago von 1970,

☐ 498 *›Kopfschmuck‹*, BAMBARA *(Mali), Holz, Höhe 69 cm. Privatsammlung.*

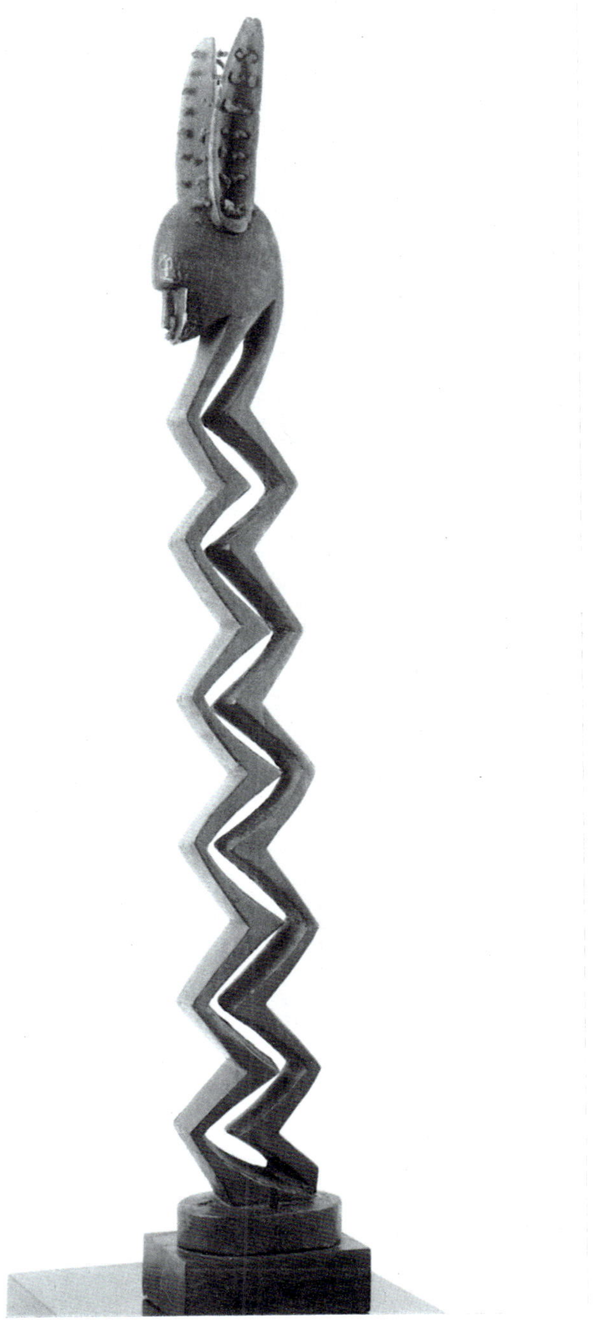

☐ 499 *Constantin Brancusi, ›Der Hahn‹ (Le Coq), 1935, polierte Bronze, Höhe 103 cm. Musée National d'Art Moderne, Paris.*

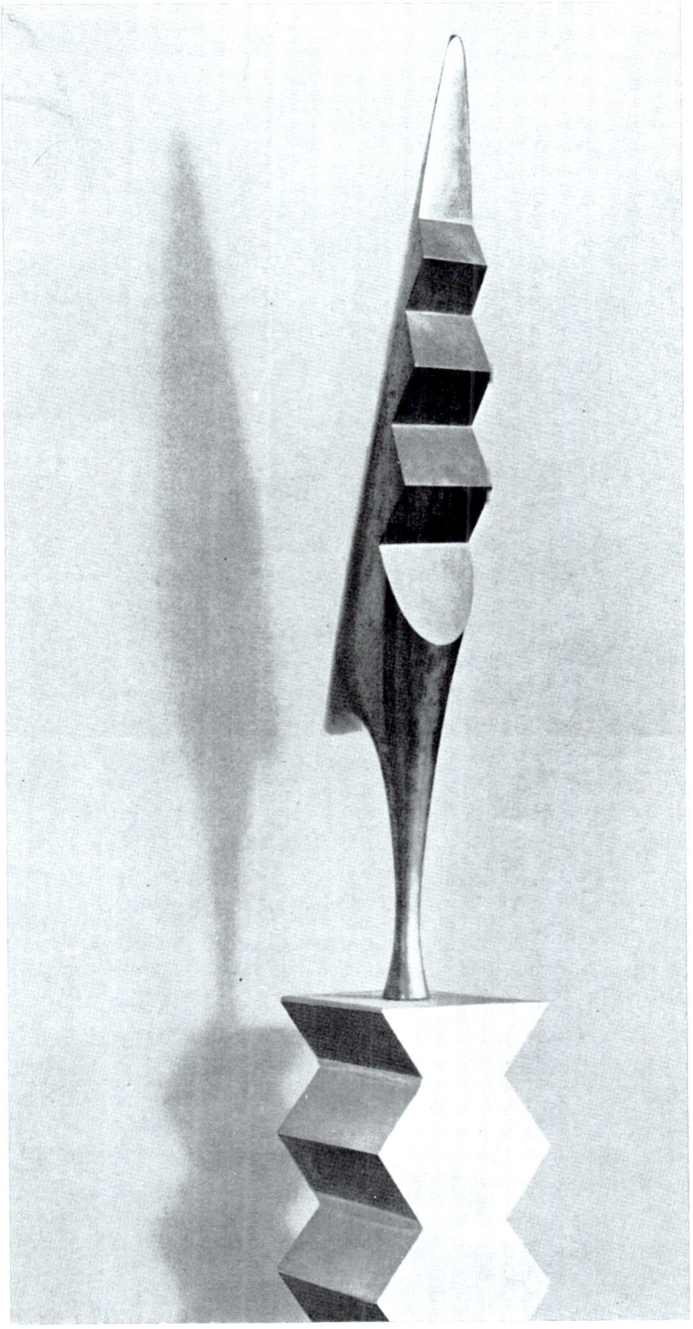

□ 500 *›Helmmaske‹*, BAULE *(Elfenbeinküste), Holz, Höhe 109 cm. Sammlung Marina Picasso. Ehemals Sammlung Pablo Picasso.*

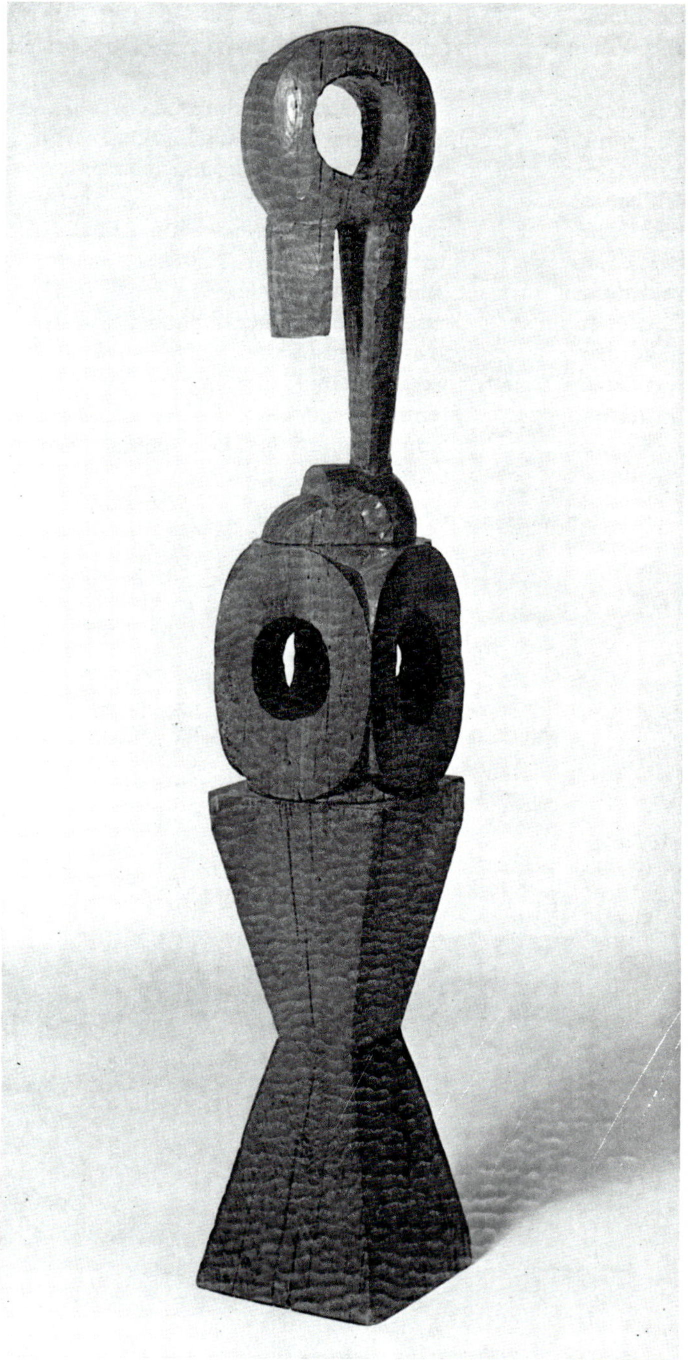

□ 501 *Constantin Brancusi, ›Die Chimäre‹ (La Chimère), 1918, Holz, 152 x 25 x 25 cm. Philadelphia Museum of Art, Sammlung L. und W. Arensberg.*

als eine Plattform, die mehrere Skulpturen trug, den Eindruck eines afrikanischen Thronraumes hervorrief.

Lange nachdem sich BRANCUSI im Gespräch mit EPSTEIN negativ über den afrikanischen Einfluß geäußert hatte, wandte er die Zähnung verschiedene Male und mit neuer Absicht in der Ende der 30er Jahre entstandenen Skulptur *König der Könige* an □ 502. Die hohe säulenhafte Figur scheint mit einer kreisförmigen Zähnung bekrönt zu sein. Auf halber Höhe ist eine Reihe von Graten vertikal angeordnet – wie ein Waschbrett von der Seite –, während auf einer daran anstoßenden Fläche eine ähnliche Gruppe von Graten die herkömmlichere horizontale Orientierung aufweist; dasselbe Motiv scheint in dem schraubenförmigen Gebilde am Fuß der Skulptur sogar noch eine andere Gestalt anzunehmen. Dieser ausgiebige Gebrauch von Spielarten der Zackung und Zähnung wie auch die betonte Segmentierung verleihen dem *König der Könige* einen afrikanischen Charakter. Die zu Beginn der 40er Jahre entstandene überlebensgroße *Karyatide* ist weniger abstrakt als die vorgenannte Arbeit, eine beeindruckende, stark vereinfachte Fassung eines Themas, das schon 1915 erprobt wurde. Es ist dies das letzte Werk BRANCUSIS, das afrikanische Einflüsse verrät – aufgrund seiner Vertikalität, Symmetrie und der formalen Unterscheidung der Teile; ebenso aufgrund der wiederholten Furchung am Hals, des einheitlich erfaßten, schwellenden Torsos; aufgrund des Standmotivs mit den angezogenen Knien und dadurch, daß die Beine getrennt sind, wobei jedes in einem Fuß (oder Fußsockel) endet. Dieses ist so gestaltet, daß die große Plastik ohne Verbindung zu einer Basis frei stehen kann.

Diese lange Liste von Arbeiten Brancusis mit afrikanischen Elementen ruft geradezu nach einer Untersuchung seiner von Epstein überlieferten Behauptung, einige afrikanisierende Werke zerstört zu haben. Die Zerstörung ist lediglich in drei Fällen dokumentiert: für *Der erste Schritt* und die Zweitfassungen von *Kleines französisches Mädchen* und *Madame L. R.* In jedem der drei Fälle blieb nur der Kopf erhalten. Für die beiden zuletzt genannten Skulpturen gilt, daß die Erstfassungen jeweils vollständig erhalten blieben, nach wie vor existieren und sich als von afrikanischer Skulptur stark beeinflußt erwiesen haben. Ich habe die Vermutung, daß die zweiten Fassungen unterdrückt wurden, weil sie zu keinem Fortschritt oder keiner lohnenden Variante gegenüber der Urfassung führten, aber keinesfalls deshalb, weil sie afrikanische Anregungen verraten hätten.[36] Angesichts der Entstehung jener spürbar afrikanischen Erstfassung von *Kleines französisches Mädchen* und *Madame L. R.* unmittelbar nach dem *Ersten Schritt* bin ich jetzt der Überzeugung, daß die letztgenannte Arbeit nicht deshalb zerstört wurde, weil sie afrikanisch war, sondern weil sie nicht afrikanisch genug war. Der Verdacht drängt sich auf, daß keine dieser Zerstörungen, von denen wir Kenntnis haben, durch sichtbare afrikanische Einflüsse ausgelöst wurde. Auch wenn es solche Zerstörungen gegeben haben sollte (und ich bezweifle, daß sie überhaupt stattfanden), dann dürften es nur wenige gewesen sein, die, verglichen mit dem umfangreichen Werk, das existiert, fast bedeutungslos sind. Dieses Œuvre spiegelt ein wunderbares Verständnis afrikanischer Kunst, die in brillanter Weise anverwandelt wurde.

Warum warnte dann Brancusi vor den Gefahren afrikanischer Einflüsse? In den 20er Jahren war er mehr und mehr in die Beschäftigung mit dem Thema des Vogels vertieft, das allmählich Gestalt annahm und in der weißen Marmorplastik *Vogel im Raum* von 1925 kulminierte. Diese Fassung war 180 cm, eine andere von 1930 188 cm hoch, polierte Bronze brachte sie zum Glänzen. 1928 schuf Brancusi *Die weiße Negerin* in weißem Marmor, um 1930 zwei monumentale Fassungen des *Großen Hahnes* in Gips □ 503 sowie die noble *Säule des Kusses,* eine über 3 m hohe Struktur in weichem, weißem Stuck. Zwischen der Helligkeit und Immaterialität dieser Arbeiten und der Intensität und Greifbarkeit der Holzplastik liegen Welten. Da Brancusis Schaffen im allgemeinen durch klare Impulse angeregt wurde, mag ihm die ständige Spannung, sich mit zwei Tendenzen seines Werkes zu befassen, unerträglich geworden sein, so daß der Ausbruch gegenüber Epstein zu einem Zeitpunkt auftrat, als die Argumente für Licht und Schatten die Oberhand gewonnen hatten. Diese Problematik bewog ihn bei einem Gespräch in Bukarest 1939 zu der Äußerung: »Ich habe Löcher eliminiert, die Schatten verursachen.«[37] Abgesehen von der dunklen Färbung des Materials besaß die Holzskulptur wegen ihrer scharfen Berechnung von Flächen eine besondere Binnenschattierung. Zum anderen rebellierte Brancusis Stolz gegen die Schuld, die er sicherlich gegenüber afrikanischer Skulptur fühlte. Es ist dies nicht das erste Mal, daß er gegenüber einem machtvollen Einfluß in dieser Weise reagiert hatte. Nach seiner frühen und kurzen, von Rodin beeinflußten Phase hatte er sich wie andere forsche Bildhauer seiner Generation gegen den Meister von Meudon erhoben. Seine Parteinahme für das direkte Meißeln erlaubte Brancusi einen, wie es schien, sauberen Bruch mit

□ 502 *Constantin Brancusi, ›König der Könige‹, Ende 1930, Holz, Höhe 300 cm. The Solomon R. Guggenheim Museum, New York.*

☐ 503 *Constantin Brancusi, ›Der Große Hahn‹ (Le Grand Coq), 1949, Gips, 479 x 57 x 100 cm. Atelier Brancusi, Musée National d'Art Moderne, Centre d'Art et de Culture Georges Pompidou, Paris.*

☐ 504 ▷
›Figur aus Holz‹, Mama (Nigeria), Höhe 53 cm. The Art Institute of Chicago.

Rodins Einfluß. Jahrzehnte später, 1952, gab er eine Erklärung für den Katalog der Ausstellung »Hommage à Rodin« ab, in der er die große Verpflichtung der modernen Skulptur gegenüber dem französischen Meister zugab. Wenn es Brancusi in den frühen Dreißigern für nötig hielt, afrikanische Kunst abzulehnen, würde er darüber später in den höchsten Tönen sprechen. Seine Anfeindung war heuristisch, sie half ihm, eine neue gedankliche Richtung zu verfolgen. Nachdem diese Bestrebungen später in Erfüllung gegangen waren, schien ihm der Zeitpunkt für einen Widerruf gekommen.

Neben den Schlußfolgerungen, die seine Werke zulassen, teilen auch eigene Aussagen Brancusis einiges über seine Einstellung gegenüber afrikanischer Kunst mit. Und so wichtig seine Bemerkungen gegenüber Jacob Epstein auch sein mögen, sollten sie nicht – wie bereits dargelegt – isoliert betrachtet werden. Im Juli 1923 veröffentlichte die Zeitschrift *The Arts* einen Artikel über Brancusi mit der Verfasserangabe M. M. Auch wenn er sich auf verschiedene Diskussionen mit dem Bildhauer in Paris berief, nahm der Artikel für sich nicht in Anspruch, eine wörtliche Reportage zu sein, sondern eine Rekonstruktion »vieler Unterhaltungen«. Darin steht zu lesen: »Christliche Primitive und schwarze Wilde lassen sich von Glaube und Instinkt leiten; der moderne Künstler entwickelt sich durch einen Instinkt, der von der Vernunft gelenkt wird.«[38] Diese Gedanken scheinen authentisch zu sein, da ihnen Brancusi auch an anderer Stelle Ausdruck verlieh, besonders in seiner Behauptung, daß primitive Künstler nicht wie er befähigt seien, mit »Präzision bis zum Ende« zu arbeiten.

Als er zu Beginn des Jahres 1926 anläßlich einer kleinen Ausstellung in der Galerie Wildenstein nach New York kam, traf ihn William Zorach und schrieb einen informativen Artikel, der gleichfalls in *The Arts* erschien und worin dieser

Brancusis Interesse an afrikanischer Kunst als selbstverständlich voraussetzte.[39] Dorothy Dudley, die im Februar 1927 für *The Dial* schrieb, teilte diesen Standpunkt – »Brancusi mag Negerkunst« – und zitierte ihn wörtlich: »Die Skulptur der Neger bringt Freude zum Ausdruck.« Ihr interessanter Bericht zitiert mehrfach den Bildhauer, der 1926 anläßlich einer wichtigen Ausstellung in der Galerie Brummer zum zweiten Mal nach New York kam. Sie ging auch auf seinen rumänischen Hintergrund ein, doch stammen diese Äußerungen von D. Dudley, nicht von Brancusi.[40] Zwei Jahre später schrieb Benjamin Fondane, ein Freund und Landsmann, von dem Brancusi ein Porträt zeichnete: »Er erkennt nur in den Primitiven, den Künstlern der Gotik und den Schwarzen seine Brüder.«[41] Innerhalb zweier Jahre beobachteten wir eine völlige Umkehr in den Gefühlen Brancusis; die innere Kraft afrikanischer Kunst, die ihn anfangs so angezogen hatte, schien nun eine Gefahr zu werden. Zu Epstein sagte er, daß man sich vor ihrem Einfluß hüten solle; gegenüber anderen sprach er von »dämonischen Mächten«.[42] Soweit dies zu beurteilen ist, hielt Brancusi zwanzig Jahre an dieser Meinung fest.

Wohl Anfang der 50er Jahre erklärte Brancusi: »Nur die Afrikaner und Rumänen verstehen es, wie man Holz schnitzt.«[43] Bevor er die Bedeutung afrikanischer Kunst wieder anerkannte, brachte er diese mit einer anderen Kunst in Verbindung, aber doch nur auf rein handwerklicher Ebene: » . . . wie man Holz schnitzt«. Zugleich weiß die Literatur von keinem anderen Beispiel zu berichten, daß Brancusi die rumänische Volkskunst erwähnt hätte, mit Ausnahme seiner Kritik zeitgenössischer Beispiele, wie dies bei Gesprächen mit Freunden in Rumänien zum Ausdruck kam.[44] Denn die beiden Kunstbereiche, die er in seiner Erklärung erwähnt, sind stark voneinander verschieden: auf der einen Seite die Tradition seiner Heimat, die ihm die Nähe und Liebe zum Holz als Medium vererbte, auf der anderen Seite die Stammeskunst, die ihm durch ihre Formenwelt und Wesensart ein neues Universum künstlerischer Möglichkeiten erschloß.

1955 besuchte Werner Münsterberger Brancusi, der bereits ein Exemplar von dessen kurz zuvor erschienenem Buch über primitive Kunst besaß. In ihrer Diskussion sprach Brancusi von der »›Befreiung‹ [der künstlerischen Vision], ein Wort, das er im Hinblick auf die Kunst der Eingeborenen mehrfach wiederholte . . .«[45] Noch über dieses Bekenntnis hinausgehend, bemerkte er: »Es ist wie mit der Luft, die man atmet, oder den Strahlen der Sonne. Man vergißt, daß sie da sind, aber man kann nicht ohne sie leben.«[46] Diese Worte, die Brancusi am Ende seines Lebens aussprach, stammen von einem Künstler, der sich im Universum afrikanischer Kunst wie zu Hause fühlte – wie in einem natürlichen Medium, das seine Ideen beflügelt. Nach dem freimütigen Afrikanisieren seiner ersten Arbeiten in Holz ist es vor allem jene Abstraktheit, die die Stammeskunst in ihm wachrief. Nach dem *Ersten Schritt* von 1913 ließ sich Brancusi nie wieder auf das nuancierte Modellieren ein, das einen der charmanten Züge des europäischen Realismus darstellt.

Seine ganz persönliche Phantasie wurde wie sein Gebrauch der fragmentierten Figur, die ein Erbe Rodins ist, dem Druck des Formalen ausgesetzt. Das Resultat davon ist die neue Eindringlichkeit von Brancusis Kunst – das Ergebnis der Vereinigung eines lokalen, zeitgenössischen Humanismus mit einer alten, andersartigen und hieratischen Strenge.

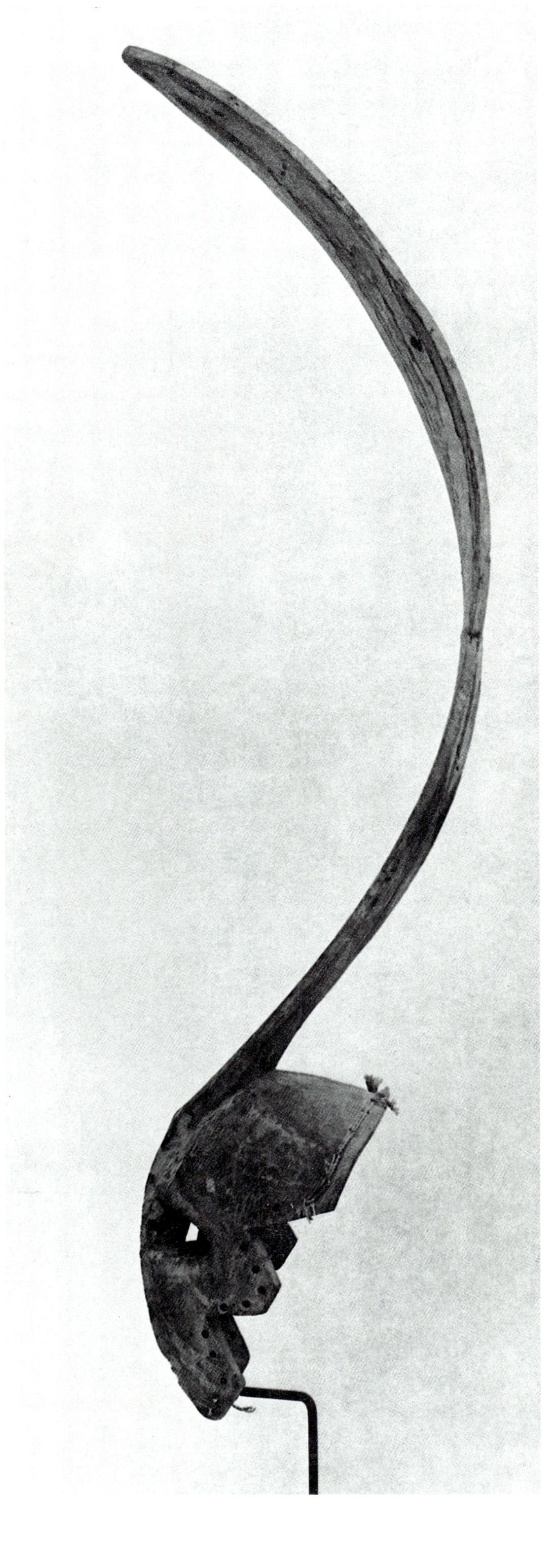

□ 505 *›Maske‹, Mossi (Obervolta), Holz, Höhe 117 cm. Sammlung E. Lustig Cohen und A. A. Cohen, New York.*

□ 506 ›Figur‹, LEGA (Zaire), bemaltes Holz, Höhe 12 cm. Sammlung M. und S. Stanoff.

□ 507 ›Figur‹, MAMBILA (Kamerun), Holz, Höhe 66 cm. ▷ Sammlung B. Holcombe.

□ 508 ›Initiationsblöcke‹, KOMO (Zaire), Holz. Feldaufnahme von Charles Henault.

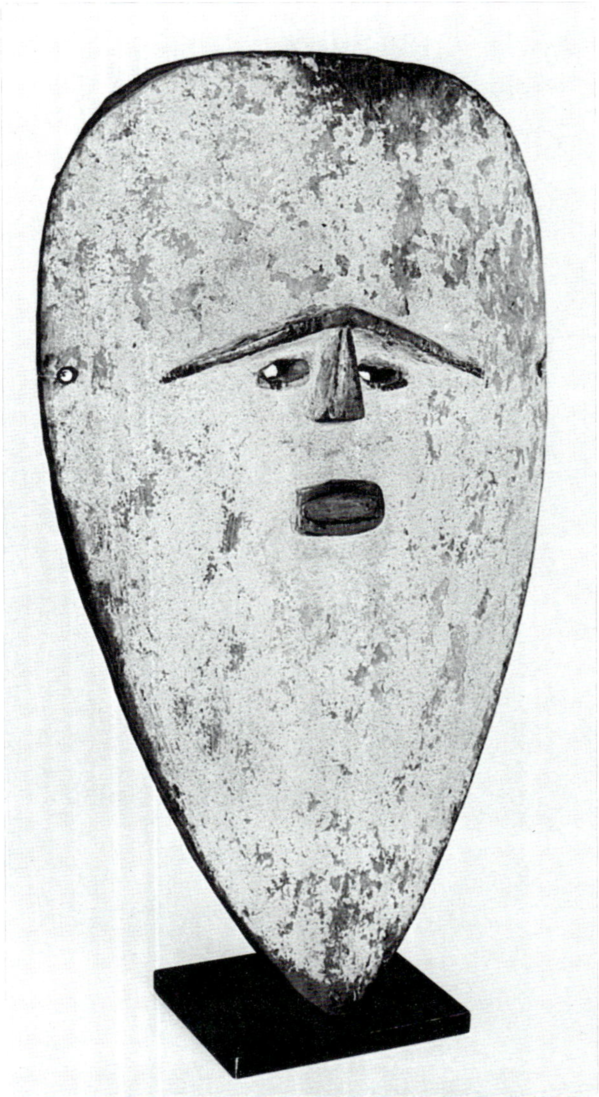

□ 509 *›Maske‹, Tsogo (Gabun), bemaltes Holz, Höhe 42 cm. The Detroit Institute of Arts.*

□ 510
›Maske‹, Chokwe (Zaire oder Angola), Holz und Fasern, Höhe 43 cm. Privatsammlung.

Anmerkungen

1. Nach 1907 schuf Brancusi gelegentlich Studien in Ton, die er jedoch zerstörte; der *Große Hahn* war in Ton, einige andere Arbeiten in Gipsformen, die von Arbeiten in Holz oder Stein abgenommen waren.

2. Die fünf Holzarbeiten von Kindern finden sich bei Geist, 1975 und 1983, unter den Nummern 42, 50, 51, 52 und 53 abgebildet.

3. Siehe *This Quarter*, 1925, Abb. 42.

4. Die Datierung des *Kusses*, die Frage nach der *taille directe* und weitere diesbezügliche Themen der folgenden drei Absätze sind bei Geist, 1978, noch ausführlicher erörtert.

5. Moffitt, J. F., »El Beso de Brancusi« in *Goya 273*, 1983, S. 296–302, vertritt die Auffassung, daß *Der Kuß* von einer Ausstellung über iberische Skulptur angeregt wurde, die im Frühjahr 1906 im Louvre eröffnet worden war. Dieser Hinweis ist zwar aufschlußreich, gibt jedoch keinerlei Auskunft darüber, warum *Der Kuß* mehr als anderthalb Jahre später erst auftauchte; auch der realistische Stil der um 1907 entstandenen Arbeiten mit dem Thema Kind ist damit nicht erklärt.

6. Siehe Kahnweiler, D. H., *André Derain*, Leipzig 1920, S. 10.

7. Siehe Kahnweilers Brief an den Verfasser vom 17. Oktober 1963, Brancusi-Archiv, Library of The Guggenheim Museum.

8. Über die Änderung des bisher geläufigen Titels *Weisheit der Erde* siehe Geist, 1976.

9. Anderson, W., *Gauguin's Paradise Lost*, New York 1971, S. 89 und Abb. 57.

10. Balasz, E., »The Myth of African Negro Art in Brancusi's Sculpture« in *Revue roumaine d'histoire de l'art 14*, 1977, S. 107–124.

11. In Balasz' Artikel, der Gemeinsamkeiten zwischen afrikanischer und rumänischer Volkskunst nachzuweisen sucht, wurde nur ein Werk Brancusis, eine Zeichnung, abgebildet. Es ist dem Leser daher unmöglich, sich von diesem Einfluß selbst zu überzeugen.

12. Michaelsen, K. J., »Brancusi and African Art« in *Artforum*, November 1971, S. 72–77.

13. Goldwater, R., *Primitivism in Modern Art*, New York 1967, S. 231. Epstein, J., *Let There Be Sculpture*, London und New York 1940, *An Autobiography*, New York 1955.

14. Epstein, 1940, S. 223.

15. Ebenda, S. 190–191.

16. *Der Kuß* von 1910 findet sich bei Geist, 1975 und 1983, unter Abb. 59.

17. De Zayas, M., *African Negro Art: Its Influence on Modern Art*, New York 1916, Abbildungen ohne Nummer. Als Provenienz der BAMBARA-Figur wird nur Obervolta angegeben. Diese Figur findet sich auch auf dem Umschlag eines russischen Buches, die sein Autor 1913 selbst aufnahm; Markow, V., *Iskusstvo Negrov* [Die Kunst der Neger], Petrograd 1919.

18. Meyer, A. E., *Out of These Roots: The Autobiography of an American Woman*, Boston 1953, S. 105.

19. Geist, 1968 und 1983, S. 155.

20. In einem Brief Werner Münsterbergers vom 10. April 1983 an den Verfasser (siehe Anm. 32 unten), veröffentlicht mit freundlicher Genehmigung des Absenders. Unter den mir bekannten westlichen Dokumenten findet sich an dieser Stelle erstmals ein eindeutiger Beweis für Matisse' Bekanntschaft mit Brancusi. So bemerkte Brancusi in einem Gespräch in Bukarest im Jahre 1939: »In Paris zählten u. a. Matisse, Erik Satie, Modigliani und vor allem Guillaume Apollinaire zu meinen Freunden«, Pandrea, P., *Portrete şi controverse*, Bukarest 1945, S. 160. Brancusi erwähnt hier außerdem »meinen Freund Picasso«, ebenda, S. 169.

21. Dr. Alexandre soll eine ganze Reihe von BAULE-Masken besessen haben, Laude, J., *La Peinture française et l'art nègre*, Paris 1968, S. 22, Anm. 15. Jüngere Nachforschungen von Jean-Louis Paudrat bestätigen dies jedoch nicht.

22. Brodzky, H., *Henri Gaudier-Brzeska*, London 1933, S. 94.

23. In einem persönlichen Gespräch mit Dr. Louise Svendsen, der früheren Kustodin des Guggenheim Museums, erwähnte diese, daß der Titel des Werkes auf James Johnson Sweeney, den ehemaligen Direktor des Museums, zurückgehe.

24. Vermutlich besteht eine Verbindung zwischen dem Werk und Mme Léone Ricou, einer Förderin der Kunst und Vertrauten des Bildhauers.

25. Aus dem Brief Münsterbergers, siehe Anm. 20.

26. Siehe etwa *Der Kuß, Schlafende Muse, Mademoiselle Pogany, Torso einer jungen Frau,* und *Vogel im Raum.*

27. Hamnett, N., *Laughing Torso,* New York 1932, S. 123–124.

28. Abgebildet in einer New Yorker Zeitung im Februar 1926. Die Abbildung wurde mir freundlicherweise von Barbu Brezianu, Bukarest, zur Verfügung gestellt.

29. Cuţescu-Storck, C., *O viaţă dăruită artei* [Ein Leben für die Kunst], Bukarest 1966, S. 50.

30. Brezianu, B., »Note pe marginea articolului ›Brancusi‹ de Michel Ragon« in *Arta plastică*, Nr. 4, 1966.

31. Im Katalog zu seiner Ausstellung in der Brummer Gallery, New York, vom 17. November bis zum 15. Dezember 1926, die er übrigens persönlich organisierte.

32. Dieser Brief – ebenso der von Münsterberger – wird im Brancusi-Archiv, Library of The Guggenheim Museum, aufbewahrt werden. In diesem Brief wird mitgeteilt, daß Brancusi über den Bildhauer Maurice Drouard – den Modigliani einmal porträtierte – bei Dr. Alexandre eingeführt wurde. Beide liebten die Natur und gingen oft gemeinsam in den Wäldern nahe Paris spazieren.

33. Siehe etwa Balas, E., »The Sculpture of Brancusi in the Light of His Rumanian Heritage«, Diss., Pittsburgh 1973, S. 35.

34. Der gezähnte Sockel einer weiteren *Maiastra*, die um 1912 entstand (Abb. 82 bei Geist, 1975 und 1983), wurde viele Jahre nach Vollendung der Skulptur geschaffen. Über den frühen Sockel siehe *Maiastra*, 1912 (ebenda, Abb. 83).

35. Brief vom 28. Mai 1922, John Quinn Sammlung, Manuscript Division, Public Library, New York.

36. Eine Photographie des *Kleinen Französischen Mädchens II* wurde bei Geist, 1975 und 1983, unter Abb. 123 veröffentlicht, eine Rekonstruktion der *Madame L. R. II* ebenda, Abb. 154.

37. Pandrea, 1945, S. 162.

38. M. M., »Constantin Brancusi: A Summary of Many Conversations« in *The Arts 4*, Nr. 1, Juli 1923, S. 15–17.

39. Zorach, W., »The Sculpture of Constantin Brancusi« in *The Arts 9*, Nr. 3, März 1926, S. 43–50.

40. Dudley, D., »Brancusi« in *The Dial 82*, Februar 1927, S. 123–130.

41. Fondane, B., »Brancusi« in *Cahiers de l'Etoile*, 1929, S. 708–25.

42. Giedion-Welcker, C., *Brancusi*, New York 1959, S. 33.

43. Geist, 1968 und 1983, S. 149. Überliefert von Etienne Hajdu in einem Brancusi-Kolloquium, das vom 13.–15. Oktober 1967 in Bukarest stattfand.

44. Pandrea, 1945, S. 155 und S. 157.

45. Aus dem Brief Münsterberger, siehe Anm. 20.

46. Münsterberger, W., *Universality of Tribal Art*, Genf 1979, S. 15.

Literaturhinweise

Geist, S.: *Brancusi: A study of the Sculpture*, New York 1968. *Brancusi, The Sculpture and Drawings*, New York 1975. »La Sagesse or Cumințenia pămîtului?« im Katalog der Ausstellung *Constantin Brancusi*, Duisburg, Wilhelm-Lehmbruck Museum, 1976, S. 90–99. *Brancusi/The Kiss*, New York 1978. *Brancusi: A Study of the Sculpture*, New York 1983. Überarbeitete und im Katalogteil aktualisierte Fassung der Ausgabe von 1968.

□ 511 *Max Pechstein, ›Afrikanische Holzskulptur‹, 1919, Öl auf Leinwand, 80 x 69 cm. Privatsammlung, New York.*

Donald E. Gordon

Deutscher Expressionismus

Während des vergangenen halben Jahrhunderts interpretierten Kunsthistoriker die Beziehungen zwischen dem deutschen Expressionismus und der Stammeskunst ganz unterschiedlich.[1] Nach Robert Goldwater waren die deutschen Expressionisten von der »Kraft und Unmittelbarkeit« primitiver Kunst fasziniert; die Reaktion der Expressionisten sei direkt und gefühlsbetont, anders als bei GAUGUIN und den Fauves, bei denen sie eher romantisch und idealisiert ausgefallen sei. Goldwaters Beobachtungen sind wichtig, doch ist zu bedauern, daß er den Ausdruck »emotionaler Primitivismus« wählte, um die Haltung der deutschen Künstler zu definieren.[2] Denn das Wort »emotional« schließt oft die Bedeutung von Antiintellektualismus oder Irrationalität mit ein. Es könnte daraus abgeleitet werden, daß die Expressionisten atavistisch waren, daß sie sich unkritisch mit der früheren Volks- oder Stammeskunst identifizierten und sogar zu ihr zurückkehrten. 1968 ging L. D. Ettlinger noch über Goldwater hinaus und behauptete, ein führender Expressionist habe nicht auf das Bild des Primitiven reagiert, sondern auf die exotische Idee: »Nicht durch eine ästhetische Erfahrung kam er zu ihrer Bewunderung, sondern durch seine Lektüre.«[3]

Goldwaters Standpunkt hat sich in den letzten Jahren immer mehr durchgesetzt. 1979 wurde von den Expressionisten gesagt, sie hätten eine »Regression« zu Stadien kindhafter Unschuld oder frühmenschlicher Animalität gesucht.[4] Und 1983 sah man »die Essenz des Expressionismus« in dem »Glauben, daß ein Inhalt über die Tradition hinaus, eine Wirklichkeit über die Darstellung hinweg existiert – kurz, eine Natur im Gegensatz zur Kultur«. Da jede Sprache kulturell ist und »der Expressionismus seinen eigenen Status als eine Sprache verleugnet«, erübrigt sich der Hinweis, daß der angebliche deutsche Glaube an die unmittelbare Naturerfahrung eine Täuschung ist.[5]

Trotzdem gab es Kritiker, die der Auffassung widersprachen, daß der expressionistische Primitivismus nur einfach emotional, regressiv sei und in der Natur gründe. Schon 1920 etwa wies ein Freund Freuds darauf hin, daß die expressionistische Regression nur ein »reculer pour mieux sauter« gewesen sei, ein taktischer Rückzug, um besser vorrücken zu können. Nach Oskar Pfister war die Regression nur eine Übergangsphase zur weiteren Entwicklung. »Jeder Schritt auf dem Weg des Fortschritts ist einzig über den Umweg einer solchen Regression möglich.«[6] Und 1947 unterschied Gustav Hartlaub zwischen einem »ursprünglichen« und einem »sekundären« Expressionismus, von denen nur der frühere unbewußt, lokal begrenzt und wirklich primitiv gewesen sei. Mittelalterliche Mystiker oder die Bildhauer der Eingeborenen seien in diesem Sinne primär Primitive, während die deutschen Expressionisten dem zweiten Typus angehörten, das heißt, sie seien »bewußt« primitiv gewesen oder hätten absichtlich primitiv gestaltet.[7] Daraus folgt, daß die modernen Deutschen über das Studium der archaischen oder der Stammeskunst zu einer kulturellen Sprache fanden – eine primitivisierende Sprache, aber doch eine Sprache.

Darüber hinaus gibt es keinen Zweifel, daß der expressionistische Primitivismus ästhetisch bedeutsam wie auch kulturell orientiert war. 1964 konnten Historiker der Kunst der Moderne und der Eingeborenen in der Suche nach formalen Beziehungen fruchtbar zusammenarbeiten: In ihrer Ausstellung »Das Ursprüngliche und die Moderne« wiesen etwa Leopold Reidemeister und Kurt Krieger auf die formalen Beziehungen zwischen diesen beiden künstlerischen Welten hin.[8] Und in der Münchner Ausstellung »Weltkulturen und moderne Kunst«, 1972, wurde, wie ich glaube, schlüssig gezeigt, daß die Reaktion der »Brücke« auf die Stammeskunst genauso »analytisch« wie auch »emotional« war. Wie es Manfred Schneckenburger im Katalog zu dieser Ausstellung formulierte, »wäre es aber falsch, ihre Begegnung als eine Art Mystik ohne Formverstand zu pauschalieren«. Heute müssen wir Schneckenburgers Feststellung bestätigen, daß das Primitive den Expressionismus in zweierlei Hinsicht beeinflußte: sowohl als Lebens- wie als Kunstidee.[9]

Der Unterschied zwischen dem Expressionismus in Deutschland und Österreich liegt in der Tat im Unvermögen der Österreicher begründet, sich wie ihre Nachbarn mit einem primitiven Ideal zu identifizieren. Mit der Kunst Eingeborener konfrontiert, räumte ihm OSKAR KOKOSCHKA 1908 emotionale Unmittelbarkeit ein, bestand jedoch auf ihrem Gegensatz zur Wiener Kultur:

»Schaute ich jedoch eine polynesische Maske mit den eingeritzten Tätowierungen an, war mir das sofort klar, weil ich an mir die Reaktionen meiner Gesichtsnerven auf Kälte und Hunger an den gleichen Stellen spürte.
Aber mir wäre nicht eingefallen, trotz meiner Sympathie für primitive Kunst, sie nachzuahmen; ich war ja kein Wilder. Ich hätte leben müssen wie diese, um echt zu sein. Und ich hatte ebensoviel Sympathie für Fossilien, für ausgestopfte Tiere, für Versteinerungen, Meteoriten, alles Dokumente einer Zeit, die nie wiederkommt.«[10]

Im Gegensatz dazu entdeckten die Expressionisten in Deutschland für sich eine Verwandtschaft mit Agrarvölkern. Während Deutschlands rascher Verstädterung in den Jahren

□ 512 *Ernst Ludwig Kirchner, ›Mädchen unter Japanschirm‹, um 1909, Öl auf Leinwand, 92 x 80 cm. Kunstsammlung Nordrhein-Westfalen, Düsseldorf.*

1910–11 oder nach dem entmenschlichenden, technisierten Krieg, wieder um 1919–20, war es leicht, solche Völker zu idealisieren. In städtischen Ateliers beschworen Künstler das Milieu eines Stammeslebens aus der eigenen Phantasie. Auf dem Lande wurde der Lebensstil der Bauern um seinetwillen geschätzt. Einige Künstler wurden sogar während der Sommerferien zu »Eingeborenen«, indem sie unbekleidet mit ihren Modellen zusammenlebten und eine sexuelle Freizügigkeit walten ließen, die nach ihrer Überzeugung die Instinktfreiheit des Stammeslebens, so wie man es sich vorstellte, nachahmte.[11]

Wie im Leben, so in der Kunst: Die deutschen Künstler eiferten dem primitiven Vorbild nach. Die Vorbilder reichten von den flachen und silhouettenhaft bemalten Reliefs der Palau bis zu den kraftvollen, plastischen Formen der Skulptur Kameruns. Jene für viele expressionistische Kunstwerke typische Härte – rechteckige Form, geometrische Einzelheiten, untersetzte Proportionen – ist ohne die primitiven Vorläufer undenkbar. Vitalismus war gleichfalls wichtig: Augen, Mund, Brüste, Genitalien traten expressiv in den Vordergrund. Sogar in Ruhestellung schienen die expressionistischen Gesichter und Figuren mit Energie geladen. Es sind dies alles deutsche Ableitungen aus der Stammeskunst. Man muß vorläufig annehmen, daß zumindest einige expressionistische Werke direkt auf identifizierbare primitive Quellen zurückgehen. Der Nachweis solcher Ableitungen hat sich aber als schwierig erwiesen. Reidemeister (1964) und Schneckenburger (1972) stellten jeweils etwa sechzig bis siebzig Werke deutscher Expressionisten und der Stammeskunst in eindrucksvollen Ausstellungen zusammen, die formale Ähnlichkeiten veranschaulichten. In einigen Fällen brachte der genaue Vergleich den Einfluß eines bestimmten primitiven Gegenstandes auf ein expressionistisches Werk zum Vorschein. Sechs oder sieben solcher Vergleiche einschließlich einiger Beispiele, die der Kenner von NOLDES Werk Martin Urban dokumentarisch belegte, sollen in der vorliegenden Studie erneut erläutert werden.[12]

Doch die meisten Vergleiche, die in diesen Ausstellungen vorgeschlagen wurden, waren ungenau oder nicht überzeugend, vor allem deshalb, weil man nicht überprüfte, ob ein bestimmtes Stammesobjekt für deutsche Künstler vor 1910 oder gar 1920 tatsächlich verfügbar war. Ein ständiges Problem ist, daß die Bestände der deutschen Völkerkundemuseen während des Zweiten Weltkriegs dezimiert wurden, wie dies vielen öffentlichen Sammlungen expressionistischer Kunst schon einige Jahre vorher widerfahren war. Eine erstaunliche Zahl solcher Gegenstände ist uns jedoch bildlich überliefert, und die Mehrzahl der Werke selbst ist noch vorhanden. Die Untersuchung der Abbildungen verlorener Gegenstände zusammen mit den noch vorhandenen kann wesentlich zur Klärung des Verfahrens beitragen, wie die Expressionisten die primitiven Quellen benutzten. Darüber hinaus müßte bei solchen Vergleichen der zu erwartende Selektionsprozeß, wie er bei der Anregung durch Vorbilder stattfindet, untersucht werden. Verdankt ein expressionistisches Werk seine Anregung mehr als einem primitiven Vorbild? Antwortete es selektiv auf ein bestimmtes Merkmal, dabei aber nicht auf alle Merkmale des Vorbildes? Solche Fragestellungen, denen in der bisherigen Literatur noch nicht nachgegangen wurde, sollen im vorliegenden Essay untersucht werden.

In seinem *Discours sur l'origine et les fondements de l'inégalité parmi les hommes* (Diskurs über den Ursprung und die Grundlagen der Ungleichheit unter den Menschen) betrachtete Jean-Jacques Rousseau den Primitiven als prärational. Seine Evolutionstheorie postulierte, was Claude Lévi-Strauss einen »dreifachen Übergang« nannte: von der Natur zur Kultur, vom Affekt zur Erkenntnis und von der Animalität zur Humanität.[13] Doch diese Kluft in der Entwicklung hinderte Rousseau im Alter nicht daran, sich bei ein oder zwei kurzen Gelegenheiten in den vorkulturellen Zustand tief einzufühlen. Er schrieb: »Ich fühle Ekstasen, unaussprechliches Vergnügen, gleichsam im System der Wesen aufzugehen, mich mit der ganzen Natur zu identifizieren.«[14]

Ein Jahrhundert später stellte in den deutschsprachigen Ländern Ferdinand Tönnies einen Unterschied zwischen natürlicher »Gemeinschaft« und einer fortgeschritteneren kapitalistischen »Gesellschaft« fest. Gemeinschaft war die Form sozialer Organisation des Volkes, die auf den familiären Gefühlen von Liebe, Verwandtschaft und Nachbarschaft gründet, während die »gebildeten« Schichten eine Gesellschaft bevorzugten, deren Grundlage Individualismus, Verträge und Warenwerte bildeten. »Organische« *Gemeinschaft* entstehe aus einer Übereinstimmung von »natürlichen Wünschen«, die »mechanische« *Gesellschaft* gewähre objektive Verbindungen zwischen »rationalen Wünschen«.[15] Tönnies' Theorie definiert jenes Phänomen, das Lévi-Strauss »kulturelle Diskontinuität« nennt. Die primitive Gemeinschaft läßt ein Bedürfnis nach Ganzheit, Respekt vor der Natur und Ablehnung historischer Zeit erkennen, wurde aber inzwischen zum Opfer der Ausbeutung konkurrenzfähigerer kolonialistischer Gesellschaften.[16]

In der expressionistischen Generation schrieb Georg Simmel sehr eindringlich über die Krankheiten der unpersönlich gewordenen modernen Städte. Noch stärker als Tönnies fand er das städtische Leben entfremdend: »Was im großstädtischen Lebensstil . . . als Dissoziation anmutet, ist in Wirklichkeit nur eine seiner grundlegenden Formen der Sozialisation«; »unter bestimmten Umständen fühlt man sich nirgends so allein und so verloren wie in der Menge der Großstadt«.[17] Trotzdem bestand Simmel im Gegensatz zu Tönnies darauf, daß Kunst an den Kreuzungspunkten von Natur und Kultur entspringe. Tönnies dagegen diskutierte Kreativität und Genie unter dem Gesichtspunkt der »natürlichen Wünsche« des einfachen Volkes; Kunst entstehe aus Gefühlen, »weiblichen« Werten und in der Gemeinschaft.[18] Simmel wiederum beobachtete, daß die Kunst nicht nur rauhes »Leben« (Natur) zu ihrer Entfaltung benötigt, sondern auch künstlerische »Form« (Kultur). Die Krise in der modernen Kultur beruhe genau auf dem Konflikt dieser beiden Faktoren:

» . . . es will, wo es [das Leben] sich ausspricht, eben nur sich selbst aussprechen und durchbricht deshalb jede Form, die ihm von einer anderen Wirklichkeit . . . auferlegt werden soll. . . . Denn kaum je erscheint in dem letzteren Falle die Brücke zwischen dem Vorher und dem Nachher der Kulturformen so ganz abgerissen wie jetzt, so daß nur noch das an sich formlose Leben zu bleiben scheint, um sich in die Lücke zu stellen . . . Aber vielleicht ist diese Formlosigkeit selbst die passende Form zeitgenössischen Lebens.«[19]

Folgt man Tönnies, so sahen Expressionisten wie NOLDE die Kunst in Beziehung zur prärationalen Gemeinschaft eines Volkes, zu den Instinkten und Gefühlen eines natürlichen Lebens, genau zu dem, was Rousseau als den primitiven Zustand der Natur betrachtete.[20] Doch wußten mit Simmel die meisten deutschen Künstler, daß Kunst ein Kulturprodukt war. In der industriellen Gesellschaft konnten Malerei und Skulptur nur einen Naturzustand beschwören; sie konnten nie ganz zu ihm zurückkehren.

Als die »Brücke« am 7. Juni 1905 in Dresden gegründet wurde, nahm sie den Namen ›Künstlergruppe‹ statt des volkstümlicheren Namens ›Gemeinschaft‹ an.[21] Als das *»Brücke«-Programm* vom Herbst 1906 die »Jugend« zum Widerstand »gegenüber den wohlangesessenen älteren Kräften« aufrief, meinte man nicht die jugendliche Unschuld von Tönnies' natürlicher Gemeinschaft,[22] sondern die »herrliche Kraft« der Jugend, wie sie 1898 von der besonders anspruchsvollen Wiener Sezession verfochten wurde.[23] Selbst der Stil des holzgeschnittenen *Programms* – elegant gestaltete Lettern in regelmäßigen Zeilenabständen – beschwört nicht ein Bild der Natur, sondern fortgeschrittener Kultur.[24]

□ 514 *Sam und Milly in Kirchners Dresdner Atelier, Photographie des Künstlers, 1911. Photoarchiv Hans Bollinger und Roman Norbert Ketterer.*

□ 513 *Ernst Ludwig Kirchner, Badende im Raum, 1909, überarbeitet 1920, Öl auf Leinwand, 151 x 198 cm. Saarland-Museum, Saarbrücken.*

Neu im *»Brücke«-Programm* ist dagegen die abschließende Einladung an jeden Künstler, »der unmittelbar und unverfälscht das wiedergibt, was ihn zum Schaffen drängt«. Der Nachdruck auf »Unmittelbarkeit und Unverfälschtheit«, wie Simmels Betonung des unverfälschten »Lebens«, spiegelt jenen dionysischen oder vitalistischen Anstoß zur Kunst, für den früher schon Friedrich Nietzsche und Walt Whitman eingetreten waren. Unter den Gründern der »Brücke« waren es ERICH HECKEL und KARL SCHMIDT-ROTTLUFF, die schon seit Jahren Nietzsche gelesen hatten,[25] während Whitman ERNST LUDWIG KIRCHNERS Lieblingsautor war.[26]

Der dionysische Impuls war allerdings mit keiner wirklich natürlichen oder »primitiven« Form von Sexualität verbunden, zumindest nicht bis zu bestimmten Werken von 1909. In *Mädchen unter Japanschirm* etwa □ 512 setzt KIRCHNER eine verführerische Nackte vor einen Ateliervorhang, der mit erotischen Spielen bedeckt ist. Auf diesem Bild und im Hintergrund von HECKELS gleichzeitigem *Mädchen mit Rose*[27] zeigt der Vorhang links oben unter anderen Nackten eine gebeugte Frau, die ihr Gesäß vorstreckt, und rechts daneben eine männliche Figur mit erigiertem Penis. Mit diesen Bildern aus dem Jahre 1909 wenden die »Brücke«-Künstler jene vage formulierte Forderung des *Programms* nach »Unmittelbarkeit« ins eindeutig Erotische.

Es gibt verschiedene Gründe für diese neue Erotik. Literarische Vorgänger spielten sicher eine Rolle. Bestimmt kannten die Dresdner Nietzsches Theorie, daß die Kunst aus der Beziehung zwischen der geistigen Idee von »Schönheit« und der körperlichen Erfahrung von »Sexualität« entstehe: »Jede ›Vollkommenheit‹, die ganze ›Schönheit‹ der Dinge erinnert unbewußt an die aphrodisische Seligkeit . . . Das Verlangen nach Kunst und Schönheit ist ein indirektes Verlangen nach den Entzückungen des Geschlechtstriebs, welche er dem Cerebrum mitteilt.«[28]

»Trieb, Trieb und Trieb
Immer der zeugende Trieb der Welt.
Immer treten aus dem Dunkel Gleiche einander entgegen, immer Stoff und Wachstum, immer Geschlecht,
Immer eine Verknüpfung der Identität, immer Unterscheidung,
Immer ein zeugendes Leben.«[29]

□ 515 *Ernst Heckel, ›Mädchen mit Ananas‹, 1910, Öl auf Leinwand, 80 x 70 cm. Verbleib unbekannt.*

Außerdem ist es möglich, die Anordnung der nackten Figuren auf dem Vorhang von den Posen der Badenden an den Moritzburger Seen aus dem Sommer 1909 abzuleiten, die KIRCHNER in seinem Stadtatelier wiederaufnimmt.[30] Weitere Werke KIRCHNERS von 1909 oder 1909–10 zeigen in der Tat männliche und weibliche Personen in sexuell aufreizenden Stellungen, am direktesten in dem Tonrelief *Liebesszene*, bei der sich Liebende gegenseitig körperlich erregen.[31] Schließlich gibt es für diesen Vorhang sehr wahrscheinlich auch einen Vorläufer aus dem Bereich der Stammeskunst. Figurenfries und phallische Erektion ähneln jenen sinnbildhaften Hausbalken der Palau – eine wichtige Quelle für die Künstler der »Brücke« nach dem Frühjahr 1910, die sie unzweifelhaft schon früher gesehen hatten □ 517, 518.

Trotzdem unternahmen KIRCHNER und HECKEL außergewöhnliche Schritte, um den primitiven Charakter einer solchen Vorlage einzuschränken. Schon die Titel der Bilder heben den »Japanschirm« und die »Rose« hervor – Sinnbilder einer modernen Sensibilität. Der Hintergrund zeigt rohes »Leben«, indes die Nackten im Vordergrund Attribute der Zivilisation halten. Während oben grober Sex angedeutet wird, finden wir unten den hochmodischen Schirm oder die Blume der romantischen Liebe. Trotz ihrer Verschiedenartigkeit beschwören beide Bilder den doppeldeutigen Lebensstil der »Brücke« – einen Stil, der dem Rohen das Verfeinerte entgegenhält, dem Natürlichen das Kultivierte.

Dieses Grundmuster wird in einer Gruppe von Werken bestätigt, die in KIRCHNERS Dresdner Atelier im Winter 1909–10 entstanden.[32] Das früheste von diesen, *Badende im Raum*, Ende 1909 gemalt □ 513, stellt anmutig und kunstvoll posierende »Badende« in einem bunten und »primitiven« Innenraum dar. Die Nackten ähneln den Aktfiguren in MATISSE' Bild *Lebensfreude* von 1906. Sie stehen, lehnen sich an, essen oder kämmen sich ihr Haar und vergegenwärtigen ein heiteres und idyllisches Arkadien.[33] Das Interieur dagegen erinnert an das Aussehen eines Raumes in einem Stammeshaus. Schlanke Figuren mit schwarzen Silhouetten schmücken den einen Durchgang, während ein Paar kräftig bemalter Vorhänge den Eingang zu einem weiteren Raum abschirmt. Die Vorhänge haben ein geometrisches Muster: Jedes Feld ist leuchtend gelb, schwarz eingerahmt und enthält grüne und gelbe Kreisfelder, die unten einen sitzenden König und oben kopulierende Paare zeigen. Der anscheinend ziemlich enge Schlafraum dahinter, der 1910 ebenfalls mit bemalten Wandbehängen ausgekleidet wurde, zeigt erneut kopulierende Paare, nun schon etwas szenischer angelegt und unter tropischen Bäumen. Während des Jahres 1911 wurde der schwarz eingefaßte Spiegel auf der rechten Seite der *Badenden im Raum* von einem Paar meterhoher Sockel flankiert, auf die schließlich KIRCHNER seine eigenen Holzskulpturen stellte.[34]

Unter den Meisterwerken KIRCHNERS aus dem Jahr 1910, die von diesen pseudoprimitiven Vorhängen und Verkleidungen Gebrauch machen, ist das bekannte Bild *Stehender Akt mit Hut* in Frankfurt das aufschlußreichste.[35] Wenn wir diese Nackte als CRANACHS *Venus* von 1532 und als KIRCHNERS Freundin, die Tänzerin Doris (»Dodo«) Grohse, identifiziert haben, verstehen wir das Bild noch immer als eine Ikone von hoher Kultur. Von CRANACHS Vorbild übernimmt der *Stehende Akt* seine elegante Pose und das modische Halsband – jetzt mit Ohrringen und einem Armreif bereichert –, während die rosaroten Ballettschuhe auf Dodos Beruf hinweisen. Doch unterstreichen der breite Hut und das abrasierte Schamhaar die Weltgewandtheit des Modells: Es ist öffentlich und auch privat von modischem Reiz. Das keilförmige Dreieck zwingt zum Blick auf die Scham – wie schon das durchsichtige Kleid bei CRANACH – und weist damit auf die Zartheit des weiblichen Geschlechts hin. Damit widerlegt die anmutige Nackte ihren Hintergrund, den grobe Formen und roher Sex bestimmen. Indem er dem Primitiven das Elegante gegenüberstellt, setzt KIRCHNER wieder die Natur der Kultur entgegen.

Auch HECKEL wandte solche Kontraste an, aber abgemildert. In seinem *Mädchen mit Ananas* von 1910 □ 515 greift er auf KIRCHNERS Thema zurück: einen anmutigen Akt vor einem primitiven Hintergrund. Doch unten ordnet nun HECKEL ein kniendes Mädchen neben einen hölzernen Hocker, den KIRCHNER nach einem Vorbild aus Kamerun geschnitzt hatte.[36] Das Lächeln des Mädchens ahmt den als Tier gestalteten Untersatz des Hockers mimisch nach, während die Ananas (als tropisches Erzeugnis) Natur und zugleich (als europäische Delikatesse) Kultur beschwört. So mildert HECKEL KIRCHNERS Gegensätze. Das Modische und das Exotische sind miteinander verbunden, nicht einander gegenübergestellt.

In der Tat waren der »Brücke« zwei ganz unterschiedliche Ideen geläufig, die zwei Annäherungsweisen an das Primitive zur Folge hatten: Natur gegen Kultur und Natur als Kultur. Die letztere Idee vertrat hauptsächlich GAUGUIN, dessen Werk im September 1910 in Dresden gezeigt wurde. Als ein Europäer in Polynesien behandelte GAUGUIN einheimische Themen Tahitis im Kontext eines hochentwickelten Stiles. Auf ähnliche Weise benutzte HECKEL einen Tierfries mit primitiver Ornamentik als Hintergrund für den farbenfrohen, doch sexuell provokativen *Akt* (*Dresden*).[37] Selbst KIRCHNER übernahm HECKELS Bildwelt und dessen Tierfries in einigen Gemälden aus dem Jahre 1910.[38] Hier erscheinen deutsche Mädchen so »primitiv« wie ihre Hintergrundfiguren.

☐ 516 *Ernst Ludwig Kirchner, ›Exotische Szene‹, Feder und Buntstift auf Postkarte, Stempel vom 20. Juni 1910. Altonaer Museum, Hamburg.*

☐ 517 *›Verzierter Holzbalken‹ (Ausschnitt), Palauinseln (Karolineninseln), bemaltes Holz. Veröffentlicht in Eckhart von Sydow, „Die Kunst der Naturvölker und der Vorzeit", 1923.*

Und doch war es ein anderer »Brücke«-Künstler, Max Pechstein, der am stärksten an Gauguin anknüpfte. 1906 hatte er sich der Künstlergruppe angeschlossen, zog jedoch schon 1908 nach Berlin. In *Negertanz-Gruppe* (*Somali-Tanz*), einem farbigen Holzschnitt von 1910, arbeitete Pechstein lieber mit schwarzen als mit weißen Modellen, auch wenn er sie nicht in einer für das Stammesleben typischen Situation darstellte, sondern im städtischen Milieu der Kabarettbühne.[39] So ist die entstandene Arbeit sowohl »primitiv« als auch zeitgemäß. Rhythmen von Stammestänzen und Muster der Stammeskleider werden auf brillante Weise beschworen, obschon der Wechsel von schwarzen und weißen Umrissen den eigentümlich modernen Sinn des Künstlers für dekorative Abstraktion verrät. Nicht unähnlich Gauguins Modellen werden Pechsteins schwarze Tänzer und Musiker zum Vermittler hoher Kultur. Sein Sinn für das Exotische, gleich dem Gauguins, veranlaßte ihn auch bald, in die Tropen zu reisen.

Kirchner jedoch, der zwischen 1909 und 1911 Negermodelle heranzog, schuf die radikalste Gestaltung dieses Themas.[40] Er unterlag jenen weißen Mythen einer instinkthaften Vitalität der Schwarzen, nicht nur im musikalischen Ausdruck (wie im Ragtime oder Jazz), sondern auch in ihrer legendären sexuellen Stärke. Solche Phantasien veranlaßten ihn, die schwarzen Zirkuskünstler Sam und Milli zu photographieren ☐ 514 und Millis ausladendes Gesäß und Sams großen Penis im Gemälde *Negerpaar* von 1911 zu malen. Kirchner vervollständigte seine Arbeit mit diesen Modellen, indem er sie sechs erotische Stellungen einnehmen ließ, wozu auch oraler und genitaler Verkehr gehörten. Davon fertigte er ebensoviele Lithographien an.[41] Da er nur wenige Abzüge von jedem Stein machte, war nicht daran gedacht, soweit es uns bekannt ist, mit Pornographie Geld zu verdienen. Sein Ziel hingegen bestand weiterhin in der »Unmittelbarkeit und Unverfälschtheit«, für die er ein halbes Jahrzehnt zuvor im *»Brücke«-Programm* eingetreten war. In der Tat kamen die Expressionisten in ihren letzten Dresdner Werken der Synthese der ursprünglichen Natur mit der hohen Kultur am nächsten. Die Leidenschaftlichkeit der Modelle und das gleich gierige zeichnerische Können des Künstler-Voyeurs treten zutage.

Mehrere geschnitzte und bemalte Hausbalken von den Palauinseln, damals eine deutsche Kolonie an der westlichen Ecke Mikronesiens, lieferten das erste wichtige Modell für den expressionistischen Primitivismus in Deutschland ☐ 517, 518.

☐ 518 *›Verzierter Holzbalken‹ (Ausschnitt), Palauinseln (Karolineninseln), Höhe 35 cm. University Museum, University of Pennsylvania, Philadelphia.*

Darauf dargestellt sind Szenen, die der Museumsführer als die »oft sonderbaren Bräuche« der Palauinseln beschreibt. Diese Balken waren im Anthropologisch-Völkerkundlichen Museum im östlichen Flügel des Zwingers in Dresden ausgestellt.[42] Sie wurden 1902[43] in einem mit Spiegeln versehenen Glasschrank plaziert, so daß sie von vorne wie hinten gut gesehen werden konnten.[44] Doch waren sie schon lange im Westen bekannt, nachdem sie erstmals 1881 veröffentlicht und in Karl Woermanns *Geschichte der Kunst aller Zeiten und Völker* (1900) dreifarbig abgebildet worden waren.[45] Es ist nicht besonders überraschend, daß Dresdner Architekturstudenten, so auch Kirchner, schon zu Beginn des Jahrhunderts auf diese bemerkenswerten Arbeiten aufmerksam wurden. Kirchner bestätigte mehrfach, daß er es war, der 1903 »im Dresdner Völkerkunde-Museum . . . die Balken der Palauinsulaner fand, deren Figuren genau die gleiche Formensprache zeigten wie meine eigene«.[46] Obwohl es durchaus denkbar ist, daß er diese Balken so früh »entdeckte«, übten sie auf sein Werk vor 1910 keinen direkten Einfluß aus.[47]

Doch müssen Vermutungen zurückgewiesen werden, daß Kirchner so früh wie die Fauves Interesse an primitiver Kunst gezeigt hätte.[48] Frühe Interpreten seines Werks wurden von den Zeichnungen Kirchners von Ende 1909 oder 1910 in die Irre geleitet, denn der Künstler datierte sie bis zu sechs Jahre vor.[49] Kirchners intensives Studium im Dresdner Völkerkundemuseum ist statt dessen in die Zeit zwischen März und Juni 1910 zu datieren. Am 31. März schrieb er aus Dresden an

□ 519 *Karl Schmidt-Rottluff, ›Zwei weibliche Akte‹, Weihnachten 1911, bemaltes Holzrelief, 19 x 27 cm. Brücke-Museum, Berlin.*

HECKEL und PECHSTEIN in Berlin: »Hier ist das Völkerkundemuseum wieder auf, nur ein kleiner Teil, aber doch eine Erholung und ein Genuß die famosen Bronzen aus Benin, einige Sachen der Pueblos aus Mexiko sind noch ausgestellt und einige Negerplastiken.«[50] Am 20. Juni 1910 sandte er eine Postkarte an HECKEL in Dangast, in der er berichtete, daß »der [Haus-] Balken wirklich wunderbar sei«.[51] Auf die Vorderseite zeichnete KIRCHNER eine *Exotische Szene* □ 516, die direkt nach einem Motiv auf einem der Palau-Balken entstand □ 517. Es ist auffallend, daß KIRCHNER das Bild der Palau nicht direkt kopierte. Er vereinfachte die regelmäßigen, dreieckigen Muster des Balkenrandes zu einer kräftigen Zickzacklinie im oberen Teil der Zeichnung. Diese Linie erinnert an die »Sprechlinien«, die auf einzelnen Palau-Balken vorkommen □ 518.[52] Ebenso wichtig ist, daß KIRCHNER die Geschlechtsteile der Palau-Figuren leicht übertreibt. Der Penis der männlichen Figur ist größer als im Vorbild, und die weibliche Figur ist in einer Dreiviertel-Rückenansicht so gezeichnet, daß das breite Gesäß wie auch das Profil der Brüste gesehen werden können, die im ozeanischen Vorbild bedeutend weniger deutlich sind.

Die eingehende Betrachtung beider Werke läßt erkennen, warum die Palau-Figuren für KIRCHNERS Betrachtungsweise von 1910 »genau die gleiche Formensprache . . . wie meine eigene« aufzuweisen scheinen. Sowohl der Palau-Fries wie die Zeichnung KIRCHNERS sind betont flach und zweidimensional angelegt, ein einfarbig glatter Grund bedingt die unräumliche Struktur, in der sich gleichermaßen flache Figuren wie Gegenstände entfalten. Diese heben sich gegen den Grund zusätzlich durch einen schmalen hellen Randstreifen ab: in einem Falle mit einer tiefen, in den Holzbalken eingeschnitzten Rille, im anderen mit einer kräftig konturierten Einfassung in weißer Farbe. Es ist, als wäre der Grund in beiden Werken das Festland, die helle Umrahmung ein endloses Wasser und die Figuren oder Gegenstände die großen Inseln, die von der Küste des Festlandes abgetrennt sind. Und da die Figuren nirgends überlappen, deuten sie auch keine Tiefenräumlichkeit an.

Kunsthistoriker bestätigen, daß dieser »Palau-Stil« die primitivistischen Arbeiten der »Brücke« anregte, die an den Moritzburger Seen im Sommer 1910 entstanden. In einem Holzschnitt wie KIRCHNERS *Mit Schilf werfende Badende*[53] sind die kantigen Figuren mit schwarzen Haarmassen von den Palau abzuleiten; selbst Unterschiede zwischen Mann und Frau hängen, wie auf den Balken, von kaum mehr als einer gebogenen Hüfte oder einem verlängerten Penis ab. Aber jetzt sind es die Umrisse des expressionistischen schwarzen Holzschnittes, die an die Stelle der weißen Umrandung der Palau-Balken treten. In beiden Fällen bleiben die Figur und der Grund ausgesprochen flach und zweidimensional. Auch in HECKELS Gemälde *Waldweiher* aus dem Sommer 1910 sind die kantig gezeichneten Figuren vor den weitgehend monochromen Hintergrund gesetzt.[54] Trotz einer gewissen Lebensnähe erscheinen die Menschen vereinfacht und ungelenk schematisiert, nicht unähnlich ihrem Vorbild aus Mikronesien. Ein gleicher »Kürzelstil« tritt uns in PECHSTEINS Moritzburger Gemälden aus demselben Sommer entgegen.[55] Selbst in einem 1912 entstandenen Werk des zuletzt zur »Brücke« gestoßenen und in Berlin lebenden OTTO MUELLER, dem *Titelblatt zur Brücke-Jahresgabe 1912*, können wir diesem Stil begegnen.[56] Eine weitere Nachwirkung der Palau-Hausbalken dokumentiert ein Werk KARL SCHMIDT-ROTTLUFFS, das Weihnachten 1911 entstand, nachdem die »Brücke«-Künstler von Dresden nach Berlin gezogen waren: das bemalte Holzrelief *Zwei weibliche Akte* □ 519. Die expressionistischen Figuren sind hier von großer räumlicher Komplexität. Die Frau links beugt sich soweit nach unten, daß das schwarze Trapez ihres Haares beinahe das schwarze Dreieck ihrer Scham erreicht. Die Frau neben ihr, die an vier Stellen von den Gliedern ihrer Nachbarin überdeckt wird, ist in einer kompliziert verkürzten Sitzhaltung dargestellt. Doch gelingt es SCHMIDT-ROTTLUFF, mit zwei Körpern und acht Gliedern eine einzige helle Masse in Orange zu schaffen, die sich gegen eine grob strukturierte tiefblaue Einfassung flächig abhebt. Diese wiederum umschließt eine mit horizontalen Kerblinien belebte Fläche, die braun bemalt ist und die hölzerne, plankenartige Struktur des Holzes betont. Obwohl SCHMIDT-ROTTLUFFS Figuren durch tief in die Oberfläche des Holzes eingeschnitzte Rillen umrissen sind, fängt das Werk den flachen, kantigen Reliefstil der Palau-Balken auch in dieser Hinsicht sehr gut ein.

Die künstlerische Entwicklung zwischen 1910 und 1911 sollte nicht außer acht gelassen werden. 1911 schuf SCHMIDT-ROTTLUFF innerhalb seiner Beschäftigung mit der Palau-Kunst eine komplexe Variation über ein vereinfachtes Thema. Sie veranschaulicht Hartlaubs Unterscheidung zwischen einer ursprünglichen Form der primitiven Äußerung und der sekundären Form der Expressionisten, die mehr oder weniger bewußt primitivistisch arbeiteten. Darüber hinaus zeigte SCHMIDT-ROTTLUFF, wie er die Auswahl seiner Vorbilder nach bestimmten Überlegungen vornahm, indem er die starken Silhouetten wählte, aber die reine Zweidimensionalität der Palau-Werke verwarf. Das gleiche gilt für andere den Palau nahestehende Arbeiten der »Brücke« in ihrem letzten Jahr in Dresden.[57]

Die Anregung eines Werkes von 1911 durch ein afrikanisches Vorbild, was für diese Zeit bei der »Brücke« noch einen Einzelfall darstellt, läßt ein ähnliches Interesse an komplexer Raumwirkung erkennen. Die *Zeichnung nach einer Benin-Bronze* □ 520 kopierte KIRCHNER nicht nach der Abbildung eines Buches, wie ich früher annahm,[58] sondern nach dem originalen Benin-Relief eines Königs mit seinem Gefolge aus dem Dresdner Völkerkunde-Museum □ 521. Donald Rosenthal, der diese Entdeckung machte, glaubt, daß »Kirchner diese Platte mit gründlicher Genauigkeit kopierte« und die Zeichnung im März 1910 oder etwas früher entstanden sei.[59] Doch ist bei genauerem Hinsehen nicht nur der »schraffierte« Strich erkennbar, den KIRCHNER wegen der Plastizität erstmals

□ 520 *Ernst Ludwig Kirchner, Zeichnung nach einer Benin-Bronze, 1911, Bleistift. Nachlaß Kirchner.*

1911 anwandte,[60] sondern auch eine ungewöhnliche Abweichung von der Räumlichkeit des afrikanischen Werks. In der Benin-Platte sind die Füße des Königs und des Gefolges genau in einer Linie; da die Füße des Königs größer sind, scheinen sie von der Basis der Platte stärker vorzustehen. Im Gegensatz dazu ist das Gefolge auf KIRCHNERS Zeichnung dem König einen Schritt voraus; den beiden Höflingen links werden die Fußknöchel durch den unteren Blattrand angeschnitten. So verlassen KIRCHNERS Figuren die Fläche des Bronzereliefs und drängen in unseren Raum vor. Mit diesem seit 1911 zu beobachtenden neuen Interesse am Raum begann der Einfluß des Reliefstils der Palau von 1910 nachzulassen.

Wenden wir unsere Aufmerksamkeit vom Dresden der Jahre 1910–11 auf das München in der Zeit von 1911–12, so erleben wir eine ganz andersgeartete expressionistische Annäherung an die Stammeskunst. Hier sind WASSILY KANDINSKY und FRANZ MARC die Schlüsselfiguren, die in diesen Jahren gemeinsam einen Almanach herausgaben und zwei Kunstausstellungen unter dem Zeichen des »Blauen Reiters« organisierten; von Interesse sind aber auch zwei weniger bedeutende Künstler dieser Gruppe, AUGUST MACKE und HEINRICH CAMPENDONK. Für sie alle, speziell aber für KANDINSKY und MARC, hatte ein einheitliches sachliches Konzept des Primitiven Vorrang vor irgendwelchen Einzelbeispielen primitiver Kunst.[61] Für den »Blauen Reiter« konnte das Primitive ohne weiteres archaische Hofkunst, Volks-, Kinder- oder Stammeskunst bedeuten. Daher wurde der Primitivismus des »Blauen Reiters« wiederholt etwa im Hinblick auf Volkskunst diskutiert.[62]

□ 521 *›Reliefplatte‹, Königreich Benin (Nigeria), Bronze, Höhe 50 cm, Staatliches Museum für Völkerkunde, Dresden.*

Nach KANDINSKY bestand eine Aufgabe des »Blauen Reiters« darin, die Vereinigung aller Ausdruckskünste zu fördern. Was ihn am meisten störte, war die scheinbar willkürliche Trennung der verschiedenen Künste und Perioden der Kunstgeschichte: »Ich träumte von Malern und Musikern in erster Linie« als »Blaue Reiter«-Mitarbeiter, schrieb er später. »Die verderbliche Absonderung der einen Kunst von der anderen, weiter der ›Kunst‹ von der Volks-, Kinderkunst, von der ›Ethnographie‹, die fest gebauten Mauern zwischen den in meinen Augen so verwandten, oft identischen Erscheinungen, mit einem Wort, die synthetischen Beziehungen – all das ließ mir keine Ruhe.«[63] KANDINSKY bestätigte, daß sein »völkerkundliches« Interesse vom »erschütternden Eindruck« herrührt, »den ich viel später (1907) im Völkerkundemuseum in Berlin von der Negerkunst erlebte«.[64] Trotzdem gibt es keinen zwingenden Beweis, daß die Stammeskunst KANDINSKYS Stil damals oder später direkt beeinflußt hätte.

Bei FRANZ MARC liegen die Dinge ganz anders. Die Exponate im Berliner Museum für Völkerkunde übten nicht nur einen allgemeinen Einfluß auf seine ästhetische Auffassung aus, sondern speziell eine starke, wenn auch nur momentane Wirkung auf seinen Stil von 1911. MARCS Brief an MACKE vom 14. Januar 1911 spricht für sich selbst:

»Ich war sehr ausgiebig im Völkerkundemuseum, um die Kunstmittel ›primitiver Völker‹ . . . zu studieren. Ich blieb schließlich staunend und erschüttert an den Schnitzereien der Kameruner hängen, die vielleicht nur noch von den erhabenen Werken der Inkas überboten werden. Ich finde es so selbstverständlich, daß wir in diesem kalten Frührot künstlerischer Intelligenz die Wiedergeburt unseres Kunstfühlens suchen und nicht in Kulturen, die schon eine tausendjährige Bahn durchlaufen haben wie die Japaner oder die italienische Renaissance. Ich bin in diesem kurzen Winter schon ein ganz anderer Mensch geworden. Ich glaube allmählich wirklich zu begreifen, auf was es für uns ankommt, wenn wir uns überhaupt Künstler nennen wollen; wir müssen Asketen werden, – erschrick nicht; ich meine dies nur in geistigen Beziehungen. Wir müssen tapfer fast auf alles verzichten, was uns als guten Mitteleuropäern bisher teuer und unentbehrlich war; unsere Ideen und Ideale müssen ein härenes Gewand tragen, wir müssen sie mit Heuschrecken und wildem Honig nähren und nicht mit Historie, um aus der Müdigkeit unsres europäischen Ungeschmacks herauszukommen. . . . Das Ziel, ›aufs innigste zu wünschen‹, ist nun natürlich . . . rein aus einem gesunden Farbeninstinkt, wie es die primitiven Völker alle hatten. Daß wir daraus ›Bilder‹ machen wollen und nicht nur bunte Säulen und Kapitäle und Strohhüte und Tongefäße, – ist unser Vorzug, unser ›Europäertum‹.«[65]

So wie KIRCHNER mit seiner Beschäftigung mit GAUGUIN im Jahr 1910 zur Untersuchung der südostasiatischen Malerei (Ajanta) kam (1910–11), so ging MARC 1911 nach seiner Untersuchung GAUGUINS (1910) zur Prüfung einer anderen Anregung GAUGUINS über – der ägyptischen Kunst. Dies ist bekannt, seit Klaus Lankheit einen Eselfries aus dem Alten Reich als Anregung für MARCS 1911 entstandenes Gemälde desselben Themas publizierte □ 525, 526.[66] Doch wies Lankheit nicht auf MARCS Übersetzung des sehr flachen Reliefs seines ägyptischen Vorbildes in die auffallend körperlichen und dreidimensionalen Tiere seines Gemäldes hin. Ich verweise nicht nur auf die Beinstellung der Esel bei MARC – in der Tiefe durch dazwischenstehendes Gras getrennt –, sondern auch auf die durchmodellierten Kinnbacken, die knochigen Köpfe und die spitzen Ohren der gemalten Tiere. Überdies sind die Gesichtszüge der Tiere wilder, sozusagen expressionistischer als die ägyptischen. Die Augen haben waagrechte Oberlider und nicht gerundete, während die Mäuler teils leicht offen und nicht wie auf dem ägyptischen Relief in zusammengedrückten Linien spröde geschlossen sind. Die einzige Erklärung für MARCS wohlüberlegtes Abweichen von der flachen und behutsamen Art seines archaischen Vorbildes ist das Eingreifen einer zweiten und echteren primitiven Anregung in seinen Stil. Die Abweichung wurde meiner Ansicht nach durch die bemalte Maske eines Ochsenkopfes aus Holz inspiriert □ 524, die seit 1899 der Sammlung des Berliner Völkerkundemuseums ange-

□ 522 *Heinrich Campendonk, ›Der Tiger‹, 1916, Holzschnitt, 25 x 32 cm, Städtische Galerie im Lenbachhaus, München.*

□ 523 *›Jagdszene‹, Benin (Nigeria), Bronze, Höhe 55 cm. Museum für Völkerkunde, Berlin.*

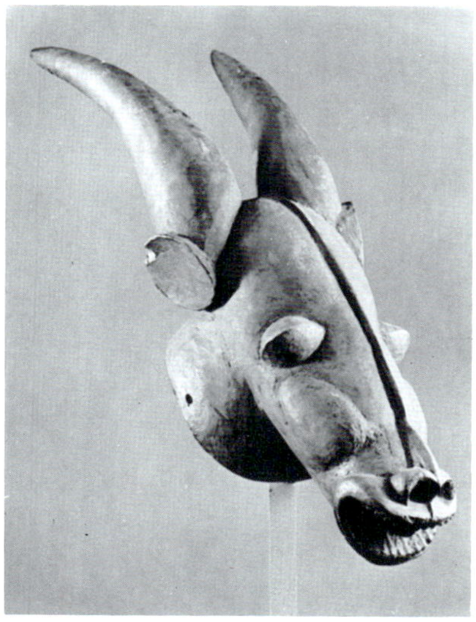

□ 524 *›Helmmaske in Gestalt eines Büffelkopfes‹, BANGWA (Kamerun), bemaltes Holz, Höhe 74 cm. Museum für Völkerkunde, Berlin.*

□ 525 *Franz Marc, ›Eselfries‹, 1911, Öl auf Leinwand, 81 x 150 cm. Sammlung Ursula Selbach, Lobberich.*

□ 526 *›Eselfries‹, altägyptisch. Rijksmuseum, Leiden.*

hört,[67] höchstwahrscheinlich im Januar 1911 ausgestellt war und den Tiermaler MARC sicherlich beeindruckte.[68] Die Kamerun-Maske ist nicht nur rundherum durchmodelliert, sondern auch ihr strenger Ausdruck und das geöffnete Maul ähneln stark den Tieren in MARCS Bild.

MARCS Verknüpfung ägyptischer mit afrikanischer Kunst ist nicht ungewöhnlich. Er folgte damit dem Hinweis von Wilhelm Worringers Studie *Abstraktion und Einfühlung* von 1908, deren Unterscheidung zwischen dem »Nachahmungstrieb« (Einfühlungsvermögen) und dem »Kunsttrieb« (Abstraktion) von einem Vergleich zwischen Volks- und Hofkunst in Ägypten ausging; denn nur die letztere ist »aus psychischen Bedürfnissen entstanden und hat psychische Bedürfnisse geweckt«.[69] Nicht zuletzt bezog Worringer das Wort »primitiv« noch entsprechend seiner Bedeutung im 19. Jahrhundert auf die vorgriechische Kunst Ägyptens und des Nahen Ostens und brachte diese primitive Kunst nur nebenbei mit der Kunst der »Wilden« und der »Orientalen« in Verbindung:

»Dabei finden wir, daß das Kunstwollen der Naturvölker, soweit ein solches überhaupt bei ihnen vorhanden ist, dann das Kunstwollen aller primitiven Kunstepochen und schließlich das Kunstwollen gewisser entwickelter orientalischer Kulturvölker diese abstrakte Tendenz zeigen.«[70]

MARC war nicht nur an ägyptischer, sondern auch an der mykenischen Kunst interessiert, und doch bezeugt sein Brief vom Januar 1911 einen größeren Respekt vor der afrikanischen Kunst als einige Jahre früher Worringer.[71] Anders als Worringer nannte nun MARC die Stämme Kameruns ein »primitives Volk« und widmete ihrem Werk jene Beachtung, die vorher Ägypten zuteil wurde.

Wie bei dem Eselfries muß die Stammesskulptur zu Beginn des Jahres 1911 einen vergleichbaren plastischen und expressiven Einfluß auf Werke MARCS ausgeübt haben. Sicherlich gilt dies für sein Gemälde *Hund im Schneefeld*, das MARC gleichfalls im Januar 1911 schuf, als er seinen begeisterten Brief schrieb. Entfernt an GAUGUINS *Der Geist der Toten wacht* □ 249 erinnernd (das er im August 1910 in München gesehen hatte), steht *Hund im Schneefeld* seinem eigenen *Akt unter Bäumen* näher (im Dezember 1910 vollendet) und unterscheidet sich von beiden durch einen besonders eckigen, vollständig modellierten und plastischen Charakter.[72] Neueste, bis jetzt noch unveröffentlichte Untersuchungen, erkennen heute Tierskulpturen aus Kamerun im Berliner Museum für Völkerkunde als mögliche Vorbilder für *Hund im Schneefeld* und weitere Werke von 1911.[73] Wie im Falle des Eselfrieses benutzte MARC jedoch die Skulptur Kameruns als formgebende Ergänzung zu anderen speziell europäischen Stilrichtungen. Die Einflüsse der Stammeskünste durchdrangen jedoch nie den expressionistischen Stil Münchens in dem Maße wie in Dresden. Außerdem betonten die Künstler der »Brücke« die primitive Erotik gerade da, wo MARC die Forderung erhob, daß die Expressionisten »Asketen werden«.

□ 527 *Emil Nolde, ›Maskenstillleben‹, 1911, Öl auf Leinwand, 73 x 77 cm. The Nelson-Atkins Museum of Art, Kansas City.*

□ 528 *Emil Nolde, ›Kanubug‹, 1911, Bleistift, 30 x 18 cm. Stiftung Ada und Emil Nolde, Seebüll.*

August Macke, Marcs bester Freund, wurde zweifellos durch dessen Brief vom Januar 1911 dazu angeregt, im Laufe dieses Jahres seine eigene Reaktion auf die primitive Kunst zu formulieren. Doch sie beschränkte sich auf einzelne Gemälde mit Indianern, die eine Art »Wildwest«-Thematik behandelten.[74] Erst im März 1912 ließ Macke Marc wissen, daß er eine Negerskulptur erworben hatte (Marc antwortete, daß auch er eine besäße),[75] doch hat sie keine Spuren in Mackes Werk von 1912 hinterlassen. Macke ging das Thema primitive Kunst in seinem Beitrag zum Almanach »Der Blaue Reiter«, in dem Artikel »Die Masken«, auch sehr vorsichtig an. Nachdem er die künstlerische Form als »Ausdruck von geheimnisvollen Kräften« definierte, beschrieb Macke die Kunstformen der »Wilden« als »stark wie die Form des Donners«.[76] Marcs 1911 durchgeführten Vergleich zwischen europäischer Kunst und afrikanischer Architekturornamentik griff Macke 1912 auf:

»Was wir als Bild an die Wand hängen, ist etwas im Prinzip Ähnliches wie die geschnitzten und bemalten Pfeiler in einer

□ 529 *Emil Nolde, ›Kopftrophäe‹, 1911, Bleistift und Farbkreide, 30 x 18 cm. Stiftung Ada und Emil Nolde, Seebüll.*

□ 530 *›Kopftrophäe‹, MUNDURUCÚ (Brasilien), Menschenkopf, Baumwolle und Federn, Höhe ohne Federn 20 cm. Museum für Völkerkunde, Berlin.*

Negerhütte. Für den Neger ist sein Idol die faßbare Form für eine unfaßbare Idee, die Personifikation eines abstrakten Begriffs. Für uns ist das Bild die faßbare Form für die unklare, unfaßbare Vorstellung von einem Verstorbenen, von einem Tier, einer Pflanze, von dem ganzen Zauber der Natur, vom Rhythmischen.«[77]

Obschon diese letzten Bemerkungen sehr romantisch klingen, war MACKES Zugang zur Stammeskunst insgesamt KANDINSKYS Auffassung der »synthetischen Zusammenhänge« ähnlich. Denn MACKE nannte nicht nur die Unterschiede zwischen afrikanischer, ozeanischer und europäischer Kunst, sondern auch die Übereinstimmungen ihrer Sprache: »Die Bronzegüsse der Neger von Benin in Westafrika (im Jahre 1889 entdeckt), die Idole von den Osterinseln aus dem äußersten Stillen Ozean, der Häuptlingskragen aus Alaska und die Holzmaske aus Neukaledonien reden dieselbe starke Sprache wie die Schimären von Notre-Dame und die Grabsteine im Frankfurter Dom.«[78] Abbildungen all dieser Werke enthielt der »Blaue Reiter«-Almanach, die meisten in MACKES Artikel.

Abgesehen von jenen, die MACKE erwähnte,[79] zeigte jedoch der Almanach überraschend wenige Beispiele aus dem Bereich der Stammeskunst.[80] Das reizvollste Werk ist vielleicht eine Ahnenfigur aus Südborneo, die auf der gegenüberliegenden Seite von KIRCHNERS Lithographie *Vier Tänzerinnen* (1911) zu sehen ist.[81] Mit dieser Gegenüberstellung wollten die Herausgeber offensichtlich eine Ähnlichkeit zwischen der Borneo-Skulptur und dem Mädchen, das auf KIRCHNERS Bild rechts zu sehen ist, andeuten. In beiden Figuren sind die Brauenbögen zu Linien zusammengefaßt, die in eine dünne senkrechte Nase auslaufen, während die Augen und der Mund aus zusammengepreßten, spitzen Ovalen bestehen. Die Ähnlichkeit bestätigt einmal mehr, was KANDINSKY »synthetische Zusammenhänge« nannte oder »so verwandte, öfters identische Erscheinungen«, und sie demonstriert, wie genau er und MARC das Bildmaterial untersuchten, das für den Almanach vorgesehen war.[82] Die Herausgeber des »Blauen Reiters« führten in der Originalausgabe mehrere solcher Bildvergleiche auf gegenüberliegenden Seiten durch, die im Layout späterer Ausgaben des Almanachs manchmal übersehen wurden.[83]

Es überrascht nicht, daß sich ein anderes Mitglied des »Blauen Reiters«, HEINRICH CAMPENDONK, tatsächlich ein ganzes Bild von einem afrikanischen Werk des Berliner Völkerkundemuseums »entlieh«. CAMPENDONKS Wappentier in einem Holzschnitt von 1916 wurde direkt von einem Bronzerelief der Benin übernommen □ 522, 523.[84] Doch verknüpfte CAMPENDONK gleichzeitig noch andere »exotische« Anregungen mit seiner Bildidee. Die Tatzen seines mythischen wilden Tieres entstammten gedruckten russischen Volksblättern, während seine gepunkteten Augenlider und das durchbrochene Muster ganz rechts von ägyptischen Schattenspielfiguren ausgingen – alle waren im »Blauen Reiter«-Almanach abgebildet.[85] Und doch hängt das Tier als Ganzes von der Benin-Bronze ab, mit ihren locker verteilten Kleeblattformen angefangen bis zur rhythmisch bewegten Silhouette. Neben der Einbindung eingeborener und volkstümlicher Elemente bestand CAMPENDONKS originellster Einfall darin, daß er einen Baumstamm an genau der Stelle plazierte, wo der Künstler der Benin den Schwanz des Tieres hochragen ließ.

□ 531 *Ausstellungsraum im Museum Folkwang, Hagen, vor 1921.*

EMIL NOLDE war der letzte wichtige Expressionist, der die Stammeskunst – wenn auch nur für einige Monate – ernsthaft untersuchte. 1906–07 gehörte er der Dresdner »Brücke« an, danach ging NOLDE seinen eigenen Weg und verbrachte später die Winter in Berlin und die Sommer in Alsen an der deutsch-dänischen Grenze. Im Herbst 1910 und erneut vom Februar bis April 1911 nahm er den Kontakt mit seinen früheren Malerfreunden wieder auf, als er mit ihnen zusammen in der »Neuen Sezession« in Berlin ausstellte.[86] Nach einem Besuch bei dem belgischen Maler JAMES ENSOR in Ostende Anfang des Jahres 1911[87] begann sich NOLDE seinerseits für volkstümliche Karnevals- wie auch Stammesmasken zu interessieren; bald studierte er auch die figürliche Plastik der Primitiven. Das bekannteste Dokument für seine neuen Interessen ist das *Maskenstilleben I* von 1911 □ 527.

Dieses Gemälde entfaltet wie viele der folgenden Stilleben NOLDES einen grundsätzlichen Widerspruch, der wiederum eine vielschichtige expressive Wirkung erzeugt. Der Widerspruch liegt zwischen Karikatur und emotionaler Intensität, und die Wirkung besteht in Gefühlen, die auf die Masken gerichtet sind und ebenso von ihnen ausgehen. Die Karikatur ist nichts Neues in NOLDES Werk, die Postkarten mit phantastischen Berggesichtern sind ein frühes Zeugnis dieser Bestätigung (das *Matterhorn* als schmunzelnder Zwerg, die *Jungfrau* als verschleierte »Jungfrau«). Diese Einfälle waren 1897–98 beim Publikum sehr beliebt. Starke Emotionalität war das Ziel seiner frühen religiösen Bilder, so des *Abendmahls* und des *Pfingstfests* von 1909 oder des Bildes *Christus und die Kinder* von 1910, in denen dem Betrachter bedeutet wird, die Seligkeit und Stärke nachzuvollziehen, die von den gemalten Heiligen ausgehen. Der *Tanz um das Goldene Kalb* aus dem Jahre 1910 fühlt sich hier einerseits in die alttestamentarischen Juden ein, die einen orgiastischen Tanz aufführen, andererseits karikiert sie dieses Bild als Dekadente und Sünder.[88]

Im *Maskenstilleben I* □ 527 sind das zweite und dritte Gesicht offensichtlich Karnevalsmasken, die eine ist verkehrt herum aufgehängt, die andere hat eine Schweineschnauze und gesträubtes Haar, wie sie NOLDE wahrscheinlich alle noch von seinem Besuch in Ostende in Erinnerung hatte. NOLDE betonte wie ENSOR weniger die humoristischen als die brutalen Aspekte dieser Gesichter.[89] NOLDES erste und vierte Maske können jedoch dank einiger Entwurfsskizzen direkt mit primitiven Objekten in Beziehung gebracht werden: dem ornamentalen Bug eines Kanus aus Vella Lavella auf den Salomoninseln □ 528 und dem Kopf eines *YORUBA*-Indianers von den *MUNDURUCÚ* aus Brasilien □ 530. Das Stilleben gibt den Kopf eines Kanubugs vollständig wieder: Das Grinsen der Zähne, die geschlitzten Augen und die dreieckige Kopfbedeckung sind dargestellt. Die Anlehnung der vierten Maske (rechts unten im Gemälde) an die Kopftrophäe ist eher auf die obere Hälfte des Gesichts beschränkt. Die Formen des Schädels, der Augen, der Nasenlöcher und der bedeckten Ohren sind beinahe identisch, weniger aber der quadratische Kiefer und der schreiende Mund.[90]

Nicht so sicher ist, ob sich NOLDE beim fünften Kopf (rechts oben) an einem Maskentyp der *IJO* aus Nigeria orientierte □ 161. Auch hier wäre seine Anleihe selektiv gewesen. Er hätte die senkrechte Nase und die halbmondförmigen Augen mit geradem Oberlid übernommen, nicht aber den Mund der Maske oder den Gesamtumriß. Während die ozeanischen und peruanischen Objekte im Berliner Völkerkundemuseum gesehen und nachgezeichnet wurden, könnte NOLDE die Maske aus Nigeria bei seinen Reisen im Jahr 1911 gesehen haben. Auf dem Weg zu ENSOR in Ostende, machte NOLDE in Brüssel, Haarlem und Amsterdam Station,[91] so daß er gut die berühmten Völkerkundemuseen von Tervuren, Leiden oder Hamburg besucht haben könnte – die beiden letzteren Städte hatten Beispiele des Maskentyps der *Ijo*.[92] Der strenge und hieratische Ausdruck der nigerianischen Maske erscheint übrigens nicht nur im *Maskenstilleben* von 1911, sondern auch im Kopfe Christi in der Mitteltafel der *Kreuzigung* aus NOLDES neunteiligem *Leben Christi* von 1911–12.[93]

Betrachtet man das *Maskenstilleben I* als Ganzes, erkennt man überraschend Gesichter aus Ozeanien, Europa, Südamerika und Afrika in einem einzigen Bild. Das Gemälde bietet sich an, Seite an Seite mit primitiven Objekten verschiedener Herkunft ausgestellt zu werden, wie es auch um 1920 im Folkwang-Museum in Hagen geschah □ 531. Doch NOLDES Anliegen war weniger völkerkundlich als vom Gefühl bestimmt. Hier ist Goldwater zuzustimmen, der behauptet, daß für NOLDE insofern ein emotionaler »Primitivismus« typisch sei, als er primitive Artefakte dazu verwandt habe, um Gefühle mitzuteilen. Er gebrauchte die Physiognomien der Stammesgegenstände als eine Enzyklopädie, aus der er emotionale Zeichen entnahm. Natürlich ist die Enzyklopädie nicht »unlokalisierbar«, wie Goldwater annahm. Seine primitiven Vorbilder sind leicht ausfindig zu machen.[94] NOLDE kannte seine Gefühlsbedürfnisse so gut, daß er die Vorbilder gegeneinander ausspielen konnte: links teuflisches Grinsen, rechts die schrecklichen blinden Augen und ein völlig konträrer Ausdruck erhabener Autorität. Dieser selektive und enzyklopädische Gebrauch primitiver Kunst im Dienste der emotionalen Gebärden ist für NOLDES Zugang zum Primitivismus während der Vorkriegsjahre charakteristisch.

□ 532
Emil Nolde, ›Hopi-Katchina‹, 1911–12, Bleistift und Farbkreide, 30 x 18 cm. Stiftung Ada und Emil Nolde, Seebüll.

□ 533 *Emil Nolde, ›Exotische Figuren II‹, 1911, Öl auf Leinwand, 65,5 x 78 cm. Stiftung Ada und Emil Nolde, Seebüll.*

□ 534 *›Katchina-Puppe‹ Hopi (Arizona), bemaltes Holz, Höhe 24 cm. Museum für Völkerkunde, Berlin.*

□ 535 *Emil Nolde, ›Der Missionar‹, 1912, Öl auf Leinwand, 79 x 65,5 cm. Sammlung Berthold Glauerdt, Solingen.*

Dies gilt auch für NOLDES Auswahl von Stammeskunst aus der Neuen Welt. *Exotische Figuren I* (oder *Fetische*) von 1911 etwa zeigt Katchina-Puppen der *HOPI*-Indianer, von denen ein Exemplar nebst der Zeichnung eines in die Länge gezogenen Holzschweines unbekannter Herkunft noch vorhanden ist.[95] Während NOLDE die Objekte zuerst einzeln zeichnete, erzeugt ihre Kombination im Gemälde eine seltsame Karikatur der deutschen Bürgerfamilie: der grimmige und schwerfällige Mann, die Frau mit ihrem dekorativen Gesichtsschmuck sowie der am Boden kauernde Dachshund. Hier hängt die gefühlsmäßige Wirkung davon ab, wie sehr wir die Stammesformen im Vergleich mit uns als zur selben Zeit gleichartig und verschieden erkennen. Das gilt auch für NOLDES *Exotische Figuren II* aus demselben Jahr □ 533, die ebenfalls eine Katchina-Puppe der *HOPI* aus dem Berliner Völkerkundemuseum zeigen □ 534. Nur daß der Künstler hier die bunte Figur mit einem Paar grimassierender heraldischer Katzen umgeben hat, die augenscheinlich von einem Stoffmuster der *INKA* stammen.[96] Das karikaturhafte Moment suggeriert die alptraumartige Begegnung zwischen bizarren, heranpirschenden Wildtieren und einem gleichfalls bizarren, aber würdevollen und bewußten Menschen. NOLDES Methode rechnet generell mit unserem rührenden Irrtum, daß Holzfiguren und andere leblose Gegenstände von menschlichen Dingen erzählen. Die Grundmethode, wie der Prozeß der Karikatur, beinhaltet sowohl künstlerische Aggression (gegen den Gegenstand) als auch psychische Regression (zu kindlichem Spiel).[97]

□ 536 *›Maske‹*, BONGO *(Sudan), Holz, Haare und Zähne, Höhe 30 cm. Museum für Völkerkunde, Berlin.*

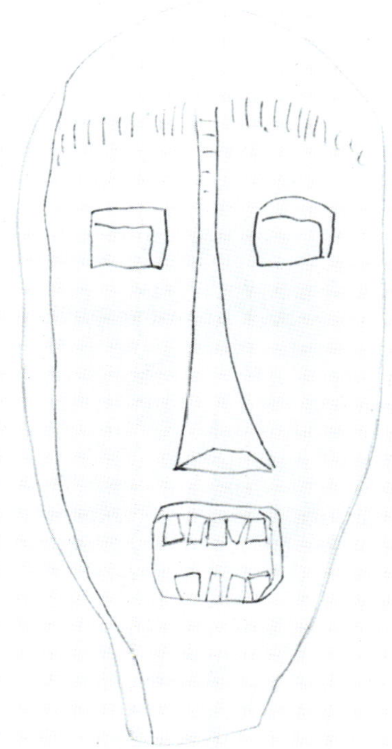

□ 537 *Emil Nolde, ›Bongo-Maske‹, 1911–12, Bleistift, 28 x 21 cm. Stiftung Ada und Emil Nolde, Seebüll.*

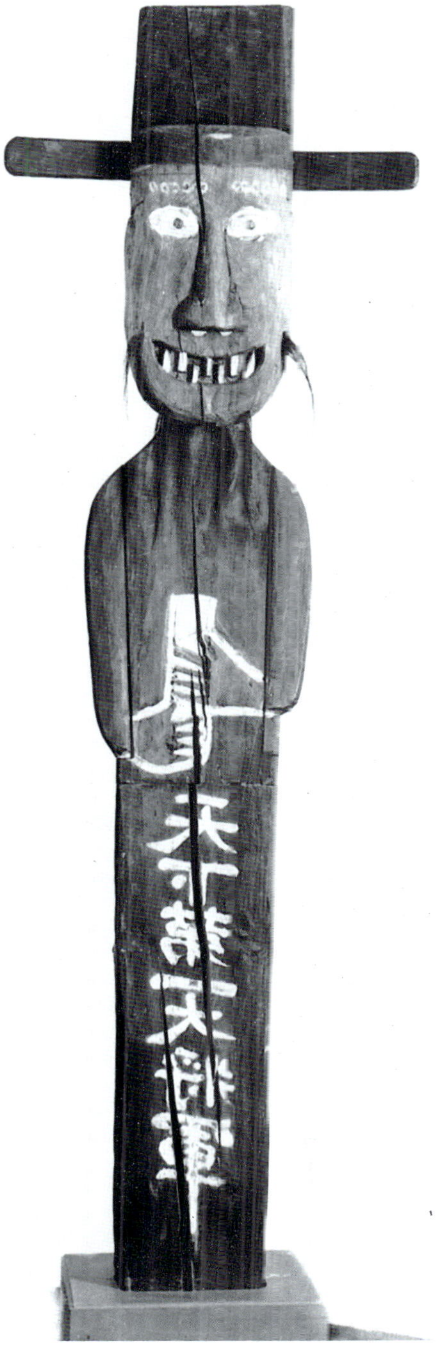

□ 538 *›Wegegott‹, Korea, bemaltes Holz, Höhe 291 cm. Museum für Völkerkunde, Berlin.*

NOLDES ehrgeizigster Versuch, außereuropäische Elemente in einem Stilleben miteinander zu vermischen, war das Gemälde *Missionar* von 1912 □ 535. Es orientiert sich an zwei primitiven Vorlagen, einer heute verlorenen *YORUBA*-Skulptur einer Mutter mit Kind[98] und einer Tanzmaske der *BONGO* □ 536 (Nordostafrika). Der schwarz berockte Missionar ist in Wirklichkeit ein koreanischer Wegegott von fast drei Metern Höhe, bemalt und aus Holz □ 538. Der Inhalt des Bildes ist klar: Die Afrikanerin kniet in der Haltung christlichen Gebets vor dem Missionar, während die entkörperlichte Maske, die ihre ursprüngliche Religion symbolisiert, den Blick voller Schrekken zwischen sie richtet. Indem er die Frau zur Aufgabe ihrer Stammesreligion bekehren will, um Christin zu werden, fördert der Priester den Untergang der alten Kultur. Aus NOLDES Sicht ist der Missionar daher zu verachten; er karikiert ihn mit den Zügen volkstümlicher Figuren des Orients. Die drolligen, koboldhaften Formen des Missionars wie auch der Maske streiten um die Seele der Frau, sie selbst aber wird von NOLDE mit Respekt und Würde wiedergegeben.

Im Gegensatz zu KIRCHNER und MARC schätzte NOLDE die Stammeskunst ursprünglich weniger aufgrund ihrer plastischen Möglichkeiten als ihrer gestalterischen Qualität wegen. Selbst die dreidimensionalsten Vorbilder gerieten dem Maler in der Kopie flächig. In der Katchina-Puppe der *TINU-HOPI* etwa zeigen die Füße nach vorne, während sie in *Exotische Figuren I* flach von der Seite dargestellt sind. Das dreidimensionale Schwein in einer vorbereitenden Skizze wird im Gemälde zu einer dunklen Silhouette. *Exotische Figuren II* trägt dem Volumen der Katchina-Puppe zwar Rechnung, die Flächigkeit des gestuften dunklen Kopfputzes wird aber im Gemälde dadurch unterstrichen, daß er im Hintergrund des Stillebens in hellen Tönen wiederholt wird. Im *Missionar* verschwindet schließlich die leichte Plastizität der beiden Vorbilder NOLDES – des koreanischen Wegegottes und der afrikanischen *BONGO*-Maske.

Die karikaturistischen und kindlichen Elemente in Bildern der Jahre 1911–12 verschwanden, als NOLDE zwei Jahre später tatsächlich Eingeborenenstämme aufsuchte. Doch blieb seine abwechslungsreiche Reaktion auf die Stammeskunst weiterhin expressiv und auch formal unverändert. Wir können die Vielschichtigkeit seiner Erwiderung NOLDES Äußerungen über primitive Kunst von 1912 entnehmen, die hier auszugsweise zitiert seien:

»Vor nicht langer Zeit waren nur einige Kunstzeiten museumsreif. Dann aber kamen hinzu: koptische und frühchristliche Kunst, griechische Terrakotten und Vasen, persi-

□ 539 *›Kopfschmuck‹, Ekoi (Kamerun), Holz, Leder und andere Materialien, Höhe 23 cm. Museum für Völkerkunde, Berlin.*

sche und islamische Kunst. Warum aber werden immer noch die indische, chinesische und javanische Kunst unter Wissenschaft und Völkerkunde eingeordnet? Und die Kunst der Naturvölker als solche überhaupt gewertet?
Wie mag es kommen, daß wir Künstler so gern die primitiven Äußerungen der Naturvölker sehen?
Unsere Zeit brachte es mit sich, daß für jedes Tongefäß oder Schmuckstück, für jeden Gebrauchsgegenstand oder jedes Kleidungsstück zuerst der Riß auf Papier entstehen mußte. – Mit dem Material in der Hand, zwischen den Fingern, entstehen die Werke der Naturvölker. Das sich äußernde Wollen ist Lust und Liebe zum Bilden.
Die absolute Ursprünglichkeit, der intensive, oft groteske Ausdruck von Kraft und Leben in allereinfachster Form, – das möge es sein, was uns die Freude gibt.«[99]

Nolde trug Stammeskunst zusammen, da er sie »unverfälscht« fand, da sie für ihn »Energie« und »Leben« ausdrückte. Doch er schätzte diese Kunst auch wegen des offensichtlichen Vergnügens, das ihre Machart widerzuspiegeln schien, und wegen des Gefühls greifbarer Stofflichkeit. Infolgedessen identifizierte sich Nolde mit dem Stammeskünstler als einem Handwerkskollegen, auch dann, wenn er auf seinem Recht bestand, im Interesse seiner eigenen Kunst von dessen Werk abzuweichen.

Im Herbst 1911 übersiedelte die Künstlergruppe »Brücke« von Dresden, der Hauptstadt Sachsens, in die deutsche Hauptstadt Berlin. Obwohl Pechstein und Mueller hier bereits einige Jahre wohnten, mußten sich die anderen erst auf die neue Umgebung einstellen. Darüber hinaus fand das Dresdner Modell des Gemeinschaftsateliers ein Ende. Einige Künstler waren verheiratet oder lebten mit ihren zukünftigen Frauen zusammen, und jeder entwickelte seinen persönlichen Stil. Die Forderung des *»Brücke«-Programms* nach jugendlicher »Unmittelbarkeit« war nicht mehr für Künstler angemessen, die zwischen 28 (Schmidt-Rottluff) und 38 Jahre alt waren (Mueller). 1912 fanden die letzten Ausstellungen der »Brücke« in Berlin und Hamburg statt; 1913 löste sich die Gruppe formell auf. Kein stilistischer Einfluß spielte 1912–13 in Berlin die große Rolle wie einige Jahre früher in Dresden die Palau-Hausbalken. Wohl stellte das Völkerkundemuseum in Berlin eine Vielfalt primitiver Gegenstände aus, die in Mitteleuropa nicht ihresgleichen hatte. Seine verschiedenen Schwerpunkte – ozeanische oder vorkolumbianische, west- oder ostafrikanische Gegenstände – verhinderten einen zu engen Blickwinkel für den nachfolgenden Primitivismus. Auch das Sammeln wurde immer wichtiger. Während im März 1912 sowohl Marc und Macke erwähnten, je eine Stammesskulptur zu besitzen, zeigten Heckels Stilleben des gleichen Jahres, daß er bereits Kunstwerke ozeanischer, ost- und westafrikanischer Herkunft besaß □ 546, 547. Zwar bezeichnete Schmidt-Rottluff einmal die Skulptur Kameruns als die »wichtigste Inspirationsquelle« für die »Brücke«,[100] doch gilt diese Feststellung eher für seinen eigenen späteren Stil als für den seiner Freunde in den Vorkriegsjahren.

Das früheste Meisterwerk, das von der »Brücke« in Berlin geschaffen wurde, stammt von der ungewöhnlichen Form einer Skulptur aus Kamerun ab: die *Vier Evangelisten*, ein Relief Schmidt-Rottluffs von Anfang 1912 □ 540.[101] Dessen Vorbild ist unter dem zu suchen, was der *Führer durch das Museum für Völkerkunde* in Berlin (1911) die »bemerkenswerten Köpfe, mit Haut überzogen« nannte,[102] nämlich den Kopfschmuck eines Tänzers des *Ekoi*-Stammes im nordwestlichen Kamerun □ 539.[103] Obwohl es die vergänglichen Materialien dieser Köpfe schwierig machen, ihr genaues Aussehen von 1912 zu rekonstruieren, dürfte das hier abgebildete Münchner Beispiel dem ähnlich gewesen sein, das Schmidt-Rottluff kannte. Über eine hölzerne Maquette in Form eines menschlichen Kopfes wurde eine Tierhaut – gewöhnlich einer Antilope – gespannt, der ein Büschel menschliches Haar hinzugefügt wurde. Zähne, die man durch die Haut in den Holzkern hämmerte, bilden den Mund. Kennzeichnend für den Kopf wie für den Mund mit den flachgedrückten Lippen waren die blinden und deformierten Augenhöhlen der tierischen Haut. Gerade die Form der Augen und des Mundes in jeder der *Evangelisten*-Tafeln bestätigen die Herkunft vom *Ekoi*-Vorbild.

☐ 540
Karl Schmidt-Rottluff, ›Vier Evangelisten: Matthäus, Markus, Lukas, Johannes‹, 1912, Öl über Messingrelief, jede Tafel 42,5 x 33 cm. Brücke-Museum, Berlin.

Ich vermute, daß SCHMIDT-ROTTLUFF von einem speziellen Objekt dieses Typus im Berliner Museum angeregt wurde und daß er darauf so selektiv reagierte wie NOLDE, wenn er Anregungen aufgriff. Grohmann findet die *Evangelisten* christlichen Werken NOLDES sogar näher als SCHMIDT-ROTTLUFFS eigenen religiösen Holzschnitten ein halbes Jahrzehnt später.[104]

Grohmann bemerkte, daß SCHMIDT-ROTTLUFF – ohne dogmatisch zu sein – von einem »tief religiösen Gefühl« motiviert war. Obwohl die traditionellen Attribute fehlen, sind die Köpfe der *Vier Evangelisten* deutlich als Matthäus und Markus, oben, als Lukas und Johannes, unten, zu erkennen.[105] Überdies halte ich es für wahrscheinlich, daß der Künstler auch bestimmte Personen im Sinne hatte: HECKEL und er selbst als Matthäus und Markus, PECHSTEIN und KIRCHNER als Lukas und Johannes – die »Brücke« als die Evangelisten einer neuen Kunst.[106]

Wie auch immer, die charakteristischen primitiven Eigenschaften des Reliefs von 1912 treten klar zutage. Die Mandelaugen von Matthäus stammen direkt von den typischen »geschlossenen« Augen des *EKOI*-Gesichtstypus ab (das linke Auge des Kopfschmuckes im abgebildeten Beispiel), während die halbgeöffneten, aber blinden, dreieckigen Augen des Johannes von den mißgestalteten Augenlöchern der *EKOI*-Tierhaut abgeleitet sind (das rechte Auge im vorliegenden Beispiel). Darüber hinaus haben die flache Nase und die vorspringenden Lippen des Markus einen negroiden Charakter, der erneut auf den *EKOI*-Typus hinweist, wie auch Lukas' Stirnhaar und selbst seine großen Lippen.

Es gibt nichts in der expressionistischen Kunst, was mit dem Relief *Vier Evangelisten* vergleichbar wäre. Seine einzigartige Wirkung beruht auf der groben, doch geistigen Intensität des afrikanischen Vorbildes. Auch wenn stärker ästhetisiert, hat das expressionistische Relief eine ähnlich beunruhigende Ausstrahlung wie das mit einer Haut überzogene Werk der *EKOI*.

Kehren wir zu KIRCHNERS Annäherung an die primitive Kunst im Jahre 1912 zurück, so entdecken wir weniger ein Interesse an der expressiven Kraft als an der skulpturalen

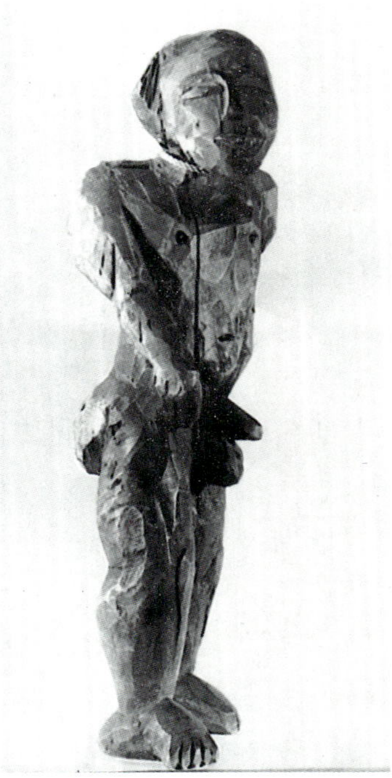

541

542

□ 541 *Ernst Ludwig Kirchner, ›Männlicher Akt‹, Holz, gebeizt, gebrannt und bemalt, Höhe 35 cm. Staatsgalerie Stuttgart.*

□ 542 *Erna Schilling und Ernst Ludwig Kirchner im ersten Berliner Atelier, Berlin-Wilmersdorf, Photographie von Ernst Ludwig Kirchner, 1912, Photoarchiv Hans Bollinger und Roman Norbert Ketterer.*

□ 543 *Ernst Ludwig Kirchner, ›Adam‹, 1912, Holz, gebeizt und gebrannt, 169 x 30 x 31 cm. Staatsgalerie Stuttgart.*

□ 544 *›Giebelplanke mit weiblicher Figur‹, Palauinseln (Karolineninseln), bemaltes Holz, Höhe 83 cm. Museum für Völkerkunde, Hamburg.*

□ 545 *›Giebelfigur‹, Palauinseln (Karolineninseln), bemaltes Holz, Höhe 65 cm. The Metropolitan Museum of Art, Michael C. Rockefeller Memorial Collection, New York.*

543

Form. Bereits früh, um 1910–11, fand er in Abbildungen der Höhlenmalerei der Ajanta in Indien das, was er »Körper« (du corps) nannte. Wie er an Henry van de Veldes Tochter Nele schrieb: »Sie sind ganz flächig und doch absolut Masse und haben somit das Geheimnis der Malerei restlos gelöst.«[107] Mit seinen ersten lebensgroßen Holzfiguren, dem *Adam* von 1912 □ 543 oder der späteren *Eva*, sah sich Kirchner dem Problem der Fläche und der Masse im plastischen Medium der Rundskulptur gegenübergestellt. Er löste es mit den Mitteln einer wichtigen, doch bis dahin nicht bemerkten Verbindung der so ganz verschiedenen Prinzipien der Palau- und der Kamerun-Formen.

Die weibliche Giebelfigur eines Palau-Männerhauses im Völkerkundemuseum Hamburg, die Kirchner bei einem seiner zahlreichen Aufenthalte in Hamburg zwischen 1910 und 1912 gesehen haben könnte, zeigt erneut die beherrschende Zweidimensionalität des Palau-Stils □ 544.[108] Obschon die Giebelfigur körperliche Masse besitzt, ist sie in Wirklichkeit in Flächen angelegt, die parallel zu den Fassadenplanken liegen, an denen sie befestigt ist. Nichts ragt weit über die Fläche der Figur hinaus; Details wie die Brüste oder die Augen sind in extrem flachem Relief gehalten. In den stilisierten Brustmuskeln des *Adam* etwa benutzt Kirchner die gleiche Art von Flachrelief wie der Palau-Künstler für die Scham der Giebelfi-

544

545

gur; die Schamgegend der *Eva* ist noch stärker dem Vorbild verpflichtet. In anderer Hinsicht jedoch sind diese Skulpturen Kirchners plastischer und deshalb mehr von afrikanischen Vorbildern abhängig. Brüste und Phallus durchbrechen die frontale Körperebene und drängen in einer Art in den Raum vor, die an die Skulptur Kameruns erinnert ◻ 560. Das gleiche gilt für die Gesichtszüge. Die Köpfe von *Adam* und *Eva* gleichen im eiförmigen Umriß, in der geradlinigen Lippen- und Nasenform sowie dem geschwungenen Bogen der Brauen der Palau-Giebelfigur. Die Augen und sogar die Pupillen, speziell die des *Adam*, sind hingegen plastisch und erinnern an afrikanische Vorbilder.

Eine andere Holzskulptur Kirchners, die heute verlorene *Weibliche Figur*, ist auf einer Photographie von Kirchner und Erna Schilling im Inneren des Wohnateliers in Berlin-Wilmersdorf sichtbar ◻ 542. Hier sind das Gesicht und selbst Augen und Brüste in der Art des Flachreliefs der Palau geschnitzt. Die Hände mit fünf gleichartig geformten Fingern scheinen direkt von der Hamburger Giebelfigur abgeleitet. Trotzdem stehen die Arme und Beine dem Palau-Stil fern. Die Schultern wie auch das Gesäß sind voll plastisch; die Schultern drängen sogar besonders stark in den Raum, ebenso das Gesäß, wie bei afrikanischen Arbeiten häufig der Fall. Selbst die Massigkeit des Kopfes und des Körpers steht dem Typus aus Kamerun

□ 546 *Erich Heckel, ›Stilleben mit Maske‹, 1912, Öl auf Leinwand, 69 x 63 cm. Saarland-Museum, Saarbrücken.*

□ 547 *›Maske‹, Ostafrika, Holz, Höhe 21 cm. Nachlaß Erich Heckel, Hemmenhofen.*

näher als dem der Palau. KIRCHNERS freistehende Skulpturen von 1912 zeigen somit eine ungewöhnliche Synthese ozeanischer und afrikanischer Stilmerkmale.[109]

KIRCHNERS Holzskulptur gewann zunehmend an plastischem Volumen und ist entsprechend mehr von Afrika als von Ozeanien inspiriert.[110] Wie er später schrieb, arbeitet sie »mit einfachen Grundformen, vor allem dem Zylinder, Kegel, Oval und der Kugel«. Diese Formen resultieren nicht aus einer »mathematischen Spekulation«, sondern aus einem »Willen zur Monumentalität«.[111] Auch hat eine solche Skulptur eine erotische und emotionale Unmittelbarkeit, sie erweitert das gemalte *Negerpaar* um die dritte Dimension und übersetzt es sozusagen aus der Wand in den realen Raum. Selbst die zweistufige Holzschüssel, die auf der Photographie des Berliner Ateliers von KIRCHNER rechts zu sehen ist, wendet das Exotische ins Nützliche, den Kunst- in den Lebensstil.

Das Innere seines Berliner Ateliers bestätigt KIRCHNERS Bedürfnis, »Kunst als Lebensentwurf« zu verwenden.[112] Exotische Wandbehänge, japanische Schirme, eine buddhistische Reproduktion und selbst ein nach koptischen Textilien gefertigtes Tischtuch trugen zu dem typisch expressionistischen Ambiente bei. Der »Atelierprimitivismus« der anderen Berliner »Brücke«-Künstler unterschied sich davon nur gering, HECKELS Atelier war noch exotischer. Ein Besucher von 1914 schrieb später: »Er [Heckel] empfing uns in einem Dachraum, der mit farbigem Stoff wie ein Zelt eingerichtet war. An den Wänden standen aus Holz geschnitzte Plastiken, Weiber und Männer mit großen Köpfen und irgendeinem starken Ausdruck in Gebärde und Bewegung. Selbstgeschnitzte Bänke und Sitze standen herum. Hinter bunten selbstgefärbten Vorhängen standen viele Ölbilder . . .«[113]

Um 1912 war HECKEL intensiv mit Stammeskunst befaßt. Sein *Stilleben mit Südsee-Plastik* aus jenem Jahr □ 548 bildet eine melanesische Holzplastik ab, die offenbar in seinem Besitz war. Es ist ein kleines Stück, das aus Neuguinea stammt (bzw. aus Papua-Neuguinea, wie es heute heißt).[114] 1912 entstand auch HECKELS *Stilleben mit Maske* □ 546, das eine geflochtene Kalebasse aus dem Kameruner Grasland und eine noch vorhandene ostafrikanische Maske darstellt □ 547.[115] Hierher gehört auch ein Gemälde von 1913, *Laute spielendes Mädchen*, das HECKELS Verlobte zeigt. Sie spielt ein Instrument, das ihr von HECKELS Bruder Manfred zugeschickt worden war, der damals in Afrika lebte[116] und zweifellos viele Kunstwerke für HECKELS Sammlung beschaffte.

Manfreds Erzählungen über Afrika könnten HECKEL auch dazu angeregt haben, dorthin zu reisen. Er äußerte den Wunsch, »nach Afrika zu gehen, um endlich das ›wilde‹ Leben zu finden, Menschen in einer natürlichen Umgebung«, ein Motiv, »nach dem er immer für seine Gemälde auf der Suche war«.[117] Ein Freund charakterisierte seine Wanderlust als eine »Sehnsucht nach der Rückkehr zur Urnatur«.[118] Solche Gefühle erklären wohl zum Teil die symbolische Funktion der primitiven Skulptur oder auch der menschlichen Figur, die in den Gemälden *Genesende* und *Gläserner Tag* als primitive Plastik dargestellt wurde.[119]

1913 waren auch die anderen »Brücke«-Künstler in das Studium der Stammeskunst vertieft. Für sein *Stilleben mit Negerplastik* □ 551 und einige spätere Gemälde[120] benutzte SCHMIDT-ROTTLUFF Pfeifenköpfe aus Kamerun des hier abgebildeten Typus □ 552. Und PECHSTEINS *Stilleben in Grau* von 1913 □ 554 zeigt einen Hocker, den er nach dem Vorbild eines kamerunischen Häuptlingsstuhls geschnitzt hatte. Dieser befand sich damals im Berliner Völkerkundemuseum.[121] Zur Illustration möchte ich hier ein anderes Beispiel heranziehen □ 553.[122] Obschon das Gemälde PECHSTEINS die Affinität zwischen dem Kubismus und Werken der primitiven Kunst ausnutzt, imitiert es trotz der Zersplitterung der Früchte und der Draperie die kamerunische Geometrie.

Als expressionistische Künstler tatsächlich in ferngelegene Stammesgebiete reisten, verschwand der primitive Lebensstil, den sie solange bewundert hatten, rasch. Vielleicht sind aus diesem Grund die künstlerischen Ergebnisse ihrer Reisen enttäuschend. Die Künstler beschränkten sich darauf, Reiseberichte zu verfassen und touristische Skizzen zu zeichnen, als sie sahen, wie die ursprüngliche Kultur vor ihren Augen unterging. Die Enttäuschung blieb nicht aus. Die »Urnatur« entpuppte sich als eine romantische Phantasie des weißen Mannes, der in Wirklichkeit die eingeborene Kultur zerstörte.

Als NOLDE 1914 nach einer Reise durch Rußland, China, Japan und über die Philippinen in Neuguinea ankam, war er in seinem Lob der Ureinwohner und in seiner Kritik an den weißen Kolonialisten freimütig:

»Wir leben in der Zeit, wo die ganzen Urzustände und Urvölker zugrunde gehen, alles wird entdeckt und europäisiert. Nicht einmal eine kleine Fläche erster Urnatur mit Urmenschen bleibt der Nachwelt erhalten. In 20 Jahren ist alles verloren. In 300 Jahren grübeln, quälen sich und graben die Forscher und Gelehrten, um tastend etwas zu fassen vom Köstlichen, das wir hatten, von der primären Geistigkeit, die wir heute so leichtsinnig und schamlos vernichten.

Die Urmenschen leben in ihrer Natur, sind eins mit ihr und ein Teil vom ganzen All. Ich habe zuweilen das Gefühl, als ob nur sie noch wirkliche Menschen sind, wir aber etwas wie verbildete Gliederpuppen, künstlich und voll Dünkel.

Ich male und zeichne und suche einiges vom Urwesen festzuhalten. Einiges möchte wohl auch gelungen sein, ich bin jedenfalls der Meinung, daß meine Bilder der Urmenschen und manche Aquarelle so echt und herb sind, daß sie unmöglich in parfürmierte Salons zu hängen sind.

☐ 548 *Erich Heckel, ›Stilleben mit Südsee-Plastik‹, 1912, Öl auf Leinwand, 70 x 50 cm. Verbleib unbekannt.*

☐ 549 *Alexej Jawlensky, ›Liebe‹, 1925, Öl auf Leinwand, 59 x 49 cm. Verbleib unbekannt.*

☐ 550 *›Maske‹, Nomoiinseln (Karolineninseln), bemaltes Holz, Höhe 52 cm. Rautenstrauch-Joest-Museum, Köln.*

☐ 552 *›Pfeifenköpfe‹, Grasland Kameruns, Terrakotta, Höhe des größten Kopfes 24 cm. Museum für Völkerkunde, München.*

◁ ☐ 551 *Karl Schmidt-Rottluff, ›Stilleben mit Negerskulptur‹, 1913, Öl auf Leinwand, 73 x 64,5 cm. Museum Ludwig, Köln.*

Gar keinen anderen bildenden Künstler weiß ich, außer Gauguin und mir selbst, der aus der unendlichen Fülle des Urnaturlebens Bleibendes brachte.«[123]

Die Bewunderung der »Urnatur« und des »Urmenschen« wurde zwei Monate später zusammengefaßt:

»Die Eingeborenen sind ein herrliches Volk, soweit sie nicht schon durch die Berührung mit der Kultur der Weißen verdorben sind. Wir haben nur einige Male Gelegenheit gehabt, ganz ursprüngliche Menschen in ihren Dörfern kennenzulernen. Aber wie war das schön . . .
Die Eingeborenen hier essen allerdings Menschenfleisch . . . Sind denn wir sogenannten Kultivierten wirklich viel besser als die Menschen hier? Hier werden bei den Fehden einzelne getötet, in Europa im Kriege Tausende, und sind die verdorbenen Großstadtmenschen, wo täglich und nächtlich die Leibesfrucht verhindert oder vernichtet wird, nicht viel schmutziger und tieferstehend als die hiesigen Naturmenschen, die viele Kinder zeugen, damit sie stark sind, damit der Nachbarstamm nicht mehr Männer hat als sie?«[124]

Nicht alle Eingeborenen wurden gepriesen. Diejenigen, die durch den kolonialen Lebensstil korrumpiert waren, schienen ihm so schlecht wie ihre weißen Arbeitgeber:

»Es gilt das Recht des Stärkeren. Alles arbeitet für die wirtschaftliche Erschließung, und dabei geht eine eigene, selten schöne Welt verloren, für immer. Die Eingeborenen an den Plätzen der Europäer sind unerträglich, verlogen, verseucht, und mit Lappen und Flitter elendster Art behangen. So gehen sie zurück an ihre Plätze, die schlechtesten Beigaben der Kultur des weißen Mannes um sich verbreitend. – Aber sage bitte nichts! – Psst! – Kein weißer Mann darf es sehen, wer es sieht, schließe hübsch die Augen, der ›wirtschaftliche Nutzen‹ überragt alle Bedenken. Wir leben in der üblen Zeit, wo die weiße Rasse sich die Bewohner der ganzen Erde dienlich macht.«[125]

Noldes eigener Vergleich mit Gauguin ist vermessen und kann nicht aufrechterhalten werden. Aquarelle wie *Eingeborene im Boot* sind betörend schön, aber sie sind im Grunde

☐ 553 *›Häuptlingsstuhl‹, westliches Grasland Kameruns, Holz, Höhe 73 cm. Staatliches Museum für Völkerkunde, Dresden.*

genommen die einzigen Ergebnisse seines Neuguinea-Aufenthalts. Keine größeren Ölgemälde wurden hier geschaffen. Um für diese »leidenschaftlichen« Werke Anregung aus der »exotischen Szenerie« zu erhalten, war kaum ein Grund, um die halbe Erde zu reisen.[126] Auch trugen NOLDES Reisen später keine Früchte. Die exotischen Kunstwerke und Artefakte, die er sammelte, wurden zu Hause als Vorlagen für Stilleben benutzt. Im *Stilleben mit Südseefigur* von 1915 etwa □ 557 steht eine Uli-Figur aus Neuirland □ 556 neben einer Porzellangruppe mit zwei Frauen, die NOLDE in Rußland gekauft hatte. Die Aussage des *Stillebens* scheint der des *Missionars* von 1912 zu widersprechen □ 535. Der melanesische Fetisch beherrscht die Komposition, wie es der koreanische Wegegott früher tat, aber das schreckeneinflößende Bild der Autorität ist nun versachlicht und in jeder Beziehung anmutig, während die Frauen, die sich miteinander unterhalten, eher galant und europäisch sind.[127]

MAX PECHSTEIN blieb nicht lange auf Neuguinea, sondern auf der bis dahin unberührten Palauinselgruppe. Wie er in seinen *Erinnerungen* schrieb, plante er, »nachdem ich dieses Paradies gefunden habe«, sich hier niederzulassen.[128] Wie schon NOLDE nahm auch PECHSTEIN seine Frau auf die tropische Reise mit, so

□ 554
Max Pechstein, ›Stilleben in Grau‹, 1913, Öl auf Leinwand. Ehemals Sammlung Dr. Karl Lilienfeld, Berlin. Verbleib unbekannt.

daß sich seine Phantasien über das primitive Leben von denen GAUGUINS deutlich unterschieden haben müssen. Und wieder wie NOLDE lernte er rasch die Mißstände des Kolonialismus kennen. Als er den Gouverneur der Palauinseln erstmals traf, »beschwor mich [der Beamte], um Gottes willen die Palauer selbst und ihre naturgebundenen Gewohnheiten nicht durch europäische Nichtigkeiten zu zerstören«. Ironischerweise wurde sein Besuch 1914 durch den Ausbruch des Krieges in Europa jäh abgebrochen. Im Oktober wurde PECHSTEIN von den Japanern interniert: »Mein Traum ist ausgeträumt.«

PECHSTEINS Tagebuch der wenigen Monate, die er auf den Inseln verbrachte, liest sich wie eine Reiseschilderung. Er kam mit vierzig Kisten persönlicher Habe an, baute einen Brotofen und – mit Hilfe der Eingeborenen – ein Segelboot sowie ein neues Dach für sein Haus. Er sah einen Stammestanz und besuchte danach eine nahegelegene Insel und ihren eingeborenen König, bevor er sich schließlich dazu entschloß, auf einer unbewohnten Insel, die man ihm überließ, sein eigenes Haus zu bauen.

Im Tagebuch drückte PECHSTEIN ein außergewöhnliches Einfühlungsvermögen den Eingeborenen gegenüber aus: »Selbst unter einfachen Menschen und mit der Natur aufgewachsen, finde ich unschwer ein Verhältnis zu dieser Fülle neuer Eindrücke. Ich muß mich nicht allzusehr umstellen . . . Aus tiefstem Gefühl der Menschengemeinschaft konnte ich mich den Südseeinsulanern brüderlich nähern. Einfache Handwerkshantierung ist mir von frühauf vertraut gewesen, so wie ich mit den Leuten von Nidden, Monterosso al Mare segelte, fischte und Netze warf. So lernte ich es auch hier leicht, ein Kanu durch die Korallenriffe zu steuern. Die wundervollste Einheit fühle ich um mich und atme sie in grenzenlosem Glücksgefühl.«

Wenn PECHSTEIN einmal mit der Arbeit an einer Holzskulptur aussetzte, führte sie ein junger Palau weiter. Der Künstler sah, daß er »mir nichts verdarb, also ließ ich ihm diese Freude«.

Nur ein Gemälde, wenige Aquarelle und mehrere Pinselzeichnungen sind von PECHSTEINS Palau-Aufenthalt bekannt.[129] *Männerhaus unter Palmen* □ 561 ist typisch für die letztgenannte Gruppe, eine schnell ausgeführte Skizze über das Leben der Eingeborenen. Die Zeichnung hält genau den Haustypus fest, von dem mehrere Hausbalken nach Dresden, Hamburg und in andere Museen gelangten:

»Holzhäuser mit hohem, spitzem Dachfirst sind ihre Behausungen, und an diesen Häusern sehe ich nun in Wirklichkeit im Gebrauch des Alltags, in der Umgebung, für die sie geschaffen sind, die geschnitzten und bemalten Balken, die einst in Dresden meine Einbildungskraft in Schwingung versetzten und den jetzt erfüllten Wunsch aufkommen ließen, sie an Ort und Stelle zu sehen. Ich sehe die primitive Ornamentik, den aus einfachstem menschlichem Bedürfnis nach Schönheit geborenen Schmuck der Hütten. Ich sehe die Kunstgriffe, mit denen dieses Urvolk seinen Körper ziert, sich an selbstherrlichen Veränderungen der Natur am eigenen Leib zu erfreuen, an diesen primären Zeugnissen des Schönheitssinnes und der Lust zur Formbildung. Ich sehe die geschnitzten Götzenbilder, in die zitternde Frömmigkeit und Ehrfurcht vor den unbegreiflichen Gewalten der Natur ihre Hoffnung und ihre Schauer, ihre Angst und ihre Unterwürfigkeit unter das unvermeidliche Schicksal eingeprägt haben.«[130]

□ 555 *›Uli-Figur‹, Neuirland, bemaltes Holz, Höhe 152 cm. Hamburgisches Museum für Völkerkunde.*

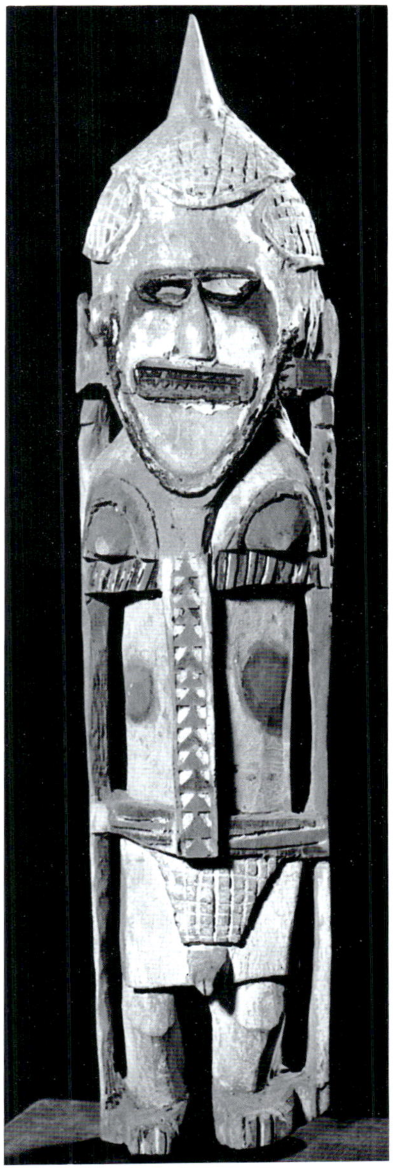

☐ 556 *›Uli-Figur‹, Neuirland, bemaltes Holz, Höhe 99 cm. Stiftung Ada und Emil Nolde, Seebüll.*

☐ 557 *Emil Nolde, ›Stilleben mit Südsee-Figur‹, 1915, Öl auf Leinwand, 88,5 x 73,5 cm. Stiftung Ada und Emil Nolde, Seebüll.*

Selbst nach seiner Rückkehr nach Deutschland, 1915, und nach seiner Entlassung aus dem Militärdienst, 1917, regten die Erinnerungen an die Palauinseln PECHSTEINS Phantasie noch lange an, wie an den Schmucknarbenmustern seiner Skulpturen zu erkennen ist. Das Gemälde *Der Götzenbildschnitzer, Palau* von 1917 ist ein echtes völkerkundliches Dokument, das einen Eingeborenen mit einem Breitbeil in der Hand zeigt, der die Arbeit eines anderen Eingeborenen studiert, bevor er seine überlebensgroße Figur vollendet.

Dieses Gemälde und andere Ölbilder von 1917 wie *Palau-Triptychon, Kopf einer Insulanerin, Palau* oder *Tanzendes Paar*[131] sind uns nur durch Photographien bekannt wie auch der große Fries, der einstmals zur Ausstattung von PECHSTEINS Berliner Atelierwohnung gehörte.[132] Obschon diese Arbeiten wirklichkeitsgetreue Darstellungen des Lebens auf den Palauinseln zu sein scheinen, enthalten sie in einem Fall einen Anachronismus. Im Bild *Im Frauenhaus, Palau*, das ebenfalls 1917 entstand, taucht unerklärlicherweise in einer melanesischen Hütte ein Häuptlingsstuhl nach einem afrikanischen Vorbild auf.[133] Auch in anderen Gemälden von 1917, einschließlich der wenig später entstandenen *Stilleben* in Mannheim und Saarbrücken, beruht die gemalte Stammesskulptur eher auf Anregungen aus Kamerun als von den Palauinseln. Vorbilder dazu gab es sehr wahrscheinlich im Berliner Museum für Völkerkunde.[134] Auch in den ersten Nachkriegsjahren sollten solche Vermischungen ozeanischer und afrikanischer Vorbilder weiterhin stattfinden.

Eine der wichtigsten Wechselbeziehungen zwischen dem deutschen Expressionismus und primitiver Kunst fand während des Krieges im Schaffen von KARL SCHMIDT-ROTTLUFF statt. In einer Reihe von Werken, die Grohmann »architekturale Figuren und Köpfe« nannte, untersuchte SCHMIDT-ROTTLUFF die formalen Strukturen westafrikanischer Plastik und machte sie seinem eigenen Schaffen zugänglich.[135] Zuerst schwankte er zwischen »untersetzten« und in die Länge gezogenen Proportionen. Der Oberkörper in *Frau mit aufgelöstem Haar*, ein Holzschnitt von 1913, ist in der Tat breiter als hoch, während im Gemälde *Mädchen vorm Spiegel* von 1915 der Rumpf, die Glieder und die Nase der Figur überlängt sind.[136] Diese beiden

□ 559 *›Reliquiarkopf‹, FANG (Gabun), Holz. Abgebildet in Carl Einstein, „Negerplastik“, 1915.*

□ 558 *Karl Schmidt-Rottluff, ›Die Drei Könige‹, 1917, Holzschnitt, 50 x 39 cm. The Museum of Modern Art, New York.*

Stile wie auch beide Werke stammen möglicherweise von einer weiblichen Reliquiarfigur der *NGUMBA* (Kamerun Fang) ab, deren Körperteile verlängert und zugleich komprimiert sind. Diese Reliquiarfigur befindet sich seit 1896 im Berliner Völkerkundemuseum □ 560.[137]

Die gerundeten Schultern sowie die jeweils ein Rechteck bildenden Finger und Füße der Figur des Holzschnittes erinnern an das Vorbild aus Kamerun; im Gemälde sind es die spitz zulaufenden Brüste, der waagrecht ausgestreckte Arm und besonders die geometrische Einpassung des kurzen Halses in die breiten Schultern sowie des zylindrischen Rumpfes in die sphärischen Schenkel. Ich betone die strukturelle Einpassung, denn sie ist der Schlüssel zu SCHMIDT-ROTTLUFFS Anleihen bei der afrikanischen Kunst während des Krieges. Es ist ein Strukturprinzip, das ihn wesentlich mehr interessierte als die Abschwächung der Form, wie sie für viele Werke der *BAMBARA* typisch ist. Die *BAMBARA*-Ahnenfigur, die Schneckenburger vorschlug, war sicherlich nicht SCHMIDT-ROTTLUFFS Vorbild: Ihr Hals und die Brüste sind zu lang, und ihr Gesicht ist frei von charakteristischen Merkmalen.[138] Außerdem hat gerade die *FANG*-Figur den eiförmig dreieckigen Kopf, der 1915 für das *Mädchen vorm Spiegel* herangezogen wurde. Es überrascht nicht, daß SCHMIDT-ROTTLUFF diese Kopfform und speziell ihren ovalen, vorspringenden Mund später in dem Holzschnitt *Christus und Nikodemus* (1919) aufgriff.[139]

Doch war SCHMIDT-ROTTLUFFS Tätigkeit als Maler zwischen diesen beiden Fällen einer direkten Anlehnung an das Exponat des Berliner Museums völlig unterbrochen. Als er vom Mai 1915 bis zum Dezember 1918 in einer Einheit in Polen stationiert war, malte er überhaupt nicht. Er schuf nur acht Holzskulpturen und eine Anzahl Holzschnitte.[140] Aber gerade diese Werke bekunden SCHMIDT-ROTTLUFFS Begeisterung für den plastischen Aufbau der Skulptur Kameruns.

Wie konnte damals ein Soldat an der Ostfront Zugang zu afrikanischer Kunst gewinnen? Er erinnerte sich natürlich der Stücke, die er früher in Berlin kennengelernt hatte, wie er auch während eines gelegentlichen Heimaturlaubs das Völkerkundemuseum besucht haben könnte. Aber nach meiner Meinung bestand keine Notwendigkeit für solch einen Besuch, wenn SCHMIDT-ROTTLUFF Carl Einsteins *Negerplastik* von 1915 gekauft hatte. Dies war in Europa das erste Buch überhaupt, das von einem Mitglied der kulturellen Avantgarde zu diesem Thema verfaßt wurde.[141] Es war für SCHMIDT-ROTTLUFF völlig irrelevant, daß die 111 Illustrationen des Buches weder Herkunftsgebiete noch Standorte vermerkten. Sicherlich kannte er bereits die meisten Stammesstile, auch kamen einige Stücke aus dem Berliner Völkerkundemuseum.[142] Wie Einstein selbst argumentierte, »sammelte man Negerkunst als Kunst«, und er fügte hinzu: »Sicherer als alle mögliche Kenntnis ethnographischer Art gilt die Tatsache: die afrikanischen Skulpturen!«[143]

Sicherlich studierte Schmidt-Rottluff 1917 die abgebildeten Gegenstände in Einsteins Buch, denn in jenem Kriegsjahr begann der Künstler trotz seiner militärischen Pflichten mit erfinderischen Varianten über die westafrikanische Kunst. Der Holzschnitt *Die Drei Könige* □ 558 ist in seiner Beziehung zu einem Reliquiarkopf der *Fang* □ 559, den Einstein von vorne und im Profil abbildete, besonders aufschlußreich. Die dreieckigen Gesichter und runden Hälse der *Drei Könige* stammen wohl entweder von diesem Vorbild oder von der oben erwähnten *Ngumba*-Figur. Während aber die stegartigen Nasen, die starren Augenbrauen und die scheibenförmigen Augen dem erwähnten *Ngumba*-Stück aus Berlin ähneln (dessen Augen aus Messingblech sind), scheinen das gefältelte Haar der rechten Figur, der Mund der Könige sowie die »Sprungschanzen«-Nase der Figur links eher vom *Fang*-Kopf abgeleitet zu sein, der in Einsteins Buch abgebildet ist.

Der *Fang*-Kopf führte wie mehrere andere Skulpturen in Einsteins Buch eine Gesichtsform ein,[144] zu der noch ein anderes typisches Merkmal westafrikanischer Bildhauerei gehört, das Hans Himmelheber »konkaves Gesicht« nannte.[145] Diese afrikanische Eigenart steht in Gegensatz zur europäischen Konvention der »runden Wangen« und der »gewölbten Stirn« und ist in der westlichen Kunst daher selten: Als Beispiel zeigt Himmelheber eine Zeichnung von Dürer, ein Gemälde von Picasso und einen Holzschnitt von Schmidt-Rottluff.[146] Schon Schmidt-Rottluffs *Blauroter Kopf* ist ein extremes Beispiel für dieses Prinzip der konkaven Gestaltung □ 566. Diese 1917 entstandene Skulptur scheint auf die *Ngumba*-Figur (mit dem ausgehöhlten offenen Mund) und den *Fang*-Kopf (mit dem röhrenförmigen Kinn) von Einsteins Abbildung abgeleitet zu sein, obwohl ihre herausragenden runden Augen und die Gesamtsilhouette auch Ähnlichkeiten mit anderen *Fang*-Köpfen hat. Das Ergebnis ist ein eindringliches Bildwerk

□ 560
›Männliche Figur‹, Ngumba (Kamerun), bemaltes Holz, 44 cm. Museum für Völkerkunde, Berlin.

□ 561 *Max Pechstein, ›Männerhaus unter Palmen‹, 1914, Tusche, 20 x 26,5 cm, Nationalgalerie, Berlin.*

mit dem passenden Untertitel ›Panischer Schrecken‹, das aber weniger eine spezifische Emotion beschwört als ein generelles Formprinzip physiognomischer Gestaltung.[147]

Nicht für alle Skulpturen Schmidt-Rottluffs, die während des Krieges entstanden, sind Vorbilder nachzuweisen. Reidemeister wie auch Schneckenburger verweisen bei dem *Grünen Kopf* von 1917 auf eine andere *Fang*-Plastik mit Messingaugen im Berliner Völkerkundemuseum.[148] Wenn überhaupt, überzeugt diese Ableitung allenfalls in der Profilansicht. Die zweistufige Nase und das mundlose Kinn der expressionistischen Arbeit weisen keine Analogie zum afrikanischen Werk auf. Außerdem gelangte das *Fang*-Stück nicht vor 1947 in das Berliner Museum und war so für Schmidt-Rottluff drei Jahrzehnte davor sicherlich nicht zugänglich.[149]

Hingegen kann ein anderes Werk Schmidt-Rottluffs aus derselben Gruppe, die Skulptur *Kopf* von 1917 □ 567, direkt auf ein ostafrikanisches Objekt bezogen werden, das in Ein-

□ 563 *›Figur‹, Teke (Volksrepublik Kongo), Holz und andere Materialien. Abgebildet in Carl Einstein, „Negerplastik", 1915.*

□ 562 *Karl Schmidt-Rottluff, ›Apostel‹, 1918, Holzschnitt, 50 x 40 cm, Brücke-Museum, Berlin. Geschenk des Künstlers.*

steins *Negerplastik* abgebildet war: eine weibliche Figur aus Tanganjika, die damals im Berliner Völkerkundemuseum war, während des Zweiten Weltkrieges aber verlorenging □ 564.[150] Die Kugelform des Kopfes, die muschelähnlichen Augen und die dreieckige Nase sind in beiden Werken ähnlich. Nur der geöffnete Mund weicht hier, wie im Falle des *Blauroten Kopfes,* von der Vorlage in Einsteins Buch ab.

Es gibt noch eine weitere Ableitung Schmidt-Rottluffs von einer Abbildung in Einsteins Buch, ein Holzschnitt von 1918, bekannt als *Apostel* (Selbstbildnis) □ 562. Die Arbeit scheint mir direkt von einem *Teke*-Objekt □ 563 aus Einsteins Buch inspiriert worden zu sein. Die scharfe Linie des Haaransatzes, das sichelförmige Ohr, die fein gestreifte Schläfe und Wange, besonders auch der vorspringende Mund oder der abstehende Bart auf dem zurückweichenden Kinn, all das sind beiden Werken gemeinsame Charakteristika.[151] Nur die Augen unterscheiden sich von Einsteins Abbildung. Sie könnten aber von einer anderen *Teke*-Figur abgeleitet sein, in diesem Falle von einer weiblichen Fetischfigur des Völkerkundemuseums in Berlin, die der alte Museumsführer erwähnte.[152] Da Schmidt-Rottluff jedoch sowohl das Geschlecht als auch die untersetzte Kopfform dieses Exponats unbeachtet ließ, kann es als

□ 564 *›Weibliche Figur‹, Luba (Zaire), Holz und Bast, Höhe 38 cm. Verbleib unbekannt. Museum für Völkerkunde, Berlin. Abgebildet in Carl Einstein, „Negerplastik", 1915.*

□ 565 *›Reliquiarkopf‹, FANG (Gabun), Holz, Höhe 43 cm. Privatsammlung.*

□ 566 *Karl Schmidt-Rottluff, ›Blauroter Kopf‹, 1917, bemaltes Holz, Höhe 30 cm. Brücke-Museum, Berlin.*

sicher gelten, daß der auslösende Impuls von Einsteins Buch ausging. Der *Apostel* von 1918 wurde wohl ebenso wie der *Heilige Franziskus* mit einem ähnlichen Bart in einem Holzschnitt von 1919[153] nach der Entlassung des Künstlers aus dem Militärdienst in Berlin geschaffen.

Stammesskulptur, schreibt Einstein in *Negerplastik*, ist charakterisiert durch ihren »religiösen« Zweck und ihre »kubische Raumanschauung«.[154] Dies sind auch Tendenzen in SCHMIDT-ROTTLUFFS Arbeit während des Krieges. Unter dem Eindruck primitiver Kunst konnte er die Körperproportionen und die Gesichtszüge beinahe nach Belieben variieren, aber er richtete sich getreu nach der plastischen Logik und der strukturellen Gliederung eines primitiven Werkes. Mit dem Waffenstillstand vom November 1918 wurde der Expressionismus in Deutschland populär. Die Bewegung war tonangebend in der Kunstszene, und die Maler übernahmen in wichtigen kulturellen Organisationen eine Führungsrolle. Dies war die »zweite Welle« des Expressionismus,[155] die heftig aber kurz war, teils bedingt durch den Tod von MARC und MACKE sowie durch die Abwesenheit KANDINSKYS (der in Rußland lebte) und KIRCHNERS (der sich in der Schweiz aufhielt). Der Versailler Vertrag von Mitte 1919 beraubte Deutschland unter anderem seiner

□ 567 *Karl Schmidt-Rottluff, ›Kopf‹, 1917, Holz. Zerstört.*

□ 568 ›*Weibliche Figur*‹, LUBA *(Zaire), Holz und Perlen, Höhe 27,5 cm. Museum für Völkerkunde, Berlin.*

□ 569 *Max Pechstein, ›Skulptur‹, 1919, Holz. Verbleib unbekannt.*

afrikanischen und ozeanischen Kolonien. Um 1920 gaben die Kritiker die Hoffnung auf einen weiteren expressionistischen Fortschritt auf, während die Künstler, die sich ihrem vierzigsten Lebensjahr näherten, über die Möglichkeiten einer künstlerischen Erneuerung in Deutschland geteilter Meinung waren. Die primitive Kunst wurde auch im späten Expressionismus noch rezipiert, doch waren diese Ableitungen oftmals modisch oder ironisch gefärbt.

Nach dem Krieg begann PECHSTEIN primitive Plastik zu sammeln, und 1919 schuf er zahlreiche Holzskulpturen.[156] PECHSTEINS *Viertelmond* ist sehr wahrscheinlich von SCHMIDT-ROTTLUFFS *Blaurotem Kopf* von 1917 beeinflußt,[157] denn beide Köpfe laufen auf ein verlängertes, vorspringendes Kinn mit einem runden, ausgehöhlten Mund zu. Während aber die geometrische Betonung bei SCHMIDT-ROTTLUFF plastisch ist, orientierte sich PECHSTEIN stärker an der Fläche. Nicht daß PECHSTEINS Werk ozeanische Linearität gegenüber afrikanischer Masse bevorzugt hätte.[158] Denn der *Viertelmond* ist auch das Werk eines Malers, der sich nur selten der Skulptur widmete. Doppelte quadratische Muster im Haar und tief eingeschnittene Bögen für die Augenbrauen und den Bart weisen darauf hin, daß PECHSTEIN zweidimensionalen Wirkungen einen besonderen Akzent verleihen wollte.

PECHSTEINS Tendenz zur Zweidimensionalität wird noch augenfälliger, wenn man eine verlorengegangene Holzskulptur von 1919 □ 569 mit ihrem vermutlichen Vorbild, einer weiblichen *LUBA*-Figur (Kongo) mit einem Halsband, vergleicht □ 568. Das Werk der *LUBA* befand sich seit 1904[159] im Berliner

Völkerkundemuseum und scheint die Gesichtszüge, das Halsband und selbst die gebogenen Arme von PECHSTEINS Figur angeregt zu haben. Doch PECHSTEINS Werk ist als Relief angelegt. Der Künstler projiziert die Brüste und das Gesäß, die in der afrikanischen Skulptur vollplastisch ausgebildet sind, in die Fläche. Des weiteren setzte der Expressionist Schmucknarben in regelmäßigen Mustern auf Gesicht und Körper, während sie der Künstler aus dem Kongo eher locker über den Bauch verteilte.[160]

Die beste Skulptur in der Reihe der verlorenen Holzarbeiten PECHSTEINS von 1919 ist der *Mond* ☐ 571. Er markiert einen Durchbruch zur Vollplastik, wie dies schon der Vergleich mit dem Titel *Viertelmond* nahelegt. Der *Mond* ist auch erheblich plastischer als die Fetischfigur der NGUMBA aus Zaire ☐ 570, auf die er wahrscheinlich zurückgeht, ein Gegenstand, der 1885 in die Berliner Völkerkundesammlung kam.[161] Einkerbungen in Kopf und Gesicht bilden bei der NGUMBA-Plastik mehrere gerade Linien, während sie bei PECHSTEIN einen runden Rahmen ergeben. Ähnlich sind die Brüste und der Unterleib im expressionistischen Werk größer und voluminöser als im Beispiel aus Afrika, obschon die Schulterfläche und der vorspringende Nabel in beiden Werken ähnlich sind. Dessen ungeachtet gab PECHSTEIN sein Interesse an der Oberflächendekoration nicht im geringsten auf. Es gibt rhombische Muster im Haar, Winkel auf dem Körper und Zickzacklinien auf den Seiten der Extremitäten. Insbesondere mittels der Streifen gelangt PECHSTEIN zu einem dekorativen Ornamentstil, der – für Deutschland recht fortgeschritten – Stammes-Art Deco genannt werden könnte.

Auch im Holzschnitt stützte sich PECHSTEIN in seiner späten expressionistischen Phase weitgehend auf die primitiven Vorbilder. So gibt das *Mappen-Umschlagblatt* eines Holzschnitt-Zyklus von 1919 »eine magische Statuette aus dem Gebiete Kameruns« partiell wieder, wie Orrel Reed beobachtete.[162] Wir können diese Statuette versuchsweise wieder als eine Figur der NGUMBA identifizieren, die sich seit 1896 im Berliner Völkerkundemuseum befindet.[163] Die Messingaugen, die entblößten Zähne und die Verschmelzung der spitz zulaufenden Brüste mit den ausgebreiteten Armen, für alle diese Charakteristika gibt es Parallelen in PECHSTEINS Holzschnitt. Daneben existiert wahrscheinlich eine andere, gleichermaßen wichtige Quelle, die uns schon bekannt ist. Die Zickzacklinien auf beiden Seiten des Kopfes ähneln dem gleichmäßig angeordneten Winkelmuster der *Mond*-Skulptur nur bedingt, die ein Jahr vorher entstand. Statt dessen strahlen sie gegen die Ohren aus wie die »Sprechlinien« auf einem Holzbalken der Palau, den KIRCHNER 1910 auf einer Postkarte skizziert hatte ☐ 516. Nach unpublizierten Untersuchungen sind überhaupt die Zickzacklinien, die Ohrringe und selbst die vollkommen ovale Form des Kopfes alles verspätete Beschwörungen der Palau-Ikonographie.[164] PECHSTEINS *Mappen-Umschlagblatt* von 1920 ist eine eindrucksvolle Synthese aus afrikanischen und ozeanischen Elementen.

Im Gegensatz zu PECHSTEIN ergründete SCHMIDT-ROTTLUFF auch weiterhin die religiöse Dimension primitiver Kunst. Einzelne Holzschnitte von 1919 wie *Christus und Nikodemus* oder *Heiliger Franziskus* sind in ihrer Verbindung von afrikanischen Formen und christlichem Inhalt der »Missionskunst« nicht unähnlich.[165] In einem Gemälde von 1920 diente die Stammeskunst hingegen einer universelleren geistigen Aussage. Die Gestalt des Menschen in *Gespräch vom Tod,* deren gestischer und mimischer Ausdruck als »angstvoll fragend«[166] charakteri-

☐ 570 *›Figur‹,* NGOMBE *(Zaire), bemaltes Holz, Höhe 63 cm. Museum für Völkerkunde, Berlin.*

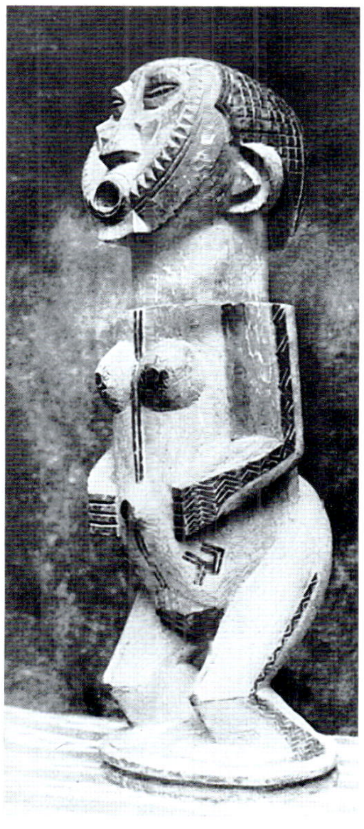

☐ 571 *Max Pechstein, ›Mond‹, 1919, bemaltes Holz. Verbleib unbekannt.*

siert wurde, scheint von einer Sargfigur aus Sumatra im Berliner Museum für Völkerkunde beeinflußt zu sein, die wenige Jahre später in Eckart von Sydows wegweisender Publikation zur Stammeskunst abgebildet wurde.[167] Maßgebend für diesen Vergleich ist das unregelmäßige Gesicht mit dem kahlen Schädel, der flachen Nase und den überlangen Lippen. Es ist bezeichnend für SCHMIDT-ROTTLUFF, daß er einen primitiven Fetisch in einem lauten und farbenreichen Gemälde verwendete, um allgemeine Fragen nach dem Tod und dem Leben danach aufzuwerfen.

Satirischer ist PAUL KLEES *Portrait des Künstlers* von 1919, das sich einer polynesischen Kultfigur bedient. Die vielfachen Linien um die Augen und den Mund, die Schultern, die Finger und der quadratische Schädel sind in KLEES Bild und der primitiven Plastik ähnlich. KLEE endet aber an der Taille, während dem großen Kopf bei der polynesischen Figur ein großer Phallus entspricht.[168] Es muß KLEE Spaß gemacht haben, auf ein exotisches Meisterwerk aus dem Völkerkundemuseum in München zurückzugreifen, das vor allem ein so auffälliges Geschlechtsteil hat. Der deutsche Künstler-Intellektuelle erkannte die vom Instinktiven her bestehende Brücke zwischen Stammesskulptur und dem modernen Menschen mit erheblicher Ironie. Vielleicht verwirklichte nur KIRCHNER, der im selbstgewählten Exil in den Schweizer Alpen lebte, so etwas wie einen »primitiven« Lebensstil, nach dem sich die anderen sehnten. Im Herbst und Winter 1919–20 schnitzte er eigene Möbel für seine Berghütte, so daß er sich fast zwangsläufig mit den eingeborenen Bildhauern verglich und dabei beobachtete, »wie viel weiter doch die Neger in diesen Schnitzereien waren«.[169] Als er einen mit Ochsenblut gefärbten Stuhl aus Nadelholz schnitzte ☐ 572, erinnerte sich KIRCHNER offenbar daran, vor dem Krieg in Berlin zusammen mit PECHSTEIN einen

Häuptlingsstuhl aus Kamerun gesehen zu haben.[170] Während aber PECHSTEIN den unteren Teil kopiert hatte, wiederholte KIRCHNER den Aufbau. Auf der Rückseite des Stuhles schnitzte er eine große hockende Frau, deren Beinhaltung der männlichen Figur auf dem Stuhl aus Kamerun glich. Über dem Kopf der Hockenden ließ KIRCHNER einen Mann und eine Frau sich die Hand reichen, in genau der gleichen V-Form, die der Bildhauer aus Kamerun benutzte, um für den Sitzenden zusätzlichen Halt zu schaffen. Mit den Schweizer Alpen vor seinem Fenster und den Möbeln – für seine Frau, die er nie mit dem bürgerlichen Ausdruck »Ehefrau« ansprechen wollte – sah KIRCHNER seine Schnitzarbeiten als einen Teil der nackten Natur selbst.[171]

»Wie viel weiter waren doch die Neger...«: Einmal mehr begegnen wir einer expressionistischen Bewunderung der Stammeskünstler, so wie einige Jahre zuvor NOLDE ausschließlich die Eingeborenen als »echte Menschen« beschrieben hatte. Eine solche Bewunderung erstreckte sich vom »Urmenschen« bis zur »Urnatur«, so wie HECKEL einst gehofft hatte, in Afrika zu leben, um in einer ursprünglichen Natur zu leben. Immerhin gelang es KIRCHNER, der für zwei Jahrzehnte eine Art »Urnatur« in den Alpen erlebte, sie in eine moderne Kultur zu integrieren. Schon um 1909–10 hatte er Natur und Kultur miteinander konfrontiert, jetzt, in der Schweiz isoliert, sollte er sich der modernen Abstraktion bedienen. Somit waren die Absichten des Expressionisten von besonderer Art. Er führte

□ 572 *Ernst Ludwig Kirchner, ›Stuhl‹, 1920, Arvenholz, mit Ochsenblut gefärbt, Höhe 87 cm. Brücke-Museum, Berlin.*

□ 573 *Max Beckmann, ›Frühe Menschen‹, um 1947, Aquarell oder Gouache und Tinte, 50,2 x 64,8 cm. Privatsammlung.* ▷

ein Zwiegespräch zwischen »Urnatur« und moderner Kunst, eine Dialektik zwischen ursprünglicher Natur und fortgeschrittener Kultur.

Die deutschen Expressionisten stellten die Natur nicht über die Kultur oder zogen die rohe Natur ihrer eigenen Kultur nicht irgendwie vor. Statt dessen betrachteten sie die Natur holistisch als den Ursprung der Kultur ihrer Zeit. Sie waren die Erben einer romantischen Tradition, in der das Leben die Kunst vital wie auch strukturell vorwegnahm. Das leitende Prinzip war die Treue der Kunst zur »inneren Wahrheit« der Natur.[172]

Was die Expressionisten dieser romantischen Tradition hinzufügten, war hingegen ein Verständnis des Bewußtseins als Bindeglied zwischen Natur und Kunst. Das Grundproblem bestand für sie in der Frage, wie der Geist den Instinkt – die Haupttriebfeder der Natur – in die Kunst als der hohen Verwirklichung der Kultur übersetzt. Die Expressionisten gingen das Problem wie Nietzsche an, indem sie ein Bindeglied zwischen dem primitiven und dem modernen Geist, zwischen dem »wilden« Geschichtenerzähler und dem träumenden Künstler unserer Zeit voraussetzten:

»Ich meine: Wie jetzt noch der Mensch im Traume schließt, so schloß die Menschheit ›auch im Wachen‹ viele Jahrtausende hindurch: Die erste ›causa‹, die dem Geist einfiel, um irgend etwas, das der Erklärung bedurfte, zu erklären, genügte ihm und galt als Wahrheit. (So verfahren nach den Erzählungen der Reisenden die Wilden heute noch.) Im Traum übt sich dieses uralte Stück Menschtum in uns fort, denn es ist die Grundlage, auf der die höhere Vernunft sich entwickelte und in jedem Menschen sich noch entwickelt: Der Traum bringt uns in ferne Zustände der menschlichen Kultur wieder zurück und gibt ein Mittel an die Hand, sie besser zu verstehen. . . . Wir können aus diesen Vorgängen entnehmen, ›wie spät‹ das schärfere logische Denken, das Strengnehmen von Ursache und Wirkung entwickelt worden ist, wenn unsere Vernunft- und Verstandesfunktion ›jetzt noch‹ unwillkürlich nach jenen primitiven Formen des Schließens zurückgreifen . . . – Auch der Dichter, der Künstler ›schiebt‹ seinen Stimmungen und Zuständen Ursachen ›unter‹, welche durchaus nicht die wahren sind; er erinnert insofern an älteres Menschentum und kann uns zum Verständnis desselben verhelfen.«[173]

Mit dem, was Nietzsche an anderer Stelle »die Logik der Träume« nannte, konnte der moderne Künstler eine Einheit zwischen dem unbewußten und dem bewußten Gefühl wiederherstellen, zwischen »Traum und Kultur« (Nietzsche).

Es sei daran erinnert, daß es bei Nietzsche drei Variablen gibt: primitives Denken, modernes Denken und den Traum des Künstlers, der zwischen ihnen vermittelt. 1919 suchte KIRCHNER eine Lösungsmöglichkeit für diese Dreiheit, indem er das primitive Denken mit der Erfahrung des nackten Daseins gleichsetzte, das Moderne mit dem erkennenden oder liebenden Intellekt und den Traum mit der kulturschöpfenden Vision. Das Ergebnis war ein ästhetisches Credo, das die expressionistische Dialektik zwischen primitivem und modernem Denken verkörpert:

»Dreifach ist das große Geheimnis der Kunst: Traum, Leben und erkennende Liebe. Der Traum gibt die Vision, die Vision bringt das Erlebnis, das durch den liebenden Geist zum Werk sich gestaltet.«[174]

Anmerkungen

1. Diese Studie ist Leopold Reidemeister gewidmet, dem Pionier in der Erforschung des Expressionismus, dessen Publikationen für alle Untersuchungen auf diesem Gebiet unersetzlich sind. Beim Formulieren meiner Gedanken profitierte ich auch von Gesprächen mit George A. Corbin, Charles W. Haxthausen, William S. Rubin und Roy Sieber sowie von den Anregungen der Studenten höherer Seminare über »Expressionismus und Primitivismus« an der Columbia University im Frühjahr 1982 und an der University of Pittsburgh im Winter 1983.

2. Goldwater, R. M., *Primitivism in Modern Painting*, New York und London 1938, Kap. 4, vor allem S. 87–90.

3. Ettlinger, L. D., »German Expressionism and Primitive Art« in *The Burlington Magazine*, April 1968, S. 195.

4. Levine, F. S., *The Apocalyptic Vision: The Art of Franz Marc as German Expressionism*, New York 1979, S. 3–5, Anmerkung 104.

5. Foster, H., »The Expressive Fallacy« in *Art in America*, Januar 1983, S. 80–81.

6. Pfister, O., *Der psychologische und biologische Untergrund des Expressionismus*, Bern und Leipzig 1920, S. 113–15, 132–33. Siehe auch die Unterscheidung zwischen einem »Ego, von der Regression überwältigt« in der Pathologie und einer »Regression im Dienste des Ego« in der Kreativität bei Kris, E., *Psychoanalytic Explorations in Art*, New York 1967, S. 177.

7. Hartlaub, G. F., *Die Graphik des Expressionismus in Deutschland*, Stuttgart 1947, S. 9–10, siehe auch Buchheim, L. G., *Die Künstlergemeinschaft Brücke*, Feldafing 1956, S. 12–13.

8. Reidemeister, L., im Katalog *Das Ursprüngliche und die Moderne*, Berlin, Akademie der Künste, 1964.

9. Schneckenburger, M., »Bemerkungen zur ›Brücke‹ und zur ›primitiven‹ Kunst« im Katalog der Ausstellung *Weltkulturen und moderne Kunst,* München, Haus der Kunst, 1972, S. 456–74, vor allem die Seiten 457–58.

10. Kokoschka, O., *Mein Leben*, München 1971, S. 51. Zu Kokoschka siehe auch Goldwater, a.a.O., S. 100, Anmerkung 1.

11. Robert Louis Stevenson und Paul Gauguin beschrieben die sexuellen Bräuche unter den Südseevölkern als freizügig. Margaret Meads berühmte Bestätigung dieser Vermutung in ihrem Buch *Kindheit und Jugend in Samoa*, 1928, wurde neuerdings von Derek Freeman in Frage gestellt, *Margaret Mead and Samoa: The Making and Unmaking of an Anthropological Myth*, Cambridge, Mass., 1983.

12. Reidemeister, L., a.a.O., Nr. 99 und 100 (Heckel); Nr. 123 und 125, 129 und 130, 131 und 133 (Nolde). Schneckenburger in *Weltkulturen*, Nr. 1777 und 1769 (Schmidt-Rottluff); Nr. 1778 und 1793 (Kirchner). Die Nolde-Vergleiche, von Reidemeister und Schneckenburger publiziert, wurden von Urban, M., *Emil Nolde: Masken und Figuren*, Bielefeld, Kunsthalle, 1971, Nr. 5 und 5b, 6 und 6a, 15 und 15a, ausführlicher vorgestellt.

13. Rousseau, J.-J., *Discours sur l'origine et les*

fondements de l'inégalité parmi les hommes, siehe Lévi-Strauss, C., *Strukturale Anthropologie*, Frankfurt a.M. 1975, Band *II*, S. 49.

14. Rousseau, *Les Rêveries*, »Siebenter Spaziergang«; Lévi-Strauss, a.a.O., S. 42–43. In den *Confessions* entdeckte Rousseau sogar die entpersönlichende Wirkung der Einfühlung; siehe Lévi-Strauss, ebda., S. 39; » . . . in Wahrheit bin ich nicht ›Ich‹, sondern der schwächste und niedrigste der ›Anderen‹.«

15. Tönnies, F., *Gemeinschaft und Gesellschaft*, Berlin 1920, erstes Buch, erster und zweiter Abschnitt; das Buch erschien erstmals 1887.

16. Lévi-Strauss, a.a.O., S. 312–17.

17. Simmel, G., »Metropolis und geistiges Leben«, 1903, *The Sociology of George Simmel*, Wolff, K. H. (Hrsg.), Glencoe 1950, S. 416, 418; siehe Lévi-Strauss, S. 320: »Diese Absonderung des Menschen von seiner natürlichen Umwelt, . . . der Zwang, dem ihn die modernen Formen des Stadtlebens unterwerfen, fast ausschließlich in einem künstlichen Milieu zu leben, bilden eine ernsthafte Bedrohung, die auf der geistigen Gesundheit der Art lastet.«

18. Tönnies, a.a.O., S. 130–32.

19. Simmel, G., *Der Konflikt der modernen Kultur*, München und Leipzig 1921, S. 13, 30. Der Titelessay erschien erstmals 1914.

20. Siehe Lévi-Strauss, a.a.O., S. 313: »Die Zukunft der Kunst, falls sie eine hat, würde vielmehr fordern, daß sie wieder mit der rohen Natur Fühlung nimmt, was im strengen Sinn unmöglich ist; . . .«

21. Reinhardt, G., »Die frühe ›Brücke‹, Beiträge zur Geschichte und zum Werk der Dresdener Künstlergruppe ›Brücke‹ der Jahre 1905 bis 1908« in *Brücke-Archiv*, Nr. 9/10, 1977–78, S. 23–24. Man beachte, daß Buchheim durch den Titel seiner Untersuchung *Die Künstlergemeinschaft Brücke* einen anderen Eindruck erweckte. Den irrtümlichen Titel übernahm Hans Konrad Roethel, *Modern German Painting*, New York 1958, S. 7.

22. Tönnies, a.a.O., S. 134–35. Mehr als die »Brücke« war es die Wandervogel-Bewegung, die die Vorstellung unschuldiger *Gemeinschaft* prägte, siehe Laqueur, W., *Young Germany: A History of the German Youth Movement*, New York 1962.

23. Reinhardt, a.a.O., S. 85–87. Es muß auch bemerkt werden, daß die darwinistischen Bezüge des *Programms* auf »Glauben an die Evolution« und an eine Jugendbewegung, »die die Zukunft in sich trägt«, mit einer echten regressiven – und volkstümlichen – Ablehnung der Geschichte wenig zu tun haben.

24. Das *»Brücke«-Programm* wurde oft abgebildet, am besten bei Selz, P., *German Expressionist Painting*, Berkeley 1957, S. 95.

25. Reinhardt, a.a.O., S. 28–31.

26. Kirchner, E. L., »Brief vom 17. April 1937« in *Ernst Ludwig Kirchner*, New York, Kurt Valentin Gallery, 1952, ohne Seitenangabe.

27. Vogt, P., *Erich Heckel*, Recklinghausen 1965, Nr. 1909/7.

28. Nietzsche, F., *Der Wille zur Macht*, Stuttgart 1980, S. 540; die Erstausgabe erschien 1901 und nicht 1906, wie von Reinhardt »Die frühe ›Brücke‹«, S. 28, behauptet.

29. Whitman, W., *Leaves of Grass*, 1855 erstmals veröffentlicht. Die populärste deutsche Übersetzung aus jener Zeit wurde von Johannes Schlaf, *Grashalme*, Leipzig 1907, verfaßt.

30. Siehe u. a. *Badende Menschengruppe in Moritzburg*, in der im Vordergrund eine weibliche Figur ihr Gesäß entblößt und die Männer darüber große Genitalien haben, in Gordon, D. E., *Ernst Ludwig Kirchner*, München 1968, Nr. 94. Reinhardts Rückdatierung dieses Gemäldes auf 1910, »Die frühe ›Brücke‹«, S. 173, Anmerkung 378 ist stilistisch nicht überzeugend.

31. Siehe u. a. den Katalog *Ernst Ludwig Kirchner, 1880–1938.*, Berlin, Nationalgalerie, 1979–80, Nr. 55–60, die *Liebesszene* hat die Nr. 62.

32. Siehe die Gruppe von Zeichnungen von 1910 und 1911, abgebildet und besprochen, im Katalog *Ernst Ludwig Kirchner 1880–1938* unter der Nr. 100–05.

33. Die einzelne männliche Figur rechts wurde übermalt, als Kirchner um 1920 die Leinwand erneuerte, obwohl er unerklärlicherweise den Kopf stehen ließ, siehe Grohmann, W., *Das Werk Ernst Ludwig Kirchners*, München 1926, Abb. 19.

34. Photographien der Vorhänge und der Wandbehänge sind abgebildet im Katalog *Ernst Ludwig Kirchner 1880–1938*, S. 18, Abb. 7, 8; die Zeichnungen, ebenda, Nr. 104, 105.

35. Der *Stehende Akt mit Hut* in Frankfurt bei Gordon, a.a.O., Nr. 163, für 1910 siehe auch *Marzella*, Stockholm, *Sitzendes Mädchen, Fränzi*, Minneapolis, *Liegender Akt mit Fächer*, Bremen, und von 1911 *Zwei Mädchen, zwei Midinetten*, Los Angeles, Gordon, Nr. 58 Rückseite, 113, 123, 189.

36. Zum Hocker, siehe Postkarte vom 24. Dezember 1910, in Schack, G. (Hrsg.), *Postkarten an Gustav Schiefler*, Hamburg 1976, Nr. 21, und eine Photographie in Gabler, K., *E. L. Kirchner: Dokumente, Fotos, Schriften, Briefe*, Aschaffenburg 1980, S. 139. Zu einem möglichen kamerunischen Vorbild siehe einen hölzernen Hocker des *BALI*-Stammes, der 1897 in das Berliner Völkerkundemuseum gelangte, abgebildet in Krieger, K., *Westafrikanische Plastik III*, Berlin, Museum für Völkerkunde, 1969, Abb. 8, S. 13. Kirchner besuchte Berlin 1910 mehrfach.

37. Vogt, a.a.O., Nr. 1910/3.

38. Siehe Gordon, a.a.O., Nr. 155, 156 und 157 von 1910. Der Tierfries erscheint 1912 als Saum eines Tischtuches in Heckels Atelier, siehe Vogt, *Erich Heckel*, Nr. 1912/46.

39. Abgebildet im Katalog *Brücke*, Cornell University, Andrew Dickson White Museum of Art, 1970, Nr. 79.

40. Gordon, a.a.O., Nr. 74 (1909), 58 Rückseite (1910), 185–87 (1911).

41. Dube, A. und W.-D., *E. L. Kirchner: Das graphische Werk*, 2 Bd., München 1967, Lithographien Nr. 185–90. Siehe auch Gabler, *E. L. Kirchner: Dokumente*, S. 70–71.

42. *Führer durch die Königlichen Sammlungen zu Dresden*, 11. Auflage, Dresden 1912, S. 88, siehe Plan S. 56.

43. Gordon, D. E., »Kirchner in Dresden« in *The Art Bulletin*, September-Dezember 1966, S. 355 und Anm. 115.

44. *Führer . . . zu Dresden*, S. 88.

45. Woermann, K., *Geschichte der Kunst aller Zeiten und Völker*, Leipzig und Wien 1900, Bd. 1, gegenüber von S. 56; die Abbildung in Woermann wurde in Ettlinger, »Primitive Art«, Abb. 42, wiedergegeben. Zur Angabe des Jahres 1881 siehe Von Sydow, E., *Die Kunst der Naturvölker und die Vorzeit*, Berlin 1923, Abb. 237 und S. 510. In meinem Pittsburgher Seminar erkannte Sara Gregg als erste die Bedeutung dieser Quelle.

46. Kirchner, »Die Arbeit E. L. Kirchners« (1925–26) in Kornfeld, E. W., *Ernst Ludwig Kirchner: Nachzeichnung seines Lebens*, Bern 1979, S. 333. Das Jahr 1903 wird auch in einem Tagebucheintrag von 1925 erwähnt, Grisebach, L., *E. L. Kirchners Davoser Tagebuch*, Köln 1968, S. 84. Die Entdeckung der Palau-Balken zusammen mit den »Federmänteln von Südseevölkern« wird in einem Brief an Botho Graef erwähnt, aber nicht datiert, in Grisebach, L. (Hrsg.), *Maler des Expressionismus im Briefwechsel mit Eberhard Grisebach*, Hamburg 1962, S. 53. »Balkenschnitzereien der Südsee« sind für 1906 in Kirchners *Chronik der Künstlergruppe Brücke* von 1913 erwähnt, 2. Textseite, u. a. in *Maler suchen Freunde*, S. 42.

47. Bolliger, H., »Die Biographie Ernst Ludwig Kirchners« im Katalog *Ernst Ludwig Kirchner*, Düsseldorf, Kunsthalle, 1960, ohne Seitenangabe.

48. Siehe Barr, A. H., Jr., *German Painting and Sculpture*, New York, Museum of Modern Art, 1931, S. 10.

49. Siehe Grohmann, W., *Zeichnungen von E. L. Kirchner*, Dresden 1925, vor allem Nr. 7, 9, 10. Siehe auch Arntz, W. F., *Paula Modersohn und die Maler der »Brücke«*, Bern, Kunsthalle, 1948, S. 13: »Schon aus dem Jahre 1904 kennen wir Zeichnungen Kirchners nach afrikanischen und Südsee-Skulpturen.«

50. Reidemeister, *Das Ursprüngliche . . .*, a.a.O., Nr. 92, in dem Kirchners Tuschskizze einer afrikanischen Plastik aus diesem Brief abgebildet ist. Obschon das genaue afrikanische Vorbild dieser Skizze noch nicht nachgewiesen worden ist, kommt die Anregung zweifelsohne aus Kamerun und könnte eine weibliche Variante einer hölzernen männlichen Figur, Höhe 52 cm, gewesen sein, die vom Dresdener Museum 1909 angekauft worden war (Inv. Nr. 24229).

51. Wietek, G. (Hrsg.), *Bemalte Postkarten und Briefe deutscher Künstler*, Hamburg, Altonaer Museum, 1962, Nr. 214. Das Wort »Balken« ist hier als »Balkon« wiedergegeben, ein in meinem »Kirchner in Dresden«, S. 354, übersehener Fehler, doch korrigiert in Reinhardt, a.a.O., S. 174, Anmerkung 381.

52. Reinhardt, a.a.O., Abb. 65, S. 91, wies auf Kirchners Interesse an solchen »Sprechlinien« hin, aber er war sich nicht bewußt, daß die Zickzackform der Zeichnung von 1910 in erster Linie eine Analogie der dreieckigen Formen der Randdekoration der Palau-Balken war. Eine weitere Ikonographie der Palau-Balken bei De-Verne Reed Smith, »The Palauan Storyboards: From Traditional Architecture to Airport Art« in *Expedition*, Herbst 1975, S. 2–17, vor allem S. 5, 11. Kathryn Kramer machte mich in meinem Columbia-Seminar auf den letzten Artikel aufmerksam.

53. Dube, a.a.O., Holzschnitt Nr. 160.

54. Vogt, a.a.O., Nr. 1910/11.

55. Siehe etwa Pechsteins *Drei Badende am Teich* von 1910, abgebildet in Reinhardt, a.a.O., Abb. 62a, S. 88. Zum »Kürzelstil« und seinem Einfluß im Sommer 1910 siehe auch Schneckenburger, *Weltkulturen*, Nr. 1777, S. 463.

56. Buchheim, L.-G., *Otto Mueller, Leben und*

Werk, mit einem Werkverzeichnis der Graphik Otto Muellers von Florian Karsch, Feldafing 1963, Karsch Nr. 5.

57. An Kirchners *Fränzi vor geschnitztem Stuhl*, 1910, Gordon, *Ernst Ludwig Kirchner* a.a.O., Nr. 122, ist die Lehne des gemalten Stuhls nach dem Palau-Reliefstil gestaltet. Körper und Gesicht sind rosafarben, umgeben von einer schwarzen Körperumrandung und einer dichten Haarmasse, alles streng zweidimensional. Doch untergräbt Kirchner diese zweidimensionale Wirkung, indem er Fränzis naturgetreu dargestellte Gestalt vor den flachen Stuhl plaziert und farbliche Spannungen zwischen Vorder- und Hintergrund schafft. Eine andere Darstellung von Kirchners geschnitztem Stuhl findet sich in Heckels Postkarte vom 16. Dezember 1910 in Schack, *Postkarten an Gustav Schiefler*, Nr. 44.

58. Gordon, *»Kirchner in Dresden«*, a.a.O., S. 357, Nr. 134. Die Kunst Benins ist natürlich ein Hofstil, doch die Expressionisten unterschieden ihn nicht von der Stammeskunst.

59. Rosenthal, D.A., »Two Motifs from Early Africa in Works by Ernst Ludwig Kirchner« in *Abhandlungen und Berichte des Staatlichen Museums für Völkerkunde Dresden*, Bd. 35, Berlin 1976, S. 169–71, vor allem S. 170. Rosenthals Datierung basiert auf Kirchners Erwähnung der Bronzen in seinem Brief vom 31. März 1910. Mein Dank gilt Sara Gregg, die mich auf diesen Artikel aufmerksam gemacht hat.

60. Gordon, *»Kirchner in Dresden«*, a.a.O., S. 358, Anmerkung 135.

61. Siehe Anmerkung 17.

62. Siehe Goldwater, a.a.O., 1938, S. 102–16, und vor allem die leicht überarbeitete Ausgabe *Primivitism in Modern Art*, New York 1967, S. 125–42. Siehe Grote, L., »Expressionismus und Volkskunst« in *Zeitschrift für Völkerkunde*, Nr. 2, 1959, S. 24–31, und Glatzel, U., »Zur Bedeutung der Volkskunst beim Blauen Reiter«, Dissertation, Ludwig-Maximilians-Universität, München 1976, vor allem S. 187–242.

63. Kandinsky, W., »Der Blaue Reiter« (Rückblick) in *Das Kunstblatt*, 1930; neu in Wassily Kandinsky, *Essays über Kunst und Künstler*, Bern 1963, 2. Aufl., S. 133–38.

64. Kandinsky, a.a.O.; für das Datum von 1907 siehe Goldwater, a.a.O., 1967, S. 127.

65. August Macke und Franz Marc, *Briefwechsel*, Köln 1964, S. 39–41.

66. Lankheit, K., *Franz Marc: Sein Leben und seine Kunst*, Köln 1976, Abb. 22, 23.

67. Krieger, K., und Kutscher, G., *Westafrikanische Masken*, 2. Aufl., Berlin, Museum für Völkerkunde, 1967, S. 56, Nr. 84, Abb. 36.

68. Kamerun-Masken in »der Form von Ochsenköpfen« waren ausgestellt; *Führer durch das Museum für Völkerkunde*, Berlin 1911, S. 70.

69. Worringer, W., *Abstraktion und Einfühlung: ein Beitrag zur Stilpsychologie*, 1908, Neuauflagen München 1959/76, S. 45.

70. Worringer, a.a.O., S. 15. Die »Raumscheu« ist typisch für die abstrakte Kunst. Sie manifestiert sich deutlich in der ägyptischen Architektur, ebenda S. 184, Anmerkung 8.

71. Zur Anlehnung von Marcs *Gelber Kuh* (1911) an einen mykenischen Goldbecher aus Vaphio, siehe Lankheit, *Franz Marc*, a.a.O., S. 78.

72. Zur Beziehung zwischen dem Werk Gauguins und den beiden Bildern Marcs siehe Gordon, D. E., »Content by Contradiction« in *Art in America*, Dezember 1982, S. 76–89.

73. Vondermuhll, A., »Franz Marc and Primitive Art«, Magisterarbeit, Institute of Fine Arts, New York 1982.

74. Vriesen, G., *August Macke*, 2. Auflage, Stuttgart 1957, Nr. 53: *Indianer im Zelt*, Nr. 260: *Indianer* und Nr. 273: *Reitende Indianer beim Zelt*.

75. Macke und Marc, *Briefwechsel*, S. 111, 114.

76. August Macke, »Die Masken« in *Almanach ›Der Blaue Reiter‹*, Wassily Kandinsky und Franz Marc, München 1912, Neuauflage München 1965, S. 53–59, vor allem S. 54–55.

77. Macke, a.a.O., S. 58.

78. Macke, a.a.O., S. 59. Vergleiche zwischen mittelalterlicher und primitiver Kunst wurden in ähnlicher Form in Wilhelm Worringer, *Formprobleme der Gotik*, 1911, angestellt.

79. Mackes Artikel begleiten Abbildungen mit den Zuschreibungen »Brasilien«, S. 53, »Osterinseln«, S. 54, »Kamerun«, S. 55, »Mexiko« und »Neukaledonien«, S. 57, »Alaska«, S. 58, »Kinderzeichnung: Araber«, S. 59. Einer Eisenplastik aus Benin, S. 109, ist eine Grabplatte aus dem Dom in Frankfurt a.M., S. 108, gegenübergestellt, während eine Tanzmaske aus Ceylon, S. 217, von Macke wie folgt beschrieben wird: »Die Maske des Krankheitsdämons aus Ceylon ist die Schreckensgeste eines Naturvolkes . . .«, S. 58.

80. Es gibt hochtrabende Überschriften wie »Marquesasinseln«, S. 66, und eine *Fang*-Maske, fälschlicherweise betitelt als »Chinesische (?) Maske«, S. 189. Zur Arbeit mit der Zuschreibung »Südborneo«, S. 31, siehe die Bemerkung weiter unten.

81. Dube, a.a.O., Lithographie Nr. 168.

82. Kirchner kannte die Skulptur aus Südborneo gewiß nicht, aber er kannte die verwandten Hartholzskulpturen der Palau, die als Vorlagen für seine eigenen Skulpturen von 1912 dienten.

83. Siehe etwa den Vergleich zwischen den Pferden in Heckels Lithographie *Zirkus* von 1910 und jenen in einem volkstümlichen russischen Druck, von Kandinsky und Marc einander gegenübergestellt, a.a.O., S. 94 und 95.

84. Sara Gregg wies erstmals in meinem Pittsburgh-Seminar auf Campendonks Verwendung dieses Benin-Reliefs hin.

85. Zu den russischen Volksblättern siehe Kandinsky und Marc, a.a.O., S. 95 und 218, zu den Schattenspiel-Figuren, S. 193 und 202.

86. Nolde nahm nicht an der ersten Ausstellung der Neuen Sezession vom Mai 1916 teil, aber an den darauffolgenden. Gordon, D. E., *Modern Art Exhibitions, 1900–1916*, München 1974, Bd. 2, S. 398, 430, 461.

87. Selz, P., *Emil Nolde*, New York 1963, S. 32. Nolde selbst gibt das Jahr 1911 an, *Jahre der Kämpfe*, Berlin 1934, S. 161 ff., aber Martin Urban datiert den Besuch auf den Beginn des Jahres 1910, *Emil Nolde: Masken und Figuren*, S. 4.

88. Siehe Gordon, »Content by Contradiction«, a.a.O., S. 81–83, wo der Widerspruch im *Tanz um das Goldene Kalb* im Sinne Nietzsches erklärt wird.

89. Die Schweinenase und die grellen Lippen von Noldes dritter Maske ähneln zwei Masken links im Vordergrund von Ensors *Intrigue*, 1890, heute im Musée Royal des Beaux-Arts, Antwerpen.

90. Das Objekt der Salomoninseln und der peruanische Kopf wurden zusammen mit Noldes Zeichnung erstmals in Reidemeister und Krieger, *Das Ursprüngliche . . .*, a.a.O., Nr. 137, abgebildet, wurden jedoch nicht mit dem *Maskenstilleben* in Verbindung gebracht. Auf diesen Zusammenhang machte mich Dr. Martin Urban aufmerksam.

91. Emil Nolde, a.a.O., S. 162–63.

92. Es gab in Leiden ein Exemplar aus Nigeria, das dem hier abgebildeten aus Hamburg »völlig gleich« war: Frobenius, L., *Die Masken und Geheimbünde Afrikas*, Halle 1898, Abb. 59 und S. 20.

93. In einer Mitteilung vom 30. August 1983 besteht Dr. Martin Urban auf dem Unterschied zwischen Masken, die Nolde in (noch vorhandenen) »Studienskizzen« kopiert hatte und jenen anderen »mehr oder weniger freien Erfindungen«, für die keine Zeichnungskopien existieren. Trotzdem kann Urban selbst bei den erfundenen Masken kaum eine »Abhängigkeit von einem Vorbild« ausschließen, wie von der hier vorgelegten Maske aus Nigeria.

94. Siehe Goldwater, a.a.O., S. 90.

95. Das Gemälde von 1911, die Katchina-Puppe und die drei vorbereitenden Zeichnungen Noldes sind abgebildet in Urban, a.a.O., Abb. 2–2d.

96. Schneckenburger, *Weltkulturen . . .*, a.a.O., Nr. 1821.

97. Kris, *Psychoanalytic Explorations in Art*, a.a.O., S. 180, 197–99.

98. Noldes Zeichnung der *Yoruba*-Skulptur ist abgebildet in Reidemeister und Krieger, *Das Ursprüngliche*, Nr. 130.

99. Nolde, a.a.O., S. 173.

100. Gordon, »Kirchner in Dresden«, a.a.O., S. 354, Anmerkung 116.

101. Das Datum ist sicher, denn das Relief war für die Kapelle der Kölner Sonderbunds-Ausstellung vorgesehen, die im Mai 1912 eröffnet wurde: Grohmann, W., *Karl Schmidt-Rottluff*, Stuttgart 1956, S. 159.

102. *Führer durch das Museum für Völkerkunde*, S. 70; ihre Funktionen als Ranginsignien und als Kopfaufsatz eines Tänzers wurden ebenfalls darin erwähnt.

103. Zur Zuschreibung dieses Objekttypus an den *Ekoi*-Stamm und zur Abbildung eines ähnlichen Beispiels siehe Himmelheber, H., *Negerkunst und Negerkünstler*, Braunschweig 1960, S. 279

104. Gleichermaßen der Nolde-Parallele folgend, schließt Reidemeister auf einen Einfluß der deutschen Gotik bei diesem Relief, Reidemeister, »Die Vier Evangelisten von Karl Schmidt-Rottluff« in *Brücke-Archiv*, Nr. 8, 1975–76, S. 13–16.

105. Grohmann, a.a.O., S. 159.

106. Man vergleiche die Köpfe der *Vier Evangelisten* mit jenen von Pechsteins *Plakat für die Brücke-Ausstellung bei Emil Richter, Dresden*, 1909.

107. Kirchner, E. L., *Briefe an Nele*, München 1961, S. 20–21.

108. Die Palau-Plastik wurde 1909 erworben. Ich danke Herrn Prof. J. Zwernemann vom Hamburger Museum für Völkerkunde für diesen Hinweis.

109. Die verlorengegangene *Weibliche Figur* ist in einem Gemälde von 1912, Gordon, *Ernst Ludwig Kirchner*, a.a.O., Nr. 268 und in einem mit einem falschen Titel versehenen Holzschnitt *Frau mit Negerplastik*, 1912, Dube, a.a.O., Nr. 205, abgebildet. Wolfgang Henze hat bezweifelt, daß dieses Werk überhaupt von Kirchner ist. Es handle sich statt dessen um »eine große ›Negerplastik‹, wahrscheinlich eine Imitation zu Übungszwecken, die im Jahre 1912 und später vielfach dargestellt wird, eine große, verhältnismäßig schlanke Figur in strenger Form und mit glatter Oberfläche, Merkmale, die wir in den Skulpturen des Jahres 1912 antreffen.« Henze, W., »Kirchner« im Katalog *Skulptur des Expressionismus*, München 1984, S. 109, Anm. 12. Dieser These widerspricht neben der Flächigkeit einiger Körpermerkmale, wie sie für Palau-Werke typisch ist, die Größe der Plastik (Höhe über 1 m). Figürliche Plastik dieser Größe ist in Afrika überaus selten.

110. Masheck, J., »Raw Art: ›Primitive‹ Authenticity and German Expressionism« in *Res* 4, Herbst 1982, S. 104, bemerkt das »Zickzackmuster einer melanesischen Holzschnitzerei« auf einem Holzschnitt Kirchners von 1911, erwähnt jedoch nicht den plastischen – und afrikanischen – Bauch und das Gesäß des darin dargestellten Akts. Darüber hinaus setzt Masheck die skulpturalen Eigenschaften sowohl des primitiven wie des expressionistischer Werkes zugunsten vorexpressionistischer Anregungen herab, wobei er dem Ornament in der Kunst oder der Vorstellung von »Flachheit« in der Kunsttheorie besondere Bedeutung beimißt.

111. L. de Marsalle (Pseudonym für E. L. Kirchner), »Über die plastischen Arbeiten von E. L. Kirchner«, *Der Cicerone* 14, 1925, S. 695–701.

112. Der Ausdruck stammt von Erika Billeter, siehe ihren Aufsatz »Kunst als Lebensentwurf« im Katalog *Kirchner 1880–1938,*, S. 16–25. Vergleiche meinen Aufsatz »Ernst Ludwig Kirchner: By Instinct Possessed« in *Art in America*, November 1980, S. 80–95, vor allem S. 90f.

113. Grisebach, E., Brief vom 8. Januar 1914, in Grisebach, a.a.O., S. 39, Zu Atelieransichten von 1912 und 1913 siehe Heckels Aquarelle, abgebildet in Reidemeister, L., *Künstler der Brücke in Berlin*, Berlin, Brücke-Museum, 1972, Nr. 111 und 112.

114. Siehe die Ahnenfiguren aus Neumecklenburg in Hausenstein, W., *Barbaren und Klassiker*, München 1922, Abb. 6 und 7.

115. Siehe die Kalebassen in Von Sydow, a.a.O., Abb. IV und 124.

116. Reidemeister, L., *Museums Discovered: The Brücke-Museum*, Fort Lee, N. J. 1981, S. 124.

117. Platte, H., »Erich Heckel: Bilder aus dem Alstertal« in *Schriften des Kunstvereins in Hamburg*, 1, 1964, Einführung. Plattes Quelle war Frau Luise Schiefler.

118. Grisebach, a.a.O., Brief vom 8. Januar 1914, S. 39.

119. Vogt, a.a.O., Nr. 1913/3 und 1913/31.

120. *Stilleben mit Vasen* im Busch-Reisinger-Museum, Harvard University; *Stilleben mit Stranddisteln* in der Kunsthalle Bremen.

121. Pechsteins Hocker erscheint erneut in einem Ölgemälde von 1917, *Im Frauenhaus, Palau*. Kirchner erinnert sich des verlorenen Berliner Originals in seinem eigenen Stuhl von 1920.

122. Der hier abgebildete Hocker wurde vom Dresdner Museum erst 1914 erworben, zu spät, um die »Brücke«-Künstler beeinflußt zu haben. Für die mir 1964 übermittelte Auskunft danke ich Herrn Dr. S. Wolf, dem Direktor des Museums. Der untere Teil des Dresdner Stücks ist hingegen dem Pechsteins sehr ähnlich.

123. Nolde, E., *Briefe aus den Jahren 1894–1926*, Sauerlandt, M. (Hrsg.), Berlin 1927, S. 98f. Ebenfalls erwähnt in Reidemeister, *Das Ursprüngliche . . .*, a.a.O., nach Nr. 149.

124. Nolde, *Jahre der Kämpfe*, a.a.O., S. 240–41.

125. Ebenda, S. 242.

126. Schneckenburger, *Weltkulturen . . .*, a.a.O., S. 473.

127. Während Uli-Figuren hermaphroditisch sind, mit Brüsten und Phallus, war Noldes Beispiel überwiegend männlich, Urban, *Emil Nolde: Masken und Figuren*, Nr. 15a. Diese Tatsache widerlegt eine Interpretation von Wentinck, C., *Modern and Primitive Art*, Oxford 1979, S. 11b, derzufolge »die Bisexualität des Uli zwischen Mann und Frau aufgeteilt ist« oder eine Darstellung »zweier Liebender« vorläge. Wentinck befindet sich ebenfalls im Irrtum, wenn er glaubt, daß Noldes Uli-Figur aus einer holländischen Sammlung stammt.

128. Pechstein, M., *Erinnerungen*, Reidemeister, L. (Hrsg.), Wiesbaden 1960, S. 77. Siehe S. 54, 91, 78 und 67 für alle in diesem und den beiden folgenden Abschnitten erwähnten Zitate.

129. Katalog *Der junge Pechstein*, Berlin, Hochschule für bildende Künste, 1959, ohne Seitenangabe; Pechstein, a.a.O., passim; Osborn, M., *Max Pechstein*, Berlin 1922, passim.

130. Pechstein, a.a.O., S. 77–78.

131. Osborn, a.a.O., S. 86–89, 97, 118.

132. Reidemeister, *Das Ursprüngliche . . .*, a.a.O., zwei Photographien. Ettlinger, »Primitive Art«, a.a.O., S. 196, betrachtet den Atelierfries als »wenig mehr als eine freie Kopie« der in Dresden gesehenen Hausbalken. Der Fries ist jedoch Pechsteins eigenen Palau-Bildern näher.

133. Ich verdanke diese Beobachtung Kathryn Kramer, einer Studentin meines Seminars von 1982 an der Columbia University.

134. Das Mannheimer *Stilleben* ist größer, 110 x 70 cm, doch wurde es fälschlicherweise »um 1913« datiert in Roethel, *Modern German Painting*, New York 1958, S. 17. Das Gemälde in Saarbrücken mißt 78 x 70,5 cm, datiert von 1917, trägt jedoch den falschen Titel *Stilleben mit afrikanischer Skulptur und Lupinen* in Reidemeister, *Das Ursprüngliche . . .*, a.a.O., Nr. 121. Die Skulptur, obwohl der Inspiration nach afrikanisch, läuft in einen rechteckigen Sockel aus, der nur von Pechstein selbst geschnitzt worden sein kann.

135. Grohmann, a.a.O., S. 75.

136. Zu diesem Holzschnitt siehe Wietek, G., *Schmidt-Rottluff Graphik*, München 1971, Nr. 72. Das Gemälde befindet sich in der Nationalgalerie Berlin.

137. Von Krieger, K., *Westafrikanische Plastik* I, 2. Aufl., Berlin, Museum für Völkerkunde, 1978, S. 83, Nr. 194, *»Ngulu melan«* genannt. Der *Führer durch das Museum für Völkerkunde*, 1911, S. 69, erwähnt »von den Ngumba die Ahnenfiguren (Ngula malang)« in Schaukasten 34b. (Die NGUMBA sind ein kamerunischer Unterstamm des Volkes der *FANG*.)

138. Schneckenburger, *Weltkulturen . . .*, a.a.O., Nr. 1780. Es ist zu beachten, daß sich das *BAMBARA*-Werk in einer Pariser Privatsammlung befindet; gleiches ist vor 1914 in Berlin nicht bekannt.

139. Wietek, a.a.O., Nr. 128. Die letztere Ähnlichkeit wurde erstmals von Christa Paula in meinem Pittsburgh-Seminar beobachtet.

140. Grohmann, a.a.O., S. 85.

141 Einstein, C., *Negerplastik*, Leipzig 1915. Einstein war Romanschriftsteller, bevor er sich der Kunstkritik zuwandte.

142. Siehe u. a. □ 564, abgebildet in Einsteins Buch von 1915, Nr. 76, ebenfalls und mit dem Standorthinweis des Berliner Völkerkundemuseums in Einstein, C., *Afrikanische Plastik*, Berlin 1922, Nr. 27. Von den 56 abgebildeten Objekten in der Ausgabe von 1922 befanden sich 21 im Berliner Museum und die meisten anderen in Privatsammlungen.

143. Einstein, *Negerplastik*, a.a.O., S. *VI*, *VII*.

144. Ebenda, Nr. 14–15, 20, 31.

145. Himmelheber, H., »The Concave Face in African Art« in *African Art*, Frühjahr 1971, S. 52–55. In meinem Columbia-Seminar machte mich Jonathan Kuhn auf diesen Artikel aufmerksam.

146. Der *Holzschnitt* von Schmidt-Rottluff wird mit einer *GURO*-Webrolle verglichen, doch der *GURO*-Kopf im Einstein-Buch, Nr. 14–15, scheint die wahrscheinlichere Anregung gewesen zu sein.

147. Schneckenburger, *Weltkulturen . . .*, a.a.O., Nr. 1783, erwähnt *GURO*-Masken als Vergleichsbeispiele für den *Blauroten Kopf*, entdeckt aber eine »mimetische Pointierung« im Mund und in den Augen, die überhaupt nicht afrikanisch ist. Für den Untertitel und seine Bedeutung siehe Reidemeister, *The Brücke Museum*, a.a.O., S. 156.

148. Reidemeister, *Das Ursprüngliche . . .*, a.a.O., Nr. 86, 88; Schneckenburger, *Weltkulturen . . .*, a.a.O., Nr. 1785, 1789.

149. Krieger, a.a.O., S. 84, Nr. 198.

150. Einstein, *Negerplastik*, a.a.O., Nr. 76 und Einstein, *Afrikanische Plastik*, a.a.O., Nr. 27. Der Verlust der Holzplastik nach 1940 wurde kürzlich von Frau Dr. Angelika Rumpf vom Berliner Völkerkundemuseum in einem Brief freundlicherweise bestätigt.

151. Diesen Vergleich verdanke ich erneut Jonathan Kuhn aus meinem Columbia-Seminar.

152. Krieger, a.a.O., S. 108, Nr. 265, Abb. 222, im Jahr 1886 erworben. »Die Reihe der Bateke-Fetische . . . sind beachtenswert«, *Führer durch das Museum für Völkerkunde*, S. 67.

153. Katalog, *Karl Schmidt-Rottluff: Das graphische Werk, zum 90. Geburtstag des Künstlers*, Berlin, Brücke-Museum, 1974, Nr. 145, Abb. 56.

154. Einstein, *Negerplastik*, a.a.O., S. 13f., 17f.

155. Miesel, V. H. (Hrsg.), *Voices of German Expressionism*, Englewood Cliffs 1970, S. 7.

156. Osborn, a.a.O., S. 157, zeigt dessen Gemälde *Um mich Gesichter* von 1920. Stilleben von Stammesobjekten sind gleichfalls bekannt.

157. Ebenda, S. 235. Schmidt-Rottluffs enge Freundschaft mit Pechstein begann im Sommer 1913, als Schmidt-Rottluff »sich auf den Spuren

von Max Pechstein in Nidden auf der Kurischen Nehrung befand. Er lebte dort in der Hütte des gleichen Fischers, mit dem 1909 Pechstein gelebt hatte«, in Reidemeister, *The Brücke Museum,* a.a.O., S. 130.

158. Der *Viertelmond* kann mit dem Ornamentband über dem Geist eines Schiffsbugs von den Salomoninseln verglichen werden.

159. Krieger, a.a.O., S. 115, Nr. 286.

160. Es sei daran erinnert, daß Pechstein 1914 bereits Schmucknarben mit dem »Schönheitssinn« der Palauinselbewohner und ihrer »Lust zur Formbildung« verband, in Pechsteins *Erinnerungen,* a.a.O., S. 78. Aber seine Anordnung der Schmucknarbenmuster in zierliche, unterteilte Streifen kann gut von den westafrikanischen Masken abstammen, speziell von der in Einstein, *Negerplastik,* a.a.O., Nr. 91, abgebildeten.

161. Krieger, a.a.O., S. 132, Nr. 327. Patricia Tanner aus meinem Pittsburgh-Seminar unternahm als erste diesen Vergleich.

162. Reed, O. P., Jr., *German Expressionist Art: The Robert Gore Rifkind Collection*, Los Angeles, University of California, 1977, S. 97, Nr. 151.

163. Krieger, a.a.O., S. 81, Nr. 191. Kathryn Kramer wies während meines Columbia-Seminars erstmals auf dieses Vorbild hin.

164. Eine Veröffentlichung von Kathryn Kramers Bericht über Pechsteins Quellen steht bevor.

165. Zur Diskussion dieser Holzschnitte, siehe den vorhergehenden Abschnitt.

166. Grohmann, a.a.O., S. 93.

167. Von Sydow, a.a.O., Abb. 252; die Ausgabe von 1923 in der Reihe der Propyläen-Kunstgeschichte war Schmidt-Rottluff gewidmet. Es war Sara Gregg in meinem Pittsburgh-Seminar, die diesen Zusammenhang erkannte.

168. Die von mir angesprochene Kultfigur ist abgebildet in Hausenstein, a.a.O., Abb. 39. Klees Zeichnung ist abgebildet in di San Lazzaro, G., *Klee*, New York 1957, S. 31, und wird dort dem »Passadena [sic] Art Institute, California« zugeschrieben. Dr. Jürgen Glaesemer von der Paul-Klee-Stiftung, Bern, informiert mich jedoch, daß der Verbleib der Zeichnung unbekannt sei.

169. Grisebach, Kirchners Davoser Tagebuch, S. 70.

170. Schneckenburger, *Weltkulturen . . .*, a.a.O., Nr. 1827, 1828, vergleicht Kirchners Stuhl mit dem Hocker aus Kamerun im Völkerkundemuseum Hamburg (Nr. 5323:1), erkennt aber nicht, daß der Hocker erst 1953 in die Hamburger Sammlung kam. Die Kenntnis des Ankaufsdatums verdanke ich Prof. J. Zwernemann vom Museum.

171. Grisebach, L., im Katalog *Kirchner 1880–1938*, S. 257, bemerkt, daß Kirchners Bemühungen, sein Haus auszustatten, »nicht von seiner Sehnsucht nach einer harmonischen Beziehung [mit Erna Schilling] zu trennen ist«.

172. Ringbom, S., »Paul Klee and the Inner Truth to Nature« in *Arts*, September 1977, S. 112–17.

173. Nietzsche, F., *Menschliches, Allzumenschliches*, München 1981, S. 25–26. Die Erstausgabe erschien 1878 (erster Teil).

174. Ausstellungskatalog *Ernst Ludwig Kirchner*, Frankfurt, Galerie L. Schames, 1919, ohne Seitenangabe.

Bandiera Futurista
MARCIARE
NON MARCIRE
DICEMBRE
6
DOMENICA
a austriaci e serb
Gli scontri sulle isole
del Danubio e della Sava
HERMANN WILD
Cav. Uff. GIULIO
LA GUERRA S
Due piroscafi ingles
silurati nell
ITALICO
Il nostro Jean Jaurès
parla ai committenti sul fronte

Ezio Bassani

Italienische Malerei

Die 1906–07 auftretende Krise der modernen Kunst, bei der die »Entdeckung« der Stammeskunst eine so entscheidende Rolle übernahm, scheint die Kunstszene Italiens nicht berührt zu haben. Die italienischen Künstler blieben dem 19. Jahrhundert treu. Selbst die impressionistische Begeisterung hatte bereits bei ihrer Ankunft einen wesentlich verhalteneren Ausdruck angenommen. Die verschiedenen Sezessionsstile des ›fin de siècle‹ und der Jahrhundertwende beschworen andere, manchmal exotische Erfahrungen, während der Pointillismus als Vereinheitlichung nationaler Unterschiede weite Verbreitung fand. Es mußten Jahre vergehen, bevor den Künstlern die Bedeutung der revolutionären »Entdeckung« der sogenannten »art nègre« durch die Vermittlung einiger weniger Futuristen bewußt wurde, die beruflich mit Pariser Kunstkreisen in Verbindung standen.

Im November 1911 hielten sich Umberto Boccioni und Carlo Carrà in der französischen Hauptstadt auf, um eine für das kommende Jahr vorgesehene Ausstellung futuristischer Malerei in der Galerie Bernheim-Jeune vorzubereiten. Zusammen mit Luigi Russolo und F. T. Marinetti kamen sie im Februar 1912 erneut nach Paris, um diese Ausstellung zu besuchen. Neben den Werken von Boccioni, Carrà und Russolo zeigte man die Arbeiten Gino Severinis, der einige Zeit in Paris verbracht und die Tochter des Dichters Paul Fort geheiratet hatte.

Severini und der damals ebenfalls in Paris tätige Modigliani regten Begegnungen zwischen ihren italienischen Kollegen und Vertretern der französischen Avantgarde an wie Picasso, Gris, Vlaminck, Derain, Matisse, Brancusi, Kahnweiler, Paul Guillaume und Guillaume Apollinaire. Allerdings war Apollinaire nach Aussage von Fernande Olivier bereits 1910 mit Marinetti zusammengetroffen und hatte sich auf eine kurze, aber intensive Verbindung mit den Futuristen eingelassen. Diese Freundschaft führte im Juni 1913 zur Veröffentlichung seines Manifests *Die futuristische Antitradition,* das der Dichter an einem Tisch des Restaurants Lapérouse schrieb, »während er« – wie Marinetti selbst überliefert – »eine köstliche Gans verspeiste«. Aber diese Freundschaft währte nicht lange. Sie wurde noch im gleichen Jahr (1913) durch bissige Polemik erschüttert.

Einige der oben erwähnten französischen Künstler, Schriftsteller und Kunsthändler, die zu den Entdeckern der »art nègre« gehörten, waren von der Manie der »Negrophilie« dieser Jahre befallen, wie andere Kapitel dieses Bandes verdeutlichen. Den italienischen Künstlern fehlte es somit nicht an Gelegenheiten, mit Arbeiten afrikanischer und ozeanischer Bildhauer in Berührung zu kommen. Zwar waren diese Arbeiten im damaligen Italien kaum bekannt und schon gar nicht in Mode, standen aber in Frankreich im Mittelpunkt der aktuellen künstlerischen Auseinandersetzung.

In den Schriften der Futuristen ist die »Entdeckung« der Stammeskunst ziemlich knapp und widersprüchlich dokumentiert. Boccioni hielt sie für ein notwendiges, schicksalhaftes Ereignis. 1913 schrieb er in der Florentiner Zeitschrift *Lacerba:* »Die Reise Gauguins nach Tahiti und das Auftreten von Fetischfiguren Zentralafrikas in den Ateliers unserer Freunde vom Montmartre sind für das Schicksal europäischen Empfindens – historisch gesehen – unvermeidlich, so wie das Eindringen einer barbarischen Rasse in den Organismus eines dekadenten Volkes.«

In der erregten Atmosphäre futuristischer Polemik gegen die Kubisten schrieb Carrà im folgenden Jahr in derselben Zeitschrift, daß in dieser Aneignung »außereuropäischer« Kunstlehren ein »gravierender Irrtum und ungewollter Betrug« lägen, »auf den die bedeutenden Künstler des heutigen Frankreich hereingefallen sind, . . . Fehler, die ihrem Trugschluß entsprangen, sich Unschuld und zeitgemäße Empfindungskraft künstlich verschaffen zu können, indem man sich dem fernen Zentrum Afrikas zuwendet, um dort Inspiration und archaische Motivik für die eigene Gestaltung gebrauchsfertig vorzufinden. Aus irgendwelchen Gründen sollen dann die Produkte durch eine Art kultureller Suggestion den ästhetischen Bedürfnissen allermodernsten Empfindens gerecht werden.«[3]

Als sich Carrà im Zusammenhang mit einer Darstellung der Kunst André Derains in *Valori Plastici* von 1921 zu den »afrikanischen Praktiken« damaliger Künstler äußerte, wurde sein Ton noch boshafter:

». . . dieser ganze sogenannte ›Negrismo‹, der während der letzten Jahre Einzug in die Malerei hielt, hat überhaupt keine ästhetische Bedeutung. Wie der Dadaismus und andere idiotische Verirrungen unserer Zeit ist der ›Negrismo‹ ein von Snobs erfundener Schwindel von kurzer Dauer. Die Ursprünge des ›Negrismo‹ liegen wie beim ›Fauvismo‹ im Literarischen, und er wird wie diese frühere Strömung unweigerlich nur kurze Zeit Bestand haben.

Besonders in Frankreich hat die literarische Behandlung des Exotischen in der Malerei eine Tradition, die sogar noch vor Baudelaire einsetzte. Die Wurzel dieser atavistischen, morbiden Entartungen – oder wie man sie sonst nennen mag – ist der

□ 574 *Carlo Carrà, ›Komposition mit weiblicher Figur‹ (Composizione con figura femminile), 1915, Tempera auf Karton, 41 x 31 cm. Puschkin-Museum der bildenden Künste, Moskau.*

□ 575 *›Maske‹,* FANG *(Gabun), bemaltes Holz, Höhe 70 cm. Musée de l'Homme, Paris.*

Eklektizismus, derselbe abscheuliche Eklektizismus, der den braven französischen Dummköpfen des letzten Jahrhunderts so viel bedeutete . . . Ich zähle den ›Negrismo‹ wie den ›Kubismus‹ zu den zahlreichen Spielarten der Salongymnastik.«[4] Eine reaktionärere Auffassung läßt sich kaum vorstellen.

Demgegenüber unternahm der toskanische Künstler und Schriftsteller ARDEGNO SOFFICI, eng mit den Futuristen verbunden (und zusammen mit Giovanni Papini Herausgeber von *Lacerba*), in seinem ebenfalls 1914 verfaßten Essay »Cubismo e futurismo« eine völlig entgegengesetzte Bewertung. SOFFICI war seit 1900 immer wieder in Paris gewesen, nahm dort aktiv am geistigen Leben teil und vermittelte so zwischen der französischen und italienischen Kulturszene.[5] Über die formbildende Rolle der afrikanischen Kunst in der kubistischen Revolution schreibt er:

»Als Picasso diese großartige, naive Kunst zu verstehen und zu lieben lernte, eine Kunst, die einfach und ausdrucksvoll, derb und subtil zugleich ist, verstand er es sofort, ihre Wesensmerkmale auszuloten. Diese bestanden für ihn in einer realistischen Deutung der Natur, die durch Umformung der äußeren Erscheinung aus einer geheimen, intuitiven Notwendigkeit heraus erfolgt und dadurch eine Steigerung des Subjektiven erzielt. Von da an arbeitete (Picasso) daran, Leben durch Umwandlung und Umformung in die Sprache seiner Kunst zu übertragen – allerdings nicht in der generalisierenden Weise seiner Lehrer, sondern indem er von jedem einzelnen Vorbild etwas lernte – d.h. seinem eigenen zeitgemäßen Empfinden folgte.«[6]

Skulptur und Malerei von BOCCIONI und SOFFICI, die beide die Rolle der afrikanischen Plastik für die Entwicklung der modernen westlichen Kunst klar erkannten, erweisen sich als von solchen Vorbildern relativ unbeeinflußt. Mit Überraschung entdeckt man statt dessen im Œuvre von CARRÀ Spuren des ›Negrismo‹, dem der Künstler doch eine so klare Absage erteilt hatte. Dieser Widerspruch zwischen öffentlichen Äußerungen und privater künstlerischer Arbeit läßt sich nur vor dem

□ 576 *Carlo Carrà, ›Bildnis Russolo‹ (Ritratto di Russolo), 1913?, Tusche, 27 x 18 cm. Privatsammlung, Florenz.*

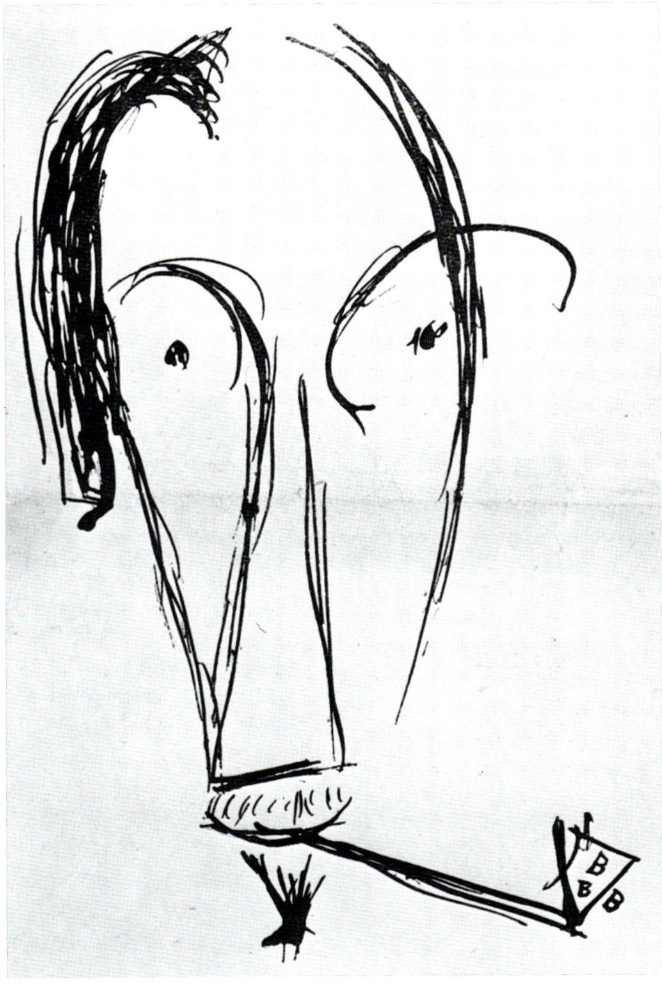

Hintergrund seiner Bemühungen erklären, den Vorrang des Futurismus über den Kubismus geltend zu machen.

Wenn man die während des zweiten Jahrzehnts unseres Jahrhunderts in Paris vorhandenen Kunstwerke aus Afrika und der Südsee genau kennt und mit der Chronologie von Carràs künstlerischem Schaffen vergleicht, entsteht die Vermutung, wenn nicht sogar die Gewißheit, daß Carrà in der Periode von 1911 bis 1916 von der Wirkung der Stammeskunst auf die europäische Kultur nicht unberührt blieb und er sich insbesondere mit afrikanischen Skulpturen mehr als nur einmal auseinandersetzte. 1899 reiste Carrà das erste Mal nach Paris, da ihm eine Stelle als Dekorationsmaler für die im Bau befindlichen Pavillons für die Weltausstellung von 1900 in Aussicht stand. In seiner freien Zeit besuchte er die Museen der Stadt, wobei ihm die Entdeckung der Impressionisten große Freude bereitete. Die ethnographischen Sammlungen im Musée du Trocadéro beeindruckten ihn hingegen überhaupt nicht. In seiner Autobiographie schrieb er später: »Was die Museen betrifft, so besuchte ich neben dem Louvre, dem Petit-Palais und dem Palais du Luxembourg den Trocadéro, der mir ziemlich langweilig und unbedeutend vorkam.«[7]

Interessant ist, daß die ersten Reaktionen von Vlaminck und Derain, die später zu den Entdeckern der Kunst der Naturvölker zählten, ebenfalls negativ ausfielen. Zweifellos waren sie – wie Carrà – noch nicht weit genug, um die Bedeutung außereuropäischer Kunst zu erfassen. Vlaminck selbst bemerkte hierzu, sein Freund Derain und er hätten bei »mehreren ausgiebigen Rundgängen durch das Musée du Trocadéro unter den ausgestellten Objekten nur solche gesehen, die man gemeinhin als Fetische von Wilden sowie als völkerkundliche Wunderlichkeiten bezeichnen würde«.[8]

Erst bei seinem zweiten Aufenthalt in Paris im Jahre 1911 und in einem noch größeren Maße während seiner späteren Besuche von 1912 und 1914 gestand es sich der nun aufgrund seiner futuristischen Erfahrungen gereifte und aufgeschlossene Carrà zu, von afrikanischer Skulptur beeindruckt zu werden, auch wenn er dies in seinen Schriften bestreitet. Nach 1911 treten denn auch Gestaltungselemente in seinem Werk auf, die sich auf afrikanische Kunst zurückführen lassen.[9]

So ist das 1913 datierte *Bildnis Russolo* □ 576 meiner Ansicht nach ganz offensichtlich von dem gebräuchlichsten *Fang*-Maskentypus aus Gabun □ 575 abgeleitet, der aus einer oft recht großen (bis zu einem Meter hohen), leicht gebogenen Holzplatte besteht und gewöhnlich weiß bemalt ist. Das Gesichtsoval der Maske ist langgestreckt und verjüngt sich zum Kinn. Die überlange, spitze Nase setzt die Wölbungen der Augenbrauen fort, die den konkaven vom rein konvexen Gesichtsteil der Stirn trennen. Die Augen sind durch zwei erhabene Punkte im Zentrum der Höhlung dargestellt. Dieselben Elemente lassen sich – sieht man von Haupthaar, Kinn- und Schnurrbart ab – im *Bildnis Russolo* finden, eines Mannes, dessen Gesichtszüge auch in Wirklichkeit ziemlich regelmäßig waren. Zudem ist die Nase einem Typus nachgebildet, den bereits die Kubisten der afrikanischen Skulptur entlehnt hatten, nämlich der Nase in »Briestückform«.

Diese Zeichnung erschien in der April-Nummer von *Lacerba*, 1914, auf Seite 127 im Anschluß an die Ankündigung eines «Concerto di Intonarumori Futuristi« (Futuristisches Lärmtonkonzert) im Theater Dal Verme in Mailand mit Russolo als Dirigenten. Auf Seite 126 ist dort unter der Anzeige ein ähnliches Porträt Russolos von Soffici abgedruckt. Severini verwendete es später in seiner Collage *La Ciociara* (1914).

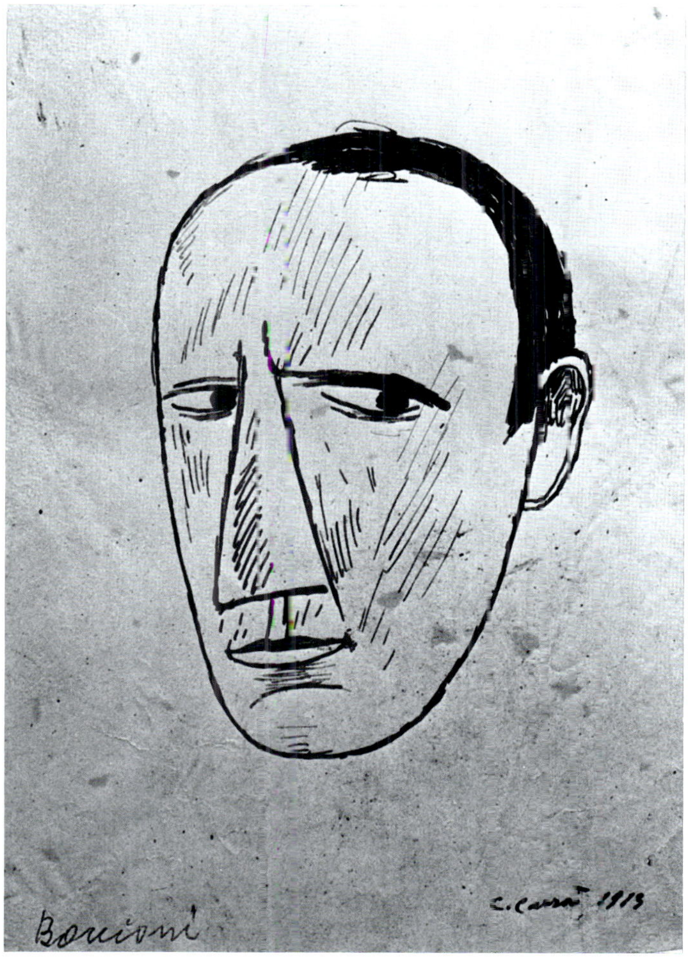

□ 577 *Carlo Carrà, ›Bildnis Boccioni‹ (Ritratto di Boccioni), 1913, Tinte, 27 x 19 cm. Privatsammlung, Reggio Emilia.*

□ 578 *Luigi Russolo, ›Selbstporträt‹ (Autoritratto), 1913, Radierung, 9,5 x 8 cm. Sammlung Marzo Constantini, Laveno.*

☐ 579 *›Maske‹, Fang (Gabun), bemaltes Holz, Höhe 48 cm. Musée National d'Art Moderne, Centre National d'Art et de Culture Georges Pompidou, Paris. Ehemals Sammlung Maurice de Vlaminck, André Derain.*

Zwei fast identische Porträts BOCCIONIS von CARRÀ aus den Jahren 1913 ☐ 577 und 1916 zeigen eine Formenvereinfachung, die zwar nicht so extrem ist, aber dem Charakter nach gerade in der Behandlung der großen, halbkegelförmigen Nase PICASSOS *Frauenkopf* von 1909 gleicht. Diese Arbeit hat ebenfalls der afrikanischen Skulptur viel zu verdanken, auch wenn das spezifische Vorbild – wenn es ein solches überhaupt gegeben hat – unbekannt bleibt. Andererseits fehlt dem Porträt Guillaume Apollinaires von 1914 jede Beziehung zur Stammeskunst, obwohl dieser sicherlich zu jenen gehörte, die CARRÀ mit dieser Kunst bekannt machten.

Die Bleistift- und Kohlezeichnung *Kopf eines jungen Mädchens* von 1909 ☐ 580 erinnert deutlich an die *FANG*-Maske, die erst VLAMINCK und dann DERAIN gehörte ☐ 579.[10] Allerdings nimmt man an, daß die Datierung dieser Zeichnung erst einige Zeit nach der Ausführung hinzugefügt wurde und sie frühestens nach 1911 entstand, d.h. nach der zweiten Parisreise CARRÀS. Auch in diesem Fall stammte die betreffende afrikanische Vorlage aus Gabun. Ihre Oberfläche hat eine etwas modulierte, leichte Krümmung, ist in einem matten Weiß gefärbt, das Licht zu absorbieren scheint, und die Nase hat die Form einer längsgeschnittenen Pyramide.

Das »Briestück« und die gleichzeitige Vereinfachung der Gesichtszüge bis zu ihrer Verwandlung in eine Maske sind auch für viele Werke CARRÀS in den folgenden Jahren typisch, so für *Frau, Figur einer Frau, Frauenbüste,* alle 1914 entstanden; für die Temperabilder *Die Tänzerin von San Martino, Clown* sowie die Zeichnungen *Frauen mit Katze* und *Kopf eines Herrn* (Frontalansicht), alle von 1915. Dazu gehören außerdem zwei Zeichnungen für den *Kopf eines Herrn,* die Zeichnungsfolgen *Weiblicher Kopf, Kopf eines Mädchens, Kopf einer Frau, Kopf eines Knaben* ☐ 582, *Boxer* und das große Ölbild *Die Romantiker* ☐ 581 mit all seinen Vorstudien.

Für die Zeichnung *Kopf eines Mädchens* von 1914 verwendete der Maler wahrscheinlich eine *BAULE*-Maske oder -Figur der Elfenbeinküste als Vorbild, von der er die Grundzüge des Gesichtsaufbaus entlehnt zu haben scheint: die regelmäßig ovale Form, die linsenförmigen Augen und die schmale, aber nicht übertrieben gestreckte Nase, die auch hier die betonten Linien der Augenbrauen fortsetzt. In der Sammlung von Paul Guillaume befanden sich mehrere Masken mit denselben Merkmalen.

Die zwei Porträts von Remy de Gourmont von 1914 und 1916 ☐ 584, die über das zu erwartende Maß an Ähnlichkeit hinaus nahezu identisch miteinander sind, erinnern unzweifelhaft an die *TEKE*-Figuren von Stanley Pool ☐ 583. Das betrifft sowohl die Gesamtform von Kopf und Hals als auch bestimmte Gesichtsteile wie etwa Nase und Ohren (letztere sind auf der Zeichnung von 1916 zu sehen) sowie besonders den flächigen, trapezoiden Bart, der direkt unter die Lippen gesetzt ist.

☐ 580 *Carlo Carrà, ›Kopf eines jungen Mädchens‹ (Testa di fanciulla), 1911 oder später, Bleistift und Kohle, 14 x 9 cm. Privatsammlung, Mailand.*

□ 581 *Carlo Carrà, ›Die Romantiker‹ (I romantici), 1916, Öl auf Leinwand, 150 x 162 cm. Privatsammlung, Turin.*

Übrigens ist auf der berühmten Photographie von Apollinaires »cabinet de travail« eine *TEKE*-Figur zu erkennen □ 429.

Die Figur in CARRÀS Temperabild *Komposition mit weiblicher Figur* (1915), jetzt im Puschkin-Museum in Moskau □ 574, ist einer kleinen *LEGA*-Skulptur aus Zaire verblüffend ähnlich, die auch zur Sammlung Paul Guillaumes gehörte □ 585. Der imposante Aufbau der kleinen Elfenbeinfigur mit ihrem kräftigen Hals – der eiförmige Kopf wird von einer Säule getragen –, rechtwinkliger Nase und Augen wie Kaffeebohnen: Das alles kehrt in Form, Anordnung und Proportion nahezu übereinstimmend auf dem jetzt in Moskau befindlichen Gemälde wieder. Die *LEGA*-Skulptur scheint CARRÀ auch bei anderen Arbeiten als Bezugspunkt gedient zu haben: Kopf und Hals der weiblichen Gestalt in *Der Stern* (1916, Sammlung Zaffino in Reggio Calabria) sind im Gemälde wie in den Vorzeichnungen offenbar nach dem Vorbild der oben beschriebenen Figur gestaltet.

Die runden Gesichter in diesen zuletzt genannten Werken und den drei Zeichnungen der Serie *Der Geiger* (1915) □ 589 nehmen eine Lösung vorweg, die CARRÀ bei dem kleinen Mädchen in *Antigrazioso* aufgriff □ 587. In diesem Werk trägt der hölzerne Puppenkörper einen wuchtigen, kugelförmigen Kopf mit betonten Augenhöhlen, Kaffeebohnenaugen und rechtwinkliger Nase. In Verbindung mit der orange-braunen Farbe erinnert dies alles an eine Reihe anderer Elfenbeinskulp-

□ 582 *Carlo Carrà, ›Kopf eines Knaben‹ (Testa di fanciullo), 1916, Aquarell, 19 x 14,5 cm. Privatsammlung, Mailand.*

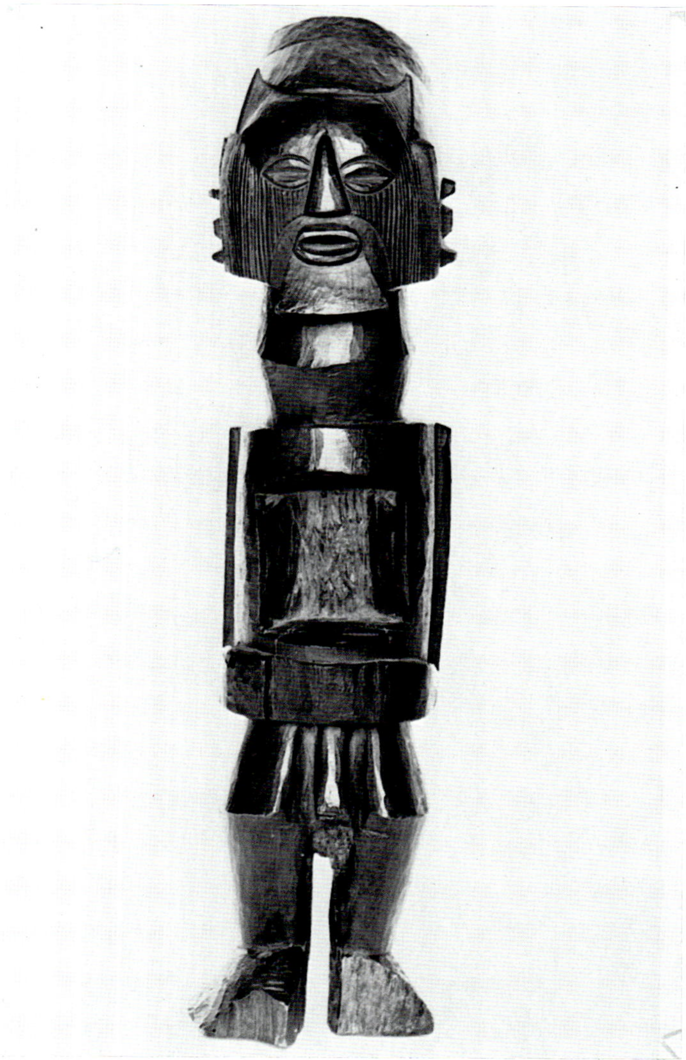

□ 583 *›Männliche Figur‹, Teke (Volksrepublik Kongo), Holz, Höhe 37,5 cm. Sammlung Louise und Michel Leiris, Paris.*

□ 584 *Carlo Carrà, ›Bildnis Remy de Gourmont‹ (Ritratto di Remy de Gourmont), 1916, Bleistift, 30 x 19 cm. Sammlung Carrà, Mailand.*

turen desselben Volkes der *Lega* (vgl. etwa den berühmten Kopf aus der ehemaligen Sammlung Ratton, Paris □ 588).

Auch bei anderen Werken Carràs lassen sich – oft nur in Einzelheiten – typische Merkmale afrikanischer Bildhauerei finden: die Büste einer Frau oder starre, zylindrische Arme, auch Finger, die wie Röhren völlig ohne Gelenke zu einem Rechteck von Parallelen aneinandergereiht sind. Als treffende Beispiele können die Frauenhände in *Akt* (1914) oder das Haar in dem Gemälde *Das Wunderkind* angeführt werden, wo die Wirkung durch den Wechsel der Licht- und Schattenzonen erreicht wird – ähnlich der Wellenbewegung des Holzes bei den kunstvollen Frisuren der *Baule*-Masken und -Figuren.

Carràs Begegnung mit afrikanischer Kunst beschränkte sich allerdings nicht auf die Übernahme einer neuen künstlerischen Sprache. Bei seiner Suche nach einem rhythmischen Gleichgewicht zwischen Ruhe und Bewegung hat er sich offenbar noch eingehender in die afrikanische Skulptur vertieft, um durch Abstreifen aller individuellen, anekdotischen Elemente grundlegende Strukturen freizulegen.

Die afrikanische Skulptur war für Carrà zweifellos ein Ansporn, solche kompakten, durch monumentale Einfachheit charakterisierten Formen zu gestalten, deren Höhepunkt der *Antigrazioso* ist. Dieses Gemälde markiert den Bruch des Künstlers mit konventioneller Eleganz, aber auch mit den vitalistisch-mechanistischen Schemata des Futurismus. Dieser Bruch war keine momentane Laune, sondern der Beginn eines Prozesses ernsthafter kritischer und selbstkritischer Reflexion. Er war für eine Periode künstlerischen Wachstums zwischen 1915 und 1920 kennzeichnend, die auf seine Begegnung mit Apollinaire, den Werken von Picasso, Derain und Cézanne (nach Carrà »der Masaccio unserer Zeit«) sowie mit den Arbeiten zahl- und namenloser Künstler Schwarzafrikas und der Südsee folgte.

Obwohl von Carrà hartnäckig geleugnet, ist es sicherlich dem Einfluß dieser Werke zuzuschreiben, daß er durch einen kaum eingestandenen inneren Gärungsprozeß die geläuterten Elementarformen von Giotto und Masaccio wiederentdeckte. Die überzeugendsten Ergebnisse dieser Wiederentdeckung sind nach meiner Ansicht *Die Dioskuren* und *Das Haus der Liebe* von 1922. Bei letzterem Gemälde erinnert die gerundete Figur der Frau – glatt wie poliertes Holz – in ihrer Ruhe und der zurückhaltenden Stellung der Arme an die Holzfiguren der Osterinsel, von denen Carrà vermutlich einige Beispiele im Hause von Paul Guillaume in Paris sah. Viele Zeichnungen von 1920 und 1921 scheinen diesen Einfluß vorwegzunehmen und teilweise noch besser zu dokumentieren.

In der Zeit vor dem Ersten Weltkrieg kamen auch zwei andere junge Künstler aus Italien nach Paris, GIORGIO DE CHIRICO und sein Bruder ALBERTO SAVINIO, der damals vorwiegend als Musiker tätig war. Vielleicht durch Vermittlung SOFFICIS entwickelten sie zu den französischen Zirkeln der Avantgarde noch stärkere Bindungen als die Futuristen. Das betraf nicht nur die sehr enge Freundschaft der zwei Brüder mit Apollinaire.[11] So war Paul Guillaume sowohl DE CHIRICOS Pariser Kunsthändler als auch der Mittelsmann bei der Beziehung des Künstlers mit MARIUS DE ZAYAS, dem mexikanischen Maler, der 1916 in New York eine Untersuchung mit dem weitsichtigen Titel »Afrikanische Negerkunst: Ihr Einfluß auf die Moderne« veröffentlichte. In den Werbeanzeigen für die Galerie Paul Guillaumes findet sich neben den Namenslisten der Künstler mit verkäuflichen Werken, unter ihnen auch DE CHIRICO, immer irgendein Hinweis auf »erstrangige afrikanische Skulptur«.

Somit hatte DE CHIRICO fast unvermeidlich die Gelegenheit, Werke der »art nègre« bald jeden Tag zu betrachten, sie anzufassen und mit anderen darüber zu diskutieren. Dennoch vermied es DE CHIRICO sorgsam, das Thema in seinen Schriften zu berücksichtigen. SAVINIO bekannte sich dagegen zu seiner Begeisterung, als er für eine Konferenz einen Vortrag über die afrikanische Kunst schrieb. In seinen Memoiren erinnert er sich daran: »1913 gründete Paul Guillaume die Société de Mélanophiles mit Büros in der Rue Navarin in Paris. Etwa zu jener Zeit verfaßte ich einen Vortrag über die afrikanische Skulptur für die Société de Mélanophiles. Er wurde auf einer Platte aufgenommen und einige Tage später in New York über ein Grammophon gehalten.«[12] Dieser knappe Hinweis ist leider alles, was wir über jene Aktivitäten wissen. Trotz ausgiebiger Nachforschungen habe ich den Text bisher nicht auffinden können. Er hätte zweifellos große historische Bedeutung, da es sich um eine der frühesten – wenn nicht die allererste – kritische Auseinandersetzung zu diesem Thema handelt. Der Anlaß für das Abspielen der Aufnahme in New York war vermutlich eine private Präsentation der Ausstellung afrikanischer Kunst (somit ein Jahr später als von SAVINIO vermerkt), die 1914–1915 in der New Yorker Galerie Alfred Stieglitz stattfand. Paul Guillaume hatte eigens dafür Skulpturen aus Paris geschickt. Es ist vielleicht in diesem Zusammenhang von Interesse, daß dieselbe Galerie Werke von DE CHIRICO zeigte, die zusammen mit der Schiffsladung afrikanischer Skulpturen eingetroffen waren,[13] und daß Stieglitz' Periodikum *291* Musikstücke und theoretische Texte von SAVINIO veröffentlichte.

Obwohl zur Genüge der Kunst der Eingeborenen ausgesetzt, ist in der Malerei der beiden Brüder kaum irgendein Echo auf diese Zeitströmungen wahrzunehmen. Dasselbe gilt auch für SOFFICI, BOCCIONI, SEVERINI und RUSSOLO. Der Einfluß der afrikanischen Kunst auf das Œuvre von CARRÀ bleibt daher ein Einzelfall.

In den folgenden Jahren war das italienische Kulturleben nicht dazu angetan, das Interesse an der Kunst der Primitiven zu steigern. Italien besaß keine Kolonien, und es gab daher keinen Markt für afrikanische und ozeanische Kunst, der die Entwicklung von Spezialsammlungen begünstigt hätte. Ich selbst kenne keine italienische Privatsammlung solcher Kunst aus dem ersten Viertel des Jahrhunderts.

☐ 585 *›Kopf‹, LEGA (Zaire), Elfenbein, Höhe 7 cm. Privatsammlung.*

☐ 586 *Carlo Carrà, ›Komposition mit weiblicher Figur‹, Farbabbildung siehe* ☐ *574.*

☐ 587 *Carlo Carrà, ›Antigrazioso‹, 1916, Öl auf Leinwand, 67 x 52 cm. Privatsammlung, Mailand.*

☐ 589 *Carlo Carrà, ›Der Geiger‹ (Violinista), 1914–15, Bleistift, 41 x 27 cm. Sammlung der Società Reale Mutua di Assicurazioni, Turin.* ▷

Nach Ansicht Paul Guillaumes waren »die aktivsten und intelligentesten Persönlichkeiten, die für die Sache der afrikanischen Kunst eintraten«, zwei Ausländer, die in Rom lebten: Edward Keeling, »ein charmanter Amateur«, und Gerald Tyrwhitt (der spätere Lord Berners), ein junger Attaché an der britischen Botschaft und zugleich Musiker.[14] Gabriele d'Annunzio, der Prinz der italienischen Dichter, qualifizierte die afrikanische Kunst als literarische Modeerscheinung ab. Leon Kochnitzky belegt dies durch ein Gespräch, das er 1920 mit dem Dichter führte: »Sehen Sie«, sagte d'Annunzio, »wenn Sie mir von Negerstatuen und Masken aus Afrika erzählen, muß ich einfach an die japanophile Besessenheit der Goncourts denken. Jede Epoche hat ihren literarischen Zeitvertreib. Exotismus und Karneval helfen einem dabei, der Trostlosigkeit der Wirklichkeit zu entfliehen, der Langeweile des Alltagslebens auszuweichen.«[15]

Für die »XIII. Internationale Kunstausstellung der Stadt Venedig« (die heutige »Biennale«) von 1922 richteten der Archäologe Carlo Anti und der Ethnologe Aldobrandino Mochi eine Ausstellung von dreiunddreißig afrikanischen – größtenteils aus dem Kongo stammenden – Skulpturen aus, die dem Ethnographischen Museum in Rom (1925 nach seinem Gründer das L. Pigorini-Museum genannt) und dem Museum für Anthropologie und Ethnographie in Florenz gehörten.[16] Die Kritiker reagierten größtenteils oberflächlich, gleichgültig oder spöttisch. Sogar der Organisator der Ausstellung, Anti, schrieb 1921 in einem Aufsatz über afrikanische Skulptur, daß er darin »nur die Ausdrucksform einer primitiven Entwicklungsstufe mit der Kindlichkeit und Einfalt aller primitiven Künste« sehe. Carrà, der der Ausstellung in Venedig vier lange Artikel in *Il Convegno* widmete, erwähnt die afrikanische Abteilung überhaupt nicht.[17]

Solch eklatante Nachlässigkeiten, ja selbst die völlige Ablehnung, setzten den durch die »Entdeckung« der außereuropäischen Kunst in Italien in Gang gesetzten Prozessen allerdings kein Ende. Eher übten solche Anregungen ihren Einfluß auf

□ 588 *›Kopf‹,* LEGA *(Zaire), Elfenbein, Höhe 13 cm. Sammlung Alain de Monbrison, Paris.*

die italienische Kunst im Verborgenen aus wie ein Karstfluß, um dann nach dem Zweiten Weltkrieg in großem Umfang wieder zum Vorschein zu kommen.

1961 schrieb CORRADO CAGLI, daß mit den Entdeckungen der Avantgarde

»den Malern und Dichtern ein grenzenloses Gebiet eröffnet wurde. Jetzt wird deutlich, daß die stilistische Komplexität der modernen Malerei – verglichen mit der der Vergangenheit, die den griechisch-römischen und den Renaissance-Regeln verpflichtet war – gerade den erworbenen Kenntnissen über primitive Kulturen und Volksbräuche viel verdankt. Alle diese Kulturen – von den Aruntas zu den Azteken, von den Nuraghen zu den Mayas, von den Höhlenbewohnern zu den Etruskern – sind letztlich in unsere moderne Zeit eingeflossen, so wie Nebenflüsse schließlich zu einem großen Strom zusammenlaufen.«[18]

Wie bei dem symbolischen Lauf des »großen Stroms« haben in die vielseitigen Schöpfungen dieses römischen Künstlers (und in die vieler anderer wie etwa MIRKO) in eindrucksvoller Weise Formen und Lösungen Eingang gefunden, die der afrikanischen, ozeanischen, indonesischen und präkolumbianischen Kunst eigentümlich sind – nicht als eklektische Anspielungen, sondern als gründlich eingearbeitete und angeglichene Bestandteile.

Doch solche Überlegungen betreffen die Geschichte unserer heutigen Zeit, die noch nicht geschrieben ist. Es ist eine Geschichte des westlichen Menschen, der sich (ein für allemal, wie wir hoffen) von der überheblichen Vorstellung befreit hat, wichtigster Urheber der Welt zu sein.

□ 590 *›Helmmaske‹, BAULE (Elfenbeinküste), Holz, Höhe 88 cm. The Metropolitan Museum of Art, The M. C. Rockefeller Memorial Collection. Schenkung Ben Heller, New York.*

□ 591 *›Krokodilmaske‹, DOGON (Mali), Holz, Höhe 63,5 cm. Sammlung Nina und Gordon Bunshaft, New York.*

Anmerkungen

1. Marinetti, F. T., *Una sensibilità nata in Egitto,* Mailand 1969, S. 288–89. Zur Verbindung von Futuristen und französischer Avantgarde siehe auch den Katalog *Apollinaire e l'Avantguardia,* Rom, Galleria Nazionale d'Arte Moderna, 1980.

2. Boccioni, U., »Fondamento plastico della scultura e pittura futuriste« in *Lacerba* 1, Nr. 6 (15. März 1913), S. 51.

3. Carrà, C., »Vita moderna e arte popolare« in *Lacerba* 2, Nr. I (1. Juni 1914), S. 167.

4. Carrà, C., »André Derain« in *Valori Plastici* 3, Nr. 3 (März 1921), S. 67–68. Carrà zufolge war Derain der erste, der afrikanische Formen verwendete: »Niemand anders als Derain verursachte die zwei Sündenfälle Fauvismus und Kubismus, indem er die paradoxe Linienführung afrikanischer Statuen in seiner Kunst nachahmte«, »Parere intorno a Matisse« in *Pittura metafisica,* Florenz 1919.

5. Siehe Richter, M., *La formazione francese di Ardengo Soffici, 1900–1914,* Mailand 1969.

6. Soffici, A., Cubismo e Futurismo, Florenz 1914, S. 14.

7. Carrà, C., *La mia vita,* Rom 1943, S. 41.

8. Vlaminck, M., *Portrait avant-décès,* Paris 1943, S. 106–07.

9. Die Werke sind dem Katalog *Carrà–Disegni* entnommen, Russoli, F., und Carrà, M., Bologna 1977.

10. Siehe Bassani, E., »La maschera bianca di Vlaminck e di Derain« in *Africa* 34, Nr. 3, Rom, September 1979, S. 286–94.

11. Fagiolo, M., *Giorgio de Chirico – Il tempo di Apollinaire – Paris 1911–1915,* Rom 1981.

12. Savinio, A., *Souvenirs,* Rom 1945, S. 150. Anmerkung 11.

13. Fagiolo, M., a.a.O., S. 113

14. Guillaume, P., »Une Esthétique nouvelle – L'Art Nègre« in *Les Arts à Paris,* Nr. 4, 15. Mai 1919, S. 4.

15. Kochnitzky, L., »Influence de la plastique nègre sur l'art contemporain« in *Synthèses,* Nr. 121, Juni 1956, S. 293.

16. Die afrikanischen Kunstwerke sind im Ausstellungskatalog auf S. 41–44 aufgeführt.

17. Carrà, C., »L'arte mondiale all'XIII Biennale di Venezia« in *Il Convegno,* 3. Mai 1922, S. 211–20, Juni 1922, S. 287–96, Juli 1922, S. 406–14, August 1922, S. 444–53. Auf der gleichen Ausstellung wurden Carràs *Die Dioskuren* und *Das Haus der Liebe* gezeigt. Die beiden Gemälde waren der Anlaß für einen heftigen Angriff von E. Thovez in der *Gazetta del Popolo* (5. Mai 1922). Er trug die Überschrift »Die Ungeheuer: Modigliani, Cézanne, Carrà«, ein Hinweis auf das kulturelle Klima im damaligen Italien.

18. Zitiert in Ragghianti, C. L., *La fondazione Cagli per Firenze,* 1979, S. 21.

□ 592 *Figur, Bangwa (Kamerun), Höhe 81 cm. Privatsammlung.*

Alan G. Wilkinson

Paris und London

Modigliani, Lipchitz, Epstein und Gaudier-Brzeska

Ähnlich wie GAUGUIN ist MODIGLIANI durch seine Gemälde viel bekannter geworden als durch seine Skulpturen, auch wenn zeitgenössische Berichte seiner Freunde bezeugen, daß der Künstler im Grunde genommen immer Bildhauer werden wollte. Der Kunsthändler Adolphe Basler stellte fest: »Die Bildhauerkunst war sein einziges Ideal, in das er große Hoffnungen setzte.«[1] Die englische Malerin NINA HAMNET, die MODIGLIANI oft in Paris besuchte, schrieb in ihren Memoiren: »Er betrachtete die Bildhauerei immer als sein eigentliches Metier.«[2] Seine Mutter adressierte ihre Briefe nach Paris: »Amedeo Modigliani, sculpteur«.[3] Und doch widmete er nur fünf bis sechs Jahre seines kurzen, tragischen Künstlerlebens – ungefähr zwischen 1909 und 1915 – der Verwirklichung dieses Ziels.

Als Maler wie auch als Bildhauer war MODIGLIANI im wesentlichen ein Porträtist. Der menschliche Kopf ist das Thema von 23 seiner 25 erhaltenen Skulpturen. MODIGLIANIS sensible Aneignung von Einflüssen afrikanischer Eingeborenenkunst finden wir gerade in diesen Skulpturen und vielen Zeichnungen aus ihrem Umkreis deutlicher als in seinen Gemälden.

Das fast völlige Fehlen dokumentarischen Quellenmaterials macht es schwierig, wenn nicht sogar unmöglich, eine Chronologie seiner Skulpturen zu erstellen und besonderen Fragestellungen im Hinblick auf primitive Einflüsse nachzugehen. Wir wissen zum Beispiel nicht, wie gut er afrikanische Plastik kannte und wann er das erste Mal mit ihr in Berührung kam. Es kann jedoch kein Zweifel darüber bestehen, daß die afrikanische Kunst eine der wichtigsten Quellen für die Entwicklung des unverwechselbar persönlichen Stils von MODIGLIANIS länglichen Köpfen war.

AMEDEO MODIGLIANI wurde am 12. Juli 1884 in Livorno in Italien geboren. Trotz seines späteren Rufs als typischer Pariser Bohemekünstler vergaß er seine bürgerlich-jüdische Herkunft nie und stellte sich anderen oft mit den Worten: »Ich bin Modigliani – Jude« vor. 1898 fing er in Livorno mit dem Zeichnen und Malen an. Seine formelle akademische Ausbildung begann 1902, als er sich an der Accademia di Belle Arti in Florenz einschrieb. Im Jahr darauf studierte er im Istituto di Belle Arti in Venedig.

Ende 1905 oder Anfang 1906 kam MODIGLIANI nach Paris und ließ sich in der Rue Caulaincourt auf dem Montmartre, unweit von Picassos Atelier im Bateau-Lavoir, nieder. Die wenigen erhaltenen Gemälde aus MODIGLIANIS ersten drei Pariser Jahren spiegeln den Einfluß von TOULOUSE-LAUTREC und PICASSOS melancholischen Bildnissen der ›Blauen Periode‹ wider. Der entscheidende Einfluß auf MODIGLIANIS malerische Entwicklung ging jedoch vom Werk CÉZANNES aus. Überdeutlich wird er in dem Gemälde *Der Bettler,* das während seiner Italienreise im Sommer und Herbst 1909 entstand.

Während der ersten sechs Monate des Jahres 1909 zog MODIGLIANI in ein Atelier in der Cité Falguière 14 auf dem Montparnasse. Er bat seinen Freund und Gönner, Dr. Paul Alexandre, ihn seinem Nachbarn BRANCUSI vorzustellen. Die Bedeutung dieses Treffens und der daraus entstandenen Freundschaft mit BRANCUSI kann gar nicht hoch genug eingeschätzt werden. Immer wenn es MODIGLIANI an Richtung und Willenskraft fehlte, seine Kraft der Bildhauerei zu widmen, gaben ihm das menschliche Beispiel BRANCUSIS und dessen Arbeit den nötigen Auftrieb. Die beiden Künstler müssen sich noch vor MODIGLIANIS Italienreise im Sommer 1909 kennengelernt haben, da BRANCUSI MODIGLIANI in Livorno besuchte, wo der Gastgeber eine Porträtzeichnung mit dem Vermerk »Brancusi« und »Livorno« anfertigte. Wahrscheinlich unternahm MODIGLIANI noch vor seiner Heimreise erste bildhauerische Versuche, so daß er während seines Aufenthaltes in Livorno an einigen Skulpturen arbeitete. Aber wieder ist es wegen fehlender Belege unmöglich, bestimmte Skulpturen in das Jahr 1909 zu datieren. Im allgemeinen wird angenommen, daß sich Modigliani im Herbst 1909, nach seiner Rückkehr nach Paris, ganz auf die Bildhauerei und die dazugehörigen Zeichnungen konzentrierte.

Die Plastik MODIGLIANIS und seines Mentors BRANCUSI weisen nicht die enge stilistische Verwandtschaft auf, die sich so oft im Schaffen von Künstlern zeigt, die eng zusammenleben und arbeiten; etwa bei PICASSO und BRAQUE zwischen 1909 und 1913 oder bei MOORE und HEPWORTH in den späten 20er und frühen 30er Jahren. MODIGLIANI wurde mit Sicherheit durch BRANCUSIS frühe Steinplastik beeinflußt, von größerer Bedeutung aber war das »moralische« Beispiel des Rumänen, der sich als Bildhauer seine Individualität und Unabhängigkeit gegenüber aktuellen Strömungen der Pariser Avantgarde bewahrte. Mit seiner ausschließlichen Vorliebe für die Steinbildhauerei folgte MODIGLIANI beharrlich dem Motto BRANCUSIS: »Der wahre Weg zur Skulptur ist die direkte Bearbeitung des Materials«,[4] während BRANCUSI selbst 1913–14 mit verschiedenen Materialien – Stein, Holz, Gips und Bronze – arbeitete. Zu berücksichtigen ist allerdings, daß 1909, als sich die beiden Künstler kennenlernten, fast alle Skulpturen BRANCUSIS aus den vergangenen zwei Jahren in Stein oder Marmor gemeißelt waren. Wie BRANCUSI, EPSTEIN und GAUDIER-BRZESKA wandte sich auch

☐ 593 *Jacob Epstein, ›Der Steinbohrer‹ (The Rock Drill), 1913–14, Bronze, 71 x 76 cm. The Museum of Modern Art, Stiftung Mrs. Simon Guggenheim, New York.*

MODIGLIANI der direkten Bearbeitung des Materials und der Kunst der Eingeborenen zu, um sich von dem übermächtigen Einfluß RODINS freizumachen. LIPCHITZ berichtete über seinen Freund: »Modigliani war wie auch einige andere Zeitgenossen der Überzeugung, daß die Bildhauerkunst in einer Misere sei und dies durch Rodin und seinen Einfluß. Es wurde zuviel in Ton modelliert, es gab zuviel ›Schmiere‹. Die einzige Möglichkeit, die Bildnerei zu retten, war, mit der direkten Arbeit am Stein wieder anzufangen. Wir führten über dieses Thema sehr viele erregte Diskussionen . . . aber Modigliani war nicht zum Nachgeben zu bewegen.«[5] 1909 konnte MODIGLIANI außer BRANCUSI keinen Bildhauer finden, der sich intensiv der direkten Methode widmete. Außerdem bot BRANCUSIS Interesse an der Stammeskunst für MODIGLIANI zweifellos eine Alternative zur griechisch-römischen Renaissance-Tradition.

Bestimmte Merkmale früherer Steinskulpturen BRANCUSIS waren mit großer Sicherheit Auslöser für MODIGLIANIS neunzehn überproportionierte Köpfe aus Stein. BRANCUSIS 1907 entstandener *Mädchenkopf* □ 477, den dieser als »erste direkte Steinarbeit« beschrieb, war bezeichnenderweise das früheste Werk des Rumänen, das MODIGLIANI beeindruckt haben muß. Sidney Geist schrieb hierzu: »Sicherlich war das ein Kopf, den Modigliani 1909, zu Beginn seiner Freundschaft mit Brancusi, sah.«[6] Von der Asymmetrie abgesehen, nehmen die anderen Charakteristika von BRANCUSIS Skulptur – das glatte, weiche Gesicht, die langgezogene Nase, der kleine Mund und die strukturierten, eingeritzten Linien der Haare – weitgehend die Serie der Köpfe MODIGLIANIS vorweg. BRANCUSIS Skulptur *Baroness R. F.* □ 596 von 1910 mit ihrer langen, schmalen und vorspringenden Nase ist als Vorbild für MODIGLIANIS überproportionierte Steinköpfe noch überzeugender als der *Mädchenkopf* von 1907, der eine ziemlich flache Nase und ausgehöhlte Wangen hat.

Die 25 Steinskulpturen, die generell als authentische Werke MODIGLIANIS anerkannt werden, stellen nur einen Teil seines Gesamtwerkes dar. Wir werden nie erfahren, wie viele Skulpturen er wirklich ausführte und wie viele verlorengingen oder zerstört wurden. Zu den erhaltenen Skulpturen gehören 23 Köpfe, eine stehende weibliche Figur und eine Karyatide □ 601, 603. Eine genaue Chronologie dieser Werke ist nicht zu erstellen. Eine Photographie von 1911 mit vier Köpfen im Atelier des Malers CARDOSO gibt jedoch den Hinweis, daß diese Werke zwischen 1909 und 1911 entstanden. Merkwürdigerweise datiert Ambrogio Ceroni alle 25 Skulpturen in die Jahre 1911–13, obwohl sich MODIGLIANI-Experten darin einig sind, daß er vor allem in den Jahren zwischen 1909 und 1915 oder 1916 als Bildhauer arbeitete.[7] Auf eine Reihe von Künstlern, die MODIGLIANIS Atelier besuchten, machten seine Steinköpfe einen großen Eindruck. Jahre später erinnerte sich LIPCHITZ an seinen Besuch des Ateliers im Jahre 1912. Dort hatte er die wichtige Beobachtung gemacht, daß die Steinköpfe so konzipiert waren, alle zusammen betrachtet zu werden, und daß sie als Gruppe eine besondere Wirkung ausstrahlten.

»Ich sehe ihn vor mir, als ob es heute wäre, wie er sich über die Köpfe beugt und mir erklärt, daß er sie als Ensemble konzipierte. Ich glaube mich zu erinnern, daß diese Köpfe noch im gleichen Jahr im Salon d'Automne ausgestellt waren, wie die Orgelpfeifen der Größe nach nebeneinander, um genau den Zusammenklang hervorzubringen, den er wünschte.«[8]

□ 594 *Amedeo Modigliani, ›Kopf‹, um 1911, Stein, 89 x 12 x 35 cm. The Trustees of the Tate Gallery, London.*

□ 595 *›Maske‹, Guro (Elfenbeinküste), Holz, Höhe 42 cm. Privatsammlung.*

Modiglianis Köpfe sind das Ergebnis einer ganz und gar persönlichen Sicht. Sie strahlen eine so kraftvolle, geheimnisvolle Präsenz aus, daß man sie, wenn man sie einmal gesehen hat, nicht so leicht wieder vergißt. Der englische Bildnismaler Augustus John, der Modigliani ebenfalls 1912 besuchte, beurteilte die Köpfe vom Standpunkt des Porträts aus. Die zwei Köpfe, die John erwarb, gehörten vermutlich zu den ersten von Modigliani verkauften Skulpturen. John schrieb: »Die Steinköpfe berührten mich seltsam. Einige Tage später hatte ich die Halluzination, auf der Straße Leuten zu begegnen, die dafür Modell gestanden haben könnten – und das, ohne daß ich zu indischem Kraut gegriffen hätte!«[9]

Der eindringlichste Bericht ist Epsteins Beschreibung der erbärmlichen Verhältnisse und der exotischen Ausstrahlung von Modiglianis Atelier:

»Sein Atelier war zu dieser Zeit [1912] ein elendes Loch in einem Hinterhof, wo er lebte und arbeitete. Es war vollgepfropft mit neun oder zehn dieser langen, durch afrikanische Masken inspirierten Köpfe und einer Figur. Sie waren in Stein gehauen; nachts stellte er Kerzen auf jeden Kopf; der Effekt war der eines primitiven Tempels.«[10]

Bis zu seiner Rückkehr nach London im Spätjahr 1912 wurde Epstein durch die Aneignung primitiver Quellen bei Künstlern wie Modigliani zu eigenen Zeichnungen und Skulpturen angeregt, die ebenfalls deutlich Bezug auf die afrikanische und ozeanische Kunst nehmen.

Es ist nicht bekannt, wann Modigliani das erste Mal mit der Kunst der Eingeborenen in Berührung kam. Sicher ist aber, daß er Picasso vor 1909 kennengelernt hatte, über sein Interesse an afrikanischer und ozeanischer Kunst Bescheid wußte und wohl auch seine Sammlung primitiver Kunst kannte. Modiglianis Freundschaft mit Lipchitz und Brancusi stellte eine weitere Verbindung zur Plastik der Eingeborenen her. Laut Alfred Werner sah Modigliani auch Beispiele afrikanischer Skulpturen in Brummers Galerie und bei Frank Burty Haviland.[11] Obwohl es keinen konkreten Hinweis gibt, kann man davon ausgehen, daß Modigliani, der 1909 »endlos über Negerkunst« sprach,[12] auch den Trocadéro besuchte.

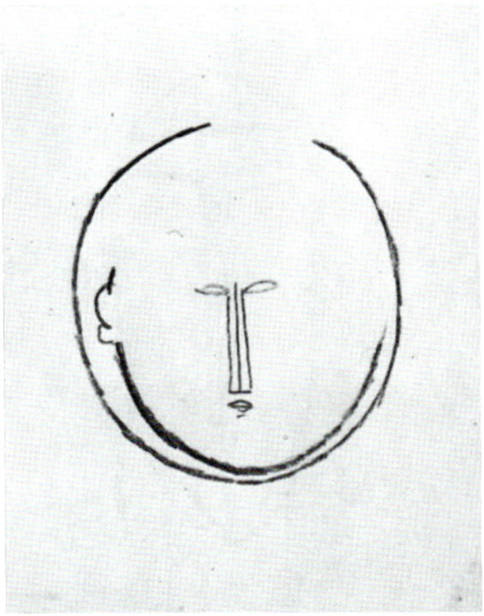

□ 596 *Constantin Brancusi, ›Baroness R. F.‹, 1910, Stein, Privatsammlung.*

□ 597 *›Maske‹, BAULE (Elfenbeinküste), bemaltes Holz, Höhe 51 cm. Indiana University Art Museum, Bloomington.*

□ 598 *Amedeo Modigliani, Seite aus einem Skizzenbuch, 1914–15, rote Kreide, 34 x 26 cm. Kunstmuseum, Kupferstichkabinett, Basel.*

Die meisten Experten sind der Ansicht, daß sich MODIGLIANI anders als PICASSO, BRANCUSI und EPSTEIN, deren Malerei und Plastik Einflüsse verschiedenster Stammesstile aufweisen, nur einem einzigen afrikanischen Regionalstil zuwandte: den *BAULE*-Tanzmasken von der Elfenbeinküste □ 597 und einigen Arbeiten benachbarter Stämme. Robert Goldwater schrieb über MODIGLIANIS Köpfe:

»Es ist ausreichend erkennbar, daß er in einer Reihe seiner Köpfe dem Beispiel des Baule-Stils (besonders seiner Masken) folgt. Bezeichnend ist das gelängte Oval des Kopfes mit dem schmalen Kinn, den mandelförmigen Augen, der scharfkantigen Form der geraden Nase, die ebenso wie der kleine rautenförmige Mund kaum die sanfte Rundung der Wangen und des Kinns unterbricht. Der zylinderförmige Hals ist ebenfalls afrikanischer Herkunft, aber sein regionales Vorbild ist weniger leicht zu bestimmen.«[13]

Die subtile Art, wie sich MODIGLIANI seine Vorbilder aneignete und transformierte, macht es jedoch schwer, einen bestimmten Stammesstil als alleinige Inspirationsquelle zu identifizieren. Obwohl die Ähnlichkeiten zwischen MODIGLIANIS Köpfen und *BAULE*-Tanzmasken überzeugend sind, muß daran erinnert werden, daß *FANG*- und *YAURE*-Masken dem Stil der *BAULE* in einigen Punkten ähneln. Im Vergleich zu der oben erwähnten *BAULE*-Tanzmaske sind denn auch die Proportionen der Köpfe MODIGLIANIS der schmalen Nase und der ausgeprägteren Längung des Kopfes bei den *FANG*- und *MARKA*-Masken □ 575, 600 ähnlicher, ebenso den vorzüglich stilisierten, wenn auch weniger gelängten *GURO*-Masken □ 595. Wahrscheinlich arbeitete MODIGLIANI aus dem Gedächtnis nach afrikanischer Kunst, die er gesehen hatte, und behielt auf diese Weise eine gewisse Distanz zu seinen Vorbildern. Wenn ein Kopf wie der aus der Tate Gallery □ 594 tatsächlich durch *BAULE*-Tanzmasken angeregt sein sollte, so änderte MODIGLIANI die ovale Gesichtsform dieser Masken entschieden ab und schuf einen schmalen, axial angelegten Kopf, der außer bestimmten *GURO*-Masken keinen stilistischen Vorgänger innerhalb dieser afrikanischen Prototypen hat. Bei MODIGLIANIS begrenztem Themenkreis ist es erstaunlich, daß jeder der Steinköpfe einen unverwechselbaren Charakter besitzt, zum Teil wohl deshalb, weil der Künstler sich nicht nur durch Stammeskunst anregen ließ. Goldwater hat auf die Ähnlichkeit zwischen der Haarbehandlung von Köpfen MODIGLIANIS und archaischer Skulptur Griechenlands hingewiesen und beobachtete, daß ihr gedämpftes Lächeln an griechische Koren oder an die sinnlicheren Gesichtszüge der Khmerplastik erinnert.[14]

Die einzigen bekannten Werke MODIGLIANIS, die höchstwahrscheinlich unmittelbar auf Vorbildern afrikanischer Skulptur basieren, sind drei Skizzen, wovon wir eine abbilden □ 598. Das Heranrücken der Augen an die Nasenwurzel, der kleine Mund und die Zeichnung des rechten Ohrs, die dem Kopf Räumlichkeit verleiht, sprechen dafür, daß diese Zeichnung auf eine *BAULE*-Maske zurückgeht. Im Unterschied zu vielen Vorstudien für die Steinköpfe und den Skulpturen selbst, in denen der Einfluß der *BAULE*-Tanzmasken absorbiert und durch andere Anregungen überdeckt ist, haben wir in dieser Skizze einen konkreten Beweis für MODIGLIANIS besonderes Interesse an den eleganten und vornehmen Skulpturen der Elfenbeinküste.

Obwohl die Gouachen, Zeichnungen und Aquarelle aus dieser Periode bezeugen, daß die Karyatide eines der Lieblingsthemen im bildhauerischen Werk des Künstlers war, ist nur eine einzige Arbeit davon erhalten □ 603. Ebenso wie die Steinköpfe als Serie konzipiert waren – sieben Exemplare wurden 1912 im Salon d'Automne als *Têtes, ensemble décoratif* gezeigt –, stellte sich MODIGLIANI auch die Karyatiden als

Gruppe vor. Er nannte sie *colonnes de tendresse,* verwirklichte sie aber nie. In den meisten von MODIGLIANIS Zeichnungen mit Karyatiden erinnern die Gesichtszüge noch entfernt an die *BAULE*-Masken, auch wenn die Gruppe der Köpfe gestrecktere Proportionen aufweist. So wie MODIGLIANI die verschiedensten stilistischen Vorbilder in seinen Steinköpfen vereinte, scheinen mir auch die Karyatiden sowohl mit der Kunst der Eingeborenen als auch mit der Europas verwandt zu sein. Die *Karyatide* im Museum of Modern Art ist mit *LUBA*-Hockern verglichen worden □ 602. Es bestehen tatsächlich gewisse Übereinstimmungen, obwohl fast nicht vorstellbar ist, daß MODIGLIANI im damaligen Paris *LUBA*-Kunst sehen konnte. Die Art und Weise, wie MODIGLIANIS Figur zwischen die flache Deckplatte – die sie

□ 599 *Amedeo Modigliani, ›Kopf‹, um 1915, Kalkstein, 56 x 13 x 37 cm. The Museum of Modern Art, Schenkung A. A. Rockefeller zum Gedenken an Mrs. Cornelius J. Sullivan, New York.*

□ 600 *›Maske‹, MARKA (Mali), Holz, Höhe 37 cm. Privatsammlung.*

mit den Armen hochstemmt – und die Basis gepreßt ist, erinnert sicherlich an entsprechende Kunstwerke der Eingeborenen. In dieser Skulptur und in allen damit zusammenhängenden Zeichnungen haben die Körper aber eine kontrapostische, gedrehte Haltung, die der frontalen Symmetrie der stehenden und knienden *LUBA*-Figuren wie auch den Karyatiden anderer afrikanischer Stämme völlig fremd ist. Auch die vollen sinnlichen Formen der *Karyatide* lassen keinen afrikanischen Einfluß erkennen. Die eher von Europa als von Afrika her zu verstehende Haltung gemahnt an so bekannte Skulpturen wie die *Kauernde Aphrodite* in Kopenhagen (römische Marmorkopie nach einer hellenistischen Bronze von ca. 275 v. Chr.) oder den *Myrtilos* aus dem Olympia-Giebel von 470–75 v. Chr. In beiden antiken Skulpturen knien die Figuren auf dem rechten Knie, während das linke Bein aufgestellt ist. Diese Beinstellung kommt in MODIGLIANIS *Karyatide* und in vielen seiner Zeichnungen des gleichen Themas vor.

Im Gegensatz zur allgemeinen Ansicht, daß die afrikanische Skulptur MODIGLIANIS primäre Inspirationsquelle war, argu-

mentiert Edith Balas, daß seine wichtigsten stilistischen Anregungen aus der altägyptischen Kunst stammen.[15] Sie zitiert aus den Memoiren der russischen Dichterin Anna Akhmatova, die 1911 in der Cité Falguière 14 die Nachbarin des Bildhauers war: »1911 war Modigliani verrückt vor Liebe zu Ägypten. Er führte mich in die ägyptische Abteilung des Louvre und versicherte mir, daß alles andere – tout le reste – keine Aufmerksamkeit verdiene. Er frisierte mich in der Art einer ägyptischen Prinzessin und einer Tänzerin.«[16]

So überzeugend sich die Argumente von Balas auch lesen, sie werden doch nur von vereinzelten Beispielen unter MODIGLIANIS Zeichnungen und Skulpturen gestützt. Balas bringt Brust und Bauch des *Stehenden Aktes* □ 601, außer der *Karyatide* MODIGLIANIS einzige erhaltene ganzfigurige Skulptur, sowie einige Zeichnungen mit ägyptischer Kunst, vor allem aus dem Louvre, in Verbindung.

Bei dem begrenzten thematischen Repertoire von MODIGLIANIS Plastik ist es nicht verwunderlich, daß sein Werk trotz des starken Eindrucks auf Künstler wie EPSTEIN, LIPCHITZ und AUGUSTUS JOHN bei seinen Zeitgenossen nur wenig Resonanz fand. Wir können jedoch auf Werke anderer Künstler hinweisen, die in enger Beziehung zu MODIGLIANIS Köpfen stehen. Die schmale Nase und der gelängte Kopf der Mutter in LIPCHITZ' Bronze *Mutter mit Kind* von 1913 □ 604 wurden zweifellos durch die Proportionen von MODIGLIANIS Köpfen beeinflußt. Der entsprechende Kopf von EPSTEINS *Mutter mit Kind* von 1913 □ 629 lehnt sich stilistisch eher an *FANG*-Plastik als an *BAULE*-Masken an, auf die MODIGLIANI zurückgriff. Trotzdem kann EPSTEIN vom Werk seines Freundes angeregt worden sein, das er ein Jahr zuvor in Paris gesehen hatte.

Es wird allgemein angenommen, daß MODIGLIANI 1914–15 die Bildhauerei aufgab und zur Malerei zurückkehrte, trotz der Behauptung seiner Tochter, daß er bis 1916 plastisch arbeitete.[17] Verschiedene Gründe wurden angeführt, warum MODIGLIANI die Bildhauerei aufgab: Krankheit, die damit verbundene physische Anstrengung oder die Schwierigkeit, während des Krieges Steinblöcke zu beschaffen. Ohne Frage haben aber die sechs, sieben Jahre, die er der Bildhauerei widmete, den Stil seiner Porträts von 1915–20 beeinflußt. Das überzeugendste Beispiel hierfür ist das Ölgemälde *Lola de Valence* von ca. 1915, das weniger ein genaues Abbild eines Modells ist, als vielmehr eine zweidimensionale Neuschöpfung seiner Steinskulpturen, etwa des *Kopfes* aus der Tate Gallery □ 594. In vielen späteren Porträts läßt er die Augen wie häufig bei den Skulpturen leer. Dieses Darstellungsmittel verleiht den Porträts eine Unnahbarkeit und Distanz zum Betrachter, die auch den geheimnisvollen Charakter seiner Skulpturen ausmacht.

Unter allen wichtigen Künstlern seiner Generation, die für primitive Kunst offen waren, vermied MODIGLIANI experimentelle Wagnisse am konsequentesten. Die dämonische Kraft und oft unverhohlene Sexualität, die außergewöhnliche formale Vielfalt und innere Logik, die von der europäischen Darstellungstradition oft völlig verschieden war, all das gehört zum Wesen der Stammeskunst, die einen so befreienden und weitreichenden Einfluß auf das Werk von PICASSO, BRANCUSI, EPSTEIN und MOORE ausübte. Aber so wie sich MODIGLIANI in seinen Gemälden die eigene Unabhängigkeit gegenüber dem Werk PICASSOS und der Avantgarde bewußt bewahrte, so behielt er auch stets zum Primitiven eine gewisse Distanz.

□ 601 *Amedeo Modigliani, ›Stehender Akt‹, um 1911–12, Stein, Höhe 160 cm. Australian National Gallery, Canberra.*

Daß ihn der *BAULE*-Stil anzog, wird zum Teil durch die weitverbreitete Annahme erklärt, diese Stammesmasken seien profane Porträts lebender Personen. MODIGLIANI verschaffte sich als Porträtist bleibendes Ansehen, vor allem dank der Bildnisse seiner Freunde, Gönner und Mitkünstler: PICASSO, BRANCUSI, LIPCHITZ, Apollinaire, FRANK BURTY HAVILAND, RIVERA, LAURENS und Guillaume. Nach einer Aussage von LIPCHITZ verlor MODIGLIANI nie sein Interesse am Menschen: »Darum wurde Modigliani, obwohl er die afrikanische Negerkunst und andere primitive Stile genauso wie wir alle bewunderte, wie der Kubismus nie tiefergehend davon beeinflußt. Er filterte bestimmte stilistische Momente heraus, wurde aber von ihrem inneren Wesen kaum berührt.«[18]

Für das Werk von JACQUES LIPCHITZ ist eine außergewöhnliche stilistische und ikonographische Vielfalt kennzeichnend. Seine frühen Bronzen (1910–11) waren biedere Porträts und Figurenstudien in der Tradition von MAILLOL und DESPIAU. 1913–14 folgten aber völlig andersartige Werke, die sein wachsendes Interesse an der Stammeskunst und anderen außereuropäischen Quellen widerspiegeln. LIPCHITZ' wichtigster Beitrag zur Geschichte der Skulptur des 20. Jahrhunderts sind zweifellos seine kubistischen Bronzen und Skulpturen aus den Jahren 1915–22. Im Gegensatz zur kühlen Reinheit und Abstraktheit seiner kubistischen Werke beeindrucken die späteren, oft dem biblischen oder jüdischen Themenbereich entnommenen Skulpturen durch ihre übersteigerte, barocke Intensität.

In seinen frühen Jahren, als die Kunst der Naturvölker eine von vielen wichtigen Einflüssen für seine Skulpturen darstellte, behielt LIPCHITZ eine absichtliche Distanz zu diesen bei. PICASSO, BRANCUSI, die deutschen Expressionisten, EPSTEIN, später MOORE und GIACOMETTI reagierten direkter und unmittelbarer auf die primitive Skulptur. Im Unterschied dazu beschrieb LIPCHITZ die Verbindung zu diesen Werken als »Begegnungen«[19] und zeigte wenig Bereitschaft, bestimmte Stile nachzuahmen. In der Einführung zum Ausstellungskatalog *The Lipchitz Collection* von 1960 versicherte er: »Ich sah mich nicht nach einer konkreten Einfluß- oder Inspirationsquelle um, sondern wollte nur meinen schöpferischen Geist anregen und bereichern.«[20]

Tatsächlich sind LIPCHITZ' Anleihen bei der Kunst der Eingeborenen so gut verarbeitet, daß wir kaum einen Stammesstil, geschweige denn eine bestimmte afrikanische oder ozeanische Plastik als möglichen Ausgangspunkt für eine seiner wenigen primitivistischen Skulpturen identifizieren können. Außerdem gibt es wenige äußere Anhaltspunkte dafür, welche Kunst-

□ 602 *›Hocker‹, LUBA (Zaire), Höhe 21 cm. Musée Royal de l'Afrique Centrale, Tervuren, Belgien.*

□ 603 *Amedeo Modigliani, ›Karyatide‹, um 1914, Kalkstein, Höhe 92 cm, Basis 41 x 43 cm. The Museum of Modern Art, Mrs. Simon Guggenheim Fund, New York.*

werke der Eingeborenen er während seiner Entwicklungsjahre von 1909–14 sah. In Skulpturen der Jahre von 1913 bis 1926 sind die Spuren primitiver Einflüsse oft durch die Dominanz des Kubismus und des Werkes seiner Freunde BRANCUSI und MODIGLIANI überschattet.

In seinen wenigen publizierten Kommentaren über den Einfluß des Primitiven auf seine einzelnen Werke äußert LIPCHITZ entweder Unzufriedenheit wegen des zu großen primitiven Einflusses oder spielt den tatsächlichen Einflußgrad herunter. Lakonisch und weitläufig stellt er bei bestimmten Skulpturen allenfalls ein *Interesse* an afrikanischer Kunst, wenn nicht überhaupt nur eine *Ähnlichkeit* fest.

So fand er etwa seine Skulptur *Mutter mit Kind* □ 604 zwar interessant, aber aufgrund des Negerhaften der Figuren, besonders der Köpfe, nie ganz zufriedenstellend. Weiter fügt er hinzu: »Obwohl ich seit meinem ersten Besuch in Paris (1909), sobald ich ein bißchen Geld hatte, afrikanische Skulpturen sammelte, gibt es nur wenige Werke von meiner Hand, in denen ich einen klaren Einfluß der Negerkunst spüre.«[21]

Als LIPCHITZ im Oktober 1909 aus seiner Heimat Litauen nach Paris kam, war er 18 Jahre alt. Im Unterschied zu anderen ausländischen Künstlern, die sich in Paris niederließen – PICASSO, BRANCUSI, ARCHIPENKO und MODIGLIANI –, hatte er keine akademische Ausbildung. 1909–10 war LIPCHITZ an der École des Beaux-Arts eingeschrieben und besuchte gleichzeitig Bildhauerklassen an der Académie Julian und Zeichenklassen an der Académie Colarossi. Zu den Werken der Impressionisten und Postimpressionisten fand er allerdings keinen Zugang. Während seiner ersten Monate in Paris nahm ihn ein Freund zu Vollards Galerie mit. Jahre später erinnerte sich LIPCHITZ:

»Damals liebte ich Rodin nicht. Ich liebte seltsamerweise die Griechen – sie verstehen die echte olympische Kunst . . . Und ich konnte Gauguin nicht verstehen . . . dort [bei Vollard] sah ich ein Gemälde von Gauguin, *Jakob ringt mit dem Engel.* Ich schwöre Ihnen, ich konnte nicht erkennen, was es darstellt. Ich war dermaßen neu in diesen Dingen, daß ich überhaupt nichts sah. Als ich das Bild später wiedersah, war ich überrascht. Wie hatte ich so blind sein können?«[22]

Die wenigen erhaltenen Werke aus LIPCHITZ' ersten zwei Pariser Jahren wie der *Sitzende Akt* von 1910 und das Bronzeporträt *Der Dichter und Maler Césare Sofianopulo* von 1911 vermitteln eher die Tradition RODINS und seiner Nachfolger als die zeitgenössischen Skulpturen und Bronzen von PICASSO, MATISSE, BRANCUSI und MODIGLIANI. Aber schon nach zwei Jahren hatte LIPCHITZ dem 19. Jahrhundert den Rücken gekehrt und nahm zeitgenössische Entwicklungen aus dem Werk von Bildhauern wie ARCHIPENKO, BRANCUSI, BOCCIONI und MODIGLIANI sowie den Kubismus PICASSOS auf.

Nach eigenen Aussagen begann sich LIPCHITZ schon 1909, seinem ersten Jahr in Paris, für die Kunst der Eingeborenen zu interessieren, obwohl sich dieser Einfluß erst 1913–14 in seiner Plastik niederschlug. In der Einleitung des Katalogs zu der Ausstellung »The Lipchitz Collection« im Museum of Primitive Art, New York, schrieb er, daß er schon 1909 anfing, afrikanische Stammeskunst zu sammeln, schon drei Jahre, bevor er PICASSO, BRANCUSI und MODIGLIANI kennenlernte. Lipchitz machte auch kein Hehl daraus, daß er sich zu Beginn seiner künstlerischen Tätigkeit kaum auskannte:

»Sie werden in dieser Ausstellung unter anderen Skulpturen einen bemalten Holzbecher aus Dahome finden, den ich vor 51 Jahren gekauft habe (1909). Ich war sicher, daß er ägyptischer Herkunft ist. Erst eineinhalb Jahre später erfuhr ich bei einem Besuch des Trocadéro, daß er aus Afrika stammt. So entdeckte ich die Negerkunst von alleine und war bald von ihr ganz begeistert.«[23]

□ 604 *Jacques Lipchitz, ›Mutter mit Kind‹, 1913–14, Bronze, Höhe 57 cm. Privatsammlung.*

Das Jahr 1913 brachte Bewegung in LIPCHITZ' künstlerische Entwicklung. Sein Freund DIEGO RIVERA stellte ihn PICASSO vor, nachdem er bereits BRANCUSI und MODIGLIANI hatte kennenlernen können. Im Jahr davor hatte LIPCHITZ im glei-

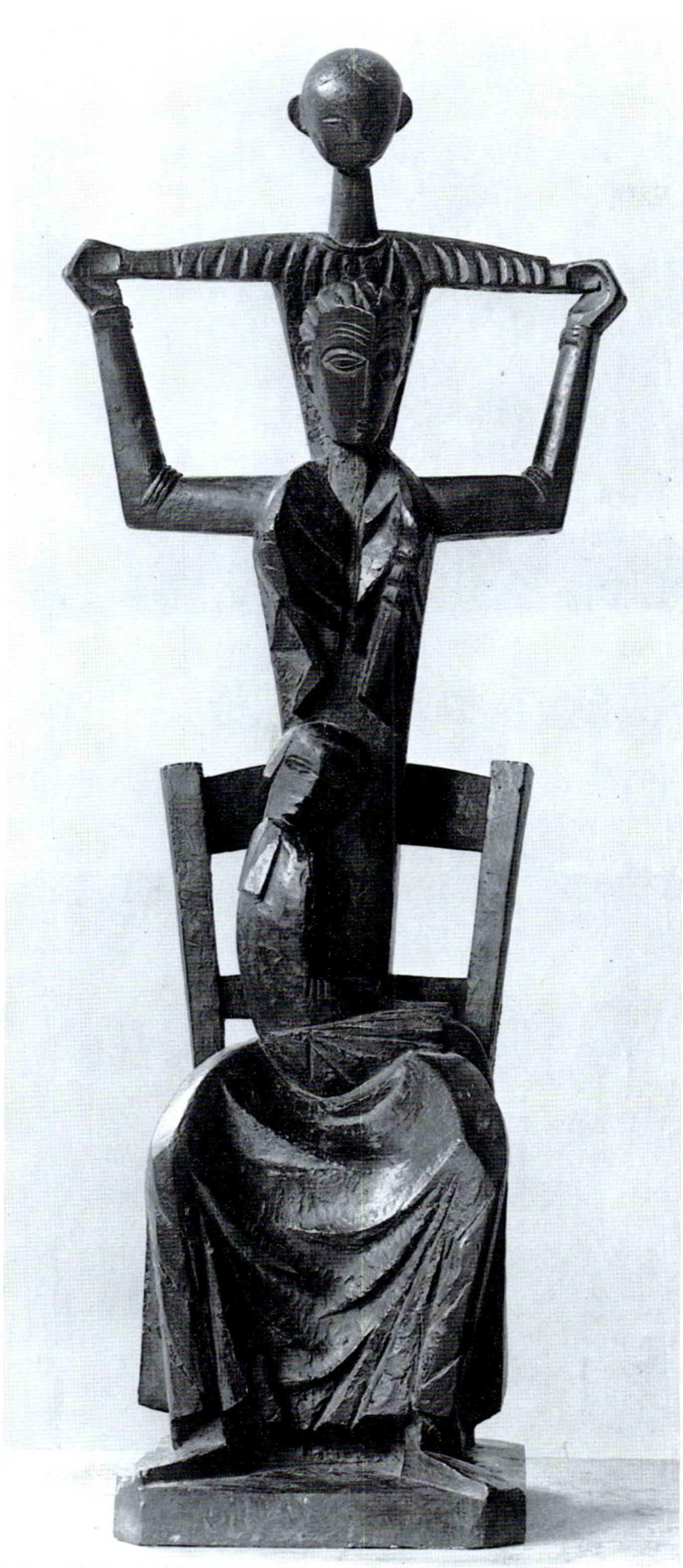

□ 605 *Jacques Lipchitz, ›Mutter mit Kindern‹, 1914–15, Bronze, Höhe 70 cm. Privatsammlung.*

chen Salon d'Automne ausgestellt, in dem MODIGLIANI sieben seiner von *BAULE*-Masken inspirierten Köpfe zeigte. 1912 oder 1913 zog LIPCHITZ in ein Atelier neben BRANCUSI. Die Skulpturen von 1913, die der Künstler »meine protokubistische Phase«[24] nannte, lassen den abrupten Richtungswechsel seiner Arbeit erkennen. Dieser war zweifellos durch seinen Kontakt mit PICASSO, MODIGLIANI und BRANCUSI ausgelöst worden. In Übergangswerken wie *Tänzerin* von 1913 wurde der ruhige, fast in der Art MAILLOLS gehaltene Naturalismus der Schwangeren des vorangegangenen Jahres – vor allem in den Flächen des Körpers – durch kantigere, einfachere Formen ersetzt.

Eine der ersten Arbeiten mit Spuren afrikanischer Kunst ist die Bronze *Mutter mit Kind*, die nach Auskunft des Künstlers wahrscheinlich vor seiner Spanienreise Ende 1913 oder Anfang 1914 entstand. LIPCHITZ' Unzufriedenheit mit diesem Werk wegen seines angeblich afrikanischen Charakters wurde schon erwähnt. Die flache, dreieckige Form der rechten Brust kennt unzählige Vorläufer in der afrikanischen Kunst. Der Künstler selbst bezeichnete die Köpfe als afrikanisch, mir scheinen sie jedoch BRANCUSI und MODIGLIANI näher zu stehen. In der Studie für *Mutter und Kind* ist die Ähnlichkeit mit den Arbeiten dieser Künstler sogar noch auffälliger. Das schmale Gesicht, die langgezogene Nase und der lange Hals der Mutter sehen aus wie eine Paraphrase von MODIGLIANIS Köpfen, die runde, vereinfachte Kopfform des Kindes steht in enger Beziehung zu BRANCUSIS zahlreichen Skulpturen dieses Themas wie etwa dem *Prometheus* von 1911.

Die Frage nach Vorbildern bei einer Skulptur wie *Mutter mit Kind* bleibt vielschichtig. Die Diskussion auf eingeborene und zeitgenössische Quellen zu beschränken, hieße das Einmalige des Werkes zu verkennen. *Mutter mit Kind* verdankt meines Erachtens der ägyptischen Kunst (die Anfang des Jahrhunderts als primitiv galt) weitaus mehr als der Stammeskunst oder der Skulptur BRANCUSIS und MODIGLIANIS. Der Kopf der Mutter zeigt im Profil ein Auge aus der Vorderansicht, wie es nur aus der ägyptischen Kunst herrühren kann. Ihr langer Hals und ihre dünnen Arme, die Art, wie der linke Oberschenkel fast waagrecht vom Körper absteht, während der Unterschenkel nahezu senkrecht auf dem Boden aufsteht, muß von der ägyptischen Skulptur angeregt sein wie etwa von dem *Kalksteinrelief* aus der 18. Dynastie im Ägyptischen Museum, Berlin, auf dem König Echnaton Prinzessin Meriton hält. Außerdem sind die Köpfe von *Mutter mit Kind* trotz ihrer stilistischen Nähe zu MODIGLIANI bzw. BRANCUSI ähnlich zueinander gestellt wie auf dem ägyptischen Relief. Es ist seltsam, daß LIPCHITZ, der die Rolle ägyptischer Kunst in seiner Bronze *Mädchen mit Zopf* (1914) eingestand, in seinen Äußerungen zu *Mutter mit Kind* nichts dergleichen erwähnte. Wenn man den ägyptischen Einfluß anstelle eines afrikanischen auf die letztgenannte Skulptur in Betracht zieht, würde seine Unzufriedenheit mit ihr weniger von ihrer »spezifischen Negerartigkeit« als von ihrem ägyptischen Eindruck herrühren.

Gegenüber der Bronze *Mutter mit Kindern* von 1914 □ 605 äußerte LIPCHITZ nicht die gleichen Vorbehalte wie gegenüber der wenig früheren Skulptur *Mutter mit Kind.*

»Unter allen Werken dieser Periode gibt es eines, das ich besonders mag. Es ist aus verschiedenen Gründen, die ich aber erst nach Jahren erkannte, sehr interessant für mich. Als erstes spielt da das Thema Mutter und Kind eine Rolle, das aus meiner Zuneigung zu meiner eigenen Mutter herrührt – ein Thema, auf das ich, wie schon erwähnt, immer wieder zurückkam. Eine Rolle spielt aber auch die absolute Frontalität der Gruppe, die sehr verschieden ist von der Drehung der Frau mit Schlange oder Tänzerin. Es mag in dieser Frontalität ein Widerschein meines Interesses für afrikanische Kunst liegen. Dennoch glaube ich sagen zu können, daß sich die ursprüngliche Idee unbewußt aus einer Erinnerung an eine russisch-byzantinische Ikone mit der Darstellung der heiligen Muttergottes mit dem Kind entwickelte.«[25]

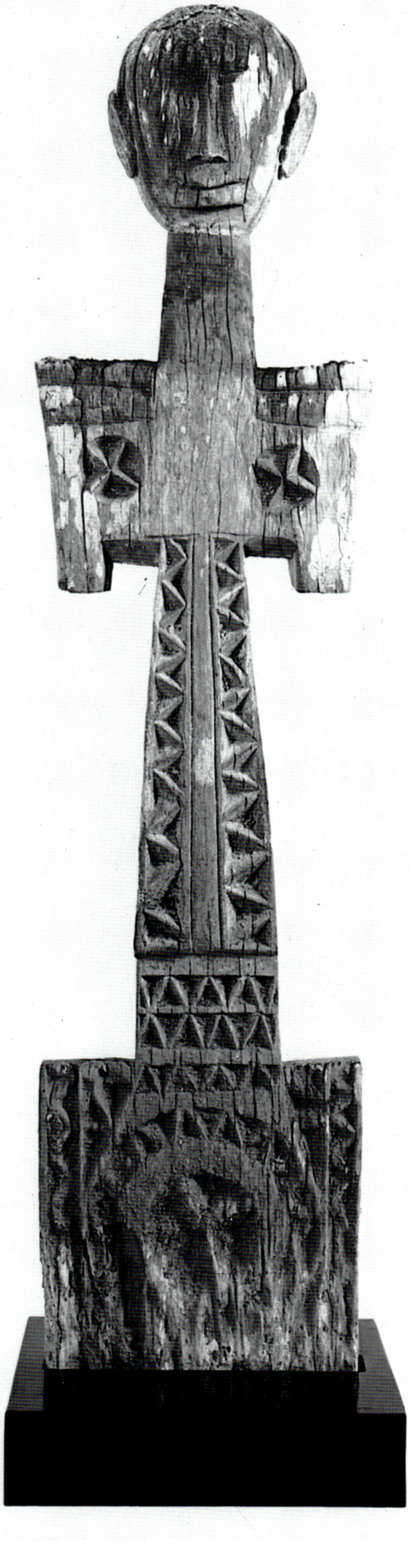

Wie immer bleibt Lipchitz' Verweis auf afrikanische Kunst im allgemeinen. Nur ungern nimmt er die stilistische Verwandtschaft zwischen *Mutter mit Kindern* und der Stammeskunst zur Kenntnis. Deborah A. Stott hat indes die Verneinung des afrikanischen Einflusses durch den Künstler in Frage gestellt: »Ein weiterer Bestandteil des Stils von *Mutter mit Kindern* muß der gemeinsame Einfluß von Brancusi und der afrikanischen Holzplastik gewesen sein. Lipchitz hat jeden derartigen Einfluß geleugnet. Die vertikale Komposition, die kantige Oberfläche, die stockartigen Arme und die Haltung mit gebeugten Knien erinnern jedoch an Brancusis frühe Holzskulpturen *Der erste Schritt* von 1913 ☐ 481 und *Kleines französisches Mädchen* von 1914 ☐ 479 sowie an ihre mutmaßlichen afrikanischen Vorbilder. Bei den Dogon gibt es einen mehrfigurigen Typus, bei dem eine Figur die andere auf der Schulter trägt. Diesem kommt Lipchitz' Komposition recht nahe. Bei einem anderen bekannten Typus der Baluba-Plastik hält eine Figur einen Häuptlingsstuhl wie die Figur von Lipchitz nach oben.«[26]

So verlockend solche Mutmaßungen sein mögen, Stott bleibt die Auskunft schuldig, wo Lipchitz so früh *Luba*-Plastik gesehen haben könnte; wir wissen nur, daß er später *Dogon*-Plastik bewunderte und sammelte.[27]

Die erhobenen Köpfe der Mutter und des Kindes in *Mutter mit Kindern* erinnern an Arbeiten von Modigliani bzw. Brancusi. *Mutter mit Kindern* und Epsteins Zeichnung *Totem* von 1913 ☐ 618 entstanden zwar mit Sicherheit unabhängig voneinander, sind sich aber darin ähnlich, wie die Figuren in einer vertikalen Komposition, bei der in beiden Fällen das Kind über den Kopf der Mutter gehalten wird, verbunden sind.

Es sei nochmals betont, daß für Lipchitz wie für Modigliani die Kunst der Eingeborenen nicht die einzige außereuropäische Anregung darstellt. Was Lipchitz ägyptischer Kunst verdankt, zeigt sich diesmal mit offenem Einverständnis in seiner Bronze *Mädchen mit Zopf* von 1914. Noch augenscheinlicher ist diese Bezugnahme in der Vorstudie aus dem gleichen Jahr *Mädchen mit geflochtenen Haaren* im Museum of Modern Art, New York.[28] Als er Jahre später über diese Skulptur schrieb, war Lipchitz viel freimütiger in bezug auf ihre formale Verwandtschaft zu ägyptischer Kunst als hinsichtlich der Beziehungen zwischen seinem Werk und primitiver Kunst.

»Ich war mir der Vorbilder ägyptischer und archaisch griechischer Skulptur wohl bewußt. In meinem Bestreben, mich von der nur anerzogenen Tradition der Klassik und Renaissance freizumachen, war es natürlich, daß ich mich unter diesen älteren Kulturen umschaute, die für die Errungenschaft der ersten Jahre des 20. Jahrhunderts besonders wichtig waren . . . Die Ägypter und die Griechen der Archaik benutzten mehrseitige Ansichten, die die Kubisten übernommen hatten . . . In *Mädchen mit Zopf* drehte ich den Kopf ins Profil und stellte die Augen in der ägyptischen Art von vorne dar. So ist es möglich, die vielen Wurzeln meines Kubismus zu sehen.«[29]

Wenn es überrascht, wie plötzlich Lipchitz 1915 kubistische Stilmerkmale in seine Skulpturen übernahm (S. 58ff.), so sei

◁ ◁ ☐ 606 *Jacques Lipchitz, ›Auseinandernehmbare Figur‹, 1915, bemaltes Holz, 86 x 22 x 15 cm. Sammlung Yulla Lipchitz, New York.*

◁ ☐ 607 *›Figur aus Holz‹, Kambe (Kenya), Höhe 112 cm, The Detroit Institute of Arts, Eleanor Clay Ford Fund of African Art.*

☐ 608 *›Stabgott‹, Mauke (Cookinseln), Holz, Höhe 23 cm. Cambridge University Museum of Archeology and Anthropology, Cambridge, England.*

daran erinnert, daß der Bildhauer im Werk von Picasso, Braque und später Gris ein fertiges Vokabular vorfand, mit dem er beginnen konnte. Während fast alle kubistischen Skulpturen und Reliefs von Lipchitz, die zwischen 1915 und 1925 entstanden, ikonographisch und stilistisch an das Werk dieser drei Künstler anschließen, scheinen einige wenige Skulpturen sehr allgemeine Anknüpfungspunkte zur Kunst der Eingeborenen aufzuweisen. Der direkte Einfluß der primitiven Kunst verschwand jedoch während dieser ganzen Periode aus dem Werk von Lipchitz keineswegs. Und wieder können wie bei den Bronzen von 1913–14 die stilistischen Bezüge auf primitive Kunst nicht bis zu ihren genauen Quellen zurückverfolgt werden. Die Proportionen der Holzplastik *Auseinandernehmbare Figur* □ 606 stehen der *Kambe*-Stele im Detroit Institute of Arts in stilistischer Hinsicht auffallend nahe □ 607: wie der Kopf, der lange Hals und der Torso senkrecht über den beiden Blöcken mit den gedrungenen Beinen aufragen. Lipchitz erwähnte in Beschreibungen seines kubistischen Werkes von 1915–25 die Kunst der Eingeborenen jedoch nie. Er bestand eher auf zeitgenössischen Quellen als dem Schlüssel zur Entwicklung seines Werkes aus dieser Periode. »Sicherlich wurde ich in meinen Ideen durch die kubistische Malerei, die mir vorausgegangen war, besonders die Picassos, beeinflußt«, schrieb Lipchitz. »Wenn Künstler so eng wie wir in diesen Jahren zusammen leben und arbeiten, werden sie selbstverständlich bis zu einem gewissen Grad wechselseitig beeinflußt; alle übernehmen Motive voneinander.«[30] Er sah darin keine Imitation: »Wir arbeiteten alle in einer gemeinsamen Sprache und untersuchten zusammen das Vokabular dieser Sprache.«[31]

Der *Sitzende* von 1922 □ 71 war, so schrieb Lipchitz, »ein wichtiger Ausgangspunkt für mich; er bestand aus vereinfachten rechteckigen Massen . . . Mit der Figur, die diagonal zur quadratischen Basis frontalisiert ist, und den vertikalen Massen, die durch die umschließenden Arme zusammengezogen sind, ist die ganze Form solide und kubisch im wörtlichen Sinne, also mehr als nur traditionell kubistisch.«[32] Nichtsdestoweniger hat die Figur Bezüge zur Stammeskunst, wenn nicht gar zu einer bestimmten Vorlage. Angefangen bei den Tikis (siehe Glossar) von den Marquesasinseln bis zu den *Fang*-Reliquiarfiguren kommen die gekurvten Arme und die eingeritzten Finger in vielen Stilen Ozeaniens und Afrikas vor, während die vereinfachte, blockartige Struktur an die geometrischen *Dogon*-Figuren erinnert □ 72, 352, 353.

Als Lipchitz 1926 die erste seiner sogenannten Transparenz-Plastiken ausführte, änderte sich die stilistische Richtung seines Werkes radikal. Wie er schrieb, gelangte er von den soliden, abstrahierten Formen in Werken wie *Sitzender* von 1922 zum »Spiel mit dem Raum durch eine Art offener, lyrischer Konstruktion, das eine wirkliche Entdeckung für mich war«.[33]

Mit einer den Transparenz-Plastiken ähnlichen Skulptur, der *Figurenstudie* von 1926, die die *Große Figur* von 1926–30 vorbereitet □ 609, rückte Lipchitz der primitiven Kunst wieder näher. Diese Maquette hatte sich aus einer kleinen Bronzeskulptur von 1926 mit dem Titel *Ploumanach* entwickelt, benannt nach dem Urlaubsort an der britischen Küste, den Lipchitz im Sommer jenes Jahres besuchte. Er war von den Felsformationen an der Küste beeindruckt, davon, wie die

◁ □ 609 *Jacques Lipchitz, ›Große Figur‹, 1926–30, Bronze, 216 x 98 cm. The Museum of Modern Art, Van Gogh Purchase Fund, New York.*

□ 610 *›Männlicher und weiblicher Kopf‹,* Baga *(Guinea), Holz, Höhe 45 cm. Sammlung Yulla Lipchitz New York. Ehemals Sammlung Jacques Lipchitz.*

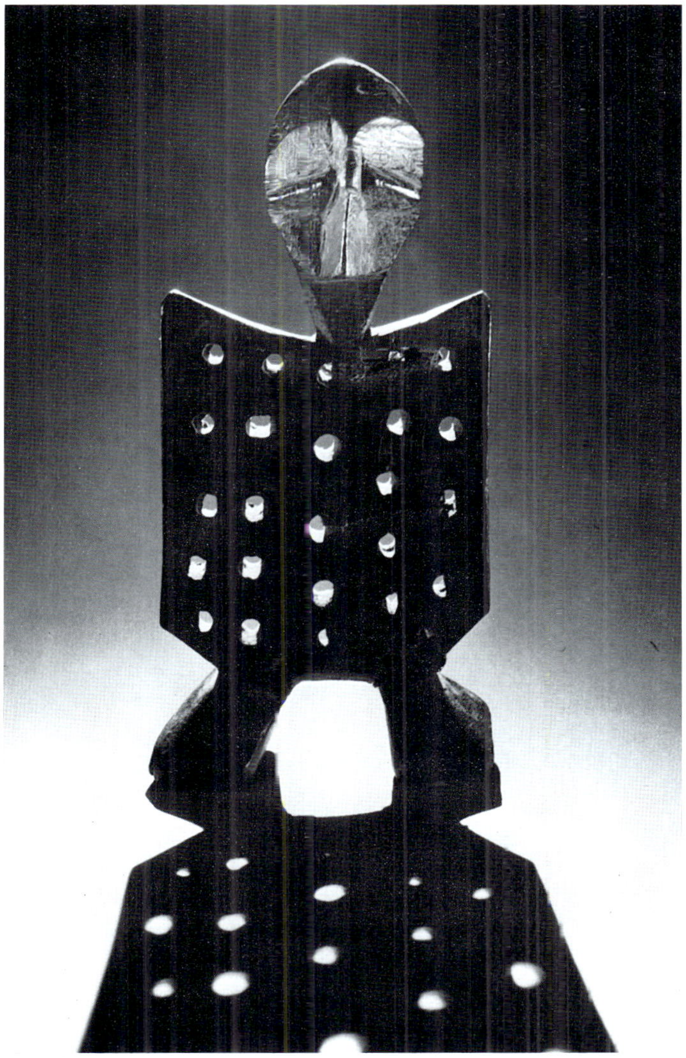

□ 611 *›Figur aus Holz und Fasern‹,* Lega *(Zaire), Höhe 25 cm. Sammlung Yulla Lipchitz, New York. Ehemals Sammlung Jacques Lipchitz.*

☐ 612 ›*Reliquiarkopf*‹, FANG *(Gabun), Holz, Höhe 58 cm, Privatsammlung. Ehemals Sammlung Jacob Epstein.*

Felsen – vom Wasser ausgehöhlt – aufeinander balancierten und schwankten. Dieses empfindliche Gleichgewicht ist in *Ploumanach* eingefangen, aus dem zwei Entwürfe für die *Große Figur* hervorgingen. Im ersten Entwurf ist die liegende Relieffigur für den oberen Teil der Skulptur übernommen worden. Dann aber, wie LIPCHITZ schrieb:

»muß ich dies plötzlich als ein primitives Totem betrachtet haben, denn in der nächsten Skizze formte ich den oberen Teil in einen Kopf mit der Andeutung von starrblickenden Augen um. Dies war die Genese der *Großen Figur* von 1926–30, ein Werk, das viele meiner Ideen seit 1915 zusammenfaßte. Insbesondere vereinte es massive Frontalität mit offener Räumlichkeit – ein Problem, an dem ich in den 20er Jahren gearbeitet hatte. Es ist ganz deutlich eine thematische Skulptur, ein Bildwerk mit einer ganz bestimmten und ziemlich erschreckenden Persönlichkeit.«[34]

Wieder scheint LIPCHITZ entschlossen, den Einfluß der Stammeskunst herunterzuspielen: »Obwohl die Figur mit afrikanischer Skulptur in Verbindung gebracht wurde und diese Ähnlichkeit offensichtlich ist, wird mir jetzt klar, daß sie sich Schritt für Schritt aus den Entdeckungen, die ich in meinen kubistischen und nachkubistischen Skulpturen der vorangegangenen fünfzehn Jahre gemacht hatte, ergab.«

Die Figur mit ihren hypnotischen, starren Augen kommt von allen Skulpturen LIPCHITZ', die den Einfluß primitiver Kunst widerspiegeln, der dämonischen Präsenz von PICASSOS Werk in den Jahren 1907–08 am nächsten. Möglicherweise stammen die vorstehenden, zylindrischen Augen der Figur von *GREBO*-Masken der Elfenbeinküste. PICASSO besaß solche Masken ☐ 29, 417, und LIPCHITZ hatte sie sicherlich gesehen. Die Proportionen der Figur und die ineinandergreifenden Bögen des Körpers zwischen Kopf und Basis lassen sich mit der Darstellung eines Gottes von den Cookinseln im Museum of Archaeology and Ethnology in Cambridge vergleichen ☐ 608. Auch die Frontalität der Figur und der rhythmische, arabeske Aufbau der Körperkonturen durch den Wechsel von ausgehöhlten Räumen und festen Volumina erinnern deutlich an bestimmte Figuren aus Neuguinea ☐ 65.

LIPCHITZ' Anleihen bei der Kunst der Eingeborenen waren, wie später bei EPSTEIN, nur von kurzer Dauer. Daß er den Einfluß afrikanischer Kunst auf sein Werk unterschätzte, sollte weniger als Verleugnung denn als ehrliches Selbstlob verstanden werden. Obwohl die Stammeskunst in seinem künstlerischen Werk keinen nachhaltigen Eindruck hinterließ, beschrieb LIPCHITZ sein Interesse am Sammeln ihrer Werke als lebenslange »Leidenschaft«.[35] Die Ausstellung seiner Sammlung im Jahre 1960 – mit Werken aus Afrika, Ozeanien, Nord- und Südamerika[36] – im Museum of Primitive Art in New York war die verdiente Anerkennung für einen der wichtigsten Künstler-Sammler des 20. Jahrhunderts.

Als der in Amerika geborene Bildhauer JACOB EPSTEIN 1902 das erste Mal nach Paris kam, war er 22 Jahre alt und hatte schon mehrere Jahre an der Art Students League in New York studiert. Er blieb drei Jahre in Paris und studierte an der École des Beaux-Arts und der Académie Julián, wo er nach dem

☐ 613 ›*Doppelgesichtiger Kopfschmuck*‹, YORUBA *(Nigeria), Holz, Höhe 61 cm. The Metropolitan Museum of Art, Fletcher and Rogers Fund, New York.*

□ 614 *Jacob Epstein, ›Sonnenblume‹ (Sunflower), 1912–13, Stein, Höhe 58,5 cm. National Gallery of Victoria, mit freundlicher Genehmigung des Council of Trustees, Melbourne.*

Modell und nach Abgüssen von Werken MICHELANGELOS modellierte und zeichnete. Aber bald begann er den akademischen Lehrbetrieb zu verachten: »Es war das gleiche wie an allen Akademien. Die deprimierenden pseudogriechischen Arbeiten sind bekannt, deren Schöpfer die Medaillen, Auszeichnungen und ein Romstipendium bekommen.«[37] Während dieser Pariser Jahre sah er das Werk von GAUGUIN und VAN GOGH, das ihm als Alternative zur Lehre der Kunstschulen erschien. In seiner Autobiographie zählt er die Skulpturen in den Pariser Museen auf, die ihn am meisten beeindruckten. Es waren nicht die Werke der griechischen Klassik oder der italienischen Renaissance, sondern die Stammesplastik, die prähistorischen und griechisch-archaischen Skulpturen.

»Besuche im Louvre öffneten mir die Augen. Die große Schatzkammer der Gemälde und Skulpturen hielt mich tagelang in Atem . . . Bei meinen Streifzügen durch den Louvre entdeckte ich damals noch völlig unbekannte Arbeiten, die aber mittlerweile zu ihrem Recht gekommen sind – frühe griechische Arbeiten, kykladische Skulpturen, die Büste der Lady of Elche und die Kalksteinbüste Echnatons. Im Trocadéro war eine Fülle primitiver Skulpturen nicht gerade vorbildlich aufgestellt, wie es in unserem Britischen Museum immer noch der Fall ist.«[38]

Wenn EPSTEIN den Trocadéro tatsächlich während seines ersten Jahres in Paris besuchte, lernte er die Kunstwerke der Eingeborenen etwa drei Jahre vor VLAMINCK, DERAIN und MATISSE kennen. EPSTEIN erinnert sich, während seiner ersten Jahre in Paris eine Privatsammlung primitiver Kunst gesehen zu haben, aber aller Wahrscheinlichkeit nach fand dieser Besuch erst 1912 statt: »Paul Guillaume hatte gerade mit einer Sammlung afrikanischer Skulptur begonnen, die noch nicht bekannt und erst von wenigen Künstlern und Schriftstellern entdeckt war.«[39] Anders als bei PICASSO und MOORE, deren Gemälde und Skulpturen bald nach ihrer Entdeckung den Einfluß primitiver Kunst verrieten, verging ein Jahrzehnt, bevor EPSTEINS Werk den Bezug zu afrikanischer und ozeanischer Kunst erkennen ließ.

1905 beschloß EPSTEIN, sich in England niederzulassen. Er zog nach London und fand ein Atelier in Camden Town. Wenn er, wie er schrieb, noch Zweifel hegte hinsichtlich seines Entschlusses, Paris zu verlassen, »so erledigte ein Besuch im Britischen Museum die Sache für mich«.[40] In Paris, so ließ EPSTEIN verlauten, war es der Louvre, wo er seine wahre Inspiration fand, in London das Britische Museum. Er erinnerte sich:

»Mein Ziel war, mich im Modellieren, Zeichnen und in der direkten Arbeit am Stein zu vervollkommnen. Zu dieser Zeit besuchte ich das Britische Museum; immer wenn ich ein neues Werkstück gemacht hatte, verglich ich es innerlich mit dem, was ich im Museum gesehen hatte. Diese reichen Sammlungen werden selten von Bildhauern besucht. Man kann dort einen ganzen Tag verbringen, ohne einen Bildhauer zu treffen . . . Stellen Sie sich einen Dramatiker oder Dichter vor, der Shakespeare und die elisabethanischen Dichter, einen Komponisten, der Bach oder Beethoven absichtlich meidet! Etwa Anfang

□ 615 *›Reliquiarkopf‹, KOTA (Gabun), Holz und Kupfer, Höhe 22,5 cm. Privatsammlung, Paris.*

□ 616 *›Aufhängehaken‹ (siehe Glossar),* Iatmul, *Provinz Ost-Sepik (Papua-Neuguinea), Höhe 65 cm. The Metropolitan Museum of Art, M. C. Rockefeller Memorial Collection, Schenkung N. A. Rockefeller, New York.*

1910 interessierte ich mich ganz besonders für die Elgin marbles und die griechische Skulptur, später für die ägyptischen Ausstellungsräume sowie die riesigen und herrlichen Sammlungen aus Polynesien und Afrika.«[41]

Rückblickend erscheint es seltsam, daß Epstein nicht die assyrische Kunst unter der von ihm im Britischen Museum bewunderten Plastik anführte. Kurz nach der Fertigstellung seiner berühmt-berüchtigten Fassadenfiguren für das Gebäude der British Medical Association (1908) erhielt er seinen zweiten Auftrag – ein großes Grabmal für Oscar Wilde, das auf dem Friedhof Père Lachaise in Paris aufgestellt werden sollte. Dieses war wahrscheinlich Epsteins erste Arbeit, die einen direkten Einfluß außereuropäischer Kunst zeigte. Wie der Künstler schrieb, »wollten Oscar Wildes enthusiastische Bewunderer lieber einen stehenden griechischen Jüngling neben einer gebrochenen Säule«,[42] aber er entschloß sich zu einem Bruch mit europäischen Vorbildern und leitete die geflügelte, waagrechte Figur des Grabsteins (vollendet 1911) von einem der kolossalen menschenköpfigen Flügelstiere aus Assyrien im Britischen Museum ab. Innerhalb von Epsteins Werk ist das Grabmal das früheste Beispiel für sein Abweichen von der griechisch-römischen Tradition. Wie die Fassadenfiguren für die Medical Association war das Wilde-Grabmal in Stein gehauen. Die Materialwahl wurde wohl zum Teil durch das assyrische Vorbild im Britischen Museum bestimmt. Schon die Vorstudie für das Grabmal (um 1910)[43] nimmt mit ihrer unverhüllten Sexualität Epsteins höchstpersönliche Interpretation der primitiven Kunst in seinen Zeichnungen und Skulpturen ab 1913 vorweg: Die phallische Gestalt der Sphinx flüstert in das Ohr des Dichters, die Zungen des sich umarmenden Paares rechts unten laufen in einer schlangenförmigen Linie zusammen, daneben streichelt die kleinere der beiden Figuren die Brust der anderen.

Im Sommer und Herbst 1912 überwachte Epstein die Aufstellung des Oscar Wilde-Denkmals in Paris. Während dieser entscheidenden Monate wurde Epsteins erneutes Interesse an der Stammeskunst, die einen tiefen wenn auch kurzlebigen Einfluß auf sein Werk von 1913–14 ausüben sollte, sicherlich durch die Sammlungen und den Primitivismus in Plastik und Malerei der Künstler angeregt, die er zum ersten Mal in der französischen Hauptstadt traf – unter ihnen Picasso, Ortiz de Zarate, Brancusi und Modigliani. Am häufigsten kam Epstein mit Modigliani zusammen. Er schrieb: »Im Verlauf von sechs Monaten sah ich ihn täglich. Wir dachten daran, einen Schuppen auf der Butte de Montmartre zu finden, wo wir zusammen im Freien arbeiten konnten. Einen ganzen Tag verbrachten wir damit, nach einem freien Grasflecken für Hütten zu suchen, jedoch ohne Erfolg.«[44] Er besuchte Modiglianis Atelier, als sich der Italiener gerade mit seinen von

□ 617 *Jacob Epstein, ›Geburt‹ (Birth), 1913, Stein, 30 x 26 cm. Art Gallery of Ontario, Toronto.*

BAULE-Masken angeregten Skulpturen und Zeichnungen beschäftigte und sah auch die länglichen Steinköpfe, die von diesem primitiven Stil beeinflußt waren. EPSTEIN besuchte auch BRANCUSIS Atelier und sah dort sicher Werke wie *Der Kuß* von 1907, die *Schlummernde Muse* von 1910 und den *Prometheus* von 1911. Er lernte auch BRANCUSIS Einstellung gegenüber der primitiven Kunst kennen. »Zweifellos war Brancusi von afrikanischer Plastik beeinflußt, aber mir gegenüber verwahrte er sich dagegen. Man darf die Afrikaner nicht nachahmen, sagte er oft.«[45] Der Kontakt zu diesen Künstlern hatte eine Neuorientierung von EPSTEINS bildhauerischem Schaffen zur Folge. Der Besuch von 1912 zog eine kurze, aber äußerst schöpferische Phase nach sich, aus der (bis 1915) unter dem Einfluß der Stammeskunst eine sehr eigenständige Gruppe von Werken hervorging.

Während der Monate in Paris schuf EPSTEIN nur wenige Skulpturen. Er fand, daß es ihm ständige Unterbrechungen erschwerten, sich auf seine Arbeit zu konzentrieren: »Ich erinnere mich, daß ich ein Atelier gemietet hatte, wo ich mit meiner Arbeit begann. Aber kaum hatte ich damit begonnen, beschwerte sich mein Nachbar unter mir über mein Hämmern.«[46] Im Herbst 1912 entschloß er sich, Paris endgültig zu verlassen und nach England zurückzukehren.

»Ich mietete an der Küste von Sussex, an einem einsamen Ort namens Pett Level einen Bungalow, von dem aus ich auf das Meer schauen und nach Herzenslust bildhauern konnte, ohne eine Menschenseele zu stören. Hier entstanden meine *Venus,* die drei Taubengruppen, die beiden Arbeiten aus Flint und die Marmorgruppe *Mutter mit Kind.*«[47]

Nach Angaben des Bildhauers dauerte die Zeit in Pett Level drei Jahre. Damals entstand ein Komplex von Zeichnungen und Skulpturen, darunter der *Steinbohrer* □ 593, die nicht nur seine primitivistischsten Werke überhaupt sind, sondern im Rückblick auch seine wichtigsten. Dazu gehören zwei Skulpturen aus Flint, *Geburt* □ 617 sowie *Mutter mit Kind,* zwei Darstellungen der Venus in Marmor, drei Taubenskulpturen □ 621 und die Gipsfassung des *Steinbohrers,* die später in Bronze gegossen wurde □ 593.

Obwohl nicht nachzuweisen ist, daß die *Sonnenblume* □ 614 schon 1910 ausgeführt wurde, wird sie seit ihrer ersten Veröffentlichung in dieses Jahr datiert.[48] Wenn dieses Datum stimmt, ist die *Sonnenblume* das früheste (und ganz vereinzelte) Beispiel für den Einfluß der Stammeskunst auf EPSTEINS Werk. Goldwater schrieb, daß der Einfluß der FANG-Plastik »schon in *Sonnenblume* (1910) – mit ihrem langen Hals, dem ovalen Gesicht, der gebogenen Nasen- und Augenbrauenlinie und dem kleinen, fest verschlossenen Mund – erkennbar ist. Mit Rücksicht auf den Gegenstand ist der blütenblattförmige Kranz gezackter als bei den *Bieri*-Köpfen, er umgibt das Gesicht aber in der gleichen Weise.«[49]

Die Gesichtszüge der *Sonnenblume* widersprechen mehreren Beobachtungen Goldwaters. Die eingeritzten Augen sind eher isoliert als mit der Nase verbunden, und einen Mund gibt es überhaupt nicht. Trotzdem ist sein Verweis auf die FANG-Skulptur wichtig. Nach den Angaben von John Donne erwarb EPSTEIN sein erstes afrikanisches Kunstwerk von Paul Guillaume wahrscheinlich während seines Parisbesuchs von 1912.[50] Lady Epstein erzählte William Fagg, daß seine erste Erwerbung eine an den Hüften abgeschnittene FANG-Büste gewesen sei.[51] Diese Information legt die Vermutung nahe, daß die *Sonnenblume* tatsächlich nach EPSTEINS Rückkehr aus Paris, gegen Ende des Jahres 1912 oder Anfang 1913 datiert werden

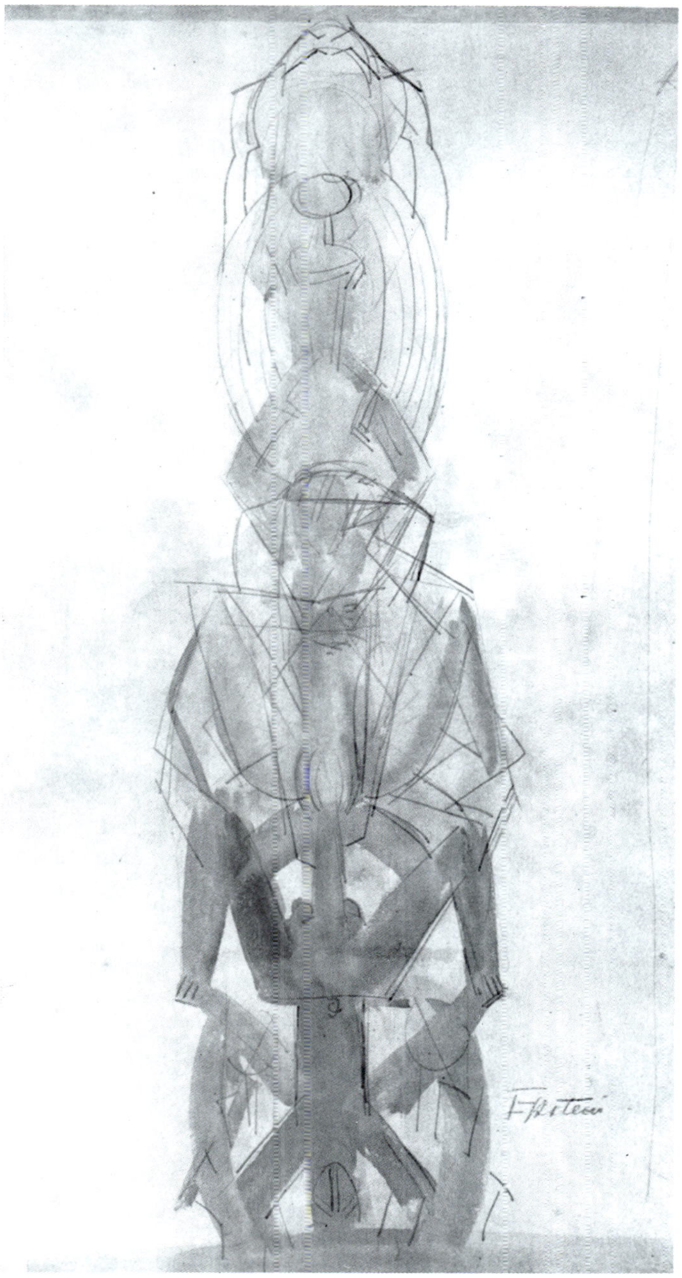

□ 618 *Jacob Epstein, ›Totem‹, um 1913, Bleistift und Lavierung, 58 x 41 cm. The Trustees of the Tate Gallery, London*

□ 619 *Holzreliefs aus Priesterwohnungen des Dorfes Koni Kombole, Zeichnung von H. Hazler nach früheren Zeichnungen von Leo Frobenius und Fritz Nansen. Veröffentlicht in Leo Frobenius, „Das unbekannte Afrika“, 1923.*

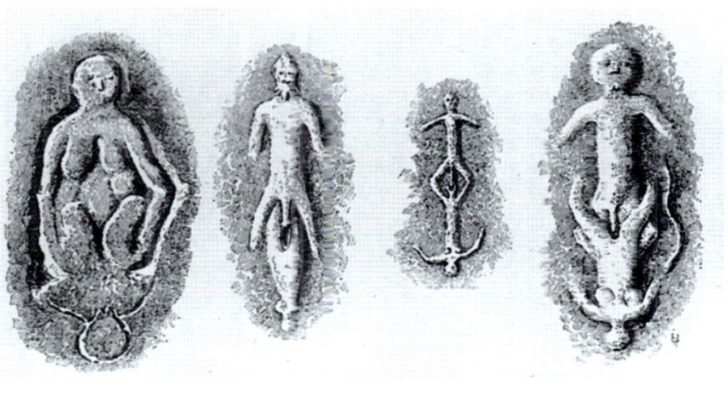

□ 620 *Jacob Epstein, ›Weibliche Figur‹ (Female Figure), 1913, Flint, Höhe 61 cm. The Minneapolis Institute of Arts, Schenkung S. H. Maslon, Ch. H. Bell, F. D. Butler, J. Cowles, B. B. Dayton und anonymer Stifter.*

könnte. Sicher besteht eine enge Verbindung zwischen dieser Arbeit und *FANG*-Kopfreliquiaren, wie dem ausgezeichneten Beispiel aus EPSTEINS eigener Sammlung □ 612.

Der zweifache Kranz aus spitzen, blütenblattartigen Formen um den Kopf der *Sonnenblume* ist für viele Stammesstile Afrikas und der pazifischen Inseln typisch: etwa für einen doppelgesichtigen *YORUBA*-Kopfschmuck □ 613, eine *BAULE*-Maske, eine Maske aus Elema am Golf von Papua (alle im Metropolitan Museum of Art). Interessant in dieser Hinsicht ist auch der ungewöhnliche Typus eines *KOTA*-Kopfreliquiars □ 615. Aus der Fülle der möglichen Vorbilder entsteht die Schwierigkeit, diesen Aspekt der *Sonnenblume* mit einem bestimmten Stammesstil in Verbindung zu bringen. Auch der Umstand, daß EPSTEIN das Blütenblattmotiv in seiner *Studie für den Steinbohrer* von 1913 in der mittleren Zeichnung oben erneut verwendete □ 633 und noch entschiedener in der Studie rechts davon ausarbeitete, läßt vermuten, daß die *Sonnenblume* ungefähr gleichzeitig und nicht schon im Jahre 1910 entstanden ist.

Fast ausnahmslos konzentrieren sich EPSTEINS Zeichnungen und Skulpturen von 1913–14 auf den Themenkreis Sexualität: Kopulation, Schwangerschaft und Geburt. Die außerordentliche Freizügigkeit, mit der EPSTEIN sexuelle und erotische Bilder darstellt, hat im frühen 20. Jahrhundert keinen Vorgänger. Sie zeugt aber von seiner Vertrautheit mit der Stammesplastik, die solche Themen zur Genüge kennt. Viele Skulpturen und Zeichnungen EPSTEINS lassen vermuten, daß ihm der unverhüllt erotische Charakter bestimmter Eingeborenenkunst Vorlagen lieferte, die er aufnahm und nach eigenen Vorstellungen zu diesen Themen umgestaltete. EPSTEIN verteidigte die offene Behandlung dieses Themas in der Stammeskunst als die natürliche Ikonographie des primitiven Rituals.

»Wenn primitive Kunstwerke das Geschlechtsprinzip ausdrücken, dann nur in einer Weise, die nicht anstößig sein kann. Erstens, weil sie offen sexuell ist, und zweitens, weil sie zu einer Haltung gehört, die nur als rituell bezeichnet werden kann. Diese bisexuellen afrikanischen Statuen sind zweifellos rituelle Werke, die das sexuelle Lebensprinzip verkörpern, sie sind in keiner Weise anstößig.«[52]

Aufgrund ihrer Nähe zu der (signierten und datierten) Zeichnung *Geburt* kann die kaum bekannte Steinskulptur mit dem gleichen Titel gewiß in das Jahr 1913 datiert werden □ 617. *Geburt* steht aufgrund des Konturs, des Reliefstils, wegen der gespreizten Beine der Mutter und der Proportionen des Kindes im Moment der Entbindung der Specksteintafel mit Relieffiguren aus Sierra Leone im Britischen Museum[53] bemerkenswert nahe. Wenn EPSTEIN dieses oder ein ähnliches Werk tatsächlich sah, so übernahm er bestimmte Merkmale – die gespreizten Beine der Figur links und das Kind in der Mitte – und ordnete diese Elemente neu an. Eine überzeugendere Quelle findet sich in ozeanischer Kunst, in der das Thema der Geburt häufiger dargestellt wird als in afrikanischer Kunst. Der figürliche Holzhaken vom Sepik ist ein gutes Beispiel □ 616. Er zeigt, wie eine Ahnenfigur einen Katzenwels gebärt.

Darstellungen der Kopulation kommen in zwei der wichtigsten und faszinierendsten Zeichnungen EPSTEINS von 1913 vor, in *Totem* □ 618 und der *Studie für den Steinbohrer* □ 633. Die totemähnliche Komposition der erstgenannten Zeichnung wird durch die ineinandergreifenden Formen von drei Figuren hergestellt. Der Mann steht während seines Eindringens in die Frau, die ein Kind über ihren Kopf hält, auf dem Kopf – ein außerordentlicher Balanceakt. EPSTEINS Totemzeichnung steht möglicherweise mit den originalen Zeichnungen nach *DOGON*-Reliefs aus Priesterhäusern des Dorfes Kani Kombole in

□ 621 *Jacob Epstein, ›Tauben‹ (Doves), um 1913, Marmor, Länge 65 cm. The Trustees of the Tate Gallery, London.*

Beziehung, die in Leo Frobenius' Buch *Das unbekannte Afrika* (München 1923) abgebildet waren □ 619.[54] Diese Skizzen von der Hand H. Hazlers basieren auf früheren Zeichnungen von Frobenius oder Fritz Nansen, die während einer deutschen Expedition im Jahre 1908 aufgenommen wurden. Auch wenn es nicht zu beweisen ist, daß EPSTEIN diese Zeichnungen kannte, sind die Ähnlichkeiten zwischen ihnen und der Totemzeichnung so auffallend, daß sie nicht zufällig sein können. In den Zeichnungen nach *DOGON*-Plastiken zeigen drei Bilder kopulierende Figuren, wobei aber immer die Frau unter dem Mann liegt. In *Totem* erinnern die Position der männlichen und weiblichen Figur und ihre schmalen, rechteckigen Körper an die dritte Illustration von Frobenius. Das Kind über dem Kopf der Mutter könnte von der oberen Figur der vierten Zeichnung der *DOGON*-Reliefs stammen. Auch die ozeanische Kunst sollte als mögliche Quelle für *Totem* in Betracht gezogen werden. Die gespreizten und dabei angezogenen Beine der Frau haben mit Arbeiten Papua-Neuguineas viel gemeinsam, etwa dem bereits erwähnten Holzhaken. Doch trotz aller Ähnlichkeiten mit der Stammeskunst ist *Totem* aufgrund der eckigen, vereinfachten geometrischen Körperformen und des hinzugefügten abstrakten Liniennetzes stilistisch dem Kubismus verwandt. Auch EPSTEINS Verbindung mit vortizistischen Künstlern, etwa WYNDHAM LEWIS, ist hier von Bedeutung. Die zwei Arbeiten in Flint, die EPSTEINS Londoner Ausstellung in der Twenty-One Gallery im Dezember 1913 präsentierte, sind die *Weibliche Figur* von 1913 □ 620 und *Weibliche Figur aus Flint* aus dem gleichen Jahr (Tate Gallery, London). Beide entstanden in Pett Level und stellen auch dasselbe Thema, eine schwangere Frau kurz vor der Geburt, dar. In seiner Zeichnung für *Weibliche Figur aus Flint* von 1913[55] ging EPSTEIN über die – in beiden Skulpturen deutlich sichtbaren – äußeren Zeichen einer fortgeschrittenen Schwangerschaft hinaus. Er stellt die Mutter dar, wie sie auf ihren riesigen, angeschwollenen Bauch sieht, in dem das Kind für die Geburt mit dem Kopf nach unten wie im Röntgenschirm zu sehen ist. In dieser Studie nehmen der gelängte Hals und Torso sowie die willkürliche Plazierung der Brüste PICASSOS erotisch besetzte, extrem verdrehte, ja zeitweise groteske Zeichnungen von Badenden in Cannes aus dem Sommer des Jahres 1927 vorweg. In EPSTEINS Zeichnung mögen die dynamischen Rundformen um die Figur die im Augenblick der Geburt geöffnete Vagina versinnbildlichen. Das Kind in der Mitte dieser Komposition ist der Strudel, den

□ 622 *›Figur aus Holz‹, Tahiti (Gesellschaftsinseln), Höhe 53 cm. The Trustees of the British Museum, London.*

WYNDHAM LEWIS so definiert hat: »Im Herzen des Strudels ist ein großer, ruhiger Ort, an dem die ganze Energie konzentriert ist. Dort im Zentrum der Konzentration befindet sich der Vortizist.«[56]

Zwei Freunde EPSTEINS, GAUDIER-BRZESKA und der Philosoph, Dichter und Kritiker T. E. Hulme, brachten die Flint-Skulpturen mit ozeanischer Kunst in Verbindung. GAUDIER, der EPSTEINS Atelier am 7. Oktober 1913 besuchte, schrieb am Tag darauf: »Er macht die außergewöhnlichsten Statuen, reine Kopien polynesischer Werke mit Nasen wie bei Brancusi.«[57] Er muß sich auf die beiden Flint-Skulpturen bezogen haben. Im Lichte von EPSTEINS späterer Bemerkung, daß es für einen europäischen Künstler absurd sei, afrikanische Idole zu ersetzen, wäre er über die Bezeichnung seiner Werke als »reine Kopien« nicht gerade erfreut gewesen. Doch die Stilmittel der weiblichen Figur – die Kopfform, die scharfen Kanten des Kinns und der Wangen, die tiefe diagonale Kerbe unter Gesicht und Hals – stehen dem Kopf einer männlichen Standfigur aus Tahiti im Britischen Museum denkbar nahe, der gut das unmittelbare Vorbild gewesen sein könnte □ 622.[58] Proportio-

□ 623 *›Schildkrötenpaar‹, Yam-Tutu-Insel, Torresstraße (Papua-Neuguinea), Holz, Höhe 9 cm. The Trustees of the British Museum, London.*

nen und Haltung der Arme, die auf dem angeschwollenen Bauch ruhen, erinnern ebenfalls stark an die Skulptur aus Tahiti. Eine der bekanntesten ozeanischen Skulpturen im Britischen Museum, die Standfigur eines Mannes von den Rurutuinseln, kommt ebenfalls als Quelle für EPSTEINS *Weibliche Figur* in Frage ☐ 465. Kopfform, Umriß und Haltung der Arme dieser Skulptur sind trotz der zahlreichen vorstehenden Figürchen der männlichen Standfigur aus Tahiti recht ähnlich.

Als diese Werke aus Flint in EPSTEINS Ausstellung von 1913 gezeigt wurden, machte sich die Presse – wie schon über die Fassadenfiguren der British Medical Association von 1908 und das Oscar Wilde-Grabmal von 1910–11 – lustig und äußerte erbitterte Kritik. Als Antwort schrieb T. E. Hulme in *The New Age* am 25. Dezember 1913 eine Rezension, in der er die Orientierung moderner Künstler an außereuropäischen Kulturen rechtfertigte. Hulme analysierte das Problem ganz philosophisch. Dem Vorwurf, daß EPSTEINS Arbeiten aus Flint vorsätzlich die Plastik der Osterinsel nachgeahmt hätten, hielt er entgegen:

»Dies scheint mir auf einer Verkennung des Wesens einer Formel zu beruhen. Da der Mensch überall der gleiche ist, gibt es Wege, in denen sich bestimmte Emotionen ausdrücken müssen und von Natur aus immer ausdrücken werden – diese müssen wir formulae nennen. Sie bilden ein stets gleichbleibendes Alphabet. Es gilt zu berücksichtigen, daß der Gebrauch dieser allgemeinen formulae nichts mit Besitz oder Mangel an Individualität seitens des Künstlers zu tun hat . . . Ausschlaggebend ist, daß bei gleicher Emotion jedes Volk gleich in welchem Jahrhundert von sich aus auf dieselben Wege kommt. Dieser Exkurs sollte anhand eines Modells verständlich machen, warum die Kritik an den Flintarbeiten zurückzuweisen ist. Der Kritiker sagt, diese seien roh, eine Mißachtung ehrwürdiger Tradition, vage Erinnerungen an dunkle Zeitalter, die vom modernen Gefühl so weit entfernt sind wie die Liebe zu den Marsmenschen. Das moderne Gefühl sei verdammt! Als wäre es jetzt nicht die Aufgabe jedes Ehrenmannes, die Welt von den kitschigen Überresten der Renaissance zu befreien.«[59]

Die Kritiker hatten völlig mißverstanden, daß für EPSTEIN wie für GAUGUIN und die Generation PICASSOS die magischen und formalen Qualitäten der primitiven Kunst eine neue Anregung waren und daß die modernen Künstler dringend der Inspiration durch die reichen und vielfältigen Bildhauertraditionen außereuropäischer und primitiver Kulturen bedurften.

In seinen drei Taubenskulpturen aus Pett Level setzte sich EPSTEINS Beschäftigung mit dem Thema der Kopulation und mit der phallischen Bildwelt fort. Während seines Parisbesuchs 1912 könnte er BRANCUSIS *Drei Pinguine* (Philadelphia Museum of Art), die wahrscheinlich 1912 entstanden, gesehen haben und von ihren ineinandergreifenden Formen angeregt worden sein. GAUDIERS Skulptur *Aufgerichtete Vögel* von 1914 wiederum könnte von EPSTEINS Taubenskulpturen beeinflußt worden sein. Es ist auch möglich, daß EPSTEIN die Anregung für seine Taubenplastiken in der Kunst der Eingeborenen fand. Wieder stehen wir den erstaunlichen, rein zufälligen Ähnlichkeiten zwischen Werken verschiedener Kulturen und Perioden gegenüber. Doch ist bei den *Tauben* ☐ 621 die symmetrische Plazierung der kleineren Taube auf dem größeren Vogel vielleicht vergleichbar mit der Skulptur zweier sich paarender Schildkröten aus Neuguinea, die 1886 vom Britischen Museum

☐ 624 *›Weibliche Sitzfigur‹, DOGON (Mali), Holz, Höhe 69 cm. Privatsammlung. Ehemals Sammlung Jacob Epstein.*

□ 625 *›Reliquiarfigur‹ (Seiten- und Vorderansicht),* Fang *(Gabun), Holz, Höhe 70 cm. Privatsammlung. Ehemals Sammlung Jacob Epstein.*

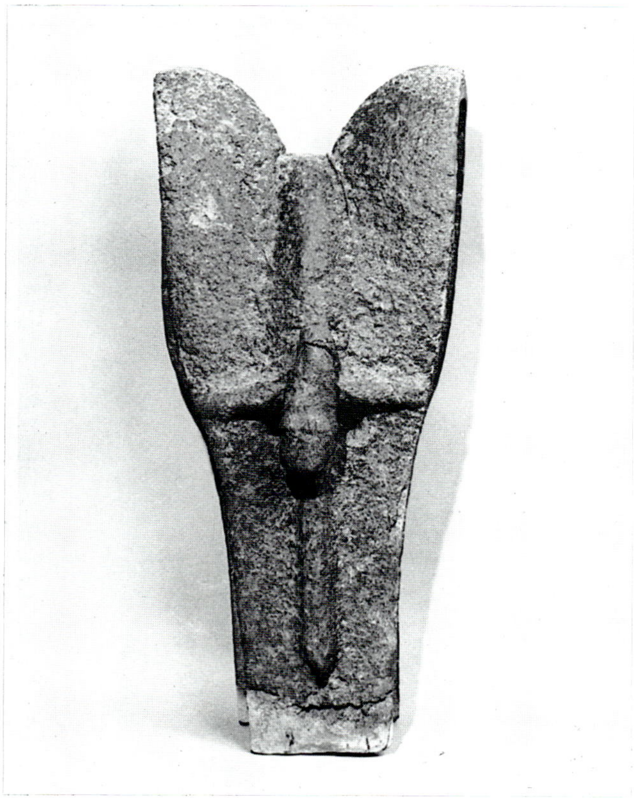

☐ 627 *›Kono-Maske‹,* BAMBARA *(Mali), Höhe 72 cm. Musée Picasso, Paris. Ehemals Sammlung Pablo Picasso.*

☐ 626 *›Reliquiarkopf‹,* FANG *(Gabun), Holz, Höhe 46 cm. The Metropolitan Museum of Art, M. C. Rockefeller Memorial Collection, Vermächtnis N. A. Rockefeller. Ehemals Sammlung Jacob Epstein.*

☐ 628 *›Affe‹, Detail,* BAULE *(Elfenbeinküste), Holz, Höhe 72 cm. Musée Africain, Lyon.*

erworben wurde ☐ 623. Obwohl wir es, wie so oft, nicht nachweisen können, ob EPSTEIN diese neuguineische Figur kannte, deuten die stilistischen und ikonographischen Ähnlichkeiten darauf hin, daß EPSTEINS Werk dieser ozeanischen Skulptur zumindest die Anregung verdankt.

Die Marmorgruppe *Mutter mit Kind* von 1913 ist eine von EPSTEINS bekanntesten Skulpturen aus der Zeit in Pett Level ☐ 629. Wie auch LIPCHITZ' Bronze *Mutter mit Kind* aus dem gleichen Jahr ☐ 604 könnte der vereinfachte Kopf des Kindes, dessen Gesichtszüge nur aus den eingeritzten Linien für Nase und Augen bestehen, erneut den Einfluß BRANCUSIS widerspiegeln – den seiner Kinderstudien, besonders des *Prometheus* von 1911 (Philadelphia Museum of Art), der bis zum Ankauf durch den großen amerikanischen Sammler John Quinn 1919 im Atelier des Künstlers blieb. Der leicht konkave Kopf der Mutter erinnert an mehrere afrikanische Stammesstile, möglicherweise an den der *SENUFO*, wahrscheinlicher aber noch an den der *FANG*.

Wie schon erwähnt, erzählte Lady Epstein William Fagg, daß das erste von ihrem Mann erworbene Werk primitiver Kunst eine *FANG*-Skulptur gewesen sei. Er besaß auch das berühmte Kopfreliquiar der *FANG*, das sich jetzt im Metropolitan Museum of Art befindet ☐ 626.

Die größten Skulpturen aus Pett Level waren die zwei Darstellungen der Venus in Marmor. Nach Berichten der Yale University Art Gallery, wo die eine Venus ausgestellt ist (die andere befindet sich im Baltimore Museum of Art), wurde die zweite, schlanker proportionierte Venus in Pett Level begonnen, aber nicht vor 1917 vollendet. Die Themen dieser Werke sind Schwangerschaft und Kopulation. Der Triumph der Venus als solcher ist ein klassisches Thema, bei dessen Darstellung die Göttin der Liebe in ihrem von Tauben oder Schwänen gezogenen Wagen thront. In EPSTEINS afrikanisch beeinflußter Interpretation steht die Venus auf kopulierenden Tauben. In den Vorstudien (1914–15) zu der zweiten Venus stammen die spitzen, hängenden Brüste sicherlich aus der Stammeskunst – wobei viele Vorbilder in Frage kommen – als auch aus der klassischen Tradition. William Fagg verglich die S-Kurve des Körpers mit der DOGON-Kultfigur im Musée de l'Homme, Paris.[60] Über die beiden Venusdarstellungen schrieb Robert Goldwater:

»Die Konturen der plumpen Gesichter, obwohl ohne Gesichtszüge, und die überlangen Hälse erinnern wieder einmal an Fang-Plastik. Die schweren Beine, die so gebogen sind, daß die Figur fast zu knien scheint, sind hingegen wie Gaudiers *Kobold* afrikanischen Arbeiten entlehnt. Die afrikanische

□ 629 *Jacob Epstein, ›Mutter mit Kind‹ (Mother and Child), 1913, Marmor, 44 × 43 cm. The Museum of Modern Art, Stiftung A. Conger Goodyear, New York.*

□ 630 *Jacob Epstein, ›Der Steinbohrer‹ (Ansicht des Kopfes), Gesamtansicht* □ *593.*

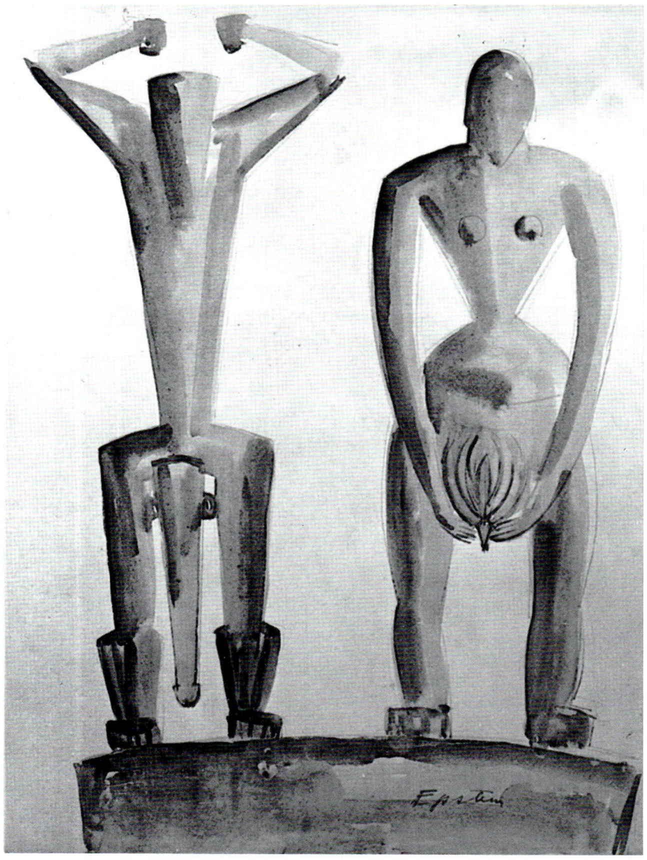

□ 631 *Jacob Epstein, ›Studie für Mann und Frau‹ (Study for Man and Woman), nach 1920, Bleistift und Lavierung, 61 x 41 cm. The Trustees of the British Museum, London.*

Holzplastik vom Sudan bis zum Kongo kennt ganz allgemein diese ungleichgewichtige Betonung der Beine und Füße. Andere moderne Bildhauer setzen dieses Stilmittel ein, weil es die Gesamtmasse der Figuren eint und festigt.«[61]

EPSTEINS fraglos wichtigste Skulptur, *Der Steinbohrer* von 1913–14 □ 593, wurde am Ende dieser kurzen Periode, in der seine Kunst entschieden durch primitive Kunst beeinflußt war, vollendet. Der Künstler selbst beschrieb die Skulptur folgendermaßen:

»Es war während der experimentierfreudigen Vorkriegstage von 1913, daß es mich dazu trieb, den *Steinbohrer* zu machen. Meine (kurzlebige) Begeisterung für maschinelle Dinge äußerte sich in der Anschaffung eines echten, gebraucht gekauften Bohrers. Aufgrund dessen schuf ich diese Konstruktion eines maschinenähnlichen Roboters mit einem Visier vor dem Gesicht, der bedrohlich ausschaute und seine Nachkommenschaft in sicherer Geborgenheit in sich trug. Das ist die wehrhafte, unheilvolle Person von heute und morgen. Keine Menschlichkeit, nur das schreckliche Frankensteinmonster, zu dem wir uns selbst gemacht haben. Ich stellte dieses Werk, das ganz aus Gips war, bei der London Group aus. Ich erinnere mich auch, daß Gaudier-Brzeska ganz begeistert war, als er 1913 mit Ezra Pound in mein Atelier kam, um es sich anzusehen.«[62]

Ich glaube, Richard Cork sieht den *Steinbohrer* ganz falsch, wenn er ihn als Signal für EPSTEINS »endgültige Ablehnung der primitiven Vorbilder zugunsten einer originelleren und herausfordernden Alternative«[63] betrachtet. Auch Goldwater unterschätzt den afrikanischen Einfluß in dieser Skulptur: »Sie ist Epsteins vortizistischstes Werk und zeigt keinerlei primitive Annäherung, allenfalls in der suggestiven Tiermaske des bedeckten Gesichts.«[64] Das letztere ist durchaus kein unwesentlicher Aspekt des Werks. William Rubin sah eine Verbindung von EPSTEINS Kopf mit Schweißermasken, bestimmten Affenköpfen der *BAULE* □ 628 sowie mit einer Kono-Maske der *BAMBARA* in PICASSOS Sammlung □ 627, die EPSTEIN vielleicht kannte. Dessenungeachtet übernahm EPSTEIN erstmals mit dem *Steinbohrer* für kurze Zeit die Ikonographie des Maschinenzeitalters, womit er vielleicht einer Idee seines Freundes T. E. Hulme folgte, der auf die Entwicklung einer »neuen geometrischen und monumentalen Kunst mit technischen Formen« drängte.[65]

Die zahlreichen Vorstudien für den *Steinbohrer* bestätigen, daß sich EPSTEIN tatsächlich nicht ganz von der Eingeborenenkunst freigemacht hatte. Es gibt mehr Vorzeichnungen für diese Skulptur als für irgendeine andere aus dieser Periode. Diese Zeichnungen veranschaulichen die Entwicklung und die komplexe Umarbeitung der ursprünglichen Ideen, von denen manche mit früheren primitivistischen Arbeiten, etwa der Zeichnung *Totem* oder der *Sonnenblume*, verbunden sind. Eine der Zeichnungen für den *Steinbohrer* □ 633, wahrscheinlich die früheste, bildet das Zwischenglied zwischen dem Primitivismus von EPSTEINS Frühwerk und den technischen Formen, die für den *Steinbohrer* kennzeichnend sind. Die rechte Skizze des Blattes zeigt eine nahezu abstrakte Figur über dem aufrechten Bohrer. Pavian und Figur sind von spitzen Formen umgeben (wie auch der Kopf in der mittleren Studie), die stark an die *Sonnenblume* erinnern. Die Skizze in der Mitte

□ 632 *›Figuren von einem Begräbnispfahl‹, Madagaskar, Holz, Höhe 101 cm. Privatsammlung. Ehemals Sammlung Jacob Epstein.*

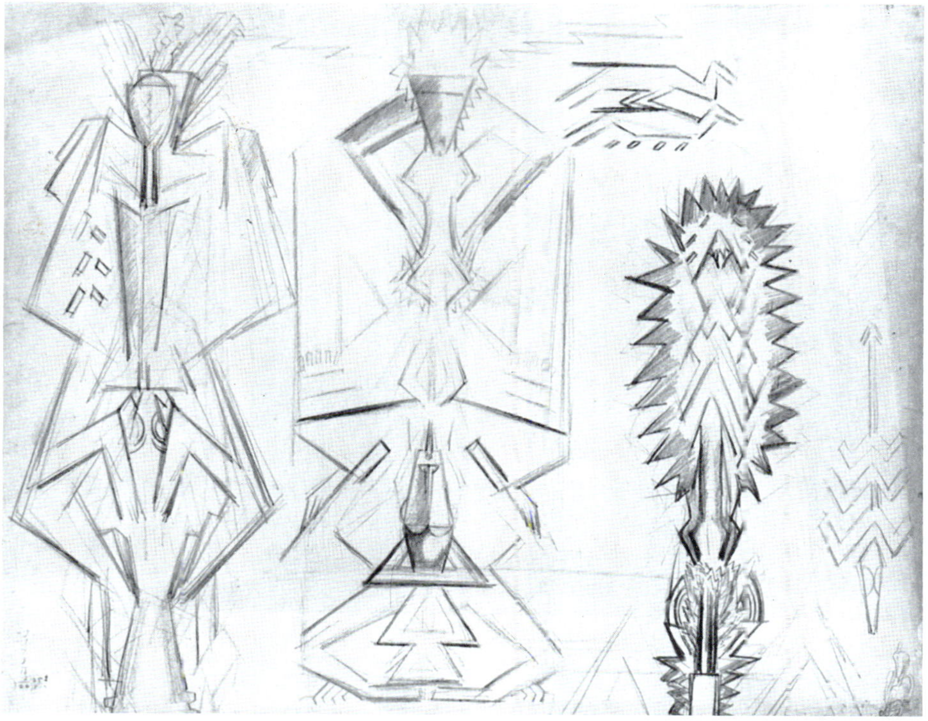

□ 633 *Jacob Epstein, ›Studie für den Steinbohrer‹ (Study for the Rock Drill), um 1913, Bleistift, rote und schwarze Kreide, 46 x 58 cm. Anthony d'Offay Gallery, London.*

□ 635 *›Spatel‹, Detail, Trobriandinseln, Provinz Milne Bay (Papua-Neuguinea), Holz mit Leim, Gesamthöhe 36 cm. Privatsammlung.*

◁ □ 634 *›Figur aus Holz‹, Tabwa (Zaire), Höhe 62 cm. Privatsammlung. Ehemals Sammlung Jacob Epstein.*

zeigt ein kopulierendes Paar – der Mann befindet sich wie in der Totemzeichnung unten, die Frau oben. Ein technoider, an einen Bohrer erinnernder Phallus dringt gerade in die große, dreieckige Vagina ein.

Wenigstens in diesen frühen Entwicklungsstadien des *Steinbohrers* hat sich Epstein erneut des Kopulationsthemas bedient, aber jetzt mit menschlichen wie auch technischen Formen dargestellt. In dieser Zeichnung scheint Epstein erfolglos zu versuchen, sich von den Vorbildern der Primitiven – zugunsten der Ästhetik des Maschinenzeitalters, die Hulme propagiert hatte – zu befreien. Der dreieckige Kopf der Frau in der mittleren Skizze nimmt ziemlich genau die Kopfform des *Steinbohrers* vorweg. Der Kopf des Mannes darunter ist aber offensichtlich afrikanischer Kunst verpflichtet. Affenmasken der *Senufo* und/oder *Baule* sind die wahrscheinlichen Vorbilder. Die Kopfform erinnert an *Senufo*-Masken in der Art der Tanzmaske, die sich früher in der Sammlung von Charles Ratton befand.[66] Die Form der Nase und Nasenflügel sowie der Spitzbart sind mit einer *Baule*-Tanzmaske aus der gleichen Sammlung, die einst Ratton gehörte, vergleichbar.[67]

In den zwei folgenden Zeichnungen mit einem ganzfigurigen Mann, der einen Bohrer hält,[68] ist die erotische Ausstrahlung in dem mächtigen, phallischen Bild des Bohrers enthalten. In diesen Studien hat sich Epstein – vom Kopf abgesehen – von der Stammeskunst freigemacht – Bohrer und Penis scheinen in Epsteins Vorstellung fast synonym zu sein.

Vielleicht kann eine andere Eigentümlichkeit des *Steinbohrers* bis zu einer primitiven Vorlage zurückverfolgt werden. Die hervorstehende und doch geschützte Fötusform der Skulptur mag Epsteins eigene Erfindung sein, sie könnte aber auch auf primitive Plastik, etwa einen Holzspatel von den Trobriandinseln (Melanesien), zurückgehen □ 635, der ein von den Armen und Beinen des Vaters umschlossenes Kind zeigt.

Epsteins Zeichnung *Studie für Mann und Frau* □ 631 ist in die Jahre 1913–15 datiert worden. Dies aufgrund der Annahme, daß sie einer unvollendeten Skulptur mit dem Titel *Mann und Frau* vorausgegangen sein könnte, die in einem

Telegramm von EPSTEINS Frau an John Quinn vom 25. Juni 1916 erwähnt ist.[69] Wenn man den außerordentlich großen, grotesken Penis betrachtet, ist man auch versucht, diese Zeichnung der mittleren Skizze von EPSTEINS Studie für den *Steinbohrer* von 1913 zuzuordnen, in der der Bohrer – ein Surrogat für Penis – ähnlich überproportioniert ist. Mehrere Gründe sprechen allerdings für eine spätere Entstehung der *Studie für Mann und Frau*. Zunächst entspricht die ausgefeilte Aquarelltechnik mehr EPSTEINS späteren Werken. Weit wichtiger ist aber die Verwandtschaft zu dem Grabpfosten aus Madagaskar ☐ 632, den EPSTEIN kurz nach 1923 oder 1924 erwarb.[70] Bestimmte Merkmale der Zeichnung – der dem *Steinbohrer* ähnliche Kopf des Mannes, der eckige Torso und die ungeheuer großen männlichen und weiblichen Geschlechtsteile – sind EPSTEINS eigene Erfindung. Doch die steifen, symmetrischen Beine der Figuren, die Haltung, in der der Mann links und die Frau rechts auf einer Basis stehen, ist der Haltung des Mannes und der Frau auf dem Grabpfosten aus Madagaskar so ähnlich, daß EPSTEIN diese Zeichnung wohl erst nach dem Erwerb dieses Kunstwerks ausführte. Mit Ausnahme weniger späterer Werke, die primitiven Einfluß zeigen – *Genesis* (1930), *Besessene Frau* (1932), *Urzeitlicher Gott* (1933), *Ecce Homo* (1934) und *Adam* (1938) –, widmete sich EPSTEIN für den Rest seiner Schaffenszeit vorrangig großen Figurendarstellungen und Porträts, darunter für viele seiner berühmtesten Zeitgenossen, die er in der Tradition von RODIN in Ton modellierte.

EPSTEIN arbeitete während dieser Periode als einsamer Künstler. Er nahm Anregungen des Kubismus, Vortizismus und der Stammeskunst auf, war aber nie von einer dieser Gruppen oder Bewegungen doktrinär abhängig. EPSTEINS Zeichnungen und Skulpturen von 1913–14 strahlen eine freizügige und oft gewalttätige Sexualität aus, die sie von den Werken anderer wichtiger Künstler unterscheidet, die Anfang des Jahrhunderts primitivistisch arbeiteten. Nur GAUDIER scheint während dieser Jahre EPSTEINS erotische Faszination in gewisser Weise zu teilen (siehe unten).

Jahre nach der Entstehung seiner primitivistischen Arbeiten erläuterte EPSTEIN das Wesen eingeborener Kunst und ihren Einfluß auf sein Werk. Über afrikanische Kunst sagte er: »Zunächst muß man sich bei der Betrachtung von Negerskulpturen darüber klar sein, daß sie von der ganzen übrigen Kunst nicht völlig getrennt ist. Es herrschen die gleichen Überlegungen wie bei jeder anderen Plastik. In jeder guten Bildhauerschule gibt es bestimmte Werte, die über das Interesse am dargestellten Objekt hinausreichen.«[71]

Aus formaler Sicht stellte EPSTEIN fest, »daß die Hauptmerkmale der Negerkunst Vereinfachung der Formen und Direktheit sind, die Vereinfachung von Naturalismus und Konstruktion sowie ihre erstaunlichen tektonischen Qualitäten«.[72] Er betonte, daß die afrikanische Kunst zwar »einem durch Stammessitten festgelegten Schema nicht restlos unterworfen ist . . der Künstler sich aber gewiß bis zu einem gewissen Grad daran gebunden fühlt, wie auch der Renaissancekünstler, wenn er eine Heilige Familie malte«.[73] Obwohl wir die Namen der Bildhauer nicht kennen, »sind die besten Beispiele afrikanischer Kunst die Werke äußerst individueller Künstler mit einer ganz persönlichen Einstellung und Technik. Ich kann aus meiner Sammlung Stücke benennen, von denen ich sicher bin, daß sie das Werk eines bestimmten Künstlers sind.«[74]

☐ 636 *›Fetischfigur‹, KUGNI (Volksrepublik Kongo), Holz und Eisen, Höhe 49 cm. Sammlung Max Granick. Ehemals Sammlung Jacob Epstein.*

EPSTEIN war sich auch der religiösen und zeremoniellen Funktionen der Stammeskunst bewußt. »Als Fetische haben sie eine religiöse oder zumindest magische Bedeutung. Sie wurden benutzt, um zu beeindrucken, zu erschrecken und den Betrachter in einen Bewußtseinszustand zu versetzen, der halluzinatorisch war oder daran angrenzte.«[75]

In seinen Schriften diskutierte EPSTEIN ausführlich die problematische Frage, wie der Einfluß primitiver Kunst auf sein Werk zu verstehen sei:

»Ich bin von der afrikanischen Kunst in der gleichen Weise beeinflußt, wie jedes primitive Werk einen Künstler beeinflussen muß. Afrikanische Kunst hat bestimmte, wichtige Erkenntnisse zu vermitteln, die bis zu den Wurzeln aller Plastik reichen. Ich habe versucht, diese Erkenntnisse aufzunehmen, ohne in der afrikanischen Formensprache zu arbeiten. Es ist für einen europäischen Künstler unserer Zeit geradezu absurd, afrikanische Idole zu machen, und jede Imitation wäre auch unaufrichtig.«[76]

EPSTEIN führt aus, daß die Sensibilität des europäischen Künstlers Einflüsse absorbiert und umwandelt, so daß er unverwechselbar eigenständige Werke hervorbringt.

»Das Wort ›Einfluß‹, wie ich es verstehe, meint mehr als ein bloß oberflächliches Studium; es meint ein völliges Begreifen von Geist und Technik, die in die Komposition eingehen, und deren Umsetzung entsprechend der Persönlichkeit des Künstlers. Letztlich eine völlige Neuschaffung durch einen neuen Geist.«[77]

In der Geschichte der englischen Skulptur des 20. Jahrhunderts waren EPSTEIN und – in einem geringeren Ausmaß – GAUDIER-BRZESKA Pioniere. MOORE und CARO erkannten EPSTEINS Bedeutung als Bildhauer an. In einer Würdigung in der *Sunday Times* vom 23. August des Jahres 1959 schrieb MOORE rückblickend über EPSTEIN: ». . . Er ertrug die Beschimpfungen und Beleidigungen, er stellte sich dem Spottgeschrei, an das sich die Künstler seit Rembrandt gewöhnt haben. Und was die Skulptur dieses Jahrhunderts angeht, so nahm er all das als erster auf sich.«

So wichtig EPSTEINS eigene primitivistische Werke auch sind, so wurden sie doch in gewissem Sinne durch den Ruhm seiner Sammlung primitiver Kunst überschattet. Über die Jahre baute er eine der erlesensten und umfassendsten Sammlungen nicht nur der Kunst Afrikas, Ozeaniens und der amerikanischen Nordwestküste auf, sondern auch der Plastik vieler anderer Kulturen wie Mexikos, Perus, Ägyptens, Griechenlands, Roms und Chinas. 1960 wurde seiner Sammlung in der Ausstellung des Art Council of Great Britain »The Epstein Collection of Tribal and Exotic Sculpture« die verdiente Anerkennung zuteil. Die Einleitung zum Katalog schrieb William Fagg. In dieser Ausstellung waren auch ein *FANG*-Kopf ☐ 612, eine *TABWA*-Figur ☐ 634 und ein wahrscheinlich neuseeländisches Tiki ☐ 642 zu sehen.[78] Im Augenblick arbeiten Mr. M. D. McLeod, Kustos im Museum of Mankind, London, und Professor Ezio Bassani an einem Katalog der EPSTEIN-Sammlung, deren Stücke seit dem Tod des Bildhauers über die Welt verstreut sind.

William Faggs Bericht über EPSTEIN und seine Sammlung bietet eine Art Epigramm von EPSTEINS eigener Erfahrung mit dem Entstehungsprozeß einer Skulptur: »Aus dieser Fundgrube pflegte er abends einige Stücke herunterzubringen und Stunden in stiller Kontemplation oder angeregter Diskussion darüber zu verbringen. Dabei beschäftigten ihn immer bildhauerische Probleme, die sich ein Künstler selbst stellt oder die

□ 637 *Henri Gaudier-Brzeska, ›Caritas‹, 1914, Bleistift, 46 x 31 cm. Kettle's Yard, University of Cambridge.*

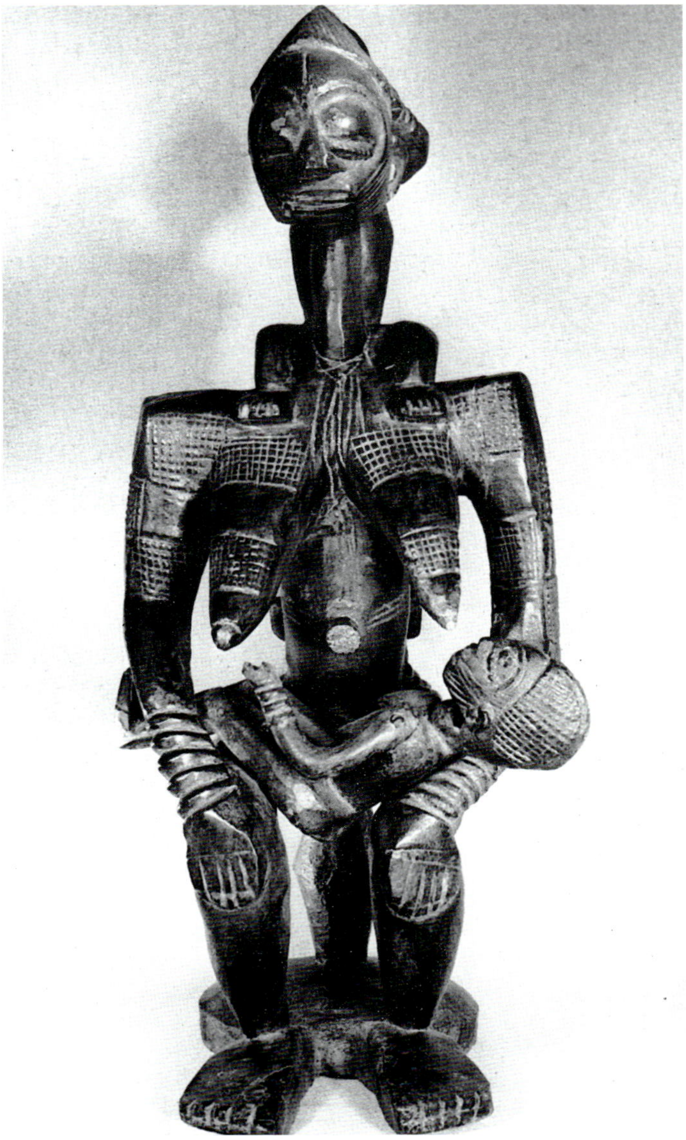

□ 638 *›Mutter mit Kindern‹, Afo (Nigeria), Holz, Höhe 70 cm. The Horniman Museum, London.*

ihm von der Tradition gestellt werden, und die Lösungsmöglichkeiten die er dafür fand.«[79]

»Der moderne Bildhauer«, schrieb Henri Gaudier-Brzeska, »ist ein Mann, der seinen Instinkt als inspirierende Kraft benutzt. Sein Werk ist emotional. Die Form eines Beines oder die Linie einer Augenbraue usw. sind für ihn völlig ohne Belang, leichtes, genußvolles Modellieren ist für ihn wertlos – was er fühlt, fühlt er intensiv, und seine Arbeit ist nichts mehr und nichts weniger als die Abstraktion von diesem intensiven Gefühl, mit dem Ergebnis, daß leblose Menschen wie Auceps über solches Schaffen in Schrecken geraten. Daß diese Skulptur mit der griechischen Klassik nichts mehr zu tun hat, daß sie aber die Tradition der barbarischen Völker der Erde fortsetzt (für die wir Sympathie und Bewunderung hegen), habe ich hoffentlich klargemacht.«[80]

Diese leidenschaftliche Darstellung der Rolle und Aufgaben des modernen Bildhauers stammt von einem Künstler, der innerhalb kürzester Zeit Wesentliches zum Primitivismus in der Skulptur des frühen 20. Jahrhunderts beitrug. Gaudier-Brzeskas Darlegung behandelt zentrale Fragen, die ihn genauso wie seine Zeitgenossen Epstein, Brancusi, Modigliani und in den 20er Jahren Moore beschäftigten: die Ablehnung des klassischen Schönheitsideals; die Freiheit zu einer Skulptur, die auf intensiven Gefühlen beruht und nicht um anatomische Genauigkeit ringt; der Verzicht auf das Modellieren zugunsten des direkten Arbeitens am Stein; die Identifikation mit der emotionalen Kraft der Stammeskunst.

Henri Gaudier wurde am 4. Oktober 1891 in Saint-Jean-de-Braye bei Orléans geboren. Nach Auskunft seines Freundes Horace Brodsky »erbte er seine bildhauerische Begabung von seinem Vater, . . . einem gewerbsmäßigen Schnitzer und Tischler. Es ist auch interessant zu erwähnen, daß seine Vorfahren einige der Figuren der Kathedrale von Chartres meißelten. Er war stolz, daß er aus einer Familie von Stein- und Holzbildhauern stammte.«[81] Gaudier hatte zwischen 1906 und 1908 einige Zeit in England verbracht, studierte Betriebswirtschaft in Bristol und arbeitete später in den Büros eines Kohlenimporteurs in Cardiff. Familiäre und persönliche Probleme, die aus seiner Beziehung zu einer 20 Jahre älteren Polin, Sophie Brzeska, herrührten (deren Nachnamen er seinem eigenen hinzufügte), und die Tatsache, daß er gegen seinen Willen zum Militärdienst eingezogen werden sollte, bewogen ihn zu dem Entschluß, Paris Ende 1910 oder Anfang 1911 zu verlassen und nach England zu ziehen, wo er dann bis zum Herbst 1914 blieb. Er kehrte also der französischen Hauptstadt zu dem Zeitpunkt den Rücken, als sie immer noch die Heimat der Künstler war, die ihn am meisten beeinflußten – RODIN und MAILLOL –, und auch derjenigen, die er künftig bewundern sollte – MODIGLIANI, BRANCUSI und ARCHIPENKO. Es blieb zum größten Teil seinem englischen Freund EPSTEIN überlassen, der 1912 Paris besuchte, GAUDIER über die neuesten Entwicklungen in seiner Heimat zu unterrichten.

GAUDIERS Bewunderung für RODIN ist in einer Reihe seiner frühen Werke sichtbar; Skulpturen wie *Kopf eines Schwachsinnigen* und *Ringer,* beide aus dem Jahre 1912, wurden zweifellos durch den großen französischen Bildhauer angeregt. Genauso wie sich BRANCUSI der beengenden Wirkung einer so kraftvollen Persönlichkeit wie RODIN bewußt war – »Im Schatten großer Bäume kann nichts wachsen«[82] – hütete sich auch GAUDIER trotz seiner Bewunderung vor einem Wettstreit. So schrieb er am 1. Januar 1910:

»Wir werden nie einen größeren Bildhauer als Rodin erleben, der sich bei dem Versuch, Phidias zu übertreffen, verausgabte . . . Rodin ist für Frankreich, was Michelangelo für Florenz war. Er wird Nachahmer aber niemals Rivalen haben . . . Solche Männer lassen durch ihre überragende Persönlichkeit eine Nation ausbluten und überlassen anderen nur die Alternative der Imitation oder Verehrung.«[83]

Auch die ruhigen, fülligen Akte MAILLOLS prägten den jungen GAUDIER, was in Skulpturen wie der Grabfigur in der Tate Gallery zu erkennen ist. Ezra Pound, sein berühmter Freund und Biograph, überliefert GAUDIERS spätere Ablehnung der beiden französischen Bildhauer:

»Gaudier selbst spricht irgendwo über die übliche ›Rodin-Maillol-Mischung‹. Die Beimischung Rodins entfernte er aus seinem Stil, als er mit den repräsentativen Büsten von Frank Harris und Col Smithers aufhörte. Ich glaube, Maillol kam als nächster an die Reihe.«[84]

Die romantische, exotische Persönlichkeit GAUGUINS machten wie sein Werk auf GAUDIER großen Eindruck, obwohl er den Künstler in seinen Schriften nicht erwähnt. GAUDIERS Freund Brodsky beschreibt jedoch ein Gemälde, das vielleicht durch die polynesischen Bilder des französischen Malers angeregt wurde:

»Bei meinem nächsten Besuch bemerkte ich, daß [Gaudier] eine tropische Phantasielandschaft in glühenden Farben mit trübem rotem Himmel und exotischen palmähnlichen Bäumen angefangen hatte – alles sehr gauguinesk. Auch das mißfiel ihm und wurde später aufgegeben. Die Leinwand wurde mit einer dünnen Gipsschicht überzogen, in die er zwei kämpfende Figuren einritzte.«[85]

GAUDIER muß die Werke GAUGUINS gekannt haben, weil er während jener Jahre in London war, als Fry und andere die britische Öffentlichkeit mit der Kunst GAUGUINS, MANETS, CÉZANNES, VAN GOGHS, REDONS, SEURATS, MATISSE' und PICASSOS bekannt machten. Abgesehen von dem von Brodsky beschriebenen Gemälde scheint GAUDIERS Werk in keiner Weise von GAUGUIN beeinflußt zu sein. Doch scheint sich GAUDIER GAUGUINS Persönlichkeit zum Vorbild genommen zu haben, als er sich nach einem tropischen Paradies sehnte und es liebte, sich als Wilder zu verkleiden. Laut Brodsky »sprach er ständig von ›wild‹ und ›barbarisch‹ und schwärmte von dem feinen und erotischen Leben in der Südsee«.[86] Während seiner kurzen ereignisreichen Freundschaft mit dem Kritiker Middleton Murry und der neuseeländischen Schriftstellerin Katherine Mansfield »sprachen sie davon, zusammen auf einer pazifischen Insel zu leben«.[87] Brodsky bezeugt auch GAUDIERS ziemlich theatralische Einfälle zum Primitiven:

»Er wollte seine Nase gerne mit einem 10 cm langen Stock durchstechen, um ihn wie ein Südseeinsulaner mit Glocken zu behängen. Er wünschte sich lange, wunderliche Ohrringe und fertigte sich tatsächlich nach Art der Maori ☐ 622 ein großes Amulett aus grünem Stein, das er um den Hals trug. Dieses Zeichen wurde auch auf dem Einband von Pounds Buch eingeprägt.«[88]

EPSTEIN, den GAUDIER im Juni 1912 in London kennenlernte, brachte ihn dazu, direkt am Stein zu arbeiten. Die erste Arbeit EPSTEINS, die GAUDIER sah, war das assyrisch inspirierte Steingrabmal für Oscar Wilde, das er in einem Brief an Dr. Uhlmayr vom 18. Juni 1912 skizzierte:

»Ein russischer [sic] Bildhauer namens Jacob Epstein arbeitet auch hier, er hat gerade ein Grab, einen Sarkophag, für Oscar Wilde in Paris vollendet. Das Ding soll im nächsten Juli auf dem Père Lachaise aufgestellt werden. Ich sah es letzten Sonntag in seinem Atelier – Oscar Wilde fliegt langsam, mit geschlossenen Augen in den Raum hinaus. Das ganz Werk – durch Ausdruck und Wahl der künstlerischen Mittel mit überzeugender, kraftvoller Bewegung und zartem Gefühlsausdruck erfüllt – ist ein Stück Skulptur, das die Zeit überdauern wird – nur der Gesamteffekt scheint zu gering.«[89]

Später behauptete EPSTEIN, daß GAUDIER nach seinem ersten Besuch »anfing, sich mit der Bildhauerei zu beschäftigen, nachdem er die Arbeiten in meinem Atelier bewundert hatte«.[90]

☐ 639 *Henri Gaudier-Brzeska, Zwei Männer mit Schüssel, 1914, Bronze, Höhe 30,5 cm. Kettle's Yard, University of Cambridge.*

Epstein förderte auch Gaudiers Interesse an primitiver Kunst. Dieselbe Wirkung hatten Gaudiers Besuche im Britischen Museum. In seinem Brief an Sophie vom 28. November 1912 (geschrieben, bevor er Epsteins primitivistische Skulpturen von 1913 sah) gestand er, in einem Übergangsstadium zu sein. Er versuchte seine Bewunderung für die Kunst der Eingeborenen mit den Errungenschaften der europäischen Plastik von den Griechen bis zu Rodin in Einklang zu bringen:

»Heute Nachmittag ging ich ins Britische Museum. Ich schaute mir besonders alle die primitiven Skulpturen an – der schwarzen, gelben, roten und weißen Rassen, gotische und griechische Skulpturen. Ich freue mich sagen zu können, daß ich schließlich von einer Sache, die mich seit langem beschäftigt hatte, überzeugt war. Ich war mir nie sicher, ob die höchst konventionelle Formgebung der Primitiven, die – immer mit großer, auf ein einziges Ziel ausgerichteter Bewegung – mir einen enormen Eindruck gelassener Freude oder übertriebenen Schmerzes vermittelt, nicht ein wahreres Verständnis der Natur aus größerer Einheitserfahrung besitzt: in anderen Worten, weiter und reicher ist als die moderne Skulptur . . . bis zu Rodin und den zeitgenössischen Franzosen. Nachdem ich beide Aspekte sorgfältig geprüft habe, glaube ich im Moment, daß dies nicht der Fall ist.«[91]

In diesem frühen Stadium seiner künstlerischen Entwicklung fand er aber, daß »mich die primitive Skulptur, wenn ich mir viel davon anschaue, langweilt, während mich die moderne europäische Skulptur, wenn ich mir genauso viel davon anschaue, unendlich interessiert«.[92] In seinen Skulpturen vom Anfang des Jahres 1913 hatte Gaudier mit Werken wie *Weiblicher Torso, Meerjungfrau, Der Ringer* und *Die Tänzerin* ganz offensichtlich noch nicht mit der Tradition Rodins gebrochen.

Zweifellos beschleunigte das Beispiel von Epsteins primitivistischen Skulpturen aus dem Jahr 1913 Gaudiers Befreiung von der griechisch-römischen Tradition und dem Einfluß Rodins und Maillols. Am 8. Oktober 1913 schrieb Gaudier

□ 640 *Henri Gaudier-Brzeska, ›Türklopfer‹, 1914, Bronze, ursprünglich Messingguß, Höhe 17 cm. Musée National d'Art Moderne, Centre National d'Art et de Culture Georges Pompidou, Paris.*

□ 641 *Henri Gaudier-Brzeska, ›Amulett‹, 1914, Stein, Höhe 10 cm. Privatsammlung.*

an Sophie über einen Besuch bei Epstein am Vortage. Epstein stelle »ganz außergewöhnliche Skulpturen her, reinste Kopien polynesischer Werke mit Nasen wie bei Brancusi«, wobei er sich wahrscheinlich auf die zwei Arbeiten Epsteins aus Flint bezog.[93] Wahrscheinlich Ende 1913 oder Anfang 1914 begann Gaudier, angeregt durch Epsteins Anverwandlung primitiver Kunst, mit eigenen von afrikanischer und ozeanischer Plastik inspirierten Werken. Endlich war Gaudier nicht mehr darin befangen, die so gegensätzlichen europäischen und primitiven Traditionen miteinander zu vergleichen. Er sah nun sein eigenes Werk und das anderer moderner Bildhauer als »Fortsetzung der Tradition der barbarischen Völker der Erde«.[94]

Hinzu kam, daß sich Gaudier jetzt ausschließlich der direkten Arbeit am Stein zuwandte. Seine Wertschätzung dieser Technik drückte er in einem Artikel über die Ausstellung der Allied Artists Association aus, die 1914 in der Holland Park Hall in London stattfand:[95]

»Die Skulptur, die ich bewundere, ist das Werk von Handwerksmeistern. Jeder Zoll der Oberfläche wurde mit dem Meißel erarbeitet – jeder Hammerschlag ist eine körperliche und geistige Anstrengung. Keine willkürlichen Übertragungen eines Entwurfs in irgendein Material mehr. Diese Leute sind sich im klaren über die verschiedenen Qualitäten und Möglichkeiten der Hölzer, Steine und Metalle. Epstein, den ich für den Besten aus der kleinen Schar guter Bildhauer Europas halte, legt darauf ganz besonderen Wert. Brancusis größter Stolz ist das Bewußtsein, ein perfekter Handwerker zu sein.«[96]

Gaudiers Skulpturen vom Ende des Jahres 1913 und von 1914 stehen im Zusammenhang mit dem Vortizismus und der Stammeskunst. Skulpturen wie *Aufgerichtete Vögel* (Museum of Modern Art, New York) und *Hirsche* (Art Institute of Chicago) sind stark facettierte, vortizistische Arbeiten. In ihrer Dreidimensionalität verwirklichen sie eigene plastische Ideen, die er im Magazin der Rebel Art Centre, *Blast,* (April 1914) vorstellte: »Bildhauerisches Gefühl ist die Wertschätzung der

□ 642 *›Zierplastik‹ (hei-tiki),* Maori *(Neuseeland), Jade und Wachs, Höhe 22 cm. The Trustees of the British Museum, London.*

□ 643 *›Jagdamulett‹, Provinz Ost-Sepik (Papua-Neuguinea), Holz, Höhe 16,5 cm. Privatsammlung.*

Massen in ihrer Beziehung zueinander. Bildhauerische Fähigkeit ist das Definieren dieser Massen durch Ebenen.«[97]

In GAUDIERS *Tänzerin* aus rotem Mansfield-Stein von ca. 1913 (Tate Gallery) hat der formale Aufbau – besonders die Herausbildung einer Art Strudel durch den Kopf mit dem Dreieck in der Mitte – mit primitiver Kunst nur wenig zu tun. Aber 1914 setzte Pound die Ausstrahlung dieser Skulptur und der beiden Flint-Skulpturen EPSTEINS mit der magischen Kraft von Medizinmännern gleich. Der Dichter identifiziert sich mit diesen Künstlern: »Wir, die wir die Erben der Medizinmänner und des Voodoo sind, wir Künstler, die wir so lange verachtet wurden, sind dabei, die Führung zu übernehmen.«[98]

GAUDIERS *Sitzende Frau* von 1914 (Musée National d'Art Moderne, Paris) verbindet europäische und primitive Stilmittel. Haltung und plumpe Gliedmaßen der Figur erinnern an MODIGLIANIS einzige erhaltene Karyatide □ 603 sowie an seine zahlreichen Zeichnungen und Aquarelle zu diesem Thema. Das maskenartige Gesicht mag wohl auf primitive Vorbilder zurückgehen, indes die asymmetrische Haltung unverkennbar europäischen Ursprungs ist.

Diese Werke mit unverhüllt primitiven Einflüssen sind den plastischen Prinzipien des Kubismus und Vortizismus weniger stark verhaftet. Eines von GAUDIERS besonders primitivistischen Werken, *Zwei Männer mit Schüssel* von 1914 □ 639, wurde sicherlich von ozeanischer Kunst beeinflußt, etwa von hawaiischen Schüsseln, die auf jeder Seite von einer menschlichen Figur gehalten werden. Eine andere Arbeit GAUDIERS, die Zeichnung *Caritas* von 1914, erinnert an mehrere Stammesstile Afrikas □ 637. Sowohl thematisch – eine Mutter, die zwei Kinder säugt – wie auch stilistisch – die Form der Füße, die zwei Babys und ihre Handhaltung – ist diese Zeichnung gewiß entweder von einer *AFO*-Plastik der Mutter mit Kind in der Art des bekannten Beispiels aus dem Horniman Museum, London □ 638, oder von einem ähnlichen Werk der *YORUBA* angeregt. Im Falle der Alabasterskulptur *Der Kobold* von 1914 ist es schwierig, ein bestimmtes Vorbild aus dem Bereich primitiver Kunst zu benennen. Robert Goldwater schlug bei der Besprechung dieses Werkes vor, daß »die ovalen Kurven der kurzen, gekrümmten Beine, deren Gewicht die ganze Figur nach unten zieht, wahrscheinlich durch afrikanische Proportionen beeinflußt sind«.[99]

Zwei kleine Werke von 1914 wurden unmittelbar durch ozeanische Kunst angeregt, die eine stärkere Wirkung auf GAUDIER ausübte als die afrikanische. Der im Original aus Messing gearbeitete *Türklopfer* von 1914 □ 640 ist eines der wenigen Werke GAUDIERS, das mit einem bestimmten Stammesstil in Verbindung gebracht werden kann, den Jadeornamenten der *MAORI* (hei-tiki) aus Neuseeland □ 642. Die vier Löcher in der unteren Hälfte des *Türklopfers* entsprechen den vier Öffnungen der neuseeländischen Zierplastiken. GAUDIER gab eine unaufrichtige Beschreibung dieser sehr figurativen, erotischen Plastik:

»Der Türklopfer ist Beispiel für eine abstrakte Struktur, die den Wert eines Objektes an sich bereichern soll. Nirgendwo sind mehr Kupidos, die auf Meerjungfrauen, Girlanden oder Vorhängen reiten. Die Technik ist unüblich – der Gegenstand wurde nicht gegossen, sondern direkt aus massivem Messing herausgehauen.«[100]

□ 644 *Henri Gaudier-Brzeska, ›Bildnis Ezra Pound‹, 1914, Holz, Höhe 73 cm. Yale University Art Gallery, New Haven.*

□ 645 *›Monolithische Steinfigur‹, Osterinsel, Höhe 255 cm. The Trustees of the British Museum, London.*

□ 646 *Henri Gaudier-Brzeska, ›Hieratischer Kopf Ezra Pounds‹, 1914, Marmor, Höhe 91 cm. Privatsammlung.*

Tatsächlich ist er kein Kupido und keine Meerjungfrau, aber ebensowenig ist der Türklopfer einfach »eine abstrakte Struktur«. GAUDIER hat die Einzelfigur der neuseeländischen Tikis in eine erotische Figur umgearbeitet. Die gegen 1914 entstandene Zeichnung für *Türklopfer* macht deutlich, was in der Messingskulptur selbst weniger sichtbar ist (Kettle's Yard, University of Cambridge).[101]

Dargestellt ist eine weibliche Figur mit erhobenen Armen, deren Kopf zwischen ihre Brüste gesunken ist. Sie sitzt oder balanciert mit überkreuzten Beinen, während gerade ein riesiger erigierter Penis in sie eindringt. Könnte GAUDIER EPSTEINS afrikanisch inspirierte Totem-Zeichnung von 1913 gesehen haben □ 618, die ebenfalls ein kopulierendes Paar mit dem Mann in umgekehrter Lage unter der Frau darstellt? Auch die mittlere Skizze in EPSTEINS Studie für den *Steinbohrer* von ca. 1913 □ 633 steht thematisch in engem Zusammenhang mit dem *Türklopfer*. Es erscheint mir sehr unwahrscheinlich, daß die unverhüllte Erotik in EPSTEINS Werk von 1913 GAUDIERS *Türklopfer* und den *Hieratischen Kopf Ezra Pounds* □ 646 nicht beeinflußt hat. Im Gegensatz zu dem harmlosen veröffentlichten Kommentar des Künstlers zur Gestaltung des *Türklopfers* erzählte er laut Brodsky im privaten Gespräch, »daß jemand einen Uhrenanhänger, einen Türklopfer oder einen Briefbeschwerer wollte – etwas ›Phallisches‹, um ihre Worte zu benutzen. Damals war das Wort ›phallisch‹ sehr beliebt und im modischen Kunstjargon weithin üblich. Brzeska schnitt für sie ein Stück Messing zurecht, das einem Freimaureramulett ähnlicher sah als irgend etwas anderem. Er erzählte ihnen dann, daß es ein Symbol für Fruchtbarkeit oder Männlichkeit sei oder irgendeinen anderen erotischen Unsinn, den er gerade im Kopf hatte. Genau das wollten sie. Sie nahmen es befriedigt mit, in dem Glauben, daß es etwas furchtbar Unanständiges sei.«[102]

Der Einfluß der Hei-Tiki-Ornamentik tritt auch in GAUDIERS *Amulett* aus grünem Stein zutage □ 641. Die gebrochenen Formen des Halsschmucks der *MAORI* vermischen sich hier – vor allem in den schräggestellten Augen – mit Gesichtszügen, die an figürliche Plastik Neuguineas, etwa Jagdamulette, erinnern □ 643.

In der kurzen künstlerischen Laufbahn GAUDIERS ist der 1914 entstandene *Hieratische Kopf Ezra Pounds* aus Marmor zweifellos die kraftvollste Skulptur. Der Dichter hat einen detaillierten Bericht über den Entstehungsprozeß des Werkes hinterlassen. Pound schrieb 1914: »Die Büste wurde begonnen, als der Winter zu Ende gegangen war.«[103] GAUDIER konnte sich keine großen Marmorblöcke leisten. »Er wollte die Büste in Gips, einem wirklich ekelhaften Material, ausführen, wogegen ich natürlich protestierte. Deshalb kaufte ich den Stein im voraus, ohne zu ahnen, was für eine Arbeit ich ihm damit aufhalste. Das Meißeln allein dauerte zwei ganze Monate. Vielleicht dauerte es auch zusätzlich noch mehrere Tage, die stumpfen Meißel wieder zu schärfen.«[104]

Brodsky schrieb über die Pound-Büste, daß »ihr Zweck und Ursprung rein pornographisch waren; der Bildhauer und das Modell hatten sich dafür entschieden. Brzeska berichtete mir, daß es ein Phallus werden sollte.«[105] Als Brodsky Pound eines Abends am Picadilly Circus traf, erzählte ihm der Dichter, daß GAUDIER an seinem Marmorporträt arbeite. »Brzeska macht mich in Gestalt einer phallischen Säule unsterblich«, äußerte Pound.[106] GAUDIER vollendete diese ehrgeizige Skulptur in bemerkenswert kurzer Zeit. Im Mai 1914 war die Arbeit in der Whitechapel Art Gallery ausgestellt.

Der *Hieratische Kopf Ezra Pounds* ist wahrscheinlich GAUDIERS einzige Skulptur, die nicht nur allgemein auf einen Stammesstil zurückgeführt werden kann, sondern auf ein bestimmtes primitives Werk – die riesige Figur von der Osterinsel Hoa-Haka-Nana-Ja □ 645, die das Britische Museum 1869 erworben hatte. Cork bemerkte hierzu:

»Gaudier konnte nicht umhin, von einem so unwiderlegbaren Beweis für die Kraft prähistorischer Kunst beeindruckt zu sein. Sein Kopf aus Marmor beweist, daß er die Figur von der Osterinsel im Kopf hatte, als er verschiedene Abschnitte seiner Skulptur in ihr noch nicht vorhersehbares Format brachte.«[107]

GAUDIER übertrug die symmetrischen Züge der Skulptur von der Osterinsel und behielt ihre Massivität und vertikale Stoßkraft bei. In Pounds Kopf ist die Nase auf einer Seite stärker angeschrägt als auf der anderen und die Einkerbung dort entsprechend tiefer. Beim Mund ist nur die Oberlippe stärker ausgearbeitet, in der Mitte flächig, rechts und links mit tiefen Einschnitten. Die streng waagrechten Augen wirken bedrohlich; die Photographie GAUDIERS am Anfang der Arbeit zeigt sie diagonal und mandelförmig auf den Marmor gezeichnet.[108] Anders als bei der Figur von der Osterinsel reicht im Kopf Pounds eine wuchtige Haarmasse unsymmetrisch in die Stirn. Für sich allein betrachtet ist der Abschnitt über den Augen eine Lektion vortizistischer Ästhetik, die in Werken GAUDIERS wie den *Aufgerichteten Vögeln* ebenfalls erscheint.

Das ganzfigurige *Bildnis Ezra Pound* ist eine von GAUDIERS wenigen Holzskulpturen □ 644. Wie der viel größere *Hieratische Kopf* aus Marmor wurde es wohl ebenfalls durch die Skulptur von der Osterinsel im Britischen Museum angeregt, enthält aber auch einige Anklänge an afrikanische Kunst. In dieser Holzskulptur ist der Kopf zu kantig gebrochenen Flächen vereinfacht. Der Bereich des Brustkorbs wurde ausgehöhlt, die vorspringende Form darunter stellt wohl den Nabel dar. Die hochstehende, dem Spitzbart der Marmorskulptur vergleichbare Form ganz unten enthält phallische Bezüge.

Im Herbst 1914 fuhr GAUDIER nach Frankreich, um in die Armee einzutreten. Seine Laufbahn als Bildhauer war alles andere als abgeschlossen. In den Schützengräben machte er mit dem gerade verfügbaren Material einige Skulpturen und Zeichnungen. GAUDIER-BRZESKA fiel am 5. Juni 1915 bei Neuville-Saint-Vaast. Im 1. Weltkrieg waren sein Tod und der von DUCHAMP-VILLON 1918 die größten Verluste für die moderne Bildhauerei.

Trotz Pounds Veröffentlichung von 1916, *Gaudier-Brzeska: A Memoir* (New York und London), und trotz der Tatsache, daß ein so bedeutender Sammler wie John Quinn mehrere seiner bedeutendsten Arbeiten erworben hatte, erhielten bis vor kurzem weder GAUDIERS bildnerisches Werk noch seine Schriften die verdiente Aufmerksamkeit. Mit EPSTEIN war er für den Eintritt der englischen Bildhauerei aus einer provinziellen Tradition in den Hauptstrom moderner europäischer Kunst verantwortlich.

□ 647 *›Hocker‹, WUTE (Kamerun), Holz, Länge 53 cm. Museum für Völkerkunde, Berlin.*

Anmerkungen

1. Werner, A., *Modigliani the Sculptor,* New York 1962, S. XIX.

2. Ebda.

3. Edinburgh International Festival, *Modigliani,* Arts Council of Great Britain, London 1963, S. 6.

4. Geist, S., *Brancusi/The Kiss,* New York 1978, S. 9.

5. Werner, *Modigliani the Sculptor,* S. XXIII.

6. Geist, S., *Brancusi: A Study of the Sculpture,* London 1968, S. 28.

7. Ceroni, A., *Amedeo Modigliani: Dessins et Sculptures,* Mailand 1965, S. 23–26.

8. Werner, *Modigliani the Sculptor,* S. XXIII.

9. *Augustus John: Autobiography,* mit einer Einleitung von Michael Holroyd, London 1975, S. 148.

10. Epstein, J., *An Autobiography,* London 1963, S. 46–47.

11. Werner, *Modigliani the Sculptor,* S. XXIV.

12. Goldwater, R., *Primitivism in Modern Art,* New York 1967, S. 236.

13. Ebda.

14. Ebda.

15. Balas, E., »The Art of Egypt as Modigliani's Stylistic Source« in *Gazette des Beaux-Arts* 97, Nr. 6, Februar 1981, S. 87.

16. Ebda.

17. *Amedeo Modigliani 1884–1920,* Musée d'Art Moderne de la Ville de Paris, Paris 1981, S. 81.

18. Lipchitz zitiert in Sichel, P., *Modigliani,* New York 1967, S. 210.

19. Jacques Lipchitz in der Einleitung zum Katalog der Ausstellung *The Lipchitz (Jacques, Yula und Lolya) Collection,* The Museum of Primitive Art, New York 1960, S. 5.

20. Ebda., S. 7.

21. Lipchitz, J. mit Arnason, H. H., *My Life in Sculpture,* New York 1972, S. 19–20.

22. Lipchitz, *The Lipchitz Collection,* S. 6.

23. Ebda., S. 7.

24. Lipchitz, *My Life in Sculpture,* S. 11.

25. Ebda., S. 16.

26. Stott, D. A., *Jacques Lipchitz and Cubism,* New York und London 1978, S. 109.

27. *The Lipchitz Collection* S. 8, Nr. 1–3.

28. Siehe Wilkinson, A. G., *Gauguin to Moore: Primitivism in Modern Sculpture,* Art Gallery of Ontario, Toronto 1981. Die Skulptur ist auf S. 214 abgebildet, die Zeichnung auf S. 215.

29. Lipchitz, *My Life in Sculpture,* S. 25.

30. Ebda., S. 40.

31. Ebda.

32. Ebda., S. 70.

33. Ebda., S. 86.

34. Ebda., S. 89–90.

35. Lipchitz, *The Lipchitz Collection,* S. 6.

36. Über sein Interesse an gleichartigen künstlerischen Ausdrucksformen verschiedenster Kunststile siehe *The Lipchitz Collection,* S. 7.

37. Haskell, A. L., *The Sculptor Speaks. Jacob Epstein to Arnold Haskell,* London 1931, S. 14.

38. Epstein, J., *An Autobiography,* London 1963, S. 12.

39. Haskell, *The Sculptor Speaks,* S. 15.

40. Epstein, *An Autobiography,* S. 18.

41. Ebda., S. 19–20.

42. Haskell, *The Sculptor Speaks,* S. 19.

43. Diese Zeichnung, das Grabmal für Oscar Wilde und der menschenköpfige Flügelstier aus Assyrien sind abgebildet in: Wilkinson, *Gauguin to Moore,* S. 170–71.

44. Epstein, *An Autobiography,* S. 46.

45. Ebda., S. 49.

46. Epstein, *An Autobiography,* S. 49.

47. Ebda.

48. Cork, R., *Jacob Epstein: The Rock Drill Period,* London 1973, S. 13, Anmerkung 10.

49. Goldwater, *Primitivism in Modern Art,* S. 239.

50. Ich danke Miss Hermione Waterfield, daß sie dieses Problem mit Mr. John Donne besprochen hat und mir die Information zukommen ließ.

51. William Fagg im Gespräch mit dem Autor.

52. Epstein, *An Autobiography,* S. 191–92.

53. Diese Skulptur aus Sierra Leone wurde vom Britischen Museum nicht vor 1920 erworben.

54. Frobenius, S. 163. Wiliam Fagg hat den Autor jahrelang bei seinen Recherchen über die Beziehung zwischen moderner und eingeborener Kunst in großzügiger Weise unterstützt. Er wies mich auch auf das Buch von Frobenius hin.

55. Siehe Wilkinson, *Gauguin to Moore,* S. 175.

56. Ebda., S. 174.

57. Ede, H. S., *Savage Messiah,* London 1931, S. 247.

58. Ich bin Barbara und Murray Frum zu großem Dank verpflichtet für ihr Interesse am Problem des Primitivismus in der modernen Kunst und für die vielen anregenden Diskussionen zu diesem Thema. Dr. Frum machte den Autor auf die enge stilistische Verwandtschaft zwischen Epsteins *Weiblicher Figur* aus Flint und der männlichen Standfigur aus Tahiti aufmerksam.

59. Epstein, *An Autobiography,* S. 64.

60. William Fagg im Gespräch mit dem Autor. Siehe Elisofon, E. und Fagg, W., *The Sculpture of Africa,* New York 1978, S. 31, Nr. 11 (dort auch eine Abbildung).

61. Goldwater, *Primitivism in Modern Art,* S. 240 und 242.

62. Epstein, *An Autobiography,* S. 56.

63. Cork, *Jacob Epstein,* S. 9.

64. Goldwater, *Primitivism in Modern Art,* S. 240.

65. Cork, *Jacob Epstein,* S. 9.

66. Elisofon und Fagg, *The Sculpture of Africa,* S. 90, Nr. 111.

67. Ebda., S. 98, Nr. 122.

68. Cork, *Jacob Epstein,* S. 45 und 47, mit Abbildung.

69. Ebda., S. 14, Anmerkung 23.

70. Ich danke Mr. M. D. McLeod für den Hinweis, daß Epsteins *Studie für Mann und Frau* auf den Grabpfosten aus Madagaskar zurückgeht.

71. Haskell, *The Sculptor Speaks,* S. 89.

72. Ebda., S. 90.

73. Ebda., S. 89–90.

74. Ebda., S. 90.

75. Epstein, *An Autobiography,* S. 188.

76. Haskell, *The Sculptor Speaks,* S. 94.

77. Ebda., S. 96.

78. Freundlicherweise übersandte Mr. McLeod dem Autor Photographien von Werken, die sich vormals in der Sammlung Epstein befanden

79. William Fagg in der Einleitung zu dem Ausstellungskatalog *The Epstein Collection of Tribal and Exotic Sculpture,* The Arts Council of Great Britain, London 1960, ohne Seitenzahlen.

80. Gaudier zitiert in Pound, E., *Gaudier-Brzeska: A Memoir,* London, New York 1916, S. 35.

81. Brodsky, H., *Henri Gaudier-Brzeska 1891–1915,* London 1931, S. 21

82. Geist, *Brancusi: A Study of the Sculpture,* S. 2.

83. Cole, R., *Burning to Speak: The Life and Art of Henri Gaudier-Brzeska,* Oxford 1968, S. 12.

84. Pound, *A Memoir,* S. 30.

85. Brodsky, *Gaudier-Brzeska,* S. 31–32.

86. Brodsky, *Gaudier-Brzeska,* S. 56

87. Ede, *Savage Messiah,* S. 141.

88. Brodsky, *Gaudier-Brzeska,* S. 56.

89. Cole, *Burning to Speak,* S. 21.

90. Ebda., S. 22.

91. Ede, *Savage Messiah,* S. 212–13,

92. Ebda., S. 213.

93. Ede, *Savage Messiah,* S. 247.

94. Pound, *A Memoir,* S. 35.

95. *The Egoist,* 16. März 1914.

96. Pound, *A Memoir,* S. 26.

97. Pound, *A Memoir,* S. 9.

98. Cork, R., *Henri Gaudier and Ezra Pound: A Friendship,* London 1982, S. 9.

99. Goldwater, *Primitivism in Modern Art,* S. 240.

100. Cole, *Burning to Speak,* S. 133.

101. Siehe Wilkinson, *Gauguin to Moore,* abgebildet S. 186.

102. Brodsky, *Gaudier-Brzeska,* S. 90.

103. Pound, *A Memoir,* S. 50.

104. Ebda.

105. Brodsky, *Gaudier-Brzeska,* S. 58–59.

106. Ebda., S. 62.

107. Cork, *Gaudier and Pound,* S. 11. Gaudier fertigte eine Reihe von Vorstudien an, die zwar zu seinen schönsten Zeichnungen gehören, die Eigenheiten des primitiven Vorbildes aber, die in der Skulptur selbst so offensichtlich sind, nicht widerspiegeln.

108. Abb. ebda., gegenüber S. 9.

☐ 648 *Marsden Hartley, ›Indianische Komposition‹ (Indian Composition), 1914, Öl auf Leinwand, 120 x 119 cm. Vassar College Art Gallery, Schenkung Paul Rosenfeld, Poughkeepsie, New York.*

Gail Levin

Amerikanische Kunst

Der Primitivismus in der amerikanischen Kunst begann unter der Ägide der europäischen Avantgarde, verschmolz jedoch bald mit amerikanischen Ansätzen und entwickelte so einen ganz eigenen Charakter. Amerikanische Künstler interessierten sich für die verschiedensten Kunstrichtungen der Eingeborenen aufgrund neuartiger stilistischer und symbolischer Anregungen, die sie in den künstlerischen Erzeugnissen exotischer Kulturen entdeckten. Einige Amerikaner wandten sich besonders der afrikanischen Kunst wegen mannigfacher formaler und suggestiver Qualitäten zu. Andere interessierten sich mehr für die abstrakten Motive und charakteristischen Themen der amerikanischen Indianerkunst, die der amerikanischen Moderne eine Antwort auf die Forderung nationalistisch orientierter Kritiker nach einem eigenständigen amerikanischen Stil und amerikanischen Bildmotiven bot.

Als Max Weber im September 1905 New York verließ, um in Paris zu studieren, war er bereits von seinem fortschrittlichen Lehrer Arthur Wesley Dow, bei dem er am Pratt Institute in Brooklyn 1899–1900 studiert hatte, dazu angeregt, sich mit außereuropäischer Kunst zu beschäftigen. Dow selbst war Schützling von Ernest Fenollosa, Kurator am Museum of Fine Arts in Boston und Kenner japanischer Kunst. Zuvor hatte Dow selbst in Paris studiert und in Pont-Aven gemalt, wo er im Sommer 1886 Gauguin kennenlernte.[1] Dow lehrte nicht nur eine neue künstlerische Sprache, die auf ästhetischen Prinzipien der Japaner aufbaute. Er regte seine Studenten auch dazu an, »die primitiven Ursprünge des Denkens, Fühlens und Handelns, die in jedem menschlichen Wesen stecken, einzubeziehen« und auf diese Weise mit sich selbst und »dem primitiven Geisteszustand eine Verbindung herzustellen«.[2] Dows sogenannte »natürliche Methode« fußte auf Erfahrungen des Ethnologen Frank Hamilton Cushing, der fünf Jahre lang bei den *Zuni*-Indianern in Neu-Mexiko gelebt hatte. Sein um mystische Gesichtspunkte erweitertes wissenschaftliches Vorgehen brachte Cushing zu der Überzeugung, daß eine weitreichende Übereinstimmung künstlerischer Ausdrucksformen östliche, westliche und primitive Kulturen verbindet.[3] Seine Lehre war die perfekte Grundlage für die neuen Ansätze, denen der junge Weber in Paris begegnen sollte.

Als Weber an der Académie Julian in Paris studierte, traf er in Jean-Paul Laurens auf einen starren, konservativen Lehrer. Aber bald stieß er auf Studienkollegen, die ihn in die fortschrittlichen Zirkel von Gertrude und Leo Stein und der Familie Delaunay einführten. Die jeden Samstag stattfindenden abendlichen Salons der Steins boten Weber die Chance, Künstler und Schriftsteller der Avantgarde zu treffen und die immer größer werdende Kunstsammlung der Steins kennenzulernen. In ihrer Wohnung, die er schon kurz nach seiner Ankunft aufgesucht haben muß, sah er zum ersten Mal ein Bild von Cézanne. Er erinnerte sich auch an die »wunderbaren japanischen Drucke« und an die »langen und engagierten Diskussionen über die neuesten Entwicklungen und Strömungen in der Kunst« unter der Leitung von Leo Stein.[4] Robert Delaunay lud Weber zu den Salons seiner Mutter ein, und bei einem dieser Treffen im Oktober 1907 traf er Henri Rousseau nach einem sonntäglichen Besuch im Salon d'Automne, wo beide Künstler ausgestellt hatten. Weber begleitete Rousseau auf seinem Heimweg, besuchte bald darauf sein Atelier, und so begann eine enge Freundschaft mit dem älteren Künstler.[5]

Im Februar 1906 verließ Weber die Academie Julian und begann, an der Académie de la Grande Chaumière und an der Académie Colarossi, wo Matisse manchmal zum Zeichnen auftauchte, ganz ohne Anleitung nach dem Modell zu arbeiten. Hans Purrmann, ein junger deutscher Maler und Freund aus der Académie Julian, der Matisse gut kannte, machte Weber den Vorschlag, eine Klasse zu organisieren, um bei Matisse zu studieren. Diese Klasse begann im Januar 1908, Weber blieb bis zum Juli. Möglicherweise lernte er erst durch Matisse afrikanische Skulptur kennen, die von jenem seit fast zwei oder drei Jahren gesammelt wurde. Auch die kühnen Farben, die flächigen Räume, sein experimenteller Stil beeindruckten ihn.[6]

Im Oktober 1908 machte Weber bei den Steins die Bekanntschaft Picassos. Als er dann beim Besuch seines Ateliers eine gemeinsame Begeisterung für Henri Rousseaus Werk entdeckte, muß er auch die Faszination verspürt haben, die afrikanische und andere primitive Skulptur in Picasso erregte.[7] Etliche Wochen später, nach einem Besuch Picassos in seinem Atelier, begleitete ihn Weber zu Rousseau. Weber nahm für sich in Anspruch, daß er Rousseau kurz darauf mit Joseph Brummer bekannt machte, der Rousseaus Händler und Mäzen wurde.[8] Weber hatte Brummer zuerst als jungen, aus Ungarn ausgewanderten Bildhauer an der Grande Chaumière kennengelernt, später als Händler japanischer Drucke und Student der Matisse-Klasse von 1908 wie auch als Händler afrikanischer Kunst (zuerst von seinem Atelier an der Rue Falguière aus und später über einen kleinen Laden am Boulevard Raspail). Weber erinnerte sich später, daß Brummer auf einem Regal immer »zwei kleine Landschaftsskizzen von Rousseau neben zwei oder drei ausgezeichneten kongolesischen Statuetten« stehen hatte.[9] Picasso, Brummer, Weber u. a. bewunderten an Rousseaus Malerei und an der afrikanischen Kunst eine ganz ähnliche Unmittelbarkeit, Einfachheit, Aufrichtigkeit und

□ 649 *Max Weber, ›Kongo Statuette‹ (auch als ›Afrikanische Skulptur‹ bekannt), 1910, Gouache auf Pappe, 34 x 26 cm. Privatsammlung, New York.*

□ 650 *›Figur aus Holz‹,* YAKA *(Zaire), Höhe 26 cm. Sammlung Joy S. Weber, New York. Ehemals Sammlung Max Weber.*

Ausdrucksstärke. WEBER nannte ROUSSEAU einen »wahrhaft Primitiven, der in unserer Zeit lebt«.[10]

Als WEBER 1909 nach New York zurückkehrte, begleiteten ihn Werke ROUSSEAUS, außerdem ein Andenken (ROUSSEAUS Spazierstock) – und seine künstlerischen Ratschläge. Möglicherweise brachte er damals auch die von oder über BRUMMER erworbene *YAKA*-Figur aus Zaire □ 650 mit, die er 1910 in ein Stilleben integrierte und das er unter zwei verschiedenen Titeln ausstellte: *Kongo Statuette* bzw. *Afrikanische Skulptur* □ 649.[11]

WEBER weckte das Interesse für ROUSSEAU und die primitive Kunst bei den New Yorker Künstlern, besonders im Kreise um Stieglitz. Als ROUSSEAU starb, veranlaßte er Stieglitz zu einer Gedächtnisausstellung in der Galerie »291« mit Bildern und Zeichnungen, die er aus Paris mitgebracht hatte. Sie fand vom 18. November bis zum 8. Dezember 1910 statt.

WEBER hatte auch begonnen, Essays und Gedichte über primitive Kunst zu schreiben, von denen Stieglitz einige in der Zeitschrift *Camera Work* veröffentlichte. So enthält etwa die Ausgabe vom Juli 1910 zwei derartige Essays. In »The Fourth Dimension from a Plastic Point of View« (Die vierte Dimension unter einem plastischen Gesichtspunkt) beobachtete er, daß »Statuetten aus Tanagra, Ägypten oder dem Kongo oftmals wie Kolossalstatuen wirken, während ein armseliges, mittelmäßiges Teil einer großen Skulptur die Ausmaße eines Stecknadelkopfes zu haben scheint, weil ihm dieser grenzenlose Sinn für Raum und Erhabenheit fehlt«.[12] In einem anderen Essay betonte er, daß er »chinesische Puppen, Katchina-Darstellungen der Hopi, aber auch indianische Decken, Körbe und andere Arbeiten der Wilden gesehen habe, viel feiner in der Farbgebung als die Werke moderner Maler-Koloristen«.[13]

Jahre später erinnerte sich WEBER an seine Besuche im Museum of Natural History in New York, wo er ein »immer größeres Verständnis für die Kunst der Primitiven und des westlichen Kontinents entwickelte«. Gerade in diesem Museum fing er an, freie Verse zu schreiben.[14] Sein erstes Gedicht war von einer präkolumbianischen Skulptur inspiriert und nannte sich »To Xochipilli, Lord of Flowers« (An Xochipilli, Herr der Blumen). Es erschien in *Camera Work* im Januar 1911.[15] 1914 folgte in London die Publikation seines Buches *Cubist Poems* (*Kubistische Gedichte*) mit einem Vorwort von Alvin Langdon Coburn. Dieser schrieb über WEBER, daß er »mit Vorliebe die Kunst der primitiven Völker studiert, die Skulpturen Ägyptens und Assyriens, die großen, einfachen Dinge, die in Stein gehauen aus der Vergangenheit vor uns stehen«.[16] Eines der Gedichte mit dem Titel »Bampense Kasai« handelt von einer afrikanischen Maske, »roh geformt und gestaltet«, die WEBER sehr bewunderte:

In the crudest geometric form,
Thy savage maker makes an art
at once untrifling big and powerful.[17]

(Selbst in roher geometrischer Form
vollbringt Dein wilder Schöpfer eine Kunst,
die bedeutend, groß und mächtig zugleich ist.)

Es ist genau diese Kraft in der Kunst des Primitiven, die WEBER in seinem Gemälde *Interieur mit Frauen* von 1917 wiederzuerwecken suchte ☐ 651. Die Komposition reflektiert sowohl WEBERS Liebe zur primitiven Skulptur als auch sein Wissen darüber, wie diese von PICASSO und anderen Künstlern aufgenommen und verarbeitet worden war. So ist etwa der Kopf der Figur mit dem eckigen Mund ganz rechts in der Formgebung nicht allein von afrikanischen Masken angeregt, sondern vermutlich auch vom Kopf der Figur rechts unten in PICASSOS *Demoiselles d'Avignon* ☐ 339. Die flache dekorative Zone in der oberen linken Bildecke scheint allerdings auf den Einfluß von WEBERS früherem Lehrer MATISSE zurückzugehen. WEBERS Synthese enthält eine Vielzahl von Elementen aus dem Kubismus: So erinnern die Felder mit Farbtupfern bei der linken Figur an viele kubistische Werke PICASSOS der Jahre 1913–1918, ebenso die vorgetäuschte Holzmaserung über der Figur links; die wiederholten Wellenlinien kommen auch bei PICASSO als Kürzel für Haare vor. Mehr als jeder andere Amerikaner war WEBER davon beeindruckt, wie PICASSO primitive Skulptur in seiner Malerei absorbierte. Dennoch ist seine dynamische Formgestaltung von der besonderen Rhythmik her ganz anders als bei PICASSO.

1926 veröffentlichte WEBER *Primitives: Poems and Woodcuts,* ein Buch, das ein »Gefühl der Verehrung«, das ihn vor den Skulpturen der Eingeborenen im Museum of Natural History ergriff, festhalten sollte.[18] Außer einem wiederholten Abdruck von »Bampense Kasai« enthielt dieses Buch Gedichte wie »Congo Form« und »The Totem Pole Man«. Die beigefügten Holzschnitte bestanden aus stark vereinfachten Formen, die eher die Kraft primitiver Skulptur als ihr Formvokabular beschworen ☐ 652.

Um dieselbe Zeit, im April 1912, kam MARSDEN HARTLEY nach Paris. Stieglitz hatte für ihn bereits zwei Ausstellungen in der Galerie »291« organisiert. HARTLEY kannte WEBERS primitivistische Gemälde und auch seine Schriften aus *Camera Work,* hatte sich aber primitive Kunst weiter noch nicht erschlossen. Im Juli 1912 schrieb HARTLEY an Stieglitz, daß er von dieser neuen Richtung in der modernen Kunst beeindruckt sei, vor allem nach der Lektüre eines Artikels in der Zeitschrift *Rhythm.* Darin wurde behauptet, daß KANDINSKY nichts als einer von GAUGUINS Schülern sei, er wurde als »Neoprimitiver« hingestellt aufgrund einer Technik, die den Verfasser an »Kunst der Primitiven und Wilden erinnert«.[19]

Möglicherweise war es das Zusammentreffen dieses Artikels mit dem Einfluß des Bildhauers JACOB EPSTEIN, den HARTLEY gerade in Paris kennengelernt hatte, aber auch die Vertrautheit mit dem Almanach *Der Blaue Reiter,* die ihn dazu bewog, den Trocadéro zu besuchen. Seine Reaktion auf das, was er dort sah, war prompt: »Die eigentlichen Dinge«, bestätigte er in einem Brief an Stieglitz, »können wir hier im Trocadéro finden.

☐ 651 *Max Weber, ›Interieur mit Frauen‹ (Interior with Women), 1917, Öl auf Leinwand, 46 x 59 cm. Forum Gallery, New York.*

□ 652 *Max Weber, ›Ohne Titel‹, Holzschnitt, 19 x 5 cm. Forum Gallery, New York. Veröffentlicht in „Primitives: Poems and Woodcuts“, New York 1926.*

Diese Menschen hatten keinen kleinlichen Ehrgeiz, sie schufen aus einer inneren Notwendigkeit heraus.«[20] Die Übernahme des Begriffes »innere Notwendigkeit« zeigt das wachsende Interesse an Kandinskys Abhandlung *Über das Geistige in der Kunst,* die Hartley zusammen mit dem Almanach *Der Blaue Reiter* in Clovis Sagots Kunstgalerie erworben hatte.[21]

Hartleys Begeisterung für die Kunst der Eingeborenen nahm bereits auf seine Werke Einfluß. »Man kann nicht länger derselbe bleiben in Anwesenheit dieser mächtigen Kinder, die der universellen Idee so nahe sind«, schrieb er an Stieglitz.[22] Er experimentierte mit dem Primitiven zunächst, indem er Stammesobjekte in seine Stilleben einbezog. Sein Bild *Indianische Töpferwaren (Gefäß und Idol)* □ 653 von 1912 zeigt einen Krug der Acoma-Indianer mit dem Bild eines Vogels und eine Holzfigur, die an geschnitzte Skulpturen der *Kwakiutl* erinnert.[23] Gleichzeitig liegt der Vergleich mit Gabriele Münters *Stilleben mit hl. Georg* von 1911 nahe, das im *Blauen Reiter* abgebildet wurde. Wie Münter ordnete Hartley eine Gruppe von primitiven Kunstgegenständen auf einer Tischplatte in einem flachen Raum an, den ein malerischer Hintergrund abschließt. Hartleys schlichte Verbildlichung indianischer Objekte und Motive entwickelte sich bald zu einer viel eigenständigeren Bildsynthese, als er sie in seine eigenen komplexen Gestaltungen aufnahm.

□ 653 *Marsden Hartley, ›Indianische Töpferwaren‹ (Indian Pottery), 1912, Öl auf Leinwand, 50 x 50 cm. The Gerald Peters Gallery, Santa Fe.*

Im Januar 1913 erfüllte sich Hartley den Wunsch, Kandinsky zu treffen und sich von der Gruppe ›Blauer Reiter‹ einen Eindruck zu verschaffen. Er reiste nach Deutschland und traf Kandinsky, Gabriele Münter und Franz Marc in München.[24] Im Mai 1913 ging er nach Berlin, wo er für längere Zeit bleiben wollte. Seine finanzielle Situation zwang ihn aber im Oktober zur Rückkehr nach New York, wo er versuchte, Geld für seine Auslandsaufenthalte aufzutreiben. Stieglitz wies den widerwilligen Hartley auf seinen amerikanischen Ursprung hin: »Deine Reise nach Europa war durch amerikanisches Geld möglich . . . Jetzt sehe ich keinen Grund, warum ein Amerikaner Dir zusätzlich Geld geben soll, ohne zu sehen, was Du gearbeitet hast.«[25]

Stieglitz seinerseits hatte schon früher die Indianer als die ureingesessenen »Exoten« der Neuen Welt erkannt, als er Gertrude Käsebiers Photographie *The Red Man* in die erste Ausgabe von *Camera Work* im Januar 1903 aufnahm und später eine Diskussion über Käsebiers wohlwollende Haltung gegenüber den Indianern in *Camera Work* vom Oktober 1907 publizierte.[26] Keine drei Jahre später erschien Webers Lob der Kunst der Indianer und anderer Primitiver in *Camera Work*. Zu den vielen Künstlern, Schriftstellern und Förderern des Stieglitz-Kreises, die schließlich zeitweilig ihr Augenmerk auf die Indianer richteten, gehörten Man Ray, Arthur Dove, John Marin, Paul Rosenfeld, William Carlos Williams und Mabel Dodge.[27]

Doves *Indianischer Frühling* von 1923 etwa enthält abstrakte Formen, die an Tipis (Indianerzelte) erinnern □ 654. Sein Interesse an primitiver Kunst war von Stieglitz gefördert worden, der ihm 1913 ein Exemplar des *Blauen Reiter* gab. Marin malte 1929 Aquarelle von Indianern wie z. B. *Tanz der Pueblo-Indianer* und *Tanz der San Domingo-Indianer* in Taos, Neu-Mexiko.

Hartley kehrte gegen Ende April 1914 über London und Paris nach Berlin zurück. Nach seiner Ankunft malte er – vielleicht als Ergebnis seiner Heimreise nach Amerika – eine Serie von abstrakten Gemälden, die sich thematisch mit den Indianern befassen. Er nannte diese Serie seine »Amerika«-Bilder, wobei er die deutsche Schreibweise benutzte.

In Deutschland interessierte man sich sehr stark für die Indianer Amerikas. Gegen Ende des 19. Jahrhunderts waren hier mehrere große Sammlungen indianischer Kunst aufgebaut worden. Deutsche Schriftsteller von Goethe bis Karl May nährten die Begeisterung der Deutschen für die Indianer.[28] In noch engerem Zusammenhang mit Hartleys Interessen stand die Tatsache, daß August Macke, einer der Mitautoren des Almanachs *Der Blaue Reiter,* schon 1910 Indianerthemen gemalt hatte. Mackes Interesse für die Indianer wurde auch in seinem Almanach-Essay »Die Masken« deutlich, in dem er auf die »Kriegsbemalung der Indianer« und den »Häuptlingskragen aus Alaska« hinwies, letzteren durch ein Beispiel aus dem Völkerkundemuseum in München illustriert.[29] Hartley kannte Macke und hatte Arbeiten von ihm gesehen, bevor er selbst mit Gemälden zu indianischen Themen begann. 1913 hatte er die Sammlung von Bernhard Koehler gesehen, zu der Mackes *Indianer auf Pferden* aus dem Jahre 1911 gehörte □ 655. Hartleys Indianerdarstellungen sind allerdings viel abstrakter und symbolischer als diejenigen Mackes.

Die flache, symmetrische und frontale Anordnung wie auch manche Formen in Hartleys Amerika-Bildern (etwa die Mandorla oder wellenförmige Linien zwischen zwei geraden Linien) verweisen auf seine Vorliebe für bayerische Hinterglas-

□ 654 *Arthur Dove, ›Indianischer Frühling‹ (Indian Spring), 1923, Öl auf Leinwand, 45 x 56 cm. The Lane Collection, Leominster, Massachusetts.*

□ 655 *August Macke, ›Indianer auf Pferden‹, 1911, Öl auf Holz, 26,5 x 35,5 cm. Städtische Galerie im Lenbachhaus, München.*

malerei, die er über den *Blauen Reiter,* Kandinskys private Sammlung und von sechs selbst erworbenen Exemplaren kannte.[30] Er fand aber auch andere Formen und Motive in der riesigen Sammlung indianischer Kunst im Museum für Völkerkunde in Berlin. Im Jahre 1914 enthielt die Nordamerika-Abteilung dieses Museums an die 30000 Objekte, die praktisch alle in überfüllten Glasvitrinen ausgestellt waren.[31] Anhand dieses Materials fand Hartley nicht nur einen Schatz neuer Formen vor, sondern entdeckte, daß manche seiner bevorzugten Symbolmotive tatsächlich bei verschiedenen Indianerstämmen gebräuchlich waren. Dazu zählten achtstrahlige Sterne und das Eiserne Kreuz.[32]

Seine *Indianische Phantasie* von 1914 greift auf Formen und Motive bayerischer Hinterglasmalerei wie auch indianische Arbeiten aus dem Völkerkundemuseum zurück □ 657. Die Farbgebung dieses Gemäldes mit der Betonung von Rot, Gelb und Grün auf schwarzem Grund mit weißen Einzelelementen entspricht einer bedeutenden Sio Hemis-Katchina (siehe

Glossar) im Berliner Museum □ 656. Von dieser übernahm HARTLEY auch den zentralen Bogen des Kopfschmuckes bzw. der Trage, die achtstrahligen Sterne in Kreisen und die Strichmännchen an den Seiten des Bogens, die er in einer Mandorla im Inneren des Tipis plazierte. In Berlin waren mehrere Tipis ausgestellt, und HARTLEYS Kanus mit ihren abstrakten Mustern stammen möglicherweise von *CHIPPEWA*-Modellen aus derselben Sammlung □ 658. Darüber hinaus erinnert der große Vogel im oberen Teil der *Indianischen Phantasie* an einen monumentalen Holzadler aus Vancouver, der sich damals im Berliner Museum befand □ 659. Andererseits erinnern die fransenartigen Schwingfedern auch an den Häuptlingskragen aus Alaska, der im Almanach *Der Blaue Reiter* abgebildet war.[33] Durch Kombination von Motiven aus der Vielfalt von Indianerstämmen ließ HARTLEY seiner Phantasie freien Lauf. Auf diese Weise ergaben sich Motive, die nie zusammen gesehen worden wären, etwa Tipis der *PRÄRIEINDIANER* und *PUEBLO*-Keramik.

Wie sehr HARTLEY vom abstrakten Charakter indianischer Motive fasziniert war, wird auch in seiner *Indianischen Komposition* von 1914 deutlich □ 648. Das Gemälde enthält verschiedene Muster und Formelemente aus den Perlstickereien der *PRÄRIEINDIANER*, die in Berlin gut vertreten sind. Eine Kindertrage der *COMANCHEN*, bei der ein rundes Medaillon neben senkrechten Linien und quadratischen Mustern angeordnet ist, mag die Komposition seines Bildes beeinflußt haben □ 661. Die schildartigen Medaillons zeigen auch, daß HARTLEY Motive der *PRÄRIEINDIANER* kannte. Das Kreuz innerhalb konzentrischer Kreise zuunterst auf der linken Seite seines Gemäldes findet man häufig bei perlenbestickten Gegenständen wie etwa auf einem Mokassin des *CROW*-Stammes □ 662. Wieder verwendete HARTLEY einen achtstrahligen Stern sowie das Strichmännchen auf einer Mandorla inmitten eines Tipi und erinnerte damit an Motive bei den Katchinas der *HOPI*. Er nahm auch weiße Formen auf wie auf der mittleren roten

□ 657 *Marsden Hartley, ›Indianische Phantasie‹ (Indian Fantasy), 1914, Öl auf Leinwand, 119 x 100 cm. North Carolina Museum of Art, Raleigh.*

◁ □ 656 *›Sio Hemis-Katchina‹, Hopi (Arizona), bemaltes Holz und Federn, Höhe 45 cm. Museum für Völkerkunde, Berlin.*

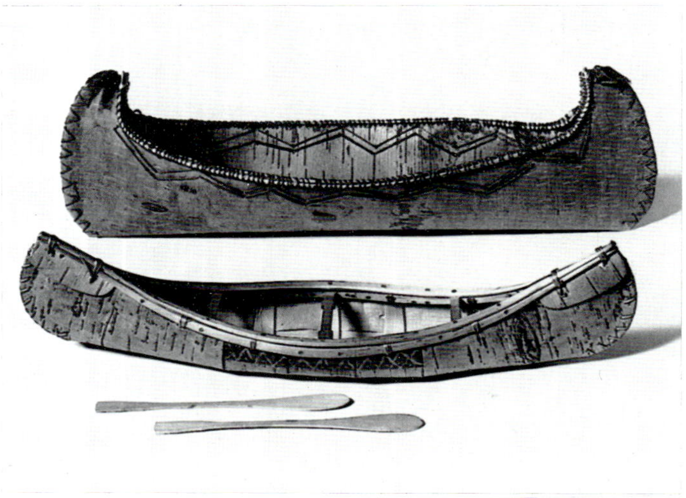

☐ 658 *›Kanumodelle‹*, CHIPPEWA, *Große Seen, Holz und Rinde, oben: Länge 39 cm, unten: Länge 42 cm. Museum für Völkerkunde, Berlin.*

☐ 659 *›Adler‹, Vancouver Island (Britisch-Kolumbien), bemaltes Holz. Ehemals Museum für Völkerkunde, Berlin. Verbleib unbekannt.*

☐ 660 *Marsden Hartley, ›Amerikanische Indianersymbole‹ (American Indian Symbols), 1914, Öl auf Leinwand, 94 x 94 cm. Sammlung John J. Brady, Jr., Des Moines.*

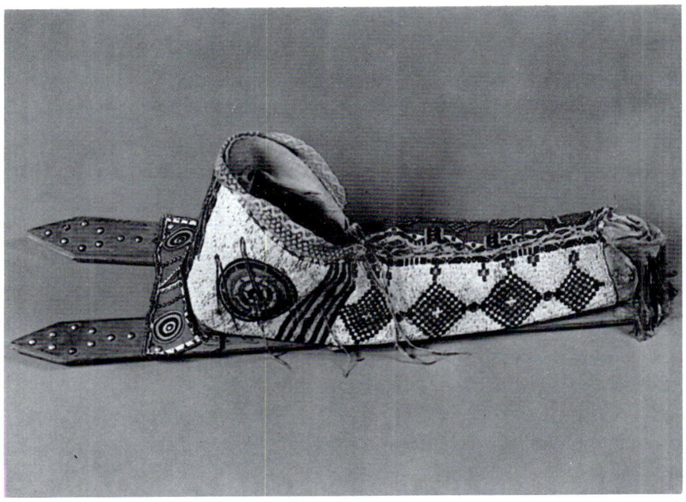

□ 661 *›Kindertrage‹, COMANCHEN (Texas), Holz, Leder, Perlen und Stickerei, Länge 105 cm. Museum für Völkerkunde, Berlin.*

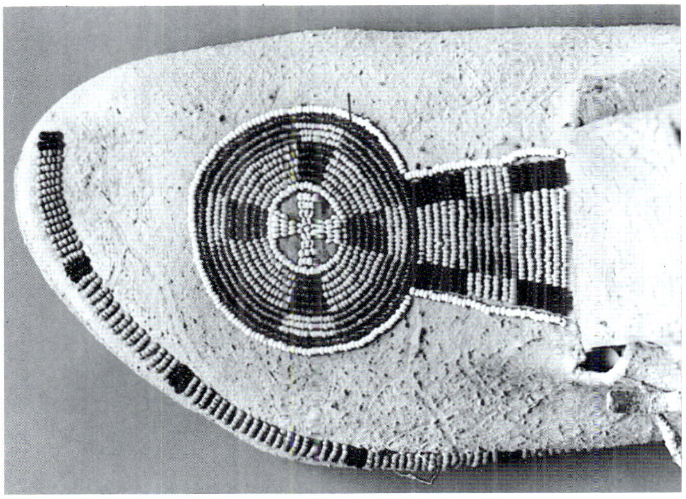

□ 662 *›Mokassin‹ (Detail), CROW (Montana oder Wyoming), Leder und Perlen, Gesamtlänge 27 cm. Museum für Völkerkunde, Berlin.*

Scheibe. Dies sind *HOPI*-Symbole für kleine Getreidepflanzen; weiße, zweigartige Symbole stehen für größere Getreidepflanzen auf einer blauen Scheibe auf dem Medaillon rechts unten. Er benutzte die gleichen *HOPI*-Zeichen für Getreidepflanzen in einer Serie von Kohlezeichnungen mit indianischen Motiven, zu denen *Berlin Symbols No. 6* oder *Primitive Art No. 2* gehören.

Amerikanische Indianersymbole ist der Titel eines anderen 1914 entstandenen Gemäldes aus HARTLEYS Amerika-Serie □ 660. Es enthält wiederum Formen, die von den Sio Hemis-Katchinas stammen, darunter die achtstrahligen Sterne in Kreisen und das Mittelkreuz unter dem Bogen des Kopfschmuckes. Der abstrakte vertikale Streifen mit Schachbrettmuster entlang der rechten Bildkante ist vermutlich auf ebensolche Motive in Perlarbeiten der *PRÄRIEINDIANER* zurückzuführen. Obwohl HARTLEY bei Ausbruch des Ersten Weltkrieges mit den indianischen Themen aufhörte, blieb er doch bei seiner Vorliebe für kühne abstrakte Muster und Formen, die er in der Kunst der Indianer gefunden hatte. Er griff auf sie noch einmal zurück in seinen späteren Serien symbolischer deutscher Militärbilder, die er als »Kriegsmotive« bezeichnete.[34]

HARTLEY sah im Indianer den »friedfertigen und unaufdringlichen Bürger« und ein Beispiel für menschlichen Adel. Vom Krieg erschüttert, wünschte sich HARTLEY, ein Indianer zu sein, und er erzählte Stieglitz, er wolle ihnen nacheifern, sein Gesicht mit ihren Symbolen bemalen und gen Westen ziehen, um die Sonne niemals untergehen zu sehen.[35] Fünf Jahre nachdem HARTLEY seine indianischen Bilder in Deutschland gemalt hatte, schrieb er einen Artikel mit dem Titel »Red Man Ceremonials: An American Plea for American Esthetics« (Zeremonien des Roten Mannes: Ein amerikanisches Plädoyer für eine amerikanische Ästhetik), der sein ungebrochenes Interesse an den Indianern dokumentiert. Er schrieb den Aufsatz während eines Aufenthaltes in Santa Fe, Neu-Mexiko, und zeigte sich sichtlich beunruhigt, daß er von der europäischen Avantgarde so übermäßig beeinflußt worden war. Entsprechend forderte er dazu auf, die Kunst der Indianer zu beachten und einen eigenen einheimischen Stil zu entwickeln:

»Das amerikanische Lebensgefühl braucht dringend ein ästhetisches Nationalbewußtsein. Wir sind lange nicht so original, wie wir uns dummerweise einbilden . . . Wir erfahren große Ermutigung durch die Ästhetik der Indianer in unserem Bestreben, ein uns eigenes ästhetisches Bewußtsein zu entwikkeln.«[36]

In einem späteren Essay zählte HARTLEY die Indianer »zu den bedeutendsten Dekorateuren der Welt« und hob besonders die Totempfähle und Gebetskleider aus Alaska hervor.[37] Er bemühte sich, die Kunst der Indianer populär zu machen, gab aber gleichzeitig zu, daß es nicht leicht sei, ihre Ästhetik zu verstehen, da sie »wie alle Primitiven, eigene Regeln und Ausdrucksformen entwickeln, die ihren eigenen ganz spezifischen psychologischen Bedürfnissen entsprechen«.[38]

Trotz seines späteren Entschlusses, niemals wieder »irgendeinem primitiven Motiv einen Einfluß auf sein Werk zu erlauben«,[39] gab es bei MAN RAY eine Phase enthusiastischen Interesses für die primitive Kunst. In einem unpublizierten Kommentar von 1957 gab MAN RAY zu, daß er in seiner Einzelausstellung in der Daniel Gallery im Jahre 1915 eine »Serie von Kompositionen« ausgestellt habe, »die von der primitiven Skulptur inspiriert« gewesen seien.[40] Die »primitiven Anregungen dauerten nur von 1913 bis 1915« äußerte er einschränkend. Während dieser Zeit lernte MAN RAY das Werk von MAX WEBER kennen. Er kannte WEBER von der Modern School des Ferrer Centers, wo er das Zeichnen nach dem Modell lernte.[41] MAN RAY, der damalige Skizzen nach einem jungen Mädchen als »einer primitiven Skulptur ähnlich« beschrieb, war WEBERS anhaltendes Interesse für die Stammeskunst sicherlich bekannt.[42] Eines seiner Gemälde, *Totem* aus dem Jahre 1914, offenbart dieses Interesse an der Kunst der Primitiven □ 663. Es ist die Darstellung eines geheimnisvoll wirkenden, gewaltigen Kopfes in lebhaften Farben, der vor einer felsigen Umgebung dramatisch in die Höhe ragt. Der große primitivistische Totem ist umgeben von einem Fries kleiner Figuren in meist geduckten Stellungen und trägt eine hügelige pastorale Landschaft auf seiner Brust. Das Gemälde mag von MAN RAYS Campingreise in den New Yorker Harri-

□ 663 *Man Ray, ›Totem‹, 1914, Öl auf Leinwand, 91 x 61 cm. Galleria Il Fauno, Turin.*

□ 664 *›Figur eines Kriegsgottes‹, ZUNI (Neu-Mexiko), Holz, Höhe 76 cm. The Brooklyn Museum, New York.*

man State Park im Herbst 1914 angeregt worden sein, die er in Begleitung seiner Frau, der Dichterin Adon Lacroix, Alison Hartpence' und anderer unternahm. MAN RAY erinnerte sich, in einem Gespräch mit Hartpence während dieser Reise die Absicht formuliert zu haben, eine Reihe von imaginären Landschaften zu schaffen, bevor er auf die Malerei nach der Natur verzichten und sich »mehr und mehr den von Menschenhand geschaffenen Quellen« zuwenden wolle.[43] *Totem* ist ein Übergangswerk, das sowohl nach der Natur als auch nach seinem handgefertigten Gegenstand gestaltet wurde, einem Gegenstand, der wahrscheinlich indianische Holzschnitzereien in der Art der *ZUNI*-Kriegsgötter □ 664 mit Totems der Indianer von der Nordwestküste verbindet, wie sie im Brooklyn Museum und dem Museum of Natural History zu sehen waren. Wie die *ZUNI*-Skulptur zeigt auch MAN RAYS *Totem* einen langen Nacken, ein eckiges Kinn und ein vereinfachtes geometrisches Gesicht mit langer Nase und linear geformten Augen.

Demzufolge war sich MAN RAY der Beliebtheit des Primitivismus voll bewußt und blieb von ihr nicht unberührt, so wie alle Mitglieder des Kreises um die Galerie »291«. Er erinnerte sich etwa, dort eine afrikanische Ausstellung gesehen zu haben.[44] Sie fand im November 1914 statt, und es war mit das erste Mal, daß afrikanische Skulptur in Amerika als Kunst präsentiert wurde. Stieglitz hatte sie mit Hilfe von MARIUS DE ZAYAS organisiert □ 665, 666. Letzterer war ein witziger und geistvoller, aus Mexiko stammender Künstler, der 1909, 1910 und 1913 in der »291« seine Karikaturen zeigte. Er hatte in

□ 665 *Ausstellung afrikanischer Skulptur in der Galerie »291«, New York, November-Dezember 1914. Abgebildet in „Camera Work", Oktober 1916.*

□ 666 *›African Savages the First Futurists‹, Ankündigung der Ausstellung afrikanischer Skulptur in Stieglitz' Galerie »291«, in ‚The World' (Magazin), 24. Januar 1915.*

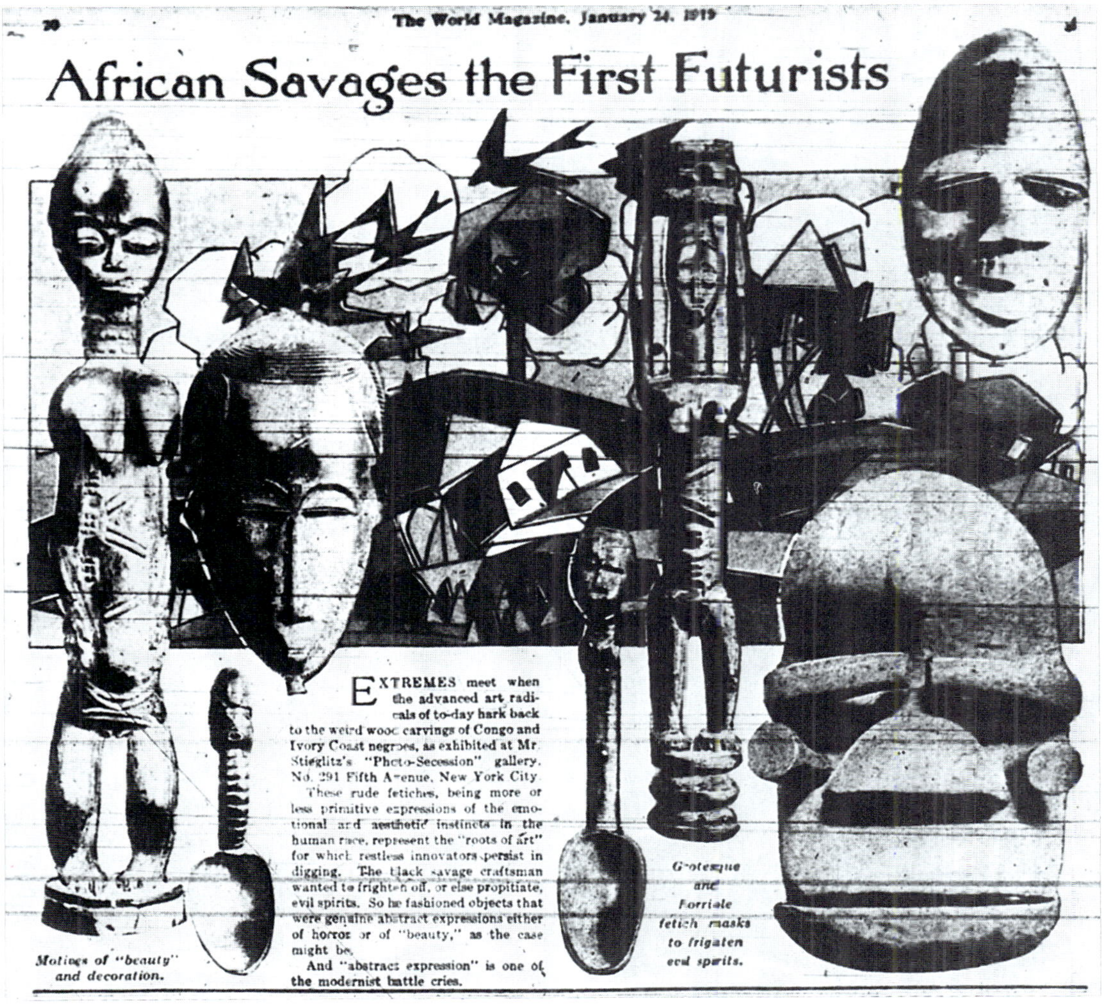

20 The World Magazine, January 24, 1915

African Savages the First Futurists

EXTREMES meet when the advanced art radicals of to-day hark back to the weird wood carvings of Congo and Ivory Coast negroes, as exhibited at Mr. Stieglitz's "Photo-Secession" gallery, No. 291 Fifth Avenue, New York City.

These rude fetiches, being more or less primitive expressions of the emotional and aesthetic instincts in the human race, represent the "roots of art" for which restless innovators persist in digging. The black savage craftsman wanted to frighten off, or else propitiate, evil spirits. So he fashioned objects that were genuine abstract expressions either of horror or of "beauty," as the case might be.

And "abstract expression" is one of the modernist battle cries.

Motives of "beauty" and decoration.

Grotesque and horrible fetich masks to frighten evil spirits.

□ 667 *Marius de Zayas, ›Alfred Stieglitz‹, um 1912, Kohle, 61 x 46 cm. The Metropolitan Museum of Art, Sammlung Alfred Stieglitz, New York.*

□ 668 *›Seelenfänger‹, Pukapuka (Cookinseln), Fasern, Höhe ca. 100 cm. The Trustees of the British Museum, London. Farbabbildung* □ *104.*

□ 669 *William Zorach, ›Der Knabe‹ (The Young Boy), 1921, Holz, Höhe 57 cm. Whitney Museum of American Art, New York.*

Europa Kunst studiert und in Paris PICASSO kennengelernt. Er sammelte Stammeskunst und versuchte sich im Kunsthandel. Schon im April 1911 schrieb er Stieglitz mit der dringenden Bitte, er solle eine Ausstellung afrikanischer Skulptur in der »291« präsentieren, da diese einen wichtigen Einfluß auf die Entwicklung der modernen Kunst in Paris habe, »besonders bei den Revolutionären«.[45] Stieglitz' Ausstellung umfaßte 18 Skulpturen, die DE ZAYAS von Paul Guillaume in Paris zur Verfügung gestellt worden waren. Sie wurden »in einer Umgebung roher und heftiger Farben« gezeigt, die Edward Steichen entworfen hatte.[46]

Auf dem Weg von Paris nach New York im Oktober 1911 machte DE ZAYAS Zwischenstation in London und besuchte dort die völkerkundliche Sammlung des Britischen Museums. Er war besonders beeindruckt von einem Objekt der Pazifikinsel Pukapuka (Danger Islands) □ 668 und berichtete darüber später:

»Es beeindruckte mich vor allem deshalb, weil es mich an die körperliche Erscheinung von Stieglitz erinnerte. Ich sage ›körperliche‹, weil die Ähnlichkeit auch eine geistige war. Das Objekt, so sagte der Katalog, stellte eine Falle zum Einfangen von Seelen dar. Das Porträt war vollständig und fing auch meine Seele ein, weil ich aus ihm eine Theorie der abstrakten Karikatur ableitete. . . Zuvor hatte ich eine Karikatur von Stieglitz mit dem Titel ›L'Accoucheur d'idées‹ gemacht. Beide Karikaturen drückten mein Verständnis der Stieglitzschen Botschaft aus: die Seelen einzufangen und die Hebamme der neuen Ideen für die Welt zu sein.«[47]

DE ZAYAS übernahm von dem primitiven Seelenfänger das Grundkonzept der Kreisformen entlang einer Mittelachse und evozierte so Stieglitz' Erscheinungsbild mit der Drahtrandbrille □ 667. Stieglitz war, so wurde DE ZAYAS klar, nicht nur Amerikas Vorkämpfer für die moderne Kunst, sondern als Photograph eine Art »Seelenfänger«, entsprechend der Vorstellung der Primitiven, daß eine Kameraaufnahme die Seele eines Menschen raube.

Stieglitz' pionierhafter Afrika-Ausstellung war eine Präsentation in Robert Coadys Washington Square Gallery vorausgegangen, die einige Beispiele afrikanischer Kunst enthielt und nur kurz vor der Ausstellung in der »291« im November 1914 stattfand.[48] Coady kämpfte für die Anerkennung des Beitrags der Schwarzen an der amerikanischen Kultur, und er stellte neben europäischer Moderne auch die Arbeiten von Negerkindern und Plastiken der Südsee aus. 1916/17 publizierte er eine Zeitschrift mit dem Titel *The Soil,* die als Forum für seine exzentrischen Ansichten über moderne Kunst in Amerika diente. In dieser Zeitschrift stellte er Abbildungen von primitiven Skulpturen, Photographien industrieller Technik sowie zeitgenössische Stadtansichten nebeneinander und begleitete diese ungleichen Paare mit ikonoklastischen Kommentaren.

Etwa zur selben Zeit, im Oktober 1915, eröffnete DE ZAYAS zusammen mit PAUL HAVILAND, FRANCIS PICABIA und Agnes Meyer in Fortsetzung von Stieglitz' Zielen die Modern Gallery. Sie zeigten moderne Kunst und Photographie neben Beispielen primitiver Kunst, um »die Beziehung zwischen diesen Dingen und der heutigen Kunst zu illustrieren«.[49] In *Camera Work* vom Oktober 1916 veröffentlichte DE ZAYAS einen Essay mit dem Titel »Modern Art in Connection with Negro Art«. Im selben Jahr erschien auch sein Buch *African Negro Art: Its Influence on Modern Art*.[50] Dort führte er aus, daß die afrikanische Kunst »in uns das Gefühl für die abstrakte Form wiedererweckt und unserer Kunst die Möglichkeit gegeben hat, unseren reinen Sinneswahrnehmungen eine Form zu geben oder neue Formen in unseren Ideen zu finden«.[51] DE ZAYAS schrieb auch die Einleitung zu Charles Sheelers Fotobuch *African Negro Wood Sculpture*, das als Folioband im Jahre 1918 erschien. Es bildet Werke aus der Modern Gallery ab, bei der bedeutende Förderer moderner Kunst wie John Quinn, Agnes Meyer und Walter Arensberg primitive Skulpturen erworben hatten.[52]

Viele der frühen amerikanischen Bildhauer der Moderne waren von primitiven und anderen außereuropäischen Kunstrichtungen beeinflußt, insbesondere von der afrikanischen Skulptur. Wie die Stammeskünstler – und ganz anders als die meisten Bildhauer seit der Renaissance – wählten viele von ihnen die Methode direkter Materialbearbeitung. Schon 1907 wurde ROBERT LAURENT von FRANK BURTY HAVILAND in das Atelier PICASSOS mitgenommen, wo er nach späteren Aussagen afrikanische Skulptur und dieser nicht unähnliche eigenhändige Arbeiten PICASSOS zu sehen bekam.[53] Als er 1910 nach Amerika zurückkehrte, begann LAURENT mit der Arbeit an Holzreliefs, die nicht nur von der primitiven Kunst und von PICASSO beeinflußt waren, sondern auch von Holzarbeiten GAUGUINS und MAILLOLS, die er in Paris gesehen hatte. Um dieselbe Zeit modellierte MAX WEBER winzige primitivistische Figürchen, die jedoch eher auf die Plastik seines Lehrers MATISSE zurückgingen als auf Arbeiten der Eingeborenen. WILLIAM ZORACH, der 1917 mit der Bildhauerei begann, erwarb Sheelers Bildband über afrikanische Skulptur und ließ sich von zwei dort abgebildeten FANG-Figuren für die Darstellung seines Sohnes Tessim in *Der Knabe* von 1921 anregen □ 669. Er war von primitiver Skulptur so begeistert, daß er gleich drei Werke aus Mahagoniholz anfertigte, das ein Schiffskapitän aus Provincetown in Massachusetts aus Afrika mitgebracht hatte.[54]

JOHN STORRS fand in der Indianerkunst Amerikas Formen, die er in seinem abstraktesten Werk, der Steinplastik *Architektonische Form* aus dem Jahre 1923, verwenden konnte □ 671. STORRS lebte abwechselnd in Frankreich und in Amerika und war in seinem Interesse für die Kunst der Indianer möglicherweise durch die Freundschaft mit MARSDEN HARTLEY bestärkt

□ 670 *›Kopfschmuck‹, HOPI (Arizona), bemaltes Holz, Fasern und Federn, Höhe 61 cm. Field Museum of Natural History, Chicago.*

□ 671 *John Storrs, ›Architektonische Form‹ (Architectural Form), um 1923, Stein, 50 x 8 x 7 cm. Galerie Robert Schoelkopf, New York.*

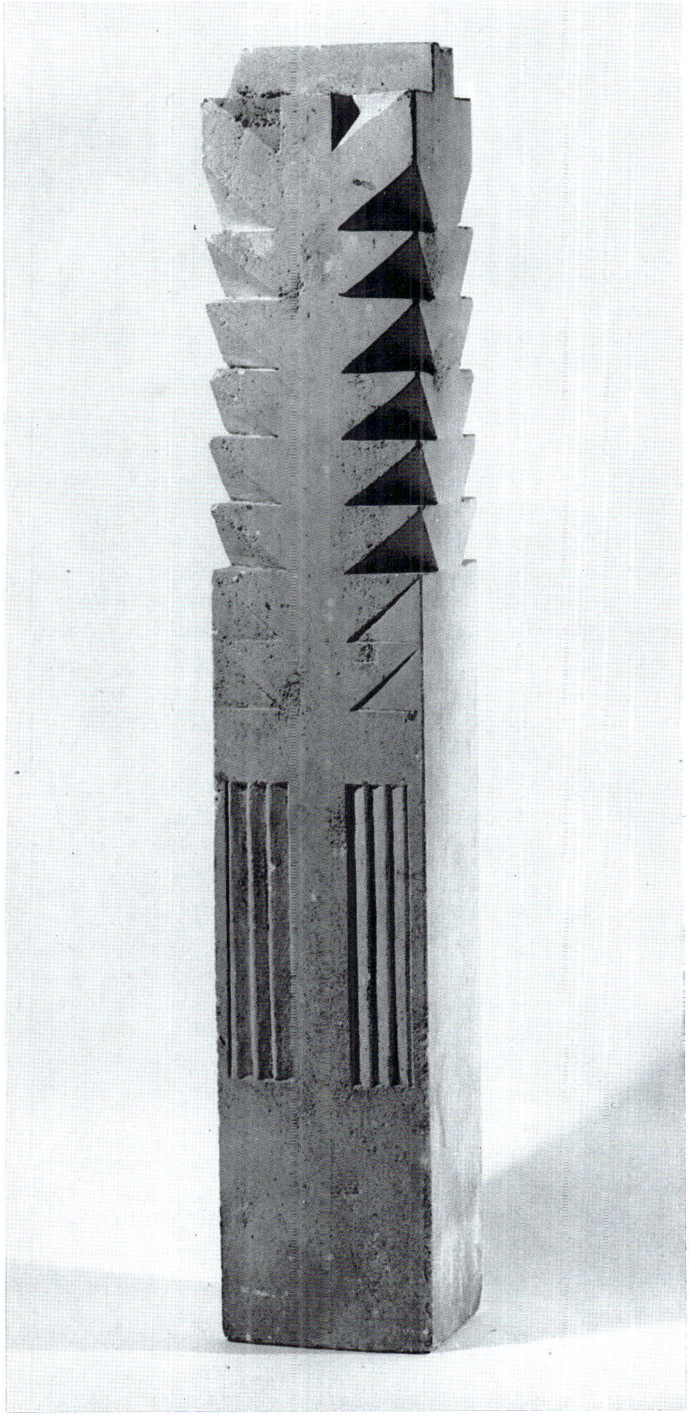

☐ 673 *Alexander Calder, ›Afrikanischer Kopf‹ (African Head), 1928, gebeiztes Holz, 38 x 12 x 18 cm. The Metropolitan Museum of Art, Schenkung Charles Oppenheim, Jr., New York.*

☐ 672 *Alexander Calder, ›Weibliche Figur‹ (Female Figur), 1929, Holz, Höhe 63 cm. Privatsammlung.*

worden, der ihn 1921 auf seinem Schloß bei Orléans besuchte. STORRS besuchte später das Field Museum of Natural History in Chicago und begann dann *NAVAJO*-Decken, indianische Keramik und andere dekorative Gegenstände zu sammeln. In den geometrischen Formen wie den Zickzackmustern und anderen Motiven entdeckte er vieles, was er für seine Skulpturen verwenden konnte. *Architektonische Form* etwa wurde mit einem *HOPI*-Kopfschmuck verglichen, bei dem das gleiche gezackte Treppenmotiv und der gleiche Sinn für aufstrebende Energie zu finden sind ☐ 670.[55] STORRS' Interesse an indianischer Kunst entspricht der Verbundenheit seines Stils mit der Art Deco-Bewegung, die ja auch sehr stark von der Kunst der Indianer Nordamerikas wie der Präkolumbiens inspiriert war.[56]

Wie STORRS lebte auch ALEXANDER CALDER abwechselnd in Frankreich und in Amerika. Seine Hinwendung zu außereuropäischer und primitiver Skulptur mochte durch JOSÉ DE CREEFT angeregt worden sein, der zu den ersten Bekanntschaften gehörte, die er nach seiner Ankunft in Paris im Jahre 1926 machte.[57] 1928/29 experimentierte CALDER mit geschnitzten Figuren im Stil der Primitiven , etwa bei *Afrikanischer Kopf* oder *Weibliche Figur* ☐ 672, 673.[58] Letztere entstand 1929 »als Gegenstück zu einer Holzarbeit aus der Südsee« im Porcellian Club in Harvard, in dem CALDERS Freund Paul Nitze Mitglied war.[59] Mit ihren verzerrten Gesichtszügen, ihrer starren Haltung und den hängenden Brüsten erinnert die Figur an ozeanische Skulpturen. Dennoch sind CALDERS primitivistische Werke mit den früheren Arbeiten von JOSÉ DE CREEFT sowohl durch die Wahl von Ebenholz und anderer exotischer Hölzer als auch in der Art der Formgebung eng verbunden.

GEORGE L. K. MORRIS begann 1929 Motive der Indianer zu malen. Er entdeckte den Primitivismus, als er im Frühling des Jahres zusammen mit FERNAND LÉGER und AMÉDÉE OZENFANT an der Académie Moderne in Paris studierte. Aber bereits 1928, damals noch Student in Yale, betonte er die Notwendigkeit einer amerikanischen Kunsttradition:

». . . die einzige Vergangenheit, die dieses Land besitzt, besteht in Wäldern und Indianern, und die Künstler müssen alle ihre Stoffe erst einmal bewußt erfinden.«[60] Im folgenden Herbst begann MORRIS sein Studium an der Art Students League, wo zwei seiner Lehrer, JOHN SLOAN und JAN MATULKA, bereits ein Interesse an den Indianern als Motive für ihre Malerei entwickelt hatten. MATULKA war ein tschechischer Einwanderer, der in Neu-Mexiko und Arizona herumgereist war. 1917/18 malte und zeichnete er Tänzer aus dem Stamm der *HOPI*-Indianer ☐ 674.[61]

SLOAN besuchte seit 1919 regelmäßig Santa Fe und entwikkelte ein ausgeprägtes Interesse für Kunst und Kultur der Indianer, die dann auch viele seiner Gemälde beeinflußten. Er beteiligte sich auch an der Organisation der großen Ausstellung indianischer Stammeskunst in den Grand Central Art Galleries in New York von 1931/32, die diese Objekte mehr unter künstlerischen und weniger unter ethnologischen Gesichtspunkten präsentierte.

MORRIS' erstes Gemälde mit indianischer Thematik, *Indianerschlacht Nr. 1,* entstand im Sommer 1929 in Lenox, Massachusetts, kurz nach seiner Rückkehr aus Paris. Es orientiert sich mehr am Stil HENRI ROUSSEAUS als an LÉGER. Nach einer weiteren Beschäftigung mit LÉGER im Herbst desselben Jahres begann MORRIS dessen Kubismus stärker aufzunehmen. Das Gemälde *Indianerschlacht Nr. 2* von 1933 ist in seiner Struktur abstrakter und flächiger und darin LÉGERS Arbeiten nicht unähnlich, greift daneben aber auf Formen der Katchina-Figuren zurück ☐ 681.[62]

MORRIS bewunderte LÉGERS Primitivismus, etwa im Dekor für *Die Erschaffung der Welt,* und nannte ihn »den wahren Primitiven, den Abenteurer, den es mehr zu neuen Horizonten

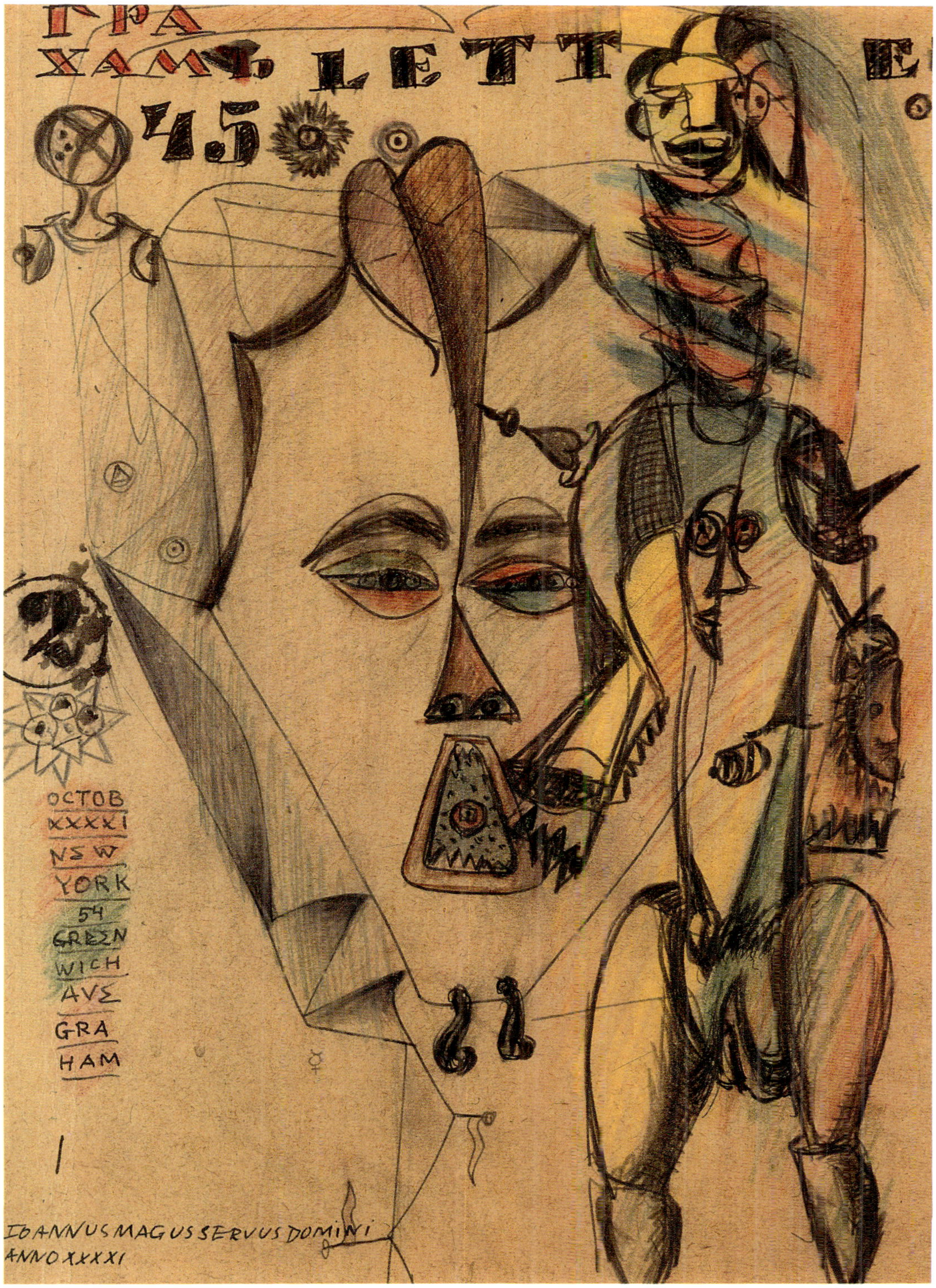

□ 675 *John Graham, ›Ohne Titel‹, 1941, Tusche, Aquarell, Bleistift und Farbkreide, 30 x 23 cm. Galerie Allan Stone, New York.*

zieht als zum Salongespräch über Kunst«.[63] In den Bildern der 30er und frühen 40er Jahre[64] beschäftigte er sich weiter mit dem Thema der Indianer und entwarf außerdem abstrakte Collagen mit Birkenrinde wie *Kämpfende Indianer* von 1935, worin das Motiv von Pfeil und Bogen mehrfach erscheint □ 680. Morris reiste nach Santa Fe, besuchte Pueblos und zeichnete dort interessante Indianermotive mit dem Ziel, das beste der amerikanischen Eingeborenenkunst mit der europäischen Idee des Primitivismus zu neuem künstlerischen Ausdruck zu verschmelzen. »Wenn eine authentische amerikanische Kultur entstehen soll, müssen wir zu den Anfängen zurückkehren«, war seine Überzeugung.[65]

Das Interesse für die primitive Kunst in Amerika wurde durch wichtige Veröffentlichungen der 20er und 30er Jahre gefördert. 1926 erschien Paul Guillaumes und Thomas Munros Buch *Primitive Negro Sculpture* mit Abbildungen von Arbeiten

◁ □ 674 *Jan Matulka, ›Schlangentanz der Hopi, Nummer I‹ (Hopi Snake Dance, Number I), 1917–18, Pastellkreide, Aquarell und Bleistift, 38 x 30 cm. Whitney Museum of American Art, Schenkung von Gertrude W. Dennis, New York.*

☐ 676 *Alexander Calder, ›Mondlicht bei einem Windstoß‹ (Moonlight in a Gust of Wind), Detail, 1966, Farblithographie, 47 x 65 cm. Privatsammlung, New York.*

☐ 677 *Alexander Calder, ›Kopf mit Ohrringen‹ (Head with Earrings), 1950, Tusche, 57 x 39 cm. Perls Galleries, New York.*

aus der Sammlung der Barnes Foundation. Der Pariser Kunsthändler Guillaume, der MARIUS DE ZAYAS für die Ausstellung afrikanischer Skulpturen in der »291« Werke zur Verfügung gestellt hatte (1914), und Munro, Professor für moderne Kunst an der Universität von Pennsylvania, betrachteten die afrikanische Kunst in ihrem »Verhältnis zu zeitgenössischer Kunst« und sahen in ihr die Möglichkeit eines »Kompromisses zwischen Darstellung und Design«.[66]

Die einflußreiche Schrift *Primitive Art* des Anthropologen Franz Boas, die in Amerika erstmals 1928 veröffentlicht wurde, setzte sich mit der weit verbreiteten Ansicht auseinander, daß die geistige Kapazität des primitiven Menschen geringer als die des westlichen sei.[67] Boas bemühte sich um die Erklärung primitiver Stile und konzentrierte sich dabei auf die Kunst der Indianer von der Nordwestküste. Sein Buch weckte großes Interesse für ihre Kunst. Das Buch, mit dem das Interesse der Künstler für primitive Kunst am stärksten angeregt wurde, war JOHN GRAHAMS *System and Dialectics of Art,* das 1937 in New York und Paris erschien.[68] GRAHAM war ein 1920 aus Rußland geflohener Maler, der kurzzeitig in Paris gelebt und dort Eluard, Breton, PICASSO und andere Künstler getroffen hatte. Nach seiner Emigration in die Vereinigten Staaten im November 1920 blieb er durch häufige Besuche über den Atlantik mit vielen seiner französischen Freunde in Kontakt. Mit der Zeit befreundete sich GRAHAM mit vielen jüngeren Künstlern, JACKSON POLLOCK, DAVID SMITH, DOROTHY DEHNER, BARNETT NEWMAN, RICHARD POUSETTE-DART, ADOLPH GOTTLIEB u.a., die sich alle für Stammeskunst interessierten. In den späten 20er Jahren hatte GRAHAM eine Sammlung afrikanischer Skulptur zusammengetragen, die er befreundeten Künstlern in seiner New Yorker Wohnung begeistert zeigte und die er auch 1930 in der Dudensing Gallery ausstellte. Die intensive Beschäftigung mit primitiver Kunst, die der Ausstellung »African Negro Art« im Museum of Modern Art von 1935 vorausging, machte ihn in Verbindung mit seinen Beziehungen zur Pariser Avantgarde zu einem bedeutenden Katalysator während der entscheidenden Jahre vieler Künstler, die später Abstrakte Expressionisten genannt wurden.

GRAHAM bestätigte sich auch als Händler und beschaffte afrikanische Skulpturen für Frank Crowninshield. Dieser bekannte Sammler beauftragte in den frühen 30er Jahren DAVID SMITH auf Anregung GRAHAMS, Sockel für seine afrikanischen Ausstellungsstücke anzufertigen. DOROTHY DEHNER erinnerte sich, daß GRAHAM sie und DAVID SMITH anläßlich eines Ausfluges nach Paris im Jahre 1935 am Tag ihrer Ankunft auf vier Ausstellungen mitnahm.[69] Im selben Jahr kaufte ADOLPH GOTTLIEB mehrere afrikanische Skulpturen von Pariser Händlern, die GRAHAM empfohlen hatte.[70]

Im Vergleich zu vielen frühen Bewunderern der Stammeskunst war GRAHAMS Ansatz eher soziologisch und anthropologisch begründet: »Primitive Kunst ist eine hochentwickelte Kunst und *Resultat einer großen Zivilisation, die auf ganz anderen Prinzipien beruht als diejenige des weißen Mannes.«*[71] An anderer Stelle hielt er die afrikanische Kunst für »einzigartig in ihrer plastischen und emotionalen Form« und sah in den

☐ 678 *›Kifwebe-Maske‹, LUBA (Zaire), bemaltes Holz und verschiedene Materialien, Höhe 44 cm. Seattle Art Museum, Sammlung Katherine White.*

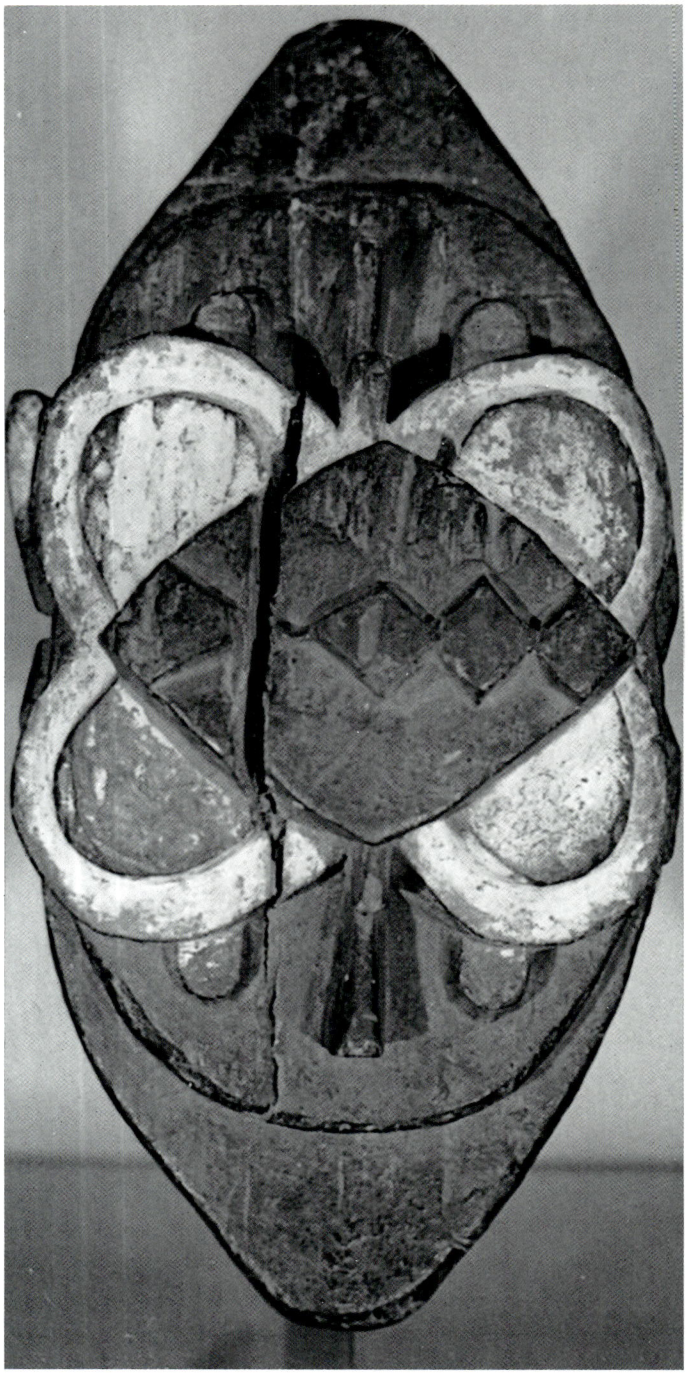

☐ 679 *›Maske‹, Igbo (Nigeria), bemaltes Holz, Höhe 38 cm. Sammlung Joseph Herman, New York.*

Stammeskünstlern die direkten Vorläufer der Abstraktion: »Afrikanische Künstler verspürten niemals den verführerischen Wunsch, die Natur nachzuahmen oder mit ihr zu wetteifern, denn sie haben vor mehr als tausend Jahren den langen Weg vom Realismus und exakter Naturwiedergabe zur Abstraktion hinter sich gebracht – eine Reise, die wir selbst gerade erst beenden.«[72] Grahams herausragende Rolle für die Durchsetzung primitiver Kunst in den 20er und 30er Jahren war vielseitig. Er befaßte sich als Sammler, Händler, Schriftsteller und Künstler mit primitiver Kunst. Eine Zeichnung von 1941 etwa zeigt ihn fasziniert von einer afrikanischen Figur und einer Maske ☐ 675. Für Graham bedeutete die Kunst der Primitiven einen zukunftsträchtigen Ansatz, und die Begeisterung, die er mit vielen anderen teilte, hatte eine nachhaltige Wirkung.

Für viele amerikanische Künstler wurden die Indianer, Afrikaner und im weitesten Sinne die schwarzen Amerikaner zu Symbolen für ein vergangenes, weniger verderbtes Zeitalter. Die Unmittelbarkeit und Schlichtheit der primitiven Kunst betrachteten bildende Künstler der Moderne als den wahren Weg zu ehrlicheren und weniger dekadenten Ausdrucksmöglichkeiten – als »universelle Idee«, wie Hartley sich gegenüber Stieglitz geäußert hatte. Kandinsky hatte in seinem Aufsatz *Über das Geistige in der Kunst,* der 1914 in englischer Ausgabe erschien, die Sympathie des modernen Künstlers für die Primitiven auf das beiderseitige Bedürfnis zurückgeführt, »nur das Innerlich-Wesentliche in ihren Werken zu bringen, wobei der Verzicht auf äußerliche Zufälligkeit von selbst entstand«.[73] Marius de Zayas behauptete, daß die Kunst der Neger in weit größerem Maße als das naturalistische Abbild in der Kunst oder gar das technische Abbild der Photographie »die Möglichkeit erkennen ließ, den Wahrnehmungen des äußeren Lebens plastischen Ausdruck zu verleihen und folglich auch neue Formen für den Ausdruck unseres inneren Lebens zu finden«.[74] Kandinsky schrieb »Der ganze Alpdruck der materialistischen Anschauungen, welche aus dem Leben des Weltalls ein böses, zweckloses Spiel gemacht haben, ist noch nicht vorbei. Die erwachende Seele ist noch stark unter dem Eindruck dieses Alpdrucks.«[75]

Es war wohl zum Teil dieser Kampf gegen die immer größer werdende Entfremdung und sterile Kühle in der modernen Gesellschaft, die so viele amerikanische Künstler dazu veranlaßte, das Primitive zu erforschen.

☐ 680 *George L. K. Morris, ›Kämpfende Indianer‹ (Indians Fighting), 1935, Collage mit Aquarell, Papierstücken und Birkenrinde, 44 x 33 cm. Meredith Long & Co., Houston.*

□ 681 *George L. K. Morris, »Indianerschlacht Nr. 2« (Battle of Indians, No. 2), 1933, Öl auf Leinwand, 71 x 126 cm. Besitz des Künstlers.*

Anmerkungen

1. Siehe Moffatt, F. C., *Arthur Wesley Dow (1857–1922),* Washington, D. C., 1977; Chisolm, L. W., *Fenellosa: The Far East and American Culture,* New Haven 1963.

2. Zitiert aus einem Bericht von Sylvester Baxter über die Sitzung der Ipswich Summer School of Art, 1902, mit dem Titel: »Handicraft and Its Extension at Ipswich«. Abgedruckt in *Handicraft 1,* Februar 1903, S. 253–54.

3. Moffatt, a. a. O., S. 93–95. Siehe Cushing, F. H., *My Adventures in Zuni.* Nachdruck aus *The Century Illustrated Monthly Magazine,* 1882–83, Santa Fe 1941. Über den Einfluß von Cushing auf Dow siehe Baxter, »Handicraft«, a. a. O.: »Cushing besaß die Fähigkeit, die primitive Sichtweise gegenüber Leben und Kunst einzunehmen . . . Indem er die primitiven Handwerksstücke genau untersuchte, gelangte er über verschlungene Wege zurück in die Vergangenheit. Indem er so ihren Entstehungsprozeß erarbeitete und sie dann in der gleichen Weise, wie sie ursprünglich auch entstanden waren, neu schuf, lernte er über ein altes und längst vergangenes Volk, was sonst durch schriftliche Überlieferung festgehalten wird.«

4. Max Weber, Interviews von Carol S. Gruber, Januar–März 1958, in *The Oral History Collection of Columbia University,* S. 73–74. Leo Stein hatte zu dem Zeitpunkt, als Weber in Paris eintraf, bereits seinen ersten Cézanne erworben. Steins Reise nach Japan im Jahre 1895 hatte das Interesse für japanische Drucke geweckt. Für meine Recherchen über Weber bin ich besonders Joy Weber, der Tochter des Künstlers, für ihre unschätzbare Hilfe zu Dank verpflichtet. Bella Fishko von der Forum Gallery gehört ebenfalls mein aufrichtiger Dank.

5. Weber, M., »Rousseau as I knew him«, 7. September 1942. Unveröffentlichtes Manuskript, Artist's file, Whitney Museum of American Art, New York, S. 1–2: »Hier, sagte ich mir, steht ein Mann, ein Künstler, ein Dichter, dessen Freundschaft und Rat ich pflegen und schätzen muß.« Vgl. die ausgezeichnete Untersuchung der Beziehung dieser beiden Künstler bei Leonard, S. E., *Henri Rousseau and Max Weber,* New York 1970.

6. Barr, A. H., Jr., *Matisse: His Art and his Public,* New York 1951, S. 139. Weber, M., »The Matisse Class«, unveröffentlichtes Manuskript, vorgetragen vor dem Matisse Symposium, Museum of Modern Art, 19. November 1951, S. 13, MoMA Archives. Dort wird berichtet, daß Matisse gelegentlich seine Studenten in sein Atelier mitnahm und ihnen unter anderem seine Sammlung afrikanischer Negerplastik zeigte. »Matisse war sehr stolz auf seine kleine, aber erlesene Kollektion afrikanischer Negerplastik und dies, bevor die Negerplastik die europäische Kunst überschwemmte, wenn nicht gar eroberte. Er pflegte eine Figurine in die Hand zu nehmen und uns die authentischen und hervorstechenden skulpturalen Qualitäten zu erklären, die außerordentliche Kunstfertigkeit, den einmaligen Sinn für Proportionen, die erregend geschmeidige Fülle und Ausgewogenheit der Formen.« Patrick Henry Bruce, ebenfalls ein amerikanischer Schüler von Matisse, entwickelte auch Interesse für afrikanische Kunst und trug schließlich eine große Sammlung zusammen. Henri-Pierre Roché erinnerte sich an Bruces »Negerobjekte« und schrieb: ». . . er begann, Negerstatuetten und Geräte zu sammeln, darunter bemerkenswerte Stößel aus Stein für Frauenhände, die geradezu erotisch waren . . .« Zitiert aus Agee, W. C., und Rose, B., *Patrick Henry Bruce American Modernist,* New York 1979, S. 223.

7. Weber, »Rousseau as I knew him«, S. 21–22. Im November zeigte Picasso Weber das *Porträt einer Frau* von Rousseau, das er gerade in einem Secondhand-Laden gekauft hatte.

8. Ebenda, S. 23–24.

9. Ebenda, S. 24–25. Weber schrieb: »Die Kunst der Neger sollte den mächtigsten Einfluß auf die Bewegung der modernen Kunst ausüben, und das Sammeln von Negerplastik wurde leidenschaftliches Hobby von Kunststudenten und Sammlern nicht nur in Paris, sondern in der ganzen Welt.«

10. Weber, M., »Eine Ausstellung mit Lithographien von Manet, Cézanne, Renoir und Toulouse-Lautrec, einigen Zeichnungen von Rodin und kleineren Bildern und Zeichnungen von Henri Rousseau«, Galerie »291«, 18. November bis Dezember 1910. Webers Vorwort wurde in *Camera Work,* Nr. 33, Januar 1911, unter »Photo-Secession Notes«, S. 46, nachgedruckt.

11. North, P., *Max Weber: American Modern,* New York 1982, S. 28. North ist der Ansicht, daß Weber 1910 »primitive Statuetten in zwei bedeutende Gouachen, auch in die *Mexikanische Statuette,* integrierte, um die Unterschiede zwischen dem zwei- und dreidimensionalen Medium dramatisch zuzuspitzen«. Weber stellte dieses Werk unter dem Titel *Kongo-Statuette* in seiner Einzelausstellung der Galerie »291« im Januar 1911 zum ersten Mal aus.

12. Weber, M., »The Fourth Dimension from a Plastic Point of View« in *Camera Work,* Nr. 31, Juli 1910, S. 25.

13. Weber, M., »Chinese Dolls and Modern Colorists« in *Camera Work,* Nr. 31, Juli 1910, S. 51.

14. Weber, *Oral History,* a. a. O., S. 94.

15. Weber, M., »To Xochipilli, Lord of Flowers« in *Camera Work,* Nr. 33, Januar 1911, S. 34.

16. Weber, M., *Cubist Poems,* London 1914.

17. Ebenda, S. 14.

18. »Woodcuts and Poems by Max Weber« in *The Art Students League News,* 15. Oktober 1948, S. 2. Weber, M., *Primitives: Poems and Woodcuts,* New York 1926.

19. Brief von Marsden Hartley an Alfred Stieglitz, Juli 1912. The Alfred Stieglitz Archives, Beinecke Rare Book and Manuscript Library, Yale University, New Haven, Connecticut. (Zit. Yale) Sadler, M. T. H., »After Gauguin« in *Rhythm, Art, Music, Literature 1,* Frühjahr 1912, S. 23–24. Über den Einfluß von Kandinsky auf Hartley siehe Levin, G., »Marsden Hartley, Kandinsky and Der Blaue Reiter« in *Arts Magazine,* November 1977, S. 156–60.

20. Hartley an Stieglitz, 9. Oktober 1912, Yale.

21. Hartley schickte Stieglitz ein zweites Exemplar des Almanachs und wies mehrmals auf seine Bedeutung hin. Vgl. die undatierte Postkarte von Hartley an Stieglitz von Anfang September 1912 und die Postkarte vom 27. September 1912, Yale.

22. Hartley an Stieglitz, 1. September 1912, Yale.

23. Ein ähnliches Acoma-Gefäß bei Frank, L., und Harlow, F. H., *Historic Pottery of the Pueblo Indians,* 1600–1880, Boston 1974, Tafel 14, mehrfarbige Kleeblattkanne, ca. 1860. Siehe auch Wingert, P. S., *American Indian Sculpture,* New York 1976, Tafel 1 a, mit einer ähnlichen *Kwakiutl*-Figur.

24. Hartley an Stieglitz, Brief Mitte November 1912. Einzelheiten für das Treffen vom 24. Januar 1913 sind in einer Postkarte und in einem 18-seitigen Brief aufgezeichnet, den Hartley Anfang Februar nach seiner Rückkehr nach Paris an Stieglitz schrieb, Yale.

25. Stieglitz an Hartley, 20. Oktober 1913, Yale.

26. Siehe *Camera Work,* Nr. 1, Januar 1903, S. 14. Vgl. Carter, N. C., »The Inner Circle: Portraits in Alfred Stieglitz's *Camera Work«,* Diss., University of Iowa 1972, S. 101–117. Keiley, J. T., »Gertrude Käsebier« in *Camera Work,* Nr. 20, Oktober 1907, S. 27. Keiley führt Käsebiers Offenheit gegenüber den Indianern auf Eindrücke zurück, die in ihre Kindheit in Colorado zurückreichen.

27. Der Kritiker Paul Rosenfeld schrieb, daß »der arme Indianer« bis in die jüngste Zeit hinein der einzige Amerikaner war, der ein »Gefühl für die Erde« entwickelt habe. Er zelebrierte die Tänze der Indianer und ihre Rituale, die ihn »in Harmonie mit der Natur« versetzen. Vgl. Rosenfeld, P., *Port of New York,* Urbana 1961, S. 94. Das Buch von William Carlos Williams, *In the American Grain,* erzählt, wie Daniel Boone zu der Einsicht gelangte, »er selbst zu sein in einer neuen Welt wie ein Indianer. Wenn das Land in Besitz genommen werden muß, dann in der Art der Indianer . . . als Blume ihrer Welt«, New York 1925, S. 137–38. Mabel Dodge, boheme-hafte Gastgeberin der führenden Maler und Schriftsteller, führte der Weg nach Taos, Neu-Mexiko, wo sie schließlich Tony Luhan, einen Indianer heiratete, ihren vierten und letzten Ehemann. Über das Bureau of Indian Affairs setzte sie sich für die Interessen der Indianer ein, vgl. Hahn, E., *Mabel: A Biography of Mabel Dodge Luhan,* Boston 1977, S. 209–10.

28. Diese Fragen sind von Ann Tempkin in ihrem Vortrag »Marsden Hartleys America: 1914 Indian Compositions« im Rahmen des Sixth Annual Whitney Symposium on American Art, 25. April 1983, sorgfältig ausgearbeitet worden. Ich hatte vorher meine eigenen Photographien und Ergebnisse bezüglich der Indianerkunst, die Hartley in Berlin gesehen hatte, dem Herausgeber des vorliegenden Buches vorgelegt. Tempkins Erkenntnisse treffen sich mit meinen eigenen nur im Hinblick auf die Kunst der Prärieindianer. Die Autorin übersah hingegen den gleichermaßen bedeutsamen Einfluß der *Hopi*-Katchinas auf Hartley. Grundsätzlich stimmen wir darin überein, daß die Motive der Prärieindianer für Hartley wichtig waren, dennoch sind die von mir vorgeschlagenen Beispiele alle der Sammlung des Museums für Völkerkunde entnommen, die Hartley 1914 in Berlin sah.

29. Macke, A., »Die Masken« in *Der Blaue Reiter,* herausgegeben von Wassily Kandinsky und Franz Marc. *Der Blaue Reiter Almanach,* von Klaus Lankheit herausgegebene dokumentarische Edition, New York 1974, S. 83–89.

30. Hartley an Stieglitz, 31. Oktober 1913, Yale. Zitiert in Levin, »Marsden Hartley, Kandinsky and Der Blaue Reiter«, S. 160. Über den weiteren Zusammenhang von Kandinskys Einfluß auf Hartley vgl. Sandra Gail Levin, »Wassily Kandinsky and the American Avant-Garde, 1912–1950«, Dissertation, Rutgers University 1976, S. 79–140.

31. Über 6000 Objekte sind während des Zweiten Weltkrieges verlorengegangen oder wurden zerstört. Herr Dr. Hartmann vom Museum für Völkerkunde danke ich für diese Information, wie auch für die kundige Unterstützung, die er mir während meiner Forschungen über die Indianerkunst Nordamerikas in Berlin zuteil werden ließ.

32. Hartley könnte diese Sterne auf dem anonymen religiösen Bild eines europäischen Malers gesehen haben, das im *Blauen Reiter,* S. 167, abgebildet war. In einem Brief an Stieglitz vom August 1913 schrieb Hartley, daß er den achtstrahligen Stern »überall in Berlin . . . (sehe) . . . alle Könige trugen ihn über ihrem Herzen – der Soldat auf der Stirn«. Arnold Rönnebeck schrieb in einem Brief an Duncan Phillips nach 1943 (Yale), daß sich Hartley für das Eiserne Kreuz interessierte, das Rönnebeck und seinem Cousin Karl von Freyburg für ihre Kriegsverdienste verliehen worden war.

33. Diese hölzerne Skulptur ging während des Kriegs verloren oder wurde zerstört. *Der Blaue Reiter,* dokumentarische Edition, S. 88.

34. Hartley an Stieglitz, 3. November 1914, Yale. Hartleys letzte Arbeiten, die von primitiver Kunst beeinflußt waren, sind abstrakte Gemälde aus dem Jahr 1925. Sie basieren auf afrikanischen Textilarbeiten. Abgebildet im Katalog *Marsden Hartley 1877–1943,* C. W. Post Art Gallery, Greenvale, Long Island, 6. November bis 14. Dezember 1977, Abb. 17 A und B.

35. Hartley an Stieglitz, 12. November 1914 (irrtümlich 1913), Yale.

36. Hartley, M., »Red Man Ceremonials: An American Plea for American Esthetics« in *Art and Archaeology,* Nr. 9, Januar 1920, S. 14. Zum Einfluß der europäischen Moderne auf Hartley siehe Levin, G., »Marsden Hartley and the European Avant-Garde« in *Arts Magazine, Nr. 54, September 1979, S. 158–63.*

37. Hartley, M., »The Red Man« in *Adventures in the Arts,* New York 1921, S. 20. Hier bezog sich Hartley auf den Häuptlingskragen aus Alaska, möglicherweise vom Stamm der *Tlingit* (Chilcat), abgebildet in *Der Blaue Reiter.*

38. Ebenda, S. 26. Hartleys Schriften über die Kunst der Indianer müssen beträchtlichen Einfluß gehabt haben. Vgl. auch Hartley, M., »Tribal Esthetics« in *The Dial,* 16. November 1918, S. 6.

39. Man Ray, *Self-Portrait,* Boston 1963, S. 75. Der in diesen Memoiren beschriebene Zeitpunkt bezieht sich auf das Jahr 1917, als Man Ray begann, mit der Spritzpistole zu arbeiten. Meine mit Francis Naumann geführten Gespräche über Man Ray trugen zu dieser Interpretation bei.

40. Dieses Zitat und auch das folgende stammen aus einem Fragebogen, den Man Ray über sein Gemälde *Fünf Figuren* (1914) ausfüllte, als es am 23. März 1957 vom Whitney Museum of American Art gekauft wurde.

41. Avrich, P., *The Modern School Movement: Anarchism and Education in the United States,* Princeton 1980, S. 155. Avrich stellt fest, daß Weber im Jahre 1912 das Ferrer Center besuchte, nachdem er dort von Robert Henri eingeführt worden war. Im Juni 1913 war Weber der Redner der Feier zum dritten Jahrestag des Ferrer Centers. Seine Gedichte und Holzschnitte wurden in der Zeitschrift *The Modern School* veröffentlicht. Man Ray erinnert sich, daß er zur gleichen Zeit an Abendklassen und geselligen Veranstaltungen am Ferrer Center teilgenommen hat. Siehe Man Ray, *Self-Portrait, S. 21-25.*

42. Man Ray, Self-Portrait, S. 23.

43. Ebenda, S. 54.

44. Ebenda, S. 74–75 und S. 18 über seine Erinnerung, afrikanische Kunst in der Galerie »291« gesehen zu haben. Siehe S. 74–75, wo er bestätigt, daß er versucht habe, seine Frau dazu zu überreden, ein Leopardenfell zu tragen mit dem Argument, daß »die Kunst der Primitiven und der Wilden moderne Menschen in allen Ländern beeinflusse und sie so viel ursprünglicher aussähe«.

45. De Zayas an Stieglitz, 21. April 1911, Yale.

46. Zitiert aus Homer, W. I., *Alfred Stieglitz and the American Avant-Garde,* Boston 1977, S. 198–99. Die Zeitschrift *Camera Work,* Nr. 48, Oktober 1916, S. 13, druckte Charles H. Caffins Bericht aus dem *New York American* ab und zitierte die Aussteller: » . . . dies ist das erste Mal in der Ausstellungsgeschichte, daß Negerplastiken von einem künstlerischen Gesichtspunkt aus gesehen werden«. Über De Zayas' eigenen Bericht über diese und andere Ausstellungen afrikanischer Kunst in New York siehe Marius de Zayas, »How, When and Why Modern Art Came to New York« in *Arts Magazine,* Nr. 54, April 1980, S. 109–12, mit Einführung und Anmerkungen von Francis

M. Naumann. Ich danke Naumann für seine hilfreichen Vorschläge bezüglich De Zayas und primitiver Kunst. De Zayas erklärte (S. 109), daß er Paul Guillaume über Guillaume Apollinaire kennengelernt habe, dessen Bekanntschaft er zuvor durch Picabia gemacht hatte.

47. De Zayas, »How, When and Why . . .«, S. 114. Für eine gründliche Analyse von De Zayas' Karikaturen und ihres Einflusses auf Picabia und andere siehe Bohn, W., »The Abstract Vision of Marius de Zayas« in *The Art Bulletin,* Nr. 62, September 1980, S. 434–52. Meine folgende Untersuchung von De Zayas' Adaption des Pukapuka-Seelenfängers basiert auf den Ergebnissen von Bohn.

48. Coady hatte Max Weber in Paris getroffen und über ihn auch Henri Rousseau. Er kannte auch die Steins. Siehe Zilczer, J. K., »Robert J. Coady, Forgotten Spokesman for Avant-Garde Culture in America« in *American Art Review,* Nr. 2, 1975, S. 77–89. Coady zeigte in seiner Galerie bereits im Frühjahr 1914 afrikanische Skulptur.

49. Zitiert aus dem Rundschreiben zur Eröffnung der Modern Gallery, 500 Fifth Avenue, am 7. Oktober 1915. Nachgedruckt in *Camera Work,* Nr. 48, Oktober 1916, S. 63 unter dem Titel »›291‹ and the Modern Gallery«. 1916 und 1918 veranstaltete die Modern Gallery wichtige Ausstellungen afrikanischer Kunst. Besprechungen bei De Zayas, »How, When and Why . . .«, S. 110–12.

50. Marius de Zayas, »Modern Art in Connection with Negro Art« in *Camera Work,* Nr. 48, Oktober 1916, S. 7. De Zayas, *African Negro Art: Its Influence on Modern Art,* New York 1916. Zur Entwicklung von De Zayas' Ideen über afrikanische Kunst: Zilczer, J., »Primitivism and New York Dada« in *Arts Magazine,* Nr. 51, Mai 1977, S. 140–42. De Zayas, der die Afrikaner als geistig tieferstehende, mit Kindern vergleichbare Wilde betrachtete, kannte wohl keine zutreffenderen anthropologischen Urteile.

51. De Zayas, *African Negro Art,* S. 41.

52. Sheeler publizierte nur 22 Exemplare dieses Buches, unter den Besitzern waren aber verschiedene Künstler, u. a. Weber und Zorach. Reid, B. L., *The Man From New York: John Quinn and His Friends,* New York 1968, S. 556–557. Noch 1922 »hielt Quinn an seinem Interesse für orientalische, afrikanische und polynesische Kunst fest, hauptsächlich waren es aber die Stammväter der Moderne«. Im Juni 1922 kaufte Quinn einen afrikanischen Torso mit einem Steinsockel für 875 Dollar von Marius de Zayas. Über primitive Kunst in der Arensberg Collection siehe Naumann, F., »Walter Conrad Arensberg: Poet, Patron and Participant in the New York Avant-Garde, 1915–20« in *Philadelphia Museum of Art Bulletin,* Nr. 76, Frühjahr 1980, S. 8–10. Dort sind Sheelers Photographien von Arensbergs Wohnung in New York abgebildet (ca. 1918), die afrikanische und aztekische Skulpturen zeigen. Naumann schrieb über Arensberg, S. 10: »Zu seiten des Kaminsimses plazierte er etwa Brancusis *Verlorenen Sohn* und eine afrikanische Figur. Auf diese Weise wollte er nicht nur einen Vergleich des Materials nahelegen – beide sind aus Holz geschnitzt und auf grauem Stein gesockelt –, sondern auch auf gemeinsame Tendenzen in der Abstraktion der Formen hinweisen. Von De Zayas hatte Arensberg 1915 seine erste präkolumbianische Skulptur erworben.«

53. Tarbell, R. K., »Sculpture in America before the Armory Show: Transition to Modern« in *Vanguard American Sculpture 1913–1939,* New Brunswick 1979, S. 4. Vgl. Kap. 4, S. 45–46; Tarbell, R. K., »Direct Carving«, mit einem Überblick über diese amerikanischen Bildhauer. Über die Genauigkeit von Laurents Erinnerungen bestehen durchaus Zweifel. Siehe Moak, P. V., »Robert Laurent (1890–1970)« in *The Robert Laurent Memorial Exhibition,* Durham 1972, S. 15. Moak schreibt, daß Laurent 1906 von Burty mit Picasso bekannt gemacht wurde und daß er Gemälde der Rosa Periode bewunderte. Während es durchaus sein kann, daß sich Laurent richtig erinnert und (laut Aussage von Tarbell) 1907 afrikanische Skulptur bei Picasso vor seiner Abreise nach Italien gesehen hat, gab er später selbst zu, die viel zitierte Geschichte von seinem Studium in Rom mit einem Holzschnitzer namens Giuseppe Doratori erfunden zu haben. Frost, R., »Laurent: Frames to Figures, Brittany to Brooklyn« in *Art News,* 1.–14. April, 1941, S. 10. Dort steht, daß Laurent Picasso 1905 kennenlernte und die Werke seiner »blauen Periode bewunderte«.

54. Tarbell, »Direct Carving«, S. 51–52. Siehe Zorach, W., *Art is my Life: An Autobiography,* Cleveland 1967, S. 66. »Ich interessierte mich für primitive Kunst. Als wir zum ersten Mal nach New York kamen, kannte ich Skulpturen der Azteken, der Mayas und Schnitzwerke der Eskimos aus dem Museum of Natural History. In der Galerie »291«, der Galerie von Stieglitz, sah ich De Zayas' Ausstellung afrikanischer Plastik. Sie besaß eine unerreichte magische und spirituelle Qualität . . . Charles Sheeler machte eine wunderbare Photoserie von diesen Plastiken, so konnte ich sie wenigstens über sein Buch besitzen. Es kostete 50 Dollar. Ich konnte das Geld kaum zusammenkratzen, aber ich kaufte das Buch.« Zorachs Gedächtnis trügt ein wenig, wenn er behauptet, Tessim in afrikanischem Mahagoni gearbeitet zu haben. In seinem Buch *The Sculpture of William Zorach,* New York 1938, S. 20, erwähnt Paul S. Wingert, daß in Provincetown *Der Knabe* aus Ahornholz geschnitzt wurde, das Zorach aus Kalifornien mitgebracht hatte. Wingert geht auch auf sein Interesse an afrikanischer Skulptur ein und ihren Einfluß auf sein Werk. Die drei Arbeiten aus Mahagoni schnitzte Zorach 1922.

55. Siehe Wechsler, J., »Machine Aesthetics and Art Deco« in *Vanguard American Sculpture, 1913–1919,* S. 102; dort auch den Verweis auf Noel Frackmans Entdeckungen in der unveröffentlichten Studie »John Storrs and the Origins of Art Deco«, New York University 1975, S. 32.

56. Hillier, B., *The World of Art Deco,* New York 1971, S. 28–32.

57. Calder, A., *Calder: An Autobiography with Pictures,* Boston 1966, S. 80. José de Creeft fertigte 1927 eine abstrakte Schnitzarbeit aus Lindenholz mit dem Titel *Voyage to Africa.* Abgebildet in Campos, J., *José de Creeft,* New York 1972, Abb. 261–262.

58. Calder begann 1926 zu schnitzen, bevor er nach Paris ging. Die ersten Holzplastiken scheinen von amerikanischer Volkskunst angeregt zu sein, weniger von primitiver Skulptur. Mein Dank gilt Joan M. Marter, die mich an ihren exzellenten Studien über den frühen Calder teilhaben ließ. Vgl. Marter, Joan M., »Interaction of American Sculptors with European Modernists: Alexander Calder and Isamu Noguchi« in *Vanguard American Sculpture,* 1913–1939, S. 106–107. Marter, J. M., »A. Calder, The Formative Years«, Dissertation, University of Delaware 1974.

59. Calder, *Autobiography,* S. 107–108.

60. Morris, G. L. K., »Contemporary Writers, British and Americans« in *The Yale Literary Magazine,* Nr. 93, März 1928, S. 103–115. Zitiert in: Lorenz, M. A., *George L. K. Morris: Artist and Critic,* Ann Arbor 1982, S. 5.

61 Matulka sammelte auch afrikanische und andere primitive Masken, die er in den 30er Jahren in seine Stilleben integrierte. Siehe Katalog *Jan Matulka 1890–1972,* Washington, 1980, S. 66, 67 und 72.

62 Lorenz, *Georges L. K. Morris, S. 13.*

63. Morris, G. L. K., »Fernand Léger versus Cubism« in *Bulletin of the Museum of Modern Art,* Nr. 1, Oktober 1935, S. 7. Eine hervorragende Analyse einiger Bilder, vor allem *Jagende Indianer No. 4.*

64. Cikovsky, N., Jr., »Notes and Footnotes on a Painting by George L. K. Morris« in *University of New Mexico Art Museum Bulletin,* Nr. 10, 1976–77, S. 3–11.

65. Zitiert bei Lorenz, *George L. K. Morris,* S. 11

66. Guillaume, P., und Munro, Th., *Primitive Negro Sculpture,* New York 1926, S. 133. Über Guillaumes Rolle als Förderer afrikanischer Kunst siehe Bell, C., »Negro Sculpture«, Nachdruck in Bell, C., *Since Cézanne,* New York 1922, S. 113–21. Bell geht auch auf den Einfluß der afrikanischen Skulptur auf moderne französische Künstler ein.

67. Boas, F., *Primitive Art,* Cambridge, Mass., 1928. Schon früher hatte Boas seine Begeisterung über die Kunst der Indianer von der Nordwestküste ausgesprochen, vgl. »Representative Art of Primitive People« in *Holmes Anniversary Volume,* Washington 1916. Für Informationen über die Künstler, die sich in den 40er Jahren für die Kunst der Indianer von der Nordwestküste interessierten, siehe: Gibson, A., »Painting outside the Paradigm: Indian Space« in *Arts Magazine,* Nr. 57, Februar 1983, S. 98–104.

68. Graham, J., *System and Dialectics of Art,* New York 1937. Neuauflage von 1971 mit einer Einleitung von Marcia Epstein Allentuck, Baltimore 1971.

69. Ebenda, Vorwort von Dorothy Dehner, S. XVIII-XIX.

70. Mac Naughton, M. D., »Adolph Gottlieb: His Life and Art« in *Adolph Gottlieb: A Retrospective,* New York 1981, S. 20

71. Graham, *System and Dialectics,* S. 116. Die Kursivschreibung stammt von mir.

72. Graham, J., Vorwort zum Ausstellungskatalog *Exhibition of Sculpture of Old African Civilisations,* Jacques Seligmann Gallery, New York 1936, zitiert bei Allentuck, *John Graham's System and Dialectics of Art,* S. 76.

73. Kandinsky, W., *Über das Geistige in der Kunst,* Bern 1952, S. 21/22. (engl. Übersetzung von Michael Sadlier, *The Art of Spiritual Harmony,* London/Boston 1914, S. 1). Über den wichtigen Einfluß der Gedanken Kandinskys in Amerika siehe Levin, »W. Kandinsky and the American Avant-Garde, 1912–1950«.

74. De Zayas, »How, When and Why . . .«, S. 109.

75. Kandinsky, *Über das Geistige . . .,* S. 22.

□ 682 *Fernand Léger, ›Vogel‹, Kostümentwurf für ›Die Erschaffung der Welt‹ (La création du monde), 1923, Aquarell, 34 x 23 cm. Dansmuseet, Stockholm.*

Laura Rosenstock

Léger

»Die Erschaffung der Welt«

Nach dem 1. Weltkrieg zeigte die Pariser Gesellschaft zunehmend Interesse an der Kunst und Kultur Afrikas und auch des schwarzen Amerika, die normalerweise häufig verwechselt werden. Die Anziehungskraft der afrikanischen Plastik, des amerikanischen Negerjazz und Negertanzes beeinflußte die Pariser Kultur in vielerlei Hinsicht, auch im Bereich von Unterhaltung, Mode und Design. Wie weit dieser Einfluß reichte, zeigt die 1923 vom Schwedischen Ballett aufgeführte *Erschaffung der Welt* besonders exemplarisch. Légers Dekoration und Kostüme waren aus seinen Zeichnungen nach afrikanischer Kunst entwickelt, das Libretto von Blaise Cendrars basierte auf afrikanischen Mythen, die Choreographie Jean Börlins auf Recherchen zur Ethnologie afrikanischer Stämme, und die Musik von Darius Milhaud war vom Jazz inspiriert, den der Komponist erst kurz zuvor in New York gehört hatte. Es sollte »das einzig mögliche ballet nègre der ganzen Welt« werden, schrieb Léger, eines, das »vorbildlich in seiner Art bleiben« würde.[1]

Zur Zeit der *Erschaffung der Welt* erreichte die Welle der schwarzen Kultur in Paris ihren Höhepunkt. »Art nègre« interessierte die Avantgarde in Paris seit 1906. Aber dem breiten Publikum blieb diese Kunst im Grunde bis nach dem 1. Weltkrieg unbekannt. Vor 1919 gab es nur einzelne Galerien, die afrikanische Skulptur ausstellten. Im Mai 1919 wurde dann eine Ausstellung primitiver Kunst unter dem Titel »Première Exposition d'Art Nègre et d'Art Océanien« von Paul Guillaume in der Galerie Devambez in Paris gezeigt. Guillaume veranstaltete in diesem Zusammenhang auch eine »Fête nègre«.[2] Obwohl die Behauptung, dies sei die »erste« Ausstellung ihrer Art, nicht ganz richtig ist, zielte diese Ausstellung erstmals auf ein breiteres Publikum, bei dem sie auf große Resonanz stieß. Zahlreiche Kolonialausstellungen sollten dieses Interesse weiter vertiefen.

Verschiedene Autoren brachten die plötzliche Popularität der afrikanischen Kunst im Paris der 20er Jahre mit der Präsenz von Truppen aus dem Senegal und Zouave in Zusammenhang, die nach Frankreich gebracht worden waren, um im 1. Weltkrieg zu kämpfen.[3] Was auch immer der unmittelbare Auslöser dieses Trends gewesen sein mag, ganz sicher war er die Antwort auf ein weit verbreitetes Bedürfnis nach neuen, unverbrauchten Kunstformen, die direkter und natürlicher sein sollten als diejenigen der Vorkriegskultur.

Avantgardistisches Theater und Ballett kamen diesen neuen Bedürfnissen des Publikums entgegen. Von 1917 bis 1926 war die Beteiligung moderner Maler an Theater- und Ballettentwürfen größer als je zuvor oder danach. Das Theater war zum wichtigsten künstlerischen Anziehungspunkt geworden. »Es hat niemals eine Zeit gegeben, die so versessen auf Schauspiel war wie die unsere. Der Andrang der Massen zur Leinwand und zur Bühne ist zu einer allgemeinen Erscheinung geworden«, schrieb Léger.[4] Zu dieser Zeit vermittelte das Theater wie keine zweite Kunstform die neuesten künstlerischen Strömungen dem breiten Publikum. So wie Picassos Ausstattung der *Parade* □ 539–545 die Öffentlichkeit mit kubistischen Ideen bekannt gemacht hatte, so machte das Theater das Publikum auch vertraut mit Dada und später mit dem Surrealismus, Kunstrichtungen, die sich besonders für die Popularisierung primitiver Kulturen einsetzten.

Die Dadaisten und in geringerem Ausmaß auch die Futuristen hatten ihre Anregungen bei Musik und Tanz der Eingeborenenstämme, vor allem in Afrika, gesucht. 1916 wurden im Cabaret Voltaire in Zürich »Afrikanische Nächte« veranstaltet, bei denen Richard Huelsenbeck seine »authentischen« Negergedichte sang (jedes endete mit »Umba-Umba«-Rufen), begleitet von Tam-Tam-Trommeln. Huelsenbeck beschrieb diese Abende folgendermaßen: »Wir kreierten gemeinsam einen wundervollen Neger-Singsang mit Klappern, Holzschlegeln und vielen primitiven Instrumenten . . . unsere kubistischen Tänze mit Masken von Janco □ 794 und selbstgemachten Kostümen aus bemaltem Pappkarton und Flitterkram.«[5] Hugo Ball bereitete eine Soiree in der Galerie Dada vor: »Ich werde einen neuen Tanz aufführen mit fünf Laban-Tänzerinnen als Negerinnen mit langen schwarzen Kaftans und Gesichtsmasken.«[6] Tristan Tzara war die treibende Kraft hinter dem Interesse der Dadaisten an Afrika. Er veröffentlichte an die 40 »afrikanische Gedichte«,[7] schrieb Artikel, in denen er primitive und westliche Kunst verglich, und hielt Vorträge über afrikanische Skulptur. Sein Stück *La Première Aventure céleste de M. Antipyrine* von 1916 war mit pseudoafrikanischen Wörtern wie »Dschilolu Mgabati Bailunda« oder »Soco Bgai Affahou« durchsetzt.

Es war keineswegs überraschend, daß sich der Primitivismus des Dada »afrikanischer« Klänge und Rhythmen bediente, denn derartige Aufführungen waren ebensogut akustische wie visuelle Ereignisse. Im Dadaismus wie Futurismus gab es auch afrikanisch inspirierte bildhauerische Ansätze. Fortunato Deperos und Gilbert Clavels *Plastische Tänze*, die 1918 im Teatro dei Piccoli in Rom aufgeführt wurden, kreisten um Deperos »Großen Wilden«, eine überlebensgroße Holzfigur, die gleich einer afrikanischen Plastik (in Deperos Parodie) Attribute wie Kopfschmuck, Stab, Nasenring und hervortretenden Bauchnabel hatte □ 583. Marcel Jancos Zeichnung

□ 683 *›Der große Wilde‹, Photographie der lebensgroßen Marionette nach dem Entwurf von Fortunato Depero für das mit Gilbert Clavel produzierte Ballett ›Plastische Tänze‹, 1918.*

zweier Negerfiguren läßt in ähnlicher Weise afrikanische Kunst anklingen □ 792. Während der Dadaismus und seine Publikationen bis 1919 in Paris weitgehend unbekannt blieben, gab es jedoch bereits eine »afrikanische« Ausstattung für das Pariser Theater in Apollinaires »Les Mamelles de Tirésias«, die 1917 aufgeführt wurden und wo ein Schauspieler als »Volk von Sansibar« auftrat. Diese stumme Rolle wurde begleitet von einer Schar von Lärmenden.

Die schwarze Kultur Amerikas wurde auch populär durch die Massen von Amerikanern, die um diese Zeit in Paris eintrafen und in den 20er Jahren die größte Gruppe von Ausländern in der Stadt bildeten. Während der amerikanische Ragtime und Cakewalk in Europa bereits um 1900 bekannt waren (1903 spielte Philip Sousa persönlich diese Musik in Paris), wurde die große Beliebtheit der amerikanischen Negerkultur – ihre Revuen, Entertainer und der Jazz – erst nach dem Krieg zu einem allgemeinen Phänomen.

Der Jazz wurde in Europa z. T. durch amerikanische Soldaten eingeführt, die während des Krieges hier stationiert waren, aber auch durch das Radio und die Dixieland-Schallplatten, die 1917 von der amerikanischen Victor Company aufgenommen wurden. Louis Mitchells Orchester, in dem Sidney Bechet spielte, war die erste schwarze Jazzband, die nach Europa kam und dort blieb. Ihr folgten 1917 andere schwarze Jazzmusiker. 1918 spielten schwarze Orchester im Casino de Paris, bei Privatfesten und vielen gesellschaftlichen Veranstaltungen. Möglicherweise fand die erste private Soiree mit amerikanischem Jazz im Haus von Etienne de Beaumont im August 1918 statt. Zum Programm dieser Veranstaltung, die als »großes Negerfest« angekündigt war, gehörte eine Aufführung von Francis Poulencs »Rhapsodie nègre«, außerdem von schwarzen amerikanischen Soldaten gespielter Jazz. 1919 kamen viele Jazzbands nach, und 1921 präsentierte das Théâtre des Champs-Elysées »The Most Famous American Southern Syncopated Orchestra«, das ein reichhaltiges Programm mit Spirituals und Schlagzeugeinlagen bot.

Die Begeisterung erreichte im Starkult um Josephine Baker ihren Höhepunkt. Wie sie in ihrer Autobiographie erzählt, war es Fernand Léger, der Rolf de Maré vorschlug, ein schwarzes Ensemble aus New York nach Paris zu holen. De Maré war Direktor und Manager des Théâtre des Champs-Elysées, das nach der Auflösung des Schwedischen Balletts im Jahr 1925 als Opern- und Musikhalle diente. *La Revue nègre,* produziert von Caroline Dudley, wurde aus Amerika geholt und im Oktober 1925 in Paris uraufgeführt. Erstmals trat Josephine Baker auf, die praktisch über Nacht zu einem europäischen Mythos wurde.[8] Die Künstler reagierten positiv auf die neue schwarze Mode und huldigten der Baker persönlich. Paul Colin gestaltete Plakate für die *Revue nègre* □ 684, und Alexander Calders erste reine Drahtplastik ist möglicherweise eine Darstellung der Josephine Baker von 1926.[9]

Die Begeisterung für die schwarze Kultur machte auch vor dem Kino nicht halt. Im Film *Princess Tam-Tam* von 1935

□ 684 *Paul Colin, ›Die Revue nègre im Théâtre des Champs-Elysées‹, 1926, Farblithographie, 155 x 118 cm. Musée de la Publicité, Paris.*

spielte J. Baker ein afrikanisches Eingeborenenmädchen, das nach Paris kommt und wie eine »Prinzessin« herumgereicht und zum Tagesgespräch des eleganten Paris wird. Schon früher zeigte Jean Renoirs stumme, phantastische Satire *Charleston* von 1927 einen schwarzen Afrikaner (gespielt von Johnny Hudgins, dem Star der *Revue nègre*), der im Jahr 2028 nach Europa kommt, die europäische Zivilisation tot vorfindet und einer weißen »Ureinwohnerin« (Catherine Hessling) begegnet, die Charleston tanzt. Partyszenen in Filmen wie Marcel L'Herbiers *L'Inhumaine* (1923) zeigten normalerweise schwarze Schauspieler in der Rolle der Unterhaltungskünstler.

In die Arbeit avantgardistischer Künstler floß oft die Begeisterung für die schwarze Kultur Amerikas, vor allem den Jazz, ein. Picabia malte 1913 in New York *Negro Song* I und II, nachdem er – wie er später erzählte – Neger in einem Restaurant gehört hatte. Gleizes malte 1915 in New York das Bild *Jazz*, und Cocteau schrieb ihm 1918 dorthin mit der Bitte, verschiedene Proben von »Negro ragtimes« zu schicken.[10] Der ausgewanderte amerikanische Maler Gerald Murphy ließ sich, solange er in Frankreich lebte, regelmäßig die neuesten Jazzplatten schicken. In ihrer Wohnung an der Riviera sangen Murphy und seine Frau ihren Freunden amerikanische Folksongs der Schwarzen und Spirituals zur Unterhaltung vor, darunter auch unveröffentlichte Lieder, die sie in Bibliotheken entdeckt hatten.

In der ernsten französischen Musik wurde der Jazz zum ersten Mal in Erik Saties Partitur für *Parade*, eine Produktion des Russischen Balletts von 1917 verwendet, die von Jazzrhythmen und Schlagermelodien aufgelockert war. Die Anleihen beim Jazz werden besonders deutlich in dem Musikstück mit dem Titel »Ragtime du paquebot« (Dampfschiff-Rag), das den Tanz des »Little American Girl« begleitete. Diese Figur mimte dabei Situationen wie Einen-Zug-Erreichen, Autofahren, Schwimmen, In-einem-Film-Mitspielen und Einen-Bankraub-Verhindern. An einer Stelle imitierte sie den Gang Charlie Chaplins, musikalisch begleitet von synkopischen Melodien und Rhythmen.[11]

Auch Strawinsky ließ sich von den neuen Klängen beeinflussen. Er hatte während des 1. Weltkrieges einige Blätter Ragtime von dem Komponisten Ernest Ansermet erhalten und integrierte Tango, Walzer und Ragtime in die Partitur seiner *Histoire du soldat* von 1918. Sein *Ragtime*, den er im gleichen Jahr komponierte, versuchte populärer Tanzmusik den Rang von Konzertmusik zu verleihen. Seine *Piano Rag Music* komponierte er 1919, nachdem er schließlich Jazzbands live gehört hatte. Dieses Stück bestätigte sein Interesse an rhythmischen Prinzipien und Improvisationsstil des Jazz.

□ 685 *Bühnenbild für ›Die Erschaffung der Welt‹ (La création du monde), Ausstattung und Kostüme von Fernand Léger. Photographie von 1923. Dansmuseet, Stockholm.*

□ 686 *Fernand Léger, Entwurf für ›Die Erschaffung der Welt‹ (La création du monde), 1922, Gouache, 28 x 44 cm. Privatbesitz.*

Nach dem 1. Weltkrieg versammelten sich in Paris verschiedene junge Komponisten um Satie und veranstalteten Konzerte inmitten der afrikanischen Skulpturen der Galerie von Paul Guillaume.[12] Jean Cocteau, der 1918 in seinem Pamphlet *Le Coq et l'harlequin* bewundernd über den amerikanischen Jazz schrieb, war ihr Poet und Publizist. Diese Komponisten – Georges Auric, Louis Durey, Arthur Honegger, Francis Poulenc, Germaine Tailleferre und Darius Milhaud – taufte der Kritiker Henri Collet später »Les Six«. Milhaud zufolge war Satie Mittelpunkt der Gruppe.

Anfang Februar 1921 besuchten Cocteau und »Les Six« die Gaya-Bar, wo der Pianist Jean Wiener mit dem schwarzen amerikanischen Saxophonisten Vance Lowry Jazz spielte. Dort sollten sich Cocteau, Milhaud und PICABIA später, als der Nachtklub als »Le Bœuf sur le Toit« bekannt wurde, als Jazz-Schlagzeuger versuchen. Obwohl Milhaud schon vorher von ähnlichen Rhythmen, die er 1917/18 in Brasilien gehört hatte, fasziniert war,[13] fand seine erste wichtige Begegnung mit dem Jazz 1920 in London statt, als Billy Arnold und seine New York Band dort spielten. 1922 hörte Milhaud bei einem Besuch in New York Paul Whitemans Orchester, und er wurde nach Harlem mitgenommen, wo man New Orleans-Jazz spielte, eine Musik, die – wie er sagte – »völlig anders war als alles, was ich je zuvor gehört hatte«.[14]

Obwohl die primitive, d.h. die traditionelle afrikanische Gesellschaft und das moderne Leben des schwarzen Amerika ganz verschiedene Kulturen hervorbrachten, wurden sie in den 20er Jahren von den Europäern häufig verwechselt. In ihrem naiven Verständnis von schwarzer Kultur betrachteten sie beides im wesentlichen als ein und dasselbe. Der Schriftsteller und Diplomat Paul Morand, der ein Jahr zuvor nach Timbuktu gereist war, bezeichnete bei einem Besuch New Yorks Harlem als »Miniatur-Afrika«. Der Film *Charleston* enthält beides: die Rolle eines Afrikaners und Jazzmusik, die den Charleston begleitet. Der Modeschöpfer Paul Poiret behauptete: »Jazz ist nicht amerikanisch, er ist schwarz.« Und Milhaud schrieb über den Jazz: »Diese ursprüngliche Musik hat ihre Wurzeln in den dunklen Ecken der schwarzen Seele, in den letzten Spuren Afrikas.«[15]

Die Tatsache, daß gewisse Elemente der afrikanischen Musik in den Grundformen des Jazz auftauchen, war u.a. die Ursache für diese Verwechslung und trübte den Blick für den urbanen Hintergrund des modernen Amerika, in dem die Sprache des Jazz eigentlich beheimatet war. Es besteht weithin Einigkeit, daß die synkopischen Rhythmen Afrikas im Jazz stets erkennbar bleiben, auch wenn sie sich mit populärer französischer und amerikanischer Musik, mit Folksongs, Marsch- und Tanzmusik verbinden. Viele Kenner des Jazz haben über die enge Beziehung dieser neuen Musik zu ihren afrikanischen Wurzeln geschrieben und bemerkt, daß die in Harlem gespielten Solostücke den gleichen Rhythmus und den gleichen Ausdruck haben wie zeitgenössische Tam-Tam-Zeremonien im Kongo.[16] Für Robert Goffin besteht kein Zweifel, daß die afrikanische Tradition im Jazz weiterlebt und die Rolle des Jazz-Schlagzeugers unmittelbar auf die afrikanischen Tam-Tam-Trommler zurückzuführen sei: »An der Basis des Jazz finden wir den Ausdruck afrikanischer Rhythmik.«[17] Marshall Stearns konstatiert Ähnlichkeiten zwischen der Rhythmik im Jazz und westafrikanischer Musik. Im Jazz entdeckt er Restelemente der Musik aus Dahome mitsamt ihren komplizierten Rhythmen, den Ruf- und Antwortmustern, der Verwendung von erniedrigten Tonstufen (blue note) und der für den Jazz so wichtigen Blues-Skala, von Schlagwerk und dem sogenannten »falsetto break«.[18]

☐ 687 *›Holzfigur‹*, Senufo *(Elfenbeinküste). Abgebildet in Marius de Zayas, „African Negro Art: Its Influence on Modern Art", 1916.*

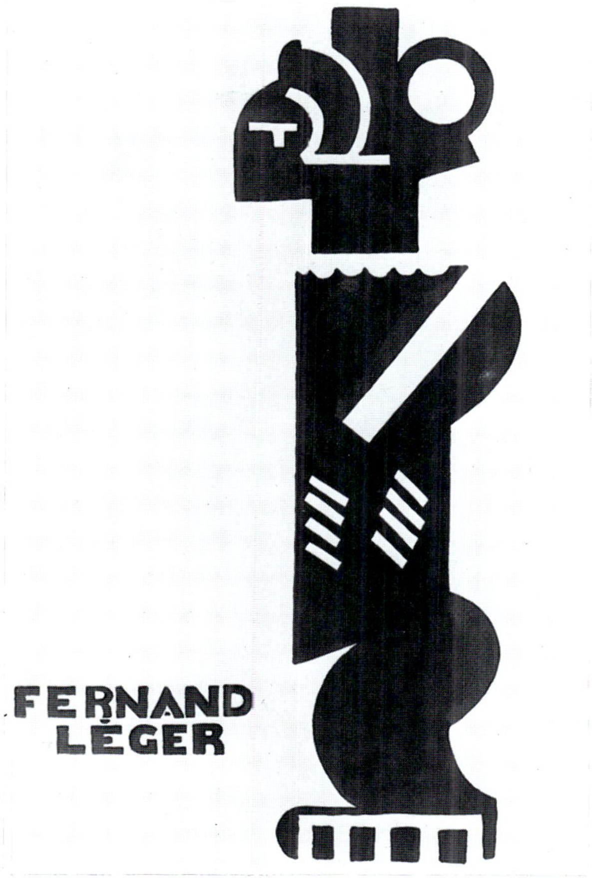

☐ 688 *Fernand Léger, Kostümentwurf für ›Die Erschaffung der Welt‹ (La création du monde), 1922/23, Gouache und Tusche, 30 x 20 cm. Sammlung Kay Hillman, New York.*

☐ 689 *›Männliche Figur‹*, Chokwe *(Angola), Höhe 42 cm. Puschkin Museum, Moskau. Abgebildet in Carl Einstein, „Negerplastik", 1915.*

Dennoch gibt es klare und substantielle Unterschiede zwischen amerikanischem Jazz und afrikanischer Musik. Kenner des Jazz bemerkten, daß das afrikanische Trommeln im Unterschied zum Jazz keinen Rhythmus kennt, wie auch afrikanischer Musik eine entwickelte natürliche Harmonie fremd ist. Außerdem sind die Elemente, die dem Jazz sein ausgeprägtes tonales System geben, europäischer Natur; er gehört somit eindeutig in den Bereich westlicher Musik.[19] Welche Verbindungen auch immer zwischen afrikanischem Trommeln und Jazz, zwischen afrikanischem Tanz und dem Cakewalk oder Charleston existieren, ihre Untersuchung würde den Rahmen der vorliegenden Studie überschreiten. Es genügt die Feststellung, daß für die französische Gesellschaft der 20er Jahre, für das breite wie für das intellektuelle Publikum, das schwarze Afrika und das schwarze Amerika unentwirrbar miteinander verknüpft waren und häufig auch gemeinsam präsentiert wurden, da man in der schwarzen Kultur Amerikas allgemein die Fortsetzung des afrikanischen Stammeslebens sah.

Ganz deutlich wird die Verwechslung und Vermischung der beiden Kulturen in der *Erschaffung der Welt,* einer Inszenierung des Schwedischen Ballets, die am 25. Oktober 1923 im Théâtre des Champs-Elysées ihre Premiere erlebte ☐ 685. Das Schwedische Ballett war im Oktober 1920 von Rolf de Maré in Paris gegründet worden.[20] Dieses Ensemble versuchte sich in experimentellem Tanz und Theaterproduktionen, in die manchmal Jazzrhythmen eingeflochten waren wie etwa in der Musik der »Six« (siehe oben) für Cocteaus 1921 kreiertes Stück

☐ 690 *Jean Börlin mit einer afrikanischen Maske bei seinem Tanz ›Sculpture nègre‹, 1920. Dansmuseet, Stockholm.*

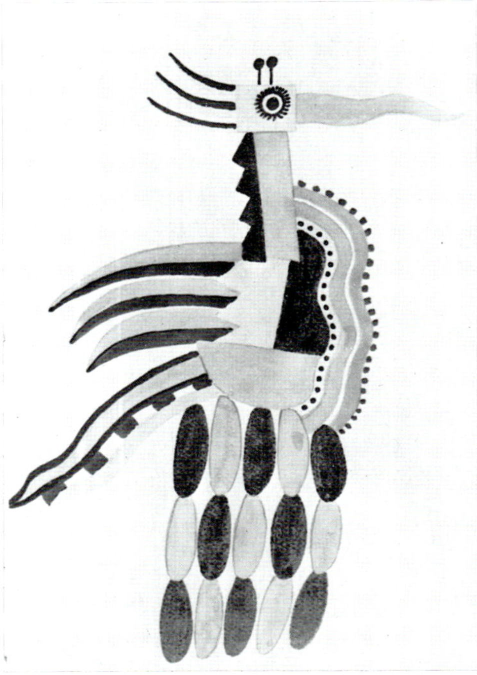

☐ 691 *Fernand Léger, ›Vogel‹, Farbabbildung* ☐ *682.*

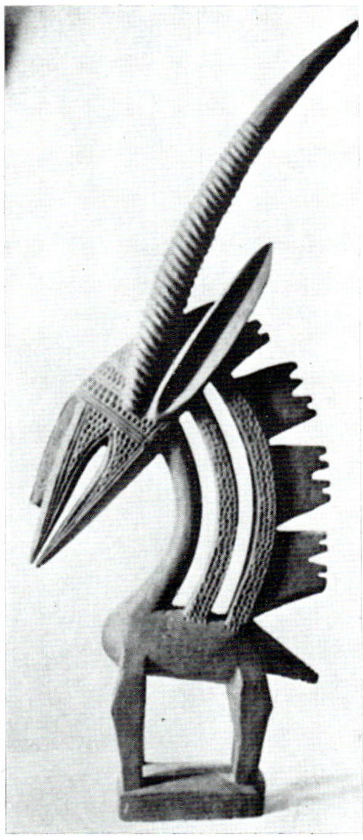

☐ 692 *›Antilopenkopfschmuck‹, Bambara (Mali). Abgebildet in Marius de Zayas, „African Negro Art: Its Influence on Modern Art", 1916.*

☐ 693 *Fernand Léger, Studie nach einem Antilopenkopfschmuck der Bambara für ›Die Erschaffung der Welt‹ (La création du monde), um 1922, Bleistift, 28 x 22 cm. Nachlaß des Künstlers.*

Les Mariés de la Tour Eiffel oder in Cole Porters Musik für *Within the Quota*, das gleichzeitig mit *Die Erschaffung der Welt* Premiere hatte.[21]

Das Regiebuch für die *Erschaffung der Welt* schrieb Blaise Cendrars, der 1921 die *Anthologie nègre*, eine Sammlung und Übersetzung afrikanischer Literatur, publiziert hatte. Cendrars bewunderte die afrikanische Literatur wegen ihrer Schönheit und Kraft und betrachtete Afrika als eine der reichsten dichterischen und sprachlichen Quellen. Er entwickelte die Geschichte der *Erschaffung der Welt* aus afrikanischen Schöpfungsmythen: Aus einer formlosen Masse entstehen Tiere, Insekten, Vögel und schließlich Mann und Frau in Gegenwart der drei gewaltigen Gottheiten der Schöpfung.

Jean Börlin, Choreograph und Erster Tänzer des Ensembles, war seit 1919 um die Gründung eines Negerballetts bemüht.[22] 1920 führte er ein Tanzsolo mit dem Titel *Sculpture nègre* in der Comédie des Champs-Elysées auf ☐ 690. Für die *Erschaffung der Welt* betrieb er völkerkundliche Studien über afrikanische Stämme in Bibliotheken und Museen und war ähnlich wie André Levinson besonders vom westafrikanischen Tanz auf Stelzen und auf allen vieren beeindruckt, den er in seine Choreographie integrierte.[23]

Milhaud seinerseits wollte seit 1922 Jazzelemente übernehmen und Musik für die »kammermusikalische« Besetzung der Bands aus Harlem komponieren: »Schließlich ergab sich für mich in der *Erschaffung der Welt* die langersehnte Möglichkeit, die Elemente des Jazz zu verwenden, denen ich so viele Studien gewidmet hatte. Ich übernahm die gleiche Orchestrierung mit 17 Soloinstrumenten wie in Harlem und machte durchgängig Gebrauch vom Jazzstil, um ein rein klassisches Gefühl auszudrücken.«[24] Die Partitur Milhauds für das Ballett spiegelt diese Adaptionen in der Fuge über ein Jazzthema und in den »Blues«-Teilen wider.

Dennoch ist das Ausmaß von Milhauds Assimilation des Jazz in seiner Ballettpartitur umstritten. Manche Kritiker betonen den grundlegenden Unterschied von Jazz und jeder symphonischen Musik und behaupten, daß trotz der Anerkennung moderner Kompositionen wie derjenigen Milhauds an die Rhythmik des Jazz sie »dennoch nicht das Wesentliche der Sprache des Jazz enthalten«,[25] vor allem nicht im Hinblick auf die Improvisation. Vorhang, Ausstattung und Kostüme für die *Erschaffung der Welt* entwarf Léger, der seine Entwürfe mit dem Studium und Kopieren von Abbildungen afrikanischer Plastik begann ☐ 688, 689.[26] Wie Jean Laude erwähnt, waren Légers Zeichnungen oft nur Durchzeichnungen nach Carl Einsteins *Negerplastik* und Marius de Zayas' *African Negro Art: Its Influence on Modern Art.* So verwandelte Léger etwa die Bleistiftzeichnung nach der Abbildung eines Antilopenkopfschmucks der *Bambara* aus De Zayas' Buch in einen Kostümentwurf für einen reichgefiederten Vogel ☐ 691–693.

Vorhang-Skizzen zeigen drei Köpfe, die von afrikanischer Skulptur angeregt sind. Das Bühnenbild bestand aus drei Figuren, die Götter darstellten ☐ 695–699. Es waren freistehende Silhouetten, beweglich und leicht tragbar ☐ 685. Sie mochten von Andrée Parrs lebensgroßen Silhouettenfiguren von Jazzmusikern angeregt worden sein, die das Bühnenbild einer früheren Aufführung des Schwedischen Balletts *L'Homme et son désir*, 1921, rahmten. Tatsächlich wurden Léger und die anderen künstlerischen Mitgestalter der *Erschaffung der Welt* zwischen Parrs Figuren im Bühnenhintergrund in einer Gruppenaufnahme photographiert ☐ 697.[27]

Während Légers frühe Dekorationsentwürfe illusionistisch modellierend vorgingen, war das Endresultat zusammengesetzt aus flachen, ineinandergreifenden Formen, unplastisch und in den Farbtönen Rostrot, Braun, Ocker, Weiß, Schwarz und Blau gehalten. Eine Reihe von flachen Kulissen mit

□ 694 *Fernand Léger, Entwurf für das Bühnenbild der ›Erschaffung der Welt‹ (La création du monde), 1923, Tusche und Gouache, 42 x 57 cm. Sammlung Bob Guccione und Kathy Keeton, New York.*

□ 695 *Fernand Léger, Entwurf zur ›Erschaffung der Welt‹ (La création du monde), 1922, Bleistift, 21 x 27 cm. The Museum of Modern Art, Schenkung John Pratt, New York.*

□ 696 *›Helmmaske‹,* BAULE *(Elfenbeinküste), Holz. Abgebildet in Carl Einstein, „Negerplastik“, 1915.*

□ 697 *Die Schöpfer der ›Erschaffung der Welt‹ (La création du monde), von links nach rechts: Darius Milhaud, Blaise Cendrars, Jean Börlin, Rolf de Maré, Fernand Léger (und Maurice Raynal). Im Hintergrund Elemente der Ausstattung von ›L'Homme et son désir‹ von Andrée Parr. Photographie, Dansmuseet, Stockholm.*

geometrischen oder landschaftlichen Motiven, möglicherweise mit dem Dekor afrikanischer Keramik verwandt,[28] umrahmte eine bemalte Bühnenleinwand, die Berge und Wolken andeuten sollte. Die Wolkenregion dieser Hintergrundszene war beweglich. Die Kostüme waren für eine Vielzahl von Rollen konzipiert: (Götter-)Boten auf Stelzen, deren ineinandergreifende Muster und Farben dem Kostüm der Gottheiten ähnelten, Figuren mit übergroßen Masken, oder die aus flachen, schwarzen Formen zusammengesetzt waren □ 688, Tiere in lebhaften Farben (rot, blau, grün und gelb) mit angehängten Armen, Schwänzen und Schnäbeln: ein Mann und eine Frau im wattierten Kostüm. Die Muster der Kostüme sollten auf Opfermale und andere charakteristische Zeichen afrikanischer Skulptur anspielen.

LÉGERS Kostümentwürfe griffen das Bühnenbild auf, besonders in den Farben und den flächigen Mustern. Dadurch verloren die einzelnen Rollen ihre individuelle Identität und wurden zu Bestandteilen der übergreifenden Bühnenausstattung. Während der Vorstellung sollte die Szenerie in das Bühnengeschehen einbezogen werden; die Kostümtänzer veränderten die Kulissen im Spielen und verwischten dadurch die Grenzen zwischen Schauspieler und Bühnenbild noch zusätzlich. In der Eröffnungsszene des Balletts ließ das dichte Ineinander von Bühnenbild und Figuren die Herrschaft des Chaos sinnfällig werden, dann wurden die Kulissen nach und nach entfernt, die Wolken verschwanden, und die Ordnung nahm ihren Anfang. Die *Erschaffung der Welt* mit ihrer Geschichte des Urbeginns der Schöpfung in einem afrikanischen Kontext spiegelte sowohl die allgemeine Sehnsucht nach einem gesellschaftlichen Neubeginn und unverbrauchten Quellen wider als auch den weit verbreiteten Glauben, daß die ägyptischen und archaisch-griechischen Wurzeln der westlichen Kunst im schwarzen Afrika ihren Ursprung hätten (siehe S. 251). LÉGER hoffte, seinen Göttern jene Mystik und Exotik verleihen zu können, wie es für ihn ein solches Thema verlangte. So beobachtete Milhaud, daß »Léger die primitive Kunst der Neger übernehmen und den Vorgang und das Bühnenbild mit afrikanischen Gottheiten voll expressiver Kraft und Düsternis bemalen wollte. Niemals waren ihm seine Entwürfe erschreckend genug.«[29]

Obwohl LÉGERS Ausstattung der *Erschaffung der Welt* von afrikanischer Skulptur angeregt war, zeigte er sich von der Kunst der Primitiven vor und nach seiner Arbeit an diesem Ballett nicht wesentlich beeinflußt. Selbst hier fiel die Anregung durch afrikanische Kunst anders aus als bei PICASSO und anderen Künstlern, die primitive Kunst wegen ihrer gestalterischen und magischen Eigenschaften schätzten und diese Momente in ihre Arbeiten aufnahmen. LÉGERS Interesse an primitiver Kunst galt grundsätzlich weniger ihrer Struktur als dem, was er als ihre spontanen, vitalen Qualitäten erachtete – letztendlich jenen Aspekten, die auch die Dadaisten interessierten. Diese Vitalität war es, die LÉGER zum Jazz und auch zu den schwarzen Revuen gezogen hatte.

LÉGER formulierte seine künstlerischen Vorstellungen der 20er Jahre in mehreren Essays, die sich mit modernem Theater, mit der Dynamik des städtischen Alltags und mit der Technologie der modernen mechanisierten Welt befaßten. Fasziniert von der Energie und Mobilität des Zirkus, Kabaretts, der Musik- und Tanzpaläste, die er mit Börlin und De Maré aufsuchte, hoffte er seinen Werken eine ähnliche Kraft und rhythmische Spannung mitzuteilen. In der Sammlung seiner Essays, erschienen unter dem Titel *Funktionen der Malerei*, betont er diese Aspekte immer wieder, erwähnt den afrikanischen Zusammenhang der *Erschaffung der Welt* aber nur ein einziges Mal. LÉGER bot das afrikanische Thema der *Erschaffung der Welt* im Grunde nur eine Möglichkeit, um sein Hauptanliegen, Dynamik und Spektakel, zur Darstellung zu bringen. Er belebte die Bühne mit einer Lichtführung, die fortwährend verdunkelt oder erhellt wurde, mit einem Bühnenbild, das ständig in Bewegung war, und dem abstrakten Muster der Kostüme, die die menschliche Gestalt verunklärten. Er wollte für dieses Ballett sogar einen komplizierten Apparat anwenden, der mit Gas Schläuche in Gestalt von Blumen, Bäumen und Tieren aufgeblasen hätte, um sie in die Luft schweben zu lassen. Das Projekt wurde schließlich fallengelassen, weil das Geräusch des einströmenden Gases die Musik übertönt hätte.

LÉGER faßte das Ziel seiner Bühnenentwürfe so zusammen: »Der Mensch wird zu einem Mechanismus wie alles andere auch. Statt Endzweck zu sein wie früher, wird er jetzt zum Mittel . . . Wenn ich das menschliche Maß zerstöre, wenn mein Bühnenbild sich ständig bewegt, erhalte ich eine maximale Wirkung. Ich erhalte etwas auf der Bühne, das völlig verschieden ist von der Atmosphäre im Saal.«[30] LÉGERS vorrangiges Ziel in der *Erschaffung der Welt* galt der Integration des Schauspielers in die Gesamtdekoration und der Verwandlung des Tänzers in ein mechanisiertes, entmenschlichtes Element. So gesehen kontrastiert LÉGERS mechanistische Struktur ironischerweise mit dem gängigen, gleichwohl falschen Urteil über die Afrikaner als ein spontanes, ungehemmtes Volk. Um dem allgemeinen Geschmack entgegenzukommen, mußte die Wirklichkeit afrikanischer Kunst in Produktionen wie der *Erschaffung der Welt* modifiziert und weniger irritierend präsentiert werden. In einem etwas anderen Zusammenhang wurde einmal geäußert, daß dieses Stück die Herbheit der primitiven Kunst aufgeweicht habe. Sein Primitivismus sei in gewisser Weise klassisch geworden, so daß primitiv die Bedeutung von archetypisch erhalten hätte.[31] In diesem Sinne wollte Milhaud den Jazz transformieren, »um ein reines klassisches Gefühl zum Ausdruck zu bringen«, und LÉGER vereinfachte und glättete seine afrikanischen Entwürfe zu dekorativen Formen. So äußerte er selbst: »Im Ballett dachte ich nur in den Kategorien des Dekorativen, der einfachen Flächen, bedeckt mit planen Farbwerten. Ich machte dies für Skating Rink und für die Erschaffung der Welt. Zusammen mit Milhaud und Blaise Cendrars schuf ich ein afrikanisches Drama. Alles darin wurde transportiert. Ausgangspunkt war für mich die afrikanische Skulptur der klassischen Periode, Grundlage waren die originalen Tänze. Im Angesicht von drei acht Meter hohen Negergottheiten wohnte man der Geburt des Menschen, der Pflanzen und der Tiere bei.«[32]

Um 1925 prägte diese stereotype Reduktion der afrikanischen Kunst ein breites Spektrum von Mode und Stil einschließlich der Innenarchitektur. So benutzte der Modeschöpfer Paul Poiret für die Ankündigung seiner Autobiographie *En Habillant l'époque* im Jahre 1931 eine afrikanische Maske.[33] Oder man nehme die berühmt gewordene Kollektion von Armreifen aus afrikanischem Elfenbein, die die wohlhabende Intellektuelle Nancy Cunard von den Handgelenken bis zum Ellbogen trug. Auch die Art Deco, die mit der »International Exhibition of Modern Decorative and Industrial Arts« im Grand Palais (Juni 1925) ihren Höhepunkt erreichte, nahm die Formen afrikanischer Kunst auf. Beide Richtungen trafen sich häufig in der Geometrie und Einfachheit der Formen. Die der Art Deco angehörenden Bildhauer JEAN LAMBERT-RUCKI □ 731 und GUSTAVE MIKLOS entwickelten ihre Kopfplastiken aus afrikanischen Masken, machten sie aber den europäischen Sammlern durch Milderung und Glättung von Form und Ausdruck und durch elegante Stilisierung schmackhafter. Designer der Art Deco verarbeiteten afrikanisches Ornament in ihren Teppichen und Stoffen und benutzten Motive aus der Kunst der Primitiven in ihren Goldschmiedearbeiten □ 698, 699. Art Deco-Möbel sind ebenfalls von Afrika beeinflußt, wie die Stühle zeigen, die aus zeremoniellen Hockern entwickelt wurden □ 700.

Der Gebrauch afrikanischer Formen in der Kunst der Art Deco verlieh der Innenarchitektur eine Tendenz zum Dramatischen und erinnert damit an den Ausgangspunkt, das Theater, das diese Formen einst populär gemacht hatte.[34] Wie wir gesehen haben, ist das große öffentliche Interesse an Afrika und darüber hinaus auch an der schwarzen Kultur Amerikas größtenteils seiner Umsetzung im Theater und Ballett dieser Jahre zu verdanken. Zuerst wurde das avantgardistische Theater von der Spontaneität und der Radikalität des Dada geprägt. Primitivismus war eines von vielen Mitteln der Provokation. Als sich die Avantgarde zusehends in den Dienst der Mode und des kulturellen Establishments stellte, konnte LÉGERS vereinfachte Spielart des Primitivismus als dekorativer Stil schließlich Aufnahme finden.[35] Erst in dieser modifizierten Spielart durfte der Primitivismus in den Gang der kulturellen Entwicklung Europas eintreten.

□ 698 *Jean Lambert-Rucki, Entwurf für eine Halskette oder ein Armband, 1936/37, schwarze, goldene, silberne Tusche und Gouache, 7 x 25 cm. Musée des Arts Décoratifs, Paris.*

□ 699 *Jean Puiforcat, ›Kanne‹, 1929–30, Silber und Ebenholz, 24 x 17 cm. Sammlung N. Manoukian, Paris.*

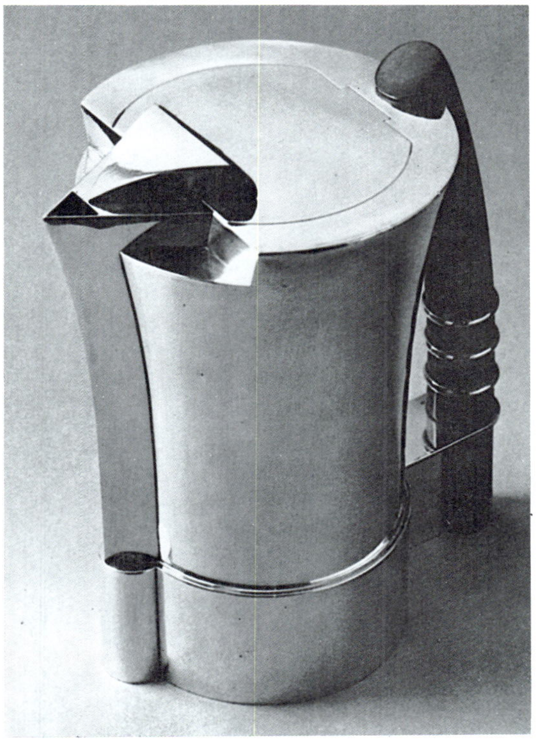

□ 700 *Marcel Coard, ›Stuhl‹, Holz, 46 x 50 x 165 cm. Privatbesitz.*

Anmerkungen

Ich danke Judith Cousins, Diane Farynyk, Beatrice Kernan und Bernice Rose vom Museum of Modern Art für ihre großzügige Mitarbeit an diesem Aufsatz.

1. Léger an Rolf de Maré, Brief vom 12. September 1922, Dansmuseet, Stockholm. Zit. bei Mc Quillan, M. A., *Painters and the Ballet, 1917–26: An Aspect of the Relationship between Art and Theatre,* Diss., New York University 1979, S. 615.

2. Guillaume Apollinaire schrieb: »M. Paul Guillaume bereitet für die nächste Saison ein choreographisches Schauspiel vor, das seiner Ankündigung zufolge eine Sensation sein wird. Er selbst wird einige Tänze mit Haltungen, Bewegungen und Gesten vorführen, die von seiner Beschäftigung mit afrikanischen Fetischen angeregt sind«, »News and Views of Literature and the Arts« in *L'Europe Nouvelle,* 20. Juli 1918. Nachgedruckt in *Apollinaire on Art: Essays and Reviews 1902–1918 by Guillaume Apollinaire,* hrsg. von Leroy C. Breunig, New York 1972, S. 472.

3. Steegmuller, F., *Cocteau,* Boston 1970, S. 171.

4. »Le spectacle lumière, couleur, image mobile, objet-spectacle« in *Bulletin de l'Effort Moderne,* 1924. Nachgedruckt in *Functions of Painting by Fernand Léger,* hrsg. von Edward F. Fry, New York 1973, S. 37. Cocteau stellte fest, daß »jeder mit Theater beschäftigt ist . . .« Cocteau, J., »Entre Picasso et Radiguet« in *Carte Blanche,* 7. April 1919. Zit. bei Mc Quillan, *Painters and the Ballet . . .,* S. 364.

5. Huelsenbeck, R., 1918. Zit. bei Rischbieter, H., *Art and the Stage in the 20th Century,* Greenwich/Conn. 1968, S. 164.

6. Ball, H., zit. bei Goldberg, R. L., *Performance: Live Art 1909 to the Present,* New York 1979, S. 42.

7. Henkin Melzer, A., »Dada Performance at the Cabaret Voltaire« in *Artforum,* November 1973, S. 76.

8. Zur Beschreibung von Josephine Bakers erstem Auftritt im Théâtre des Champs-Elysées siehe: Flaner, J., *Paris Was Yesterday,* 1925–1939, New York 1972, S. XX–XXI.

9. Arnason, H.H., *Calder,* Princeton 1966, S. 17. Vgl. Bourdon, D., *Calder,* New York 1980, S. 29.

10. Cocteau an Albert Gleizes, Brief vom 30. Januar 1918, abgedruckt bei Steegmuller, *Cocteau,* S. 201.

11. Zur Beschreibung dieser Rolle siehe Steegmuller, *Cocteau*, S. 185. Zu den Rollen in *Parade* gehörten französische und amerikanische Manager und ein Pferd (von zwei Tänzern dargestellt), dessen Kopf afrikanischen Masken nachgebildet war □ 539–545. Eine schwarze Reiterattrappe sollte ursprünglich auf diesem Pferd reiten, ging aber während der Proben verloren. Die Rollen der beiden Manager und des Negers sollten

□ 701 *›Maske‹,* Kuba *(Zaire), bemaltes Holz und Fasern, Höhe 54 cm. Museum für Völkerkunde, Berlin.*

grundlegend für die Besetzung in der französischen »music hall« des 20. Jahrhunderts werden; siehe McQuillan, *Painters and the Ballet,* S. 418.

12. Steegmuller, *Cocteau,* S. 201.

13. Nachdem Milhaud aus Südafrika nach Paris zurückgekehrt war, stellte er ein paar volkstümliche brasilianische Rhythmen wie Tango, Samba usw. zu seinem Stück zusammen mit dem Titel *Le Bœuf sur le Toit* (1919), benannt nach einem brasilianischen Karnevalslied. Cocteau erfand dazu ein passendes Szenarium, und das sich daraus ergebende Ballett wurde im Februar 1920 aufgeführt.

14. Milhaud, D., *Notes without Music,* New York 1953, S. 136.

15. Milhaud, ebda., S. 137. Diese Tendenz, anderen Kulturen afrikanische Eigenschaften zuzuschreiben, beschränkte sich nicht auf das schwarze Amerika. Auf andere Beispiele für die Verwechslung der verschiedenen künstlerischen Quellen sollte hingewiesen werden. 1910 hatte sich Strawinsky mit einem heidnischen russischen Ritus beschäftigt. Er wurde die Grundlage für *Le Sacre du Printemps,* der am 29. Mai 1913 im Théâtre des Champs-Elysées aufgeführt wurde. Strawinskys Mitarbeiter und Erfinder der visuellen Umsetzung dieses Themas war Nicolas Roerich, Maler und Archäologe, der sich mit alten slawischen Volksstämmen beschäftigte. Obwohl die Musik eigentlich nicht traditionell russischen Ursprungs ist – bis auf die Melodie des Solo-Fagotts am Anfang des ersten Akts, die litauischer Volksmusik entlehnt ist –, klingt sie doch volkstümlich, auf russische Themen und Melodien bezugnehmend. Dennoch wird diese Musik häufig und fälschlicherweise als primitive afrikanische Rhythmen beschrieben. Der amerikanische Pianist und Komponist George Antheil schrieb: »Seit Wagner hat die Musik zwei große Bluttransfusionen bekommen, zuerst die slawische und dann die schwarze. Im Hinblick auf letztere waren es die beiden epochemachenden Daten des *Sacre du Printemps* von Strawinsky und seinem revolutionären Primitivismus im Jahre 1913 und die Ankunft der ersten schwarzen Jazzband in Paris 1917.« Zit. bei Locke, A., *The Negro and His Music,* New York 1969, S. 109 (Nachdruck der Ausgabe von 1936). Vgl. auch Shattuck, R., *The Banquet Years,* New York 1968, S. 155. »Nachdem Strawinsky seine ganz primitiven afrikanischen Rhythmen in den *Sacre du Printemps* von 1913 eingeführt hatte . . .«

16. Dem Tanz wurde eine ähnliche Verwandtschaft zugeschrieben. »Die Vorläufer der Sambas und Rumbas sind afrikanische Tänze.« Raab, C., »Lateinamerikanische Tänze« in *Weltkulturen und moderne Kunst,* Ausstellungskatalog, Haus der Kunst, München 1972, S. 571 (englische Ausgabe: *World Cultures and Modern Art,* S. 330). Wegen ihrer Ähnlichkeit mit zeitgenössischen nigerianischen Tänzen waren die Zuschauer der 30er Jahre von den aus verschiedenen karibischen Tanzmotiven zusammengesetzten Tänzen der Katherine Dunham beeindruckt. Vgl. *Katherine Dunham: Her Dancers, Singers, Musicians,* hrsg. von R. Buckle, London 1949, S. 23. Auch der Ragtime enthielt Elemente von afrikanischen rhythmischen Kombinationen. Es ist darauf hingewiesen worden, daß, während sich die Ragtimespieler in den 90er Jahren des vorigen Jahrhunderts in Chicago versammelten, »die Musiker aus Dahome die Besucher der World's Fair (World's Columbian Exposition, Chicago) mit den original afrikanischen Formen des gleichen Rhythmus verblüfften.« Blesh, R./Janis, H., *They All Played Ragtime,* New York 1950, S. 149. Zit. bei Feather, L., *The Book of Jazz,* New York 1976, S. 25.

17. Goffin, R., *Jazz from the Congo to the Metropolitan,* übersetzt von W. Schapp und L. G. Feather, Garden City 1944, S. 14.

18. Stearns, M. W., *The Story of Jazz,* London 1978, S. 3–15.

19. Zur Diskussion über diese Differenzen siehe Ulanov, B., *A History of Jazz in America,* New York 1952, S. 11–12. Zit. bei Feather, *The Book of Jazz,* S. 25–26. Vgl. auch Hodeir, A., *Jazz: Its Evolution and Essence,* übersetzt von David Noakes, New York 1979, S. 40–44.

20. Rolf de Maré reiste nach Afrika und sammelte afrikanische Kunst.

21. *Within the Quota* war einem amerikanischen Thema gewidmet und von einem amerikanischen Komponisten vertont worden. Bühnenbild und Kostümentwürfe stammten von Gerald Murphy. Die Rollen umfaßten den »Colored Gentleman«, der einen Vaudeville, und das »Jazz Baby«, das einen Shimmy tanzte. *Within the Quota* hatte zusammen mit *Die Erschaffung der Welt* am 25. Oktober 1923 Premiere.

22. *Les Ballets Suédois dans l'art contemporain,* Paris 1931, S. 67.

23. Levinson, A., »La Création du Monde« in *Comoedia,* 28. Oktober 1923. Zit. bei Blondel, E., *F. Léger et les arts du spectacle,* Diss., Université de Paris 1969, S. 45. Gedankt seien Judi Freeman und Judith Cousins, die mich über diese Doktorarbeit in Kenntnis setzten.

24. Milhaud, *Notes without Music,* S. 148–149.

25. Hobson, W., *American Jazz Music,* New York 1976, S. 82–83. Siehe auch Hodeir, *Jazz: Its Evolution and Essence,* S. 260–263 und Raab, C., »Schwierigkeiten der Verbindung von Jazz und symphonischer Musik« in *Weltkulturen und moderne Kunst,* S. 556. Milhaud u. a. europäische Musiker wie Strawinsky, die mit Jazzelementen experimentierten, machten davon nicht lange Gebrauch. Auf einer Reise in die USA im Jahre 1926 ließ Milhauds Begeisterung für den Jazz nach, nachdem er erlebt hatte, was aus dem volkstümlichen Harlem-Jazz geworden war. Vgl. Willett, J., *Art and Politics in the Weimar Period: The New Sobriety, 1917–1933,* New York 1978, S. 159–160. Vgl. Milhaud, *Notes without Music,* S. 192.

26. Sacks, L., »F. Léger and the Ballets Suédois« in *Apollo,* Juni 1970, S. 465.

27. McQuillan, *Painters and the Ballet,* S. 290. Milhaud schrieb die Musik für das Ballett *L'Homme et son désir,* als er in Europa war. Die folgende Beschreibung der *Erschaffung der Welt,* ebda. S. 614–29, ist in vieler Hinsicht der Arbeit von McQuillan verpflichtet.

28. Blondel, *F. Léger et les arts du spectacle,* S. 45.

29. Milhaud, *Notes without Music,* S. 148.

30. »Le Ballet-Spectacle, l'Objet-Spectacle« in *Bulletin de l'Effort Moderne,* 1925. Nachgedruckt in *Functions of Painting by F. Léger,* S. 72.

31. McQuillan, *Painters and the Ballet,* S. 614.

32. »L'Estétique et la Machine: l'Ordre géométrique et le Vrai« in *Propos d'artistes,* 1925. Nachgedruckt in *Functions of Painting by Fernand Léger,* S. 63.

33. Laude, J., *The Arts of Black Africa,* übersetzt von Jean Decock, Berkeley 1971, S. 20. In seiner Autobiographie schreibt Poiret interessanterweise: »In New York fragte ich an die zwanzigmal, in jeder Gesellschaftsschicht, nach der Adresse des Völkerkundemuseums, keiner konnte sie mir sagen. Ich entdeckte es am oberen Ende des Broadway und fand es vollkommen leer.« Poiret, P., *My First Fifty Years,* übersetzt von Stephen Haden Guest, London 1931, S. 266–67.

34. Theater und Ballett trugen nicht nur dazu bei, dem Publikum afrikanische Kunstformen vorzustellen, sondern lösten 1909 in Paris auch den Art Deco-Stil aus durch die Formen und Farben des Russischen Balletts.

35. Zur weiteren Diskussion bezüglich des Niedergangs der Pariser Avantgarde in den 20er Jahren und ihrer Absorbierung durch das kulturelle Establishment siehe Willett, *Art and Politics in the Weimar Period,* S. 168–171. Vgl. auch McQuillan, *Painters and the Ballet,* S. 373–377.

☐ 702 *Paul Klee, ›Schauspielers Maske‹, 1924, Öl auf Leinwand, 37 x 34 cm. The Museum of Modern Art, Sammlung S. und H. Janis, New York.*

Jean Laude

Paul Klee

Paul Klee formulierte seine Gedanken über die eigene Auseinandersetzung mit dem Primitivismus in zwei bemerkenswerten Stellungnahmen. Im Jahre 1912, als er sich bereits Kandinsky und der Gruppe »Blauer Reiter« angeschlossen hatte, schrieb er an einen Schweizer Kollegen: ». . . die dritte Ausstellung der neuen Vereinigung und deren noch radikaleren Sezession, genannt der Blaue Reiter. Mich an die Idee haltend und nicht an die momentane Zufälligkeit oder mir scheinbare Zugehörigkeit mancher Leistung, möchte ich Leute beruhigen wollen, die da nicht an irgendeinen Museumsliebling, und wäre es selbst ein Greco, anknüpfen konnten. Es gibt nämlich noch Uranfänge von Kunst, wie man sie eher in ethnographischen Sammlungen findet oder daheim in seiner Kinderstube. Lach' nicht, Leser! Die Kinder können es auch, und es steckt Weisheit darin, daß sie es auch können! . . . Parallele Erscheinungen sind die Arbeiten der Geisteskranken . . . Alles das ist tief ernst zu nehmen, ernster als sämtliche Pinakotheken, wenn es gilt, heute zu reformieren . . .«[1] Jahre später äußerte Klee in einem Gespräch mit Lothar Schreyer, das dieser aufzeichnete: »Ich sage es oft, aber es wird manchmal nicht ernst genug genommen, daß sich uns Welten geöffnet haben und öffnen, die auch der Natur angehören, aber in die nicht alle Menschen hineinblicken, vielleicht wirklich nur die Kinder, die Verrückten, die Primitiven. Ich meine etwa das Reich der Ungeborenen und der Toten, das Reich dessen, was kommen kann, kommen möchte, aber nicht kommen muß, eine Zwischenwelt . . . Dorthin vermögen die Kinder, die Verrückten, die Primitiven noch oder wieder zu blicken. Und was diese sehen und bilden, ist für mich die kostbarste Bestätigung. Denn wir sehen alle das gleiche, wenn auch von verschiedenen Seiten. Es ist im ganzen und einzelnen das gleiche, über den ganzen Planeten, keine Phantasterei, sondern Tatsache um Tatsache.«[2] Diese beiden Aussagen sind um so interessanter, als die erste aus dem Jahre 1912 stammt, in dem Klee den Almanach »Der Blaue Reiter« kennenlernte, in dem Kinderzeichnungen und primitive Kunst abgebildet waren, das zweite Zitat aus den Jahren von Lothar Schreyers Lehrtätigkeit am Weimarer Bauhaus (1921–23), als die Frage des Primitivismus keine großen Diskussionen mehr auslöste.

Zwischen diesen beiden Stellungnahmen liegen mindestens zehn Jahre, ein Zeitraum, in dem sich in Klees Kunst tiefgreifende Wandlungen vollzogen. Klees Äußerung aus der Weimarer Zeit spricht ein Thema an, das in künstlerischen Debatten und der Kritik später, um 1930, in stark verändertem Sinn an der Tagesordnung war: die heute in Mißkredit geratene Zusammenfassung primitiver Kunst mit Schöpfungen der Irren und Kinderzeichnungen unter einer einzigen ästhetischen Kategorie. Ein Zusammenhang zwischen primitiver Kunst und Kinderkunst war früher schon von S. Levinstein gesehen worden, der sie in dem 1904 in Leipzig erschienenen Buch *Kinderzeichnungen bis zum 14. Lebensjahr* miteinander verglich. Klee besaß auch ein Exemplar des Buches *Bildnerei des Geisteskranken* von H. Prinzhorn, das 1922 in Berlin erschien. Es liefert uns einen Anhaltspunkt dafür, daß sein Gespräch mit Lothar Schreyer frühestens während dieses Jahres stattgefunden haben kann.

In ihrer Untersuchung über Masken und Marionetten in Klees Werk bemerkt Calliope Rigopoulu, daß in *Schauspielers Maske* von 1924 □ 702 »Robert J. Goldwater . . . kongolesischen Einfluß wahrzunehmen glaubt. James Pierce Smith hingegen findet sie den Masken Ozeaniens näherstehend. Margaret Plant erkennt den Einfluß Hokusais, insbesondere von (dessen Bild) *Der Laternengeist* aus seinen *100 Geschichten*, der in Wilhelm Michels Buch *Das Teuflische und Groteske in der Kunst* abgebildet war, das Klee kannte.«[3] Hier drängt sich natürlich die delikate Frage nach den Grenzen vergleichender Studien generell auf, wenn drei als seriös bekannte Autoren dasselbe Gemälde drei verschiedenen Quellen zuschreiben können. Doch es geht eigentlich nicht darum, nur mögliche oder lokalisierbare Einflüsse nachzuweisen. Die in Frage kommenden Quellen sind nicht ohne Ähnlichkeiten, doch sind nur ihre Gemeinsamkeiten, wie sie bei *Schauspielers Maske* deutlich werden, relevant. Klee kopierte nie einen Gegenstand oder ein Werk, das er irgendwo sah, in einer Abbildung oder als Original besaß. Im Augenblick des Malens oder Zeichnens hatte er solche Werke nie vor sich. Er machte sich vielmehr ein geistiges und dadurch im Verhältnis zu einem bestimmten Form- und/oder Inhaltsproblem umgestaltetes Bild davon. Die Lösung sucht er dann innerhalb der allgemeinen Problematik, die sich bei ihm empirisch von einem Werk zum anderen verfolgen läßt. Klee wurde sich dieser Tatsache sehr früh, schon 1908, bewußt und zog alsbald theoretische und praktische Konsequenzen daraus: »Wie der Mensch, so hat auch das Bild Skelett, Muskeln und Haut. Man kann von einer besonderen Anatomie des Bildes sprechen. Ein Bild mit dem Gegenstand: ›nackter Mensch‹ ist nicht menschen-anatomisch, sondern bild-anatomisch zu gestalten. Man konstruiert fürs erste ein Gerüst der zu bauenden Malerei. Wie weit man über dieses Gerüst hinausgeht, ist frei, es kann vom Gerüst schon eine Kunstwirkung ausgehen, eine tiefere als von der Oberfläche allein.«[4]

Für ein Werk Paul Klees eine spezifische Quelle zu ermitteln, ist außerdem aus folgendem Grund schwierig. Wenn er das Werk eines anderen Künstlers zum Ausgangspunkt seiner Arbeit nahm, beschränkte er sich auf einen einzigen Aspekt, den er aus dem Gesamtzusammenhang löste. Er übernahm nur das, was ihm gerade in diesem Augenblick sein eigenes künstlerisches Schaffen anzuregen oder zu bestätigen schien. Das Ergebnis ist, daß die Bildquelle, von der die Anregung ausging, Teil einer neuen Vision wird, in der sie nicht mehr dieselbe Bedeutung besitzt wie in ihrem ursprünglichen Zusammenhang. Ihre Wirkung bestand in den durch sie möglich gewordenen Übergängen und Fortschritten, in dem Entwicklungsweg, der nun über sie hinausschreitet, in dem sie nurmehr ein Moment ist und den sie bereichert.

Bei Klee stützt sich Theorie auf Erfahrung, nicht auf ein vorgefaßtes System. Sie schöpft ganz aus der Praxis, die ihr vorausgeht und aus der sie sich herleitet. Aber Theorie ist auch Teil der geistigen und kulturellen Umgebung, in der sie entsteht und auf die sie zurückwirkt.

Fest steht, daß Klee Werke primitiver Kunst kannte (im weitesten Sinn des um die Jahrhundertwende geläufigen Begriffes) einschließlich der Werke nichtklassischer und außereuropäischer Kunst. Bereits im Jahre 1906 hatte er solche Arbeiten bei einem Besuch des Museums für Völkerkunde in Berlin gesehen. Er sah unweigerlich auch jene Werke, die im Almanach »Der Blaue Reiter« sowie in Levinsteins Buch abgebildet waren, von dem er ein Exemplar besaß. Überdies kannte er wahrscheinlich auch die Illustrationen von Hermann Bahrs *Expressionismus* (München 1916). Andererseits wird Primitivismus in Klees eigenen Schriften wie auch in den Schriften seiner Freunde vom »Blauen Reiter« als eine Rückkehr zu den Ursprüngen, genauer: zur Kunst *vor* und *neben* der Renaissance, und als der Beginn einer neuen »geistigen Ära« bestimmt. Primitivismus wird daher eher als eine *Idea* im Sinne Goethes verstanden, als eine Art *Analogon* zur Urpflanze aus der »Metamorphose der Pflanzen« denn als ein spezifisches Formenrepertoire, aus dem einige wenige Formen bevorzugt wären, weil sie rein formalen Interessen entgegenkommen.

□ 703 *Paul Klee, ›Zimmerperspektive mit Einwohnern‹, 1921, Aquarell über Ölfarbezeichnung auf französischem Ingres, 48,5 x 32 cm. Paul-Klee-Stiftung, Kunstmuseum, Bern.*

Ein anderer wichtiger Aspekt von Klees Kunst ist ihre Beziehung zwischen Form und Inhalt, die ganz anders ist als bei Picasso, Braque, Matisse oder gar Robert Delaunay, mit dem sich Klee wohl kurzzeitig verbunden fühlte. Wesentlich durch die einheitschaffende ›Stimmung‹ determiniert, steht das Verhältnis Form/Inhalt mit Novalis' Vorstellung vom »magischen Ich« in Zusammenhang oder mit Iwanows ähnlicher Idee des »Kryptogramms des Unsagbaren« und der »Hiroglyphe des Erlebnisses«.[5] Solche Gedanken konnte Klee entweder durch Kandinsky persönlich oder über dessen Schriften kennengelernt haben. Es sei ebenfalls darauf verwiesen, daß Klee 1905 bereits Ernst Machs Forschungen kannte und seine lebhaften Eindrücke davon Carl Einstein mitteilte, der seinerseits daraus gewisse Grundsätze für sein Buch *Negerplastik* und die Interpretation der Werke Picassos, Braques und Gris' ableitete. Das von Mach behauptete Wechselverhältnis von Innenwelt und Außenwelt wirft Licht auf Klees Verhältnis zur Natur nach 1905: Es rechtfertigt seine Weigerung, die Natur nachzuahmen und muß im Sinne Hermann Bahrs verstanden werden, der, ausgehend von Goethes Vorstellung der »Erfahrung als dem Mittler zwischen Subjekt und Objekt«, den Impressionismus als die Darstellung »des überwiegenden Teils des Objekts« auf Kosten des Subjekts und den Expressionismus als Bekenntnis zum »überwiegenden Teil des Subjekts« auf Kosten des Objekts beschrieb.[6] Was Klee angeht, ist der »überwiegende Teil des Subjekts« nicht im Sinne einer Überbewertung des Egos zu verstehen, sondern eher als eine Aufnahmebereitschaft für manifeste oder latente Geschehnisse, die sich in der äußeren Welt ereignen oder dort Form annehmen. Hier taucht wiederum die Problematik des »Zeichens«, genauer des »magischen Zeichens« auf, durch das laut Bahr der moderne Mensch – in einer historisch unerträglichen Situation – sich wieder dem »primitiven« Menschen annähert: das dekadente Thema des ›Weltschmerzes‹ erhält eine neue Bedeutung.

Aus diesen verschiedenen Andeutungen, die sich alle um die Idee des Primitivismus drehen und sowohl Klees eigenem Denken wie den Diskussionen seiner Zeit entnommen sind, lassen sich einige Grundprinzipien ableiten. Mit ihrer Hilfe werden formale Analysen möglich; sie weisen uns die Richtung unseres Vorgehens und bieten schließlich eine bessere Vergleichsgrundlage. Dies will nicht heißen, daß der Primitivismus die Gesamtheit von Klees Werk und Theorie betrifft. Er bildet jedoch einen integralen Bestandteil des Ganzen. Seine Werke – wie Klee in Übereinstimmung mit den Vorstellungen seiner Zeit darlegte – betonen das Vermögen zu sehen (und folglich das Gesehene sichtbar zu machen) und bestätigen die Richtung seiner Bestrebungen. Dies sind die Kernpunkte seines Gesprächs, das er 1922 mit Lothar Schreyer führte.

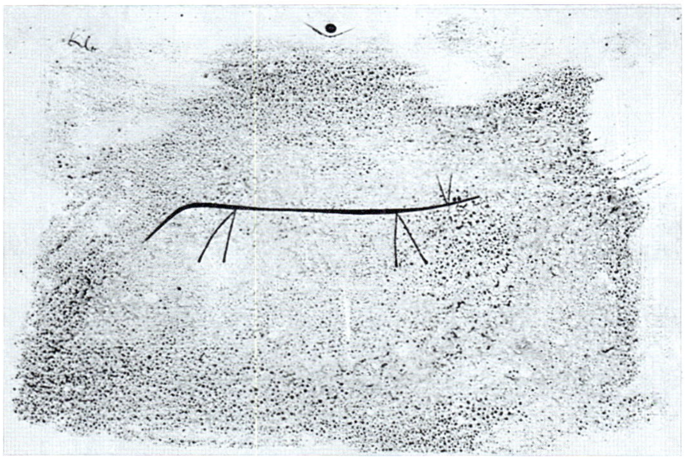

☐ 704 *Paul Klee, ›Tier, einen Geruch witternd‹, 1930, Aquarell und Tusche, Papier, 32 x 48 cm. Paul-Klee-Stiftung, Kunstmuseum Bern.*

☐ 705 *›Tierfigur‹, Königreich Karagwe, Bukoba (Tansania), Eisen, Höhe 20 cm. Linden-Museum, Stuttgart.*

Klees Gemälde, Zeichnungen und Radierungen haben im allgemeinen die Tendenz, von der Bildfläche vor allem mit den Mitteln der Linie Besitz zu ergreifen. Das Problem zweidimensionaler Darstellung auf der Bildfläche löst Klee anders als etwa Picasso, Braque oder Delaunay; auch die Geschichte des Problems ist bei ihm eine andere.

Für Picasso und Braque entsteht der Bildraum als Ergebnis eines schrittweisen, methodischen Vorgehens, in dem das Malerische zuallererst besteht; der Raum wird durch einen Prozeß gewonnen – insbesondere durch das Studium der Masken und figürlichen Skulpturen der Afrikaner südlich der Sahara –, der alle verfügbaren Mittel ausschöpft: die Wirkung des Lichts auf die Volumina, die größtmögliche Bewahrung der lokalen Farben, die bewußte, doch umfunktionierte Anwendung der Cézanneschen »Übergänge«, das Streben nach einer »Poesie des Gegenstandes«. Robert Delaunay (dessen Arbeit Klee vor seiner Reise nach Tunesien genau verfolgte) wollte seinerseits »neue Medien« schaffen, da seiner Meinung nach Cézanne schon »die schönsten Früchte geerntet« hatte. Klee ging zumindest in seinen Lehrjahren ganz anders vor; Ausgangspunkt und Problematik waren nicht die gleichen.

Zu betonen ist, daß sich Klees Stil aus einer Radiertechnik entwickelte, bei der das lineare Element, das der Jugendstil bereits in seinem reich entwickelten Arabeskenstil bevorzugte, zusammen mit floralen Arabesken vorherrscht. Folglich kann die Bedeutung, die er der Bildoberfläche beimaß, nur als Ergebnis von Methoden verstanden werden, die sich grundsätzlich von jenen der in Paris arbeitenden Maler unterschieden. Untersucht man, wie es seine Theorie der Genese nahelegt, die Entwicklung von Klees Kunst genauer, so finden wir den Maler – trotz der »Tunesischen Offenbarung«, die sich, wie wir heute wissen, lange vorher anbahnte[7] – um die Gesetze der Linie bemüht, über die er in seinem *Pädagogischen Skizzenbuch* von 1925 eine methodische Untersuchung durchführte. Von den 43 Abschnitten der Abhandlung sind nur die letzten drei Probleme der Farbe gewidmet. Sie stehen am Ende einer ausführlichen Untersuchung der »Bewegung«, die durch Linearität beschleunigt werde und für die der Pfeil ein Ideogramm darstelle. Das Werk schließt folgendermaßen: »Wir sind beim spektralen Farbkreis angelangt, wo jeder Pfeil sich erübrigt. Denn hier heißt er nicht mehr ›dorthin‹ – sondern ›überall‹, also auch ›dort‹.«[8]

Hier sind zum besseren Verständnis der technischen Probleme zwei Faktoren zu berücksichtigen, die auch bei der Theorie der künstlerischen Arbeit als Genese eine Rolle spielen. Erstens entwickelte Klee durch seine Entdeckung der Hinterglasmalerei im Jahre 1906 – also vor Wassily Kandinsky und Gabriele Münter – eine Technik, die er wiederholt in seinen *Tagebüchern* beschreibt.[9] Zum anderen führten ihn die Kinderzeichnungen – die er studierte, von denen er sich später aber distanzierte, als sein eigenes Werk damit verglichen wurde – zu anderen Experimenten mit der Raumillusion (*Zimmerperspektive mit Einwohnern,* 1921 ☐ 703) und mit der perspektivischen Verkürzung von Figuren sowie zu einer sparsameren Anwendung der Mittel, schließlich zum reinen Symbol (*Tier, einen Geruch witternd,* 1930 ☐ 704). Letzteres Werk kann übrigens auch mit Gegenständen wie der aus Eisen geschmiedeten Kuh der *Bukoba* (Tansania) aus der Sammlung des Linden-Museums in Stuttgart in Beziehung gebracht werden ☐ 705.[10] Volkskunst wie Kinderzeichnungen kennzeichnet die besondere Rücksicht auf die Oberfläche, die Linear- und Luftperspektive ausschließt. Einige der im Almanach »Der Blaue Reiter« abgebildeten Hinterglasmalereien bestehen aus einem Nebeneinander getrennter Bildelemente, die mit dem Ganzen keinen Zusammenhang bilden. In *Die Dreifaltigkeit oder die fünf Wunden Christi*[11] komponierte der Hinterglasmaler sein Werk um das strahlende Herz, das von einer Dornenkrone umwunden ist und von einem Kreuz gekrönt wird, unter dem zwei ausgebreitete Flügel dargestellt sind. Die Verbindungen der Teile sind hier nicht logisch wie in der klassischen europäischen Malerei. Trotz der kohärenten Wirkung, die durch die formale Ordnung erzielt wird, ist ihnen auch und vor allem – selbst in der Anordnung auf der Bildfläche – eine symbolische Ordnung zu eigen. Einige Werke Klees aus den Jahren 1920 bis 1940 verfolgen eine ähnliche Strategie.

Wenn Paul Klee zu Lothar Schreyer sagt, daß Kinder und Naturvölker eine besondere Wahrnehmungskraft besitzen, so versteht er darunter nicht deren Fähigkeit, durch den dargestellten Gegenstand etwa eine transzendente Realität sichtbar zu machen, sondern das, was frei zwischen Innen- und Außen-

□ 706 ›*Padaung-Frau mit Halsringen*‹, *Burma. Veröffentlicht in Victoria Ebin, „The Body Decorated", 1979.*

□ 707 ›*Kifwebe-Maske*‹, Luba *(Zaire), Höhe 35 cm. Sammlung G. und F. Schindler, New York.*

□ 708 ›*Muschel mit eingeritztem Muster*‹, *Collingwood Bay, (Papua-Neuguinea), Höhe 8 cm. The Trustees of the Australian Museum, Sydney.*

welt fließt, wofür die ›Stimmung‹ sowohl Zeichen als auch Signal ist. Ehe wir unsere Betrachtung fortsetzen, müssen wir auf diese Frage näher eingehen. Führen sie auf Ähnlichkeiten zwischen Klees Technik und dem mythischen Denken zurück, dann sollten auch einige der Auswirkungen auf die Form untersucht werden. Denn frei fließen können Bedeutungen nur dann, wenn sich die Bildelemente, die die Bedeutung tragen, leicht von den Objekten oder Figuren, mit denen sie ein Ganzes bilden, ablösen lassen und gleichsam in ein anderes Ganzes übergehen können; d.h., wenn sie imstande sind, neue Objekte oder Figuren zu bilden, so als stellte ihr Zusammenhang eine natürliche Ordnung dar; sie müssen also in sich selbst Einheiten sein, deren Bedeutung von einer Reihe von Kombinationen abhängt. Jene Werke, die Einflüsse von Stammeskunst oder sogar von Volkskunst aufweisen – obwohl bei letzteren die symbolische Kraft schwächer oder ganz gering ist –, bestehen aus Zusammenstellungen einfacher »Zeichen«, die für sich genommen relativ neutral sind, jedoch einander aktivieren, wenn sie zusammen in Konfiguration treten.

Folglich waren es nicht so sehr die sichtbare Struktur oder der architektonische Charakter primitiver Kunst, die Klee in seinem Vorgehen bestätigten, als vielmehr ihr Vermögen, einfache Zeichen ohne Abbildcharakter zu schaffen, die eher stellvertretend für eine äußere Wirklichkeit als von ihr abgelei-

□ 709 *Paul Klee, ›Bilderbogen‹, 1937, Gouache auf Leinwand ohne Grundierung, 59 x 56,5 cm. The Phillips Collection, Washington.*

tete Abstraktionen sind. Daher kann eine Beziehung zwischen KLEES Werk und diesem oder jenem Werk aus Schwarzafrika, Ozeanien oder Altamerika nur auf der Ebene spezifischer Anleihen oder einer Anordnungsweise von Bedeutungseinheiten auf der Bildfläche hergestellt werden, wobei er lediglich die Gestaltungsart beibehielt.

KLEES Interesse nicht nur am Primitivismus im allgemeinen, sondern an spezifischen Aspekten der Stammeskunst, muß im Verhältnis zur Geschichte seiner eigenen Malerei gesehen werden. Denn nach unserer Kenntnis seines Œuvres kann man behaupten, daß KLEE (mit sehr wenigen Ausnahmen) nicht zur Zeit des »Blauen Reiters« – als das Interesse der Avantgarde ganz bewußt außereuropäischer Kunst galt – aus dem Zeichenschatz verschiedener primitiver Kulturen schöpfte, sondern erst zwischen 1920 und 1940. Erst jetzt konnte er die Prinzipien ihrer Bildgestaltung begreifen und nachbilden.

Es ist an dieser Stelle nützlich, kurz auf die komplexe Bedeutung des Zeichens im Werk PAUL KLEES einzugehen. Er verwendet das Zeichen im transitiven wie im intransitiven Sinn. Wird es intransitiv verwendet, so ist es in erster Linie reine Linienschrift ohne Umrißfunktion, eine Spur, die auf der Bildfläche spielt oder zur Konstituierung einer Ebene beiträgt. In seiner transitiven Verwendung *bezeichnet* das Zeichen etwas. Manchmal ist es ein Piktogramm, manchmal sogar ein

Ideogramm. In bestimmten Teilen von KLEES Werk kann man es erst dann untersuchen, wenn die semantischen Veränderungen, die das Zeichen durchmacht, innerhalb des ikonographischen Ganzen, dem es angehört, geklärt sind. Dasselbe Zeichen kann in verschiedenen Werken unterschiedliche Bedeutungen haben.

Nach der tunesischen Reise nähern sich bestimmte Werkreihen KLEES der Grenze zwischen Sichtbarem und Lesbarem, ohne sie indes nach der einen Seite oder anderen Seite hin zu überschreiten. In Tunis, in St. Germain oder Kairouan sah KLEE arabische Inschriften. Wahrscheinlich fielen ihm auch Nabeul-Keramik oder *azulejos* auf.[12] In dieser Zeit hatte die touristische Nachfrage die Keramikproduktion noch nicht zur ausschließlichen Darstellung exotischer Motive (Kamel, Palme usw.) auf Kosten der traditionellen »abstrakteren« Motive geführt. Vielleicht regten diese *azulejos,* Teppiche der Beduinen oder aus Kairouan KLEE dazu an, bestimmte Werke aus quadratähnlichen Formen aufzubauen und in einige davon Zeichen einzutragen. *Azulejos,* Teppiche und Kalligraphie, die KLEES Aufmerksamkeit fesselten, sind Kunstäußerungen, bei denen die Flächengestaltung und das Zeichen im Mittelpunkt stehen.

Der Einfluß der *azulejos* auf KLEE ist daran erkennbar, daß er gegen Mitte seines Aufenthaltes in Tunesien begann, die Bildfläche, anders als DELAUNAY, in unregelmäßige Vierecke mit gemischten Farben zu unterteilen und wiederum mit abgekürzten Zeichen zu versehen.[13] Dieses formale Thema setzte er dann in anderen Serien fort, etwa in den »Architekturen« und »magischen Vierecken« der 20er Jahre. KLEE arbeitete in diesem Stil mit Variationen bis ungefähr 1938, als er anfing, ihn gelegentlich mit einer von östlichen Vorbildern angeregten Ikonographie zu verbinden.[14] Auf die Beduinen- und sogenannten Kairouan-Teppiche konnte KLEES Aufmerksamkeit um so leichter gelenkt werden, als 1910 eine große Ausstellung islamischer Kunst in München stattfand, die in ganz Europa starkes Interesse hervorrief und über die in allen größeren Publikationen, in der Presse und in den Kunstzeitschriften ausführlich berichtet wurde.[15] Es ist unwahrscheinlich, daß der Maler diese Ausstellung versäumte, zumal er sich nach Will Grohmanns Aussage bereits vor seiner Reise nach Tunesien vom Nahen Osten und seiner Kultur angezogen fühlte. Teppiche und gemusterte Stoffe □ 716, 718, ja sogar primitive Tapas (siehe Glossar) bestätigten den Künstler in seinem Bestreben reiner Flächengestaltung. Sie lieferten ihm eher Beispiele als Modelle für die besondere Behandlung der glatten Oberfläche, bei der das Feld in geschlossene Segmente unterteilt wird, etwa durch unregelmäßige Vierecke unterschiedlicher Größe und Farbe, aber auch durch eingezeichnete Rechtecke mit parallelen Seiten.

Darf man sagen, daß der Primitivismus, indem er neue Quellen erschloß und in einem »imaginären Museum« zusam-

□ 710 *Paul Klee, ›Östlich-süß‹, Öl auf Holz, 49,8 x 66 cm. Privatsammlung.*

mentrug, Werke unterschiedlichster Art, deren einzige Gemeinsamkeit ihr Gegensatz zu klassischer und abendländischer Kunst war, eine entscheidende Rolle für die Kunst des 20. Jahrhunderts spielte? Oder war der Primitivismus nur eine Zwischenstation auf einem Wege, der in jeder Hinsicht über ihn hinausging? War er nur ein Vorwand, um einen viel radikaleren Bruch herbeizuführen?

In diesem Zusammenhang verlangt ein bestimmtes Aquarell KLEES unsere Aufmerksamkeit. Es veranschaulicht eine Technik des Malers, die man ähnlich bei Stammesobjekten antreffen kann. Das Bild *Bauchredner* □ 715 von 1923 mit dem rätselhaften Untertitel *Rufer im Moor* entstand in KLEES Zeit am Bauhaus, als seine Schrift »Wege des Naturstudiums«[16] erschien.

Es ist ein komplexes Werk, insofern als KLEE in ihm zwei Verfahren von besonderer Gegensätzlichkeit verbindet. Der »Hintergrund« besteht aus Rechtecken, die in horizontalen Streifen gleicher Länge aber unterschiedlicher Breite und Farbe angeordnet sind. Diese Gestaltungsweise setzt sich in einer ganzen Reihe von Werken fort, angefangen mit bestimmten tunesischen Aquarellen,[17] den »Gemälde-Gedichten«,[18] schließlich den »Architekturen«[19] bis hin zu jenen Blättern, die, wären sie ohne Titel, als »abstrakt« gelten könnten.[20] Es wäre unrichtig, diese Gestaltungsweise ausschließlich mit der strukturell orientierten Arbeit am Bauhaus zu verbinden, da sie bereits nach 1914 immer häufiger auftritt. Zudem ist darin eine musikalische Konzeption enthalten; die Anordnung der Rechteckstreifen erinnert an Notenlinien, die der Farbtöne und -werte ist »polyphon«: Grüntöne, Rottöne und Violettöne.

Auf diesen gestreiften Hintergrund ist mit Tusche und Feder eine menschliche Figur von transparenter Erscheinung gesetzt, die jedoch in entschieden helleren Farbtönen gehalten ist (blasse, leuchtende Grün- und Rosatöne); diese Figur mag gewisse Ähnlichkeiten mit Kinderzeichnungen haben, doch sind ihre Hauptzüge höchst präzise und von meisterhafter Gestaltung. Der Kopf hat die Form einer Glocke oder eines Helms und erinnert entfernt an Masken, die bei den Initiationsriten der Mädchen vom Stamm der *MENDE* in Guinea und Sierra Leone getragen werden. Der gesamte Rumpf besteht aus einer unspezifischen Form mit geschwungener Kontur. Darauf sind fünf ebenso transparente imaginäre Tiere dargestellt. Solche Motive sollten in einer Reihe von »organischen« Werken bis 1939 wiederkehren □ 713, 714.[21]

Die transparenten Tierformen erinnern an die »Röntgen«-Malereien, die man unter den auf Baumborke gemalten Bildern in Arnhemland im Norden Australiens fand □ 712, ebenso bei den *TLINGIT* Kanadas und in der ozeanischen Kunst. Es besteht aber auch ein wesentlicher Unterschied. Während in den Borkengemälden ein Fötus, Eingeweide und Rückgrat relativ realistisch dargestellt werden, zeigt PAUL KLEES Werk monströse, imaginäre Wesen, die durch den Bauchredner sprechen sollen. In gleicher Weise wird der Kopf des Verliebten in der etwa gleichzeitig entstandenen Lithographie *Der Verliebte* □ 713 von seiner Geliebten mit gespreizten Beinen bewohnt. PAUL KLEE benutzt also die »Röntgen-Technik« im wesentlichen dazu, um Wunschphantasien darzustellen. Die Stammeskünstler wie auch KLEE verwenden die Technik, um das dem Auge Verborgene sichtbar zu machen; was jedoch gezeigt wird, beweist im ersteren Fall Kenntnisse der Anatomie und im zweiten eine persönliche Bildwelt oder Besessenheit.

Obgleich in Ton, zeichnerischen und malerischen Techniken ganz verschieden, ist das junge Mädchen im Bild *Der Verliebte* (1922) wie der *Bauchredner* (1923) ein Opfer von Monstern, die es verfolgen und unterjochen. Beide Werke stehen in direktem Bezug zur außereuropäischen Kunst – im ersten Fall durch Anverwandlung der Form, im zweiten durch Übernahme einer Darstellungsweise. Ganz offensichtlich erfolgten KLEES Ausbrüche aus dem Abendland aus »magischen« Absichten heraus – soweit diese durch die Psychoanalyse erklärbar sind. Selbstverständlich lassen sich die Bezüge zu exotischer Kunst in seinem Werk auch aus rein formalen und malerischen Gründen erklären, die selbst wiederum durch die Auffassung von Form als Genese gerechtfertigt sind. Die Bezüge können im Kontext des Werkes neue Sinnzusammenhänge herstellen, so daß eine Untersuchung hier ansetzen sollte. In dieser Funktion scheint ihnen die Bedeutung von Archetypen zuzukommen. Die Übernahmen können mit anderen Worten in zwei Dimensionen erfolgen: als elementare Zeichen, die aus ihrer ursprünglichen Bedeutung gelöst wurden, oder im Hinblick auf die Bedeutung, die ihnen der neue Zusammenhang verleiht oder in ihnen entdeckt. Ein Zeichen oder eine Form, die aus einem unklassischen, außereuropäischen Werk entlehnt wurden, haben etwas Elementares, weswegen ihre Herkunft nicht leicht feststellbar ist. Dieses Elementare übt selbst die Funktion eines Zeichens aus, eines Zeichens der Primitivität, der Ursprünglichkeit. Diese Ursprünglichkeit ist natürlich eine psychische Eigenschaft des Künstlers; zugleich aber wird sie jenen Kulturen zugeschrieben, die künstlerische Darstellung nicht als Kommunikationsmittel sehen, sondern als Zeugnis einer gegenseitigen Durchdringung von Innen- und Außenwelt.

□ 711 *›Maske aus Holz‹, SHIRA-PUNU (Gabun), bemaltes Holz Höhe 34 cm. Bernisches Historisches Museum, Bern.*

Wiederum sind wir mit dem diffizilen Problem konfrontiert,

□ 712 *›Känguruh‹, australische Ureinwohner, bemalte Rinde, Höhe 50 cm. Museum für Völkerkunde, Basel.*

□ 715 *Paul Klee, ›Der Bauchredner (Rufer im Moor)‹, 1923, Aquarell auf gefärbtem Papier, 39 x 29 cm. Sammlung Heinz Berggruen, Genf.* ▷

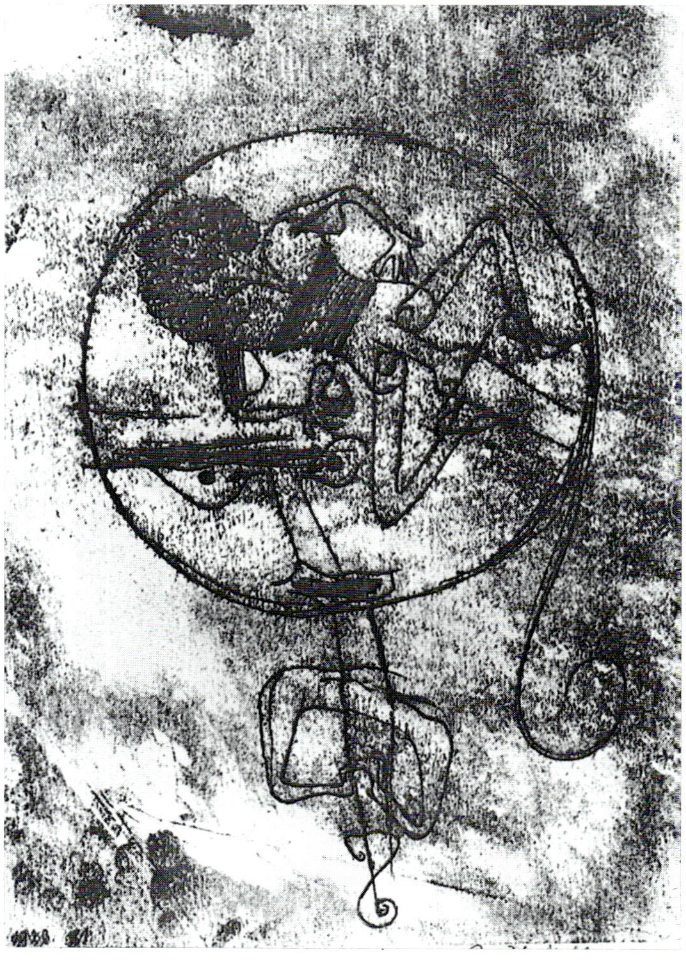

□ 713 *Paul Klee, ›Der Verliebte‹, 1922, Lithographie mit roter Tonplatte, 27,5 x 19 cm. Sammlung Karl Djerassi, Stanford.*

□ 714 *Paul Klee, ›Der Torso und die Seinen (bei Vollmond)‹, 1939, Wasserfarben, gewachst, auf gipsgrundierter Jute, 65,5 x 50,5 cm. Paul-Klee-Stiftung, Kunstmuseum Bern.*

Klee

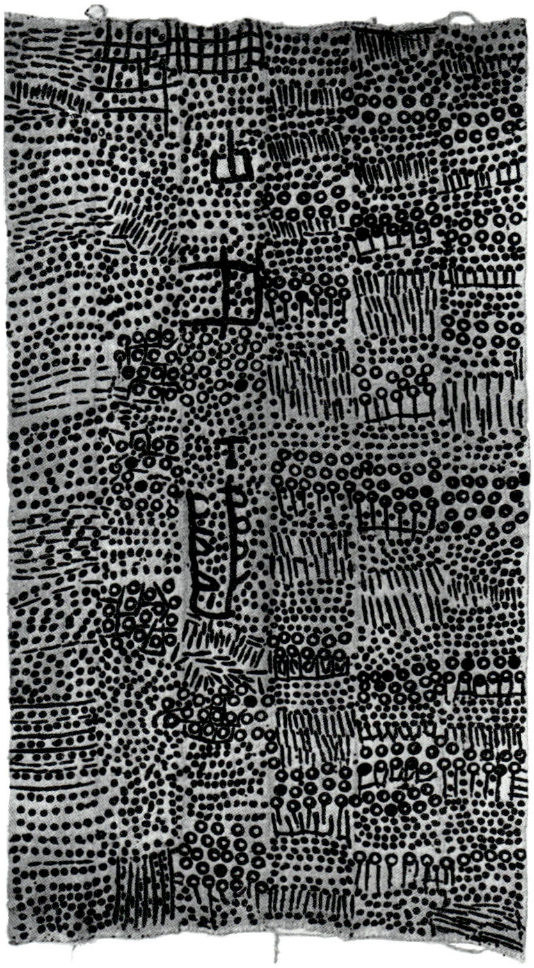

□ 717 *›Maske‹*, Bwa *(Obervolta), bemaltes Holz, Höhe 38,5 cm. Privatsammlung. Ehemals Sammlung Tristan Tzara.*

□ 716 *›Stoff mit Muster‹*, Bambara *(Mali), gefärbte Baumwolle. Veröffentlicht in Henri Clouzot, „Tissus nègres", ohne Erscheinungsjahr.*

□ 718 *›Stoff mit Muster‹*, Bambara *(Mali), gefärbte Baumwolle. Veröffentlicht in Henri Clouzot, „Tissus nègres", ohne Erscheinungsjahr.*

eine spezifische »exotische« Quelle in Klees Werk ausfindig zu machen, die der Künstler in seinem Werk als Anregung aufnahm. Diese Quelle könnte sich zum Beispiel schon Jahre, bevor sie in seinem Werk zur Anwendung kam, in das künstlerische Bewußtsein eingeprägt haben. In diesem Falle wäre sie durch das unbewußte Wirken des Gedächtnisses und durch den neuen formalen und ikonographischen Zusammenhang umgestaltet worden, in den das übernommene Element gestellt und dann integriert wurde und verwandelt wieder auftaucht. Es kann sogar so elementar sein, daß es in Wirklichkeit von zahlreichen Objekten, die zeitlich und räumlich voneinander getrennt sind, zugleich abstrahiert wurde. Aufgrund fehlender dokumentarischer Hinweise kann die Quelle daher nicht mit Gewißheit identifiziert werden. Nicht zuletzt verlangt Klee von der unklassischen, außereuropäischen Kunst keine Systematisierung der Form, die in der syntaktischen Struktur lokalisierbar wäre: Wie er Schreyer anvertraute, suchte Klee in solcher Kunst eine Bestätigung. Je nach dem Phantasiegesetz des jeweiligen Werkes verwendet und erweitert er andererseits ein Vokabular an Formen und Zeichen, die er seinen jeweiligen Absichten anpaßt.

Man sollte sich davor hüten, vorschnell zu verallgemeinern und diese Technik der Aneignung fremder Formen und Zeichen a priori auf alle Werke KLEES zu übertragen. Denn der Künstler scheint in zahlreichen Fällen mehr als nur eine eigene Bestätigung in exotischer Kunst gefunden und seine künstlerischen Intentionen manchmal bestimmten Objekten angepaßt zu haben.

Eine formale Analyse kann nur dann heuristisch erfolgreich sein, wenn sie sich dem Gegenstand ihrer Untersuchung anpaßt. Deshalb müssen wir Methoden finden, mit denen eine formale Analyse für jedes einzelne Werk durchführbar ist; um zu diesen Methoden zu gelangen, müssen wir uns dem jeweiligen bildnerischen, graphischen oder ikonographischen Komplex so weit als möglich nähern, um dessen Beziehung zu seiner Umgebung und seiner Zeit besser beurteilen zu können. Dank Mathilde Klee sind einige Seiten und Hefte aus KLEES Grundschultagen erhalten, die den künstlerischen Werdegang ihres Bruders von früher Kindheit bis zum Erwachsenenalter in anschaulicher Weise aufzeigen.

In einem Heft von 1897 machte KLEE einige Bemerkungen über Goethes Gedicht »Harzreise im Winter« und zeichnete unzählige Köpfe in Frontal- und Profilansicht auf den Rand. Eigenartigerweise besteht jedoch keinerlei Beziehung, weder illustrativer noch sonstiger Art, zwischen diesen ziemlich sorgfältig ausgearbeiteten Zeichnungen und dem Text, den KLEE gerade studierte.[22] Diese Zeichnungen, die der junge KLEE wahrscheinlich halb bewußt ausführte, während er abwesend dem Lehrer zuhörte, sind weniger Karikaturen als vielmehr »Grotesken«, für die viele seiner Werke, ja sogar Spätwerke, Beispiele liefern. Wenigstens zwei dieser Köpfe, die sich unter der Gruppe von Köpfen links oben befinden, verdienen Beachtung. Einer davon zeigt Ähnlichkeiten mit den sogenannten »Masken mit verzerrtem Mund«, die bei Volksfesten oder der Fastnacht getragen werden. Der andere Kopf erinnert ein wenig an bestimmte Masken der *TLINGIT* und *HAIDA*. Ein drittes Gesicht, das über dem Kopf mit verzerrtem Mund zu

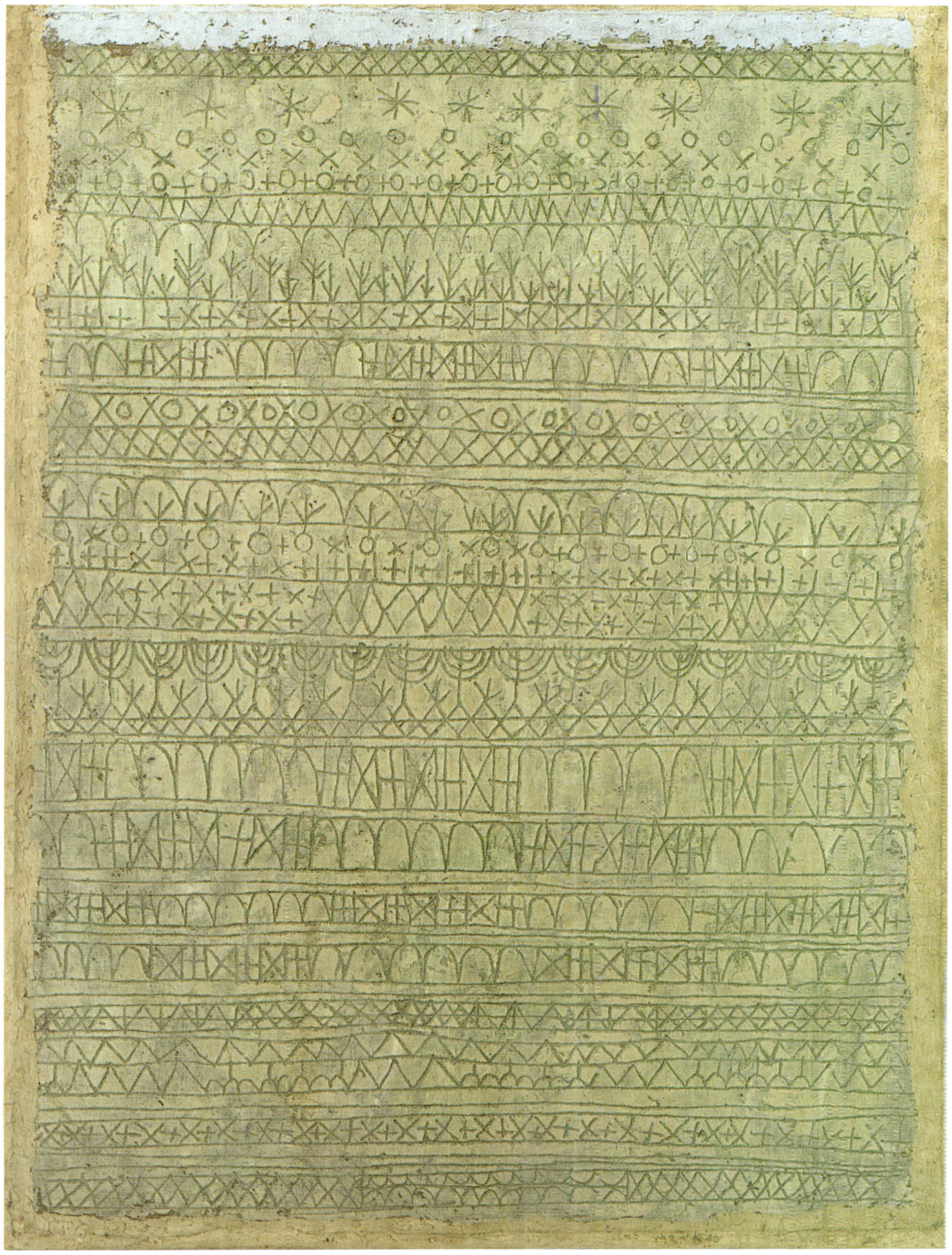

□ 719 *Paul Klee, ›Pastorale‹, 1927, Tempera auf Leinwand, 69 x 52 cm. The Museum of Modern Art, A. A. Rockefeller-Fund, New York.*

sehen ist, teilt gewisse Merkmale modellierter Totenschädel □ 50 und sogar melanesischer Masken.

Obwohl Klee meines Wissens in seinen *Tagebüchern*, seinem Briefwechsel oder den »theoretischen« und pädagogischen Schriften darüber nichts vermerkt, können wir mit Sicherheit annehmen, daß er das Berner Historische Museum und dessen völkerkundliche Abteilung besuchte. Dort muß er Objekte gesehen haben, die einige seiner Zeichnungen anregten und seine Vorstellung von Primitivismus prägten. Von den »exotischen« Gegenständen, die im Almanach »Der Blaue Reiter« gezeigt werden, stammten überdies fünf aus der Sammlung in Bern □ 711,[23] die meisten anderen aus dem Staatlichen Museum für Völkerkunde in München. Dies rechtfertigt die Annahme, daß Klee bei der Auswahl der Illustrationen für den »Blauen Reiter« mitwirkte, wobei er Stücke aus der Sammlung des Berner Museums heranzog, während Wassily Kandinsky und Franz Marc die für sie interessanten Stücke der Münchner Sammlung aufnahmen.[24] Sein Besuch 1906 im Berliner Museum für Völkerkunde ging auf die Anregung durch »exotische« Werke zurück, die er als Heranwachsender in Bern entdeckt hatte. Nach Mitteilung Ladislas Segys (zitiert von J. S. Pierce)[25] sammelte Klee eine Zeitlang Pfeile und Bögen aus Schwarzafrika und bewahrte in seinem Münchner Atelier zwischen 1906 und 1914 offenbar einige afrikanische Masken auf. Segy macht jedoch keinerlei Angaben über deren Herkunft oder Art.[26]

□ 721 *›Reliquiarfigur‹*, KOTA *(Gabun), Holz, Kupfer, Messing und Eisen, Höhe 54 cm. Sammlung Philippe und Maryse Dodier, Avranches, Frankreich.*

◁ □ 720 *Paul Klee, ›Götzen‹, 1913, Feder und Tusche, 13 x 10 cm. Sammlung Joshua und Leda Natkin, West Redding, Connecticut.*

□ 722 *Paul Klee, ›Zeichnung eines Reliefs mit exotischem Phantasietier‹, 1897, Feder und Tusche, 5 x 5 cm. Paul-Klee-Stiftung, Kunstmuseum, Bern.*

□ 723 *Paul Klee, ›Zeichnung eines Reliefs mit exotischer Figur‹, 1897, Feder und Tusche, 9 x 5 cm. Paul-Klee-Stiftung, Kunstmuseum, Bern.*

Mit Recht wäre einzuwenden, daß die Köpfe auf dem Rand von Klees Schulheft sozusagen mechanisch, ohne besondere künstlerische Absicht gezeichnet wurden und so für unser Thema nur bedingt relevant sind. Gleichwohl scheinen sie jedoch ein Beweis dafür zu sein, daß Klee zu jener Zeit schon außereuropäische Kunst kannte. Noch wichtiger ist, daß sie uns zeigen, wie Klee als junger Mann erstmals exotische Kunstwerke in sich aufnahm. Erste Beweise dafür, daß er das Berner Museum so früh besuchte, würden allerdings mehr Gewißheit in die Sache bringen. Jürgen Glaesemer wies mich kürzlich auf einige Zeichnungen aus jenem Jahr hin, darunter *Zeichnung eines Reliefs mit exotischem Phantasietier* □ 722 und *Zeichnung eines Reliefs mit exotischer Figur* □ 723. Klee selbst gab ihnen den Titel *»Zeichnungen nach Reliefs«*: Sie wären demzufolge Nachahmungen oder Zeichnungen nach Ausstellungsstücken, die er möglicherweise im Bernischen Museum gesehen hatte.

Selbstverständlich sind diese Skizzen nur Jugendwerke, und es wäre falsch, daraus zu große Schlußfolgerungen zu ziehen. Klee wurde durch seine frühe, frühreife Begegnung mit außereuropäischer, unklassischer Kunst zu einer phantasiebestimmten Zeichnung angeregt oder fühlte sich zumindest in dieser Orientierung bestärkt. Die Vorliebe für die satirische Zeichnung und Karikatur bestärkte außerdem Klee darin, sich von der idealen Kunst loszusagen, die ihm schon sehr früh als nicht mehr zeitgemäß erschienen war.[27] Seine Distanzierung vom klassischen Abendland war selbstverständlich nicht die einzige Auswirkung dieses Bruches. Mittlerweile völlig unsatirisch, war sie gleichfalls einem phantasievollen Schaffen förderlich, das sich nach 1903 in zunehmendem Maße durchsetzte.

Dieser Bruch erfolgte nicht nur auf der Ebene formaler Systeme. Als Klee ideale Kunst fortan für überholt hielt, war er sich durchaus bewußt, daß er einem Nihilismus folgte, den er als scharfsinniger Leser Nietzsches als das beherrschende Merkmal seiner Epoche betrachtete. Der bloße Gedanke daran war für Kandinsky und Franz Marc Grund tiefer Beängstigung. Obwohl er wie seine beiden Freunde an die Notwendigkeit eines neuen Menschen glaubte und sich die Grundzüge der Utopie des Bauhauses zu eigen machte (von denen die letzten Abschnitte des Jenaer Vortrags zeugen), war sein Standpunkt im Vergleich zu dem seiner Freunde und späteren Kollegen in Weimar und Dessau deswegen nicht weniger originell. Er unterschied sich vom Mystizismus Kandinskys und Marcs sowie dem Soziologismus des Bauhauses durch die bahnbrechende Praxis der Karikatur und der satirischen Zeichnung, durch solide klassische Bildung und realitätsnähere und kritischere Lektüre.

Aus dieser Perspektive hat der Primitivismus im Falle Klees zwei verschiedene Nebenbedeutungen, die sich stets überlagern. Zum einen bedeutete er, wenn auch metaphorisch, einen Neubeginn, für den die Künstler als seine Begründer die Verantwortung zu tragen hatten. Zum anderen scheint der Primitivismus als Vorstellung, aber auch als Phänomen gesehen, das sich in unterschiedlichen Werken manifestiert, in Paul Klees künstlerischer Entwicklung eine Schlüsselrolle zu spielen. Untrennbar mit dem Begriff der Genese verbunden, soll er nicht als alternatives Modell das klassische ersetzen: Er enthält in sich selbst die Entwicklung, die unendliche Vielfalt von Variationen und Transformationen, denen Klee alle seine Vorbilder unterzieht.

Anmerkungen

Jean Laude, ein Experte für die Kunst der Naturvölker und der Moderne, der an der Universität von Paris Oberseminare über das Werk Klees hielt, war der gegebene Autor für das vorliegende Kapitel. Er wurde schwerkrank, als der Artikel zu schreiben war, und starb einige Monate nach Zusendung eines ausführlichen Manuskriptes, das offensichtlich ein Buch über Klee werden sollte. Mit Laudes Zustimmung grenzte sein Freund Pierre Daix diesen Text auf die Passagen, die sich auf primitive Kunst beziehen, ein. Er konnte damals den Autor im Krankenhaus konsultieren. Weil Laude wegen seines schlechten Gesundheitszustandes auf bestimmte Fragen nicht eingehen konnte und sein Kapitel nur auf wenige Werke Bezug nimmt, haben wir uns erlaubt, noch zusätzliches Bildmaterial aufzunehmen. Dazu zählt eine Gegenüberstellung von Klees *Götzen* □ 720 mit einer KOTA-Reliquiarfigur □ 721, ein Vergleich, der in *Paul Klee and Primitive Art* von James Smith Pierce (New York und London 1976) vorkommt.

1. Klee, F. (Hrsg.), *Tagebücher von Paul Klee 1898–1918,* Köln 1957, S. 274–75.
2. Schreyer, L., *Erinnerungen an Sturm und Bauhaus,* München 1956, S. 170–71.
3. Rigopoulu, C., »Masques et marionettes chez Paul Klee«, Dissertation bei Fanette Roche, Université de Paris 1981, S. 23.
4. Klee, F., *Tagebücher von Paul Klee 1898–1918,* Köln 1957, S. 241.
5. Siehe Haxthausen, C. W., »Klees künstlerisches Verhältnis zu Kandinsky während der Münchner Jahre« in *Paul Klee: Das Frühwerk, 1883–1922,* München 1979.
6. Bahr, H., *Expressionismus*, München 1916, S. 45.
7. Siehe Suter-Raeber, R., »Der Durchbruch zur Farbe und zum abstrakten Bild« in *Paul Klee: Das Frühwerk,* S. 131–65; und Güse, E.-G., *Die Tunisreise (Klee, Macke, Moilliet),* Stuttgart 1982.
8. Klee, P., *Pädagogisches Skizzenbuch,* München 1925. Zitat entnommen aus Wingler, H. M. (Hrsg.), *Paul Klee – Pädagogisches Skizzenbuch,* Mainz und Berlin 1965, S. 51.
9. Klee, F., *Tagebücher,* S. 197–99. Tatsächlich hatte er um 1902 eine Technik entwickelt, die der Hinterglasmalerei ähnlich war; ebda. S. 136, 180, 188.
10. O. K. Werkmeister analysierte die Beziehungen zwischen Klees Werk und Kinderkunst in »The Issue of Childhood in the Art of Paul Klee«, *Arts Magazine,* September 1977, S. 138–51.
11. Abgebildet im *Blauen Reiter Almanach,* Paris 1981, S. 256.
12. August Macke, der zusammen mit Louis Moilliet Klee begleitete, hinterließ ein Zeugnis von Klees Interesse an einheimischer Töpferei in *Marchand et cruches,* 1914. Man kann hier auch die Aufteilung der Fläche in Quadrate nach Art der Beduinenteppiche feststellen. Siehe Güse, E.-G., »Raum und Fläche – Europa und der Orient zu August Mackes Tunisaquarellen« in *Die Tunisreise,* a.a.O., S. 144.
13. Hierfür nur zwei Beispiele: *Motiv aus Hammamet,* 1914, und *Südliche Gärten,* 1914, abgebildet in Güse, *Die Tunisreise,* S. 192, 193.
14. Siehe besonders *Nillegenden,* 1937 (Pastell), abgebildet in *Paul Klee par lui-même et par son fils Felix Klee,* Paris 1963, dritte Bildtafel nach S. 56.
15. »Meisterwerke mohammedanischer Kunst«, München Mai/Oktober 1910. Im ersten Band des Kataloges sind sechsundvierzig Teppiche verschiedener Herkunft abgebildet.
16. Klee, P., »Wege des Naturstudiums« in *Staatliches Bauhaus in Weimar 1919–1923,* Weimar 1923.
17. Vor allem in *Rote und weiße Kuppeln,* 1914/15, Kunstsammlung Nordrhein-Westfalen, Düsseldorf, abgebildet in Güse, *Die Tunisreise,* S. 73; und *Über ein Motiv aus Hammamet,* 1914, Kunstmuseum Basel, abgebildet in *Paul Klee: Das Frühwerk,* S. 403, Nr. 337.
18. Vor allem in *Hoch und strahlend steht der Mond,* 1916/20, Galerie Beyeler, Basel, abgebildet in *Paul Klee: Das Frühwerk,* S. 456, Nr. 337.
19. Die »Architekturen« beginnen 1919 mit *Herbstlicher Ort,* 1921, Privatsamml., abgebildet in *Paul Klee: Das Frühwerk,* S. 534, Nr. 449, werden fortgesetzt in *Orange-Violett grüne Stufung, Orange Vergehend-Grün-Violett gegen Orange (liegend),* 1922/71, abgebildet in *50 Werke von Paul Klee,* Kornfeld und Klipstein Verkaufskatalog, Bern 11.–13. Juni 1975, und gehen bis zu *Drei Türme,* 1923, Felix Klee-Samml., Bern, abgebildet in *Paul Klee*, St. Paul-de-Vence, Maeght Foundation, Juli-September 1977, S. 77, Nr. 55, und bis *Architektur,* 1923, Hermann Rupf-Samml., Bern, abgebildet in Grohmann, W., *Paul Klee,* Köln 1966, S. 201.
20. Hauptsächlich *Freundlicher Blick,* 1923, abgebildet in *Klee,* Ausstellungskatalog, Paris, März–Mai 1974, Nr. 20; *Alter Klang,* 1925, Kunstmuseum Basel, abgebildet in *Paul Klee,* Katalog, Paris, M.N.A.M., November 1969–Februar 1979, Nr. 73, *Harmonie der nördlichen Flora,* 1927/58, abgebildet in *Paul Klee, Opere 1900–1949, dalla collezione Felix Klee*, a.a.O., S. 115, Nr. 78.
21. Mangels eines besseren Ausdrucks bezeichnete ich diese Serie »organisch« wegen der undefinierbaren Art ihrer Formen, die in einem undifferenzierten Raum schweben. Die Serie beginnt mit einer Darstellung von Bäumen in *Park am See, ohne Häuser,* 1920, abgebildet bei Paul Klee, *Opere,* S. 94, Nr. 41. Marie Bonaparte schrieb 1933: »Hier wirft die Psychoanalyse etwas Licht darauf, indem sie uns zeigt, zu welchem Entwicklungsstadium die »Magie« gehört; was ich meine, ist der Moment in der menschlichen ontogenetischen und phylogenetischen Evolution, in dem die Magie vorherrschend ist.« In »La Pensée magique chez le primitif«, *Revue française de psychoanalyse* VII, 1, 1934, S. 13.
22. Abgebildet bei Grohmann, Paul Klee, S. 34. Ich überprüfte diese Beziehungslosigkeit anhand von Goethe, *Poésies*, übers. v. Betz, M., Paris 1949; das Gedicht befindet sich auf S. 68–71.
23. Folgende Stücke kommen aus Bern: die DAYAK-Skulptur (Borneo); drei polychrome Statuetten aus Bali und die *SHIRA-PUNU*-Maske □ 711 aus Gabun, im *Blauen Reiter Almanach,* S. 87, Abb. 114. Der Irrtum in der Bildunterschrift, die die Maske aus Gabun für chinesisch erklärt, ist bezeichnend für die überaus große Beachtung, die man China um 1912 schenkte.
24. Ein interessantes Forschungsprojekt auf diesem Gebiet wäre, ein Inventar der Überreste des Archivs vom »Blauen Reiter« anzulegen und die Kataloge der Museen von Bern und München zu konsultieren. Wahrscheinlich wurden dort die Photographien erworben und die Rechte für deren Veröffentlichungen eingeholt. Die reproduzierten Werke wurden sicher aus einem größeren Bestand ausgewählt, den man unbedingt kennen sollte, um die exotischen Werke bestimmen zu können, die Klee, Kandinsky und Marc zugänglich waren.
25. Siehe Klees Aufzeichnungen zu seinem Kurs am Bauhaus, 3. April 1922, veröffentlicht bei Splilller, J., *Das Bildnerische Denken,* S. 409. Zitiert von Pierce, *Paul Klee and Primitive Art,* New York und London 1976, S. 35.
26. Segy, L., *African Sculpture Speaks*, New York 1952, S. 35.
27. Christian Geelhaar berichtet eingehend über Klees intellektuelles Erwachen während einer Reise nach Italien: »In Genua, Rom, Neapel und Florenz wurde ›ein Stück Geschichte lebendig‹, wenngleich es [dem Künstler] schmerzlich bewußt wurde, ›daß das Idealische im Bereich der bildenden Kunst total überholt ist‹. Ihn befiel eine Ratlosigkeit, die er durch Satire und Karikatur zu bezwingen suchte.« Geelhaar fügt hinzu, daß der junge Klee in dieser seelischen Verfassung sofort nach seiner Rückkehr, zwischen 1903 und 1905, mehrere Radierungen mit dem Titel »Erfindungen« anfertigte: ». . . was sie im wahrsten Sinn des Wortes sind – unabhängig von irgendeinem natürlichen, direkten Modell« (Klee, *Dessins,* Paris 1975, S. 12). Ich sollte noch ergänzen, daß zu der Zeit Rom, Florenz, Neapel und in geringerem Maße Genua in ihren Völkerkundemuseen bedeutende Sammlungen ozeanischer Kunst hatten, die Paul Klee jedoch nicht besuchte.

□ 724 *Paul Klee, ›Eskimo mit weißen Haaren‹, Handpuppe, 1924, Holz, Gips, Farbe und Pferdehuf, [illegible]5 x 8 x 6 cm. Privatsammlung, Bern.*

Rosalind Krauss

Alberto Giacometti

Beschreibt man Alberto Giacomettis Bronzeplastik *Unsichtbarer Gegenstand* ☐ 725, 729 als »ein junges Mädchen mit leicht angezogenen Knien, das den Anschein erweckt, es wolle sich dem Betrachter darbringen (eine Pose, zu der der Bildhauer durch die Haltung angeregt wurde, die einst ein kleines Mädchen seiner Heimat eingenommen hatte)«, dann beteiligt man sich an dem von Giacometti in den 40er Jahren unternommenen Versuch, sein Frühwerk umzudeuten. Daß Michel Leiris hierbei mitwirkte, als er diesen Text für den Katalog der Giacometti-Ausstellung von 1951 verfaßte und darin den *Unsichtbaren Gegenstand* in den Dienst einer reinen Wiedergabe der sichtbaren Welt stellt, zeigt die Brüche und Verschiebungen, die das Paris der Nachkriegszeit verwandelten.[1] Denn diese Beschreibung ist ein Affront gegen André Breton.

Wer kann das Lehrbeispiel für das seltsame, doch eindrucksvolle Wirken des objektiven Zufalls vergessen, mit dem Breton das *Reich von L'Amour fou* eröffnet? Giacometti und Breton besuchen den Flohmarkt, wo jeden ein scheinbar nutzloser Gegenstand gefangennimmt und sich beide ganz gegen ihre Absicht zu dessen Kauf gezwungen fühlen. Giacometti erwirbt eine scharfeckige, kriegerähnliche Maske ☐ 727, deren ursprüngliche Verwendung beiden ein Rätsel bleibt.[2] Das Lehrbeispiel will auch nicht den eigentlichen Zweck des Objekts aufklären, sondern seine tiefere Bestimmung. Der Schilderung Bretons zufolge diente es nämlich der Lösung von Problemen, die Giacometti lähmten, als er die einzelnen Teile des *Unsichtbaren Gegenstandes* zu einem Ganzen zusammenzufügen versuchte. Vor allem der Kopf hatte der Einfügung in das übrige Werk widerstanden. In diesem kritischen Moment schien sich die Maske wie von selbst anzubieten. »Das Eingreifen der Maske«, schrieb Breton, »hatte anscheinend den Sinn, Giacometti bei der Überwindung seiner Unentschlossenheit zu helfen. Es sollte uns auffallen, daß die Entdeckung des Gegenstandes hierbei genau denselben Zweck wie ein Traum erfüllt, nämlich das Individuum von lähmenden emotionalen Hemmungen zu befreien, Ausgleich zu schaffen und zu verstehen zu geben, daß das von ihm für unüberwindlich gehaltene Hindernis beseitigt worden ist.«[3] In Bretons Schilderung hat die Welt der realen Gegenstände des weiteren nichts mit einer Kunst der Mimesis zu tun; die Objekte sind keinerlei Modelle für das bildhauerische Schaffen. Die Welt ist vielmehr wie ein großer Fundus, unter dessen Oberfläche dem Wirken des Unbewußten nachzuspüren ist; wie ein Lackmuspapier, mit dem sich die ätzende Schärfe der Begierde erfassen läßt. Giacometti hätte nach Bretons Ansicht den *Unsichtbaren Gegenstand* ohne die Maske, den Traum, ebensowenig vollenden können, wie es ihm selbst nicht gelungen wäre, ohne seine eigene ›trouvaille‹ vom Markt die literarische Welt von *L'Amour fou* zu betreten.

Das kleine Schweizer Mädchen in Giacomettis späterer Erinnerung und Leiris' Darstellung haben mit diesem Schlüsselbeispiel für den erstaunlichen, objektiven Zufall nichts zu tun. In den Dienst einer direkten, auf die reale Welt bezogenen Modellfunktion gestellt, entzieht das kleine Schweizer Mädchen den *Unsichtbaren Gegenstand* dem Bereich des Surrealismus und versetzt es in die Sphäre von Giacomettis Atelier nach dem Kriege, als er sich Monat für Monat in immer neuen Versuchen bemühte, in seinem Werk eine Ähnlichkeit mit dem vor ihm stehenden Modell herzustellen.[4] Indem Leiris das Werk in einen neuen Kontext stellt, den ein neuer Freundeskreis und Verbündete wie Sartre und Genet bilden, führt er es an die Problematik der Schrift *Die Phänomenologie der Wahrnehmung* heran und entfernt es von *Les Vases communicants.*

Der Historiker kann eine solche Mißachtung der Chronologie natürlich nicht gelten lassen, und darum erwähnt der führende Interpret von Giacomettis Werk, Reinhold Hohl, mit keinem Wort die Erinnerung an das Schweizer Kind bei der Besprechung dieses Meisterwerks aus der Vorkriegsperiode des Bildhauers. Doch Bretons Geschichte erscheint ihm ebenso fragwürdig: »Entgegen der Schilderung Bretons, ein geheimnisvoller Gegenstand vom Flohmarkt habe dem Künstler bei der Gestaltung geholfen (tatsächlich handelte es sich um das erste Modell einer eisernen Schutzmaske, die der französische Sanitätsdienst im Ersten Weltkrieg entworfen hatte), entlehnte Giacometti die stilisierten Körperformen der *Sitzfigur einer Verstorbenen* von den Salomoninseln, die er im Museum für Völkerkunde in Basel gesehen hatte, und verband sie mit anderen Elementen der ozeanischen Kunst wie etwa dem Todesdämon in Vogelgestalt.«[6]

Trotz der Bestimmtheit, mit der Hohl diesen Zusammenhang darstellt, sind seine Belege spärlich und indirekt. Giacometti sprach 1963 in einem Interview über ein rekonstruiertes Haus Ozeaniens aus dem Baseler Museum.[7] Da die Figur der Salomoninseln seit den frühen 30er Jahren in derselben Galerie stand, konnte Hohl zumindest vermuten, daß Giacometti das Objekt kannte.[8] Am stärksten wird Hohls These durch die schematische Rahmenkonstruktion der halb sitzenden Figur gestützt, die für Südseestatuen dieser Art typisch ist und sonst normalerweise nirgendwo auftritt.[9] Da Giacomettis Skulptur

☐ 725 *Alberto Giacometti, ›Der unsichtbare Gegenstand‹ (L'Objet invisible), 1934, Bronze (Abguß von 1935), 154 x 32 x 28 cm. Albright-Knox Art Gallery, Edmund Hayes Fund, Buffalo.*

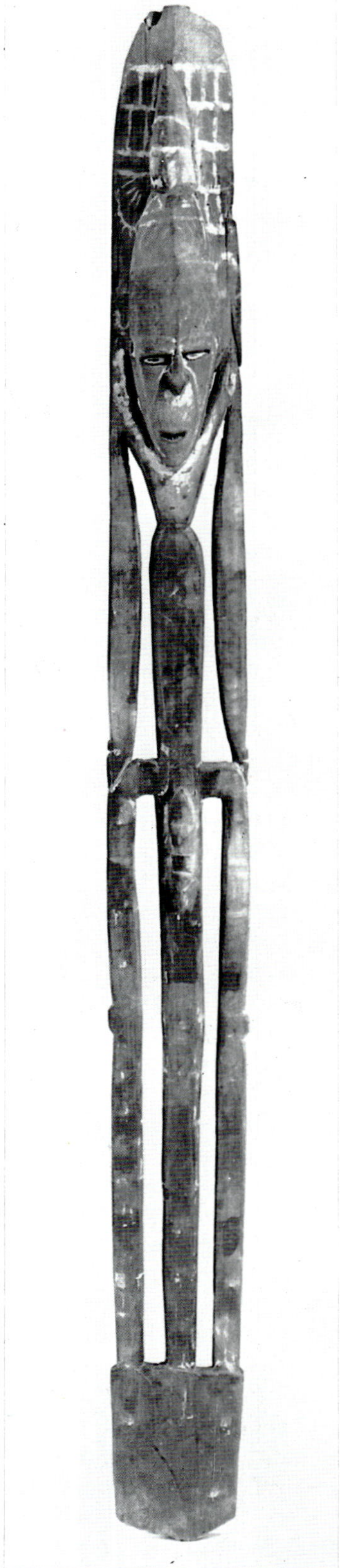

□ 726 ›*Figur aus Holz*‹, *Kopar, Provinz Ost-Sepik (Papua-Neuguinea), bemalt, Höhe 161 cm. Museum Rietberg, Sammlung Von der Heydt, Zürich.*

□ 727 ›*Eiserne Maske*‹, *Photographie von Man Ray. Veröffentlicht in André Breton, „L'Amour fou", Paris 1937.*

ihre Ausdruckskraft teilweise der rätselhaften Beziehung zwischen der halb knienden Haltung und den Strukturelementen verdankt, die sie zu umschließen scheinen – eine flache Scheibe an den Schienbeinen auf der Vorderseite der Figur und das sonderbare Gerüst hinter ihr –, und diese Konstruktion für ein Modell im Atelier nicht »natürlich« ist, lag es schon immer nahe, ihren Ursprung in einem anderen Kunstwerk zu suchen. Aufgrund des Stützaufbaus, der Haltung, des vorspringenden Kopfes und der deutlichen Formung der Brüste wäre die von Hohl vorgeschlagene Statue der Salomoninseln hier eine durchaus mögliche Quelle.[10]

Hohls These, diese Statue sei das Vorbild für den *Unsichtbaren Gegenstand,* gründet sich natürlich auf einer umfangreichen Kenntnis zur Rolle der primitiven Kunst in der Arbeit des Bildhauers in den Jahren vor 1934. Der Primitivismus war von grundlegender Bedeutung für GIACOMETTIS frühe Befreiung nicht nur von der klassischen Bildhauerei, sondern auch von den kubistischen Konstruktionen, die in den frühen 20er Jahren als die einzige logische Alternative erschienen. GIACOMETTIS Kunst reifte aufgrund seiner Fähigkeit, in sehr enger Beziehung zu den primitiven Quellen schöpferisch tätig zu sein, so daß ihm schon zwei Jahre nach Verlassen des Ateliers von BOURDELLE eine großformatige Skulptur gelang, die aufgrund ihres tiefgreifenden Bezuges zur afrikanischen Stammeskunst als sein eigenes Werk zu betrachten ist.

Diese Figur, die lebensgroße *Löffelfrau* □ 737, entstand Ende 1926 oder Anfang 1927. In ihrer über das unmittelbar zuvor geschaffene Werk *Das Paar* hinausgehenden Auffassung läßt sich GIACOMETTIS Intuition erahnen, skulptural auf primitive Kunst zu reagieren.[11] *Das Paar,* die erste Reaktion GIACOMETTIS auf afrikanische Quellen, wurde durch die Mode des »style nègre« beeinflußt, die in den frühen 20er Jahren außergewöhnlich weit verbreitet war □ 733. Die Zeichnungen, die LÉGER 1924 in einer Ausgabe von *L'Esprit nouveau* als *personnages* für *Die Erschaffung der Welt* □ 732 veröffentlichte, weisen dieselben Grundformen – Trapez, Oval – für die Gesamtform des Körpers wie *Das Paar* auf, und auch die ornamentalen Details für die Darstellung der Anatomie sind in ihrer Art gleich: So stammt ein sowohl von GIACOMETTI als auch von LÉGER verwertetes Einzelmotiv von den Ritzmustern auf afrikanischen Masken, die die beiden als dekoratives Ausdrucksmittel für anatomische Formen (wie bei den Händen in *Das Paar*) verwendeten. Stilgemäß sind diese primitivisierenden Elemente mit graphischen Mitteln vor einen vereinfachten,

□ 728 ›*Figur aus Holz, Haar und Muscheln*‹, *Santa Cruz (Salomoninseln), Höhe 37 cm. The Trustees of the British Museum, London.*

□ 730 *›Figur aus Holz‹, Bougainville (Salomoninseln), bemalt, Höhe 175 cm. Museum für Völkerkunde, Basel.*

□ 729 *Alberto Giacometti, ›Der unsichtbare Gegenstand‹ (L'Objet invisible), 1934, Gips, Höhe 153 cm. Photographie von Dora Maar. Veröffentlicht in André Breton, „L'Amour fou", Paris 1937.*

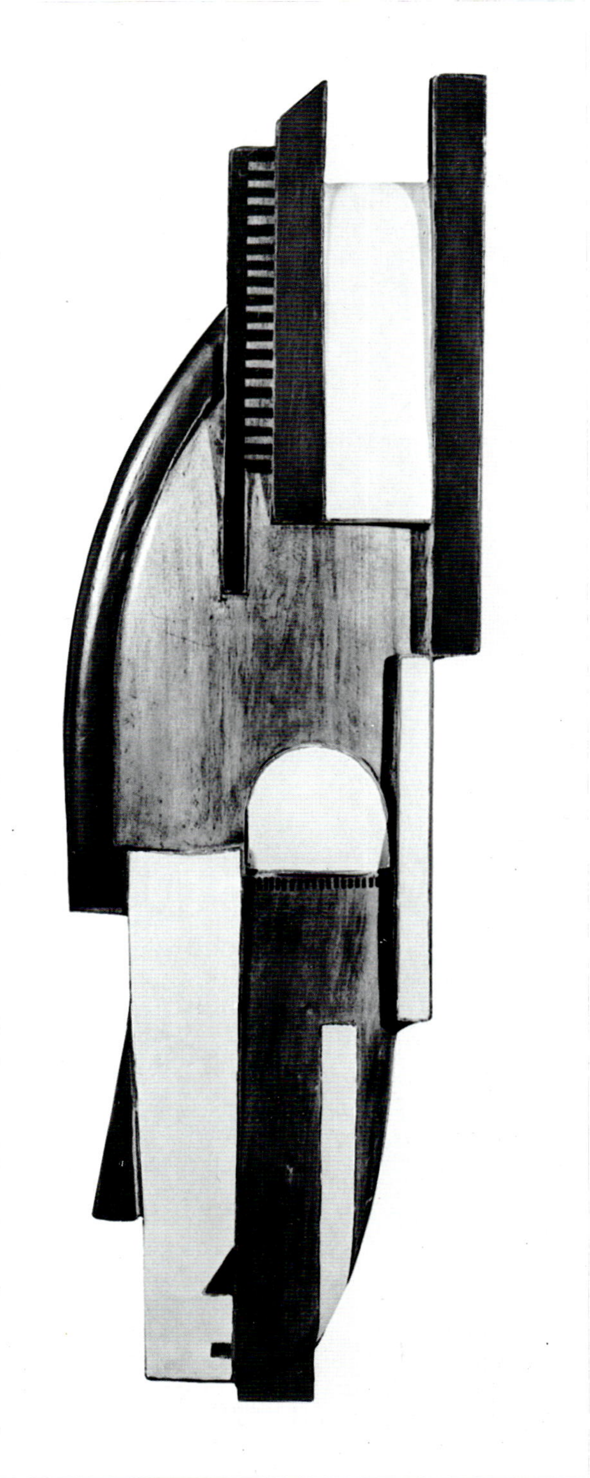

□ 731 *Jean Lambert-Rucki, ›Maske‹, Holz. Privatsammlung.*

flachen Hintergrund gesetzt. Auch die Formen dieser Grundflächen könnten der afrikanischen Kunst entlehnt sein (es ist daher eine Beziehung zwischen dem Umriß der männlichen Figur von *Das Paar* und jenem Typ von Stammesschilden denkbar, die auch PICASSO interessierten). Selbst die Zusammenstellungen der Figuren könnten – wie in *Das Paar* – auf afrikanische Vorbilder bezogen sein, in diesem Fall auf das dem Brauchtum der *BAGA* und *DOGON* geläufige »erste Paar« □ 71, 610. Das Ergebnis solcher Verwendung von zufälligen und umgestalteten Elementen ist jedoch eine verallgemeinerte Darstellung des Afrikanisch-Primitiven ohne eine bestimmte bildnerische Quelle.

Das Mittel der Stilisierung, das die spielerischen Verwandlungen und neuen Kombinationen der initialen Vorbilder ermöglicht, verbindet diese Darstellungen von GIACOMETTI und LÉGER mit einem größeren Komplex, der Neger-Deco genannt werden könnte. Bildhauer wie MIKLOS und LAMBERT-RUCKI schufen in diesem Kontext um 1925 stilisierte »afrikanische« Masken und figurative Skulpturen □ 731. Der Designer PIERRE LEGRAIN entwarf elegante Möbel nach dem Muster afrikanisch-primitiver Sessel und Hocker für Kunden wie Jacques Doucet. Die vielen widersprüchlichen Vermutungen, die in der GIACOMETTI-Literatur zur ethnographisch korrekten Quelle für *Das Paar* geäußert wurden,[12] beweisen, daß es der Neger-Deco gelungen ist, die Erfahrung von Afrikanität – so hätte es Roland Barthes genannt – zu vermitteln, ohne dabei die Vorbilder zu verraten. Während *Das Paar* an diesem stilisierenden Umgang mit dem Primitiven noch teilnimmt, wird bei der *Löffelfrau* darauf verzichtet.

Die *Löffelfrau* zielt auf eine wesentlich tiefgreifendere Aneignung der Strukturen afrikanischer Bildschnitzkunst. Sie offenbart eine Metaphorik, die uns bei den Getreideschaufeln der *DAN* häufig begegnet, deren Aushöhlung dem weiblichen Unterleib – aufgefaßt als Gefäß, Beutel oder Höhle – angenähert ist □ 734–736.[13] In den Jahren vor 1927 waren diese Löffel – viele davon sind geradezu »abstrakt« – ziemlich bekannt. Auf der großen Ausstellung afrikanischer und ozeanischer Kunst im Musée des Arts Décoratifs im Winter 1923/24 wurden sechs Löffel aus der Sammlung Paul Guillaume gezeigt.[14] Indem GIACOMETTI die Metapher übernahm und sie umkehrte – aus »ein Löffel ist wie eine Frau« wurde »eine Frau ist wie ein Löffel« –, konnte er die Idee verstärken. Universell wurde sie dadurch, daß er die Formen der manchmal recht naturalistischen Schnitzereien aus Afrika zu einer prismatischeren Abstraktion hin verallgemeinerte. Indem er dem Modell der *DAN* ein Frauenbild aufzwang, das fast nur aus einem Mutter-

□ 732 *Fernand Léger, Entwurf für ›Die Erschaffung der Welt‹ (La Création du monde). Veröffentlicht in „L'Esprit nouveau", Nr. 18, 1924.*

□ 733 *Alberto Giacometti, ›Das Paar‹ (Le Couple), 1926, Bronze, Höhe 64 cm. Sammlung Sylvia und Joe Slifka, New Jersey.*

leib besteht, paßte GIACOMETTI die formale Eleganz des afrikanischen Gegenstandes den Fruchtbarkeitsgöttinnen der Steinzeit mit ihrer roheren Durchbildung an.[15]

Mit dieser Verherrlichung der weiblichen Urfunktion, gesehen aus der Perspektive einer primitiven formalen Logik, hatte sich GIACOMETTI der aggressiven antiwestlichen Haltung der bildnerischen Avantgarde angeschlossen. Verbalen Ausdruck fand diese Haltung z. B. bei Georges-Henri Rivière, der bald stellvertretender Direktor des Trocadéro werden sollte, und in dessen Lobschrift auf die Archäologie, der »elternmordenden Tochter des Humanismus«, veröffentlicht im ersten Band der *Cahiers d'art.*[16] Nach der nüchternen Behauptung, das Ideal der griechischen Kunst sei überlebt, schrieb Rivière, wenn Louis Aragon und Jean Lurçat jetzt nach Spanien fahren würden, wäre ihr wichtigstes Ziel nicht der Prado wie noch bei ihren Vätern, sondern die Höhlen von Altamira. Diese These bestätigt auch die zur selben Zeit geschaffene *Löffelfrau.*

Aber die *Löffelfrau* ist außerdem noch etwas anderes: nämlich das, was eine andere Gruppe der intellektuellen Avantgarde als »weichen« Primitivismus bezeichnet hätte, also ein formal und damit kraftlos gewordener Primitivismus. Die *Löffelfrau* in Verbindung mit den *Cahiers d'art* zu bringen, bedeutet in der Tat, sie in den Kontext einer formalisierenden Konzeption des »Primitiven« zu stellen, so wie sie etwa in Christian Zervos' Lob von BRANCUSI zum Ausdruck kommt, wenn er diesen als den erfolgreichsten Bildhauer der Nach-

□ 734 *›Löffel aus Holz‹*, DAN *(Liberia oder Elfenbeinküste), Höhe 52 cm. Indiana University Art Museum, Bloomington.*

□ 735 *›Löffel aus Holz‹*, DAN *(Liberia oder Elfenbeinküste), Höhe 45 cm. Privatsammlung.*

□ 736 *›Löffel aus Holz‹*, WOBE *(Elfenbeinküste), Höhe 30 cm. Musée de l'Homme, Paris.*

kriegszeit bezeichnet. Seit dem großen Zustrom schwarzer Kultur, so schrieb Zervos 1929, »hat Brancusi alle Perspektiven erforscht, die die Neger ihm eröffnet haben und die ihm das Erreichen der reinen Form ermöglichten«.[17] Die *Löffelfrau* teilt sowohl den Sinn für den Größenmaßstab als auch die Eigenart der formalen Reduktion, zu der GIACOMETTI zweifellos in Kenntnis des Brancusischen Werkes gelangte. Ein Jahr vor dem Entstehen von GIACOMETTIS Skulptur veröffentlichte Paul Guillaume ein Buch, welches das Extrem einer die primitive Kunst ästhetisierenden Bewegung darstellte.[18] *Primitive Negro Sculpture,* das unter der Ägide von Albert Barnes entstand, mit Unterstützung der Barnes Foundation geschrieben und in englischer Sprache herausgegeben, ließ unter den bisherigen Veröffentlichungen nur Roger Frys Analyse der formalen Struktur afrikanischer Kunst gelten.[19] Aufgrund Guillaumes hervorragender Stellung in der Kunstwelt war das Buch mit Sicherheit schon vor seiner Übersetzung ins Französische in Paris gut bekannt, und es ist denkbar, daß eine darin vorkommende Illustration GIACOMETTIS Konzeption der *Löffelfrau* nachhaltig beeinflußte.

Unter der Voraussetzung, daß jedes Werk afrikanischer Kunst als Lösung eines formalen Problems verstanden werden kann, präsentiert *Primitive Negro Sculpture* jedes seiner Objekte als »eine rhythmische, variierte Abfolge eines Themas in Masse, Linie oder Oberfläche« und beschreibt, wie die geometrisch erfaßten Elemente zuerst artikuliert und dann zu einer Ganzheit verbunden werden. Worauf der gesamte Text immer wieder hinweist, ist die fortwährende Präsenz eines Willens zur Kunst, einer ästhetischen Triebkraft, die als ursprünglich begriffen wird. Allen religiösen oder sonstigen Ideen zugrundeliegend, sei dieser Instinkt die gemeinsame Eigenschaft der Kinder aller Rassen wie der »Kinder« der menschlichen Spezies: der primitiven Männer und Frauen. Somit ermögliche das kreative Spiel westlicher Kinder mit Farben, Ton und Stiften einen Zugang zu den Triebfedern primitiver Kunst. Guillaume schließt mit der Gewißheit, es sei »also nicht schwierig, sich die ständige Entwicklung der Negerkunst aus dem freien, naiven Spiel des ästhetischen Impulses vorzustellen«. Damit stellt er eine Verbindung her zwischen den ästhetisierenden Interessen der Kunstwelt und der überaus euphorischen Phase in der Entwicklungspsychologie der späten zwanziger Jahre und gelangt so in Übereinstimmung mit dem Psychologen G. H. Luquet.[20]

Zweifellos war die Überzeugung Luquets, daß die Kunst von Kindern und Eingeborenen eine Kategorie für sich bilde, die ihrerseits die Werte der »zivilisierten« Kunst in Frage stelle, für Georges Bataille das Interessante an diesem Buch, was ihn letztlich auch zu einer Besprechung in der Zeitschrift *Documents* veranlaßte.[21] Bataille weicht jedoch von Luquets Verklärung der primitive Gestaltungen motivierenden Kräfte scharf ab und artikuliert damit den von diesem Flügel der radikalen Avantgarde geführten Angriff auf die L'art pour l'art-Auffassung des Primitivismus. Weil Batailles Position – wie ich zeigen werde – mit GIACOMETTIS endgültiger Konzeption und der Verwendung primitiver Vorbilder viel zu tun hat, lohnt es sich, auf Batailles Kritik an Luquet einzugehen.

Für Luquet hat das Kind anfangs keinerlei Bildintentionen, sondern manifestiert seine Existenz aus reiner Lust, indem es mit seinen schmutzigen Fingern Wände beschmiert oder weiße Papierbögen mit Kritzeleien vollmalt. Später beginnt das Kind Teile dieser ersten Spuren mit gegenständlichen Bedeutungen zu versehen. Mit diesem »Lesen« der von ihm geschaffenen

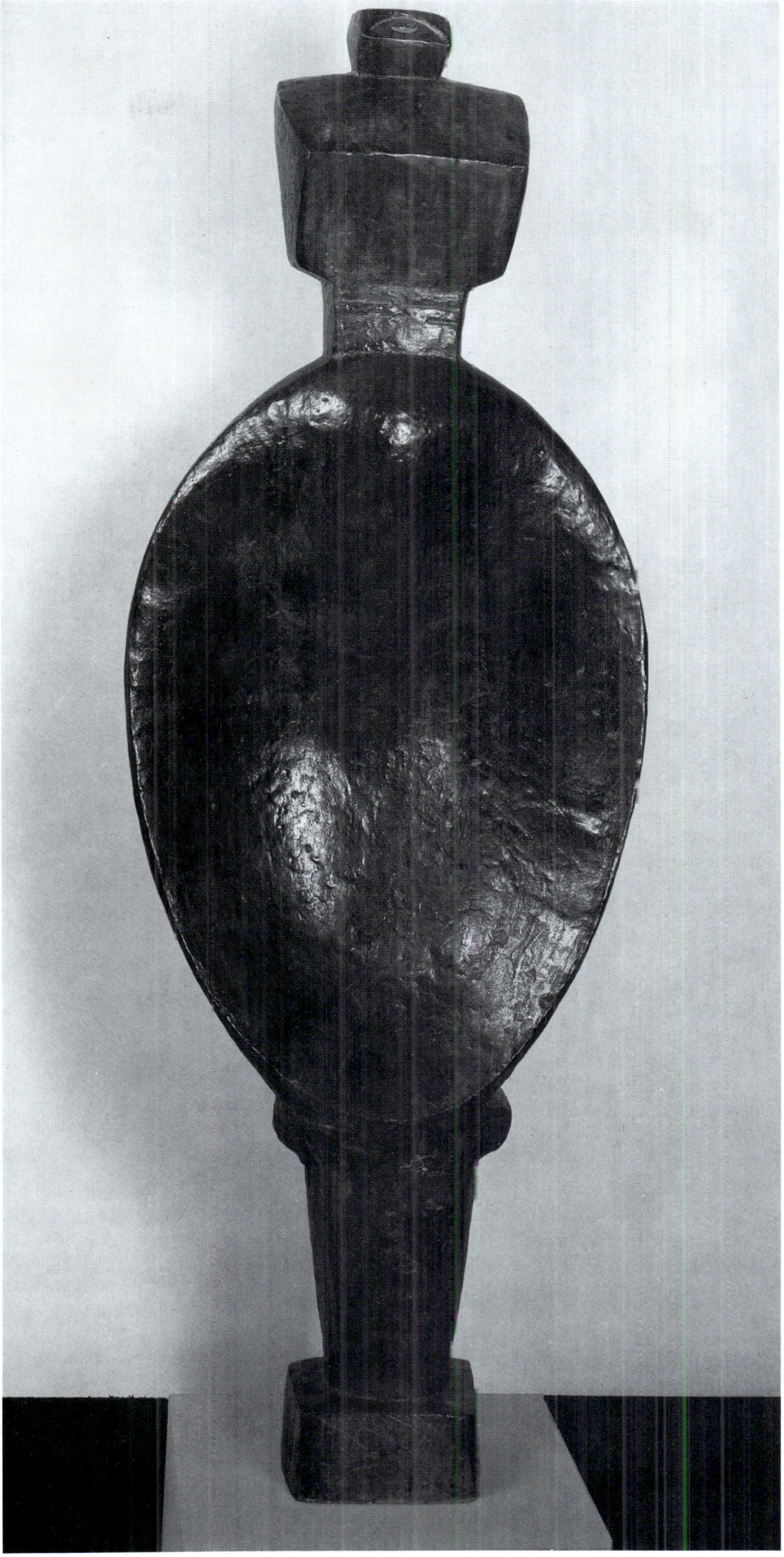

☐ 737
Alberto Giacometti, ›Löffelfrau‹ (Femme cuillère), 1926, Bronze, 144,5 x 51 x 17,5 cm. Sammlung Mr. and Mrs. Burton Tremaine, Meriden, Connecticut.

□ 738 *Alberto Giacometti, ›Schwebende Kugel‹ (Boule suspendue), Ausschnitt, 1930–31, Gips und Metall, 61 x 36 x 34 cm. Kunstmuseum, Alberto Giacometti-Stiftung, Basel.*

Linien kann das Kind schließlich die Bilder bewußt wiederholen. Da das Begriffsvermögen noch sehr schematisch ist, werden die Zeichen mit der Idee eines Gegenstandes verknüpft, ein Vorgang, der mit Konzeption und nichts mit Ähnlichkeit zu tun hat. Deshalb bezeichnet Luquet die primitive Gestaltung als *geistigen Realismus,* während er den Terminus *visueller Realismus* dem mimetischen Verfahren des westlichen Erwachsenen vorbehält.

Die Entwicklung der prähistorischen Höhlenmalerei erklärt Luquet natürlich analog zur Malerei heutiger Kinder: Zufälliges Malen entwickelt sich langsam zu intentionalen Mustern, die ihrerseits ein figuratives Lesen nach sich ziehen. Die zuerst noch in den nichtfigurativen Mustern »erkannte« Ähnlichkeit mit Objekten der Außenwelt kann mit der Zeit immer weiter ausgearbeitet und vervollkommnet werden.

Nach Luquet sind es also absolute Freiheit und Lust, die den Impuls zum Zeichnen auslösen, und dieser Instinkt – nicht der Wunsch, Realität abzubilden – steht am Anfang. Auf dieser Grundlage bildet sich nach und nach ein Verfahren, um die Zeichen den Darstellungsbedingungen anzugleichen, wobei ein Gestaltungs-»System« mit konstanten Merkmalen im gesamten Bereich der primitiven Kunst entsteht – ob es sich hier nun um Graffiti, Zeichnungen von Kindern, Eingeborenen oder Bauern handelt. Charakteristika wie Gesichtsprofile mit zwei Augen und zwei Ohren oder die Wiedergabe von Häusern und Körpern als durchsichtig, um ihren Inhalt zu zeigen, oder die freie Kombination von Grund- und Aufriß blieben in der Praxis des »geistigen Realismus« – unabhängig von Zeit und Ort – konstant. Luquet zufolge gesellte sich der Freude so das Wissen großzügig hinzu.

Die Chronologie prähistorischer Kunst unterstützt Luquets unbeschwertes Fortschrittsdenken sicherlich nicht. Die Höhlen von Lascaux mit ihrem erstaunlichen Naturalismus sind älter als die viel gröberen Darstellungen späterer Zeiten. Wenn Bataille seine Leser auf diesen offensichtlichen Fehler in Luquets System aufmerksam macht, geschieht dies aber nicht historischer Genauigkeit zuliebe, sondern wegen eines Gedankens, der ihm schon während seiner Zeit als Herausgeber der *Documents* gekommen war und danach an Bedeutung gewonnen hatte. Worauf Bataille nämlich aufmerksam macht, ist die unterschiedliche Art der Wiedergabe von Menschen und Tieren in derselben Periode: »Das Rentier, der Bison oder die Pferde sind mit einer solchen Detailgenauigkeit dargestellt, daß – hätten wir ebenso naturgetreue Abbildungen von den Menschen – die dunkelste Epoche der Avatare der Menschheit ihre Verschlossenheit umgehend preisgeben müßte. Aber die Zeichnungen und Skulpturen, die die Aurignac-Menschen selbst verkörpern sollen, sind fast alle *informe* und viel weniger menschenähnlich als die Darstellungen der Tiere; andere, wie die Hottentotten-Venus, sind unwürdige Karikaturen der menschlichen Gestalt. Mit dem gleichen Gegensatz haben wir es in der Zeit des Magdalénien zu tun.«[22]

Da »diese rohe und verzerrende Kunst der menschlichen Gestalt vorbehalten war«, unterstreicht Bataille ihre Vorsätzlichkeit, ihren Status als eine Art ursprünglichen Vandalismus, dem die menschlichen Abbilder unterworfen waren. Tatsächlich möchte Bataille an die Stelle von Luquets heiterer Sicht eines Lustprinzips als des Initialimpulses zum Zeichnen das Prinzip der Destruktivität setzen. Das kindliche Bemalen von Mauern, die Kritzeleien auf Papier entstammten einem Wunsch nach Zerstörung und Verstümmelung der Malfläche. In jeder aufeinanderfolgenden Entwicklungsphase bei Luquet sieht Bataille die Verkörperung einer neuen Lust, das zu ändern und zu deformieren, was vor dem Subjekt existiert: »Kunst, denn auch das ist unbestritten Kunst, vollzieht sich mithin durch eine Zerstörungsabfolge. Insofern sie also Instinkte freisetzt, sind diese sadistischer Natur.«[23]

Der Begriff, den Bataille wählt, um das Phänomen des Sadismus gleichzeitig auf Kinder- und Höhlenkunst anzuwenden, ist *Alteration* (Änderung), und dieses Wort ist in seiner präzisen Doppeldeutigkeit für ihn typisch. Denn *Alteration* stammt vom lateinischen *alter,* das sowohl den Wechsel eines Zustandes als auch den Wechsel (oder das Voranschreiten) von Zeit bezeichnet und dadurch die divergierenden Bedeutungen von *Devolution* und *Evolution* umfaßt. Bataille betont, daß Alteration auf den Zerfall von Kadavern hinweist und gleichzeitig auf »den Übergang zu einem völlig heterogenen Zustand, der . . . dem ›tout autre‹ entspricht, d.h. dem Geweihten, das sich z.B. durch einen Geist vergegenwärtigt«.[24] Alteration – das den ursprünglichen Impuls der menschlichen Selbstdarstellung beinhaltet – wird so zu einem Konzept, welches zugleich auf- und abwärts gerichtet ist: wie *altus* und *sacer,* die gegensätzlichen Urbegriffe, die Freud interessierten. Das Ursprüngliche ist daher unauflösbar diffus, gebrochen durch eine unaufhebbare Dualität an der Wurzel der Dinge, auf die Bataille in seiner Nähe zu Nietzsches Denken Wert legte. Während die Logik es verwirft, Begriffe wie hoch und tief, unrein und heilig als polare Gegensätze zu begreifen, erlaubt dieses Spiel mit dem Widersprüchlichen das Aufspüren der Wahrheit, die Bataille nie müde wurde, immer wieder hervorzuheben: daß sich Gewalt, historisch gesehen, schon immer im Zentrum des Heiligen befand; daß, um wahrhaftig zu sein, der bloße Gedanke des Kreativen zugleich eine Todeserfahrung sein muß und daß es nicht einen Moment echter Intensität ohne eine genauso extreme Grausamkeit gibt.[25]

Bataille ist sich vollkommen bewußt, daß der zivilisierte Mensch des Westens die Gewalt in alten religiösen Riten am liebsten ignorieren möchte: Vor der Bedeutung der deformierten Anthropoiden in den Höhlen verschließt er entweder die Augen oder macht sich keine Gedanken – oder er ästhetisiert die gesamte afrikanische Kunst. In seinem allerersten Essay über primitive Kultur wies Bataille auf den Widerstand von Forschern hin, die sich das Schreckliche und Grausame an der Götterdarstellung bestimmter Völker nicht eingestehen wollten. Dieser Text ist in einer Sammlung ethnologischer Essays für die erste große Ausstellung präkolumbianischer Kunst in Paris (1928) enthalten und trägt den Titel »L'Amérique disparue«. Hier unternimmt Bataille den Versuch (nach dem früher üblichen Verfahren, präkolumbianische Kultur dem Primitiven zuzurechnen), die Wirklichkeit hinter der Darstellung der aztekischen Götter als Karikatur, monströs und deformiert zu erfassen.[26] Obwohl sein Wissen über präkolumbianische Kultur noch ziemlich oberflächlich war, wies seine Analyse doch weit über den damaligen Kenntnisstand hinaus – so sieht es jedenfalls der Ethnologe Alfred Métraux in einem Rückblick auf diese frühe Arbeit Batailles.[27] Bataille sah in diesen Abbildern die Vergegenwärtigung unheilvoller, verhehlender Götter voller Verschlagenheit. Ihnen wurde mit einem religiösen Eifer gehuldigt, der unbarmherzige Grausamkeit mit schwarzem Humor verband, um einen Kult des Deliriums zu errichten: »Zweifellos ist nie eine blutigere Ausartung menschlichen Wahns ersonnen worden: immer wieder in hellstem Sonnenlicht begangene Verbrechen zu dem einzigen Zweck der Befriedigung götzenbesessener Alpträume, schrecklicher Geister! Die kannibalischen Mahlzeiten der Priester, die Zeremonien mit Kadavern und Strömen von Blut – viele solche historischen Ereignisse erinnern an die überwältigenden Orgien, die der illustre Marquis de Sade beschrieb.«[28] Den Bezug von Mexiko auf de Sade auszudehnen, war für das ethnologische Denken der 20er Jahre, besonders im Kreise um Marcel Mauss, typisch. Mauss' Seminar über die Religionen der Primitiven hob besonders die gewalttätigen Götterriten Afrikas, Ozeaniens und Amerikas hervor. Nicht nur Bataille wurde hierdurch angeregt, sondern auch Michel Leiris, was ein Werk wie *Les Rites de possessions des Ethiopiens de Gondar et ses aspects théâtraux* beweist.

Aber während er von der unersättlichen Blutgier der Azteken spricht, von ihren Praktiken, in denen der Priester am Altar lebendigen Opfern das Herz herausschnitt und dieses noch zuckende Organ hochhielt, betont Bataille den »erstaunlich fröhlichen Charakter dieses Horrors«. Wie beim Konzept der Alteration erlauben die Opferpraktiken der Azteken die Erfahrung der Doppelnatur des Sakralen. »Mexiko war nicht nur der blutigste Schlachthof der Menschheit«, schreibt Bataille in einem Vergleich der Azteken mit der Inkakultur, die er als bürokratisch und starr empfand, »es war auch eine wohlhabende Stadt, ein echtes Venedig der Kanäle und Brükken, prächtiger Tempel und schöner Blumengärten an jeder Ecke.«[29] Es war eine Blutkultur, auf deren Boden Blumen und Fliegen zugleich gediehen.

Hatte Giacometti in seiner Auffassung des Primitiven 1926–27 noch zum Lager Luquets gehört, wurde er 1930, dem

□ 739 *Alberto Giacometti, ›Schwebende Kugel‹ (Boule suspendue), 1930–31, Gips und Metall, 61 x 36 x 34 cm. Kunstmuseum, Alberto Giacometti-Stiftung, Basel.*

Jahr der Veröffentlichung von »L'Amérique disparue«, ein Anhänger Batailles. Denn in der Zwischenzeit hatte sich Giacometti der *Documents*-Gruppe angeschlossen.

1928, im Jahr nach der Vollendung von *Löffelfrau*, zeigte Giacometti seine Arbeiten zum ersten Mal. Er stellte zwei der plattenähnlichen Köpfe und Figuren aus, die er in jenem Jahr geschaffen hatte, Objekte, die die reine Frontalität der *Löffelfrau* zu einer neuen Einfachheit und Eleganz steigerten. In Übereinstimmung mit der seinem ästhetisierenden Primitivismus impliziten Tendenz wurden nun präklassische Objekte zum Vorbild für Abstraktion und Reduktion der Form. Daß er in seiner Praxis von solchen Vorbildern beeinflußt war, fiel den Betrachtern dieser Werke sogleich auf. In einem der frühesten Kommentare zu Giacomettis Plastiken sprach Zervos von ihrer Beziehung zur kykladischen Kunst.[30]

Aufgrund dieser beiden ausgestellten Objekte bat André Masson Giacometti um ein Treffen. Daraufhin erfolgte die Einführung Giacomettis in die Gruppe, der Masson, Desnos, Artaud, Queneau, Leiris und Bataille angehörten, jene als abtrünnig geltenden Surrealisten, deren geistiger Mittelpunkt die *Documents* darstellten. Drei der Herausgeber waren Bataille – der sich besonders für die Entwicklung der ethnographischen Theorie einsetzte, wie sie in den Seminaren von Marcel Mauss an der »Ecole des Hautes Etudes« formuliert wurde[31] – Michel Leiris – der 1931 Völkerkundler geworden war – und Carl Einstein – der 1915 seine Studie über primitive Bildhauerei veröffentlicht hatte. Somit lag das Interesse ihrer Zeitschrift an diesem Thema auf der Hand. Während seiner engen und dauerhaften Freundschaft mit Leiris wurde Giacometti nicht nur mit Einzelfragen und Theorien der Völkerkunde, sondern auch mit deren Verwendung durch die *Documents*-Gruppe vertraut.[32] 1930 – nach seiner Aufnahme in die *Documents* – schuf Giacometti *Schwebende Kugel* □ 738, 739. Obwohl diese Skulptur für die orthodoxen Surrealisten eine Sensation war – sie verschaffte Giacometti sofort Zugang zu Breton und Dali – und obwohl sie die große surrealistische Begeisterung für erotisch besetzte Objekte auslöste, war sie doch ein Werk, das mit dem Surrealismus viel weniger als mit den Theorien Batailles zu tun hatte.[33]

Maurice Nadeau erinnert sich an die ersten von der *Schwebenden Kugel* provozierten Reaktionen: »Jeder, der dieses Objekt in Aktion sah, empfand eine starke, doch undefinierbare sexuelle Emotion aus unbewußten Wünschen. Dieses Gefühl war keineswegs eine Befriedigung, sondern eher beunruhigend – ähnlich dem irritierenden Gewahrwerden eines Versagens.«[34] Mithin ist *Schwebende Kugel* eine erotische Maschine zur Nichterfüllung von Lust, wie Duchamps *Das große Glas* ein Apparat zur Trennung der Geschlechter ist. Dabei ist *Schwebende Kugel* noch expliziter sadistisch als *Das große Glas*. Denn die gleitende Bewegung, die die gefurchte Kugel zu ihrem keilförmigen Gegenstück deutlich in Beziehung setzt, erinnert nicht nur an eine Liebkosung, sondern auch an ein Schneiden und erweckt damit etwa Assoziationen an den Film *Un Chien andalou* (1928) mit seiner erschreckenden Anfangsszene, in der ein Rasiermesser ein geöffnetes Auge durchschlitzt.[35]

Mit dieser, Liebe und Gewalt zugleich verkörpernden Doppelgeste entsteht eine grundlegende Ambivalenz der sexuellen Identität der Elemente von *Schwebende Kugel*. Nach der einen Lesart ist der von der Kugel bearbeitete Keil dessen weiblicher Partner; nach einer anderen ist er – geschwollen und scharf – das phallische Aggressionsinstrument gegen die verwundbare Rundheit der Kugel. Er ist nicht nur das Rasiermesser von *Un Chien andalou,* sondern auch das Horn des Stiers in Batailles *L'Histoire de l'Œil,* das den Matador durchbohrt und durch Herausreißen eines Auges tötet.[36]

Der Keil ist vielleicht noch in dritter Weise Phallusersatz und noch ganz anders mit dem Reich der sakralen Gewalt verbunden, das um 1930 Giacometti und Bataille gemeinsam interessierte. Der Keil hat die Form der Palmettensteine des alten mexikanischen Ballspiels – keilförmige Elemente, die wahr-

□ 740 *Alberto Giacometti, ›Stachel ins Auge‹ (Pointe à l'œil), 1932, Holz und Metall, 12 x 61 x 35,5 cm. Musée National d'Art Moderne, Centre National d'Art et de Culture Georges Pompidou, Paris.*

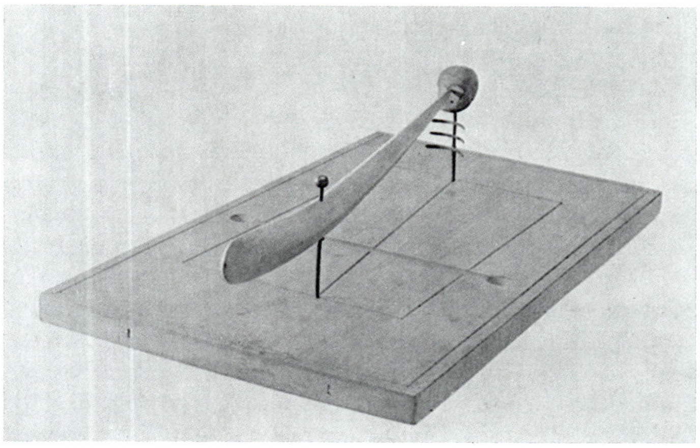

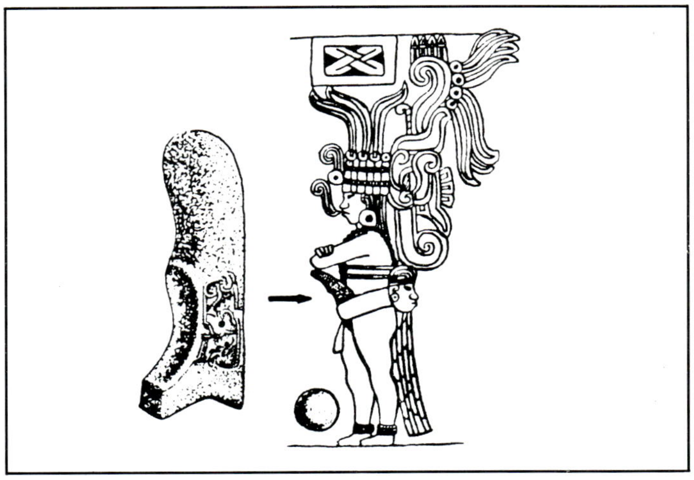

□ 741 *›Ballspieler‹, Vega de Aparicio, Veracruz (Mexiko), Zeichnung nach einer Steinskulptur im Museo Nacional de Antropologia, Mexiko. Aus Borhegyi, „The Rubber Ball Game of Ancient America", 1963.*

scheinlich als Schutz von den fast nackten Teilnehmern des Spiels getragen wurden, bei dem der Ball mit Knien und dem Gesäß gestoßen wurde □ 741.

Die im Zusammenhang mit dem Spiel stehenden Bezeichnungen machen den Gebrauch des Gesäßes deutlich (in Molinas Nahua-Lexikon von 1571 wird »ollama« als »Spielen des Balles mit dem Gesäß« definiert, »olli« als »ein Gummi von Heilbäumen, aus dem sie Bälle herstellen, die mit dem Gesäß gespielt werden«).[37]

Wie alles andere in dem von Bataille so verehrten Mexiko, war dieses toltekische Ballspiel eine Mischung aus Überschwang und Grausamkeit. Berichten zufolge brachte der Ball den Spielern blutige Wunden bei und manchmal sogar den Tod noch auf dem Spielfeld. Der Einsatz des Gesäßes als Spielinstrument gab diesem Ballspiel darüber hinaus eine homoerotische Note. Wenn, wie ich vorschlage, das mexikanische Ballspiel ein Faktor bei der Entstehung von *Schwebender Kugel* war – direkt danach sollte Giacometti Skulpturen als Spielfeld oder Spielbrett auffassen, wie *Stachel ins Auge* □ 740, *Kreislauf* □ 788 und *Das Spiel ist aus* □ 743 –, dann muß man der Serie von Unbestimmtheiten sexueller Zeichen im Werk ein »drittes Geschlecht« hinzufügen.

Schon Giacomettis frühe Plastik hatte sein Interesse an präkolumbianischer, afrikanischer und kykladischer Kunst veranschaulicht. Jacques Dupin, dessen Studie noch zu Lebzeiten des Künstlers entstand, macht darauf aufmerksam, daß Giacomettis frühe »exotische« Quellen aus Afrika, Ozeanien und Mexiko stammten.[38] Zwei Werke, die diesen frühen mexikanischen Einfluß bezeugen, sind der *Kauernde* von 1926 und die vielleicht noch frühere Gipsplastik *Kopf* □ 747.[38] Über eine rein ästhetische Beziehung zu Mexiko hinaus geht eine dritte Skulptur, *Stunde der Spuren* von 1930, die im Verständnis des aztekischen Ethos Bataille sehr nahesteht □ 748. Die Bildwelt von »L'Amérique disparue« und die anderen Berichte über die aztekische Kultur, die die *Documents* veröffentlichten – Giacometti bewahrte die gesamte Heftfolge sein Leben lang sorgfältig auf[39] –, legen es nahe, *Stunde der Spuren* als ekstatische Verbildlichung des Menschenopfers zu deuten. Die Figur an der Spitze drückt mit ihrem aufgerissenen Mund entweder tiefste Ekstase oder Schmerz aus (Bataille würde sagen, beides). Sie steht wie auf einem Altar, unter dem die Form eines aus dem Körper gerissenen Herzens hin- und herschwingt.[40]

□ 742 *›Spielbrett‹, Gio (Liberia), Holz, Länge 56 cm. Peabody Museum of Archaeology and Ethnology, Harvard University, Cambridge.*

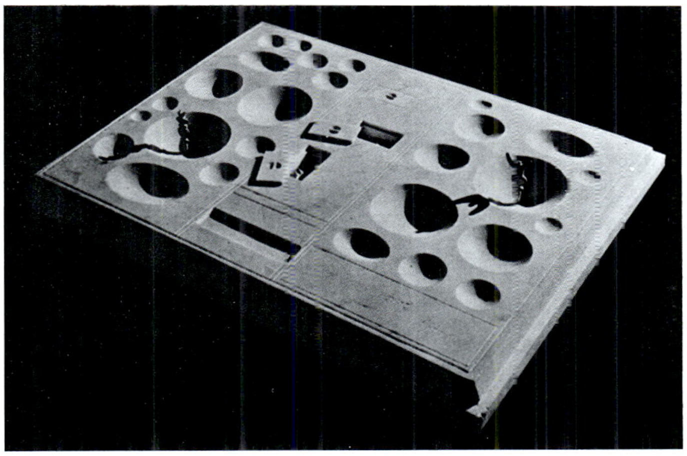

□ 743 *Alberto Giacometti, ›Das Spiel ist aus‹ (On ne joue plus), 1933, Marmor, Holz und Bronze, 5 x 40 x 30 cm, Privatsammlung.*

Stunde der Spuren ging *Schwebender Kugel* unmittelbar voraus. Strukturell sind sie durch das Spiel mit einem hängenden Element verbunden, das an einem käfigähnlichen Gerüst hin und her pendelt. Im Rahmen der Vorstellungen, die man damals über die aztekische Kultur hatte, können diese beiden Werke Giacomettis wohl auch thematisch miteinander in Beziehung stehen.

Unbestreitbar ist aber, daß man beide auf Giacomettis detaillierte Schilderungen seiner eigenen sadistischen und gewalttätigen Vorstellungen beziehen kann. Ein Text wie »Hier, sables mouvants« mit seinen Phantasien von Vergewaltigung und Schlächterei (»ihr Schreien und Stöhnen durchhallte den ganzen Wald«) hat, obwohl zuerst in Bretons Zeitschrift publiziert, mit den vom Surrealismus zugelassenen Vorstellungen einer erschütternden Schönheit wenig zu tun.[41] Der Text verweist auf Bataille, dessen Schriften und Forschungen es Giacometti anscheinend erlaubten, solchen Phantasien des Brutalen Ausdruck zu verleihen. So wie seine lebenslange Vorliebe für die Zeitschrift Batailles, setzten sich auch Giacomettis Schriften zur Gewalt – wie in seinem Aufsatz zu Jacques Callot oder seinem Text »Le Rêve, le Sphinx et le mort de T.« – weit über die dreißiger Jahre und den Bruch mit dem Surrealismus hinaus fort. In Struktur und bildhaftem Ausdruck lassen diese Texte oft an Bataille denken.[42]

Wie bereits erwähnt, fungiert Alteration als ein Begriff Batailles, der den Urwiderspruch beschreibt, der in der Beziehung zur Bedeutung liegt, insofern als die Bedeutung ständig zwischen zwei Polen oszilliert. Dieselbe Bedeutungsschwankung – wegen der hier angelegten Komplexität wäre ›Wanderung‹ die treffendere Bezeichnung – wird auch bei *Schwebender Kugel* ins Spiel gebracht. Denn das Werk ist zwar als gepaarter Gegensatz strukturiert, indem männlich und weiblich neben- und gegeneinandergestellt sind, doch ist der Gehalt dieser Begriffe nicht festgelegt. Jedes Element kann entweder als männliches oder als weibliches Symbol interpretiert werden (und für die Kugel gibt es neben einer Interpretation als Hoden noch die möglichen semantischen Werte Gesäß und Auge, die beide grammatisch neutral sind). Für jede der Lesarten gilt, daß die Deutung einer Einzelform nur in Opposition zu ihrem Gegenstück erfolgen kann. Diese Lesarten bewegen sich in einem ständig wechselnden Feld der Beziehungen, von der metaphorischen Darstellung einer heterosexuellen Verbindung bis in die Bereiche grenzüberschreitender Sexualität – Masturbation, Homosexualität, Sadismus – und wieder zurück. (Es wäre anzumerken, daß die in dem charakteristischen Ausdruck der Skulptur enthaltene Grenzüberschreitung das Werk zugleich von Bretons unerbittlicher Ablehnung des sexuell Perversen und von Picassos eher harmlosem »jeux d'esprit« der Verwandlungen des menschlichen Körpers in den späten 20er Jahren, mit denen *Schwebende Kugel* verglichen wird, unterscheidet.[43]) Mit seiner ständigen Bewegung, seiner konstanten »Alteration« ist dieses Bedeutungsspiel die auf eine Symbolebene erhobene faktische Pendelbewegung des Werkes.

Obwohl die Alter(n)ation in *Schwebende Kugel* ständig geschieht, ist sie durch die Möglichkeiten der metaphorischen Reichweite der beiden Bestandteile, Keil und Kugel, und durch deren sexuellen Bedeutungswechsel dennoch geregelt. Mit diesem erotischen Spiel innerhalb eines geschlossenen Systems nimmt die Plastik an der dämonischen Logik von Batailles *L'Histoire de l'œil* teil. In Batailles Werk – nach Roland Barthes ist es buchstäblich die Geschichte eines Objektes, des Auges, und dessen, was ihm widerfährt (und nicht den Personen der Geschichte) – wird die Voraussetzung für eine Bedeutungswanderung geschaffen, bei der das Objekt sozusagen durch verschiedene Wortstadien »dekliniert« wird. Als kugelförmiges Element wird das Auge durch eine Kette von Metaphern gewandelt und in bestimmten Phasen der Erzählung durch andere kugelförmige Objekte ersetzt: Eier, Hoden, die Sonne. Als flüssigkeitshaltiges Objekt ermöglicht das Auge zugleich eine zweite, mit der ersten verwandte Assoziationsreihe: Eidotter, Tränen, Urin, Sperma. Die beiden metaphorischen Ketten bilden also ein Kombinationssystem, in dem Begriffe interagieren können, um eine schier unendliche Bildfolge hervorzubringen. So kann die als Auge und Eidotter versinnbildlichte Sonne als »schwaches Leuchten« beschrieben werden und die Formulierung von der »urinigen Verflüssigung des Himmels« hervorbringen. Es ist jedoch korrekter, die beiden metaphorischen Reihen als zwei Ketten von Bedeutungsträgern zu charakterisieren, »weil jeder dieser Begriffe offensichtlich nur der Bedeutungsträger seines Nachbarbegriffes ist«.[44] Wenn man diese *combinatoire* als eine Art Maschine zur Erzeugung von Metaphern auffaßt, da sich ein Teil der einen Kette mit dem einer anderen verbindet, muß man berücksichtigen, daß es wegen der logischen Zwänge, die die Ketten regeln, nichts Surrealistisches bei diesen »Begegnungen« gibt – sie kommen nicht zufällig zusammen.

☐ 745 *Alberto Giacometti, ›Kopf‹ (Tête), 1934, Gips. Verbleib unbekannt.*

☐ 744 *›Karnevalsmaske‹, Photographie von Jacques-André Boiffard. Veröffentlicht in Georges Limbours Aufsatz ›Eschyle, le carnaval et les civilisés‹, „Documents", Nr. 2 (1930).*

☐ 746 *›Menschenschutz‹, Photographie. Veröffentlicht in ›Aboutissements de la mécanique‹, „Variétés", Januar 1930.*

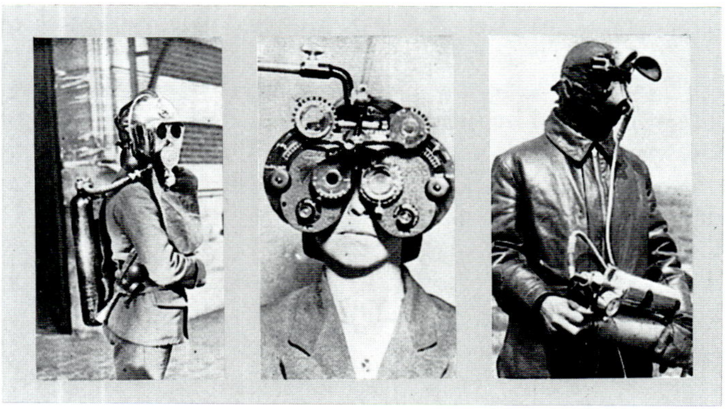

Die Struktur dieser metaphorischen Ergänzungen bestimmt mithin nicht nur den Verlauf der erotischen Handlung der Erzählung, sondern ebenso das Wortgewebe, aus dem der *récit* besteht. Es ist wichtig, diesen Aspekt der *L'Histoire de l'œil* mit der Aktion von der *Schwebenden Kugel* zu vergleichen. Als Handlung auf metaphorischer Ebene ist die Geschichte des Auges nämlich nicht die eines wirklichen Auges. Ohne Bezug zur realen Welt, zu einem Moment, der den metaphorischen Verwandlungen vorausginge, ihren Ausgangspunkt bilden und ihnen Sinn verleihen würde, besäße die Geschichte keinen hervorgehobenen Begriff. Zur Struktur des Werkes sagt Barthes: »Das Paradigma hat nirgendwo einen Anfang.« Da die sexuelle Zuordnung des Auges völlig zweideutig bleibt (ein runder Phallizismus), gibt es auch in den tieferen Schichten der Erzählung keinerlei Hinweis auf eine bestimmte sexuelle Vorstellung, deren endgültige Bedeutung sich fassen ließe. »Wir haben keine andere Möglichkeit, als über die Existenz einer völlig sphärischen Metapher innerhalb von ›L'Histoire de l'Œil‹ zu reflektieren: Jeder der dortigen Begriffe ist auch immer Träger eines anderen Begriffes (und kein Begriff ist nur einfach in seiner Bedeutung), ohne daß dieser Rundlauf angehalten werden könnte.«[45]

Dieser runde Phallizismus, dieser Zusammenbruch der Unterscheidung zwischen dem korrekt Männlichen und dem korrekt Weiblichen, das Auslöschen der Unterschiede verhält sich zur Logik wie die Perversion zur Erotik, nämlich grenzüberschreitend. Wie Bataille in seinem »lexikalischen Eintrag« in den *Documents* zum Wort *informe* erklärt, ist es die Aufgabe der Philosophie sicherzustellen, daß alles seine richtige Form, seine eindeutigen Umrisse und Begrenzungen hat. Aber manche Wörter – eines davon ist *informe* – haben ein gegenteiliges Ziel. Ihre Aufgabe besteht darin zu deklassifizieren, die »mathematischen Gehröcke«, die die Philosophie über alles stülpt, wegzureißen. Indem sich *informe* der Formlosigkeit, dem Zusammenbruch der Differenz öffnet, »suggeriert es eine Welt, die in gewissem Sinne einer Spinne oder Spucke – ›crachat‹ – ähnelt«.[46] *Informe* bezeichnet das, was Alteration hervorbringt, nämlich eine Bedeutungs- oder Wertreduktion, die nicht durch Widerspruch – was dialektisch wäre –, sondern durch die Zersetzung der Grenzen des Begriffs vonstatten geht. Es ist die Reduktion auf eine Identität des Kadavers, die grenzüberschreitend wirkt. Der runde Phallizismus ist eine Zerstörung von Bedeutung/Sein. Das heißt aber nicht, daß den Objekten und Bildern in *L'Histoire de l'œil* und *Schwebende Kugel* die Form durch ihre Ähnlichkeit mit Spucke fehlen würde, sondern sie führen wie eigens dafür eingesetzte Maschinen zur Zerstörung der Differenz.

Batailles »Lexikon« verfolgte das Ziel, die Aufgaben der Wörter aufzudecken.[47] Seine Zeitschrift *Documents,* in der das »Lexikon« enthalten war, hatte ebenfalls eine Aufgabe zu erfüllen. Zu ihr gehörte es, völkerkundliche Daten zu nutzen, um die sauberen Begrenzungen der Kunstwelt und ihre auf *Form* basierenden Kategorien zu überschreiten. Dies ist die »harte« Verwendungsweise des Primitivismus – im Gegensatz zu der zuvor genannten »weichen« oder »ästhetisierenden« Richtung. Sie kann sich keinesfalls darauf beschränken, dieses oder jenes Formelement aus dem Repertoire »primitiver« Objekte zu entlehnen, so wie es selbst von Kunststudenten (vor allem in der angewandten Kunst) in den 20er Jahren erwartet wurde.[48] Statt dessen wird das Primitive in einem erweiterten Sinne verwendet (jedoch unter strikter Beachtung des ethnographischen Details), um Kunst in ein Netzwerk einzuflechten, das in seiner philosophischen Dimension radikal antiidealistisch und antihumanistisch ist. Bataille schließt seinen Artikel »Primitive Kunst« mit dem Hinweis auf die von ihm verehrte moderne Kunst, eine Kunst, die »ziemlich rasch einen Prozeß der Auflösung und Zerstörung eingeleitet hat, der für die meisten Menschen nicht weniger schmerzhaft war, als es der Anblick der Zersetzung und der Zerstörung eines Kadavers gewesen wäre«.[49] Der »geistige Realismus« – die ästhetisierende und dem konstruktiven Denken verpflichtete Kategorie Luquets, die der frühen Verteidigung kubistischer Malerei viel verdankt[50] – geht nicht mehr auf die Bedingungen dieser »niedergehenden Malerei« ein, genausowenig wie auf die Bildhauerei insgesamt, betont Bataille. Wenn Bataille in den *Documents* PICASSOS Werke erörtert, geschieht dies bezeichnenderweise unter der Rubrik »Soleil pourri«.[51]

Nur aufgrund eines besseren Verständnisses der Rolle, die der Primitivismus für die abtrünnigen Surrealisten spielte, können wir das Brillante einer Skulptur wie *Schwebende Kugel* und die Thesen zu den Vorbildern von *Der unsichtbare Gegenstand* richtig beurteilen. Denn das reichverzweigte Netzwerk des Primitiven, das sich zu Beginn der 30er Jahre entwickelt hatte, stellt eine Plastik wie *Der unsichtbare Gegenstand* in viele miteinander verzahnte Bezüge, unterstützt damit nicht nur die Thesen Hohls zu dem Werk, sondern auch die Bretons und Leiris' und läßt noch weitere für die Entstehung des Werks wichtige Bedingungen erahnen.

Der Bericht von Leiris über das kleine Schweizer Mädchen ist im Kontext von GIACOMETTIS damaliger Kunst sicherlich der fragwürdigste Hinweis, zeigt aber dennoch, daß er in die Umstände bei der Entwicklung des Werks hineinpaßt. Breton zufolge war die erste Fassung des Kopfes, der schließlich durch die Maske vom Flohmarkt ersetzt wurde, flach und ungegliedert, obwohl die Gestaltung der Augen als große Räder – das rechte unversehrt, das linke gebrochen – auch in der zweiten und dritten Fassung zu finden war.[52] Eine Gipsplastik von 1934, kurz vor dem *Unsichtbaren Gegenstand* entstanden, bestätigt Bretons Beschreibung □ 745. Sie war zweifellos der Entwurf für eine erste Fassung des Kopfes. Während die endgültige Version durchgegliedert ist, ist der Gipsentwurf weich und nahezu formlos. Beiden Konzeptionen ist (über die räderartigen Augen hinaus) das Maskenhafte gemeinsam.[53] Der Gipskopf ist eindeutig von einer der Karnevalsmasken nach Photographien von JACQUES-ANDRÉ BOIFFARD kopiert worden, die in den *Documents* Limbours Text »Eschyle, le carnaval et les civilisés« abbildete □ 744.[54]

□ 747 *Alberto Giacometti, ›Kopf‹ (Tête), um 1925, Gips. Musée National d'Art Moderne, Centre National d'Art et de Culture Georges Pompidou, Paris.*

□ 748 *Alberto Giacometti, ›Stunde der Spuren‹ (L'Heure des traces), 1930, Holz, Gips und Metall. Verbleib unbekannt.*

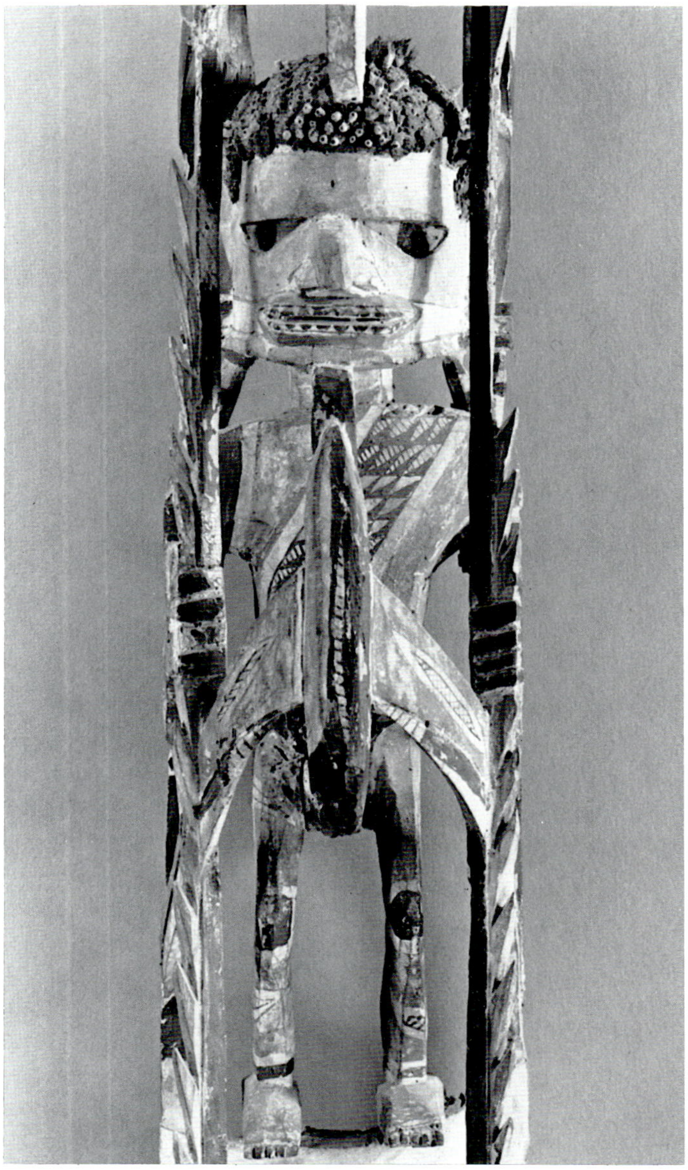

□ 749 *›Malanggan‹ (Detail), Neuirland, bemaltes Holz, Höhe 176 cm. Privatsammlung, New York. Ehemals Sammlung Max Ernst.*

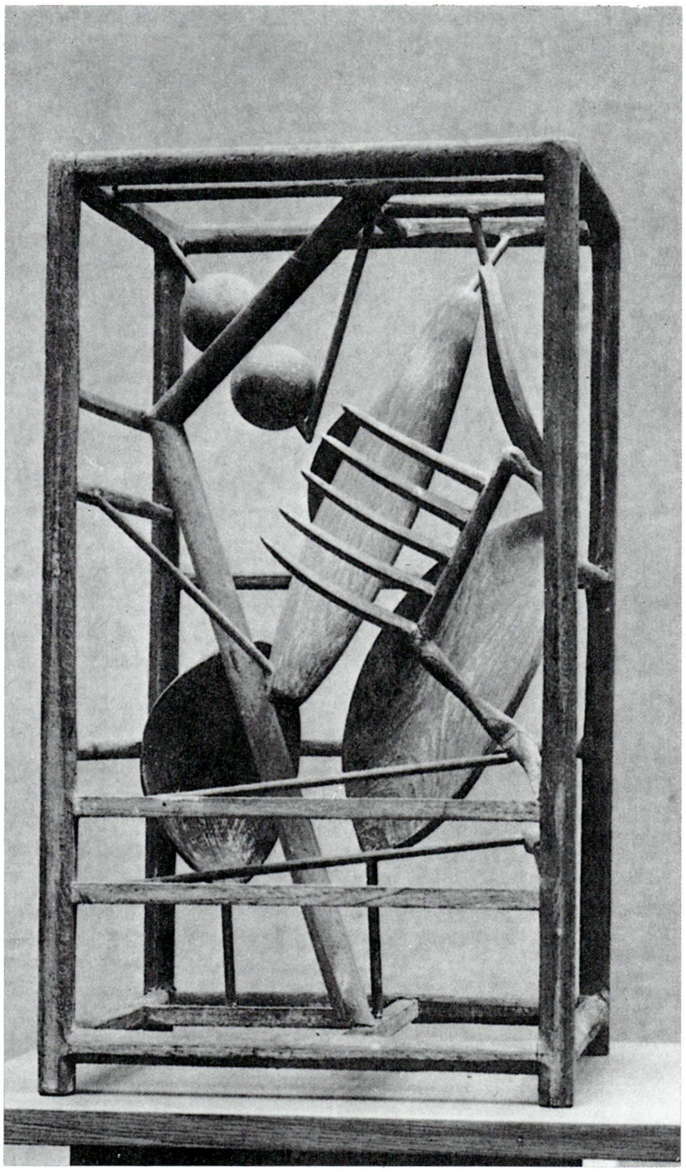

□ 750 *Alberto Giacometti, ›Käfig‹ (Cage), 1931, Holz, Höhe 49 cm. Moderna Museet, Stockholm.*

Der Schauplatz von Limbours Betrachtung zu diesem Thema ist eine chaotische Gemischtwarenhandlung, wo der Autor beobachtet, wie ein kleines Mädchen eine Karnevalsmaske mit Bart schüchtern in die Hand nimmt und sich beim Anprobieren in eine Art Lolita verwandelt, die ihre Zunge lasziv über die Lippen des Papiermaché-Gesichts gleiten läßt. Die lebendige Beschreibung dieser »Salome der Straßen« könnte zu einer Assoziation mit dem kleinen Schweizer Mädchen geführt haben.

Auch das übrige in Limbours Artikel verdient Beachtung. Nachdem er zuerst die Todesvorstellung beschreibt, die in den grimassierenden Masken der griechischen Tragödie die Lebendigkeit des menschlichen Gesichts erstarren läßt, wendet sich der Autor primitiven Masken zu. Das bevorzugte Gebiet primitiver Kunst war für die *Documents*-Gruppe wie auch für die orthodoxen Surrealisten nicht mehr Afrika, das sie als zu rational, zu formalistisch empfanden, sondern Ozeanien, und darauf geht auch Limbour ein.[55] In einer für die streng antikolonialistische Haltung beider Gruppen typischen Textstelle prangert Limbour die Vergewaltigung dieser Gebiete durch den weißen Mann an, der seine »Fastenmissionare, seine Papiermaché-Jesuiten« an die Stelle der unglaublichen Kraft der melanesischen Maskenkultur setzt.[56] Mit einem direkt aus Batailles Idee der *soleil pourri* stammenden Bild spricht er von den Gesichtern, die in die großen, in der Erde steckenden Pfähle geschnitzt sind und »direkt in die Sonne blicken«.[57] Nachdem der Westen die Südsee überfallen hatte, um ihre Heiligtümer auf die Kunstmärkte und die Trocadéros der »Zivilisation« zu bringen, brachte er seine eigenen Masken hervor – Masken, so Limbour, die eines Aischylos würdig sind. Er meint die Gasmasken, sie allein entsprächen unserer Zeit. »Denn wenn Religion, Todeskult und dionysische Feste die Maske bei den verschiedenen Völkern des Altertums in einen geheiligten, rituellen Schmuck verwandelt haben, besitzen auch wir unsere eigene Religion, unsere Gesellschaftsspiele und mithin unsere eigenen Masken. Nur verlangt die allgemeine Standardisierung unseres Zeitalters, daß wir alle die gleiche tragen.«

Der Avantgarde der 20er Jahre war das Bild der Gasmaske, die die »Menschlichkeit« des Gesichts durch einen furchterregenden Ausdruck der Brutalität des industrialisierten Krieges

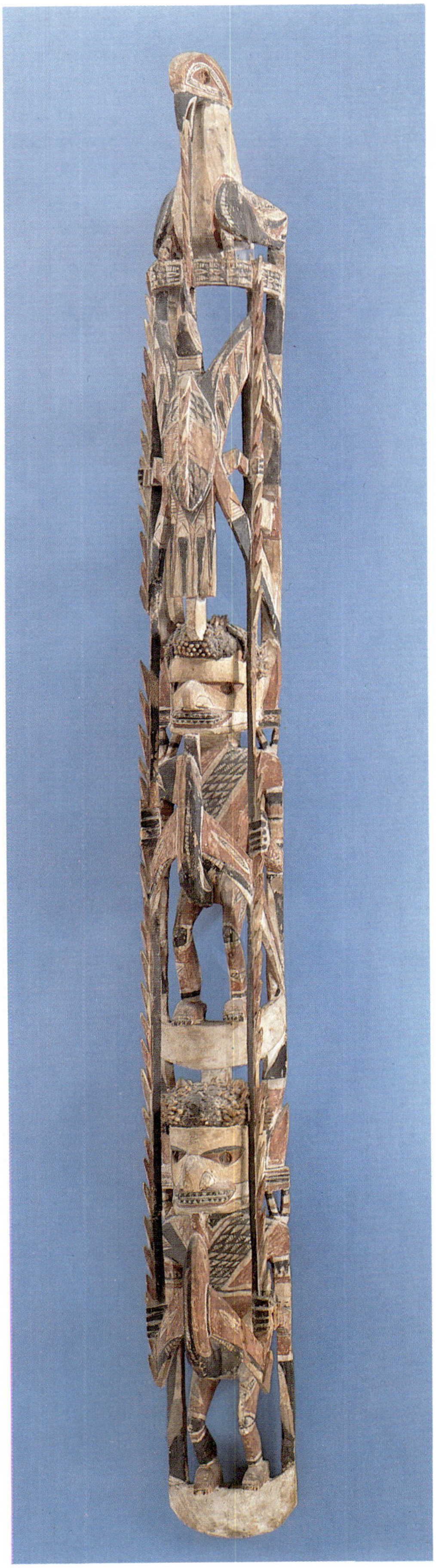

□ 751 ›*Malanggan*‹, *Neuirland, bemaltes Holz, Höhe 176 cm. Ehemals Sammlung Max Ernst.*

□ 752 ›*Malanggan*‹, *Neuirland, bemaltes Holz, Höhe 134 cm. Musée National des Arts Africains et Océaniens, Paris.*

□ 753 *Max Ernst, Collage aus ›Une Semaine de bonté‹, fünftes Buch, 1934. Element: Finsternis. Vorbild: Osterinsel.*

□ 754 *Alberto Giacometti, ›Drei Personen auf einer Wiese‹ (Trois Personnages dans unpré), 1930. Zerstört.*

ersetzte, weithin bekannt. Eine Photoserie in *Variétés,* die Träger von Gasmasken wie auch anderer mechanischer Gerätschaften zeigt, läßt eine Faszination erkennen für alles, was moderner Erfindungsgeist ersonnen hatte, um den menschlichen Kopf zu ersetzen □ 746.[58] Wie bei aller Mechanistik, hier nur viel eindringlicher, läßt dieser Ersatz keinesfalls höhere Stufen menschlicher Evolution erkennen, sondern sehr viel niedrigere, weil der Träger der Gasmaske im Aussehen einem Insekt so ähnlich wird.

Der Mensch mit dem Insektenkopf ist *informe,* ist verändert. Was das Zeichen seiner höchsten Fähigkeiten – seines Verstandes, seines Geistes – sein sollte, ist niedrig geworden, einer zertretenen Spinne oder einem Wurm ähnlich. Wie die deformierten Anthropoiden in der Höhlenmalerei ist der Mensch mit dem Insektenkopf *acéphale,* eine das Menschliche überschreitende Vorstellung.[59] Der Begriff stammt natürlich von Bataille und wird in seinem Werk als eine Art Schlüssel zum Eintritt in das fiktive Theater verwendet, in dem die Menschheit die Fülle ihrer Widersprüche zur Schau stellt. *Acéphale* weist nämlich auf die Erfahrung der menschlichen Vertikalität hin, auf seine Erhebung im biologischen und moralischen Sinne, in der Negation aber auf eine Entwicklung hin zum Primitiven, dem Aufstieg nach unten. Wie noch gezeigt wird, hat diese konzeptuelle Umkehrung auch bei der Neudefinition von Skulptur eine Rolle gespielt, die GIACOMETTI in jener Zeit versuchte. Aber ihre nachhaltigste Wirkung auf ihn und andere zeitgenössische Künstler lag im Thematischen.

Innerhalb der schöpferischen Logik dieser Jahre ist der Mensch mit dem Insektenkopf auch die *Frau* mit dem Insektenkopf: die Gottesanbeterin. Als Symbol der Aufhebung des Unterschieds zwischen Leben – oder Zeugung – und Tod faszinierte die Gottesanbeterin die um *Variétés, Documents* und *Minotaure* gruppierte Avantgarde wegen einer Besonderheit: Vom Weibchen dieser Spezies wußte man, daß es den Partner nach oder sogar noch während der Kopulation verschlang. Wegen der Ähnlichkeiten dieses Insekts mit dem menschlichen Körperbau empfanden die Surrealisten sein Paarungsverhalten als besonders unheimlich. Roger Caillois berichtet in seinem 1934 im *Minotaure* veröffentlichten Essay über die Gottesanbeterin, der zur Grundlage für seine späteren Studien über Funktion des Mythos und Ambivalenz des Sakralen wurde, daß Breton, Eluard und DALI große Sammlungen dieser Tiere in Käfigen hielten.[60]

Caillois' Essay ließ einen Schwarm von Gottesanbeterinnen über die Leinwände surrealistischer Malerei ziehen.[61] Aber schon vor 1934 hatte das Insekt im Werk von GIACOMETTI und MAX ERNST eine Rolle gespielt. GIACOMETTIS *Frau, Kopf, Baum* von 1930 stellt die Frau als eine Gottesanbeterin dar und scheint die zwei *Käfige* □ 750 des folgenden Jahres angeregt zu haben. Beide zeigen eine abstrahiert dargestellte Gottesanbeterin innerhalb der alptraumartigen Grenzen der Plastik beim Angriff auf ihren männlichen Partner – letzterer durch eine simple Kugel oder einen Schädel dargestellt.[62] Diese Gottesanbeterinnen scheinen außerdem von den extremen Formentrennungen beeinflußt zu sein, die man als Hauptmerkmal ozeanischer Kunst, damit als deren Quelle für Kraft und wilde Poesie betrachtete. Einige der Mallanggan aus Neuirland, die GIACOMETTI damals möglicherweise kannte, regten ihn mit großer Wahrscheinlichkeit zur Idee einer in ihren Gliedmaßen unverbundenen, eingesperrten Figur an □ 749, 751, 752.[63] Carl Einstein veröffentlichte in den 20er Jahren eine Analyse melanesischer Bildmotive. Besonders aufschlußreich für die Deu-

□ 755 *Alberto Giacometti, ›Kopf/Landschaft‹ (Tête/Paysage), 1930–31, Gips, 24 x 68 cm. Verbleib unbekannt.*

□ 756 *›Kindersarg‹, Nouméa (Neukaledonien), Holz, Pflanzenfasern, Höhe 40 cm. Musée de l'Homme, Paris.*

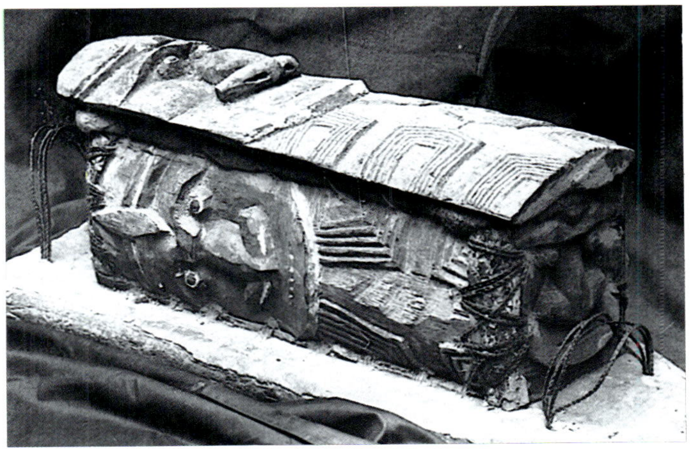

□ 757 *Das Dorf Goulfé (Kamerun). Veröffentlicht in André Gides Aufsatz ›Architectures nègres‹, „Cahiers d'art", Nr. 7–8, 1927.*

□ 758 *Alberto Giacometti, ›Projekt für einen Durchgang‹ (Projet pour un passage), 1930–31, Gips, 15 x 127 x 43 cm. Alberto Giacometti-Stiftung, Kunsthaus Zürich.*

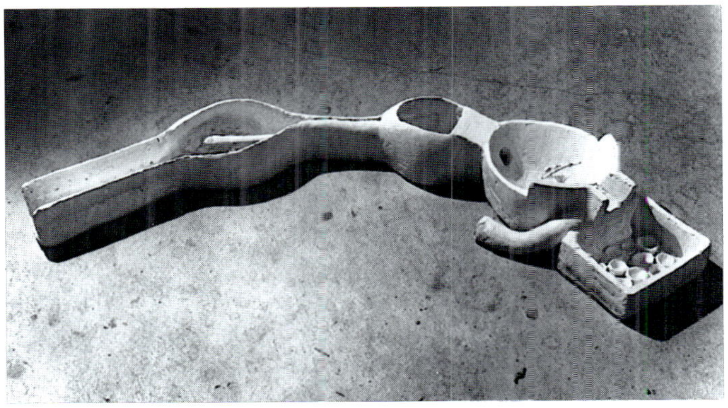

tung der *Käfige* ist der darin beschriebene Aufbau des Malanggans als eines in einem Knochengerüst befindlichen Schädels, entsprechend der primitiven Vorstellung von einem Skelett.[64]

Später griff Max Ernst das Thema der Gottesanbeterin auf. In *Une Semaine de bonté* von 1933 ist sie Bestandteil einer ganzen Bildserie, die den Bedingungen des *acéphale* gewidmet ist.[65] Dieser Roman aus Collagen, in denen der menschliche (männliche) Kopf durch alles mögliche – vom Wurm über Vögel bis zum Löwen – ersetzt ist, zeigt in einem Kapitel die Hauptfiguren mit Köpfen der großen Statuen von der Osterinsel. Neben einer solchen Figur, die sich im Spiegel betrachtet, sitzt eine Gottesanbeterin, die gerade ihren Partner verschlingt □ 753.[66]

Die in den frühen 30er Jahren entstandene Freundschaft zwischen Giacometti und Max Ernst veranlaßte letzteren im

□ 759 *›Figur aus Holz‹, Nukuoro (Karolineninseln), Höhe 50 cm. Rautenstrauch-Joest-Museum für Völkerkunde, Köln.*

□ 760 *›Figur aus Holz‹, Marquesasinseln, Höhe 35 cm. Museum für Völkerkunde, Berlin.*

□ 761 *›Figur aus Holz‹, Marquesasinseln, Höhe 33,5 cm. Etnografiska Museet, Stockholm.*

Jahr 1934, das Sommerhaus von GIACOMETTIS Familie in Maloja zu besuchen. Hier schuf er mit GIACOMETTIS Hilfe eine Skulpturenfolge aus großen Steinen, die von den beiden aus einer Moräne herbeigeschleppt und dann von MAX ERNST leicht überarbeitet wurden □ 40. Als figürliche Motive auf diesen Skulpturen wählte er Vögel aus Kulten der Osterinsel und den Papua-Vogel aus Neuguinea, mit dem sich MAX ERNST identifizierte und den er als sein Alter ego Loplop verwendete.[67] Viele seiner Skulpturen aus den folgenden Jahren zeigen die Auswirkungen dieses Besuchs. So ist sein *Mondspargel,* 1935 □ 837, deutlich von *Drei Personen auf einer Wiese* beeinflußt □ 754, ein assoziationsreich mit dem Primitiven verbundenes Werk, das GIACOMETTI 1930 in die Schweizer Landschaft stellte.[68] Aber die Einflußnahme war wohl wechselseitig, wie GIACOMETTIS *Projekt für einen Durchgang* (1930–31) beweist □ 758, das Bildern von MAX ERNST wie *Anatomie einer Braut* oder *Die schöne Gärtnerin* nahesteht.

Daß MAX ERNST die Gottesanbeterin in *Une Semaine de bonté* mit Ozeanien und der Herkunft des Papua-Geistervogels in Zusammenhang bringt, wirkte neben anderen Faktoren auf die Entstehung des *Unsichtbaren Gegenstands* ein, dessen Vogelkopf an Loplop erinnert. Vor diesem Hintergrund wird verständlich, wie in der Logik des *Unsichtbaren Gegenstandes* die Todesauffassung der Salomoninseln mit dem mythisch/biologischen Todesboten in Gestalt der Gottesanbeterin verknüpft wird. In Bretons Bericht über den Austausch einer Version des Kopfes gegen eine andere bleibt, wie sich jetzt herausstellt, die Darstellung des Kopfes als Maske gleich, folglich der Figur als *acéphale.* Je grausamer die Maske anmutet, desto ähnlicher wird sie dem spitzen Gesicht der Gottesanbeterin mit ihren großen, starrenden Augen.[69] Daß GIACOMETTI von der Maske auf dem Flohmarkt angezogen wurde, war, um mit Freud zu sprechen, überdeterminiert.

Eine Richtung innerhalb der GIACOMETTI-Forschung konzentriert sich fast ausschließlich auf die psychobiographischen Hintergründe seiner Kunst.[70] Diesem Interpretationsansatz zufolge wäre den oben genannten Einflußfaktoren für den *Unsichtbaren Gegenstand* zweifellos die halluzinatorische Präsenz der Mutter hinzuzufügen, die sich hinter dem Todesgeist der Salomoninseln verbirgt. Die schwarzgekleidete Frau, die GIACOMETTI in seinen Jünglingsphantasien vergewaltigt und abschlachtet, ist dieselbe Frau, die den *Palais de quatre heures* betritt und dessen erotische Idylle zerstört. Die große Ächterin seiner Sexualität ist Annetta Stampa Giacometti.[71] Es läßt sich nachvollziehen, wie diese mütterliche Gewalt gleichzeitig mit den Todesgedanken, die GIACOMETTIS Arbeit durchziehen, und mit der ebenso starken Fixierung auf Schwangerschaft und Geburt in Zusammenhang stand. GIACOMETTI war von der Vorstellung besessen, der Fels würde Früchte tragen, oder in den Worten ARPS: »Die Steine sind voller Eingeweide. Bravo. Bravo.«[72] So interessant die Auswertung dieses Ansatzes auch sein mag, ist er für unser Thema doch nur von peripherem Interesse, obwohl ein weiteres Zeugnis dieser persönlichen, biographischen Motivation bei den folgenden Ausführungen zum Aspekt des Todes und des Monuments nicht ungelegen käme.

Jedes künstlerische Œuvre läßt sich von zwei möglicherweise gegensätzlichen Gesichtspunkten her beurteilen. Der eine

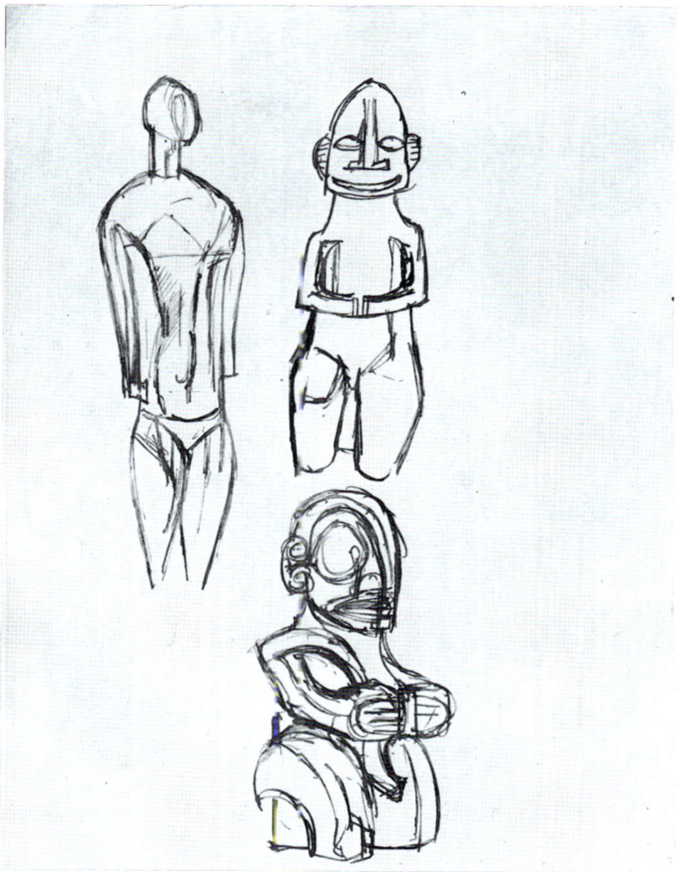

☐ 762 *Alberto Giacometti, ›Stammesskulpturen‹, Feder auf Papier, 27 x 21 cm. Privatsammlung.*

erfaßt das Werk aus der Totalität des Individuums heraus. Der andere, viel unpersönlichere historische Ansatz geht vergleichend vor, d. h. in Beziehung zu den Werken anderer und zur Gesamtentwicklung des jeweiligen Mediums. Oft überschneiden sich die beiden Blickwinkel. So stimmt etwa der Verlauf von MONDRIANS Entwicklung bei der Suche nach den neoplastischen Elementen in der Malerei überein mit seiner Stellung an der Spitze der allgemeinen Entwicklung der Abstraktion in der Kunst des 20. Jahrhunderts.

Bei GIACOMETTI ist das anders. Aus der Perspektive des individuellen Œuvres betrachtet, ist seine Skulptur fast ausschließlich die des Monuments: die einzelne, vertikale Figur, die wie ein Denkmal in den Raum ragt, hieratisch, unbeweglich, hoch. Von *Löffelfrau* über *Unsichtbarer Gegenstand* bis zu seinen stehenden Figuren aus den 50er Jahren läßt sich diese Thematik kontinuierlich verfolgen, so daß man dem Œuvre eine innere Geschlossenheit zusprechen kann. Von der Geschichte der Bildhauerei her gesehen – ein unpersönlicher und viel weniger wohlwollender Maßstab – ist GIACOMETTIS Schaffen vertikaler Monumente jedoch von geringerem Interesse, d. h. innovatorisch weniger reich als seine Arbeiten aus den Jahren 1930–33, denn zu jener Zeit war sein Werk horizontal ausgerichtet.

Das formal Neue an diesen Skulpturen, das in der historischen Entwicklung dieses Mediums durch nichts vorbereitet worden war, bestand in der Drehung der Achse des Monuments um neunzig Grad, um dessen Vertikalität in die Horizontalität der Erde zu überführen. Bei Objekten wie *Projekt für einen Platz, Kopf/Landschaft* ☐ 755 und den außergewöhnlichen Spielbrett-Skulpturen wie *Kreislauf* ☐ 788 oder *Das Spiel ist aus* ☐ 743 wird das Werk selbst ganz einfach und direkt als Sockel verstanden. Man könnte den innovatorischen Charakter dieser Erfindung in Frage stellen, wenn man daran erinnert, daß bereits DEGAS bei seiner *Badenden* (um 1886) auf den Sockel als Bindeglied verzichtete und die Skulptur direkt auf den Boden stellte oder daß BRANCUSI schon nach 1910 die Unterscheidung zwischen Figur und Sockel aufgab. Damit würden wir jedoch das Besondere an GIACOMETTIS höchst origineller Idee verkennen. Denn die *Badende* von DEGAS ist – wie auch GIACOMETTIS *Ermordete Frau* (1932) – als Skulptur ohne Sockel und daher als eine von oben gesehene Figur konzipiert. Das Werk selbst wird jedoch nicht als Sockel verstanden. Und obwohl BRANCUSI oft an eine solche absolute Verschmelzung dachte, bleiben seine Sockel/Skulpturen im Gegensatz zu GIACOMETTI vertikal. Sie bleiben dem grundlegenden Gegensatz zwischen dem Nichtkünstlerischen – dem Grund – und dem Künstlerischen – der Skulptur – verpflichtet. Die Vertikale trennt den Darstellungsbereich der Skulptur von der realen Welt, was traditionell der aufrechte Sockel signalisiert, der das Werk vom Boden erhebt und dem Realraum entrückt. Wie ein Bilderrahmen trennt der Sockel den Bereich künstlerischer Vorstellung vom Umfeld der Wirklichkeit ab.

Besteht das Bild aber »nur« aus seinem Rahmen, dann ist diese Unterscheidung nicht mehr so leicht zu treffen. Das Dargestellte beginnt dann mit der realen Umgebung zu verschmelzen. Diese Transformation des Skulpturalen vollzog GIACOMETTI zwischen 1930 und 1933. Die Drehung der Achse in die Horizontale war auch inhaltlich als »Erniedrigen« des Objekts gemeint, das hierdurch dem Grund und dem Realen zugleich verbunden wurde – dem wirklichen Raum und der

☐ 763 *Alberto Giacometti, ›Nimba-Maske und Frauen‹, Feder auf Papier, 30 x 21 cm. Privatsammlung.*

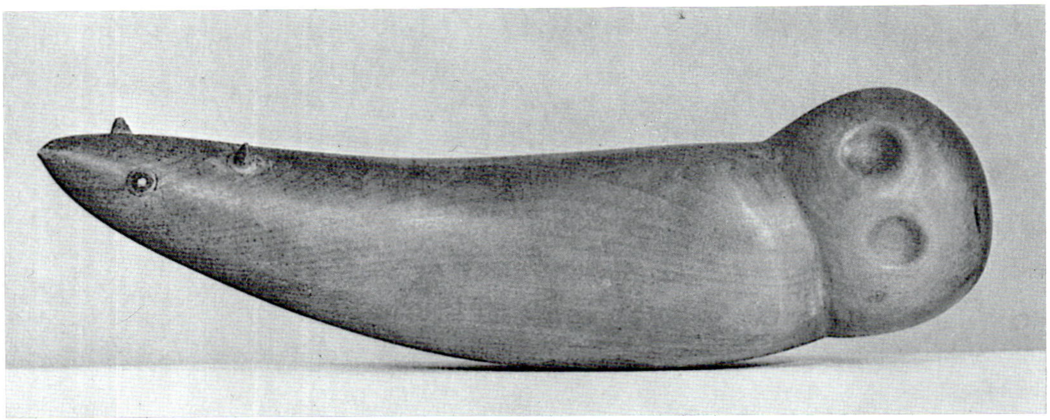

☐ 764 *Alberto Giacometti, ›Unangenehmer Gegenstand‹ (Objet desagréable), 1931, Holz, Länge 48 cm. Privatsammlung, New York.*

☐ 765 *›Fisch‹, Osterinsel, Holz, Länge 17 cm. Ehemals Museum für Völkerkunde, Berlin. Verbleib unbekannt.*

☐ 766 *Alberto Giacometti, ›Unangenehmer Gegenstand zum Wegwerfen‹ (Objet desagréable à jeter), 1931, Holz, Länge 22 cm. Privatsammlung, London.*

☐ 767 *›Ohrschmuck‹, Marquesasinseln, Elfenbein, Höhe 9 cm. Privatsammlung. Ehemals Sammlung Tristan Tzara.*

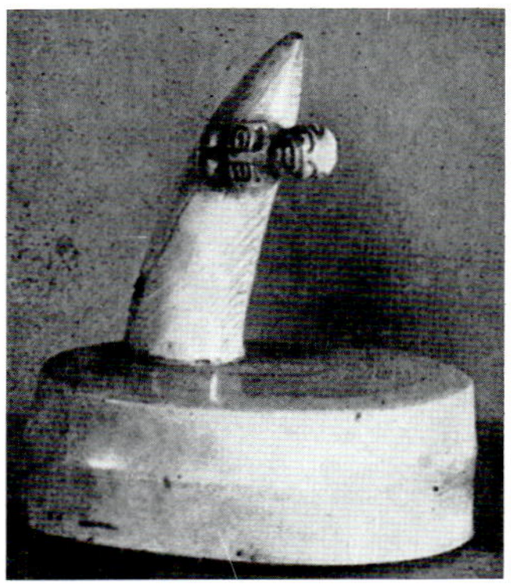

tatsächlichen Bewegung in realer Zeit. Aus der Perspektive der Geschichte moderner Skulptur betrachtet, stellt dieser Vorgang die Inauguraltat von Giacomettis Kunst dar. Sie hatte Auswirkungen auf vieles, was nach dem Zweiten Weltkrieg im Rahmen der neuen Überlegungen zur Skulptur geschehen sollte. Gerade in dieser bewegten Szene begegnet uns Giacomettis Verhältnis zur Stammeskunst und zum Primitiven aufs neue.

Die früheste dieser Skulpturen ist *Projekt für einen Durchgang* (1930–31), die den »Anatomien« von Max Ernst und der ethnographischen Metapher vom Körper als einer Ansammlung afrikanischer Lehmhütten gleichermaßen verpflichtet ist ☐ 757.[73] Giacomettis alternativer Titel für das Werk – *Das Labyrinth* – unterstreicht den Bezug zur Welt des Primitiven.[74] Denn für das von der Idee des Minotaurus besessene Denken der frühen 30er Jahre stellte sich das Labyrinth als diametraler Gegensatz zu den Maximen von Klarheit und Raumbeherrschung, wie sie die klassische Architektur kennt, dar. Der in einem Labyrinth gefangene Mensch wird beherrscht, ist hilflos und verloren.[75]

Mit der zweiten dieser Horizontalskulpturen wird der Aspekt einer ›Rotation‹ der Achse noch deutlicher. *Kopf/Landschaft* (1930–31) trug zuerst den Titel *Fall eines Körpers über ein Diagramm.* Diese Vorstellung von einem fallenden

Körper bestätigt verbal, was die Skulptur visuell zum Ausdruck bringt.[76] Das Strukturprinzip von *Kopf/Landschaft* beruht auf der metaphorischen Beziehung zwischen den zwei räumlich-anamorph verknüpften Elementen: In die Horizontale gedreht, ähnelt das Gesicht einer Landschaft. Genau diese Beziehung wurde von DALI bei einer Vorführung des »paranoid-kritischen« Denkens zum Ausdruck gebracht: Er »las« eine Photographie, die afrikanische Eingeborene vor ihren Hütten sitzend zeigte, als PICASSO-Kopf. Wie er erklärte, resultierte diese (falsche) Lesart aus einer Orientierungslosigkeit gegenüber der Photographie. Während DALIS Demonstration war das Bild wie *Kopf/Landschaft* um neunzig Grad gedreht.[77] Aber GIACOMETTIS Skulptur ähnelt eher einer Maske oder irgendeiner flachen Bedeckung als einem gedrehten Gesicht. Auch die Landschaft als alternative Lesart ähnelt mit ihren rechtwinkligen, wie Gräber aussehenden Öffnungen eher einer Totenstadt als dem neutralen Gelände in DALIS Beispiel.[78] (Im folgenden Jahr sollte die Verbindung von Grab und Totenstadt durch die in den Boden von *Das Spiel ist aus* versenkten Särge noch präzisiert werden.)

Eine Reihe liegend photographierter und so publizierter afrikanischer Masken mag als Anregung für die Gestaltung von *Kopf/Landschaft* eine Rolle gespielt haben.[79] Der Gegenstand, auf den die meisten Assoziationen hinweisen, die das metaphorische Spiel des Werkes erweckt, ist jedoch der im Musée de l'Homme befindliche Deckel eines Kindersarges aus Neukaledonien □ 756. Er kommt als Bildquelle stärker in Betracht. Der Kindersarg gehörte zu den vielen Abbildungen in der Sonderausgabe der *Cahiers d'art* von 1929 über Ozeanien. GIACOMETTI besaß dieses Sonderheft, aus dem er vieles abzeichnete. Er wies immer wieder darauf hin, daß sein häufiges Abzeichnen anderer Kunstwerke meist nach Illustrationen, weniger nach den Objekten selber geschah.[80] Dies beweisen seine Zeichnungen ozeanischer Objekte vor 1945, denn sie stammen fast alle aus der gleichen Veröffentlichung □ 759–762.[81] Diese Hilfsquelle, die zur damaligen Zeit die größte und zugänglichste Fundgrube für ozeanische Bildwerke darstellte (sie enthielt zudem viele Stücke aus den surrealistischen Sammlungen von Breton, Aragon, Tzara), könnte GIACOMETTI noch andere Anregungen geliefert haben außer der durch den Sargdeckel erfolgten für *Kopf/Landschaft* von Abbildung 122. Der Fisch von der Osterinsel in Abbildung 180 □ 765 könnte die Entwicklung der phallischen *Unangenehmen Gegenstände* von 1931 □ 764 beeinflußt haben, und der stoßzahnähnliche Ohrring von Abbildung 169 aus dem Besitz Tzaras □ 767 zeigt starke Bezüge zu *Unangenehmer Gegenstand zum Wegwerfen* □ 766 derselben Werkserie.[82] Ferner erinnert die Vogel/Frau-Statue von Abbildung 46 an eine der beiden Figuren, die die Totenstadt von *Das Spiel ist aus* bewohnen. Wie schon weiter oben im Zusammenhang mit dem Objekt von MAX ERNST besprochen, enthalten die verschiedenen Malanggane, vor allem jene aus dem Besitz Louis Aragons (Abbildung 65), die Vorstellung des skulpturalen Gerüsts, das sich bei GIACOMETTI in der Ausprägung als Käfig wiederholt nachweisen läßt.

Angesichts der fast ausschließlichen Identifikation der Surrealisten mit Ozeanien könnte das Überwiegen dieser Quellen gegenüber allen anderen primitiven Bildern in GIACOMETTIS damaliger Vorstellungswelt die allgemeine Einstufung seines damaligen Schaffens (1930–32) als »surrealistische Periode« untermauern.[83] Jedoch begann GIACOMETTIS Beziehung zu den orthodoxen Surrealisten eigentlich nicht 1930. *Die Schwebende*

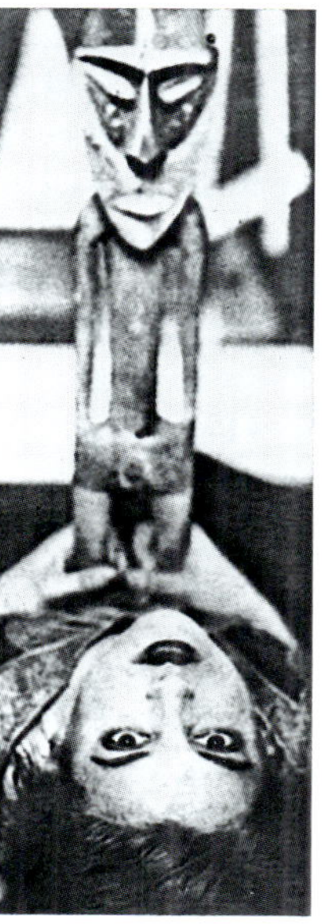

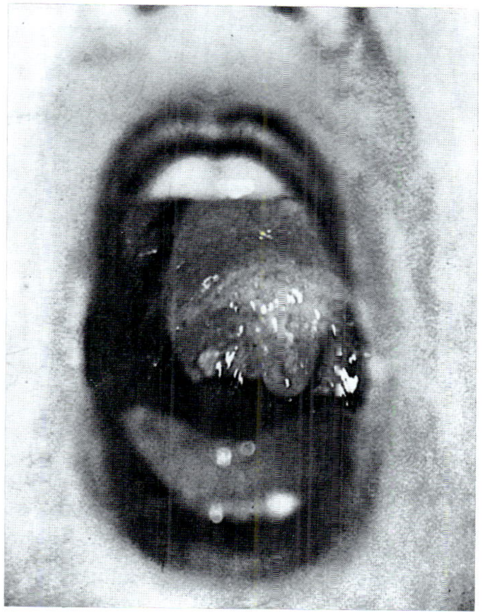

□ 768 *Jacques-André Boiffard, Photographie ohne Titel, um 1930. 8 x 28 cm. Privatsammlung*

□ 769 *Jacques-André Boiffard, Photographie. Veröffentlicht in Georges Batailles Aufsatz ›Bouche‹, „Documents“, Nr. 5, 1930.*

□ 770 *Man Ray, Photographie. Veröffentlicht in „Minotaure“, Nr. 7, 1935.*

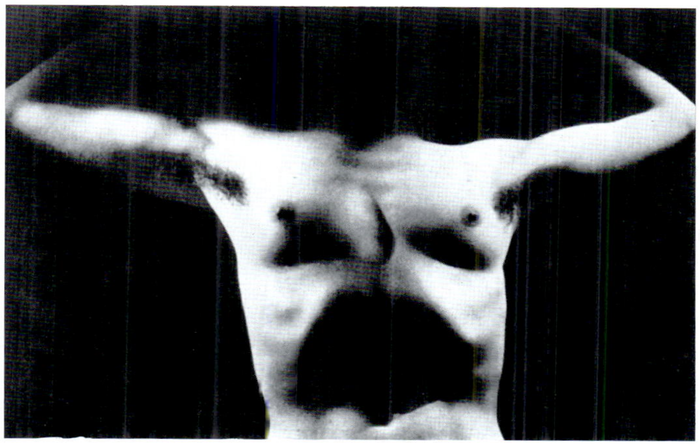

Kugel, das Werk, das ihre Aufmerksamkeit erregte, wurde erst am Ende jenes Jahres ausgestellt. Es sind nicht die Ideen der Surrealisten, ihre Begeisterung für die Aleatorik, für Zufallsspiele und das ›objet trouvé‹, unter denen der Ursprung der Gedanken GIACOMETTIS zu suchen wäre, oder das Muster für die Achsendrehung in der Skulptur, das horizontale Spielbrett, die Bewegung in realer Zeit, die Skulptur als Sockel und den Sockel als Totenstadt. Diese Entwicklungen nahmen erst 1930 ihren Anfang, als sich GIACOMETTI noch mit den *Documents* verbunden fühlte. Die Beschäftigung mit realer Zeit, die mit *Schwebender Kugel* und *Stunde der Spuren* beginnt, zieht die Berücksichtigung des Realraumes nach sich, und dieser wird durch eine Skulptur, die nichts anderes ist als ihr Sockel, als eine Vertikale definiert, die in die »gemeine« Niedrigkeit gedreht ist. Genauso ging Bataille vor, als er in den *Documents* das Konzept der »bassesse« – eines niedrigen, gemeinen Materialismus – entwickelte.[84]

In der anatomischen Geographie des Batailleschen Denkens symbolisiert die vertikale Achse den Anspruch des Menschen auf das Höhere, das Geistige, das Ideale wie auch seine

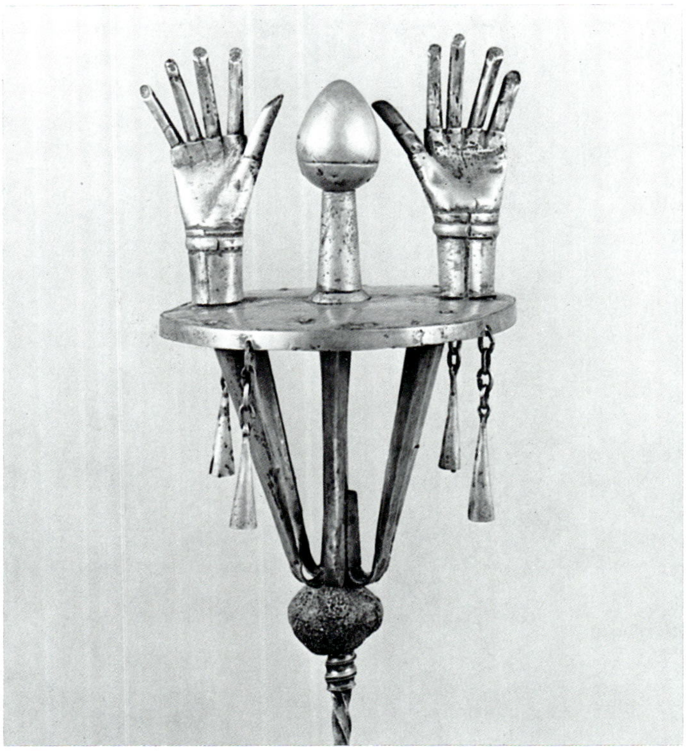

☐ 771 ›*Stab mit plastischer Verzierung*‹, *Detail*, Fon *(Volksrepublik Benin), Silber, Gesamthöhe 117 cm. Höhe des Ausschnitts 30 cm. Sammlung Charles Ratton, Paris.*

Forderung, daß ihn das Aufrechte nicht nur biologisch, sondern auch ethisch über das Tier erhebe. Natürlich glaubt Bataille nicht an diese Unterscheidung und betont die Präsenz des Niedrigen als wahre Quelle der Libido – hinter der repressiven Aneignung der Vertikalität. Hier ist Niedrigkeit Achse und Richtung in einem, die Horizontalität des Schlamms in der Realität. In »Le Gros Orteil« betont der Autor, daß die große symbolische Betrachtung der Füße als Brennpunkte von Ekel und Eros daraus resultiere, daß sie der Körperteil seien, der im schmutzigen Boden stecke. »Eine Rückkehr zur Wirklichkeit bedeutet kein neues Akzeptieren, sondern daß wir auf gemeine Weise Verführte sind, so daß wir ohne symbolische Surrogate mit weit geöffneten Augen ins Weinen geraten: angesichts eines großen Zehs.«[85]

In dem »lexikalischen« Eintrag *Bouche* wird dieses Gegenüber von vertikaler und horizontaler Achse speziell mit dem Rotationsvorgang herausgearbeitet. Die geistige Achse ist diejenige, die Augen und Mund verbindet und sich durch Sprache ausdrückt, jenem Vermögen, das den Menschen auszeichnet. Dagegen verbindet die biologische Achse den Mund mit dem After – sie betrifft die Stoffwechselfunktionen der Nahrungsaufnahme und des Ausscheidens. Die Senkung der geistigen oder spirituellen Achse auf die biologische läßt an die tatsächliche Verschiebung menschlicher Laute von klarer Artikulation zu tierischem Schreien denken, die in Augenblicken größter Qual oder Lust auftritt. Diese Äußerungen sind ihrer wahren Natur nach Ausscheidungen. Somit hat der Leib an seiner Spitze eine Öffnung, die nichts mit dem Ideellen zu tun hat, sondern eher ein Loch ist, das dem After ähnelt. *Documents* illustrierte diesen Text mit einem ganzseitigen Photo von Boiffard, das einen weit geöffneten, speicheltriefenden Mund zeigt ☐ 769.[86]

Die Vorstellung eines Loches am Ende des menschlichen Kopfes, die entidealisierend, entrationalisierend und verunsichernd ist, führte Bataille zu dem Versuch eines legendenhaften anatomischen Mythos vom Zirbeldrüsenauge. Er sieht diese Drüse im Hirn des Menschen als einen blinden Fleck an. In diametralem Gegensatz zu Descartes' Vorstellung, daß das Zirbeldrüsenauge jenes Organ sei, das die Seele mit dem Körper verbinde, sieht Bataille die Funktion der Drüse darin, den Menschen nach oben zu treiben, ihn zum Lichthimmel – dem Sinnbild alles Erhabenen – streben zu lassen, ihn aber auch zu verleiten, direkt in die Sonne zu starren und daher irr und blind zu werden.[87] Die durch das (blinde) Zirbeldrüsenauge hervorgerufene Besessenheit von der Sonne stellt also ein weiteres Beispiel für den Fall des Vertikalen in die Horizontale dar – so wie der verwirrte Mensch seinen Kopf symbolisch und tatsächlich verliert.[88] Das Menschenbild mit dem Loch auf dem Schädel – eine andere Form des *acéphale* – verbindet sich so mit der Erfahrung des Labyrinths, dem Raum der Implosion. Die Unterscheidung innen/außen, Anfang/Ende verschwimmt.

Die blendende, in den Wahnsinn treibende Sonne ist die *soleil pourri,* in die die Götzen der Osterinsel starren und der Bataille einen Essay über Picassos »verderbende Kunst« widmete. Bataille zufolge entspricht die ganze Problematik der modernen Malerei seiner Vorstellung von den Anfängen der Kunst als einer Darstellung des Opferaktes, als symbolische Ergänzung zur Verstümmelung des menschlichen Körpers. Ursprünglich ist der Ort dieser Verstümmelung die Höhle oder Grotte der prähistorischen Maler, der ersten Bewohner des Labyrinths gewesen. Dort nahm die Kunst ihren Anfang, aber nicht als Akt der Selbstverdoppelung, wie es der Narziß-Mythos nahelegt. Die Malerei sei vielmehr aus der Ablehnung des Menschen, sich zu reproduzieren, und aus einem Akt der Selbstverstümmelung heraus geboren.[89]

☐ 772 *Alberto Giacometti, ›Tisch‹ (Table), 1933, Bronze, Höhe 143 cm. Musée National d'Art Moderne, Centre National d'Art et de Culture Georges Pompidou, Paris.*

Bataille beschreibt dieses Verbindungsnetz zwischen Malerei, Sonnenkult und Körperverstümmelung in einem Akt von Opferwahn in seinem Essay »La Mutilation sacrificielle et l'oreille coupée de Vincent van Gogh«. Es versteht sich, daß Van Goghs Tat für Bataille nicht abartig war, sondern die wesentliche, archaische Funktion der Kunst verkörpert. Ein Kenner Batailles erklärt hierzu: »Selbstverstümmelung muß man sich als einen Akt, den bildnerischen Akt par excellence vorstellen. Denn Malerei ist nichts, wenn sie nicht auf die Architektur des menschlichen Körpers trifft, und diese Architektur ist nicht einfach, weil Selbstverstümmelung zu ihr gehört.«[90] Der Minotaurus, nicht Narziß, bestimmt die Geburt einer Kunst, in der die Darstellung Alteration verkörpert.

Giacomettis horizontale Spielbrett-Skulpturen verkörpern eine nach der anderen die Verschmelzung der Darstellungsebene mit den Bedingungen des Sockels, des Bodens, der Erde. Diese Drehung der Achse in die physische Dimension ist der Richtungswechsel des *acéphale*. Aber diese gedrehten Werke haben mit dem Thema des Kopflosen und des Labyrinths noch eine weitere Gemeinsamkeit, denn mit einer Ausnahme tragen sie alle Todesbedeutung in sich. In *Das Spiel ist aus* wird die »Skulptur« als ein Spiel aufgefaßt, dessen Brett halbkreisförmige Mulden im Stil des afrikanischen Kieselsteinspiels ›i‹ aufweist □ 790.[91] In seiner Mitte sind allerdings zwei winzige Särge mit schräg aufliegenden Deckeln eingelassen. Der konkrete Raum des Bretts, auf dem man die Steine in realer Zeit bewegen kann, verschmilzt auf diese Weise mit der Vorstellung einer Nekropole.

Als eine der Bedeutungen von *représentation* führt das Lexikon Littré das mit einem Totentuch bedeckte, sargartige Gerüst in Gedenkgottesdiensten auf. Repräsentation als Zeichen des Todes ist somit von der Idee her zwischen den symbolischen und den tatsächlichen Verfall gespannt – die

□ 774 *Alberto Giacometti, ›Drei Augen – zwei Arme‹, 1931–32, Marmor, Höhe 37 cm. Privatsammlung, Paris.*

□ 773 *›Puppe aus Holz‹, Mossi (Obervolta), Höhe 40 cm Privatsammlung.*

richtige Bedingung für Alteration. Batailles Konzept eines »niederen Materialismus« bewegt sich genau in diesem Zwischenbereich zwischen Wirklichkeit und Symbolik, weil es das gesamte Geflecht sozialer Beziehungen als völlig durch die Bedingungen der Repräsentation, d.h. durch Sprache strukturiert versteht. Sprache wird dabei als ein richtungsloses Gewirr verstanden, in dem etwa das Sakrale die Funktion genau der Bedingungen des Wortes selbst ist: *Sacer* weist wie *altus* in zwei Richtungen, zum Heiligen und zum Verfluchten. Die klassische Philosophie möchte diese Dualität unterdrücken und statt dessen eine Sprache rekonstruieren, in der jedes Element eine spezifische und einzige Bedeutung hat. Sie will vertikale Monumente schaffen, um die Totenstadt zu verdekken, wo Bedeutung in den Schmutz des Verfalls, der Unreinheit und des Todes einsinkt. Der Ort dieser linguistischen Totenstadt, wo Sprache die realen Bedürfnisse des *acéphale* zugleich gestaltet und widerspiegelt, ist das Labyrinth.

Das Spielbrett von *Das Spiel ist aus* ist kein Ready-made. Seine Horizontalität ist mit dem weiter nicht gestalteten Umkippen der Schneeschaufel in Duchamps *In Advance of a Broken Arm* nicht zu vergleichen. Das Spielbrett mit den kleinen Figuren ist eine Darstellung, in der das Symbolische zu einer Funktion des Sockels im Batailleschen Sinne *(basesse)*

☐ 775 *›Figur aus Holz‹, MBOLE (Zaire), Höhe 94 cm. Sammlung Jacques Blanckaert, Brüssel.*

☐ 776 *Figur, ZULU (Republik Südafrika), Holz, Höhe 62 cm. The Trustees of the British Museum, London.*

□ 777 *Alberto Giacometti, ›Mann‹ (Homme), 1929, Bronze, 40 x 31 x 9 cm. Sammlung Ruth und Frank Stanton.*

wird – ein von surrealistischer Poetik weit entferntes Konzept, das statt dessen einer Vision des Primitiven entstammt.

1935 änderte sich GIACOMETTIS Kunst schlagartig. Er begann nach der Natur, mit Modellen im Atelier zu arbeiten, statt Skulpturen zu schaffen, die – wie er einmal rückblickend auf sein Werk der frühen 30er Jahre sagte – »ganz aus dem Geiste entsprungen waren«.[92] Der dadurch beschleunigte Bruch mit den Surrealisten führte bei GIACOMETTI zu einer feindseligen Einstellung. Er erklärte, daß »alles, was er bis zu jener Zeit gemacht hatte, Masturbation gewesen sei und daß er kein anderes Ziel habe, als einen menschlichen Kopf wiederzugeben«.[93] Als Teil dieser Ablehnung soll er seine Beziehungen zur primitiven Kunst mit der Bemerkung verleugnet haben, daß er diesen Objekten – wenn überhaupt – nur deshalb etwas entnommen habe, weil die »art nègre« in seiner frühen Schaffenszeit in Mode war.[94]

GIACOMETTI lehnte nicht einfach den Surrealismus oder eine vergleichbare Verbindung zur primitiven Kunst ab, sondern – in einem tieferen, strukturellen Sinne – das Horizontale in all seinen Bedeutungen: als ein Feld für neue Lösungen von Formproblemen der Skulptur und gleichzeitig als eine Matrix zur »Änderung« der menschlichen Anatomie. Seit 1935 befaßte er sich nur noch mit Vertikalplastik. Mit diesem Entschluß ließ er die beiden Themen hinter sich, deren Zusammenspiel die Brillanz seines Werks in den frühen 30er Jahren hervorgebracht hatte: das Niedere und das Primitive.

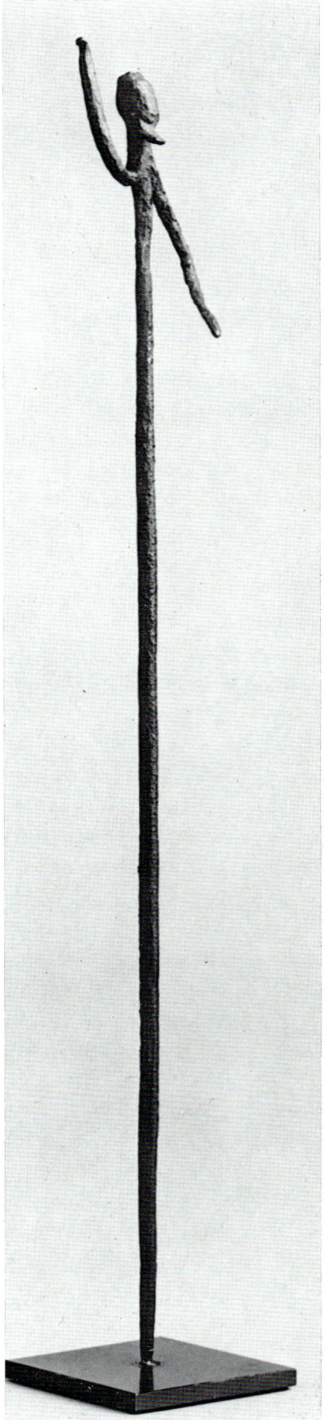

□ 778 *›Stab mit menschlicher Figur‹, Detail, MBUUN (Zaire), Holz und Metall, Höhe 84 cm. Sammlung Erle Loran, Berkeley.*

□ 779 *›Taktstock‹, BAMBARA (Mali), Holz, Höhe 108 cm. Sammlung M. und R. Garcia, Paris.*

□ 780 *›Stab mit figürlicher Verzierung‹, DOGON (Mali), Eisen, Höhe 48 cm. Sammlung L. Winderman, New York.*

□ 781 *›Figur aus Holz‹, KULANGO (Elfenbeinküste), Höhe 46 cm. Sammlung Friede, New York.*

□ 782 ›Figur aus Holz‹, MUMUYE (Nigeria), Höhe 121 cm. Privatsammlung.

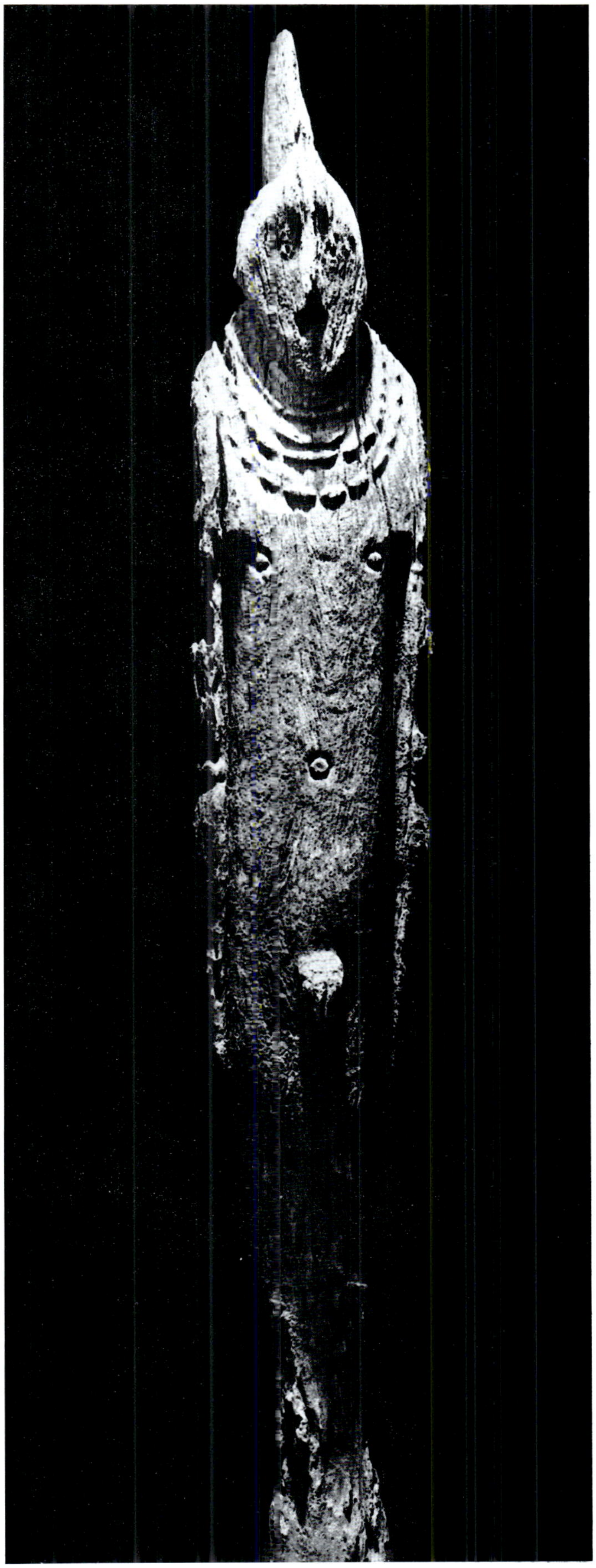

□ 783 ›Begräbnispfahl‹, KONSO (Äthiopien), Holz, Höhe 213 cm. Privatsammlung, Paris.

Anmerkungen

1. Leiris, M., »Pierres pour un Alberto Giacometti« in *Brisées,* Paris 1966, S. 149.

2. Breton, A., *L'Amour fou,* Paris 1937, S. 40–57. Erstveröffentlichung unter dem Titel »L'Equation de l'objet«, *Documents 34,* Nr. 1, 1934, S. 17–24.

3. Breton, »L'Equation«, S. 20.

4. Eines dieser Modelle schrieb dazu einen detaillierten Bericht und bemerkte darin, daß, »soweit es damals bei den einzelnen Handlungen des Malens und Modellsitzens zum Ausdruck kam, etwas Sadomasochistisches in unserer Beziehung lag . . . [obwohl] es schwierig wäre, genau zu bestimmen, welche Handlungen von wem und warum sadistisch und/oder masochistisch waren«, Lord, J., *A Giacometti Portrait,* New York, Museum of Modern Art 1965, S. 36.

5. Siehe de Beauvoir, S., *La Force de l'âge,* Paris 1960, S. 409–503.

6. Hohl, R., *Alberto Giacometti,* New York, Guggenheim Museum 1974, S. 22. Siehe auch Hohl, *Alberto Giacometti,* Lausanne 1971, S. 298, Anm. 15.

7. Clay, J., *Visages de l'art moderne,* Paris 1969, S. 160.

8. Die Statue stammt von einer Expedition, die Felix Speiser in den Jahren 1929–30 durchführte, und wurde 1933 im *Führer durch das Museum für Völkerkunde Basel, Salomonen* (Abb. 11, *Totenstatue, Bougainville,* S. 21) veröffentlicht. Mit der Kunst der Salomoninseln befaßte sich 1930 ein Essay in *Documents,* der sich mit visueller und religiöser Bedeutung ihrer Werke beschäftigte. Siehe Clarke, L., »L'Art des Iles Salomon« in *Documents* 2, Nr. 5, 1930.

9. Siehe etwa die Duka-Figur im Britischen Museum, 1944, Oc. 2. 1177 □ 728.

10. Hohl veröffentlichte die Figur der Salomoninseln in seiner Monographie von 1972 (S. 291, Abb. 30) ohne das »Gerüst«, obwohl diese Stütze in der Publikation des Museums für Völkerkunde, Basel 1933, wiedergegeben wurde. (Nach dieser Veröffentlichung gingen die Stützstäbe verloren.) Statt dessen glaubt Hohl in den architektonischen Elementen von *Der unsichtbare Gegenstand* vor allem den Einfluß der ägyptischen Bildhauerkunst zu sehen (Hohl, 1972, S. 300, Anm. 34). William Rubin zufolge könnten die Geisterfiguren vom Sepik-Strom eine andere mögliche Quelle für das Gerüst hinter dem Frauenkörper in Giacomettis Skulptur darstellen/sein. Eine von ihnen □ 726, jetzt im Rietberg Museum (RMe 104), gehörte zu jenem Teil der Von der Heydt-Sammlung, der 1933 dem Musée de l'Homme übergeben und dort ausgestellt wurde. Giacometti könnte sie somit dort gesehen haben. (Diese Information verdanke ich Philippe Peltier, der mir freundlicherweise seine Kenntnis über die bedeutenden Sammlungen ozeanischer Kunst der damaligen Zeit vermittelt hat.) Vertikale Strukturen, die den Körper entweder flankieren oder zu umfassen scheinen, lassen sich allerdings auch bei den neuirischen Malanggan nachweisen, ozeanischen Kultfiguren, die von den Surrealisten bewundert und gesammelt wurden □ 76, 77. Doch morphologisch sind weder die Skulpturen vom Sepik-Strom noch die aus Neuirland dem glattflächigen, anatomisch generalisierenden Stil von *Der unsichtbare Gegenstand* verwandt. Evan Maurer spricht von Einflüssen des Figurentypus der Karolineninseln aufgrund gewisser stilistischer Ähnlichkeiten und der Tatsache, daß eine der Zeichnungen Giacomettis nach ozeanischen Artefakten eine solche Figur darstellt. Siehe Maurer, *In Quest of the Myth. An Investigation of the Relationships between Surrealism and Primitivism,* Diss., University of Pennsylvania 1974, S. 318. Der Figurentypus der Karolineninseln besitzt jedoch weder die in *L'Objet invisible* so eindringlich wirkende, halb kniende Haltung noch irgendeinen stützenden Zusatz. Ein Vorläufer für die stilisierte Körperauffassung in *Der unsichtbare Gegenstand* und dessen rätselhafte Geste ist schon in der modernen Bildhauerei nachzuweisen. Georg Kolbes *Himmelfahrt Mariens,* ein Werk von 1921, bei dem die Jungfrau ihre überlängten Hände in einer eigentümlichen Gebetshaltung hält, siehe Spalding, J., *Max Ernst from the Collection of Mr. and Mrs. Jimmy Ernst,* 1979, S. 12. Nicht nur aufgrund mangelnder Information darüber, ob Giacometti dieses Werk kannte, sondern auch wegen der Verschiedenheit des Themas beider Skulpturen ist dieser Vorschlag nur bedingt zutreffend. Giacomettis nach primitiven Vorstellungen gestaltetes Thema steht Ideen der traditionell-christlichen Lehre äußerst fern.

11. *Löffelfrau* wird im allgemeinen auf 1926 datiert, außer in Hohls Monographie, wo es ohne nähere Begründung dem Jahre 1927 zugeordnet wird, und Brenson, B., *The Early Work of Alberto Giacometti, 1925–1935,* Diss., The Johns Hopkins University 1974, S. 225. Der Datierung von Hohl und Brenson folgend, glaube ich eine größere stilistische Reife und Vollkommenheit zu erkennen und nehme daher eine spätere Entstehung von *Löffelfrau* eben wegen Giacomettis wachsender Beziehung zu »primitiven« Quellen an.

12. Als Vorbild für den weiblichen Teil von *Das Paar* schlägt Maurer eine Reliquiarfigur der *Mahongwe* vor, Cowling dagegen die Körperschilde der *Makonde*, siehe Maurer, a.a.O., S. 316, und Cowling, E. N., *The Primitive Sources of Surrealism*, Magisterarbeit, London, The Courthauld Institute 1970, S. 46. Auf der Ebene des konzeptuellen und morphologischen Vergleichs überzeugt beides nicht. Doch auch wenn die jeweiligen »Quellen« kaum überzeugen, beweisen die Vermutungen der Autoren, daß sie den »afrikanisierenden« Charakter der Figuren von *Das Paar* verspürt haben. Diese Eigenschaft läßt wiederum Vermutungen anderer gelehrter Experten, das Werk habe ein neolithisches Vorbild, etwas fragwürdig erscheinen. Zwischen der weiblichen Figur von *Das Paar* und einer der Menhir-Figuren von Saint-Sernan-sur-Rance, abgebildet im Katalog des Carnac-Museums von 1927, sind zwar durchaus bedeutende kompositionelle, jedoch keine konzeptuellen Ähnlichkeiten nachzuweisen. Als erste wies Stephanie Poley auf diesen Zusammenhang hin (Alberto Giacomettis Umsetzung archaischer Gestaltungsformen in seinem Werk zwischen 1925 und 1935, *Jahrbuch der Hamburger Kunstsammlungen* 22, 1977, S. 177), später auch Alan Wilkinson, *Gauguin to Moore, Primitivism in Modern Sculpture,* Art Gallery of Toronto 1981, S. 222. Die Wirkung prähistorischer Kunst auf Giacomettis Œuvre zeigt sich bei anderen Werken, am deutlichsten bei der Skulptur *Die Liebkosung* von 1931. Dort waren die schablonierten Hände der Höhlenmaler – selbst geradezu ein Symbol der Moderne, wie ihr sinnbildliches Erscheinen auf dem Einband von Ozenfants *Foundations of Modern Art* (1931) beweist – zweifellos Vorbild für die Radierung der gespreizten Hand auf der Oberfläche der Skulptur. Doch bei *Das Paar* ist das Prähistorische, wenn es die Komposition tatsächlich beeinflußt haben sollte, offenkundig in einen »style nègre« umgewandelt worden.

13. Das Vorbild der *Dan* wurde zuerst von Jean Laude erkannt in *La Peinture Française (1905–1914) et l'art nègre,* Paris 1968, S. 13. Michael Brenson schlug den Einfluß einer Begräbnisstatue der *Kota* vor, die Giacometti von dem Malerbildhauer Serge Brignoni in den Jahren 1926–30 geliehen bekam (a.a.O., S. 56–57). In einem Gespräch mit William Rubin im Januar 1984 gab Brignoni den zusätzlichen Hinweis, daß er die *Kota*-Figur an Giacometti eigentlich verkauft hatte und sie nach seiner Ansicht die Gestaltung der weiblichen Hälfte des *Paares* beeinflußt habe. Diese Ansicht wird zusätzlich erhärtet durch eine verlorengegangene Gipsfigur, die den Übergang zwischen den von Léger angeregten kubistischen Arbeiten der Jahre 1925/26 und dem *Paar* bildet (wie auch Diego Giacometti bestätigt hat, daß die verlorene Gipsarbeit dem *Paar* unmittelbar vorausgegangen sei). Die Verbindung der ovalen Form der *Kota*-Statuette mit einer plakettenartigen, rechteckigen Fläche für den Körper der Figur läßt diese recht architektonische Auffassung der menschlichen Gestalt auch auf die Kenntnis anthropomorpher Schließen vermuten, die von westafrikanischen Stämmen hergestellt wurden und in Sammlungen mit Werken der *Bambara, Dogon* und anderen eine gewisse Rolle spielen.

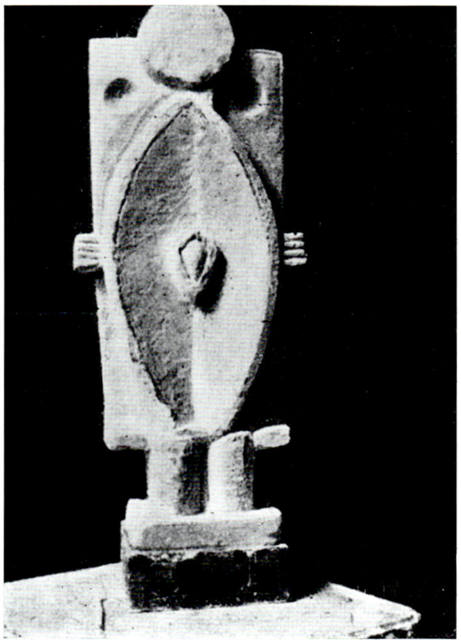

□ 784 *Alberto Giacometti, ›Frau‹ (Femme), 1926, Tusche, 18 x 13 cm. Kunsthaus Zürich.*

14. Die »Exposition de l'art indigène des colonies d'Afrique et d'Océanie«, Musée des Arts Décoratifs (November 1923–27. Januar 1924), wurde von André Level zusammengestellt. Für die Ausstellung wurden u. a. folgende Sammlungen herangezogen: Félix Fénéon, André Lhote, Patrick Henry Bruce, Paul Guillaume und natür-

lich die des Trocadéro. Guillaume steuerte neunundsiebzig Objekte bei, davon sechs Löffel unter der Rubrik »Elfenbeinküste«. Jean-Louis Paudrat ist davon überzeugt, daß sich darunter auch Objekte der DAN befunden haben. Zwei andere Löffelfrauen, die Giacometti gesehen haben könnte, sind: der *LEGA*-Löffel in Einstein, C., *La Sculpture Africaine,* Paris 1922, S. 42, und das auf Tafel 3 abgebildete Gerät in Guillaume, P., und Munro, Th., *Primitive Negro Sculpture,* New York 1926. Die französische Ausgabe erschien 1929.

15. Siehe die Kopie, die Giacometti von der Venus von Laussel anfertigte, veröffentlicht in Carluccio, L., *A Sketchbook of Interpretive Drawings,* New York 1968, Taf. 2. Die Datierung dieser Zeichnungen ist schwierig, auf demselben Blatt befindet sich jedoch auch die Skizze für Giacomettis *Trois Personnages dehors* von 1929.

16. Rivière, G. H., »Archéologismes« in *Cahiers d'art* 7, 1926, S. 177.

17. Zervos, Ch., »Notes sur la sculpture contemporaine« in *Cahiers d'art* 10, 1929, S. 465.

18. Guillaume und Munro, a.a.O.

19. Fry, R., »Negro Sculpture« in *Vision and Design*, New York 1920.

20. Ein Beispiel von vielen für die ästhetisierende Sehweise, bei dem die primitive Kunst nur als ein Moment kollektiver Kunstdarstellung, also des allen Menschen vertrauten ästhetischen Impulses betrachtet wird, ist Ozenfant, A., *Foundations of Modern Art. The Ice Age to 1931,* London 1931. Französische Ausgabe 1928.

21. Luquet, G. H., *L'Art primitif,* Paris 1930. Für Batailles Besprechung siehe »L'Art primitif« in *Documents 2,* Nr. 7, 1930, S. 389–97, gesammelt in Bataille, G., *Œuvres complètes,* Paris 1970, Bd. 1, S. 247–54.

22. *Œuvres complètes,* Bd. 1, S. 251. Die Übersetzung von *informe* lautet »ungestalt«, Bataille will mit diesem Begriff jedoch die aristotelische Differenz zwischen Form und Inhalt aufheben.

23. *Œuvres complètes,* Bd. 1., S. 253.

24. Ebenda, S. 251. Diese Idee der Doppeldeutigkeit, die in der ethnologischen Wurzel eines bestimmten Begriffs enthalten ist, berücksichtigt das Interesse Freuds an einer solchen etymologischen Untersuchung, bei der gerade »altus« und »sacer« als Beispiele verwendet werden. Siehe Freuds »Antithetische Bedeutung von Hauptwörtern«, veröffentlicht 1910 im *Jahrbuch für psychoanalytische und psychopathologische Forschungen,* Bd. 1, als Besprechung von Karl Abels *Gegensinn der Urworte.* Zu Batailles Kenntnis dieses Textes siehe Hollier, D., *La Prise de La Concorde,* Paris 1974, S. 240.

25. Bataille war offensichtlich auf die ihm damals zugänglichen ethnologischen Daten angewiesen, aus denen er eine eigene Auswahl zur Stützung seiner Philosophiekritik traf. Zu Batailles Verbindung zur Ethnographie in den 20er und 30er Jahren siehe Métraux, A., »Rencontre avec les ethnologues« in *Critique, 195–6,* 1963, S. 677–84.

26. In Babelon, J., *L'Art précolumbien,* Paris 1930. Diese Aufsatzsammlung führte in die *Exposition de l'art de l'Amérique* von 1928 im Pavillon de Marsan ein und enthielt u. a. Texte von Alfred Métraux und Paul Rivet. Daß man die präkolumbianische Kunst damals mit der afrikanischen und ozeanischen in eine Reihe stellte, läßt sich z. B. dem Text »L'Art nègre« entnehmen, den Zervos als Einleitung einer Sonderausgabe der *Cahiers d'art* (Nr. 7–8, 1927) schrieb. Zur »Vorliebe unserer Generation für die ›art nègre‹« führt er aus: »Das, was vor zwanzig Jahren mit Hilfe von Negerskulpturen geschaffen wurde, wird heutzutage unter dem Eindruck melanesischer und präkolumbianischer Kunst erzeugt« (S. 230). Zum gleichen Thema schrieb Breton »Das besondere Interesse, das die Maler zu Beginn des zwanzigsten Jahrhunderts für afrikanische Kunst verspürten, wendet sich heute der amerikanischen Kunst vor der Eroberung zu, die – zusammen mit der ozeanischen Kunst – einen besonderen Einfluß auf die Künstler ausübt« (Breton, *Mexique,* Paris 1939, Vorwort). Die 1931 versteigerten Sammlungen von Breton und Eluard umfaßten mindestens so viel präkolumbianische wie ozeanische Stücke. Zur Ausstellung surrealistischer Objekte in der Galerie Charles Ratton im Jahre 1936 gehörten neben ozeanischen auch amerikanische Objekte, die im Katalog als eskimoisch, peruanisch und präkolumbianisch aufgeführt sind.

27. Métraux, a.a.O.

28. Bataille, *Œuvres complètes,* Bd. 1, S. 152.

29. Ebenda, S. 157.

30. Zervos, »Notes sur la sculpture contemporaine«, S. 472.

31. Eine Darstellung, wie Batailles Denken von Mauss geprägt wurde, findet sich bei Métraux, a.a.O. Eine andere Untersuchung zu diesem Verhältnis liefert James Clifford, »On Ethnographic Surrealism« in *Comparative Studies in Society and History,* Oktober 1981, S. 543–64.

32. Hohl hebt hervor, daß Giacometti die genauen ethnographischen Informationen zum Kontext der Stammeskunst, die ihm über seine Beziehung zu Leiris leicht zugänglich waren, kannte und verwendete (Hohl, 1972, S. 79). In einem Interview mit dem Autor (24. Februar 1983) steuerte Leiris hierzu keine genaueren Informationen bei, doch er bejahte, daß Giacometti bei den ethnographisch orientierten Diskussionen der *Documents*-Gruppe anwesend war.

33. Im Herbst 1930 stellte Giacometti zusammen mit Miró und Arp in der Galerie Pierre aus. Georges Sadoul erinnert sich: »Ende 1930 traf ich Alberto Giacometti. Man hatte ihn gerade in die Surrealistengruppe aufgenommen. Mit seinen Skulpturen aus beweglichen Objekten führte er 1930 eine neue Gestaltungsweise in den Surrealismus ein. Damit wurden surrealistische Objekte mit symbolischer oder erotischer Funktion zur Mode, sie herzustellen, praktisch eine Verpflichtung« (zitiert in Hohl, 1972, S. 249). Die Datierung von Dalís »Objets à fonctionnement symbolique« in *Le Surréalisme au service de la révolution 3,* 1931, 16–17, veranschaulicht diese spätere Bemühung, Giacomettis Neuerungen in den Kern der surrealistischen Bewegungen aufzunehmen.

34. Nadeau, M., *Histoire de Surréalisme,* Paris 1945, S. 176.

35. Batailles Artikel »L'Œil«, *Documents 1,* Nr. 4, 1929 – in derselben Ausgabe erschien der erste Aufsatz zu Giacomettis Werk (Leiris, M., »Alberto Giacometti«, S. 209–10) – beginnt mit einer Diskussion dieses Bildes und führt die verschiedenen Filmeinstellungen von *Un Chien andalou* als die Orte auf, an denen das Bild reproduziert wurde. Batailles Konzentration auf das Thema Auge ist nicht nur eine Fortsetzung eigener Interessen seit *L'Histoire de l'œil.* Der in derselben Ausgabe veröffentlichte Artikel von Marcel Griaule über den bösen Blick und seine Bedeutung für die religiösen Systeme der Pri-

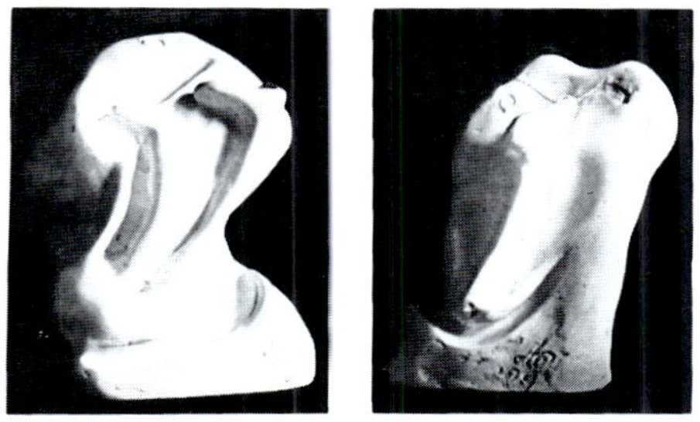

□ 785 *Hans Arp, ›Kopf‹, 1929, Gips, veröffentlicht in „Variétés", Juni 1929, Sonderausgabe „Le Surréalisme en 1929".*

□ 786 *›Aztekische Pyramide‹, Castillo de Teayo, Mexiko. Aus „Cahiers d'Art", Nr. 10, 1929.*

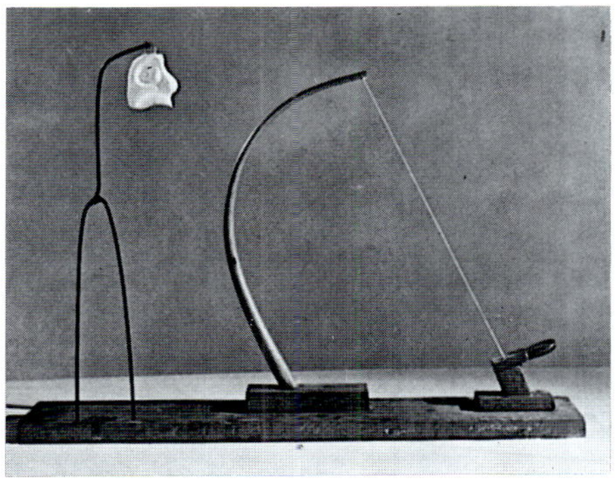

□ 787 *Alberto Giacometti, ›Blume in Gefahr‹, 1933, Holz, Metall und Gips, 56 x 78 x 18 cm. Alberto Giacometti-Stiftung, Kunsthaus Zürich.*

□ 788 *Alberto Giacometti, ›Kreislauf‹ (Circuit), 1931, Holz, 5 x 47 x 47 cm. Henriette Gomès, Paris.*

mitiven festigt das Band zwischen ethnographischer Analyse und moderner Thematik aufs neue.

36. In seinem Artikel »La Pointe à l'œil d'Alberto Giacometti« in *Cahiers du Musée National d'Art Moderne 11*, 1983, S. 64–100, vertritt Jean Clair die These einer direkten Verbindung zwischen Batailles erotisierter, phallischer Vorstellung vom Auge, wie sie sich in *L'Histoire de l'œil* und den Aufsätzen der *Documents* findet, und Giacomettis Skulptur *Stachel im Auge*. Seine Besprechung dieses Werks wendet sich teilweise Batailles Begriff des Sehens zu, der sich an den Begrenzungen des vom Körper getrennten Auges konkretisiert.

37. Unabhängig von unseren gegenwärtigen ethnographischen Kenntnissen über dieses Ballspiel wird der Wissensstand der dreißiger Jahre in einem Bericht wie Blom, F., »The Maya Ball-Game Pok-Ta-Pok« in *Middle American Papers*, (Tulane University 1932) dokumentiert, wo die lexikalischen Stichwörter dieses Spiels veröffentlicht sind. Diese Art Material stand Bataille zur Verfügung. Die Verbindung von Ballspiel und Tod wird gestützt durch die Reliefplatte vom Spielfeld in El Tajin, Veracruz, die eine Opferszene auf dem Spielfeld darstellt.

38. Dupin, J., *Alberto Giacometti*, Paris 1962, S. 88.

39. Jacques Dupin teilte mir mit, daß Giacometti ihm zu Beginn der Arbeit an seiner Monographie seine sorgsam gehütete, vollständige Reihe der *Documents* als Arbeitsgrundlage auslieh. Einer der *Documents*-Artikel zu diesem Thema, der mit den Darstellungen der Opfer und der Hinrichtungsstätten wie in einer Handschrift illustriert ist, stammt von Hervé, R., »Sacrifices humains du Centre Amerique«, *Documents* 2, Nr. 4, 1930.

40. *Cahiers d'Art 10*, 1929, S. 456, zeigt die Photographie einer aztekischen Pyramide mit einem Altar an der Spitze, dessen Bauweise an *L'Heure des traces* erinnert □ 248.

41. Alberto Giacometti, »Hier, sables mouvants« in *Le Surréalisme au service de la révolution 5*, 1933.

42. Giacometti, A., »A propos de Jacques Callot« in *Labyrinthe 7*, 15. April 1945, S. 3. Dieser Essay schildert die Faszination, die für Callot, Goya und Géricault von Schrecken und Zerstörung ausging. »Für diese Künstler besteht in jeder Lebenssphäre ein rasendes Bedürfnis nach Zerstörung sogar bis zu der des menschlichen Bewußtseins.« In einem Gedankengang, der offensichtlich Bataille nahe steht, folgert Giacometti, daß es zum Verständnis nötig ist, »einerseits von der Zerstörungsfreude und Grausamkeit bei Kindern und andererseits von der Thematik der Kunst« zu sprechen. »Le Rêve, le Sphinx et la mort de T.«, *Labyrinthe 22/23*, 15. Dezember 1946, S. 12–13. Es ist nicht nur die dort erzählte Traumgeschichte von der Spinne, die an Batailles »informe« erinnert. Die Beschreibung des Kopfes von T., wie er durch den Tod auf schreckliche Weise zum Ding wird, könnte von Bataille stammen. »Ein Objekt, ein kleines, abmeßbares, unbedeutendes Gehäuse« geworden, sieht er den Kopf als verwesenden Kadaver – »erbärmlicher Abfall zum Wegwerfen« –, dem zu Giacomettis Entsetzen eine Fliege in den Mund fliegt.

43. Hohl erklärt z. B.: »Es ist sicher, daß die von Picasso im *Projekt für ein Monument* entworfenen Keulen- und Kugelformen den Aufbau von *Schwebende Kugel* beseelten« (Hohl, 1972, S. 81).

44. Barthes, R., »La Métaphore de l'œil« in *Critique, 195–96*, 1963, S. 772. Meine Argumentation zur Struktur der Metapher in Batailles Novelle schließt sich der von Barthes an.

45. Ebenda, S. 773.

46. »Informe« war Batailles Beitrag im »Dictionnaire« von *Documents 1*, Nr. 7, 1929.

47. Eine Besprechung von Batailles »Lexikon« im Kontext der verschiedenen Avantgarde-Lexika findet sich bei Denis Hollier, a.a.O., S. 59–65.

48. So wurde z. B. eine vierbändige Reihe mit photographischen Reproduktionen speziell für die Ausbildung von Kunst- und Designstudenten unter dem Titel *La Décoration primitive* veröffentlicht (Paris 1922). Die Bände behandelten Skulpturen und Textilien der afrikanischen, ozeanischen und präkolumbianischen Kunst mit gleichem Interesse.

49. Bataille, *Œuvres complètes*, Bd. 1, S. 253.

50. Apollinaire besteht z. B. in *Les Peintres cubistes* (Paris 1913) darauf, daß der Kubismus »keine Kunst der Nachahmung, sondern eine Kunst der Konzeption ist«. Und in Légers Artikel »Les Origines de la peinture et sa valeur représentative« (*Montjoie 8*, Mai 1913, S. 7) konzentriert sich der Autor auf den Unterschied zwischen »visuellem Realismus« und einem »Realismus der Konzeption«.

51. Dieses erschien in der Sonderausgabe zu Picasso, *Documents 2*, Nr. 3, 1930.

52. Breton, *L'Équation*, S. 20.

53. Im Jahr vor der Herstellung des Gipsentwurfs der Maske für *Der unsichtbare Gegenstand* schuf Giacometti eine andere »Maske« in Gips, den deformierten Kopf von *Blume in Gefahr* (1933) □ 787. Diese Skulptur gleicht mit ihren Bildern der beginnenden Enthauptung der Blume (bzw. des Kopfes) einer kleinen Maschine zur Produktion von *acéphale*. Ein Gipskopf von Arp □ 785, der in der Sonderausgabe über Surrealismus von *Variétés* (Juni 1929) erschien, hat möglicherweise zur Idee des Kopfes als Maske im Prozeß des Zerfalls beigetragen.

54. *Documents 2*, Nr. 2, 1930, S. 97–102.

55. Siehe die Texte von Evan Maurer und Philippe Peltier in diesem Band.

56. 1931 organisierte Louis Aragon in einem Versammlungssaal in der Rue de la Grande-Batelière eine antikolonialistische Ausstellung, um gegen die offizielle Exposition Coloniale zu protestieren. Giacometti beteiligte sich mit politischen Karikaturen. In *Le Surréalisme au service de la révolution 4* (Dezember 1931) erschienen zwei Aufnahmen des Saales, den Aragon, Eluard und Tanguy für die Ausstellung »La Vérité sur les colonies« gestalteten.

57. »Soleil pourri« konzentrierte sich auf den Mithraskult und auf die beim direkten Blick in die Sonne hervorgerufenen Verkrampfungen. Diese Thematik wurde in der Textfolge »L'Œil pinéal« weiterentwickelt, siehe Anm. 87 ff.

58. »Aboutissements de la mécanique«, *Variétés 2*, Nr. 9, Januar 1930.

59. Batailles Konzentration auf *acéphale* führte 1936 zur Gründung einer gleichnamigen Zeitschrift, deren Titelbild von Masson entworfen wurde. Eine seiner frühen Abhandlungen zur Menschendarstellung im Altertum als *acéphale* war der Text »Le Bas Matérialisme et la gnose«, *Documents 2*, Nr. 1, 1930, S. 1–8. Leo Frobenius behandelt das Thema in »Bètes hommes ou dieux«, *Cahiers d'art 10*, 1929.

60. Caillois, R., »La Mante religieuse«, *Minotaure 1*, Nr. 5, Mai 1931, S. 25. Siehe auch »La Nature et l'amour«, *Variétés 2*, Nr. 2, Juni 1929.

61. Pressly, W., »The Praying Mantis in Surrealist Art«, *Art Bulletin 55*, Dezember 1973, S. 600–15.

62. Hohl geht der Verwendung der Kugel als sinnbildlicher Verkörperung des Mannes in den Werken dieser Jahre nach (Hohl, 1972, S. 81–82).

63. Dieses sind D 62.2.10 des Musée des Arts Africains et Océaniens, früher in der Sammlung M. Girardin, und der wichtige Malanggan aus der Sammlung von Max Ernst □ 749, 751.

64. Einstein, C., »Sculptures mélanésiennes« in *L'Amour de l'art 8*, 1926, S. 256.

65. *Femme 100 Têtes* (1929) von Ernst war diesem Thema dem Namen nach gewidmet, obwohl es keine direkten Illustrationen liefert.

66. *Une Semaine de bonté*, S. 168.

67. Siehe Maurers Argumentation, S. 579 ff. Den Nachforschungen von Philippe Peltier zufolge war Max Ernsts umfangreiche Sammlung ozeanischer Kunst auf Objekte vom Papua-Golf (Neuguinea) spezialisiert, obwohl sie auch anderes umfaßte.

68. Das jetzt zerstörte Werk wurde in *Minotaure* 3/4, 1933, S. 40, veröffentlicht. Diese direkt in den Boden getriebenen, an Pfähle erinnernden Figuren haben eine unverkennbare Ähnlichkeit mit den damals sehr bekannten Holzpfosten der Eingeborenen, die, mit Totem-Schnitzereien verziert, vor die Eingänge von Dörfern oder Häusern in die Erde gesteckt wurden, um das jeweilige Gebiet zu schützen.

69. Giacometti erklärte die Anziehungskraft ozeanischer Skulptur mit dem Hinweis auf die Überbetonung der Augen. »Die Skulptur der Neuen Hebriden ist wahrhaftig und mehr als das, weil sie einen Blick hat. Es ist keine Nachahmung eines Auges, es ist der reine, einfache Blick. Alles übrige dient nur der Unterstützung des Blicks.« Charbonnier, G., *Le Monologue du peintre*, Paris 1959, S. 166.

70. Das gilt nicht nur für Hohls Monographie, sondern auch für die Methode von Yves Bonnefoy, der eine größere Studie über den Künstler vorbereitet. Siehe »Études comparées de la Fonction poétique« in *Annuaire du Collège de France*, 1982, S. 643–53.

71. Giacometti, »Le Palais de quatre heures« in *Minotaure* 3/4, 1933, S. 46.

72. Dies ist das Epigramm des Kapitels *Une Semaine de bonté*, das den Abschnitt über die Osterinsel enthält. Giacomettis Text »Hier, sables mouvants« berichtet eingangs von dem großen Felsen, in den er als Kind hineinkroch und dort Stunden verbrachte.

73. Siehe Gide, A., »Architecture nègres« in *Cahiers d'art* 7/8, 1927, besonders das Bild auf S. 265.

74. *Die Sammlung der Alberto-Giacometti-Stiftung*, Zürich 1971, S. 94.

75. Den Namen für die Zeitschrift *Minotaure* steuerte 1933 Bataille bei.

76. Dieses Werk mit der Inschrift »La vie continue« wurde in Zervos' »Quelques notes sur les sculptures de Giacometti« in *Cahiers d'art*, 1932,

S. 337–42, unter dem Titel *Chute d'un corps sur un graphique* veröffentlicht. Als Giacometti die Kunst jener Jahre später schilderte, bezeichnete er diese jetzt verlorene Skulptur als *Paysage – Tête couchée.* Siehe »Lettre à Pierre Matisse« in *Alberto Giacometti,* New York 1948. Carola Giedion-Welcker, die Giacometti kannte, publizierte eine etruskische Votivbronze aus dem Museum von Piacenza als mögliche Anregung für *Projekt für einen Platz* (in Giedion-Welcker, *Contemporary Sculpture,* New York 1969). Hohl zufolge steht dieses Objekt eher mit *Fall eines Kopfes über einem Diagramm* in Verbindung und erklärt dessen Titel, weil das etruskische Werk mit Runen bedeckt ist (Hohl, 1972, S. 299, Anm. 29).

□ 788a *›Figur aus Holz‹,* NAMSHI *(Kamerun), Höhe 37 cm. Privatsammlung.*

77. Dalí, S., »Communication, visage paranoïaque« in *Le Surréalisme au service de la révolution 3,* Dezember 1931, S. 40.

78. Siehe Hohl, 1972, S. 82.

79. Vgl. die Sonderausgabe zu »art nègre« von *La Nervu, 9–10,* 1926, Abb. 9.

80. Giacometti, A., »Notes sur les copies«, *L'Ephémère 1,* 1966, S. 104–08. Diego Giacometti bestätigt mir, daß die bei Carluccio, a.a.O., wiedergegebenen Zeichnungen ozeanischer Objekte nach der Ausgabe der *Cahiers d'art* von 1929 angefertigt wurden.

81. Carluccio, a.a.O., Taf. 5, zeigt drei Skulpturen aus dem Baseler Museum: Abb. 104, 105 und 114 in den *Cahiers d'art* von 1929. Taf. 6 bildet Statuen der Osterinsel ab, Abb. 188 und 187 in *Cahiers d'art.* Taf. 8 von Carluccio zeigt zwei Objekte aus Neuguinea als Nachzeichnungen von Abb. 43 und 41, Taf. 9 von Abb. 2, 153 und 157 der *Cahiers d'art.* Die späten Zeichnungen nach primitiven Vorbildern bei Carluccio sind im Sinne von Giacomettis Übergang zur Arbeit nach der Natur (seit 1935) wahrscheinlich aus der unmittelbaren Begegnung mit den Gegenständen entstanden.

82. Möglich ist auch der Einfluß der außergewöhnlich phallischen *casse-têtes* aus Neukaledonien und den Fidschiinseln, von denen sich viele seit dem Ende des 19. Jahrhunderts im Musée de l'Homme befanden □ 838.

83. Hohl, 1972, S. 81.

84. Bataille, »Le Bas Materialisme et la gnose«.

85. Bataille, »Le Gros Orteil«, *Documents 1,* Nr. 6, 1929, S. 302.

86. In der Zeichnung einer Nackten von 1926, Kunstmuseum, Zürich □ 789, bringt Giacometti diese Achsendrehung durch das Verschmelzen von Mund und Genitalien zum Ausdruck. Ein solches Verhältnis ist auch für die weibliche Figur von *Das Paar* aus demselben Jahr formbestimmend und tritt in der afrikanischen Kunst häufig auf.

□ 789 *Alberto Giacometti, ›Nackte‹, 1926, Tusche, 18 x 13 cm. Privatsammlung.*

87. Die fünf Texte über das Zirbeldrüsenauge wurden zwischen 1927 und 1930 geschrieben und nicht veröffentlicht. Sie sind in den *Œuvres complètes,* Bd. 2, S. 13–50, enthalten.

88. Siehe »Soleil pourri«, wo Bataille von »un être anthropomorphe *dépourvu de tête*« spricht (S. 174). Hollier erörtert diesen Gedanken des Achsenwechsels a.a.O., S. 137–54.

89. In »La Mutilation sacrificielle et l'oreille coupé de Vincent van Gogh«, *Documents 2,* Nr. 8, 1930, kritisiert Bataille etwa, daß Luquet die Hypothese der »übereinandergelegten Finger« akzeptiert, die die Höhlenmalereien unter Zuhilfenahme von Schablonenhänden mit fehlenden Fingern erklären soll (*Œuvres complètes,* Bd. 1, S. 267). Als besonders faszinierendes Motiv ist die Schablonenhand bei *Caress* (1930) verwendet worden.

90. Hollier, a.a.O., S. 148.

□ 790 *Das Spiel ›i‹,* DOGON *(Mali), veröffentlicht in Marcel Griaule, „Jeux dogons", 1938.*

91. Hohl führt die hölzernen Spielbretter aus Benin, die Giacometti in der Galerie Charles Ratton gesehen haben könnte, als mögliches Vorbild für dieses Werk auf (Hohl, 1972, S. 299, Anm. 27). M. Ratton hingegen bezweifelt die Existenz von Benin-Objekten dieser Art. Man braucht statt dessen nur die hölzernen Spielbretter für ›i‹ zu betrachten, die auch heute noch hergestellt werden. Die Spielfläche war oft improvisiert: in die Erde oder in Stein gehöhlt. Marcel Griaules Abhandlung zeigt eine solche Steintafel (Griaule, *Jeux Dogons,* Paris 1938 Abb. 95, □ 790).

92. James Lord, a.a.O., S. 48. Siehe Giacomettis Schilderung in »Le Palais de quatres heures«, a.a.O.

93. Marcel Jean, *Histoire de la peinture surréaliste,* Paris 1959, S. 227.

94. Giacometti soll dies in den späten 30er Jahren zu Greta Knutson gesagt haben, der damaligen Gattin von Tristan Tzara, als er ihr Porträt saß (wie mir Knutsons Schwiegertochter, Frau Tzara, berichtete).

□ 791 *Wifredo Lam, ›Der Dschungel‹ (The Jungle), 1943, Gouache auf Papier über Leinwand, 238 x 230 cm. The Museum of Modern Art, New York.*

Evan Maurer

Dada und Surrealismus

Pressenotiz vom 5. Februar 1916:
»Cabaret Voltaire. Unter diesem Namen hat sich eine Gesellschaft junger Künstler und Literaten etabliert, deren Ziel es ist, einen Mittelpunkt für die künstlerische Unterhaltung zu schaffen. Das Prinzip des Cabarets soll sein, daß bei den täglichen Zusammenkünften musikalische und rezitatorische Vorträge der als Gäste verkehrenden Künstler stattfinden, und es ergeht an die junge Künstlerschaft Zürichs die Einladung, sich ohne Rücksicht auf eine besondere Richtung mit Vorschlägen und Beiträgen einzufinden.«[1]

Es ist ironisch, daß diese harmlose Bekanntmachung für Europa das Startzeichen jenes revolutionären Kunstphänomens bedeutete, das die »Voltairisten« Dada nennen sollten. Vorweggenommen von Marcel Duchamp und einigen New Yorker Künstlern, erweiterten und forderten die lebhaften Dada-Aktivitäten die Literatur und bildende Kunst in Europa und Amerika für die nächsten acht Jahre heraus (vom Beginn des Ersten Weltkrieges bis in die frühen zwanziger Jahre). »Das Programm des Dada bestand darin, keines zu haben . . .«, schrieb Hans Richter, »und es gab dieser Bewegung in jenem geschichtlichen Augenblick die explosive Kraft, sich nach *allen* Seiten ohne ästhetische und soziale Bindungen frei zu entfalten. Diese absolute Voraussetzungslosigkeit war in der Tat ein Novum in der Geschichte der Kunst. Die Schwäche der menschlichen Natur sorgte dafür, daß ein solch paradiesischer Lebenszustand nur von kurzer Dauer war.«[2] Denn 1924 verkündete der Kreis um André Breton in Paris seine Hinwendung zum Surrealismus und führte die leidenschaftliche Hingabe an die Ursachen künstlerischen, politischen und sozialen Wandels, die die Gruppe ursprünglich zusammengeführt hatte, in Übereinstimmung mit verwandten, doch andersartigen Ideen fort.

Der Name Dada wurde von einer Gruppe deutscher, französischer und rumänischer Schriftsteller ersonnen, die zu Beginn des Ersten Weltkrieges nach Zürich gekommen waren. Obwohl gleichzeitig und unabhängig davon eine ähnliche Entwicklung in New York stattfand, müssen wir uns zunächst auf die Schweizer Gruppe konzentrieren, um ihre stärkere Verknüpfung mit Primitivismus und primitiver Kunst zu untersuchen.[3] Nicht zufällig entwickelte sich Dada in Zürich, dem weltoffenen geistigen Zentrum der Schweiz, die neutraler Zufluchtsort inmitten des weltweiten Blutbades war, das den Lauf der politischen und sozialen Geschichte unwiederbringlich ändern sollte. Dadas scharfer Sinn für das Absurde und sein Beharren auf künstlerischer und sozialer Freiheit wurde von den bürgerlichen Gesellschaften provoziert, die für einen Krieg verantwortlich waren, der auf unvorstellbare Weise Menschenleben vernichtete. Hugo Ball, der eigentliche »Impresario« der Dada-Veranstaltungen, beschrieb die Haltung seiner Kollegen als zynische Revolte gegen das Establishment:

»Es ist in dieser heruntergekommenen Zeit unmöglich, daß wir ihr Respekt bezeugen. Was setzt es denn voraus, daß wir darüber so respektvoll sein sollten? Ihre Kanonen? Unsere Trommeln übertönen sie. Ihr Idealismus? Es dauerte lange, um zu einem Subjekt der Verachtung zu werden . . . die großartigen Schlächter-Festivals und der kannibalische Heroismus? Unsere vorsätzliche Verrücktheit, unser Enthusiasmus für Illusionen wird sie beschämen.«[4]

Die Zermürbungskriege der ersten beiden Kriegsjahre verschlissen Heere mit Millionen von Menschen, die sich gegenseitig in schier endlosen Artilleriegefechten entlang der Europa durchschneidenden Frontlinie vernichteten. Am 21. Februar 1916, wenige Wochen nach der Eröffnung des dadaistischen Cabarets Voltaire, griffen die deutschen Armeen in einem planmäßig vorbereiteten Manöver die schwer befestigten Stellungen um die kleine Stadt Verdun an. Sie zwangen damit die Franzosen zu einer bis dahin unerreichten Konzentration von Artillerie, um sie durch das Heranziehen ihrer Reserven in dieser Todesfalle zu dezimieren. Das zunehmende Grauen von Verdun dauerte zehn Monate, in denen auf einem kleinen Gebiet die gemeinsamen Verluste der Deutschen und der Franzosen auf 420000 Tote und 800000 Gasgeschädigte und Verwundete geschätzt werden.[5]

Die Spannungen dieser einmaligen und sinnlosen Tragödie hatten eine starke Wirkung auf die Zürcher Bevölkerung, vor allem die jungen Künstler und Schriftsteller, die hier aus vielen europäischen Ländern zusammengekommen waren. Die psychologische und emotionale Wirkung des Krieges auf die Zivilbevölkerung war in dieser neutralen Enklave stärker als man annehmen könnte. Die Nähe der Kampfplätze brachte den Schlachtenlärm bis zu den Außenvierteln der Stadt. Wie sich Marcel Janco erinnerte, konnte man die Kanonen bereits einige Kilometer hinter Zürich hören.[6] Der dadaistische und surrealistische Maler und Dichter Hans Arp wies auch auf die unmittelbar physische Bedrohung durch die Auseinandersetzung hin, als er schrieb: »Angeekelt von den Schlächtereien des Weltkrieges, gaben wir uns 1915 in Zürich den schönen Künsten hin. Während in der Ferne der Donner der Geschütze grollte, sangen, malten, klebten, dichteten wir von ganzer Seele.«[7]

Die Ablehnung der miteinander verquickten ästhetischen und sozialen Werte der etablierten Ordnung durch die Dadaisten führte sie zur Kunst der Primitiven als auch zu verwandten

□ 792 *Marcel Janco, ›Einladung zu einer Dada-Soiree‹, 1916, Kohle, 73 x 55 cm. Kunsthaus, Graphische Sammlung, Zürich.*

Gebieten wie der Volkskunst, der naiven Kunst und der Kinderkunst. Diese Formen galten als Äußerung elementarer Gefühle und Ideen, die von traditionellen westlichen Werten unverdorben geblieben waren und alternative künstlerische Mittel gebrauchten. Arp ging auf diese Fragen ein, als er sagte, daß die Dadaisten Zürichs ganz am Anfang »eine elementare Kunst suchten, die den Menschen vom Wahnsinn der Zeit heilen würde. Wir sehnten uns nach einer neuen Ordnung, die das Gleichgewicht zwischen Himmel und Hölle herstellt.«[8]

Ähnlich wie am Montmartre um die Jahrhundertwende war die Kleinkunstbühne Mittelpunkt der frühen Dada-Aktivitäten in Zürich. Hier erzeugte die gesellige Umgebung von Essen und Trinken, Lärm und Gespräch, eine lebendige Atmosphäre für Aufführungen und Ausstellungen, für die Veröffentlichung von Flugblättern und Schriften. Erregung und Dramatik der Dada-Soireen bestanden aus einer ausgelassenen Mischung von Nonsens-Versen, Laut-Gedichten, Rezitationen in verschiedenen Sprachen, Klaviermusik, Trommeln und Jazz. Afrikanische Musik und Gedichte, afrikanisch inspirierte Masken, Schreie und Gelächter, Pantomimen und Beschimpfungen wurden alle mit großem Ernst dargeboten in der erklärten Absicht, die Zuhörer zu aktivieren und einzubeziehen.

Das einzige Bilddokument dieser ersten Dada-Soireen ist das 1916 entstandene Gemälde *Cabaret Voltaire* von Marcel Janco □ 793, das nicht nur die Erregung und Spannung, wie sie Richter beschrieben hatte, festhält, sondern auch einen deutlichen Beweis für das Interesse der Zürcher Dadaisten am Primitivismus liefert. An der Wand hinter der Bühne schielt bedrohlich eine übergroße Gesichtsmaske auf das Publikum herab, eine der vielen Masken, die Janco für diese Aufführungen herstellte, ein junger Rumäne, der nach Zürich gekommen war, um Architektur zu studieren. Nach eigenen Aussagen der Dadaisten bildeten Jancos Masken einen wichtigen Bestandteil ihrer Aufführungen. Obwohl aus verschiedenartigstem Alltagsmaterial hergestellt, war ihre Wirkung verwirrend und eindringlich □ 794. 1948 schrieb Arp an Janco: »Ich habe die Masken nicht vergessen, die Du für unsere Dada-Vorstellungen zu machen pflegtest. Sie waren erschreckend, die meisten mit blutigem Rot beschmiert, aus Karton, Papier, Pferdehaar, Draht und Stoff . . .«[9] Jancos Vorliebe für bis dahin unübliche, vergängliche Materialien hatte mit der Auffassung der Dadaisten von Kunst in primitiven Gesellschaften zu tun, speziell Ozeaniens. Seine eigenen Collagen erläuternd, verglich Arp sein Werk mit dem Künstler der Südsee: »Anstatt das Papier zu zerschneiden, zerriß ich es mit meinen Händen, ich gebrauchte Gegenstände, die ich am Strand fand, und ich stellte natürliche Collagen und Reliefs zusammen. Ich arbeitete so wie die Ozeanier, die sich nie um die Dauer ihrer Materialien kümmern, wenn sie Masken anfertigen, und die verderbliche Materialien wie Muscheln, Blut und Federn verwenden.«[10]

□ 794 *Marcel Janco, ›Maske‹, 1919, Papier, Karton, Schnur, Gouache und Pastell, 45 x 22 x 5 cm. Musée National d'Art Moderne, Centre National d'Art et de Culture Georges Pompidou, Paris.* ▷

Auch wenn es nicht nachzuweisen ist, daß originale afrikanische oder ozeanische Masken in die Vorstellungen einbezogen wurden oder man einen direkten Bezug zu ihnen herstellen wollte, wurden Jancos Masken von seinen Dada-Freunden sehr häufig »Neger-Masken« genannt. »Neger« wurde in diesem Zusammenhang gleichermaßen auf die Kunst Afrikas und Ozeaniens angewandt.[11] Während Jancos Masken nie ein bestimmtes afrikanisches oder ozeanisches Vorbild nachahm-

□ 793 *Marcel Janco, ›Cabaret Voltaire‹, 1916, Öl auf Leinwand. Verbleib unbekannt.*

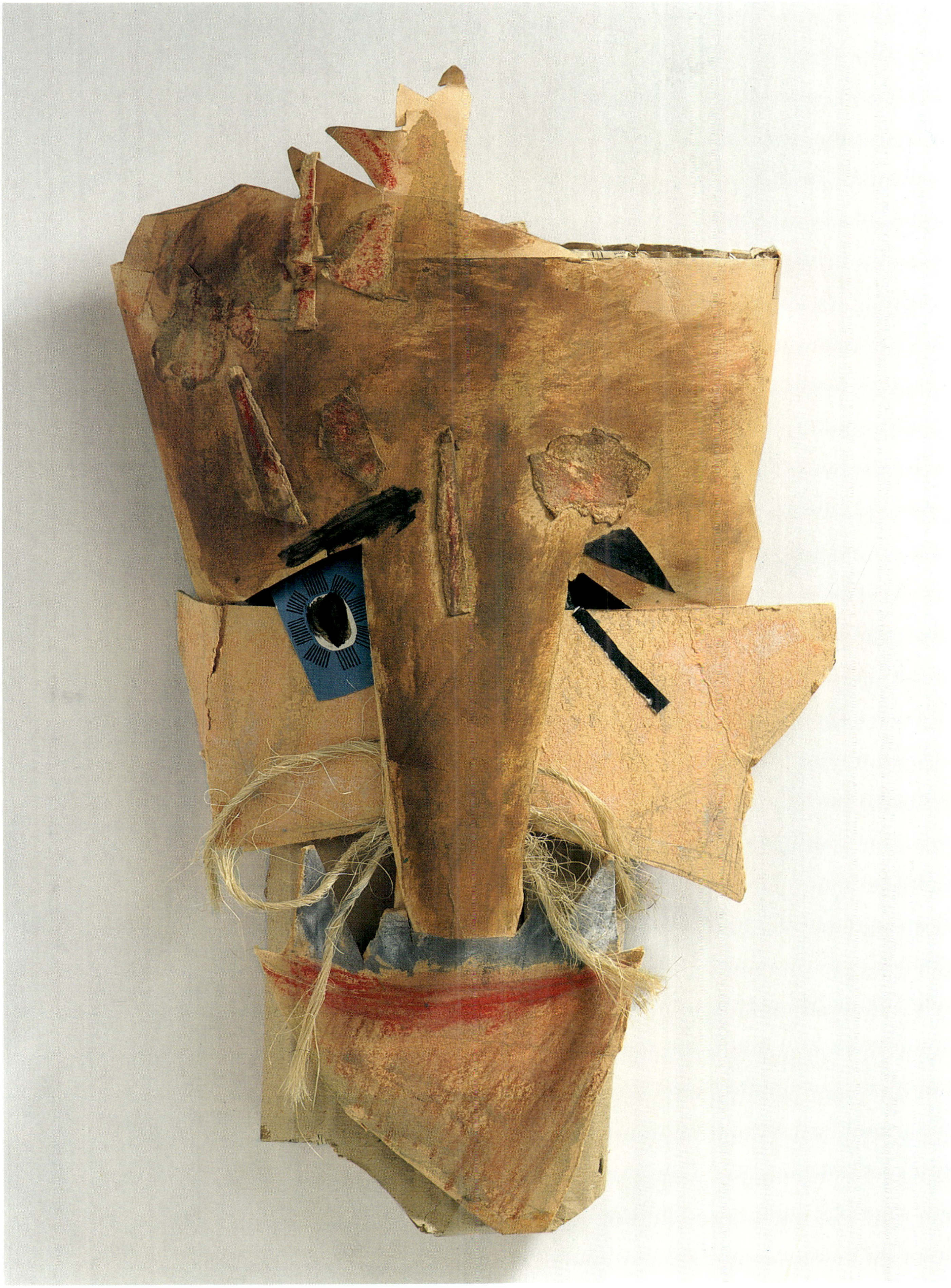

□ 795 *Hannah Höch, ›Die Süße‹, aus der Serie ›Aus einem Völkerkundemuseum‹, 1926, Collage, 30 x 15,5 cm. Sammlung Rössner, Backnang.*

ten, erweckten sie bei seinen Kollegen die unmittelbare Assoziation mit dem, was sie als die angeborene geistige Kraft der primitiven Kunst verstanden. Für HANS RICHTER war die beschwörende Kraft verkörpert in »den abstrakten Negermasken von Janco, die das Publikum aus der Ursprache der neuen Gedichte in den Urwald künstlerischer Visionen versetzten«.[12]

Für JANCO stellte die primitive Kunst eine von mehreren Anregungen aus traditionslosen Quellen dar, die über Formen und Techniken frei verfügten, um die Welt darzustellen. In einem Interview erklärte der Künstler kürzlich, »daß wir nicht nur die primitive Kunst als die eigentliche Kunst ansahen, sondern auch die Kunst der Kindheit. Wir kamen sogar auf die Idee, die Kunst der Geisteskranken auszustellen.«[13] Ein tiefgreifendes Interesse an diesen drei Gebieten – der Kunst der Primitiven, des Kindes und Geisteskranken – sollte später zu einem wichtigen Aspekt in Literatur und Kunst des Surrealismus werden.

Wie die Masken der Primitiven – JANCOS hauptsächliche Inspiration – waren auch seine Masken dazu bestimmt, von Tänzern bei musikalischen Darbietungen getragen zu werden. Trägt ein afrikanischer Tänzer eine Maske bei einem geheiligten Ritual, wird er gleichzeitig zum Medium des Geistes, den die Maske darstellt.

Die Maske ist deshalb ein bedeutsames Element bei der Umwandlung des individuellen Bewußtseins vom Menschlichen zum Mythischen. Hugo Ball, der Gründer des Cabarets Voltaire, verstand dieses Phänomen und war fasziniert, wie JANCOS Masken die Aktion der Darsteller, die sie trugen, beeinflußten. Er schrieb:

»Wir waren alle zugegen, als Janco mit seinen Masken ankam, und jeder band sich sogleich eine um. Da geschah nun etwas Seltsames. Die Maske verlangte nicht nur sofort nach einem Kostüm, sie diktierte auch einen ganz bestimmten pathetischen, ja an Irrsinn streifenden Gestus. . . . Die motorische Gewalt dieser Masken teilte sich uns in frappierender Unwiderstehlichkeit mit. Wir waren mit einem Male darüber belehrt, worin die Bedeutung einer solchen Larve für die Mimik, für das Theater bestand. Die Masken verlangten

□ 796 *Hannah Höch, ›Denkmal II – Eitelkeit‹, aus der Serie ›Aus einem Völkerkundemuseum‹, 1926, Collage, 26 x 17 cm. Sammlung Rössner, Backnang.*

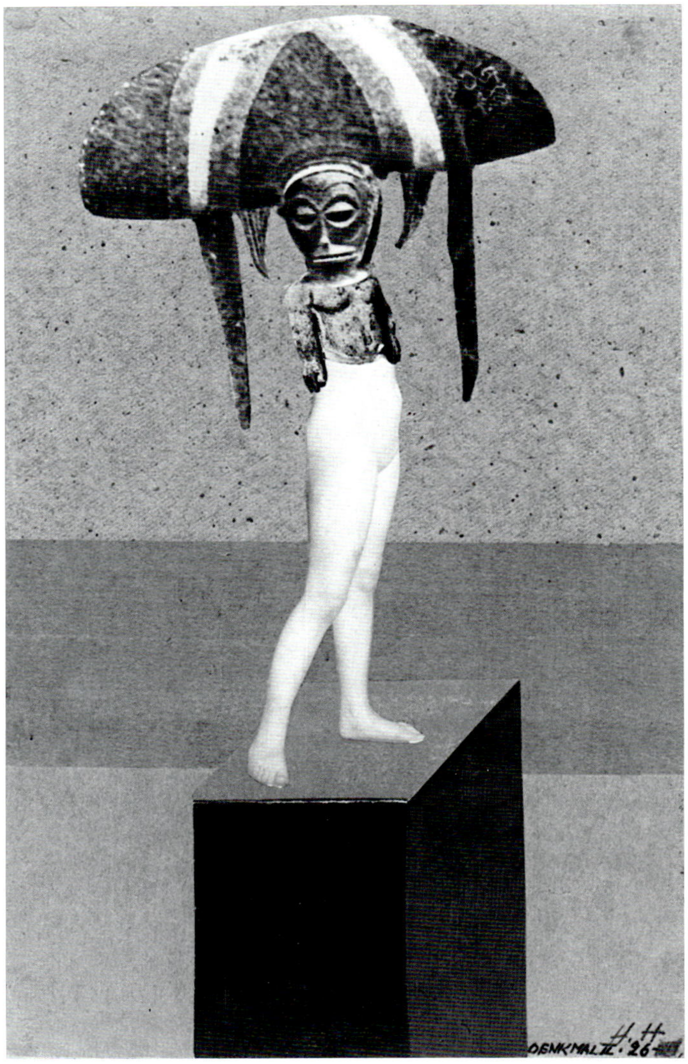

einfach, daß ihre Träger sich zu einem tragisch-absurden Tanz in Bewegung setzten. . . . Was an den Masken uns allesamt fasziniert, ist, daß sie nicht menschliche . . . Charaktere und Leidenschaften verkörpern.«[14]

Zusätzlich zu seinen Masken stellte Janco eine kraftvolle Zeichnung her, die direkt von der afrikanischen bildhauerischen Ästhetik beeinflußt war. *Einladung zu einer Dada-Soiree* □ 792 zeigt eine sitzende Figur von vorn und eine stehende in der Rückenansicht. Beide Körper bestehen aus breiten schwarzen Flächen, die Beine, Arme und Oberkörper abstrahieren und vereinfachen, wie es für den Stil und die Bemalung afrikanischer Figurenplastik charakteristisch ist. Der Kopf der sitzenden Figur ist gleichfalls zu Flächen abstrahiert, wobei der große ovale Mund mit den gebleckten Zähnen, die dominierende Nase, die breiten dreieckigen Augen sowie eine sorgfältig ausgearbeitete Wellenfrisur betont werden. Dieser Gesichtstypus ist dem sehr ähnlich, der von den Bildhauern Kameruns, speziell denen aus dem Stamm der *Bangwa*, bevorzugt wird. Es ist nicht ganz sicher, ob Janco die strenge Tradition der Skulptur Kameruns kannte, aber diese kraftvollen Figurenbilder und Masken waren der interessierten Öffentlichkeit in Völkerkundemuseen, besonders in Deutschland, und in Publikationen zugänglich.[15]

Einen direkten Bezug zwischen dem Dadaismus und den öffentlichen Sammlungen von Stammeskunst stellt eine Serie von Photocollagen von Hannah Höch her, die den Titel *Aus einem Völkerkundemuseum* trägt und von denen wir *Die Süße* und *Denkmal II – Eitelkeit,* beide 1926 entstanden, abbilden □ 795, 796. Diese verspotten die überkommenen europäischen Schönheitsideale durch Kombination von Photographien afrikanischer Skulptur mit gezeichneten und gemalten menschlichen Körperteilen. Jenes Völkerkundemuseum, auf das der Titel der Serie anspielt, ist nicht zu benennen, da Höch im Jahr der Entstehung dieser Collagen von Berlin nach Holland zog. Die afrikanischen Bildwerke, die sie benutzte, können dagegen identifiziert werden. Es handelt sich wahrscheinlich um eine *Chokwe*-Skulptur (Zaire) in *Denkmal II – Eitelkeit* und eine Maske in einem gabunischen Stil, möglicherweise der *Sogo*, in *Die Süße*.

Man Ray war auch ein Dadaist, dessen Werk primitiver Kunst nahesteht. Seine *Sculpture by Itself I* von 1918 □ 798 ist zu minimaler Figürlichkeit abstrahiert, die an primitive Stile, etwa die sparsame Ästhetik der *Dogon*-Masken, erinnert.[16] 1921 zog er von New York nach Paris, wo er sich an den Aktivitäten der Dadaisten beteiligte, die bald den Kern der surrealistischen Bewegung bilden sollten. Während dieser Zeit begünstigte der vorherrschende Stil der Art Deco modische Wiedergaben primitiver Formen. Man Rays Photographie *Noire et Blanche* von 1926 □ 797 ist ein eleganter und zugleich unheimlicher Kommentar zur Anwendung der »Art nègre« in der Art Deco. Das entkörperlichte, maskenhafte Gesicht des Modells kontrastiert gegen eine Maske im *Baule*-Stil mit überfeinerten Proportionen und auf Hochglanz polierter Oberfläche, die wohl zu der Vielzahl gewerblich hergestellter afrikanischer Objekte gehört, die damals populär waren.

Ein anderer wichtiger primitivistischer Aspekt des Dadaismus in Zürich war das Interesse an afrikanischer Figurenplastik, Dichtung und den sogenannten »chants nègres«, von Afrika inspirierte Lieder mit Trommelbegleitung. Der bedeutendste Vertreter dieser Richtung war Jancos Landsmann Tristan Tzara, der später auch eine wichtige Rolle in der Pariser Dada-Bewegung spielen sollte.

□ 797 *Man Ray, ›Noire et blanche‹, 1926, Silberdruck auf Seidenpapier, 22 x 28 cm. Galerie Zabriskie, New York.*

□ 798 *Man Ray, ›Sculpture by Itself I‹, 1918, Eisen, Holz und Kork, 43 x 18,5 x 19 cm. Westfälisches Landesmuseum für Kunst und Kulturgeschichte, Münster.*

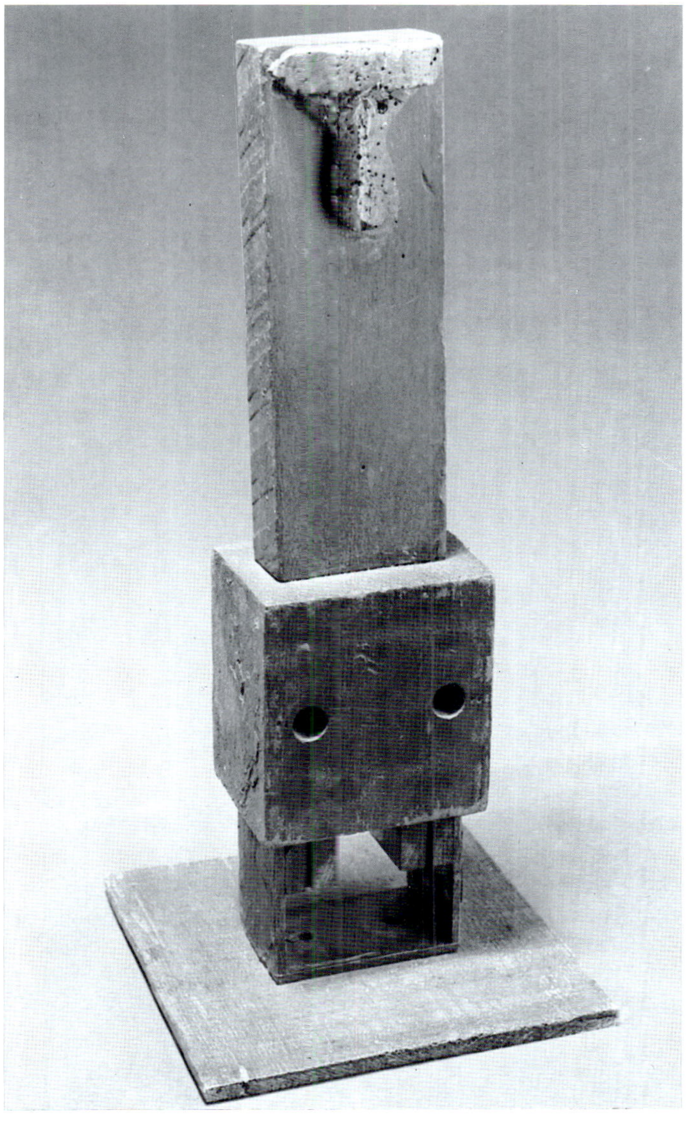

☐ 799 *›Bekrönung eines Kopfschmucks‹, Senufo (Mali), Holz, Höhe 60 cm. Sammlung Pierre Harter, Paris.*

Tzara, in der Zürcher Dada-Bewegung eines der aktivsten Mitglieder, war unter den Dada-Persönlichkeiten am stärksten an afrikanischer, ozeanischer Kunst und an der Idee des Primitivismus interessiert. Er scheint in Zürich auch der einzige Dadaist gewesen zu sein, der selbst eine afrikanische Skulptur besaß. Emmy Hennings, zusammen mit Hugo Ball Mitbegründer des Cabarets Voltaire, erzählte von einer Ausstellung in der Dada-Galerie von 1917, die, wie sie schreibt, um eine sehr schöne und teure afrikanische Skulptur, die Tzara gehörte, aufgebaut war. Dieses Werk war so eindrucksvoll, daß sich seine Präsenz in einem Raum, der mit Bildern von Kandinsky, Feininger, Klee und Campendonk vollhing, behauptete.[17]

Im gleichen Jahr publizierte Tzara einen kurzen Aufsatz zur afrikanischen und ozeanischen Kunst, dem 1929 Artikel über ozeanische und präkolumbianische Kunst folgten.[18] Der Aufsatz, »Note sur l'art nègre«, erschien in *SIC,* der futuristisch orientierten Pariser Kunstzeitschrift.[19] In diesem kurzen Essay unterstrich Tzara das Bedürfnis nach einer neuen Art der Darstellung von Gegenständen, die von den Beschränkungen traditioneller Definitionen und Assoziationen befreit sind. Kunst müsse auch über die bloße Darstellung von Oberflächenwerten und die sklavische Beschränkung auf äußere Naturformen hinausgehen, um ihre essentiellen inneren Werte in aller Wahrheit auszudrücken. Zur Illustration dieser Idee benutzte Tzara den Vergleich zweier Brüder, von denen einer das langweilige und begrenzte Vertrauen auf die Formen der Vergangenheit verkörpert, während sich der andere über die künstlerische Freiheit und kreative Kraft des Primitiven freut. Der primitive Bildhauer war nicht an westliche Proportionsregeln gebunden, er fühlte sich – wie die Dadaisten fälschlicher-

□ 800 *›Figur aus Holz‹, San Cristobal (Salomoninseln), bemaltes Holz und Federn, Höhe 72 cm. The Trustees of the British Museum, London.*

weise glaubten – keinen Formkonventionen unterworfen und schuf deshalb Skulpturen, die einem organischen Prozeß assoziativer Freiheit entsprangen. Hieraus leitete sich die Grundidee dadaistischen und surrealistischen Schaffens ab.

Tzara war von der Kunst der Primitiven nicht nur aus formalen Gründen heftig angezogen worden, sondern betrachtete sie auch als Ausdruck einer integrierten Lebensauffassung. In »Note sur l'art nègre« legte er die damals allgemein verbreitete Ansicht dar, daß die Kunst der Stammeskulturen das erste Beispiel menschlicher Kreativität in ihrer frühesten und reinsten Form darstellt. Tzara empfand, daß die Kunst auf dieser machtvollen Elementarstufe gleichermaßen die wechselseitigen Beziehungen der Dinge mit der Natur und die Assoziationskraft der Formen widerspiegle, um andere Bilder, Gefühle oder Ideen anzuregen, die auf den Prinzipien universeller Entsprechung beruhten. Besonders aufschlußreich ist, daß Tzara in dieser frühen Erklärung die schöpferischen Kräfte des Mundes wie die der Hand erwähnt. Hierin spiegelt sich sein eigenes Wirken als Dichter und eine weitere Verknüpfung zwischen Dada und Primitivismus auf dem Gebiet der Literatur und der darstellenden Künste.

»Negermusik«, Tanz und Dichtung zählten regelmäßig zu den Hauptbestandteilen Zürcher Dada-Aufführungen. Begleitet vom ununterbrochenen Trommeln Richard Huelsenbecks, der von afrikanischer Musik besessen war, trugen Tzara und andere ihre eigenen, von Afrika inspirierten Lieder vor. Später erklärte Tzara das Interesse, das Dada an den elementaren Eigenschaften primitiver Kunstäußerungen hatte, und ihre grundlegende soziale Notwendigkeit als Ausdruck der bewußten wie auch unbewußten schöpferischen Kräfte:
». . . die Kunst der primitiven Völker war ein wesentlicher Bestandteil ihrer sozialen und religiösen Struktur und erschien als der eigentliche Ausdruck ihres Lebens. DADA, das die ›dadaistische Spontaneität‹ befürwortete, wollte aus der Dichtkunst eher einen Lebensstil als den zufälligen Ausdruck von Intelligenz und Willen machen. Für DADA war Kunst eine Form jenes dichterischen Schaffens, das – allen Menschen gemeinsam – in seinen tiefen Wurzeln mit den primitiven Strukturen des Gefühlslebens verbunden ist. DADA versuchte diese Theorie in die Praxis umzusetzen, indem er die afrikanische und die ozeanische Kunst mit dem geistigen Leben in unmittelbarem Ausdruck vereinigte . . . durch Veranstaltung von NEGER-SOIREEN mit improvisiertem Tanz und Musik. DADA ging es darum, die herrlichen Quellen dichterischen Wirkens in den Tiefen des Bewußtseins wiederzuentdecken.«[20] Tzara bedeutete diese »primitive Dichtkunst« ein echter künstlerischer Ausdruck des Lebens, da diese im Dienste all seiner Tätigkeiten stand. In seiner »Note sur la poésie nègre« von 1918 faßte Tzara diesen Standpunkt in der Feststellung zusammen, daß »man dann einen Organismus erschafft, wenn die Bestandteile dem Leben ganz nahe sind. Die Dichtkunst lebt zuerst bezogen auf die Aufgaben von Tanz, Religion, Musik und Arbeit.«[21]

In seinem großen Enthusiasmus für den Primitivismus übersetzte Tzara auch ozeanische Gesänge für die Zeitschrift *Dada*. Die Gesänge dienten als Muster »primitiver Kunst« und als Modell für die »pseudoafrikanische« Sprache des Dada, wie es einige Kommentatoren ausdrückten.[22] Alle drei »poèmes nègres« stellten Fassungen totemistischer Mythen aus der mündlichen Überlieferung der Stämme australischer Ureinwohner dar.[23] Die Gesänge werfen nicht nur ein Licht auf das Interesse des Dada an den Elementarformen des Primitiven, sondern auch am Mythischen als einer wesentlichen Vorbedingung künstlerischer Tätigkeit. Der Dadaismus suchte nach einer philosophischen und künstlerischen Alternative zu den traditionellen europäischen Verfahren, die er als psychologisch und ästhetisch einengend ansah. Der Primitivismus bot dem Dadaismus ein überzeugendes Modell, das später auch der surrealistischen Bewegung von Nutzen sein sollte.

Der Surrealismus wurde in den frühen zwanziger Jahren von einer Gruppe französischer Schriftsteller und Dichter begründet, die als Mitglieder der Dada-Bewegung neue Wege suchten, um die soziale und künstlerische Umgebung, die sie als bedrückend und unerträglich empfanden, aufzurütteln. Auf ihrer Suche nach einem frischen Zugang zum Leben, nach einer

neuen Weltsicht, konnten sich die Surrealisten auf eine starke Avantgarde-Tradition stützen, bei der Veränderungen hoch im Kurs standen. Die Surrealisten waren entschlossen, eine umfassende Philosophie des Lebens wie auch der Kunst zu entwickeln. Ihre Interessen, die in erster Linie literarisch waren, schlossen einen engen Kontakt nicht nur mit den zeitgenössischen Entwicklungen in der Literatur und der bildenden Kunst ein, sondern auch mit Philosophie, Anthropologie, Psychologie und Politik. Dieser etwas eklektische intellektuelle Hintergrund setzte sie weitreichenden und oftmals disparaten Einflüssen aus, die auf ihre Entwicklung ganz unterschiedlich einwirkten. Viele dieser Einflüsse resultierten aus einem direkten Interesse am Primitiven, während andere zu Ideen über die Elementarformen menschlichen Bewußtsein anregten, worin sich Auffassungen ähnlich jenen widerspiegelten, die man an der Basis primitiver Erfahrungen zu wissen glaubte.

Drei Grundzüge der surrealistischen Philosophie waren die Überzeugung, daß der Traum einen gültigen und integralen Bestandteil menschlicher Erfahrungen darstellt, der Glaube an die schöpferische Kraft des Unbewußten sowie die Überzeugung, daß eine universale Notwendigkeit für den Mythos besteht, der – einer allen Menschen gemeinsamen geistigen Instanz entspringend – die Völker aller Zivilisationen verbindet. Vom Beginn der Bewegung an studierten die Surrealisten die Ideen und Schöpfungen der Philosophen und Künstler, um Anregungen zu erhalten und bei der Formulierung und Rechtfertigung ihrer eigenen Philosophie historisch unterstützt zu werden.

Auf ihrer Suche nach Vorgängern wurden die Surrealisten nicht nur von den Erzeugnissen des primitiven Menschen angezogen, sondern auch von seinem Weltbild, einem Thema, das während des 19. und 20. Jahrhunderts von einer Vielzahl von Völkerkundlern, Anthropologen, Psychologen und Philosophen immer eingehender untersucht worden war. Nach Auffassung der damit befaßten Gelehrten verkörpert die Mentalität des Primitiven gerade jene Qualitäten, die die Surrealisten verzweifelt in ihr eigenes Leben und ihre Kunst zu integrieren versuchten. Wir können das Wesen dieser von Europa ausgehenden Deutung des Primitiven, die den Hintergrund der surrealistischen Theorie bildete, stellvertretend mit den Schriften von vier wichtigen Autoren näher definieren, mit denen die Surrealisten vertraut waren: Sir James Frazer, der umfangreiche Studien zur Mythologie betrieb, Lucien Lévy-Bruhl, Sigmund Freud und Henri Bergson.

Frazer glaubte an das Vorhandensein einer gemeinsamen menschlichen Mentalität, die sich in der Ähnlichkeit offenbart, wie Völker verschiedener geographischer Standorte, Kulturen und Zeitperioden ihre Beziehung zur Welt, in der sie leben, zu Bildern verdichten und ausdrücken. Unter den Surrealisten sehr beliebt war *The Golden Bough (Der goldene Zweig)*, ein gewaltiges kulturelles Quellenbuch, in dem eine Anzahl von Grundthemen menschlichen Denkens von Tausenden von Beispielen illustriert wird, angefangen bei den Mythen und Legenden der Antike des Orients, der europäischen Volkskultur bis hin zu den primitiven Kulturen Afrikas, Ozeaniens, Nord- und Südamerikas.

Einer von Frazers wichtigsten Beiträgen zum Studium des primitiven Geistes war seine Untersuchung über die Funktion

□ 801 *›Figürliches Brett‹, Sawos, Provinz Ost-Sepik (Papua-Neuguinea), bemaltes Holz, Höhe 208 cm, Sammlung Milton und F. Rosenthal.*

des Traumes. Mit vielen verblüffenden und oft reizvollen Darstellungen demonstrierte *The Golden Bough* den unausgesprochenen Glauben des primitiven Menschen, daß seine Träume ein wesentlicher und wichtiger Bestandteil des alltäglichen Lebens sind und daß diese Erfahrungen der Seele und des Geistes auf sein Verhalten genauso einwirken wie die Ereignisse und Gedanken, die seine wachen Stunden aktivieren. Darüber hinaus führte Frazer zahlreiche Beispiele an, die belegen, daß das Traumleben des primitiven Menschen als Ausdruck einer höheren Ebene von Wahrheit als die der Erfahrungen seines wachen Bewußtseins betrachtet wird. Am Beispiel des *Gran Chaco*-Stammes berichtet er, daß »die Indianer fest davon überzeugt sind, was [die Träume] erzählen, denn diese wundervollen Abenteuer sind einfach ihre Träume, die sie von erlebten Realitäten nicht unterscheiden.«[24]

In *The Golden Bough* zeigte Frazer auch, daß die Menschen in den primitiven Kulturen sich selbst als Lebewesen in einem Universum erfahren, in dem jeder Gegenstand und alle Naturkräfte von einer Seele oder einem als gleichrangig anerkannten Geist angeregt sind.

Solch ein Weltbild führte diese Menschen zwangsläufig zu einem viel engeren Verhältnis gegenüber ihrer Umgebung, denn sie betrachteten die Gegenstände, die Flora und die Fauna, mit denen sie zusammenlebten, als Träger einer geistigen Kraft. Diese schienen ihnen zur gleichen Art von Reaktion und Aktion befähigt wie die Lebenskraft, die ihrer eigenen Existenz Energie spendete. So unterhält das glückliche Mitglied einer primitiven Kultur eine harmonische Beziehung zu den Kräften der Natur, ganz im Gegensatz zum modernen westlichen Menschen, der dazu neigt, seine Spezies als der Natur überlegen zu betrachten und sich deshalb von ihr physisch und psychisch abgrenzt. Frazers Untersuchung der dualistischen Struktur der primitiven Weltsicht und der Bedeutung des Traumes war ein großer Schritt in der Entwicklung des europäischen Bewußtseins und Verständnisses für die Kultur der Primitiven.

Während der ersten drei Jahrzehnte des 20. Jahrhunderts begründeten französische Wissenschaftler eine einflußreiche Tradition anthropologischer Forschung. Einer der geistigen Väter dieser Bewegung war Lucien Lévy-Bruhl, der sich großer Popularität erfreute und besonders unter den Surrealisten einflußreich war. In seinen zwei wichtigsten Veröffentlichungen, *Les Fonctions mentales dans les sociétés inférieures*, 1910, und *La mentalité primitive*, 1922, suchte Lévy-Bruhl die grundlegenden Unterschiede zu definieren, wie die Angehörigen der primitiven und der zeitgenössischen westlichen Kulturen die Welt betrachten und wie sie ihre Beziehungen zu ihr gestalten. Seine Hauptthese war, daß der primitive Mensch die Welt auf einem dualistischen Prinzip aufbaut, das großen Wert auf die mystischen spirituellen Kräfte legt, die alle Dinge beleben und jede Art von Kausalität aufrecht erhalten. Wie Frazer und andere, die über dieses Thema schrieben, behauptete auch Lévy-Bruhl, daß der Traum der wichtigste Berührungspunkt zwischen physischer Realität und den kausal nur schwer faßbaren geistigen Wesenheiten sei.[25] Er betrachtete es als eines der wichtigsten Merkmale der primitiven Gesellschaft, daß sich ihre Mitglieder in einem Zustand ununterbrochenen Austausches zwischen materieller zeitlicher Realität und den Bereichen der Geister erlebten.[26] Aus diesen Gründen waren Lévy-

☐ 802 *›Figur aus Holz‹*, *Abelam*, *Provinz Ost-Sepik (Papua-Neuguinea), bemaltes Holz, Höhe 305 cm. Sammlung Friede, New York.*

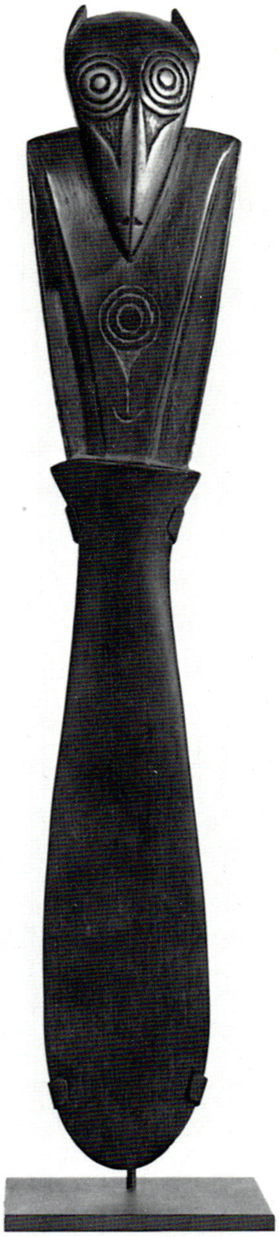

☐ 803 *›Spatel mit fliegendem Fuchs‹, Trobriandinseln, Provinz Milne Bay (Papua-Neuguinea), Holz, Höhe 26 cm. Sammlung Friede, New York.*

Bruhls Theorien für die Surrealisten besonders attraktiv, die die Fähigkeit zu entwickeln suchten, den Traum und das unbewußte Denken als Mittel zu benutzen, um die bewußte Erfahrung zu erhellen und den kreativen Prozeß zu bereichern.

In seinen Untersuchungen über primitive Wahrnehmungen und Erkenntnisse legte Lévy-Bruhl besonderen Nachdruck auf die Bedeutung des Totemismus – eines Systems, bei dem sich eine bestimmte gesellschaftliche Einheit mit einem Naturelement, Pflanze und Tier, identifiziert und dieses als seinen Leitgeist und Wächter anerkennt. Obwohl sich der Einzelne mit nur einem bestimmten Naturelement in Verbindung bringt, ist er sich bewußt, daß die anderen Tiere, Pflanzen und Naturkräfte in der Welt auf dieselbe mystische Weise mit anderen Gruppen verbunden sind. Das daraus entstehende von allen getragene Einvernehmen unterliegt dem, was Lévy-Bruhl den Vorgang der kollektiven Darstellung nannte. Er erläuterte, daß »für den Primitiven, der einer totemistischen Gemeinschaft angehört, jedes Tier, jede Pflanze, selbst jeder Gegenstand wie etwa die Sonne, der Mond, die Sterne am Totem Anteil hat . . . Selbst in Gemeinschaften, in der diese Form nicht lebendig ist, ist die kollektive Darstellung bestimmter Tiere (wahrscheinlich aller, wenn die Forschung vollständiger wäre) von ihrem Wesen her mystisch.«[27]

Die totemistische Rolle von spirituell verlebendigten Pflanzen- und Tierformen, wie sie Lévy-Bruhl beschrieb, ist – so werden wir noch sehen – für das Werk surrealistischer Künstler, allen voran André Masson und Max Ernst, von großer Bedeutung.

Die Beziehung zwischen Lévy-Bruhls Theorie des primitiven Weltbildes und den Interessen der Surrealisten wurde 1945 von Jules Monnerot in »La poésie moderne et le sacré« zur Diskussion gestellt, worin der Autor den Traum und den Mythos als die wichtigsten gemeinsamen Elemente von Primitivismus und Surrealismus hervorhob. Monnerots Schrift ist insofern besonders wichtig, als sie von André Breton sehr freudig begrüßt wurde, der schrieb, daß sie einen »hervorragenden Nachweis der Verwandtschaft zwischen surrealistischem Denken und jenem der Indianer« erbringe.[28]

Die Persönlichkeit, die den stärksten Einfluß auf die Entwicklung der ideologischen Verbindungen der Surrealisten mit dem Primitivismus ausübte, war Sigmund Freud. Die *Traumdeutung*, 1905 publiziert, schenkte der modernen Psychoanalyse den Glauben an die Gültigkeit der Phänomene des Traumes, die hier in bezug auf das primitive Denken untersucht werden. Freud postulierte, daß all die verborgenen Empfindungen und Gefühle, denen der Mensch in seinem wachen Bewußtsein aus dem Wege gehe, während der Traumperiode metaphorisch verkleidet Gestalt annähmen. Der Schlüssel zu seinen traumkritischen Theorien war deshalb die Verbindung der Prozesse freier Assoziation mit der Interpretation der Traumsymbole. Diese beiden Methoden waren für die Surrealisten von großer Bedeutung, deren Interesse an Träumen und Traumsymbolismus den Wunsch nährte, die Quellen des Unbewußten für Kunstwerke zugänglich zu machen, um ihnen die tiefe suggestive und bewußtseinserweiternde Kraft wirklicher Traumerfahrungen zu geben.

Auch Freuds *Totem und Tabu* von 1913 hatte auf viele Surrealisten sowie auf deren Interesse und Verständnis für das Primitive großen Einfluß. In diesem Werk versuchte Freud, die Kluft zwischen sozialer Anthropologie, Folklore und Psychologie zu überbrücken, um aus den in der westlichen Kultur nurmehr im Kindheitsalter rudimentär erkennbaren Überresten des Totemismus auf seine ursprüngliche Bedeutung zu schließen. Dementsprechend versuchte diese Schrift, eine Beziehung zwischen dem Denken der Primitiven und gewissen psychologischen Phänomenen herzustellen, die in der westlichen Gesellschaft noch lebendig sind, um beide besser zu verstehen. Freuds Vorwort zu *Totem und Tabu* wies darauf hin, daß heute noch Menschen leben, die in ihrer psychologischen Struktur den frühesten Menschen, den »ersten« Primitiven nahestehen:

»Es leben Menschen, von denen wir glauben, daß sie den Primitiven noch sehr nahestehen, viel näher als wir, in denen wir daher die direkten Abkömmlinge und Vertreter der früheren Menschen erblicken. Wir urteilen so über die sogenannten Wilden . . . deren Seelenleben ein besonderes Interesse für uns gewinnt, wenn wir in ihm eine gut erhaltene Vorstufe unserer eigenen Entwicklung erkennen dürfen. Wenn diese

☐ 804 *›Maske‹*, SULKA *(Neubritannien), bemaltes Mark, Holz und Federn, Höhe 120 cm. Übersee-Museum, Bremen.*

□ 805 *Ausstellung surrealistischer Objekte in der Galerie Charles Ratton, Paris, 1936.*

Voraussetzungen zutreffend sind, so wird eine Vergleichung der ›Psychologie der Naturvölker‹, wie die Völkerkunde sie lehrt, mit der Psychologie des Neurotikers, wie sie durch die Psychoanalyse bekannt geworden ist, zahlreiche Übereinstimmungen aufweisen müssen und wird uns gestatten, bereits Bekanntes hier und dort in neuem Licht zu sehen.«[29]

Indem er vielfach auf die Ideen von Frazer und Lévy-Bruhl wie auch anderer namhafter Völkerkundler Bezug nahm, bestätigte Freud das dualistische Weltbild der Primitiven, das er in den Begriffen Volk, Körperseele, Ding oder Ding-Seele sprachlich faßte. Er schrieb auch, daß Ursächlichkeit in der Gesellschaft der Primitiven geistigen Kräften zugeschrieben wird, und, Frazers *The Golden Bough* folgend, betonte er nachdrücklich die Macht homöopathischer Zauberei oder den Glauben der Primitiven an die Macht geistiger Kräfte, um auf die Welt einzuwirken. Freud nannte diese Energie die »Allmacht der Gedanken«.

Im Kapitel »Animismus, Magie und Allmacht der Gedanken« zu *Totem und Tabu* behandelte Freud die Rolle der Kunst in ihrer Beziehung zur menschlichen Psychologie:

»Nur auf einem Gebiete ist auch in unserer Kultur die Allmacht der Gedanken erhalten geblieben, auf dem der Kunst. In der Kunst allein kommt es noch vor, daß ein von Wünschen verzehrter Mensch etwas der Befriedigung Ähnliches macht . . . Mit Recht spricht man vom Zauber der Kunst und vergleicht den Künstler mit einem Zauberer. Aber dieser Vergleich ist vielleicht bedeutsamer, als er zu sein beansprucht. Die Kunst, die gewiß nicht als ›l'art pour l'art‹ begonnen hat, stand ursprünglich im Dienste von Tendenzen, die heute zum großen Teil erloschen sind. Unter diesen lassen sich mancherlei magische Absichten vermuten.«[30]

Daß dieses Bild des Künstlers als eines Magiers, das im vergangenen Jahrhundert von Baudelaire und Mallarmé gebraucht wurde, gerade für den surrealistischen Künstler zutrifft, wird sich bei der Erörterung des Werkes von MAX ERNST und WIFREDO LAM erweisen. Im Kapitel »Die infantile Wiederkehr des Totemismus« in *Totem und Tabu* fand Freud mit der Theorie des Ödipuskomplexes eine Erklärung für das Phänomen des totemistischen Clans. Diese Deutung sah zwischen bestimmten geistigen Zuständen des modernen Menschen und dem primitiven Geist eine klare Analogie. Die Auswirkungen dieser Theorie werden, wie noch zu zeigen sein wird, einen großen Einfluß auf das Werk von ERNST ausüben, der Freuds Schriften aus den Jahren vor dem Ersten Weltkrieg, als er an der Universität Bonn Psychologie studierte, gut kannte.

Henri Bergson untersuchte das Unbewußte und den Traum zur gleichen Zeit, als Lévy-Bruhl und Freud ihre Ergebnisse veröffentlichten. Er stützte viele seiner Theorien auf das Primat der Intuition im geistigen Prozeß des Menschen. Vorläufer dieser Auffassung war eine Reihe von Denkern des 19. Jahrhunderts, von denen die Symbolisten beeinflußt waren und die nun gleichermaßen die Surrealisten inspirierten, als sie nach schöpferischen Alternativen zu dem beschränkten Rationalismus der traditionellen westlichen Gesellschaft Ausschau hielten. Bergsons Philosophie, die den Surrealisten in ihrer Ganzheit vertraut war, setzte eine dualistische Welt voraus, in der die Kräfte des Verstandes und der abstrakte Intellekt dem »élan vital« fremd waren, jener schöpferischen Lebenskraft, die durch die Intuition geleitet wird. So wie der primitive Mensch seine Welt als ein räumliches und zeitliches Amalgam von Geist und Materie erlebt, so erkannte Bergson im gegenseitigen Durchdringen von Raum und Zeit zu einer großen wogenden Masse ewigen Wandels – dem eigentlichen Rhythmus des Lebens – das Hauptmerkmal der aufwärtsgerichteten Lebensbewegung und Evolution. »La durée«, dieses Stadium unbestimmbarer Dauer, in dem sich der Geist des Lebensimpulses frei bewegen kann, steht der europäischen Auffassung des primitiven Geistes sehr nahe, derzufolge sich Vergangenheit, Gegenwart und Zukunft in einem Zustand ständiger Kommunikation befinden. In dieser Hinsicht können die surrealistischen Künstler und die Menschen primitiver Gesellschaften, wie sie von den hier erwähnten Gelehrten geschildert wurden, als die Verwirklichung von Bergsons einflußreicher Philosophie der Lebenskraft gesehen werden, die sich für ihn in der positiven Richtung bewegt.

In den frühen Jahren des Surrealismus entwickelte sich das Interesse an primitiver Kunst auf der Seite der Galerien und Kunstzeitschriften parallel zur wachsenden Bewunderung bei den Mitgliedern der surrealistischen Gruppe. Unter den vielen Autoren, die über primitive Kunst schrieben, hatte der Dichter Guillaume Apollinaire den direktesten Draht zu den Surrealisten. Bereits 1912 erwähnte Apollinaire die primitiven Künste Ozeaniens und Afrikas in seinem Gedicht »Zone«. Hier beschreibt er eine Person, die wenig Wert auf die traditionellen Formen westlicher Kultur legt. Nach einem Tag aufmerksamen Suchens »gehst Du zu Fuß nach Auteuil nach Hause, um inmitten Deiner Fetische aus Ozeanien und Guinea zu schlafen, sie sind wie Christus in anderer Gestalt oder anderen Glaubens, sie sind weniger ein Christus dunkler Erwartungen«.[31] Apollinaires Interesse an primitiven Gegenständen und an der Glaubenswelt jener Kulturen, aus denen sie kamen, bestätigt sein Vorwort zu dem Buch *Sculptures nègres*, das der Pariser Kunsthändler Paul Guillaume 1917 veröffentlichte. Im April des gleichen Jahres schrieb Apollinaire einen Artikel über »Fetischistische Skulptur der schwarzen Rassen«, dem in der populären Zeitschrift *Mercure de France* eine größere Leserschaft bestimmt war.

Während der Pariser Frühzeit des Surrealismus vervielfachte sich die Zahl der Bücher und Artikel, die der primitiven Kultur

□ 806 *›Maske‹*, BAINING *(Neubritannien), bemalter Rindenstoff, Rahmen aus Rohr, Höhe 99 cm. Hamburgisches Museum für Völkerkunde.*

□ 807 *›Maske und Tanzkostüm‹,* ASMAT *(Irian Jaya), bemaltes Holz, Bambus, Fasern und andere Materialien, Höhe 170 cm. The Metropolitan Museum of Art, The M. C. Rockefeller Memorial Collection, Schenkung N. A. und M. C. Rockefeller, New York.*

und Kunst gewidmet waren. Als die Galerie Devambez 1919 eine der ersten Ausstellungen afrikanischer und ozeanischer Kunst in Paris organisierte, veröffentlichten André Clouzot und René Level *L'Art nègre et l'art océanien.* Dieser Trend setzte sich im folgenden Jahr mit dem Erscheinen des Artikels »Opinions sur l'art nègre« in der Zeitschrift *Action* fort, der auf Erklärungen PICASSOS, GRIS', LIPCHITZ', COCTEAUS und anderer ausführlich einging.[32] Die wachsende Popularität der primitiven Kunst und des sie begleitenden Primitivismus spiegelt sich in der Folge auch in der steigenden Veröffentlichung von Material über die Primitiven in den Kunstzeitschriften der späten zwanziger und dreißiger Jahre, vor allem den *Documents, Cahiers d'art, La Révolution surréaliste* und *Minotaure.*[33]

Während sich dieses zunehmende Interesse am Primitivismus auf wissenschaftlichem und literarischem Gebiet zeigte, waren auch viele Mitglieder der surrealistischen Gruppe selbst aktive Sammler primitiver Kunst. Es wurde bereits darauf hingewiesen, daß Tzara eine afrikanische Skulptur besaß, als er sich in Zürich aufhielt. Als er Ende 1919 nach Paris zog, hielt sein Interesse am Sammeln an – das nun von vielen seiner Kollegen geteilt wurde. Zwei hervorragende frühe Sammlungen waren die von Breton und Paul Eluard. Die Vorliebe der Surrealisten für die Kunst Ozeaniens, der nordamerikanischen Indianer und der ESKIMOS vor derjenigen Afrikas belegt die Auktionsliste der beiden vereinigten Sammlungen, die als Folge der äußerst schwierigen Finanzlage im Juli 1931 im Hôtel Drouot zum Verkauf angeboten wurden. Bei einer Gesamtzahl von 312 Objekten stammten 30 aus Afrika, 134 aus Ozeanien, 124 aus Nord- und Südamerika, 14 aus Malaysia, 7 waren »diverser« Herkunft.[34] Die Breton-Eluard-Auktion war eine der wichtigsten Versteigerungen primitiver Kunst, die zwischen den beiden Weltkriegen in Paris stattfand. Ihr Umfang weist darauf hin, daß neues Material viel leichter zugänglich war und dessen Vielfalt den unterschiedlichsten Vorlieben entsprach.

Primitive Kunst war auch in verschiedenen Ausstellungen vertreten, die die Surrealisten selbst organisierten. Die erste in dieser Reihe war die Eröffnungsausstellung der Galerie Surréaliste in Paris am 16. März 1926, die das Werk von MAN RAY vorstellte, daneben eine Auswahl von ozeanischen Objekten aus den Sammlungen Bretons, Eluards, Louis Aragons und anderer. Ein anderes wichtiges Ereignis dieser Art war die »Ausstellung surrealistischer Objekte« von 1936, die zwischen dem 22. und 29. Mai in der Galerie von Charles Ratton stattfand, dem bekannten Pariser Händler für primitive Kunst □ 805. Zwischen den bunt zusammengewürfelten Stücken befand sich eine große Auswahl von Objekten der primitiven Kulturen Ozeaniens und Amerikas. Sie standen unmittelbar neben Naturgegenständen, interpretierten Objekten sowie Objekten von surrealistischen Künstlern und Dichtern.[35] Demselben Muster folgte 1936 die »International Surrealist Exhibition« in London, die von einer Gruppe englischer Künstler mit Unterstützung von Breton, Eluard und MAN RAY organisiert wurde. Die Ausstellung umfaßte über vierhundert Gemälde, Skulpturen und Gegenstände, darunter viele Objekte aus Afrika, Ozeanien, Nord- und Südamerika.[36] Die meisten Exponate beider Ausstellungen waren Leihgaben aus den Sammlungen surrealistischer Künstler.

Die primitive Gesellschaft fand die Antwort auf Lebensfragen in der geistigen Welt und im Bereich des Traumes. Die Surrealisten begaben sich auf einen ähnlichen Weg, indem sie primitive Künste und Kulturen studierten. Man erkannte, daß in den primitiven Gesellschaften die Beziehung zwischen der Kunst und dem schöpferischen Akt stark von der Magie beeinflußt wird, ein Thema, das eine weitere Verbindung zwischen den Surrealisten und den Primitiven eröffnet. Für den Primitiven ist ein Gegenstand insofern magisch, als er eine Kraft verkörpert. In der surrealistischen Philosophie ist die Fähigkeit eines Objektes, geistige Bilder und durch sie kraftvolle Gefühle zu beschwören, ein Maß für das »Wunderbare«. Breton sucht nach einer Methode, mit deren Hilfe der zeitgenössische Künstler Formen schaffen könnte, die den gleichen Grad von psychischer Kraft und assoziativer Bedeutung hätten wie die Gegenstände des primitiven Künstler-Magiers. In seiner Künstlerrolle kommt daher der Surrealist der primitiven Kultur am nächsten, denn in seiner Kunst, in der sprachlichen wie der bildenden, vermag er seine Bestrebungen und Ideale am besten zu verwirklichen.

In seiner Rolle als »l'homme révolté« war Breton Lautréamonts Maldoror sehr ähnlich, einer Figur, die er bewunderte und imitierte, indem er sein eigenes Leben in eine Suche nach neuen Wegen umwandelte, um ein besseres Verhältnis zur Welt zu gewinnen. Diese Suche führte Lautréamonts Maldoror und Breton in einen Zustand des Seins, der eine engere Verbindung und eine geistige Vereinigung mit den grundlegenden Elemen-

☐ 808 *André Masson, ›Apollo und Daphne‹ (Apollo et Daphne), 1933, Öl auf Leinwand, 89 x 116 cm. Privatsammlung.*

☐ 809 *André Masson, ›Die Legende vom Mais‹ (La légende du mais), 1943, Tempera auf Holz, 50 x 61 cm. Privatsammlung.*

ten der Welt zur Folge hatte, dies auf eine Weise, die beide den primitiven Menschen zuschrieben. Clifford Browder schrieb 1967 über André Bretons Verhältnis zur Kunst und Kultur der Primitiven:

»Es ist nicht überraschend, daß Breton schon früh ein Interesse an primitiver Kunst entwickelte . . . und daß er amerikanische Indianerreservate besuchte und Zeuge von Voodoo-Zeremonien auf Haiti war, die den lebendigen Beweis erbrachten, daß jener besondere Geisteszustand, den der Surrealismus kultivieren wollte, bei den Wilden überlebt hatte. Insofern als sie der ›Ansteckung‹ durch das Christentum entgangen waren, boten die primitiven Gesellschaften Breton das Schauspiel des in Harmonie mit der Natur lebenden Menschen, der den sprudelnden Lebensimpulsen, die in der westlichen Kultur unterdrückt wurden, ungehinderten Ausdruck verlieh. Konsequenterweise lag für letztere die Hoffnung nicht im anthropologischen Studium solcher Gesellschaften, sondern in der Erneuerung ihrer Erlebnisfähigkeit. Durch Anwendung dieser kühnen Phantasie und Naivität, die dem Kind und dem wilden Menschen eigen sind, entdeckte man wieder das verlorene Paradies des *surréel.*«[37]

Breton rühmte die Kunst der Indianer und Ozeaniens wegen des mutigen Nebeneinanders von skulpturaler Plastizität und zweidimensionaler Dekoration, mit der sie natürliche und

□ 810 *André Masson, ›An den Ufern der Langeweile‹ (Sur les rives de l'ennui), 1938, Feder und Tusche. Aus den „Mythologies", 1946.*

□ 811 *André Masson, ›Die Erde‹ (La terre), 1939, Sand und Öl auf Holz, 43 x 53 cm. Musée National d'Art Moderne, Centre National d'Art et de Culture Georges Pompidou, Paris.*

geistige Sinnbilder ausdrückten. Er fühlte, daß ihm hier ein Modell für die beschwörende Bildersprache vorlag, die er in seiner Dichtung suchte. »Sie sehen, welche Beweiskraft diese Gegenstände für die surrealistische Vision haben, welche neuen geistigen Flüge sie sogar für uns bereithalten«, sagte er von seiner Sammlung. »Diese Eskimo-Maske stellt einen Schwan dar, der den Jäger in den Frühling führt. . . . In der zinnenartigen Frisur [einer Katchina-Figur der *Hopi*] finden Sie die Wolken über dem Berg, in der Mitte dieses Schachbrettes eine kleine Kornähre, einen Regenbogen um den Mund, in den senkrechten Streifen ihres Kleides sehen Sie, wie der Regen ins Tal fällt.«[38]

Die Beschwörung der natürlichen Umgebung primitiver Kulturen findet sich als Thema in vielen Werken Bretons. Die fremdartigen und verlockenden Bilder von wilder, unberührter Natur spielen eine große Rolle in *Martinique charmeuse de serpents (Reizendes Martinique, voll von Schlangen),* das er 1948 zusammen mit Masson schrieb. 1937 veröffentlichte Breton das Buch *L'Amour fou (Die verrückte Liebe),* in dem er exotische Pflanzen und Szenerien beschrieb, die für ihn die Verkörperung wundervollen Widersinns und geheimnisvoller Wunder waren, die einzig die von moderner Künstelei verschonte Natur hervorbringen kann. Die Natur, die er verherrlicht, ist zeitlos, liegt in Ozeanien und ist tief in einer ursprünglichen Vergangenheit verwurzelt – eine Natur, die den Menschen transzendiert und ihn doch über die Barrieren und Begrenzungen augenfälliger täglicher Realitäten hinausführen kann. Breton sah in diesen primitiven und beschwörenden Naturszenerien eine »Traumwelt« (»un pays de rêve«),[39] in der die Einschränkungen der Gesellschaft gebrochen sind und ein Zustand natürlicher Harmonie herrscht, die dem Menschen erlaubt, die tiefen, angeborenen Wünsche des Traumes und des Unbewußten auszuleben.

Bretons lange und gründliche Beschäftigung mit der Kunst und dem Leben der primitiven Kulturen erreichte 1957 mit *L'Art magique (Die magische Kunst)* ihren Höhepunkt. Ein langatmiges, abschweifendes und leider an vielen Stellen unzusammenhängendes Buch, das nicht viele neue Informationen zum überlieferten Wissen über die Verbindungen zwischen Surrealismus und Primitivismus beisteuert. Aber es hilft Bretons tiefes Gefühl und Verständnis, die Vielschichtigkeit und den Typenreichtum primitiver Kunst, insofern als es um Theorien des Magischen geht, vor Augen zu führen. Es erläutert auch, wie Breton die primitiven Kunstformen mit den Bildern in Beziehung brachte, die von den Magiern, den Okkultisten und Alchimisten der europäischen Geschichte benutzt wurden, wodurch er ein weiteres Bindeglied zwischen westlichen und primitiven Kulturen herstellte.

Wie Breton beschäftigte sich auch ANDRÉ MASSON mit dem Primitivismus sowohl intellektuell wie auch künstlerisch. 1943 schuf MASSON ein Gemälde, das jene überkulturellen Verbindungen zwischen klassischen und primitiven Mythen widerspiegelt, die seit den zwanziger Jahren einen so großen Einfluß auf seine Entwicklung hatten. Das Gemälde *Die Legende vom Mais* □ 809 behandelt eine Legende der *IROKESEN* über die mystische Beziehung zwischen der Korngöttin und der Sonne. MASSONS Quelle für den Mythos war Frazers *The Golden Bough*,[40] doch zog ihn zum Teil auch die Analogie zur klassischen Legende von Apollo und Daphne an, die er bereits 1933 malerisch umgesetzt hatte □ 808. Es ist bezeichnend, daß MASSON *Die Legende vom Mais* malte, als er in den Vereinigten Staaten lebte – als hätte ihm die Nähe zur Heimat der indianischen Legende die notwendige Inspiration für dieses Bild gegeben, das von seiner Komposition der früheren Fassung dieses klassischen Mythos sehr ähnelt.[41] In beiden Bildern geht die Bewegung von links nach rechts, indem der Sonnengott das unwillige weibliche Wesen verfolgt, das im Schrecken zurückschaut, während es dem Rand des Gemäldes entgegen flüchtet. Beide Mythen folgen dem gleichen Grundmuster von Wunsch, Konflikt, Jagd, Anziehung und der Verwandlung, die zur Bindung der anthropomorphen Wesen an die pflanzlichen Formen des Lorbeers und des Korns führt. Der Reiz beider Mythen lag für MASSON in der Darstellung der menschlichen Fähigkeit zu physischer Vereinigung mit anderen Aspekten der Natur. Beide setzen voraus, daß nicht nur Pflanzen und Bäume, Erde und Steine einen Geist als bewegende Kraft besitzen, dessen Quelle und Macht mit der des Menschen identisch ist, auch die Menschen selbst stehen in einer physischen Verwandtschaft mit den Naturelementen und haben die Fähigkeit der körperlichen Verwandlung, die von der Metamorphose symbolisiert und offenbart wird.

Die Legende vom Mais ist das Werk, das immer zuerst genannt wird, um MASSONS Interesse an den primitiven Mythologien zu illustrieren. Es gibt jedoch noch andere Mythen und Märchen primitiver Kulturen, die MASSON gut kannte und die ihm als Anregung für viele seiner Darstellungen der menschlich-pflanzlichen Metamorphose dienten. Wir brauchen uns nur MASSONS bevorzugter Quelle primitiver Mythologie – *The Golden Bough* – zuzuwenden, um mehrere Stellen zu finden, die sich auf die symbolische und rituelle Umwandlung des Menschen in eine Pflanze beziehen. In seinem Kapitel »Menschliche Darstellungen der Baumgeister« leitet Frazer eine Anzahl von Beispielen mit folgender Bemerkung ein:

»Die Darstellung des Baum- oder Vegetationsgeistes durch einen Baum, einen Zweig oder eine Blume wird manchmal ganz fallengelassen, während seine Darstellung durch eine lebende Person übrigbleibt. In diesem Fall wird der darstellende Charakter der Person normalerweise dadurch gekennzeichnet, daß er oder sie wie eine Pflanze mit Blättern oder Blumen bekleidet ist . . .«[42]

Wir werden die Bedeutung dieser Auffassung für MASSONS Werk nachweisen, wenn wir zwei andere wichtige Quellen für seine Bilder der Mensch-Pflanzen-Metamorphose betrachtet haben. Diese beziehen Gegenstände der primitiven Kunst – vor allem der ozeanischen – mit ein, ebenso die Literatur, worin diese behandelt werden.

□ 812 *André Masson, ›Morgenröte bei Montserrat‹, 1935, Öl auf Leinwand, 51 x 66 cm. Snite Museum of Art, Universität Notre Dame. Ständige Leihgabe von Dr. R. H. Stern.*

□ 813 *›Osterinsel‹, Feder- und Tuschezeichnung von Pierre Loti, 1872.*

☐ 814 *Max Ernst, ›Der Elefant von Celebes‹, 1921, Öl auf Leinwand, 125 x 108 cm. The Trustees of the Tate Gallery, London.*

Seit dem Beginn des 20. Jahrhunderts hat die wissenschaftliche Untersuchung der primitiven Kunst zur Erkenntnis geführt, daß primitive Kulturen ihre magisch-religiösen Bilder in einem begrifflichen Kontext betrachteten, der von dem, den Europa auf sein eigenes künstlerisches Schaffen seit jeher anwandte, völlig verschieden ist. In einer primitiven Kultur werden die Masken, Statuen und anderen Objekte, die Teil ihres künstlerischen Erbes sind, nicht von ihrem Erinnerungswert oder ihrer ästhetischen Wirkung her gesehen, sondern eher als Verkörperungen von Geistwesen, die während des Rituals eine gewaltige und unmittelbare geistige Kraft ausüben.[43] Diese Deutung trifft vor allem auf die Zeremonialmasken und -kostüme zu, die eine wichtige Rolle im geistigen und künstlerischen Leben dieser Gesellschaft spielen. Während des religiösen Rituals verliert die Person, die die Maske mit der Absicht aufsetzt, ein bestimmtes Geistwesen darzustellen, für diese Zeit ihre persönliche Identität und wird selbst zum Geistwesen. Nach Ansicht der Primitiven hat der Mensch so die Fähigkeit, zeitweise in ein anderes Wesen verwandelt zu sein, sei es in einen Ahnen, in ein Tier oder in einen Baum. Die Verwandlung geschieht sowohl optisch wie auch psychologisch, denn das Maskenkostüm verwandelt die Erscheinung des am Ritual Beteiligten meist völlig. Ein gutes Beispiel dafür sind die aus Fasern bestehenden Kostüme der *Asmat* von Neuguinea ☐ 807, die, indem sie die Gestalt des Trägers verhüllen, Kopf, Gesicht und Arme noch so weit erkennen lassen, daß dieses Gebilde aus Peddigrohr, Sennit und anderen natürlichen Bestandteilen aus dem Lebensraum der *Asmat* zu einem eindringlichen Bild des mythischen Baummenschen wird, der zum Leben erweckt ist.

Masson hat das Bild des vermenschlichten Baumes in den Zeichnungen aus den späten dreißiger und frühen vierziger Jahren am konsequentesten verfolgt, speziell in den *Mythologien* von 1938, einer Folge von Zeichnungen, die der Erforschung des Mythos gewidmet sind.

Im Kapitel »Mythologie der Natur« zeigen sieben der fünfzehn Zeichnungen Bilder des Frauen-Baumes. *An den Ufern der Langeweile* ☐ 810 ist ein bezeichnendes Beispiel dafür, die sinnlichen Frauenkörper im Vordergrund weisen baumhafte Züge auf. Die Baumstämme sind Körper; Äste und Zweige bilden Arme und Finger, Beine und Zehen; die Haare sind das Laubwerk. Masson gelingt eine täuschende Synthese von Pflanzen und menschlichen Formen, indem er jedes Element in seiner zweifachen Funktion integriert, so daß das Ergebnis schließlich weder als die eine Funktion noch die andere zu deuten ist.

Man könnte auch das vielen Kulturen vertraute Bild der Mutter Natur, Verewigung der uralten Idee der Frau als der symbolischen Quelle erneuernder Kraft in der Welt, anführen. Frazer hielt diesen Aspekt früher Religion für so wichtig, daß er in seiner Schrift von 1926, *The Worship of Nature,* in sechs Kapiteln die Verehrung der Erde unter den Kulturen untersuchte, die von den indogermanischen Völkern der Antike über Afrika bis zu den verschiedenen indianischen Stämmen Amerikas reichen.[44] Diese Kapitel beinhalten verschiedene Erzählungen über die Rolle der weiblichen Gottheit, die die Erde – Mittelpunkt des immerwährenden Lebenszyklus im Glauben vieler Kulturen – als Mutter und Nahrungsspenderin verkörpert. Als ein Beispiel dafür zitierte Frazer eine alte Quelle, die besagt, daß »die Indianer die Erde als ihre universelle Mutter betrachten. Sie glauben, daß sie inmitten ihres Schosses erschaffen worden sind, wo sie für lange Zeit ihren Aufenthaltsort hatten, bevor sie auf ihrer Oberfläche zum Leben kamen.«[45]

☐ 815 *›Getreidespeicher‹, Konkombwa (Ghana oder Togo). Veröffentlicht in Roland Penrose, „Max Ernst's Celebes", 1972.*

☐ 816 *Marquesaner mit Körpertätowierung, Zeichnung, 1804. Veröffentlicht in Kapitän A. J. von Krusenstern, „Voyage around the World“, 1913.*

☐ 817 *Max Ernst, ›Die schöne Gärtnerin‹ (La Belle Jardinière), 1923, Öl auf Leinwand. Wahrscheinlich zerstört.*

Frazer und Lévy-Bruhl erkannten, daß der Glaube an eine lebenserhaltende Erdmutter in vielen primitiven Kulturen der Welt tief verwurzelt ist. MASSON übernahm diese alte und ursprüngliche Vorstellung von der Frau als Idol mit ihrem Versprechen ewiger Fruchtbarkeit als eines der zentralen Elemente seiner symbolischen Darstellungen. In vielen Bildern MASSONS begegnen wir diesem Thema. Eines der bezeichnendsten unter ihnen ist *Die Erde* von 1939 ☐ 811, bei dem MASSON Sand unter die Farbe mischte. Die Gestalt der Frau, die die Erde darstellt, ist deutlich sichtbar. Ihren großen Brüsten in der oberen Bildhälfte entspricht die entblößte Scham, die durch eine Kreisfläche mit dunkel gefärbtem Sand betont wird. Der rechte Arm der Figur reicht über den Körper und preßt mit einer sonderbar krallenartigen Hand Milch aus der linken Brust – ein weiteres Symbol ihrer lebensspendenden Fähigkeiten. MASSONS Anwendung eines natürlichen Stoffes, Sand, als künstlerisches Mittel beschwört die Idee der Frau als einer Verkörperung der Erde selbst, eine Vorstellung, die auch häufig im primitiven Glauben zu finden ist.[46]

Während seiner langjährigen Beschäftigung mit der primitiven Kunst war MASSON immer dazu fähig, sich einen gewissen intellektuellen Abstand und eine vorurteilsfreie Aufrichtigkeit den kulturellen und ästhetischen Qualitäten gegenüber zu erhalten, die ihn schöpferisch anregten. Er war sich bewußt, daß zwischen der Bewunderung des westlichen Menschen für die primitive Kunst und seiner Fähigkeit, diese zu entziffern und so zu begreifen, wie sie von den Kulturen verstanden wird, die sie schufen, für immer eine Kluft bestehen würde.[47] In *Le Plaisir de peindre* (*Das Vergnügen zu malen*) warnte MASSON vor den Gefahren, »ein in Paris gemaltes Werk mit der Arbeit eines Eingeborenen der Neuen Hebriden zu vergleichen, mit dem . . . wir auf dem Gebiet der Kunst, der Metaphysik oder vom Lebensstil her nichts gemeinsam haben«.[48] Aus diesen Gründen könne der westliche Mensch, obwohl dazu fähig, die plastischen Qualitäten der primitiven Kunst zu schätzen, nicht darauf hoffen, all die inhärenten, tief intuitiven und emotionalen Bedeutungen zu verstehen, die auf den Ebenen des Magischen und des Geistigen wirkten. Jedoch ist es neben einer Reihe anderer Ursachen gerade diese Fremdartigkeit und Zweideutigkeit, die diese Kunstformen für die westliche Gesellschaft so anziehend und so wichtig machen.

Wie bereits erwähnt, zogen die Surrealisten die Kunst der ozeanischen Kulturen gegenüber derjenigen Afrikas vor. Das Erscheinen der Kunst der Südsee in Paris während der zwanziger Jahre kommentierend, behauptete MASSON, daß das Interesse der Surrealisten mehr ein ästhetisches als ein anthropologisches sei und daß sie »diese Kunst für die Künstler entdeckten, nicht für die Ethnographen, sondern für die kulturelle Welt«.[49] Bei der Definition, worin genau die ästhetische Anziehung der ozeanischen Kunst liege, wies MASSON auf die Weite Ozeaniens und die Vielfalt der Kulturgruppen hin, die sie bewohnen, und erwähnte nicht nur die Inselgruppen Polynesiens, sondern auch Neuseeland, Neuguinea, die Marquesasinseln, den Bismarckarchipel und Australien.[50] Indem er ihre Vielfalt erkannte, entdeckte er auch einen vielen Typen der ozeanischen Kunst gemeinsamen Stilwillen, der diese von afrikanischen Formen trenne. Als Beispiel für diese Beobachtung wies MASSON auf die anthropomorphen Skulpturen der *MAORI* Neuseelands hin.

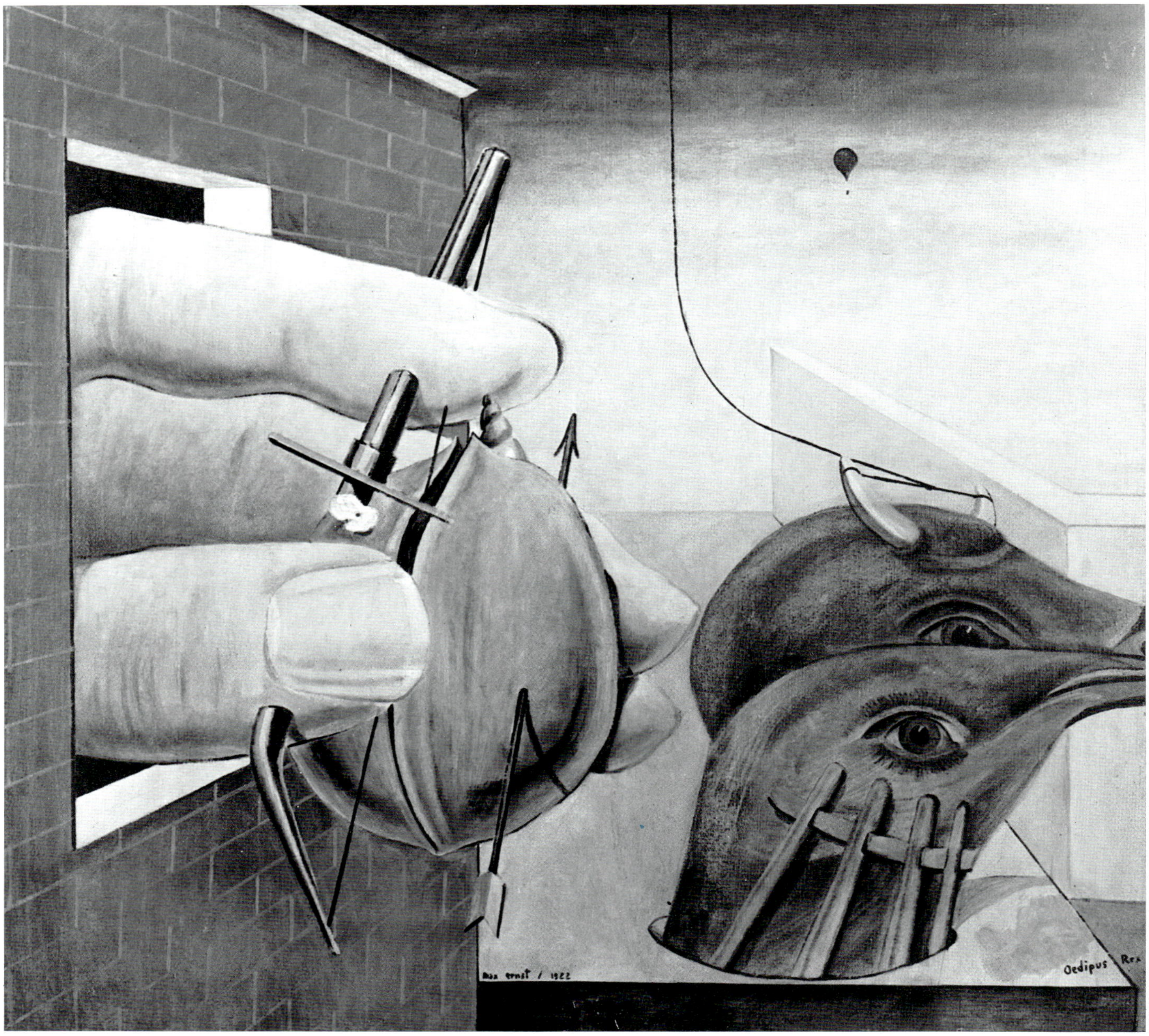

□ 818 *Max Ernst, ›Ödipus Rex‹, 1922, Öl auf Leinwand, 89 x 116 cm. Privatsammlung.*

Diese Werke fand er besonders wirkungsvoll, vor allem wegen »der verwickelten Darstellung des Körpers – der viszeralen Verschmelzung, die in der afrikanischen Kunst nicht auftritt«.[51]

Wie bei den meisten Künstlern der Fall, die Formen oder Themen primitiven Vorbildern entlehnen, gibt es nur wenige direkte Beziehungen zwischen MASSONS Werk und einem bestimmten Beispiel primitiver Kunst. Im Gegenteil, die Weise seiner Anverwandlung von Stammesformen oder -stilen in seinem eigenen Werk ist mit dem Erlernen des Wortschatzes einer neuen Sprache vergleichbar, bei dem die Worte oder Bilder innerhalb einer persönlichen syntaktischen Struktur angewendet werden. Die indirekten Auswirkungen des primitiven Einflusses sind in MASSONS Werk der dreißiger und vierziger Jahre zu erkennen, auch in seinen drei wichtigen Zeichnungsbänden *Mythologien, Anatomie meines Universums* und *Nächtliches Notizbuch* – wie auch in anderen Zeichnungen, Drucken und Gemälden.

1935 schuf MASSON zwei Werke, die seine Philosophie der kosmischen Einheit in visueller Form zusammenfassen: *Landschaft der Wunder* und *Morgenröte bei Montserrat* □ 812. In diesen Werken sind Erde, Luft, Feuer und Wasser in einer gänzlich zerstörten Landschaft dargestellt, belebt von einem wilden, elementaren Gefühl für Bewegung. Kosmische Gebilde rotieren und wirbeln durch den Himmel, während die Erde selbst wie im ersten Moment der Schöpfung in einem vulkanischen Ausbruch aufgerissen wird.

Daß die *Morgenröte bei Montserrat* Assoziationen an die Genesis erweckt, ist ebenfalls Zeugnis für MASSONS Beschäftigung mit dem Primitivismus. Dieses Bild ist eines der wenigen Beispiele für direkte Anlehnungen an bestimmte Werke primitiver Kunst. In die Landschaft gestellt sind Darstellungen der rätselhaften Steinfiguren der Osterinsel, die MASSON sowohl von Publikationen wie von dem Exponat des Musée de l'Homme in Paris kannte. Dieser berühmte und ungedeutete Typus polynesischer Großplastik ist als stiller Zeuge für seine Urlandschaft passend gewählt. Diese Figuren, die so dargestellt sind, wie sie in Wirklichkeit von den Hängen der Insel den

Pazifik überblicken □ 813, sind von einer Ahnung zeitlosen Mysteriums erfüllt. In *Morgenröte bei Montserrat* stellen diese gigantischen primitiven Figuren die Menschheit dar, wie sie war und wie sie sein wird, ein integraler Bestandteil und ein bewußter Beobachter der geistigen und schöpferischen Kräfte der Welt.

»Die Kraft, Halluzinationen zu schaffen, ist die Kraft, das Leben zu verherrlichen. Sie kann als eine Form von Verrücktheit verstanden werden, aber ich denke, Max Ernst akzeptiert dies als einen Teil der Aufgabe des Künstlers . . . In diesem Sinne ist Max Ernst ein Primitiver, selbst wenn er nicht in einer primitiven Landschaft lebt.«[52]

Diese Aussage von Matta charakterisiert die Weise, wie Max Ernst von surrealistischen Freunden mit der Mentalität primitiver Gesellschaften und deren Schaffensweisen in Verbindung gebracht wurde. Ernsts lange und produktive Laufbahn begann vor dem Ersten Weltkrieg und dauerte bis zu seinem Tode im Jahre 1976. Sie zeichnete sich durch ein tiefes intellektuelles und ästhetisches Interesse an den Primitiven aus. Als Student der Psychologie und der Philosophie an der Bonner Universität zwischen 1909 und 1914 las er die Schriften Hegels, Nietzsches und Freuds wie auch Frazers (*Der goldene Zweig*) und die des deutschen Ethnographen Wilhelm Wundt.[53] Ernst blieb auch nach seinen Universitätsjahren der Völkerkunde verbunden. Er lernte die wissenschaftlichen Arbeiten von Lévy-Bruhl und Claude Lévi-Strauss, der später ein enger Freund wurde, und anderer Ethnologen kennen, die sein Grundwissen auf diesem Gebiet erweiterten. Er begann auch früh die vielen außerordentlichen Sammlungen der deutschen Völkerkundemuseen zu besuchen und baute sich eine Bibliothek über dieses Thema auf. Was er von den primitiven Kulturen lernte, war von großem Einfluß auf seine Schriften wie auch auf seine Kunst. Roland Penrose wies nach, daß Ernst schon früh, 1921, die Abbildung eines afrikanischen Getreidespeichers aus einer englischen anthropologischen Zeitschrift als Vorlage für das Gemälde *Der Elefant von Celebes* □ 814, 815 benutzte.[54] Zu einer anthropologischen Quelle kehrte er auch zwei Jahre später für das Bild der tätowierten Figur in *Die schöne Gärtnerin* zurück □ 817, das deutlich von der marquesanischen Körperverzierung angeregt ist □ 816.

Als eines der Gründungsmitglieder der surrealistischen Bewegung entwickelte Ernst ein komplexes Bild seiner selbst, das er in knapper Form in seinem berühmtesten Essay, *Beyond Painting,* beschrieb (1936 erstmals veröffentlicht). Diese Schrift gliedert sich in drei Hauptteile. Im dritten mit dem Titel »Unmittelbare Identität« beschreibt *Ernst* eindrucksvoll, wie er die primitive Weltsicht übernahm.

Wie Breton und Masson und in Übereinstimmung mit ihren Vorgängern bis zurück zu Gauguin fühlte Ernst, daß der surrealistische Künstler die mythische, geistige Harmonie mit der Natur wiedergewinnen müsse, die während der Entwicklung des Christentums, des westlichen Rationalismus und der Technik verlorenging. Natur in allen ihren Formen wurde wichtigstes Motiv seiner Arbeit. Als er dann sein Verhältnis zum Primitiven definierte, waren seine Gefühle zur Natur ausschlaggebend. In »Unmittelbare Identität« schrieb er in der dritten Person über sich:

»Zum Beispiel die ›Natur‹ betrachtend, kann man in ihm zwei Haltungen unterscheiden, anscheinend unvereinbar: die des Gottes Pan und die des Menschen Papou, der alle Geheimnisse besitzt und das spielerische Vergnügen in seiner Vereinigung mit ihr realisiert (›er heiratet die Natur, er verfolgt die Nymphe Echo‹, sagen sie), und jene des bewußten und gestaltenden Prometheus, des Räubers des Feuers, der, von Gedanken geleitet, sie mit unversöhnlichem Groll und schweren Kränkungen verfolgt. ›Dieses Monstrum ist nur von den Antipoden der Landschaft befriedigt‹, wiederholen sie. Und ein neckisches kleines Mädchen fügt hinzu: ›Er ist zur gleichen Zeit ein Gehirn und ein Gemüse.‹«[55]

□ 819 *Max Ernst, Collage aus „Une Semaine de bonté", 1934. Viertes Buch: Mittwoch, Element: Blut, Beispiel: Ödipus.*

Ernst definierte die erste Hälfte seiner zweifachen Beziehung zur »Natur« im Sinne zweier Figuren, die die Traditionen der klassischen Mythologie und des primitiven Menschen darstellen, denn Ernst nahm wie Masson beide als Quelle der Inspiration und der Identifikation wahr. Seine Begeisterung für die Mythologie entsprang der Erkenntnis, daß der Westen dringend eines neuen Systems von Glaubensvorstellungen bedarf. Nachdem er die kulturellen Einflüsse auf seine Kindheit beschrieben hatte, drückte er die Hoffnung aus, daß »eines Tages einige Elemente einer neuen Mythologie diesem Drama entspringen werden«.[56]

Pan ist der klassische arkadische Gott der Wälder und Hirten, eine schillernde und komplexe Figur, deren physische Merkmale Mensch und Tier verbinden. Man glaubte ihn im Besitz von Kräften der Inspiration und Wahrsage.[57] Als Ernst sich selbst – den Gott Pan ergänzend – mit »Papou« gleichsetzte, benutzte er das französische Wort für »Papua«. Die Kunst des Papua-Golfes war einer seiner bevorzugten Stile,[58] und mit dem »Menschen Papou« ist der Stammesmensch schlechthin gemeint. Für Ernst lebte er in einer harmonischen Beziehung mit der Natur und hielt die mythischen Strukturen

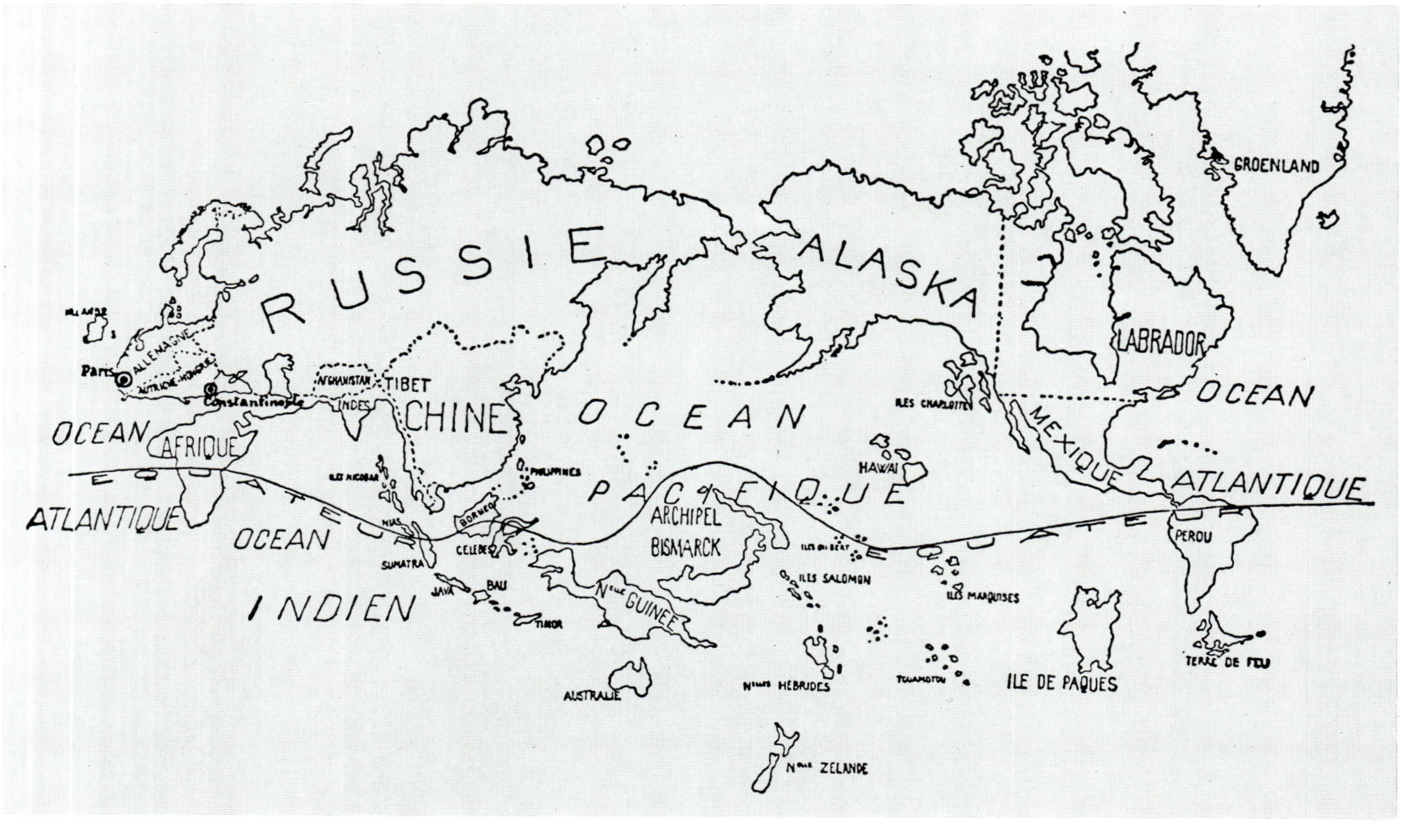

△ ◻ 820 *›Surrealistische Weltkarte‹. Veröffentlicht in „Variétés“, 1929.*

◻ 821 *›Figur eines Vogelmenschen‹, Osterinsel, Holz, Höhe 33 cm. American Museum of Natural History, Department of Anthropology, New York.*

◻ 823 *Max Ernst, ›Nach uns die Mutterschaft‹ (Après nous, la Maternité), 1927, Öl auf Leinwand, 142 x 115 cm. Kunstsammlung Nordrhein-Westfalen, Düsseldorf.* ▷

◻ 822 *›Rückenschmuck‹, Osterinsel, Holz, Höhe 9,5 cm. Congregazione di SS. Cuore, Rom.*

lebendig, die dieses Verhältnis ermöglichen und bestimmen. So entspricht der »Papou« dem Gott Pan insofern, als auch er »alle Geheimnisse besitzt und das spielerische Vergnügen in seiner Vereinigung mit ihr [der Natur] realisiert (›er heiratet die Natur, er verfolgt die Nymphe Echo‹, sagen sie)«.[59] Der Aspekt des Primitiven, den ERNST in sich selbst erkannte, ermöglichte ihm in der Folge, nicht nur mit der Natur in Harmonie zu leben, sondern half ihm auch, alle ihre Rätsel zu ergründen und sich die Geheimnisse ihrer schöpferischen Kräfte anzueignen.

In der klassischen wie in der Stammesmythologie erscheinen Tiere und ihre vermenschlichten Spielarten als Symbole sowohl der geistigen Kräfte der Natur als auch der mystischen Beziehung des Menschen zu diesen Kräften. Diese Bildersprache durchzieht das ganze Werk von MAX ERNST – eine bizarre Menagerie von Insekten, Fischen, Tieren und phantastischen Mischwesen, die sein persönliches Bestiarium darstellen. Der Vogel jedoch ist bei weitem sein bevorzugtes Geschöpf, und gerade in seiner persönlichen Beziehung zu den Vögeln fühlte sich ERNST dem Primitiven am stärksten verbunden.

1948 schrieb ERNST eine autobiographische Phantasie, die mit einer Beschreibung seiner Geburt in ornithologischen Begriffen beginnt: »Am 2. April (1891) um 9.45 Uhr schlüpfte Max Ernst aus dem Ei, das seine Mutter in eines Adlers Nest gelegt und auf dem der Vogel sieben Jahre lang gebrütet hatte.«[60] In seiner Kindheit blieben die Vögel die entscheidenden Symbole. Im gleichen Text beschrieb er den Tod seines Lieblingsvogels, dessen Leiche er am nächsten Morgen fand, genau in dem Moment, als ihm sein Vater die Geburt einer neuen Schwester mitteilte. »Die *Erschütterung*«, so erinnerte sich ERNST, »war so stark, daß er in Ohnmacht fiel.«

□ 824 *Max Ernst, ›Vogeldenkmal‹ (Monument aux oiseaux), 1927, Öl auf Leinwand, 162,5 x 30 cm. Privatsammlung.*

»In seiner Phantasie verknüpfte Max beide Ereignisse und machte das Baby für den Tod des Vogels verantwortlich. Eine Serie von mystischen Krisen, Anfällen von Hysterie, Taumelzuständen und Depressionen folgte. Eine gefährliche Verwirrung zwischen Vögeln und Menschen machte sich in seinem Geist breit und kam später in seinen Zeichnungen und Gemälden immer wieder zum Vorschein. Später identifizierte sich Max selbst mit Loplop, dem Vogelobersten.«[61]

Nach Auffassung von ERNSTS Freund und Biograph, Patrick Waldberg, wurde der Vogel sein »Totem«.[62] ERNSTS Erzählung gibt uns das klassische Beispiel für eine totemistische Beziehung, die von Frazer, Wundt, Lévy-Bruhl und anderen als eines der Grundelemente primitiver Kultur verstanden wurde. Doch die vielleicht einflußreichste Quelle, die ERNST zu diesem Thema gelesen hatte, war Freuds *Totem und Tabu* von 1913, nach dem ERNST 1941 ein Gemälde betitelte, das Vögel und weibliche Formen vor einem Hintergrund zeigt, der an Gruppen von Totempfählen der Indianer der Nordwestküste Amerikas erinnert. In Freuds Texten finden sich Beschreibungen totemistischer Beziehung, die ERNSTS Identifikation mit den Vögeln genau entsprechen. Freud wies nach, daß das Totem in der Regel nicht nur Clan-Tier war, sondern auch »ihr Schutzgeist und Helfer, der ihnen Orakel sendet«.[63]

Freuds Hauptanliegen bestand darin, den Ursprung des Ödipuskomplexes bis zum Totemismus der primitiven Kulturen zurückzuverfolgen. Aus den biographischen Quellen und aus ERNSTS eigenen Schriften geht deutlich hervor, daß er sehr starke ödipale Neigungen hatte, da er seinen Vater verachtete, zu seiner Mutter hingegen enge gefühlsmäßige Bindungen unterhielt.[64] Sein Versuch, diese Gefühle im Lichte von Freuds Theorie künstlerisch auszudrücken, führte zu einem seiner interessantesten Gemälde, *Ödipus Rex,* in dem das totemistische Bild des Vogels erstmals wirkungsvoll zur Geltung kommt □ 818.[65]

Ödipus Rex, vielleicht ERNSTS letztes wichtiges Gemälde, bevor er sich im Sommer 1922 in Paris niederließ, verdankt die

☐ 825 *und* ☐ 826 *Reliefs mit Vogelmenschen auf den Felsen von Orongo (Osterinsel).*

☐ 827 *Max Ernst, ›Natur im Morgenlicht‹ (La nature à l'aurore), 1936, Öl auf Leinwand, 24 x 35 cm. Städelsches Kunstinstitut, Frankfurt.*

□ 828 *Max Ernst, ›Das innere Gesicht: das Ei‹, 1929, Öl auf Leinwand, 77 x 79 cm. Menil Foundation Collection, Houston.*

□ 829 *›Schild‹, Sioux (Dakota oder Minnesota), bemaltes Leder und Federn, Höhe 45 cm. Denver Art Museum, Schenkung C. W. Douglas.*

□ 830 *Max Ernst, ›Die Geburt der Turmuhr‹ (L'origine de la pendule), 1925, Frottage, Bleistift auf Papier, 42 x 26 cm. Cabinet des Estampes de Strasbourg.*

räumliche Inszenierung und geheimnisvolle Bildsprache Giorgio de Chirico. Durch runde Löcher im Boden schauen zwei Vogelköpfe heraus. Links greifen die Finger einer riesigen (linken) Hand aus dem Fenster einer roten Backsteinmauer. Die Finger halten eine sehr große, teilweise geöffnete Walnuß, die von einem Pfeil durchbohrt ist. Auch Daumen und Zeigefinger der Hand sind durchbohrt, in diesem Fall von zwei Hälften eines mechanischen Instruments, dessen Enden – wie bei einem Bogen – durch eine Sehne verbunden sind. Schließlich ist das Ganze durch die Form hinter der Nuß vervollständigt, die gegen den Zeigefinger drückt. Ihr spiraliges Aussehen erinnert an gewisse Arten von Schneckenmuscheln oder an die Spitze einer großen Schraube. Die Umgebung besteht lediglich aus dem geometrisch geordneten Grundriß, der glatten Backsteinmauer, dem klaren Himmel sowie einem Freiballon.

Wenn wir bei unserer Interpretation von Freuds Text und Ernsts autobiographischem Bericht ausgehen, können wir die beiden Vögel als die Eltern des Künstlers deuten – der kleinere mit Zaun, der »gefangen« ist, einen anmutigeren Kopf und weiblichere Augen hat, steht für seine Mutter, der größere, gehörnte für seinen Vater. Die teilweise geöffnete Nußschale läßt sich als weibliches Geschlecht deuten, so wie der Pfeil, der sie durchbohrt, unverkennbar ein phallisches Symbol ist. Der Daumen und der Zeigefinger, die die Nuß halten, sind von einem Metallinstrument durchbohrt sowie von einem hornartigen Gegenstand, die durch eine gespannte Sehne miteinander verbunden sind. Sie bilden eine Bogenform, eine Ergänzung zum Pfeil, und schaffen so eine Beziehung zwischen dieser Gruppe und der ähnlichen Anordnung der Hörner des Vogels. So wie die Vögel das Totem darstellen, stehen die durchbohrte

□ 831 *Max Ernst, Collage aus „Une Semaine de bonté“, 1934. Fünftes Buch, Element: Dunkelheit, Beispiel: Osterinsel.*

□ 832 *›Monumentaler Steinkopf‹, Osterinsel. Veröffentlicht in Stéphen Chauvet, „L'Ile de Pâques et ses mystères“, 1935.*

Hand und die Nußschale für die Wünsche und Verbote des Tabus.[66] In *Ödipus Rex* wendet ERNST Freuds Theorien über die Beziehung zwischen dem Ödipuskomplex und dem Totemismus an, um seine eigenen gemischten Gefühle gegenüber seinen Eltern und die totemistische Identifikation mit dem Vogel zum Ausdruck zu bringen. Diese Interpretation stützt auch sein Collagen-Roman *Une Semaine de bonté* von 1934, in dem ERNST Menschen mit Vogelkopf als Hauptmotiv seines Mittwoch-Zyklus anwendet, der Ödipus gewidmet ist. Unser Beispiel zeigt zwei der Mischwesen □ 819, über denen eine große Hand mit einem scharfen Instrument aus dem offenen Fenster herausragt – ein direkter Bezug zu dem Bild *Ödipus Rex,* das zwölf Jahre vorher entstanden war.

ERNSTS berühmte Frottagen-Serie von 1925, *Histoire Naturelle,* enthält vier Arbeiten, deren Hauptmotiv große Vögel in der Mitte des Bildes sind. Das schlagendste Beispiel, *Die Geburt der Turmuhr* □ 830, zeigt eine Ähnlichkeit mit Bildern von Vögeln mit ausgestreckten Flügeln, wie sie in der Kunst der nordamerikanischen Indianer vorkommen. Die Anregung zu dieser Form könnte von einer der vielen Darstellungen des Donnervogels, entweder der Stämme der Nordwestküste oder der *PLAINS-INDIANER,* ausgegangen sein. Ein schönes Beispiel für den letzteren Typ ist ein Kriegsschild der *SIOUX* □ 829. Die Kraftströme, die hier von den Vogelflügeln ausgehen, stehen ERNSTS Komposition und den zwei Baumformen mit dem wellenförmigen Maserungsmuster nahe, die hinter seinem ähnlich angeordneten Vogel erscheinen. Der Schild war für ERNST möglicherweise auch insofern von Interesse, als er dem indianischen Prärie-Krieger als eine Art persönliches Totem diente.

ERNSTS Reihe der *Vogeldenkmäler* von 1927 führte zu einem neuen Bild des Vogels, das auf seiner persönlichen Identifikation mit Vögeln wie auch auf seinem Jugendtrauma basierte, das er beim Tod seines Lieblingsvogels und der Geburt seiner Schwester erlitten hatte. Das Ergebnis, »die gefährliche Kombination von Vögeln und Menschen«, über die er sich selbst geäußert hatte, wird in dem Bild *Nach uns die Mutterschaft* offensichtlich □ 823, in dem die Flügel und der Schwanz der Vögel die Gestalt von menschlichen Armen und Beinen annehmen. Hauptmotiv ist ein sitzender anthropomorpher Vogel, der einen kleineren Vogel an seine Brust drückt, eine Andeutung von ERNSTS metamorphischer Geburt aus einem Ei in einem Adlernest wie auch der Geburt der Schwester, deren Ankunft er mit dem Tod seines Lieblingsvogels verband.

In *Max Ernst: Loplop* präsentierte Werner Spies eine gültige Untersuchung zur komplizierten Beziehung des Künstlers zur Bildwelt des Vogels. Dessen ungeachtet ist eine verblüffende Bildquelle für ERNSTS anthropomorphe Vögel in der Kunst der polynesischen Kulturen der Osterinsel zu finden, die einen entscheidenden Einfluß auf viele Aspekte seines Werkes ausübte. Der Grad der Wertschätzung für die Osterinsel bei den Surrealisten ist an der Größe dieser winzigen Insel auf der »Surrealistischen Weltkarte« abzulesen, die 1929 in *Variétés* erschien □ 820. Seit ihrer Entdeckung durch eine holländische Expedition am Ostertag 1722 haben die Osterinsel und ihre Kunst eine große Anziehungskraft für westliche Wissenschaftler, Sammler und Künstler. Die Bibliographie über die Insel

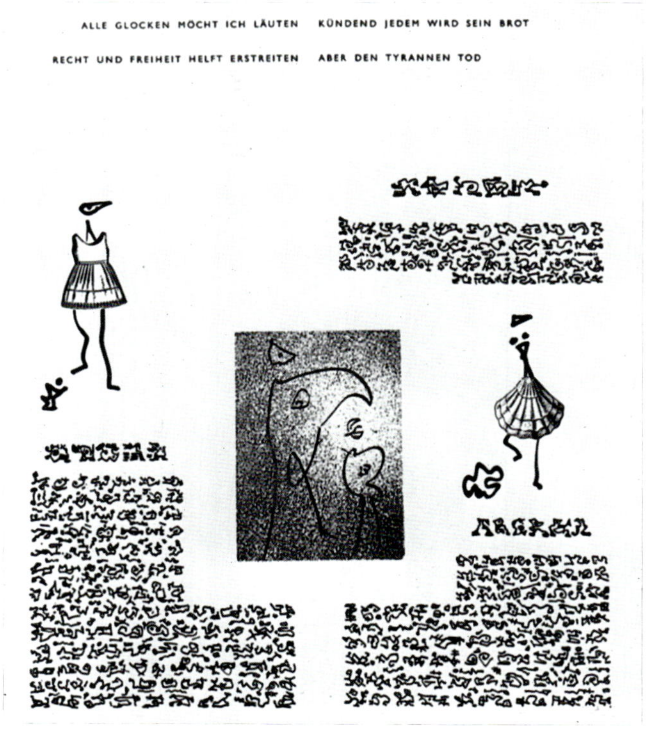

☐ 833 *Max Ernst, Seite aus „Maximiliana", Paris, 1964. New York Public Library.*

☐ 834 *›Figur aus Holz‹, Era River, Golfprovinz (Papua-Neuguinea), bemaltes Holz, Höhe 54 cm. Sammlung Dorothea Tanning, New York. Ehemals Sammlung Max Ernst.*

und ihre Kultur ist umfangreich und enthält mindestens 65 Beiträge, die zwischen 1900 und 1927 erschienen.[67] MAX ERNST fühlte sich durch die Kultur der Osterinsel stark angesprochen, und ihre Kunst regte, wie noch zu zeigen ist, seine Bildwelt in den verschiedensten Medien vielfach an.[68]

Die wichtigste Gottheit der Osterinsel führte den Namen MakeMake. Sie wurde in Figuren dargestellt, die gleichermaßen Züge des Menschen und des Vogels aufweisen ☐ 821. MakeMake wurde mit der dunklen Seeschwalbe in Verbindung gebracht, die samt ihren Eiern eine wichtige Nahrungsquelle für die Inselbewohner war. Jeden Frühling wurde derjenige, der zu ihren Nistplätzen auf den kleinen Felsinseln in Küstennähe hinausschwamm und das erste Ei der Saison zurückbrachte, als die Reinkarnation des Gottes betrachtet – eine wichtige zeremonielle Stellung, die er ein Jahr lang innehatte.[69] Bilder von MakeMake wurden vollplastisch und als Relief in Stein und Holz gehauen wie auch auf Stein gemalt. Neben den berühmten Monumentalfiguren und Steinköpfen waren sie die populärsten Kunstwerke jener Kultur. Unter diesen Werken sind die wichtigsten Bildquellen für ERNSTS anthropomorphe Vögel zu finden.

ERNSTS erste Adaption der Vogelformen der Osterinsel findet man in den runden, aufgeblähten Körpern der schwebenden Vögel in seiner Serie der *Vogeldenkmäler*, die den geschnitzten Rückenornamenten ähnlich sind, die vergleichbare Vögel der Osterinsel darstellen ☐ 822. Der segmentierte Körper wie auch das Aussehen des Kopfes, des Auges und des Schnabels der Skulptur finden einen Widerhall in den zwei Vögeln, die das größte Gemälde in ERNSTS Serie beherrschen ☐ 824. Seine anthropomorphen Vogelbilder treten kurze Zeit später auf und sind in *Nach uns die Mutterschaft* voll entwickelt. Einzelne Züge und die Komposition rufen deutlich die Reihe ähnlicher Bilder, die in die Felsen von Orango gehauen oder gemalt wurden, in Erinnerung ☐ 825, 826.

Zu einer der interessantesten Phasen von ERNSTS Anwendung des anthropomorphen Vogels kam es in den dreißiger Jahren. In *Natur im Morgenlicht* von 1936 ☐ 827 erscheint der vogelköpfige Mensch als Profil in einer Dschungellandschaft, mit großen Armen, am Ellbogen eingeknickt, und übergroßen gestikulierenden Händen.[70] Diese Haltung (und den Körpertyp) wählte ERNST für viele Bilder. Er ist unzweifelhaft von den anthropomorphen Vogelbildern der Osterinsel abgeleitet, wie sie auf Photographien der Felsskulpturen zu sehen sind, die 1935 – ein Jahr vor *Natur im Morgenlicht* – in Paris veröffentlicht wurden.

Es wurde bereits darauf hingewiesen, daß ein Hauptaspekt des Vogelkultes auf der Osterinsel das Auffinden und Einbringen der ersten Seeschwalbeneier war. Ein faszinierendes Beispiel, das dieses Thema illustriert, ist ein eiförmiger Stein ☐ 39, in dem die bekannte kauernde Figur des Vogelkopf-Gottes eingraviert und aufgemalt ist, der ein anderes Ei in seinen Händen hält. Dieser Stein wurde 1914 entdeckt und 1919 erstmals in einem Buch publiziert und abgebildet, das ERNST entweder in Deutschland oder in Paris zugänglich war.[71] Mit dem Jahre 1927 begann ERNST eine Reihe von großen eiförmigen Kompositionen, ausgefüllt mit runden, stilisierten Vögeln und anthropomorphen Vogelfiguren, die dem Bild von der Osterinsel sehr nahe kommen. 1929 malte ERNST dann eine Serie von acht Werken mit dem gleichen Titel, *Das innere Gesicht: das Ei* ☐ 41, die jeweils ein großes ovales Feld aufweisen, das mit einer Vielzahl krummliniger Vogelformen ausgefüllt ist. ERNST fügte bei vier Bildern der Serie einen weiteren Bezug auf die Osterinsel hinzu, indem er ein oder zwei kleinere Eier in oder um die Vogelschnäbel malte ☐ 828. 1934 griff ERNST auf das Objekt von der Osterinsel erneut zurück, als er im Sommer mit GIACOMETTI in Maloja, Schweiz, weilte und eine Gruppe von Skulpturen aus Granitsteinen von Gebirgsbächen meißelte und bemalte. Während mehrere dieser ovalen

Steine mit abstrakten Vögeln verziert sind, kam ERNSTS Skulptur mit dem Titel *Ovaler Vogel* □ 40 den Formen der Skulptur von der Osterinsel am nächsten, denn in der Form und in den Proportionen des einem Ei ähnlichen Steines und der einzelnen Vogelmenschenfigur sind sich die beiden Arbeiten beinahe gleich. ERNST vermied die direkte Nachbildung, indem er das geknickte Bein und den Fuß wegließ und durch eine kleine Vogelform anstelle des Eis ersetzte. Doch obschon Details der Darstellung geändert wurden, haben die zwei Skulpturen wesentliche Züge gemeinsam.

Ein anderes Beispiel für den direkten Einfluß der Kunst der Osterinsel auf ERNSTS Werk enthält der Collagen-Roman *Une Semaine de bonté* von 1934, der in Kapitel unterteilt ist, die jeweils für einen Wochentag stehen. Der Donnerstag hat zwei Themen, von denen das erste den Titel »Das Lachen des Hahnes« trägt. Dargestellt sind Hahnenköpfe, die an Menschenkörpern befestigt sind, ähnlich den Vogelmenschenformen der Osterinsel. Das zweite Thema ist »Die Osterinsel« mit neun Collagen, deren Hauptfiguren mit Köpfen des populärsten Figurentyps von der Osterinsel ausgestattet sind. Reproduktionen dieser monumentalen Steinskulpturen wurden vielfach publiziert, und originale Beispiele dafür waren in öffentlichen Museen ausgestellt, so jenes, das seit 1930 im

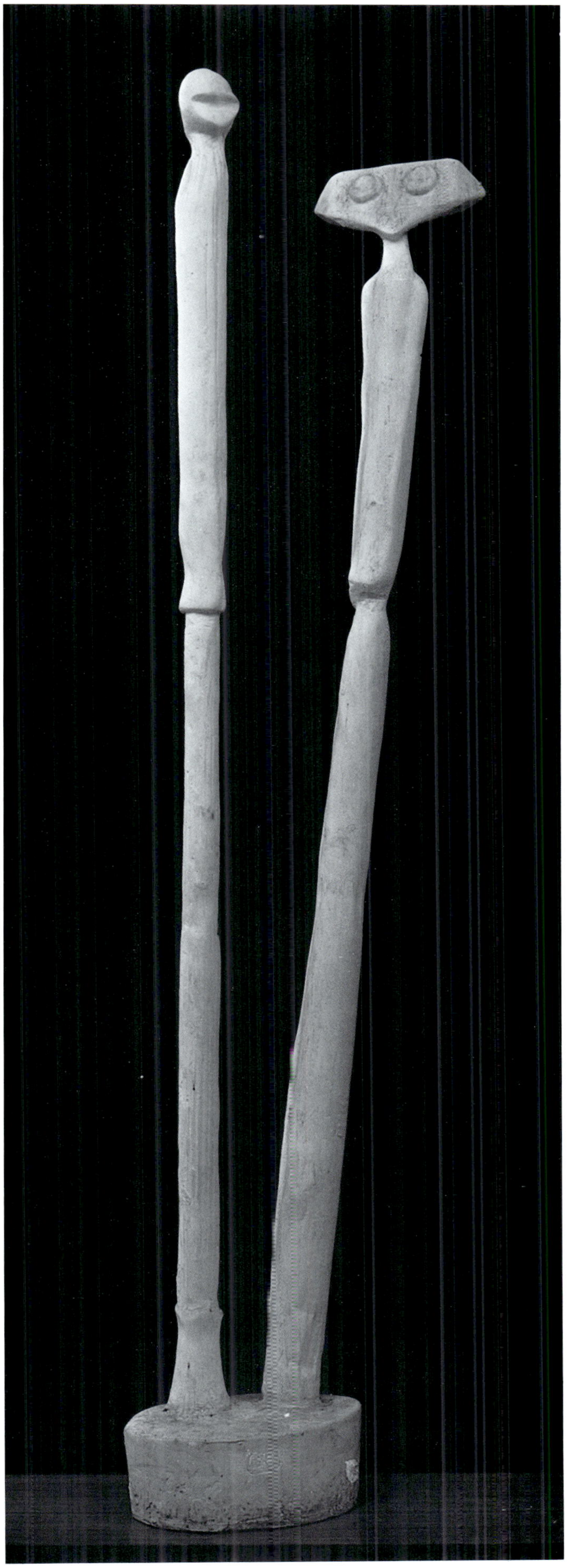

□ 835 *Max Ernst, ›Mondspargel‹ (Les asperges de la lune), 1935, Gips, Höhe 166 cm. The Museum of Modern Art, New York.*

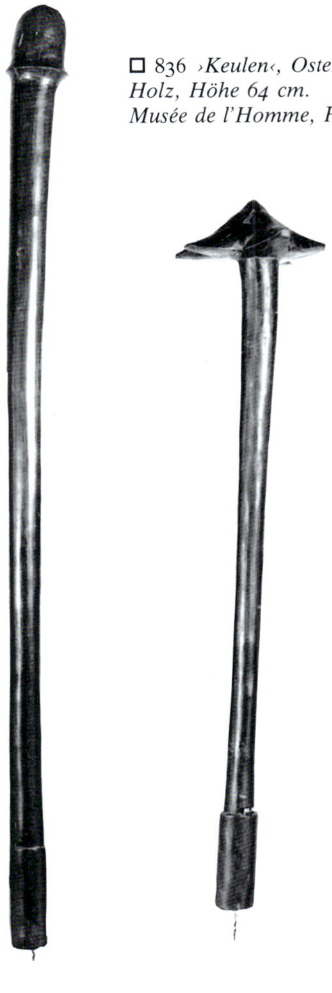

□ 836 *›Keulen‹, Osterinsel, Holz, Höhe 64 cm. Musée de l'Homme, Paris.*

☐ 837 *Max Ernst mit seiner Katchina-Sammlung, Photographie von James Thrall Soby, 1942. Sammlung A. A. und E. Cohen, New York.*

☐ 838 *Max Ernst, ›Die Horde‹ (La horde), 1927, Öl auf Leinwand, 46 x 55 cm. Sammlung Dr. H. Roland, Woking, England.*

Trocadéro (Musée de l'Homme) in Paris zu sehen war ☐ 832. Profilansichten dieser Köpfe der Osterinsel kommen häufig in diesen Serien ERNSTS vor, so etwa in der Collage, die den »Osterinsel-Menschen« und eine sinnliche Frau zeigt ☐ 831. 1935 benutzte ERNST erneut ein Vorbild der Osterinsel in seiner geheimnisvollen Skulpturengruppe *Mondspargel* ☐ 835. Die Übereinstimmung geht so weit, daß die schlanken Spargel von abstrakten anthropomorphen Köpfen gekrönt werden, die von ganz ähnlichen Formen der Keulen von der Osterinsel inspiriert sind. Unter diesen gibt es Beispiele mit menschlichen Köpfen, die gleiche Proportionen aufweisen und gleich hoch sein können ☐ 836.

Daß ERNST in der Bildwelt der Osterinsel auch später noch Anregung fand, belegt sein 1964 veröffentlichtes illustriertes Buch *Maximiliana* ☐ 833.[72] Es vereint Radierungen, Collagen, Kalligraphien und einen sparsamen Text zu einer Hommage an Wilhelm Leberecht Temple (1821–1889), einem Amateurastronomen, der einen vorher unbekannten Asteroiden entdeckte, den er Maximiliana taufte. Ein Großteil des Buches besteht aus einer fremdartigen Bilderschrift, die der Künstler für diese Publikation entwickelt hatte. Diese wunderbare, aber

□ 839 *Max Ernst, ›Einwohnerin von Tours‹, 1960, Bronze, Höhe 26 cm. Sammlung Dorothea Tanning, New York.*

□ 840 *›Kopf‹, Asante (Ghana), Terrakotta, Höhe 50 cm. Privatsammlung.*

bedeutungslose Handschrift entstammt einer gleichfalls interessanten Bilderschrift der Osterinsel, die in Holztafeln geschnitzt ist □ 227. Während Ernsts Formen weniger präzise umrissen sind als die primitiven Bildzeichen, haben sie einen ähnlichen Stil in der Anordnung der Zeichnung und Linien.

Es wurde schon darauf hingewiesen, daß Ernst in *Beyond Painting* seine Vorliebe für die melanesische ozeanische Kultur, die des Gebietes des Papua-Golfes in Neuguinea, bestätigte. In den frühen sechziger Jahren erreichte seine Sammlung von Skulpturen dieser Region die stattliche Zahl von über 25 Werken, die Mehrzahl davon ausgeschnittene Figuren aus dünnen Holzbrettern in flachem Relief geschnitzt und bemalt. In einem Beispiel aus Ernsts Sammlung □ 834 können wir sehen, daß sich diese Figuren durch einen markanten Umriß und eine starke Binnengliederung auszeichnen, die Gesichtszüge, Knochen, Rippen und innere Organe schematisch angibt.

Solche Figuren vom Papua-Golf, die Ernst als Sammler besonders faszinierten, scheinen auch die beinahe fünfzig Figurenbilder angeregt zu haben, die er 1927 schuf (einschließlich der Serie mit dem Titel *Die Horde*). Typische Beispiele aus diesen Serien □ 838 haben figürliche Konturen und ein inneres Linienmuster, das mit der »Grattage«-Technik erzielt wurde. Wie die Papua-Figuren sind die Körper in Ernsts *Horden* frontal gesehen und zeigen eine ähnliche Vielfalt von Posen und Kopf- oder Körperumrissen. Ihre klaren Konturen und ihr System der inneren Zeichnung lehnen sich deutlich an die Linien der Papua-Künstler an, die Einzelheiten der Anatomie bezeichnen. Ernst griff auch zu starken Übermalungen, die die Wirkung der automatischen Linie verringern, zugleich aber die des Flachreliefs verstärken, die ebenfalls für die Flachrelieffiguren der Papua charakteristisch ist. In allen *Horden*-Gemälden versuchte Ernst den mysteriösen und erschreckenden Gehalt der Papua-Bildwelt einzufangen, indem er ihre geisterhaften und gliederlosen Formen für seine eigenen in gleicher Weise besessenen und bedrohlichen Phantome heranzog.

Wie so viele Europäer war Ernst von den Indianern fasziniert, denen er als Kind erstmals in den populären Erzählungen von Karl May begegnet war. Obschon er sich später der indianischen Bildwelt der Prärie und der Nordwestküste bediente, galt sein größtes Interesse den *Hopi* und den *Zuni* des Südwestens. Breton war der erste, der Ernsts Werk mit den *Pueblo*-Göttern in Verbindung brachte, als er 1927 in seinem

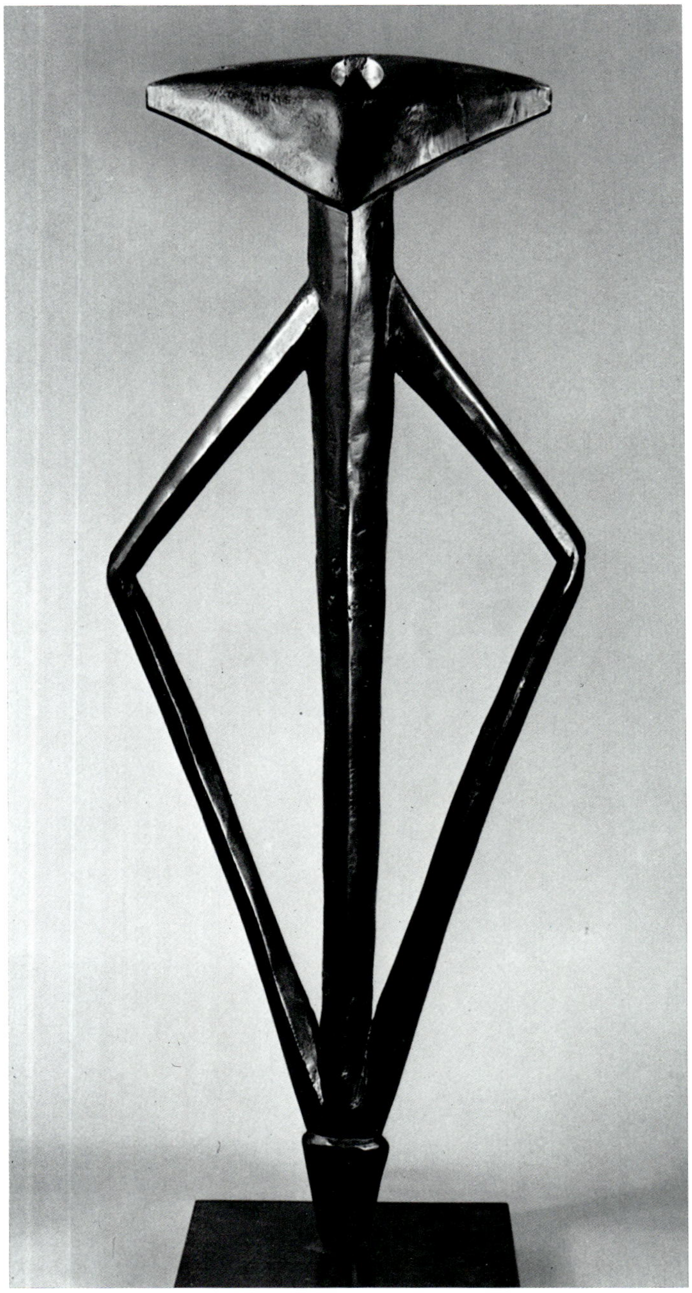

□ 841 ›Pfeife‹, Mossi (Obervolta), Holz, Höhe 57 cm. Privatsammlung.

□ 843 Max Ernst, ›Der König spielt mit seiner Königin‹ (Roi jouant avec la reine), 1944, Bronze, Guß aus dem Jahr 1954 nach der originalen Gipsplastik, Höhe 98 cm, Sockel: 48 x 52 cm. The Museum of Modern Art, Schenkung D. und J. de Menil, New York. ▷

□ 842 ›Katchina‹, Hopi (Arizona), Pappelholz, Wurzeln, Farbe, Leder und andere Materialien, Höhe 51 cm. Nachlaß Jimmy Ernst. Ehemals Sammlung Max Ernst.

□ 844 *Max Ernst, ›Kopf eines Mannes‹, 1947, Öl auf Leinwand, 51 x 30 cm. Privatsammlung, Paris.*

□ 845 *›Kopf einer Reiterfigur‹, SENUFO (Elfenbeinküste), Holz, Gesamthöhe 34 cm. Privatsammlung, New York. Gesamtansicht* □ *877.*

Essay über ERNST von den »Puppen von Neumexiko« sprach, den Katchinas der *HOPI-* und *ZUNI*-Indianer. Diese kleinformatigen bemalten Holzschnitzereien von Göttern sind in Wirklichkeit Lehrobjekte für Kinder mit der Darstellung von mehr als 200 Katchinas, übernatürlichen Wesen, die dem Götterhimmel der *HOPI* und *ZUNI* angehören. Sie sind den Katchina-Tänzern ähnlich: Die spezifischen Kostüme bezeichnen einzelne Katchina-Geister, wie sie im festgelegten Ablauf der Zeremonialtänze auftreten, die acht Monate lang im Jahr abgehalten werden.

Nach seiner Emigration nach Amerika im Jahr 1941 war es ERNST möglich, eine große Sammlung von Katchina-Figuren zusammenzutragen, von denen viele in einer Aufnahme des Künstlers zu sehen sind, die der Photograph James Thrall Soby 1942 in New York machte □ 837. Daß ihm nun die Kunst der *HOPI* zugänglich war, hat sich sicherlich auch auf die 1944 geschaffenen Skulpturen ausgewirkt. Die größte Arbeit, *Der König spielt mit seiner Königin* □ 843, spielt bildhaft auf das Schach an – Thema einer Ausstellung in der Galerie Julien Levy. Der rechteckige Kopf der Hauptfigur, überragt von einem Paar stark gebogener Hörner, gleicht einer Gestaltung wie der Büffel-Katchina der *ZUNI*, die ERNST in der Photographie von Soby in Händen hält □ 837, 842.[73] Natürlich war ERNST in dieser Zeit weiterhin an deren Formen von Stammeskunst interessiert. Auch zeigt das gleiche Werk, wie William Rubin hinwies, eine Ähnlichkeit mit den anthropomorphen *MOSSI*-Pfeifen aus Afrika □ 841. Andere auffallende Ähnlichkeiten seines Werks mit afrikanischer Kunst sind in seiner

□ 846 *›Kono-Maske‹, Bambara (Mali), Holz, Höhe 48 cm. Privatsammlung, Frankreich.*

Einwohnerin von Tours (1960) deutlich erkennbar □ 839,840, aber auch im verblüffenden Vergleich seines Gemäldes *Kopf eines Mannes* von 1947 □ 844 und einer ähnlich abstrakten Kono-Maske der *Bambara* aus Mali □ 846, von der sich ein Beispiel in seiner Sammlung befand.

Nach seiner Heirat mit der Malerin Dorothea Tanning, 1946, kaufte Ernst in der Stadt Sedona, Arizona, ein Grundstück, wo er und Dorothea bis 1953 in einem selbsterbauten Haus wohnten. Obschon Ernst bereits vorher den Südwesten bereist hatte,[74] war es das erste Mal, daß er wirklich in nächster Nähe der Indianer lebte, die er so bewunderte. »Die Indianer waren etwas von dem, was Max Ernst am stärksten nach Arizona zog . . .«, bemerkte John Russell. »Die Zähigkeit, mit der die Hopi-Indianer an ihren alten Bräuchen festhielten und es ablehnten, mit Geld korrumpiert zu werden, gehörte mit zu dem Großartigsten, dem Max Ernst in Arizona begegnete.«[75] Auch Waldberg unterstrich die Bedeutung von Ernsts Umzug nach Arizona mit dem Hinweis, daß Ernsts Kunst »wie die der Hopi-, Navajo- und Apachen-Indianer, die für mehr als zehn Jahre seine Nachbarn waren, weder realistisch noch abstrakt ist, sondern emblematisch«.

»Von wenigen Ausnahmen abgesehen hat er nie versucht, die Gestalt des Menschen zu erfassen (auch nicht von Dingen). Während seines ganzen langen Schaffens wird der Mensch durch etwas anderes, ihn Vertretendes, wiedergegeben, eine erfundene Form oder Maske, am häufigsten durch einen Vogel, manchmal auch durch eine schematisierte Person, deren Kopf ein Rechteck, ein Dreieck oder ein Kreis sein kann. Auf

□ 847 *Max Ernst, Photographie von Arnold Newman, 1942.*

□ 848 ›Katchina‹, ZUNI (Arizona oder Neu-Mexiko), bemaltes Holz und verschiedene Materialien, Höhe 81 cm. Sammlung Rollings, Tucson. Ehemals Sammlung Max Ernst.

□ 849 *Max Ernst, ›Lustige Hunde‹, 1958, bemaltes Holz und Federn, 81 x 19 cm. Sammlung Dorothea Tanning, New York.*

□ 850 *Max Ernst, ›Kopf‹ (Tête), aus der Serie der Miniaturmasken, 1959, Gold (Guß 1960), Höhe 7,5 cm. Privatsammlung.*

□ 851 *›Miniaturmaske‹, eskimoisch (Alaska), Knochen, Höhe 9,5 cm. Sammlung Dorothea Tanning, New York. Ehemals Sammlung Max Ernst.*

□ 852 *›Fingermaske‹, eskimoisch (Alaska), Holz und Federn, Höhe ca. 8 cm. Sammlung Matta, Paris.*

☐ 853 *Max Ernst, ›Der Seher‹, um 1935, Öl auf Leinwand, 24 x 19 cm. Privatsammlung.*

☐ 854 *Max Ernst im Vogelkostüm. Photographie von John Pewald, 1958. Sammlung Dorothea Tanning, New York.*

☐ 855 *Leonora Carrington, ›Bildnis Max Ernst‹ (Portrait of Max Ernst), 1940, Öl auf Leinwand, 50,8 x 26 cm. Privatsammlung, New York.*

ähnliche Weise benutzen die Indianer einfache geometrische Formen in ihren Bildern, Figuren und Masken. Hier kann der Kopf ein Kreis sein, dort ein Quadrat oder anderswo ein Dreieck, während die umgebenden ornamentalen Motive – viereckige Muster, Wellenlinien und parallele Bänder – das Meer, die Wolken, die Tage oder die Jahreszeiten symbolisieren können. Solche Formen stellen nicht Erscheinungen dar, sondern Ideen.«[76]

Während ERNST in den vierziger Jahren viele *personnages* mit Hörnern schuf, die den Einfluß der Katchinas belegen, ist deren volle Wirkung auf sein Werk am besten in *Capricorne* (*Steinbock*) von 1948, seiner beeindruckendsten Skulptur, greifbar ☐ 859. *Capricorne* besteht aus einer sitzenden, gehörnten Figur, die in ihrer rechten Hand einen Stab hält, in ihrer linken eine Kreatur mit einem Fischschwanz und ein Tier auf ihrem Schoß. Neben ihr steht ein armloses weibliches Wesen, dessen miteinander verschmolzene Beine von einem Fischschuppenmuster bedeckt sind. Lucy Lippard nannte diese Gruppe ein »Familienporträt von Ernst, seiner Frau Dorothea und ihren beiden langhaarigen Tibeter-Hunden ... Es ist im wesentlichen eine Wächtergruppe mit der barbarischen Würde, die zu dieser Rolle gehört.«[77] Lippard wies auch darauf hin, daß das alte Symbol des Steinbocks mit der Metamorphose und Wiedergeburt verknüpft war, primitiven Glaubensvorstellungen, die ERNSTS Gefühle über sein neues Leben in Arizona widerspiegeln würden. Die gehörnte Maske der sitzenden Figur ist deutlich von Katchinas abhängig, wie etwa dem großen Beispiel im Vordergrund links in der Photographie von ERNST inmitten seiner Katchina-Sammlung ☐ 837. Die Frisur des weiblichen Wesens von *Capricorne* ist gleichfalls von den Katchinas angeregt, speziell von einhörnigen Typen wie die des *ZUNI*-Regenmachers des Nordens. Die Köpfe der zwei kleinen Tiere erinnern auch an die Katchina-Formen. Im Hinblick auf Lippards Interpretation dieser beiden als die zwei Hunde ERNSTS, sei darauf verwiesen, daß der eine tatsächlich »Katchina« genannt wurde.[78] Katchinas halten häufig auch

□ 856 *›Maske‹*, KWAKIUTL *(Britisch-Kolumbien), bemaltes Holz, Muscheln und Haar, Höhe 38 cm. Sammlung Dorothea Tanning, New York. Ehemals Sammlung Max Ernst.*

□ 857 *Max Ernst, Collage aus „La femme 100 têtes", 1929.*

□ 858 *›Maske‹*, YAKA *(Zaire), bemaltes Holz, Höhe 22 cm. Sammlung D. und J. de Menil, Houston.*

□ 859 *Max Ernst, ›Capricorne‹, 1948, Bronze (Guß 1964), 240 x 205 cm. Menil Foundation Collection, Houston.*

□ 860 *›Totempfahl‹, TLINGIT (Alaska), bemaltes Holz, Saxman Totem Park, Alaska.*

□ 861 *›Totempfahl‹, zum Gedenken an Mungo Martin, Schnitzerei von Tony und Henry Hunt, KWAKIUTL, Cemetery, Alert Bay (Britisch-Kolumbien), bemaltes Holz.*

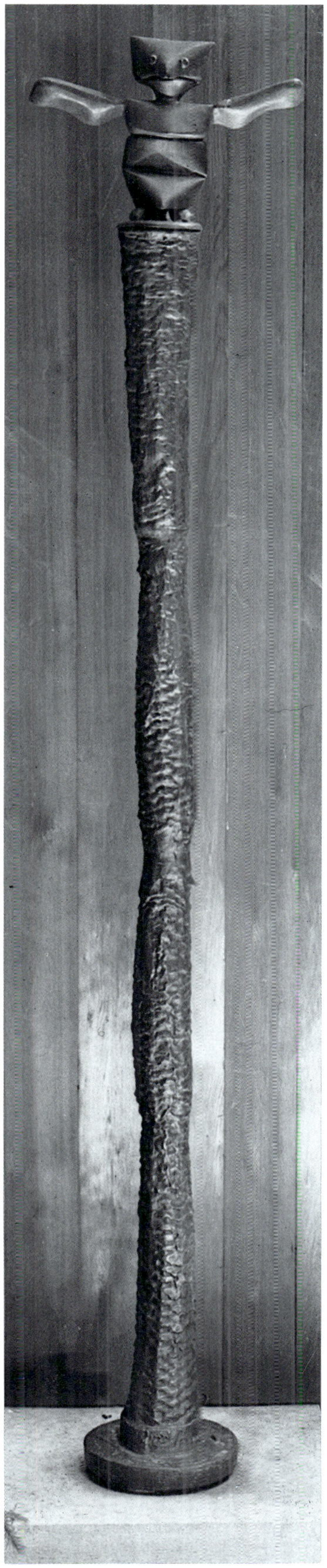

□ 862 *Max Ernst, ›Der Genius der Bastille‹ (Le génie de la Bastille), 1960, Bronze (Guß 1961), Höhe 313 cm. Menil Foundation Collection, Houston.*

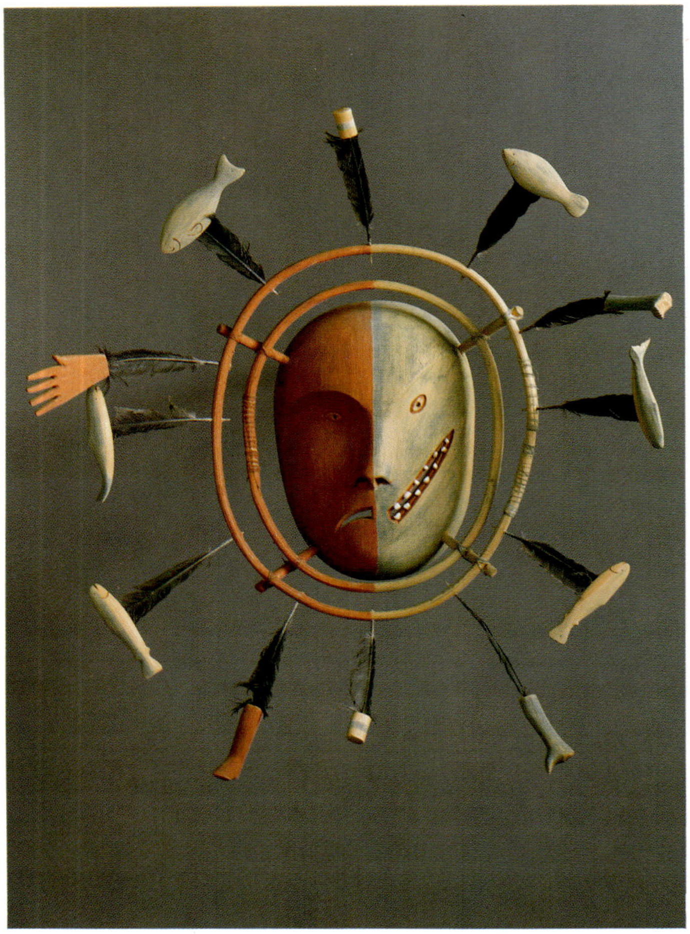

□ 863 *›Maske‹, eskimoisch, Nunivakinsel (Alaska), bemaltes Holz, Federn, Höhe 32 cm. Thomas Burke Memorial Washington State Museum, Seattle.*

□ 864 *›Maske‹, eskimoisch (Alaska), bemaltes Holz, Federn, Höhe 35,5 cm. Lowie Museum of Anthropology, University of California, Berkeley.*

große Stäbe in Händen, und in der *Hopi*-Kultur ist der Stab oftmals Symbol geistiger Kraft und Autorität.[79] So ist die Geste der Hauptfigur von *Capricorne* noch ein weiteres Beispiel dafür, wie Ernsts Kunst Anklänge an eine hohe Kultur, die der *Pueblo-Indianer*, enthält.[80]

Ernsts Skulptur ist wie einige seiner früheren Gemälde auch den Totem-Bildern der Stämme der Nordwestküste verpflichtet. Es war ihm möglich, deren Kunstwerke bei New Yorker Adressen wie Julius Carlebach oder der Heye Foundation käuflich zu erwerben □ 856, Gelegenheiten für Sammler, die sich in Europa nicht boten. Das beste Beispiel für diesen Einfluß ist *Der Genius der Bastille* von 1960 □ 862, in dem der Künstler den Typus der stehenden Vogelfigur in Analogie zu den entsprechenden Werken von der Nordwestküste anwendet. Hier wie dort sitzt der Vogel hoch auf der Spitze eines Pfostens. Ein Totempfahl der *Tlingit* □ 860 mit einem bekrönenden Vogel, der die Flügel weit ausgebreitet hat, sei als Vergleichsbeispiel angeführt. Ernst hat auch westliche Bilder der *Plains-Indianer* in seinen frühen Collagen-Roman *La femme 100 têtes* (1929) integriert □ 857, als er Radierungen mit der Darstellung eines Sonnentanzes benutzte, wie ähnlich schon einmal bei den Köpfen von der Osterinsel für die Collagen von *Une Semaine de bonté.*

Natürlich offenbaren Ernsts Skulpturen auch den Einfluß anderer Stammeskulturen. Ein Motiv, das er vornehmlich von den vierziger bis in die sechziger Jahre anwandte, ist der runde Kopf mit runden Augen und Mund, der in *Mondsüchtig* von 1944 wie auch in vielen Beispielen der Serie der Miniaturmasken aus dem Jahre 1959 auftritt □ 850. Diese elegant abstrahierten Gesichter stehen den eskimoischen »Finger«-Masken □ 852 wie auch einer kleinen eskimoischen Knochenmaske recht nahe, die zu Ernsts Privatsammlung gehörte □ 851. Ein anderes Werk aus dieser Zeit mit auffälliger Ähnlichkeit zur Kunst der *Eskimos* ist Ernsts *Lustige Hunde* von 1958 □ 849. William Rubin wies darauf hin, daß diese Holzskulptur mit der eskimoischen Maske, die auf dem Photo der Sammlung Bretons rechts außen zu sehen ist, verglichen werden kann □ 867.

In seiner Ernst-Biographie beschrieb Waldberg den Künstler als einen Schamanen, »als einen Anrufer der verborgenen Geister, Vermittler der großen Geheimnisse«.[81] Seit ungefähr 1880 war der Schamane Gegenstand großen wissenschaftlichen Interesses. Gerade in Frankreich und Deutschland wurden während der ersten drei Jahrzehnte dieses Jahrhunderts viele Untersuchungen publiziert.[82] Lévy-Bruhl erwähnte Schamanen als Beispiele für primitive Hellsichtigkeit,[83] als Traumdeuter[84] und als Verkörperung übernatürlicher Kräfte,[85] während Frazer in seinem *Goldenen Zweig* Anekdoten schildert, die den Schamanen als einen magischen Bildner erkennen lassen, der menschliche Figuren schnitzt.[86] In einem Interview mit dem Autor bekannte Ernst sein lebenslanges Interesse am Schamanismus und seine Vertrautheit mit der Literatur über dieses Thema, die Eliades große Studie von 1951 zusammenfaßte.[87] Der Schamane ist vor allem Heiler und Seher, der dank seiner Fähigkeit, mit Elementen der geistigen Welt zu kommunizieren, wirksam handeln kann. Die Einweihung des Schamanen stellt Bedingungen, die Ernst in seinen eigenen Autobiographien nachvollzog. Eliade schreibt:

»Welches nun die Art der Erwählung gewesen sei, anerkannt ist ein Schamane erst nach einer doppelten Unterweisung, die 1. durch Ekstase (Träume, Trance usw.), 2. durch Überlieferung (schamanische Techniken, Namen und Funktionen der Geister, Mythologie und Genealogie des Clans, Geheimsprache usw.) geschieht. Diese doppelte Unterweisung durch Geister und durch alte Schamanenmeister kommt einer Initiation gleich.«[88]

Wie schon erwähnt, schrieb Ernst in den ersten Zeilen seiner Autobiographie: »Am 2. April (1891) um 9.45 Uhr schlüpfte Max Ernst aus dem Ei, das seine Mutter in eines Adlers Nest gelegt und auf dem der Vogel sieben Jahre lang gebrütet hatte.«[89] Der Gedanke, daß ein Mensch aus einem Ei geboren wird, das von einem Vogel ausgebrütet worden ist, zieht sich durch die gesamte schamanistische Literatur. Eliade: »Festzuhalten wäre auch das Motiv vom Riesenvogel, welcher auf den Ästen des Weltenbaumes die Schamanen ausbrütet; es hat in den nordasiatischen Mythologien, speziell den schamanistischen, eine große Tragweite.«[90] Daß Ernst den Vogel, der sein Ei ausbrütete, als Adler ausgab, ist ein weiterer wichtiger Hinweis dafür, daß er sich mit dem Schamanen identifizierte. Eliade bemerkte:

»Andererseits ist an die mythischen Beziehungen Adler – Schamane zu denken. Erinnern wir uns, daß der Adler als Vater des ersten Schamanen gilt, eine bedeutende Rolle bei der Initiation des Schamanen spielt und schließlich im Mittelpunkt

□ 865 *›Maske‹, eskimoisch, Kuskokwim River (Alaska), bemaltes Holz, Walroßzahn, Federn und Fasern, Höhe 91 cm. Hamburgisches Museum für Völkerkunde.*

□ 866 *Joan Miró, ›Karneval des Harlekin‹, 1924–25, Öl auf Leinwand, 66 x 93 cm. Albright-Knox Art Gallery, Buffalo.*

□ 867 *›Eskimoische Masken‹, Sammlung André Breton, Paris, um 1955.*

□ 868 *Victor Brauner, ›Die Rückforderung des Symbols‹, 1959, Öl auf Leinwand, 54 x 65 cm. Privatsammlung.*

eines mythischen Komplexes steht, der den Weltenbaum und die ekstatische Reise des Schamanen mitumfaßt.«[91]

Auch mit der Zahl 7 – die Brutzeit des Adlers – spielte Ernst auf den Schamanismus an. Viele schamanistische Riten kennen die Sieben als magische Zahl.[92] Die Autobiographie fährt fort, die bedeutendsten Ereignisse aus Ernsts Kindheit aufzuzählen: »Erster Kontakt mit Halluzinationen: Masern . . . Eine Fiebervision: Vor ihm eine Vertäfelung aus Mahagoniimitation, grob gemalt, schwarz auf rot. Die groben Striche erwekken im Fieberhirn Vorstellungen organischer Art – drohende Augen, lange Nasen, ein enormer Vogelkopf mit dichtem, schwarzem Gefieder . . .«[93] In seiner Studie über die schamanistische Initiation schrieb Eliade: ». . . meistens jedoch bilden Krankheiten, Träume und Ekstasen schon selbst eine Initiation, haben also den Zweck, den profanen Menschen aus der Zeit vor der ›Erwählung‹ in einen Handhaber des Sakralen zu verwandeln.«[94] Es sei geradezu die Empfänglichkeit für solche »›Krankheiten‹, Anfälle, Träume und Halluzinationen, welche in kurzer Zeit einen Menschen zum Schamanen bestimmen«.[95] Es ist bezeichnend, daß zu Ernsts erster halluzinatorischer Erfahrung die dem Schamanen wie dem Künstler eigene Fähigkeit gehörte, gewöhnliche Gegenstände transformiert wahrzunehmen. Von Bedeutung ist auch die Tatsache, daß in den beiden ersten Visionen Vögel vorkamen. Die Bedeutung des Vogels als persönliches totemistisches Zeichen Ernsts wurde bereits erörtert, aber seine Wahl erhält eine zusätzliche Bedeutung, wenn wir erfahren, daß der Vogel auch im Leben des Schamanen eine große Rolle spielte. Hierauf werden wir später zurückkommen.

Ernst schrieb, daß die Nacht von 1906, in der sein Lieblingsvogel starb und seine Schwester geboren wurde, seinen »ersten Kontakt mit okkulten, magischen und Hexenkunst-Kräften« bedeutete.[96] Das Ereignis führte zu einer Anzahl von mystischen Krisen und einer Verwirrung zwischen Vögeln und Menschen, die, wie er sagte, in seinen späteren Zeichnungen und Gemälden zum Vorschein kam. Von diesen Gefühlskrisen und geheimnisvollen Kontakten ausgehend, faßte Ernst die folgenden acht Jahre seines Lebens in einem Satz zusammen, der initiatorischen Traumerfahrungen der Schamanen entspricht, in denen sie Tieren, Hexen und Hellsehern begegnen und in die Wälder, Berge, zu abgelegenen Plätzen und zur Welt der Geister »reisen«, um die Geheimnisse ihrer Berufung zu lernen.[97] Ernsts Entdeckung der mystischen Erfahrung ist diesem Phänomen zu ähnlich, um zufällig zu sein: »(1906–1914) Ausflüge in die Welt der Wunder, Chimären, Phantome, Dichter, Ungeheuer, Philosophen, Vögel, Frauen, Irren, Magier, Bäume, Erotik, Steine, Insekten, Berge, Gifte, Mathematik usw. . . .«[98]

Unmittelbar nach dieser Aufzählung schrieb Ernst den vielleicht merkwürdigsten Abschnitt seiner sehr unorthodoxen Autobiographie:

»(1914) Max Ernst starb am 1. August 1914. Er erlebte seine Wiederauferstehung am 11. 11. 1918 als ein junger Mann, der

□ 869 *›Maske‹, eskimoisch (Alaska), bemaltes Holz, Federn, Höhe 48 cm. Privatsammlung. Ehemals Sammlung André Breton.* ▷

□ 870 *Joan Miró, ›Malerei‹, 1933, Öl auf Leinwand, 174 x 196 cm. The Museum of Modern Art, Schenkung des Advisory Committee, New York.*

□ 871 *›Felszeichnungen‹, Taghtania (Algerien). Veröffentlicht in „Cahiers d'art", Nr. 2, 1930.*

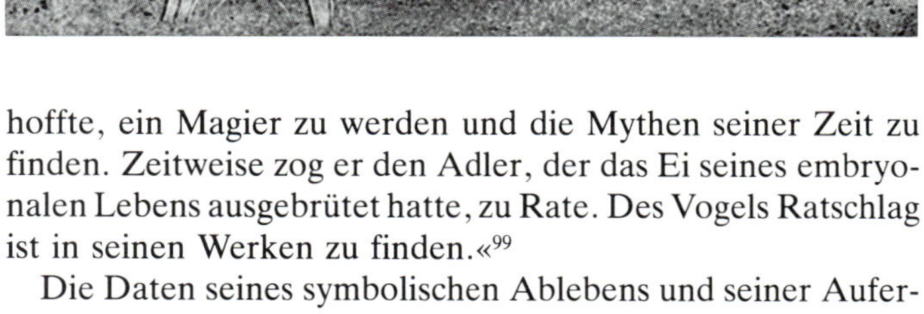

hoffte, ein Magier zu werden und die Mythen seiner Zeit zu finden. Zeitweise zog er den Adler, der das Ei seines embryonalen Lebens ausgebrütet hatte, zu Rate. Des Vogels Ratschlag ist in seinen Werken zu finden.«[99]

Die Daten seines symbolischen Ablebens und seiner Auferstehung sind jene von Ernsts Eintritt und Entlassung aus der deutschen Armee während des Ersten Weltkrieges. Wenn Ernst schrieb, daß er starb und wieder auferstand »als ein junger Mann, der hoffte, ein Magier zu werden und die Mythen seiner Zeit zu finden«, nahm er auf seine symbolische Transformation in einen Schamanen-Künstler Bezug. Ritueller Tod gefolgt von der Wiedergeburt ist Kernpunkt aller wahren schamanistischen Initiationen, denn solange der Aspirant nicht stirbt und wiedergeboren wird, kann er kein Wissen von der geistigen Welt und dem Magischen haben, keinen Zugang zu verborgenen Wahrheiten, die Grundlage für die Ausübung seines heiligen Berufes sind.

Ernsts Bemerkung über das Befragen des Adlers, der ihn zur Welt brachte, ist gleichermaßen bedeutungsvoll, denn die Fähigkeit, sich mit Tieren zu verständigen, ist eine der bedeutsamsten Kräfte eines Schamanen. Dazu bemerkte Eliade: »Die Sprache der Tiere, an erster Stelle die der Vögel, zu erlernen, heißt auch, überall auf der Welt die Geheimnisse der Natur zu kennen und damit auch prophezeien zu können.«[100] Forschungen über schamanistische Phänomene zeigen uns auch Parallelen zu dem ungewöhnlichen Ereignis im Zusammenhang mit dem Vogel, auf den Ernst im letzten Abschnitt seiner Autobiographie zu sprechen kommt: »(1941) Der Vogel folgte dem Flugzeug, das Max am 14. Juli in dieses Land brachte und baute sein Nest in einer Wolke über dem East River.«[101] Im Hinblick auf die schamanistische Beziehung zu Vögeln schrieb Eliade, daß die Verfolgung durch einen Vogel Symbol sei für die geistige Reise zu Wissen und Macht, »von einem Vogel begleitet zu sein, bezeichnet die Fähigkeit, schon im Leben die ekstatische Reise zum Himmel, ins Jenseits zu tun«.[102] Die Untersuchung von Ernsts Autobiographie läßt die Verbindungen zwischen seinen höchst unkonventionellen und rätselhaf-

□ 872 *Victor Brauner, ›Die Konzentrationskraft des M. K.‹, 1934, Öl auf Leinwand, Objekte, 150 x 300 cm. Privatsammlung, Paris.*

□ 873 *›Figur aus Holz (Gott A'a)‹, Rurutu (Australinseln), Höhe 112 cm. The Trustees of the British Museum, London. Vorderansicht* □ *465.*

ten Aussagen und jenen Ritualen und Glaubensbekenntnissen erkennen, die der Berufung und Initiation des Schamanen dienen; auch die Ernsthaftigkeit, mit der er sich mit diesem Aspekt des Primitiven identifizierte.

Max Ernsts Vorliebe für den Vogel als persönliches schamanistisches Symbol wird auch dadurch bestätigt, daß er sich selbst in Gestalt seines Totems darstellte oder von anderen so dargestellt wurde. Leonora Carringtons *Bildnis Max Ernst* von 1940 □ 855 zeigt ihn in einem Gewand aus Vogelfedern, und 1958 erschien er in einem aufwendigen Vogelkostüm, das Dorothea Tanning für den Kostümball mit dem Thema »Mittsommernachtstraum« geschaffen hatte □ 854. Seine bewußte Identifikation mit dem Vogel verweist erneut auf Gemeinsamkeiten mit dem Schamanismus, für den Kostüme ein wichtiger Aspekt der rituellen Praxis sind. Von den drei wichtigsten Wesen, deren Formen Schamanen imitieren, ist der Vogel das häufigste.[103]

Ernst selbst beschrieb sich einmal als eine vogelköpfige Gestalt: »Ich sah mich selbst mit einem Kopf einer Gabelweihe, einem Messer in der Hand, in der Haltung des *Denkers* von Rodin. Doch war es eigentlich die befreite Haltung von Rimbauds Seher.«[104] Ernst bezieht sich dabei auf den *Seher* □ 853, ein Selbstporträt von 1935, in dem er Elemente der symbolistischen Vision und der primitiven Mystik verknüpfte. Wie der primitive Schamane suchte Ernst mit Halluzinationen und Visionen Seher zu werden, der fähig sein würde, hinter die Erscheinungen zu schauen, um den surrealen Visionen seiner schöpferischen Vorstellung Gestalt zu verleihen. Nachdem er

☐ 874 *Roberto S. A. Matta, ›Being With‹, 1946, Öl auf Leinwand, 223,5 x 456 cm. Sammlung des Künstlers.*

☐ 875 *Roberto S. A. Matta, ›Wundbefragung‹, 1948, Öl auf Leinwand, 150 x 196 cm. The Art Institute of Chicago, Sammlung M. und E. Ludgin.*

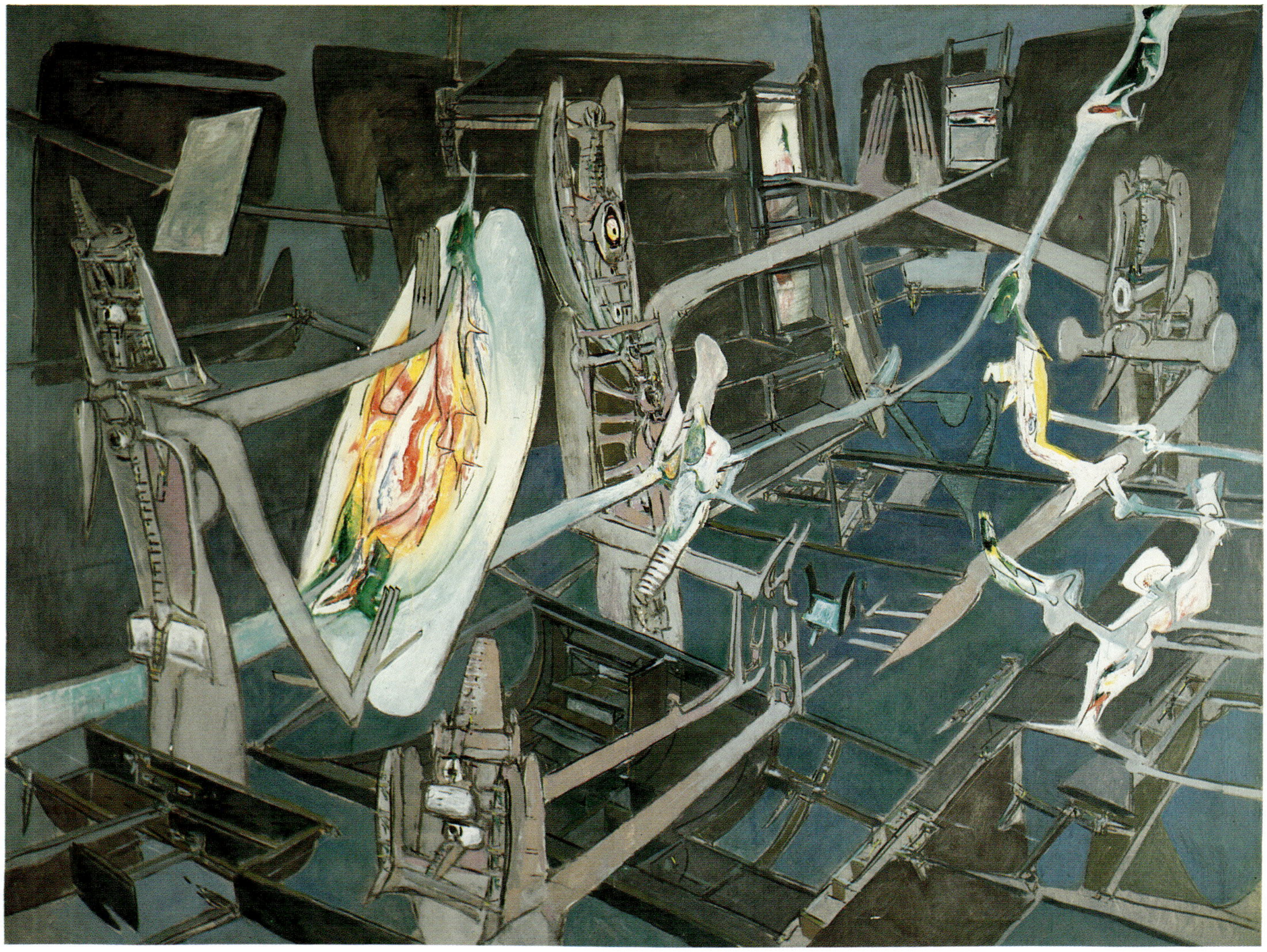

die metamorphische visuelle Entwicklung beschrieben hatte, die zu seinen Collagen führte, schrieb ERNST: »So erhielt ich ein getreues festgelegtes Bild meiner Halluzinationen und wandelte meine geheimsten Wünsche in offenbarende Träume um.«[105] Er suchte keine tatsächliche Kommunikation mit Geistern und übernatürlichen Kräften, statt dessen eher die Fähigkeit, den Bildern Gestalt zu verleihen, die aus den Tiefen des schöpferischen Bewußtseins des Menschen entspringen.

In den frühen Jahren des Surrealismus war ERNST derjenige unter den Künstlern, der sich dem Primitivismus und der Bildwelt der primitiven Kunst am stärksten zuwandte. In unterschiedlichem Maße wurde sein Interesse auch von anderen Surrealisten geteilt, von JOAN MIRÓ genauso wie von MASSON. Obwohl sich MIRÓ mit der Theorie dieses Themas nicht befaßte, stehen seine Bilder der primitiven Ästhetik strukturell sehr nahe. Überdies suchte MIRÓ wie die primitiven Künstler die vitale Essenz der Dinge einzufangen. Dieses Anliegen drückte sich 1939 in der Forderung aus, daß der Künstler »versuchen muß, den religiösen Gehalt, den wesentlichen Sinn der Dinge zu entdecken . . . den der primitiven Völker«.[106]

Elizabeth Cowling sah in eskimoischen Masken mit die frühesten Anreger für MIRÓs Werk, speziell für *Karneval des Harlekin* von 1924–25 □ 866.[107] Es gibt viele Ähnlichkeiten zwischen seinen wunderlich abstrakten Figuren und diesen Masken. Cowling vergleicht etwa den großen runden Kopf der Figur auf der linken Seite von *Karneval* mit einer zusammengesetzten eskimoischen Maske der Nunivakinsel □ 863. Obwohl die Gemeinsamkeiten in Form und Farbe überzeugend sind, ist es unmöglich zu beweisen, daß der Künstler schon so früh solche Objekte gekannt hat. William Rubins Untersuchungen haben gezeigt, daß MIRÓ eskimoische Masken dieses Typs nicht gesehen haben konnte, ehe er *Karneval des Harlekin* gemalt hatte.[108] Auch zu anderen eskimoischen Masken können Parallelen gezogen werden, etwa zu jener mit dem bizarren Gesicht, das in einen tropfenförmigen Körper gestellt ist □ 864, oder zu den Beispielen auf der 1955 aufgenommenen Photographie von Bretons Sammlung □ 867. Diese Ähnlichkeiten können indes nur als Verwandtschaften gedeutet werden, nicht als Einflüsse.

MIRÓs Werk offenbart auch eine enge Beziehung zu prähistorischen Höhlenmalereien.[109] Er bewunderte diese Tier- und Menschenbilder, über die in *Cahiers d'art* allein zwischen 1929 und 1930 fünf Artikel erschienen. Der Einfluß dieser Höhlenmalereien auf MIRÓ wird in seinen gewundenen Figuren der dreißiger Jahre und in seinen Darstellungen vereinfachter Tierformen auf einer wandartigen Oberfläche oftmals deutlich. Ein glänzendes Beispiel für seine Nähe zur paläolithischen Bildwelt sind die anmutig stilisierten Tiere und Horngebilde seiner *Malerei* von 1933 □ 870 im Vergleich mit einer Darstellung ganz ähnlicher und genauso komponierter Formen, die 1930 in dem Artikel »Les origines de l'art et de la culture« in den *Cahiers d'art* erschien □ 871.

Auch andere dem Surrealismus in den 30er und 40er Jahren nahestehende Künstler brachten der Stammeskunst ihre Bewunderung entgegen. Neben ALBERTO GIACOMETTI, der in diesem Buch gesondert behandelt wird, sind es vor allem BRAUNER, MATTA, PAALEN und LAM, die auf jeweils ganz individuelle Weise primitive Anregungen verarbeiteten.

□ 876 *›Yipwon-Figur‹, ALAMBLAK, Karawari River, Provinz Ost-Sepik (Papua-Neuguinea), Holz, Federn und Stoff, Höhe 205 cm. Privatsammlung, New York.*

□ 877 ›*Lendentuch*‹, *Sentani-See (Irian Jaya), bemalter Rindenstoff, Höhe 56 cm. Tropenmuseum, Amsterdam.*

□ 878 ›Liebesszene‹, australische Ureinwohner, bemalte Rinde, 86 cm. Sammlung Friede, New York.

□ 879 Joan Miró, ›Mann und Frau‹, 1935, Öl auf Karton, 106 x 75 cm. Privatsammlung.

□ 880 ›Figur aus Holz‹, Lega oder Baule (Zaire), Höhe 20 cm. Sammlung D. und J. de Menil, Houston.

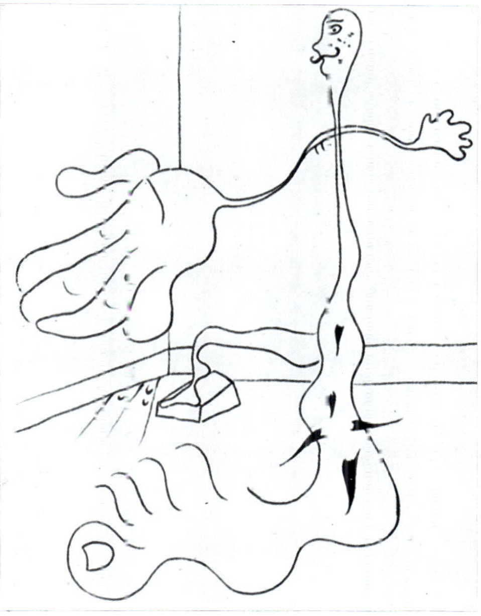

□ 881 Joan Miró, ›Statue‹, 1926, Contékreide, 62 x 48 cm. The Museum of Modern Art, New York.

☐ 885 *Wifredo Lam, ›Begegnung‹, 1946, Tusche, 30,5 x 24,5 cm. Sammlung H. Benitez, Saarbrücken.* ▷

☐ 882 *›Reiterfigur‹, SENUFO (Elfenbeinküste), Holz, Höhe 34 cm. Privatsammlung, New York.*

☐ 883 *›Goli-Maske‹, BAULE (Elfenbeinküste), Holz, Höhe 99 cm. Privatsammlung.*

☐ 884
Wifredo Lam, ›Das Omen‹, 1947, Öl auf Leinwand, 100 x 105 cm. Sammlung R. Morone, Turin.

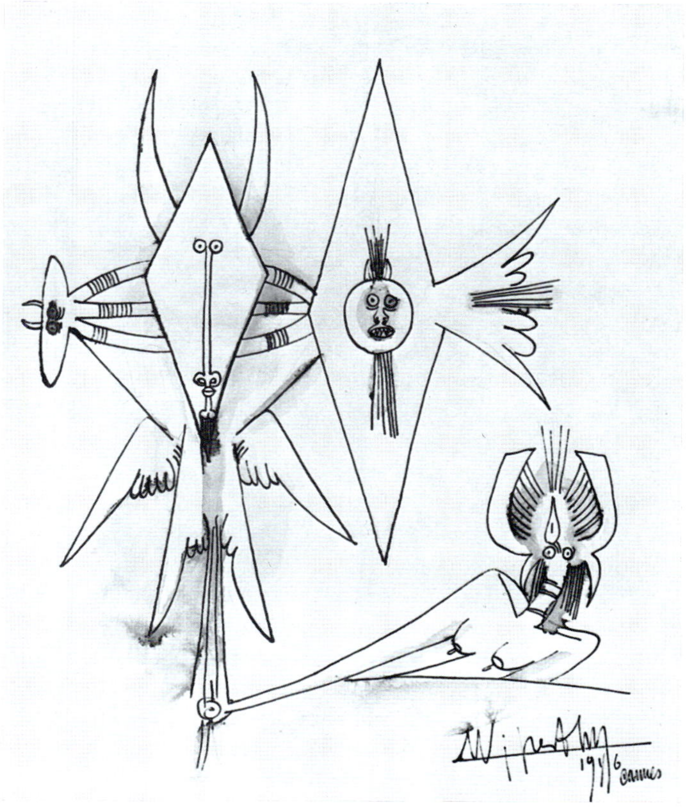

Victor Brauners Kunst ist vom gleichen Geist geheimnisvoller und ikonischer Kraft durchdrungen, den viele primitive Kunstwerke ausstrahlen. Während etwa viele seiner Bilder an altägyptische oder präkolumbianische Kunst nur weitläufig erinnern, offenbaren andere ganz überraschende Übereinstimmungen mit bestimmten Typen primitiver Objekte. So ist etwa die Hauptfigur in *Die Konzentrationskraft des M. K.* von 1934 □ 872, über deren nackten Körper kleine Figuren krabbeln, von der berühmten Skulptur der Australinseln im Britischen Museum inspiriert □ 873, einem Werk, das auch Picasso (siehe S. 343 und □ 465) und später Henry Moore bewundern sollten.

Brauner war auch an den zweidimensionalen anthropomorphen Tierfiguren interessiert, die in der Kunst Südamerikas und Mexikos wie unter den Indianern Nordamerikas weitverbreitet waren. Eines der besten Beispiele seiner Begeisterung für diese Bildwelt ist sein *Vorspiel zu einer Zivilisation* von 1954 □ 886, das das »Schattenbild« eines großen Tieres darstellt. Darin eingeschlossen sind viele stilisierte Darstellungen von Pferden und Reitern, Kriegern, Tieren, Masken und abstrakten Symbolen. Die Idee hierfür entnahm Brauner den mit Bildzeichen übersäten Gewändern der *Plains-Indianer* □ 888, die die Taten eines Kriegers auf einer Tierhaut darstellten, deren Umriß ein Tier wiedergibt. Seine geheimnisvollen Figuren zeigen auch starke Ähnlichkeiten mit prähistorischen Steininschriften des Südwestens und mit altmexikanischen Buchmalereien, etwa jenen in der Bibliothèque Nationale in Paris □ 887.

Unter den späteren Surrealisten war Matta der begeistertste und belesenste Kenner der primitiven Kunst, der seine große Sammlung primitiver Objekte mit einem Gespür für erfinderische Phantasie wie auch Qualität aufbaute. Mattas Beziehung zur Stammeskunst zeigt sich in einer allgemeinen ästhetischen und emotionalen Verwandtschaft wie auch in punktuellen Anleihen. Seine Verarbeitung von Aspekten des Primitiven ist

□ 886 *Victor Brauner, ›Vorspiel zu einer Zivilisation‹, 1954, Enkaustik auf Holz, 130 x 195 cm. Privatsammlung.*

□ 887 *›Sonnenkult‹ (Aubin-Manuskript Nr. 20), präkolumbianisch, Mixteken (Mexiko), bemaltes Leder, Höhe 51 cm. Bibliothèque Nationale, Paris.*

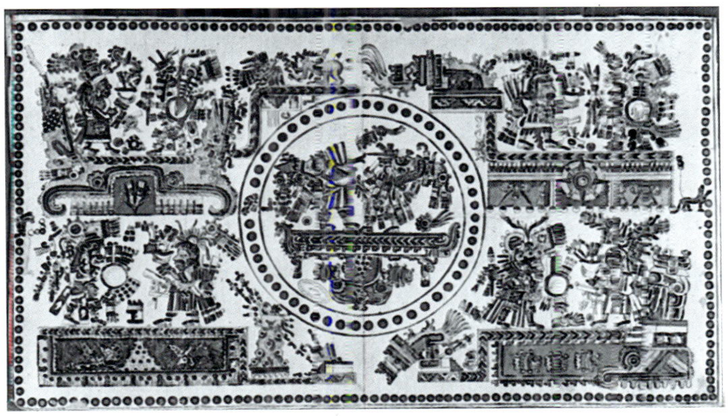

□ 888 *›Umhang‹, Hidatsa (Norddakota), bemaltes Bisonleder und Federn, Höhe 300 cm. Linden-Museum, Stuttgart.*

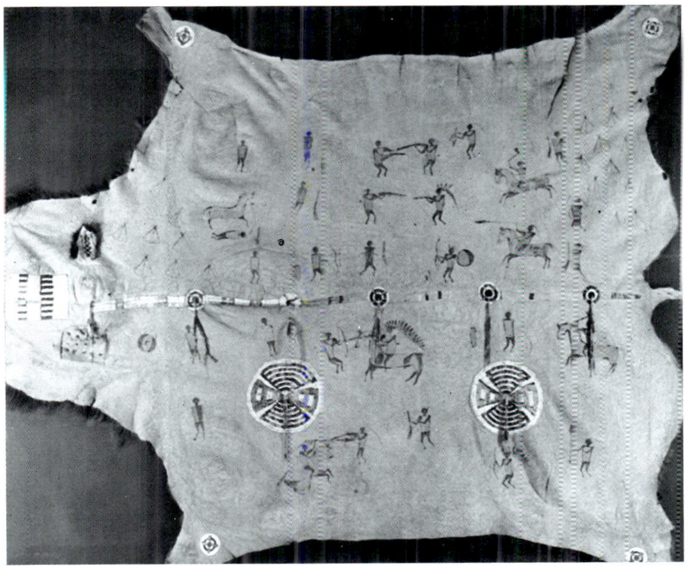

☐ 889 *›Kopf‹, Neubritannien, bemaltes Holz, Höhe 157 cm. Musée Barbier-Müller, Genf.*

in den monströsen »personnages« seiner Gemälde der späten vierziger und frühen fünfziger Jahre besonders augenfällig. Beispiele hierfür wurden von William Rubin in der Einführung des vorliegenden Buches behandelt (siehe S. 61 ff.). Zu jener Zeit schuf MATTA eine Vielfalt von Geschöpfen, deren Körper oftmals entlang einer vertikalen Achse angeordnet sind, wie in *Being With* von 1946 ☐ 874. Die Figuren im Vordergrund rechts und in der Mitte, die von pfahlartigen Formen flankiert sind, zeigen eine starke Ähnlichkeit mit den Malanggan-Skulpturen aus Neuirland, von denen MATTA eine Anzahl besaß und sich ein hervorragendes Exemplar in der Sammlung von MAX ERNST befand ☐ 751. Diese Beziehung ist besonders auffällig, wenn man die Mittelfigur von *Being With* mit einem Teil des Malanggan vergleicht ☐ 749, denn beide enthalten eine Figur, die eingeschlossen ist und darüber hinaus von parallelen Gruppen flankierender Elemente gehalten wird. Diese Elemente und ein auffälliger Sinn für dramatische Gestik sind auch kennzeichnend für eine andere Skulptur, die als Modell für diese Bildwelt diente: ALBERTO GIACOMETTIS Skulptur *Der unsichtbare Gegenstand* ☐ 725, deren originale Gipsform MATTA besaß. Viele von MATTAS Gestalten, wie etwa in *Wundbefragung* von 1948 ☐ 875, zeichnen sich durch eine Aggressivität aus, die von ihrer packenden Gestik wie von den scharfen, zackenförmigen Elementen herrührt, die ihre durchbrochenen Körper und Köpfe bilden. Die Anregung für diese machtvolle Bildwelt kam u. a. von den Figuren aus dem Gebiet des Karawari (Neuguinea). MATTA hatte eine besondere Vorliebe für diese Skulpturen und besaß auch einige Werke dieser Region ☐ 876.

Auch WOLFGANG PAALEN war ein begeisterter Sammler primitiver Kunst, obschon seine Annäherung an diesen Komplex akademischer als bei MATTA war. Einen großen Teil seiner Energie investierte er in deren Studium. Während sein eigenes Werk unspezifische Formen des Totemismus erkennen läßt, finden die eigentlichen Auswirkungen seines Primitivismus in seinen Schriften ihren Niederschlag. Auf das künstlerische Erbe von Nord- und Südamerika konzentriert, wandte sich PAALEN vor allem den reichen Traditionen der Nordwestküste Amerikas zu. 1945 publizierte seine Zeitschrift *DYN* mehrere Nummern, in deren Mittelpunkt Artikel über die Kunst Mexikos und Nordamerikas standen.[110] Nicht zuletzt wegen seiner Belesenheit und seiner wissenschaftlichen Neigungen wurde PAALEN zum Wortführer der Surrealisten in ihrer Parteinahme für die Naturvölker und deren Kunst. In der Einführung zu der Ausgabe von *DYN,* die die Indoamerikaner behandelte, formulierte er beredt die wichtigsten Ziele der Gruppe am Ende des Zweiten Weltkriegs und unterstrich Amerikas neue kulturtragende Rolle für das vom Krieg verwüstete Europa:

»Bis heute haben die Phasen kulturellen Wandels ihre Orientierung nur intuitiv gefunden; so wurde die Kunst des Okzidents abwechselnd von der Asiens, Afrikas und Ozeaniens befruchtet, heute ist es verständlich geworden, weshalb jetzt der Augenblick gekommen ist, den enormen Reichtum der indianischen Formen in das Bewußtsein der modernen Kunst zu integrieren . . .«[111]

Surrealisten wie Breton, MASSON, ERNST, TANGUY, PAALEN und LAM suchten während des Zweiten Weltkriegs politischen Schutz in Nord- und Südamerika. Ihre Erfahrungen auf Kuba, in Mexiko und den Vereinigten Staaten verstärkten ihr Bewußtsein von der Bedeutung der altamerikanischen Kulturen und der zeitgenössischen Künstler.

Breton unterstrich in seinem 1941 erschienenen Artikel über

den kubanischen Maler WIFREDO LAM die Verbindungen zwischen dem Surrealismus und dem Primitiven, als er bemerkte, daß »das moderne Auge die unendliche Vielfalt jener Objekte der sogenannten ›Wilden‹ allmählich entdeckte . . . und im Bewußtsein der unvergleichlichen Ressourcen der primitiven Vision sich schließlich in diese Vision so verliebte, daß es das Unmögliche wünscht und sich mit ihm vereinigen will«.[112] Aus Bretons Sicht war LAM der Künstler, der diese Assimilation der visuellen und symbolischen Grundlagen der primitiven Kunst am besten verwirklichen konnte. Michel Leiris, der surrealistische Dichter und führende französische Afrika-Ethnologe, hat ausführlich über LAM geschrieben und wie Breton die engen Beziehungen des Künstlers zur primitiven Bildwelt und Magie wiederholt erläutert. Leiris führte aus, daß LAMS persönliche Verbindung mit dem Primitiven von dem frühen Kontakt mit seiner Patin herrührte, einer »professionellen Zauberin« im Voodoo-Kult, der auf Kuba und anderen karibischen Inseln sehr populär war.[113] Schon als Kind war er Augenzeuge von Visionen, Trancezuständen und Tieropfern. Er entwickelte ein rituelles Bewußtsein für die Kräfte des Dschungels und die Naturgeister, und er war mit afrikanischen oder von Afrika beeinflußten Gegenständen vertraut, die in den magisch-religiösen Zeremonien benutzt wurden.[114] Breton schrieb in seiner schon erwähnten Schrift über LAM:

»Die reichen Quellen der primitiven Vision sind bei Wifredo Lam nicht versiegt; aufgrund seiner Herkunft . . . hat er die einmalige Chance, instinktiv aus ihnen zu schöpfen, während er gleichzeitig vom Gefühl her dem sozialen Bewußtsein dieses Zeitalters tief verhaftet bleibt und die am höchsten entwickelte Technik beherrscht.«[115]

Dies war LAMS große Synthese als Surrealist: Er verband eine enge Anlehnung an das Stammesritual mit der kulturellen und künstlerischen Weltklugheit des westlichen Intellektuellen.

Als Erwachsener wurde LAM erstmals 1928, während seiner Studienzeit in Madrid, von afrikanischer Stammesskulptur gefesselt.[116] Obwohl er die Völkerkunde dieser Kultur nie studierte, nahm er begierig und gründlich ihre Formen figuraler Abstraktion auf. LAM war sich bewußt, wieviel er primitiver Kunst verdankte, als er einmal im Hinblick auf eine BAULE-Maske in seiner Sammlung ausrief: »Sie sehen – ich habe diese Formen ganz spontan wiedergewonnen! Sie sind in mir wie eine angestammte Überlieferung lebendig geworden.«[117]

1938 übersiedelte LAM nach Paris, wo er sich bald mit PICASSO anfreundete, dessen »afrikanische« Werke der Jahre 1907–08 auch den jungen kubanischen Maler beeinflußten. 1941 und 1942 vollzog sich in LAMS Werk ein größerer Wandel. Er ersetzte seine früheren Figuren, die flache, ovale Köpfe hatten, durch ein abwechslungsreicheres Formenrepertoire und durch Gesichtstypen, die er mit einer üppigen Dschungellandschaft neu verschmolz. Diese Veränderung seiner Malerei hängt mit LAMS Rückkehr in seine karibische Heimat zusammen, zu der ihn die Situation Frankreichs während des Zweiten Weltkriegs zwang. Zurück auf den Antillen vermochte LAM die künstlerischen Lektionen, die er in Europa gelernt hatte, seinen künstlerischen Intentionen dienstbar zu machen, um ein mächtiges Empfinden des primitiven Bewußtseins im Herzen seines Erbes auszudrücken. »Nach den vielen Jahren, die er weit entfernt von den Tropen verbrachte«, schrieb Leiris, »war die Wiederentdeckung seiner Heimat, die er antraf, als die Welt von einem globalen Krieg überzogen war, sicherlich ein großer Schock für Lam. Er regte ihn zu einer Neueinschätzung von allem an, so daß die Malerei nicht nur zu einem Mittel der Selbstbestätigung

□ 900 *›Gestell für Opfergaben‹, Mangareva (Gambierinseln), Holz, Höhe 178 cm. Musée de l'Homme, Paris.*

□ 901 ›*Maske*‹, GUERE *(Elfenbeinküste), Holz, Höhe 28 cm. Privatsammlung.*

chen weiblichen Figuren bevölkert, die im Vordergrund des für LAM typischen flachen, nichtillusionistischen Raumes stehen. LAM huldigt der geläufigen »Vereinfachung« der primitiven Kunst und PICASSOS *Demoiselles d'Avignon* □ 301. In beiden Bildern steht nahe dem linken Bildrand eine Figur, die einen Arm über den Kopf hält, um das Auge des Betrachters auf die anderen Figuren der rechten Seite zu lenken. Eine weitere kompositionelle Beziehung besteht zwischen LAMS und PICASSOS Frau unmittelbar rechts neben der ersten Figur, die in beiden Fällen den Betrachter mit einem hocherhobenen rechten Arm anblicken, wobei der Ellbogen nach oben zeigt. Eine weitere Verwandtschaft zwischen den beiden Bildern besteht in der großen Frau auf der äußersten Rechten von *Der Dschungel,* deren Kopf in Form einer Mondsichel LAM direkt der roten Sichelform des Stillebens entlehnte, das im Vordergrund der *Demoiselles* erscheint. Ihr Körper erinnert auch an die Figur im oberen rechten Teil von PICASSOS Gemälde, denn in beiden sind die Arme angehoben, so daß ihre Ellbogen auf die Bildmitte zurückweisen.

Von PICASSOS früher Erwiderung auf die primitive Skulptur künden die Gesichter der beiden Frauen auf der rechten Seite der *Demoiselles.* Wie Rubin ausführte, können diese nicht mit

wurde, sondern auch zur Gestaltung eindringlicher Bilder dessen, was es sei, ein Mensch unter Menschen zu sein und ein lebendes Wesen inmitten des Kosmos.«[118]

LAMS wichtigstes Symbol natürlicher Kraft und Präsenz wurden das üppige Laubwerk des Dschungels und die undurchdringlichen Zuckerrohrfelder, die für die kubanische Landschaft so charakteristisch sind, wie auch allgemeine Anspielungen auf seine Nähe zu Afrika. Das beste Beispiel für diese Bildwelt des Urwaldes ist *Der Dschungel* aus dem Jahr 1943 □ 791, in der schnell trocknenden Technik der Gouache ausgeführt, die es LAM ermöglichte, viele dünne, transparente Farbschichten aufzutragen, so daß mehrere Bilder übereinander zu sehen sind. Dadurch entstanden nicht nur eindrucksvolle Effekte von Transparenz, sondern auch die Wirkung einer gegenseitigen Durchdringung von Phänomenen, die ein zentraler Aspekt der primitiven Naturauffassung ist. *Der Dschungel* erweckt den Eindruck von undurchdringlicher Urwaldvegetation, in deren Mitte weibliche Figuren stehen, deren röhrenförmige Beine und runde Knie, Gesäß, Körper und Brüste so angelegt sind, daß sie vom umgebenden Laubwerk beinahe nicht unterschieden werden können. So getarnt bilden sie einen wesentlichen Bestandteil ihrer natürlichen Umgebung – eine vom Primitiven inspirierte Darstellung der Vereinigung der Menschheit mit der Natur. LAM selbst erläuterte diese Synthese, als er schrieb, daß wir in seinen Dschungelszenen Augenzeuge sein können von »Lebewesen auf ihrer Reise vom pflanzlichen zum tierischen Zustand, dem Wald noch in Resten verhaftet«.[119]

Der Dschungel führt nicht nur LAMS Anwendung der primitiven Bildlichkeit exemplarisch vor, sondern auch Einflüsse PICASSOS, zu dem er als Lehrer und geistig verwandten Menschen aufschaute. Das dichte Laubwerk ist von vier totemglei-

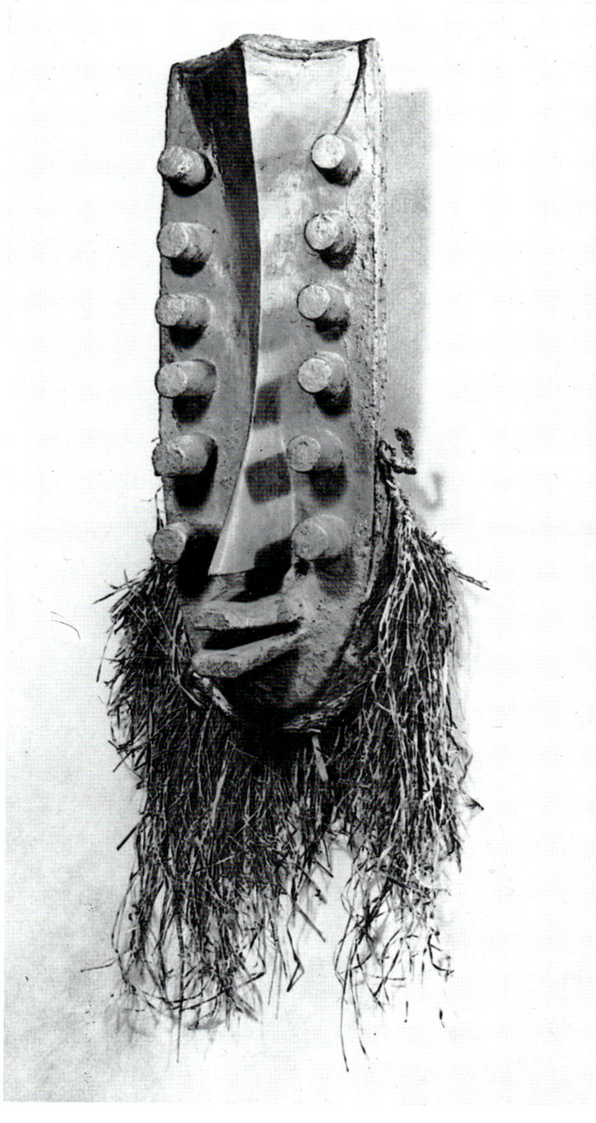

□ 902 ›*Maske*‹, GREBO, *Guigloregion (Elfenbeinküste), Holz und Fasern, Höhe 42 cm. Musée d'Art Africain (I.F.A.N.), Dakar, Senegal. Ständige Leihgabe des Musée des Arts Africains et Océaniens, Paris.*

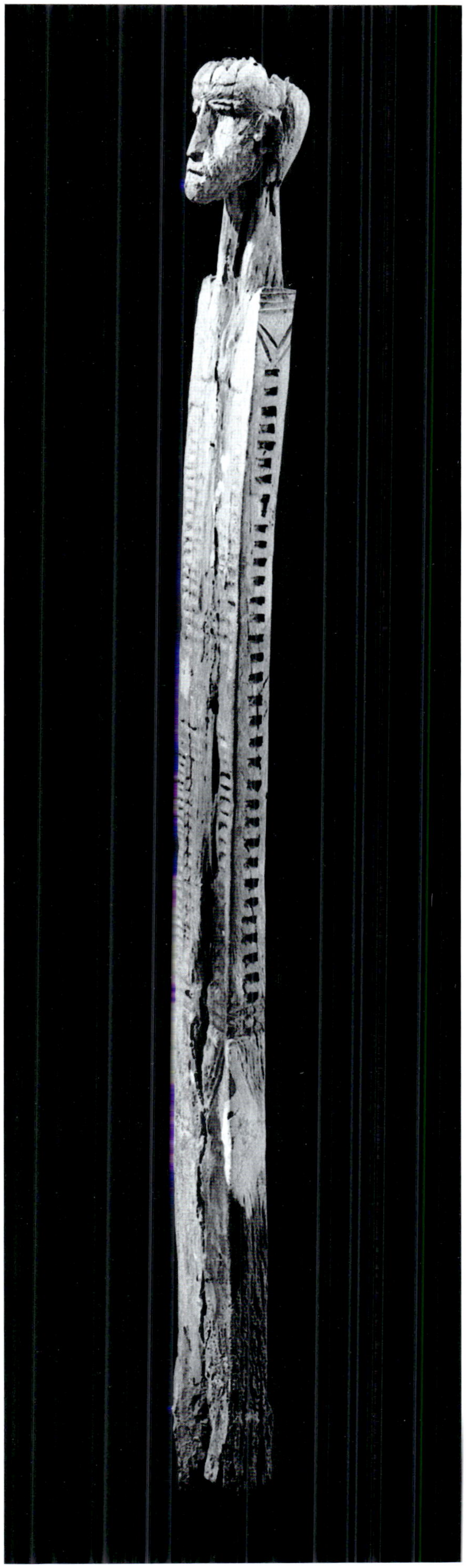

□ 903 ▷
›Grabfigur‹, KAMBE *(Kenia), Holz, Höhe 220 cm. Privatsammlung, Belgien.*

□ 904 ▷ ▷
›Grabfigur‹, GIRYAMA *(Kenia), Holz, Höhe 152 cm. Privatsammlung, Belgien.*

□ 905 *›Figur aus Holz‹*, FON *(Volksrepublik Benin), Höhe 43 cm. Privatsammlung, Paris.*

bestimmten Stammesskulpturen in Verbindung gebracht werden, die PICASSO gesehen haben könnte. Anders bei LAM, der sich von einer Reiterfigur der SENUFO anregen ließ □ 882. Der nach vorn geneigte Kopf, die Schmucknarben oder die lange Nase und der vorspringende Mund des *SENUFO*-Objekts finden sich bei der sitzenden und stehenden Figur auf der linken Seite von *Der Dschungel* wieder: Die genitalförmigen Anhängsel am Kinn dieser Gesichter treten in LAMS Werk häufig auf und sind auch mit den stilisierten Bärten wie etwa in Skulpturen der *DOGON* oder der *TEKE* vergleichbar.[120] Andere Züge afrikanischer Stile, die LAM in *Der Dschungel* übernahm, sind die Betonung von Gesäß und Brüsten wie auch die Vereinfachung der Glieder, Hände und Füße.

Ein weiteres Beispiel für LAMS synkretistische Anwendung der primitiven Bildsprache ist *Omen* von 1947 □ 884. Hier weichen die zusammengedrängten Formen des tropischen Dschungels einem kargen Hintergrund, in dem LAMS mythische Gestalten bedrohlich umherschweben. Ihr geheimnisvolles Wesen wird durch Formen erreicht, die LAM von zwei anderen Typen afrikanischer Masken ableitete, die er besonders schätzte. Der runde Kopf mit den starren Augen in der unteren Bildmitte des Gemäldes stammt von der Goli-Maske der *BAULE* □ 883, ein Einfluß, den LAM, wie oben erwähnt, selbst bezeugte. Die Figuren in der oberen rechten Ecke von *Omen* haben gestreckte, kantige Gesichter, die auf die Masken des Kono-Bundes der *BAMBARA* zurückgehen □ 846.

Die Surrealisten versuchten einzeln wie als Gruppe ihre Ideen sowohl auf das Leben wie auf die Kunst anzuwenden – »die Welt umzugestalten, das Leben zu ändern, aus dem Nichts menschliches Verständnis zu erneuern« (Breton).[121] In ihrem Bemühen, Einsicht und Wahrnehmung zu erweitern und die schöpferischen Kräfte neu zu beleben, suchten sie den elementarsten Energiebereich der Menschheit nutzbar zu machen: das unbegrenzte Potential des Unbewußten, das sich in Träumen und in Mythen manifestiert. Von Anfang an waren sich die Surrealisten bewußt, daß diese mächtigen Kräfte die primitiven Gesellschaften so stark durchdringen, daß sie alle Schranken zwischen Leben und Kunst aufheben; diese Erkenntnis erklärt die Anziehungskraft, die das Primitive auf sie ausübte.

Obwohl Breton unter den Surrealisten einer der frühesten und glühendsten Verfechter des Primitivismus war, erkannte er schließlich die große Schwierigkeit der westlichen Gesellschaft, sich tatsächlich mit den Stammeskulturen zu verbinden. 1955, elf Jahre vor seinem Tod, drückte er seine Skepsis gegenüber dem Stand des Primitivismus aus, den er infolge mangelnder Unterstützung von seiten der völkerkundlichen Forschung in einem desolaten Zustand sah.

»Leider war die Ethnographie trotz unserer Ungeduld nicht in der Lage, ausreichende Schritte zu unternehmen, um die Entfernung zwischen uns und den alten Maya oder der zeitgenössischen Kultur der Ureinwohner Australiens zu verringern. Nach wie vor kennen wir zum großen Teil ihre Wünsche nicht, und wir haben von ihren Bräuchen ein nur sehr bruchstückhaftes Wissen. Die Inspiration, die wir aus ihrer Kunst ziehen konnten, blieb letztlich unwirksam, weil es uns an dem fundamentalen organischen Kontakt fehlt, so daß ein Gefühl von Wurzellosigkeit bleibt.«[122]

Obschon Breton an der westlichen Fähigkeit zweifelte, eine mit den primitiven Kulturen vergleichbare geistige Integrität wiederherzustellen und zuletzt zu einer Rückbesinnung auf die frühen europäischen Wurzeln riet, sahen Surrealisten im Primitiven auch weiterhin eine reiche Quelle der Inspiration.

□ 906 *›Figur aus Holz‹*, Abelam, *Provinz Ost-Sepik (Papua-Neuguinea), Höhe 108 cm. The Metropolitan Museum of Art, The M. C. Rockefeller Memorial Collection, Schenkung N. A. Rockefeller, New York.*

☐ 907 *›Ahnenfigur‹, Geelvink Bay (Irian Jaya), Holz und Schädel, Höhe 44 cm. Museum voor Land-en Volkenkunde, Rotterdam.*

Anmerkungen

1. Neue Zürcher Zeitung, 5. Februar 1916.

2. Richter, H., *Dada-Kunst und Antikunst,* Köln 1964, S. 33.

3. Alfred Stieglitz' Galerie für moderne Kunst in der Fifth Avenue Nr. 291 in New York veranstaltete 1914 und 1916 die ersten Verkaufsausstellungen für afrikanische und präkolumbianische Kunst. Die Februar-Ausgabe seiner Zeitschrift *291* des Jahres 1916 zeigte als Titelbild eine Reliquiarfigur der KOTA und enthielt einen Artikel von Marius de Zayas unter dem Titel »Modern Art . . . Negro Art«.

4. Browning, G. F., *Tristan Tzara: The Genesis of the Dada Poem, or From Dada to Aa,* Stuttgart 1979, S. 11.

5. Horne, A., *The Price of Glory: Verdun, 1916,* New York 1962, S. 328.

6. Naumann, F. M., »Janco/Dada: An Interview with Marcel Janco« in *Arts Magazine,* November 1982, S. 81.

7. Arp, J., *Arp on Arp: Poems, Essays, Memories,* Jean, M. (Hrsg.), New York 1970, S. 39.

8. Arp, ebenda, S. 39.

9. Motherwell, R. (Hrsg.), *The Dada Painters and Poets: An Anthology,* New York 1967, S. xx.

10. Arp, a.a.O., S. 338.

11. Richter, a.a.O., S. 20, 23, 77, 79.

12. Ebenda, S. 18–19. Jancos Masken haben auch Ähnlichkeiten mit den Masken aus Rindentuch von den Neuen Hebriden und Neubritannien wie auch mit bestimmten Masken der *MARKA* und *BAMBARA.*

13. Naumann, a.a.O., S. 83.

14. Richter, a.a.O., S. 23.

15. German, P., »Das plastisch-figürliche Kunstgewerbe im Graslande von Kamerun« in *Jahrbuch des Museums für Völkerkunde, Leipzig,* Leipzig 1911.

16. Man Rays Gemälde *Totem* aus dem Jahre 1914 teilt diesen primitiven Minimalismus.

17. Hennings, E., »Das Cabaret Voltaire und die Galerie Dada« in *Als Dada begann, Eine Dada-Chronik,* Zürich 1957, S. 42.

18. Tzara, T., »L'Art et l'Océanie« in *Cahiers d'art* 1, 1929, S. 59–60; »A propos de l'art précolumbien« in *Cahiers d'art* 4, 1929, S. 170–72.

19. Tzara, T., »Note sur l'art nègre« in *SIC,* Nr. 21–22, September-Oktober 1917.

20. Peterson, E., *Tristan Tzara: Dada and Surrational Theorist,* New Brunswick 1971, S. 46.

21. Tzara, a.a.O.

22. Peterson, a.a.O., S. 11.

23. Siehe »Chanson de cocadou« in *Dada,* Nr. 1, Juli 1917 und »Tribu Loritja«, »Le Chanson de Serpent« in *Dada,* Nr. 2, Dezember 1917.

24. Frazer, J. G., *The New Golden Bough,* Gaster, T. H. (Hrsg.), New York 1964, S. 196.

25. Diese Theorien sind auch von Andrew Lang und Wilhelm Wundt entwickelt worden. Siehe Maurer, E. M., *In Quest of the Myth. An Investigation of the Relationships between Surrealism and Primitivism,* Diss., University of Pennsylvania, 1969, S. 28–30, 34–39.

26. Lévy-Bruhl, L., *Primitive Mentality,* Boston 1966, S. 98.

27. Ebenda, S. 8–9.

28. Breton, A., *Entretiens (1913–52),* Paris 1952, S. 245.

29. Freud, S., *Totem und Tabu,* Frankfurt a. M. und Hamburg 1956, S. 7.

30. Ebenda, S. 102–103.

31. Apollinaire, G., *Alcools,* Berkeley 1965, S. 12.

32. »Opinions sur l'art nègre« in *Action 1,* April 1920.

33. Siehe Maurer, *In Quest of the Myth,* a.a.O., S. 12–15.

34. *Sculptures d'Afrique, d'Amérique, d'Océanie,* Paris, Galerie Paul Guillaume, 1931.

35. Jean, M., *The History of Surrealist Painting,* New York 1960, S. 247–52.

36. Ray, P. C., *The Surrealist Movement in England,* Ithaca 1971, S. 135.

37. Browder, C. H., *André Breton: Arbiter of Surrealism,* Genf 1967, S. 61.

38. Breton, a.a.O., S. 244–45.

39. Breton, A., *L'Amour fou,* Paris 1937, S. 106.

40. Leiris, M., und Limbour, G., *André Masson et son univers,* Paris 1947, S. 127–28, und Interviews mit André Masson von Evan M. Maurer, 8. Dezember 1970.

41. *Irokesische Landschaft* von 1942 ist ein anderes Beispiel für Massons Hinwendung zu indianischen Themen.

42. Frazer, a.a.O., S. 120–24.

43. Basler, A., *L'Art chez les peuples primitifs,* Paris 1929, S. 9

44. Frazer, J. G., *The Worship of Nature,* New York 1926, S. 316–440.

45. Ebenda, S. 427.

46. Ebenda, S. 378–80, 402–03, 427.

47. Interview mit André Masson von Evan M. Maurer, 8. Dezember 1970.

48. Masson, A., *Le Plaisir de peindre,* Nizza 1950, S. 180.

49. Interview mit André Masson von Evan M. Maurer, 8. Dezember 1970.

50. Ebenda.

51. Ebenda. Dieser Typus von »Röntgen«-Bildern wird gewöhnlich auch in der Skulptur und Malerei der Stämme der Nordwestküste Amerikas gefunden, wo er in besonderer Weise mit dem Phänomen des Schamanismus verknüpft ist. Siehe Maurer, E. M., *The Native American Heritage,* Chicago 1977, S. 290, 310.

52. Ernst, M., *Beyond Painting, and Other Writings by the Artist and His Friends,* Motherwell, R. (Hrsg.), New York 1948, S. 194.
Einzelne Abschnitte wurden zitiert aus dem Ausstellungskatalog *Max Ernst,* Köln und Zürich, 1962–63, aus *Max Ernst – Jenseits der Malerei, das graphische Œuvre,* Hannover 1972, und aus dem Ausstellungskatalog *Max Ernst,* München und Berlin 1979.

53. Waldberg, P., *Max Ernst,* Paris 1958, S. 60.

54. Penrose, R., *Max Ernst's Celebes,* University of Newcastle upon Tyne 1972, S. 14–15. Ernsts Interesse für Völkerkundemuseen zeigt sich auch an dem Titel seiner Skulptur *Das Völkerkundemuseum (Le Musée de l'homme)* aus dem Jahr 1965. Dargestellt ist ein Mann, der auf dem Boden sitzt und mit den Armen die Knie umfaßt, eine Haltung, die von Steinskulpturen aus Ecuador und Costa Rica (ca. 1000–1500 n. Chr.) direkt übernommen ist. Derselbe Titel taucht in einem Katalog der Galerie Alexandre Iolas des Jahres 1965 auf.

55. Ernst, a.a.O., S. 19.

56. Ebenda, S. 27.

57. *Encyclopaedia Britannica,* 11. Auflage, Stichwort »Pan«.

58. Interview mit Max Ernst von Evan M. Maurer, 24. Mai 1974.

59. Ernst, a.a.O. Die Nymphe Echo verweist auch auf Pan. Echo war eine Oreade, eine Nymphe der Grotten und Wälder. Sie soll die Liebe Pans verschmäht haben, der sie in einem Wutanfall von ihren Schafhirten zerreißen ließ. Frazer beschrieb auch primitive Riten, in denen Menschen symbolisch mit Personifikationen der Natur vermählt werden. Siehe *The New Golden Bough,* S. 110.

60. Ebenda, S. 26.

61. Ebenda, S. 28.

62. Waldberg, a.a.O., S. 42. 1973 schuf Ernst die Skulptur *Stehende Figur (Totem),* die den Totem der *Haida* von der Nordwestküste Amerikas stark ähnelt.

63. Freud, a.a.O., S. 8.

64. Siehe Maurer, *In Quest of the Myth,* a.a.O., S. 182–85.

65. Ebenda, S. 222–29.

66. Sala, C., *Max Ernst et la démarche onirique,* Paris 1970, S. 33.

67. Stephan-Chauvet, *L'Ile de Pâques et ses mystères,* Paris 1935, S. 83–86.

68. Interview mit Max Ernst von Evan M. Maurer, 2. Mai 1974.

69. Linton, R., und Wingert, S., *Arts of the South Seas,* New York, Museum of Modern Art, 1946, S. 42–43.

70. 1938 schuf Ernst große Figuren aus Zement, um die Mauern seines Hauses in Saint-Martin d'Ardèche zu schmücken.

71. Stephan-Chauvet, a.a.O., Tafel 28, Abb. 66 und Anmerkungen. Der Stein wurde abgebildet in Scoresby Routledge, *The Mystery of Easter Island,* London 1919.

72. Ernst, M., *Maximiliana ou l'exercice illégal d'astronomie* [Maximiliana oder die illegale Ausübung der Astronomie], Paris 1964.

73. Die Ausgabe des Jahres 1903 von Fewkes' wunderbar illustriertem *Bulletin of American Ethnology* über die Katchinas stand in Ernsts Bibliothek.

74. Guggenheim, P., *Out of This Century,* New York 1946, S. 297.

75. Russell, a.a.O., S. 146.

76. Waldberg, P., »Max Ernst in Arizona« in *Homage to Max Ernst,* di San Lazzaro, G. (Hrsg.), Sonderausgabe von *XXe Siècle Review,* New York 1971, S. 57. Teilweise in deutscher Übersetzung im Ausstellungskatalog *Max Ernst,* Köln und Berlin 1979, S. 128. In Ernsts Bibliothek befand sich eine häufig benutzte französische Taschenbuchausgabe von *Sun Chief* von Don Talayesva. Diese bewegende autobiographische Erzählung über die *Hopi*-Kultur begeisterte Ernst so stark, daß er sie in Leder binden ließ.

77. Lippard, L. R., »The Sculpture« in *Max Ernst: Sculpture and Recent Painting,* New York, Jewish Museum, 1966, S. 44.

78. Levy, J., »A Summer in Long Island« in *Homage to Max Ernst,* di San Lazzaro, G. (Hrsg.), a.a.O., S. 61.

79. Waters, F., *Book of the Hopi,* New York 1966, S. 171.

80. Unter vielen anderen von Katchinas beeinflußten Werken Max Ernsts sind *Die schöne Deutsche,* 1934–35; *Mondsüchtig,* 1944; *Zwei und zwei macht eins,* 1956; *Mensch,* 1960.

81. Waldberg, *Max Ernst,* a.a.O., S. 363.

82. Eliade, M., *Schamanismus und archaische Ekstasetechnik,* Frankfurt a. M., 3. Auflage 1982.

83. Lévy-Bruhl, a.a.O., S. 216–17.

84. Ebenda, S. 269.

85. Ebenda, S. 345.

86. Frazer, *The New Golden Bough,* a.a.O., S. 39.

87. Interview mit Max Ernst von Evan M. Maurer, 24. Mai 1974.

88. Eliade, a.a.O., S. 22–23.

89. Ernst, *Beyond Painting,* a.a.O., S. 26.

90. Eliade, a.a.O., S. 48.

91. Ebenda, S. 158–59.

92. Ebenda, S. 126, 263 ff, 446.

93. Ernst, *Beyond Painting,* a.a.O., S. 28.

94. Eliade, a.a.O., S. 43.

95. Ebenda, S. 45.

96. Ernst, a.a.O.

97. Eliade, a.a.O., S. 43–73.

98. Ernst, *Beyond Painting,* a.a.O., S. 39.

99. Ebenda.

100. Eliade, a.a.O., S. 105.

101. Ernst, *Beyond Painting,* a.a.O., S. 29.

102. Eliade, a.a.O., S. 105.

103. Ebenda, S. 91.

104. Ernst, *Beyond Painting,* a.a.O., S. 10.

105. Ebenda, S. 14.

106. Duthuit, G., »Enquête« in *Cahiers d'art,* 14, Nr. 1–4, 1939, S. 75.

107. Cowling, E., »The Eskimos, the American Indians and the Surrealists« in *Art History* 1, Nr. 4, Dezember 1978.

108. Cowling ist sich bewußt, daß Miró im Musée de l'Homme in Paris oder in der Sammlung Pinart, die jetzt dem Musée des Beaux-Arts et d'Archéologie von Boulogne-sur-Mer gehört, keine zusammengesetzten eskimoischen Masken gesehen haben kann. Sie hält es aber für möglich, daß er Abbildungen in deutschen Veröffentlichungen oder den Berichten der Smithsonian Institution gesehen haben könnte. In einem Gespräch William Rubins mit André Masson, Mirós engem Freund und Nachbar im Jahr 1924, wurde auch Mirós Beziehung zu eskimoischen Masken erörtert. Masson behauptete, daß Miró bis in die dreißiger Jahre keine Maske der Eskimos gekannt habe, auch keine wissenschaftlichen Veröffentlichungen, wie Cowling annimmt.

109. Rubin, W., *Miró in the Collection of the Museum of Modern Art,* New York, Museum of Modern Art, 1973, S. 60.

110. Paalen, W. (Hrsg.), *DYN* 4–5, Dez. 1945.

111. Ebenda, Einführung.

112. Breton, A., *Surrealism and Painting,* New York 1972, S. 171.

113. Leiris, M., *Wifredo Lam,* N.Y. 1972, S. 7.

114. Ebenda.

115. Breton, *Surrealism and Painting,* S. 73.

116. Charpier, J., *Lam,* Paris 1960, S. 26.

117. Rousseau, M., »Wifredo Lam – peintre cubain« in *Présence africaine* 4, 1948, S. 59[illegible].

118. Leiris, a.a.O., S. 9–10.

119. Wifredo Lam, »Œuvres récentes de Wifredo Lam« in *Cahiers d'art* 26, 1951, S. 186.

120. Dieses besondere Merkmal scheint auch mit den bei Picasso in den späten zwanziger Jahren vorkommenden genitalen Darstellungen in Beziehung zu stehen, wie etwa in den Studien zu seiner *Kreuzigung* von 1929. Siehe auch Rosenblum, R., »Picasso and the Anatomy of Eroticism« in *Studies in Erotic Art,* New York 1970, S. 339–93.

121. Balakian, A., *Surrealism: The Road to the Absolute,* New York 1970, S. 49.

122. Breton, *Surrealism and Painting,* S. 333.

Alan G. Wilkinson

Henry Moore

Nur wenige Bildhauer des 20. Jahrhunderts besitzen Henry Moores enzyklopädisches Wissen über die Geschichte der Plastik, und nur wenige haben so kenntnisreich wie er über das Wesen der Plastik im allgemeinen – die der primitiven Völker eingeschlossen – und über einzelne Künstler und Kunstwerke geschrieben. Es gibt nur spärliche äußere Anhaltspunkte dafür, inwieweit Modigliani, Epstein, Gaudier und Lipchitz mit einzelnen Werken primitiver Kunst vertraut waren. Moore dagegen überliefert, besonders mit seinen Skizzenbüchern aus den 20er Jahren, ein wertvolles Verzeichnis der ihm bekannten Skulpturen.

Moore wurde 1898 in Castleford, im nordenglischen Industriegebiet Yorkshire, als siebtes Kind eines Bergarbeiters geboren. Schon früh beschloß er, Bildhauer zu werden, und wurde glücklicherweise von seiner Zeichenlehrerin an der Mittelschule, Miss Alice Gostick, in seiner Absicht bestärkt. 1917 ging er zur Armee und kämpfte in den Schützengräben an der Westfront. Im Unterschied zu zwei anderen jungen Bildhauern – Gaudier-Brzeska und Duchamp-Villon – überlebte er, obwohl er in einen Gasangriff geriet und deshalb einige Zeit im Lazarett verbringen mußte. Er war schon 21 Jahre alt, als er sich 1919 in einen zweijährigen Kursus an der Leeds School of Art einschrieb.

Moores erste Begegnung mit der primitiven Kunst erfolgte zweifellos über Roger Frys Buch *Vision and Design* (1920), das er während seines letzten Studienjahres an der Leeds School of Art las. Frys Kapitel über »Negerplastik« beginnt mit einer Verurteilung der akademischen Tradition, die während Moores Studentenzeit immer noch verbindlich war.

»Was für eine wohlgeordnete, enge, abgeschlossene, kleine Welt war das, als Griechenland die einzige Quelle der Kultur war und die griechische Kunst, abgesehen von einigen Nachbildungen der Renaissance, sogar in Gestalt römischer Kopien unbestritten die einzige Kunst war.«[1]

Sowohl durch die sarkastischen Bemerkungen über die Beschränktheit der griechischen Kunsttradtion als auch durch das Lob afrikanischer und präkolumbianischer Plastik gab Frys Buch den entscheidenden Anstoß für Moores künstlerische Entwicklung: seine häufigen Besuche im Britischen Museum während der 20er Jahre.

»Ich stieß durch Zufall auf dieses Buch, als ich in der Leeds Reference Library nach einem anderen Werk suchte. Fry betonte in seinem Essay über Negerskulptur die charakteristische ›Dreidimensionalität‹ und ›Materialgerechtheit‹ der afrikanischen Kunst. Darüber hinaus eröffnete mir Fry den Zugang zu anderen Büchern und zu den Schätzen des Britischen Museums. Das war der eigentliche Anfang.«[2]

Moore kam im Herbst 1921 nach London, nachdem er während seiner Zeit in Leeds mit einem Stipendium für das Royal College of Art ausgezeichnet worden war. Wie vor ihm Epstein war er von den Skulpturensammlungen im Britischen Museum überwältigt: »Im Britischen Museum erfüllte mich ein Raum nach dem anderen mit Begeisterung. Das Royal College of Art bedeutete im Vergleich dazu nichts.«[3] Die Skulpturen, die ihn besonders interessierten, beschrieb er genauer: ägyptische, assyrische, sumerische, afrikanische, ozeanische, nord- und südamerikanische, eskimoische Werke und besonders die monumentale präkolumbianische Steinskulptur der Azteken, Mayas und Tolteken.[4] Moores eigene, weit gefaßte Definition primitiver Kunst, die mehr vom Geiste des 19. als des 20. Jahrhunderts geprägt war, umfaßt Werke all dieser Perioden und Kulturen: »Der Begriff ›primitive Kunst‹ wird im allgemeinen für die Erzeugnisse der verschiedensten Rassen und Geschichtsperioden sowie die unterschiedlichsten sozialen und religiösen Systeme benutzt. Im weitesten Sinne scheint er die meisten außereuropäischen Kulturen und die großen orientalischen Zivilisationen zu umfassen.«[5]

Moores Ablehnung des griechischen Kunstideals und der akademischen Tradition war eine Fortsetzung von Gauguins Position in den Jahren um 1890. Er schrieb: »Das Griechische ist der große Irrtum, so schön es auch sein mag.«[6] In ähnlicher Weise erinnerte sich Moore vor kurzem, wie er sich in den Jahren seiner künstlerischen Entwicklung bewußt von der klassischen Kunsttradition befreite. »Es gab eine Periode, in der ich es zu vermeiden suchte, griechische Skulpturen auch nur anzusehen; und ebenso Renaissancekunst. Damals dachte ich, daß die Kunst Griechenlands und der Renaissance der Feind sei, daß man das alles ablehnen und wieder am Anfang der primitiven Kunst beginnen müsse.«[7]

Während der 20er Jahre befaßte sich Moore nicht nur mit der Kunst der Eingeborenen Afrikas und Ozeaniens, sondern mit vielen Traditionen, vorwiegend solchen außereuropäischer Plastik. Später, im Jahre 1937, behandelte er die Geschichte der Bildhauerkunst auf der ganzen Welt, wobei er nachdrücklich betonte, daß die griechische Skulptur nur während einer kurzen Periode bedeutsam und nur eine unter vielen großen bildhauerischen Traditionen gewesen sei:

»Die Welt hat mindestens dreißigtausend Jahre lang Skulpturen hervorgebracht. Durch die moderne Entwicklung der Nachrichtenübermittlung kennen wir heute einen großen Teil

□ 908 *Henry Moore, Maquette für ›König und Königin‹ (Maquette for King and Queen), 1952, Bronze, Höhe 27 cm. Privatsammlung.*

□ 909 *Henry Moore, ›Reliefkopf‹ (Relief Head), 1923, Schiefer, Höhe 32 cm. Privatsammlung.*

davon, und die paar Bildhauer Griechenlands aus einem Zeitraum von wenigen hundert Jahren machen unsere Augen nicht mehr blind für die bildhauerischen Leistungen des Rests der Menschheit. Paläolithische und neolithische Skulptur, sumerische, babylonische, ägyptische, frühgriechische, chinesische, etruskische, indische Werke, Skulpturen der Mayas und mexikanische, peruanische, romanische, byzantinische und gotische Plastiken, Skulpturen der Afrikaner, von den Südseeinseln und den nordamerikanischen Indianern – Originalwerke oder zumindest Photographien sind von allen verfügbar und geben uns einen nie zuvor möglichen Überblick über die Bildhauerkunst der ganzen Welt.«[8]

In den zahlreichen Zeichnungen seiner Skizzenbücher aus den 20er Jahren zeigt sich, daß MOORE ein umfassendes Studium der Plastik vieler dieser Epochen und Kulturen betrieb. Er kopierte einige der frühesten bekannten Skulpturen, etwa die jungsteinzeitliche *Venus von Grimaldi,* die er in Herbert Kühns Buch *Die Kunst der Primitiven* (1923) abgebildet sah, ebenso, wie er sumerische, ägyptische, etruskische, indische, präkolumbianische, gotische und eskimoische Kunstwerke, vor allem aber Skulptur der Eingeborenen Afrikas und Ozeaniens zeichnete.[9]

Der Einfluß primitiver Kunst auf PAUL GAUGUINS Werk, der sich vor allem in seinen Holzplastiken geltend macht, ging ausschließlich von der ozeanischen Skulptur aus, besonders derjenigen der Marquesasinseln. PABLO PICASSO interessierte sich 1907–08 stärker für afrikanische als für ozeanische Kunst. Im Vergleich zu anderen Bildhauern des 20. Jahrhunderts spielten diese Kunstrichtungen einzig bei HENRY MOORE eine weniger große Rolle als die präkolumbianische Steinskulptur – sowohl in formaler Hinsicht wie bei der Wahl des Materials, besonders in seinen Plastiken der 20er Jahre. Seinen Höhepunkt erreichte der präkolumbianische Einfluß auf den englischen Bildhauer in den zwei Steinskulpturen *Liegende Figur* aus dem Jahre 1929, Leeds City Art Galleries, und *Liegende* von 1930, National Gallery of Canada.

Im vorliegenden Buch konzentrieren wir unsere Untersuchungen jedoch auf die Stammeskunst, die im allgemeinen heute ausschließlich als primitiv gilt. Im Gespräch über seine Skulpturen der 20er Jahre stellten MOORE und ich nur in wenigen Werken den Einfluß afrikanischer Kunst fest. Die deutlichsten Beispiele dafür sind seine beiden einzigen Holzskulpturen aus dieser Periode, *Mädchenkopf* von 1922 und *Stehende* von 1923 □ 910, beide in der City Art Gallery, Manchester. Das charakteristische Material der meisten afrikanischen Skulpturen ist Holz, und in diesem Falle ist MOORES Auswahl des Mediums bezeichnend. Keine der beiden Arbeiten scheint sich auf einen bestimmten Stammesstil zu beziehen, und im Fall der *Stehenden* mag der Einfluß sogar aus zweiter Hand sein. Die kurzen gebeugten Beine, die eher in eine Art Basis als in Füße auslaufen, könnten direkt durch GAUDIERS Skulptur *Der Kobold* angeregt worden sein: Diese muß MOORE in Ezra Pounds Buch *Gaudier-Brzeska: A Memoir* (1916), das er 1922 oder 1923 las, gesehen haben. MOORE schrieb darüber: »Ein anderes Buch, das mir viel half und Anregung gab, war Ezra Pounds Buch über Gaudier-Brzeska. Es war mit großer Unbefangenheit und Sachkenntnis geschrieben. Gaudier spricht wie ein junger Bildhauer, der die Gegenstände gerade neu entdeckt.«[10] Sogar in seinen eigenen Schriften wiederholt MOORE mehrere Feststellungen GAUDIERS aus Ezra Pounds Erinnerungen. GAUDIER hatte geäußert: »Die Inder erfuhren den hamitischen [afrikanischen] Einfluß gefiltert durch die Brille der griechischen Künstler.«[11]

MOORE schrieb über seine entschiedene Ablehnung des griechischen Kunstideals: »Diese Beseitigung der griechischen Brille von den Augen des modernen Bildhauers (in Verbindung mit der Richtung, die durch Werke solcher Maler wie Cézanne und Seurat eingeschlagen worden war) half ihm, erneut die wahre emotionale Bedeutung von Gestaltwerten zu erkennen, anstatt den Darstellungswert als so wichtig zu erachten . . .«[12] Die wahre emotionale Bedeutung der Gestaltwerte – das ist, kurz gesagt, die überzeugende Alternative zur griechisch-römischen Tradition, die die Kunst der Eingeborenen anbot. Die Eingeborenenplastik bot den Malern und Bildhauern des 20. Jahrhunderts mit ihrer erstaunlichen Freiheit und Vielfalt

□ 910 *Henry Moore, ›Stehende‹ (Standing Woman), 1923, Holz, Höhe 30,5 cm. City Art Gallery, Manchester.*

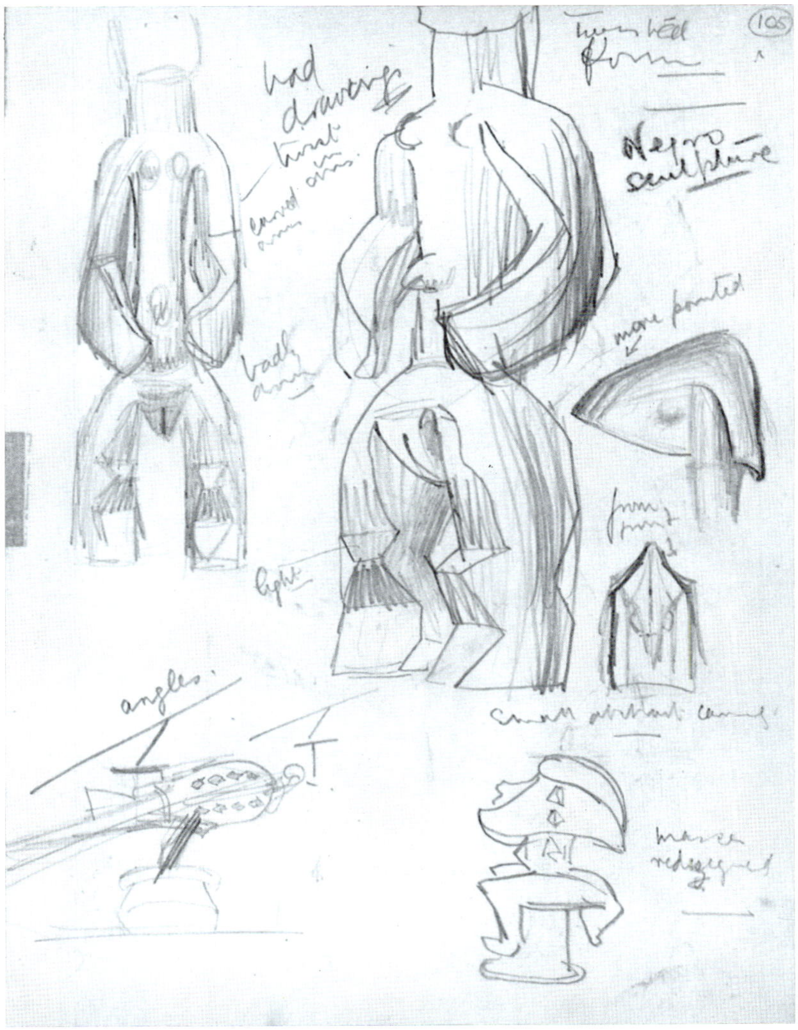

□ 911 *Henry Moore, Seite 105 aus dem Skizzenbuch Nr. 3, 1922–24, Bleistift, 22,5 x 17 cm. The Henry Moore Foundation, Much Hadham, England.*

Rechts oben: □ 912 *›Figur aus Holz‹, MUMUYE (Nigeria), Höhe 48 cm. The Trustees of the British Museum, London.*

□ 913 *›Kopf‹, BAGA (Guinea), Holz. Höhe 61 cm. The Trustees of the British Museum, London.*

der Formerfindung, ihrer Intensität und Unmittelbarkeit des Ausdrucks und ihrer immanenten Logik unbegrenzte formale Anregungen, aus denen sie schöpfen konnten, um die menschliche Figur neu zu gestalten. In einem jüngeren Kommentar zu zwei Skulpturen im Museum of Mankind, London, – einer männlichen und einer weiblichen Holzfigur der *ZANDE* im Südsudan – schrieb MOORE: »Die Entdeckung, daß die afrikanischen Plastiker die menschliche Figur so weit interpretieren und zugleich ihren Ausdruck erhalten und steigern konnten, ermutigte mich als junger Student, kühner und experimentierfreudiger zu sein.«[13]

MOORE berichtete, daß er sich während seiner Studentenzeit in Leeds (1919–21) intensiv mit dem Werk GAUGUINS auseinandersetzte, obwohl er sich dessen besonderer Leistungen als Plastiker nicht bewußt war. »Ich hatte das Glück, die Bekanntschaft von Michael Sadler zu machen, der damals Vizepräsident der Universität Leeds war. Ein Mann, der Werke von Cézanne und Gauguin schon vor 1914 gekauft hatte, Kandinsky übersetzte und der wirklich wußte, was in der modernen Kunst vor sich ging.«[14] Tatsächlich waren MOORES einzige Skizzen europäischer Kunst aus dem späten 19. und frühen 20. Jahrhundert Studien nach Werken CÉZANNES und GAUGUINS. Die Henry Moore Foundation besitzt eine Bleistiftzeichnung von drei ›Badenden‹ CÉZANNES, die an die Figuren der *Großen Badenden* von 1898–1905 erinnern (Philadelphia Museum of Art). Diese hatte MOORE während seines ersten Parisaufenthalts im Jahr 1922 in der Sammlung Pellerin gesehen.[15] Auf

□ 915 *Henry Moore, Seite 103 aus dem Skizzenbuch Nr. 3, 1922–24, Bleistift, 23 x 17 cm. The Henry Moore Foundation, Much Hadham, England.*

□ 914 *›Figur aus Holz‹, Jukun (Nigeria), Höhe 88 cm. The Trustees of the British Museum, London.*

Links unten: □ 916 *›Mutter mit Kind‹, Nootka, Vancouver Island (Britisch-Kolumbien), Holz, Höhe 27 cm. The Trustees of the British Museum, London.*

Seite 52 des Skizzenbuchs Nr. 2 von 1921–22 befindet sich eine Skizze in Feder und Tinte mit der Beschriftung »Gauguin«, die wahrscheinlich auf der Kohlezeichnung *Weiblicher Akt* von 1892 basiert.[16] Diese Zeichnung einer Figur in orientalischer Pose, wie sie in vielen Gemälden und graphischen Arbeiten Gauguins erscheint, ist in Charles Morice' Buch *Paul Gauguin* (Paris 1919, S. 172) abgebildet, vermutlich der Ausgangspunkt von Moores Skizze. Wie für Gauguin stellten Bücher, Reproduktionen und Photographien auch für Moore wichtiges Quellenmaterial bereit. Gauguins Zeichnung *Weiblicher Akt* geht ihrerseits auf eine der Figuren auf einem Photo zurück, das er mit nach Tahiti genommen hatte, eine Abbildung des javanischen Tempels von Borobudur.[17] Moores Schieferarbeit *Reliefkopf* von 1923 □ 909 ist wahrscheinlich seine einzige Plastik, die den Einfluß von Gauguins bildhauerischem Werk widerspiegelt. In den frühen 70er Jahren beschrieb Moore dem Autor diese Arbeit als ziemlich gauguinesk, und vor kurzem sagte er zu Ann Garrould: »Als ich an diesem Kopf arbeitete, bemerkte ich nicht, wie sehr ich von Gauguin beeinflußt worden war.«[18] Die wahrscheinlichste Inspirationsquelle war das bemalte Gipsrelief *Selbstbildnis Gauguin*, das auf Seite 78 in Charles Morice' Buch über den Künstler abgebildet ist.

Ein anderer Künstler, der Moore während der 20er Jahre beeinflußte, war Epstein – nicht nur der Mensch und sein Werk, sondern auch seine Sammlung. Jacob Epstein war schon damals dabei, den Grundstock für eine der erlesensten privaten

Sammlungen primitiver und exotischer Kunst zu legen. »Der einzige aktive Bildhauer der zwanziger Jahre in England, für den ich Anerkennung empfand, war Epstein . . . Nachdem ich meine Ausbildung abgeschlossen hatte und in den Lehrkörper des Royal College (1924) berufen worden war, wurde ich mit Epstein enger bekannt und habe nie vergessen, wie er mich in sein Schlafzimmer führte, um mir seine Sammlung primitiver Schnitzarbeiten zu zeigen – es war so vollgestopft mit Negerplastik etc., daß ich mich fragte, wie er ins Bett kam, ohne etwas umzustoßen.«[19]

Mitte der 20er Jahre zeichnete MOORE viel nach afrikanischer, ozeanischer, eskimoischer, mexikanischer und peruanischer Plastik. Seine Skizzenbücher dieser Jahre stellen ohne Zweifel das umfassendste Verzeichnis dar, das je ein Künstler des 20. Jahrhunderts über solche Werke primitiver Kunst anlegte, die ihn besonders faszinierten. Wir haben nicht nur konkrete Belege über viele Werke, die MOORE besonders bewunderte, sondern oft auch seine Jahre später verfaßten Beschreibungen der Skulpturen. Zeichnungen nach afrikanischer Kunst übertreffen zahlenmäßig die Zeichnungen nach Werken aus Ozeanien, Nordamerika (Nordwestküste und Arktis) und Peru. Im Britischen Museum war die afrikanische Plastik weit zahlreicher vertreten als die Skulpturen aus Ozeanien und Nordamerika (Nordwestküste und Arktis), was der Grund dafür sein mag, daß MOORE viel mehr Zeichnungen nach afrikanischer Kunst anfertigte als von Werken aus anderen Erdteilen. (Erstaunlicherweise existieren nur wenige Nachzeichnungen präkolumbianischer Plastik, die MOORE in den 20er Jahren so sehr bewunderte.) MOORES Zeichnungen waren großenteils ziemlich einfache, in einigen Fällen sehr detaillierte Studien der Vorbilder. Wie der Künstler oft hervorgehoben hat, beobachtet und analysiert man beim Zeichnen genauer als beim bloßen Betrachten.

MOORE zeichnete die Kunstwerke der Eingeborenen entweder im Britischen Museum oder nach Illustrationen aus Büchern über primitive Plastik. Höchstwahrscheinlich sind alle Studien auf Seite 105 des Skizzenbuchs Nr. 3 von 1922–24 nach Werken im Britischen Museum entstanden □ 911: links unten ein *BAGA*-Kopf;[20] rechts unten das Ornament eines Kanubugs von den Salomoninseln; rechts in der Mitte zwei Studien einer Keule aus Neukaledonien, die in Form eines Vogels endet,[21] sowie zwei Ansichten einer *MUMUYE*-Figur, die 1922 vom Britischen Museum erworben wurde. Während des »Festival of Britain« 1951 finanzierte das »Colonial Office« eine wichtige Ausstellung über die Kunst der Eingeborenen mit dem heutzutage merkwürdig klingenden Titel »Traditional Art from the Colonies«. In dieser Ausstellung war unter anderem die *MUMUYE*-Plastik zu sehen. William Fagg konnte MOORE zu einem gemeinsamen Besuch der Ausstellung überreden. Der Künstler beantwortete ihm eine Reihe von Fragen über das Wesen der Stammeskunst. Auf die Frage Faggs, welche von den Skulpturen für ihn den besten Gebrauch der besonderen Eigenschaften des Holzes zur Anschauung bringen würde, antwortete MOORE: »Diese [Mumuye-Skulptur] scheint mir unter diesem Aspekt betrachtet am gelungensten zu sein. Dem primitiven Schnitzer ist dadurch, daß er die Arme frei gestaltet hat und sie doch den Kern des Körpers umhüllen, etwas Besonderes geglückt.«[22]

Auf Seite 103 desselben Skizzenbuches von 1922–24 □ 915 geht die Profilfigur unten auf eine männliche Figur aus der Region Neuguineas zurück, die vor dem 1. Weltkrieg von Deutschland kontrolliert wurde. Sie wurde nach einer Repro-

□ 917 *›Kopf eines Affen‹, Ubangi? (Republik Zentralafrika), Holz, Höhe 18 cm. Privatsammlung, New York. Veröffentlicht in Carl Einstein, „Negerplastik", 1915.*

□ 918 *Henry Moore, Seite 120 aus dem Skizzenbuch Nr. 3 1922–24, Bleistift, Feder und Tinte, 23 x 17 cm. The Henry Moore Foundation, Much Hadham, England.*

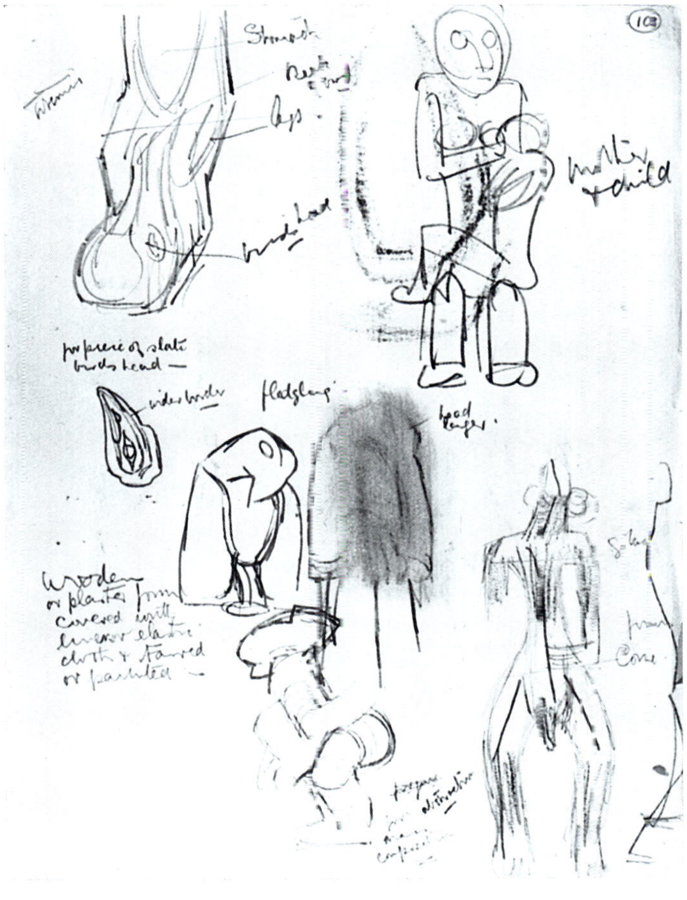

□ 919 *Henry Moore, Seite 90 aus dem Skizzenbuch Nr. 3, 1922–24, Bleistift und Kreide, 23 x 17 cm. The Henry Moore Foundation, Much Hadham, England.*

duktion auf einem losen Blatt aus einem bis jetzt nicht identifizierten deutschen Buch oder einer Zeitschrift kopiert, das der Autor unter MOORES Papieren entdeckte. Rechts davon befindet sich die Studie einer männlichen *JUKUN*-Figur (Nordnigeria), die 1909 vom Britischen Museum erworben wurde □ 914. Weiter oben rechts befindet sich eine Zeichnung MOORES zu einem seiner zwei wichtigsten Themen – Mutter und Kind –, wahrscheinlich kopiert nach einer Holzplastik der *NOOTKA* aus Vancouver Island (Britisch-Kolumbien) □ 916. 1981 schrieb MOORE über diese Skulptur und verwandte Werke der Nordwestküste, daß das Thema der Mutter mit Kind »für den Bildhauer das Problem der Beziehung zwischen einer großen und einer kleinen Form mit der Abhängigkeit der kleinen Form von der großen stellt. Sein Reiz liegt besonders im Ausdruck zweier Grunderfahrungen des Menschen, nämlich Kind zu sein und Mutter zu sein. Diese nordamerikanischen Mutter- und Kindfiguren sind bemerkenswert. Sie strahlen ein starkes Gefühl mütterlicher Fürsorge aus, ohne sentimental zu sein.«[23] Zwei andere Hauptquellen für MOORES Kopien nach Werken der Eingeborenenplastik waren die Illustrationen in zwei wichtigen frühen deutschen Publikationen über afrikanische Kunst, Carl Einsteins *Negerplastik* (1920) und Ernst Fuhrmanns *Afrika* (1922). Der kleine Kopf genau rechts über der Mitte auf Seite 120 des Skizzenbuchs Nr. 3 □ 918 rührt von einem Vorbild her, das wahrscheinlich den Kopf eines Affen[24] darstellt und in Einsteins Buch auf Tafel 15 erscheint □ 917. Die Köpfe links davon sind freie Interpretationen der Köpfe auf dem Halsstück eines Gefäßes der *INKA* aus Trujillo, das in Ernst Fuhrmanns *Reich der Inka* (1922) auf Tafel 15 wiedergegeben ist. Das im Besitz des Künstlers befindliche Exemplar der Bücher trägt auf dem Vorsatzblatt die Aufschrift: »Henry Spencer Moore 1923«. Alle Zeichnungen auf der Seite 143 des Skizzenbuches Nr. 3 basieren auf Illustrationen in Fuhrmanns *Afrika*.[25]

Mehrere Zeichnungen MOORES machen deutlich, daß bestimmte primitive Arbeiten nicht nur zu Studienzwecken, sondern mit der Absicht kopiert wurden, sie in neue Ideen für Skulpturen umzusetzen. Auf Seite 107 des Skizzenbuches Nr. 3 von 1922–24 □ 920 stammen die zwei größten Skizzen von dem prähistorischen Steinstößel in Form eines Vogels aus dem Nordosten Papua-Neuguineas im Britischen Museum □ 490, der wahrscheinlich auch BRANCUSI angeregt hat. Die langgezogenen Proportionen des kleinen Vogels scheinen MOORE Schwierigkeiten bereitet zu haben, da er zu der Zeit an massiven, blockartigen Steinskulpturen arbeitete. So schrieb er auch über eine seiner eigenen Skulpturen *Mutter mit Kind* aus Stein von Hornton, 1924–25 (City Art Gallery, Manchester): »Sie hat keinen Hals, weil ich mich davor fürchtete, den Stein zu schwächen.«[26] Seine kleine Skizze in Bleistift, Feder und Tinte zeigt einen viel kompakteren, weniger gelängten Vogel und beweist damit, daß MOORE eine unproblematischere Form ausarbeitete, die er eventuell in eine Steinplastik umsetzen konnte.

Die Studien auf Seite 106 desselben Skizzenbuches □ 922 veranschaulichen, wie der Künstler den Steinstößel als Ausgangspunkt benutzte. Er zeichnete nicht länger eine einfache Kopie des Originals, sondern – wie die Beschriftung des Blattes festhält – eine »Abstraktion« davon. Die vier Studien in den oberen beiden Dritteln dieser Seite erinnern an GAUDIER-BRZESKAS Skulptur *Aufgerichtete Vögel* von 1914 (The Museum of Modern Art, New York).

□ 920 *Henry Moore, Seite 107 aus dem Skizzenbuch Nr. 3, 1922–24, Bleistift, Feder und Tinte, 23 x 17 cm. The Henry Moore Foundation, Much Hadham, England.*

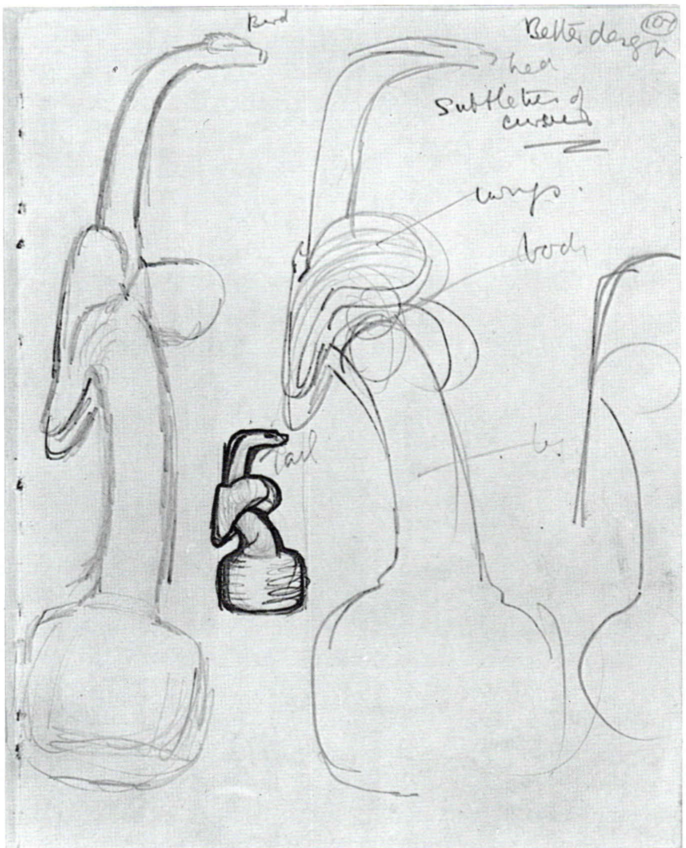

Die Art und Weise, wie MOORE den Steinstößel in den Studien auf Seite 106 veränderte, enthält den Schlüssel für unser Verständnis seiner Arbeitsmethode. Das ganze Beweismaterial liegt vor uns: die identifizierte prähistorische Skulptur und MOORES Antwort – ein seltenes Ereignis im Studium der Zusammenhänge zwischen dem Primitiven und dem Modernen. In diesen Zeichnungen schuf er nicht nur weniger langgezogene und damit kompaktere Proportionen als die des Stößels, sondern setzte gleichzeitig die glatten Oberflächen der neuguineischen Skulptur in eine komplexe Verbindung zwischen Ebenen und Winkeln um, die offensichtlich dem Einfluß des Vortizismus und der Skulptur GAUDIER-BRZESKAS von 1914 viel verdankt. Obwohl diese Studien nicht ins Plastische umgesetzt wurden, stehen sie in enger Verbindung mit der kantigen Oberfläche von MOORES Marmorplastik *Hund* von 1922.

Wie wir gesehen haben, spiegeln einige in den 20er Jahren entstandene Zeichnungen MOORES nach Stammeskunst seine Beschreibung der ziemlich chaotischen Präsentation völkerkundlicher Objekte in den Sälen des Britischen Museums wider, mit »ihrem unerschöpflichen Reichtum und ihrer Vielfalt an bildhauerischen Leistungen (aus Afrika, Ozeanien, Nord- und Südamerika); es war aber so vollgestopft und so wahllos zusammengewürfelt aufgestellt wie alter Kram im Hafentrödel, daß ich nach Hunderten von Besuchen auf bislang unentdeckte Skulpturen stieß«.[27] In anderen Zeichnungen, etwa jenen auf Seite 90 des Skizzenbuches Nr. 3 □ 919 richtete er seine Aufmerksamkeit auf ein oder zwei Werke. Die kriechende Figur oben auf dem Blatt geht auf den *ARAWAK*-Sitz im Britischen Museum zurück (Dominikanische Republik), der die Gestalt einer männlichen Figur hat.[28] MOORE erinnerte sich

□ 922 *Henry Moore, Seite 106 aus dem Skizzenbuch Nr. 3, 1922–24, Bleistift, 23 x 17 cm. The Henry Moore Foundation, Much Hadham, England.*

□ 921 *›Figur aus Holz‹, Hawaiinseln, Länge 67 cm. The Trustees of the British Museum, London.*

vor kurzem daran, daß die karibischen Skulpturen während seiner Studentenzeit – als diese Zeichnung entstand – im Britischen Museum hoch auf einem Regal aufgestellt waren, so daß man sie nur schlecht betrachten konnte. Doch diese *ARAWAK*-Plastik hatte einen besonderen Reiz für ihn: »Ich mochte sie zum Teil deshalb, weil sie eine liegende Figur war und zum Teil wegen der freien Auffassung der Beine; sie strahlen so viel Leben aus.«[29] Von hier aus führt eine direkte Verbindung zu seinem anderen Hauptthema – der liegenden Figur –, das MOORE wie das Thema der Mutter mit Kind seit den späten 20er Jahren bis heute nicht mehr losgelassen hat.

Die Studien im mittleren und unteren Teil des Blattes haben eine der kraftvollsten und dynamischsten Arbeiten ozeanischer Kunst im Britischen Museum zum Vorbild – die hawaiische Figur einer Hockenden, die wohl eine Tänzerin darstellt □ 921. »Seit meiner Studentenzeit war diese eine meiner Lieblingsfiguren«, schrieb MOORE. »Sie war immer in einer großen Vitrine mit 30 oder noch mehr Stücken ausgestellt, aber selbst in dieser Zusammenstellung fiel sie durch ihre bezaubernde Formstrenge auf, und ich fühlte das Bedürfnis, sie zu skizzieren. Sie hat den flach abfallenden Rücken und die mächtigen Muskeln eines Gorillas in Verbindung mit der Straffheit und Anspannung eines Ringers.«[30]

Aus Hunderten von Beispielen primitiver Kunst, die im Britischen Museum ausgestellt waren, hat MOORE viele Werke ausgewählt und gezeichnet, die mittlerweile zu den qualitätvollsten Exponaten afrikanischer und ozeanischer Kunst gezählt werden. Die *MUMUYE-*, *JUKUN-*, *ARAWAK-*, *NOOTKA-* und hawaiischen Skulpturen, die gerade besprochen wurden, waren 1970 alle in William Faggs Ausstellung »The Tribal Image« im Britischen Museum vertreten, für deren Auswahl die bildhauerische Qualität allein ausschlaggebendes Kriterium war. Das Auge des Bildhauers hatte diese Qualität schon Mitte der 20er Jahre erkannt.

Sidney Burney, in den 20er und 30er Jahren Londons wichtigster und einflußreichster Händler eskimoischer, afrikanischer und ozeanischer Kunst, hatte die Zusammenhänge

☐ 923 *Henry Moore, ›Mädchen‹ (Girl), 1932, Buchsbaum, Höhe 30 cm. Privatsammlung.*

☐ 924 *Henry Moore, ›Studien nach afrikanischer und eskimoischer Plastik‹, 1931, Bleistift und Kreide, 27 x 19 cm. Privatsammlung.*

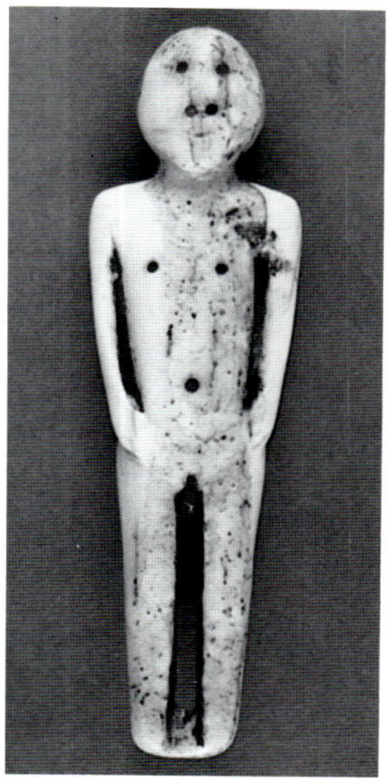

☐ 925 *›Figur aus Elfenbein‹, eskimoisch (Alaska), Höhe 10 cm. The Trustees of the British Museum, London.*

zwischen der Kunst der Eingeborenen und der Moderne klar erkannt. Moore zählte sicher zu den Besuchern seiner Galerie. Burney organisierte 1928 eine bahnbrechende Ausstellung, in der er afrikanische Skulpturen zusammen mit Werken zeitgenössischer Künstler wie Zadkine, Epstein, Dobson, Hepworth und Skeaping zeigte. Ein sachkundiger Kommentar in der *Times* lautete: » . . . was durch die Ausstellung so deutlich wird, ist die Traditionsgebundenheit jeder guten Skulptur unabhängig von Ort und Zeit«.[31] Vier Jahre später stellt der englische Bildhauer Leon Underwood[32] eine ähnliche aber anspruchsvollere Ausstellung in Burneys Galerie zusammen, deren Ziel es war, Werke aus Mexiko, Indien, China, Ägypten, Afrika, Persien und Neuseeland modernen Skulpturen von Degas, Gaudier-Brzeska, Modigliani, Moore und Hepworth sowie zwei eigenen Werken gegenüberzustellen.

Während der 30er Jahre hielt Moores Interesse für Eingeborenenkunst an, aber ihr Einfluß auf sein Werk war im Gegensatz zum vorausgegangenen Jahrzehnt sporadischer. Die radikale Richtungsänderung in Moores Kunst, ablesbar anhand von Skulpturen wie *Komposition* von 1931, *Kopf und Kugel*

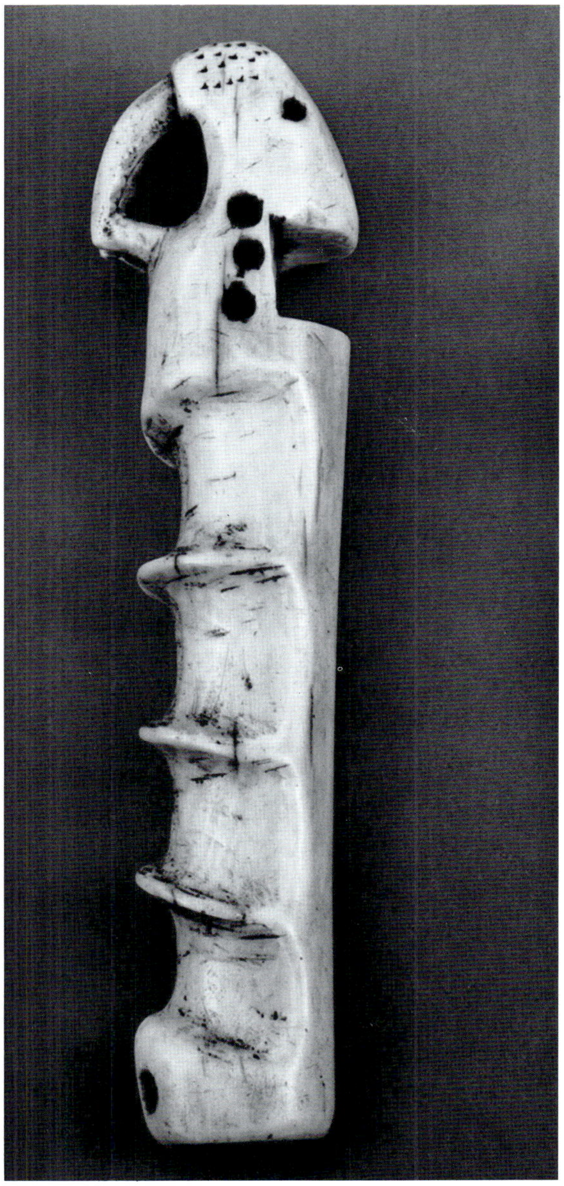

□ 926 *›Trommelschläger‹, eskimoisch (Alaska), Elfenbein, Höhe 16 cm. The Trustees of the British Museum, London.*

□ 927 *Henry Moore, ›Aufrechtes Motiv: Maquette Nr. 11 (Upright Motive: Maquette No. 11), 1955, Bronze, Höhe 31 cm. Privatsammlung.*

von 1934 und *Vier-Stücke-Komposition* aus dem gleichen Jahr, hat dem befreienden Einfluß der Skulptur PICASSOS, ARPS und GIACOMETTIS viel zu verdanken. Als Vergleichsbeispiele seien genannt: PICASSOS *Metamorphose* von 1928, ARPS *Glocke/Röhre und Nabel* von 1931 und GIACOMETTIS *Frau mit durchschnittener Kehle* von 1934. Obwohl er sich seine künstlerische Unabhängigkeit bewahrte, lehnten sich MOORES Skulpturen und Zeichnungen der 30er Jahre stark an das Werk der Surrealisten an, mit denen er auf der »International Surrealist Exhibition« in den New Burlington Galleries in London im Juni 1936 ausstellte. Und wie die Surrealisten suchte nun MOORE in der ozeanischen und eskimoischen Skulptur nach Inspiration.

MOORE hatte nur wenige Zeichnungen nach eskimoischer Plastik angefertigt. Ihr Einfluß auf sein Werk war, verglichen mit dem ozeanischer Kunst, nur verschwindend gering. Auf Seite 100 des Notizbuches Nr. 3 von 1922–24 stammen die drei Studien in der Mitte, bezeichnet mit »Fischschwanz« und »Bohrloch«, wahrscheinlich von elfenbeinernen Harpunenspitzen der *ESKIMOS*; dazwischen ist eine Skizze einer eskimoischen Nadelschachtel zu sehen.[33] Weiter oben rechts befindet sich die Zeichnung einer Indianerpfeife von der Nordwestküste aus der Christy Collection im Britischen Museum.

Die Zeichnung *Studien nach afrikanischer und eskimoischer Plastik* von 1931 □ 924 ist in mehrfacher Hinsicht interessant. Die Beschriftung am oberen Rand der Blätter, »Erinnere dich an die mexikanische Mutter mit Kind bei Burneys – einfache Ausdruckskraft und Intensität – und an die Negerfigur für Vitalität und Lebenslust . . .«, bezeugt, daß MOORE Burneys Londoner Galerie besuchte, wo er in UNDERWOODS Ausstellung von 1932 eigene Werke zeigte. Die Fortsetzung der Beschriftung beweist, daß MOORE immer noch Kontakt zu EPSTEIN und seiner Sammlung hatte: ». . . und an die Figur, die Epstein gehört – Negermutter mit Kind für große primitive Stärke«. Die zwei größten Studien sind nach *DOGON*-Standfiguren mit gebeugten Knien entstanden. Die zwei Standfiguren in der unteren Hälfte des Blattes stehen in engem Zusammenhang mit figürlichen Knochen- und Elfenbeinschnitzereien der *ESKIMOS* wie etwa der Figur aus Elfenbein im Britischen Museum □ 925. Aus diesen Studien ging MOORES aus Buchsbaum

☐ 928 *›Malanggan‹, Neuirland, bemaltes Holz und Fasern, Höhe 104 cm. The Trustees of the British Museum, London.*

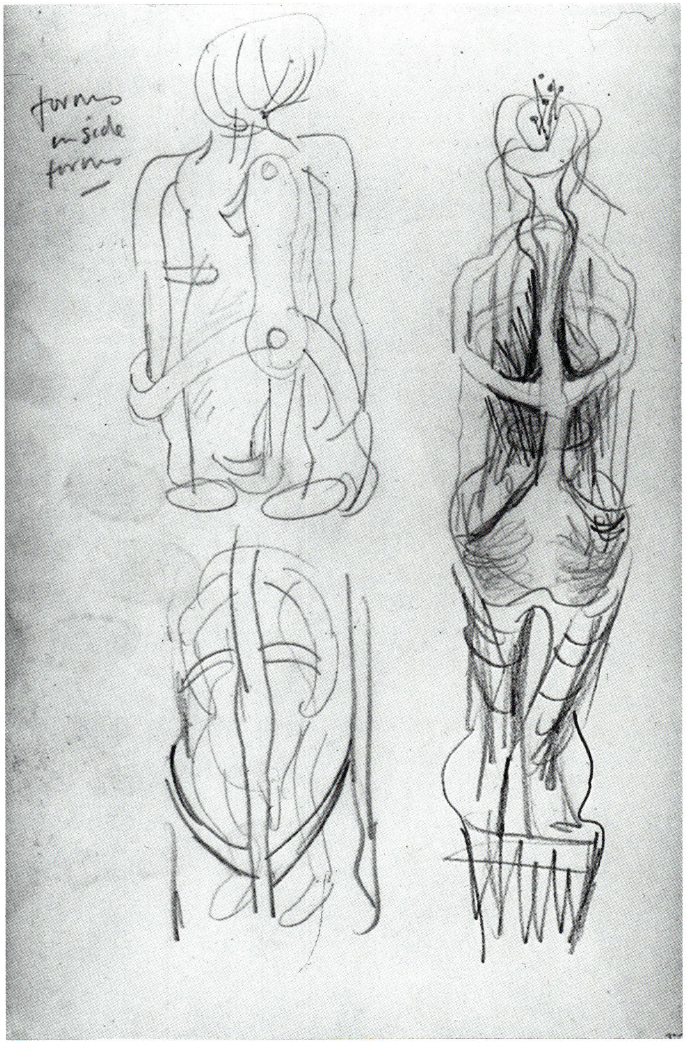

☐ 929 *Henry Moore, Seite aus dem Skizzenbuch B, ›Formen in Formen‹, 1935, Bleistift, 22 x 14 cm. The Henry Moore Foundation, Much Hadham, England.*

gefertigte Figur *Mädchen* von 1932 hervor ☐ 923, eine seiner wenigen von eskimoischer Kunst angeregten Skulpturen. In einem viel späteren Werk, *Aufrechtes Motiv: Maquette Nr. 11* von 1955 ☐ 927, vereinigte Moore organische Formen mit Einzelformen, die wahrscheinlich der Kunst der *Eskimos* entliehen sind. Die beiden horizontalen Verlängerungen im Entwurf sind entsprechenden Merkmalen, wie man sie bei eskimoischen Trommelknäufen antrifft, auffallend ähnlich ☐ 926.

Der Haupteinfluß auf Moores Skulpturen und Zeichnungen in den 30er Jahren ging von der ozeanischen Kunst aus. Er wertete die vielschichtige, groteske und erotische Bilderwelt, die für die Kunst der Pazifischen Inseln vielfach typisch ist, nicht in dem Grad aus wie die Surrealisten. Das heißt nicht, daß er ihre Besonderheiten nicht wahrnahm. 1941 schrieb er:

»Die vielen Inseln Ozeaniens brachten alle Bildhauerschulen mit ganz unterschiedlichen Formideen hervor. Die Skulpturen Neuguineas mit ihren dünnen, spinnenbeinigen Überdehnungen und vogelschnabelartigen Verlängerungen stehen im unmittelbaren Kontrast zu den gesichtslosen Köpfen und glatten Oberflächen der Nukuoro-Plastik; oder die schwerfälligen Steinfiguren der Marquesasinseln, die in direktem Gegensatz zu den weichlichen, gerippten Holzfiguren der Osterinsel stehen.«[34]

Vor kurzem verglich Moore die markanten Merkmale von afrikanischer und ozeanischer Kunst:

»Während afrikanische Skulptur massig, ausdrucksvoll, von großer Festigkeit ist und offensichtlich eine erdverbundene Lebenshaltung widerspiegelt, scheinen mir die ozeanischen Völker ein ängstlicheres, nervöseres und in hohem Maße imaginäres Weltbild zu haben, das sich in phantastischen, vogelähnlichen und käferartigen Gebilden von alptraumartigem Charakter ausdrückt.«[35] Moores in Blei gegossene *Liegende Figur* von 1931 war wahrscheinlich seine erste von ozeanischer Kunst angeregte Skulptur.[36] Während die verdrehten, biomorphen Formen der Figur deutlich dem Werk Picassos verpflichtet sind, haben sich die drei parallelen Stützen zweifellos von Formen der neuirischen Skulptur anregen lassen ☐ 928, wie etwa dem Malanggan aus dem Britischen Museum, den Moore Mitte der 30er Jahre skizzierte. Die Skulptur Neuirlands übte von allen Stilrichtungen ozeanischer Stammeskunst den größten formalen Einfluß auf Moores Werk aus.

Die Seite *Formen in Formen* des Skizzenbuches B von 1935 läßt uns über Moores Begeisterung für neuirische Skulptur nicht im Zweifel ☐ 929. Die Studie links unten, bei der die Beine durch ein äußeres Netzwerk aus horizontalen und gebogenen Streben geschützt sind, erinnert deutlich an neuirische

□ 930 *Henry Moore, ›Studie für Skulpturen: innere/äußere Formen‹ (Study for Sculpture: Internal/External Forms), 1950, Kreide, Bleistift, Gouache, Feder und rote Tusche, 29 x 24 cm. Privatsammlung.*

□ 931 *Henry Moore, ›Arbeitsmodell für aufrechte innere und äußere Formen‹ (Working Model for Upright Internal and External Forms), 1951 Bronze, Höhe 64 cm. Art Gallery of Ontario.*

Bildhauerarbeiten.[37] Die Studie direkt darüber zeigt die obere Hälfte der neuirischen Skulptur. In der größeren Zeichnung rechts benutzte MOORE die primitive Plastik für eine Idee zu einer eigenen Skulptur. Diese Zeichnung ist die erste von vielen Studien über den inneren Formenaufbau, die MOORE zwischen 1935 und 1940 ausführte. Vor kurzem beschrieb er eine andere aus Neuirland stammende Malanggan-Plastik des Britischen Museums wie folgt:

»Neuirische Skulpturen wie diese machten durch die Einlagerung einer Form in eine andere einen ungeheueren Eindruck auf mich. Ich erkannte, was für eine geheimnisvolle Aura erreicht werden konnte, wenn das Innere teilweise verborgen blieb, so daß man erst um die Skulptur herumgehen mußte, um sie zu verstehen. Ich war auch von dem handwerklichen Können verblüfft, das nötig ist, um diese Meißelarbeit im Inneren der Skulptur auszuführen.«[38]

MOORES erste Skulptur zum Thema der inneren und äußeren Form, *Der Helm* von 1939–40, stand keinesfalls mit ozeanischer Kunst in Beziehung, sondern ging auf eine Abbildung zweier prähistorischer griechischer Werkzeuge oder Geräte zurück, die er in den *Cahiers d'art* (1934) gesehen hatte.[39] Erst 1948 kehrte er in der Zeichnung *Studie für Skulpturen: innere/äußere Formen* □ 930 wieder zu einem von Ozeanien angeregten Motiv zurück, einer Fortsetzung der Zeichnungen von 1935–40. Diese Zeichnung geht der definitiven plastischen Studie für die erste Skulptur dieses Themas voraus, der Bronze *Arbeitsmodell für aufrechte innere und äußere Formen* von 1951 □ 931. Sie hat ihren Ursprung in der neuirischen Plastik, die er 1935 in sein Skizzenbuch kopierte.

Eine von MOORES schönsten Holzarbeiten aus den späten 30er Jahren, *Vogelbauer* von 1939 □ 935, scheint wiederum dieses fortgesetzte Interesse an ozeanischer Kunst zu belegen. Die Verwendung von Schnüren in den Arbeiten dieser Periode wurde nach Aussage des Künstlers durch mathematische Modelle, die er im Naturwissenschaftlichen Museum (und meiner Meinung nach auch im Werk von GABO) gesehen hatte, angeregt. Dagegen zeigen die hochschießenden Formen der Plastik, obwohl sie einen größeren räumlichen Abstand zueinander haben, deutliche Gemeinsamkeiten mit neuirischen Reibetrommeln □ 934. Sogar MOORES eigener Titel, *Vogelbauer*, enthält eines der Worte, die er benutzte, um die Raumidee neuirischer Skulptur zu beschreiben: »eine Vogel-im-Käfig-Form«.[40]

Drei Spitzen von 1939–40 □ 932 war eine der letzten Skulpturen MOORES, die er vollendete, bevor er sich für zwei Jahre auf seine Bunker- und Kohlegrubenzeichnungen (1940–42) konzentrierte. Wie fast alle seine Skulpturen von 1921 bis in die frühen 50er Jahren geht diese Arbeit auf eine vorbereitende Zeichnung zurück, eine der vielen Studien für *Spitze Formen* von 1939, die sich heute in der Albertina befindet. *Drei Spitzen* ist ein problematisches Werk, für das außerordentlich disparate Quellen einschließlich der Stammeskunst als Anreger in Frage kommen. David Sylvester schlug vor, daß MOORE die stachelige Form in der Mitte von den spitzen, herausgestreckten Zungen des Pferdes und der Frau auf der linken Seite von PICASSOS *Guernica* (1937) möglicherweise unbewußt übernommen habe. Offensichtlich erteilte jedoch MOORE Sylvester die Auskunft, daß die genaue Quelle der Skulptur ein Gemälde im Louvre gewesen sei: das im 16. Jahrhundert aus der Schule von Fontainebleau hervorgegangene Doppelbildnis der badenden Gabrielle d'Estrées und ihrer Schwester, die Gabrielles Brustwarze zwischen Zeigefinger und Daumen hält: eine doch wohl kaum in Betracht kommende Bildquelle.[41] Als ich das Portrait aus Fontainebleau dann mit MOORE besprach, löste er die Streitfrage ziemlich verschmitzt auf und gab zu, daß er Sylvester sozusagen an der Nase herumgeführt habe. In Kenntnis von MOORES offensichtlichem Interesse an ozeanischer Kunst, das Mitte und Ende der 30er Jahre in den von Neuirland angeregten Zeichnungen zur inneren und äußeren Form und im *Vogelbauer* von 1939 seinen Höhepunkt erreichte, scheint primitive Kunst hier noch eher in Frage zu kommen. Ich verweise auf die »Haken«-Figuren, die Yipwons, aus der Karawari-Region □ 933, bei welchen der Penis oben und unten von zwei spitzen, rippenartigen Formen »geschützt« wird. Wenn man sich den Penis und die beiden gewölbten Formen von der neuguineischen Plastik getrennt denkt, könnte sie fast mit MOORES *Drei Spitzen* verwechselt werden. Auch hier geben wieder seine Vorstudien für die Skulptur unschätzbare Hinweise auf die Art und Weise, wie MOORE seine Vorbilder transformierte. Neben der Zeichnung aus der Albertina verrät auch *Sitzende Figur und spitze Formen* von 1939 MOORES kurzzeitige Leidenschaft für spitze Formen am Ende der 30er Jahre. In der größten Studie rechts oben dürften die zwei aufwärts und abwärts gerichteten dornenartigen Formen, die sich fast berühren, weniger durch ein Werk der ozeanischen Kunst als durch eine afrikanische Plastik angeregt sein wie etwa die *PERE*-Figur, deren ausgehöhlter Torso aus einer Serie von aufwärts und abwärts gerichteten spitzen Formen besteht □ 11. Allerdings ist es recht unwahrscheinlich, daß MOORE eines dieser Objekte vor 1939 sah.

Zwischen August 1940 und 1943, als er an einem Auftrag für eine Madonna mit Kind für St. Matthew's in Northampton arbeitete, wandte sich MOORE zeitweise von der Bildhauerei ab und konzentrierte sich als offizieller Kriegskünstler zunächst auf Bunker- und später Kohlegrubenzeichnungen. Im Sommer 1942 hatte er die Zeichnungsfolgen von Bergarbeitern beendet und fing damit an, ein Skizzenbuch mit Ideen für Skulpturen zu füllen. 1942 fertigte er auch mehrere großformatige, bis ins Detail ausgearbeitete Zeichnungen von Skulpturen in freier Umgebung an, darunter die berühmteste seiner Malerzeichnungen, die er *Menschenmenge vor einem verschnürten Gegenstand* nannte □ 939. Mit ihren surrealistischen Anklängen liegt sie chronologisch genau zwischen MAN RAYS *Das Rätsel der Isidore Ducasse* von 1920 (eine mit einem Leintuch verschnürte Nähmaschine) und CHRISTOS *Verpackte Gebäude in Lower Manhattan* von 1964–66.

MOORE wies den Autor darauf hin, daß die Idee eines verschnürten Gegenstandes durch eine allgemein in den Bildhauerateliers geübte Praxis entstanden sein könnte. Er erinnerte sich, daß er als Student in der Modellierklasse des Royal College of Art in den frühen 20er Jahren den Ton feucht hielt, indem er ihn in ein nasses Tuch wickelte und einschnürte. Die

□ 932 *Henry Moore, ›Drei Spitzen‹ (Three Points), 1939–40, Bronze, Länge 19 cm. Privatsammlung.*

□ 933 *›Yipwon-Figur‹ (siehe Glossar), Ausschnitt,* ALAMBLAK, *Karawari-Fluß, Provinz Ost-Sepik (Papua-Neuguinea), Holz, Gesamthöhe 215 cm. Sammlung Friede, New York. Ehemals Sammlung Matta. Gesamtabbildung in Farbe* □ *108.*

□ 934 ›Reibetrommel‹, Neuirland, bemaltes Holz, Länge 47 cm. Privatsammlung.

□ 935 Henry Moore, ›Vogelbauer‹ (Bird Basket), 1939, Holz und Schnur, Länge 42 cm. Privatsammlung.

□ 936 ›*Kopfschmuck*‹, Ausschnitt, IGBO (Nigeria), Holz, Gesamthöhe 83,5 cm. National Commission for Museums and Monuments, Lagos.

□ 937 *Henry Moore, Maquette für ›König und Königin‹, Detail, siehe* □ *908.*

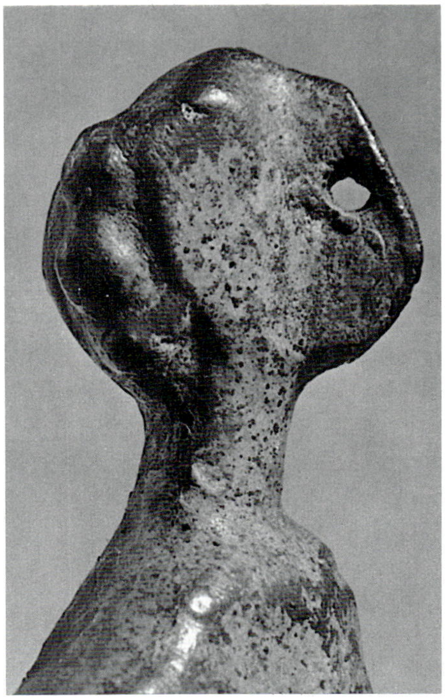

□ 938 *Henry Moore, Maquette für ›König und Königin‹, Detail, siehe* □ *908.*

präzise Quelle für *Menschenmenge vor einem verschnürten Gegenstand* erwähnte er jedoch nicht. Diese ist eine Photographie in Leo Frobenius' *Kulturgeschichte Afrikas* (1933), von der MOORE ein Exemplar besaß. Sie zeigt *NUBA* aus Nordnigeria, die um zwei verhüllte (aber nicht verschnürte) Dako-Kulttanzkostüme herumstehen □ 940. In der Geschichte des Primitivismus vor dem 2. Weltkrieg ist MOORES Zeichnung eine der wenigen Arbeiten, die nicht durch ein Kunstwerk, sondern durch die Photographie einer Stammeszeremonie angeregt wurden. Obwohl MOORES Zeichnung ohne Zweifel auf diese Photographie zurückgeht, gestaltete er die Umgebung und die dramatische Erwartungssituation neu. Eine im Vergleich zu dem riesigen verschnürten Objekt zwergenhaft kleine Menge hat sich in Erwartung des Enthüllungsrituals auf einer öden Ebene versammelt. Die Zeichnung ist geheimnisvoller als die Arbeiten von MAN RAY und CHRISTO, denn bei diesen wissen wir, was bedeckt und verschnürt wurde. In MOORES Zeichnung bleibt die Identität der Form unter der Leinwand im Dunkeln.

Seit 1942 hat MOORE nur wenige Werke geschaffen, die in Zusammenhang mit primitiver Kunst stehen. Für *König und Königin* von 1952–53 □ 908, wahrscheinlich MOORES bekannteste und beliebteste Skulptur, übernahm er Einzelheiten aus zwei afrikanischen Schnitzarbeiten. Als er mit William Fagg 1951 die Ausstellung »Traditional Art from the Colonies« besuchte, betrachteten sie vor allem den *IGBO*-Haarschmuck aus dem Nigerianischen Museum □ 936. Fagg schrieb, daß sich MOORE besonders dafür interessierte, »wie der Igbo-Künstler den menschlichen Kopf geöffnet hatte. Dies mag ihn veranlaßt haben, seine Idee von 1930 aufzugreifen. Sie scheint nicht nur in *König und Königin* von 1952 durch, sondern in vielen seiner Hauptwerke der 50er Jahre.«[42] Dies ist ein Hinweis auf das Loch in den schmalen Köpfen des Königs und der Königin □ 937, 938. Fagg deutete auch an, daß die Krone des Königs von einem anderen Werk aus der Ausstellung von 1951 herrühren könnte, und zwar von der *YORUBA*-Plastik eines Widderkopfes.[43] Die Haltung von *König und Königin* wurde durch ägyptische Sitzstatuen im Britischen Museum angeregt.

Mondkopf von 1964 □ 943 scheint fast die letzte Skulptur MOORES zu sein, die durch die Kunst der Eingeborenen beeinflußt ist. Die beiden Teile stellen eine Hand (die hier gezeigte Ansicht) und einen Kopf dar. Die frühere, kleinere Fassung hieß *Kopf in der Hand.* Als MOORE an der größeren Fassung arbeitete, fand er, daß »mich die ganze Wirkung so stark an Licht und Form des Vollmonds erinnerte, daß ich sie seither *Mondkopf* nannte«.[44] Obwohl *Mondkopf* manchmal mit den dünnen Formen figürlicher kykladischer Plastik verglichen wurde, war der genaue Ursprung der handähnlichen Form – nach Mitteilung William Faggs – die *MAMA*-Maske eines Büffels aus Nigeria, die in Faggs *Nigerian Images* (1963) abgebildet ist □ 942. Laut Fagg gab der alte Harry Fischer, MOORES Freund und Händler, dem Bildhauer ein Exemplar dieses Buches, bald nachdem es erschienen war. MOORE setzte die symmetrische *MAMA*-Maske □ 941 in ein Formgebilde um, das an einen abstrakten, gehörnten Kopf erinnert bzw. an eine asymmetrische Riesenhand. Nachdem die primitive Kunst schon seit Jahren ihre dominierende Wirkung auf sein Schaffen eingebüßt hatte, zeigt *Mondkopf,* daß MOORE Mitte der 60er Jahre immer noch für die Formen der Stammeskunst empfänglich war, die einen so tiefen Einfluß auf seine künstlerische Entwicklung während der 20er und 30er Jahre ausgeübt hatten.

Die Abbildungen von MOORES Werk, die hier afrikanischen und ozeanischen Plastiken gegenübergestellt werden, erbringen den sicheren Nachweis, daß die Kunst der Naturvölker eine der wichtigsten Quellen für seine Skulpturen und Zeichnungen darstellt. Der in Wechselwirkung stehende Einfluß der Kunst der Primitiven, Präkolumbiens und exotischer Hofkunst hat wahrscheinlich in MOORES Werk eine nachhaltigere Wirkung gezeigt als im Werk irgendeines anderen großen Bildhauers oder Malers des 20. Jahrhunderts. Die Anleihen bei der Eingeborenenplastik sind in vielen Holz- und Bronzeskulptu-

□ 939 *Henry Moore, ›Menschenmenge vor einem verschnürten Gegenstand‹ (Crowd Looking at a Tied-Up Object), 1942, Bleistift, schwarze und farbige Kreiden, Pastell, mit Lavierung, 40 x 55 cm. Privatsammlung.*

ren von Henry Moore, die in diesem Essay besprochen wurden, so offensichtlich, daß Goldwaters Behauptung ganz klar widerlegt ist, daß »nur wenige direkte formale Übernahmen erfolgten und . . . nur ein kleiner Teil der modernen Plastik an die allgemeinen Proportionen und Rhythmen eines bestimmten primitiven Stammesstils entfernt erinnert«.[45] Wie wir gesehen haben, *erinnert* eine Reihe von Skulpturen Moores nicht nur an Stammesstile, sondern wurde in einigen Fällen durch primitive Werke, die wir identifizieren konnten, unmittelbar angeregt.

Daß *Mondkopf* (1964) bis heute Moores letzte primitiv inspirierte Skulptur ist, soll nicht heißen, daß er in den letzten 20 Jahren das Interesse an afrikanischer und ozeanischer Kunst verloren hätte. Im Gegenteil, er hat seiner bescheidenen Sammlung von Eingeborenenplastik die bemerkenswertesten Erwerbungen hinzugefügt: eine wichtige *Luba*-Maske, eine *Mumuye*-Standfigur, zwei *Mangbetu*-Figuren und eine bronzene *Asante*-Kudo-Schachtel aus dem 18. Jahrhundert. Moores Begeisterung für eine der größten ozeanischen Skulpturen im Britischen Museum, der berühmten Figur von den Rurutuinseln □ 465, war so groß, daß er vor kurzem, wie schon Picasso vor ihm, einen Bronzeabguß des Originals herstellen ließ. Die 1981 erschienene Veröffentlichung *Henry Moore at the British Museum* bezeichnet den Höhepunkt von Moores seit über fünfzig Jahren immer wieder gepflegter schriftstellerischer Auseinandersetzung mit der Bildhauerei. Diese begann 1920 mit Moores unveröffentlichtem Manuskript *History of Sculpture: Notes,* das sich jetzt in »The Henry Moore Centre for

□ 940 *Der Stamm der Nuba (Nigeria) neben zwei verhüllten Tanzkostümen für den Dako-Kult. Veröffentlicht in Leo Frobenius, „Kulturgeschichte Afrikas", 1933.*

the Study of Sculpture« in Leeds befindet. Moores wichtigste Schrift über Stammeskunst war bis zur oben genannten Publikation von 1981 ein Artikel mit dem Titel »Primitive Art«, der am 24. August 1941 im *Listener* erschien. In *Henry Moore at the British Museum* kommentiert der 84jährige Künstler 50 Skulpturen der Sammlung und entdeckt viele Werke wieder, die er als Student in den 20er Jahren zum ersten Mal gesehen hatte. Unter den Illustrationen zur Eingeborenenkunst befinden sich vier Skulpturen, die er in seinen Skizzenbüchern aus der Mitte der 20er Jahre kopiert hatte.

□ 943 *Henry Moore, ›Mondkopf‹ (Moon Head), 1964, Bronze, 58 x 44 x 25 cm. The Trustees of the Tate Gallery, London.* ▷

□ 941 *›Maske‹, MAMA (Nigeria), Holz, Gesamthöhe 46 cm. Sammlung R. Reinhardt Bedford, New York.*

In der Einleitung zu diesem Buch schrieb MOORE: »Die abgebildeten Werke sind eine sehr beschränkte persönliche Auswahl, . . . aber genauso, wie ich davon fasziniert gewesen wäre zu wissen, was, sagen wir, Picasso im Louvre am liebsten mochte und welche Werke ihn beeinflußt haben könnten, hoffe ich, daß die Leser daran Interesse haben zu wissen, was mich im Britischen Museum beeinflußt hat.«[46] Wir würden wirklich gerne mehr darüber erfahren, welche primitiven Arbeiten die anderen wichtigen Künstler des 20. Jahrhunderts sahen und bewunderten.

MOORES Beitrag zur Geschichte des Primitivismus ist einzigartig. Seine Kopien von Eingeborenenplastik stellen ein faszinierendes Verzeichnis besonderer Werke dar, auf die er reagierte. Seine Skulpturen lassen weitreichende Ähnlichkeiten und Umdeutungen der afrikanischen und ozeanischen Kunst erkennen, angefangen bei den afrikanischen Proportionen seiner *Stehenden* von 1924 bis zu einer Arbeit wie *Mondkopf* von 1964, die unmittelbar von einer *MAMA*-Maske angeregt ist. Bei Künstlern wie MODIGLIANI und – in geringerem Ausmaß – LIPCHITZ muß die Untersuchung primitiver Einflüsse wegen der Eigenart ihrer Arbeiten und aufgrund des Fehlens dokumentarischer Belege über afrikanische Skulpturen, die ihnen bekannt waren, spekulativ und allgemein bleiben. Im Gegensatz dazu hat uns MOORE in seinen Skizzen, Zeichnungen und Skulpturen viel Grundlagenforschung abgenommen und dabei sowohl unser Verständnis für seine eigene Arbeit als auch unsere Wertschätzung der Eingeborenenplastik als einer eigenständigen Kunst vergrößert.

□ 942 *›Maske‹, MAMA (Nigeria), Holz, Höhe 50 cm. National Commission for Museums and Monuments, Lagos. Veröffentlicht in William Fagg, „Nigerian Images", 1963.*

Anmerkungen

1. Fry, R., *Vision and Design,* 1920, Neuauflage Middlesex 1961, S. 85.

2. Moore, H., *Henry Moore on Sculpture.* Hrsg. mit einer Einleitung von Philip James, London 1966, S. 49. (Erscheint in den folgenden Anmerkungen als Moore.)

3. Ebenda, S. 33.

4. Ebenda, S. 155–74.

5. Ebenda, S. 155.

6. Goldwater, R., *Primitivism in Modern Art,* New York 1967, S. 66.

7. Nairne, S., und Serota, N. (Hrsg.), *British Sculpture in the Twentieth Century,* Whitechapel Art Gallery, London 1981, S. 104.

8. Moore, S. 57.

9. Ein genaues Verzeichnis der Zeichnungen Moores nach primitiver Kunst und außereuropäischer Skulptur bei Wilkinson, G., *The Drawings of Henry Moore,* Tate Gallery/Art Gallery of Ontario, London 1977, S. 143–50. (Erscheint in den folgenden Anmerkungen als Wilkinson.)

10. Moore, S. 49.

11. Pound, E., *Gaudier-Brzeska: A Memoir,* London, New York 1916, S. 10.

12. Moore, S. 57.

13. Moore, H., *Henry Moore at the British Museum,* mit Photographien von David Finn, London 1981, S. 96 (Erscheint in den folgenden Anmerkungen als *Henry Moore at the British Museum.)*

14. Moore, S. 32.

15. Siehe Wilkinson, S. 67, Abb. Nr. 62.

16. Ebenda, S. 146, Abb. 112 und 115.

17. Siehe Wilkinson, A. G., *Gauguin to Moore: Primitivism in Modern Sculpture,* Art Gallery of Ontario, Toronto 1981, S. 52, Abb. 15.

18. Dem Autor durch Ann Garrould (Moores Nichte) zitiert, Juni 1983.

19. *Henry Moore at the British Museum,* S. 10.

20. Ich bin William Fagg zu Dank verpflichtet, der diese Skizze als Kopie nach der BAGA-Skulptur identifiziert hat.

21. Siehe Cranstone, B. A. L., *Melanesia: A Short Ethnography,* British Museum, London 1961, S. 68, Abb. 23. In Abb. 23 sind die drei Keulen rechts Beispiele für den ›vogelköpfigen‹ Typus, den Moore kopierte.

22. Moore, S. 173.

23. *Henry Moore at the British Museum,* S. 125.

24. William Fagg wies den Autor darauf hin, daß dieser Kopf wahrscheinlich vom Ubangi stammt.

25. Siehe Wilkinson, S. 148, Abb. 120.

26. Moore, H., *Henry Moore,* photographiert und herausgegeben von John Hedgecoe, London 1968, S. 45.

27. Moore, S. 157.

28. Siehe Fagg, W., *The Tribal Image: Wooden Figure Sculpture of the World,* British Museum, London 1970, Abb. Nr. 4.

29. *Henry Moore at the British Museum,* S. 112.

30. Ebenda, S. 86.

31. Nairne und Serota, S. 79.

32. Leon Underwood (1890–1975) war ein Künstler, dessen Ruhm durch das Werk von Moore und Hepworth überschattet wurde, denen er in den frühen 20er Jahren das Modellzeichnen beigebracht hatte. Sein Schaffen ist jedoch im hier vorgegebenen Kontext aus verschiedenen Gründen wichtig. Seine eigenen Skulpturen, Ölgemälde und Druckgraphiken zeigen den zeitweiligen Einfluß primitiver Kunst. Seit 1919 sammelte er afrikanische Skulpturen und stellte im Laufe der Jahre eine bedeutende Sammlung zusammen. Zu Underwoods wichtigsten Veröffentlichungen über afrikanische Kunst gehören: *Figures in Wood of West Africa,* 1947; *Masks of West Africa,* 1948, und *Bronzes of West Africa,* 1949.

33. Abbildung von S. 100 des Skizzenbuchs Nr. 3 bei Wilkinson, S. 150, Abb. 131.

34. Moore, S. 159.

35. *Henry Moore at the British Museum,* S. 91.

36. Nairne und Serota, S. 120. Ann Gruetzner schrieb: »Moore sagte vor kurzem, daß die merkwürdigen, nebeneinander gestellten Formen der in Blei gegossenen *Liegenden Figur* (Privatsammlung) unmittelbar durch ozeanische Skulpturen inspiriert wurden.«

37. Christa Lichtenstein stellte in ihrem Artikel »Henry Moore and Surrealism«, *Burlington Magazine* 123, Nr. 944, November 1981, S. 645–58, erstmals heraus, daß Moores Zeichnungen zum Problem innerer und äußerer Form auf das Vorbild neuirischer Skulpturen zurückgehen.

38. *Henry Moore at the British Museum,* S. 81.

39. Abbildung der griechischen Bronzefiguren und von Moores Studie von 1937 bei Wilkinson, S. 144, Abb. 93 und 94.

40. Moore, S. 159.

41. Sylvester, D., *Henry Moore,* The Arts Council of Great Britain, London 1968, S. 36.

42. Fagg, W., und Plass, M., *African Sculpture: An Anthology,* London 1964, S. 30. Der IGBO-Kopfschmuck ☐ 936 ist dort ebenfalls abgebildet.

43. Siehe Wilkinson, A. G., *Gauguin to Moore: Primitivism in Modern Sculpture,* S. 298 Abb. 112.

44. Moore, H., *Henry Moore,* photographiert und herausgegeben von John Hedgecoe, London 1968, S. 466.

45. Goldwater, S. 246.

46. *Henry Moore at the British Museum,* S. 7.

☐ 944 *›Seehund‹, eskimoisch (Alaska), Walknochen, Höhe 45 cm. Privatsammlung. Ehemals Sammlung Henry Moore.*

□ 945 *Theodoros Stamos, ›Klänge im Felsen‹, 1946, Öl auf Holz, 122 x 72 cm. The Museum of Modern Art, New York.*

Kirk Varnedoe

Abstrakter Expressionismus

Für viele amerikanische Künstler, die um 1940 in eine Sackgasse geraten waren, bot der Primitivismus – möglichst umfassend verstanden – die Lösung eines verwirrenden Rätsels: Welche Grundlage konnte für eine neue Kunst gefunden werden, die weder eine Ableitung noch provinziell, die individuell und doch universal, frei von akademischen Normen und doch absolut war? Mehrere Künstler fanden ihre Antwort in einer Erscheinungsform des Primitiven, die eher ein allgemeines Ambiente als einen eigenen Stil bedeutete – einen weiten Bereich bildlicher Darstellungen und Themen, die weniger an Stammeskunst als an die Ursprünge der Natur- und Menschheitsgeschichte denken ließen.

Dieser neue Tenor war bereits in den späten dreißiger Jahren sichtbar und fand in den frühen vierziger Jahren in Bildern wie Adolph Gottliebs *Bildzeichen* von 1942 □ 947 und Jackson Pollocks *Wächter des Geheimen,* 1943 □ 948, mit ihrer Andeutung von Mythen, Archetypen und totemistischen Zeichen weite Verbreitung. Gegen Mitte des Jahrzehnts waren solche Anklänge zum Kennzeichen eines großen Teils avantgardistischer Kunst in Amerika geworden. Sie begegneten in so unterschiedlichen Werken wie Mark Rothkos Bildern von Lebensanfängen, etwa *Urlandschaft,* 1945 □ 949, und David Smiths versteinerten Ungeheuern, *Juravogel,* 1945 □ 951, oder – aufgrund anderer Bezüge zu Evolution und Untergang, zu vergangenen Kulturen und lebendigem Ritual – in den Werken von Barnett Newman, Theodoros Stamos, Mark Tobey, William Baziotes, Isamu Noguchi und zahlreichen anderen.

Einige dem Primitivismus verpflichtete Ideen waren in den zwei Jahrzehnten vor 1940 in amerikanischen Kunstkreisen aufgekommen. Jedoch von einer ganz anderen Ausprägung, waren sie oft mit einer Romantisierung heimatlichen Erbes und materialistisch politischen Vorstellungen verbunden. So waren etwa die mexikanischen Muralisten – Rivera, Orozco, Siqueiros u. a. – wegen der Wiederbelebung der Mythen und Formen ihrer alten Landeskultur und weil sie dieses Erbe in den Dienst der nationalen Einheit und sozialen Erneuerung stellten, sehr bewundert worden. In den späteren Dreißigern folgte jedoch Unzufriedenheit mit dieser Art volkparteilichen Archaisierens. Grund dafür war eine allgemeine Enttäuschung über den Marxismus, der jene Kunstrichtung begünstigt hatte (eine politische Wende, die der Hitler-Stalin-Pakt von 1939 noch beschleunigte). Als das Museum of Modern Art die Vereinigung von Archaik und Moderne 1940 mit der Ausstellung »Twenty Centuries of Mexican Art« feierte, war die Blütezeit der Muralisten bereits vorbei. Ihr rhetorisch vereinfachter Naturalismus schien sogar in seinen expressionistischsten Momenten für die Suche nach kosmischeren Welten in den vierziger Jahren unzulänglich geworden zu sein.[1] Die neu aufkommende Form des Primitivismus suchte primitive Mythen und Zeichen tiefer zu erfassen und gebrauchte sie nicht als Gegenstände einer kollektiven Soziologie, sondern einer Universalpsychologie, die zu den Grundlagen der modernen Psyche vorstieß. Die frühere Vorliebe für mexikanische Archaik in der Kunst war auch symptomatisch für das Bedürfnis, der Dominanz der europäischen Moderne durch Rückbesinnung auf die eigene Kunstvergangenheit entgegenzuwirken. Bei dem neuen Primitivismus, der um 1940 entstand, bedeutete die wiederholte Berufung auf das »Universelle« unter anderem auch eine konstruktive Antwort auf die Herausforderung durch die europäische Kunst. Die immer häufigere Bezugnahme auf Prähistorie, Primitive und die Archaik fiel insbesondere mit einem zunehmenden Interesse an den Werken der europäischen Surrealisten zusammen. Die Amerikaner betrachteten primitive Kunst auch mit einem Verständnis, das hauptsächlich durch die Formen, die man in den jüngsten Arbeiten Picassos, Klees, Mirós, Ernsts, Massons und Mattas vorfand, geprägt war. Der Surrealismus beeinflußte nicht nur die Erscheinung des Primitivismus der amerikanischen Künstler, sondern auch deren beharrlichen Wunsch, die zeitgenössischen Kunstideale mit dem Schöpfertum des frühen Menschen zu verbinden.

Maler wie Gottlieb, Rothko und Newman hatten sich vom Bereich abstrakter Malerei abgewandt, der ihrer Meinung nach besonders in Amerika im trivialen Sinn dekorativ oder formal geworden war. Bei ihren tastenden Schritten, einen eigenen abstrakten Stil zu formulieren, hoben sie deshalb nachdrücklich ihr Interesse am Inhaltlichen hervor. Durch die Identifikation mit dem Primitiven konnten sie ein weniger willkürliches, zeitlos gültiges Vokabular abstrakter Formen für sich beanspruchen. Damit war es ihnen auch möglich, ihren Primitivismus von der, wie es ihnen schien, lediglich oberflächlichen, formalen Aneignung der Stammeskunst durch einige europäische Moderne abzugrenzen. In ihren Stellungnahmen, die die Ideale der Künstler verkündeten, zugleich aber deren eingefahrene Bahnen oft verbargen, verurteilten sie deshalb die moderne Abstraktion, um Forderungen nach einer tieferen Beziehung zum primitiven Künstler zu erheben. Gottlieb verkörperte dieses Bedürfnis nach Differenzierung, als er 1943 sagte: »Obwohl moderne Kunst durch die Entdeckung primitiver Kunstformen erste Impulse erhielt, meinen wir, daß die wahre Bedeutung primitiver Kunst nicht vorrangig im formalen Bereich zu suchen ist, sondern in dem geistigen Gehalt, der allen archaischen Werken zugrunde liegt.«[2] Obwohl Gottlieb

□ 948 *Jackson Pollock, ›Wächter des Geheimen‹ (Guardians of the Secret), 1943, Öl auf Leinwand, 123 x 191,5 cm. San Francisco Museum of Modern Art, A. M. Bender Bequest Fund.* ▷

□ 946 *John Graham in seinem Atelier. Photographie von 1938. Links eine Reliquiarfigur der* FANG. *Galerie Allan Stone, New York.*

□ 947 *Adolph Gottlieb, ›Bildzeichen‹ (Pictograph), 1942, Öl auf Leinwand, 122 x 91 cm. Adolph and Esther Gottlieb Foundation, New York.*

bezeichnenderweise all das übergeht, was man europäischen Vorgängern verdankte (denen fälschlicherweise rein formale Interessen unterstellt werden), gibt er die Sehnsucht der amerikanischen Künstler nach dem Mythos und der religiösen oder magischen Ausdruckskraft des Primitiven wieder. Diese Betonung einer allgemeinen Geisteshaltung jenseits bestimmter Stile oder Formen kennzeichnet ihre Sehnsucht nach den elementaren Grundlagen menschlicher Erfahrung, die regionale, nationale und andere Grenzen künstlerischer oder politischer Gegensätze überschreiten.

GOTTLIEBS Gebrauch des Wortes »archaisch« ist außerdem bezeichnend für die Art, wie diese Künstler in ihren Stellungnahmen oft Vorklassisches mit Vorgeschichtlichem, die *INKA* und die *ESKIMOS* zu einem synthetischen Konzept des Primitiven vereinten und größeren Nachdruck auf die universalen Gemeinsamkeiten der Psyche legten als auf die unterschiedlichen Stile der Kunst. Zahllose Artikel in Zeitschriften wie *Cahiers d'art* und *Documents* zeigten ihm und gleichgesinnten amerikanischen Künstlern – selbst den Künstlern, die französische Texte nicht lesen konnten und nur die Abbildungen studierten –, daß den Surrealisten letztlich weniger an Stammesstilen an sich gelegen war als an einem fundierten Verständnis des Geistes und der Bedeutung primitiver Kunst. Für dieses beinahe ethnologische Ethos und für die Propagierung der primitiven Mentalität als Vorbild modernen Kunstschaffens durch die Surrealisten waren die Amerikaner sehr empfänglich.

In anderer Hinsicht jedoch war ihnen der surrealistische Geist fremd, und die surrealistischen Ideen über das Primitive konnten den Wünschen solcher Künstler wie GOTTLIEB, NEWMAN und POLLOCK nicht gerecht werden. Das surrealistische Interesse an Parallelen zwischen dem primitiven Geist und dem modernen Unbewußten war vorwiegend freudianischen Vorstellungen über die Pathologie der menschlichen Psyche verbunden. Natürlich war Freud für die amerikanischen Künstler der frühen vierziger Jahre genauso wichtig. Aber die Amerikaner beschworen häufig eine Vorstellung von Archetypen, die eher mit dem Konzept eines »kollektiven Unbewußten« im Sinne Jungs verbunden war – dem Glauben an ein angeborenes »kollektives Gedächtnis«, das aus dem modernen Unbewußten einen Hort an Formsymbolen werden läßt, die den frühesten Erfahrungen der Menschen entstammen. Diese vagen »Jungschen« Ideen findet man im Vokabular amerikanischer Künstler, wenn sie auf das Unbewußte und auf primitive Kunst Bezug nehmen. Freilich ist deren Verbreitung mehr dem Werkstattgespräch und solch selbsternannten Theoretikern wie JOHN GRAHAM als einem genauen Studium Jungscher Schriften zu verdanken.

GRAHAM, ein russischer Emigrant mit erstklassigen Kenntnissen der modernen europäischen Kunst, war als Maler und sensibler Ästhet in der New Yorker Kunstszene der zwanziger und dreißiger Jahre eine prominente Gestalt. Er besaß außerdem primitive Kunst, über die er schrieb und mit der er handelte. Als Berater New Yorker Sammler und Partner der wichtigsten Händler in Europa trug er dazu bei, DAVID SMITH, GOTTLIEB, POLLOCK und andere mit qualitätvollen Stammesobjekten bekannt zu machen und diesen Künstlern einen Begriff von der Funktion und dem Entstehungszusammenhang primitiver Kunst zu vermitteln. Er betonte, wie sehr sich die prähi-

storische Kunst aller Völker und Zeiten ähnlich sei, und vertrat die Auffassung, daß die Stile der afrikanischen Skulptur den Errungenschaften der früheuropäischen Zivilisationen gleichwertig und vermutlich zeitlich vorausgegangen seien. Außerdem betrachtete er eine Kultur, die solche Skulpturen schuf, als hoch entwickelt, zudem um die »Expansion des unbewußten Geistes« bemüht.[3] In seinem theoretischen Traktat *System and Dialectics of Art* (1937) vertrat GRAHAM die Ansicht, daß ein Hauptziel moderner Kunst die Erforschung des Unbewußten sein sollte, um den Kontakt »mit der ursprünglichen Vergangenheit des Volkes« wiederherzustellen. Er definierte Kunstschöpfung als »Schaffung neuer authentischer Werte durch Eintauchen in die Erinnerung an unvordenkliche Zeiten und deren Gestaltung in reiner Form . . .«[4]

Solche Ausführungen über das Primitive und Unbewußte brauchten in den späten dreißiger Jahren nicht noch durch die Jungsche Lehre unterstützt zu werden (und GRAHAM berief sich auch nicht auf sie). Außerdem erwuchs die amerikanische Haltung, die vom früheren Freudianismus nicht völlig abwich, nicht primär aus gelehrten Differenzen über psychoanalytische Theorie, sondern aus Veränderungen in der allgemeinen Einstellung zu Stil und Ethos, im Leben ebenso wie in der Kunst. Das Freudsche Modell der Psyche und eine marxistisch-materialistische Sicht der Gesellschaft führten bei vielen Surrealisten (wie Irving Sandler bemerkte) zu einer Verbindung von metaphysischem Skeptizismus und radikalen politischen Idealen, die schlecht zu dem geradezu religiösen und fatalistischen Tenor des neuen amerikanischen Interesses an Mythos und

□ 949 *Mark Rothko, ›Urlandschaft‹ (Primeval Landscape), 1945, Öl auf Leinwand, 139 x 89 cm. Sammlung P. G. Peterson.*

Archetypus paßten.[5] Auch zog die Lehre Freuds bei den Surrealisten amoralische Gewagtheiten nach sich, eine Obsession der *amour fou* und sophistische Wortspielereien, die damit dem überzogenen europäischen Lebensstil anzugehören schienen, für den die meisten der weniger wohlhabenden amerikanischen Künstler eine (notgedrungen auch etwas neidische) Antipathie empfanden. Die Jungschen Ideen erfüllte eine feierliche Spiritualität, die den Amerikanern sympathischer war und ihrer Meinung nach auch den Umständen der Kriegsjahre besser entsprach.[6]

Diese unterschiedlichen Auffassungen gehörten in den größeren Zusammenhang, in dem die spezifischen Faktoren der amerikanischen Situation und die Ereignisse der Kriegsjahre den neuen Primitivismus der vierziger Jahre von seinen europäischen Vorgängern abgrenzten. Was immer seine formalen und geistigen Vorläufer in Europa gewesen sein mögen, der neue amerikanische Primitivismus war sichtlich ein Kind seiner Zeit und seiner Umgebung und eine Reaktion auf bestimmte unmittelbare Bedürfnisse. Im Grunde bot die neue »Regression« einen Ausweg für die amerikanischen Künstler, die in jahrzehntelanger Auseinandersetzung zwischen Nationalismus und Internationalismus und der unüberhörbaren Forderung nach sozialpolitischer Verantwortlichkeit der Kunst hin und her gerissen waren. Die Welt der Höhlen und Indianerzelte bot eine Vielzahl abstrakter Formen, deren Bedeutungsbereich, über die klare Widerlegung der verhaßten Beschränktheit amerikanischer Regionalschulen hinaus, die ganze Tagespolitik hinter sich zu lassen oder zumindest zu umgehen schien. Im Bereich dieser Aura des Elementaren konnten viele Diskussionen der dreißiger Jahre durch Hinwendung zu philosophischen Absolutheiten und letzten Naturwahrheiten, die man im wissenschaftlichen Stil anging, auf ein höheres Niveau gehoben werden.

Die amerikanischen Künstler, die primitive Stile übernahmen oder ihre neuen abstrakten Stile unter Berufung auf primitive Vorläufer verteidigten, suchten etwa das überkommene Patt zwischen den »Massen« und dem »Unbewußten« zu überwinden. Diese beiden Begriffe waren, wie ein Leitartikel von 1943 bestätigt, die Schlagworte in der Kunst der vorhergehenden zwanzig Jahre gewesen.[7] In den dreißiger Jahren hatte die scheinbar unüberbrückbare Kluft zwischen moderner Originalität, eingestimmt auf die Inspiration des »Unbewußten«, und öffentlicher Verantwortlichkeit (eine verständliche Kunst für die »Massen«) eine Sehnsucht nach primitiven Gesellschaften geweckt, in denen der Künstler durch praktische Aufgaben für das Gemeinwohl unersetzlich war.[8] Die Aussagen der Avantgarde der vierziger Jahre betonten jedoch vor dem sozialen Vorteil die geistige und psychologische Kraft der primitiven Kunst und unterstrichen die ahistorischen Verbindungen zwischen dem modernen und primitiven Künstler mehr als die historischen Faktoren, die sie trennten.[9] Diese Betonung kollektiver Wahrheiten, die eher zeitlos/psychisch als historisch/sozial waren, entsprach und unterstützte Forderungen nach einer neuen »apolitischen« Künstlerindividualität.[10] Das Unbewußte des modernen Künstlers sah man als die direkte Verbindung zur lebenden Quelle des kollektiven Gedächtnisses, und die schwierige, sichtlich nicht kommunikative, moderne Abstraktion hielt man für die wahre Verkörperung ewiger gemeinsamer Wahrheiten. Man berief sich auf primitive Vorläufer und verteidigte damit den modernen Individualismus als Wiederherstellung einer Universalität, die über Klasse oder Nation hinausgehen sollte. Zur Eingeborenenkunst der amerikanischen Nordwestküste schrieb BARNETT NEWMAN 1946: »Es gibt in diesen Werken eine Antwort für alle jene, die moderne abstrakte Kunst für das esoterische Vergnügen einer versnobten Elite halten. Denn bei diesen einfachen Völkern war abstrakte Kunst eine normale, von allen verstandene und vorherrschende Tradition. Sollen wir sagen, daß der moderne Mensch die Fähigkeit verloren hat, auf so hohem Niveau zu denken?«[11]

Obwohl man in primitiven Formen diese Qualität scheinbarer Zeitlosigkeit erkannte, schienen sie vielen Künstlern dem

□ 950 *Robert Motherwell, ›Indianer‹ (Indians), 1944, Tusche, Verbleib unbekannt.*

□ 951 *David Smith, ›Juravogel‹ (Jurassic Bird), 1945, Stahl, 64 x 89,5 x 19 cm. Privatsammlung.*

historischen Zeitpunkt der vierziger Jahre besonders geeignet. Mit der Ausbreitung des Faschismus und dem Beginn des Weltkrieges schien die moderne Welt durch das bösartige Wiederaufleben menschlicher Irrationalität einerseits und durch die neuen Möglichkeiten des mechanisierten und (später) atomaren Terrors andererseits gezeichnet. Dies versetzte den Menschen des 20. Jahrhunderts in eine ähnliche Lage erniedrigender Verwundbarkeit wie den Menschen vor der Zivilisation. Es wurde behauptet, daß nur die Kunst, die im tiefsten instinktiven Leben Gründe und Gefühle des Urschmerzes anspreche, angemessener Ausdruck des Zeitalters sein könnte. »Wenn wir eine Verwandtschaft zur Kunst des primitiven Menschen bekennen, liegt es daran, daß die Gefühle, die er ausdrückte, eine besondere Aktualität besitzen. In Zeiten der Gewalt scheinen persönliche Vorlieben für Feinheiten der Farbe und Form irrelevant. Jeder primitive Ausdruck enthüllt das ständige Bewußtsein mächtiger Kräfte, die unmittelbare Gegenwart von Terror und Angst und das Eingeständnis der Furcht vor der Tierwelt genauso wie vor den ewigen Ungewißheiten des Lebens. Daß diese Gefühle gerade heute von so vielen Völkern in der Welt erfahren werden, ist eine bedauernswerte Tatsache, und für uns ist eine Kunst, die diese Gefühle beschönigt oder verdrängt, oberflächlich und bedeutungslos.«[12]

Solche Bemerkungen enthüllen eine Wahrheit über die vierziger Jahre, eingeschlossen in eine falsche Vorstellung vom Primitiven; denn indem Gottlieb erklärte, wie sehr die Gegenwart der vorhistorischen Vergangenheit ähnlich sei, erfand er eine Vergangenheit nach dem Bild der Gegenwart. Seine Vorstellung der Nähe zum Primitiven enthält eine geläufige, wenn auch falsche Projektion moderner Ängste auf die Seele des frühen Menschen (siehe S. 44ff.). Dem Gesagten fügte Gottlieb hinzu: »Heute, da unsere Wünsche auf den verzweifelten Versuch, dem Bösen zu entrinnen, reduziert sind und die Zeit aus den Fugen geraten ist, sind unsere obsessiven, unheimlichen, mit Zeichen übersäten Bilder Ausdruck der Neurose, die heute unsere Realität darstellt.«[13] Nicht nur die Gefühle, auch die Sprache selbst – geologisch, philologisch und psychologisch zugleich – kennzeichnet den Ton des neuen Primitivismus.

In seiner aufrichtig feierlichen Reaktion auf die grellen freudianischen Elemente im Surrealismus mag dieser Ton nicht nur als kriegsbedingt, sondern auch – in Verbindung mit zusätzlicher Entpolitisierung – als provinzieller Konservativismus kritisiert werden. Doch machte sich diese Einstellung zunehmend in der Kunstpraxis bemerkbar. Die überzeugte Ablehnung surrealistischer Spitzfindigkeiten ging Hand in Hand mit einer Abneigung gegen technische Überfeinerung bei Surrealisten wie Salvador Dali. Diese Haltung gab den primitivistischen Tendenzen der Amerikaner einen besonderen

□ 952 *Mark Tobey, ›Eskimo Idiom‹, 1946, Tempera auf Holz, 110,5 x 70,5 cm. Seattle Art Museum, Schenkung Rubinstein.*

Auftrieb und machte sie empfänglich für die gröberen, mehr gestischen Aspekte im Werk solcher Künstler wie PICASSO und MIRÓ. Während die Amerikaner einen schwerfälligen emotionalen Stil vortrugen, ohne ihn durch spielerische oder sinnliche Elemente aufzulockern, suchten sie auch eine rauhe und vitale Kunst, die von »zivilisierter« Glätte frei war. In einem solchen Klima konnte das Gefühl der Unterlegenheit, das zuvor viele amerikanische Künstler gegenüber den europäischen Leistungen empfunden hatten, in wortreiche Erklärungen über die Tugenden der jugendlichen »Barbarei« Amerikas umgewandelt werden. Die scheinbaren Beschränkungen der europäischen Sensibilität analysierend (und allzu verallgemeinernd), schrieb NEWMAN 1948: »Alles [an Europa] ist so hoch kultiviert. Der Künstler in Amerika ist im Vergleich dazu wie ein Barbar. Er besitzt nicht die überfeinerte Sensibilität gegenüber dem Gegenstand, die europäisches Empfinden beherrscht. Er besitzt nicht einmal die Gegenstände. Dies ist daher unsere Gelegenheit, frei von altem Tand näher an die Ursprünge der tragischen Empfindung zu kommen. Sollen wir nicht als Künstler neue Gegenstände zur Darstellung suchen?«[14]

Bei der Suche nach diesen »neuen Gegenständen« setzte sich der neue amerikanische Primitivismus, was die Vorbilder betrifft, von den europäischen Vorläufern noch weiter ab. Überblickt man die Zeugnisse der vierziger Jahre (Aussagen, Artikel und Bücher ebenso wie die Werke selbst), stellt man beeindruckt fest, daß vor allem Bezüge zur Kunst des amerikanischen Kontinents, sowohl zu Stammestraditionen der *ESKIMOS* und der Indianer der Nordwestküste oder anderer amerikanischer Gebiete als auch, wenn auch in geringerem Umfang, zu den großen, untergegangenen Reichen Zentral- und Südamerikas vorherrschen. Als Europa durch das Kriegschaos zu dauerndem kulturellen Niedergang verdammt schien, war der Moment für andere Quellen eines Neubeginns gekommen. Eine besondere Chance hatten dabei die Kulturen, die nicht mit dem Niedergang Europas in Verbindung gebracht werden konnten, und Formen, die unabhängig waren von den primitiven Quellen (vor allem afrikanischen), die bereits mit europäischer Kunst verknüpft waren.

In den dreißiger Jahren waren Regionalisten wie Marxisten der Meinung, daß nur eine autochthone Mythologie, die aus

□ 953 *›Maske‹, eskimoisch (Alaska), bemaltes Holz, Höhe 99 cm. Sammlung G. Terasaki, New York.*

dem gleichen Boden, aus dem gleichen Volk stammt, eine verantwortungsvolle Kunst ermöglichen könne.[15] Mit dem Beginn des Krieges und dem gestiegenen Prestige einer psychologisch begründeten Vorstellung von Kunstschaffen und künstlerischer Wirkung wurden solche Ideale verbunden zu einer neuen Form der Bewunderung für die amerikanische Urkultur und den modernen Individualismus. Sie fanden Ausdruck in der allgemeinen Vorstellung, daß nur durch die tiefste Versenkung in das Eigene – die eigene Nation genauso wie das eigene Unbewußte – die Elemente einer wirklich universalen Kunst gefunden werden könnten.[16] Ironischerweise brachte dieses neue amerikanische Selbstvertrauen die Ursprünge des traditionellen europäischen Denkens buchstäblich »nach Hause« zurück, denn – von Montaigne bis zur Entdeckung Polynesiens 1767 – war man von den neuentdeckten Völkern Amerikas fasziniert. Mehr noch, in der Betonung von »Neuem« und »Eingeborenem« waren die Surrealisten den amerikanischen Künstlern wieder einmal vorausgegangen.[17] André Breton, Max Ernst und andere waren nicht nur von dem ursprünglichen Interesse der Kubisten an Afrika abgerückt und hatten sich der Südsee zugewandt, sondern sie bewunderten auch die Kunst der Stämme der Nordwestküste und der Eskimos – lange bevor es unter New Yorker Künstlern Mode geworden war.

Wie im Primitivismus der vierziger Jahre vielfach zu beobachten, tat sich der altamerikanische »Einfluß« mehr in der Idee kund, in den Worten der Künstler, als in ihren Bildern und Skulpturen. Bevor er im Werk einiger wichtiger Künstler voll verarbeitet wurde und sich fruchtbar auswirkte, war der Primitivismus Mitte der Vierziger mehrere Jahre lang als vernunftgemäße allgemeine Anschauung führend; er befriedigte einen weiten Bereich oft verhältnismäßig oberflächlicher Bedürfnisse bei Künstlern unterschiedlichster Begabung und Zielsetzung. In dieser Atmosphäre waren rein künstlerische Belange oft weniger wichtig als die mittelbaren strategischen Vorteile, die sich aus der Förderung alter amerikanischer Kunst ergaben.

Ein in erster Linie praktischer Vorteil war, daß die einheimischen Kulturen ein Erbe überlieferten, in dem sich der Wunsch amerikanischer Künstler nach Abgrenzung zur europäischen Kunst erfüllen ließ, ohne die Verwechslung mit dem starren Regionalismus der dreißiger Jahre zu riskieren. In dieser Hinsicht rückten die vierziger Jahre nicht nur von unmittelbaren europäischen Vorläufern ab, sondern eine seit langem bestehende Richtung amerikanischen primitivistischen Denkens lebte in neuer Form wieder auf. Seit dem 1. Weltkrieg war die Moderne in der amerikanischen Literatur und Kunst wiederholt mit einer Verherrlichung amerikanischer Eingeborenenkultur einhergegangen – die alte ironische Identifikation eines Avantgardekünstlers mit den Völkern, die zu den Außenseitern und Opfern der Staatsgründung gemacht worden waren. Die Verbindung zwischen dem »untergehenden Volk«, das im Land verwurzelt war, und der Avantgarde, dem Träger des neuen Geistes, der sich gegen das Establishment richtete, war bereits vor 1940 in Werken so unterschiedlicher Künstler wie Marsden Hartley, John Storrs und George L. K. Morris hergestellt worden (wie Gail Levin in einem vorhergehenden Kapitel des vorliegenden Buches bemerkt). Der Ort, wo die Synthese aus international-progressiven und indianischen Tendenzen am konsequentesten betrieben wurde, war die Künstler- und Intellektuellenkolonie in Taos, Neu-Mexiko. Die Tänze, die Martha Graham in den dreißiger Jahren kreierte und die die besondere Mischform aus eingeborenem und kolonial-christlichem Mystizismus, wie sie im amerikanischen Südwesten anzutreffen ist, beschworen (z. B. *Primitive Mysterien,* 1931), verbanden diese ausgesprochen primitivistische Tradition mit den neuen Entwicklungen der New Yorker Kunst. Grahams Werk stand dem neuen Primitivismus nicht nur im dunkel »archaischen«, Jung und dem Mythos verpflichteten Tenor ihrer Choreographie der vierziger Jahre nahe – auch in manchen Bühnenbildern, die Noguchi für sie entwarf (z. B. *Höhle des Herzens*) –, sondern auch in der Gesamtkonzeption ihrer Auseinandersetzung mit widerstreitenden Forderungen nach Aktualität und Zeitlosigkeit, internationaler Moderne und dem Wunsch nach authentischer, tief persönlicher Erfahrung während der dreißiger und der vierziger Jahre.[18] Solche künstlerischen Probleme, die sich bezeichnenderweise hinter der Beschwörung von Stammeslehren und alten Mythen verstecken, bildeten einen wichtigen Unterbau der primitivistischen Tendenzen der vierziger Jahre.

Unbestreitbar gibt es große Unterschiede zwischen *Azteken* und *Irokesen,* zwischen den alten Reichen Mittel- und Süd-

□ 954 *David Smith, ›Der Brief‹ (The Letter), 1950, Stahl, geschweißt, Höhe 28 cm. Munson-Williams-Proctor Institute, Utica, New York.*

amerikas, wo die mexikanischen Muralisten Anregung gesucht hatten, und den Stammesgemeinschaften Nordamerikas: Für den künstlerischen Primitivismus im Amerika der vierziger Jahre hatten diese unterschiedlichen Kulturen jedoch einige Gemeinsamkeiten. Als die amerikanischen Künstler nach einer Kunst suchten, um elementare Wahrheiten, die sie mit ihren Urahnen gemeinsam hatten, zu beschwören, begünstigten verschiedene Faktoren, darunter nicht zuletzt ein rassischer Gesichtspunkt, die einheimischen Kulturen. Für die europäischen Nationen, die (trotz ihrer Kolonialpolitik) nie eine eigene afrikanische Sklavenbevölkerung entwickelt hatten, besaß die »art nègre« nicht den problematischen sozialen Aspekt, den er in den Vereinigten Staaten hatte. Die Europäer – in ihrer Distanz zur schwarzen amerikanischen wie auch afrikanischen Bevölkerung – neigten dazu, beide Kulturen zu ignorieren. Den Primitivismus afrikanischer Prägung verband man in Europa mit dem Chic des schwarzen Blues und dem Jazz (Josephine Baker u. a.) in einer Form, wie er in das Amerika vor dem Weltkrieg nicht übertragen werden konnte. Wenngleich Künstler wie Gottlieb afrikanische Objekte besaßen und bewunderten, hätte es für weiße Maler in New York – im Gegensatz zu Picasso und Modigliani in Paris Jahrzehnte früher – im Jahr 1940 etwas anderes bedeutet, eine Urbeziehung zwischen ihren künstlerischen Neuerungen und der afrikanischen Kunst zu propagieren. Obwohl sich viele amerikanische Künstler, um ihren Arbeiten Gewicht zu geben, nachdrücklich auf primitive Vorläufer beriefen, hätte eine spezielle Verbindung – vermittels erkennbarer afrikanischer Vorbilder – zwischen einer bereits in Frage gestellten modernen Minderheit und der unterdrückten schwarzen Mehrheit zu sehr spezifisch sozialen Fragen geführt, die die meisten der Künstler geflissentlich aus ihrer Kunst tilgten. Die amerikanischen Ureinwohner, deren Bevölkerungszahl kleiner war und die als eher folkloristisches Phänomen ein geringeres soziales Problem

□ 955 ›Kopfschmuck‹, SENUFO (Elfenbeinküste), Holz, Höhe 142 cm. Museum für Völkerkunde, Berlin.

darstellten, konnten von den Künstlern leichter als vorzeitliche Quelle in Anspruch genommen werden.

Der amerikanische Primitivismus erwuchs aus einer bewußten Idealisierung primitiver Kulturen. Sowohl das Gefühl, einem reinen Wunder gegenüberzustehen, das die früheren Modernen gegenüber Stammeskunst empfunden hatten, als auch der zwielichtige Schein, der den trivialeren Primitivismus der zwanziger Jahre umgab, hatte sich verloren. Die dunkle Wildheit und Wollust, die man zu Unrecht lange mit vielen »Fetischen« der »art nègre« assoziiert hatte, wurde durch ein neues, synthetisches Ideal des Primitiven ersetzt, das sich leicht auf jene Gesellschaften, deren mythologische und soziale Strukturen bekannter waren, anwenden ließ. GOTTLIEB sagte: »Der Grund, daß diese dämonischen und wilden Bilder uns heute faszinieren, liegt nicht in ihrer Exotik. Sie erwecken in uns auch keine Sehnsucht nach einer Vergangenheit, die aufgrund ihrer Ferne bezaubernd erscheint. Es ist im Gegenteil die Unmittelbarkeit ihrer Bilder, die uns unwiderstehlich zu den Phantasien und dem Aberglauben, den Fabeln der Wilden und der seltsamen Glaubenswelt hinzieht, die der primitive Mensch so lebendig ausgedrückt hat.«[19] (»Dämonisch« und »wild« tendieren ironischerweise zur alten Fehlinterpretation der Stammeskunst als expressionistisch, auch wenn GOTTLIEBS Aussage dies nicht bestätigt.) Solche Bekenntnisse zu einer neuen Ernsthaftigkeit sollen nicht bedeuten, daß die Künstler der vierziger Jahre eifrige Anthropologen wurden; die amerikanischen Künstler waren in der Regel über anthropologische Dinge schlechter informiert als surrealistische Vorgänger wie MAX ERNST. Das Zitat verweist freilich auf eine bewußte mythologische »Verpackung«, das ihr Interesse an primitiven Objekten zunehmend bestimmte.

Diese wesentlich gelassenere Einstellung gegenüber Mythen und Praktiken der Stammeskunst bekundet einen Wandel, den wir in der amerikanischen Szene dieser Jahre bereits feststellen

□ 956 *David Smith, ›Royal Incubator‹, 1949, Stahl, Bronze und Silber, 94 x 97,5 x 25 cm. Sammlung B. Wright.*

□ 957 *›Maske‹, eskimoisch, Kuskokwimfluß (Alaska), bemaltes Holz, Walroßzahn, Federn und Fasern, Höhe 91 cm. Hamburgisches Museum für Völkerkunde. Farbabbildung* □ *865.*

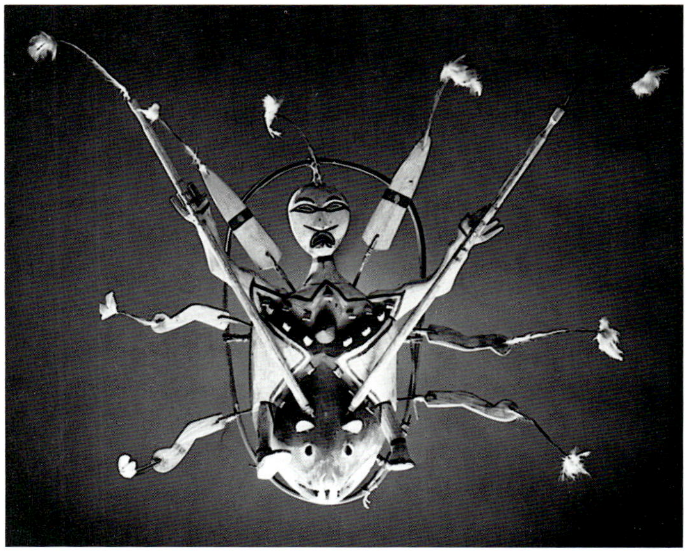

konnten. Wiederum war die marxistische Ästhetik der zwanziger und dreißiger Jahre Voraussetzung für die eher antimaterialistischen Betrachtungsweisen der Vierziger: Die Deutung menschlichen Schaffens im sozialen Kontext wurde abgelöst durch ein Verständnis aus dem geistigen Kontext heraus, das mehr von Glaubenssystemen als von wirtschaftlichen Faktoren ausging. (Dieser Wandel läßt sich, was »Kontext« und »Ästhetik« betrifft, auch an Veränderungen in der Präsentation primitiver Objekte in Museen und Galerien ablesen.)[20] Man bevorzugte die Eingeborenenkulturen Amerikas, da deren zeremonielle und kosmologische Systeme der Fachwissenschaft wie dem Allgemeinverständnis vertraut waren und die Grundlage zur Würdigung ihrer Kunst darstellen konnten. Ob die primitiven Stämme Nordamerikas oder die archaischen Hofkulturen Mittelamerikas, man assoziierte die Kunst der Eingeborenen mit zeremonieller Würde und mythologischen Vorstellungen über das Zusammenspiel von Mensch und Kosmos in einer Weise, wie sie besonders die neue Generation der primitivistischen Künstler ansprach.[21]

Afrikanische Kunst war für die amerikanischen Künstler der vierziger Jahre weniger anziehend – nicht nur aus sozialpolitischen Gründen oder weil man deren Mythologien weniger kannte, sondern auch aufgrund formaler Anschauungen. Mit ihrem zergliedernden Aufbrechen der plastischen Gestalt des Menschen (und entweder neutraler oder leicht vereinfachter Farbigkeit) hatte afrikanische Skulptur die frühe Avantgarde beeindruckt, die sich mit der von Cézanne begründeten Strukturierung der Masse und der Verschränkung von Körper und Raum befaßte. Wie William Rubin hervorhebt (S. 48, 61 ff.), hatte die surrealistische Generation einen Interessenwandel hin zu einer neuen Würdigung der eher malerischen und anscheinend phantasievolleren Seite der Südseekunst bewirkt. Die primitivistischen Maler im Amerika der vierziger Jahre suchten jedoch die endgültige Loslösung von der Gegenständlichkeit. Das bedeutete, entweder die plastische Präsenz des menschlichen Körpers zugunsten eines eher landschaftlichen Raumes zu vermeiden oder zoomorphe und andere abstrakte, pseudobiologische Organismen an ihre Stelle zu setzen. Die zeichenhafte Einfachheit der Kunst amerikanischer Eingeborener sprach ihr Interesse an isolierten archetypischen Bildern an. Die Suche nach neuen Möglichkeiten des Formats und der Oberfläche, wie sie die Maler der New Yorker Schule betrieben – man denke vor allem an die Allover-Malerei –, führte sie außerdem eher zu zweidimensionalen als plastischen Vorbildern. Das Wandformat von Zeichnungen der vorgeschichtlichen Menschen und des Buschmannes sowie die Muster indianischer Stoffe und Totems erregten mehr Neugier als afrikanische Figuren. Jackson Pollock sagte 1944: »Ich war immer sehr beeindruckt von den plastischen Qualitäten der Indianerkunst. In ihrer Fähigkeit, adäquate Bilder zu finden, und ihrem Verständnis für den malerischen Gegenstand besitzen die Indianer den Zugang echter Maler. Ihre Farbigkeit ist im wesentlichen westlich, ihre Vorstellungskraft hat die Universalität großer Kunst.«[22] Auch Mark Tobey huldigte in Werken wie *Eskimo Idiom* von 1946 □ 952 dem indianischen Erbe. Er vereinfacht in diesem Bild die Komplexität eskimoischer Masken □ 953, bei denen die Gesichter und Körper, Menschen und Tiere in erfinderischen Systemen von Öffnung und Kontraktion verbunden werden. In Tobeys *Trommeln, Indianer und das Wort Gottes* von 1944 □ 962 – das von Objekten der Nordwestküste aus seiner eigenen Sammlung beeinflußt ist – zeigt sich nicht nur ein Interesse an indianischen Mustern, sondern auch daran, wie deren Kunst mit geistigen und zeremoniellen Inhalten verbunden ist.

Selbst in der Skulptur wandten sich Künstler wie David Smith von reinen Monolithen ab zu einer offenen »Zeichnung im Raum«, die mit den bekannteren afrikanischen Formtypen weniger gemeinsam hat. Nur selten zeigen Formen wie der Kopfschmuck der *Senufo* (von den in den vierziger Jahren in New York Beispiele verfügbar waren, die Smith möglicherweise sah □ 955) Affinitäten zu den stark malerischen Arbeiten Smiths wie *Der Brief* □ 954. Eskimoische Masken zeigten jedoch eine formale Aufsplitterung der Teile und eine Einbeziehung des Raums, die für den Schöpfer von *Royal Incubator* von 1949 □ 956, 957 interessant gewesen sein könnten. Louise

□ 958 *Frederick J. Kiesler, ›Totem für alle Religionen‹ (Totem for All Religions), 1947, Holz und Seil, 285 x 87 x 78 cm. The Museum of Modern Art, Schenkung A. P. Bartos, New York.*

Bourgeois scheint eine Ausnahme gewesen zu sein, als sie, zumindest in Arbeiten der späten vierziger Jahre wie *Schwangere* □ 966, Skulpturen schuf, die afrikanischen Formen nahestehen. Für Smith und andere Künstler wie Frederick Kiesler war der schichtende Aufbau der Totems der Nordwestküste ein wichtigeres Vorbild für seine additiv konzipierte Skulptur, die teils menschlich, aber nicht traditionell figürlich wie die surrealistischen *personnages* gestaltet war – wie Kieslers *Totem für alle Religionen* von 1947 □ 958. Isamu Noguchi bezog noch ein größeres Spektrum des indianischen Erbes ein. Ähnlich Barnett Newman bewunderte er indianische Erdformen wie die der Mound-Building People des Ohio- und Mississippitals □ 959. Offensichtlich zählten sie zu den Inspirationsquellen seiner Landschaft/Skulptur-Projekte der dreißiger Jahre wie *Konturiertes Spielfeld* □ 961 und *Monument für den Pflug.* Obwohl *Diese gequälte Erde* von 1943 □ 960 ganz unmittelbar durch Luftaufnahmen von Kriegsschäden in Afrika angeregt war, spiegelte sich darin auch das Studium indianischer Erdmonumente. Noguchis Anregung durch indianische Erdformen verbindet den künstlerischen Primitivismus mit wissenschaftlich-naturgeschichtlichen Interessen, wie es für die fortschrittlichen Künstler seiner Generation typisch ist; denn darin mischt sich nostalgische Verehrung des kollektiven Kunstschaffens früher Gesellschaften mit einer Bewunderung der zeitlos natürlichen Künstlerschaft der geologischen Erosion.[23] Noguchi verstand Erdmäler als Mittel gegen die Sterilität moderner Denkmäler wie auch gegen die Aushöhlung der künstlerischen Kraft durch den Kunsthandel. Er nahm damit in den dreißiger und vierziger Jahren Vorstellungen der Land Art der siebziger Jahre vorweg.

Alle diese Bezüge auf indianische Kunst führten jedoch nicht zu einem besonderen Stileinfluß. Der neue Primitivismus bedeutete eine Synthese aus ausgewählten Elementarformen von geradezu anonymer, archetypischer Allgemeingültigkeit und vermied dadurch die kulturspezifische Kunstform, die frühere primitivistische Kunst oft begleitet hatte (wie Marsden Hartleys »indianischer« Stil □ 648). Ihren erklärten Zielen entsprechend, auf vielerlei Traditionen aufzubauen, betrachteten diese Maler primitive Kunst nicht vorrangig als Formenrepertoire, sondern als Zeugnis formgebender Energien, die ästhetische Fragen beiseite drängten. Anfänglich nahmen primitivistische Werke amerikanischer Künstler in ikonographischer Hinsicht stärker auf primitive Lehren und Zeichen Bezug. Diese Bezüge wichen jedoch bald einem stärkeren Interesse am künstlerischen Prozeß, bei dem der Geist des Primitiven – die formgebende Energie – in zwar weniger spezifischer, aber grundlegender Weise auf modernes Kunstschaffen übertragen wurde.

Obwohl die Amerikanische Avantgarde der vierziger Jahre zu Anfang gelegentlich formale Anregungen der Stammeskunst aufnahm, bekundet ihr Primitivismus letztlich ein Ethos der Eliminierung, ein Bedürfnis, alle tradierten Stilübernahmen beiseite zu räumen. Sie suchten nach Strukturen, die eine Aura der Determination besaßen, naturgeschichtlichen Formen und der elementaren Kommunikation mehr angehörten als dem Bereich der Ästhetik. Infolgedessen wurden formale Anregungen durch primitive Kunst zusammen mit anderen Quellen aus den Bereichen linguistischer Zeichen und der Naturwissenschaft oft zu Bildern, die einen breiten, kulturell unspezifischen, atavistischen Zug besaßen. Häufig scheint bei diesen Bildern eine Metapher aus dem Bereich der Geologie und/oder Archäologie vorzuliegen – beide Male ein Freilegen tiefer Schichten biologischer wie auch geistiger Existenz, wobei eher der äußerste Zwang der Notwendigkeit als kulturell determinierte Einfälle die Form bestimmten. Entsprechende Lobesworte wählte der Katalogtext zu einer Gottlieb-Ausstellung 1947: »Die Fragmente, die er bei der Erforschung unseres gemeinsamen Untergrunds – eines Untergrunds der den Menschen der Maya-Kultur, Ozeaniens, des paläolithischen und des atomaren Zeitalters verbindet – aufdeckte, hat er zu einem mächtigen und beeindruckenden Zeichen zusammengeschlossen.«[24]

□ 959 *Erdaufschüttung in Form einer Schlange (The Great Serpent Mound), 6 x 1,5 x 225 m. Adams County, Ohio.*

□ 960 *Isamu Noguchi. ›Diese gequälte Erde‹ (This Tortured Earth), 1943, Bronze, 71 x 71 x 10 cm. Sammlung Isamu Noguchi Foundation, New York.*

Diese archäologische Metapher im Primitivismus der vierziger Jahre teilt sich in zwei komplementäre Richtungen. Einerseits lassen zahlreiche Darstellungen an genetische Anfänge, prähistorische Formen der Evolution oder Zerstörung sowie an Phänomene der Mikrobiologie denken. ROTHKOS Werk von 1940–1946 ist das beste Beispiel dafür (z. B. *Ritual,* 1944, *Langsamer Strudel am Rande der See,* 1944 □ 964, und zahlreiche Gemälde und Aquarelle ohne Titel). Aber NEWMANS früheste Zeichnungen und Gemälde von 1944–45, die an Amöben und Samen erinnern, gehören ebenfalls dazu (z. B. *Gea,* 1944–45). Ebenso sind die Hinweise in Arbeiten von DAVID SMITH, THEODOROS STAMOS und WILLIAM BAZIOTES auf versteinerte Tiere und die Lehre geologischer Gesteinsschichten ebenfalls mit der Naturgeschichte interpretierbar.[25] Daneben und gelegentlich in Verbindung damit findet man ein Repertoire an Chiffren und schematischen Bildzeichen, die an unbekannte Alphabete, originäre Geometrie und primitive Schriftformen erinnern. GOTTLIEBS Bildzeichen und DAVID SMITHS *Der Brief* □ 954 sind prominente Beispiele dafür. Auch in der Malerei POLLOCKS finden sich Anklänge an Höhlenschriften (etwa in *Verwundetes Tier* von 1943 □ 980 und in *Wächter des Geheimen,* 1943 □ 948); Zeichnungen SMITHS, das spätere Werk GOTTLIEBS und Gemälde von FRANZ KLINE und MARK TOBEY verraten eine Begeisterung für kalligraphische Zeichen.

Ein zentraler Gedanke innerhalb der primitivistischen »Rückwendungen« der vierziger Jahre war die Annäherung dieser beiden Formen – ursprüngliche, auf die Oberfläche geschriebene Zeichen und die in die Erde eingebettete Naturgeschichte – als sinnbildhafte Wiedervereinigung des menschlichen Geistes mit Naturvorgängen. Diese Bildsprache und Metaphorik ist weder zweitrangig noch den Aussagen über primitive Kunst fremd. Im Mittelpunkt aller Bestrebungen der amerikanischen Avantgarde der vierziger Jahre stand das Sondieren der Grundlagen menschlicher Darstellungsweisen und ihres Zusammenhangs zu den Naturgesetzen. Eher im Bereich dieser Bildsprache und auf dieser tieferen Bedeutungsschicht als in den Statements antwortete der neue amerikanische Primitivismus auf allgemeinere Fragen. Hier reicht er über seine Ursprünge im Surrealismus und über einzelne pragmatische oder politische Belange seiner Zeit hinaus und schließt sich Grundströmungen an, die im modernen Primitivismus seit GAUGUIN und im umfassender verstandenen Primitivismus europäischer Künstler und Intellektueller seit dem 18. Jahrhundert bekannt sind.

Die Wiedervereinigung von Geist und Natur auf der Ebene frühester Anfänge war – allgemein gesprochen – ein Ideal, das sich auf ethnologische Theorien über primitive Mentalität stützen konnte, die zwischen den beiden Weltkriegen großen Einfluß ausübten und den Surrealisten geläufig waren. Der

□ 961 *Isamu Noguchi, ›Konturiertes Spielfeld‹ (Contoured Playground), 1941, Gips, 8 x 66 x 66 cm. Sammlung Isamu Noguchi Foundation, New York.*

□ 962 *Mark Tobey, ›Trommeln, Indianer und das Wort Gottes‹ (Drums, Indians, and the Word of God), 1944, Tempera auf Holz, 47 x 35 cm. Verbleib unbekannt.*

□ 963 *›Totempfahl‹,* HAIDA *(Britisch-Kolumbien), bemaltes Holz, Höhe 111 cm. Privatsammlung. Ehemals Sammlung Mark Tobey.*

französische Anthropologe Lévy-Bruhl glaubte am Anfang des Jahrhunderts im Geist des »Wilden« das Fehlen klarer Unterscheidungssysteme zu erkennen, die das logische Denken des zivilisierten Menschen kennzeichnen.[26] Später sollte diese Ansicht durch Lévi-Strauss' Betonung der logischen Struktur primitiver Gedanken, die zwar anders, aber der Rationalität westlichen Denkens gleichwertig seien, widerlegt werden (vgl. meine Ausführungen im letzten Kapitel dieses Buches). Lévy-Bruhls Ansicht war vor den fünfziger Jahren weit verbreitet und wurde von Jung und zahlreichen anderen Autoren der Anthropologie vertreten. Nach Lévy-Bruhl erfuhr der primitive Mensch die Welt in einer weniger zerteilten Form; die Grenzen zwischen Tieren, Pflanzen und Menschen waren für ihn durchlässig und frei zu überschreiten. Diese Form des »Partizipierens«, wo Bedeutung und Gestalt unwillkürlich und ohne Hindernisse miteinander verbunden sind, bot dem modernen Künstler einen erträumten Ausweg vor der verfremdenden Wirkung der Rationalität. BARNETT NEWMAN äußerte, als er 1947 das Werk von STAMOS würdigte, daß der moderne Künstler die Attitude der »Sensibilität« überwunden hätte, die den Menschen von der Natur trenne, ihn isoliere und Natur nur zum Gegenstand der Betrachtung mache. Über Gemälde wie *Klänge im Felsen* von 1946 sagte er, daß sie »eine Naturempfindung offenbaren, die mehr an wahre Vereinigung grenzt. Seine [Stamos'] Bildzeichen erfassen den Augenblick totemistischer Affinität zu Fels und Pilz . . . Stamos fußt auf der gleichen Grundlage wie der primitive Künstler, der . . . ein Phänomen abbildete . . . immer als Ausdruck des ursprünglichen Mysteriums an sich, wo Fels und Mensch gleich sind.«[27]

Unvermeidlich erinnern solche Aussagen an JACKSON POLLOCKS berühmte Ablehnung der Naturnachahmung: »Ich bin Natur.« William Rubin sieht diese prahlerische Aussage (die auch in den Worten anderer Künstler der Generation POLLOCKS begegnet) zu Recht in Verbindung mit einer romantischen Tradition des natürlichen oder naiven Dichters,[28] eine Tradition, die seit langem mit primitivistischen Gedanken im literarischen und philosophischen Bereich verbunden ist. Dieser Zusammenhang wiederum ermöglicht es uns, die tieferen Verbindungen in den Vorstellungen der amerikanischen Künstler der vierziger Jahre nicht nur zu Lévy-Bruhl und Jung, sondern auch zu zentralen, historischen Positionen des europäischen Primitivismus zu erkennen.

Die dreifache Verbindung von »unverbildeten« Ausdrucksformen, innersten Schaffensquellen und grundlegenden Naturkräften geht als Konstellation mindestens auf die Schriften von Herder zurück. Im gleichzeitig auftretenden Interesse an

□ 964 *Mark Rothko, ›Langsamer Strudel am Rande der See‹ (Slow Swirl by the Edge of the Sea), 1944, Öl auf Leinwand, 191 x 215 cm. The Museum of Modern Art, Vermächtnis Mrs. Mark Rothko, New York.*

Schriften über die Vorgeschichte, wissenschaftliche Naturgeschichte und Stammeskunst bei den Künstlern der vierziger Jahre wird dieser wiederkehrende Zusammenhang erneut evident. So gesehen, erscheint die primitive Kunst – die unbewußte Poesie der Stammeshymne oder die Zeichenfigurationen des Buschmannes – von überpersonaler emotional/psychologischer Notwendigkeit gestaltet und zu einer integralen Rolle im Gemeinschaftsleben bestimmt. In ihren Formen sieht man daher die große Sehnsucht der modernen abstrakten Kunst nach allgemeingültigen Zeichen verwirklicht, die gleichzeitig kulturell (vom Menschen stammend, ohne sklavisch die Naturerscheinungen nachzuahmen) und natürlich sind (in unmittelbarer, den Zufall ausschließender Weise mit universalen Bedeutungen verbunden). Solche Zeichen würden von Bewußtseinsebenen aufsteigen und sich an solche wenden, in welchen die problematischen Barrieren zwischen Körper und Geist, Ich und Gesellschaft, Naturgesetzen und Menschenwerk durchlässig wenn nicht aufgehoben sind. Der Primitivismus stand damit, solange er als Richtung europäischen Denkens bestand, mit dem Nachdenken über die Herkunft von Sprache und Naturzeichen und mit der Suche nach einer absoluten oder »natürlichen« Kunst, die mit unwandelbaren, allgemeingültigen Formen und Bedeutungen in Einklang steht, wiederholt in Beziehung (siehe hierzu meine Ausführungen im Kapitel Gauguin, S. 201, 216).

Dieser Wunsch, kulturelle und natürliche Grundlagen zu vermischen, zeigt sich in den vierziger Jahren nicht nur darin, daß man allgemein von alten Alphabeten und Versteinerungen fasziniert war, sondern auch im Zusammenspiel von Bildtiteln und Bild – wie man am Werk Rothkos sieht. Seine Bilder, entstanden aus der Vereinigung surrealistischer Phantasie mit mikroskopisch/biologischen Strukturen, wurden mit Bildtiteln versehen, die an griechische Mythologie (*Die Opferung der Iphigenie,* 1942), christliche Mysterien (*Gethsemane,* 1945) und an jüdische Dämonenlehre (*Die Riten der Lilith,* 1945) erinnern. Rothko verband seine leichtflüssig gemalten, sanft wogenden Formen auf diese Weise mit Assoziationen intensiver, traditionsgebundener Schwere; die großen Themen menschlichen Denkens wurden mit den höchsten Momenten der Menschheitsgeschichte verbunden. Die dramatische Abkehr der Kunst Rothkos von zeitgenössischen sozialen Themen (etwa seine Serie New Yorker U-Bahnszenen) und seine Hinwendung zur Verschmelzung des Epischen und Elementaren ist weniger der Anregung außereuropäischer Kunst zu verdanken als vielmehr formalen Vorbildern bei Masson oder noch früher bei Redon und seiner Ausbildung in Yale.[29]

Dieser Wandel vom Proletarischen zur Urexistenz war jedoch programmatisch und von der geistigen Orientierung her durch das Ideal des Primitiven bestimmt. ROTHKO sprach mit Neid von dem Privileg des »archaischen« Künstlers, in einer Gesellschaft zu leben, in der transzendentale Kunst in allseits bekannten Mischwesen von Mensch und Tier ausgedrückt werden konnte. Es war die Aufgabe des modernen Künstlers, in neuen Formen, frei von Assoziationen mit vertrauten Dingen, Äquivalente für diese »Ungeheuer und Götter« vergangener Zeitalter zu schaffen.[30]

Mehrere Gelehrte fanden in den bei ROTHKO Mitte der vierziger Jahre verwendeten Formen Hinweise auf indianische Sandbilder oder Gewänder und auf Gerätschaften primitiver Rituale.[31] Seine Kunst scheint jedoch für die Form des Primitivismus in der Kunst der vierziger Jahre charakteristisch zu sein, die jenseits spezifischer stilistischer Einflüsse lag und deren Bedeutungsbereiche kaum direkte primitivistische Aussagen berührten. ROTHKO vertrat, ohne ausdrücklich Jung zu nennen, eine aus dem Unbewußten abgeleitete, zeitlose Gültigkeit der Kunst.[32] Bilder wie *Langsamer Strudel am Rande der See*

◁ ☐ 965 *Adolph Gottlieb, ›Bildzeichen-Symbol‹, 1942, Öl auf Leinwand, 137 x 102 cm. Privatsammlung, New York.*

☐ 964 und *Figur am archaischen See*, die das Element Wasser behandeln, können mit Jungs Aussage übereinstimmen, daß »Wasser das gängigste Symbol für das Unbewußte ist«.[33] Die zarten, mit Flimmerhärchen versehenen Organismen, die auf der Leinwand schweben, verwenden die fragilen, doch entschiedenen Bewegungen frühester Evolution als Äquivalent für die erzeugende Kraft der tiefsten Bewußtseinsschicht. Sie bewegen sich quer durch Schichten, die gesprungene Horizonte zwischen Verwurzeltsein und Aufsteigen, Potentiellem und Entstehendem, vorbewußtem Denken und höherer Entwicklung darstellen. Die fragmentarische Vision dieser Bilder betont bezeichnenderweise die Kontinuität zwischen solcher Einteilungen sowie die organische Integrität einer Umwandlung, mit der verschiedene Formen zu einer einzigen treibenden Energie zusammengefaßt werden. Diese Formen seien, sagte Rothko, »Organismen mit Willen und einem Wunsch nach Selbstbehauptung«, moderner Ersatz für die »Ungeheuer und Götter«, ohne die »Kunst unser Dasein nicht darstellen kann«.[34] Es werden hier Metaphern für jene Gedanken und frühesten Archetypen angesprochen, die nach Rothko sein Werk bestimmen sollten, aus den Tiefen des Bewußtseins auftauchen mit unentschieden potentiellem, doch vorbestimmtem, »natürlichem« inneren Impuls nach Selbstbestimmung. »Unser Bewußtsein«, schrieb J. Graham Ende der 30er Jahre, »enthält Aufzeichnungen all unserer vergangenen, individuellen und kollektiven Erfahrungen seit der ersten Zellbildung . . .«[35]

Adolph Gottlieb teilte Pollocks Interesse an Mythen und seine Art, sich mit dem Primitiven zu identifizieren; die gemeinsamen Interessen der beiden Maler zeigen sich an den verwandten Bildthemen der Zeit von 1943–1945. Gottlieb wählte für sich jedoch eine ganz andere Ausdrucksform. Während Rothkos Rückwendung einen ursprünglichen Zustand flüssig organischer Metamorphose beschwor, stellte Gottlieb mit seinen Bildzeichen von 1941–51 ☐ 947, 965 ein Feld linguistischer Fragmente, eine Art Urschriftsatz an Zeichen dar. Die Ursprünge dieser linearen Gerüste und schematischen Zeichen sind unterschiedlich. Auch wenn man dem kaum zustimmen muß, der Künstler selbst bestand darauf, daß die Aufteilungen christlicher Erzählungen auf Predellenbildern und Freskenzyklen der Frührenaissance wichtigere Quellen waren als die Vorbilder, die er – aus früheren Quellen primitiver Schriften und Textilien bereits umgewandelt – in der Kunst Paul Klees und Joaquin Torres-Garcías gesehen haben konnte ☐ 719.[36] Auf jeden Fall formten moderne europäische Vorbilder seinen Stil genauso wie ähnliche Strukturen in den Decken der *Tlingit*-Indianer der Nordwestküste ☐ 968. Als Gottlieb zum ersten Mal ein Bildzeichen ausstellte – *Bildzeichen-Symbol,* in einer Gruppenausstellung von 1942 ☐ 965 –, wies die Kritik sofort auf dessen indianischen Ursprung, genauer: auf dessen Herkunft von der Nordwestküste, hin.[37] Obgleich Gottlieb sich schon lange vorher für amerikanische Indianerkunst interessierte (spätestens 1937, als er die Sammlung des State Museum in Tucson, Arizona, bewunderte), erwarb er seine eigene *Tlingit*-Decke erst nach jener Ausstellung ☐ 968.[38] Sie hat möglicherweise die Strukturen späterer Arbeiten wie *Nachtformen* von 1949/50 beeinflußt ☐ 967.

☐ 966 *Louise Bourgeois, ›Schwangere‹ (Pregnant Woman), um 1947–49, bemaltes Holz und Gips, 133 x 18,5 x 24,5 cm. Privatsammlung.*

□ 967 *Adolph Gottlieb, ›Nachtformen‹, um 1949–50, verschiedene Materialien auf Holzfaserplatte, 60 x 76 cm, Adolph and Esther Gottlieb Foundation, New York.*

Das Interesse der Primitivisten an Bildzeichen reicht jedoch über einzelne Stilfragen hinaus zu allgemeinen, substantiellen Dingen, tiefsten Schichten menschlichen Geistes, wie sie früheste Schriftformen aufdecken. GOTTLIEB versuchte sein Werk mit einer frühen Entwicklungsperiode menschlicher Zeichen zu verknüpfen, als die Grundelemente der Kommunikation noch nicht einer konventionellen Grammatik unterworfen waren und eine ungeformte Eigenständigkeit behaupteten – gedankliche, aus der Natur entstandene Einheiten, deren neue Bedeutung nur dem vorlogischen Geist verständlich war. Titel dieser Schriftzeichen wie *Augen des Ödipus* verbinden diese Vorstellung von der frühen Entstehung der Sprache ausdrücklich mit den großen Mythen der europäischen Tradition und lassen sich darin mit Lehren des Philosophen Ernst Cassirer vergleichen. Cassirers Arbeiten der vierziger Jahre, wie der Aufsatz *Language und Myth,* untersuchten verwandte Phänomene religiöser und sprachlicher Ursprünge und betonten außerdem – darin den gefühlsmäßigen Aussagen New Yorker Künstler sehr ähnlich –, daß »Kunst wie Sprache ursprünglich gänzlich im Mythos eingebunden ist. Mythos, Sprache und Kunst entstehen als konkrete, ungeteilte Einheit, die sich nur nach und nach in drei unabhängige Bereiche geistiger Kreativität auflöst.«[39]

Das Interesse für die Strukturen primitiven Schreibens ist letztlich so alt wie der Primitivismus selbst und geht bis auf GAUGUIN zurück, den Rongorongo-Symbole der Osterinsel faszinierten und die er in seine Bilder aufnahm □ 227. Wichtiger für GOTTLIEB und seine Generation waren jedoch zahlreiche Werke JOAN MIRÓS und PAUL KLEES, in denen die sichtbare Verbindung von Bild und Schrift auf nachhaltiges Interesse an prähistorischen Bildzeichen hinweist.[40] Typisch für GOTTLIEB ist die im wesentlichen kubistische Aufteilung und Fragmentierung der Bildzeichen. Seine Bildzeichen stehen in einem auffällig geteilten Zeichenfeld. Das Fließen des automatischen »Schreibens« gilt nicht GOTTLIEBS Zeichen, sie beschwören weniger den spontanen Ausbruch eines tiefen Bewußtseinsstromes, sondern einen ersten ordnenden Impuls und das Vermögen des primitiven Geistes, seine Bedeutungselemente eher in der Schwebe zu halten, als sie in einem ununterbrochenen Fluß aufzulösen. GOTTLIEBS »Sprache« stützt sich auf ein Gesamtraster und unterscheidet sich darin von der Vorliebe MIRÓS und KLEES für raumoffene Zeichenmuster. »Wie jene frühen Maler, die ihre Bilder auf rechteckigen Grundeinteilungen anbrachten«, sagte er 1944, »stellte ich meine Bildzeichen nebeneinander, jedes für sich in ein Rechteck des Malers eingeschlossen, damit sie sich schließlich in der Vorstellung des

☐ 968 *›Decke‹, TLINGIT (Alaska), gefärbte Wolle und Fasern der Zedernrinde, Höhe 175 cm. Sammlung Esther Gottlieb, New York. Ehemals Sammlung Adolph Gottlieb.*

Betrachters verbinden.«[41] Durch diese Ordnung sollte die Rezeption des Betrachters in einer Weise dezentralisiert und zerstreut werden, wie es nach GOTTLIEB den frühesten und grundlegendsten Formen der Wahrnehmung und des Selbstausdrucks entsprach. GOTTLIEB: »Wenn ich sage, daß ich eine totale Erscheinungsform anstrebe, meine ich, daß ich Dinge nehme, die ich kenne – Hand, Nase, Arm –, und sie, getrennt von ihrem Assoziationsbereich und ihrer Anatomie, in meine Gemälde einbringe. Ich benütze sie als eine Gesamtheit dessen, was sie für mich darstellen. Dies ist eine primitive Methode und ein primitives Ausdrucksbedürfnis, das sich nicht aus herkömmlichen Arbeitsweisen ableitet . . . Es führt uns zu den Anfängen des Sehens zurück.«[42] Wie diese Bemerkung zeigt, wollte GOTTLIEB mit der tiefsten Vergangenheit seine Kunst unmittelbarer erfahrbar machen und über entliehene Symbole des Primitiven zu Grundebenen menschlicher Wahrnehmung gelangen. Die Treue gegenüber entliehenen Formen schien aber in seinem Werk und besonders in seinen Bildschriftzeichen das Ziel, zu den »Anfängen des Sehens« zu gelangen und einen machtvollen abstrakten Stil auszubilden, eher behindert als gefördert zu haben. Auch wenn seine Aussagen über primitive Kunst sehr überzeugend klingen, scheint GOTTLIEB in der Tat die paradoxe Regel zu verkörpern, die für amerikanische Kunst dieser Zeit weithin gilt: Je deutlicher und bewußter sich die Arbeiten gegenüber primitiven Formen aufgeschlossen zeigten, desto geringer war letztlich ihr Erfolg. Erst als GOTTLIEBS Primitivismus in den späten vierziger Jahren an Dichte gewonnen hatte, erreichten die Bildzeichen ihre höchste Vollendung.

Wenngleich dem biomorphen Automatismus stärker verhaftet, wich ROTHKO wie GOTTLIEB von surrealistischen Vorbildern ab. Er wandelte die gegenständlichen und inneren Anklänge an Bilder der Surrealisten und PICASSOS stark ab, um den Bruch mit der sichtbaren und sinnlichen Welt deutlicher zu vollziehen – eine Rückwendung, die den menschlichen Bereich verließ und sich eher der (durch Mikrostrukturen angeregten) Welt ODILON REDONS und den Photodiagrammen der Biologie zuwandte.[43] Gleichzeitig mit der Ablehnung der Freudschen Richtung im Surrealismus wollte man auch anatomische Bezüge vermeiden; sexualpathologische oder traumdeuterische Vorstellungen wurden zugunsten neutraler, allgemeiner Kennzeichen organischen Lebens aufgegeben.

Trotz dieser Parallelen gibt es in den Bildern ROTHKOS und GOTTLIEBS Unterschiede – zwischen der Vorstellung eines organischen Bewußtseins, das in der frühesten Entwicklungsstufe verwurzelt und dadurch im wesentlichen gefühlsmäßig und umfassend ist, und der Vorstellung, daß bewußtes Denken

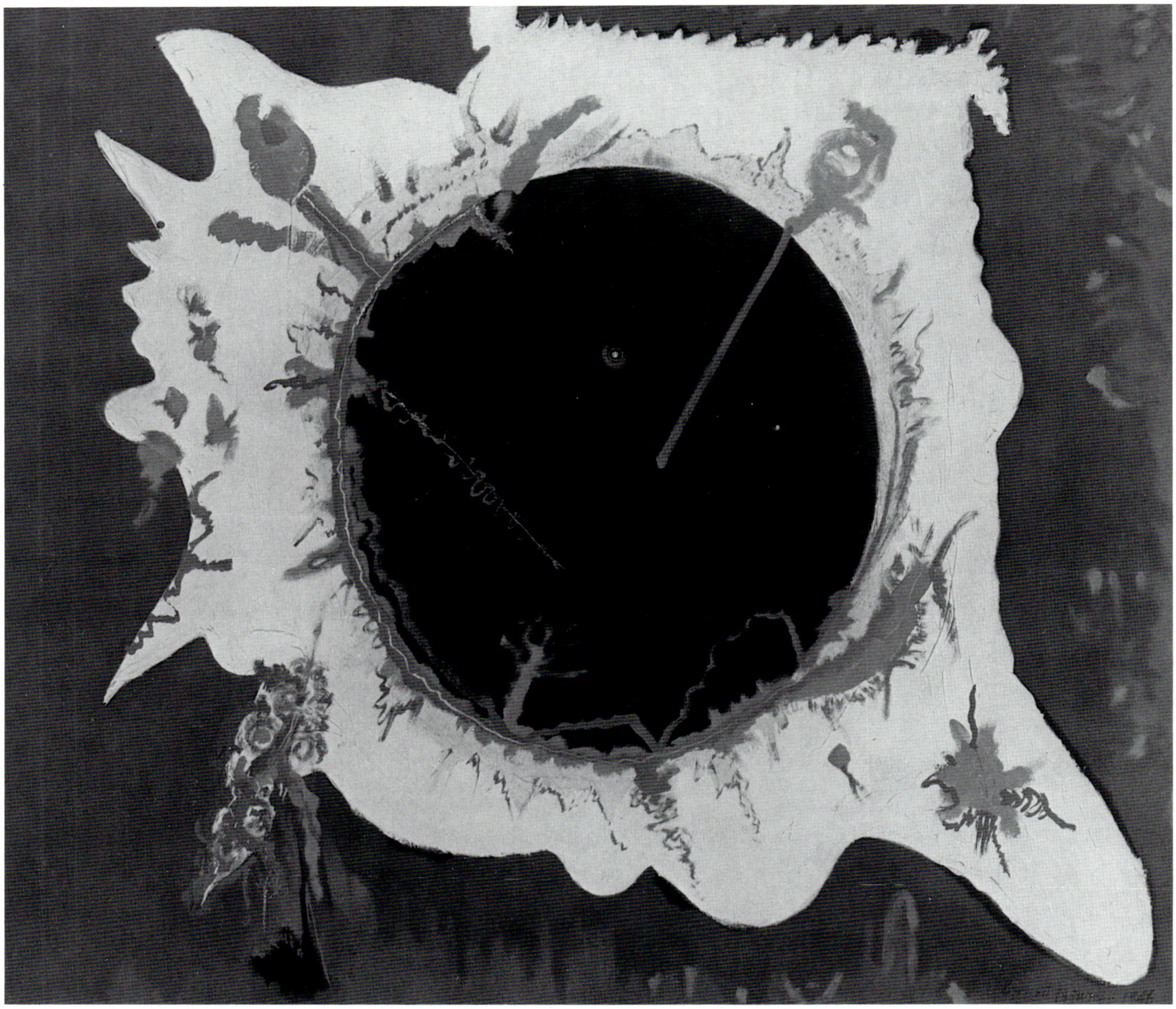

□ 969 *Barnett Newman, ›Heidnische Leere‹ (Pagan Void), 1946, Öl auf Leinwand, 84 x 96,5 cm. Sammlung Annalee Newman.*

von ursprünglicher Trennung der Erfahrung und ihrer Einordnung in ein konstruiertes Sprachgebäude abhängt. Es verwundert daher nicht, daß GOTTLIEBS Kunst weiterhin zumindest teilweise auf der sichtbaren Welt aufbaute (reduzierte Zeichen etwa für landschaftlichen Raum, Kalligraphie), indes ROTHKO nach und nach Formbezüge wirksam eliminierte und sich eher einer geläuterten Sinneserfahrung zuwandte. Damit ließ er die primitive Erscheinungsform hinter sich und wandte die Idee »primitiver« Reduktion entschiedener und fruchtbarer auf grundlegendere Bereiche visueller Erfahrung an. Die Gegensätze in ihren Arbeiten aus der Mitte der vierziger Jahre erklären sich jedoch nicht nur aus Unterschieden des Temperaments und der Begabung. Fast den gleichen Gegensatz zwischen »natürlichen« und »geistigen« Grundlagen findet man auch im frühen Œuvre BARNETT NEWMANS, als er zusammen mit ROTHKO und GOTTLIEB 1943 den berühmten Brief an die *New York Times* schrieb.[44]

Paradoxerweise ist BARNETT NEWMAN für ein Verständnis des Primitivismus der New Yorker Schule von zentraler Bedeutung – paradox deshalb, weil er einerseits zwar der kenntnisreichste und profilierteste Sprecher für das neue Interesse am Primitivismus war, seine eigenen Gemälde und Skulpturen andererseits aber keine nachweisbare Verbindung zu irgendeinem primitiven Stil, weder eingeboren noch vorgeschichtlich, aufweisen – wie er überhaupt auch recht spät zu malen anfing (1945–46). Oft und mit großer Bewunderung sprach er von solchen Stammeskünstlern wie den indianischen Erbauern der Erdhügel. Als eifriger Propagandist schrieb er mehrere Aufsätze und manifestartige Bekenntnisse, in denen er die primitive Kunst zur Verteidigung der neuen Abstraktion heranzog. Nicht zuletzt kannte er die primitiven Stile besser als andere Künstler seiner Generation. Primitivismus war in seinem Frühwerk (1945–1947) jedoch nicht gleichbedeutend mit Bezügen zu bestimmten primitiven Werken, sondern beinhaltete nur allgemeinere Anklänge an das Ursprüngliche und Suggestive von Technik und Stil MAX ERNSTS (z. B. *Genetischer Moment* □ 970) und, was die Ikonographie betrifft, eine Konfrontation emblematischer, genetischer und geometrischer Zeichen (z. B. *Euklidischer Schlund* □ 971). Nach 1947 begegnet das »primitive« Element in seinem Werk nur als konzeptueller Faktor, als ein Ethos reduzierender Läuterung.[45] Gerade

□ 970 *Barnett Newman, ›Genetischer Moment‹ (Genetic Moment), 1947, Öl auf Leinwand, 96,5 x 71 cm. Sammlung Annalee Newman.*

am Beispiel NEWMANS stellen sich eine Reihe von Fragen, die in allem, was zu GOTTLIEB, ROTHKO und anderen gesagt wurde, enthalten sind: Fragen nach dem Auseinanderklaffen von Aussagen und Werk im amerikanischen Primitivismus, nach den unterschiedlichen Ebenen, in denen sich der Primitivismus in den vierziger Jahren bewegte – formales Zitat, synthetische Metapher und schließlich unsichtbares assimiliertes Ideal.

Neben linearen, fließenden Formen, die an ROTHKOS filigrane Organismen erinnern, findet man in NEWMANS frühen Zeichnungen und Bildern (um 1945/46) Kern- oder Samenformen, Zeichen eingeschlossener Kraft (*Gea,* 1945); später entwickeln sich diese zu explosiveren Formen, die an kosmische wie an zellulare Vorgänge erinnern (*Heidnische Leere,* 1946 □ 969). Andererseits beinhalten viele dieser Werke eckige oder geradlinige Elemente, die sich auf die idealen, geometrischen Produkte des Geistes beziehen. Bilder wie *Der Tod des Euklid* und *Euklidischer Schlund* □ 971 sind Sinnbilder für NEWMANS Unzufriedenheit mit der sterilen, säkularisierten Geometrie, wie sie ihm in der griechischen Tradition gegeben schien, und für seine Bewunderung von Formen, die enger mit irrationalen und ursprünglichen Mysterien der Naturwelt verknüpft waren.[46] Es überrascht nicht, daß ihn sein Studium der Naturwissenschaften (ermutigt durch seinen Freund Tony Smith) zur Synthese dieser Gegensätze von Geist und Natur geführt haben soll – in Form von beinahe mystischen Geometrien, die deutlich auf Gesetzen natürlichen Wachstums beruhen.[47] Die Synthese, die er suchte und die er in der ägyptischen Kunst und bestimmten primitiven Stilen bewunderte, war die eines formalen Systems kompromißloser, abstrakter Klarheit, geistig verbunden mit einer Achtung vor der Natur und der ihr

zugrundeliegenden Ordnung. Wie ROTHKO und andere war er der Ansicht, daß solche geklärten, universalen Formen das moderne Mittel seien für eine Erfahrung mit den großen mythologischen und religiösen Themen.

Es wurde die Ansicht vertreten, daß der »Spalt« als Kennzeichen NEWMANS späterer Arbeiten letztlich von den scharfen, vertikalen Unterteilungen in den Mustern der Indianer der Nordwestküste herrühre.[48] Als man den Künstler jedoch einmal bat, etwas zu diesem »Spalt« zu sagen, meinte er, daß er wie der Schrei einer Möwe in der Weite der nördlichen Tundra sei.[49] Die adäquate Bestimmung der Rolle des Primitivismus im Werk NEWMANS liegt sicherlich irgendwo zwischen solch allzu spezifischen formalen Eigenschaften einerseits und der eigenen, dichterischen Umschreibung andererseits. Umfassender als jeder andere Künstler seiner Zeit zeigt NEWMAN in der Bewunderung des Primitiven ebenso sprachliches Ausdrucksvermögen wie künstlerisches Engagement. Zwischen beiden scheint es aber keine direkte Verbindung zu geben, und man muß dabei indirekt vorgehen. Der Hinweis auf den verzweifelten Schrei einer Möwe entspricht in der Tat einer wesentlichen Vorstellung NEWMANS vom Primitiven: Die Erfahrung der Urangst, des Ausgeliefertseins gegenüber der Natur, ließ nach seiner Ansicht die tiefreichende Spiritualisierung der primitiven Welt entstehen.[50] Der »Spalt« als Zeichen steilen vertikalen Aufragens in einem weiten, offenen Feld hat analoge Bedeutungen. Die Energien der metamorphischen Urorganismen ROTHKOS ersetzt er durch mystisch reine, undifferenzierte

□ 971 *Barnett Newman, ›Euklidischer Schlund‹ (Euclidian Abyss) 1946–47, Öl und Gouache über Leinwand auf Holz, 71 x 56 cm. Sammlung Tremaine, Meriden, Connecticut.*

□ 972 *›Helmmaske‹*, WITOTO *(Kolumbien), verschiedene Materialien, Höhe 28 cm. Museum für Völkerkunde, Berlin.*

□ 973 *›Maske‹, Ramu-River, Provinz Madang (Papua-Neuguinea), Holz, Muscheln und Lehm mit Fasern, Höhe 34 cm. Sammlung Friede, New York.*

Kraft, die von dem Gedanken evolutionären Wandels frei ist. Das wiederum ist – neben der rigoros ahistorischen Vorstellung von primitiver Spiritualität – ein Gedanke, der für antimarxistische wie existenzialistische Positionen, die NEWMAN als Grundlage moderner Kunst vertrat, wichtig war.

NEWMANS verschiedene Schriften über primitive Kunst spiegeln den dramatischen Ideenwandel wider, der andernorts in den dreißiger und frühen vierziger Jahren stattfand. Sozialbewußte Autoren der dreißiger Jahre hatten die Wirksamkeit primitiver Kunst als ein Element praktischen oder/und magischen kollektiven Nutzens hervorgehoben; wie bereits erläutert, tendierten primitivistische Künstler der dreißiger und vierziger Jahre dazu, ihre Abstraktionen unter Berufung auf die größere, kollektive Allgemeingültigkeit des Mythos zu verteidigen.

In Texten wie »The First Man Was an Artist« trat NEWMAN indes für eine ursprüngliche Freiheit der Kunst vom Nützlichkeitsdenken ein und trennte die Anfänge der Kunst sogar von ihrem ursprünglichen kommunikativen Impuls (vermittelst GOTTLIEBS linguistischer Zeichen). NEWMAN vertrat die Ansicht, daß die frühesten Darstellungen grundsätzlich keine Abbildungsfunktion gehabt hätten – ein Gedanke mit einer langen Tradition im anthropologischen Denken. Er beschrieb das solipsistische, geistige Bedürfnis des Menschen, Skulpturen früher als Töpferwaren, Kunst früher als Sprache auszubilden. Solche Argumente wandten sich direkt gegen die marxistische Theorie von Ursprüngen, Zielen und Determinanten künstlerischer Produktion. Sie setzten an ihrer Stelle einen imaginären ursprünglichen Künstler, in dem sich Willensfreiheit und direkte Konfrontation mit schrecklichen, unkontrollierbaren Kräften vereinen und ihn damit zum legitimen Vater existentieller Abstraktion machen. Der Stammeskünstler, bemerkte NEWMAN, sei weder durch »soziale Bedingungen« noch durch irgendein reines Formgefühl bewegt; seine Gestaltungen seien durch »einen rituellen Willen zum metaphysischen Verständnis diktiert«.[51]

Diese Theorie NEWMANS verkörpert das eine Extrem im Gegensatz zwischen einem Primitivismus, wie er in der amerikanischen Avantgarde unmittelbar nach dem 2. Weltkrieg verstanden wurde, und einem Primitivismus, wie er zur selben Zeit in Europa in der Kunst JEAN DUBUFFETS auftauchte. NEWMAN betrachtete den primitiven Künstler als Prototyp geklärter Spiritualität, als Schöpfer von Abstraktionen, die grundlegende Ordnungen der Natur verkörperten. DUBUFFET dagegen hob den aggressiv-entstellenden, obsessiven und fetischistischen Charakter primitiven Denkens und die intensive physische Auseinandersetzung des Primitiven mit den groben Materialien der Natur hervor. Seine Aussagen über primitive Kunst betonten die radikale Herausforderung, die sich europäischen Gebräuchen durch die »Werte des Wilden« – »Instinkt, Leidenschaft, Stimmung, Gewalt und Verrücktheit« – stellte und die er als überlegen bewunderte.[52]

Dubuffet handelte dementsprechend nach der Devise, daß der moderne Künstler sich dem Geist der »Wildheit« zuwenden solle, indem er das tägliche Leben in seiner ganzen aggressiven Energie umfaßt und die Objekte ungeachtet irgendwelcher diskriminierender Schönheitsnormen oder reduktiver, ästhetischer Vereinfachung aufnimmt. Dubuffet wandte sich nicht nur gegen die analytischen, skulpturalen Interessen des ganz frühen Primitivismus, sondern auch gegen die zunehmende Tendenz zeitgenössischer amerikanischer Kunst, von einem primitivistischen Ethos ausgehend sich ausschließlich abstrakter Formen zu bedienen. Die inkrustierten Oberflächen seiner Leinwände (etwa *Der Kellermann,* 1946 □ 975) erinnern an die eingebackene Schicht aus Schlamm und Kieselsteinen, wie sie Objekte und Zierat verschiedener Stammeskulturen kennen (wie etwa die *Witoto*-Maske aus dem Amazonasgebiet □ 972). Die rohen Beimischungen seiner fetischistischen Objekte (z. B. *Der Zauberer,* 1954 □ 974, in dem Wurzeln und Schlacken grob vermischt sind) beschwören groteske Physiognomien und zeigen darin deutliche Affinität nicht nur zu Materialprozessen der Stammeskunst, sondern auch zu primitiven Phantasiebildern von anthropomorphen Formen der Natur. In solchen Werken suchte Dubuffets buchstäbliche *nostalgie de la boue* die ungezügelte, physische und emotionale Aggressivität, die er in Stammesobjekten wahrnahm, mit der rauhen Kraft der Graffiti und der wertlosen Dinge moderner Städte zu verbinden. Ganz im Gegensatz zu Newmans distanzierter Einstellung behauptete er, daß man den primitiven Geist innerhalb europäischer Kultur nicht über die »tote Sprache« eines vertrockneten, hehren Humanismus wiedergewinnen könne, sondern im gesellschaftlichen Randbereich und im Dialekt, der »Sprache, die auf der Straße gesprochen« wird. Dubuffet nimmt die heutigen Graffiti-Künstler vorweg, auch indem er an den primitivistischen Geschmack Gauguins erinnert, der auf ähnliche Weise in den urbanen Randgruppen der modernen Gesellschaft die wertvollsten Residuen des Primitiven und deshalb die größten Schaffenskräfte verkörpert sah. (Unter Benützung einer linguistischen Metapher hatte Gauguin die Spontaneität des Verbrecher-Slangs gepriesen und der traditionsbelasteten, überzivilisierten Ausdrucksweise vorgezogen »In Mazas [einem berüchtigten Pariser Gefängnis] findet man noch den Genius einer Sprache; dort wird ein neues Wort geschaffen und ein für allemal verstanden. An der Akademie kann man nur etymologisch vorgehen, und ein Jahrhundert vergeht, ehe ein neuer Ausdruck übernommen wird.«)[53]

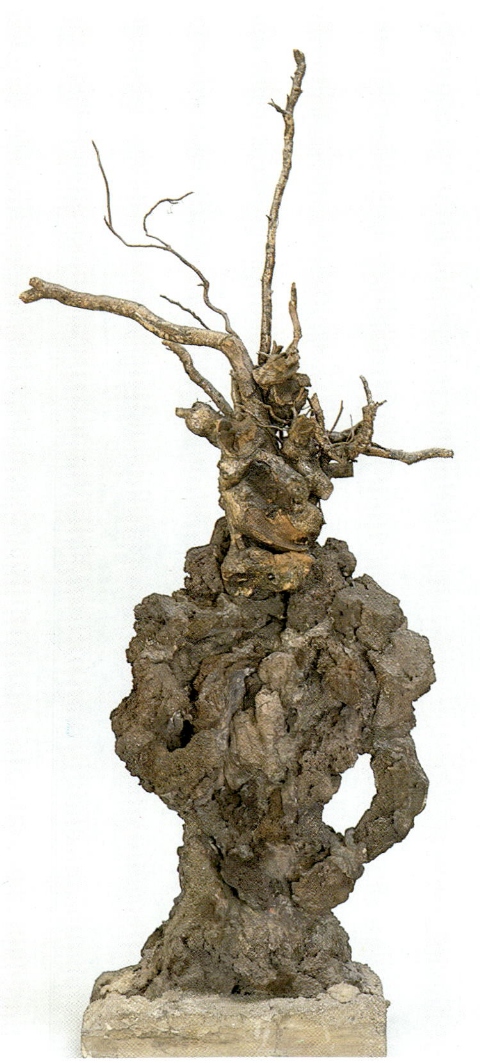

□ 974 *Jean Dubuffet, ›Der Zauberer‹, 1954, Schlacke und Wurzeln, Höhe mit Sockel 110 cm. The Museum of Modern Art, Schenkung N. R. Miller, A. L. Hillman und Samuel Girard Funds, New York.*

□ 975 *Jean Dubuffet, ›Der Kellermann‹, 1946, Öl und verschiedene Materialien auf Leinwand, 46 x 38 cm. Privatsammlung, Schweiz.*

☐ 976 *›Figur aus Holz‹, Wapo Creek, Golfprovinz (Papua-Neuguinea), bemaltes Holz und Muscheln, Höhe 63,5 cm. Sammlung Friede, New York.*

☐ 977 *Jean Dubuffet, ›Der Zecher‹, 1964, Öl auf schwarzer Akrylgrundierung, 195 x 130 cm. Dallas Museum of Art, Schenkung J. H. Clark.*

□ 978 *Jackson Pollock, ›Kreis‹ (Circle), um 1938–41, Öl auf Holz, 32 x 30,5 cm, Durchmesser 30 x 28 cm, unregelmäßig. The Museum of Modern Art, Schenkung L. Krasner zum Gedenken an Jackson Pollock, New York.*

DUBUFFETS Idee des Primitiven sieht im modernen Künstler und seinen Stammesvorfahren eine geistige Verwandtschaft zu Kindern, Verrückten sowie anderen Randgruppen und Häretikern. Die primitivistischen Arbeiten der Künstler sind in dieser Hinsicht notwendigerweise antagonistisch und wenden sich ausdrücklich gegen die Strukturen der konformistischen und repressiven Gesellschaft des Westens, um die anarchische Energie des frühen Menschen wiederzubeleben. Diese Tendenzen stehen in scharfem Kontrast zu dem Ideal, das viele Aussagen der amerikanischen Künstler der vierziger Jahre andeuten, die im modernen Künstler den Erben des Stammespriesters oder Schamanen sehen, der den gemeinsamen Mythen der Zeit Ausdruck verleiht. Die Amerikaner waren der Meinung, daß die Erforschung des Unbewußten und die resultierende Rückgewinnung des Primitiven für den Künstler mehr ein erlösender als ein revolutionärer Akt sei. Nirgendwo wird diese Vorstellung vom Künstler als Mythenschaffer oder Schamane deutlicher oder problematischer als in der Vorstellungswelt JACKSON POLLOCKS, dem eindrucksvollsten Vertreter der neuen amerikanischen Ästhetik. Einerseits fühlte sich POLLOCK intensiv und ursprünglich dem Primitivismus verpflichtet, was nachhaltig sein Kunstschaffen beeinflußte. Andererseits scheint vieles, was über POLLOCKS Primitivismus und über POLLOCK als modernen Primitiven gesagt worden ist, ungenau und einem angemessenen Verständnis seiner Kunst hinderlich.

POLLOCKS Interesse an indianischer Kunst zeigt sich in der Koloristik einiger Werke der späten dreißiger Jahre (besonders in der vorherrschenden Verwendung von Gelb, Rot und Schwarz), in den schamanistischen Zügen des Bildes *Nackter Mann* □ 979 und gelegentlich in spezifischeren Formen wie dem ungewöhnlichen Schild und den schlangenartigen Bildungen des *Kreises* □ 978. In den vierziger Jahren wiederholen sich solche Bezüge in Beispielen wie dem Federkopfschmuck der rechten Figur in *Die Mondfrau durchschneidet den Kreis* von 1943 □ 981.[54] Diese Affinität war offensichtlich allgemein durch seine Jugendzeit im amerikanischen Westen geprägt. Entscheidende Anregungen zum Primitivismus erfuhr POLLOCK im Studium europäischer Künstler, besonders PICASSOS und MASSONS, und durch die enthusiastischen, exzentrischen Vorstellungen JOHN GRAHAMS. POLLOCKS Interesse an dem 1937 geschriebenen Artikel GRAHAMS, »Primitive Art and Picasso«, ist bekannt. Irving Sandler hat den Einfluß dieser Bekanntschaft hervorgehoben und auf Ähnlichkeiten zwischen der eskimoischen Maske, die GRAHAM dort abbildet □ 983, und den gewundenen Formen im mittleren Kopf von POLLOCKS *Geburt* von 1939 □ 982 hingewiesen.[55] Einerseits ist die Verbindung ungewöhnlich, denn es ist eines der wenigen Male, daß POLLOCK mehr oder weniger direkt bei einer bestimmten Stammesform Anleihen macht. Andererseits ist es ausgesprochen charakteristisch, wie POLLOCK dabei eine Stammesform mit einem Bild der Entstehung in einer Weise verbindet, die für sein wiederkehrendes primitivistisches Bildinteresse am Seelenkampf zwischen Urkräften des Männlichen, Weiblichen, des Todes und der Fruchtbarkeit typisch ist.

POLLOCKS Beschwörungen von Mythen und Archetypen in der Zeit von 1942–1946 zeigen eine individuelle psychologische Intensität, die sich jedem Betrachter offenbart, aber genauso problematisch und kontrovers wäre für jene, die die Bilder nach psychologischen Theorien Freuds und Jungs interpretieren wollten. POLLOCK unterzog sich von 1939–1941 einer

□ 979 *Jackson Pollock, ›Nackter Mann‹ (Naked Man), um 1938–41, Öl auf Leinwand über Holz, 127 x 61 cm. Privatsammlung, New Jersey.*

psychoanalytischen Therapie, mit der er wiederholte, von Alkoholismus begleitete Depressionen zu bewältigen versuchte; seine Ärzte waren Anhänger der Lehre Jungs. In den siebziger Jahren wiesen mehrere Kunsthistoriker auf diese Psychoanalyse und seine Freundschaft mit Jungianern hin, um Interpretationen einer spezifisch Jungschen Ikonographie in den Werken der frühen vierziger Jahre zu unterstützen.[56] Es ist anzunehmen, daß Pollock auf die eine oder andere Weise mit Grundbegriffen der Archetypenlehre vertraut wurde, zu der die Vorstellung gehört, daß die archetypische Form eine Brücke zwischen persönlicher Vorstellungskraft und globaleren Dimensionen menschlicher Erfahrung darstellt. Donald Gordon hat jedoch gezeigt, daß Pollocks psychiatrische Behandlung mit Jungschen Theorien nichts zu tun hatte.[57] Auch hat William Rubin zu Recht hervorgehoben, daß sich der Künstler nur begrenzt mit Jung beschäftigt, der daher nur bedingt zur Interpretation seiner Gemälde herangezogen werden könne.[58] Jungsche Ikonographie aus den Bildern Pollocks herauslesen zu wollen, ist vielleicht nicht abwegiger als andere Interpretationen. Es gibt jedoch dafür keine äußeren Hinweise, und man riskiert, den Maler verzerrt als eine Art Illustrator hinzustellen.

Im allgemeinen scheint es trotzdem gerechtfertigt, Pollocks Beschäftigung mit mythischen Themen, primitiven oder vorhistorischen Zeichen in Verbindung mit der »Archäologie seiner eigenen Person«, seiner Suche nach Selbsterfahrung als Mensch und Künstler, zu sehen. Selbst Rubin verbindet Form wie Inhalt des primitivistischen Bildes *Geburt* mit diesem Versuch der Selbstfindung, besonders was die Auseinandersetzung des Künstlers mit Picasso anbelangt. Nach Rubins Meinung wurde die Maske, die Graham abbildete, zum passenden und sinnvollen Bezugspunkt für den Versuch Pollocks im Jahre 1939, »über Picasso hinauszugehen« – speziell als Reaktion auf Picassos *Demoiselles d'Avignon* □ 301, die seit Mai jenes Jahres in New York ausgestellt waren und deren Wirkung Rubin neben anderen Spuren von Arbeiten Picassos der dreißiger Jahre in *Geburt* nachweist. Die Maske, die Graham mit dem europäischen Künstler verbinden wollte, ist um vieles verzerrter als die extremsten der maskenhaften Gesichter in Picassos *Demoiselles* und glücklicherweise nordamerikanisch. Wie Rubin ausführt, wurde sie von Pollock als Mittel eingesetzt, als er in der Auseinandersetzung mit Picasso um einen eigenen Stil rang. Die Maske war außerdem ein ideales Mittel, um die Schmerzen der Geburt darzustellen (ein Trauma, das nach Rubins Ansicht in der Phantasie Pollocks aufgrund seiner oft schmerzvollen und problematischen Mutterbeziehung eine wichtige Rolle spielt).[59]

Paradoxerweise ist es vermutlich Picasso selbst, dem Pollock in seiner intensiven, persönlich gefärbten Verbindung primitiver Kunst mit ursprünglichen Energien der Sexualität, Fruchtbarkeit und Kreativität – Assoziationen, die nirgends deutlicher werden als in der gewaltigen Lebenskraft von *Geburt* – am nächsten stand. Hier wie bei den *Demoiselles* fühlt man eine Verbundenheit mit Quellen der Stammeskunst, die über unkonventionelle Formen hinaus an Intuitionen magischer Bereiche grenzt, die an der Entstehung eines neuen künstlerischen Selbst teilhaben. Durch diese persönliche Prägung erhält Pollocks primitivistische Phase eine Intensität, die uns bei seinen Zeitgenossen nicht begegnet. Die eindrucksvollste Verbindung primitiver und moderner Formen des Kunstschaffens fand jedoch nicht in dieser Reihe archetypischer Bilder und mythischer Themen von 1942–1946 statt, sondern in den späteren Abstraktionen, die er mittels »dripping« schuf. Dort findet man eine weniger deutliche, tieferreichende, formal und geistig umfassendere Verarbeitung der Stammeskunst.

Pollocks spezifische malerische Interessen machten ihn für die Möglichkeiten der Höhlenzeichnungen und Wandbilder empfänglich, dies nicht nur im Hinblick auf das Wandformat, sondern auch auf die Vorliebe des primitiven Künstlers, innere Bildeinteilung zu vernachlässigen, Zeichen übereinanderzulagern und auf die wechselnde Gestalt der Maloberfläche sensibel zu reagieren. Pollocks »getropfte« Bilder stehen all diesen Formen indianischer Kunstpraxis nahe. Es wäre jedoch falsch,

□ 980 *Jackson Pollock, ›Verwundetes Tier‹ (Wounded Animal), 1943, Öl auf Gips über Leinwand, 96,5 x 76 cm. Privatsammlung.*

□ 981 *Jackson Pollock, ›Die Mondfrau durchschneidet den Kreis‹ (The Moon-Woman Cuts the Circle), 1943, Öl auf Leinwand, 109,5 x 104 cm. Musée National d'Art Moderne, Centre National d'Art et de Culture Georges Pompidou, Paris, Schenkung F. Lloyd.*

daraus zu schnelle Schlußfolgerungen zu ziehen. Einige Autoren verglichen etwa POLLOCKS innovative Methode, Farbe direkt auf die flach ausgebreitete Leinwand zu gießen, mit der Gießtechnik der Sandmaler der *NAVAHO* und fügten die Bekanntschaft damit den jugendlichen Erfahrungen des Künstlers im amerikanischen Westen hinzu.[60] POLLOCK wußte zweifellos von den indianischen Sandmalern, obwohl er wahrscheinlich nie vorher die Entstehung eines solchen Werkes gesehen hatte, ehe das Museum of Modern Art 1941 im Zusammenhang mit einer Ausstellung indianischer Kunst Demonstrationen von indianischen Künstlern veranstaltete. Diese Künstler führten aber streng vorgeschriebene, vorwiegend geometrische Entwürfe aus, ganz im Gegensatz zur Erscheinungsform und zum Geist von POLLOCKS eigenen Bildern.

Wenn POLLOCK von Sandbildern beeindruckt war, so zeigte sich darin vermutlich eine allgemeine Wertschätzung der »Choreographie« des rituellen Kunstschaffens und der Vorstellung – die in den späten vierziger Jahren John Cage vertreten sollte –, daß ephemere aktionsorientierte Kunst, die in primitiven und anderen außereuropäischen Gesellschaften eine wichtige Stellung einnimmt, realisierbar ist. POLLOCK fühlte sich der Natur und der Erde stark verbunden und empfand ebenso starke Gefühle für den sorgfältigen rituellen Aufbau der Oberflächen in den gegossenen Bildern – Eigenschaften, die Rubin als »tellurischen« Instinkt und den Wunsch, die Leinwände »wie ein Gärtner« zu behandeln, bezeichnet hat.[62] In einem solch tieferen, weniger direkten, aber potentielleren Bereich wird POLLOCKS Nähe zum Primitiven am überzeugendsten. Ein Gemälde wie *Verwundetes Tier* von 1943 □ 980 zeigt bereits POLLOCKS Interesse an der primitiven Herstellung von Zeichen. Er sah sie, in welchem Format auch immer, als magisch intendierte Aktion, mit der die Kluft zwischen Darstellung und Wirklichkeit, Malen und Tun überwunden werden kann. Die groben Pinselzüge und Bogenformen wiederholen dabei ähnliche Zeichen bei Tierdarstellungen vorgeschichtlicher Höhlen wie Altamira. In diesen Zeichen schien sich ihm der Glaube des prähistorischen Menschen zu zeigen, daß gegen das Bild gerichtete Zeichen wirksame Schläge gegen das lebende Ziel der Jagd sind. Solche Bilder verweisen auf eine Vorstellung, die im Einklang steht mit POLLOCKS aufkommender Neudefinition moderner Malerei: das Ideal eines Künstlers, der tief im kollektiven Mythos wurzelt, sich aber auch gleichzeitig auf die physische Erfahrung des entstehenden Kunstwerks richtet; der in intensiver ritueller Aktion eine unbegrenzte Fläche mit Zeichen bedeckt und sein Bild mit einem Gefühl physischer, psychischer wie auch ästhetischer Befriedigung schafft.[63]

Wie zur Bestätigung dieses Modells eines physischen und psychischen Partizipierens setzte POLLOCK bei einigen »dripping«-Bildern wie *Nummer 1, 1948* □ 984 seinen Handabdruck in das Farbgeflecht. Er vervielfältigte dieses Zeichen auch, so daß Bezüge zu den prähistorischen Handformen – etwa an den Wänden der Castillo-Höhle in Spanien – deutlicher wurden □ 985. Mit beeindruckender Spontaneität und ohne sich mit mythischem Symbolismus zu belasten, macht POLLOCK hier wie MIRÓ und andere vor ihm □ 989, 988, 990 vielleicht das elementarste Zeichen von Verwandtschaft mit dem primitiven Künstler geltend, das, persönlich und dem Augenblick verhaftet, zugleich universal erfahrbar und zeitlos ist.[64] Der Handabdruck bestätigt einen Primitivismus, der über stilistische Neugestaltung der sichtbaren Welt hinausreicht und dem fundamentalen Kern des Mythischen näherkommt.

◻ 982 *Jackson Pollock, ›Geburt‹ (Birth), 1939–40, Öl auf Leinwand über Sperrholz, 117 x 55 cm. Sammlung L. Krasner Pollock, New York.*

◻ 983 *›Maske‹, eskimoisch, Hooper Bay (Alaska), bemaltes Holz und Federn, Höhe 21,5 cm. The University Museum, University of Pennsylvania, Philadelphia. Abbildung aus John D. Graham, ›Primitive Art and Picasso‹, „Magazine of Art", April 1937.*

□ 984 *Jackson Pollock, ›Nummer 1, 1948‹ (Number 1, 1948), 1948, Öl auf Leinwand, 173 x 264 cm. The Museum of Modern Art, New York.*

Die Internationalisierung einer primitiven Person bei POLLOCK sollte man jedoch mit Vorsicht betrachten. Seit seinen frühen primitivistischen Phasen gab POLLOCK seine Identifikation mit dem primitiven Mythenschöpfer und Mysterienträger, dem Schamanen, zu verstehen. Der *Nackte Mann,* der um 1938–41 entstand □ 979, zeigt eine solche Gestalt mit den Attributen des Mannes und des totemistischen Tieres. Wenn auch die »dripping«-Bilder deutlichere Bezüge herstellten als die früheren primitivistischen Gemälde, so war auch ihre irreführende Interpretation schließlich erfolgreich, die – problematisch und unbeabsichtigt – einen Mythos für ihre Zeit schuf. Dies geschah mit der populär werdenden Darstellung POLLOCKS bei der Arbeit und mit der bedenklichen Konstruktion einer Rolle mit den unwillkürlichen Gesten einer verfremdeten Freiheit in einer existentiellen Leere, angepaßt an die intellektuelle Stimmung Amerikas nach dem 2. Weltkrieg.[65]

Durch die voreilige, bedenkliche »Zustimmung« wie der Harold Rosenbergs und auch durch die ungewöhnlichen Photos HANS NAMUTHS vom »dripping«-Verfahren wurde POLLOCK zu einem Mann der einsamen, zwingenden Aktion, und man identifizierte ihn mit einem Sinn für Maß, Energie und Freiheitsverlangen, das für essentiell modern und spezifisch amerikanisch gehalten wurde.[66] Besonders sein gewaltsamer Tod schien ihn zu dem Jungschen Heros zu machen, der die dunkle Zeit der Suche nach dem Unbewußten überwunden hatte, um triumphierend und erhöht, wenn auch gequält, wiederaufzuerstehen – der Künstler als der beispielhaft Leidende, ein Schamane unserer Zeit.

Wie überzeugend er auch sein mag, wir sollten uns jedoch bewußt sein, wie verzerrend dieser Mythos POLLOCKS als moderner Primitiver ist. Zu oft sah man in ihm die Karikatur eines Cowboy-Existentialisten und verband mit seinen Arbeiten der Zeit von 1947–1950 – den wundervoll schwingenden, lyrischen Farbbändern, die buchstäblich auf die Leinwand getanzt sind – das Klischee einer gemarterten Psyche, das sich aus den ganz andersartigen, sichtlich gequälten primitivistischen Arbeiten von 1939–1946 herleitet.[67] In weit positiverer und erfüllterer Weise – in der befreienden Wirkung des Vorrangs der Aktion und als Beispiel intensiver Auseinandersetzung mit der Kunst als Prozeß – hat POLLOCK den Geist des Primitivismus in seinen »dripping«-Bildern genuin aufgenommen – fruchtbar für ihn und für die Nachwelt. Als legitimes Vermächtnis POLLOCKS können nicht nur Arbeiten von Malern wie MORRIS LOUIS und FRANK STELLA, sondern auch die späteren Happenings und die am Rituellen orientierte Performance Art der siebziger Jahre gelten.

Auf jeden Fall ging der Primitivismus – wenn er überhaupt eine Nachfolge fand – eher auf einer solchen geistigen Ebene als in formalen Zitaten oder suggestiven Bildthemen in die reifsten Arbeiten der Künstler ein, die um 1946 seine wichtigsten Träger waren. In den frühen fünfziger Jahren schien es allgemein so, als sei der Primitivismus nur Teil einer Episode in der Auseinandersetzung mit dem Surrealismus gewesen, ein notwendiger Übergang hin zu einem unabhängigeren abstrakten Stil für die junge amerikanische Malerei. Einem ähnlichen Muster folgte auch die Entwicklung der Skulptur dieser Zeit.

Es hatte in der amerikanischen Skulptur vor 1940 einzelne Beispiele des Primitivismus gegeben, Werke wie JOHN STORRS' Zwitterbildungen aus Wolkenkratzern und Totems □ 671 oder

□ 984a *Jackson Pollock, ›Nummer 1, 1948‹ (Number 1, 1948), Ausschnitt von* □ *984.*

ALEXANDER CALDERS *Apfelmonster* □ 82 – das sich, wie William Rubin zeigte, mit den Imunus Neuguineas □ 81 vergleichen läßt (siehe S. 66). Wie die amerikanische Malerei befaßte sich die Skulptur in der Zeit um 1946/47 mit dem Mythos und der Beschwörung des Ursprünglichen besonders eingehend, um in den fünfziger Jahren abstraktere und zurückhaltendere Formen zu bevorzugen.

Wie verschiedene andere Maler ihrer Generation (z.B. ROTHKO) kamen die amerikanischen Bildhauer wie HERBERT FERBER und SEYMOUR LIPTON in den späten dreißiger und frühen vierziger Jahren vom naturalistischen Stil und sozialen Themen der Gegenwart zu einer abstrakteren, auf mythische Themen konzentrierten Formensprache. Wie schon in der Malerei war der Surrealismus vor allem bei der Verwandlung des Erscheinungsbildes der Skulptur wirksam. Bei einigen Bildhauern machte sich dies in logischer, allmählicher Entwicklung bemerkbar; für andere bedeutete es eine drastische Umkehr, nicht nur als Reaktion auf europäische Vorbilder und die Forderungen der Weltereignisse, sondern auch auf die schnellen Veränderungen in der amerikanischen Malerei. DAVID HARE setzte sich nachhaltig mit europäischen Vorbildern auseinander und schuf in den vierziger Jahren Arbeiten, die eine individuelle Anpassung surrealistischer Vorbilder an die neuen mythisch-magischen Themen zeigten (z.B. *Das Spiel des Zauberers,* 1944 □ 986). Mitte der vierziger Jahre, meist als Reaktion auf Krieg und Atombombe, wandten sich sogar Bildhauer wie THEODORE ROSZAK, der in seinen konstruktivistisch inspirierten Arbeiten der dreißiger Jahre moderne Technologie verherrlicht hatte, den expressiveren, prozeßorientierten Seiten surrealistischer Kunst und dem rohen, oft grotesken, am Surrealismus geschulten Formenschatz zu, um Urängsten

□ 985 *›Höhlenmalerei‹, Ausschnitt, Castillo (Spanien). Veröffentlicht in G. Baldwin Brown, „The Art of the Cave Dweller“, 1928. Dieses Buch befand sich in Pollocks Bibliothek.*

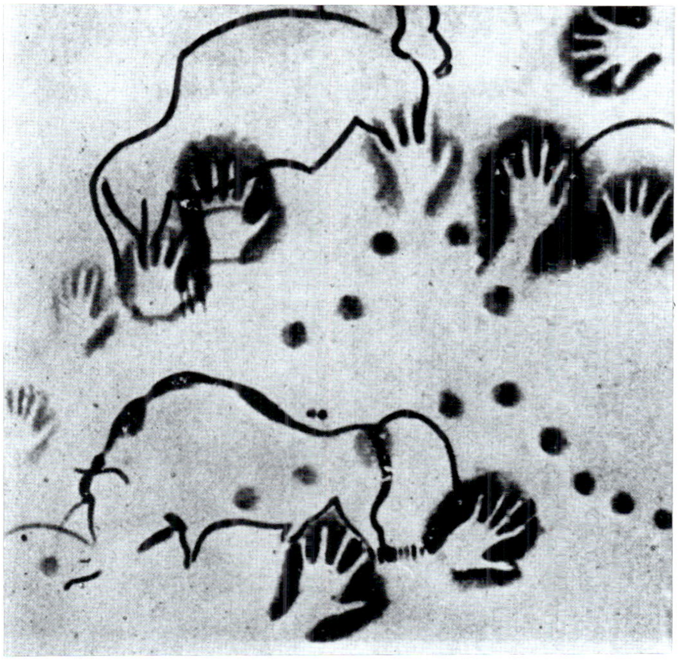

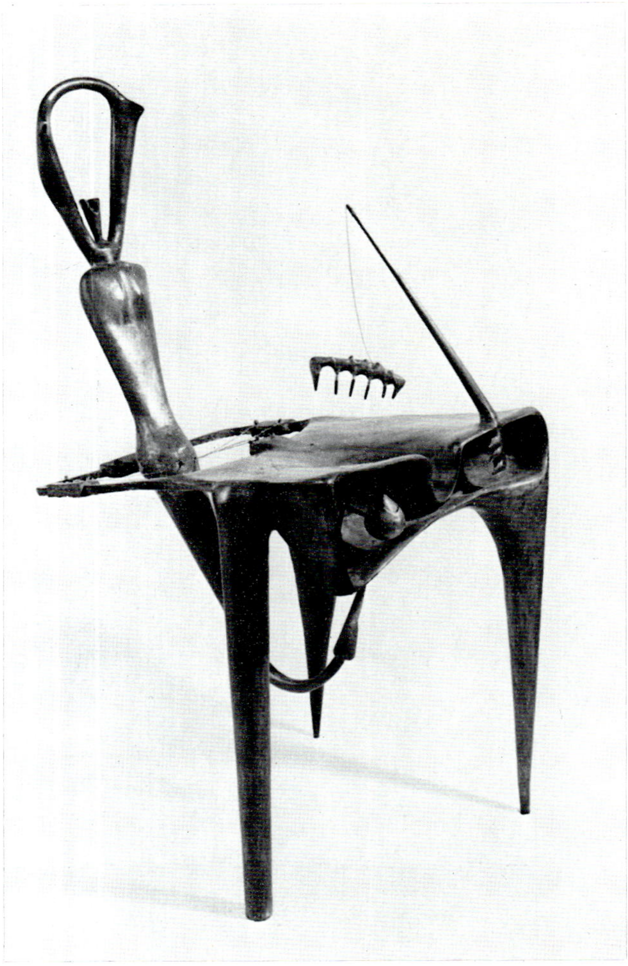

□ 986 *David Hare, ›Das Spiel des Zauberers‹ (Magician's Game), 1944, Bronze (Guß 1946), 102 x 47 x 64 cm. The Museum of Modern Art, anonyme Schenkung, New York.*

□ 987 *Theodoros Stamos vor Felszeichnungen in Sandia (Neu-Mexiko), 1947.*

□ 988 *Theodore J. Roszak, ›Geist der Kitty Hawk‹ (Spectre of Kitty Hawk), 1946–47, Stahl, geschweißt und geschmiedet, mit Bronze und Messing überzogen, Höhe 102 cm, Sockel 46 x 38 cm. The Museum of Modern Art, New York.*

Ausdruck zu verleihen. In diesem Klima wurden die surrealistischen Traumgebilde (besonders die empfindlichen, oft sadistischen Formen in der Plastik GIACOMETTIS aus den frühen dreißiger Jahren) in aggressive Alpträume verwandelt. Knochen und Vögel wurden zu spitzen Skelettmonstern und schrecklichen Lufträubern. Der einfache Vorgang des Metallschweißens wurde zum Medium gequälter, gewundener Formen des Schmerzes (etwa LIPTONS *Moloch* von 1946 oder ROSZAKS *Geist der Kitty Hawk,* 1946–47 □ 987). Es kam soweit, daß man eine primitiv-rohe Schlußbearbeitung einer Skulptur oder die »archaische« Beschwörung mythischen Schreckens, sogar formelhafte Seiten eines Großteils amerikanischer Metallskulpturen um 1950 voraussagen konnte. Ein Werk wie FERBERS *Er ist kein Mann* von 1950 □ 991 erinnert in seiner geschundenen Würde an die Gewalt dieser archaisierenden Zeit. Gleichzeitig gehört es jedoch zu dem weniger körperlichen Vokabular von ikonischen Naturformen, wie man es im Werk von Malern wie STAMOS antrifft □ 945, und kündigt einen neuen, zurückhaltenderen Gefühlston und eine formale Klärung an. LIPTON hat einst bestätigt, daß er selbst Primitives in

□ 989 *Joan Miró, ›Frau, die von der Flucht träumt‹, 1942, Öl auf Leinwand, 130 x 195 cm. Sammlung M. Neumann, Chicago.*

diesem allgemeinen Sinn aufnehme, aber nicht bewußt nach »allgemeinen Formanalogien zu prähistorischen, primitiven Skulpturen oder anderen Ideen moderner Plastik« strebe. Er nahm für sich in Anspruch, bei seiner Erforschung instinktiver, unterbewußter Bereiche »das Urzeitliche im Menschen« entdeckt zu haben: »Das Knochengerüst des Dinosauriers wurde für mich lebendig. Es ist der Keim, das Innerste, der Ursprung, das Dunkel der Erde, der tief animalische Quell menschlicher Kräfte, was mich als Nährboden künstlerischer Substanz am meisten interessiert.«[68] LIPTONS Aussage ist bezeichnend für die Art, wie in der Skulptur der Zeit die Idee des Primitiven mit dem Gedanken an die urzeitliche Evolution verbunden wurde. In dieser Hinsicht wie auch für andere Aspekte der amerikanischen Kunst der vierziger Jahre war jedoch die Entwicklung DAVID SMITHS beispielhaft. In ihr finden sich mit bezeichnenden Abweichungen viele der Aussagen, die wir bereits bei der primitivistischen Malerei untersuchten.

Erste primitivistische Interessen SMITHS fielen zusammen mit ersten Versuchen in der Skulptur. Er und DOROTHY DEHNER verbrachten 1931 acht Monate auf den Jungferninseln, weil sie, wie die Künstlerin später sagte, »Gauguin sein wollten«.[69] SMITH begann dort kleine Objekte aus Draht und Naturmaterial wie Korallen zu formen. In dieser Zeit wurde er auch der Stammeskunst gewahr und befreundete sich in den späten zwanziger und frühen dreißiger Jahren mit JOHN GRAHAM. 1933 vermittelte er SMITH den Auftrag, Sockel für afrikanische Objekte in der Sammlung Crowninshield zu entwerfen, eine Sammlung, die GRAHAM als Berater und Händler mit aufgebaut hatte.[70] Die Sammlung Crowninshield stand ihm vor Augen, als er die Sockel gestaltete, und vier Holzskulpturen jenes Jahres (z. B. *Ohne Titel* □ 992) zeigen, daß er Methoden und Formen afrikanischer Bildhauer studiert hatte. Es sind jedoch wenig ausdrucksvolle Gegenstände, die wenig mit dem Primitivismus zu tun haben, wie er im Werk SMITHS in den vierziger Jahren entsteht.

Primitivistische Züge traten in der Skulptur SMITHS vor allem in den späten dreißiger Jahren auf, als er in sein Repertoire

□ 990 *Adolph Gottlieb, ›Schwarze Hand‹ (Black Hand), 1943, Öl auf Leinwand, 76 x 61 cm. Privatsammlung, New York.*

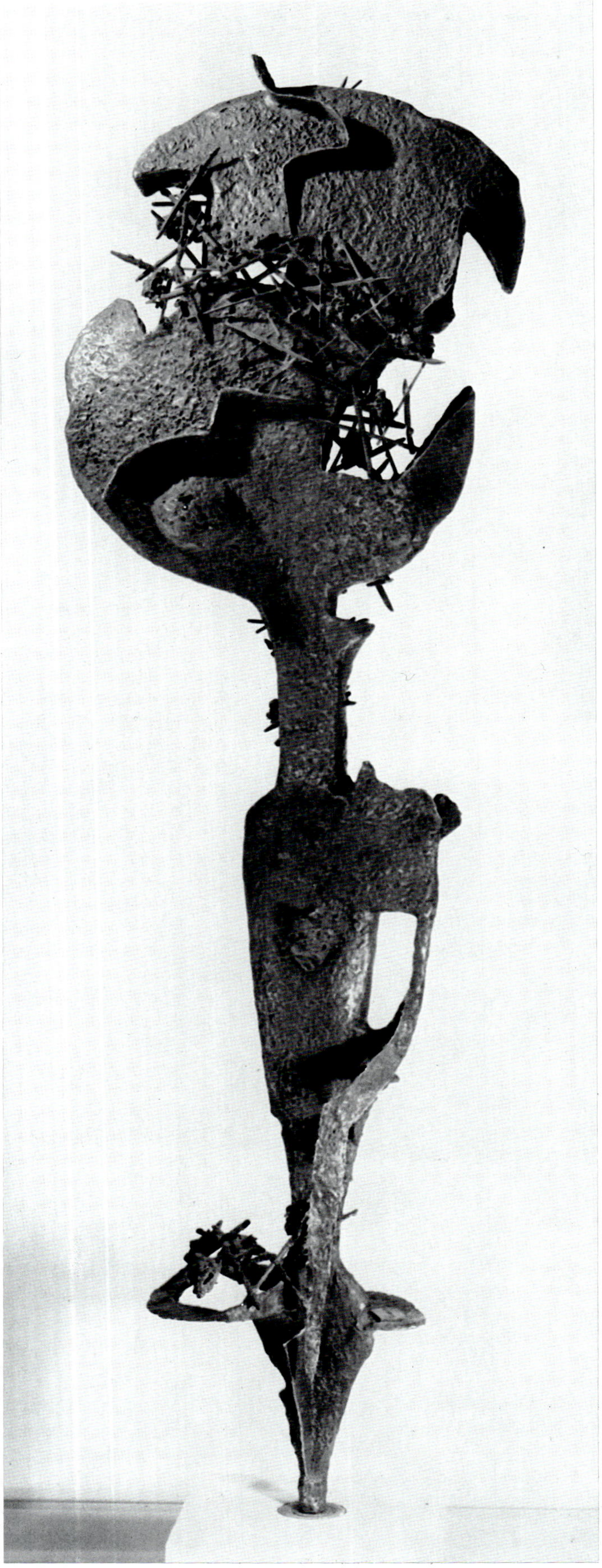

□ 991 *Herbert Ferber, ›Er ist kein Mann‹ (He is Not a Man), 1950, Bronze mit Metallstäben (einziger Guß vom Bleioriginal), 171 x 49 x 34 cm. The Museum of Modern Art, Schenkung William Rubin, New York.*

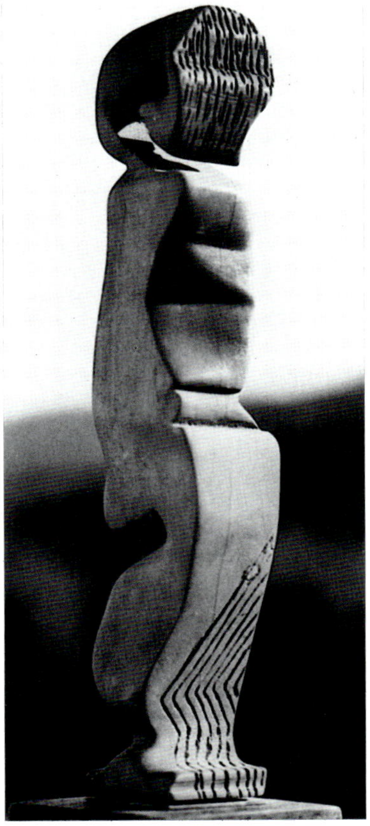

□ 992 *David Smith, Ohne Titel, 1933, Holz, 31 x 9 x 4 cm. Besitz des Künstlers.*

moderner Formen (besonders der Verarbeitung von Vorbildern PICASSOS und GONZALES') einen Gestalt- und Zeichenschatz aufnahm, der besonders von den großen archaischen Kulturen Ägyptens, Babyloniens und dem vorklassischen Griechenland beeinflußt war. Diese Vorliebe für die Archaik machte ihn für einen zeichenhaften, erzählenden Reliefstil aufgeschlossen (besonders bei den *Medaillen der Unehre,* 1939–1940) und bot gleichzeitig eine Kontrolle für die biomorphen Grotesken, von denen er sich in seiner persönlichen Fassung des Surrealismus angezogen fühlte. SMITHS Arbeiten der vierziger Jahre kreisen um heftige Themen und Empfindungen und lassen sich darin den Werken POLLOCKS dieser Zeit vergleichen – im Gegensatz zu der passiveren, neosymbolischen Poesie ROTHKOS, STAMOS', BAZIOTES' und anderer. Doch scheint er Stammeskunst weder als Vorbild für expressionistische Verzerrungen betrachtet zu haben noch an zerfurchten Oberflächen oder obsessivem Anhäufen von Fetischobjekten interessiert gewesen zu sein. Wenn sich in den *Medaillen der Unehre* die eine Seite SMITHS widerspiegelt – seine erzählende, zeichenhafte Tendenz –, so zeigt sich in *Der Held,* 1952 □ 993, die andere Seite: seine Bewunderung des Ikonischen, der monumentalen vereinfachten Würde und Klarheit der vorklassischen Skulptur wie jene der Kykladen. Beide Seiten verbanden sich mit dem Interesse an der europäischen Moderne – die eine mit den ausdrucksvolleren, freien Interpretationen PICASSOS und des frühen GIACOMETTI, die andere – wenn auch weniger deutlich – mit Aspekten BRANCUSIS und dem späteren GIACOMETTI.

SMITH war ein unermüdlich forschender Autodidakt, und es besteht kaum Zweifel, daß er sich in vielen außereuropäischen Kunstformen auskannte. Wie andere seiner Generation ließ er sich von indianischen Vorbildern anregen. Am stärksten fühlte er sich wohl von Totempfählen der Nordwestküste angezogen, vielleicht deshalb, weil diese genau das Prinzip der Addition verschiedener Teile, wie es SMITHS freierer, improvisierender Seite entgegenkam, mit einer unspezifischen, aber monumental vereinfachten Figürlichkeit vereinte. In *Pfeiler des Sonntags* von 1945 ☐ 995 zeigt sich die Vorstellung eines persönlichen Totems, ein regelmäßiges formales System aus einer eher improvisierten Häufung fast automatischer Zeichen mit autobiographischem Bezug – die ironische Verbindung einer religiösen Stammesform mit der persönlichen Phantasie seiner in die Kirche gehenden Mutter.[71] (Auf eine Vorzeichnung zu diesem Werk schrieb SMITH das Wort »Totem« ☐ 994.) Mit den Tanktotem-Serien waren Anklänge an die übereinander angeordneten Bilder der Stammespfähle wieder aufgegeben. Nur allgemeine Assoziationen mit Stammesritualen und dem Sakralen blieben bestehen, die über den Bildtitel unser Verständnis der aufrechten Skulpturen beeinflussen.[72] Im allgemeinen war auch SMITHS Primitivismus eine synthetische »Rückwendung«, die eher im thematischen Bereich und auf der Ebene unsichtbarer Anregungen lag als in evidenter Abhängigkeit zu primitiven oder archaischen Vorbildern. Wie bei den bereits erwähnten Malern finden sich in seinen Arbeiten vielfach die gleichen Mischformen, die Elementares und Unbewußtes, Naturgeschichte und ein »sprachwissenschaftliches« Interesse an frühen Zeichen verbinden – jedoch mit anderen Aussagen.

Nicht nur Arbeiten wie *Juravogel* ☐ 951 und *Landschaft mit Schichten*, 1946, sondern auch zahlreiche Skizzenbücher belegen, wie bei ROTHKO und NEWMAN, SMITHS intensives Studium der Naturwissenschaften. Wie viele Maler seiner Generation besuchte er oft das American Museum of Natural History in New York. Die Abteilung Biologie – nicht die der Ethnologie – regten ihn nachhaltig an, und er besaß Photos zur Unterstützung seiner Arbeit ☐ 997. Lebhaftes Interesse zeigte er für einzelne Formen aus den Bereichen der Tiermorphologie, der Embryologie und der Paläontologie. NEWMAN und ROTHKO hatten sich für den mikroskopischen Bereich und die Entstehung des Lebens interessiert; die Arbeiten SMITHS hingegen bezeugen oft ein Interesse an Versteinerungen – mehr an reduzierten Resten und verkürzten Diagrammen als am puristischen Keim undifferenzierten Potentials. Alle drei Künstler sahen in der Evolution eine Metapher für Prozesse im Unbewußten. SMITH interessierte sich jedoch nicht für die im Stillen stattfindende genetische Transformation, sondern für den Bereich der Evolution, der das Machtstreben, den Überlebenskampf und die Selektion der einzelnen Arten betrifft. Seine schwergliedrigen Raubvögel der Urzeit wie *Königlicher Vogel* ☐ 998 und *Jura-Vogel* ☐ 951 beschwören eine Zeit der elementaren Gewalt und des Überlebenskampfes, denen in der modernen Welt die Phantome des Krieges – siehe SMITHS Werk *Überlebenskampf (Das Profitstreben)* – entsprechen.[73]

SMITH suchte weniger die gemeinsamen Elemente des prähistorischen, primitiven und modernen Menschen in den »inneren Universalien« des Mythos und den Naturgesetzen der Evolution, sondern wies kritisch auf die Zustände des menschenunwürdigen Wettkampfs und der Gewalt hin, worin die zeitgenössische Gesellschaft der frühgeschichtlichen ähnlich ist. Seine monströsen Vögel und Skelettformen bedeuteten etwas anderes als die häufigen Knochenformen und gelegentlichen Versteinerungen im Surrealismus (z.B. die den Flugsauriern ähnlichen Wesen in GIACOMETTIS *Palast um 4 Uhr*, eine Skulptur, die SMITH in den späten 30er Jahren mit Gewinn studiert hatte). In formaler Hinsicht befreiten sie ihn von den

☐ 993 *David Smith, ›Der Held – 1952‹ (The Hero – 1952), 1951–52, bemalter Stahl, 187 x 65 x 30 cm. The Brooklyn Museum, Dick S. Ramsey Fund, New York.*

Fesseln des Anthropomorphismus und ermutigten dadurch Experimente mit einer kühneren und offeneren Zeichenform. Indem auf die Evolution bezogene gedankliche Metaphern vermieden wurden, führten diese Kreaturen auch von der Vorstellung eines abgeschlossenen Unbewußten mit ewig unveränderlichen Symbolen weg. Seine Verbindung evolutionären Kampfes und gegenwärtigen Leidens – kapitalistische Ausbeutung und faschistischer Totalitarismus – übte auch implizit Kritik an jenem primitivistischen Idealismus, der sich mehr mit der »natürlichen und universalen« als mit der sozialpolitisch materialistischen Seite des Menschen befaßte. Anstatt sich von politischen Dingen auf eine hypothetische Frühzeit zurückzuziehen, projizierten SMITHS Ungeheuer die Konflikte der Gegenwart auf die früheste Geschichte des Lebens auf der Erde zurück und sprachen demgemäß eine weniger feierliche, weniger archetypische bestimmte Bildwelt des modernen Unbewußten an.

Ähnlich politisch gefärbt war SMITHS »Rückwendung« im sprachlichen Bereich und in seinen Interessen an Urzeichen, wie man an *Der Brief* □ 954, *Brief nach Australien, Das Bankett* und zahlreichen anderen Skulpturen, Zeichnungen und Skizzen sieht. Sein Interesse an einer hypothetischen Frühzeit, wo Bedeutung und Zeichen unauflösbar in Bildzeichen verbunden waren, entstand aus einem Mißtrauen gegenüber dem Wort, das auf eine Abneigung gegen verbale »Erklärungen« von Kunst zurückgeht. Daraus leitet sich das Prinzip ab, Formen von einer Klarheit auszuwählen, deren Aussagekraft noch von ideologischer Verfälschung verschont war. In einem Prosagedicht, das einer plastischen Figuration mit den Buchstaben *y* und *h* beigegeben war, beschwor er die »Rückkehr zu den Ursprüngen, als das Reine noch nicht durch Wörter befleckt war«; als die Künstler in den Buchstaben »Objektsymbole« schufen, »bevor Wörter gemacht wurden, die Moralisten,

□ 994 *David Smith, Studien zu ›Pfeiler des Sonntags‹ (Pillar of Sunday), 1945, Graphit, Feder, blaue und schwarze Tinte, schwarze Tempera, 25 x 18 cm. Fogg Art Museum, Harvard University, Schenkung des Künstlers, Cambridge.*

Pragmatiker, Geldwechsler und dumpfe Erzieher mißbrauchten«.[74] Hier wird eine andere, eher inhaltliche als formale Ebene relevant, von der aus SMITHS *Brief* □ 954 eine Bewunderung von Stammesformen wie dem teils figürlichen, teils ideographischen Kopfschmuck der *SENUFO* □ 955 widerzuspiegeln scheint. Allgemeiner ausgedrückt verbindet dieses Verhältnis zur Sprache seine Bewunderung für Primitives wie Modernes. Sie liegt seiner Verehrung von James Joyce zugrunde, der das Wort aus seinen konventionellen Zwängen befreit und wieder das freie, kreative Spiel in der Kommunikation eingeführt hatte. SMITH entwickelte und vertrat später in seiner Schrift »The Language Is Image« von 1952 den gleichen Gedankengang, nach dem die ursprüngliche Einheit von Vision und Bedeutung durch die moderne westliche Zivilisation zerteilt und das kreative Potential unterdrückt wurde: »Nach der Keilschrift und chinesischen oder anderen alten Texten zu urteilen, verkörperten die Objektsymbole eine Identität, aus der später die Buchstaben und Wörter entwickelt wurden. Der poetisch-kommunikative Gebrauch der Sprache wurde zusehends von einem an Geschäft und Nutzen orientierten Gebrauch beherrscht, woraus sich eine Seite ihrer Unzulänglichkeit erklärt. Der primitive Mensch vor dreißig- oder vierzigtausend Jahren hatte weder das Wort Bild, noch bestand eine Notwendigkeit zu einer begrenzten Vision. Durch Selektion oder eidetische Vorstellung umfaßte sein Verhältnis zum Objekt alle seine Teilbereiche und Funktionen . . . Die Höhlenmenschen von Altamira bis Rhodesien hatten durch das eidetische Bild wirkliche Realität geschaffen.«[75]

SMITHS Verweise auf das wahrnehmungspsychologische Phänomen des eidetischen Bildes, die sich in allen seinen Schriften und Skizzenbüchern finden, entsprachen seinem Ideal, daß es ein Band zwischen dem primitiven und dem modernen Künstler gäbe. Eidetische Bilder sind Formen der Halluzination des Wachbewußtseins, in denen die normalen Grenzen zwischen geistiger Produktion und sinnlicher Wahrnehmung aufgehoben sind und das Subjekt ein Bild in außerordentlicher Vollständigkeit und Eindringlichkeit sieht, ohne die betreffende Person oder den Gegenstand real vor Augen zu haben. In anthropologischen Abhandlungen und Schriften der zwanziger und dreißiger Jahre wird diese Kraft zu bildlicher Vorstellung besonders den Kindern, »Wilden« und Künstlern zuerkannt.[76] Die eidetische Fähigkeit stellte das »geistige Auge« der visuellen Wahrnehmung gleich und hob die Grenzen zwischen Vorstellung und Wahrnehmung, Mythos und Realität auf. Sie brachte Darstellungen hervor, die man in der Mitte zwischen Subjektivität und Objektivität, zwischen dem kollektiven Unbewußten und der persönlichen Erfahrung glaubte. Es ist verwirrend, daß SMITH uns hier, in der psychologischen Sprache seiner Zeit, wieder an GAUGUIN erinnert. Dieser hatte auf ähnliche Weise den primitiven Geist als Sitz höherer, persönliche Wahrnehmung transzendierender Bildkraft (und deshalb als Sitz einer Urkreativität) bewundert und sich von den abergläubischen Phantasien bretonischer Frauen und tahitischer Eingeborener faszinieren lassen □ 220, 249. Bei SMITH kommt eine soziale Dimension hinzu, wenn er betont, daß die Kraft seiner Kunst wie das eidetische Bild auf einer präverbalen Gestaltungsebene wirkt – in einem Wahrnehmungsbereich, der »jedem Menschen, jedem Stand offensteht und Sprachbarrieren überwindet«.[77] Hier zeigt sich erneut der alte Traum der Linguisten und Künstler von einer Sprache Adams, einem System der Zeichen, das die Menschheit verbindet, statt sie zu trennen, und eine Fülle von Bedeutungen umfaßt.

□ 995 *David Smith, ›Pfeiler des Sonntags‹ (Pillar of Sunday), 1945, bemalter Stahl, 73 x 44 x 24 cm. Indiana University Art Museum, Bloomington.*

Bezeichnenderweise lassen weder Aussagen noch die Arbeiten SMITHS erkennen, daß solch ein System der Zeichen einfach durch Ausgrabung archaischer Formen oder Nachahmung der Stammeskunst wiederzugewinnen ist. In der wiederholten Berufung auf eidetische Erfahrung wie in der Entwicklung seiner Formenauswahl strebte SMITH eine »Universalität« an, die weniger auf latent konservativen, halb Jungschen Lehren von gemeinsamen, ewigen Symbolen beruhte, als auf einem neurologischen Ideal universaler visueller Fähigkeiten. Seine Vorstellung von visueller Wahrnehmung als klassenunabhängiger, zeitloser menschlicher Fähigkeit entfernt sich vom Symbol hin zum Schauen als der Grundlage für ein Interesse am Primitiven und als Basis für eine moderne Kunst. Diese Verschiebung steht im Einklang mit dem Wunsch nach einem absoluten Neubeginn, der in den späten vierziger Jahren die Suche nach archetypischen Symbolen, die den neuen amerikanischen Primitivismus anfangs motiviert hatte, verdrängte. In dieser Hinsicht wiederholen die Arbeiten SMITHS der Zeit um 1949/50 die gleiche Absorption und Transzendenz, die man bei POLLOCK, NEWMAN und ROTHKO beobachten konnte.

Der Primitivismus der vierziger Jahre hob sich in seiner stärksten Ausprägung selbst wieder auf. Denn jenen Künstlern, die sich genauer mit dem Beispiel des primitiven Künstlers befaßten, stellte sich die Übernahme von Stammesformen und die gezielte Beschwörung alter Mythen als Verfälschung ihres Hungers nach Absolutem und ihrer Sehnsucht nach Universalität – die größte Herausforderung der primitivistischen Bewegung – dar. Ein neuer primitivistischer Zug, der die Schwerfälligkeit der Kriegsjahre verdrängte, taucht um 1948 in den Arbeiten und Aussagen der New Yorker Schule auf. BARNETT NEWMAN sprach es am deutlichsten aus:

»Mit unserer Beziehung zu absoluten Gefühlen dokumentieren wir den natürlichen Wunsch des Menschen nach dem Höheren. Wir benötigen dazu nicht die überholten Requisiten einer altmodischen und ausgedienten Legende. Wir schaffen Bilder, deren Realität in sich evident ist und die ohne Requisiten und

□ 996 *Enrico Baj, ›Zorniger General mit Orden‹, 1961, Öl und Collage auf Leinwand, 129,5 x 96,5 cm. Museum of Contemporary Art, Chicago, als Schenkung von Joseph und Jory Shapiro in Aussicht gestellt.*

Gedankenstützen auskommen, die Assoziationen an ausgediente Bilder erwecken. Wir befreien uns von den Fesseln der Erinnerung, Assoziation, Nostalgie, der Legende und des Mythos . . .«[78]

Diese veränderte Einstellung erklärt u. a. auch, warum CLYFFORD STILL, dessen Arbeiten der späten dreißiger und vierziger Jahre die emotionale Wertigkeit und mitunter auch die für den Primitivismus seiner Zeit typischen Züge aufweist, später alle Verantwortung für Bildtitel wie *Totemistische Phantasie* ablehnte, die seinen frühen Bildern gegeben worden waren[79] – und dies, obwohl er sich diese Titel ausgedacht oder ihnen zumindest zugestimmt hatte, als die Bilder das erste Mal gezeigt oder verkauft wurden. Bei all diesen Malern zeigte sich um 1950 die allgemeine Tendenz, die ominösen (und mitunter ziemlich willkürlich erdachten) Bildtitel, die für die vierziger Jahre charakteristisch waren, zugunsten einfacher Zahlen oder Gattungsnamen aufzugeben oder überhaupt auf Bildtitel zu verzichten. Eine neue Nomenklatur läßt auf einen neuen Inhalt schließen. Die Neutralisierung ging einher mit dem Eliminieren übernommener Formen und Zeichen; und dies zeigt am deutlichsten die Enttäuschung in bezug auf das Ideal eines Archetypus oder einer Urchiffre als Träger einer universalen Bedeutung.

Diesen Wandel signalisiert eine weitverbreitete Abkehr von den surrealistischen Resten und insbesondere von der Vorstellung, daß das mit Symbolen beladene Unbewußte Quelle künstlerischer Erfahrung und die Grundlage für die Rezeption des Betrachters sei. Ein nachdrücklicher Empirismus ersetzte die Diskussion über Vorformen höchster Erkenntnis und menschlicher Tradition, die noch für die vierziger Jahre typisch gewesen war. Zur gleichen Zeit beginnen ROTHKO, NEWMAN, GOTTLIEB und in geringerem Umfang auch POLLOCK eng zusammengehörende Werke in erkennbaren oder von ihnen selbst dazu deklarierten Serien zu schaffen – ein weiteres Beispiel für den universalen oder sogar klinisch-klaren Zug der »Experimente« der neuen Abstraktion.

Die symbolische und mythische Phase des Primitivismus war nicht notwendigerweise der Auftakt zur fortgeschrittenen Abstraktion in der New Yorker Schule gewesen; denn wie die Beispiele DE KOONING und GORKY zeigen, konnten einige Künstler auch von der europäischen Tradition aus direkt zu einer neuen Kunst von hoher Originalität und Kraft gelangen. (GORKY lehnte den Primitivismus auch offen als Selbstbetrug und Eskapismus ab und betrachtete primitive Kunst als schlechtes Vorbild für eine der dynamischen Komplexität moderner Erfahrung gemäßen Kreativität.)[80] Einem Großteil der Künstler diente der Primitivismus als ein notwendiges Mittel, die eigene Originalität voll zu entfalten, und er bot Gelegenheit zur Auseinandersetzung mit einigen der dringendsten Fragen der Zeit. Es wäre zu einfach, das Phänomen als Übergangsphase unreifer oder weniger talentierter Künstler abzutun oder seine Bedeutung ausschließlich als Ausdruck individualpsychologischer Entwicklungen bei einigen wichtigen Künstlern zu sehen.

Man sollte die Episode des Primitivismus in der amerikanischen Kunst statt dessen in seinen weiten, kulturellen Bezügen, im Zusammenhang mit dem Kampf zwischen Faschismus und Marxismus und besonders in der Auseinandersetzung mit dem Faschismus sehen. Allgemein könnte man sagen, daß sich darin die Situation, die vorher im Zusammenhang mit Gauguin besprochen wurde, wiederholt (siehe S. 184 ff.): Ein moderner Primitivismus, an universalen Grundlagen der Kultur interessiert, steht einer Ideologie menschlicher Evolution gegenüber, die auf einer historizistischen, rassischen Verfälschung der Naturwissenschaften gründet. Wie Gauguins Bewunderung für primitive Kreativität eine Reaktion auf den vorherrschenden, falsch angewandten Darwinismus war, so verstanden sich die primitivistischen Interessen der abstrakten Expressionisten bis zu einer sehr bezeichnenden Stufe als Alternative zu den jüngsten darwinistischen Ideen einer rassisch determinierten Geschichte, wie sie der Nationalsozialismus vertrat.

Es sei nachdrücklich betont, daß es in den vierziger Jahren in der Welt mehr als nur eine Spielart des Primitivismus gab und mehr zur Debatte stand als nur Fragen des Stils. Von allen primitiven Zeichen, die die menschliche Vorstellung im 20. Jahrhundert gefangennahmen, war das Hakenkreuz sicherlich mit am prägendsten. Dieses alte kosmologische Symbol, das auf den Fahnen des nationalsozialistischen Deutschland zu sehen war, bezeugt eine erschreckend erfolgreiche Wiederbelebung archaisch-mythischer Macht. Für jede denkende Person im Leben der dreißiger und vierziger Jahre war es eine höchst beunruhigende Herausforderung, wie der Faschismus mit dem Bollwerk kollektiver, sozialer Integration gegen die entfremdenden Ungewißheiten des modernen Lebens anging und primitive Volksmythen mit aggressiver Wissenschaft und Technologie verband. Wie Erich Kahler kurz nach dem Krieg in der Zeitschrift *Chimera* zum Mythos anmerkte: »Der Faschismus enthüllte ein tiefes Bedürfnis der menschlichen Psyche, das man im Zeitalter des Rationalismus nicht wahrhaben wollte.«[84] Die Diskussionen über das Wesen des Mythos als Thema der Kunst, die für Wandlungen in der amerikanischen Kunst um 1940 so große Bedeutung haben, spiegeln die nationalsozialistische Herausforderung wider. Der marxistische Materialismus als unnachgiebiger Feind aller Mystik und Transzendenz verunglimpfte alles Mystische. Aber das wirtschaftlich bestimmte »wissenschaftliche« Ideal einer Gesellschaftsordnung, die die Marxisten dem entgegenhielten, empfanden viele Künstler und Intellektuelle angesichts der demonstrierten Macht irrationalen, die Weltordnung bedrohenden Atavismus als ungenügend. Wie Kahler es später formulierte: »Wir begegnen diesen Gefahren, die diese menschliche Neigung birgt, nicht, indem wir sie leugnen, als Überreste alten Aberglaubens hinstellen, die überwunden sind oder überwunden sein sollten, sondern nur indem wir sie sehen und mit ihnen rechnen.«[85] Den

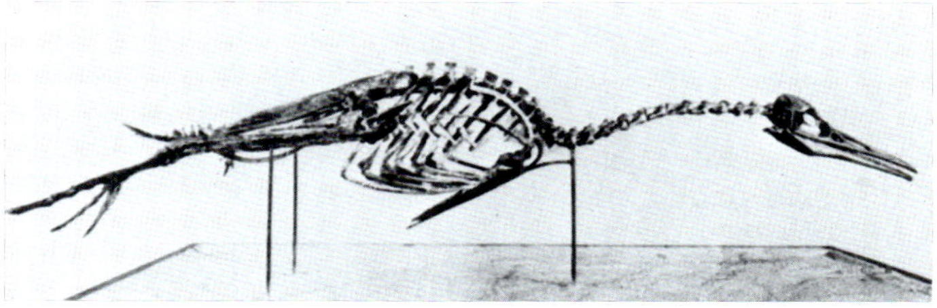

□ 997 *Fossiles Skelett des prähistorischen, vogelähnlichen ›Hesperornis regalis‹ aus der Sammlung des American Museum of Natural History, New York. Photographie aus dem Archiv von David Smith.*

□ 998 *David Smith, ›Königlicher Vogel‹ (Royal Bird), 1947–48. Edelstahl, geschweißt, 55 x 150 x 23 cm. Walker Art Center, Minneapolis, Schenkung T. B. Walker Foundation.*

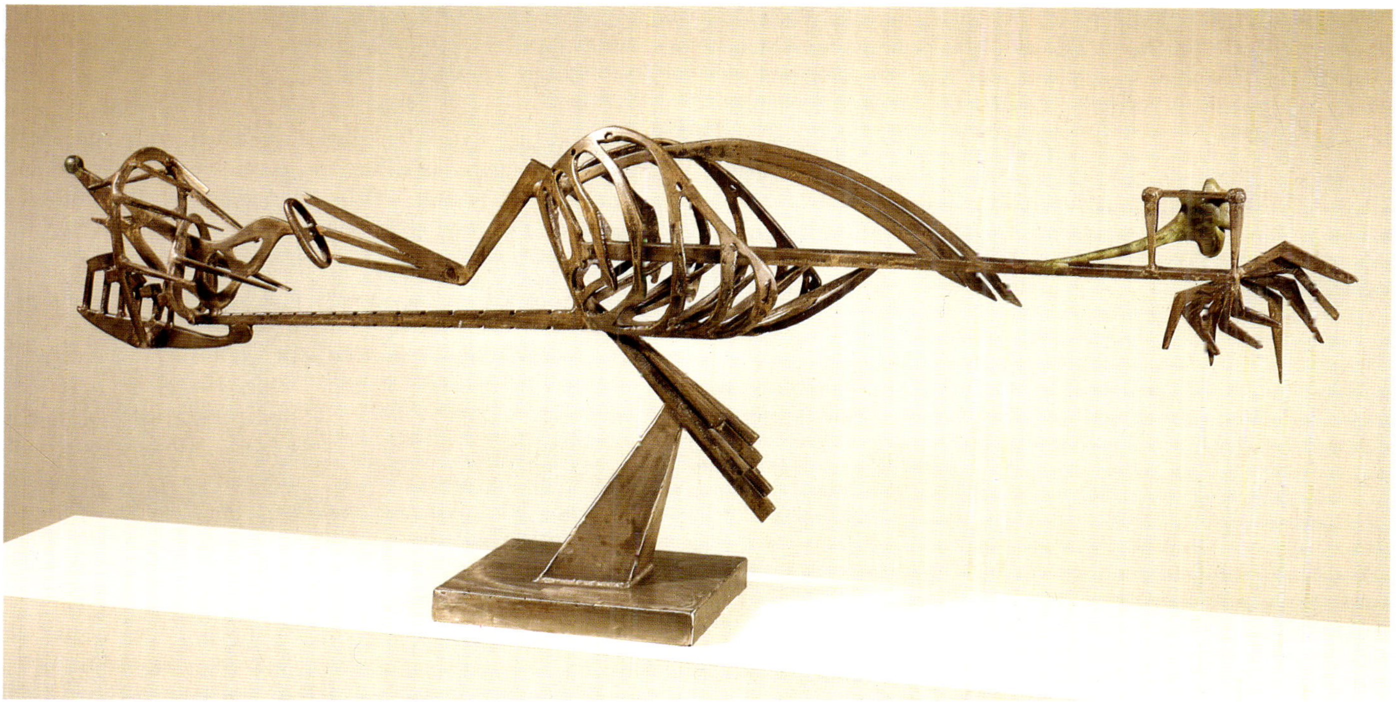

Primitivismus der frühen New Yorker Schule und seinen Drang, mythische zeitgemäße Ausdrucksformen zu finden, sollte man im Zusammenhang mit der Abkehr vom Materialismus sehen, die dazu befähigte, der Herausforderung durch den Nationalsozialismus zu begegnen und ihn mit seinen eigenen Mitteln zu schlagen. Dem Mißbrauch von Wissenschaft und Mythos im Faschismus stellten die amerikanischen Künstler in ihren primitivistischen Idealen eine positive Verbindung von Mythos und Wissenschaft entgegen.

Während sich die Nationalsozialisten auf archaische Mythen als dauerhafte Grundlage völkischer Einheit und der Klassifizierung der Kulturen beriefen, betonten die New Yorker Künstler einen synkretistischen Geist des Mythos, der an universale Grundlagen aller menschlichen Erfahrung heranreicht. Ihre Bewunderung primitiver Kunst betonte die antirassistische, kulturelle Gleichwertigkeit, die unhierarchische Verherrlichung menschlicher Kreativität, während sich die Deutschen kulturspezifisch ausschließlich der arischen Kultur zuwandten. Ebenso sahen die Deutschen in der Wiederbelebung von Mythos und Ritual die Möglichkeit, die Individualität des Einzelnen dem modernen Gesamtstaat unterzuordnen. Die amerikanischen Vorstellungen fußten auf einem komplexeren psychoanalytischen Modell der Analogie zwischen der positiven Integration des Individuums und dem Zusammenhalt der Gesellschaft.[83] Im Individuum wie in der Kultur sollte ein Gewahrsein für bleibende Symbole des Unbewußten gefördert werden, nicht die bloße Unterwerfung unter eine Tyrannei der genetischen Erinnerung, sondern die befreiende Fähigkeit zu spontaner Erfahrung. Primitivismus als Vorbedingung für Individualität, Archetypen als Katalysator für Kreativität – diese Kombinationen aus Atavismus und aggressivem Experiment, die ich, etwa anhand der Entwicklung POLLOCKS, aufzeigte, bildeten eine spezifische Alternative zum totalitären Primitivismus. Im Deutschland des Nationalsozialismus wurde diese negative Version der Tyrannei menschlicher Tradition durch eine korrumpierte Naturwissenschaft unterstützt, für die eherne Rassengesetze Vorrang hatten. Der Primitivismus der Amerikaner versuchte dagegen seine Auffassung von Tradition mit einem anderen Wissenschaftsbegriff zu verbinden; einer Wissenschaft, die mehr nach Wundern als nach versklavenden Gesetzmäßigkeiten forscht. Der amerikanische Primitivismus der vierziger Jahre verband sich mit dem Ideal der Wissenschaft als einem Modell für eine ungespaltene Gesellschaft im Dienste der Wahrheit und als Zugang zu den Mysterien und den ehrfurchtgebietenden, gewaltigen Naturkräften. Die biologische und menschheitsgeschichtliche Bildwelt ROTHKOS, SMITHS, NEWMANS und anderer beschwor im Gegensatz zum teleologischen Eliteideal der genetischen Theorie des Nationalsozialismus nicht nur eine Lebensenergie vor der Aufteilung in Arten, sondern auch eine spezifisch wissenschaftliche Sicht der archäologischen, paläontologischen und mikrobiologischen Forschung. (In der Tat könnte man in der Verwendung von Versteinerungen und Zellen, von ideographischen und amöboiden Formen in diesen Kunstwerken eine Entsprechung zu fortschrittlichsten Vorstellungen in der Evolutionsforschung der vierziger Jahre sehen, die gleichfalls nach einer Synthese genetischer Mutation und sozialer Auslese suchte.)[84]

WOLFGANG PAALEN, ein surrealistischer und primitivistischer Autor und Künstler der vierziger Jahre, vertrat 1945 die Ansicht, daß man »einer bereits universalen Wissenschaft, die jedoch per definitionem unseren emotionalen Bedürfnissen nicht gerecht werden kann, als Ergänzung eine universale Kunst hinzufügen muß; beide Seiten werden zur Erschaffung eines neuen, des notwendigen Weltbewußtseins beitragen.«[85] Diese Betonung eines wissenschaftlichen Ideals als Vorbild für neue, überkulturelle Ausdrucksformen zeigte sich bereits 1944, als POLLOCK auf die Frage nach der Entstehung einer neuen amerikanischen Kunst erwiderte: »Die Vorstellung einer isolierten amerikanischen Malerei, die in den dreißiger Jahren bei uns populär war, erscheint mir ebenso absurd wie die Vorstellung, eine rein amerikanische Mathematik oder Physik zu schaffen.«[86] Zu diesem Prinzip der Universalität, das mit der dringenden Suche der Amerikaner nach letztem, originär Absolutem in Mythos und Sprache in Einklang steht, kam das Gefühl, daß die moderne Wissenschaft in ihrer Konfrontation mit dem Unbekannten zudem an dem Aufbruch zum Primitivismus teilnahm. Diese Vorstellung von einer weit fortgeschrittenen Wissenschaft ist in dem allgemeinen Gefühl von einem neuen Zeitalter des Mythos genauso wie in den spezifisch primitivistischen Themen ROTHKOS (organische Energie als Grundlage des Lebens), NEWMANS (abstrakte Form als höhere Wahrheit), SMITHS (eidetische Wahrnehmung) und anderer enthalten. Ein Text dieser Zeit macht die Verbindungen besonders klar. In der Abhandlung »The Persistence of Myth« von 1946 kam Erich Kahler zu dem Schluß, daß »sogar an der äußersten Front menschlichen Wissens eine Situation erreicht wurde, wo eine extreme Ausweitung menschlicher Macht ihn zur selben Zeit erneut den ganzen Umfang seiner alten Ohnmacht, den Kosmos zu begreifen, erkennen läßt«.

Die Grenzen unserer Vernunft werden immer deutlicher, und das rationalistische, allzu große Vertrauen in eine unbegrenzte Herrschaft der Vernunft über die Natur ist durch die Naturwissenschaft selbst erschüttert worden. Mit dem beeindruckenden Fortschritt der jüngsten Zeit ist die Physik zu einem Grenzbereich vorgedrungen, der sich selbst rationaler Erkenntnis zu verweigern scheint. Sie ist in Mikrobereiche vorgestoßen, wo Phänomene nicht mehr abgebildet, sondern nur schematisch, das heißt mit Symbolen erfaßt werden können; sie ist so tief in die innerste Struktur der Elemente vorgedrungen, daß sie die Übergangsformen der Elemente entdeckte und zu der Erkenntnis kam, daß die Elemente selbst ganz spezifische Anordnungen, Bindungen allgemeiner Energien sind . . .

»Die Physik vereinigt auf einer neuen Ebene die innere und äußere Welt und fordert auf erkenntnistheoretischer Grundlage eine Einheit, von der man auch in früheren, religiösen Zeiten überzeugt war. Die Forschungsergebnisse haben, indem sie ein Objekt vollständig in einen Komplex von Beziehungen auflösen, die Physiker noch weiter von der Sphäre der sinnlichen Wahrnehmung in die Sphäre abstrakter Begriffe geführt . . . Indem die Physik vom Äußeren ausging, korrespondiert sie seltsamerweise mit der vorausgegangenen Theorie der Psychoanalyse, die, vom Inneren ausgehend, zu einer Verschmelzung der inneren und äußeren Welt gelangte: Sie erkannte nach außen gerichtete Reaktionen als Projektionen innerer Situationen. Die Physik hat in ihren höchsten Triumphen im Menschen angesichts der undurchdringlichen Ausdehnung, die an den Grenzen der äußeren Welt wieder entsteht, das Urschaudern erzeugt; die Psychoanalyse hat die verhehlte Angst des Menschen vor inneren Abgründen enthüllt. Sowohl die Physik als auch die Psychoanalyse haben gezeigt, daß sich diese Ängste gegenseitig bedingen und ein und derselben Furcht vor dem Unbekannten entspringen, die der wahre Ursprung des Mythos ist.«[87] Mythos und Wissenschaft, das

☐ 999 *›Maske‹*, Pueblo *(Arizona oder Neu-Mexiko), Leder und andere Materialien, Höhe 29 cm. Sammlung Lebel, Paris.*

Primitivste und das Modernste, sah man als spiegelbildlich aufeinander bezogen; und man erkennt im Primitivismus der New Yorker Künstler den Wunsch nach einer Kunst, die solche offensichtlichen Gegensätze versöhnt: einer Kunst, die alte Zeichen und Mythen verkörpert und zudem Begegnungen mit universalen, abstrakten Wahrheiten und fundamentalen Energien ermöglicht. Ebenso wie man das Gefühl hatte, daß die Finsternis des Krieges den Menschen in die Ohnmacht der Urzeit zurückwarf, so sprachen viele Autoren in den späteren vierziger Jahren das Empfinden aus, daß der Mensch durch die Entdeckung der modernen Wissenschaft in einen Zustand mythischen Schreckens vor dem Kosmos zurückversetzt würde. Dieser Zusammenhang wurde besonders mit den Folgen der Atombombe deutlich. Die Kommentare, die beim Öffnen dieses furchtbaren Tores zu unbekannten Bereichen geäußert wurden, waren den Aussagen Newmans und anderer Künstler über moderne Erfahrung als geistiger Nachklang des Primitiven auffallend ähnlich.[88]

Die Vorstellung, daß adäquate Vorbilder der Zukunft in einem Verständnis der Vergangenheit liegen, gibt es natürlich nicht nur in der Kunst. Auch ist das Bestreben, die frühere Ganzheit von Wissen und Intuition, Kunst und Wissenschaft wiederzugewinnen, ein grundlegendes Thema abendländischen Denkens. Diese Vorstellungen schienen aber im 20. Jahrhundert den Intentionen der Avantgarde besonders nahe zu kommen – in ihrer Bewunderung primitiver Kunst wie auch in ihrer Haßliebe gegenüber dem Fortschritt der Wissenschaft. Was diese oder andere, früher behandelte Fragen betrifft, scheint die primitivistische Phase der New Yorker Schule nicht nur weitreichende und dringliche Probleme der westlichen Kultur der 40er Jahre, sondern auch Fragen nach der Rolle der Kunst in Gesellschaft und Geschichte aktualisiert zu haben, die für die Kunst des 20. Jahrhunderts generell symptomatisch sind. Die Suche nach unbewußten Wurzeln menschlicher Darstellungen, die Faszination, die vom Ideal universaler Zeichen ausging, oder die Verbindung der tiefen irrationalen Vergangenheit des Menschen mit der aktuellen wissenschaftssüchtigen Kultur sind keineswegs nur kurzlebige Launen oder irrelevante Themen der Kunst. Diese wiederkehrenden Hauptkennzeichen des modernen Primitivismus nahmen durch die verschiedenen abstrakten Stile, die die auffälligen primitiven Bezüge in der amerikanischen Kunst am Ende der 40er Jahre ersetzten, eine einheitliche Gestalt an und blieben eine ständige Herausforderung der modernen Kultur – eine Herausforderung, der sich Künstler der folgenden Generation erneut zu stellen hatten.

□ 1000 ›*Vogel*‹, SENUFO (*Elfenbeinküste*), *Holz, Höhe 135 cm. Sammlung E. Loran, Berkeley.*

Anmerkungen

Für die wertvolle Unterstützung meiner Forschungen, die zum Gelingen dieses Aufsatzes wesentlich beitrugen, möchte der Autor Joan Pachner seinen Dank aussprechen.

1. Man vergleiche die Diskussion über den Einfluß der mexikanischen Muralisten auf Pollock in Sandler, I., *The Triumph of American Painting*, New York 1971, S. 103–04. Die Bedeutung der Mexikaner für Pollock und andere hebt auch Robert Carleton Hobbs hervor, »Early Abstract Expressionism: A Concern with the Unknown Within« in Hobbs, R. C., und Levin, G., *Abstract Expressionism: The Formative Years*, Ithaca 1978, S. 14.

2. Adolph Gottlieb aus »The Portrait and the Modern Artist«, Rundfunkmanuskript über »Art in New York«, WNYC, 13.10.1943, zitiert in MacNaughton, M. D., »Adolph Gottlieb: His Life and Art« in *Adolph Gottlieb, A Retrospective*, New York 1981, S. 42. Auch Barnett Newman kritisierte die falschen Auffassungen europäischer Moderner über primitive Kunst und sah dabei einen Zusammenhang mit den Mängeln abstrakter Malerei in Europa. Seine Aussagen erschienen in »The Plasmic Image«, ein Manuskript, an dem er von 1943 bis 1945 arbeitete. Man vergleiche die umfangreichen Auszüge aus diesem Text und die Anmerkungen von Thomas Hess, in Hess, T. B., *Barnett Newman*, New York, Museum of Modern Art, 1971, vor allem S. 37, 39.

3. Graham, J., »Introduction« in *Exhibition of Sculpture of Old African Civilizations*, New York, Jacques Seligmann Gallery, 1936, S. 3.

4. Graham, J., *System and Dialectics of Art*, New York 1937, S. 15. Zu John Graham und seiner Bedeutung für die Künstler der New Yorker Schule siehe Sandler, I., »John D. Graham: The Painter as Esthetician and Connoisseur« in *Artforum*, Oktober 1968, S. 50–53, und Sandlers Diskussion über den Einfluß Grahams auf Pollock in *Triumph*, S. 105–06.

5. Siehe die von Irving Sandler durchgeführte Analyse des Bruches der New Yorker Maler mit den Surrealisten, Sandler, I., *Triumph*, a. a. O., S. 63–64.

6. Zum psychologischen Gehalt der frühen Arbeiten des abstrakten Expressionismus siehe Hobbs, »Early Abstract Expressionism: A Concern with the Unknown Within«, a.a.O., S. 8–40.

7. Leitartikel in *View*, Reihe 3, Nr. 1, 1943, zitiert in Ashton, D., *The New York School: A Cultural Reckoning*, New York 1980, S. 20.

8. Barr, A., schrieb in der Einleitung zu Frobenius, L., und Fox, D. C., *Prehistoric Rock Pictures in Europe and Africa*, New York, Museum of Modern Art, 1937: »Technische und ästhetische Qualitäten sind nicht erstrebenswerter als der unbestreitbare Sinn für sozialen Nutzen, den diese prähistorischen Bilder erkennen lassen . . . Heute sind die Wände so bemalt, daß sie dem Künstler nützen, aber in prähistorischer Zeit waren sie zum Nutzen für die Gemeinschaft.«

9. Zur Abkehr von der Geschichte hin zu einer mythisch orientierten Psyche siehe Hobbs, a.a.O., und Sandler, *Triumph*, a.a.O., S. 63–64.

Die nachdrücklichste Ablehnung der materialistischen Sicht der Stammeswelt zeige sich in B. Newmans »The First Man Was an Artist« in *Tiger's Eye,* Nr. 1, 1947, S. 57–60. Die antimarxistische Sicht von Newman war aber bereits in den Aussagen Wolfgang Paalens enthalten, in »The New Image« in *DYN,* Nr. 1, April/Mai 1942, S. 7: »Engels war im Irrtum, als er schrieb ›Der Mensch muß essen, trinken, gekleidet sein und Obdach finden, bevor er sich mit Politik, Kunst, Wissenschaft und Religion beschäftigen kann . . .‹ Unbestreitbar zeigen Anthropologie und Psychologie, daß Kunst, Wissenschaft und Religion untrennbar die sichtbare Welt und die Anfänge des Denkens verdeutlichen.« Paalens Aussagen sind nicht nur für die zunehmende Ablehnung des Marxismus charakteristisch, sondern auch für die Tendenz, die Autorität der Wissenschaft zur Bestätigung der neugepriesenen, ahistorischen Universalien menschlicher Erfahrung heranzuziehen.

Die Vorstellung, daß die Anfänge der Kunst vom Nützlichkeitsdenken frei waren, gab es bereits bei Luquet, G. H., in *L'Art et la religion des hommes fossiles,* 1926: »Es scheint mir unvorstellbar, daß bildende Kunst in der Anfangsphase etwas anderes als uneigennützige Aktivität gewesen sein sollte. Wie Breuil [Abbé Breuil, der früheste und beste Kenner der Höhlenmalerei] schreibt: ›Wenn Kunst nicht um der Kunst willen entstanden wäre, hätte es nie magische oder religiöse Kunst gegeben . . .‹« Luquets Ansicht, daß der primitive Künstler vorrangig aus der Lust am Schaffen tätig wurde, ist wiederum eine Reaktion auf die primitivistische Einstellung von Coleridge gegenüber den Anfängen der Wissenschaft. Für Coleridge, zitiert von Peter Medawar in *Pluto's Republic,* New York 1982, S. 31, war jener »der erste Mensch der Wissenschaft, der einen Gegenstand nicht danach beurteilte, ob er als Nahrung, Obdach, Waffe, Gerät, Ornament oder *Spielzeug* dienen könne, sondern der, der ihn um des Wissens willen verstehen wollte«.

10. Eine Analyse der »apolitischen«, individualistischen Einstellung im politischen Denken der vierziger Jahre bei Guilbaut, S., *How New York Stole the Idea of Modern Art,* Chicago 1983, z. B. S. 75–79.

11. Newman, B., »Northwest Coast Indian Painting«, New York, Betty Parsons Gallery, 1946.

12. Gottlieb in »The Portrait and the Modern Artist«, a.a.O., zitiert bei Sandler, *Triumph*, a.a.O., S. 64, und bei MacNaughton, a.a.O., S. 42.

13. Gottlieb in *Tiger's Eye,* Nr. 2, Dezember 1947, S. 43, zitiert bei MacNaughton, a.a.O., S. 44.

14. Newman, »The Object and the Image«, in *Tiger's Eye,* Nr. 3, März 1948.

15. »Nur eine autochthone Mythologie, die aus dem gleichen Boden, dem gleichen Volk, der gleichen kulturellen Substruktur und der gleichen ökonomischen Grundlage stammt, kann wirkungsvoll zwischen Kunst und materieller Produktion vermitteln . . .« Lloyd, A. L., »Modern Art and Modern Society« in *Art Front,* Oktober 1937, zitiert bei Ashton, a.a.O., S. 71.

16. Als Martha Graham 1937 über das »Bewußtsein des Landes« sprach, das ihr Frühwerk charakterisierte, bezeichnete sie es »als vorübergehende, aber unumgängliche Isolation, um so etwas wie grundlegende Volkswahrheiten zu finden, von denen man ausgehen kann«. Siehe »Affirmations 1926–1937« in Armitage, M. (Hrsg.), *Martha Graham,* 1937. Die Kontroverse zwischen Einheimischem und Universalem wurde seit den Anfängen im Symbolismus des späten 19. Jahrhunderts mit moderner Kunst verbunden, besonders im Hinblick auf einen Gegensatz zwischen einer regionalistisch/naturalistischen Betonung des Ländlichen und der symbolistischen Betonung eines weitgefaßten völkisch geistigen Mystizismus derselben »Primitiven«. Die Ansicht, daß wirkliche Universalität nur von einem Künstler, der tief mit seinem Land verwurzelt ist, erreicht werden kann, zeigte sich besonders in der aufkommenden nordischen Romantik des letzten Jahrzehnts des 19. Jahrhunderts. Man vergleiche dazu den Aufsatz des Autors über »Nationalism, Internationalism, and the Progress of Scandinavian Art« in *Northern Light: Realism and Symbolism in Scandinavian Painting, 1880–1910,* New York, Brooklyn Museum, 1982, und die Besprechung von Marcia Vetrocq, die Ähnlichkeiten mit der New Yorker Schule herausstellt, »Souls on Ice« in *Art in America,* September 1983, S. 116–23.

17. Man vergleiche dazu die Aussagen von Evan Maurer über die Surrealisten und die Indianer im vorliegenden Buch, S. 579, und die »surrealistische Weltkarte«, in der Alaska eine besondere Rolle einnimmt ☐ 820. Bekannt wurde die Kunst und Kultur der Nordwestküste vor allem durch den Surrealisten Wolfgang Paalen; man vergleiche seinen Aufsatz »Paysage Totemique« in *DYN,* Nr. 1, April/Mai 1942, Nr. 2, Juli/August 1942 und Nr. 3, Herbst 1942. Ebenso »Totem Art« in *DYN,* Sonderausgabe zum Thema Indianer, Nr. 4–5, 1943–44.

18. Zu Graham und der New Yorker Schule siehe Ashton, a.a.O., S. 143. Ashton zitiert Grahams Aussagen zu dem Tanz *Dark Meadow,* die in Lloyd, M., *The Borzoi Book of Modern Dance,* 1949, angeführt werden: »Er geht auf unsere frühen Vorfahren, auf barbarische, primitive Lebensursprünge zurück, die unserer kollektiven Erinnerung entspringen, und befaßt sich mit dem psychologischen Hintergrund der Menschheit.«

19. Gottlieb, »The Portrait and the Modern Artist«, zitiert bei Sandler in *Triumph,* a.a.O., S. 63.

20. Es scheint geboten, auf die Änderungen in der Präsentationsweise von Stammeskunst während der 20er, 30er und 40er Jahre ausführlicher einzugehen. Die Rolle der Händler, die Stammesobjekte als rein ästhetische Gegenstände auffaßten, war – angefangen mit Stieglitz im Jahr 1914, siehe S. 466 – prägend für die Verbreitung eines formalen, nichtethnologischen Zugangs, wie ihn zum Beispiel die kubistische Auffassung von Stammeskunst beinhaltete. Die New Yorker Ausstellungen des Museum of Modern Art zu prähistorischer Kunst und Stammeskunst waren wichtige Etappen. Für die Konzeption einer neuen Ausstellungsästhetik bei Stammeskunst hat René d'Harnoncourt entscheidende Anregungen gegeben. Eine treffende Zusammenfassung der Änderungen der Museumspraxis gibt Thomas, T., »Artists, Africans, and Installation« in *Parnassus* 12, Nr. 1 und 4, Januar und April 1940: »Als es modern wurde, sich mit eingeborener Kunst zu beschäftigen, als Privatsammlungen aufgebaut wurden und deshalb der Marktwert der einzelnen Stücke stieg, begannen die Museen ihre Sammlungen mit einem neuen Gefühl für diese Schätze aufzustellen. Für die Ausstellungskonzeptionen waren nicht mehr ethnologische, sondern ästhetische Vorstellungen entscheidend.« Weiter meinte Thomas vorausschauend: »Die nächste Phase in der Ausstellungspraxis eingeborener Kunst wird vermutlich wiederum etwas der alten ethnologischen Vorstellung nicht Unähnliches bringen, aber viel von der ästhetischen Wertschätzung beibehalten.« Über die Präsentationsweise bei der Ausstellung »Twenty Centuries of Mexican Art« im Museum of Modern Art urteilte Nicolas Calas, daß sie »die Kunstschätze manchmal . . . wie Gegenstände im Schaufenster eines eleganten Geschäftes der Fifth Avenue erscheinen lasse. Wenn der Ausstellungsbesucher das Erdgeschoß mit den Aztekenstatuen verläßt, um die spanischen Räume oder die Abteilungen moderner mexikanischer Kunst zu betreten, hat er weniger die Empfindung, zehn oder zwanzig Jahrhunderte zu durchschreiten, sondern eher in eine andere Abteilung von Saks oder Macy's zu gehen . . .«, »Mexico Brings Us Art« in *View 1,* Nr. [illegible], September 1940, S. 2. Größere Kontroversen erregte jedoch die Ausstellung der Kunst der Südsee im Museum of Modern Art 1946. In einer Besprechung im *Art Bulletin* 28, Nr. 2, Juni 1946, betrachtete der Anthropologe Gregory Bateson genau die Voraussetzungen für diese Form der Präsentation, die selbst wiederum Kunst bedeute. Bateson untersucht die Aufstellung, Beleuchtung und Abfolge in D'Harnoncourts Präsentationsweise im Zusammenhang mit jüngsten Veränderungen in der anthropologischen Theorie, besonders D'Harnoncourts Art, »Stimmung« zu erzeugen, die Bateson mit aktuellen Vorstellungen zur Psychologie primitiver Gesellschaften verglich. Der Artikel analysiert und lobt, wie D'Harnoncourt Beleuchtung, Farbveränderung usw. einsetzte, um die unterschiedlichen Kunstformen der Südsee zu unterstreichen. Dieser Wandel von der Darstellung rein ethnologischer Zusammenhänge zu einem abstrakten Symbolismus scheint der Malerei von D'Harnoncourts Zeitgenossen genau zu entsprechen. In einer weiteren, weniger detaillierten Ausstellungsbesprechung in *View,* Reihe V-VI, 1945–46, setzte Leon Kochnitzky die Präsentationsform im Museum nicht nur mit dem ästhetischen Vorbild einer modernen Rezeption primitiver Kunst in Beziehung, sondern auch mit der Ablehnung einer früheren, positivistischen Anthropologie zugunsten eines eher am Mythischen orientierten Akzents auf Magie und Psychologie bei der Beschäftigung mit dem primitiven Menschen.

21. Ein gutes Beispiel für die unterschiedliche Bewunderung von Südamerika, Mittelamerika und der Indianerkultur ist die Sammlung von Artikeln in der Sonderausgabe von *DYN* zum Thema der Indianer, Nr. 4–5, 1943–44. Man beachte besonders die Betonung von Themen aus Kosmologie, Mythologie, Astrologie u. a. bei Aufsätzen wie »Totem Art«, »The Enigma of Maya Astronomy« und »New Discoveries in the Temple of the Sun in Palenque«. Zu Veränderungen in der Sicht der Indianer und dem zunehmenden Interesse an Schamanentum und Mystizismus in den dreißiger und vierziger Jahren siehe Jonaitis, A., »Creations of Mystics and Philosophers: The White Man's Perception of Northwest Coast Indian Art from the 1930s to the Present« in *American Indian Culture and Research Journal* 5, Nr. 1, 198[illegible], S. 1–45. Ein weiteres Beispiel für das besondere Interesse an indianischer Kunst in den vierziger Jahren unter-

sucht Ann Gibson in »Painting outside the Paradigm: Indian Space« in *Arts,* Februar 1983, S. 96–103. Es handelt sich dabei um die »Semiologie« oder »indianische Raumauffassung«. Bei den beteiligten Künstlern verband sich Aufgeschlossenheit gegenüber der Kunst der Indianer von der Nordwestküste mit der Bewunderung für einen neuen Raumbegriff, den die moderne Physik erschloß. Diese Verbindung von primitivistischen Interessen und moderner Physik zeigt sich auch bei anderen Autoren und Künstlern der Zeit. Siehe unten Anm. 87.

22. Pollock, J., »Jackson Pollock« in *Arts and Architecture,* Februar 1944, S. 14, zitiert von Sandler in *Triumph,* a.a.O., S. 65.

23. Siehe Hess, T., »Isamu Noguchi '46« in *Art News,* September 1946, S. 34f.

24. Wolfson, V., Katalog der Kootz Gallery, New York, Januar 1947, zitiert von Guilbaut, a.a.O., S. 148.

25. Zu Stamos siehe Pomeroy, R., *Stamos,* New York, o.J. Zu Baziotes siehe Hadler, M., *The Art of William Baziotes,* Diss., Columbia University, 1977; ebenso *William Baziotes: A Retrospective Exhibition,* Newport Beach, Newport Harbor Art Museum, 1978, mit Aufsätzen von Barbara Cavaliere und Mona Hadler; ebenso Cavaliere, B., »An Introduction to the Method of William Baziotes« in *Arts,* April 1977, S. 28–29; und Hadler, M., »William Baziotes: A Contemporary Poet-Painter« in *Arts,* Juni 1977, S. 102–10. Ein weiterer Maler des abstrakten Expressionismus, der sich in seinem Frühwerk zum Primitivismus hingezogen fühlte, war Richard Pousette-Dart; man vergleiche die Untersuchung zu seinen primitivistischen Themen und die Abbildungen seiner frühen, maskenartigen Bilder bei Levin, G., »Richard Pousette-Dart's Emergence as an Abstract Expressionist« in *Arts,* März 1980, S. 125–29.

26. Lévy-Bruhl, L., *Les Fonctions mentales dans les sociétés inférieures,* 1910. Englische Ausgabe u.d.T. *How Natives Think,* London 1926. Darin werden die positivistischen Theorien des 19. Jahrhunderts zurückgewiesen, besonders die von Tylor, der in dem Bedürfnis nach Erklärungen oder in praktischen Zwängen die Ursache der Stammespraktiken sah. Lévy-Bruhl ging von der durch Dürkheim hervorgehobenen Bedeutung »kollektiver Darstellungen« aus und behauptete, daß »Mythen, Bestattungsriten, Anbauweisen und die Ausübung der Magie . . . eine Reaktion des primitiven Menschen auf kollektive Bedürfnisse und Gefühle darstellen, die tief und gewaltig und von zwingender Kraft sind« (S. 25). Lévy-Bruhl stellt fest, daß »ihre geistige Aktivität zu wenig differenziert sei, um Ideen oder Abbildungen von Gegenständen getrennt von den Emotionen und Leidenschaften zu betrachten, die sie hervorrufen oder durch die sie hervorgerufen sind« (S. 36). Da »die umgebende Realität des primitiven Menschen selbst mythisch ist, ist für die primitive Mentalität der Unterschied zwischen belebten und unbelebten Dingen nicht genauso wichtig wie für uns« (S. 40). »Es ist keine Frage der *Assoziation.* Die mystischen Eigenschaften, die Dinge und Wesen erfüllen, sind wesentlicher Bestandteil der Vorstellung des primitiven Menschen, der in ihnen ein einheitliches Ganzes sieht« (S. 44–45). Siehe besonders das Kapitel »The Law of Participation«, S. 68ff. Zu Jungs verwandten Vorstellungen eines undifferenzierten primitiven Denkens siehe »The Psychology of the Child Archetype« in *The Collected Works of C. G. Jung,* Bd. 9, Teil 1, New York 1959, vor allem S. 153–54. Solche Vorstellungen trifft man in den vierziger Jahren in Aussagen der Künstler häufig an. Frederick Kiesler etwa sagte zu seinem Entwurf für Peggy Guggenheims Galerie »Art of This Century«, daß er in der Zeit zurückreiche, »um die physischen und geistigen Grenzen aufzuheben, die die Menschen von der Kunst, mit der sie leben, trennen. Er strebt nach einer Einheit von Vision und Realität, wie sie in primitiven Zeiten bestand, als scheinbar gegensätzliche Erfahrungen harmonierten, als Gott und die Darstellung von Gott, der Dämon und das Bild des Dämon gleich unmittelbar und real waren . . .«, *VVV,* Nr. 2–3, 1943, S. 76. Allgemeines zu Kieslers Ideal einer »ursprünglichen Einheit« bei Goodman, C., »Frederick Kiesler: Designs for Peggy Guggenheim's Art of This Century Gallery« in *Arts,* Juni 1977, S. 90–95, und Lader, M. P., »Peggy Guggenheim's Art of This Century: The Surrealist Milieu and the American Avant-Garde, 1942–1947«, Diss., University of Delaware, 1983, vor allem S. 114.

27. Newman, B., Einleitung zu *Stamos,* New York, Betty Parsons Gallery, 1947, zitiert bei Hobbs, a.a.O., S. 26, Anm. 5.

28. Rubin, W., »Pollock as Jungian Illustrator: The Limits of Psychological Criticism« in *Art in America,* Dezember 1979, S. 86. Zur Idee der Verwandtschaft zwischen Kunst und Natur stellte eine Reihe von Epigrammen in *DYN,* Nr. 1, April-Mai 1942, S. 27, unter dem Titel »Sehen und Darstellen« das Prinzip dar, das Pollock vertrat: das Prinzip, »nicht nach der Natur zu malen, sondern sich an den großen Rhythmen der Natur zu orientieren, nicht ihren zufälligen Erscheinungen zu folgen, sondern allgemeine Vorgänge der Natur aufzugreifen«. Smith, D., »Second Thoughts on Sculpture« in *College Art Journal 13,* Nr. 3, Frühjahr 1954, S. 203–07, griff diesen Gedanken auf, der in Pollocks Aussage und Newmans Beschreibung von Stamos' Werk, siehe Anm. 27 oben, angesprochen wird. »Der Künstler ist jetzt selbst Natur, sein Werk ist die totale Kunst. Es gibt kein vermittelndes Objekt . . . und sein Werk kommt dem Totalen, Letzten näher. Die neue Stellung des Künstlers läßt sich mit der des primitiven Menschen vergleichen. Er ist nicht der wissenschaftliche Betrachter der Natur. Er ist Teil der Natur. Er ist die Natur im Kunstwerk«, zitiert bei Rose, B., *Readings in American Art since 1900,* New York 1975, S. 250.

29. Eine Untersuchung der Vorbilder, die Rothko prägten, vor allem bei Polcari, S., »The Intellectual Roots of Abstract Expressionism: Mark Rothko« in *Arts,* September 1979, S. 124–34; Rosenblum, R., »Notes on Rothko's Surrealist Years« in *Mark Rothko,* New York, Pace Gallery, 1981, und Ward, J., »The Function of Science as Myth in the Evolution of Mark Rothko's Abstract Style«, unveröffentlichte Abschlußarbeit, Institute of Fine Arts, New York University, 1977. Ward untersuchte den Lehrplan und die Schriften während Rothkos Jahren in Yale und zeigt mögliche Verbindungen zwischen einzelnen Textillustrationen und Rothkos Formenwelt auf.

30. Rothko, »The Romantics were Prompted . . .« in *Possibilities,* Nr. 1, Winter 1947–48, S. 84.

31. Rosenblum, a.a.O., S. 8, vergleicht *Langsamer Strudel am Rande der See* □ 964 mit einem NAVAJO-Sandgemälde bei der Ausstellung des Museum of Modern Art im Jahre 1941 über »Indian Art of the United States«. Sandler, in *Triumph,* a.a.O., S. 179, schreibt: »Obwohl die hybriden Formen in Rothkos mystisch inspirierten Bildern abstrakt sind, zeigen sie Anklänge an sichtbare Phänomene – Organismen im Wasser oder Geräte, die in primitiven Ritualen verwendet werden.« In einer Fußnote äußert sich Sandler über den Vergleich von Bildern Rothkos mit »Schilden, Bögen und anderen Gegenständen des primitiven Lebens«, den William Seitz durchführte, in »Abstract Expressionist Painting in America«, Diss., Princeton 1955.

32. In dem Interview »The Portrait and the Modern Artist«, siehe Anm. 2 oben, sagte Rothko, daß die Mythen der alten Zeit »Symbole der Ängste und Motivationen des primitiven Menschen sind, gleich in welchem Land oder welcher Zeit sie entstanden. Sie mögen griechisch, aztekisch, isländisch oder ägyptisch sein, sie unterscheiden sich nur im Detail, aber nie in der Substanz. Und unsere moderne Psychologie zeigt, daß sie noch in unseren Träumen, unserem Dialekt, unserer Kunst fortbestehen trotz aller Veränderungen der äußeren Lebensbedingungen.« Zitiert bei Sandler, *Triumph,* a.a.O., S. 63.

33. Siehe die Interpretation von Wasser als Symbol in der Mythologie, in Jung, C. G., »Archetypes of the Collective Unconscious«, 1934, in *The Collected Works of C. G. Jung,* Bd. 9, Teil 1, S. 17–22.

34. In »The Romantics Were Prompted . . .« gab Rothko einen weiten Bedeutungsbereich seiner Formen an:
»Über Formen:
Sie sind einzigartige Elemente in einer einzigartigen Situation.
Sie sind Organismen mit eigenem Willen und einem Wunsch nach Selbstbehauptung.
Sie bewegen sich mit innerer Freiheit, ohne mit der Welt in Harmonie stehen oder verletzen zu müssen, was wahrscheinlich in ihrer Nähe ist.
Sie lassen sich mit keiner bestimmten Seherfahrung verbinden, aber sie lassen das Prinzip und die Leidenschaft der Organismen erkennen.«

35. Graham, *System and Dialectics of Art,* a.a.O., S. 19. Die Vorstellung kann teilweise von Freud abgeleitet sein. In der Einleitung zur *Traumdeutung* schreibt er: »Es gibt zwei Formen von [archaischer] Vorgeschichte, in die uns die Beschäftigung mit dem Traum zurückführt – sie führt uns einerseits in die individuelle Vorgeschichte, die Kindheit, andererseits – insofern als jedes Individuum in abgekürzter Form irgendwie die Entwicklung der Menschheit nachvollzieht – auch in die phylogenetische Vorgeschichte . . . Ich finde, zum Beispiel, daß symbolische Zusammenhänge, die der Mensch nie durch Lernen erworben hat, genau als phylogenetisches Erbe betrachtet werden wollen.« Auszug aus *The Standard Edition of the Complete Psychological Works of Sigmund Freud,* Bd. 15, S. 199, zitiert von Sulloway, F. J., in *Freud, Biologist of the Mind,* New York 1979, S. 338. Diesen Hinweis genauso wie weitere, wertvolle Informationen zur Verbindung zwischen Mikrobiologie und der Symbolisierung des Unbewußten verdanke ich einem unveröffentlichten Manuskript von Weiss, J., »Microbiology in Art: Symbolism to Biomorphism«, Institute of Fine Arts, New York University, 1983.

36. Eine ausführliche Untersuchung der Vorbilder dieser Kompositionen mit Bildzeichen bei

MacNaughton, a.a.O., S. 32–35. Zu Klee siehe Kagan, A., »Paul Klee's Influence on American Painting: New York School« in *Arts*, Juni 1975, S. 54–59, und *Arts*, September 1975, S. 84–90. Gottlieb bestätigte seine Aussage, daß die Kompositionseinteilungen der Schriftzeichen seine Vorliebe für italienische Malerei wiedergeben, in einem Interview mit Martin Friedman, August 1962 (S. 5 des Manuskripts im Archiv der Adolph und Esther Gottlieb Foundation, New York). Torres-Garcías Interesse an altamerikanischen Kulturen wird erklärt in seinem Buch *Metafisica de le Prehistoria Indoamericana,* Montevideo 1939.

37. In einer Besprechung der Ausstellung in der Galerie Wildenstein (wo auch ein Werk von George L. K. Morris gezeigt wurde, *Indianische Komposition*, das wirkliche Zweige, Rinde und Nägel enthielt) berichtete A. Z. Kruse vom *Brooklyn Eagle* am 24. Mai 1942: »Adolph Gottlieb zeigt eine Vorliebe für modernen französischen Symbolismus und indianische Themen und bietet eine sorgfältig durchdachte Verbindung beider Richtungen.« In einem nicht näher bestimmbaren Zeitungsausschnitt, jetzt im Archiv der Gottlieb Foundation, mit einer Besprechung derselben Ausstellung meint Carlyle Burrows am 31. Mai 1942, daß von den abstrakten Bildern der Ausstellung »Adolph Gottliebs Alaska-Motiv mit Anklängen an indianische Kultur die reichste Erfindung, was ihren Symbolgehalt betrifft, darstellt . . .« Bedanken möchte ich mich bei Sanford Hirsch, der mich auf diese Zeitungsausschnitte hingewiesen und meine Forschungen im Archiv der Gottlieb Foundation unterstützt hat.

38. Zum Kauf der Decke siehe MacNaughton, a.a.O., S. 38. Das Schlüsseldokument zu Gottliebs früherer Wertschätzung alter amerikanischer Kunst während seines Aufenthalts im Südwesten Amerikas ist sein Brief an Paul Bodin vom März 1938, jetzt im Archiv der Gottlieb Foundation; der Künstler erwähnt darin das »State Museum, das eine wundervolle Sammlung indianischer Objekte besitzt«.

39. Cassirer, E., *Language and Myth,* New York 1946, S. 98.

40. Zu Mirós Interesse an primitiven Zeichensystemen siehe vor allem Stitch, S., *Joan Miró: The Development of a Sign Language,* St. Louis, Washington University Gallery of Art, 1980, ebenso Levin, G., »Miró, Kandinsky, and the Genesis of Abstract Expressionism« in Hobbs and Levin, a.a.O., S. 27–40. Zu Klee siehe Smith Pierce, J., *Paul Klee and Primitive Art,* New York 1976; ebenso Kagan, A., »Paul Klee's Influence on American Painting«, a.a.O. Gottliebs Interesse an primitiven Schriftformen wurde untersucht von Wilkin, K., *Adolph Gottlieb: Pictographs,* Edmonton, Edmonton Art Gallery, 1977. Ihr Anhang führt einen Artikel des *American Magazine of Art* vom Juni 1935 an, mit dem Titel »Phases of Calligraphy«, in dem moderne europäische Kunst mit Hieroglyphen, Felsbildern und Felsinschriften verglichen werden.

41. Gottlieb in Janis, S., *Abstract and Surrealist Art in America*, New York 1944, S. 119.

42. Gottlieb, *Untitled Edition – MKR's Art Outlook,* Nr. 6, Dezember 1945, S. 4, 6, zitiert bei Sandler, *Triumph,* S. 196, und bei MacNaugthton, a.a.O., S. 34.

43. Rosenblum, a.a.O., S. 9, behandelt Rothkos Verbindungen zum Symbolismus nicht nur bezüglich Redon, sondern in umfassenderer Weise. Siehe auch die Untersuchung zu mikrobiologischen Strukturen in Rothkos Werk bei Ward, a.a.O.

44. Siehe die Untersuchung dieses Briefes bei MacNaughton, a.a.O., S. 40–41, vollständig wiedergegeben im Anhang, S. 169. Der Brief wurde von Gottlieb, Rothko und Newman unterschrieben. Sie verteidigen darin ihre Arbeit gegenüber einer verständnislosen Kritik Edward Alden Jewells in der *Times*, bekräftigen ihren Glauben an eine zeitlose Gültigkeit »archaischer« Symbole und heben ihre »geistige Verwandtschaft zu primitiver und archaischer Kunst« hervor.

45. Über die Idee des Primitivismus und ihres Zusammenhangs mit der Tendenz zu reduktiv klärender Vereinfachung siehe Gibson, A., »Regression and Color in Abstract Expressionism: Barnett Newman, Mark Rothko, and Clyfford Still« in *Arts,* März 1981, S. 144–53.

46. Siehe Newmans Vergleich zwischen ägyptischer und griechischer Formauffassung in Hess, a.a.O., S. 42.

47. Zum Nachweis von Newmans speziellem Interesse am Goldenen Schnitt und einer Bibliographie von Arbeiten Cooks, Hambridges, Ghykas u. a., die diese Gedanken unterstützen, siehe Cavaliere, B., »Barnett Newman's *Vir Heroicus Sublimis:* Building the Idea Complex« in *Arts,* Januar 1981, S. 144–52. Zu Tony Smiths Anteil an Proportionstheorien und Zahlenmystik siehe den Vortrag von Margi Cohen Conrads »Mathematical Systems in Tony Smith's Sculpture«, Goodson Symposium, Whitney Museum of American Art, 1977. Zu einer Zeit, als Smith und Newman von solchen Theorien fasziniert waren, kritisierte sie Milton Brown, siehe »Twentieth-Century Nostrums: Pseudo-Scientific Theory in American Painting« in *Magazine of Art* 41, Nr. 3, März 1948, S. 98–101.

48. Richardson, B., *Barnett Newman: The Complete Drawings, 1944–1969,* The Baltimore Museum of Art, 1979, S. 20–22.

49. Persönliche Mitteilung Herbert Ferbers an den Autor im November 1983.

50. Die Theorie, daß Kultur tiefen Ängsten des primitiven Menschen entspringe, hat eine lange Tradition, siehe meine Untersuchung zu Gauguins Beschäftigung mit tahitischem Aberglauben, S. 207. Newman legte besonderen Nachdruck auf seine Vorstellung, daß »alle primitive Kunst . . . aus der Angst entstand«, siehe hierzu die Ausführungen von Hess, a.a.O., S. 43. Ebenso die einfühlsame Abhandlung über diese Auffassung primitiver Mentalität im weiteren Kontext von Newmans Interesse am Mystizismus, ebda., passim.

51. Newman, »The First Man Was an Artist«, a. a. O., zitiert bei Sandler, *Triumph, a. a. O., S.* 187. Zum Hintergrund von Newmans antimaterialistischer Vorstellung über das Primat des künstlerischen Impulses im Leben des frühen Menschen siehe Anm. 9 oben.

52. Dubuffet, J., »Anticultural Positions«, Notizen für einen Vortrag im Arts Club of Chicago am 20. Dezember 1951, in Franzke, A. (Hrsg.), *Jean Dubuffet,* übersetzt von Joachim Neugroschel, Basel 1976. Mein Dank gilt Phyllis Hattis, die mir diese spezielle Übersetzung zugänglich machte.

53. Gauguin, P., *Cahiers pour Aline,* Paris 1963: »C'est encore à Mazas où se trouve le génie d'une langue; là un mot nouveau est créé et compris à tout jamais. A l'Académie on ne peut procéder que par étymologie et il faut un siècle pour adopter une nouvelle expression «

54. Siehe die Zusammenfassung von Interpretationen dieses Bildes durch Robertson, Alloway, Read und Langhorne in Rubin, »Pollock as Jungian Illustrator: The Limits of Psychological Criticism« in *Art in America,* November 1979, S. 102–05. Zur Frage, ob der betreffende Kopfschmuck eine männliche oder weibliche Person darstellt, siehe Elizabeth Langhornes Stellungnahme zu Rubins Aussagen in *Art in America,* Oktober 1980, S. 62.

55. Zum Einfluß John Grahams auf Pollocks Primitivismus siehe Irving Sandlers Brief in *Art in America,* Oktober 1980, S. 57–58; ebenso Anm. 4 oben.

56. Einen vollständigen Überblick zu den Jungschen Interpretationen von Pollocks Ikonographie gibt Rubin, »Pollock as Jungian Illustrator . . .«, Teil 1 und 2, a.a.O. Zu den Reaktionen auf Rubins Thesen siehe Anm. 54 und 55 oben.

57. Gordon, D., »Pollock's *Bird,* or How Jung Did Not Offer Much Help in Myth-Making« in *Art in America,* Oktober 1980, S. 43–53.

58. Rubin, »Pollock as Jungian Illustrator . . .«, Teil 1 und 2, a.a.O.; siehe ebenso Rubins Antwort auf Langhorne und andere in *Art in America,* Oktober 1980, S. 65–67.

59. Diese Gedanken zu Pollock, Picasso und dem Primitivismus verdanke ich einer freundlichen Mitteilung William Rubins, der sie in seiner demnächst erscheinenden Monographie über Pollock behandeln wird.

60. Siehe etwa die Untersuchung Bryan Robertsons in *Jackson Pollock,* New York 1960 S. 82–83.

61. Sandler bemerkt: »Es gab möglicherweise einen Einfluß der Navajo-Indianer auf Pollock Nicht weil sie ihm das »dripping«-Verfahren zeigten, sondern weil sie ihre Bilder am Ende der rituellen Zeremonie auslöschten. Die magische Bedeutung beim Akt des Malens war für sie wichtiger als die Herstellung eines Bildes. Ihre Einstellung mag Pollock bestärkt haben, sich von konventionellen Malauffassungen zu befreien.« *Triumph,* a.a.O., S. 113.

62. Siehe Rubin in »Pollock as Jungian Illustrator . . .«, Teil 1 und 2, a.a.O.

63. Sandler, *Triumph,* a.a.O., S. 106, zitiert einen langen Abschnitt aus Grahams *System and Dialectics of Art* über die Vorstellung, daß der primitive Künstler mythische Bezüge und Spontanität umfasse.

64. Pollocks Methode des Handabdrucks hat in der modernen Kunst zahlreiche Vorläufer. MacNaughton behandelt einen davon, Gottliebs *Schwarze Hand* von 1943 [illegible] 90 und eine Aquatinta Picassos von 1936, die einen Handabdruck zeigt. Hobbs, a.a.O., S. 10, 25, Anm. 3, bezieht sich ebenfalls auf Gottlieb und nennt weitere mögliche Vorbilder für Pollock im Werk von Miró (Umschlag des Katalogs zu Mirós Ausstellung in der Galerie Pierre Matisse, 1936) und von Hans Hofmann (*The Third Hand,* 1947). Meyer Schapiro behandelte Pollocks Handabdruck in einer BBC-Sendung, veröffentlicht unter dem Titel »Younger American Painters of Today« in *The Listener,* 26. Januar 1955, S. 146–47. Auch Charles Stuckey befaßte sich mit Pollocks Handabdruck und möglichen Vorbildern, »Another

Side of Jackson Pollock« in *Art in America,* Dezember 1977, S. 80–91. Den Hinweis auf die vorliegende Abbildung □ 985 aus einem Buch über Höhlenmalerei, das im Inventar von Pollocks Bibliothek aufgeführt war, erhielt der Autor aus einem Seminarbericht von Claude Cernuschi über Pollock und den Primitivismus, Institute of Fine Arts, New York University. Der Handabdruck offenbart in seinen möglichen Doppelbezügen zum okkulten Symbolismus eine spezielle Mischung aus Schicksal und Freiheit. Hier ist die Chiromantie relevant, mit der sich die Surrealisten zeitweise beschäftigten, und der Prozeß, besonders was Automatismus und instinktiven Ausdruck der Person betrifft, der durch kein Darstellungssystem eingeschränkt wird.

65. Zur Entstehung des Pollock-Mythos siehe William Rubin, »The Myth and the Paintings« in »Jackson Pollock and the Modern Tradition«, Teil 1, *Artforum,* Februar 1967, S. 14–22; zum weiteren theoretischen und politischen Zusammenhang dieser Aussagen siehe Guilbaut, vor allem Kapitel 3 und 4.

66. Rose, B., »Hans Namuth's Photographs and the Jackson Pollock Myth – Part One: Media Impact and the Failure of Criticism« in *Arts,* März 1979, S. 112–16.

67. Siehe Sandlers Aussagen zu »Ekstase« und »Angst« in der »dripping«-Malerei in *Triumph,* a.a.O., S. 112. Auch Rubin hebt das »ganze Gefühlsspektrum« in Pollocks »dripping«-Malerei hervor, »die viel mehr an Leidenschaft, Freude, Überschwang, Ekstase, Lust, Ernst, Zärtlichkeit, Leiden, Anmut, Zartheit und zuweilen sogar Charme enthalten«, in »Jackson Pollock and the Modern Tradition«, a.a.O., S. 17.

68. Lipton, S., »Some Notes on My Work« in *Magazine of Art 40,* Nr. 7, November 1947, S. 264, zitiert bei Lubar, R. S., in »Prehistoricism in Sculpture, 1940–1955: David Smith, Theodore Roszak, Seymour Lipton«, unveröffentlichtes Manuskript, Institute of Fine Arts, New York University, 1983.

69. Dehner, D., zitiert von Wilkin, K. in *David Smith: The Formative Years,* Edmonton Art Gallery, 1981, S. 9.

70. Krauss, R., *The Sculpture of David Smith: A Catalogue Raisonné,* New York 1977, S. 4.

71. Siehe die Untersuchung zu *Pillar of Sunday* bei Fry, E., *David Smith,* New York 1969, S. 43, und bei Wilkin, a.a.O., S. 14. Eine ganz ähnliche Skulptur und Aussage bei Paalen, W., *Paysage totémique de mon enfance,* 1937, abgebildet in *DYN,* Nr. 3, Herbst 1942, S. 29. Beide Arbeiten wurden vermutlich durch die flügelartigen Vorsprünge bei Stammespfählen der Nordwestküste angeregt.

72. Siehe Krauss, R., *Terminal Iron Works,* Cambridge 1971. Sie versteht das Konzept des Totemismus, besonders wie in Freuds *Totem und Tabu* dargelegt, als Verbindung zwischen der sexuellen Ikonographie in Smiths Frühwerk und einer aktuellen formalen und erkenntnistheoretischen Problematik der »Wahrnehmung und Abneigung«, die ihrer Meinung nach für dessen Auseinandersetzung mit moderner Skulptur zentral war. Krauss stützt sich zum großen Teil auf die eigene Lesart der Fragen moderner Skulptur und auf ihre eigene formale Analyse der Rezeption von Smiths Skulptur durch den Betrachter. Obwohl sich Smith in Aussagen über sein Werk verschiedene Male auf das Primitive bezog, gibt er keine Hinweise auf eine psychologische und anthropologische Auffassung von der Rolle des Totems, die die Theorie von Krauss unterstützen würde. Einige seiner Assoziationen der primitiven Weltsicht mit der eidetischen Vorstellung (siehe Anm. 75 unten) lassen außerdem vermuten, daß er mit dem Primitiven nicht die Erfahrung einer durch Tabusysteme eingeschränkten und unterteilten Welt verband. Vielmehr betrachtete er die primitive Mentalität als Sitz einer höheren Wahrnehmungsform, zu der eher eine umfassendere als begrenztere Weise der »Inbesitznahme« der Welt durch Erkennen gehörte, und als den Ort unentfremdeter Gemeinschaft mit der Natur, siehe Anm. 28 oben.

73. Zu den Assoziationen mit Überlebenskampf siehe Fry, a.a.O., S. 63; Krauss, R., a.a.O., S. 126; und Wilkin, K., a.a.O., S. 14–15. Hilfreich war dem Autor auch das unveröffentlichte Manuskript von Lubar, R. S., a.a.O., siehe Anm. 68 oben.

74. Dieses Blatt wird als »Page from a Willard Gallery exhibition announcement« abgebildet bei McCoy, G. (Hrsg.), *David Smith,* New York 1973, S. 71.

75. Smith, D., »The Language Is Image« in *Arts and Architecture,* Februar 1952, S. 21.

76. Über eidetische Bildvorstellungen siehe Jaensch, E. R., *Die Eidetik und die typologische Forschungsmethode,* und ders., *Eidetische Anlage und kindliches Seelenleben,* Leipzig 1934. In dem erstgenannten Werk schrieb Jaensch: »Die eidetische Forschung hat bereits gezeigt, daß die Vorstellung des Kindes nicht mit der Vorstellungsstruktur des Logikers, sondern mit der des Künstlers die größte Ähnlichkeit aufweist. Es gibt in der Tat zahlreiche Künstlerpersönlichkeiten, die beständig Charakteristika einer jugendlichen Entwicklungsstufe beibehalten«, S. 47. Aldrich, C. R., *The Primitive Mind and Modern Civilization,* 1931, Neuauflage New York 1969, bezieht sich auf die Arbeiten von Jaensch und anderen. Eine seiner Aussagen zur Vorstellungswelt des primitiven Menschen faßt viele der Meinungen zusammen, die in Äußerungen so unterschiedlicher Künstler wie Gauguin, Newman und Smith wiederkehren: »Die primitive Gesellschaft fühlt sich jederzeit und unvermeidlich der Gefahr ausgesetzt . . . Der Wilde gleicht einem Kind, das von frühester Kindheit an mit Gespenstergeschichten gefüttert wurde und meint, in einem von Gespenstern heimgesuchten Haus zu leben. Die Welt des Wilden wird wirklich heimgesucht; denn er hat nicht den Kontakt mit seinem Unbewußten verloren, zumindest nicht in dem Ausmaß wie der zivilisierte Mensch. Wenn er daher an seine tote Mutter denkt, glaubt er das Bild der Mutter aus seiner Erinnerung so lebendig vor sich zu sehen, daß es ihm wie die Erscheinung einer Vision, wie ein Geist vorkommt. Vermutlich ist dies eine Form der *image eidetique,* die jüngst die Aufmerksamkeit der Psychologen erregt hat«, S. 98–99. Aldrich zitiert ferner die Arbeit von E. Tripp über experimentelle Erzeugung eidetischer Nachbilder, indem man den Blick auf Gegenstände mit neutralem Hintergrund konzentriert, S. 99. (Smith bezog sich im Grunde gleichzeitig auf eidetische Vorstellungen und Nachbilder als identische Phänomene, siehe McCoy, G., »The Artist and Nature« in *David Smith,* S. 117. Man kann annehmen, daß die anhand von Arbeitsphotos der fünfziger Jahre dokumentierte Methode Smiths, die Silhouetten der Skulpturen gegen einen eigens hergerichteten neutralen Hintergrund zu stellen und so zu studieren, durch die Ansicht, zwischen eidetischer und nachbildnerischer Wahrnehmung bestehe ein Zusammenhang, ermutigt wurde.) Aldrich verbindet außerdem das eidetische Phänomen mit der Jungschen Idee einer angeborenen kollektiven Erinnerung und nennt die »Ähnlichkeit dieser Produkte [das heißt der Halluzinationen eidetischer Wahrnehmung] bei Menschen unterschiedlichster Kulturen« als »Beweis, daß die Grundzüge der Psyche in einer bestimmten Tiefe, jenseits einer rein persönlichen Erfahrung bei allen Menschen gleich sind. Die eidetischen Phänomene verweisen auf ein ursprüngliches Entwicklungsstadium, das weit niedriger war als jeder heute noch existierende primitive Entwicklungsstand, als der Mensch noch nicht das tatsächlich Gesehene von dem, was ihm lebendig im Gedächtnis war, unterscheiden konnte«, S. 102. Verbindungen solcher Ideen zu jenen, die Gauguin in Arbeiten wie *Der Geist der Toten wacht* □ 249 anregten, sind ganz direkt. Mit dem Interesse am eidetischen Bild tauchen viele der Themen wieder auf, die Gauguin beschäftigten – die Unabhängigkeit des Geistes von der Versklavung durch die Eindrücke der Wahrnehmung, die Ursprünge der Darstellung in innerlich erzeugter Vorstellung. Kurz vor dem Kapitel über »Darstellung«, in dem eidetische Phänomene behandelt werden, legt Aldrich das theoretische Konzept fest: »Die Frage, ob Wahrnehmung nur eine fast mechanische Reaktion auf eine Stimulation der Sinne darstellt oder ob sie voll subjektiver Elemente wie Wert und Bedeutung ist, ist äußerst wichtig. Es ist offensichtlich, je subjektiver die menschliche Wahrnehmung ist, desto mehr ist die sichtbare Welt der Gegenstände, in der wir leben, eine von uns selbst geschaffene Welt«, S. 57. Smiths Interesse für eidetische Phänomene stand jedoch vermutlich den Interessen der Surrealisten näher, die in dieser Form von Halluzination die Möglichkeit einer gleichzeitigen Vereinnahmung und Umgestaltung der Welt sahen. In dem Aufsatz »Le Message automatique« in *Minotaure,* Dezember 1933, bezog sich André Breton auf Forschungen Jaenschs und anderer über eidetische Phänomene. Diese Experimente sollten beweisen, sagte er, daß »Wahrnehmung und Darstellung – vom Erwachsenen gewöhnlich als diametral entgegengesetzt empfunden – nur als die getrennten Produkte einer *einzigen, ursprünglichen Fähigkeit* verstanden werden sollten, deren wir uns im eidetischen Bild bewußt werden und von der wir Spuren im Primitiven und im Kind entdecken«, S. 65. Automatismus, meinte Breton, führe zurück zu diesem »Zustand der Gnade«, in dem Subjektivität und Objektivität eins waren. Mein Dank gilt Jeffrey Weiss, der mich auf Bretons Artikel hingewiesen hat.

77. Smith, »The Language Is Image«, a. a. O., S. 33.

78. Newman, »The Sublime Is Now« in *Tiger's Eye,* Nr. 6, Dezember 1948, S. 53, zitiert von Sandler, *Triumph,* a. a. O., S. 149.

79. Polcari, S., »The Intellectual Roots of Abstract Expressionism: Clyfford Still« in *Art International,* Mai–Juni 1982.

80. In einem Brief vom 24. November 1940 an seine Schwester schrieb Gorky: »Ästhetik oder höchste Kunst sind das, was empfindlich auf komplexe Dinge reagiert und uns diese Komplexität dadurch besser verstehen läßt. Deshalb sehe ich in primitiver Kunst keine hohe Kunst, statt dessen eine interessante Kunst. Große Kunst entsteht meiner Ansicht nach aus Kom-

plexität, aus dem Zusammenprall vieler neuer und gegensätzlicher Ideen. Primitive Kunst resultiert weitgehend aus Isolation und aus der Isolation kann, da ihr die alles umfassende Erfahrung fehlt, keine Ästhetik oder hohe Kunst entstehen. Fortgeschrittene Kulturen bieten wegen ihrer komplexen Gegensätze das größte Potential für große Kunst«, Mooradian, K., *The Armenian Correspondence of Arshile Gorky: 1937–148,* Chicago 1978, S. 265.

81. Kahler, E., »The Persistence of Myth« in *Chimera* IV, Nr. 6, Frühjahr 1946, S. 9.

82. Ebenda. Zur Diskussion über die Angemessenheit des Mythos in moderner Kunst siehe Lloyds Leitartikel in *Art Front,* zitiert in Anm. 15 oben, und Rosenberg, H., »Breton – A Dialogue« in *View,* Reihe 2, Nr. 2, Mai 1942.

83. Die Vorstellung, daß zwischen dem Individuum und der Kultur Analogien bestehen, war, speziell unter dem Gesichtspunkt der Integration als Maßstab für Gesundheit, ein Hauptaspekt von Ruth Benedicts einflußreichem anthropologischen Werk *Patterns of Culture,* 1934, Neuauflage mit einem Vorwort von Margaret Mead, Boston 1959. Der antirassistische Tenor in der Anthropologie Franz Boas' und seiner Studenten scheint sich hier genau gegen die rassistischen Kulturvorstellungen zu richten, die damals in Deutschland aufkamen. Siehe auch Boas, F., *Anthropology and Modern Life,* New York 1928, wo allein ein Blick auf die Kapitelüberschriften genügt, um seine Auseinandersetzung mit rassistischen Ideologien zu zeigen.

84. Zur neodarwinistischen Synthese aus Mendelscher Vererbungslehre und Vorstellungen natürlicher Auslese durch sozialen Wettbewerb siehe Mayr, E., *The Growth of Biological Thought,* Cambridge 1982, S. 566–70.

85. Aus Wolfgang Paalens Einleitung zur indianischen Sonderausgabe von *DYN,* Nr. 4 und 5, 1943–44, zitiert von Maurer, E., »In Quest of the Myth: An Investigation of the Relationships between Surrealism and Primitivism«, Diss., University of Pennsylvania, 1974, S. 327.

86. Jackson Pollock in einem Interview mit *Arts and Architecture,* Februar 1944, S. 14, Nachdruck bei Tuchman, M., *The New York School: The First Generation,* New York, o. J., S. 117.

87. Kahler, a. a. O., S. 9–10.

88. Zum Einfluß der Atomkriegs-Diskussion auf die Vorstellung der New Yorker Schule vom Primitiven und zur Verbindung von Primitivismus und wissenschaftlicher Gesinnung im Interesse der Künstler für das American Museum of Natural History siehe Weiss, J., »Science and Primitivism: A Fearful Symmetry in the Early New York School« in *Arts,* März 1983, S. 81–87.

☐ 1001 *Walter de Maria, ›Blitzfeld‹ (Lightning Field), Quemado, Neu-Mexiko, 1971–77, 1,6 x 1 km; 400 in einem rechtwinkligen Gitter angeordnete Masten aus Edelstahl, durchschnittliche Höhe 6,27 m. Dieses große Mastengitter in einem hügeligen Wüstengebiet dient als Bühne für sensationelle meteorologische Darbietungen. Das streng angeordnete Gitter ist charakteristisch für die zeitgenössische rationale Ästhetik; das Gefühl für den Ort und besonders für die Beziehung Erde–Himmel weist jedoch Bezüge auf zu primitiven Stätten und Systemen der Naturverehrung.*

Kirk Varnedoe

Zeitgenössische Tendenzen

Seit dem 2. Weltkrieg hat sich das Gleichgewicht zwischen Ideen und Objekten im künstlerischen Primitivismus verschoben. Für Picasso, Miró, Ernst und die anderen führenden Künstler Europas vor dem Krieg entstanden Vorstellungen über das Primitive aus der Begegnung mit konkreten Beispielen der Stammeskunst. Die Generation der abstrakten Expressionisten jedoch zog eine weitergefaßte, synthetische Idee des Primitiven vor. Ihre Sicht (wie im vorhergehenden Kapitel besprochen) wandte sich dem Geist der Mythen und der Magie mehr zu als bestimmten Einzelphänomenen und fand einen vollendeten Ausdruck in Formen der Abstraktion, die keine offensichtliche Verbindung mit Stammesstilen zeigten. Eine noch deutlichere Tendenz, das Primitive unter eher begrifflichen als konkreten Bedingungen zu sehen, war seit den späten 60er Jahren sichtbar geworden. Werke der Land Art wie Robert Smithsons *Spiral-Mole* von 1970 □ 1003, der Performance wie die Rituale von Joseph Beuys □ 1037 und zahllose andere zeitgenössische Werke verdanken ihre Gestalt nicht der primitiven Malerei oder Skulptur, sondern dem Strukturgefüge von prähistorischen und eingeborenen Gesellschaften, den Vorstellungen über die Mechanismen primitiven Denkens und Glaubens oder kollektiven Ausdrucksformen wie Architektur und Tanz. Untergegangene religiöse Systeme, neue Theorien über primitives Bewußtsein und rätselhafte Monumente wie Stonehenge □ 1002 haben das einzelne Objekt als wichtigste künstlerische Quelle für primitivistische Künstler heute weitgehend verdrängt.[1]

Diese Interessenverlagerung scheint aber die Affinitäten zwischen zeitgenössischer und primitiver Kunst nicht vermindert zu haben. Im Gegenteil, die Verbindungen scheinen noch vielgestaltiger und in einiger Hinsicht tiefgreifender zu sein als in der frühen Moderne – aber in Form und Bedeutung sind sie ganz anders. Die Avantgarde unseres Jahrhunderts führte, bildhaft gesprochen, die Stammeskunst aus den ethnologischen und naturhistorischen Museen heraus; die neuen Primitivisten haben die westliche Kunst in genau die gleichen Bereiche zurückgestoßen. Robert Smithson, Joseph Beuys, Nancy Graves □ 1031, 1033, 1034, Charles Simonds und viele andere Künstler aus den vergangenen zwei Jahrzehnten haben eine Kunst geschaffen, die sich direkt auf die Ausstellung naturgeschichtlicher Museen bezieht und sowohl von den Methoden als auch von den Gegenständen anthropologischer und paläontologischer Forschungen zeugt.[2] In solchen Arbeiten scheint der Primitivismus zu seinem Ausgangspunkt zurückgekehrt zu sein: vom Objekt ohne Kontext zum Kontext ohne Objekt. Simonds' kleine Zivilisationen, die Lehrdioramen zum Verwechseln ähnlich sind □ 1035, bilden den Gegenpol zu Picassos Anfängen, als er afrikanische Skulpturen aus ihrer didaktischen Präsentation im Trocadéro herausholte.

Im Zentrum dieser Änderungen steht ein neuer Typ von Künstler und eine umfassendere Vorstellung von moderner Kunst. In den 60er Jahren begann eine neue Generation von vorwiegend bürgerlichen, akademisch gebildeten, in ihrem kunsthistorischen Bewußtsein sehr differenzierten und befangenen Künstlern mit der Systems und Process Art, Concept Art, Performance Art, Land Art und anderen unorthodoxen Richtungen, die viele Prämissen der früheren Moderne ablehnten. In einem gewissen Sinne war es die Absicht dieser Künstler, eine Kunst zu schaffen, die durch ihre Neuheit schockierend und schwer zugänglich war und damit die avantgardistische Aggressivität wiederbelebte, die sie durch die breite Aufnahme der abstrakten Malerei in den 50er Jahren erstickt glaubten. Jedoch suchte die aktuelle Diskussion vielfach die Kluft zwischen der Kunst und ihrem Publikum zu schließen, anstatt zu verbreitern. Mit der Ablehnung dessen, was als begrenzende, letztlich marktkonforme Ideale des individuellen Stils (im Sinne des Connaisseurs) und autonomer Objekte gesehen wurde, strebte diese neue Richtung danach, eine erkannte Entfremdung zwischen der modernen Kunst und der Gesellschaft im allgemeinen zu überwinden. Von ihren Produzenten und Bewunderern wurde sie treffend in Begriffen beschrieben, die weniger aus der bildenden Kunst als aus der Anthropologie stammen. In Anlehnung an traditionelle (wenn auch ungenaue) Berichte über eingeborene Künstler, in denen diese als gleichgültig gegenüber Fragen der Ästhetik dargestellt werden, prophezeiten die neuen Künstler und ihre Befürworter unter den Kritikern eine Kunst, die sich – wie die primitive Kunst in der Vergangenheit – mehr mit umfassenderen Systemen der Natur, der Magie, des Rituals und der sozialen Organisation beschäftigen würde.

Diese veränderte Vorstellung einer modernen Kunst wiederum traf auf ein verändertes Bild vom Primitiven. In den 60er und 70er Jahren wurde der Taschenbuchladen – eher als der Trödelladen, die Galerie oder das Völkerkundemuseum – der wichtigste Ort für den Kontakt vieler Künstler mit Stammesskulpturen. Hier begegnete der Künstler einer ethnologischen Betrachtungsweise, die durch den Strukturalismus, wie ihn Claude Lévi-Strauss in *Tristes Tropiques* (1955), *The Savage Mind* (1962) oder *The Raw and the Cooked* (1964) formulierte, eine neue Orientierung gewonnen hatte. Diese Schriften waren methodisch wie inhaltlich einflußreich. Sie übten harte Kritik an den Anmaßungen der modernen technologischen Gesell-

□ 1002 *Stonehenge, Ebene von Salisbury, Wiltshire, 1800–1400 v. Chr., Durchmesser 29,5 m, Höhe der Steine über dem Boden 4,10 m.*

schaft und würdigten andererseits das primitive Leben und Denken mit einer intellektuellen Schärfe, die frei war von Sentimentalität oder Romantik. LÉVI-STRAUSS' strukturalistische Anthropologie hielt die westliche Kultur nicht für ›fortgeschrittener‹ als die der Stammesgesellschaften, sondern nur für anders und betrachtete sie sogar in entscheidender Hinsicht als unterlegen. LÉVI-STRAUSS beschrieb den primitiven Geist überdies nicht als Ort des Magischen und der Halluzinationen, wie zuvor von Schriftstellern wie Lévy-Bruhl heraufbeschworen (siehe S. 555 ff.) und von den Surrealisten verehrt, sondern als Stätte machtvoller Formen der Logik, die vom wissenschaftlichen Denken zwar entfernt, mit diesem aber vergleichbar sind. Der kritische Rationalismus solcher Ansätze entmystifizierte und adelte das Primitive in den Augen der Künstler, die ihre künstlerische Reife nach 1960 erreichten und auf die Ideale des abstrakten Expressionismus ablehnend reagierten. Dieser hatte immer noch Mythos mit Mysterium gleichgesetzt und das Ideal einer alogischen Vorstellungsgabe und Spontaneität in bezug auf den schriftlosen Menschen gepriesen. Die strukturalistische Perspektive eröffnete demgegenüber eine andere Art primitiver Mentalität, die als Schöpfer einer in allen materiellen und geistigen Belangen gültigen, streng binomischen Ordnung durchaus Vorläufer der Minimal und Systems Art sein könnte. Die vom Strukturalismus gepflegte Totalperspektive, in der Fetische und Angelhaken, Totems und Tischsitten gleichbedeutsame Ausdrucksweisen dieser kollektiven Ordnung sind, entsprach ebenfalls den Zielen von Künstlern, die die etablierte Kategorisierung und Wertbestimmung von Kunst ablehnten.[3]

All das führte zu einem Primitivismus, der sich selbst für hinreichend kenntnisreich hielt. Dabei stellt sich die Frage, ob seine Ergebnisse nicht oft reines Bücherwissen sind oder wirklich als radikaler und authentischer gelten können als die angeblich »bloß formale« Übernahme von Stammeskunst durch die frühen Modernen wie PICASSO. Die ästhetischen und ideologischen Quellen, aus denen sich die jüngste Anziehungskraft primitiver Kulturen speist, sind sicherlich reich genug, um künstlerische Leistungen von Tiefe und Kraft zu stützen, aber auch befangen und formalistisch genug, um eine Menge von banalen, schlechten und mitunter finsteren Werken anzuregen. Um hier differenzieren zu können, müssen wir kritischer prüfen, woher der neue Primitivismus kam, was er versprach, was er für Ergebnisse zeitigte und was er bedeuten könnte. Warum Stonehenge im Raumzeitalter?

Eine scheinbar naheliegende Antwort wäre, daß der Primitivismus als Gegenreaktion der 70er Jahre auf die hochtechnisierte, hart abgrenzende Ästhetik der 60er Jahre entstand (Pop Art, Minimal Art und Hard-edge Malerei) und dabei die unpersönliche Rationalität zugunsten neuer Ideale von künstlerischer, persönlicher und politischer Befreiung ablehnte. Dies schloß einen engeren Kontakt sowohl mit der irdischen Natur als auch mit der Natur des Universums ein. Wie zutreffend diese Deutung auch sein mag, sie deckt sich vielleicht zu sehr mit klischeehaften Vorstellungen über die jüngste Kulturgeschichte und ist in mehrerer Hinsicht auch falsch. Die wichtigsten Aspekte und bedeutendsten Künstler des neuen Primitivismus entwickelten sich in den 60er Jahren; dem Erbe rationalistischer Ästhetik kommt dabei eine große Bedeutung zu. Außerdem verhilft die Polarisierung zwischen einem kalten, modernen Rationalismus und einem struppigen primitiven Instinkt genausowenig zum Verständnis der zeitgenössischen Kunst wie zur Annäherung an die Stammesgesellschaften. Die

□ 1003 *Robert Smithson, ›Spiral – Mole‹ (Spiral Jetty), Großer Salzsee, Utah, 1970, schwarzes Gestein, Salzkristalle, Erde, rotes Wasser, Länge der Spirale 457 m, Breite ca. 4,50 m.*

□ 1004 *Bodenzeichnung in Form eines halben Labyrinths, Nazca, Pompa Ingenio (Peru), 300 v. Chr.–700 n. Chr.*

□ 1005 *Michael Heizer, ›Doppeltes Negativ‹ (Double Negative), Virginia River Mesa, Nevada, 1969–70, 487 x 15 x 9 m.*

□ 1006 *Michael Heizer, ›Doppeltes Negativ‹, Luftaufnahme, siehe* □ *1005.*

□ 1007 *Michael Heizer, ›Komplex Eins/Stadt‹ (Complex One/City), nahe bei Hiko im mittleren Süden Nevadas, 1972–76, Zement, Stahl und Erde, 7,20 x 33,50 x 42,60 m.*

vielfältigen und irritierenden Aspekte des neuen Primitivismus müssen mit Begriffen eines komplexeren Zusammenhangs zwischen Wissenschaftlichem und Sinnlichem, Unfreiem und Freiem charakterisiert werden. Werke der Land Art, das frappierendste Beispiel der Verwandtschaft zwischen neuer und primitiver Kunst, scheinen dafür ein guter Ausgangspunkt zu sein.

Mit ihrer Diskussion über Grundformen der Wahrnehmung und elementare Organisationssysteme beinhaltete schon die reduktionistische Ästhetik der frühen 60er Jahre eine Vorstellung des *primitif* – im französischen, philosophischen Sinne des Begriffs –, die elementare Ursprünge und essentielle Erfahrungen beschwor. Das minimalistische Ideal neutraler Formen am Urgrund der Wahrnehmung schuf eine implizierte Verbindung zwischen Reduktion und Regression, zwischen scharfkantiger Geometrie und den geistigen Urformen. Es schuf eine Verbindung des Unberührten mit dem Ursprünglichen, die populär gemacht wurde durch STANLEY KUBRICKS Verwendung einer minimalistischen Steintafel, mit der er in den Anfangsszenen des Films *2001* (1968) den Ursprung aller menschlichen Errungenschaften darstellen wollte. Es war dann nur noch ein kleiner Schritt vom Monolithischen zum Neolithischen, von ganz reiner Leere zu Formen einer expliziteren archaisierenden Strenge. Diesen Schritt machten ROBERT SMITHSON (der sich schon als minimalistischer Bildhauer einen Ruf verschafft hatte) und MICHAEL HEIZER in ihren frühen Werken der Land Art. HEIZERS *Doppeltes Negativ* von 1969–70 □ 1005–06 und *Komplex Eins/Stadt* von 1972–76 □ 1007 erinnern an die monumentalen Geometrien mittelamerikanischer Ruinen, SMITHSONS *Spiral-Mole* (1970) □ 1003 in ähnlicher Weise an prähistorische Bodenzeichnungen □ 1004. In diesen Arbeiten konzentrierte sich die Beschäftigung mit prozeßhaften Vorgängen auf geologische Veränderungen; das Interesse an »Realzeit-Systemen« umfaßte eine Dauer von Jahrtausenden. Der minimalistische Absolutismus wurde mit Assoziationen an extreme Überlebens- und Vernichtungssituationen verbunden, die das Drama der menschlichen Vergangenheit mit den Grundkräften der Naturgeschichte verschmolzen.

Durch die implizit enthaltene Flucht vor den Zwängen der Zeit (besonders denen des Kunstmarkts) und durch die Konfrontation mit dem Elementaren thematisierten diese Arbeiten viel von der momentanen Unzufriedenheit mit der städtischen Umgebung. Indem sie erneut die Ideale von Weiträumigkeit und titanischer gestischer Freiheit verkörperten, die für die Mythologisierung der abstrakten Expressionisten bezeichnend gewesen waren, beschworen die frühen Werke der Land Art in lebhafter Weise eine neue Art von heroischem Wildwestkünstler und einen spektakulären Weg, den großen Geist vortechnischer Gesellschaften zu vergegenwärtigen. Rückblickend jedoch prägten sie genauso einen romantisch-schwülstigen Pessimismus. Nicht nur Freiheit, auch der Widerhall von Ozymandias klingt in diesen Monduntergängen. Mit unnahbarer Autorität beherrschte HEIZERS Werk unmenschlich weite Wüstenräume und geologische Zeiträume; SMITHSONS *Mole* war (in der Kombination mit Rhetorik und Film) sogar noch bewußter ein Schauplatz von unerbittlichem Verfall.[4] Ihre archäologische Metaphorik bezog sich nicht auf das schöpferische Handwerk von Stammeskünstlern, sondern auf Spuren untergegangener Gesellschaften, die unermeßliche kollektive Anstrengungen und das Streben nach kosmischem Wissen verkörperten – in einem Maßstab, der eher den Autobahnbauer als den Maler oder Bildhauer als modernes Pendant empfiehlt. Solche Metaphorik verschmolz Hybris und Vanitas, transzendentales Ziel und entropisches Schicksal, indem sie zeitgenössische Ideen von überwältigender Wucht und ökonomischer Verzweiflung in die Zeit zurückprojizierte.

Die epische Gewichtigkeit dieser ersten Werke der Land Art reflektiert die rhetorische Tonlage in den letzten Jahren des Vietnamkrieges (obwohl ihre Ödland-Romantik sicherlich andere persönliche und gesellschaftliche Quellen hatte).[5] In Freilandprojekten der späten 70er Jahre war die Etablierung dieser künstlerischen Form mit einer nicht zu leugnenden Verminderung der schöpferischen Energie verbunden, aber auch mit einer vermehrten Konzentration auf die Zeit- und Naturerfahrung des primitiven Menschen aus antiepischen, rein persönlichen Vorstellungen. Spätere Werke wie zum Beispiel Richard Fleischners *Rasenlabyrinth* □ 1008 von 1974, Richard Longs weitflächige Steinsetzungen □ 1009 oder Martin Puryears bound structures □ 1017 beziehen sich in weniger monumentaler Weise auf ähnliche prähistorische Quellen. Was zunächst nur als Domestizierung des Maßstabs erscheinen mag, läßt eher einen ganz anderen Geist des Primitiven als Anreger vermuten.

Das Konzept der räumlichen Orientierung ist für viele dieser Earthworks und anderer Freilandprojekte aus den 60er und 70er Jahren entscheidend und kann unser Verständnis der angesprochenen Probleme vertiefen. Stonehenge □ 1002 und vor allem die riesigen Zeichnungen auf den Nazca-Ebenen in Peru □ 1004, 1011, 1041 sind dafür Schlüsselbeispiele. Solche Monumente vermitteln – besonders aus der Luft gesehen – die erregende Vorstellung von einer utopischen, ja geradezu unbegrenzten Macht. Mit der Darstellung der Ordnung des Universums im Dienste der Religion, die schon die moderne Wissenschaft ankündigt, bewirken sie einen Schauer von zeitlosem Rätsel. Wenn sie jedoch unmittelbar vom Boden aus erfahren werden, haben diese Strukturen eine andere, stark subjektive und bewegungsästhetische Wirkung, indem sie eine gesteigerte persönliche Empfindung für den Ort in der Natur, der nahegelegenen wie der globalen, hervorrufen. Von den Arbeiten Smithsons und Heizers bis zu den Freilandprojekten von Walter de Maria □ 1001, 1012, Robert Morris □ 1016, Nancy Holt □ 1013–14, Michelle Stuart □ 1015, Richard Long □ 1010 u.a. können wir eine wiederkehrende Beschäftigung mit solchen Orientierungsstrukturen feststellen. Dieses Interesse oszilliert zwischen astronomischer Mathematik und unmittelbarer Erfahrung, Kartographie und Bereichen der Wahrnehmung, zwischen dem Kosmischen und dem Chthonischen. Für diese Künstler bildeten oft die Geomantik alter Anlagen und primitive Ordnungssysteme, die Sterne und Steine aufeinander ausrichteten, die entscheidende Anregung.[6]

Solche Modelle können natürlich zur Imitation genauso wie zur Innovation ermuntern. In der Tat sind Irrgärten zum Wandern und selbstgebaute »Observatorien«, die man auf Planeten und Sterne ausrichtete, am Ende der 70er Jahre nur allzu geläufig. Doch das beste Werk dieser Art ging über den druidischen Exotismus hinaus, um die Gerichtetheit primitiver Anlagen

□ 1008 *Richard Fleischner, ›Rasenlabyrinth‹ (Sod Maze), 1974, Newport, Rhode Island, Durchmesser 43 m.*

□ 1009 *Richard Long, ›Steine in Island‹ (Stones in Iceland), 1974.*

in einem umfassenderen Sinne zu begreifen. Es war darum bemüht, eine Erfahrung anzuregen, in welcher die beiden Orientierungsmöglichkeiten ineinander übergehen: durch die Strukturierung der kinästhetischen Erfahrung des Ortes verbunden mit der Humanisierung und Vergegenwärtigung des Gefühls, in einem größeren Gefüge von Raum und Zeit zu stehen. Die Verwirklichung solcher Ziele kann außer den innersten Bezügen zu primitiven Vorläufern alles außer acht lassen. In JAMES TURRELLS *Roden Crater Project* in Arizona □ 1021 – bei dem der ganze vulkanische Krater in ein nahtloses, objektfreies Sehfeld umgeformt werden soll, das sich rasiermesserscharf gegen den Himmel öffnet – werden die wesentlichen Prämissen der Fusion zwischen Erde und Himmel, zwischen individueller Sinneswahrnehmung und universalem geistigem Bewußtsein neu formuliert. Dies geschieht auf eine moderne Weise, ohne Imitation. Damit werden insgesamt die be- und entgrenzenden Urgefühle der Ehrfurcht in machtvoller Weise angesprochen.[7]

In diesen unterschiedlichen Antworten auf archaische und primitive Orientierungssysteme können wir allmählich eine fundamentale Ambivalenz im Konzept des Primitiven erkennen. Auf der einen Seite brachten neuere Künstler prähistorischen und archaischen Gestaltungen ihre Bewunderung entgegen, die offensichtlich zu unpersönlich im Maßstab oder zu sehr mathematisch bestimmt waren, um den frühen Modernen zu gefallen. Die Begeisterung für kollektive Monumentalwerke (wie für die Erbauer von Erdhügeln, für die Menschen von Stonehenge und für die präkolumbianischen Gesellschaften von Süd- und Zentralamerika) wurde implizit und explizit von einer Bewunderung begleitet für die rigorose soziale Integration, für das ritualisierte Verhalten und für den Willen zu kosmischem Determinismus, Phänomene, die hinter solchen Monumenten zu liegen scheinen. Gleichzeitig wurde auch das Modell primitiver Gesellschaften, oft im Hinblick auf dieselben Phänomene, als Quelle für künstlerische Befreiung und persönliche Erfüllung beschworen. Damit ging die Ablehnung grundlegender Konventionen einher, die die früheren Vertreter der Moderne im allgemeinen noch beachtet hatten (Einzelobjekte, individueller Stil u.a.), sowie eine Hinwendung zur unmittelbaren, persönlichen Erfahrung, die als besonders irrational, intuitiv und antiautoritär angesehen wurde. Diese Schwankungen zwischen dem Kollektiven und Persönlichen, zwischen Vernunft und Instinkt, höherer Ordnung und kindlicher Spontaneität sind für den zeitgenössischen Primitivismus weitgehend typisch.

Es mag axiomatisch erscheinen, daß eine rigide Sozialstruktur und riesige kollektive Geometrien die Vehikel und Zeichen von Einschränkungen und Unterdrückung darstellen, während andererseits zwanglos aufgehäufter Schlamm und Zweige eher ein Ausdruck der Befreiung improvisierter, innovativer Energien sind, die im allgemeinen als das wichtigste Ergebnis des Primitivismus gelten können. Doch die zeitgenössische Kunst gab vielfach zu verstehen, daß diese ambivalenten Lesarten des primitiven Geistes in sich nicht unvereinbar sein müssen. Die beiden Aspekte scheinen statt dessen häufig miteinander verflochten, etwa im zweifachen Sinne des Ideals räumlicher Orientierung, aber auch innerhalb der Grundverfahren vieler neuer Werke. Auf der einen Seite erkennen wir normative

□ 1010 *Richard Long, ›In Peru eine Linie gehen‹ (Walking a Line in Peru), 1972.*

□ 1011 *Bodenzeichnung in Form eines Dreiecks, Nazca, Pompa Ingenio, Peru, 300 v. Chr. – 700 n. Chr.*

□ 1012 *Walter de Maria, ›Meilenlange Zeichnung‹ (Mile Long Drawing), Ausschnitt, Mohave Wüste, 1968. Zwei parallele 10 cm breite Kreidelinien, Abstand 3,60 m, Länge 1,6 km.*

□ 1013 *Nancy Holt, ›Sonnentunnels‹, siehe* □ *1014, Blick durch die nordwestliche Röhre. In die Wandung eingeschnittene Löcher projizieren das Muster des Sternbildes Drache in das schattige Innere.*

□ 1014 *Nancy Holt, ›Sonnentunnels‹ (Sun Tunnels), in der Großen-Salzsee-Wüste, nahe bei Lucin, Utah, 1973–76, vier Betonröhren, Länge jeweils 5,40 m, Durchmesser 2,40 m, Abstand von einem Ende zum anderen jeweils 26 m. Die Röhren sind nach dem Sonnenstand während der Sonnwenden (Sonnenaufgänge und -untergänge) ausgerichtet.*

□ 1015 *Michelle Stuart, ›Steinmarkierungen/Sonnwend-Steinhügel‹ (Stone Alignments/Solstice Cairns), Rowena Dell Plateau, Schlucht des Columbia River, Oregon, 1979.*

□ 1016 *Robert Morris, ›Observatorium‹ (Observatory), Oostelijk Flevoland, Niederlande, 1970–77. Vergrößert nachgebaut an einem anderen Ort, 1977, Erde, Holz und Granit, Durchmesser des äußeren Rings 91,40 m.*

Rituale und strenge Organisationsmuster, auf der anderen scheint eine heftigere, flexiblere Reaktion auf Materialien und Umwelt sowie, damit einhergehend, ein unmittelbares persönlich-psychisches Engagement beabsichtigt zu sein. Diese Verschmelzung verweist uns nicht nur auf eine bereicherte Idee vom Primitiven, sondern auch – über die recht direkten Verbindungen der Land Art mit dem Minimalismus hinaus – auf ein komplexeres Vermächtnis der Ästhetik der 60er Jahre.

Unter funktionalen und anderen Gesichtspunkten stellt die Kunst der frühen 60er Jahre die Voraussetzungen für den Primitivismus in mindestens zwei wichtigen Bereichen. Der generelle Wunsch, daß Werke ihren Entstehungsprozeß ausdrücken sollten, und das Aufkommen mathematischer Systeme als Ausgangsformeln für Kunst öffneten einerseits den Weg zu neuen, regelgebundenen Schaffensmethoden, in denen sterile Wiederholungen leicht in unverhülltes Ritual übergingen. Auch und gerade in der Skulptur verhalf die Ablehnung der Metaphorik zugunsten unmittelbar wahrgenommener Eigenschaften der Masse, Größe, Gestalt und Orientierung andererseits zu einer geläuterten Poesie des rohen Materials und körperlichen Bewußtseins. In beiden Gebieten führte die Rückkehr zu den Grundlagen der geistigen Struktur und der physischen Erfahrungen von Kunst dazu, daß Einfachheit neu bewertet wurde und Voraussetzungen für neue Wege entstanden, um sich den Geist und die Formen primitiver Kreativität dienstbar zu machen. Hier erkennen wir die gemeinsamen Wurzeln so verschieden orientierter Künstler wie Richard Long und Carl Andre. Beredte Kunst und stumme Kunst, Computergitter und Kinderspiele, das Raffinierte und das Archaische bildeten oft seltsame Gefährten in diesem wichti-

□ 1017 *Martin Puryear, ›Installation‹, 1977, Zedern- und Fichtenholz, Rohleder, 540 x 495 cm. Corcoran Gallery of Art, Washington. Puryears Holz- und Lederarbeiten beschwören oft primitive Hütten, Kultstätten und Gerätschaften.*

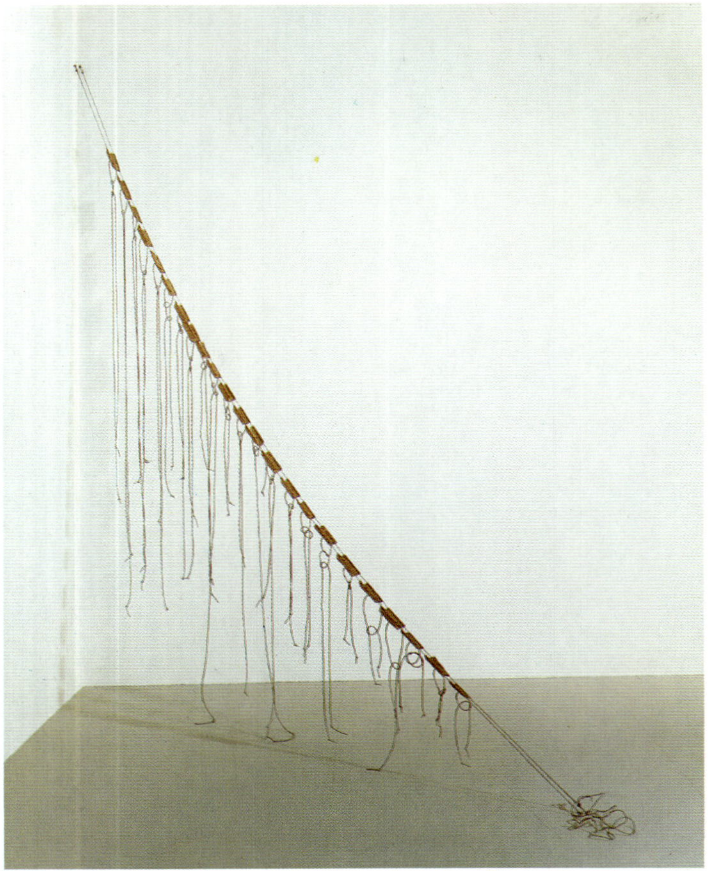

□ 1018 *Eva Hesse, ›Band II‹ (Vinculum II), 1969, 23 gummierte Maschendrahtplatten, an ummantelten Draht geheftet (591 x 7,6 cm), mit 23 herabhängenden Gummifäden verknotet, Länge zwischen 18 und 157 cm. The Museum of Modern Art, The Gilman Foundation Fund, New York.*

Obwohl die von Hesse verwandten Materialien oft industriell vorgefertigt sind, ruft ihr Gebrauch häufig Assoziationen mit dem Körper und mit dem groben oder rituellen Aussehen von primitiven Artefakten hervor. Diese Tendenz und das persönliche psychologische Moment ihres Werks trugen zu einem Vokabular bei, das von primitivisierenden Künstlern in den 70er Jahren vielfach benutzt wurde.

□ 1021 ▷
James Turrell, ›Roden Crater Project‹, in Arbeit. Ein vulkanischer Krater nahe der Painted Desert in Arizona wird vom Künstler teilweise neu gefaßt. Innerhalb des vulkanischen Randes werden unterirdische Räume entstehen, die nach täglichen und jährlichen astronomischen Zyklen sowie nach einmaligen Ereignissen wie Eklipsen, die über mehr als 12 000 Jahre im voraus berechnet wurden, ausgerichtet sind. Der Krater soll in einen parabolischen Teller umgeformt werden, in dem das ganze Himmelsgewölbe mit großer Unmittelbarkeit erfahren werden kann. Der Blick vom Rand wird diese Erfahrung mit der des Horizonts und der Wahrnehmung der unzerstörten, ursprünglichen Geologie der Landschaft verbinden.

□ 1019 *Eva Hesse, Ohne Titel, 1970, Fiberglas auf Polyäthylen über Aluminiumdraht, sieben Einheiten, Höhe jeweils 218 bis 281 cm. Sammlung Victor W. Ganz, New York.*

□ 1020 *Eva Hesse, ›Ischtar‹ (Ishtar), 1965, Holz, Kork, Farbe und Gummi, 91 x 19 x 6 cm. Privatsammlung.*

gen Ursprungsbereich des neuen Primitivismus. Zwei Künstler, deren Werke eine solche Interessenverbindung besonders deutlich verkörpern und die verschiedene ästhetische Auffassungen verbinden, sind die späte Eva Hesse und Jackie Winsor.

In der Blütezeit der Minimal Art und Pop Art entwickelte Hesse als Außenseiterin ein Vokabular aus geschmeidigen Materialien und Strukturen mit besonders viszeralen, sexuellen Assoziationen □ 1018–20. Innerhalb der Schemata und Serienfolgen der Kunst der frühen 60er Jahre fand sie andererseits nicht nur fremde, sterile Logik vor, sondern auch eine autobiographische, poetische Komponente, mit der sie ihr Anliegen darstellte. In Verbindung mit unheimlichen, taktilen Oberflächen und faserigen oder welligen Formen gesehen, scheinen Hesses Wiederholungen eher zwanghaft oder therapeutisch als bloß mechanisch zu sein.[8] In ähnlicher Weise werden in den wenig später entstandenen Strukturen von Jackie Winsor musterartige Verfahren und geometrische Formen zum Mittel für eine Arbeit, die eine rituelle Besessenheit durch den Arbeitsprozeß und absichtlich derbe Körperlichkeit zur Geltung bringt. Besonders in ihren frühen Werken aus unbearbeitetem Holz und Schnur □ 1022–23 artikulierte Winsor die Grunderfahrungen von Gewicht und Größe mit groben, keineswegs »schön« wirkenden Mitteln und zeigte, wie einfache festgelegte Aufgaben durch Beharrlichkeit eine persönliche Erfahrung der Mühe ausdrücken können.[9] Wie bei Hesse ging Mathematik hier in Mantra über: Ästhetische Verfahrensweisen, dazu bestimmt, die zen-artigen, gestischen Freiheiten des abstrakten Expressionismus zum Schweigen zu bringen, erwiesen sich am Ende als neue Wege, um die Freisetzung psychischer Energien in veränderter und verständlicher Form durch die Hingabe an den künstlerischen Prozeß wiederzugewinnen. In den Werken dieser und anderer Künstler der späten 60er und frühen 70er Jahre war die Syntax der Minimal Art Grundlage wie auch Hintergrund für die Entstehung von Arbeiten, die ohne besonderen Verweis auf primitive oder prähistorische Kulturen die Möglichkeiten eines neuen, beziehungsreichen Primitivismus erprobten.

Nicht nur in der Begeisterung für alte Ingenieurleistungen wie Stonehenge oder Avebury, sondern auch in den grundlegenden Mitteln und Methoden von Hesse, Winsor und einem breiten Spektrum anderer neuer Werke sind Instinkt und Körperlichkeit deutlich mit Intelligenz und begrifflichem Schema in einer Weise gepaart, die eher fruchtbar als verhängnisvoll ist. Künstler wie Richard Long und Michelle Stuart beschäftigen sich in äußerst physischer, unmittelbarer Art und Weise mit der Erde und rohen Materialien. Longs Wanderungen und Steinsetzungen drücken die Einfachheit eines Kinderreims und die Freiheit einer von Zäunen verschonten Topographie aus □ 1009–10. Seine Arbeiten für Galerien und Museen übertragen dieses Gefühl in elementare Anordnungen aus Steinen und Holzstücken □ 1025 oder in Fingermalereien aus Schlamm □ 1024. Stuarts Steinabdrücke und Erdabreibungen verbinden ihren Körper mit den archaischen und prähistorischen Stätten, die sie besucht □ 1028–29. Im Werk jedes der genannten Künstler ersetzt der ursprüngliche Kontakt alles, was traditionellerweise Technik genannt werden könnte. Doch in der Organisation und Darbietung ihrer Kunst zeigen sie sich gleichermaßen um Systeme kartographischer Erfassung, Katalogisierung und Berechnung bemüht – Long in den maßstabgerechten Beziehungen von Entfernung und Zeit, die seine Bewegungen und Markierungen bestimmen □ 1030, und Stuart in den Netzsystemen und Buchformen, die ihre zu Papier gebrachten Erinnerungen strukturieren. Auch im Werk

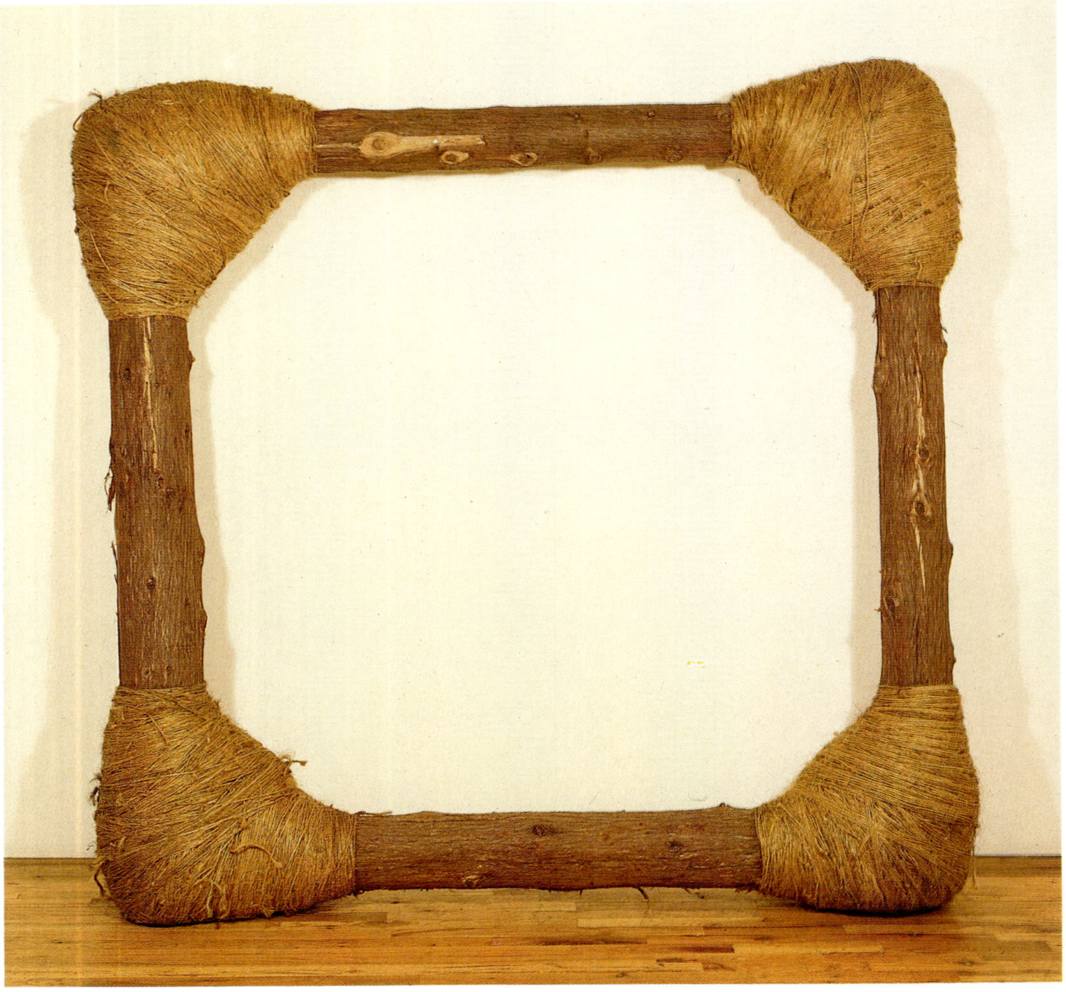

□ 1022 *Jackie Winsor, ›Gebundenes Viereck‹ (Bound Square), 1972, Holz und Schnur, 192 x 193 x 37 cm. The Museum of Modern Art, New York.*

□ 1023 *Jackie Winsor, ›Vier Ecken‹ (Four Corners), 1972, Holz und Hanf, 76 x 122 x 122 cm. Allen Memorial Art Museum, Oberlin College, Ohio. Schenkung Donald Droll in Erinnerung an Eva Hesse.*

□ 1024 *Richard Long, ›River Avon Schlammkreis‹ (River Avon Mud Circle), 1982, Schlamm auf weißer Wand (zerstört), Durchmesser 279 cm. Sperone Westwater, New York.*

□ 1025 *Richard Long, ›Marmorsteinkreis‹ (Marble Stone Circle), Marmor, Durchmesser ca. 240 cm. Galerie Jean Bernier, Athen.*

□ 1026 *Michael Singer, ›First Gate Ritual Series 4/79‹, Dayton, Ohio, 1979. Zerstört.*

□ 1027 *Michael Singer, ›First Gate Ritual Series 10/78‹, 1978, weißes Kiefernholz, Steine und Schilfrohr, 254 x 426 x 604 cm. The Fort Worth Art Museum.*

von MICHAEL SINGER beherrscht der Geist eines dominanten Musters, oft eines begrabenen Netzes, kurzlebige Geflechte aus Stöcken und Ästen □ 1026–27. Seine Reaktion auf erkannte Eigenschaften von Gewicht und Form hat etwas von den Rezepturen eines Rituals. Nicht nur zwischen Kieselsteinen und einem Zweig läßt er ein Gefühl von Balance entstehen, sondern auch zwischen der rauhen Notwendigkeit eines Vogelnests und der verfeinerten Sparsamkeit der Shintozeremonie. Im Werk von LONG, STUART und SINGER ist die primitive Erfahrung als eine sich wechselseitig steigernde Kombination systematisierten Verhaltens und reagierenden sinnlichen Bewußtseins verinnerlicht. Gerade in der tiefen, persönlichen Struktur der Aktivitäten taucht mehr als in irgendwelchen formalen Verweisen auf prähistorische oder eingeborene Stätten und Monumente eine entschieden zeitgenössische Poesie des Primitivismus auf. Es ist eine Poesie, in der die Grundlagen der Logik und Dokumentation die gefühlsbetonten Assoziationen mit der fernen Vergangenheit fernhalten wie auch anregen.

Diese Künstler scheinen auf eher schöpferische als hinderliche Weise »wissend« zu sein. Die veränderten Maßstäbe der neuesten Kunst und neue Ideen bezüglich primitiver Kultur fördern nicht nur eine andere Art des Zitierens, sondern auch eine neue komplexe Art der Identifikation über kulturelle Barrieren hinweg. Solche Arbeiten laufen einer allzu einfachen Trennung zwischen rationalistischer und primitivistischer Ästhetik zuwider. Sie lassen Möglichkeiten erkennen, wie der jüngste Primitivismus etwas mehr darstellen kann als die einfache Flucht oder Opposition gegenüber der modernen westlichen Kultur. Der synthetische Charakter dieser Kunstformen läßt die mögliche Schlußfolgerung zu, daß das Primitive und das Moderne nicht so sehr antagonistisch sind, sondern sich vielmehr gegenseitig bereichern. Diese Erkenntnis beschränkt

☐ 1028 *Michelle Stuart, ›Nazca-Linien-Sternkarte‹ (Nazca Lines Star Chart), 1981–82, Erde aus Nazca, Peru, auf Papier, 304 x 426 cm. Privatsammlung.*

☐ 1029 *Michelle Stuart, ›Nazca Lines Southern Hemisphere Constellation Chart Correlation‹, 1981, Tusche auf Pergament, 43 x 56 cm. Privatsammlung.*

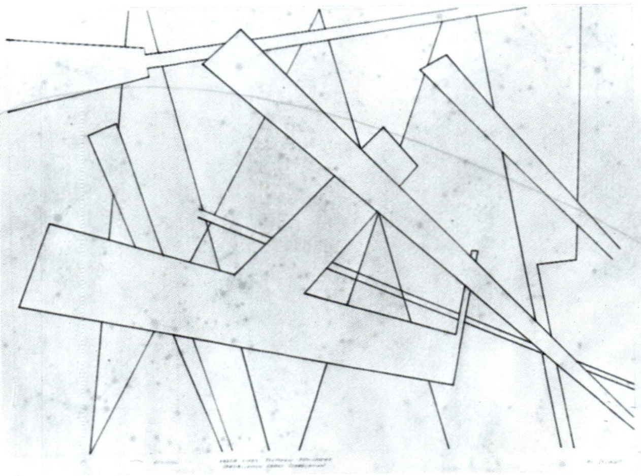

☐ 1030 *Richard Long, ›Cerne Abbas-Begehung (Eine sechs Tage dauernde Wanderung über alle Straßen, Wege und Pfade innerhalb eines 6 Meilen großen Kreises um den Giganten von Cerne Abbas)‹, Detail, 1975. Zwei Teile: Tinte und Photographie auf einer Vermessungskarte, 72,5 x 73,6 cm, Schwarzweißphotographie 36 x 53,5 cm. The Tate Gallery, London.*

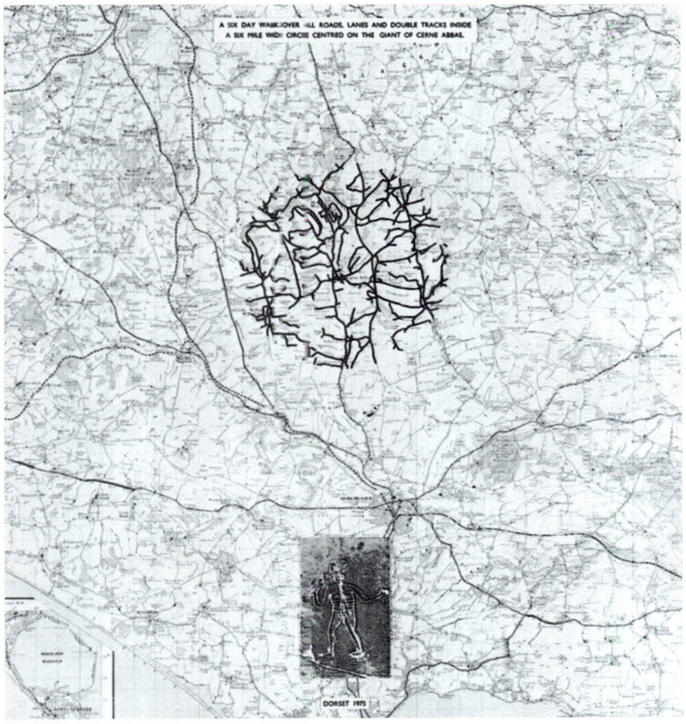

□ 1031 *Nancy Graves, ›Totem‹ (Totem), 1970, Tierfell, Stahl, Gaze, Wachs, Ölmalerei, Latex und Acryl, 259 x 91 x 91 cm. Sammlung der Künstlerin.*

sich nicht allein auf die Kunst. Sie ist breiten intellektuellen Strömungen der jüngsten Vergangenheit zugehörig: Strömungen, die mit allem in Verbindung stehen, was wir in Betracht gezogen haben, und uns helfen können, der Grundfrage nach der heutigen Relevanz des Primitivismus näher zu kommen.

Wie paradox es auch scheinen mag, eine moderne Theorie behauptet, daß uns technische Fortschritte – im Guten oder Schlechten – unseren primitiven Pendants näherbringen. Die negative Version dieser Ansicht vergleicht die Angst moderner Zeit mit dem hypothetischen Bild vom primitiven Menschen, der von Furcht verzehrt wird. Eine Variante des gleichen Pessimismus betrachtet die Konflikte und Zerstörungen unserer Zeit als Wiederkehr der Brutalität eines gewalttätigen Naturzustandes, in dem sich mit modernen Waffen der darwinsche Überlebenskampf wiederholt. Beide Vorstellungen dieses deprimierenden Zusammenhangs waren in den 40er Jahren geläufig (siehe das Kapitel über den abstrakten Expressionismus, S. 632ff. und S. 662ff.) und sind seitdem erweitert worden. Mit seiner Gleichsetzung von Dinosauriern und Bulldozern sowie der umfassenderen Metapher vom kulturellen Untergang, der mit der Entropie der Natur in einer ewigen Spirale der Geschichte verbunden ist, lag SMITHSONS Film zu seiner *Spiral-Mole* auf der gleichen Wellenlänge.[10] Wir haben uns auch alle an die Vorstellungen gewöhnt, daß uns unsere neuesten Technologien in einer verheerenden Umwälzung der Schwelle zu einem neuen Steinzeitalter immer näher bringen.

Dem Bild dieser Zusammenhänge sind aber auch positive Seiten abgewonnen worden, die ein gegenseitiges Geben und Nehmen zwischen der primitiven Vergangenheit und der technologischen Gegenwart hervorheben. Sicherlich haben in den 60er Jahren nur wenige neue Ideen eine breitere Resonanz gefunden als Marshall McLuhans Vorstellung eines »global village«, in dem uns erfolgreiche Systeme der Telekommunikation buchstäblich zu unseren Sinneswahrnehmungen zurückführen und eine primitive Bewußtseinsfülle und ursprüngliche Vertrautheit in weltweitem Maßstab herstellen würden.[11] Es hat sich auch gezeigt, daß uns Fortschritte in der Elektrotechnik und Datentechnik näher an das primitive Denken heranbringen, als sie uns davon entfernen. Die Metapher von Stonehenge als Computer ist Ausdruck einer Korrelation, in der wir, je klüger wir werden, bemerken, wie klug sie – oder wir – schon immer waren.[12] An Albernheit grenzt dieser Optimismus mit dem Glauben, daß die *HOPI*-Sprache für das Verständnis des Quantum-Universums besser ausgerüstet sei, um schließlich ein modernisiertes Atlantis zu erreichen, in dem vorzeitliche Raumfahrer megalithische Startbahnen errichten. Es passiert hier jedoch etwas sehr Wichtiges, das, wie mir scheint, direkt mit einem Großteil neuerer primitivistischer Kunst zusammenhängt. Es trägt dazu bei, die häufige Verbindung zwischen neuem Primitivismus und Wissenschaft und die Beschwörung des primitiven Menschen als eines Wissenschaftlers zu verstehen. Dieses geschieht in der wiederbelebten Archäoastronomie und der Geomantik, Methoden, die das Schema des Archäologen und die Strukturen des Anthropologen erkennen lassen; ebenso in merkwürdigen Verbindungen von Interessen, wie sie im Werk von NANCY GRAVES auftauchen □ 1031, 1033–34. Dort liegt die Welt des Schamanentums und der Hautbemalung neben der von Muybridge und der Mondkarten.[13] Der gemeinsame Nenner ist die Bewunderung der Ordnungssysteme des Menschen, die im Dialog mit der Naturordnung gesehen werden, die er in diesen Systemen zu erfassen sucht. Die neuen Sprachen der Wissenschaft werden als anderer Weg der Erkenntnis gefeiert, der uns nicht der Natur entfremdet, sondern unsere Bewunderung steigert, indem er uns mehr Natur und mehr Geheimnisse verständlich macht. Damit eröffnen sich Wege des Wiederfindens, neue Möglichkeiten, um sich mit fernen und verlorenen Kulturen zu verständigen. Solche Arbeit sieht es offenbar als eine Aufgabe der Kunst in einem hochwissenschaftlichen Zeitalter, diesen tieferliegenden universellen Forschergeist zu humanisieren, ein Urgefühl für das Wunder in einer unmittelbar zugänglichen Form zu isolieren und mitzuteilen, eine geistige Reichweite

□ 1032 *Romare Bearden, ›Das Vorherrschen des Rituals: Taufe‹ (The Prevalence of Ritual: Baptism), 1964, photomechanische Reproduktion, synthetisches Polymer und Bleistift auf Pappe, 23 x 30,5 cm. Hirshhorn Museum and Sculpture Garden, Smithsonian Institution, Washington.*

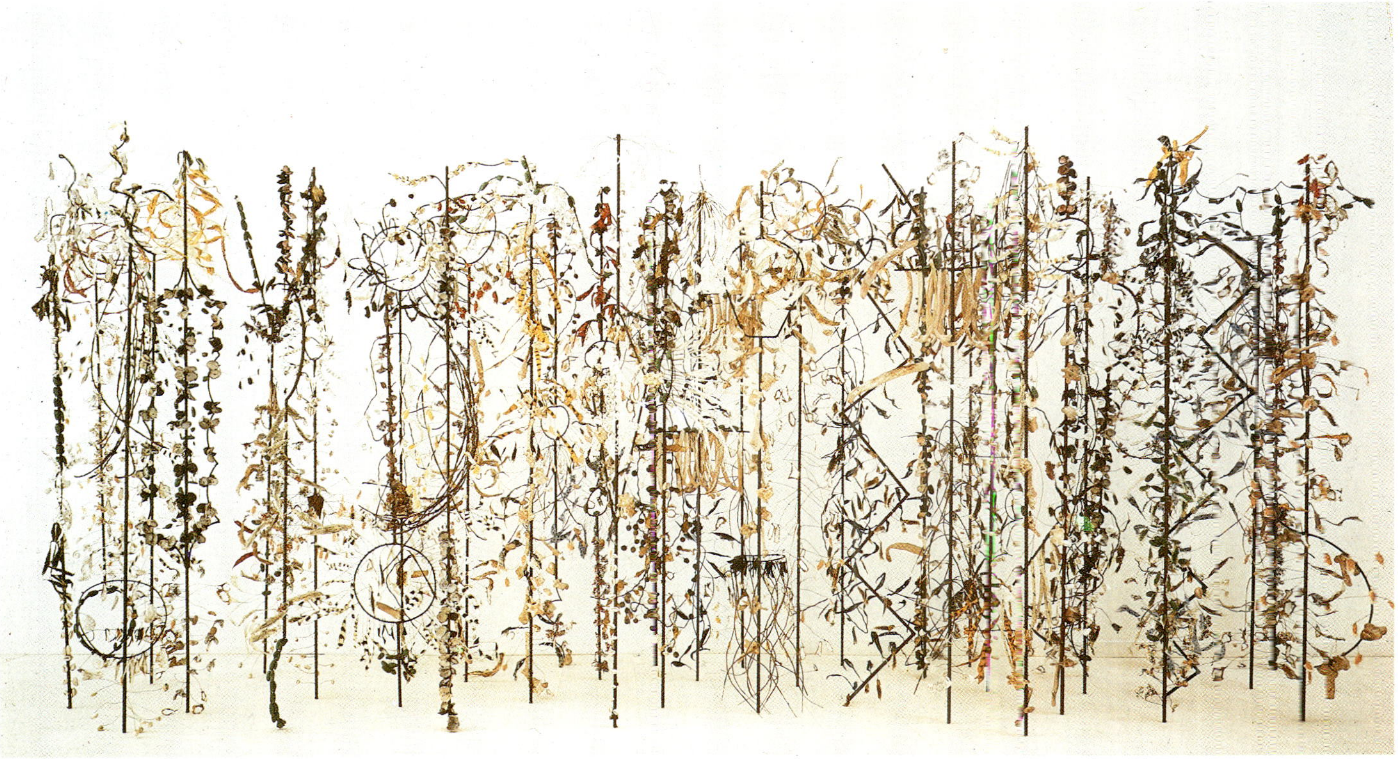

☐ 1033 *Nancy Graves, ›Variabilität und Wiederholung variabler Formen‹ (Variability and Repetition of Variable Forms), 1971, Stahl, Wachs, Marmorstaub, Acryl, Gipsgaze und Latex, 38 Einheiten. Gesamtformat 305 x 457 x 1067 cm. National Gallery of Canada, Ottawa. Die Bildsprache natürlicher Formen in diesem Bild – Zweige, Weinreben, Beeren, Käfer und Kaurimuscheln – spiegelt die Erfahrung der Künstlerin mit den Artefakten primitiver Kulturen der südpazifischen Inseln wider. Das Werk steht mit einer anderen Arbeit, ›Schamane‹, 1972, Wallraf-Richartz-Museum, Köln, in enger Beziehung, das durch die Kultur der Indianer von der Nordwestküste angeregt ist.*

zu vermitteln, die den gegenwärtigen Menschen mit seinen scheinbar weit entfernten menschlichen Pendants verbindet. Wenn wir eine positive Antwort auf die früher gestellte Frage »Warum Stonehenge im Raumzeitalter?« finden wollen, so bringen uns diese Beobachtungen zum Kern der Sache.

Aber dieses Problem hat auch eine negative Seite, die mit mehr als schlechter oder sogar pessimistischer Kunst zu tun hat. Sie betrifft den Primitivismus als solchen und die Politik. Alle Fragen, die wir gerade betrachtet haben, von kollektiver gegenüber individueller Erfahrung, von kontrollierender Ordnung gegenüber instinktmäßiger Freiheit, haben letzten Endes Auswirkungen im Bereich des Politischen. Insoweit er per definitionem eine Kritik an der modernen westlichen Gesellschaft gewesen ist, hat der Primitivismus schon immer solche Implikationen gehabt, die sich bei guter und sensitiver Kunst genauso sicher auswirken wie bei den vielfältigen Formen neoprimitiver Agitprop, die die letzten zwei Jahrzehnte erlebt haben. Solche Arbeiten, in denen politische Belange in aggressiver Weise selbstbewußt vorgetragen werden, zwingen sehr schnell zu den unbequemen Fragen über den letztlichen Gehalt aller Ideale, die die Flucht vor der westlichen Tradition in einen primitiven Zustand beabsichtigen.

Während der vergangenen zwei Jahrzehnte, spätestens seit die Hippies indische Kleidung entdeckten, trug eine lockere Allianz ideologischer Interessen – Feminismus, Ökologie, Antiimperialismus, Antiatombewegungen und Selbstbewußtsein rassischer Minderheiten – dazu bei, Stile und Aufmachung primitiv zu gestalten. Gleichzeitig haben sich die Nationen der Dritten Welt um die Integrität ihrer eigenen Stammeskünste verstärkt bemüht. Dieses neue Klima des Selbstbewußtseins hat in fruchtbarer Weise den Weg für viele Künstler geebnet, den Kontakt mit ihrem eigenen Erbe wieder aufzunehmen, wie etwa in ROMARE BEARDENS ☐ 1032 Hommage an die afrikanische Kultur; auch hat es westliche Künstler für die rassischen und historischen Fragen, die Verweise auf fremde Kulturen betreffen, sensibilisiert (was teilweise der Grund sein mag für

☐ 1034 *Nancy Graves, ›Fossilien‹ (Fossils), 1970, Wachs, Gaze, Marmorstaub, Acryl und Stahl, 91 x 762 x 762 cm. Sammlung der Künstlerin.*

☐ 1035 *Charles Simonds, ›Menschen, die in einem Kreis leben. Sie graben ihre Vergangenheit aus und bauen sie in ihre Gegenwart auf. Ihre Wohnfunktionen als eine persönliche und kosmologische Uhr, jahreszeitlich, harmonisch, zwanghaft‹, 1972, Lehm auf Holzunterlage, Lehmaufbauten: 22 x 66 x 66 cm, Unterlage: 81 x 81 x 81 cm. The Museum of Modern Art, Kay Sage Tanguy Stiftung, New York.*

die Mode »neutralerer« prähistorischer anstelle afrikanischer oder anderer eingeborener künstlerischer Quellen). Der sich daraus ergebende Bewußtseinswandel hat in der Kunst zu unterschiedlichen Ergebnissen geführt. In seiner banalsten Form zeitigte der selbstgebastelte politische Primitivismus ein harmloses Rollenspiel, Taschenspielereien mit Phantasien über Atlantis sowie astrologischen oder alchimistischen Mystizismus. In anderen Äußerungen war er jedoch Arena für Ikonographien der Regression, die mehr zu denken geben und im Hinblick auf die politischen Komponenten des alten und neuen Primitivismus zu untersuchen sind.

Schon sehr früh enthielt die westliche Wertschätzung des primitiven Menschen eine immanente Ambivalenz von Freiheit und Determinismus. Primitive Ausdrucksformen wurden etwa als ursprünglichen Kommunikationsstrukturen und ursprünglichem Denken nahestehender angesehen und damit als Ausdruck einer innewohnenden Notwendigkeit, die die Launen stilistischer Veränderungen hinter sich läßt. Diese Vorstellung einer Notwendigkeit unterstellt gleichermaßen eine unbewußte Spontaneität und eine unfreiwillige Bindung an tiefliegende Strukturen des Denkens oder der Natur. Die Bewunderung für die offensichtlich festgelegten und beständigen Gemeinschaftsstile des eingeborenen oder prähistorischen Menschen konnte so paradoxerweise die Befreiung moderner Spontaneität propagieren (wie etwa im Falle POLLOCKS, vgl. S. 654 ff.) oder noch direkter die Sehnsucht nach der Sicherheit überpersönlicher Absolutheiten ansprechen.[14] Wie im Falle der abstrakten Expressionisten haben moderne Künstler beide Möglichkeiten oft gleichzeitig verfolgt, indem sie sich vorstellten, daß eine Universalsprache, »Mythos für unsere Zeit«, aus einer befreiten, tiefreichenden Selbstverwirklichung erfolge. Ein ideologisch eingefärbter neuer Primitivismus hat vielfach das gleiche Ideal wieder aufgegriffen, um persönliches Psychodrama mit weitreichenden politischen Interessen gleichzusetzen, dies am Beispiel des primitiven Priesters oder Schamanen, der einmal als harmloser Verrückter und ein anderes Mal als Kollektivheiler erscheint.[15] Was natürlich in einer modernen pluralistischen Gesellschaft wesentlich fehlt, ist ein allgemeiner Konsens, der dem Schamanen sein Format und seine Mitteilungskraft gibt. Wie als Antwort auf dieses Fehlen einer kultischen Einheit neigten einige der bekanntesten Manifestationen dieser Kunst bis zu einem beunruhigenden Grad zur Sehnsucht nach Kollektivismus oder ursprünglichem Determinismus als Heilmittel für moderne Leiden.

In mehreren Fällen des feministischen Primitivismus zum Beispiel schien die einfachere, unterdrückte und von den primitiven Gesellschaften erhellte Wahrheit eine Reduktion der Identität auf das Geschlecht und der Kultur auf das Biologische zu beinhalten. Eine Ikonographie aus Blut, Haaren und Organen als Reaktion auf einen früheren Formalismus, der mit männlicher Vorherrschaft verbunden war, zeichnet zahllose neuere Werke aus, die feministisches Bewußtsein als wesentlich mit körperlichem Bewußtsein verbunden ausdrükken. Gebärmutterähnliche Räume und Eingeweidesymbole, die genausogut zum männlichen Sadismus des Surrealismus passen würden, sind in Objekte und Riten eingefügt, die – häufig unter ausdrücklicher Betonung eines Zusammenhangs mit eingeborenen oder prähistorischen Kulturen und Kunstarten – eine »natürliche« Ordnung des Stammeslebens feiern, das dem Imperium von Blut und Boden unterworfen ist.[16]

Solch eine Metaphorik ist nicht die ausschließliche Domäne einer bestimmten Art von Politik. CHARLES SIMONDS' frühe Demonstrationen von primären Beziehungen zwischen Erde, Körper und Architektur waren persönlich und direkt; seine »kleinen Leute« schienen zunächst eine Art Tolkienschen Charme mit befreienden politischen Idealen einer flüchtigen, gemeinschaftsorientierten Kunst zu verbinden □ 1035. Aber die Spenglerschen Zyklen, die anschließend für sie konstruiert wurden, und die unerbittlich erläuternde Dokumentation, die sie einschloß, haben den Humor in dem Maße trostloser gemacht, als die Phantasien einer totalitären sozialen Geschlossenheit und eines biologischen Determinismus, die ihre sexualisierte Anthropologie durchdringen, immer offenkundiger zutage traten.[17]

Nirgends jedoch ist die politische Problematik der jüngsten primitivisierenden Kunst so deutlich wie in dem ungewöhnlichen Werk des Deutschen JOSEPH BEUYS □ 1036–37. Durch seine merkwürdige Produktion aus Rede und Talg zieht sich ein selbstproklamiertes Programm sozialer Erneuerung ebenso wie ein weniger bemerkter symbolistischer Zug, der auf die deutsche chthonische Mythologie zurückweist. BEUYS' ganz persönlicher Mythos des Überlebens und der Wiedergeburt (der um den Absturz des von ihm gesteuerten Jagdfliegers und seine Rettung durch tartarische Nomaden kreist, 1943) ist die

□ 1036 *Joseph Beuys, ›Objekt aus „Eurasia", 32. Satz der Sibirischen Symphonie 1963‹, 1966, Kreide auf Tafel, Filz, Fett und Hase, 180 x 230 x 55 cm. Sammlung L. Schirmer, München.*

□ 1037 *Joseph Beuys, ›Ich liebe Amerika und Amerika liebt mich‹, 1974. Eine einwöchige Performance in der Galerie René Block in New York. Beuys (hier eingehüllt in eine Decke) lebte in einem Käfig mit einem Koyoten, der speziell als ein für die Indianer wichtiges Tier ausgewählt worden war, von den amerikanischen Weißen aber verachtet wird.*

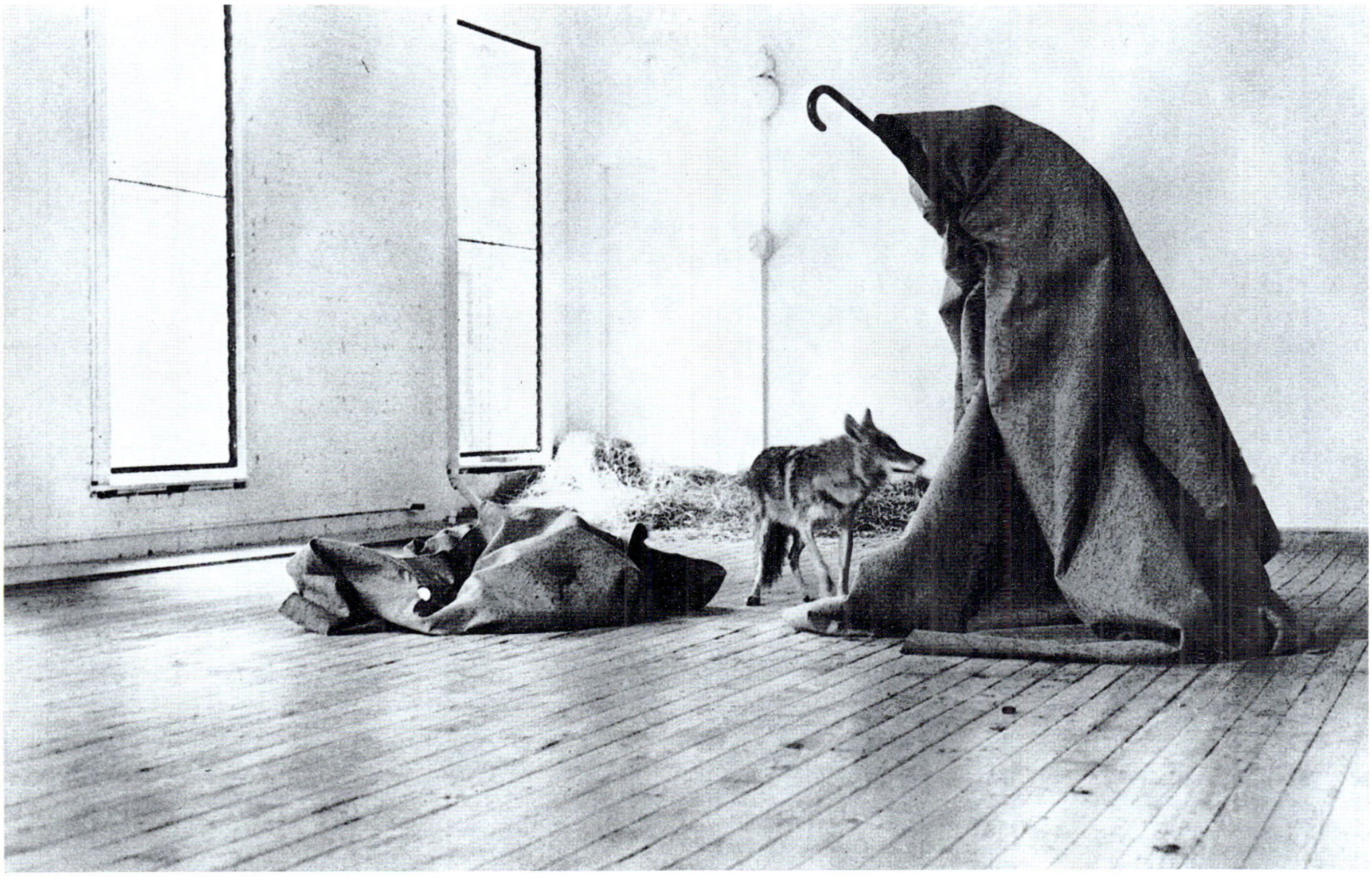

Seele in seiner metaphorischen Maschine – einem sperrigen Apparat aus wattiertem Eisen, Vitrinen der Jahrhundertwende und verrückten Diagrammen, die auf pseudoalchimistischen Rezepturen von Ursubstanzen, besonders Filz, Fett und Honig, basieren. Seine Performances mit (totemistischen?) toten und lebenden Tieren sind nur die offensichtlichen Beispiele seiner selbstbewußten Inszenierung in der Rolle des Schamanen, die in diesem Fall beabsichtigt und propagiert ist, als die eines erlösenden Zentrums neuerwachten deutschen Nationalbewußtseins. Stimme der neuen Linken und Advokat der Befreiung, sind BEUYS und sein Mythos nichtsdestoweniger unbequeme Erinnerung an ältere Beschwörungen eines nördlichen Eins-Seins des Menschen mit der Natur, die durch den Nationalsozialismus für einen üblen Zweck ausgenutzt wurden.[18]

Es wurde bereits deutlich gemacht, daß geometrische Ordnung und verbindliches Muster nicht notwendigerweise Unterdrückung bedeuten müssen. Ebenso sollte es auch klar sein, daß Biologie nicht Freiheit ist und daß das Ideal der Regression zur Natur hin seine Gefahr hat. Aber das ist ein Gemeinplatz und verhilft uns nicht zum Verständnis dessen, was im jüngsten Primitivismus unheilverkündend ist. Jenseits der Bewunderung für die Monumente unbarmherzig autoritärer Kollektivgesellschaften (öfter archaischen als eingeborenen Gepräges) oder eines sozio-biologischen Atavismus, die beide ziemlich deutliche Warnsignale sind, gibt es feinere, tiefergehende Strömungen in der neuen primitivistischen Kunst, die vermuten lassen, daß es dafür in der jüngeren Vergangenheit beunruhigende Vorgänger gab.

Wie wir zum Beispiel sagten, hat sich ein Werk, das sich selbst als postmodern stilisierte, an anthropologischen Modellen eingeborener und prähistorischer Integration von Kunst und Gesellschaft orientiert. In ihnen wurde ein Heilmittel gegen die Trennung oder Entfremdung der Kunst von ihrem Betrachter und gegen den daraus resultierenden Schwund ihrer Relevanz und Kraft gesehen. Hinter vielen Werken der Land Art und der Earthworks stand nach unserer Analyse der Wunsch, gerade diese Barriere zu überwinden, die Erfahrung des Betrachters umfassender einzubeziehen und ein Gefühl für Raumorientierung zu schaffen, das das Bewußtsein für Ort und Zeitpunkt steigern sollte. In Verbindung mit astralen und irdischen Ausrichtungen und Verweisen auf Menhire oder megalithische Monumente verfolgten viele dieser Werke außerdem die Absicht, auf einem persönlichen, das Ich auflösenden Niveau einen Sinn für Gemeinschaft mit uralten Rhythmen natürlicher Ordnung und menschlicher Tradition zu fördern. Wie positiv dies auch zu bewerten ist, an fast das gleiche dachte ALBERT SPEER in seinem Entwurf für die Zeremonienfelder (Zeppelinfelder) und Paradeflächen des Dritten Reiches. In der Tat war eines der deutschen Monumente, das von den Nazis besonders bewundert wurde, ein großer Kreis aus Monolithen. Bewußt Stonehenge nachgebildet, blieb er absichtlich ohne autonome figürliche Skulpturen und diente besonders den Sonnwendfeiern, bei denen der entfremdende Atomismus der modernen Gesellschaft in einer stärkenden Fusion von Blut und Boden, des Volkes mit dem Zyklus der Jahreszeiten und der Erde aufgehen sollte.[19]

Wenn auch totale Kunst und totalitaristische Kunst von unterschiedlichen Voraussetzungen ausgehen, so haben sie doch gemeinsame Feinde und können dabei enden, daß sie sich gegenseitig annähern. Insofern als sich der Primitivismus selbst

□ 1038 *Robert Smithson, ›Kreis‹, 1973, Fossilienschiefer, 46 x 28 cm. Sammlung Harris Weston, Cincinnati.*

□ 1039 *Keith Haring, Ohne Titel (Totem), 1983, Emaille auf Holz, 262 x 109 cm. Sammlung des Künstlers.*

□ 1040 *A. R. Penck, ›Verteidigung‹, 1983, Harz auf Leinen, 247 x 346 cm. Galerie Mary Boone/Galerie Michael Werner.*

als der rechtschaffene Feind des Modernen darstellt (wie viele seiner jüngsten Fürsprecher zu verstehen gaben), gerät er in eine gefährliche Gesellschaft mit anderen derartigen Feinden und erlaubt wenig schmeichelhafte Vergleiche. Wenn wir eine negative Antwort auf die Frage »Warum ein modernes Stonehenge?« haben wollen, dann ist sie hier zu suchen.

Reicher und mehr im Einklang mit dem Grundanliegen dieses Buches wäre es indes, den Primitivismus – sei er modern oder postmodern ausgerichtet – nicht nur als Symptom kultureller Entfremdung, sondern als Ausdruck des Lebens zu sehen. Nur in seinen einfallslosesten Momenten, nur für ein konventionelles Gemüt und den Uniformierten kann die Bewunderung des 20. Jahrhunderts für die Stammeskultur als rundum negative oder rein affirmative Antwort auf das moderne Leben gesehen werden. Wie primitivistisches Denken seit jeher, war es ein Dialog der Selbstprojektion, der Entdekkung und Selbstkritik, mit dem das moderne Leben für notwendige Alternativen wie auch für Mittel, diese zu entdecken und zu verstehen, Vorsorge trifft. Daumier und volkstümliche Graphik gaben Gauguin sein Verständnis für Hokusai und für die Kunst der Marquesasinseln, die ihrerseits Giotto für ihn lebendig werden ließen (vgl. S. 193). Dann führte Gauguin zusammen mit Cézanne Picasso zu seiner entscheidenden Begegnung mit der Stammesskulptur, was diesem wiederum half, aus seiner Bewunderung für Rousseau und seiner eigenen Leistung auf dem Gebiet der Karikatur größeren Nutzen zu ziehen.[20] Unter allen Erscheinungen der neuesten neoprimitivistischen Malerei, der nationalistischen Rhetorik, die ihr das Wort redet, oder der auf Neuaufnahme älterer Formen zielenden Tendenzen (A. R. Penck □ 1040 u.a.), erkennt man erfreulicherweise eine wenn auch schwache Fortsetzung dieser Art des Dialogs in der neuen Begeisterung für Graffiti. Hier verbinden sich die ausgeklügelten Mittel der modernen internationalen Zeichensprache mit den Konventionen des Cartoon und den Erfindungen der Straße in entweder grell auftrumpfenden oder ominösen unterirdischen Piktogrammen modernen Lebens (z. B. Keith Haring □ 1039). Kommunikationstheorie und Höhlenmalerei treffen sich in der südlichen Bronx. Tiefergehend und gehaltvoller manifestiert sich dieser essentielle Austausch in den besten Werken der Kunst, die wir besprochen haben. Minimal Art, Strukturalismus und moderne Technologie haben nicht einfach die Gegensätze hervorgebracht, denen sich der jüngste Primitivismus entzog, sie haben auch nicht einfach dazu ermutigt, eine vitale Originalität mit Bücherwissen zu erzielen. Sie haben genausogut neue Wege zum primitiven Denken und der primitiven Gesellschaft eröffnet, neue Bereiche der Gemeinsamkeit, die wiederum unsere Kunst erneuern und zur Rückbesinnung auf die vernachlässigten Vorbilder und Quellen innerhalb unserer eigenen Kultur verweisen.

Die Idee des Primitivismus als Flucht vor der Zivilisation oder die der primitiven Kunst als einer entlegenen Herausforderung ist eine späte Folge der romantischen Vorstellung, daß wirklicher Fortschritt, wirkliche Revolution, überhaupt Wahrheit in ihrem tiefsten Sinne nur möglich ist, wenn wir über die engen Grenzen der eigenen Kultur hinausgehen.[21] Moderne Erkenntnisse über das Denken und die Begrenztheit der Sprache legen nahe, daß diese Fluchtphantasie ewig unerfüllt bleibt. Dies muß nicht bedeuten, daß die Macht des Primitivismus reine Täuschung ist oder wir Gefangene von Konventionen sind, die uns den Kontakt mit irgend etwas jenseits unseres vertrauten Gesichtskreises versperren. Modernes Denken und moderner Stil verengen nicht nur, sondern erweitern auch unsere Sicht. Die Geschichte des modernen Primitivismus und der Charakter der besten unter den neueren Beispielen sind ein Beleg dafür. Dies ist ein Prozeß der Revolution, der mit der modernen Kultur beginnt und endet. Deswegen – nicht trotzdem – kann sich unsere Begegnung mit dem, was weit entfernt und verschieden von uns ist, ständig ausdehnen und vertiefen und unser Selbstverständnis stets bedrohen, herausfordern und erneuern.

Anmerkungen

Der Autor möchte Elyn Zimmerman und Adam Gopnik für viele wertvolle Gespräche danken, die diesem Essay zu seiner Entstehung verhalfen.

1. Der Wandel, auf den hier verwiesen wird, hatte seine Parallelen auch auf vielen anderen Gebieten. Primitivistische Tendenzen tauchten in transformierter und neubelebter Gestalt in Tanz, Dichtung und Musik der letzten zwei Jahrzehnte auf. Wichtiges Material zur Dichtung siehe Rothenberg, J., und Rothenberg, D., *Symposium of the Whole: A Range of Discourse toward an Ethnopoetics,* Berkeley 1983, besonders das Kapitel über »Contemporary Moves«. Zu Schlüsselbeispielen in der Musik siehe Reich, S., »Postscript to a Brief Study of Balinese and African Music« und »Notes on Music and Dance« in Reich, S., *Writings about Music,* Halifax 1974. Reichs Unterscheidung, S. 40, zwischen Einfügungen von *Klangmotiven* der eingeborenen Instrumente in früherer Zeit und den augenblicklichen Bemühungen, die *Struktur* solcher Musik zu assimilieren, wird von seiner eigenen Trommelmusik, die auf seinen Untersuchungen in Afrika basiert, beispielhaft vorgeführt. Seine Einfälle veranschaulichen den Gegensatz zwischen oberflächlichem Exotismus und dem Bedürfnis nach eingehendem Studium primitiver Kulturen, die einen großen Teil des neuesten Primitivismus motiviert haben.

2. Naturgeschichtliche Museen waren natürlich eine ständige Inspirationsquelle für moderne Künstler; zum Teil deswegen, weil sie oft naturwissenschaftliche Ausstellungen mit ethnologischen Ausstellungen verbinden. Siehe Weiss, J., »Science and Primitivism: A Fearful Symmetry in the Early New York School« in *Arts,* März 1983. Das American Museum of Natural History war für die Kunst seit 1945 eine besonders fruchtbare Fundstätte. In den 40er Jahren wird die Faszination, die sowohl von ethnologischen als auch biologischen Exponaten ausging, in den Plastiken von David Smith sichtbar □ 997, 998. Dies gilt auch für Claude Lévi-Strauss, siehe dessen Aufsatz »The Art of the Northwest Coast at the American Museum of Natural History« in *Gazette des Beaux-Arts,* 1943, S. 75. Robert Smithson setzte diese Tradition in seinem Film *Spiral-Mole* durch die Darstellung der Halle der Dinosaurier fort, siehe Childs, E. C., »Robert Smithson and Film: The Spiral Jetty Reconsidered« in *Arts,* Oktober 1981, S. 68–81. Eine Untersuchung zur Knochenverwendung in Nancy Graves' Werk mit den Methoden vergleichender Morphologie siehe *Nancy Graves: Sculpture, Drawings, Films, 1969–1971,* Aachen, Neue Galerie im Alten Kurhaus 1971, und Cathcart, L., *Nancy Graves: A Survey, 1969/1980,* Buffalo, Albright-Knox Art Gallery 1980. Zu Beuys siehe Tisdall, C., *Joseph Beuys,* New York, Solomon R. Guggenheim Museum 1979 – obwohl der Katalog in seinen Reproduktionen der Praxis von Beuys nicht gerecht wird, seine Werke in schweren Glasvitrinen auszustellen, die in ihrer Art an die ältere Museumspraxis in naturwissenschaftlichen Museen erinnern (siehe besonders den riesigen Aufbau seines Werks im Hessischen Landesmuseum Darmstadt). Zu Charles Simonds siehe Neff, J., u. a., *Charles Simonds,* Chicago, Museum of Contemporary Art 1982. Dort sagt Neff von Simonds, S. 10, daß »er zum Zeitpunkt der Drucklegung dieses Katalogs gerade die Möglichkeiten eines visionären Umweltmuseums der Naturgeschichte erforscht«.

3. Lévi-Strauss' Bezug zur modernen Kunst ist ein Thema, das einer eigenen Untersuchung bedarf. Es scheint klar zu sein, daß seine Bewunderung für Picasso eng mit seiner Reaktion auf die Stammeskunst verknüpft ist (siehe seine Bemerkungen zur Kunst der Nordwestküste, zitiert oben in Anmerkung 2). In der Tat scheint sein einflußreiches Modell des primitiven Denkens, wie es in »The Science of the Concrete« in *The Savage Mind,* 1962, formuliert ist, von einem Begriff der Kreativität auszugehen – dem des *bricoleur* –, der unter dem Eindruck von Picassos Collagen und des surrealistischen Denkens entstand und auf den Stammesmenschen projiziert wurde. Lévi-Strauss' Anleihen bei der Ästhetik der frühen Moderne ergibt in Verbindung mit seinem Einfluß auf das Denken jüngerer Künstler ein aufschlußreiches Modell des Primitivismus als Selbstprojektion der Moderne und als selbsterneuernde Kritik. Leider ist Lévi-Strauss' persönliche Einstellung gegenüber jüngerer Kunst weit weniger ergiebig. Wichtig in dieser Hinsicht war auch George Kublers *The Shape of Time,* New Haven 1962. Kublers antiorganisches Modell historischer Entwicklung in formalen Sequenzen und seine Beschäftigung mit Objektfamilien ungeachtet traditioneller Vorstellungen von künstlerischer Leistung spiegelte sich in der minimalistischen Ästhetik der 60er Jahre. Das Zusammentreffen von Kublers persönlichem Interesse an der präkolumbianischen Kunst mit dem zeitgenössischen Wiederaufleben künstlerischen Interesses an Stätten wie Nazca, Chichén Itzá und Tikal ist ein weiterer Berührungspunkt zwischen diesem archäologisch/historischen Denken und der Ästhetik der Gegenwart.

4. Zu Smithson und der Ikonographie der Kristallisation, der Auslöschung und des Verfalls siehe Childs, »Robert Smithson and Film«, a. a. O., und Gopnik, A., »Basic Stuff: Robert Smithson, Science and Primitivism« in *Arts Magazine,* März 1983. Die grundlegenden Texte dazu in Holt, N. (Hrsg.), *The Writings of Robert Smithson,* New York 1979. Allgemein zu Werken der Land Art siehe Beardsley, J., *Probing the Earth: Contemporary Land Projects,* Washington 1978, und Beardsleys in Kürze erscheinendes Buch *Earthworks and Beyond,* New York 1984. Zu den Berührungspunkten zwischen modernen und primitiven Werken der Land Art siehe vor allem das Sonderheft des *Art Journal,* herausgegeben von Robert Hobbs, über »Earthworks: Past and Present«, Herbst 1982.

5. Die negative Tendenz bestimmter Richtungen innerhalb der Minimal Art und einiger Werke der Land Art mag aus einer Haßliebe zu öden Stadtsiedlungen herrühren, die sich auch in bestimmten Aspekten des Werks von Richard Serra offenbart. Aufschlußreich ist in dieser Hinsicht Smithsons früher Artikel über »Entropy and the New Monuments«, siehe Holt (Hrsg.), *The Writings of Robert Smithson.* In einer unpublizierten Schrift des Institute of Fine Arts, New York University, interpretierte Robert Knafo auch Smithsons Metaphorik der Umweltverschmutzung, des Ödlands und des Verfalls als zugehörig zu seinen früheren blutbesudelten Kreuzigungen und stellte eine Beziehung zu Smithsons Engagement für den gescheiterten Katholizismus und seine Vorliebe für die trostlosen Visionen T. S. Eliots her. Die Idee von Zerstörung und Verfall bildet einen interessanten Gegensatz zu den »reineren« minimalistischen Vorstellungen einer antihistorischen Zeit, die der Synchronie gegenüber der Diachronie den Vorzug geben. Zu George Kublers antihistorischer, antiindividueller Theorie von Entwicklungsmustern von Objekten in vergangenen Zivilisationen siehe oben Anm. 3, und zu ihrem Einfluß auf solche Fragen der Ästhetik in den 60er Jahren steht eine Untersuchung noch aus.

6. Eine grundlegende Untersuchung zu den Theorien über die Beziehung des Betrachters zu zeitgenössischer Skulptur unter besonderer Berücksichtigung des Modells prähistorischer Anlagen siehe Morris, R., »Aligned With Nazca« in *Artforum,* Oktober 1975.

7. Zum Werk Turrells siehe Haskell, B., *James Turrell: Light and Space,* New York, Whitney Museum of American Art 1980.

8. Zu Hesse siehe Lippard, L., *Eva Hesse,* New York 1976.

9. Zu Winsor siehe Johnson, E. H., *Jackie Winsor,* New York, The Museum of Modern Art 1979.

10. Siehe Childs, »Smithson and Film« und Gopnik, »Basic Stuff«.

11. Siehe vor allem McLuhan, *Understanding Media: The Extensions of Man,* 1964, und *War and Peace in the Global Village,* 1968.

12. Siehe Hawkins, G. S., *Stonehenge Decoded,* Garden City 1965.

13. Zu Graves' Bewunderung der photographischen Bewegungsanalyse von Eadweard Muybridge und zu ihren Werkserien, die auf NASA-Mondkarten basieren, wie auch zu ihrer Serie über prähistorische Kunst siehe Cathcart, *Nancy Graves* (z. B. *Paleo-Indian Cave Painting,* 1971, S. 16).

14. Diese beiden Tendenzen innerhalb des primitivistischen Denkens decken sich weitgehend mit zwei altbekannten philosophischen Vorstellungen über die Zugänglichkeit der Wahrheit, die von Karl Popper als optimistische und pessimistische Wissenslehre behandelt wird. »Jede bildet die Basis für eine der beiden diametral entgegengesetzten Philosophien von Staat und Gesellschaft: auf der einen Seite ein antitraditionalistischer, antiautoritärer, revolutionärer und utopischer Rationalismus kartesianischer Prägung und auf der anderen Seite ein autoritärer Traditionalismus«, siehe Popper, »Sources of Knowledge and Ignorance« in *Conjectures and Refutations,* New York 1968, S. 11. Poppers Unterscheidung und seine Identifikation des grundlegenden Erbes des Rationalismus steht mit meinen früheren Bemerkungen im Hinblick auf Gauguins Rationalismus und dessen Abkehr von romantischen Traditionen in Bezug, siehe S. 209ff.

15. Eine Untersuchung über neueste Selbstmanipulation und schamanistische Praxis in der Kunst bei McEvilley, Th., »Art in the Dark« in *Artforum,* Sommer 1983, und bei Billeter, E., *Mythos und Ritual in der Kunst der 70er Jahre,* Zürich, Kunsthalle, 1981. Die Entwicklung des modernen Interesses am Schamanismus untersuchte Jonaitis, A., »Creations of Mystics and Philosophers: The White Man's Perceptions of Northwest Coast Indian Art from the 1930s to the Present« in *American Indian Culture and Research Journal* 5, 1, 1981. Siehe auch »Stones, Bones, and Skin: Ritual and Shamanic Art« in

□ 1041 *Bodenzeichnung in Form einer Spirale und Zickzacklinie, Nazca, Pompa Ingenio (Peru), 300 v. Chr. – 700 n. Chr.*

einem Sonderheft von *Artscanada,* Dezember 1973/Januar 1974 und *The Coming and Going of the Shaman: Eskimo Shamanism and Art,* The Winnipeg Art Gallery 1978.

16. Siehe Lippard, L., über »Feminism and Prehistory« in *Overlay: Contemporary Art and the Art of Prehistory,* New York 1983. Zu weiteren Zusammenhängen zwischen biologischer und soziologischer Polemik siehe zwei Bände, die unter der Schirmherrschaft der Dialectics of Biology Group entstanden, Rose, S. (Hrsg.), *Against Biological Determinism and Toward a Liberatory Biology,* London 1982.

17. Siehe Neff u. a., *Charles Simonds,* besonders wegen Simonds' eigener Texte über seine »little people«.

18. Über den Schamanismus in seinem Werk sagte Beuys: »Ich nehme diese Form altertümlichen Verhaltens als die Idee der Transformation durch konkrete Lebens-, Natur- und Geschichtsprozesse. Meine Absicht ist offensichtlich nicht die, zu solchen früheren Kulturen zurückzukehren, sondern die Idee der Transformation und der Substanz hervorzuheben. Das ist genau das, was der Schamane tut, um Veränderung und Entwicklung herbeizuführen: seine Natur ist therapeutischer Art.

»Natürlich kann der Schamane tatsächlich nur in einer Gesellschaft operieren, die noch intakt ist, weil sie sich in einem früheren Entwicklungsstadium befindet. Unsere Gesellschaft ist weit davon entfernt, intakt zu sein, aber auch das ist ein notwendiges Stadium. Es ist der Höhepunkt der Krise, der – wie wir in der Vergangenheit beobachten können – in jedem Geschichtsstadium einsetzt. Wenn die Intaktheit nicht mehr vorhanden ist, beginnt eine Art Metamorphose. So zeigt der Schamanismus, indem er einen Punkt in der Vergangenheit kennzeichnet, auch eine Möglichkeit für historische Entwicklung auf. Dies könnte beschrieben werden als die tiefste Wurzel der Idee geistigen Lebens, sogar tiefer noch als das mythische Niveau der späteren Stadien etwa der griechischen und ägyptischen Kulturen . . .

»Wenn wir unser eigenes Stadium des historischen Materialismus und alle Dinge, die wir in unserer gegenwärtigen Krise als negativ erfahren, in Betracht ziehen, so müssen wir zugeben, daß auch dieses Stadium eine historische Notwendigkeit ist. Ich erfuhr es im Krieg, und ich fühle es jetzt jeden Tag: Dieses Stadium des Verfalls entsteht mit einem einseitigen Verständnis der Idee des Materialismus. Wenn die Leute sagen, daß schamanistische Praxis atavistisch und irrational sei, so könnte man antworten, daß die Haltung der zeitgenössischen Wissenschaftler genauso altmodisch und atavistisch ist, weil wir jetzt in einem anderen Entwicklungsstadium in unserer Beziehung zum Materiellen angelangt sein sollten.

»Wenn ich als eine Art schamanistische Figur erscheine oder darauf anspiele, tue ich es, um meinen Glauben an andere Prioritäten zu betonen und die Notwendigkeit für einen völlig anderen Umgang mit Natursubstanzen hervorzuheben. Zum Beispiel ist es an Orten wie den Universitäten, wo jedermann so rational daherredet, nötig, daß eine Art Zauberer auftritt.« Tisdall, a. a. O., S. 23. Zum Beuysschen Mythos siehe besonders Buchloh, B., »Beuys: The Twilight of the Idol; Preliminary Notes for a Critique« in *Artforum,* Januar 1980, S. 35–43.

19. Das zur Debatte stehende Monument ist das *Tannenberg-Denkmal* von 1927, entworfen von Johannes und Walter Krüger. Seine Bedeutung für die Neuorientierung des deutschen Denkmals sowie sein Bezug zu späteren Nazi-Idealen behandelt George Mosse in *The Nationalization of the Masses,* New York 1977, vor allem auf S. 68–71.

20. Zu Gauguin und Picasso siehe mein Kapitel und das von William Rubin in diesem Buch. Zu Picasso und der Wechselbeziehung zwischen Karikatur, afrikanischer Kunst und Kubismus siehe Gopnik, A., »High and Low: Primitivism, Caricature and the Cubist Portrait« in *Art Journal,* Winter 1984.

21. Unter denen, die sich über die Eigenart der Entdeckung und Erfindung geäußert haben, ist Stephen Jay Gould derjenige, der stets die formative und tragende Rolle der Kultur hervorgehoben hat. Siehe u. a. seine Untersuchung von Darwins Entdeckungen, die die Galapagos-Finken betreffen, in »Darwin at Sea« in *Natural History,* September 1983. Zur affirmativen Rolle der Gesellschaft bei Entdeckungen siehe auch Brannigan, A., *The Social Basis of Scientific Discoveries,* New York 1981.

Weiterführende Untersuchungen zu diesem Themenkomplex in *Primitive Presence in the '70s* Poughkeepsie, N. Y., Vassar College Art Gallery 1975, und in der Besprechung von Carter Ratcliff, »On Contemporary Primitivism« in *Artforum,* November 1975, sowie bei Kardon, J., »The Ethnographic Model« in *Masks, Tents, Vessels Talismans,* Philadelphia 1979.

Photonachweis

Die Abbildungsvorlagen wurden überwiegend von den in den Bildlegenden genannten Besitzern zur Verfügung gestellt. Weitere Photos stammen von den nachfolgend genannten Photographen, Galerien und Institutionen (die Zahlen beziehen sich auf die Bildnummern).

Frontispiz: Museum für Völkerkunde, Berlin (Dietrich Graf); The Museum of Modern Art, New York (Mali Olatunji).

1 Creative Photography Ltd., Parnell, Neuseeland
2 Margit Baumann, Bern
5 © Foto Wettstein und Kauf, Museum Rietberg, Zürich
6 Mit freundlicher Genehmigung des Museum Rietberg, Zürich
7 Mit freundlicher Genehmigung des Museum Rietberg, Zürich
8 Ken Cohen, New York
9 Ken Cohen, New York
10 Hubert Josse, Paris
11 Speltdoorn, Brüssel
12 © Colorphoto Hans Hinz, Allschwil-Basel
13 Studio Contact, Paris
15 Jerry L. Thompson, Amenia, N.Y.
18 Larousse, Paris
20 © Malcolm Varon, New York, 1983
22 Ken Cohen, New York
23 © the Trustees of the British Museum, London
24 Ken Cohen, New York
25 André Koti, Paris
26 © Malcolm Varon, New York, 1983
27 Jean-Luc Mabit, Paris
29 André Koti, Paris;
30 MoMA (Kate Keller)
31 Lee Boltin, Croton-on-Hudson, N.Y.
32 MoMA (Mali Olatunji)
34 Mit freundlicher Genehmigung der Forum Gallery, New York
35 eeva-inkeri, New York
39 © the Trustees of the British Museum, London
42 MoMA (Mali Olatunji)
43 Museum für Völkerkunde, Berlin (Dietrich Graf)
44 Museum für Völkerkunde, Basel (Peter Horner)
46 Musée de l'Homme, Paris (J. Oster)
47 © Museum für Völkerkunde, Basel
48 © Colorphoto Hans Hinz, Allschwil-Basel
49 © Colorphoto Hans Hinz, Allschwil-Basel
50 © Museum für Völkerkunde, Basel (Peter Horner)
51 Roger Asselberghs, Brüssel
52 Igor Delmas, Paris
53 James Mathews, New York
54 Indiana University Art Museum, Bloomington (Ken Strothman and Harvey Osterhoudt)
56 Roger Asselberghs, Brüssel
58 Musée de l'Homme, Paris (J. Oster), Ken Cohen, New York
59 Jerry L. Thompson, Amenia, N. Y.
62 Mario Carrieri, Mailand
63 Mit freundlicher Genehmigung von M. Knoedler and Co., New York
65 André Morain, Paris
66 Igor Delmas, Paris
67 Poro, Mailand
69 Musée Barbier-Müller, Genf (Pierre-Alain Ferrazzini)
70 André Koti, Paris
71 Eric Pollitzer, New York
72 Mit freundlicher Genehmigung der Art Gallery of Ontario, Toronto
74 Soichi Sunami
78 André Koti, Paris
79 © Malcolm Varon, New York, 1983
81 MoMA (Mali Olatunji)
82 A.S.C. Rower, New York, © A.S.C. Rower, New York, 1984
84 Mit freundlicher Genehmigung des Metropolitan Museum of Art, New York
85 Soichi Sunami
86 © Appollot Photographie, Grasse
87 Hubert Josse, Paris
88 Indiana University Art Museum, Bloomington (Ken Strothman and Harvey Osterhoudt)
90 Little Bobby Hanson, New York
91 Musée de l'Homme, Paris (P. Destable)
92 The Metropolitan Museum of Art, New York, alle Rechte vorbehalten
93 MoMA (Kate Keller)
94 © Speltdoorn, Brüssel
95 Museum für Völkerkunde, Berlin (Dietrich Graf)
96 Michael Arthur, San Diego
97 MoMA (Mali Olatunji)
98 Musée de l'Homme, Paris (J. Oster)
100 David Reynolds, New York
101 Jerry L. Thompson, Amenia, N.Y.
102 Robert Griffin, Los Angeles
103 Igor Delmas, Paris
104 A. C. Cooper Ltd., London
105 Eric Pollitzer, New York
106 A. C. Cooper Ltd., London
107 © Speltdoorn, Brüssel
108 A. C. Cooper Ltd., London
109/111 Mit freundlicher Genehmigung der Perls Gallery, New York
110 Mit freundlicher Genehmigung der Archive Denyse Durand-Ruel, Rueil-Buzenval, Frankreich
113 O. E. Nelson, New York
114 © the Trustees of the British Museum
115 Appollot Photographie, Grasse
116 © The Metropolitan Museum of Art, New York, 1984
117 Mit freundlicher Genehmigung des Museums für Völkerkunde, Wien
118 Mit freundlicher Genehmigung des Museums für Völkerkunde, Wien
119 Mit freundlicher Genehmigung des Museums für Völkerkunde, Wien
121 Mit freundlicher Genehmigung des Museums für Völkerkunde, Wien
122 © the Trustees of the British Museum, London
123 The National Museum of Denmark, Kopenhagen (Lennart Larsen)
124 Mit freundlicher Genehmigung des Museums für Völkerkunde, Wien
126 Mit freundlicher Genehmigung des Museums für Völkerkunde, Wien
127 Museum of the American Indian, Heye Foundation, New York (Carmelo Guadagno)
130 © American Museum of Natural History, 1984 (R. P. Sheridan)
133 Eric Pollitzer, New York
135 Bibliothèque Nationale, Paris
137 © The Metropolitan Museum of Art, New York, 1984
138 Bibliothèque Nationale, Paris
139 Musée de l'Homme, Paris
140 Hubert Josse, Paris
141 Bibliothèque Nationale, Paris
142 Bibliothèque d'Art et d'Archéologie, Fondation Jacques Doucet, Paris
143 Little Bobby Hanson, New York
144 Musée de l'Homme, Paris (D. Ponsard)
146 Bibliothèque Nationale, Paris
147 Mit freundlicher Genehmigung der Galerie Albert Loeb, Paris
148 Musée de l'Homme, Paris (Jacques Viot)
149 Hubert Josse, Paris
150 Hubert Josse, Paris
151 Eric Pollitzer, New York
152 Rheinlander Photoatelier, Hamburg
154 Mit freundlicher Genehmigung der Pierre Matisse Gallery, New York
155 Musée de l'Homme, Paris (van de Broek)
160 Denise Colomb, Paris
161 In Focus Production, Tucson
162 Musée de l'Homme, Paris
163 Roger Asselberghs, Brüssel
166 Jerry L. Thompson, Amenia, N. Y.
167 A. C. Cooper Ltd., London
168 Barnes and Bradforth, London
172 Speltdoorn, Brüssel
173 Igor Delmas, Paris
174 Musée Royal de l'Afrique Centrale, Tervuren
177 Igor Delmas, Paris
178 Berriet, Paris
179 Berriet, Paris
180 Mit freundlicher Genehmigung des Kunstmuseums Basel
182 René-Jacques, Paris
183 Poro, Mailand
184 Igor Delmas, Paris
185 Bob Kolbrener, St. Louis
186/187 Nationalgalerie, Budapest
190 Vladimir Markow (V. I. Matrei)
193 Alfred Stieglitz
195 Poro, Mailand
197 Mit freundlicher Genehmigung des Minneapolis Institute of Arts
198 Hubert Josse, Paris
200 MoMA (Mali Olatunji)
201 André Koti, Paris
202/3 Roger Asselberghs, Brüssel
208 Soichi Sunami
209 Poro, Mailand
S. 92/3 Mit freundlicher Genehmigung des Sterling and Francine Clark Art Institute, Williamstown, Mass.
216 © The Metropolitan Museum of Art, New York, 1983
221 Tom Scott, Edinburgh
222 Ole Woldbye, Kopenhagen
223 The Metropolitan Museum of Art, New York, alle Rechte vorbehalten
224 © The Metropolitan Museum of Art, New York, 1983
229 © Colorphoto Hans Hinz, Allschwil-Basel
234 Mit freundlicher Genehmigung des Musée Gauguin, Tahiti (Dominique Charnay)
236 A. C. Cooper Ltd., London
239 A. C. Cooper Ltd., London
240 Mit freundlicher Genehmigung der Art Gallery of Ontario, Toronto
242 A. C. Cooper Ltd., London
243 Mit freundlicher Genehmigung der Art Gallery of Ontario, Toronto
246 Jan and John F. Thomson, Los Angeles
248 Musée Barbier-Müller, Genf (Pierre-Allain Ferrazzini)
252 Speltdoorn, Brüssel
253 The Metropolitan Museum of Art, New York, alle Rechte vorbehalten
255 John Webb, Cheam, Surrey, England
255b © Museum für Völkerkunde, Basel
256 Mit freundlicher Genehmigung von M. Knoedler and Co., New York
260 Hubert Josse, Paris
268 Bruce C. Jones, Rocky Point, N.Y.
271 The Metropolitan Museum of Art, New York, alle Rechte vorbehalten
272 Ray Manley, Tucson
275 Mit freundlicher Genehmigung des National

Museum of African Art, Eliot Elisofon Archives, Smithsonian Institution (Eliot Elisofon)
276 Mit freundlicher Genehmigung von Michel Kellerman
283 Larry Ostrom
284 André Koti, Paris
285 André Koti, Paris
286 Mit freundlicher Genehmigung von M. Knoedler and Co., New York
288 André Koti, Paris
290 Eric Pollitzer, New York
291 MoMA (Kate Keller)
292 Ken Cohen, New York
294 Mit freundlicher Genehmigung des Historischen Museums, Bern
295 © The National Museum of Ireland
298 Hubert Josse, Paris
301 MoMA (Kate Keller)
307 The Metropolitan Museum of Art, New York, alle Rechte vorbehalten
311 Soichi Sunami
313 Nic Tenwiggenhorn, Düsseldorf
315 Malcolm Varon, New York
316 MoMA (Mali Olatunji)
319 © Colorphoto Hans Hinz, Allschwil-Basel
320 Eric E. Mitchell
321 MoMA (Kate Keller)
324 Musée de l'Homme, Paris (D. Ponsard)
325 MoMA (Kate Keller)
328 André Koti, Paris
330 Musée de l'Homme, Paris (J. Oster)
334 MoMA (Kate Keller)
335 Musée de l'Homme, Paris (D. Ponsard)
336r/337 MoMA (Kate Keller)
338 Speltdoorn, Brüssel
339 MoMA (Kate Keller)
340 Bruno Piazza, Brüssel
341 © Michel Laurent
344 © Malcolm Varon, New York, 1984
345 André Koti, Paris
346 Mit freundlicher Genehmigung der Acquavella Galleries, New York
349 Ken Cohen, New York
350 Speltdoorn, Brüssel
355 Eric Pollitzer, New York
362 Appollot Photographie, Grasse
363 Mit freundlicher Genehmigung der Galerie Jan Krugier, Genf
364 Appollot Photographie, Grasse
365 MoMA (Kate Keller)
367 Nic Tenwiggenhorn, Düsseldorf
370 André Koti, Paris
372 Mit freundlicher Genehmigung der Galerie Louise Leiris, Paris
373 André Koti, Paris
374 Mit freundlicher Genehmigung von Michel Kellerman
376 Appollot Photographie, Grasse
378 André Koti, Paris
379 © University Museum, University of Pennsylvania
383 A. Lauro, Marseille
385 John Webb, Cheam, Surrey, England
387 MoMA (Kate Keller)
391 Nic Tenwiggenhorn, Düsseldorf
392 André Koti, Paris
393 Malcolm Varon, New York
395 Mit freundlicher Genehmigung der Galerie Jan Krugier, Genf
400 Malcolm Varon, New York
401 Speltdoorn, Brüssel
402 Mit freundlicher Genehmigung von Dr. Stanley Jernow
403/404 Musées Nationaux, Paris
406 Jacqueline Hyde, Paris
408 Musées Nationaux, Paris
409 Appollot Photographie, Grasse
412 Mit freundlicher Genehmigung der Galerie Louise Leiris, Paris
415 Eric Pollitzer, New York
416 MoMA (Mali Olatunji)
417 André Koti, Paris
422/423 Speltdoorn, Brüssel
425 André Koti, Paris
429 René-Jacques, Paris
430 André Koti, Paris
432 André Koti, Paris
438 MoMA (Mali Olatunji)
439 Herbert Migdoll, New York
440 Chevallier, Troyes
447 Mit freundlicher Genehmigung von Alex Maguy, Paris
450 Nic Tenwiggenhorn, Düsseldorf
453 André Koti, Paris
456 Nic Tenwiggenhorn, Düsseldorf
457 Mit freundlicher Genehmigung der Nationalgalerie Berlin (Reinhard Friedrich)
458 André Koti, Paris
459 MoMA (Kate Keller)
460 Appollot Photographie, Grasse
462 © Edward Quinn, Nizza
465 © The Trustees of the British Museum, London
466 © André Ostier, Paris
467 André Koti, Paris
468 © Roger Asselberghs, Brüssel
470 Appollot Photographie, Grasse
472 Musées Nationaux, Paris
473 Malcolm Varon, New York
475 © Brassaï, 1943
483 Soichi Sunami
486 Carmelo Guadagno
487 Hubert Josse, Paris
490 © the Trustees of the British Museum, London
493 Brancusi Archives, Musée National d'Art Moderne, Paris
498 Eric Pollitzer, New York
500 Jacqueline Hyde, Paris
502 Carmelo Guadagno und David Heald
505 Dennis Barna, Brooklyn, N.Y.
508 Charles Henault
511 Eric Pollitzer, New York
519 © Henning Rogge, Berlin
528 Ralph Kleinhempel, Hamburg
529 Ralph Kleinhempel, Hamburg
530 Museum für Völkerkunde, Berlin (Dietrich Graf)
531 Bildarchiv Foto Marburg
532 Gerd Remmer, Flensburg
537 Gerd Remmer, Flensburg
540 Henning Rogge, Berlin
545 The Metropolitan Museum of Art, New York, alle Rechte vorbehalten
547 Hepp und Hepp, Konstanz
551 Rheinisches Bildarchiv, Köln
552 Hamburgisches Museum für Völkerkunde (Brigitte Claassen)
556 Gerd Remmer, Flensburg
557 Ralph Kleinhempel, Hamburg
558 Soichi Sunami
561 © Staatliche Museen Preußischer Kulturbesitz, Berlin (Jörg Anders, Berlin)
562 © Henning Rogge, Berlin,
566 Henning Rogge, Berlin
567 Mit freundlicher Genehmigung des Brücke-Museums, Berlin (Emy Frisch)
572 © Henning Rogge, Berlin
573 Mit freundlicher Genehmigung von Christie, Manson and Woods International, New York
574 Studio Parvum Photo, Mailand
575 Musée de l'Homme, Paris (D. Ponsard)
576 Studio Parvum Photo, Mailand
577 Studio Parvum Photo, Mailand
580 Studio Parvum Photo, Mailand
581, 582 Studio Parvum Photo, Mailand
583 Mit freundlicher Genehmigung der Galerie Louise Leiris, Paris
584 Studio Parvum Photo, Mailand
585 Studio Parvum Photo, Mailand
587 Studio Parvum Photo, Mailand
588 André Koti, Paris
590 The Metropolitan Museum of Art, New York, alle Rechte vorbehalten
593 MoMA (Mali Olatunji)
594 © The Tate Gallery, London
595 Eric Pollitzer, New York
599 Soichi Sunami
600 Walker Evans
601 Mit freundlicher Genehmigung von Franyo und Gustave Schindler, New York
603 Adolph Studly
606 MoMA (Mali Olatunji)
609 MoMA (Mali Olatunji)
610 MoMA (Kate Keller)
612 Foto, Mailand
613 © The Metropolitan Museum of Art, New York, 1980
615 Igor Delmas, Paris
616 The Metropolitan Museum of Art, New York, alle Rechte vorbehalten
622 © the Trustees of the British Museum, London
623 © the Trustees of the British Museum, London
624 Mario Carrieri, Mailand
625 The Metropolitan Museum of Art, New York, alle Rechte vorbehalten
627 Musées Nationaux, Paris
630 MoMA (Mali Olatunji)
631 Mit freundlicher Genehmigung der Anthony d'Offay Gallery, London
636 Ken Cohen, New York
642 A. C. Cooper Ltd., London
644 Derek Balmer, Bristol, England
645 © the Trustees of the British Museum, London
646 Mit freundlicher Genehmigung der Anthony d'Offay Gallery, London
649 Mit freundlicher Genehmigung des Joslyn Art Museum, Omaha, Nebraska
650 eeva-inkeri, New York
653 Mit freundlicher Genehmigung der Babcock Galleries, New York
656 Museum für Völkerkunde, Berlin (Dietrich Graf)
658 Museum für Völkerkunde, Berlin (Dietrich Graf)
661/662 Museum für Völkerkunde, Berlin (Dietrich Graf)
663 Mit freundlicher Genehmigung von Cordier and Ekstrom, New York (Geoffrey Clements, New York)
667 The Metropolitan Museum of Art, New York, alle Rechte vorbehalten
668 A. C. Cooper, Ltd., London
669 Jerry L. Thompson, Amenia, N. Y.
671 John D. Schiff
673 The Metropolitan Museum of Art, New York, alle Rechte vorbehalten
674 Geoffrey Clements, New York
676 A.S.C. Rower, New York, © 1984 A.S.C. Rower, New York
680 Chisholm, Rick and Assoc., Houston
681 Clemens Kalischer, Stockbridge, Mass.
686 Mit freundlicher Genehmigung des Musée National Fernand Léger, Biot
693 Mit freundlicher Genehmigung des Musée National Fernand Léger, Biot
694 Eric Pollitzer, New York
695 David Allison, New York
702 MoMA (Kate Keller)
703 © COSMOPRESS, Genf, und ADAGP, Paris, 1984
704 © COSMOPRESS, Genf, und ADAGP, Paris, 1984
707 © Malcolm Varon, New York
713 Mit freundlicher Genehmigung des Milton and Sally Avery Center for the Arts, The Bard College Center, Annandale-on-Hudson N.Y.
714 © COSMOPRESS, Genf, und ADAGP, Paris, 1984
717 Walker Evans
719 MoMA (Kate Keller)
720 Mit freundlicher Genehmigung der Saidenberg Gallery, New York

722/23 © COSMOPRESS, Genf, und ADAGP, Paris, 1984
728 © the Trustees of the British Museum, London
731 Mit freundlicher Genehmigung von Audap-Godeau-Solanet, Paris
733 Eric Pollitzer, New York
734 Indiana University Art Museum (Ken Strothman und Harvey Osterhoudt)
736 Mit freundlicher Genehmigung des Museum Rietberg, Zürich
737 Eric Pollitzer, New York
742 © President and Fellows of Harvard College, 1984 (Hillel Berger)
749 © Malcolm Varon, New York
751 © Malcolm Veron, New York, 1984
758 Walter Drayer, Zürich
762 Mme Sabine Weiss, Paris
763 Mme Sabine Weiss, Paris
765 Mit freundlicher Genehmigung des Museums für Völkerkunde, Berlin
771 Routhier, Studio Lourmel, Paris
773 Roger Asselberghs, Brüssel
774 Mme Sabine Weiss, Paris
775 Roger Asselberghs, Brüssel
776 © the Trustees of the British Museum, London
777 MoMA (Kate Keller)
783 Igor Delmas, Paris
784 Mit freundlicher Genehmigung von Reinhold Hohl, Magden, Schweiz
792 Mit freundlicher Genehmigung von Francis M. Naumann, New York
797 Richard di Liberto, Fresh Meadows, N.Y.
799 Hubert Josse, Paris
800 © the Trustees of the British Museum, London
801 Eric Pollitzer, New York
802 Little Bobby Hanson, New York
805 Mit freundlicher Genehmigung von Charles Ratton, Paris
806 Hamburgisches Museum für Völkerkunde (Brigitte Claassen)
807 The Metropolitan Museum of Art, New York, alle Rechte vorbehalten
818 Soichi Sunami
821 The American Museum of Natural History, New York (Rota)
827 © Städtisches Kunstinstitut, Frankfurt am Main (Ursula Edelmann, Frankfurt am Main)
829 © The Denver Art Museum
834 Eric Pollitzer, New York
835 Soichi Sunami
839 © Malcolm Varon, New York
840 Eric Pollitzer, New York
842 Glenbow Photograph, Calgary, Alberta
843 MoMA (Mali Olatunji)
844 Mme Sabine Weiss, Paris
845 MoMA (Kate Keller)
846 André Koti, Paris
847 © Arnold Newman
848 Ray Manley, Tucson
849 Eric Pollitzer, New York
851 © Malcolm Varon, New York
856 Eric Pollitzer, New York
859 Hickey-Robertson, Houston
861 Bill Holm, Seattle
862 Taylor and Dull
865 Hamburgisches Museum für Völkerkunde (Brigitte Claassen)
867 Mit freundlicher Genehmigung von *L'Œeil,* Lausanne
868 Mit freundlicher Genehmigung von Richard L. Feigen und Co., New York
869 André Koti, Paris
870 Soichi Sunami
872 Studio Marion-Valentine, Paris
873 © the Trustees of the British Museum, London
879 Mit freundlicher Genehmigung der Pierre Matisse Gallery, New York (Oliver Baker)
881 Soichi Sunami
882 MoMA (Kate Keller)
885 Mit freundlicher Genehmigung der Pierre Matisse Gallery, New York (Eric Pollitzer, New York)
886 Walter J. Russel, New York
888 Linden-Museum, Stuttgart (Ursula Didoni)
889 Musée Barbier-Müller, Genf (Pierre Alain Ferrazzini)
901 Mit freundlicher Genehmigung der Henri Kamer Gallery, New York
902 Mit freundlicher Genehmigung des Musée des Arts Africains et Océaniens, Paris
903/904 Roger Asselberghs, Brüssel
905 Igor Delmas, Paris
906 The Metropolitan Museum of Art, New York, alle Rechte vorbehalten
909 Mit freundlicher Genehmigung der Marlborough Fine Art Ltd., London
910 © City Art Gallery, Manchester
912/913 © the Trustees of the British Museum, London
914/915 © the Trustees of the British Museum, London
921 © the Trustees of the British Museum, London
923 Mit freundlicher Genehmigung der Henry Moore Foundation, Much Hadham, England
925 © the Trustees of the British Museum, London
926 © the Trustees of the British Museum, London
927 Mit freundlicher Genehmigung der Henry Moore Foundation, Much Hadham, England
928 A. C. Cooper Ltd., London
933 A. C. Cooper Ltd., London
934 Jean-Luc Mabit, Paris
936 Mit freundlicher Genehmigung der Art Gallery of Ontario, Toronto
941 Ken Cohen, New York
945 MoMA (Mali Olatunji)
947 © Adolph and Esther Gottlieb Foundation, New York, 1980 (Robert Emates, New York)
948 Don Myer
949 Mit freundlicher Genehmigung der Pace Gallery, New York, © Besitz Mark Rothko
951 Mit freundlicher Genehmigung von Christie, Manson and Woods International, New York
953 © Justin Kerr, New York, 1983
956 Mit freundlicher Genehmigung der Smithsonian Institution, Washington
957 Hamburgisches Museum für Völkerkunde (Brigitte Claassen)
958 James Mathews, New York
960 Eric Pollitzer, New York
961 Rudolph Burckhardt, New York
962 Adolph Studly
964 MoMA (Mali Olatunji)
965 © Adolph and Esther Gottlieb Foundation New York, 1980 (O. E. Nelson, New York)
966 Rudolph Burckhardt, New York
967 © Adolph and Esther Gottlieb Foundation, New York, 1979 (O. E. Nelson, New York)
968 Mit freundlicher Genehmigung der Adolph and Esther Gottlieb Foundation, New York
969 Malcolm Varon, New York
970 Malcolm Varon, New York
971 Mit freundlicher Genehmigung von Wadsworth Atheneum, Hartford
973 Little Bobby Hanson, New York
974 MoMA (Mali Olatunji)
975 Pierre-Alain Ferrazzini, Genf
977 David Wharton
978 MoMA (Kate Keller)
979 Courtesy Richebourg/Mc Coy Gallery, New York
980 Mit freundlicher Genehmigung von E. V. Thaw, New York
982 Mit freundlicher Genehmigung der Tate Gallery, London
984 MoMA (Kate Keller)
986 Geoffrey Clements, New York
988 Soichi Sunami
989 Michael Tropea, Chicago
990 ©Adolph and Esther Gottlieb Foundation, New York, 1979 (O. E. Nelson, New York)
991 Eric Pollitzer, New York
995 University of Indiana Art Museum, Bloomington (Ken Strothman und Harvey Osterhoudt)
996 Tom van Eynde, Berkeley, Ill.
999 D.A.D./R. W. Dreyfus, Paris
1001 © Dia Art Foundation, 1980 (John Cliett)
1004 © Marilyn Bridges, 1979
1007 Mit freundlicher Genehmigung der Xavier Fourcade, Inc., New York
1008 Mit freundlicher Genehmigung des Künstlers
1010 © Marilyn Bridges, 1979
1012 © Walter De Maria, 1968
1015 Mit freundlicher Genehmigung des Künstlers
1016 © Pieter Boersma GFK, Amsterdam, mit freundlicher Genehmigung der Leo Castelli Gallery, New York
1017 Mit freundlicher Genehmigung des Künstlers (Maryanne Caruthers-Akin, Portland, Oregon)
1019 Christos Gianakos, New York
1029 Mit freundlicher Genehmigung des Künstlers (Leslie Harns)
1032 Lee Stalsworth
1033 Joe Schopplein, San Francisco
1034 Peter Moore, New York
1035 Rudolph Burckhardt, New York
1037 Mit freundlicher Genehmigung der Ronald Feldman Fine Arts, New York (Caroline Tisdall)
1038 Mit freundlicher Genehmigung der John Weber Gallery, New York (J. Ferrari)
1039 Mit freundlicher Genehmigung der Mary Boone Gallery, New York (Alan Zindman/ Lucy Fremont, New York)
1040 Ivan Dalla-Tana, New York
1041 © Marilyn Bridges 1979

Anhang

Lexikon der Stämme und Stammesgebiete

Das folgende Lexikon gibt Auskunft über Siedlungsgebiete, Geschichte, Lebensweise, Kultur und Kunst aller in den Beiträgen genannten Stämme Afrikas, Ozeaniens, Nord- und Südamerikas. Völkergruppen, in deren Gesellschaftsstruktur die Kennzeichen der Hofkultur überwiegen, wurden entsprechend dem Verständnis von Primitivismus nicht aufgenommen. Präkolumbische Kulturen, die noch Traditionen von Stammeskulturen bewahrten (z. B. die Inka), sind indes in einigen Ausnahmefällen vertreten.

Die nach den Stammesnamen jeweils in Klammern gesetzten Bezeichnungen geben weitere in der völkerkundlichen Literatur geläufige Schreibweisen wieder. Ziffern, die nach dem Stammesnamen stehen, sind allgemeine Seitenverweise, solche mit einem Künstlernamen verweisen auf Textstellen, wo eine spezifische Beziehung zwischen dem Stamm und dem genannten Künstler hergestellt wurde. Die im Buch abgebildeten Kunstwerke der Stämme sind jeweils am Ende des Artikels mit Titel und Abbildungsverweis zusammengefaßt.

Zur Erläuterung von Fachbegriffen wie ›Deszendenz‹ siehe das Glossar. Hinweise auf wichtige Publikationen zu den Stämmen und primitiven Kulturen finden sich am Schluß des Lexikons der Stämme und Stammesgebiete.

A

Abelam 48

Stamm in NO-Neuguinea, dem jetzigen Staat Papua-Neuguinea. Siedlungsort sind die südlichen Vorberge des Prinz-Alexander-Gebirges und das südwärts anschließende Savannenland nördlich der Sepik-Niederung. Die *Abelam* sprechen eine zur Ndu-Familie gehörige nichtmelanesische Sprache. Sie sind relativ kleinwüchsig und gehören physisch zu den »Voraustronesiern«. Metall- und schriftlose Kultur. Die *Abelam* leben in zu lockeren Dorfschaften zusammengeschlossenen Weilern auf Hügelkämmen und Bergkuppen. In jeder Dorfschaft leben zwei nichtexogame, nichttotemistische, vorwiegend patrilineare Gruppen *(aras)*, innerhalb derer jeder Mann mit seinen Söhnen seinen zeremoniellen Tauschpartner für Yams und Schweine hat. In gut gepflegten, klaneigenen Gärten Anbau von Yams (Dioscorea esculenta), Taro, Bananen, Zuckerrohr u. a. Abernten von meist wildwachsendem Sago. Wichtigste Anbaupflanze ist der in kleinen »heiligen Gärten« kultivierte Pfahlyams, dessen Anbau mit zahlreichen kultischen und magischen Praktiken umgeben ist und der nach der Ernte mit Masken, Kopfputz und Würdesymbolen der »großen Männer« zur Schau gestellt wird. Die Pflanzen gelten als geisterhafte Wesen, die sehen und hören, aber nicht reden können. Kulthaus mit bis zu 25 m aufragender, turmartiger Vorderfront, die weithin sichtbare Geisterbildnisse in leuchtenden Farben sowie vollplastisch beschnitzte, reich bemalte Giebelbalken mit Gesichtsdarstellungen oder Figurenreihen, die bestimmte Verstorbene symbolisieren sollen, trägt. Weitere eindrucksvolle Schnitzwerke sind Geisterfiguren, Nashornvögel, Schlangen u. a. *Lit.:* Koch 1968.

Bemalte Figur aus Holz □ 61; Figur aus Holz □ 802, 906

Acoma 484
Hartley 468

Siedlung der → *Puebloindianer* im Südwesten der USA.

Adjukru (Ajukru, Ayukru) 141

Elfenbeinküste, ca. 25 000 Stammesangehörige. Gruppe der Lagunen-Völker in der Region des Ortes Dabu (westlich Abidjan). Die bei ihnen vorherrschende Kleinwüchsigkeit wird als Folge der Vermischung mit den autochthonen Pygmäen erklärt. Sie dürften von den nördlich benachbarten → *Baule* und → *Akan*-Völkern, von denen sie kulturell beeinflußt wurden, an die Küste abgedrängt worden sein. Die *Adjukru* leben vornehmlich von der Lagunenfischerei, ergänzt durch Hackbau (Bananen, Maniok und Yams, dem eine wichtige kultische Rolle zukommt). Matrilineare Deszendenz; aus Pfahlbauten bestehende Kleindörfer unter der Herrschaft eines Ältestenrats und Dorfvorstehers. Hochstehendes Kunsthandwerk (Holzschnitzerei, Schmiedewesen).

Aduma (Duma, Badouma) 139, 140, 143, 181

S-Gabun, sprachlich den → *Teke*, kulturell den → *Shira* nahestehend.

Afo (Afao, Afu, Eloi)
Gaudier-Brzeska 460

Nigeria, ca. 8 000 Stammesangehörige, die der Kwa-Sprachengruppe zugehören. Die *Afo* sind Hackbauern in den Feuchtsavannen nördlich des Benue und bauen Hirse und Knollenfrüchte an, patrilineare Deszendenz, Seniorat mit Bevorzugung der Brudernachfolge. Ahnenkult und Agrarriten. Bekannt sind vor allem religiöse Lehmplastiken in Tier- und Menschenform mit stark stilisierten, z. T. gänzlich abstrakten Gebilden.

Mutter mit Kindern □ 638

Akan 135, 136, 142

Sammelbezeichnung für verschiedene Twi sprechende Gruppen, die den Großteil der heutigen Bevölkerung Ghanas ausmachen. Manchmal mit den → *Asante*, dem 700 000 Menschen umfassenden Hauptstamm der *Akan*, gleichgesetzt. Die *Akan* dürften in mehreren Wellen aus den Trockensavannen des nördlichen Nigergebietes in die tropischen Regenwälder des Südens gewandert sein. Legendäre Königslisten der *Akan* reichen mit den beiden Staatsgründungen Bono und Banda ins 13. Jahrhundert zurück. Der im 17. Jahrhundert blühende Denkera-Staat wurde von den ihnen ursprünglich tributpflichtigen *Asante* erobert (1720).

Figur aus Holz □ 210; Bekrönung eines Stabes □ 471

Alamblak (Arambrak)

Nebenfluß des → Karawari und Bezeichnung für die dort ansässige papuanische Bevölkerung.

Yipwon-Figur □ 108, 876, 933; Jagdamulett □ 159

Alaska

→ *Eskimo*

Aleuten 101, 105

Algerien Felszeichnungen 871

Ambete (Mbete, Mbede) 141, 181

Gabun, Kongo-Brazzaville, von den → *Kota* kulturell assimilierte Gruppe.

Anago 140, 141

→ *Yoruba*

Angmagssalik 106

Eskimoische Siedlung an der Ostküste Grönlands, deren Bewohner heute fast völlig europäisiert sind. Kunst und Religion sind nahezu vergessen. Immerhin fertigen diese *Eskimos* noch Figuren an, die böse Geister oder Gespenster darstellen. Die Qualität dieser Erzeugnisse dokumentiert den Niedergang einer einstmals intakten Kultur. In der Kunst Grönlands sind Spuren der normannischen Besiedlung, etwa im 12. Jahrhundert n. Chr., festzustellen. Ausgrabungen förderten Masken zutage, die normannisch-westeuropäischen Einfluß zeigen könnten.

Maske □ 128

Angola 174

→ *Chokwe*

Anyi (Anji, Agni) 135, 140, 141, 142, 180

Östliche Elfenbeinküste. Die *Anyi* umfassen mit verschiedenen Untergruppen ca. 100000 Mitglieder. Sie siedeln am Mittellauf des Comoé, relativ junge Volksbildung durch Vermischung mit → *Akan*-Gruppen, die nach der Eroberung ihres Königreiches Denkera durch die → *Asante* 1720 nach Westen und Süden abwanderten. Sie schufen kleine Feudalherrschaften mit absolut regierenden Herrschern. Feldbau von vornehmlich Yams, Taro und Hirsen, bescheidene Viehzucht. Verehrung einer höchsten männlichen Himmelsgottheit, die das Leben der Menschen bestimmt und der eine weibliche Erdgottheit gegenübersteht. Aus der Verbindung der beiden entstand ein reiches Pantheon. Matrilineare Deszendenz, Streusiedlung, Fertigung von kultischen Bronzegefäßen in Gelbgußtechnik. Wie die benachbarten, ebenfalls Twi sprechenden → *Asante* und → *Baule* sind die *Anyi* bekannt für ihre Goldgewichte.

Apachen 581

Indianerstamm, der teils zu den → *Prärie*-, teils zu den → *Puebloindianern* gehört.

Äquatorial-Guinea → *Fang*

Arawak Moore 615

Sprachgruppe im nördlichen Südamerika und der Karibik.

Arnhemland (Australien)
Klee 505

Asante (Ashanti) 136, 180, 623
Moore 623

Südliches Zentralghana. Hauptstamm der → *Akan*, 700000 Stammesangehörige. Die *Asante* sind seit Beginn des 16. Jahrhunderts als Träger eines mächtigen Staates nachweisbar. In einer Konföderation unter Osai Tutu (ca. 1695–1731) zerstörten sie 1720 das Denkera-Reich und bauten in der Folge einen Staatenverband auf, der im 19. Jahrhundert fast die Ausdehnung des heutigen Ghana erreichte. Quelle ihres Wohlstands waren die bedeutenden Goldminen und der über die Küstenstämme abgewickelte Handel mit den Europäern. Konflikte mit diesen handelsvermittelnden Stämmen lieferten den Engländern den Vorwand zu Krieg und zur Annektion des Reiches (1901). Absolutes zentralistisches Gottkönigtum, das deutlich mediterrane Züge aufweist, die über die Großstaaten des Sudan nach Süden und Westen ausstrahlten. Die Herrscher – Mittler zwischen dem Volk und den Königsahnen – waren durch zahlreiche Tabus und sakrale Privilegien ausgezeichnet. Symbol des Staates und Verkörperung seiner »Lebenskraft« war der »Goldene Stuhl«, ein mit Goldblech beschlagener Holzschemel, der wie der König die Erde nicht berühren durfte. Eine wichtige Rolle spielte die Königinmutter – ein Hinweis darauf, daß die herrschende patrilineare Nachfolgeregelung eine ursprünglich matrilineare Deszendenz überlagert hatte. Verschiedene Staatsräte und auf unterer Ebene Volksversammlungen beschränkten die absolute Macht des Herrschers. Die *Asante* sind Meister des Kunsthandwerks in Metall (Goldgewichte, Kleinplastiken, Goldschmuck) und der Holzschnitzkunst: Charakteristisch sind kleine, stilistische Fruchtbarkeitspuppen (*akua ba*, → *Fante*) mit übergroßen, scheibenförmigen Köpfen auf langen, mit Ringwülsten versehenen Hälsen. Ihre ohne Töpferscheibe gefertigten Tongefäße dienten dem Alltagsgebrauch und kultischen Zwecken. Die Religion der *Asante* kreist um ein Gottheitspaar (männlicher Himmel, weibliche Erde), dem ein reiches Pantheon mit z.T. androgynen Gottheiten entstammt.

Kopf □ 840

Asmat 70, 128, 564

Urtümliche Papua-Kultur in den sumpfigen Küstenländern Südwest-Neuguineas zwischen Lorenz-Fluß und Digul, jetzt in Irian Jaya (West-Irian) zu Indonesien gehörig. Etwa 30000 Menschen, die in Dschungel-Dörfern an zahllosen Flüssen wohnen. Bis zu 50 m lange Kulthäuser für Zeremonien und Kultfeste der Männer und als Junggesellenhäuser. Diese Holzbauten dienen auch als Aufbewahrungsort für die heiligen Masken, Trommeln. Ahnenfiguren oder Zeremonialschilde (Schilde wurden auch als Repräsentanten für einen vom Feind getöteten Angehörigen zum Eröffnungsfest für eine Rache-Kopfjagd geschnitzt) sowie für Trompeten und andere mit der Kopfjagd verbundene Kultobjekte. Zur Vertreibung der Totengeister und als Mahnmal für die Rache-Kopfjagd wurden *bisj*-Pfähle aus Mangroven-Stämmen errichtet. Sie tragen unten stilisierte Bootsdarstellungen, darauf übereinanderstehende Totenfiguren; oben befindet sich der weit ausladende »Vordersteven« oder die »Fahne« aus einer Brettwurzel. *Lit.:* Koch 1976, S. 37–39.

Schild □ 90, 294; Maske und Tanzkostüm □ 807

Athapasken 101

Sprachgruppe im nördlichen Teil Kanadas

Äthiopien

→ *Konso*

Attie (Atie, Attje, Akye) 180

Elfenbeinküste, ca. 55000 Stammesangehörige. Die *Attie* leben im Hinterland der eigentlichen Lagunenvölker zwischen Anjeby und dem unteren Comoé und betreiben Fischfang mit Wanderhackbau (Yams, Maniok, Bananen). Charakteristische Straßendörfer mit Dorfvorstehern und Ältestenrat. Mutterrechtliche Züge, erblicher Sklavenstand, der eine eigene Klasse bildet. Die *Attie* haben alte metallurgische Traditionen sowie eine bemerkenswerte Holzschnitzkunst (Thronstühle, Zeremonialschemel).

Australien 114

Känguruh □ 712; Liebesszene □ 885

Siehe auch Arnhemland

Australinseln (Tubuaiinseln) 70, 89
Brauner 579

Polynesien, östlich der Cookinseln, zu denen deutliche Beziehungen im Schnitzstil bestehen (geometrische Kerbschnitt-Ornamentik auf den Zeremonialpaddeln von Tubuai und den Zeremonialbeilen von Mangaia, Cookinseln).

Siehe auch Rurutu

Azteken 11, 86, 523–525
Zorach 485 – Giacometti 544

Das Reich der Azteken in Mexiko, das von etwa 1200 n. Chr. bis zur Ankunft der Spanier am 8. November 1519 bestand, trat in gewisser Weise das Erbe des Mayareiches an. Die Azteken waren ein kriegerisches Volk, das langsam einen straff organisierten Staat aufgebaut hatte. Aztekische Kunst weist realistischere Züge auf als die der Maya. Erhalten sind vor allem Masken aus graugrünem Stein. Bekannt sind auch die Schilde, mit aufgeklebtem Federmosaik dekoriert, die schon von Cortez gesammelt wurden. Als Inkunabeln aztektischer Plastik gelten die *Gottesmutter Tlazoltéotl*, die bei der Geburt des Maisgottes dargestellt ist (Privatsammlung, Washington), oder die Darstellung der aztekischen Gottheit Xolotl als Skelett (Linden-Museum, Stuttgart). Die aztekische Religion beinhaltet einen Glauben an verschiedene Götter. Die Spanier wurden als Verkörperung des Gottes Quetzalcoatl betrachtet, der aufgrund einer

Weissagung von Osten kommend das Land betreten sollte. Der »Zufall« wollte es, daß die Spanier genau an dem astrologisch geweissagten Datum die Küste Mexikos betraten.

Figur des Gottes Xochipilli □ 114; Aztekische Pyramide □ 786

B

Bafo 143

Stamm Kameruns, der im Küstenhinterland am Oberlauf des Mungo siedelt.

Baga (Bago) 25, 29, 70, 138, 140, 158, 167, 180, 349, 352, 353
Giacometti 518 – Matisse 351, 352 – Moore 613, 627 – Picasso 87, 275, 282, 283, 285, 286, 303, 308, 336, 349, 351

Republik Guinea, Küstenstreifen südlich der → *Nalu*. Die *Baga* zählen mit ihren Untergruppen, die zum geringen Teil islamisiert sind, ca. 45 000 Menschen. Wichtigste Kulturpflanze ist der Reis; bekannte Holzschnitzer (Masken) und Töpfer, Geheimbundwesen *(Simo)*, Ahnenverehrung, patrilineare Deszendenz. Kompaktdörfer mit Kleinhäuptlingen, die die politische Autorität darstellen.

Vogelkopfschmuck □ 33, 206; Schlangenfigur □ 78; Nimba-Maske □ 360, 454, 458; Figur aus Holz □ 365; Figur aus Holz und Stoff □ 366; Männlicher und weiblicher Kopf □ 610; Kopf □ 913

Bahoulé 167

→ *Baule*

Baining 43
Giacometti 43

Voraustronesische *Papua* der Gazelle-Halbinsel auf Neubritannien, jetzt zu Papua-Neuguinea gehörig. Halbnomadische Pflanzer. Sie fertigten die größten »Masken« der Erde an, die 10–12 m lang sein konnten und mittels Bambusstangen getragen wurden: großgesichtige Masken aus Baststoff (Tapa) über einem Stabgestell, mit runden Augen und vorstehendem Maul, die angeblich Krokodildarstellungen sind. Diese Masken wurden für Zeremonien beim Totenkult und anderen Anlässen gebraucht. *Lit.:* Koch 1976, S. 84, 86, 122.

Helmmaske □ 47; Kopfschmuck □ 152; Maske □ 806, 150 (oben Mitte)

Siehe auch Neubritannien

Bakoutos 167

Untergruppe der → *Ngombe*.

Balante 141, 180

Guinea-Bissau, zusammen mit den kulturell von ihnen nicht zu unterscheidenden *Kunante* ca. 170 000 Menschen. Sie siedeln an der Geba-Mündung und bis zum Casamance und leben vom Reisbau und der Fischerei. Wie die → *Baga* sind sie als gute Töpfer bekannt. *Balante*-Jünglinge bedecken ihre Geschlechtsteile mit Schildkrötenschalen oder Holzplatten, für die Frauen ist eine relativ große sexuelle Freizügigkeit bezeugt.

Balong 143

Stamm in Kamerun, der am Unterlauf des Mungo lebt.

Baluba → *Luba*

Bambara (Banmana) 25, 138, 140, 141, 158, 161, 180, 349, 350, 414
Brancusi 27, 360, 377 – Braque 153, 356, 357 – Derain 153 – Epstein 452 – Ernst 581 – Giacometti 542 – Janco 606 – Lam 604 – Léger 492 – Matisse 153, 238 – Picasso 282, 283, 295, 327, 329 – Schmidt-Rottluff 404

Mali, zusammen mit der islamischen Fischerkaste der *Somono* ca. 1 Million Mitglieder. Mande sprechende Gruppe der Sudan-Neger, ihr Hauptwohngebiet liegt zwischen Niger und Bani, in Ausläufern bis Nioro im Norden und Odienné im Süden (Elfenbeinküste), im Osten bis Macina, im Westen mit kleinen abgesplitterten Gruppen im Senegal und Guinea-Bissau. Karger Feldbau (Hirsen, Mais), z. T. mit künstlicher Bewässerung, im Nigerüberschwemmungsgebiet auch Reis, gute Weiden für Rinderzucht. Die wichtigste Hausform ist das runde Lehmhaus mit grasgedecktem Kegeldach. Gesellschaftliche Grundeinheit ist die erweiterte Familie, die eine Wohn- und Wirtschaftsgemeinschaft bildet und an deren Spitze der Älteste steht. Zu größeren Verbänden zusammengeschlossene Familien werden vom Oberhaupt der herrschenden Familie (fama) geleitet. Sein Status zeigt Spuren sakralen Königtums. Neben der vorherrschenden patrilinearen Deszendenz ein wohl überlagertes altes matrilineares System. Entwickelte Färbekunst und religiöse Holzschnitzerei (Antilopenmaskenaufsätze). Die *Bambara* entwickelten ausgeprägte Schöpfungsmythen mit Fruchtbarkeitsmotiven und Ahnenkult. Beschneidungszeremonie, um nach traditioneller Vorstellung die ursprüngliche Bisexualität aufzuheben. Im 17. Jahrhundert machten sich die *Bambara* von den → *Malinke* unabhängig und gründeten mit Ségou und der Landschaft Kaarta als Zentren zwei Staaten, die sich bis zur Eroberung durch die Franzosen (1890/91) behaupten konnten. In jüngster Zeit setzt sich der Islam, der seit alters einen starken Einfluß ausübte, immer mehr durch.

Figur □ 187; Figur aus Holz und Metall □ 209; Weibliche Sitzfigur □ 285; Antilopenkopfschmuck □ 354, 355, 356, 357, 692; Männliche Figur □ 372; Maske □ 394; Figur aus Holz □ 482; Kopfschmuck □ 498; Stoff mit Muster □ 716; Stoff mit Muster □ 718; Taktstock □ 779; Kono-Maske □ 627, 846

Bamileke

Kamerun, eine der drei Hauptgruppen der *Semi-Bantu* im → Kameruner Grasland (→ *Bantu*). Sammelbezeichnung für ca. 450 000 Menschen, die in etwa 90 Häuptlingsschaften organisiert sind. Sie siedeln westlich des Nunflusses, der Ostgrenze der benachbarten → *Bamum*. Pflanzbau von Mais und Kokoyams. Relativ hohe Siedlungsdichte trotz der isoliert über das Land verstreuten, umzäunten Gehöftanlagen. Zusammenhängende Häusergruppen nur in den Residenzen der Häuptlinge und hoher Würdenträger. Patrilineare Deszendenz mit Lokalexogamie. Die männlichen Nachkommen errichten ihre Gehöfte meist in der Nähe des väterlichen Hofes. Die Felder liegen häufig weit von den Höfen entfernt. Die patrilineare Gruppe stammt vom gemeinsamen Ahnen ab, der in Form eines Schädelkultes verehrt wird. Die göttlich gedachten Kräfte des »Urahns« gehen auf den jeweils herrschenden Häuptling über, der im Zentrum der rituellen Handlungen (vornehmlich Agrarkulte) steht. Die Herrscherinsignien (Schädel, Ahnensteine, Raphiataschen mit Zaubermedizin, eiserne Doppelglocken, sakrale Haumesser und Tonpfeifen sowie dem König vorbehaltene Kleider und Schmuckstücke) werden als heilige Attribute verehrt. Komplexes Rangzeremoniell, das sich in reichbeschnitzten Stühlen ausdrückt, die nur vom Häuptling verliehen werden dürfen: Die Stühle der Obersten haben vier Beine, drei Beine sind Zeichen niederen Ranges, zweibeinige Stühle sind Neuankömmlingen vorbehalten, während die gewöhnlichen Stammesmitglieder auf Bänken sitzen. Töpferei ist Domäne der Frauen, nur Figuren oder Masken aus Ton sowie Holztöpfe (häufig mit Tierdarstellungen) werden von Männern angefertigt.

Maske □ 176

Bamum (Mum, Mom, Banum)

Semi-Bantu des → Kameruner Graslandes (→ *Bantu*), setzen sich aus zwei Bevölkerungsgruppen zusammen: den *Tikar* im Sudan, von denen sich die *Bamum* unter der Führung des Häuptlingssohnes Nsare vor 250 Jahren abspalteten, und den autochthonen → *Bamileke*, mit denen sich die *Bamum* nach ihrer Einwanderung vermischt hatten. Das gegenwärtige Siedlungsgebiet wird von den Flüssen Nun und Mbam (im S und SW) und Nigeria (im N) begrenzt. Feldbau von Mais und Yams. Mehrere patrilineare Gruppen bilden eine Dorfgemeinschaft, deren Häuptling als Vertreter des Königs fungiert; Glaube an ein höchstes Wesen *(Ninyi oder Nyui*, »der überall ist, der alles sieht und alles hört«) sowie ausgeprägter Ahnenschädelkult. Entwickelte Holzschnitzkunst (Masken, Trommeln, Häuptlingsfiguren), Skulpturen aus Elfenbein (ein dem König vorbehaltenes Material) sowie geschnitzte Holzstühle, die die Stellung der Häuptlinge symbolisieren. In der Hauptstadt Fumban wurde bereits zu Beginn des 20. Jahrhunderts unter dem bedeutenden König Njoya eine für den Export arbeitende

Kunsthandwerksindustrie gefördert, die bis heute blüht.

Kopfschmuck □ 198

Bangwa 143
Janco 551

Kamerun, Häuptlingsschaft im Unterbezirk Bangante der Region der → *Bamileke*.

Holzmaske □ 284; Helmmaske in Gestalt eines Büffelkopfes □ 524; Figur □ 592

Banks Islands → Neue Hebriden

Figur eines Männerbundes (Rangstatue) □ 44, 46

Bantu

Sammelbezeichnung für einige hundert Stämme und Völker in Zentral-, Ost- und Südafrika. Ca. 90 Millionen Menschen. Mit ihrem Siedlungsraum umfassen die *Bantu* etwa ein Drittel Afrikas. Ihre Zusammengehörigkeit wird durch sprachliche Kriterien und weniger durch kulturelle Merkmale bestimmt. Die Sprache der *Bantu* kennt mehrere Untergruppen, z. B. das Semi-Bantu, das zwischen den Mittelbantu-Sprachen und den westsudanesischen Sprachen einzuordnen ist. Die *Bantu* werden in fünf Gruppen eingeteilt: *Nord-*, *Mittel-*, *Ost-*, *Südwest-* und *Südost-Bantu*.

Basa (*Bassa*, *Abo-Bassa*) 181

Kamerun, östliche und südöstliche Nachbarn der → *Duala* zwischen Wuri und Nyong, Bantu sprechend.

Bassa 180

Kru sprechende Gruppe in Liberia → *Kru*.

Basutoland 135

Baule (Baoule, Bahoulé) 25, 26, 87, 89, 141, 142, 158, 162, 167, 180, 219, 233
Brancusi 377 – Carrà 420, 422 – Epstein 434, 435, 446, 452, 453 – Lam 601, 604 – Matisse 231, 238, 303 – Modigliani 432, 433 – Ray 551

Elfenbeinküste, ca. 400000 Stammesmitglieder, die mit den → *Anyi*, → *Asante* und → *Attie* zur → *Akan*-Gruppe gerechnet werden. Um 1730 verließen die *Baule* nach Thronstreitigkeiten unter Führung der Königinmutter Aura Poku das Reich der *Asante* und zogen westwärts in die Savannen zwischen Bandame und dem in ihn einmündenden Nzi-Fluß. Zu der aus der *Asante*-Tradition mitgebrachten hochentwickelten Feinschmiedekunst (Goldarbeiten, Gelbguß) trat nun über Vermittlung der → *Guro*, ihren neuen Nachbarn, die Holzschnitzkunst: in der Tradition der → *Senufo* stehende Masken mit langgezogenen, herzförmigen Gesichtszügen und figurale Skulpturen. Diese relativ junge Entwicklung, die v. a. die westlichste *Baule*-Gruppe der *Atutu* erfaßte, erfuhr durch die frühe Wertschätzung und Nachfrage der europäischen Sammler seit etwa 50 Jahren wohl auch rückwirkende stilistische Veränderungen. Die meist kleinen Kultfiguren aus Holz (Höhe zwischen ca. 20 und 50 cm) stellen oft sog. »spirituelle Sexualpartner« dar, die jedem *Baule* bereits im Jenseits vor seiner Geburt zugedacht werden.

Maske □ 15, 186, 192, 597; Figur aus Holz □ 25, 880; Weibliche Figur □ 272; Helmmaske □ 440, 444, 500, 590, 696; Affe □ 628; Goli-Maske □ 883

Baya (Gbaya, Baja) 143

Zentralafrikanische Republik, ca. 200000 Stammesmitglieder, die von manchen Autoren der östlichen nigritischen Sprachgruppe (mit dem Hauptstamm der *Zande*) zugeordnet werden. Ihr Siedlungsraum erstreckt sich in den Feuchtsavannen zwischen der Grenze zu Kamerun und dem 600 km östlich liegenden Ubangiknie. Die *Baya* sind vermutlich in den letzten 200 Jahren aus dem Osten (Sudan) eingewandert und leben in ständiger Auseinandersetzung mit den islamischen, rinderzüchtenden *Fulbe*. Vorwiegend Feldbauern (Hirsen, Mais), Streudorfsiedlungen, patrilineare Deszendenz. Ihre Kultur ist z. T. durch den Einfluß der *Fulbe* geprägt: straffes, zentralisiertes Häuptlingstum mit sakralen Zügen, Geheimbundwesen. Beschneidungs- und Exzisionspraktiken. Glaube an einen Hochgott *(So)*, mit deutlichen Ahnenzügen. Entwickelte Töpferei (Frauen) und hochgeachtete Stellung der Schmiede.

Bella-Coola 105

→ *Indianer der Nordwestküste*

Vorführung eines Tanzes aus dem Winterzeremoniell-Zyklus □ 126

Benue River – Gebiet 181

Bembe (Bemba, Babemba, Wawemba) 26, 142, 181
Matisse 153

Sambia, ca. 150000 Stammesmitglieder. Zusammen mit zahlreichen anderen, ebenfalls Bemba sprechenden Stämmen (→ *Tabwa* u. a.) bilden sie die bedeutendste Gruppe der *Mittel-bantu* (→ *Bantu*) zwischen den → *Luba*- und Nyassa-Völkern. Sie bewohnen das bergige Hochland NO-Sambias mit seiner vorherrschenden Trockenwaldvegetation und betreiben v. a. Brandrodungshackbau (Hirsen, Mais). Eine Besonderheit stellt das Citimene-Düngeverfahren dar: Abgeschlagene Baumäste und Unterholz werden verbrannt und die Asche zu Saatbeeten aufgehäuft. An größeren Gewässern und in Sumpfgebieten spielt der Fischfang eine wichtige Rolle. Die *Bembe* gelten seit alters als vorzügliche Jäger. Die Herrscherschicht der *Bembe* führt ihre Abstammung auf die *Luba-Lunda*-Reiche zurück und dürfte Anfang des 18. Jahrhunderts aus dem südlichen Kongo eingewandert sein, deren politische Organisation (Zentralstaat mit einem König an der Spitze, jedoch matrilineare Nachfolge) sie mitgebracht hatten. Die Bemba-Sprache (das Ci-Bemba) ist Lingua franca in der gesamten Region, dem sog. »copper belt«.

Doppelgesichtige Maske □ 163

Benin 143, 146, 172, 174, 180, 413
Campendonk 389 – Giacometti 545 – Kirchner 384

Nigeria, vermutlich seit dem 12. Jahrhundert bestehendes Königreich in der Region westlich des Nigerunterlaufs (um die heutige Stadt Benin City). Seine Träger waren die *Edo* oder *Bini* (ca. 200000 Stammesmitglieder), zu den Sudan-Negern gehörender Zweig Kwa sprechender Gruppen. Nahe verwandt sind die *Ishan* (auch Esa, ca. 200000), die *Kurukuru* (ca. 190000) und die *Sobo* (ca. 400000); die *Itsekiri* (ca. 35000), die als Fischer auf den Inseln westlich des Nigerdeltas leben, zählen der Sprache nach zu den → *Yoruba*. Ob die Macht der Zentralherrscher sich über alle diese Völker in gleichem Maße erstreckte, ist zweifelhaft. Ursprungsort der noch heute herrschenden Beninkönige ist Ife, die heilige Stadt der *Yoruba*, die auch den *Edo* als religiöses Zentrum galt. Ende des 13. Jahrhunderts kam aus Ife ein *Yoruba*-Prinz, dessen Sohn und Nachfolger Eweka als der eigentliche Gründer von Benin verehrt wird. Auf ihn geht auch der bis heute übliche Herrschertitel Oba zurück. Einigen tatkräftigen Herrschern gelang es, weitere Kleinfürstentümer der *Edo* zu erobern und das Großreich zu schaffen. Bestimmend für die dauerhafte Blüte des Reiches waren neben der erfolgreichen Militärpolitik die einträglichen Handelskontakte mit den *Yoruba*, den östlich des Nigers lebenden *Igala* und → *Ibo* sowie den islamischen Handelszentren im Norden. Über den Fernhandel gelangten mit den exotischen Gütern und wertvollen Metallen (Kupfer, Zinn, Zink) auch fremde Motive und künstlerische Anregungen zu den Handwerksgilden. Von einschneidender Wirkung waren die Handelsbeziehungen mit den Portugiesen seit etwa 1470. Formen, Ornamente und Motive europäischer und asiatischer Objekte (z. B. Waffen, illustrierte Bücher, vermutlich auch chinesische Textilien) beeinflußten auf diese Weise die Handwerker und Künstler Benins, die diese Anregungen mit ihren eigenen Traditionen vereinigten und eigenständig weiterentwickelten. Der prachtvoll ausgestaltete Hof war das Zentrum der künstlerischen Aktivität, zugleich der bedeutendste Auftraggeber und Sammler der Gegenstände. Die von den Portugiesen seit alters gerühmte Benin-Kunst verfiel im 18. Jahrhundert (konventionalisierte Motive, erstarrte Formen) und geriet auch in Europa, wo sie früher durchaus bekannt gewesen war, in Vergessenheit. Thronwirren schwächten die Macht der Könige, und 1897 eroberten die Engländer die Hauptstadt und plünderten den Palast mit seinen Schätzen: Zahlreiche Kunstwerke kamen als Beute auf den europäischen Markt und führten zur Wiederentdeckung der Benin-Kunst. 1914 setzten die Engländer die Dynastie mit beschränkten Rechten wieder ein. Die überaus reichhaltige Produktion der Benin-Künstler umfaßt v. a. Gelbgußarbeiten

(Porträtköpfe der Ahnen, Reliefplatten vom Königspalast – mit Darstellungen von Europäern und mythologischen Szenen –, Kultstäbe, Aquamanile in charakteristischer Leopardenform), Elfenbeinschnitzereien sowie Terrakotten.

Reliefplatte □ 521; Jagdszene □ 523

Benin, Volksrepublik

→ *Fon*, *Yoruba*

Bete 180

Elfenbeinküste, mit Untergruppen ca. 150000 Stammesmitglieder. Zu den → *Kru* gehörig, siedeln nördlich von Daloa zwischen Sassandra und den Quellgebieten des Nioumourou und Boubo.

Bijogo (Bidyogo, Bissago) 138, 360

Guinea-Bissau, ca. 20000 Stammesmitglieder. Zur Westatlantik-Gruppe gehörender Stamm der Sudan-Neger, die auf den der Geba-Mündung vorgelagerten Bijagósinseln leben. Neben Hackbau (Reis), Gartenbau und Sammelwirtschaft betreiben sie vornehmlich Fischerei: Zwischen kilometerlangen Zäunen werden die Fische zusammengetrieben und bei Niedrigwasser aufgesammelt. Bekannt als hervorragende Bootsbauer und Holzschnitzer. Die Frauen tragen charakteristische gelbrote Baströcke und Lehmknötchenfrisuren. Die *Bijogo* leben in Dorfgemeinschaften mit patrilinearer Deszendenzregelung. Für Initiationen werden Tätowierungen durchgeführt.

Figur aus Holz □ 189; Puppe aus Holz und Perlen □ 485

Bismarckarchipel 114, 116, 117, 120, 122, 127, 128

Melanesische Inseln vor NO-Neuguinea, früher deutsche Kolonie, jetzt zu Papua-Neuguinea gehörig.

Biwat (Mundugumor)

Stamm am mittleren Yuat, dem südlichen Nebenfluß des unteren Sepik, Ostsepik-Provinz, Papua-Neuguinea. Nach der amerikanischen Anthropologin Margaret Mead »von geradezu selbstzerstörerischer Aggressivität«. Sie schufen ausdrucksstarke Kultmasken und Schutzpfropfen für Kultflöten. *Lit.*: Stöhr 1972, S. 80, 114, 115.

Figur zur Bekrönung eines Daches □ 136

Boa

Zaire, Gruppe der *Mittel-Bantu* (→ *Bantu*), die im tropischen Regenwald der bergigen Region östlich von Kisangani (ehem. Stanleyville) leben.

Maske □ 401

Bobo (Bwa) 141, 180

Mit 290000 Menschen die größte Ethnie in Obervolta, im östlichen Teil *Bobo-Uli*, im westlichen *Bobo-Fing* genannt. Starke altnigritische Traditionen mit Einflüssen der *Mande* und, wenn auch in geringem Maß, des Islam. Im Gegensatz zu den benachbarten → *Dogon* kaum künstlerische Traditionen. Hackbauern (v. a. Hirsen) der Trockenwaldsavanne mit bescheidener Viehzucht; Lehmhäuser. Die wichtigste soziale Einheit ist die erweiterte Großfamilie mit patrilinearer Nachfolge. Kultbundwesen (*Do*) mit drei Altersklassen: Alle sieben Jahre werden die Initianden mit Maskentänzen und religiösen Weihen in die Gemeinschaft eingeführt. Durch die Feiern soll auch die Fruchtbarkeit der Felder, Menschen und Tiere gefördert werden. Die weibliche Schutzgottheit des Bundes wird als »Mutter des Dorfes« sowie als »Mutter der (ranghöchsten) Affenmaske« bezeichnet. Die beim Tanz verwendeten Holz- und Laubmasken werden in eigenen Maskenhäusern im Busch verborgen. Das Bundwesen steht in enger Beziehung mit den Schmiedekasten. Sakrales Häuptlingstum, Glaube an vergöttlichte Himmel und Erde, Buschgottheit als »Herr des Wildes«. Auch der Ahnenkult spielt eine bedeutende Rolle. Die Holzmasken der *Bobo* sind reich ornamentiert.

Maske □ 717

Bobo – Fing

→ *Bobo*

Bongo (Dor) 136
Nolde 393

Sudan, um 1870 ca. 100000 Menschen, heute nur noch ca. 5000. Vertreter der Bongo-Bagirmi-Sprachgruppe (→ *Sara*) der Sudan-Neger. Die *Bongo* leben als Feldbauern (Hirsen) der Feuchtsavannen auf dem Eisensteinplateau (SW-Sudan). Das Jagdwesen ist von hoher sozialer (Trophäenkult) und religiöser Bedeutung (Jagdkulte für den »Herrn der Tiere«). Umfangreiche Eisenindustrie, z. T. sind die *Bongo* in Schmiededörfern organisiert.

Maske □ 536

Borneo
Kirchner 389

Siehe auch *Dayak*

Bougainville 122

Kopf □ 255b; Figur aus Holz □ 730

Siehe auch Salomoninseln

Boyo 70

Zaire, Maniema sprechende Untergruppe der → *Hemba*, westlich des Tanganjika-Sees.

Figur aus Holz □ 79

Bozo 180

Mali, kleinere ethnische Einheit der *Mande* am Niger und Bani mit ca. 30000 Mitgliedern. Sie leben vornehmlich als Fischer und Bootshändler. Daneben betreiben sie in den Flußniederungen Ackerbau. Die *Bozo* haben wie die → *Bambara* am stärksten von allen *Mande*-Völkern dem Islamisierungsdruck widerstanden. Ausgeprägtes Geheimbundwesen mit Maskenkult.

Tierkopf □ 472

Britisch-Kolumbien

→ *Haida*, *Kwakiutl*

Bukoba 501

→ Königreich Karagwe

Tierfigur □ 705

Burma

Padaung-Frau mit Halsringen □ 706

Bwa → *Bobo*

C

Chamba (Camba, Tsamba) 44, 46

Nigeria, mit Untergruppen ca. 20000 Stammesmitglieder, davon etwa 15% Moslems. Kulturell nicht einheitliche Gruppen, die südlich des Benue in den Schebschi- und Alantika-Bergen siedeln und im Süden z. T. den Donga-Fluß erreichen. Hackbauern (Hirsen, Yams, daneben Gemüse in Hausgärten); patrilineare Deszendenz mit mutterrechtlichen Spuren; Glaube an einen mit der Sonne assoziierten Hochgott. In der Mythologie hat der Schmied eine bedeutende Stellung als Kulturheros. Ahnenverehrung mit Schädelkult, rituelle Beschneidung bei der Initiation, sakrales Häuptlingstum. Holzmasken und Pfahlskulpturen sind die wichtigsten künstlerischen Erzeugnisse.

Männliche Figur □ 51; Figur aus Holz □ 109

Cherokesen (Cherokee) 98

Indianerstamm, der vor Ankunft der Europäer in Süd- und Nord-Carolina, Tennessee und Georgia lebte. Die *Cherokesen* waren sehr zahlreich, lebten in Dörfern und Städten und ernährten sich vom Pflanzenanbau. Im späteren 19. Jahrhundert wurden sie von der Regierung der USA nach Oklahoma umgesiedelt – ihre blühende Kultur zerbrach. Die gesellschaftliche Organisation bestand aus sieben matrilinearen Clans. Ihre Religion beinhaltete einen Glauben an sieben Himmel und sieben Himmelsrichtungen. Die *Cherokesen* fertigten Geflechte, Malereien, Trommeln und vor allem Masken. Es gab aus Holz geschnitzte Masken und solche aus Kürbissen. Sie wurden bei dem rituellen Booger-Tanz getragen. Infolge des raschen Niedergangs sind die Kenntnisse über die *Cherokesen* wie auch über die Creek, einen benachbarten und kulturell ähnlich strukturierten Stamm, insgesamt relativ lückenhaft.

Cheyenne → *PRÄRIEINDIANER*

Maske für ein Pferd □ 127

Chibcha 86

Ca. 45 Sprachen umfassende indianische Sprachfamilie im nördlichen Südamerika (Kolumbien, Ecuador) und im südlichen Mittelamerika (Panama, Costa Rica).

Chippewa
Hartley 470

→ *PRÄRIEINDIANER*

Kanumodelle □ 658

Chiriqui 86

Nach der Provinz Chiriqui in Panama benannte indianische Kultur Südamerikas, die im westlichen Panama und im Südosten von Costa Rica von ca. 300 bis um 1500 bestand. Die letzten Jahrhunderte der Chiriquikultur sind gekennzeichnet durch das Eindringen der → *CHIBCHA*. Bemerkenswert vor allem die Blüte einer monumentalen Steinskulptur mit überlebensgroßen Doppelfiguren und großen Altaranlagen in der 1. Jahrtausendhälfte.

Chokwe (Cokwe, alte portugiesische Benennung Kioko) 139, 142, 143, 181
Höch 551 – Matisse 153

NO-Angola, südliches Zaire, Teile von Sambia, ca. 600000 Menschen, zu den *MITTEL-BANTU* (→ *BANTU*) gehörend. Die *CHOKWE* haben ihr Stammland im hohen Trockenwald am oberen Kasai und an den Oberläufen seiner westlichen Nebenflüsse. Lange Zeit dem Lunda-Reich unterworfen, konnten sie dieses jedoch Ende des 19. Jahrhunderts selbst erobern. Durch ihre Nordexpansion nahmen sie viele Kulturzüge der Kongoprovinz an: großstaatliche Organisation, Gottkönigtum, Knabenweihe. Regenzeitfeldbau (v.a. Maniok und Mais) mit starken jägerischen Elementen; matrilineare Deszendenz; intensiver Ahnenkult. Auch das Orakelwesen spielt eine wichtige Rolle. Das Gebiet der *CHOKWE* ist eine der bekanntesten Kunstprovinzen Afrikas: Die Schnitzereien von Stäben, Stühlen, Kämmen, Musikinstrumenten und Masken (in Verbindung mit einem ausgeprägten Geheimbundwesen) zeigen eine stark geometrisierte Ornamentik.

Figur aus Holz □ 188; Maske □ 211, 510; Männliche Figur □ 689

Chrotega 86

Collingwood Bay

Muschel mit eingeritzem Muster □ 708

Comanchen
Hartley 470

→ *PRÄRIEINDIANER*

Kindertrage □ 661

Cookinseln 114
Lipchitz 442

Polynesien. Nördliche Gruppe mit den Atollen
→ Pukapuka, Manihiki, Rakahanga, Tongareva u. a., südliche mit → Raratonga, Mangaia u. a. Zunächst vielleicht von Tahiti und den → Marquesasinseln, später von Tonga und Samoa besiedelt: Verbindungen zu den Australinseln (u. a. Rurutu). Polynesische Dialekte, lokale Varianten der altpolynesischen Basiskultur. Auf Raratonga und Mauke Göttersymbole mit streng stilisiertem Gesicht und brett- bzw. pfahlartigem Körper (Stab- bzw. Pfahlgottheiten); auf Mangaia Kultbeile mit Basaltklinge und einem Holzstiel, der rundum mit regelmäßiger Kerbschnittornamentik (K-Motiv) bedeckt ist, als Symbol des Gottes Tane-mata-ariki, des Schutzpatrons der holzbearbeitenden Handwerker. Diese Kultbeile wurden vor allem zum Ritual bei Friedensverhandlungen gebraucht, wobei man die turmartigen Schäfte mit rechteckigen Öffnungen wohl erst nach der Missionierung (nach 1823) entwickelte und ihnen keine kultische Bedeutung beimaß. *Lit.:* Koch 1976, S. 172–173.

Siehe auch Australinseln, Mauke, Pukapukainsel, Raratonga

Creek 98

→ *CHEROKESEN*

Cross River – Gebiet 181

Von *SEMI-BANTU* (→ *BANTU*) besiedeltes Waldland, das mit dem → Kameruner Grasland eine gemeinsame Kulturprovinz bildet. Es erstreckt sich über die dichten Wälder an der Grenze zwischen Kamerun und Nigeria und gilt als ein Rückzugsgebiet mit vielen kleinen autonomen Dorfgemeinschaften. Das soziale Leben ist durch Altersklassen und Kultbünde (»Leopardenbund«) geregelt. Die Frau nimmt eine relativ hohe gesellschaftliche Stellung ein. Hauptgruppen sind die → *IBIBIO* und → *EKOI*.

Siehe auch EJAGHAM, EKET

Crow
Hartley 470

→ *PRÄRIEINDIANER*

Mokassin □ 662

D

Dahome 140, 141, 172

Dan (Da) 13, 141, 163, 180
Braque 153 – Giacometti 43, 518, 542, 543 – Picasso 272

Zusammen mit den verwandten → *GIO, TURA* und *YAKUBA* ca. 150000 Stammesmitglieder im Hinterland von Liberia und der mittleren Elfenbeinküste (im Osten bis zur Stadt Man). Mande sprechende Gruppen, die nach Süden in den westafrikanischen Regenwald vordrangen und sich kulturell stark an die benachbarten → *KRU* und *TEMNE* anglichen. Hackfeldbau (v. a. Reis) mit Sammelwirtschaft und bescheidener Rinderhaltung; patrilineare Deszendenz mit mutterrechtlichen Spuren. Die Dorfgemeinschaft als größte politische Einheit steht unter der Herrschaft eines Häuptlings und eines Ältestenrats. Reiche bildhauerische Tradition: Masken, die mit einem ausgeprägten Geheimbundwesen in Verbindung stehen, stellen Buschgeister dar, die nach mythischer Tradition die frühesten Landbesitzer vor den Menschen waren. Die Autorität dieser Geister wird durch Kulte, die das Privileg bestimmter Familien sind, immer wieder erneuert. Die Zahl der Geister und der sie repräsentierenden Masken ist unbegrenzt. Der klassische *DAN*-Stil zeichnet sich durch ruhige, klare Formen, weiche Wölbungen und die Betonung von Längs- und Querachse (Augenlinie) aus.

Masken □ 4–9; Maske □ 335; Löffel aus Holz □ 735

Dayak
Blauer Reiter 513

Kulturgruppen im Nordteil der Insel Borneo (Indonesien und Malaysia), See-Dayak (Iban) und Land-Dayak.

Siehe auch Borneo

Delaware

Indianer, die zu einer kleineren Gruppe von Stämmen in der Umgebung von New York gehören (*MAHICAN, MOHIKANER* u. a.). Ihre Kunstwerke sind Malereien auf Birkenrinde, meist in Gestalt von Tieren, die gut verglichen werden können mit den Tierdarstellungen auf Felsbildern – hier wirkt die jägerische Vergangenheit nach. Berühmt sind die mit Perlstikkereien geschmückten sogenannten Wampungürtel. Der Vertrag mit William Penn im Jahre 1682 wurde auf einem solchen Gürtel niedergeschrieben.

Keule □ 123

Dinka (Denkawi) 136

Sudan, ca. 500000 Stammesangehörige. Zur westlichen Gruppe der Niloten gehörend, einer etwa 4 Millionen umfassenden, relativ einheitlichen Völkergruppe der Sudan-Neger mit eigenständiger Sprache, vornehmlich großem und schlankem Körperbau und charakteristischen Kulturmerkmalen. Die *DINKA* leben in den Trockensteppen längs des Nils zwischen den Orten Shambe und Malek, im Westen bis ins südliche Kordofan-Gebiet. Vorrecht der Männer ist die Viehzucht (neben Rindern auch Ziegen und Schafe), die besonderes soziales Ansehen genießt und die wirtschaftliche Grundlage darstellt. Ergänzend wird auch Feldbau betrieben (Hirsen, Mais, Hülsenfrüchte). Die Deszendenz ist patrilinear geregelt. Größte politische Einheit ist eine Gruppe von Dorfgemeinschaften, die unter der Führung des Oberhauptes der vornehmsten Familie steht. Zentrum der religiösen Verehrung ist ein mit dem Himmel assoziierter Hochgott, Nyalic. Die *DINKA* haben (wie alle Niloten) religiöse Einflüsse von außen (Islam, Christentum) strikt abgelehnt. Die Eisengewinnung war zwar bekannt, doch ist das Kunsthandwerk in Metall (wie auch aus Holz) kaum entwickelt.

Djibete

Maske □ 197

Dogon (Habe, Habbe) 32, 58, 59, 63, 70, 141, 172, 179, 180, 282
Capek, Josef 158 – Epstein 446, 447, 451 – Giacometti 518, 542 – Lam 604 – Lipchitz 90, 439, 441 – Moore 617 – Ray 551

Mali, ca. 225000 Stammesmitglieder, die im felsigen Bergland von Bandiagara und Hamborie sowie in den Trockensavannen der Ebene im Nigerknie siedeln. Unter dem Druck der Islamisierung und der frühen sakralen Königreiche wurden sie zurückgedrängt und bewahrten so altertümliche, autochthone Traditionen. Patrilineare Deszendenz mit Spuren eines alten, überlagerten matrilinearen Systems; große Claneinheiten, die nebeneinander existieren und unter dem System einer Kantonalverfassung zusammengefaßt sind und von einem politischen und religiösen Oberhaupt zusammen mit dem Ältestenrat regiert werden. Die *DOGON* sind Hackbauern (Hirsen), die z. T. Terrassen anlegen. Auch die Rinderzucht spielt eine gewisse Rolle. Die *DOGON* tradieren detaillierte Urzeitmythen mit einem Schöpfergott und einem Zwillingspaar, dem eine wesentliche Bedeutung zukommt. Sie kennen komplexe Seelenvorstellungen in Verbindung mit der Weitergabe der Lebenskraft bei der Zeugung. Von zentraler Bedeutung ist auch der Ahnenkult. Neben dem Adel und den Freien existiert ein endogames Handwerkskastenwesen mit Schmieden, Schnitzern, Lederarbeitern und Musikanten, die nicht versklavt werden durften. Alle beschnittenen *DOGON*, die nicht einer Kaste angehören, sind Mitglieder des Maskenbundes, der bei Bestattungen und Totenfeiern für Initiierte rituelle Tänze aufführt. Anläßlich dieser Feiern werden neue Masken angefertigt. Alle 60 Jahre findet an jeweils verschiedenen Orten ein großes Maskenfest (*sigi*) statt, in dessen Mittelpunkt eine Schlangenmaske steht. Die *DOGON* haben eine außergewöhnlich entwickelte Holzschnitzkunst (Pfahlskulpturen und Masken) mit einer Tendenz zu strenger Symmetrie und Stilisierung.

Sitzendes Paar □ 72; Figur aus Holz und Metall □ 209; Holzfigur □ 352, 353; Figur aus Holz □ 215 a; Maske □ 437; Krokodilmaske □ 591; Weibliche Sitzfigur □ 624; Stab mit figürlicher Verzierung □ 780; Das Spiel ›i‹ □ 790

Duala (Douala) 143, 181

Kamerun, mit verschiedenen Untergruppen ca. 80000 Mitglieder. Die *DUALA* sind der bedeutendste Stamm der sog. Kameruner *KÜSTEN-BANTU* (→ *BANTU*). Sie wichen um 1750 unter dem Druck der *PANGWE* (→ *FANG*) zur Küste hin aus und ließen sich an den Mündungen des Wuri und des Sanaga nieder (nahe der heutigen Stadt Douala). Aus den ursprünglichen Hackbauern des tropischen Regenwaldes (Maniok, Yams, Taro) und Fischern wurden unter der Kolonialherrschaft Händler. Die Duala-Sprache war Lingua franca und wurde durch den Einfluß der Mission zur Schriftsprache Kameruns. Die häufigen Handelskontakte mit den Europäern ließen in der Kunst einen eigenartigen Mischstil entstehen, der sich vor allem in den bunt bemalten und reichbeschnitzten Booten (Schiffschnäbel) und Paddeln zeigt. Dagegen gerieten die ehemals bedeutenden Masken und Ahnenfiguren aus Holz nach und nach in Vergessenheit.

E

Edo 135
→ Benin

Ejagham

Stamm im südlichen Grenzgebiet zwischen Kamerun und Nigeria, Hauptgruppe der *EKOI*, ca. 90000 Mitglieder, die auch als »eigentliche Ekoi« bezeichnet werden. Zusammen mit den → *IBIBIO* sind sie typische Vertreter der *WALDLAND-SEMI-BANTU* am Cross River (→ *BANTU*). Ihre Gehöfte bestehen aus vier Häusern, die einen Hof umschließen. Patrilinear; besondere Bedeutung der Altersklassenverbände (das Ansehen der Männer wuchs mit dem Alter). Die *EJAGHAM* haben Priesterhäuptlinge, die an sakrale Könige erinnern. Sie glauben an eine höchste Gottheit; wichtige Rolle des Ahnenkultes, in dem die aus Holz geschnitzten Masken als Repräsentanten der Verstorbenen verwendet wurden.

Ekpe-Stammesemblem □ 101

Eket

SO-Nigeria, *SEMI-BANTU* des Cross River-Gebietes (→ *BANTU*), die zu den → *IBIBIO* gehören und im Süden der Provinz Calabar siedeln.

Figur aus Holz □ 66

Ekoi 413
Schmidt-Rottluff 394, 395

→ *EJAGHAM*

Kopfschmuck □ 539

Elek 138

Elfenbeinküste 159, 167, 171, 172, 274, 325
Picasso 294, 319 – Vlaminck 221

Weibliche Figur □ 390

Siehe auch OST-AKAN (→ AKAN), BAULE, DAN, GREBO, GUERE, GURO, KULANGO, SENUFO, WOBE, YAURE

Era River

Golf-Provinz, Papua-Neuguinea
Figur aus Holz □ 834

Eskimo 11, 48, 53, 95, 96, 99, 101, 340, 634, 635
Hartley 484 – Ernst 588 – Miró 595, 607 – Moore 617, 618 – Smith 638 – Tobey 638 – Zorach 485

Das nördlichste Volk der Erde lebt in kleinen Gruppen an der Küste Alaskas, Kanadas und Grönlands. Grundelement der sozialen Organisation ist die Familie. Die Religion trägt eindeutig schamanistische Züge. Masken, *Inua*, stellen dementsprechend die Doppelnatur des Menschen, Mensch und Geist oder Mensch und Tier, dar; eine andere Form, *Tunghat*, stellt die Hilfsgeister dar. Der Schamane erwirbt Hilfsgeister, die ihn unterstützen bei der Heilung von Kranken und bei der Reise zur »Mutter der Seetiere«, von der er Fangtiere erbittet. Die eskimoische Kultur ist bis heute lebendig geblieben, bekannt sind vor allem Specksteinschnitzereien der *ESKIMO* von Alaska.

Eskimoische Maske □ 62, 115, 129, 132; Eskimo-Frau mit ihrem Kind □ 119; Ejakintomino □ 120; Maske von Inuk Elio □ 128; Fingermaske □ 852; Miniaturmaske □ 851; Maske □ 363, 864, 865, 869, 953, 957, 983; Masken □ 867; Figur aus Elfenbein □ 925; Trommelschläger □ 926; Seehund □ 944

Etoumbi 271, 274
Picasso 39

Maske □ 337

Ewe (Eibe, Krepe) 180

SO-Ghana, S-Togo, mit Untergruppen ca. 700000 Stammesmitglieder. Die *EWE* sind vor allem Ackerbauern mit dem Kernland zwischen unterem Volta und Mono-Fluß (auch *WEST-EWE* genannt). Sie sind in kleinen Häuptlingsschaften mit straffer Führung organisiert. Neben dem Himmelsgott Mawu, der in der Vorstellung der *EWE* eher vage bleibt, und der Erdgöttin Li wird v. a. das Götterpaar Sgble (männl.) und Sodza (weibl.) verehrt. Diese beherrschen Donner und Blitz und fördern dadurch Regen und Fruchtbarkeit. Das Götterpaar ist vermutlich aus der Aufspaltung eines androgynen Gewittergottes entstanden. Im weiteren Sinne bezeichnet Ewe eine Sprachengruppe innerhalb der *KWA*, zu denen auch die *GUN* und → *FON* (auch *OST-EWE* genannt) gehören, die im Süden der heutigen Republik Benin im 17. Jahrhundert das Königreich Dahome gründeten.

Bekrönung eines Stabes □ 471

F

Fang (Fan, Pahouin) 21, 22, 25, 36, 72, 89, 141, 151, 158, 162, 172, 173, 181, 219, 233, 432, 455
Braque 22, 153, 316 – Carrà 419, 420 – Derain 21, 22, 87, 153, 226, 227, 420 – Epstein 434, 445, 446, 450 – Lipchitz 441 – Matisse 153, 240 – Picasso 22, 275, 295, 313, 327, 329, 348 – Schmidt-Rottluff 404, 405 – Vlaminck 87, 153, 221, 223 – Weber 36 – Zorach 477

Süd-Kamerun und Nord-Gabun, ca. 840000 Stammesmitglieder. Unter dem Sammelbegriff *Pangwe-Fang* werden eine Vielzahl ethnisch und sprachlich unterschiedlicher Gruppen zusammengefaßt, die die Tropenwälder im Hinterland der Küste bewohnen. In mehreren Wanderungswellen drangen sie aus der Sudanzone nach Süden vor – im 18. Jh. waren sie noch nördlich des oberen Sanaga bezeugt – und nahmen die heutigen Siedlungsgebiete ein. Sie übten auf die authochthone Bevölkerung einen starken Assimilationsdruck aus. Wegen ihrer kriegerischen Tradition waren die *Fang* gefürchtet und galten früher als Kannibalen. Sie leben vom Feldbau (Maniok, Yams, Taro) und sind als hervorragende Eisenschmiede bekannt. Die *Fang* zeichnen sich durch eine höchst eigenständige Holzschnitzkunst (Masken und Figuren) aus. Berühmt sind ihre weißen Masken: aus hellem, leichtem Holz in Herzform geschnitzt, sind sie großflächig angelegt und von geringer Plastizität. Nur die lange, schmale Nase ist erhaben. Die Masken sind häufig mundlos, die Augen zu schmalen Schlitzen reduziert. Die Frisuren sind den kunstvollen Haartrachten der *Pangwe* nachgebildet, am unteren Rand wurden meist Bastkrausen befestigt. Ein fester Typus in der Kunst der *Fang* sind auch die Wächter der Ahnenschädel (Byeri-Figuren, siehe Glossar), Holzskulpturen, die die Knochen- und Schädelreliquien hervorragender Ahnen beschützen sollen, die in Rindenschachteln oder Körben aufbewahrt werden.

Maske mit Bronzereplik □ 17, 18; Maske □ 20, 91, 257, 370, 392, 398, 409, 419, 443, 575, 579; Doppelgesichtige Helmmaske □ 92; Reliquiarfiguren □ 190; Reliquiarfigur □ 191, 275, 289, 383, 385, 625; Reliquiarkopf □ 288, 559, 565, 612, 626; Kopf □ 386; Harfe □ 405

Fante (Fanti) 136

Ghana, ca. 200000 Stammesangehörige. An der Küste lebende Gruppe der → *Akan*-Völker. Sie standen unter starkem kulturellen Einfluß der nördlich benachbarten expansiven → *Asante* (v. a. Anstoß zur staatlichen Organisation) und hatten mit diesen ständig kriegerische Auseinandersetzungen. Die *Fante* vereitelten jedoch bis zur Kolonialisierung durch die Engländer alle Versuche der *Asante*, zur Küste vorzustoßen und mit den Europäern direkte Handelsbeziehungen aufzunehmen. *Fante* und *Asante* sind bekannt für ihre charakteristischen Holzpuppen (*akua ba*): ca. 30 cm hohe Schnitzwerke, die sich durch einen relativ großen Kopf auszeichnen (rechteckig, brettförmig bei den *Fante*, rund, scheibenförmig bei den *Asante*), der auf einem langen, mit mehreren Ringkerben versehenen Hals sitzt. Der Körper besteht aus einem stilisierten Rumpf, erst seit der Jahrhundertwende mit rudimentären Armen (kreuzförmig eingesetzt) und Beinen. Die überwiegend weiblichen Puppen sollten vermutlich die Fruchtbarkeit der Frauen günstig beeinflussen.

Fidschiinseln 113, 128
Giacometti 545

Fon (Fong, Fo) 76, 140, 141, 174, 180
Apollinaire 157

Republik Benin, die östlichsten Vertreter der → *Ewe*-Gruppen; mit Untergruppen zählen sie etwa 1 Million Menschen. Um 1625 gründeten die *Fon* nach der Eroberung mehrerer Kleinstaaten das Königreich Dahome. Dank der straffen Militärorganisation (vermutlich Einsatz von Frauenheeren) und rücksichtsloser Gewaltherrschaft dehnten die *Fon* das Reich im 18. Jahrhundert bis an die Küste aus und nahmen mit den Europäern unmittelbare Handelsbeziehungen auf. Wirtschaftliche Grundlage war der Sklavenhandel, den die *Fon* bis zur Kolonisierung durch die Franzosen (1894) im Austausch gegen Waffen und Munition betrieben. Ihre Bedeutung liegt eher in ihrer militärischen Macht als in kulturellen Leistungen, die sich in einer maßlosen Prunkentfaltung am Königshof erschöpften. Die kulturelle Abhängigkeit der *Fon* von den → *Yoruba* ist unübersehbar. Die höchste Gottheit der *Fon* hat androgyne Züge; sie überträgt dem ihr entstammenden Zwillingspaar (Mann und Frau oder Mutter und Sohn) die Herrschaft über die Welt. Das jüngste und klügste der 14 Kinder dieses Paares ist Legba, der göttliche Trickster, der den Menschen am nächsten steht und als Vermittler zu den Göttern fungiert. Er wird mit einem großen Phallus dargestellt, der Zeichen seiner Funktion als Förderer der Fruchtbarkeit ist. Naturerscheinungen (Blitz, Donner, Regen) werden als göttliche Mächte angesehen, die Pocken gelten als Strafe der Erdgottheit.

Fetisch □ 97, 103; Affenschädel □ 113; Figuren □ 162; Figur aus Metall □ 452; Stab mit plastischer Verzierung □ 771; Figur aus Holz □ 905

Fong → *Fon*

G

Gabun 167, 172, 348
Carrà 420 – Matisse 240

Siehe auch Fang, Kota, Ongwe, Punu, Shira-Punu, Tsogo

Gambierinseln

Mangareva, Polynesien.

Gestell für Opfergaben □ 900

Geelvink-Bai

West Irian. ›Korwar-Stil‹; Typisch sind Ahnenfiguren und Behälter für Ahnenschädel.

Ahnenfigur □ 907

Gesellschaftsinseln 117

Zentraler Archipel Polynesiens, früher wichtigstes Expansionszentrum polynesischer Kultur mit Tahiti als größter und wichtigster Insel. Streng gegliederte Gesellschaft: Häuptlinge (*ari'i*, Groß- und Exekutivhäuptlinge), die als Abkömmlinge der Götter gelten, freie Großgrundbesitzer bzw. Kleinbauern (*ra'atira*) sowie »besitzlose« Gemeine (*manahune*). Die Bewohner legten Kultplätze z. T. mit rechteckigen Stufenpyramiden in Trockenmauerwerk an. Brustschmuck für Priester und Häuptlinge wurde aus Kokosfasergeflecht mit Haizähnen, Federn und Hundehaaren gefertigt. Bekannt sind auch Trauergewänder, Göttersymbole mit eingeflochtenen roten Papageienfedern, Fliegenwedel, Tapas (siehe Glossar) mit ornamentalen Blattabdrücken für Kleidung, Schlafdecke sowie als Prestigegut. *Lit.:* Koch 1976, S. 175–178.

Siehe auch Tahiti

Ghana → *Asante, Akan*

Gilbertinseln 113, 114

Inselgruppe Mikronesiens.

Gio 180

Liberia, Untergruppe der Mande sprechenden → *Dan*.

Spielbrett □ 742

Giryama

Kenia, mit Untergruppen (darunter die → *Kambe*) ca. 155000 Menschen. *NO-Bantu* (→ *Bantu*). Die zu den sog. *Mijikenda* (»Neun Siedlungen«) gehören und am Unterlauf des Tana-Flusses leben, von der Küste jedoch durch Suahili sprechende Gruppen abgeschnitten sind. Bei den *Mijikenda*-Gruppen sind hölzerne Grabpfosten verbreitet, die nur besonders verdienten Mitgliedern der Gemeinschaft beim Grab oder in der Hütte des Verstorbenen – teilweise erst Jahrzehnte nach dessen Tod – gesetzt werden. Die ca. 2 m hohen Pfosten mit vollplastischem Kopfaufsatz oder Bretter mit rundem Aufsatz, in den stilisierte Augen und Mund eingeschnitzt sind, zeigen Kerbornamente (florale und geometrische Elemente), die islamische Einflüsse vermuten lassen. Sie wurden über die islamisch geprägten Suahili-Stämme der Küste vermittelt, vielleicht auch über die alten Wohnbereiche in Somalia (17. Jh.) oder über noch ältere, arabisch-persische Kontakte in Ostafrika.

Grabfigur □ 904

Golf-Provinz

Papua-Neuguinea.
→ Papua-Golf, Era River, *Kerewa*, *Namau*, Wapo Creek

Grebo 25, 28, 29, 31, 32, 43, 142, 180, 319
Lipchitz 442 – Picasso 25, 27–29, 43, 88, 313, 314, 319, 347, 351, 352

Grenzregion Liberia/Elfenbeinküste, Kru sprechende Gruppe (→ *Kru*), die im Regenwald des Cavally als Fischer und Reisbauern leben. Im regierenden Ältestenrat besitzt der Älteste das höchste Ansehen; kleine Dorfgemeinschaften. Patrilineare Deszendenz mit starken matrilinearen Traditionen.

Maske □ 29, 31, 332, 417, 902

Großen Seen, Gebiet der 99

Guere 180, 325
Picasso 313, 352

Maske □ 431, 901

Guinea 136, 140, 167

Siehe auch Baga, Susu

Guinea-Bissau

→ *Bijogo*

Guro (Kweni) 25, 26, 180, 432
Schmidt-Rottluff 414

Mittlere Elfenbeinküste, mit Unterstämmen ca. 150 000 Stammesmitglieder. Mande sprechend; die *Guro* wanderten aus dem Nigerbecken südwärts und verdrängten die autochthonen → *Kru*-Stämme. Ihr Siedlungsbereich erstreckt sich zwischen dem Sassandra und dem Weißen Bandama. Sie bauen verschiedene Reissorten an und sind daneben Jäger. Die *Guro* leben in Rechteckhäusern mit abgerundeten Ecken. Dorfdistrikte werden von mehreren Familienverbänden geführt, Oberhaupt ist das älteste Mitglied des Ältestenrats; patrilineare Deszendenz; Glaube an eine Erdgottheit und Vorstellung eines Totenlandes, das die Seele erst auf einem beschwerlichen Weg erreicht. Die *Guro* pflegen einen ausgeprägten Ahnenkult mit Geheimbundwesen. Sie sind bekannte Holzschnitzkünstler (Masken, Skulpturen), deren Stil mit den benachbarten → *Baule* viele gemeinsame Züge aufweist, obgleich die beiden Gruppen weder sprachlich noch kulturell eine Einheit bilden.

Maske □ 595

Gurunsi (Grusi, Grunshi, Gorensi) 180

Obervolta, Ghana. Sammelbezeichnung für verschiedene Gruppen mit besonders altertümlichen voltaischen altnigrischen Zügen, ca. 110 000 Menschen. Sie wurden von den *Mossi*, mit denen sie in dauernden Konflikten lebten, in das Grenzgebiet zwischen Obervolta und Ghana abgedrängt (Schwarzer und Weißer Volta). Relativ kleine soziale Einheiten (Großfamilien, Klane), die sich nur in Kriegszeiten zu losen Konföderationen zusammenschlossen.

H

Haida
Klee 509 – Ernst 607

→ *Indianer der Nordwestküste*

Totempfahl □ 963

Hawaiinseln 110, 113, 119, 120, 460
Moore 615

Figur aus Holz □ 921

Hemba (meist als Luba-Hemba bezeichnet) 47

Zaire, lubaisierte Gruppen (→ *Luba*) in den Savannen des südöstlichen Katanga (zwischen Tanganjika-See und Lualaba-Fluß). Im 15. Jahrhundert eroberte Ilunga Kalala, ein *Hemba*-Häuptlingssohn Reiche der *Luba* und führte in seinem Königreich von Kongolo das sakrale Königtum ein. Dies gilt als Beginn des eigentlichen *Luba*-Reiches (→ *Luba*). Die *Hemba* leben in weit verstreuten, kleinen politischen Einheiten, deren Häuptlinge relativ große Macht innehaben. Sie betreiben Feldbau mit Brandrodung in Wechselwirtschaft (v. a. Mais und Maniok); matrilineare Nachfolgeregelung; Glaube an einen Schöpferahnen und ausgeprägte Ahnenverehrung. Verbreiteter Hexenglaube, geringe Ausbildung von Mythen. Seit dem 17. Jahrhundert sind sie als Schöpfer figuraler Skulpturen (Ahnen-, Schalenträgerfiguren) bekannt.

Figur aus Holz □ 56

Hidatsa

→ *Prärieindianer*

Umhang □ 888

Hopi 105
Ernst 577, 580, 581, 588, 607 – Hartley 470, 473, 484 – Matulka 478 – Nolde 392 – Storrs 478

→ *Puebloindianer*

Katchina-Puppe □ 534; Sio Hemis-Katchina □ 656; Kopfschmuck □ 670; Katchina □ 842

I

Iatmul (Yatmül) 54, 55

Wichtigste Vertreter der wohl bedeutendsten Kunstregion Neuguineas am mittleren Sepik, jetzt zur Provinz Ost-Sepik von Papua-Neuguinea gehörig, etwa 8 000 Menschen. Voraustronesische Papua-Sprachen; Anbau von Knollenfrüchten, Yams und Taro sowie Bananen und Kokospalmen; Sagogewinnung, Fischfang. Politisch selbständige Dorfgemeinschaften, die in jeweils zwei Gruppen aus mehreren Klanen gegliedert waren, von denen jede ihr eigenes Tambaran-Kulthaus besaß. Dieses war bis zu 30 m lang (mit Firstenden) und hatte ein bis zu 20 m hohes Giebeldach auf baumstammdicken beschnitzten Pfosten. Im Kulthaus befanden sich figürlich beschnitzte »Kulthocker«, wohl Symbole der Klan-Ahnen, auf deren Sitzfläche Redner bei wichtigen Beratungen mit Dracaena-Zweigen (einer kultisch wichtigen Pflanze) schlugen. Zur Ausstattung des Kulthauses gehörten Kultbretter mit stilisiertem menschlichen Gesicht über einem durchbrochen gearbeiteten, in Ornamente aufgelösten Körper, »Schädelwände« aus einem mit Palmblattscheiben besetzten Gestell aus Palmholzstäben, die mit Gesichtern und männlichen Figuren (einer riesenhaften in der Mitte) bemalt sind. Auf diese »Schädelwände« wurden mit Ton naturalistisch übermodellierte Schädel von verstorbenen Familienangehörigen oder Kopfjagdopfern gesteckt. Bekannt sind auch figürlich geschnitzte Doppelhacken als Aufhängehacken für Gebrauchsgut, ferner Nackenstützen für die ruhenden Männer oder Schlitz-, Hand- und Wasser-Stampftrommeln. Die *Iatmul* kennen holzgeschnitzte und aus Rattanstreifen geflochtene Masken und geflochtene Tanzanzüge, die zur Darstellung übernatürlicher Wesen, mythischer Vorfahren und Klan-Ahnen vor allem bei Initiationsriten getragen wurden. *Lit.:* Koch 1976, S. 45–50.

Bemalte Figur aus Holz □ 65, 149 (2. v. l.); Aufhängehaken aus Holz □ 616

Ibibio (Agbisherea) 44, 180

SO-Nigeria, Provinz Calabar, mit Untergruppen ca. 1 Million Menschen. Die *Ibibio* haben kulturell große Gemeinsamkeiten mit ihren westlichen Nachbarn, den → *Ibo*, gehören aber aufgrund ihrer Sprache (das dem Semi-Bantu angehörige Efik) zu den → *Ekoi* und zählen mit ihnen zu den typischen → Cross River-Bewohnern. Hackbauern (Maniok und Yams, der im Zentrum der jährlichen Kultfeste steht). Patrilineare Deszendenz, der gemeinsame männliche Ahn bestimmt die Zugehörigkeit zu einer Verwandtschaftsgruppe. Die Führer der eher zersplitterten Häuptlingsschaften haben politische und sakrale Funktionen. Ansehen und Privilegien richten sich nach dem Senioratsprinzip. Altersklassensystem und Geheimbundwesen (*Ekpe*-Bund, siehe Glossar): Bei den Yamsemtefesten verkörpern die Mitglieder mit schwarzen Masken die wiederkehrenden Ahnen. Bei diesen Festen wird auch der Ahnenpfosten erneuert.

Maske □ 52

Ibo
Moore 622

Nigeria, ca. 5–6 Millionen Stammesmitglieder. Am östlichen Unterlauf des Niger lebende, Kwa sprechende Sudan-Neger, die politisch nur locker organisiert sind und in Streudörfern siedeln (im Gegensatz zu den benachbarten → *Yoruba* und → *Ewe*). Die *Ibo* wurden in ihrer Geschichte immer wieder von Sklavenjägern überfallen. Ihr Versuch, einen eigenen Nationalstaat zu gründen, wurde 1967 von der nigerianischen Zentralregierung blutig unterdrückt. Träger der politischen Gewalt sind Großfamilien. Im von Savannen unterbrochenen Regenwald bauen die *Ibo* v. a. Yams und Taro an, in jüngerer Zeit auch Maniok. Daneben ist der Fischfang von Bedeutung. Sie glauben an einen höchsten Schöpfergott im Himmel, der sich mit der Erde als Trägerin der Fruchtbarkeit vermählt. Sie kennen zahlreiche Geister, die die natürliche Umwelt beleben; Ahnenkult und wichtige Rolle von Weissagepraktiken. Die *Ibo* fertigen Holzmasken und Tonfiguren an, die in Gruppen von Menschen und Tieren als Schutzgeister an Altären aufgestellt werden.

Igbo 67, 68, 136, 138, 180, 627

Nigeria, östlich des Nigerunterlaufs siedelnde Kleingruppe, die zu den Bantu sprechenden *Mbembe* (ca. 38000) gezählt werden (Murdock), nach anderen Autoren auch Bezeichnung für die → *Ibo*.

Yam-Maske □ 88; Figur aus Holz □ 173; Maske □ 679; Kopfschmuck □ 936

Ijo (Idjo, Ijaw)
180

Nolde 390, 391

Nigeria, ca. 175000 Menschen, die sich auf ca. 20 Gruppen verteilen (darunter die → *Kalabari*). Der Überlieferung nach stammen sie aus → Benin und gründeten seit dem frühen 17. Jahrhundert Kleinhandelsstaaten im Nigerdelta (die bekanntesten »Deltastaaten« waren Bonny, Neu-Calabar, auch Owome genannt, und Brass). Ursprünglich wurden die kleinen Fischerdörfer von Männerversammlungen regiert, später übernahmen die wirtschaftlich erfolgreichsten Händlerfamilien die Verwaltung. Dauerfeldbau von Yams, Taro, seit jüngerer Zeit auch Maniok sowie Fischfang. Glaube an eine im Himmel lebende und z. T. mit ihm identifizierte Schöpfergöttin (»Tamuno«), die als Spenderin der Empfängnis gilt und durch einen mit schwarzer Erde gefüllten Tontopf repräsentiert wird. Sie wird gemeinsam mit der beim Yamsfest lebensgroß dargestellten Erdgottheit Amakiri verehrt. Sie soll Frieden und reiche Ernte bringen und Unheil abwehren; daneben existieren niedere Gottheiten (häufig in Pythongestalt gedacht). Die *Ijo* kennen ein Geheimbundwesen und den Ahnenkult, deren Maskenwesen die Sujets der Schnitzkunst bestimmen: Nilpferd- und Fischmasken (die für den Wasserkult waagerecht auf dem Kopf getragen werden) sowie weißbemalte weibliche und schwarzbemalte männliche Totenmasken.

Ilanda 143

Indianer 11, 48, 95, 97–101, 105, 106, 173, 469, 480, 484, 556, 564, 585, 600, 634
Ernst 577 – Hartley 469, 470, 473 – Matulka 478 – Morris 478, 480 – Noguchi 639 – Pollock 638, 654, 656 – Rothko 644 – Sloan 478 – Smith 662 – Tobey 638

Erdaufschüttung in Form einer Schlange □ 959

Siehe auch Acoma, *Apachen*, *Bella-Coola*, *Cherokesen*, *Comanchen*, *Creek*, *Crow*, *Delaware*, *Indianer der Nordwestküste*, *Iowa*, *Irokesen*, *Mohawk*, *Navajo*, *Prärieindianer*, *Tlingit*

Indianer der Nordwestküste 570, 573, 607, 634, 671, 672
Ernst 577, 588 – Kiesler 639 – Newman 632, 649 – Paalen 600 – Smith 662 – Tobey 638

Diese amerikanischen Ureinwohner sind eine kulturell sehr einheitliche Gruppe, deren einzelne Stämme jedoch unterschiedlichsten Sprachgruppen angehören. Zu ihnen gehören u. a. die Stämme der *Bella-Coola*, *Haida*, *Kwakiutl*, *Nootka*, *Tlingit* sowie die *Salish*, die an der Küste leben. Das Häuptlingswesen ist kennzeichnend für die soziale Ordnung der Nordwestküste. Grundlage für die Ernährung war der Fischfang. Häuser, Boote und Geräte bestanden aus Holz, auch Metall wurde verwendet, vor allem das Kupfer. Kennzeichnend für die Religion der Nordwestküste war ein hochentwickelter Schamanismus mit Ahnenverehrung. Ahnen und Hilfsgeister, die man sich in Tiergestalt vorstellte, wurden als Tiere abgebildet. Die Indianer der Nordwestküste sind die künstlerisch produktivsten unter den Indianern Nordamerikas. Berühmt sind die riesigen Totempfähle, in denen Ahnen und ganze Genealogien aus übereinandergesetzten Tier- und Menschenfiguren dargestellt wurden. Mit den Masken konnten Ahnen- und Tiergeister tänzerisch dargestellt werden. Die Ornamentik stellt in Varianten immer die gleichen Motive dar: hockende Menschen- oder Tierfiguren. Bekannt sind auch die ornamentierten Dekken aus Zedernbast und Wildziegenhaar, in denen die gleichen Motive wie in der übrigen Kunst vorkommen, die aber noch stärker abstrahierte Formen verwenden. Die riesigen, seetüchtigen Ruderboote der Küstenindianer (Einbäume mit aufgesetzten Planken) sind mit Reliefs verziert.

Objekte von Indianern der Nordwestküste □ 124; Figur aus Holz □ 131

Siehe auch Bella-Coola, *Haida*, *Kwakiutl*, *Nootka*, *Salish*, *Tlingit*, Vancouver Island.

Inka 11, 86, 523
Moore 614 – Nolde 392

Die Inka sind kein Stamm oder eine Volksgruppe, sondern ein Herrschergeschlecht, das Peru von etwa 1440 bis 1532, dem Jahr der Ankunft der Spanier unter Pissarro, regierte. Die Inka erweiterten ihr Reich von Ecuador bis weit nach Chile. Die Kontinuität der Herrschaft, eine absolute Diktatur (»theokratischer Sozialismus«), wurde durch ein ausgeklügeltes Verwaltungssystem gesichert. Der Straßen- und Brückenbau machte die entferntesten Landesteile rasch zugänglich, auch wenn das Rad und das Pferd noch nicht bekannt waren. Die Kunst diente ausschließlich der Verherrlichung des Herrschers und der Toten. Riesige Tempel- und Festungsanlagen sind von Mauern umschlossen, die aus behauenen Steinen ohne Mörtel gefügt wurden. Diese Technik sicherte die Widerstandsfähigkeit gegen Erdbeben. Die Kunst der Inka ist außer durch die Architektur nur durch Grabbeigaben aus Gold, Silber und Keramik bekannt. In der trockenen peruanischen Wüste haben sich sogar Textilien – aus Lama- und Vikunawolle gearbeitet – erhalten. Sie lassen ahnen, welche Vielfalt textiler Techniken die Indianer des Inkareiches beherrschten. Die oft weitgehend abstrahierte Ornamentik zeigt mythologische Szenen. Keramik wurde ohne den Gebrauch der Töpferscheibe angefertigt und ist bemalt. Besonders typisch sind Gefäße in Kopfgestalt und mit Tierformen. Dem spanischen Einbruch konnte kaum Widerstand entgegengesetzt werden. Nachkommen der indianischen Bevölkerung haben sich in Peru erhalten, vor allem im Stamm der *Quetchua*.

Iowa 101

→ *Prärieindianer*

George Catlins Iowa-Truppe beim Auftritt für Louis-Philippe in den Tuilerien □ 125

Irian Jaya (West-Irian)

Westlicher Teil Neuguineas, früher holländische Kolonie, jetzt als Provinz zu Indonesien gehörig.

→ *Asmat*, Geelvinck-Bai, Sentani-See

Irokesen
Masson 563

Eigentlich kein Stamm, sondern eine Konföderation von Stämmen (*Onondaga*, *Cayuga*, *Mohawk*, *Oneida* und *Seneca*), die bei Ankunft der Europäer in der Gegend der großen nordamerikanischen Seen lebten. Die irokesischen Siedlungen waren in Schutzlagen auf Hügelkuppen errichtet und durch mehrere Palisadenreihen und Erdwälle befestigt. Solche Dörfer waren im Durchschnitt von mehr als 1000 Personen besiedelt. Die soziale Organisation bestand aus matrilinearen und matrilokalen Gruppen. Die Religion war im Grunde dualistisch, neigte aber – vielleicht unter christlichem Einfluß – zu einer Hochgottvorstellung. Das religiöse Leben war in den Händen von Geheimgesellschaften, die für ihre Kulte Masken aus Maisstroh benutzten, die Krankheiten abwehren sollten, und Holzmasken, sogenannte Falschgesichter, mit verzerrten Gesichtszügen. Als Pflanzenbauer waren die *Irokesen* die nördlichste Ausstrahlung der pflanzenbauerischen Hochkulturen Mittelamerikas. Ihre nächsten nördlichen Nachbarn waren bereits Jäger. Die heute noch lebenden *Irokesen* sind gesuchte Arbeiter bei Hochbauten, da sie völlig schwindelfrei sind. Die Frisur der *Irokesen*, der »Hahnenkamm«, ist das Vorbild der modernen Punkfrisur.

Keule □ 123

Siehe auch Mohawk

J

Jukun (Kororofa, Yukun) 68, 91, 143
Moore 614, 615 – Picasso 330

Nigeria, mit verschiedenen Untergruppen ca. 30000 Stammesmitglieder, Bantu sprechende Feldbauern in der Benue-Ebene (um Wukari). Wahrscheinlich aus dem NO kommend, gelangten sie entlang des Mandara-Gebirges über das Gongola-Gebiet in den Benue-Raum, wo sie das Reich Kwararafa mit der gleichnamigen Hauptstadt südlich des Benue gegründet haben sollen. Ihre ständigen kriegerischen Auseinandersetzungen mit den *Haussa* im Norden (seit dem 14. Jahrhundert) sind uns aus den *Haussa*-Chroniken bekannt. Im 17. Jahrhundert erreichte das Reich Kwararafa als expansive Militärmacht seinen Höhepunkt, seit dem 18. Jahrhundert Verfall und schließlich Eroberung durch die *Fulbe*. Heute existieren die *Jukun* nur mehr in verstreuten Gruppen, die jedoch die Erinnerung an das sakrale Königtum in ihren Kulten lebendig halten.

Maske □ 446; Figur aus Holz □ 914

K

Kalabari

Nigeria, zusammen mit den *Brass* Unterstämme der → *Ijo*, ca. 175000 Stammesangehörige.

Maske □ 112; Kopfschmuck □ 161

Kambe (Wakambe)
Lipchitz 441

Kenia, kleine Gruppe mit ca. 3100 Menschen, westlich von Mombasa, die als Unterstamm der → *Giryama* zu den küstennahen *Nordost-Bantu* zählen, die früher *Nyika* (»Buschleute«) hießen, heute weniger diskriminierend als *Mijikenda* (»Neun Siedlungen«) bezeichnet werden. Die *Kambe* sind von der Küste durch die *Suahili* abgeschnitten. Sie bauen u. a. Hirsearten an, daneben hat die Rinderzucht eine große Bedeutung. Sie leben in kleinen Kompaktdörfern mit Häuptlingen und haben ein ausgeprägtes Altersklassensystem.

Figur aus Holz □ 607; Grabfigur □ 903

Kamerun 174, 380
Janco 551 – Kirchner 382, 396, 415 – Marc 386, 387 – Pechstein 398, 403, 409, 410 – Schmidt-Rottluff 394, 398, 404

Siehe auch Bamum, Bangwa, Ejagham, Ekoi, Fang, Bamileke, Mambila, Namshi, Mfumte, Ngumba, Wute

Kameruner Grasland 181

Bezeichnung für die offenen Savannen im Süden des Zentralhochlandes von Kamerun, die von *Semi-Bantu* (→ *Bantu*) bewohnt werden und eine zusammengehörige Kulturprovinz bilden. Die stark zersplitterte Bevölkerung stellt jedoch keine ethnische, politische oder kulturelle Einheit dar. Die zahlreichen kleinen Häuptlingstümer zeigen Spuren sakralen Königtums, die auf die benachbarten Großreiche (Mali, Ghana, Guinea-Küste) weisen. Das Kunstschaffen (Holzplastiken, Pfeifenköpfe) hat relativ ausdrucksstarke, fast derbe Züge.

Häuptlingsstuhl □ 553; Pfeifenköpfe □ 552

Kanioka 163

Große Häuptlingsschaft der → *Luba-Hemba* um 1500.

Karagwe, Königreich

Tansania, Zwischenseengebiet. Nachfolgereich des alten Bunyoro-Königreiches (seit dem 13. Jahrhundert).

Tierfigur □ 705

Siehe auch Bukoba

Karawari 620

Der Karawari (Korowori) ist der südliche Nebenfluß des Sepik und Siedlungsgebiet der *Alamblak* und anderer Papua-Gruppen. Typisch für die Karawari-Region sind Kultkrokodile und sog. Hakenfiguren, Yipwon (siehe Glossar). *Lit.:* Tischner, H., *Das Kultkrokodil vom Korowori,* Wegweiser zur Völkerkunde, Heft 7. Hamburgisches Museum für Völkerkunde 1965.

Siehe auch Papua-Golf, Papua-Neuguinea, *Alamblak.*

Karolinen 116
Giacometti 542

Inselgruppe Mikronesiens.
→ Nomoinseln, Nukuoro, Palauinseln

Kasingo
Figur aus Holz □ 473

Keaka

Untergruppe der → *Ekoi.*

Figur aus Holz □ 215

Kenia

→ *Giryama, Kambe*

Kerewa

→ Papua-Golf

Schädelgerüst □ 137

Kissi (Kisi, Gissi) 180

Ca. 200000 Stammesmitglieder, Sudan-Neger der Temne-Gruppe (wie die benachbarten → *Sherbro, Bulom* u. a.), die vornehmlich in Guinea (südlich von Kissidougou) und mit Ausläufern bis nach NW-Liberia und dem östlichen Sierra Leone siedeln. Brandrodungsfeldbau im tropischen Regenwald (das Hacken muß z. T. wegen Erosionsgefahr unterbleiben). Angebaut werden u. a. Reis, von dem mindestens neun Arten bekannt sind. Daneben Sammelwirtschaft und Fischfang. Kleine politische Organisationseinheiten (Dörfer). Patrilineare Deszendenz mit bemerkenswerten mutterrechtlichen Einflüssen. Vorstellung eines Totenreiches jenseits des Flusses oder auf dem Grund von Gewässern. Verehrung von heiligen Fischen (Wels). Große Bedeutung des Ahnenkults und der Geheimbünde (*Kono*).

Komo (Kumu)

Zaire, ca. 21000 Stammesmitglieder. Hackbauern (u. a. Bananen, daneben Maniok, Yams) in den Waldgebieten südöstlich des Kongo-Oberlaufs um den Ort Lubutu. Die *Komo* sind die bedeutendsten Holzschnitzer dieser Region, deren Plastik (geschnitzte Pfeiler, Masken aus Holz oder Baumrinde) mit dem Initiations- und Bundwesen in Verbindung steht.

Initiationsblöcke □ 508

Kongo (Gebiet) 159, 167, 172, 179

Kongo, Volksrepublik

→ *Kota, Kugni, Kwele, Shira, Punu, Teke, Vili, Yombe*

Kongo 22, 89, 135, 143, 181, 348
Matisse 153

Sammelbezeichnung für die *Mittel-Bantu*-Stämme, die in einem sich südlich an den tropischen Regenwald anschließenden Gürtel zwischen Atlantischem und Indischem Ozean leben (→ *Bantu*). Das bedeutende Königreich Kongo (Bakongo) ist seit dem 15. Jahrhundert durch enge Beziehungen mit den Portugiesen bekannt: Die Oberschicht des Reiches trat zum Katholizismus über, und unter König Affonso I. erlebte das Reich Mitte des 16. Jahrhunderts seine größte Blüte und Macht. Seit dem 17. Jahrhundert Verfall und »Verwilderung« des Christentums, das sich nur in rudimentären Spuren (»Kreuz«-Embleme, Rosenkranz) erhält. Zu den *Kongo* gehörten nach Schätzungen 2,5 Millionen Menschen. Sie betrieben extensiven Brandrodungsfeldbau. Matrilineare Deszendenz; Hochgottglaube und in den Häuptlingsschaften Spuren sakralen Königtums.

Siehe auch Kota, Teke, Etoumbi, Yombe, Shira, Punu, Kugni

Koniagi (Konyagi, Awunlen) 180

Senegal, Guinea, ca. 10–15000 Menschen, die in der Ebene von Younkounkoun leben und zu der altertümlichen Gruppe der *Tenda* gerechnet werden, obwohl sie verschiedene Sprachen sprechen. Neben dem vorherrschenden Reisanbau reger Handel mit den benachbarten Gruppen. Sie leben in kompakten Dörfern in Rundhäusern mit Bambuswänden. Von den Zentren aus werden Filialdörfer gegründet. Politisch sind sie in Kleinhäuptlingstümern organisiert. Die Schmiede nehmen eine besonders geachtete Stellung ein. Traditionell trugen die Männer Penisfutterale, belegt sind auch mannigfaltiger Perlschmuck, Aluminiumohrringe und Nasenschmuck aus den Stacheln von Stachelschweinen. Matrilineare Deszendenzregelung; vage Vorstellung eines Himmelsgottes. Einen Wassergott (Fato) stellt man sich in Gestalt eines Widders oder einer Schlange vor, die sich bei Gewässern zeigen. Geheimbundwesen, das in enger Verbindung zum Ahnenkult steht.

Konkombwa

Hackbauern am Mittellauf des Oti (Grenzgebiet von Togo und Ghana). Mit Untergruppen 50000 Stammesmitglieder.

Getreidespeicher □ 815

Kono (Konor) 180

Im äußersten Süden Guineas um den Mount Nimba siedelnd, Nachbarn der → *Mano* und → *Dan*, ca. 80000 Stammesmitglieder.

Konso

S-Äthiopien, zu den kushitischen Völkern zählende Gruppe, die in ca. 40 stadtähnlichen Dörfern südlich des Camosees siedelt. Sie betreiben in den umliegenden Bergen intensive Terrassenwirtschaft mit künstlicher Bewässerung; Hauptpflanzen sind Hirsen, daneben Baumwolle, Hülsenfrüchte und Knollenpflanzen, die z. T. im selben Beet gezogen werden. Die Dörfer genießen einen autonomen Status. Hohepriester, die nur religiöse Funktionen hatten und auf Berghöhen residierten, gliederten das Land jedoch nach ihrem Einflußbereich in vier Bezirke. Ein Himmels- und Erdgottheitenpaar dominiert; wichtige Rolle der Verdienstfeste mit Errichtung von Grab- und Erinnerungsmalen, schwach entwickelte Seelenvorstellung. Blutige Tieropfer, Getreide- und Trankopfer, die die Fruchtbarkeit der Saat und des Viehs sichern sollen. Die *Konso* rezitieren charakteristische litaneienhafte Gebete. In ihren Erzählungen und Legenden kommen zahlreiche alttestamentliche Motive vor.

Begräbnispfahl □ 783

Kopar

Dorf am Unterlauf des Sepik (Papua-Neuguinea). Es zählte im Jahr 1909 80 Einwohner.

Figur aus Holz □ 726

Korea

Wegegott □ 538

Kota (Bakota, Okota, Kuta) 16, 25, 135, 138, 139, 181, 275, 276, 295, 348, 349, 606
Epstein 446 – Giacometti 330, 542 – Gris 22 – Matisse 352 – Picasso 87, 275, 276, 283, 287, 290, 303, 308, 313, 330, 331, 334, 336, 349, 351, 352

NO-Gabun, NW-Kongo (Brazzaville), zwischen den Flüssen Ogooué und Sangha. Sammelbezeichnung für verschiedene Gruppen (darunter → *Ndasa* und → *Mbamba*) der kulturell relativ einheitlichen *Äquatorial-Bantu*. (→ *Bantu*). Feldbeuter des tropischen Regenwalds (u. a. Maniok, Yams, Taro). Patrilineare Deszendenz. Die *Kota* sind Schöpfer von sog. Wächterfiguren: Wie die benachbarten → *Fang* bewahrten sie Knochen der Männer und Frauen von hohem Ansehen in Rindenschachteln oder Körben auf, an deren Rand Figuren oder Holzköpfe gesetzt wurden. Die *Kota* schufen v. a. flache, stilisierte Kopfplastiken, die reich mit Kupfer- oder Messingblech beschlagen waren. Auch Künstler wurden durch solche Gedächtnisfiguren geehrt.

Hütte mit Kota-Reliquiarfiguren □ 164; Reliquiarfiguren und andere Objekte □ 165; Reliquiarfigur □ 193, 331, 343, 344, 347, 349, 410, 411, 413, 721; Reliquiarkopf □ 615

Kpelle (Kpwessi, Kpese) 180

Ca. 250000 Stammesmitglieder, → Mande sprechende Gruppen im Hinterland von Liberia und dem benachbarten Guinea (wo sie als *Guerzé* bekannt sind). An Dörfer gebundene Hackbauern (u. a. Reis) mit patrilinearer Deszendenz. Geheimbundwesen (*Poro*). Kulturelle Homogenität mit anderen Mande-Gruppen dieser Regenwaldregion wie → *Dan*, → *Guro*, → *Kono* und → *Toma*.

Kran (Bush Kru, Kraa) 180

Liberia, Elfenbeinküste (wo sie auch als *Guere* oder *Ngere* bekannt sind), Untergruppe der → *Kru*, mit Untergruppen ca. 15000 Menschen. Die *Kran* siedeln v. a. östlich des mittleren Cavally.

Kru (Krao) 180

Sammelbezeichnung für Gruppen, die zu den Sudan-Negern gehören und zwischen Monravia (Südliberia) und dem unteren Bandama (Elfenbeinküste) leben, u. a. *Bassa*. Kennzeichnend ist die starke Zersplitterung in Kleinstaaten und Dialekte (vermutlich unter dem Druck der → *Dan*). Sie werden von manchen Autoren als eigenständige Sprachgruppe, von anderen als Unterabteilung der Kwa-Sprachen bezeichnet. Die *Kru*-Stämme zeichnen sich durch kulturell altertümliche Züge aus. Sie sind vorwiegend Hackbauern mit Brandrodung im tropischen Regenwald (Bananen, Yams, Taro, in jüngerer Zeit auch Reis). Bei den Küstenstämmen, die auch vorzügliche Bootsbauer sind, ist der Fischfang von Bedeutung. Die *Kru* sind bekannt für Holzschnitzereien und Gelbgußschmuck. Patrilineare Deszendenz. Die politische Herrschaft wird vom Ältestenrat ausgeübt, in dem das älteste Mitglied die höchste Autorität genießt. Neben den eigentlichen *Kru* (auch Crau, Krawi, Nana genannt), zu denen ca. 1 Million Menschen gehören, zählen zu dieser Gruppe unter anderen auch die → *Grebo* (am Cavally), die → *Kran* und die → *Bete*.

Kuba (Bakuba) 25, 26, 143, 168, 181
Braque 153 – Matisse 153 – Weber 36

Zaire, mit Unterstämmen ca. 75000 Menschen. Volk der *Mittel-Bantu*, das im Einzugsgebiet des Kasai siedelt, einem südlichen Nebenfluß des Kongo. Anfang des 16. Jahrhunderts errichteten sie auf der Grundlage eines Kleinstaatenbundes ein hochorganisiertes Großreich mit prächtiger Hofhaltung, das nach ihrer charakteristischen Waffe, einem Wurfmesser (*Shongo*), auch Bashongo-Reich genannt wird. Die ausführlichen, mündlich überlieferten Herrschergenealogien umfassen 120 Namen. Die legendären ältesten Könige haben kulturheroische Züge: Einer der bedeutendsten Herrscher (ca. 1600–1629) soll Kulturkontakte mit den westlich am oberen Kwango siedelnden → *Pende* gepflegt und von dort künstlerische Anregungen (Ornamente und Motive der Holzschnitzerei, Weberei und Korbflechterei) eingeführt haben. Die *Kuba* betreiben Feldbau mit Brandrodung (Mais, Maniok) und sind matrilinear organisiert. Ihre Dörfer mit mehreren Sektionen von matrilinearen, unabhängigen Klans werden von einem Rat und einem Häuptling beherrscht. Sie glauben an einen Schöpfergott, Ahnenverehrung ist nur rudimentär vorhanden. Die *Kuba* und die in ihrem Einflußbereich lebenden Gruppen sind durch die Erzeugnisse ihrer Kunst und ihres Kunsthandwerks berühmt: Maskenschnitzerei, Elfenbeinminiaturen und Gewebe. Das von den Königen geförderte, sozial sehr angesehene Kunsthandwerk (die Künstler wurden am Hof geschult und in Gruppen organisiert) strahlte seit dem 19. Jahrhundert auf alle Bereiche der Gesellschaft aus. So zeigen die meisten Kultobjekte und Alltagsgegenstände ähnliche Motive und Stilmerkmale: diagonal verlaufende Ornamente (Einfluß der Korbflechterei?) aus Dreiecken, Rauten, Zickzacklinien, Flecht- und Schlingbändern.

Sitzender König □ 23; Maske □ 111, 701

Kugni (Bakougni, Kunyi) 139

Kongo-Brazzaville, kleine Gruppe der → *Vili-Kongo* südlich des Kouilou.

Fetischfigur □ 636

Kulango (Pakhala, Kolambo) 135, 180

Elfenbeinküste, ca. 40000 Stammesmitglieder. Seit dem 16. Jahrhundert als Hackbauern in den Feuchtsavannen zwischen Comoé und Schwarzem Volta bezeugt. Mit den → *Senufo* ethnisch verwandt. Bekannt als Schöpfer stark ornamentierter Masken.

Figur aus Holz □ 781

Kundu 143

Kamerun, mit Untergruppen ca. 50000 Stammesmitglieder. Die *Kundu* sind *Küstenbantu* des Hinterlandes im Gebiet der Rumpi-Berge.

Kurumba (Koromba, Fulse) 141, 180

Obervolta, ca. 86000 Stammesmitglieder, sprachlich den *Gurunsi* verwandt. Die *Kurumba* leben in zerstreuten Siedlungen und sind größtenteils vermischt mit den *Fulbe*, → *Mossi* und *Songhai* zwischen Aribinda (im Osten) und Wahuguya (im Westen).

Kuyu (Koyo) 181

Kongo-Brazzaville, Gruppe der *Mboshi*, die an den Kongozuflüssen Likoula, Kouyou und Alima auf den höher gelegenen trockenen Landstreifen (meist schon außerhalb der Urwaldzone) als Feldbauern leben. Hochstehende Kunst: u. a. Pfahlplastik mit polychromer Bemalung. Sozioreligiöse Dualismen (Zweiteilung des Landes mit verschiedenen Schutztieren), Schöpfergottglaube und ausgeprägtes Maskenwesen.

Siehe auch Mboshi

Kwakiutl 340, 484
Hartley 468

→ *Indianer der Nordwestküste*

Maske ☐ 461; Totempfahl, zum Gedenken an Mungo Martin ☐ 861

Kwele (Kuel[l]e, Bakwele, Bakwil) 67, 68, 141, 181

N-Gabun, SO-Kamerun, zu den insgesamt 30000 zählenden Bantu sprechenden *Dzem* gehörig. Feldbeuter des äquatorialen Regenwalds. Mit den verwandten → *Kota* besonders bekannt für ihre künstlerische Fertigkeit (v. a. Masken).

Maske ☐ 87

L

Landuma (Landoma) 140, 180

Republik Guinea, vermischt mit den *Tyapi* siedeln sie am mittleren Rio Nunez und zählen gemeinsam ca. 20000 Menschen. Reisbauern und Fischer. Kennzeichnend für das religiöse Leben sind Ahnenverehrung und Geheimbundwesen (*Simo*).

Lega (Zaire) 181
Carrà 421, 422 – Giacometti 543 – Picasso 341

Die *Lega* kamen im 16. Jahrhundert aus dem NO und drangen in das Waldgebiet von Manieme (westlich des Kivu-Sees) ein, wo sie als Hackbauern (Bananen), Jäger und Sammler leben. Eines der wenigen Völker Zaires, das Erz im Stollenbau gewann. Glaube an einen Schöpfergott (Kalaga) mit Zügen eines Ersten Ahnen und Kulturheros. Die *Lega* sind berühmt für ihre Statuetten und Masken aus Holz und Elfenbein mit charakteristischen konkaven Gesichtern.

Doppelgesichtige Figur ☐ 166; Maske ☐ 196; Figur ☐ 506; Kopf ☐ 585, 588; Figur aus Holz und Fasern ☐ 610; Figur aus Holz ☐ 880

Lele

Harfe ☐ 405

Liberia → *Dan, Grebo*

Loango-Küste

Figuren ☐ 171

Lobi 141, 180

Obervolta, Ghana, ca. 200000 Menschen, die an der Schwarzen Volta und in Nordghana leben. Sie betreiben Regenzeitfeldbau, Viehzucht und Jagd. Patrilineare Deszendenz; Dorfgemeinschaften mit Ältestenrat, wobei das Oberhaupt nach dem Senioratsprinzip bestimmt wird. Eine wichtige Rolle im religiösen Leben der *Lobi* spielen die »Bateba«, menschengestaltige Figuren aus Holz, Lehm oder Metall: Sie gelten als lebendige, sich bewegende Wesen, deren besondere Kraft gegen Schadenzauber und Hexerei hilft. Sie unterstützen auch die im Rang unter ihnen stehenden Schutzgeister des Dorfes gegen unheilvolle Mächte.

Luba (Baluba) Zaire, Sambia 25, 26, 143, 181, 238, 294, 349
Lipchitz 439 – Modigliani 433 – Moore 623 – Pechstein 408

Sammelbezeichnung für verschiedene Stämme der *Bantu-Neger*, die erst durch die politisch-historische Entwicklung zu einer kulturellen und sprachlichen Einheit zusammenwuchsen. Zu den *Luba* zählen u. a. die *Kanioka*, die → *Kete*, die → *Lulua*, die → *Songge* sowie die → *Hemba*. Das eigentliche *Luba*-Reich, das vermutlich schon im 13. Jahrhundert bestand, erstreckte sich in den Savannen zwischen dem Fluß Kasai und dem Tanganjika-See (mit dem Kerngebiet in Süd-Katanga). Das *Luba*-Reich hielt sich bis zum Ende des 19. Jahrhunderts und war eher eine Art Konföderation als ein fest geeinter Staat. Trotz seiner großen Assimilationskraft (»Lubaisierung«) erhielten sich zahlreiche regionale Traditionen mit unterschiedlichen Kunststilen und thematischen Schwerpunkten. Lediglich die verbreiteten Frauendarstellungen, die das hohe Ansehen der Frau bezeugen, sind den meisten Stämmen gemeinsam. Auffallend sind idealisierte Menschendarstellungen mit stilisierten und ausdrucksstarken Gesichtszügen sowie die Detailfreudigkeit (Frisuren, Narbenschmuck). Bekannt sind auch Häuptlingsstühle, die nur für hervorragende Persönlichkeiten angefertigt werden und auch als vorübergehender Sitz der Ahnengeister gelten, sowie sog. Schalenträger-Figuren (*mboko*), sitzende oder kniende Frauen (selten Männer), die eine Schale in Händen halten. Die Figuren scheinen (als Geistersitz) v. a. mit dem Orakelwesen in Verbindung zu stehen.

Hocker ☐ 24, 602; Figur aus Holz und Metall ☐ 202; Figürliche Verzierung eines Holzstabes ☐ 280, 281; Weibliche Figur ☐ 564, 568; Kifwebe-Maske ☐ 678, 707

Siehe auch Kanioka

Lulua (Luluwa) 143, 181

Zaire, am Mittellauf des gleichnamigen Flusses siedelnde Gruppe der → *Luba*.

Lunda 143

→ *Mbala*

Lwalwa (Zaire) 39
Picasso 338

Gruppe der → *Lunda*, die als Abspaltung von den → *Luba* ein großes Reich im südlichen Zaire beherrschten, bis sie Ende des 19. Jahrhunderts von den → *Chokwe* erobert wurden. Die *Lwalwa* haben Doppeldeszendenz.

Maske ☐ 45, 455

M

Madagaskar 159, 455

Figuren von einem Begräbnispfahl ☐ 632

Mahican → *Delaware*

Mahongwe → *Ongwe*

Makonde (Wakonde, Wamakonde) 47, 181
Giacometti 542

Grenzgebiet zwischen Tansania und Moçambique. Östlich des Malawi-Sees siedelnde Ethnie der *Nyassa*-Völker, die sprachlich zu den → *Bantu* gehören; unter dem Einfluß der Ostküste z. T. islamisierte Kultur. Die *Makonde* leben vom Feldbau (Mais, Hirsen) und der Rinderhaltung. Matrilineare Deszendenz. Dorfsiedlung ohne angestammte Herrschaftsorganisation. Betonter Ahnen-Hochgott-Glaube. Hochentwickelte Flecht- und Schnitzkunst: Ahnenfiguren, Masken, die bei den Schlußfesten der Knaben- und Mädcheninitiation getragen werden und Geister darstellen. Bei den südlichen *Makonde (Mawia)* gibt es Medizin- und Schnupftabaksbehälter aus Holz oder Bambus (*mtete*) mit dekorativen Deckeln in Menschen- oder Tierkopfform.

Helmmaske ☐ 57

Malaita → Salomoninseln

Malekula 126

→ Neue Hebriden

Figur eines Männerbundes (Rangstatue) ☐ 327 (Mitte), 329

Mali → *Bambara, Bozo, Dogon, Marka, Senufo*

Malinke (Manding, Mandinke, Mellenka) 138, 140, 141, 180

Liberia, Elfenbeinküste, Senegal, Guinea und Guinea-Bissau, ca. 1 Million Menschen. Neben den → *Bambara* die wichtigste Mande sprechende Gruppe der Sudan-Neger. Ausgedehntes Siedlungsgebiet am oberen Senegal, Niger und Gambia. Hackfeldbauern, z. T. mit künstlicher Bewässerung, v. a. Hirsen, Mais und Reis. Die *Malinke* sind die Nachkommen des großen Handelsreiches Mali (ca. 11.–17. Jahrhundert), das große Teile Senegambiens und des Westsudan beherrschte. Die Oberschicht des hervorragend organisierten Staates – Kerngebiet mit der Hauptstadt am Sankarani, drei Außenprovinzen, die in je zwölf Bezirke unterteilt waren und von Beamten verwaltet wurden – war islamisiert. Ende des 17. Jahrhunderts wurde Mali von den → *Bambara* zerstört. Seitdem sind die *Malinke* in drei relativ zusammenhanglose Gruppen geteilt (Gambia – Niger/Senegal – Hinterland von Liberia und Elfenbeinküste). Sie sind bekannt für ihre religiöse Holzschnitzkunst.

Mama 68, 91, 330
Moore 27, 622, 624

Nigeria, ca. 15 000 Stammesmitglieder, Bantu sprechende Gruppe von Hackfeldbauern (v. a. Hirsen) im zentralnigerianischen Plateau. Erbliches Dorfhäuptlingstum.

Figur aus Holz □ 504; Maske □ 941, 942

Mambila (Mabila, Mambere)

Nigeria, Kamerun, Hackbauern (v. a. Hirsen) in z. T. terrassierten Feldern in der Region des Mambila-Plateaus.

Figur aus Holz □ 213; Figur □ 507

Mambwe 53

NO-Sambia, *Ost-Bantu*-Volk des Malawi-Tanganjika-Zwischenseegebietes. Neben Feldbau mit Brandrodung bedeutendes viehzüchterisches Element. Matrilineare Deszendenz. Hochgottglaube mit ausgeprägter Ahnenverehrung. Glaube an eine Wiedergeburt in Tierform, bei den Adligen in der besonderen Ausformung des »Fanany«: Der Häuptling wird über das Zwischenstadium einer aus dem Leichnam sich nährenden Made als Schlange oder Löwe inkarniert.

Figur aus Holz □ 68

Mangbetu (Monbuttu) 136, 181
Moore 623

NO-Zaire, mit verschiedenen Untergruppen ca. 500 000 Stammesmitglieder, Sudan-Neger, die am Oberlauf von Uelle und Ituri im Übergangsgebiet zwischen Feuchtsavanne und Regenwald siedeln und vom Anbau von Maniok, Bananen und Ölpalmen leben. *Mangbetu* bezeichnet eigentlich ein Herrschergeschlecht, das (ähnlich wie die benachbarten *Bandia* und die → *Zande*) im 18. Jahrhundert einen straff organisierten Staat aufbaute. Die *Mangbetu* konnten sich gegen die expansiven *Zande* behaupten und prägten ihrerseits die autochthonen Stämme (ihre Sprache wurde zur Lingua franca der Region). Durch die Überlagerung ergab sich eine Schichtung der Bevölkerung in Herrscherklans, Freie und Hörige. Absolutes Königtum mit komplexer Hofetikette. Würdezeichen (Schädeldeformation) und Herrschaftsinsignien (Schmuck). Die *Mangbetu* sind bekannt als vorzügliche Holzschnitzer und Töpfer.

Muster mit figürlichen Elementen □ 83; Harfe □ 422

Mano (Mah, Mana) 180

Im Grenzgebiet von NO-Liberia, Guinea und Elfenbeinküste. Sie gehören zu den Mande sprechenden → *Guere* und sind Nachbarn der → *Dan*.

Maori 117, 121, 215
Gauguin 216 – Gaudier-Brzeska 460, 462 – Masson 565, 566

Voreuropäische Bevölkerung von Neuseeland, den beiden großen Inseln südlich Australiens, die vermutlich vor etwa 1000 Jahren von polynesischen Seefahrern der etwa 2000 Seemeilen entfernten Gesellschaftsinseln besiedelt wurden. Sie ernährten sich durch Fischen, Sammeln u. a. eßbarer Farnwurzeln und durch die Jagd auf Moas, bis zu 3 m große Laufvögel (ausgerottet). Mitte des 14. Jahrhunderts Ankunft einer »großen Flotte« (ebenfalls aus Tahiti) mit Nutzpflanzen und dem Hund als Haustier; auf die Häuptlinge in den einzelnen Booten führen die *Maori* seither ihre Genealogien zurück. Anpassung an die veränderten subtropischen Umweltbedingungen: anstelle von Tapa mittels »Fingerweben« geknüpfte Umhänge aus neuseeländischem »Flachs« zum Schutz gegen Regen und Kälte (auch als Schlafdecken) und als Körperschutz gegen Stichwaffen. Die *Maori* errichteten Prunkbauten mit festen Wänden aus überreich beschnitzten Bohlen: schematisierte menschliche Ahnenfiguren mit heraushängender Zunge, die plastisch gearbeitet und ganz von reliefartigen Bogen- und Spiralornamenten überzogen sind. Der gleiche Dekor (z. T. durchbrochen) auf Kriegsbooten, Keulen, Häuptlingsstäben, Schmuckkästen, Musikinstrumenten, Grabstocktritten oder Särgen. Diese Gegenstände wurden in voreuropäischer Zeit mit Querbeilen und Meißeln aus Nephrit gearbeitet. Nephritmeißel traten als Ohranhänger der Schnitzmeister auf. Eine besondere Bedeutung hatte Brustschmuck, *hei-tiki* (siehe Glossar). Als Häuptlingsschmuck verwendete man die Spiralornamente der Schnitzkunst in Form von Tätowierungen (Tatauierungen); tätowierte menschliche Köpfe wurden präpariert. Die *Maori* sind heute dem modernen Staatswesen der zugewanderten Weißen angepaßt, ihre traditionelle Kultur ist auf Museen und staatlich subventionierte Kultstätten beschränkt. *Lit.:* Koch 1976, S. 189–184.

Brustschmuck (hei-tiki) □ 642

Marka 180, 432
Janco 606 – Picasso 352

Mali, verstreut siedelnder Unterstamm der Mande sprechenden *Sononke*-Gruppe im Sahel nördlich des Senegal und des Niger, insgesamt 350 000 Stammesmitglieder. Die *Marka* haben durch Vermischung starke kulturelle Elemente der → *Malinke* angenommen und sind fast durchweg islamisch. Die Bezeichnung ›Marka‹ wird vielfach für alle *Sononke* gebraucht.

Maske □ 600

Marquesasinseln 11, 16, 87, 114, 119, 120, 122, 127, 128, 158, 201, 215, 226, 351
Ernst 567 – Gauguin 201, 202, 216, 610, 699 – Lipchitz 441 – Moore 618 – Picasso 25, 294, 304

Polynesien. Schon sehr früh vom melanesisch-polynesischen Grenzgebiet her besiedelte gebirgig-schroffe Inseln mit tiefen und engen, daher schwer zugänglichen Tälern sowie ungünstigen Anbauverhältnissen und beschränkten Fischfangmöglichkeiten. Überliefert sind ständige Fehden unter den relativ isoliert lebenden, von Häuptlingen »demokratisch-liberal« regierten Stämmen. Verehrung vergöttlichter Stammesahnen, ruhmreicher Häuptlinge oder Priester auf speziellen Kultplätzen (*me'ae*). Die *Marquesaner* besaßen hölzerne oder steinerne Standbilder (Tikis) mit uniform stilisiertem Totenkopf als zeitweiligem Aufenthaltsort der vergöttlichten Ahnen. Das Tiki tritt auch als Dekor bei Fächergriffen, Ohrschmuck, Schildpatt-Diademen, Stelzentritten, Kampfkeulen, Schüsseln für das Kawa-Getränk auf sowie bei Steinstößeln zum Zerstampfen des Brotfruchtteiges oder steinernen Netzsenkern u. a. Die *Marquesaner* sind bekannt für ihre große Schmuckfreudigkeit. Außer Kopf-, Ohr- oder Brustschmuck aus Walzahn, Menschenknochen, Eberzähnen, Schildpatt, Schneckengehäusen wurde und wird auch der ganze Körper – in Form von Tätowierungen – mit komplizierten Mustern jeweils besonderer Bedeutung verziert. *Lit.:* Koch 1976, S. 178–181.

Zwei Tikis □ 142; Ohrschmuck □ 232, 767; Griff eines Paddels □ 236; Keule aus Holz □ 244, 246; Marquesanische Tätowierung □ 245; Steinfigur □ 248; Tiki □ 373; Fächergriffe □ 379; Figur aus Holz □ 382, 760, 761; Monumentale Steinfigur □ 234; Körpertätowierung □ 816

Marschallinseln 79

Mikronesien, seit 1976 amerikanisches Commonwealth.

Stabkarte □ 106

Maryland 98

Massim-Region 117, 128

→ Trobriandinseln

Mauke

Eine der → Cookinseln

Stabgott □ 608

Maya 11, 86
Zorach 485

Die klassische mexikanische Hochkultur, die von ca. 900 bis 1100 n. Chr. bestand. Berühmt sind die Maya durch Tempelbauten, Mathematik und Astronomie, ihre immer noch nicht entzifferte Schrift. Unter ihren künstlerischen Leistungen ragen besonders die bemalten Gefäße und Terrakottafiguren heraus, die außerordentlich lebendig und detailreich in Rot,

Grün und Blau bemalt sind. Technisch gesehen bestehen sie aus einem schlecht gebrannten Ton, der porös und zerbrechlich ist. Es handelt sich dabei meist um Götterfiguren oder Darstellungen von Priestern. Die reiche Ornamentierung zeigt Symbole in einer Art Kurzschrift. Die Kultur der Maya verschwand ungefähr um 1100, ohne daß die Wissenschaft bisher plausible Gründe dafür gefunden hätte. Die riesigen Städte und Tempel der Maya, Teotiahuakan, Uxmal, Palenque, Chichen Itza u. a., die den Architekten Frank Lloyd Wright anregten, bezeugen eine hohe, noch längst nicht befriedigend erforschte Kultur.

Mbala (Bambala) 26, 181

Zaire. zwischen Kwango und Kasai lebende Feldbauern mit Brandrodung (Mais, Maniok). Nach der Gründung des Yaka-Reiches durch die *Lunda* (um 1700) wurden die *Mbala* nach Norden abgedrängt und nahmen in ihre autochthonen Traditionen *Lunda*-Einflüsse auf. In zahlreiche kleine Häuptlingstümer zersplittert. Die *Mbala* sind in drei Schichten geteilt: Adel – Freie – Sklaven; patrilineare Nachfolgeregelung.

Siehe auch Lunda

Mbamba (Mbama) 139, 348

Gabun, Gruppe der → *Kota*.

Mbembe

SO-Nigeria, mit Untergruppen 38000 Menschen (1921), zu den *Semi-Bantu* des Waldlandes am → Cross River zählende Gruppe, die in der Grenzregion zu Kamerun im Küstenhinterland lebt.

Figur aus Holz □ 177

Mbete → *Ambete*

Mbole 181

Zaire, ca. 100000 Stammesmitglieder, zu den Bantu sprechenden *Mongo* gehörende Gruppe am Galonga (südl. Nebenfluß des Kongo). Jäger, Fischer und Feldbauern des tropischen Waldlandes (Knollenfrüchte). Zum Teil sind sie mit Pygmäen vermischt. Besonders bekannt sind die *Mbole* für ihre sorgfältig geschnitzten Nackenstützen aus Holz. Bundwesen (*Ekofo*).

Maske □ 350; Figur aus Holz □ 775

Mboshi 142

Volksgruppe im Bereich der Kongozuflüsse Likonala, Konyon und Alima. Sie bewohnen die höher gelegenen trockenen Landstreifen, die zum Großteil bereits außerhalb der eigentlichen Urwaldzone liegen. Kulturelle Verwandtschaften zu den → *Kota*. Ungewöhnlich für afrikanische Kunst ist die Bemalung der *Mboshi*-Skulptur.

Mbum 143

Stamm im Adamana-Massiv, im Grenzgebiet zwischen Kamerun und Zaire.

Mbunda

Nordangola, unter starkem kulturellen Einfluß der → *Lunda* stehend.

Maske □ 183

Mbuun

Zaire, am unteren Kasai siedelnd; matrilinear, mehrere Matrilinien unabhängiger Klans bilden ein Dorf, das von einem Häuptling und einem Rat regiert wird.

Stab mit menschlicher Figur □ 778

Melanesien

»Schwarze Inseln«: → Neuguinea mit Admiralitätsinseln und → Bismarckarchipel, → Salomonen, → Neue Hebriden, → Neukaledonien.

Mende (Mendi, Kossa) 180
Klee 505

Sierra Leone, zusammen mit Untergruppen ca. 1 Million Stammesmitglieder, die den größeren Teil des Südens des Landes einnehmen. Feldhackbauern (Reis, Hirsen) und Kleinviehhalter. Patrilineare Deszendenz mit alten matrilinearen Spuren. Die Klans siedeln in Hauptdörfern, von denen aus Filialgründungen erfolgen. Erbliches Häuptlingswesen. Große Rolle des Ahnenkultes und damit verbunden des Geheimbundwesens. Wie andere Mande sprechende Gruppen (→ *Dan*, → *Kran*) bekannte Holzschnitzer (Skulpturen, Masken).

Mexiko 95, 100, 629
Gauguin 216 – Giacometti 524 – Paalen 600

Ballspieler □ 741

Mfumte 48

Nigeria, mit den → *Mbembe* zu den bantoiden *Tigon* gehörend, insgesamt ca. 15000 Stammesmitglieder, die im bergigen Grenzland zwischen Nigeria und Kamerun leben.

Figur aus Holz □ 59

Mikronesien

»Kleine Inseln« (Atolle) im Nordpazifik: Marianen, → Karolinen mit → Palauinseln, Yap, Truk, Ponape und → Marschallinseln (alle seit 1976 amerikanisches Commonwealth) sowie die → Gilbertinseln, Guam und Nauru.

Minianka (Banmana, Bamana) 180

Mali, 170000 Menschen, siedeln südlich des Bani im Gebiet der → *Senufo*, von denen sie sich trotz sprachlicher Verwandtschaft kulturell unterscheiden.

Mixteken

Bei Ankunft der Spanier das in kultureller Hinsicht führende Volk Mexikos, indes die → Azteken in administrativer und strategischer Hinsicht den ersten Rang einnahmen. Die Grenzen zwischen mixtekischer und aztekischer Kultur sind fließend. Berühmt sind die Mixteken durch ihre Goldschmiedekunst und die Buchmalerei. Die Bücher bestanden aus Hirschleder und waren sorgfältig ausgemalt. Dargestellt wurden vor allem Herrschergenealogien, die von 670 bis 1511 n. Chr. lückenlos dokumentiert sind und insofern für die Erforschung der mixtekischen Kultur besondere Aufschlüsse geben.

Sonnenkult □ 887

Moche

Lokale Kultur in Peru, die sich durch einen eigenen Stil in der Keramik und eine hohe Entwicklung der Metallurgie auszeichnet. Eine einfache und urtümliche Gestaltungsweise ist insgesamt besonders charakteristisch. Wie in anderen südamerikanischen Kulturen waren Gefäße in Menschengestalt besonders verbreitet. Die Moche-Kultur ging später im Inkareich auf.

Bügelkanne □ 223

Mohawk 98

→ *Irokesen*

Stirn-Tragriemen □ 122

Mohikaner 98

→ *Delaware*

Montol

Nigeria, tschadisch sprechende Gruppe im Norden des Nigerianischen Plateaus, die zu den *Angas* (insgesamt 200000 Menschen) gezählt werden.

Kultische Heilfigur □ 54

Mossendjo-Gebiet 348

Mossi (Mosi, Moie, Yatenca) 141, 180
Ernst 580

Obervolta, 1,5 bis 1,8 Millionen Menschen zählendes Volk der Sudan-Neger, die in den Savannen zwischen Schwarzem und Weißem Volta als Brandrodungshackbauern (Hirsen) und Viehzüchter (Rinder, Pferde) leben. Vermutlich drangen die *Mossi* vor 1000 Jahren mit gepanzerten Reitern (die später übliche Rüstung der Leibwache des Herrschers dürfte auf diese Zeit zurückgehen) aus dem Osten in das nördliche Ghana ein und gründeten den Staat Dagomba (1332/33). In der Folge kriegerische Expansionszüge nach Timbuktu und weitere Staatengründungen (Mamprusi, Ouagadougou, Yatenga). Dank ihrer hervorragenden staatlichen Organisation konnten sie sich bis zur Kolonisierung durch die Franzosen (Ende 19. Jahrhundert) halten. Sakrales Königtum, patrilineare Deszendenz; in ihrer Plastik und Maskenschnitzerei dominieren abstrahierende und ornamentalisierte Motive.

Maske □ 505; Puppe aus Holz □ 773; Pfeife □ 841

Mumuye 25, 48
Moore 40, 613, 615, 623

Nigeria, Sammelname für mehrere Gruppen (insgesamt ca. 70000 Menschen), die im Bergland östlich von Jalingo bis zur Grenze von Kamerun als Hackbauern leben. Größtenteils extensiver Regenzeitfeldbau, in dichter besiedelten Gebieten auch intensive Terrassenkulturen, vornehmlich von Hirsearten. Absolutes Königtum mit Staatsratskontrolle des Herrschers und Verwaltung der Provinzen durch Häuptlinge. Patrilineare Deszendenz. Hochgottglaube, ausgeprägter Ahnendienst mit Schädelkult und Agrarriten. Ihre religiösen Holzschnitzwerke (Figuralplastiken, Masken, Kopfaufsätze) werden v. a. bei Totenfeiern verwendet.

Figur aus Holz □ 60, 782, 912

Mundurucú
Nolde 86, 390

Indianerstamm am Rio Tapajoz, Brasilien. Die *Mundurucú* waren gefürchtete Kopfjäger, berühmt bei Sammlern durch ihre Federarbeiten. Gute Beispiele im Staatlichen Museum für Völkerkunde in München, Sammlung Spix und Martius. *Lit.:* Zerries, O., *Indianer vom Amazonas*, Ausstellungskatalog, München 1960.

Kopftrophäe □ 530

Myene

Völkergruppe an der Küste von Südgabun, am Unterlauf des Ogwe.

Harfe □ 405

N

Nafana 180

Teil der → *Senufo*, südöstliche Nachbarn der → *Kulango* in den Feuchtsavannen des Grenzgebietes zwischen Elfenbeinküste und Ghana.

Nalu 180

Im Küstenstreifen zwischen Rio Cumbija in Guinea-Bissau und dem Rio Nunez in der Republik Guinea siedelndes Volk mit ca. 10000 Stammesmitgliedern. Anbau von Reis, daneben Fischfang; wichtige Rolle des Ahnenkultes und von Geheimbünden (*Simo*). Die *Nalu* sind bedeutende Holzbildhauer (Masken).

Namau

→ Papua-Golf

Imunu □ 81; Maske □ 295

Namshi (Namchi, Namdji, Doayo)

Kamerun, ca. 20000 Menschen (mit Untergruppen), die im nördlichen Adamaua-Bergland an der nigerianischen Grenze leben.

Figur aus Holz □ 788 a

Navajo (Navaho) 672, 673
Ernst 581 – Pollock 656 – Storrs 478

Indianerstamm, der zu den → *Puebloindianern* gehört. Die *Navajo* wanderten ursprünglich von Norden ein und übernahmen den Ackerbau von den bereits ansässigen *Puebloindianern*, die Schafzucht von den Spaniern. Sie sind heute bekannt durch ihre Silberarbeiten, die von Mexiko angeregt sind. Von besonderer Ausstrahlung sind ihre Sandgemälde aus gestreutem farbigen Sand. Rituelle Vorschriften regeln die Ausübung dieser religiösen Zeremonie, die als Erntedank, zur Regenbeschwörung u. ä. sitzend und auf dem nackten Erdboden vollzogen wird. Auch für die Heilung werden Sandgemälde gestreut. Dabei setzt sich der Kranke auf die Bilder, die eine Aktivierung des Weltbildes und damit die Gesundung bewirken sollen.

Ndasa 348

Teil der → *Kota*

Neubritannien 116
Janco 606

Maske □ 134; Kopf □ 889

Siehe auch *Baining*, *Sulka*

Neue Hebriden 39, 113, 114, 116, 120, 122, 128, 265, 266, 293
Giacometti 544 – Janco 606 – Matisse 247 – Picasso 343, 347, 351

Jetzt Vanuatu. Melanesische Inselgruppe südöstlich der Salomoninseln: Banksinseln, Santo, Malekula, Ambrym, Oba u. a. Gesellschaftsstruktur mit deutlicher Rangfolge, die nicht erblich ist. Der soziale Aufstieg der Männer erfolgt in »Verdienstfesten« durch regelmäßiges Spenden von Reichtümern, v. a. Ebern mit kreisförmigen Hauern, wodurch Prestige und Rang in der Welt der Lebenden und der Toten erworben werden. Aus Baumfarn geschnitzte Rangstatuen, auf Ambrym mit übergroßem Kopf, scheibenförmigen Augen und hervortretender Nase. Die Rangstatuen der Banksinseln haben (z. T. übereinander angeordnete) Gesichter mit stegförmig hervortretender Nase, Augen und Mund sowie eine blütenartige eingekerbte Umrandung. Typisch für die Neuen Hebriden sind auch Totenstatuen mit übermodelliertem Schädel und einem Körper, der aus Kokosfasern und Ton geformt ist, sowie bemalte Masken aus Baumrinde und Fasern (auf Oba) bzw. Palmholz (auf Malekula). *Lit.:* Koch 1976, S. 95–97.

Figur eines Männerbundes (Rangstatue) □ 156, 329; Maske □ 324, 326; Körpermaske □ 467

Siehe auch Banks Islands, Malekula, Oba

Neuguinea 53, 54, 66, 83, 89, 113, 114, 116, 117, 119, 120, 122, 123, 124, 127, 128, 159, 162, 265, 293
Brancusi 362 – Calder 659 – Epstein 448, 450 – Ernst 532 – Gaudier-Brzeska 462 – Lipchitz 442 – Matta 600 – Moore 613, 618 – Nolde 401

Größte Insel Melanesiens mit zwei Staaten, → Papua-Neuguinea und → West Irian.

Objekte aus der »La Korrigane«-Expedition □ 155; Ahnenfigur □ 907

Neuirland 29, 63, 114, 116, 122, 126, 127, 128, 316
Giacometti 43, 530, 542 – Heckel 398 – Matta 63, 600 – Matisse 247, 351 – Moore 618–620, 627 – Nolde 401

Insel nördlich von Neubritannien, jetzt ebenfalls zu Papua-Neuguinea gehörig. Im NW der Insel und auf den Tabarinseln mehrere Monate dauernde Totenfeiern mit Tänzen, Prozessionen und Festessen, veranstaltet von den Hinterbliebenen zum Wohle ihrer Toten, zur Sicherung der Existenz der Sippe und zur Mehrung ihres Ansehens. Malanggan-Kulthütten bzw. -höfe, Zurschaustellung von Malanggan-Schnitzereien (siehe Glossar), Tanz mit *tatanua*-Stülpmasken mit Scheitelkamm (ursprüngliche Trauerhaartracht), *kepong*-Masken mit flügelartigen Ansätzen bei Heischegängen (zum Einsammeln von Muschelgeld für die Festessen), Vogel- und Eberkopfmasken. Im mittleren Neuirland blühte ein Geheimkult für die Toten mit Uli-Figuren (siehe Glossar), großen Sonnensymbolen aus Stäben und Bast mit durch Bienenwachs überformten Schädeln mit Deckeln der Turbo-Schnecke als Augen sowie Kreidefiguren. Typisch sind auch *kapkap*-Brustschmuck (siehe Glossar) und Geldstränge aus rundgeschliffenen Muschelscheibchen sowie Streichtrommeln aus einem länglichen Holzblock in Tiergestalt mit eingeschnittenen Zungen, die durch Reiben mit der Handfläche eine Tonfolge erzeugen (Stimme vom Totenvogel bzw. Geistern). *Lit.:* Koch 1976, S. 79–83.

Malanggan □ 2, 77, 531, 749, 751, 752, 928; Modellierter Kopf □ 50; Reibetrommel □ 423, 934; Uli-Figur □ 149, 531, 555, 556, 557

Neukaledonien 113, 114, 116, 117, 119, 120, 127
Giacometti 535, 545 – Moore 613 – Picasso 294, 305, 318

Große Insel am Südrand Melanesiens (französisch). Zu den ältesten Menschentypen gehörige paläo-melaneside Bewohner, oft als »Kanaken« bezeichnet. Naßtaro-Anbau auf bewässerten Terrassen in Gemeinschaftsarbeit des ganzen Stammes. Besonders großes, mit allerlei Zierrat ausgestattetes Rundhaus mit Kegeldach, das gemeinsames Eigentum aller Männer einer Sippe und repräsentatives Zentrum des Dorfes ist. Es wird bekrönt von hohen Schnitzwerken (Symbolen der Sippenahnen oder mythischer Ahnengeister), zu seiten des Eingangs mächtige, bohlenartige Reliefschnitzereien. Darstellungen der Sippenahnen-Schutzgeister mit realistisch gearbeitetem Gesicht und in schematischer Ornamentik angedeutetem Körper. Die Neukaledonier fertigten auch Holzmasken mit Haaraufsatz,

Bart und Federbehang, Prunkbeile mit großen, scheibenförmigen Nephritklingen (Würdezeichen der Häuptlinge) oder Vogelkopf- u. a. Hartholzkeulen an. *Lit.:* Koch 1976, S. 98–100.

Mannequin mit der Maske eines Kanakenhäuptlings ☐ 135; Kanakendorf ☐ 140; Figur zur Bekrönung eines Daches ☐ 160, 403, 404, 425; Kindersarg ☐ 756

Neuseeland 113, 114, 116, 119, 120, 124, 127, 128, 201, 455
Gaudier-Brzeska 460, 461

Siehe auch Maori

Ngbandi (Wangandi, Mogwandi) 181

N-Zaire, aus dem Norden in den tropischen Regenwald zwischen Ubangi und Kongo zugewandert. Dominierende Gruppe dieser Region, die von den → *Zande* sprachlich assimiliert wurde. Sie leben vornehmlich vom Fischfang und vom Handel an den Flüssen, daneben Anbau von Bananen, Yams und Taro. Patrilineare Deszendenz, Dorfhäuptlingswesen, Streusiedlungen.

Figur aus Holz, Muscheln und Bast ☐ 194

Ngombe (Gombe, auch Waldmenschen, »hommes de la forêt«, genannt) 143

Zaire, ca. 170000. Bantu sprechende Ethnie, deren Mitglieder vornehmlich Fischfang sowie Jagd und Feldbau betreiben. Ihr weit verstreutes Siedlungsgebiet erstreckt sich zu beiden Seiten des Kongobogens (etwa zwischen den Orten Lolanga und Lisala) und am oberen Giri-Fluß.

Figur ☐ 570

Ngumba (Nzumba, Mgoumba, Nvumba) 47, 48
Pechstein 409 – Schmidt-Rottluff 404, 405

SO-Kamerun, zusammen mit den *Mabea* ca. 12000 Menschen. *Ngumba* und *Mabea* gehören zu den wenigen Stämmen der Maka-Nzimu-Gruppe, die von den *Pangwe* (→ *Fang*) weder ausgelöscht noch assimiliert wurden. Tropische Hackbauern (Knollenfrüchte), wobei der Raubbau am Boden zu weit entfernten Neurodungen zwingt, die später zum Nachzug der Siedlung führen (»Wanderfeldbau«). Familienverbände mit patrilinearer Deszendenz, die in Dorfgemeinschaften mit Ältestenrat zusammengefaßt sind. Geheimbundwesen und kollektive Initiationsfeiern. Der Ahnenkult ist von größerer Bedeutung als die Verehrung von Gottheiten. Mit der Verbreitung des Christentums Neudeutung bestehender Gottesvorstellungen in Form eines personifizierten Schöpfergottes (*Nzambi*).

Reliquiarfigur ☐ 58; Männliche Figur ☐ 560

Nias 122

Insel vor der Westküste Sumatras, Indonesien. Im Süden, der durch den Sklavenhandel reich geworden war, befanden sich große Dörfer mit den staatlichen Häusern der Adligen. Im armen Norden trifft man auf grob gearbeitete, im mittleren Gebiet der Insel auf ornamentale megalithische Zeugnisse (Sarkophage, Ahnenfiguren, Steinsitze u. a.). Kopfjagd mit magisch-religiösem Hintergrund. Ständisch gegliederte Gesellschaft: Adlige konnten durch Erfolg in der Kopfjagd und Verdienstfeste zwanzig, Gemeine (Krieger) fünf Grade durchlaufen. Ahnenkult: holzgeschnitzte, sitzend dargestellte Ahnenfiguren mit spitzem Kopfschmuck, rechts einem Ohrring, Kopfjägerhalsschmuck und (Betel?-) Schale in den Händen. Auf Nias wurden auch Schilde, Schwerter, Speere, Dolche (als Waffen) gefertigt. *Lit.:* Barbier, J. P., *Indonésie et Mélanésie,* Genf 1977.

Nigeria 172, 174
Nolde 413

Maske ☐ 195

Siehe auch Afo, Benin, *Chamba, Djibete, Eket, Ibibio, Igbo, Ijo, Jukun, Kalabari, Mama, Mambila, Mbembe, Montol, Mumuye, Nuba, Urhobo, Wurkun, Yoruba*

Njawi (Njabi) 181

S-Gabun, → *Shira.*

Nomoiinseln (Mortlockinseln)

Einziger Ort Mikronesiens, wo Masken existieren. Tapuana-Masken, Verkörperung guter Geister, für rituelle Tänze am Meer, die die Taifungefahr bannen sollen. *Lit.:* Stöhr 1971, Abb. 51.

Maske ☐ 550

Nootka
Moore 614, 615

→ *Indianer der Nordwestküste*

Mutter mit Kind ☐ 916

Nordwestküste

→ *Indianer der Nordwestküste*

Nuba
Moore 622

Republik Sudan, ca. 570000 Stammesmitglieder. ›Nuba‹ ist die von den Sudan-Arabern gebrauchte Sammelbezeichnung für alle negroiden, nichtislamischen Völker, die in den Bergen leben. Im ethnographischen Sinne handelt es sich um die Bergvölker von Kordofan, die kulturell und sprachlich äußerst zersplittert sind und zahlreiche kleinere Gruppen umfassen, darunter die *Katla, Tagali, Talodi* und *Temain.* (Die *Nuba* sind nicht zu verwechseln mit den ägyptisch beeinflußten Nubiern.) Die einheitliche Wirtschaftsform ist charakterisiert durch Hackbau (v. a. Hirsen, in jüngerer Zeit auch Mais und Baumwolle) sowie Rinderzucht. Die *Nuba* leben in Streu- oder Kompaktsiedlungen und bewohnen Rundhäuser mit Lehmwänden. Die Deszendenz ist im Süden matrilinear, im Norden patrilinear geregelt. Unterschiedlich stark ausgeprägte Gottesvorstellungen, verbreitete Ahnenverehrung, Geisterkulte und Glaube an magische Praktiken (bedeutende Rolle des Regenmachers).

Tanzkostüme ☐ 940

Nukuoro
Moore 618

Polynesische Exklave in Mikronesien. Atoll, nach alten Traditionen von Samoanern besiedelt. Verehrung von Familien-Schutzgöttern, die unter Vermittlung von Priestern bzw. Sippenhäuptlingen bei Haus- und Bootsbau, Hochzeit, Geburt sowie bei Naturkatastrophen, Krankheit oder Tod angerufen wurden. Langwährende Zeremonien zu Ehren der hohen Götter, deren Bildnisse im großen Kulthaus aufgestellt waren: vollendet stilisierte, auf ihre Grundformen abstrahierte, bis lebensgroße menschliche Figuren mit annähernd tropfenförmigem Kopf ohne Andeutung von Mund, Nase, Augen oder Ohren. *Lit.:* Koch 1976, S. 131–132; Stöhr 1971, Abb. 50.

Weibliche Figur ☐ 1; Figur aus Holz ☐ 759

Nupe 143, 180

NW-Nigeria, ca. 350000 Stammesmitglieder, Sudan-Neger mit Kwa-Sprachen, die im weitesten Bereich der Mündung des Kaduna in den Niger leben. Die staatliche Einigung erfolgte im 15. Jahrhundert, der traditionelle Reichsgründer Tsoede oder Edegi (ca. 1400) genoß später religiöse Verehrung. Seine Nachkommen unterwarfen in der Folge benachbarte Stämme, die sich auch sprachlich den *Nupe* assimilierten. Der Islam konnte sich erst im 18. Jahrhundert und zunächst nur in der aristokratischen Oberschicht durchsetzen. Nach Thronwirren unterwarfen um 1830 die *Fulbe* das Land, die die *Nupe* kulturell gänzlich überlagerten. Um 1900 eroberten die Engländer das Gebiet. Die *Nupe* zeichneten sich weniger durch ihre politische Macht als durch ihre hochentwickelten Handwerkstechniken aus (Zinn- und Messingarbeiten, Weberei, Steinschneiderei; Glasherstellung, Holzmasken und Kopfaufsätze); daneben nahmen sie im Fernhandel zwischen Nord- und Südnigeria eine wichtige vermittelnde Stellung ein. Die *Nupe* sind Hackbauern (Yams, Hirsen) und Viehzüchter (Buckelrinder). Eine geringe Rolle spielen die Jagd (doch kennen sie ein Berufsjägertum) und der Fischfang. Patrilineare Deszendenz und Klassengesellschaft unter einem absoluten, sakralen König als dem Erben der traditionellen staatlichen Organisation.

Nyamwezi (Banyamezi, Wanyamezi) 72

Tansania, bedeutendes, ca. 3 Millionen Menschen umfassendes Volk der *Ost-Bantu*, die vornehmlich als Hackbauern und in geringerem Maße als Viehzüchter zwischen Ruaha- und Viktoria-See leben. Die *Nyamwezi* stellen die größte sprachlich und kulturell einheitliche Gruppe Tansanias dar. Traditionell bauen sie Hirsen, Bohnen, Erbsen und Kürbis an, in jüngster Zeit auch Mais und Maniok. Ausgeprägtes Häuptlingswesen; Hochgottglaube mit solaren Zügen.

Figur aus Holz □ 94

O

Oba 143

→ Neue Hebriden

Maske □ 324

Obervolta

→ *Bobo, Mossi, Tusyan*

Ojibwa 101

→ *Prärieindianer*

Okande 140

Mit den → *Shira* verwandte Gruppe auf dem gabunischen Zentralplateau.

Olmeken 86

Die Olmeken herrschten schon seit ca. 800 v. Chr. an der südamerikanischen Ostküste, wahrscheinlich Vorläufer der Maya. Sie sind kulturell faßbar durch die sog. La Venta-Kultur, einen Ausgrabungsort an der Ostküste von Mexiko. Bedeutend vor allem Skulpturen und Schmuck aus Jadeit. Großartigstes Zeugnis olmekischer Kunst sind die bisher ungedeuteten bis zu 2,50 m hohen Riesenköpfe, die im Urwald ohne äußeren Zusammenhang (Siedlung oder Kultanlage) aufgestellt wurden.

Ondumbo 139, 141

Ongwe (Hongwe, Hungue, Mahongwe) 139, 143
Brancusi 27, 361 – Giacometti 542 – Picasso 259, 275, 303

Im Grenzgebiet zwischen Gabun und Kongo-Brazzaville. Teil der → *Kota*, tropischer Hackbau mit Brandrodung (Maniok, Yams, Taor), »Wanderfeldbau«.

Reliquiarfigur □ 27, 342, 487

Ostafrika

Maske □ 547

Osterinsel 11, 16, 37, 40, 43, 48, 117, 120, 122, 123, 124, 126, 127, 128, 198, 536
Carrà 422 – Ernst 37, 39, 40, 42, 531, 532, 573–576 – Gaudier-Brzeska 462 – Gauguin 202, 203, 646 – Giacometti 535 – Masson 566 – Moore 618 – Picasso 40, 343

Die am weitesten östlich gelegene Insel Polynesiens und eine der isoliertesten Inseln der Erde (polynesischer Name: Rapanui). Sie war möglicherweise schon früh von Westen her (etwa von den Marquesasinseln) besiedelt. Polynesische Bevölkerung, deren Stämme ihre Herkunft auf je einen »Klan-Ahnen«, meist ein Sohn oder Enkel des Hotomatua, zurückführten. Die Gesellschaft war in Häuptlinge, Priester, Krieger und Gemeine gegliedert; geachtete Stellung der Steinbildhauer, Holzschnitzer und Rezitationsexperten für Genealogien. Die Kultobjekte aus Holz hatten die Gestalt leicht gekrümmter männlicher Figuren mit hervortretenden Rippen, eingesunkenem Bauch, ausgeprägter Wirbelsäule sowie dünnen Gliedmaßen und stellten die Totengeister vergöttlichter Ahnen (*moai kavakava*) dar. Bekannt sind Eidechsen (*moko*) mit menschlichen Gliedmaßen, Fisch- und Vogelmenschen. Die Skulpturen wurden mittels Querbeilen mit Steinklingen und Obsidiansplittern bearbeitet. »Sprechende Bretter« (siehe Glossar) fanden als Gedächtnisstütze der Experten beim Rezitieren der traditionellen Kultgesänge Verwendung. Die eindrucksvollsten Zeugnisse des religiös motivierten Kunstschaffens der Osterinsel sind die berühmten »Statuen«, riesige 3,50 bis 5,50 m hohe Büsten aus leicht zu bearbeitendem Tuffstein vor allem vom Kraterrand des erloschenen Vulkans Ranoraraku. Von dort aus waren die Skulpturen auch relativ leicht zu den Hängen der Insel bzw. zu den Kultstätten transportierbar. Mit langgezogenem Kopf und den scharfgeschnittenen Gesichtszügen über einem massigen Rumpf sind diese Werke zu Symbolen polynesischer Kunst schlechthin geworden. Ein Teil dieser Skulpturen bekrönte einst die Rückseite der gemauerten rechteckigen Zeremonialplattformen (ahu). Dort nahmen die Götter- und Ahnengeister, sobald sie von den Priestern gerufen wurden, in den Figuren ihren Sitz. Unter den Waffen waren die Speere und Lanzen mit Obsidian-Spitzen versehen. Lange, flache Keulen, beidseitig mit Gesichtern, die aus Knochenringen und Obsidian eingelegte Augen haben, dienten als Häuptlingszeichen und Waffe, kurze, flache Keulen mit Griff in Form eines menschlichen Kopfes neben anderen als Hauptwaffe im Nahkampf. Die traditionelle Kultur der Osterinsel erlosch u. a. durch die Verschleppung des größten Teils der männlichen Bevölkerung zur Arbeit in den Guano-Gruben durch peruanische Sklavenfänger (1859–62), wo die meisten umkamen. Seit 1863 wurde die Osterinsel christlich missioniert. *Lit.:* Helfrich, K., *Führungsblatt des Museums für Völkerkunde*, Berlin; Koch 1976, S. 186–189.

Relief mit einem Vogelmenschen □ 39; Zeichnung von Pierre Loti □ 139; Tafel mit Schriftzeichen □ 227; Figur aus Holz □ 239, 242; Tanzstab □ 252; Arm in Arm □ 475; Monolithische Steinfigur □ 645; Fisch □ 765; Rückenschmuck □ 822; Figur eines Vogelmenschen □ 821; Reliefs mit Vogelmenschen auf den Felsen von Orongo □ 825, 826; Monumentaler Steinkopf □ 832; Keulen □ 836

P

Pahouin 167

→ *Fang*

Palauinseln 116, 380, 383, 384, 412
Heckel 384 – Kirchner 384, 385, 396, 413 – Mueller 384 – Pechstein 401–403, 409, 415 – Schmidt-Rottluff 384

West-Mikronesien. Vielfältig gegliederte Bevölkerung mit Bezirks-, Dorf- und Unterhäuptlingen, Männer- und Frauenklubs. Die Männer-Klubhäuser, die nagel- und bindungslos verzapft waren, trugen auf Giebeln und innerem Querbalken bemalte Reliefdarstellungen aus Sagen und Märchen sowie eine weibliche Giebelfigur mit gespreizten Beinen. Jedes Dorf hatte zwei bis zehn Klubhäuser mit jeweils bis zu hundert Mitgliedern, etwa gleichaltrige Männer einer Generation, die dort wohnten und schliefen. *Lit.:* Koch 1976, S. 100–102, 139–140.

Verzierter Holzbalken □ 517, 518; Giebelplanke mit weiblicher Figur □ 544; Giebelfigur □ 545

Papua

Bezeichnung für ältere Bevölkerungsgruppen Melanesiens und deren Sprachen.

→ Papua-Golf, Papua-Neuguinea

Papua-Golf 66, 116, 117, 119, 544
Epstein 446, 447 – Ernst 567, 577 – Gauguin 216

Die weiten Schwemmlandgebiete in Papua-Neuguinea. Kulturgruppen der *Elema, Namau, Gope* und *Kerewa*. In dramatischen Zeremonialfesten Verehrung von Meeres- und Buschgeistern, Ahnen (auch Tier-Stammahnen) und mythischen Heroen. Die Bewohner schufen über 6 m hohe Masken aus Baumbast über einem Stabgestell, die mit aufgenähtem Rohr und Malereien verziert wurden. Bekannt sind Schädelaltäre mit (wohl von Feinden stammenden) an der Stirn beschnitzten Schädeln. Zeremonial- oder Kraftschilde mit eingekerbten Gesichtsdarstellungen, Schwirrhölzer, gegabelte Kampfschilde für Bogenschützen oder sanduhrförmige Handtrommeln, die in aufgesperrten Rachen enden. Im Papua-Golf-Gebiet wurden auch breite Rindengürtel (Bauchpanzer), stabartige Tanzkeulen mit kugeligem Kopf oder kleine Kokosnüsse mit krokodilartiger Maulöffnung (Kraftträger) hergestellt – alle sind mit den Klanahnen-Zeichen, der typischen schematisierten Reliefdarstellung der menschlichen Figur bzw. des Gesichts, beschnitzt. *Lit.:* Koch 1976, S. 42–45.

Siehe auch Papua-Neuguinea, Era River, *Kerewa, Namau*, Wapo Creek

Papua-Neuguinea 201
Moore 614

Seit 1975 unabhängiger Staat mit 20 Provinzen, u. a. Golf-Provinz, Ost- und Westsepik-Provinz, Provinz Ost-Hochland, Madang. Ehemalige deutsche Kolonien Kaiser-Wilhelm-Land, Bismarckarchipel, Admiralitätsinseln und Bougainville sowie Britisch-Neuguinea, später unter australischem Mandat.

Bemalte Figur aus Holz □ 12, 62; Haarschmuck □ 67; Figur aus Holz □ 70, 157, 834; Schädelgerüst □ 160; Figur □ 160; Stößel aus Stein □ 490; Jagdamulett □ 643; Maske □ 973; Figürliches Brett □ 801

Siehe auch *ABELAM*, *ALAMBLAK*, Bismarckarchipel, *BIWAT*, Era River, *IATMUL*, *KEREWA*, Kopar, *NAMAU*, Neuirland, Papua-Golf, *SULKA*, Torresstraße, Torricelliberge, Trobriandinseln, Wapo Creek

Pende (Baoende) 47, 181, 274, 348
Matisse 153

Zaire, zwischen den Kongo-Nebenflüssen Kwango und Kasai siedelnd, *MITTEL-BANTU*-Gruppen, ca. 27 000 Stammesmitglieder, sehr stark kulturellen Einflüssen der → *LUNDA* ausgesetzt, unter deren Herrschaft sie zeitweilig standen. Traditionellerweise Hackbau mit Brandrodung von Hirsen, in jüngerer Zeit auch Mais und Maniok; die Dörfer mußten alle fünf bis zehn Jahre verlegt werden. Patrilineare Deszendenz, Dreiklassensystem: Aristokratie, Freie, Sklaven. Verehrung der Ahnen, die z. T. mit Naturgeistern identifiziert werden. Die *PENDE* sind bekannt für ihre Holzschnitztradition.

Maske □ 207; Mbuya-Maske □ 340

Pere (Babili, Bapere) 26, 70
Moore 620

Zaire, gemeinsam mit den *BIRA* ca. 45 000 Stammesmitglieder. Bantu sprechende Gruppe des tropischen Regenwalds, der das Bergland des östlichen Zaire bedeckt (zwischen Kisangani, ehem. Stanleyville, und dem Albert-See). Kulturell verschiedenen Einflüssen des Nordens und Ostens ausgesetzt. Im Unterschied zu den anderen Stämmen der Region betreiben die *PERE* neben dem üblichen Bananenanbau vor allem die Jagd. Wenig entwickelte sozialpolitische Institutionen (Grundeinheit ist die erweiterte, patrilineare Familie). Naturgeisterglaube, Ahnenkult, Initiationsbünde, große Bedeutung der Jagdriten.

Musikinstrument □ 11

Peru

Bodenzeichnung in Form eines halben Labyrinths □ 1004; Bodenzeichnung in Form eines Dreiecks □ 1011; Bodenzeichnung in Form einer Spirale und Zickzacklinie □ 1041

Siehe auch Inka, Moche

Plains-Indianer 100, 101, 105

→ *PRÄRIEINDIANER*

Brauner □ 599 – Ernst □ 573, 588

Prärieindianer (Plains-Indianer)
Hartley 470, 473, 484

Gruppe von Indianern, zu denen vor allem die *SIOUX*, *IOWA*, *OJIBWA* sowie *CHEYENNE*, *COMANCHEN*, *CHIPPEWA*, *HIDATSA*, *CROW* und *APACHEN* gehören. Diese Stämme wurden früh von den Stämmen der *ALGONKIN* (eine kanadische Sprachgruppe) nach Süden abgedrängt. Sie lebten ursprünglich vom Ackerbau in den Flußtälern. Das Pferd, das die Spanier Mitte des 18. Jahrhunderts mitbrachten, führte einen Kulturwandel herbei. Die *PRÄRIEINDIANER* wurden zu berittenen Büffeljägern, so wie sie in der europäischen Vorstellung weiterleben. Typisch für diese Indianer sind vor allem ornamental bemalte und bestickte Lederkleidung aus Hirschhaut sowie aus Büffelhaut gefertigte Zeremonialdecken. *Lit.:* Maximilian Prinz zu Wied-Neuwied, *Reise in das innere Nord-America in den Jahren 1832–1834*, Koblenz 1938. Dieser Reisebericht enthält Malereien des Schweizer Malers Bodmer, der das Aussehen und die Trachten der *PRÄRIEINDIANER* detailgenau festhielt.

Siehe auch *SIOUX*, *IOWA*, *OJIBWA*, *CHEYENNE*, *COMANCHEN*, *CHIPPEWA*, *HIDATSA*, *CROW*, *APACHEN*

Puebloindianer
Ernst 577, 588 – Hartley 470

Indianerstämme im Südwesten der USA: *HOPI*, → *ZUNI*, → *NAVAJO* und *APACHEN*. Diese Indianer werden nach ihren stadtartigen Siedlungen, den sogenannten Pueblos, benannt. Die *HOPI*, die Ackerbau betreiben, sind matrilokal organisiert: Der Mann zieht nach der Heirat zur Frau, deren Eigentum das Haus und Land sind. Rituale und Zeremonialgeräte sind Eigentum der verschiedenen Klans. Die Religion und das rituelle Leben konzentrieren sich auf Regenzeremonien. Obwohl die Indianer Christen sind, werden die Regenzeremonien im alten Stil abgehalten – vor den von spanischen Missionaren erbauten Kirchen – »Jesus Christus bringt keinen Regen«. Die *HOPI* sind Schöpfer der sogenannten Katchina-Puppen, Personifizierungen von Göttern und der Seelen, die die Boten zwischen Menschen und Göttern sind – auch im Regen- und Fruchtbarkeitskult spielen sie eine wichtige Rolle. Insgesamt sind etwa 300 verschiedene Typen von Katchinas bekannt, von denen etwa dreißig bei jedem Hauptfest in Erscheinung treten. Es handelt sich um kubisch gestaltete menschliche Figuren mit aufwendigem Kopfschmuck, der mit geometrischen Zeichen verziert ist. Die Feste, zu denen die Katchina-Puppen und -Masken angefertigt werden, haben einen deutlichen Bezug zur Winter- bzw. Sommersonnenwende.

Maske □ 999

Siehe auch *HOPI*, *APACHEN*

Pukapukainsel 79

→ Cookinseln

Seelenfänger □ 104, 668

Punu (Puno) 303
Matisse 87 – Picasso 87, 307, 308

Grenzgebiet Kamerun/Gabun, ca. 40 000 Stammesmitglieder, südöstliche Nachbarn der → *SHIRA*.

Harfe □ 405

Q R

Queensland 113

Raratonga

→ Cookinseln

Stabgott □ 255

Rurutu (Rorutua) 343
Epstein 448 – Moore 623

Australinseln, Nordpolynesien. Rurutu ist Heimat von A'a, der Gottheit Tangaroa bei der Erschaffung des Götter- und Menschengeschlechts. Viele kleine Figuren dringen aus Körper und Gliedmaßen des Gottes und formen auch Mund, Nase und Ohren seines scheibenförmigen Gesichts.

Figur aus Holz (Gott A'a) □ 465, 873, 462

Siehe auch Australinseln

S

Salampasu

Zaire, Gruppe der *LUNDA* (→ *MBALA*)

Maske □ 214

Salish

→ *INDIANER DER NORDWESTKÜSTE*

Figur □ 130

Salomoninseln 113, 114, 124, 127, 128, 542
Giacometti 515, 532 – Moore 613 – Nolde 390

Melanesischer Inselarchipel südöstlich des Bismarckarchipels (Neubritannien, Neuirland) mit Bougainville, Malaita u. a.

Zeremonialschild □ 158; Figur aus Holz, Haar und Muscheln □ 728; Figur aus Holz □ 800

Siehe auch Bougainville

Sambia

→ *MAMBWE*

Samoa 113, 114

Sango 141

Zaire, ca. 2 500 Stammesmitglieder, Fischergruppe am Ubangi.

Sao (Saho, Shiho, So) 181

Somalia, ca. 50 000 Stammesmitglieder, großteils muslimisch (Sunniten), die 10 000 Mitglieder zählende Untergruppe der *IROB* ist christianisiert. Mit den *AFAR* verwandt. Sie leben am Horn von Afrika und betreiben Feldbau (Hirsen, Mais, Hülsenfrüchte) und Viehzucht.

Sara 181

Tschad, ca. 750000 Stammesmitglieder. Sammelbezeichnung für eine Vielzahl von Ethnien, die zwischen dem Oberlauf des Logone im Westen und dem Irosee im Osten (in der Gegend von Fort Archambault) leben und durch die Zugehörigkeit zur Bongo-Bagirmi-Sprachengruppe verbunden sind. Vorherrschender Rodungsfeldbau (Hirsen, in jüngerer Zeit auch Reis und Maniok), daneben Kleinviehzucht (Ziege, Schaf, Huhn). Runde, meist grasgedeckte Kegeldachhäuser mit Wänden aus Matten oder luftgetrockneten Ziegeln. Eingangsöffnung in charakteristischer Schlüssellochform. Gruppen von umzäunten Gehöften, die jeweils mehrere Häuser (für die einzelnen Frauen) und Speicher umfassen, bilden ein Dorf, mehrere Dörfer sind zu territorialen Einheiten zusammengefaßt, als deren politisches und religiöses Oberhaupt ein »Erdherr« fungiert, der jedoch an die Entscheidung der Klanoberhäupter gebunden ist. Es bestehen starke Bestrebungen, die politische Unabhängigkeit dieser Einheiten zu wahren. Die *Sara* gelten als geschickte Schmiede und Töpfer. Strenge Initiationsprüfungen, die vor allem Knaben auferlegt werden (Gesichtsnarben, unter dem Einfluß des Islam auch Beschneidung und Exzision). Geheimbundwesen mit terroristischen Zügen (»Löwenmenschenbund«). Von größter Wichtigkeit sind die Agrarriten des Erdherrn, die als Erdkult verstanden werden. Zu den religiösen Feiern werden rohgeschnitzte Masken und Grabpfähle verwendet. Glaube an einen Kulturheros *Su*, der den *Sara* die Feldfrüchte, Waffen, Werkzeuge, Feuer und Kultobjekte gebracht hat.

Sentani-See 124
Matisse 247

Im Norden von West-Neuguinea, dem jetzigen Irian Jaya, gelegenes, etwa 30 km langes Seengebiet mit ca. 6000 Menschen. Pfahlhausdörfer wurden in einiger Entfernung vom Ufer über dem Wasser angelegt. Die Häuptlinge (*ondoforo*) nahmen eine besondere Stellung ein. Sie organisierten Initiationsrituale (Einweihung der Novizen in den Kult, Aufnahme in die Gruppengemeinschaft) und bewahrten in den *ondoforo*-Häusern die Kultobjekte auf: freistehende, stark stilisierte Kultfiguren, auch Doppelfiguren, z. T. überlebensgroß als Abschluß der Pfosten, die den Boden der Häuser stützten, sowie Bambustrompeten, Trommeln. Bekannt sind auch flache Speiseschüsseln für Sago und Fisch, Knochendolche, Kalkkalebassen zum Betelkauen und Bambus-Tabakdosen. Diese Arbeiten wurden häufig mit »Haken-Spiralen« verziert. Die Tapas (siehe Glossar) vom Sentani-See sind mit figürlichen Motiven bemalt: fliegende Hunde, Eidechsen, Fische u. a. *Lit.:* Koch 1976, S. 35–36.

Doppelfigur □ 148; Tapa □ 151, 298; Lendentuch □ 877

Senufo (Sene, Siena) 25, 141, 158, 180, 219
Brancusi 360 – Derain 153 – Epstein 450, 453 – Lam 604 – Picasso 294 – Smith 29, 638, 664

Mali, Elfenbeinküste, ca. 680000 Menschen, Gruppe von Sudan-Negern, die zwischen Bani (Nebenfluß des oberen Niger) und der nördlichen Elfenbeinküste siedeln. Die *Senufo* verteilen sich auf ca. 30 kleinere Stämme, die sich nach linguistischen und kulturellen Kriterien unterscheiden, darunter die →*Nafana*, →*Kulango*, →*Minianka*. Unter dem Einfluß westlich benachbarter *Mande*-Gruppen schufen sie Kleinstaaten, von denen das Reich um die Stadt Sikasso im 19. Jahrhundert am bedeutendsten war. 1898 wurde es von den Franzosen zerstört. Die *Senufo* betreiben vor allem Hackbau (Hirsen, Trocken- und Naßreis, z. T. auch mit künstlicher Bewässerung), daneben halten sie Vieh (kleinwüchsige Kurzhornrinder). Als Behausung dienen Rundbauten aus Lehm mit kegelförmigem Strohdach. Patrilineare Deszendenz; Haupteinheit ist die erweiterte Großfamilie. Von besonderer politischer und religiöser Bedeutung sind die Ältesten. In der Stellung der Gauhäuptlinge haben sich Spuren sakralen Königtums erhalten. Der Himmel wird als höchstes Wesen verehrt, seine Gattin ist die Erde, Buschgeister gelten als »Herren der Tiere«. Die Ahnen vermitteln zwischen Geister- und Menschenwelt. In neuerer Zeit verstärkte Islamisierung der *Senufo*. Sie zeichnen sich durch eine sehr spezifische Holzschnitzkunst aus: phantasievolle Holzmasken und Rundplastiken mit stark abstrakten Formen, die trotz verzerrender Stilisierung ausgewogen und klassisch erscheinen. Auffallend ist die Fähigkeit der Künstler, den relativ kleinen Figuren Monumentalität zu verleihen. Solche meist paarweise aufgestellten Skulpturen stellen Ahnen von Wahrsagerinnen dar. Verbreitet sind auch kleine Gelbguß-Anhänger in Form von mythischen Tieren, Menschen oder anthropomorphen Buschgeistern, die vor Krankheit und Unheil schützen sollen.

Weibliche Figur □ 115; Weibliche Figur, Rhythmusgeber □ 167, 168; Figur eines Vogels □ 185; Trommel □ 389; Maske □ 470; Helmmaske □ 484; Holzfigur □ 687; Bekrönung eines Kopfschmucks □ 799; Kopf einer Reiterfigur □ 845; Reiterfigur □ 882; Kopfschmuck □ 955; Vogel □ 1000

Sepik-Region 126, 128
Epstein 446 – Giacometti 542 – Picasso 341

Siehe auch Papua-Neuguinea, Ostsepik-Provinz, *Iatmul*

Shango
Picasso 351

Gabun, *NW-Bantu*, verwandt mit den → *Shira*, von deren Siedlungsbereich sie durch die → *Tsogo* getrennt sind.

Sherbro (Mampua) 135, 180

Sierra Leone, mit den verwandten *Krim* zusammen ca. 200000 Menschen. Feldhackbauern mit Brandrodung (zahlreiche Arten von Naß- und Trockenreis). Eine bedeutende Rolle spielt der für alle Männer obligatorische *Poro*-Geheimbund, der bei den meisten Nachbarvölkern in Sierra Leone und Liberia verbreitet ist und an dessen Spitze ein auch politisch höchst einflußreicher Bundmeister steht. Die von ihm getragene Maske des Bunddämons gilt als Verkörperung aller Ahnenseelen. Daneben existiert eine Vielfalt von Masken, deren Träger bestimmte Gesten, Bewegungen und Sprechweisen beherrschen müssen. Das Trägeramt wird in den jeweiligen Familien vererbt, wobei immer mehrere Mitglieder als Träger ausgebildet sind. In den Urwaldgebieten Sierra Leones und Guineas, die heute von *Sherbro*, →*Kissi*, *Bulom* und *Temne* bewohnt werden, stellte man zwischen dem 13. und 18. Jahrhundert kleine Steinstatuen aus Steatit her (*Kissi: pomdo*; →*Mende: nomoli*), die heute als kraftgeladen gelten und die Fruchtbarkeit fördern sollen. Ursprünglich handelte es sich wohl um Grabmale. Stilistische Parallelen lassen sich in den sog. »afro-portugiesischen« Elfenbeinschnitzereien finden, die im 15. und 16. Jahrhundert in europäischem Auftrag von den *Sherbro* und Bulom hergestellt wurden und stark autochthone Züge aufweisen.

Shilluk 136

Sudan, ca. 110000 Stammesmitglieder. Nach der eigenen Überlieferung siedeln die *Shilluk* seit dem 15. Jahrhundert in einem hierarchisch organisierten Königreich nordwestlich des Nil. Sie leben vor allem als Großviehzüchter; eines der wenigen Völker der Niloten, die eine nur gering entwickelte Holzschnitzkunst haben (Masken).

Shira (Echira, Ashira) 16, 22, 142, 181, 513
Matisse 153, 240 – Picasso 308, 351 – Vlaminck 22

Gabun, Gruppe der *Bantu*-Neger, wie die im gleichen Raum lebenden *Punu*, *Tsogo*, *Aduma*, *Mbete*, *Njawi*, *Teke*. (Über alle diese Gruppen gibt es kaum ethnographische Informationen oder Bevölkerungsangaben. Sie sind vermutlich nördlicher Herkunft und siedeln jetzt im Regenwald des unteren Ngunie. Brandrodungshackbau von Knollenfrüchten (Maniok, Yams, Taro) mit häufiger Verlegung der z. T. weit von den Siedlungen entfernten Felder (»Wanderfeldbau«); daneben bescheidene Kleinviehhaltung. Die *Shira* leben in relativ zersplitterten Kleindörfern.

Maske □ 13, 287, 408; Harfe □ 405; Maske aus Holz □ 711

Siehe auch Punu, Tsogo, Vuvi, Aduma, Mbete, Njawi, Teke

Sierra Leone
Epstein 446

Sioux
Ernst 573

→ *Prärieindianer*

Schild □ 829

Sogo → *Tsogo.*

Songge (Songe, Songye, Basonge, Wasonga) 25, 26, 44, 76, 143, 181, 273, 274

Zaire, ein zu den → *Luba* gehörender Stamm, mit denen sie sprachlich und kulturell eng verwandt sind. Seit dem 16. Jahrhundert zwischen Lubefu und Lomami (südliche Nebenflüsse des Kongo) in größeren Häuptlingsschaften organisiert und politisch aktiv. Entwickelter Feldbau mit Brandrodung (ursprünglich Hirsen, in neuerer Zeit v. a. Mais und Maniok). Patrilineare Deszendenz. Die Häuptlinge gehen auch inzestuöse Verbindungen mit nahen Verwandten und ihren Schwestern ein (Theorie des »heiligen Blutes«); die Gesellschaft ist in drei Klassen – Sklaven, Freie, Aristokraten – geteilt. Stadtorganisation. Besondere Bedeutung der *bakishi*: Bünde von Männern und Frauen, die die Fruchtbarkeit fördern und Zauberei bannen sollen. Zusätzlich stellen diese Bünde einen wichtigen politischen Machtfaktor dar. Die *Songge* zählen zu den kunstfertigsten Völkern der Region: Ihre Holzmasken, Kifwebe (siehe Glossar), fallen durch ihre stark geometrischen Muster auf, die in weiß eingefärbten Kerben Zickzacklinien und Bögen beschreiben, sowie durch ihre großen umrandeten Augen, die vorspringende Nase und den viereckigen Mund. Die Masken treten häufig paarweise (Mann und Frau) auf und scheinen mit Gefahren für den Stamm in Beziehung zu stehen (Naturkatastrophen, Seuchen, Krieg, Tod des Häuptlings). Eine Untergruppe der *Songge*, die *Zappo-Zap*, galten als die besten Schmiede im südlichen Zaire. Sie stellten dekorative Prunkäxte (Würdezeichen hoher Beamter und Herrscher) her, die durch Fernhandel weite Verbreitung fanden.

Kifwebe-Maske □ 26, 212, 338, 469; Fetisch □ 107; Figur aus Holz, Metall und Federn □ 172; Figur aus Holz und Metall □ 201

Sudan 140, 159, 167, 172
Moore 611

Zwei Figuren aus dem Sudan □ 169

Siehe auch Bongo, Dinka, Nuba, Shilluk

Südmalekula Matisse 153 – Picasso 153

→ Malekula, Neue Hebriden

Suku (Basuku, Bapindi) 181

Zaire, gemeinsam mit den *Samba* ca. 80 000 Menschen. *Suku*, → *Pende* und → *Yaka* sind Mittel-*Bantu* im Einzugsgebiet des Kwango, einem südlichen Nebenfluß des Kongo. Regenzeitfeldbau (Maniok, Reis) und Ölpalmenkultur. Unter dem politischen Einfluß des Königreichs Lunda übernahmen sie die organisatorische Struktur in Häuptlingsschaften. Die *Suku* verfügen über eine alte Holzschnitztradition.

Sulka

Alte Bevölkerungsgruppe mit nichtmelanesischer Sprache südlich der Gazelle-Halbinsel auf Neubritannien, jetzt zu Papua-Neuguinea gehörig. Masken aus mit Baummarkstreifen besetzten Rohrgeflechten, rot gefärbt und schwarz-weiß-grün gemustert, mit Faserbehang zum Verhüllen des Trägers. Diese Masken stellen jenseitige Wesen dar und wurden bei der Aufnahme von Novizen in die geheimen Männerbünde verwendet. Bekannt sind auch Kampfschilde aus leichtem Holz, die mit stilisierten Gesichtsornamenten bemalt und mit Rattanstreifen überspannt wurden sowie einen Rand aus Federn haben. *Lit.:* Koch 1976, S. 84–86.

Schild □ 153; Maske □ 804, 150 (rechts oben)

Siehe auch Neubritannien

Sumatra
Schmidt-Rottluff 410

Sundi (Nsundi) 143

Zaire, nördliche Nachbarn des alten Kongo-Reiches (→ *Kongo*). Ihr Territorium war Anfang des 17. Jahrhunderts vorübergehend in der Hand der *Jaga*

Susu (Soso, Soussou) 180

Sierra Leone, Guinea ca. 30 000 Stammesmitglieder, sie bilden sprachlich gesehen den Übergang von den Mande-Tan zu den Mande-Fu. Vermutlich siedelten sie bereits bei Ankunft der Portugiesen (1462) im heutigen Sierra Leone. Hackbau mit Brandrodung (Reis, Hirsen). Dorfgemeinschaften mit Häuptlingen auf Klanbasis. Wichtiges Geheimbundwesen (*Poro*) mit Masken und Kostümen; der Bundmeister nimmt eine wichtige politische Stellung ein.

Maske □ 333

T

Tabwa 455

Zaire, Sambia, Bemba sprechende *Bantu*-Gruppe, die östlich des Mwerusees bis zum Tanganjikasee lebt. Seit 1740 unter der Herrschaft der *Lunda*, die als Eroberer eine aristokratische Oberschicht mit dem königlichen Klan an der Spitze bildeten. Im Gegensatz zu dem patrilinear organisierten Adel behielten die Unterworfenen ihre matrilineare Nachfolgeregelung. Hackfeldbau, v. a. von Maniok und Hirsen, Kleinviehhaltung. Hochgottglaube; entwickelte Vorstellung vom Weiterleben nach dem Tode sowie ausgeprägter Ahnenkult, im besonderen hinsichtlich der königlichen Vorfahren, mit Figuralplastiken aus Holz. Kennzeichnend für die stehenden Figuren sind die ungewöhnten Proportionen (lange Oberkörper, kurze Beine); fein gearbeitete Details: Gesicht, Narben, Finger und die abgestuft geschnitzten Zehen.

Figur aus Holz □ 634

Tahiti 87, 109, 110, 113 114, 117, 127, 187, 188, 196–198, 214, 216
Epstein 447, 448 – Gauguin 198, 202 – Matisse 243, 247

→ Gesellschaftsinseln

Tahiti-Pavillon auf der Weltausstellung 1900 □ 141; Tapa □ 144; Figur aus Holz □ 622

Tanganjika
Schmidt-Rottluff 406

Tansania 174

Siehe auch Karagwe, *Makonde, Nyamwezi*

Teke (Bateke) 55, 139, 141, 158, 163, 181
Carrà 420, 421 – Lam 604 – Schmidt-Rottluff 406

Mit den → *Shira* verwandte, wenig erforschte Gruppe der *Bantu*-Neger im südlichen Gabun, die einige 100 000 Menschen zählen dürfte. Sie siedeln vermischt mit den zahlreichen Pygmäen dieser Region, mit denen sie in wirtschaftlicher Symbiose stehen. Als einziger Stamm im südlichen Gabun haben die *Teke* wohl unter dem Einfluß der → *Vili* eine über die Dorfgemeinschaft hinausgehende staatsähnliche Organisation aufgebaut. Brandrodungshackbau (v. a. Maniok), Fischfang, Jagd, Kleinviehhaltung und Sammelwirtschaft.

Bemalte Maske aus Holz □ 69; Holzfigur □ 330; Figur □ 563; Männliche Figur □ 583

Tinu-Hopi
Nolde 393

Gruppe der → *Hopi*

Tiv 143

Nigeria, Bantu sprechender Stamm von ca. 800 000 Mitgliedern im mittleren Benue-Becken.

Tlingit
Ernst 588 – Gottlieb 645 – Hartley 484 – Klee 505, 509

→ *Indianer der Nordwestküste*

Decke □ 133, 968; Totempfahl □ 860

Tolteken 86, 524

Das Reich der Tolteken bestand von 856 bis 1168 im Hochland von Zentralmexiko. Häufigster Typus ihrer bedeutenden Steinplastik ist der sog. Chac Mool, eine lebensgroße toltekische Götterfigur, die in liegender Haltung dargestellt wird und im Bauch eine als Schale dienende Aushöhlung hat.

Toma (Busy, Lomy) 180

Liberia, Guinea, ca. 150 000 Stammesmitglieder. Die Mande sprechenden *Toma* leben im äußersten NO von Liberia und im angrenzenden Teil von Guinea südlich der Stadt Macenta. Brandrodungshackbau (Reis). Matrilineare Deszendenz; relativ große Dorfsiedlungen mit Kleinhäuptlingen, die vom Ältestenrat unterstützt und vom *Poro*-Geheimbund kontrolliert werden. Wichtige Rolle des Ahnenkults, der mit Gewässern in Verbindung steht (im Wasser liegendes Totenreich, Verehrung heiliger Welse). Die *TOMA* sind bekannt für ihre Schmiedearbeiten in Eisen, Gold und Silber sowie Skulpturen und Masken aus Holz.

Tongainseln 113

Zentralpolynesien. »Tausendjähriges Königreich« mit Herrschaftssitz des als Halbgott angesehenen *Tu'i Tonga* auf Tongatapu. 159 Inseln, davon 36 bewohnt, die über 50000 qkm Meeresfläche verstreut sind. Alles Land Eigentum des Königs, der es an seine Häuptlinge vergab, diese wiederum an die *matapule* und Gemeinen; Tributpflicht der Landnutzer. Gürtelmatten dienten als Würdezeichen; Häuptlingsgewänder wurden aus Tapa, Hängekörbe für kleines Gebrauchsgut und Kostbarkeiten aus Kokosfasergeflecht hergestellt. Solche Korbwaren wurden auch mit Zierscheiben aus Seeschneckenhäusern bedeckt. Kawa-Becher sind aus Kokosschale, Kriegskeulen aus schwerem hartem Kasuarinenholz hergestellt. *Lit.:* Koch 1976, S 165–168.

Tapa □ 145

Torresstraße 127, 273
Picasso 89, 351

Mit dieser Herkunftsangabe sind die zwischen Neuguinea und Australien gelegenen Inseln der Torresstraße gemeint, die jetzt zu Papua-Neuguinea gehören. In wenigen Museen befinden sich als Zeugen der längst erloschenen alten Kultur hölzerne Schnitzmasken, die zu Fruchtbarkeitsriten für gute Ernten gebraucht wurden (Insel Saibai), sowie vor allem Masken aus Schildpatt, die unter Hitzeeinwirkung aus miteinander »verschweißten« oder zusammengenähten Schildpattstücken zu menschlichen Gesichtern oder Tierfiguren – z. B. Krokodilen oder Fischen – zurechtgebogen wurden. Man trug sie als Ahnendarstellung bei Bestattungszeremonien auf dem Kopf. *Lit.:* Koch 1976, S. 111–112.

Maske □ 143, 432; Schildkrötenpaar □ 623

Trobriandinseln
Epstein 453

Mit den Louisiaden, d'Entrecastaux-Inseln und der Südostspitze Neuguineas zum »Massim-Distrikt« zählende Inselgruppe, wo infolge des *kula*-Zyklus, eines prestigesteigernden zeremoniellen Tauschhandels mit festen Partnern, bei dem aus Conusschnecken geschliffene Armringe in die eine, aus Muschel- und Schneckenmaterial bestehender Halsschmuck in die Gegenrichtung weitergegeben werden, eine weitgehende Ähnlichkeit des materiellen Besitzes entstand. Dokumente hochstehender künstlerischer Tätigkeit sind die schildartigen Stevenverzierungen der für den *kula*-Handel verwendeten seegängigen Boote mit scharfkantig eingeschnittenen Kurven- und Spiralornamenten, mit ähnlichen Motiven verzierte Tanzschilde oder ovale Kampfschilde mit federstrichartigem schwarzem Dekor auf weißem Grund. Bekannt sind auch Kalkspatel (zum Betelkauen) aus schwarzem Holz mit figuralem Griff (menschliche Figuren wie Trommler u. a., Tiere wie fliegende Hunde etc.) und mit eingeschnittenem, mit Kalk ausgelegtem Dekor. *Lit.:* Koch 1976, S. 63–64; Stöhr 1972, S. 122–123.

Spatel □ 635; Spatel mit fliegendem Fuchs □ 803

Tsogo (Sogo) 141, 181, 551
Braque 153 – Matisse 153

S-Gabun, Nachbarn der → *SHIRA*.

Maske □ 509

Tuareg 238 (männl. *TARGI*, weibl. *TARGIA*, Eigenbezeichnung *IMUHAR*)

Mali, Niger, Algerien, Libyen, ca. 300000 Menschen. Verschiedene Gruppen, die von den Trockenzonen der zentralen Sahara bis in den südlichen Sahel mit regelmäßigen Trocken- und Regenzeiten leben. Ursprünglich im tripolitanischen Hinterland beheimatet und ihrer Sprache und Herkunft nach mit den Berbern verwandt. Ihre Schrift (Tifinar), die aus 25 Zeichen besteht, ist aus dem altlibyschen Alphabet abgeleitet. Seit dem 11. Jahrhundert wichen sie unter dem Druck der arabischen Beduinen nach Süden bis in den Nigerbogen aus. Die *TUAREG* sind nomadische Viehzüchter mit Kamelen als Transport- und Reittieren sowie als Milchlieferanten, mit Pferden, Rindern und großen Herden von Ziegen und Schafen. Neben Milchprodukten ist Hirse die wichtigste Nahrungsquelle, die ihnen von abhängigen Ackerbauern geliefert wird. Eine wichtige wirtschaftliche Rolle spielt ihre Tätigkeit als transsaharische Karawanenhändler. Die gesellschaftliche Struktur der *TUAREG* ist durch ein ausgeprägtes Kastensystem bestimmt: An der Spitze stehen die europiden Adligen, die die politische und militärische Führung innehaben und durch Endogamiegebote ihre rassische Identität bewahren. Fast ebenbürtig sind die Marabuts (moslemische Gelehrte und Prediger), die jede kriegerische Tätigkeit ablehnen. Eine dritte Gruppe bilden die Nachkommen aus Verbindungen von *TUAREG* mit Arabern. Die breite Masse sind die dunkelhäutigen Vasallen (die sog. »Ziegenleute«), die mit den negriden Sklaven und den abhängigen Bauern mehr als die Hälfte der Bevölkerung ausmachen. Gesellschaftlich verachtet werden die ebenfalls negriden Schmiede und Lederarbeiter. Die Nachfolgeregelung der *TUAREG* ist matrilinear. Ein Stamm besteht aus mehreren durch Heirat verbundene Matrilinien, die ein abgegrenztes Territorium einnehmen und ein gewähltes Oberhaupt haben. Die *TUAREG* sind vollständig islamisiert, ein Naturgeisterglaube hat sich in Spuren erhalten (möglicherweise auch christliche Komponenten).

Tupinamba

Indianerstamm an der Ostküste Brasiliens, in der Provinz Bahia. Er ist einer der ersten südamerikanischen Indianerstämme, der mit Europäern in Berührung kam. Bekannt wurden die *TUPINAMBA* vor allem durch den Bericht von Hans Staden, der eine Zeitlang ihr Gefangener war (*Wahrhaftig Historia und beschreibung eyner Lantschafft der Wilden, Nacketen Grimmigen Menschefresser Leuthen Cap. XXIII, Marpurg uff Fastnacht 1557*, Frankfurt 1925). Dieser Bericht ist durch seine genauen Beobachtungen ein unersetzliches Zeugnis der Sitten und Lebensformen der *TUPINAMBA*. Der Autor beschreibt darin vor allem den Kannibalismus, den dieser Stamm pflegte, wobei es sich nicht allein um »Menschenfresserei« handelt, sondern um einen zeremoniellen Kannibalismus, der in komplexe religiöse Vorstellungen eingebunden ist.

Die Leute von Calicut □ 117; Scheingefecht zwischen zwei brasilianischen Stämmen □ 118

Tusyan (Tusya)
Ernst 37, 39

Obervolta, ca. 15000 Stammesmitglieder. Im Quellgebiet des Schwarzen Volta siedelnde, Lobi sprechende (→ *LOBI*) Hackbauern der Trockenwaldsavanne (v. a. Hirseanbau); daneben Jagd für den Fleischbedarf und Sammelwirtschaft. Sie bewohnen Rundbauten mit Lehmwänden und regeln die Nachfolge nach der Patrilinie. Die soziale Grundeinheit ist die erweiterte Großfamilie. In der Stellung der Häuptlinge haben sich alte Züge sakralen Königtums erhalten. Verehrung einer Himmels- und Erdgottheit. Geheimbundwesen und wichtige Rolle des Ahnenkults.

Maske □ 37

U V W

Ubangi
Moore 627

Größter Nebenfluß des Kongo und Grenzfluß zwischen Zaire und der Republik Zentralafrika bzw. der Volksrepublik Kongo.

Kopf eines Affen □ 917

Siehe auch *YAKOMA*

Urhobo 143

Nigeria, Untergruppe der *ISOKO* (insgesamt 435000 Stammesmitglieder), die zu den → *EDO* gehört.

Mutter mit Kind □ 468

Vancouver Island

Adler □ 659

Vanuatu

→ Neue Hebriden

Vili (Vili-Kongo, Bawili) 139, 140, 141, 143, 151, 181
Matisse 87, 153, 303, 351

Zaire, Sammelbezeichnung für die *Bantu*-Stämme im westlichen (unteren) Kongogebiet. Zur Zeit der Landung Diego Caos hatten sie nördlich des Kongo das Königreich Loango gegründet. Ihre südlichen Nachbarn längs der Küste waren die → *Woyo* (mit dem Fürstentum Ngoi), die sich rühmten, die Vorfahren der *Vili* zu sein.

Hundefetisch □ 95, 98; Figur aus Holz □ 178; Statuette aus Holz □ 260

Siehe auch *Kongo*

Virginia 97, 98

Vuvi 181

Stamm im Grenzgebiet zwischen Südgabun und Kongo-Brazzaville, im Quellgebiet des Ngunie.

Waja 25

Nigeria, tschadisch sprechende Gruppe im Osten des nigerianischen Plateaus.

Wapo Creek

Fluß in der Golfprovinz von Papua-Neuguinea.

→ Papua-Golf

Figur aus Holz □ 976

West Irian (Irian Jaya)

→ *Asmat*, Geelvink-Bai, Sentani-See

Westsudan 136

Siehe auch Sudan

Witoto 86, 651

Tupi sprechender Indianerstamm am Rio Putomajo (oberes Amazonasgebiet) an der Grenze von Brasilien und Peru. Bekannt v. a. durch seine zur Erinnerung an Verstorbene angefertigten Totenfiguren.

Helmmaske □ 972

Wobe (Ouobe)

Mittlere Elfenbeinküste, ca. 30000 Menschen. Stamm der → *Kru* und nördlichste Untergruppe der → *Kran* (→ *Guere*). Im tropischen Regenwald östlich der Stadt Man betreiben sie Hackbau mit Brandrodung (v. a. Reis, der über die Vermittlung der Araber schon um das Jahr 1500 am Niger nachzuweisen ist und sich in der Folge nach W und SW ausbreitete), daneben Anbau von Maniok, Taro, Yams, Bananen.

Löffel aus Holz □ 736

Woyo 141, 181

Zaire, seit den ersten Kontakten der Portugiesen mit den Königreichen am unteren Kongo (→ *Kongo*, → *Vili*) Ende des 15. Jahrhunderts bekannt. Die *Woyo* waren Träger des an der Küste gelegenen Fürstentums Ngoi und rühmten sich, die Wiege der *Vili* zu sein. Wie bei vielen anderen Gruppen dieser Region nimmt die Königin eine besondere Stellung ein und übernimmt z. B. bei Abwesenheit des Herrschers die Regierungsgeschäfte.

Fetischfigur □ 430

Wumbu 348

Gabun, Untergruppe der → *Kota*.

Wurkun 25

Nigeria, ca. 45000 (mit Unterstämmen). Heterogene Gruppen, die vornehmlich tschadische Sprachen sprechen und nördlich des Benue-Mittellaufes in den Wurkun-Bergen leben. Sie zählen zu den Völkern des nigerianischen Plateaus.

Maske □ 184

Wute (Bute, Babute, Bafute) 143

Kamerun, ca. 40000 Stammesmitglieder. Ihre sprachliche Stellung zwischen → *Zande* und *Semi-Bantu* (→ *Bantu*) ist ungeklärt. Sie siedeln in mehreren Gruppen zwischen den Flüssen Mbam, Dyerem und Sanaga (Feuchtsavannen und Regenwald). Anfang des 19. Jahrhunderts gerieten sie unter die Herrschaft der *Fulbe*, die sie zwar Ende des Jahrhunderts abschütteln konnten, eine dauerhafte politische Stabilität blieb ihnen indes versagt. Traditioneller Hirsefeldbau, in jüngerer Zeit auch Mais und Maniok; daneben Viehzucht und Jagd. Patrilineare Deszendenz; Kompaktdörfer. Spuren sakralen Königtums mit besonderer Rolle der Königinmutter.

Hocker □ 647

Y

Yaka (Bayaka, Yagga) 181
Weber 36, 466

Zaire. Der bedeutendere der *Mittel-Bantu*-Stämme (→ *Bantu*) im Gebiet des Kwango und Kwilu (südliche Nebenflüsse des Kongo, vgl. die verwandten → *Suku*, → *Pende*). Östliche Nachbarn des Königreichs der → *Kongo* (→ *Vili*), dessen Hauptstadt sie 1569 eroberten. In der Folge gerieten die *Yaka* vermutlich unter die Herrschaft des *Lunda*-Reiches. Sie sind nicht identisch mit den berüchtigten *Jaga* oder *Djaga*, kriegerischen Völkern, Die im 16. Jahrhundert weite Bereiche Zentralafrikas unter ihre Herrschaft brachten und schließlich von den → *Kongo* (gemeinsam mit den zu Hilfe gerufenen Portugiesen) vertrieben wurden. Die *Yaka* betreiben Feldbau mit Brandrodung (Mais, Maniok). Sie verehren einen Schöpfergott, der auch als Erster Ahn gilt, und Naturgeister. Verbreitet sind Hexerei und der Glaube an die Wirksamkeit magischer Stoffe. Die *Yaka* sind bekannte Holzschnitzkünstler: Ihre Masken und figürlichen Plastiken zeigen kräftige Gesichtszüge mit aufgeworfenen Nasen, kaffeebohnenartigen Augen mit Sehschlitzen und markante Ohren.

Figur aus Holz □ 35, 650; Maske □ 858

Yakoma 181

Zentralafrikanische Republik, ca. 25000 Stammesmitglieder, spezialisierte Fischer am Ubangi.

Siehe auch Ubangi

Yangere (Jangere, Ngere, Yangeli) 141, 181

Enklave der *Banda* im SW der Zentralafrikanischen Republik mit ca. 3000 Menschen. Die kulturell und sprachlich relativ einheitlichen, azandeisierten *Banda* (→ *Zande*) leben verstreut im Gebiet der *Gbaya* und *Mandja* (Zentralafrikanische Republik). Grund hierfür sind die Raubzüge der Araber und die Expansion der → *Zande*.

Yaure 26, 180, 432

Elfenbeinküste, Stamm am Oberlauf des Bandama. Starken kulturellen Einflüssen der benachbarten → *Baule* (im Osten) und der → *Guro* (im Westen) ausgesetzt. *Yaure*-Masken sind häufig von einer stilisierten zickzackförmigen Bartkrause eingerahmt. Auf den Wangen sind Ziermetallplättchen befestigt. Vogelfiguren oder gegenständige Vogelpaare bilden den Aufsatz

Maske □ 16

Yombe (Bayombe, Mayumbe) 16, 22, 25
Matisse 303 – Picasso 22, 307, 308

Zaire, ca. 170000 Stammesmitglieder (1933). Zur Zeit der portugiesischen Entdeckungen an der Küste Äquatorialafrikas (15. Jahrhundert) waren die *Yombe* Träger des kleinen Königreiches Bunga und vermutlich auch Gründer des *Kongo*-Reiches. Sie siedeln im Küstenhinterland in der Region der Wasserfälle des unteren Kongo. Die *Yombe* stellten (ähnlich wie die benachbarten frühen Königreiche der → *Vili* und → *Kongo*) verschiedenartige magische Figuren, Reliquiare (siehe Glossar), sog. »Spiegel-« oder »Nagelfetische« her. Ihr Verbreitungsgebiet deckt sich etwa mit der Region der frühen erfolgreichen Missionierung im 16./17. Jahrhundert. Daneben finden sich bei den *Yombe* häufig weibliche Figuren aus Holz, deren Funktion unklar ist (Assoziation mit Wahrsagerei, Abwehr von Krankheiten?).

Mutter mit Kind □ 22; Fetisch □ 80; Gruppe □ 406; Fetischfigur □ 430

Yoruba (Joruba) 16, 89, 140, 180, 264
Epstein 446 – Gaudier-Brzeska 460 – Matisse 303 – Moore 622 – Nolde 390, 393, 413 – Picasso 294, 307 – Vlaminck 221, 223

Im südwestlichen Nigeria sowie in Teilen von Benin und Togo, ca. 15 Millionen Stammesmitglieder. Kwa sprechende Sudan-Neger, die in vorkolonialer Zeit zahlreiche Kleinstaaten gründeten. So bezeichnen Untergruppen der *Yoruba* wie die Anago, Oyo, Ife, Ketu, Owe, Ekiti oder Ijebu keine eigenständigen Ethnien, sondern politische Herrschaftsbereiche. Nach eigenen Überlieferungen der *Yoruba* erfolgte ihre Einwanderung aus dem Norden in zwei Wellen zwischen dem 6. und 10. Jahrhundert und im 11. Jahrhundert. Die Gründung eines einheitlichen Reiches fand vermutlich schon im 13. Jahrhundert statt. Das ursprüngliche Zentrum Ife blieb auch später das religiöse Zentrum, in dem v. a. der Reichsgründer und Gewittergott Schango (meist als Reiter dargestellt) verehrt wurde. Dagegen verlagerte sich das politische Zentrum nach Oyo. Nachdem sich schon früher Randgebiete losgesagt hatten, zerfiel schließlich im 18. Jahrhundert auch die Zentralmacht von Oyo, und 1893 errichteten die Engländer ein Protektorat. An der Spitze der einzelnen *Yoruba*-Reiche stand ein sakraler König, dessen politische Macht jedoch von den Ratsversammlungen der Adligen und den regionalen Machthabern z. T. stark beschnitten wurde. Die *Yoruba* leben vorwiegend als Hackbauern (Yams, Taro, in jüngerer Zeit Maniok) in den Savannen und im tropischen Regenwald des Tieflandes. Ihre Religion ist geprägt durch ein umfangreiches, hierarchisch gegliedertes Pantheon, das sich um den Hochgott Olorun (»Besitzer des Himmels«) gruppiert; Olorun zeigt die charakteristischen Züge eines Deus otiosus, der sich nach Erschaffung der Welt zurückzieht und nicht mehr unmittelbar in das Weltgeschehen eingreift. Das Pantheon umfaßt eine Fülle von Gottheiten (*orisha*), die nach Machtbereichen und Richtungen eingeteilt und nach formalen Kriterien zugeordnet werden, jedoch unschwer die ursprüngliche Vielfalt der Naturgottheiten und Ahnengeister erkennen lassen. In der reichen Mythologie spielen androgyne Gottheiten, häufig in inzestuösen Beziehungen lebend, eine wichtige Rolle. Hier sind Einflüsse aus den archaischen Hochkulturen des Mittelmeerraums zu vermuten. Von großer Bedeutung ist das Orakelwesen, das nach dem Gott des Schicksals *Ife* genannt wird. Die *Yoruba* gelten als einer der bedeutendsten Kulturträger Afrikas. Ihre künstlerischen Arbeiten stellen neben religiösen Themen auch Szenen aus dem Alltag dar. Verbreitet sind u. a. kultisch bemalte Darstellungen der Gottheiten und mythischen Helden (Egungun, Epa, Gelede – siehe Glossar), Ritualstäbe (Eisen), Orakelbretter und -schalen aus Holz sowie Zwillingsfiguren.

Gelede-Maske □ 14; Doppelgesichtiger Kopfschmuck □ 613

Z

Zaire

→ *Bembe, Boa, Boyo, Chokwe, Hemba, Kasingo, Komo, Kuba, Lega, Luba, Lwalwa, Mangbetu, Mbole, Mbuun, Ngbandi, Ngombe, Pende, Pere, Salampasu, Songge, Tabwa, Yaka, Yombe, Zande*

Zande (Sande, Azande, Niam-Niam) 26, 53, 136, 168, 181

Moore 611

NO-Zaire, im SO der Zentralafrikanischen Republik und im Sudan, ca. 1 Million Menschen. Sudan-Neger, die Ende des 18. Jahrhunderts von N her vorstießen und mit ihrer überlegenen politisch-militärischen Organisation die autochthone Bevölkerung (bis auf die → *Mangbetu*) verdrängte oder sprachlich und kulturell assimilierte (»Azandeisierung«). Die Kerngruppe der *Zande* stellten die *Ambomu* mit ihrer abgeschlossenen Adelskaste dar (*Vungura, Avongare*). In sieben Generationen wuchs dieser Herrscherklan auf ca. 10000 Mitglieder an, aus denen sich die Verwalter der unterworfenen Stämme, die Provinzbürokratie und Heerführer rekrutierten. An der Spitze des Reiches stand der König, der seine Residenz in der zentralen Königsprovinz hatte. In abgestufter Form wiederholte sich diese Zentralisierung in den umliegenden Provinzen, die mehr oder minder unter der direkten Autorität des Königs standen. Bei militärischer Bedrohung von außen konnte der König als oberster militärischer Befehlshaber die Truppen aus allen Landesteilen einberufen. Da es kein geregeltes Nachfolgerecht gab, kam es häufig zu blutigen Machtkämpfen unter den Königssöhnen. Entwickelte Schmiedekunst (Waffen, mehrarmige Wurfmesser, *pinga*), und sozial hoher Rang der Schmiede. Die *Zande* betreiben Gartenbau (Mais, Süßkartoffel) und Wanderfeldbau (Hirsen). Sie sind patrilinear organisiert und leben in isolierten Gehöften oder Streusiedlungen. Das religiöse Leben beschränkt sich im wesentlichen auf Ahnenverehrung. Auffallend sind die Armut an Mythen und die besondere Bedeutung des Orakelwesens sowie des Hexenglaubens. Von hohem Niveau zeugen die Holzschnitzereien der *Zande*-Völker: Schemel, Schüsseln, Spielbretter, Musikinstrumente (Schlitztrommeln in Tiergestalt, die an den Fürstenhöfen aufgestellt wurden, beschnitzte Bogenharfen).

Figur aus Holz □ 200, 215b; Wurfmesser □ 292; Sanza □ 424

Zentralafrika, Republik

→ Ubangi, *Yakoma*

Zulu (Amazulu, Sulu) 181

Republik Südafrika (Provinz Natal), mit verschiedenen Untergruppen mehr als 2 Millionen Stammesmitglieder. Die *Zulu* sind Teil der Nguni-Gruppe, den seit dem 14. Jahrhundert am weitesten nach Süden vorgedrungenen *Bantu*-Negern. Unter ihrem Häuptling Chaka (Shaka), dem »schwarzen Napoleon«, waren sie von größter politischer Bedeutung in Süd- und Ostafrika. Chaka organisierte die *Zulu* in militärischen Altersklassen mit strenger Heiratsregelung, führte neue Nahkampftaktiken (Stoßspeere) ein und schuf in zehnjähriger kriegerischer Expansion ein diktatorisch regiertes Großreich, das mit seiner Ermordung (1828) und der entscheidenden Niederlage gegen die Buren (1838) zerfiel. Die politischen und kulturellen Auswirkungen durch abgespaltene und umherziehende Teile der *Zulu* waren bis nach Tanganjika zu spüren. Die *Zulu* sind zu gleichen Teilen Ackerbauern (Mais, Hirse) und Viehzüchter (Rinder, Ziege). Erbliches Häuptlingstum und ausgeprägter Ahnenkult, der die Verehrung der Gottheiten in den Hintergrund drängt.

Figur aus Holz □ 776

Zuni 465

Ernst 577, 578, 585 – Klee 40, 41 – Ray 474

→ *Puebloindianer*. Die *Zuni* waren die ersten Indianer im heutigen Gebiet der USA, deren Siedlungen von den Spaniern 1540 erobert wurden. Von ihrer Kunst sind vor allem die Darstellungen der Kriegsgötter bekannt, Figuren, die aus dem Holz eines lebenden Baumes, den ein Blitz getroffen hatte, angefertigt wurden.

Figur eines Kriegsgottes □ 43, 664; Katchina □ 848

Literaturhinweise

Afrika

Agthe, J., *Luba Hemba, Werke unbekannter Meister,* Ausstellungskatalog des Museums für Völkerkunde, Frankfurt am Main 1983

Baumann, H., (Hrsg.), *Die Völker Afrikas und ihre traditionellen Kulturen,* 2 Bände, Wiesbaden 1975, 1979

Himmelheber, H., *Negerkunst und Negerkünstler,* Braunschweig 1960

Kecskési, M., *Kunst aus dem alten Afrika,* Ausstellungskatalog des Staatl. Museums für Völkerkunde München, Innsbruck, Frankfurt am Main 1982

Kecskési, M., Stößel, A., *Keramik aus Afrika südlich der Sahara,* Ausstellungskatalog des Staatl. Museums für Völkerkunde, München 1984

Krieger, K., *Westafrikanische Plastik I–III,* Veröffentlichungen des Museums für Völkerkunde Berlin, N. F. 7, Berlin 1965–1969

Leuzinger, E., *Die Kunst von Schwarz-Afrika,* Zürich 1970

Menzel, B., *Goldgewichte aus Ghana,* Veröffentlichungen des Museums für Völkerkunde Berlin, N. F. 12, 1968

Murdock, G. P., *Africa – Its People and their Culture History,* New York 1959

Stößel, A., u. a., *Afrikanische Keramik. Traditionelle Handwerkskunst südlich der Sahara,* Ausstellungskatalog des Staatlichen Museums für Völkerkunde, München 1984

Schweeger-Hefel, A., *Plastik aus Afrika,* Ausstellungskatalog des Museums für Völkerkunde Wien, 1969

Ozeanien

Bodrogi, T., *Die Kunst Ozeaniens,* Budapest 1960

Bühler, A., *Kunststile am Sepik,* Basel 1960

Bühler, A., Barrow, T., und Mountford, Ch. P., *Ozeanien und Australien,* Baden-Baden 1961

Gathercole, P., Keppler, A., Newton, B., *The Art of the Pacific Islands,* National Gallery of Art, Washington 1979

Helfrich, K., *Malanggan. Bildwerke von Neuirland,* Band 1, Veröffentlichungen des Museums für Völkerkunde Berlin, N. F. 25, 1973

Kelm, H., *Kunst vom Sepik,* Bd. I–III, Museum für Völkerkunde Berlin, 1966–68

Koch, G., *Kultur der Abelam. Die Berliner Maprik-Sammlung,* Museum für Völkerkunde Berlin, 1968

Koch, G., *Südsee. Führer durch die Ausstellung der Abteilung Südsee.* Museum für Völkerkunde, 2. Auflage, Berlin 1976

Nevermann, H., *Masken und Geheimbünde in Melanesien,* Berlin 1933

Parkinson, R., *Dreißig Jahre in der Südsee,* Stuttgart 1907

Schlesier, E., *Die melanesischen Geheimkulte,* Göttingen 1958

Steinen, K. v. d., *Die Marquesaner und ihre Kunst,* 3 Bände, Berlin 1925–28

Stöhr, W., in *Exotische Kunst im Rautenstrauch-Joest-Museum,* herausgegeben von Fröhlich, W., 2. erweiterte Auflage, Köln 1971

Stöhr, W., *Melanesien. Schwarze Inseln der Südsee,* Rautenstrauch-Joest-Museum, Köln 1972

Amerika

Disselhoff, H.-D., *Alt-Amerika,* Baden-Baden 1976

Dockstader, F. J., *Kunst in Amerika,* Stuttgart 1968

Hoffmann, G. (Hrsg.), *Indianische Kunst im 20. Jahrhundert,* München 1984

Krickeberg, W., »Die Völker Amerikas außerhalb der Hochkulturen« in Weigert, H., *Kleine Kunstgeschichte der Welt,* Bd. 1, S. 229–256, Stuttgart 1956

Kroeber, A. L., *Cultural and Natural areas of native North America,* University of California Publications in Archaeology and Ethnology, Vol. 38, Berkeley 1939

Lommel, A., *Masken, Gesichter der Menschheit,* Zürich 1970

Lommel, A., *Schamanen und Medizinmänner,* München 1980

Rasmussen, K., *Thulefahrt,* Frankfurt 1926

Siebert, E., Forman, W., *Indianerkunst,* Prag 1967

Swanton, J. R., *The Indians of the southeastern United States,* Bureau of American Ethnology, Bulletin 137, Washington 1946

Ubbelohde-Doering, H., *Die Königsstraßen der Inka,* Berlin 1941

Zerries, O., *Unter Indianern Brasiliens. Sammlung Spix und Martius 1817–1820,* Innsbruck, Frankfurt am Main 1980

Glossar

Aufhängehaken

Figürlich gestaltete Holzhaken (Menschen und Tiere) zum Aufhängen von Gegenständen als Schutz gegen Ratten u. ä. Charakteristisch für Neuguinea, besonders die Sepik-Region und angrenzende Gebiete → *Iatmul.*
☐ 616

Bundwesen

Zusammenfassende Bezeichnung für soziale Institutionen, die nicht auf den üblichen verwandtschaftlichen Kategorien beruhen. Die Völkerkunde unterscheidet Männer-, Frauen-, Geheim-, Medizin-, Zauber-, Kult-, Kriegerbünde u. a. In allen Fällen ist das religiöse Element von großer Bedeutung (z. B. in Form von Jagdzauber, Fruchtbarkeitskulten, Ahnenverehrung), wobei die Mitglieder des Bundes mit Gottheiten, Schutzgeistern oder Ahnen in Kontakt treten oder diese repräsentieren (Maskentänze). Bünde sind meist nach sozialem Rang oder Alter gegliedert. Die Aufnahme erfolgt durch Initiationsfeiern, durch die das neue Mitglied (oder die Gruppe von neuen Mitgliedern) in die Geheimnisse des Bundes eingeweiht wird. Häufig existieren eigene Versammlungshäuser, in denen die Zusammenkünfte stattfinden und die Bundesinsignien aufbewahrt werden. Bünde sind in der ganzen Welt verbreitet, besonders in Nordamerika, Westafrika und der Südsee.

Byeri-Figuren (Malan)

Sog. »Wächterfiguren« der → *Fang.* Die Schädel- und Knochenreliquien der Ersten Ahnen der *Fang* und der → *Kota* wurden in zylinderförmigen Schachteln aus Rinde oder geflochtenen Körben aufbewahrt, auf deren Rand holzgeschnitzte Köpfe oder Figuren gesetzt wurden (siehe ☐ 164). Die Figuren haben Metallauflagen aus europäischen Messinggefäßen, wobei die männlichen Gestalten häufig ein mit magisch wirksamen Objekten gefülltes Antilopenhorn in der Hand tragen. Der Oberkörper der Byeri-Figuren ist im Verhältnis zu den sehr gedrungenen Beinen langgestreckt.
Diese Figuren bewachen die Ahnen und schützen die Lebenden vor Unheil. Ihre aus Glas gefertigten, mit Metallringen eingefaßten Augen vermögen nach dem Glauben der *Fang* in die Vergangenheit und Zukunft zu sehen.

Deszendenz

Verwandtschaftsregelungen einer Gemeinschaft in absteigender Folge, die nicht mit der biologischen oder genealogischen Abstammung verwechselt werden darf. Grundsätzlich spricht man von 3 Deszendenztypen: 1. patrilinear (nach der väterlichen Linie), 2. matrilinear (nach der mütterlichen Linie) und 3. bilinear (Doppeldeszendenz). Damit verbinden sich im allgemeinen jeweils festgelegte Vorschriften der Nach- und Erbfolge, des Wohnortes, der Familiengründung, der Autoritätsausübung etc. Zu unterscheiden ist die Patri- bzw. Matrilokalität, der Brauch, daß der Sohn nach der Heirat innerhalb oder in der Nähe der Familiengemeinschaft des Vaters bleibt (entsprechend die Tochter bei der Familiengemeinschaft der Mutter): Die Heiratswohnfolge muß sich nicht mit der Deszendenzfolge decken.

Ekpe (Egbo, Ngbe)

»Leoparden-Bund«, Bezeichnung überregionaler Kultbünde (→ Bundwesen) verschiedener → Crossfluß-Stämme (→ *Ejagham,* → *Ibibio*). Sie haben wichtige politische, soziale sowie religiöse Funktionen, stehen – getrennt – sowohl Männern wie auch Frauen offen und sind traditionell nach zahlreichen Klassen und Rängen geordnet. Bei den anläßlich der Yamsernte veranstalteten Festen verkörpern ihre schwarze Masken tragenden Mitglieder die zur Erde zurückgekehrten Ahnen. Masken, Bundinsignien, Musikinstrumente und Schädeltrophäen werden in besonderen Häusern (Ekpe-Häusern) aufbewahrt. Die Masken weisen großen Formen- und Stilreichtum auf. Beeindruckend sind v. a. die meist überlebensgroßen Helm- und Kopfaufsatzmasken, die mit oft nachgefärbter Antilopenhaut überzogen sind und durch Menschenhaarbesatz, realistische Bemalung und Tätowierung extrem naturalistisch wirken.
☐ 101

Fetisch

Von portug. feitiçao: Machwerk. Ältere Bezeichnung für magisch wirksame Figuren.
☐ 80, 95, 97, 98, 107, 430, 636

Gelede

In den westlichen → *Yoruba*-Provinzen verbreiteter Kultbund (→ Bundwesen), der v. a. bei der Felderbestellung, beim Begräbnis eines Mitglieds oder bei Naturkatastrophen aktiv wird. Die magische Wirkung des Gelede-Maskenkults wird auf die Muttergöttin Iya Nla zurückgeführt, deren Kraft allen Frauen, besonders Müttern, innewohnt. Die Mitglieder sind ausschließlich Männer, die bei den Tänzen Frauenkleider und häufig künstliche Brüste aus Holz tragen. Die Masken stellen nur weibliche Gesichter dar und werden helmartig auf dem Kopf getragen, wobei das Gesicht von einem durchsichtigen Tuch bedeckt ist.
☐ 14

Hakenfiguren

Brettartige Figuren mit stark stilisiertem Gesicht, deren Körper ganz in Haken aufgelöst sind. Hakenfiguren werden in der → Karawari-Region (Neuguinea) angefertigt. *Siehe auch* Yipwon.

Hei-tiki

Ahnensymbol der Maori Neuseelands, ursprünglich wohl für den ersten Menschen (tiki). Es wurde – vor allem von Frauen hohen Ranges – als Brustschmuck getragen, als geschätztes Erbstück Toten mit ins Grab gegeben und bei der Sekundärbestattung vom Erbberechtigten wieder in Besitz genommen. *Siehe auch* Neuseeland. *Lit.:* Schubert, R., *Wittelsbach und Bayern, 400 Jahre Sammeln und Reisen,* Staatl. Museum für Völkerkunde, München 1980, S. 38. G. Koch, *Südsee. Führer durch die Ausstellung der Abteilung Südsee,* Museum für Völkerkunde Berlin, 2. Aufl., Berlin 1976, S. 24.
☐ 642

Imunu

Wurzelskulptur mit menschlichem Kopf, die in Neuguinea u. a. zum Schutz der Frisur oder des Kopfschmucks im Schlaf als Nackenstütze verwendet wurde. Siehe auch *Namau.*
☐ 81

Kanaken

Bezeichnung für die Bewohner → Neukaledoniens, gelegentlich auch auf andere Südseeinsulaner übertragen.
☐ 140 Kanakendorf

Kapkap

Brustschmuck aus zugeschliffener, runder Muschelscheibe mit durchbrochen gearbeiteter Schildpattauflage → Neuirland u. a.

Katchina

→ S. 557 ff.
☐ 534, 656, 837, 842, 848

Kifwebe (Tschifwebe)

Wörtlich »Maske«, Bezeichnung für die Masken der → *Songge.*
☐ 26, 212, 338, 469, 707, 923

Malanggan-Figuren

Durchbrochen geschnitzte Menschen- und Tierfiguren, Bildfiguren und -friese, die Weiß, Rot, Schwarz und Gelb bemalt sind. Die Verschlußdeckel der Turbo-Seeschnecke dienen als Augen. Bei den Malanggan-Figuren handelt es sich um Darstellungen von Verstorbenen, mythischen Vorfahren und Ereignissen, Sippengeistern in Tiergestalt (Vögel, Hähne, Schweine, Fische, Schlangen), von Mond und Sonne. Monatelang im Geheimen geschnitzt, wurden sie bei Totenfeiern in Malanggan-Schauhütten oder -Kulthöfen ausgestellt.
☐ 2, 77, 749, 751, 752

Nimba-Maske, -Figur

→ S. 28[illegible] ff.
☐ 360, 454, 458

Reliquiarfigur

Auch als »Spiegel-« oder »Nagelfetisch« bezeichnet. Typus von figuraler Plastik, der am unteren Kongo verbreitet ist. Medizinmänner ergänzen die von Handwerkern aus Holz gefertigten Skulpturen, indem sie in einer Höhlung im Bauch oder Rücken (die häufig durch Spiegel verschlossen wird) magische Gegenstände deponieren. Die darin verborgene latente Kraft kann durch bestimmte Worte oder Praktiken (etwa das Einschlagen eines Nagels) aktiviert werden. Auf diese Weise versuchte man sich gegen Schadenzauber, Unheil oder Krankheit zu schützen, oder man bekräftigte eine feierliche Kulthandlung. Meist wurden männliche, manchmal weibliche Figuren dargestellt (unter besonders sorgfältiger Ausarbeitung der Gesichtszüge), seltener Tiere.
☐ 27, 58, 164, 165, 190, 191, 342, 343, 344, 347, 349, 383, 385, 413, 487, 559, 612, 615, 625, 626, 721

»Sprechende Bretter« (kohau rongorongo)

Auf der → Osterinsel angefertigte längliche Holzstücke mit mittels Obsidianmessern oder Haizähnen sorgsam eingeschnittenen »Schrift-

zeichen« (Pictogrammen) in Form von Menschen, Vögeln und anderem Getier, Pflanzen und schematisierten Symbolen als Gedächtnisstütze der Experten beim Rezitieren der traditionellen Kultgesänge.
□ 227

Schamanismus

Meist als Religion bezeichnete besondere psychische Verfassung in Verbindung mit einem intensiv tierbezogenen Weltbild der frühen Jäger, d. h. des späteren Paläolithikums.
Der Schamanismus hat sich in Nordsibirien und bei den → *Eskimos* bis in unsere Zeit erhalten. Schwächere Varianten finden sich bei fast allen Naturvölkern. Der Schamane wirkt in Trance als Krankenheiler und versetzt dabei auch seine Patienten in diese Geistesverfassung – eine besondere nachzuvollziehende frühe Form von Psychosomatik.
Seine Fähigkeiten erwirbt der Schamane durch eine qualvolle Vorbereitungszeit, durch Leiden, die ihm von den »Geistern« zwangsweise auferlegt werden. Er kann sich dem Schamanenamt nicht entziehen – es aber auch nicht freiwillig wünschen.
Der Schamane ist auch befähigt, Jagdwild beizuschaffen. Psychische Störungen der Gruppe, die den Erfolg der Jagd gefährden könnten, werden durch Aktivierung des jeweiligen Weltbildes behoben. Schamanen üben auch ausgesprochen künstlerische Tätigkeiten aus: Theater, Anfertigung von Gewändern und Masken und vor allem Felsbildern, in denen die Tierseelen gefangen bzw. gehalten werden sollen. *Lit.:* Lommel, A., *Schamanen und Medizinmänner,* München 1980.

Tapa

Polynesische Bezeichnung für Stoff aus Rindenbast. Solche Stoffe wurden in vielen tropischen Gebieten hergestellt, besonders qualitätvolle in Polynesien. Das Rohmaterial wurde vor allem aus der Pflanzenfamilie der Morazeen gewonnen, in Polynesien vorwiegend vom Papiermaulbeerbaum. Die zwischen Rinde und Holzteil sitzende Bastschicht wurde in einem Streifen herausgelöst, getrocknet, gewässert und auf einer hölzernen Unterlage mit Holzschlegeln bearbeitet, wobei der Baststreifen von 4–8 auf 60–80 cm Breite gedehnt wurde. Zur Verzierung dienten Pflanzenfarben, Tonerden und Ruß, die mittels Matrizen, Stempeln, Naturabdrücken von Blättern u. ä. oder einfach mit einem Pflanzenpinsel aufgetragen wurden. Verwendet wurden die Baststoffe vor allem für Kleidung, aber auch als Zudecke (→ *Baining, Namau,* Sentani-See, Tahiti, Tongainseln). *Lit.:* Schubert, R., a. a. O.; Koch, G., a. a. O.
□ 144, 145, 150, 151, 152, 295, 298, 806, 877

Tellem-Figuren

Von den *Dogon* verehrte Holzskulpturen hohen Alters (über 200 Jahre), die sich in abgelegenen Teilen des Hombori-Gebirges im Nigerbogen erhalten haben. Ihre Oberfläche ist z. T. durch Umwelteinflüsse mit einer aschgrauen Kruste überzogen. Als Schöpfer der Tellem-Figuren werden die *Dogon* bzw. ihre Vorgänger angenommen. Die *Dogon* selbst sehen in mysteriösen Vorbewohnern des Landes deren Urheber und bezeichnen sie als ›Tellem‹ (kleine Ahnen).

Tiki

Ahnenfiguren mit stilisierten Darstellungen des Totenkopfes (mit großen Augenhöhlen, Nasenstumpf und breiter Mundöffnung, gelegentlich auch vorquellender Zunge), aus Stein und Holz gearbeitet bzw. als Dekorelement auf Keulen, Fächergriffen, Ohrpflöcken u. a. angebracht → Marquesasinseln u. a.
□ 142, 373, 760

Uli-Figuren

Darstellungen vergöttlichter Ahnen, mit ihren betonten Brüsten und Penis vermutlich besonders mächtiger Häuptlinge.
□ 555, 556

Yam-Maske (knife yam-Maske, mma-ji)

V. a. in Schwarz, Weiß und Rot bemalte Holzmasken der *Igbo* mit Augenschlitzen und ohne Mund. Ihre Bezeichnung rührt von dem Aufsatz her, der die Form eines Haumessers hat. In der Verlängerung des Aufsatzes sind im Gesicht drei oder vier hervorstehende Holzzapfen angeordnet. Die Yam-Masken werden von Jünglingen bei den traditionellen, jährlich in den Dörfern stattfindenden Sing- und Tanzspielen satirischen Charakters getragen.
□ 88

Yipwon

Aus Holz geschnitzte → Hakenfiguren, Darstellungen gleichnamiger Geister, die als Erfolgsbringer für Jagd und Kriegszüge galten und in Zeremonialhäusern oder Höhlen aufbewahrt wurden → *Karawari-Region, Alamblak.*
□ 108, 159, 876, 933

Künstler- und Personenregister

D

E

F

G

H

S

T

U

V

W

Z